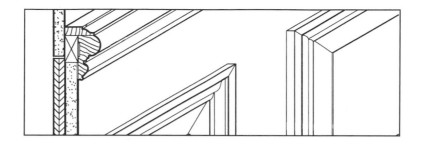

# INTERIOR GRAPHIC STANDARDS

## STUDENT EDITION

**MARYROSE McGOWAN, AIA**
EDITOR IN CHIEF

**KELSEY KRUSE, AIA**
GRAPHICS EDITOR

WILEY

## JOHN WILEY & SONS, INC.

Published by John Wiley & Sons, Inc., Hoboken, New Jersey

Published simultaneously in Canada

For general information on our other products and services or for technical support, please contact our Customer Care Department within the United States at (800) 762-2974, outside the United States at (317) 572-3993 or fax (317) 572-4002.

Wiley also publishes its books in a variety of electronic formats. Some content that appears in print may not be available in electronic books. For information about Wiley products, visit our website at www.wiley.com

**Library of Congress Cataloging-in-Publication Data:**

Interior graphic standards / Maryrose McGowan, editor-in-chief,
Kelsey Kruse, graphics editor. — Student ed.
          p. cm.
    ISBN 0-471-46196-2 (Cloth)
  1. Building—Details—Drawings. 2.
Building—Details—Drawings—Standards. I. McGowan, Maryrose. II.
Kruse, Kelsey.
TH2031 .I55 2004
721'.028'4—dc22
                                2003020623


Printed in the United States of America

10  9  8  7  6  5  4  3  2  1

# CONTENTS

# 2 INTERIOR BUILDING COMPONENTS 141

# PREFACE

John Wiley & Sons, Inc., the American Institute of Architects, and the Department of Interior Architecture at Rhode Island School of Design (RISD) are pleased to present this first edition of *Interior Graphic Standards, Student Edition.* It is our hope that students of interior design will find in this volume a companion for all aspects of their design education. The student edition serves as a reference for the core classes required by all curriculums, including construction methods and materials, professional practice, construction specification writing, furniture selection and specification writing, design studio, acoustics, lighting, mechanical and electrical systems, construction detailing and documentation, color theory, and human factors.

Although this student edition is an abridgment of the first edition of *Interior Graphic Standards,* it contains more than 20 original pages whose content was guided by the Student Edition Advisory Board: Barbara G. Anderson, Kansas State University; Brian Davies, University of Oregon; Rebecca Foss, University of Minnesota; Rhonda Gilmore, Cornell University; Jane Kielb, College of DuPage; Tim Shea, AIA, UCLA Extension; Steve Smith, AIA, Pratt Institute; and Tom Witt, Arizona State University.

The vitality of the first edition of *Interior Graphic Standards, Student Edition,* has been established by the contributions and inspiration of the students in the Department of Interior Architecture at RISD. The six detailing concepts were developed and refined under the guidance of Jeffrey Meese, AIA, during the Scheme Detailing seminar in fall 2002, with the following students: Minkyong Choe, Mayura Dhume, Douglas Flandro, Caitlin Gaiewski, Lei Yun Goh, Youn Mi Kang, Sabrina Macedo, Signe Skjaerlund, and Robert C. Smith. These detailing concepts explore the manner by which construction detailing further refines a design concept.

Students of interior design are at the beginning of a lifetime of building the skills and acquiring the knowledge and resources required for an inspired design practice. It is our hope that *Interior Graphic Standards, Student Edition,* will serve as both a launchpad and touchstone in these endeavors to all who seek its guidance.

MARYROSE McGOWAN, AIA
*Editor in Chief*
Cambridge, Massachusetts

# INTRODUCTION

*Interior Graphic Standards, Student Edition,* is based on *Interior Graphic Standards,* a professional reference compiled from the contributions of more than 200 industry experts and researchers. Material appropriate for learning was retained, and more than 20 pages of original material has been added.

The student edition of *Interior Graphic Standards* is loosely organized according to the three principles of well-designed space as set forth by Vitruvius, the first-century Roman architect, in *10 Books on Architecture:*

- **Commodity,** or *convenience* (Part 1, Design Data), supporting its intended function and extending its occupants' abilities.
- **Firmness,** or *durability* (Part 2, Interior Building Components), serving as sound shelter.
- **Delight,** or *beauty* (Part 3, Interior Typologies), providing an aesthetic image representing societal function and purpose.

Achieving these three purposes through design involves bringing to bear substantial knowledge to the process of design decision making. This book assists students of interior design in their wide variety of studies with design data and criteria organized in a manner that is familiar to design professionals. In this way, *Interior Graphic Standards, Student Edition,* supports students in organizing their reference materials and design inspirations, and prepares them for the rigors of professional practice. If the course taught is for senior students, it may be appropriate to use *Interior Graphic Standards* as a text so that graduating students have the professional reference to use as they begin their practice.

The presentation of the material in Part 2 is consistent with the standard organization of construction and furniture contract documentation and with product literature storage and retrieval methods used in most design firms in the United States and Canada. This ordering system is based on MasterFormat™, a master list of titles developed to organize information about construction requirements, products, and activities into a standard sequence. MasterFormat is promulgated by the Construction Specifications Institute.

# ACKNOWLEDGMENTS

## JOHN WILEY & SONS, INC.

ROBERT C. GARBER
Vice President and Group Executive Publisher

AMANDA L. MILLER
Publisher

JULIE M. TRELSTAD
Senior Editor

DIANA CISEK
Production Director

EILEEN G. CHETTI
Production Manager

MICHAEL OLIVO
Senior Production Editor

JENNIFER ACKERMAN
Assistant Developmental Editor

ROSANNE KONEVAL
Senior Editorial Assistant

LAUREN LaFRANCE
Editorial Assistant

JANICE BORZENDOWSKI
Copy Editor

LISA STORY
Proofreader

JENNIFER RUSHING-SCHURR
Indexer

LUCINDA GEIST
Graphic Designer

## RHODE ISLAND SCHOOL OF DESIGN

ROGER MANDLE
President

DAWN BARRETT
Dean, Division of Architecture & Design

BRIAN KERNAGHAN
Department Head, Interior Architecture

WENDY ABELSON
Department Assistant, Interior Architecture

SCHEME DETAILING STUDENT CONTRIBUTORS
Mia Alwen
Elizabeth Aukamp
Pyinerl S. Chang
Winnie Cheng
Jason Dickerson
Carl Henschel
Yon-Hwa Jang
Min Kyeng Kang
Tonu Lensment
Tanya Nachia
Manami Nakabayashi
May Sophonpanich
Merve Yoneymen
Thitapa Youngcharoen

INTERIOR TYPOLOGIES STUDENT CONTRIBUTORS
Lalana Assawamunkong
Michael Blankenship
Pyinerl S. Chang
Leonor De Lope Friedeberg
Mayura Dhume
Douglas Flandro
Meryl Grant
Natasa Jelic
Sunyoung Kwon
Ted Milligan
Tanya Nachia
Natasza Naczas
Betty Ng
Shawn Parks
Soyploy Phanich
Sukamorn Prasithrathsint
Heidi Rhodes
Anna Rosete
Mette Shenker
May Sophonpanich
Perry Sye
Brian Tan
Nancy Vayo
Thitapa Youngcharoen
Ji-Seong Yun

## INTERIOR GRAPHIC STANDARDS STUDENT EDITION

INTERIOR GRAPHIC STANDARDS
STUDENT EDITION ADVISORY BOARD

Barbara G. Anderson
*Kansas State University, Manhattan, Kansas*

Brian Davies
*University of Oregon, Eugene, Oregon*

Rebecca Foss
*University of Minnesota, Minneapolis, Minnesota*

Rhonda Gilmore
*Cornell University, Ithaca, New York*

Jane Kielb
*College of DuPage, Glen Ellyn, Illinois*

Tim Shea, AIA
*UCLA Extension, Los Angeles, California*

Steve Smith, AIA
*Pratt Institute, Brooklyn, New York*

Tom Witt
*Arizona State University, Tempe, Arizona*

INTERIOR GRAPHIC STANDARDS
ADVISORY BOARD

Eric Alch
*SOM, New York, New York*

Stephen Apking, AIA
*SOM, New York, New York*

Sarah Bader
*Gensler, Chicago, Illinois*

Jan Bishop, AIA
*The Hillier Group, Princeton, New Jersey*

Jane Clark, AIA
*Zimmer Gunsul Frasca Partnership, Seattle, Washington*

John L. Hogshead, AIA
*Perkins and Will, Atlanta, Georgia*

Ted Kollaja, AIA
*lauckgroup, Dallas, Texas*

Elizabeth Niedzwiecki, AIA
*The Hillier Group, Princeton, New Jersey*

Tim Shea, AIA
*Richard Meier & Partners, Los Angeles, California*

MARYROSE McGOWAN, AIA
*Editor in Chief*

KELSEY A. KRUSE, AIA
*Graphics Editor*

# COURSE TOPIC PAGE FINDER

*Interior Graphic Standards, Student Edition,* can be readily adapted as a reference text for several commonly required courses of studies, including the following:

- Construction Methods and Materials
- Furniture Design, Selection, and Specification
- Construction Detailing and Documentation
- Construction Specifications
- Design Studio

For these courses, a detailed list of lecture topics, with required reading page numbers shown in parentheses, is provided below. Lectures and other supporting pedagogical materials are available at www.wiley.com/college/mcgowan.

## CONSTRUCTION METHODS AND MATERIALS

### Frame Construction
1. Wood: wood roof and wood floor truss construction (123) and wood frame construction (124)
2. Steel: light-gauge steel frame construction (125, 127)

### Partitions
1. Partition construction: gypsum board assemblies and details (218–224), concrete masonry units (143–145), plaster (214–215), and glass-reinforced gypsum (GRG) (216–217)
2. Wall finishes: paints and coatings (277–279), wallcoverings (268–270), acoustical wall panels (266–267), upholstered wall systems (271), ceramic tile (226–230), and stone facing (272–276)
3. Wood finishes: wood and wood composite panels (154–155), wood veneers (180–183), interior architectural woodwork (184–188), and examples of wood veneer panels (190–191)

### Windows
1. Glazing: glass (208–211), glazing (212–213), and glass unit masonry (glass block) assemblies (146)
2. Window treatments and exterior glazing considerations (292–296)

### Flooring
1. Carpet: carpet and carpet tile (251–262) and oriental rugs (263–265)
2. Resilient flooring: vinyl, rubber, linoleum, and cork (247–249), and resilient base and transitions (250)
3. Hard flooring: ceramic tile (226–230), tile setting accessories (225), terrazzo (231–233), wood (243–246), and stone (240–242).
4. Access floors (280)

### Ceilings
1. Stretched ceiling systems (234)
2. Acoustical ceilings: acoustical panel ceilings (236), acoustical tile ceilings (235), and acoustical ceiling detailing (237)
3. Glass-reinforced gypsum (GRG) (216–217)

### Casework
1. Countertops (172–179)
2. Standard casework (160–169)
3. Custom casework examples (170–171)

## FURNITURE DESIGN, SELECTION, AND SPECIFICATION

Furniture, Furnishings, and Equipment Contract Documents (75–80)

Uniform Commerical Code, Article 2 (421–433)

Seating Design and Selection Criteria (299–301)

Wood-Frame Furniture Design and Selection Criteria (302–303)

Plastics (156–158)

Wood (154–155)

Metals (149–153)

Conference Tables (304)

Booth Construction and Layout and Banquette Seating (305–306)

Textiles and Leather (281–290)

Systems Furniture (307–316)

Metal File Cabinets (297–298)

Task Lighting (291)

## CONSTRUCTION DETAILING AND DOCUMENTATION

Construction Contract Documents (75–80)

Building Systems (123–140)

Frame Construction: wood roof and wood floor truss construction (123), wood frame construction (124), and light-gauge steel frame construction (125, 127)

Partitions: gypsum board assemblies (218–223), concrete masonry units (143–145), plaster (214–215), and glass-fiber-reinforced gypsum (GRG) (216–217)

Detailing Concepts (121–122)

Stair Design (102–110)

Interior Architectural Woodwork (184–188)

Countertops (172–179)

Standard Casework (160–169)

Custom Casework Examples (170–171)

Conveying Systems: elevators (317–319), and escalators and moving walks (320)

Mechanical Systems (321–327)

Plumbing Systems (328–329)

Electrical Systems (330–333)

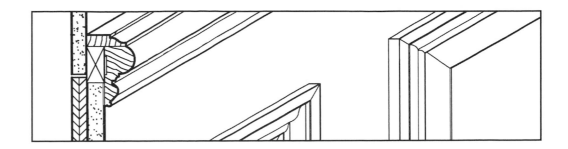

# GENERAL PLANNING AND DESIGN DATA

Vitruvius' first principle of architectural design is *commodity,* or convenience. For a space to support human endeavors and extend human capability, it must accommodate both activities and occupants. The strengths and limitations of human beings to perceive, to work efficiently, to be productive, to maintain robust health, and to thrive are discussed in Part 1, "General Planning and Design Data." Project management and construction and furniture contract execution discussions, as well as life safety and health and welfare issues are also described here.

Human Factors

Design Principles

Historic Preservation

Color

Principles of Perception

Acoustics

Interior Lighting

Programming

Life-Cycle Costing

Contract Administration

Interior Landscape Design

Sustainable Design Criteria

Indoor Air Quality

Stair Design

Life Safety Considerations

Detailing Concepts

Building Systems

# HUMAN FACTORS

Human factors information refers to the variables that affect human performance in the built environment, such as human physiology and human psychology. Data accumulated from the fields of engineering, biology, psychology, and anthropology are integrated in this multidisciplinary field.

*Fit* describes a design that uses human factors information to create a stimulating but nonstressful environment for human use. Some areas of fit are physiological, psychological, sensual, and cultural.

## ANTHROPOMETRICS AND ERGONOMICS

The field of anthropometrics provides information about the dimension and functional capacity of the human body. *Static anthropometrics* measures the body at rest; *dynamic anthropometrics* measures the body while performing activities defined as "work." Dimensional variation occurs in anthropometric data because of the large range of diversity in the human population. To utilize anthropometric charts effectively, a designer must identify where a subject user group falls in relationship to these variables. The factors that cause human variations are gender, age, ethnicity, and race. Patterns of growth affected by human culture cause variation in human measure as well. Percentiles that refer to the frequency of occurrence describe dimensional variation on anthropometric charts: that is, the mean percentile (50%), the small extreme percentile (2.5%), and the large extreme percentile (97.5%).

Ergonomics is the application of human factors data to design. This term was coined by the U.S. army when it began to design machines to fit humans, rather than trying to find humans to fit machines.

## HUMAN BEHAVIOR

Human behavior is motivated by innate attributes such as the five senses and by learned cultural attributes. Each human has a unique innate capacity to gather sensual information. How that information is understood is determined by personal and cultural experience.

*Proxemics* is the study of human behavior as it relates to learned cultural behavior. Human behavior is motivated by the innate nature of the animal, and this behavior is expressed and modified by each person's learned culture and traditions.

### Innate Human Attributes

The five senses determine human comfort levels in the environment and are a part of human factors studies.

- *Sight.* Behavioral scientists agree that, for human beings, seeing is the most engaged sense for gathering information. Physical form is perceived when visual data is organized into patterns, and that data is integrated with memories and emotions. Visual form is perceived as having a context with boundaries. Visual form can be understood to be a dynamic system of directional lines of forces that are innate, kinetic, and independent of the representational content of a form. Once a form's attributes have been perceived, humans tend to give the perceived form symbolic meaning. This meaning is cultural and personal, resulting from associations and past experiences.

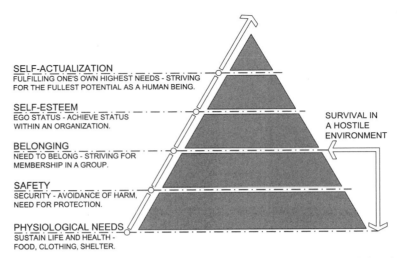

Maslow's diagram attempts to explain human behavior motivated by innate drives. It is a theoretical model that describes human needs and motivations. This "need hierarchy system" is presented as a constantly evolving process, such that when a person satisfies one need, another presents itself, and the individual will be driven to satisfy that set of needs. This is a nonlinear process. Most building programming efforts focus on human behavior that addresses the areas of belonging, self-esteem, and self-actualization.

**HIERARCHY OF NEEDS (AFTER MASLOW)** *Source: Forrest Wilson,* A Graphic Survey of Perception and Behavior for the Design Professions; *New York: Van Nostrand Reinhold, 1984 (p.163).*

- *Touch.* Touch is essential to human development and growth. Texture is learned most completely through skin contact. Human skin is sensitive to temperature, pain, and pressure. Vision and touch are interwoven in sighted humans. Memory of tactile experiences allows humans to understand their environment through visual scanning.
- *Hearing.* Humans can use hearing to determine distances. Sound moves in concentric circles and in horizontal and vertical planes. The ear transmits these airborne vibrations to the brain where it is processed and assigned meaning. The ability to focus hearing is called *sensory gating*. The ability to gate sound varies, and diminishes with aging.
- *Smell and Taste.* Research about smell is difficult to conduct because human sensitivity to smell is highly variable over time and from person to person. A person's sense of smell to an odor can fatigue quickly during exposure. Smell is defined in terms of commonly perceived odors such as flowery, putrid, burned, resinous, and spice. Taste and smell are closely related in human experience.

## UNIVERSAL DESIGN

Good design that works with respect to human factors issues can result in *universal design*. Principles of universal design are:

- Equitable use
- Perceptible information
- Flexibility
- Tolerance of error
- Simple and intuitive use
- Low physical effort

Universal design differs from *accessible design*. Universal design functions equally well for as inclusive a group of users as is possible; accessible design addresses the requirements of only one user group, people with disabilities. By limiting the user group description, accessible design can be exclusive and can segregate people with disabilities from others.

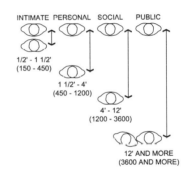

**DISTANCE RELATIONSHIPS AMONG PEOPLE**

## DISTANCE RELATIONSHIPS

Some aspects of human behavior related to territoriality are cultural. The space between objects has form but the space between people is kinetic. The dimension of human territoriality varies in dimension due to cultural forces.

- *Defensible space* occurs when designed form reinforces meaning for the user and where boundary and ownership are visible in public space.
- *Intimate space* is where lovers, family, small children, and close friends are allowed to enter.
- *Personal space* is a protected area where strangers are not welcome.
- *Social space* is a range of space in which most public interactions occur. Speech and expression are clear and communications are efficient and accurate.
- *Public distance* is the range of space where it is not considered rude to ignore someone; and it does not allow interaction.

*Faith Baum, AIA, IIDA; Faith Baum Architect; Lexington, Massachusetts*

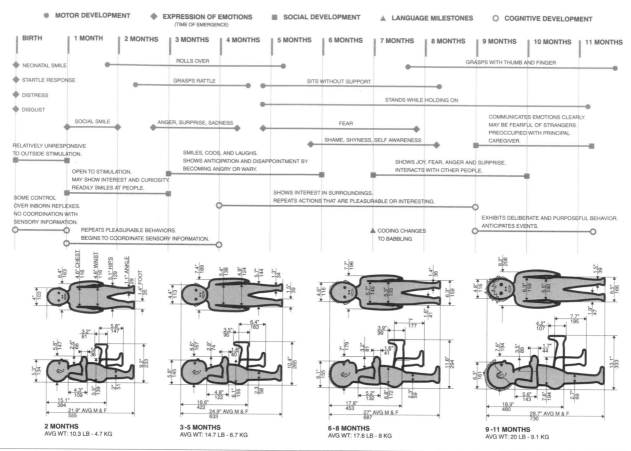

**MEASURE AND DEVELOPMENT OF INFANTS—BIRTH TO 11 MONTHS**

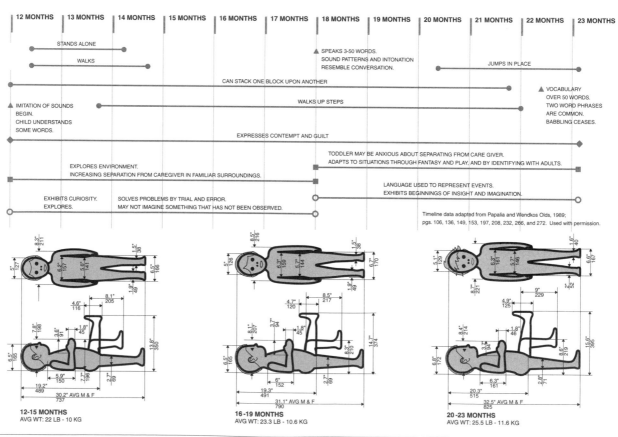

**MEASURE AND DEVELOPMENT OF INFANTS—12 TO 23 MONTHS**

1    ☐    **HUMAN FACTORS**

*Henry Dreyfuss Associates, The Measure of Man & Woman (Alvin R. Tilley, Ed.). John Wiley & Sons, Inc., New York. 2001.*

● MOTOR DEVELOPMENT   ■ SOCIAL DEVELOPMENT   ▲ LANGUAGE MILESTONES   ○ COGNITIVE DEVELOPMENT

**2.5 - 3 YEARS**

● CANNOT TURN OR STOP SUDDENLY OR QUICKLY

● CAN JUMP A DISTANCE OF 15 TO 24 INCHES

● CAN ASCEND STAIRWAYS UNAIDED, ALTERNATING THE FEET

BEGINNINGS OF CONVERSATION; BREAKTHROUGH IN ATTENTION TO COMMUNICATION.

▲ NEW WORDS ARE LEARNED ALMOST EVERY DAY.
COMPREHENSION IS EXCELLENT, ALTHOUGH CHILD
STILL MAKES MANY MISTAKES IN GRAMMAR.

**4 YEARS**
**GIRLS TALLER THAN BOYS**

● MORE EFFECTIVE CONTROL OF STOPPING, STARTING, AND TURNING

● CAN JUMP A DISTANCE OF 24 OR 33 INCHES

● CAN DESCEND LONG STAIRWAYS ALTERNATING THE FEET, IF SUPPORTED

CHILD THINKS THAT HIS OR HER POINT OF VIEW IS THE ONLY ONE POSSIBLE

▲ VOCABULARY REACHES 1,000 WORDS, ABOUT 80% ARE INTELLIGIBLE.
GRAMMAR IS CLOSE TO ADULT SPEECH, AND SYNTACTIC MISTAKES ARE FEWER.

GROUNDWORK FOR LOGICAL THINKING: CHILDREN CAN THINK ABOUT OBJECTS, PEOPLE, OR EVENTS IN THEIR ABSENCE
BY USING MENTAL REPRESENTATIONS OF THEM, BUT THEY CANNOT YET MANIPULATE THESE REPRESENTATIONS.

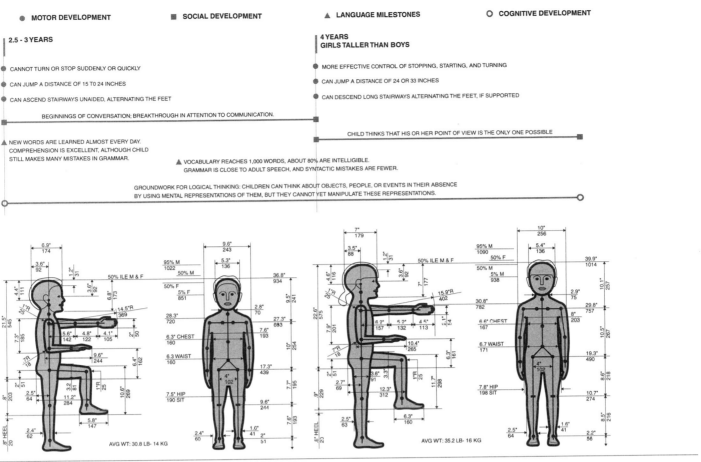

**MEASURE AND DEVELOPMENT OF TODDLERS—2.5 TO 4 YEARS**

**5 YEARS**

● CAN START, TURN, AND STOP EFFECTIVELY IN GAMES

● CAN MAKE A RUNNING JUMP OF 28 TO 38 INCHES

● CAN DESCEND LONG STAIRWAYS UNAIDED, ALTERNATING THE FEET

**6 YEARS**

● GIRLS ARE SUPERIOR IN ACCURACY OF MOVEMENT.
BOYS ARE SUPERIOR IN FORCEFUL, LESS COMPLEX ACTS.

● CAN THROW WITH PROPER WEIGHT SHIFT AND STOP

CHILD THINKS THAT HIS OR HER OWN POINT OF VIEW IS THE ONLY ONE POSSIBLE

CHILD LEARNS NOT ONLY BY SENSING AND DOING, BUT BY THINKING AS WELL.
BASIC UNDERSTANDING OF CAUSE AND EFFECT.

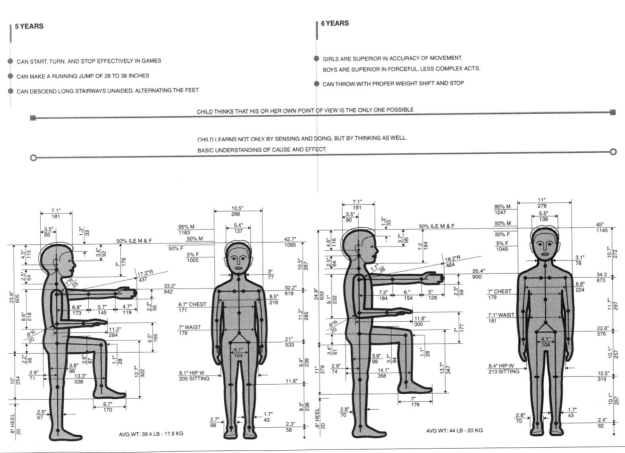

**MEASURE AND DEVELOPMENT OF YOUTHS—5 TO 6 YEARS**

*Henry Dreyfuss Associates, The Measure of Man & Woman
(Alvin R. Tilley, Ed.). John Wiley & Sons, Inc., New York. 2001.*

● MOTOR DEVELOPMENT ■ SOCIAL DEVELOPMENT ○ COGNITIVE DEVELOPMENT

**7 YEARS**

● BALANCING ON ONE FOOT WITHOUT LOOKING BECOMES POSSIBLE
● CAN HOP AND JUMP ACCURATELY INTO SMALL SQUARES
● CAN ACCURATELY PERFORM JUMPING JACK EXERCISES

**8 YEARS**

● GRIP STRENGTH PERMITS STEADY 12-POUND PRESSURE
● GIRLS CAN THROW A SMALL BALL 40 FEET

■ CHILD REALIZES THAT OTHERS MAY INTERPRET A SITUATION IN A WAY DIFFERENT FROM HIS OR HER OWN

○ CHILDREN CAN THINK LOGICALLY ABOUT "HERE & NOW", BUT NOT YET ABOUT ABSTRACTIONS

AVG WT: 50.4 LB - 22.9 KG

AVG WT: 56.1 LB - 25.5 KG

**MEASURE AND DEVELOPMENT OF YOUTHS—7 TO 8 YEARS**

**9 YEARS**

● GIRLS CAN JUMP VERTICALLY TO A HEIGHT OF 8 1/2 INCHES; BOYS, 10 INCHES
● BOYS CAN RUN 16 1/2 FEET PER SECOND
● BOYS CAN THROW A BALL 70 FEET

**10 YEARS**

● CAN JUDGE AND INTERCEPT PATHWAYS OF SMALL BALLS THROWN FROM A DISTANCE
● GIRLS CAN RUN 17 FEET PER SECOND

■ CHILD HAS RECIPROCAL AWARENESS, REALIZES OTHERS HAVE A POINT OF VIEW AND THAT OTHERS ARE AWARE THAT HE OR SHE HAS A PARTICULAR POINT OF VIEW.

■ CHILD UNDERSTANDS IMPORTANCE OF LETTING OTHERS KNOW THAT THEIR REQUESTS HAVE NOT BEEN IGNORED OR FORGOTTEN.

○ GAINING PROFICIENCY AT CLASSIFYING, MANIPULATING NUMBERS, DEALING WITH CONCEPTS OF TIME AND SPACE, AND DISTINGUISHING REALITY FROM FANTASY

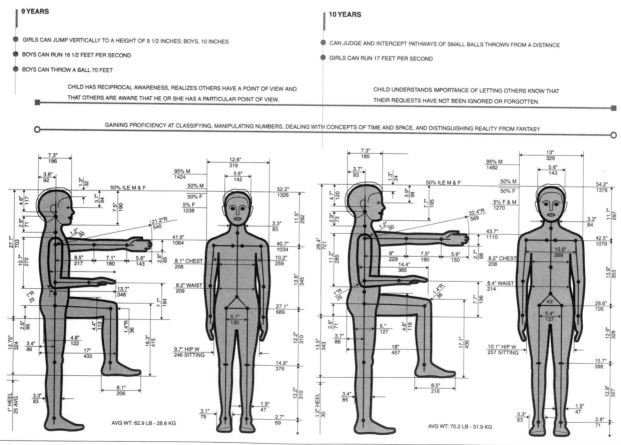

AVG WT: 62.9 LB - 28.6 KG

AVG WT: 70.2 LB - 31.9 KG

**MEASURE AND DEVELOPMENT OF YOUTHS—9 TO 10 YEARS**

*Henry Dreyfuss Associates, The Measure of Man & Woman (Alvin R. Tilley, Ed.). John Wiley & Sons, Inc., New York. 2001.*

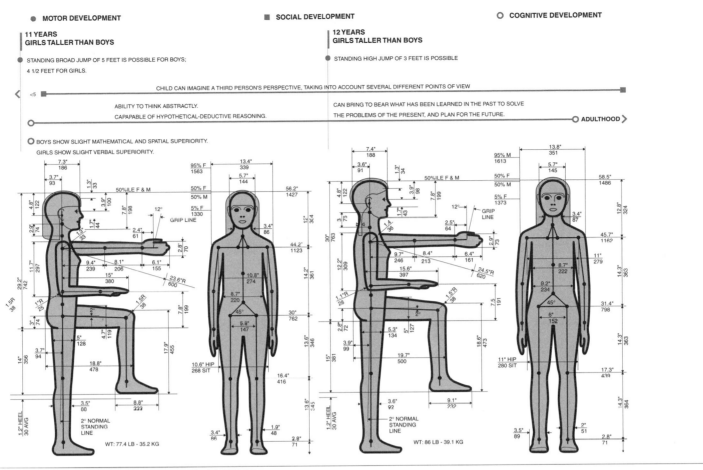

**MEASURE AND DEVELOPMENT OF YOUTHS—11 TO 12 YEARS**

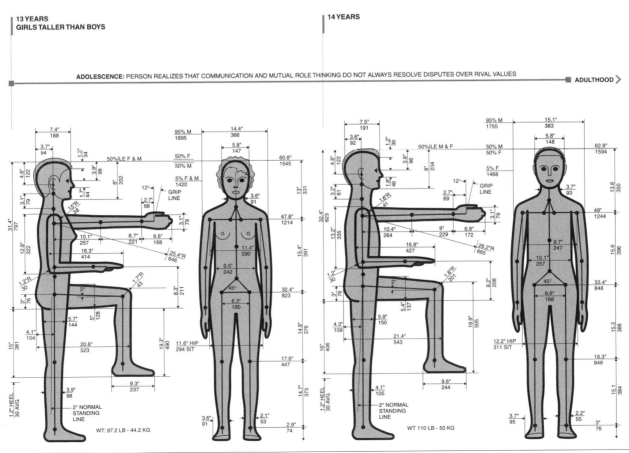

**MEASURE AND DEVELOPMENT OF YOUTHS—13 TO 14 YEARS**

*Henry Dreyfuss Associates*, The Measure of Man & Woman
*(Alvin R. Tilley, Ed.). John Wiley & Sons, Inc., New York. 2001.*

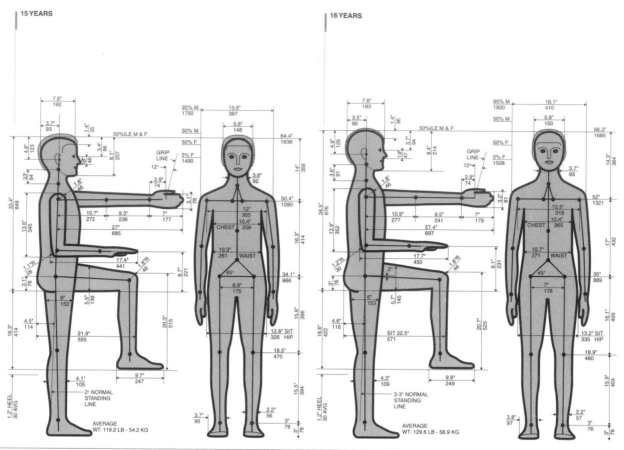

**MEASURE OF YOUTHS—15 TO 16 YEARS**

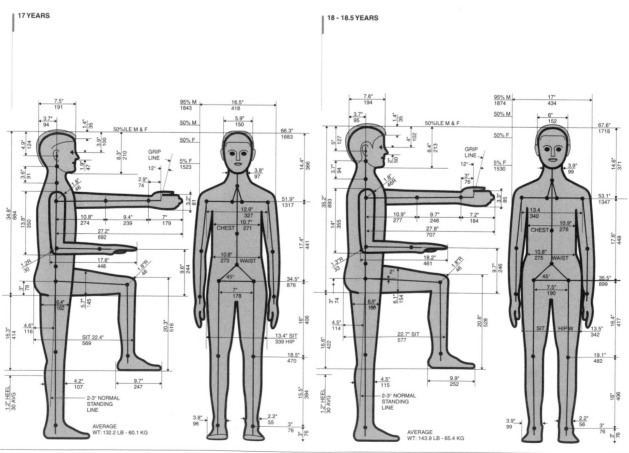

**MEASURE OF YOUTHS—17 TO 18.5 YEARS**

*Henry Dreyfuss Associates,* The Measure of Man & Woman
*(Alvin R. Tilley, Ed.). John Wiley & Sons, Inc., New York. 2001.*

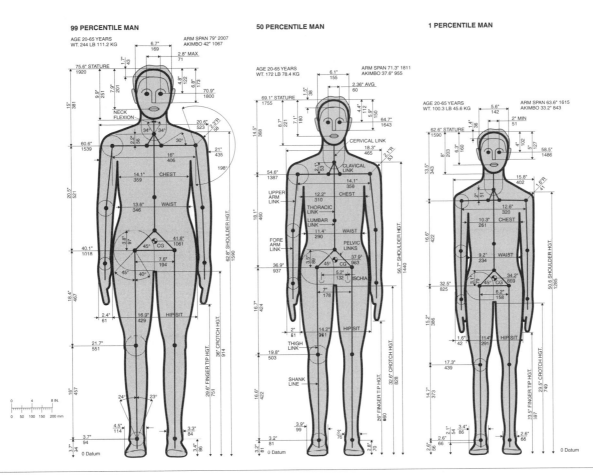

**MEASURE OF MAN—FRONT VIEW**

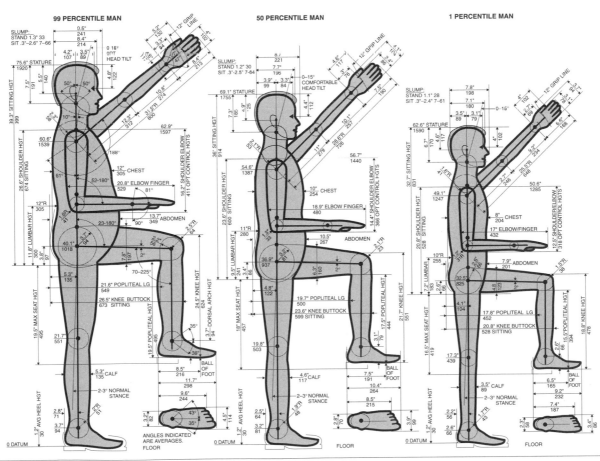

**MEASURE OF MAN—SIDE VIEW**

*Henry Dreyfuss Associates,* The Measure of Man & Woman *(Alvin R. Tilley, Ed.). John Wiley & Sons, Inc., New York. 2001.*

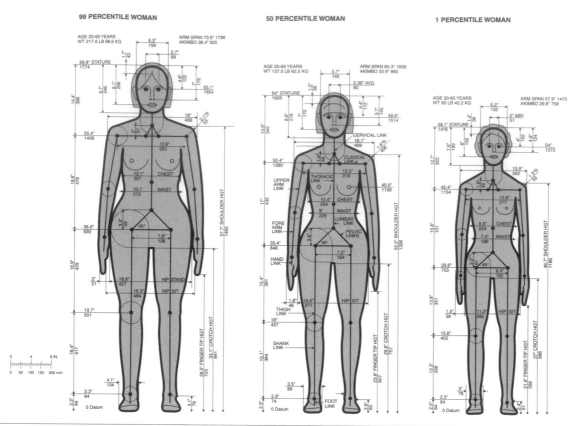

**MEASURE OF WOMAN—FRONT VIEW**

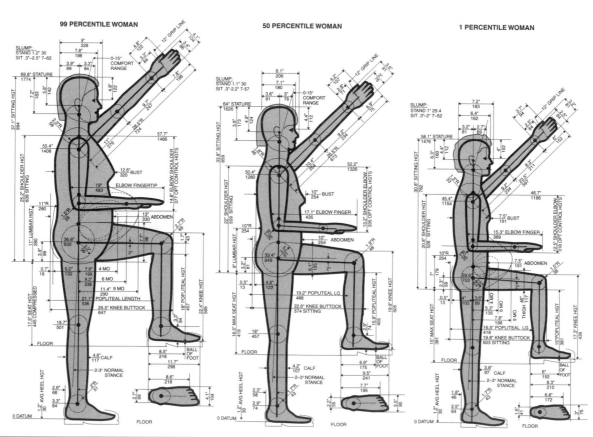

**MEASURE OF WOMAN—SIDE VIEW**

*Henry Dreyfuss Associates, The Measure of Man & Woman
(Alvin R. Tilley, Ed.). John Wiley & Sons, Inc., New York. 2001.*

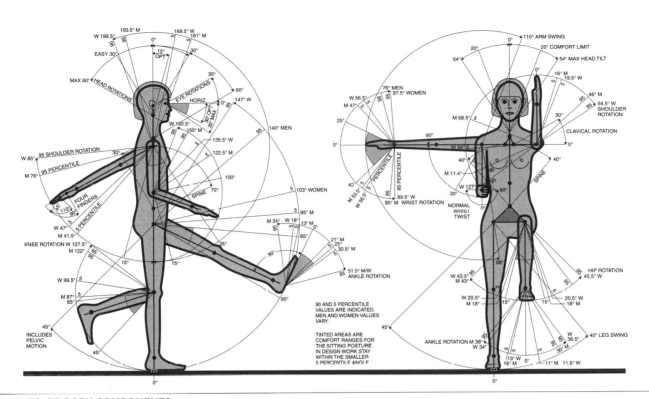

**ANGLE MOVEMENTS OF BODY COMPONENTS**

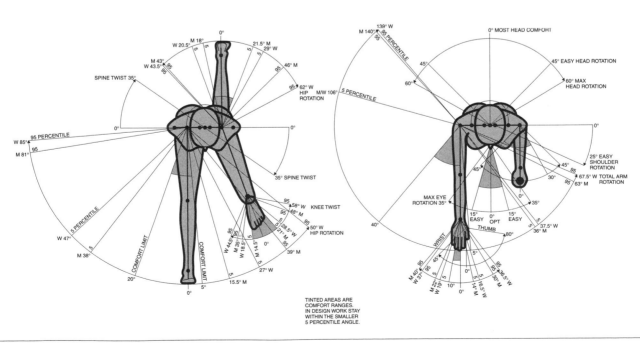

**ANGLE MOVEMENTS OF BODY COMPONENTS—TOP VIEW**

*Henry Dreyfuss Associates,* The Measure of Man & Woman
*(Alvin R. Tilley, Ed.). John Wiley & Sons, Inc., New York. 2001.*

# ACCESSIBILITY

## DEFINITION

*Accessible* is a design term that was first introduced in the 1950s to describe elements of the physical environment that can be used by people with disabilities. Originally, the term described facilities that could be accessed by wheelchair users, but it has evolved to include designs for a wider group of people with more diverse functional requirements.

Society's need for accessible design has increased as a result of continuing medical advances. Concurrently, the development of new building technologies, such as residential elevators, wheelchair lifts, and power door operators, has made the provision of accessible facilities more practical and less expensive.

From a designer's perspective, there is a difference between appropriate accessible design for public facilities and the best approach for private, custom-accessible projects. Public accessibility standards establish general design specifications that broadly meet the targeted population's needs. By contrast, custom-accessible design should address the specific needs of an individual user.

## REGULATORY HISTORY

The American National Standards Institute (ANSI) published the first national standards for accessible design in 1961. After its initial publication, many state and local jurisdictions began to adopt ANSI A117.1, *Accessible and Usable Buildings and Facilities,* as their accessibility code, although they often modified selected standards to suit their communities. ANSI has periodically revised the A117.1 standard since it was first published. In 1980, it was expanded to include housing standards focused primarily on the needs of wheelchair users (specifically paraplegics).

The 1968 Architectural Barriers Act was the first federal legislation that required accessible design in federal facilities. To address the absence of federal accessibility standards and the lack of an enforcement mechanism, Congress enacted the 1973 Rehabilitation Act. In addition, the act required facilities built with federal funds, and facilities built by entities that receive federal funds, to be accessible.

Section 502 of the 1973 Rehabilitation Act created a new federal agency, the Architectural and Transportation Barriers Compliance Board (ATBCB) to develop and issue minimum guidelines for design standards to be established by four standard-setting agencies. In 1984, the ATBCB issued the Uniform Federal Accessibility Standards (UFAS), which were established by the Department of Defense (DoD), the Department of Housing and Urban Development (HUD), the General Services Administration (GSA), and the U.S. Postal Service (USPS). UFAS is similar to the format and content of ANSI A117.1, 1980.

In 1988, Congress enacted the Fair Housing Amendments Act (FHAA). Although the act's guidelines include design requirements, it is a civil rights law, not a building code. Two years later, in 1990, President George Bush signed the Americans with Disabilities Act (ADA). This landmark legislation provided new civil rights protections for people with disabilities, and its guidelines included new federal accessibility stan-

**FHAG: FAIR HOUSING ACCESSIBILITY GUIDELINES**

**UFAS: UNIFORM FEDERAL ACCESSIBILITY STANDARDS**

**ADAAG: AMERICANS WITH DISABILITIES ACT ARCHITECTURAL GUIDELINES (TITLE III)**

**CABO/ANSI: AMERICAN NATIONAL STANDARDS INSTITUTE A117.1**

**SBCCI: SOUTHERN BUILDING CODE CONGRESS INTERNATIONAL**

**BOCA: BUILDING OFFICIALS AND CODE ADMINISTRATORS INTERNATIONAL**

dards. ADA addresses the design and operation of privately owned public accommodations and state and local government facilities and programs. ADA design standards are very similar to the 1986 ANSI standards. ADA did not include housing design requirements because they were addressed in the earlier Fair Housing Amendments Act.

## CIVIL RIGHTS LAWS AND BUILDING CODES

Enactment of the 1988 Fair Housing Amendments Act and 1990 Americans with Disabilities Act created a complex relationship between federal laws and the local building codes that already existed throughout the United States. Although many of the accessible design requirements in the civil rights laws and the codes are similar, there are major differences.

Building codes are specific to a legal jurisdiction, such as a state, county, township, or city. These state/local regulations are usually based on national model codes (BOCA, UBC, SBCCI, IBC) that a jurisdiction elects to adopt. The state and local jurisdictions typically modify the model codes and, as part of their review and enforcement process, make administrative rulings and interpretations. Over time, these modifications and interpretations make the design requirements of each municipality unique even though the underlying code is based on a national model.

Building officials use local codes to review architectural and engineering plans before they permit construction.

They also perform on-site inspections to verify that the completed construction is in compliance.

Unlike municipal officials, federal agencies do not issue building permits and typically do not inspect construction. Neither does the federal government issue rulings or interpretations for individual projects. Civil rights law enforcement is a "complaint-based process" that HUD administers for Fair Housing, and the Department of Justice administers for ADA. These agencies may choose to act on a citizen complaint, or a complainant may elect to seek direct relief through federal courts.

As civil rights laws, Fair Housing and ADA include both provisions both for facility design and construction and for facility operation and management. Provisions that address operation and management create new legal responsibilities that are shared between facility designers and facility operators.

Terminology common to both civil rights law and building code standards can be confusing because the same words often have different meanings. The term *dwelling,* for example, has a much different meaning in the Fair Housing design guidelines than it does in building codes. Similarly, building use and occupancy categories such as *transient lodging* and *assembly areas* (places of assembly) are not consistent between ADA and the building codes. Because designers must deal with both types of standards, they should carefully review the definitions included in each.

## MANEUVERING CLEARANCES

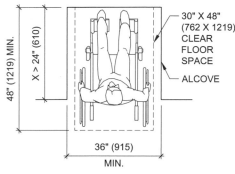

30" X 48" (762 X 1219) CLEAR FLOOR SPACE

ALCOVE

48" (1219) MIN.

X > 24" (610)

36" (915) MIN.

**FORWARD APPROACH—ALCOVE**

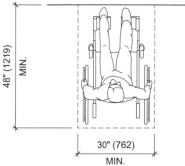

48" (1219) MIN.

30" (762) MIN.

**FORWARD**

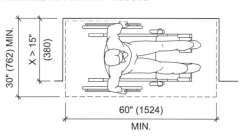

30" (762) MIN.

X > 15" (380)

60" (1524) MIN.

**PARALLEL APPROACH—ALCOVE**

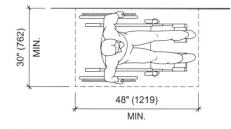

30" (762) MIN.

48" (1219) MIN.

**PARALLEL**

## MANEUVERING CLEARANCES

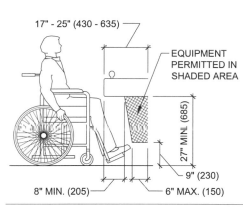

17" - 25" (430 - 635)

EQUIPMENT PERMITTED IN SHADED AREA

27" MIN. (685)

9" (230)

8" MIN. (205)

6" MAX. (150)

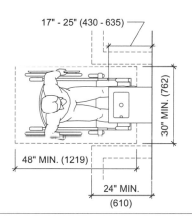

17" - 25" (430 - 635)

30" MIN. (762)

48" MIN. (1219)

24" MIN. (610)

**SAMPLE MANEUVERING CLEARANCES—DRINKING FOUNTAIN**

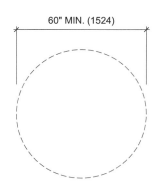

60" MIN. (1524)

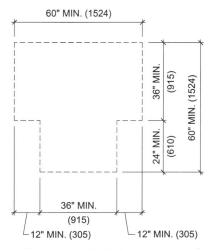

60" MIN. (1524)

36" MIN. (915)

60" MIN. (1524)

24" MIN. (610)

36" MIN. (915)

12" MIN. (305)

12" MIN. (305)

Knee and toe clearance can be included as part of the wheelchair turning space and clear floor space at accessible elements. However, the extent and location of knee and toe clearance can affect the usability of the space.

Knee and toe clearance that is included as part of a T-shaped turning space should be provided only at the base of the T or on one arm of the T. In some configurations, the obstruction of part of the T-shape may make it impossible for a wheelchair user to maneuver to the desired location.

## WHEELCHAIR TURNING SPACE

*Lawrence G. Perry, AIA; Silver Spring, Maryland*

---

THIS AREA MAY BE USED AS PART OF MANEUVERING CLEARANCE OR WHEELCHAIR TURNING SPACE

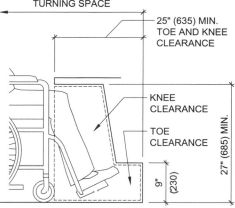

25" (635) MIN. TOE AND KNEE CLEARANCE

KNEE CLEARANCE

TOE CLEARANCE

27" (685) MIN.

9" (230)

**MAXIMUM CLEARANCE**
Additional space can be provided beneath the table, desk, or other element, but that space is not considered knee and toe clearance.

THIS AREA MAY BE USED AS PART OF MANEUVERING CLEARANCE OR WHEELCHAIR TURNING SPACE

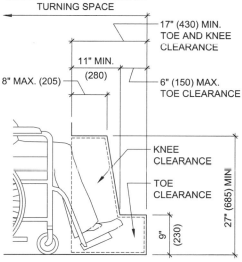

17" (430) MIN. TOE AND KNEE CLEARANCE

11" MIN. (280)

8" MAX. (205)

6" (150) MAX. TOE CLEARANCE

KNEE CLEARANCE

TOE CLEARANCE

27" (685) MIN.

9" (230)

**MINIMUM CLEARANCE**
Clearances shown are required at specific accessible elements. Knee and toe clearance must always be at least 30 in. (762 mm) wide.

THIS AREA MAY BE USED AS PART OF MANEUVERING CLEARANCE OR WHEELCHAIR TURNING SPACE

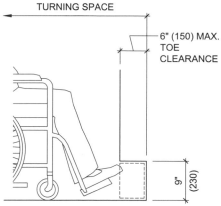

6" (150) MAX. TOE CLEARANCE

9" (230)

**TOE CLEARANCE ONLY**

## KNEE AND TOE CLEARANCES

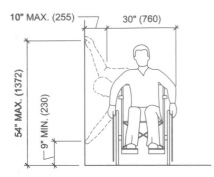

**HIGH AND LOW SIDE REACH LIMITS**

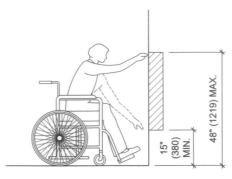

**UNOBSTRUCTED FORWARD REACH**

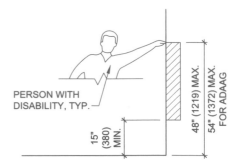

PERSON WITH DISABILITY, TYP.

**UNOBSTRUCTED SIDE REACH**

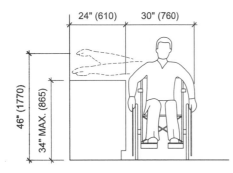

**MAXIMUM SIDE REACH OVER OBSTRUCTION**

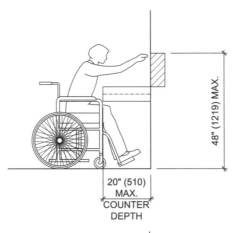

20" (510) MAX. COUNTER DEPTH

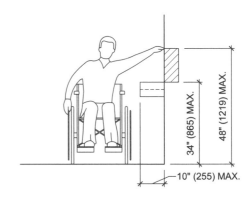

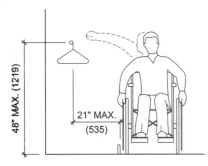

**CLOSET**

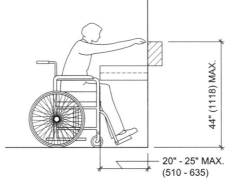

**UNOBSTRUCTED HIGH FORWARD REACH**

ANSI A117.1 provides exception for existing elements located 54 in. (1,372 mm) maximum above the floor or ground.

A117.1 provides exception for elevator car controls, allowing buttons at 54 in. (1,372 mm) maximum, where the elevator serves more than 16 openings.

A117.1 does not apply the 48-in. (1,219-mm) restriction to tactile signs. Tactile signs must be installed so

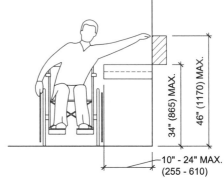

**OBSTRUCTED SIDE REACH**

the tactile characters are between 48 and 60 in. (1,219 and 1,524 mm) above the floor.

FHAG allows inaccessible controls in covered dwelling units if "comparable" accessible controls are provided.

Floor outlets are permitted if an adequate number of accessible wall outlets isare provided.

Electric outlets above kitchen counters can be located in corners, provided additional outlets are located within reach.

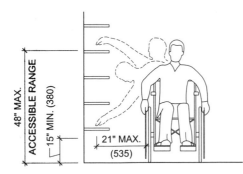

**SHELVES**

Accessible controls and operating mechanisms should be operable with one hand and not require tight grasping, pinching, or twisting of the wrist, with the following exception: FHAG does not regulate the operating force or type of operation required for controls and operating mechanisms in dwelling units.

**PARALLEL/SIDE REACH LIMITS**

**REACH RANGES**

**SPECIFICATIONS FOR WATER CLOSETS SERVING CHILDREN**

| DIMENSION | PRE-K–K (AGES 3 AND 4) IN. (MM) | GRADES 1ST–3RD (AGES 5-8) IN. (MM) | GRADES 4TH–7TH (AGES 9-12) IN. (MM) |
|---|---|---|---|
| Water closet centerline | 12 (305) | 12–15 (305–380) | 15–18 (380–455) |
| Toilet seat height | 11–12 (280–305) | 12–15 (305–380) | 15–17 (380–430) |
| Grab bar height | 18–20 (455–510) | 20–25 (510–635) | 25–27 (635–685) |
| Dispenser height | 14 (355) | 14–17 (355–430) | 17–19 (430–485) |

**CHILDREN'S REACH RANGES FROM A WHEELCHAIR**

| FORWARD OR SIDE REACH | AGES 3 AND 4 IN. (MM) | AGES 5-8 IN. (MM) | AGES 9-12 IN. (MM) |
|---|---|---|---|
| Maximum | 36 (915) | 40 (1,015) | 44 (1,120) |
| Minimum | 20 (510) | 18 (455) | 16 (405) |

*Lawrence G. Perry, AIA; Silver Spring, Maryland*

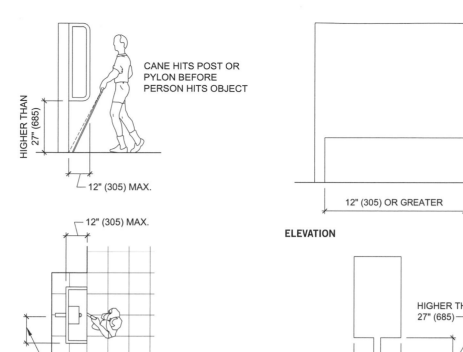

CANE HITS POST OR PYLON BEFORE PERSON HITS OBJECT

HIGHER THAN 27" (685)

12" (305) MAX.

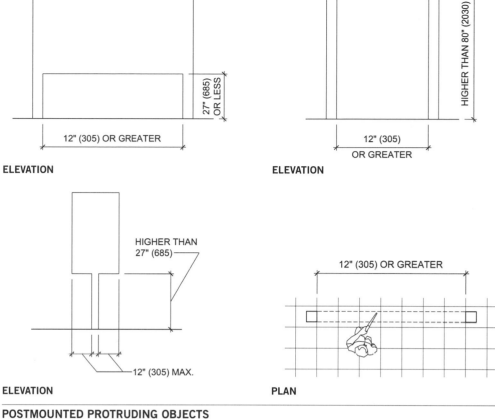

27" (685) OR LESS

12" (305) OR GREATER

**ELEVATION**

HIGHER THAN 80" (2030)

12" (305) OR GREATER

**ELEVATION**

12" (305) MAX.

THIS OVERHANG CAN BE GREATER THAN 12" (305) BECAUSE THE OBJECT CANNOT BE APPROACHED FROM THIS DIRECTION

**OBJECTS MOUNTED ON POSTS OR PYLONS**

**FREESTANDING OBJECTS**

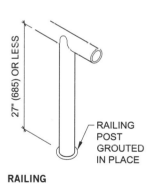

HIGHER THAN 27" (685)

12" (305) MAX.

**ELEVATION**

12" (305) OR GREATER

**PLAN**

**POSTMOUNTED PROTRUDING OBJECTS**

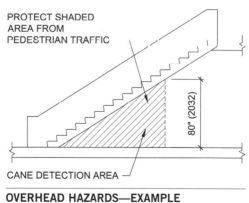
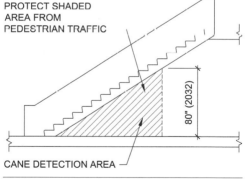

PROTECT SHADED AREA FROM PEDESTRIAN TRAFFIC

80" (2032)

CANE DETECTION AREA

**OVERHEAD HAZARDS—EXAMPLE**

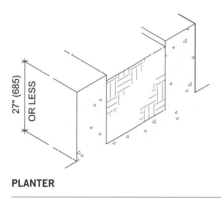

27" (685) OR LESS

27" (685) OR LESS

RAILING POST GROUTED IN PLACE

**PLANTER**   **RAILING**

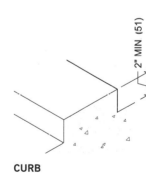

2" MIN (51)

**CURB**

**OVERHEAD HAZARD PROTECTION—EXAMPLES**

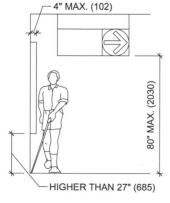

4" MAX. (102)

80" MAX. (2030)

HIGHER THAN 27" (685)

**WALKING PARALLEL TO A WALL**

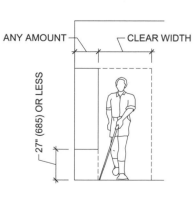

ANY AMOUNT    CLEAR WIDTH

27" (685) OR LESS

**WALKING PARALLEL TO A WALL**

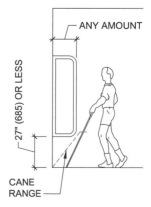

ANY AMOUNT

27" (685) OR LESS

CANE RANGE

**WALKING PERPENDICULAR TO A WALL**

**DIMENSIONS OF PROTRUDING OBJECTS**

## PROTRUDING OBJECTS

Wall sconces, fire alarm appliances, environmental controls, door hardware, signs, and suspended lighting fixtures are examples of protruding objects.

Some standards specify the extent to which doorstops and door closers may protrude into the 80-in. (2,032-mm) vertical clearance, generally allowing a 2-in. (51-mm) maximum projection.

Protruding objects are not permitted to reduce the required width of an accessible route (36 in. (915 mm), with this exception: a 32-in. (813-mm) width is permitted for a 24-in. (6,100-mm) length).

*Lawrence G. Perry;, AIA; Silver Spring, Maryland*

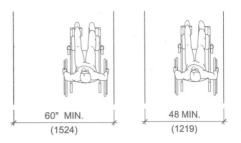

| 60" MIN. (1524) | 48 MIN. (1219) |
|---|---|
| **TWO WHEELCHAIRS** | **ONE WHEELCHAIR AND ONE AMBULATORY PERSON** |

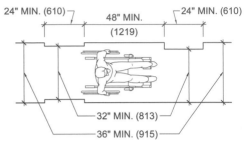

**SINGLE WHEELCHAIR**

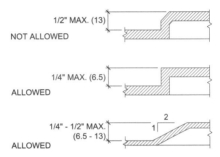

**CHANGES IN LEVEL**

Changes in level greater than ½ in. (13 mm) must be ramped. Some standards prohibit changes in level in clear floor space, maneuvering clearances, wheelchair turning space, and access aisles.

## CLEAR WIDTH OF AN ACCESSIBLE ROUTE

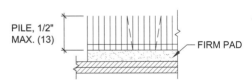

**CARPET ON FLOOR OR GROUND SURFACES**

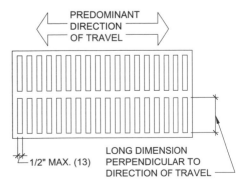

**OPENING IN FLOOR OR GROUND SURFACES**

All surfaces must be firm, stable, and slip-resistant. Other openings, such as in wood decking or ornamental gratings, must be designed so that a ½-in. (13-mm) diameter sphere cannot pass through the opening. The potential for wood shrinkage should be considered.

## FLOOR AND GROUND SURFACES

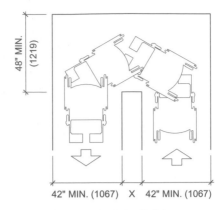

42" MIN. (1067)   X   42" MIN. (1067)

**U-TURN AROUND AN OBSTRUCTION**

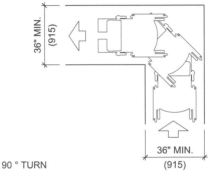

90 ° TURN          36" MIN. (915)

Dimensions shown apply when *X* is less than 48 in. (1,219 mm).

## TURNS

## REQUIREMENTS FOR INTERIOR ACCESSIBLE ROUTES

Accessible routes are generally required as follows:

*Multilevel buildings and facilities:* Required between all levels, including mezzanines, in multistory buildings, unless exempted.

- *ADA elevator exception:* Buildings with only two floors are exempt from providing an accessible route to the upper or lower level. Buildings with less than 3,000 sq ft (279 sq m) per floor, regardless of height, are exempt from providing an accessible route to upper or lower floor levels. Neither exception applies to shopping centers, offices of professional health care providers, public transportation terminals, or state and local government facilities.
- *Building code elevator exception:* Model building codes generally exempt a maximum aggregate area of 3,000 sq ft (279 sq m), regardless of the number of levels. Similar to the ADA restrictions, this exception cannot be used in offices of health care providers, passenger transportation facilities, or mercantile occupancies with multiple tenants. Consult the applicable local code.

*FHAG elevator requirements:* Required for buildings containing dwelling units, and not public or common-use spaces, FHAG does not require accessible routes to all levels. Instead, the existence or lack of an elevator determines the extent of units covered. When elevators are provided, they generally must serve all

floors; an exception is provided for elevators serving only as a means of access from a garage to a single floor. When elevators are not provided, only the "ground floor" units are subject to the FHAG requirements. In mixed-use construction, an accessible route is required to the first level containing dwelling units, regardless of its location. Consult FHAG for specific requirements.

*Levels not containing accessible elements or spaces:* For facilities in which only a percentage of the spaces provided are required to be accessible (assembly, residential, institutional, and storage), the model codes do not require an accessible route to serve levels not containing required accessible spaces. Separate requirements for dispersion of accessible elements and spaces may still require multiple accessible levels. Consult the applicable local code.

*Accessible spaces and elements:* To all spaces and elements that are required to be accessible.

- *Toilet rooms and bathrooms:* ADA generally requires that all toilet and bathing rooms be accessible. This does not trigger a requirement for accessible routes if the floor level is not otherwise required to have an accessible route.
- *Alterations:* ADA and the model building codes generally do not require that altered elements trigger a requirement for accessible routes to the elements, unless covered under specific "primary function" requirements. Consult ADA and the applicable local code.

## COMPONENTS OF ACCESSIBLE ROUTES

Accessible routes are permitted to include the following elements: (1) walking surfaces with a slope of less than 1:20, (2) curb ramps, (3) ramps, (4) elevators, and (5) platform (wheelchair) lifts. The use of lifts in new construction is limited to locations where they are specifically permitted by the applicable regulations. Lifts are generally permitted to be used as part of an accessible route in alterations.

Each component has specific technical criteria that must be applied for use as part of an accessible route. Consult the applicable code or regulation.

## LOCATION OF ACCESSIBLE ROUTES

Accessible routes must be located as follows:

*Interior routes:* Where an accessible route is required between floor levels, and the general circulation path between levels is an interior route, the accessible route should also be an interior route.

*Relation to circulation paths:* Accessible routes should "coincide with, or be located in the same area as, a general circulation path." Avoid making the accessible route a "second- class" means of circulation. Consult the applicable regulations for additional specific requirements regarding location of accessible routes.

Where the accessible route departs from the general circulation path, and is not easily identified, directional signs should be provided as necessary to indicate the accessible route.

*Lawrence G. Perry, AIA; Silver Spring, Maryland*

# ACCESSIBLE RAMPS

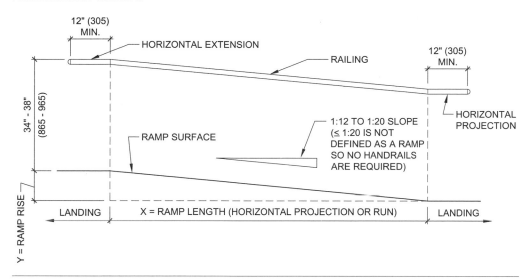

12" (305) MIN.
HORIZONTAL EXTENSION
RAILING
12" (305) MIN.
HORIZONTAL PROJECTION
1:12 TO 1:20 SLOPE (≤ 1:20 IS NOT DEFINED AS A RAMP SO NO HANDRAILS ARE REQUIRED)
RAMP SURFACE
34" - 38" (865 - 965)
Y = RAMP RISE
LANDING
X = RAMP LENGTH (HORIZONTAL PROJECTION OR RUN)
LANDING

## COMPONENTS OF A RAMP

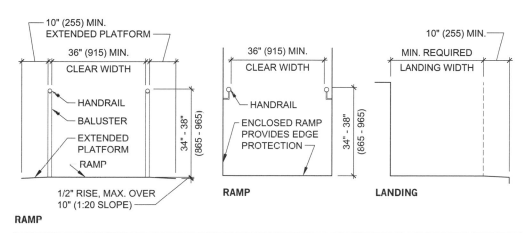

10" (255) MIN. EXTENDED PLATFORM
36" (915) MIN. CLEAR WIDTH
HANDRAIL
BALUSTER
EXTENDED PLATFORM
RAMP
1/2" RISE, MAX. OVER 10" (1:20 SLOPE)
34" - 38" (865 - 965)

**RAMP**

36" (915) MIN. CLEAR WIDTH
HANDRAIL
ENCLOSED RAMP PROVIDES EDGE PROTECTION
34" - 38" (865 - 965)

**RAMP**

10" (255) MIN.
MIN. REQUIRED LANDING WIDTH

**LANDING**

## RAMP AND RAMP LANDING EDGE

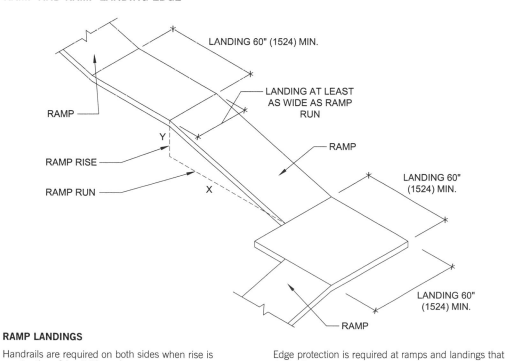

LANDING 60" (1524) MIN.
LANDING AT LEAST AS WIDE AS RAMP RUN
RAMP
RAMP
Y
RAMP RISE
RAMP RUN
X
LANDING 60" (1524) MIN.
LANDING 60" (1524) MIN.
RAMP

**RAMP LANDINGS**

Handrails are required on both sides when rise is greater than 6 in. (152 mm).

Edge protection is required at ramps and landings that drop off.

## RAMPS AND LANDINGS—SECTIONS

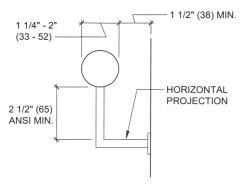

1 1/4" - 2" (33 - 52)
1 1/2" (38) MIN.
HORIZONTAL PROJECTION
2 1/2" (65) ANSI MIN.

**CIRCULAR**

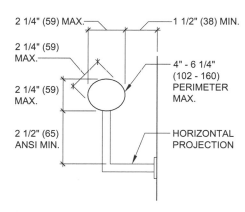

2 1/4" (59) MAX.
1 1/2" (38) MIN.
2 1/4" (59) MAX.
4" - 6 1/4" (102 - 160) PERIMETER MAX.
2 1/4" (59) MAX.
2 1/2" (65) ANSI MIN.
HORIZONTAL PROJECTION

**NONCIRCULAR**

Provide continuous handrails at both sides of ramps and stairs and at the inside handrail of switchback or dogleg ramps and stairs. If handrails are not continuous at bottom, top, or landings, provide handrail extensions as shown in the ramp and stair example; ends of handrails must be returned smoothly to floor, wall, or post.

## HANDRAIL DESIGN

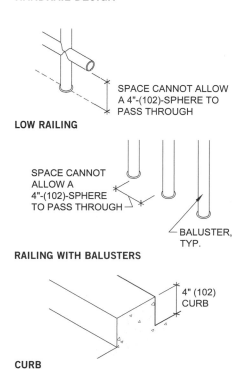

SPACE CANNOT ALLOW A 4"-(102)-SPHERE TO PASS THROUGH

**LOW RAILING**

SPACE CANNOT ALLOW A 4"-(102)-SPHERE TO PASS THROUGH
BALUSTER, TYP.

**RAILING WITH BALUSTERS**

4" (102) CURB

**CURB**

## RAMP AND RAMP LANDING EDGE PROTECTION DETAILS

*Lawrence G. Perry, AIA; Silver Spring, Maryland*

## RESIDENTIAL BEDS

For wheelchair users who can independently transfer themselves between bed and chair, bed heights should facilitate their access from a sitting position.

Quadriplegics or other wheelchair users who cannot independently transfer themselves between bed and chair are typically assisted by attendants, who use a portable lift mounted on a metal stand. The lift base typically requires approximately 8 in. (203 mm) of clearance under the bed.

## DRESSERS, CHESTS, AND CABINETS

Dressers and chests for wheelchair users should be situated so there is a clear access aisle of approximately 42 in. (1,067 mm) in front.

Cabinets, tables, stands, and other furniture with doors should have relatively narrow leaves so the arc of the swing when they are opened is small. This makes the leaf easier to operate without moving the wheelchair as the door is opened.

## DESKS, TABLES, AND WORKSTATIONS

Knee space is integral to the use of desks, tables, and workstations. Furniture must offer knee space that can accommodate the wheelchair in a position that places the user's legs fully beneath the horizontal surface and his or her upper body close to the front edge of the top.

The recommended minimum width for a knee space of 2 ft 6 in. (762 mm) requires an aisle of approximately 3 ft 4 in. (1,016 mm) in order for most wheelchairs to easily complete a 90° turn.

## CHAIRS

For ambulatory people who have difficulty maintaining their balance, chairs should be stable in order to provide support. Chairs equipped with armrests help ambulatory users to sit and rise, and are generally more comfortable to sit in. Chair leg supports and cross-bracing should not obstruct kick space below the seat. Kick space allows the chair occupant to position his or her feet partially beneath the body in order to rise.

Ergonomic work chairs allow many aspects of the chair, such as seat height and angle of incline, to be adjusted to suit each individual. Wheelchair users who transfer diagonally can use chairs with armrests, while those who transfer from a parallel position must have clear side access without fixed armrests.

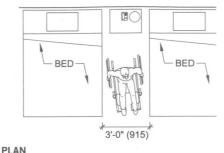

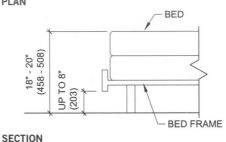

**PLAN**

**SECTION**

**BEDS**

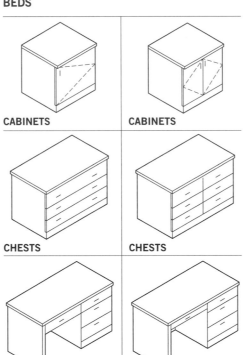

| CABINETS | CABINETS |
| CHESTS | CHESTS |
| DESKS | DESKS |
| **DIFFICULT TO OPERATE** | **EASY TO OPERATE** |

**FURNITURE OPERATION FOR ACCESSIBILITY**

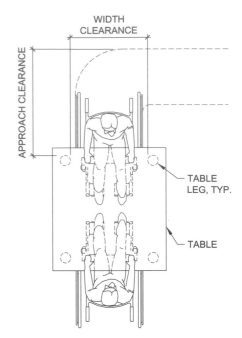

For knee space below a tabletop with a minimum width of 2 ft 6 in. (762 mm) between obstructions (e.g., table legs), the approach clearance should be 3 ft 6 in. (1,067 mm). A knee space width of 3 ft 0 in. (915 mm) or more should have an approach clearance of 3 ft 0 in. (915 mm).

**TABLE CLEARANCES**

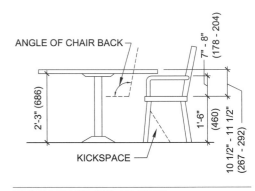

**CHAIR FOR DINING OR DESK**

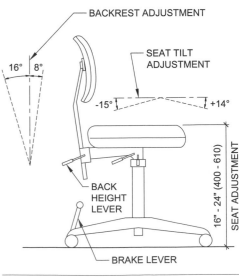

**ERGONOMIC WORKSTATION CHAIR**

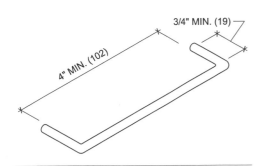

**ACCESSIBLE DRAWER PULL**

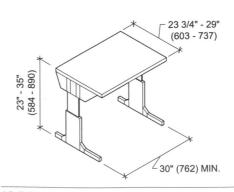

**ADJUSTABLE HEIGHT WORK SURFACE**

*Kim A. Beasley, AIA, and Thomas D. Davies, Jr., AIA; Paralyzed Veterans of America Architecture; Washington, D.C.*

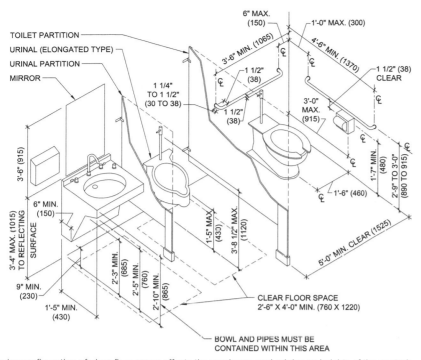

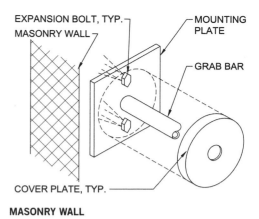

**MASONRY WALL**

The particular configuration of clear floor space affects the maximum and minimum heights of the controls. If the partition is greater than or equal to 2 ft 0 in. (610 mm) deep, urinal clear floor space must be 3 ft 0 in. (915 mm) wide. If less than 1 ft 5 in. (430 mm) deep, it may be 29 in. (737 mm) wide.

## LOCATION OF ACCESSIBLE FIXTURES AND ACCESSORIES

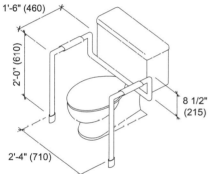

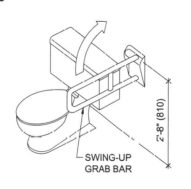

SWING-UP GRAB BAR

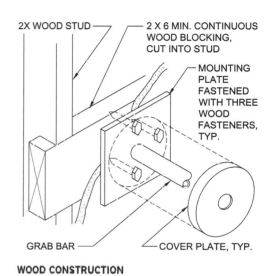

**WOOD CONSTRUCTION**

These configurations do not comply with UFAS or ADAAG.

## OPTIONAL GRAB BAR CONFIGURATIONS

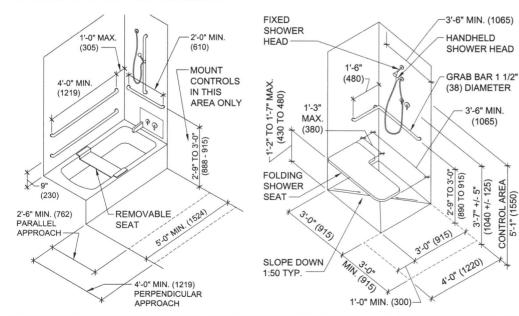

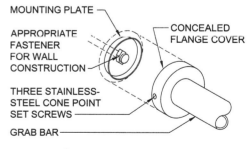

**CONCEALED FLANGE**

Size: 1½ in. (38 mm) or 1¼ in. (32 mm) O.D. with 1½ in. (38 mm) clearance at wall.

Material: Stainless steel or chrome-plated brass with knurled finish (optional).

Installation: Concealed or exposed fasteners; return all ends to the wall, intermediate supports at 3 ft 0 in. (915 mm) maximum. Use heavy-duty bars and methods of installation.

Other grab bars are available for particular situations.

Consult ANSI and ADAAG requirements, as well as applicable local and federal regulations.

## ACCESSIBLE BATHTUB AND SHOWER

## GRAB BAR ATTACHMENT DETAILS

*Mark J. Mazz, AIA; Hyattsville, Maryland*

## ACCESSIBLE TOILET ROOMS

All dimensional criteria on this page are based on ANSI A117.1, and on adult anthropometrics.

In new construction, all public and common- use toilet rooms are generally required to be accessible. Where multiple single-user toilet rooms or bathing rooms are clustered in a single location, and each serves the same population, only 5%, but not less than one, of the rooms must be accessible. The accessible room(s) must be identified by signs.

Single-user toilet and bathing rooms provided within a private office are permitted to be adaptable. Making the room accessible is permitted to involve replacement of the water closet and lavatory, changing the swing of the door, and installing grab bars in previously reinforced walls.

Doors are not permitted to swing into the required clear floor space at any fixture, except in single-user rooms, where a clear floor space is provided beyond the swing of the door.

### Unisex Toilets

Recent model codes require accessible unisex toilets in certain assembly and mercantile occupancies. These unisex rooms are beneficial for parents with small children and for persons with disabilities who require personal assistance in using toilet facilities. This requirement applies when a total of six or more water closets (or water closets and urinals) is provided in the facility.

Unisex facilities must be located within 500 ft (152 m), and within one floor, of separate-sex facilities. Doors to unisex toilet and bathing rooms must be securable from within the room.

Accessible unisex toilet and bathing rooms are permitted in alterations in lieu of altering existing separate-sex facilities in certain conditions. Unisex rooms must be located in the same area and on the same floor as the existing inaccessible facilities.

### Toilet Room Layouts

Some of the toilet room layouts shown are similar. Variations are in the direction of the door swing and based on whether the width or depth is the more constraining dimension. Dimensions show comfortable minimums and preferred dimensions.

Overall room dimensions include a 2-in. (51-mm) construction tolerance.

Each layout shows the required clear floor space for the fixtures and the doors.

For door maneuvering clearances, see ADAAG (Section 4.13.6 and Figure 25) for various requirements and conditions. Variables include direction of swing, direction of approach, size of door, and door hardware.

Doors to bathrooms are assumed to be 36 in. (915 mm) wide, with a closer and latch for privacy.

Maneuvering clearances at the base of water closets and below lavatories may vary due to fixture design. Confirm actual water closet and lavatory dimensions for other makes and models.

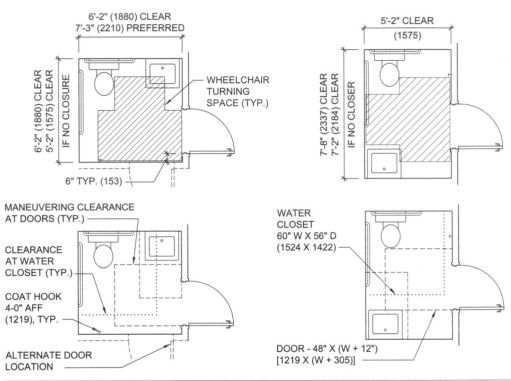

**SHORT AND COMPACT—OUTSWINGING DOOR**

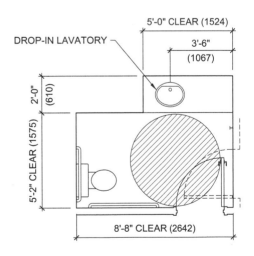

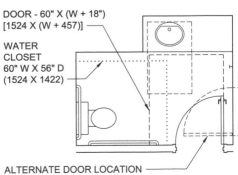

**LAVATORY ON SIDE WALL**

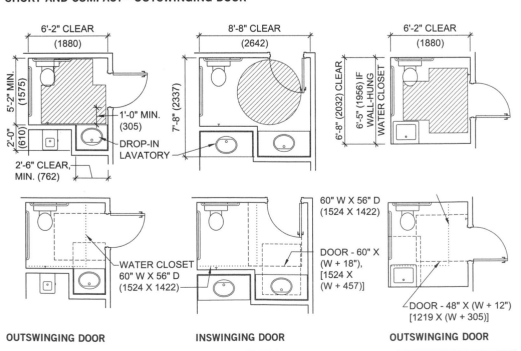

OUTSWINGING DOOR   INSWINGING DOOR   OUTSWINGING DOOR

**LAVATORY ON OPPOSITE WALL**

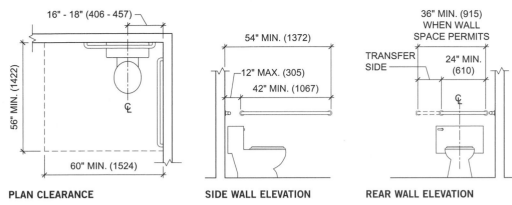

**PLAN CLEARANCE**

ANSI 117.1-1998 requires the water closet clearance to be unobstructed by lavatory or other fixtures. Other regulations allow configurations with a lavatory within the water closet clearance.

**SIDE WALL ELEVATION**

**REAR WALL ELEVATION**

The dashed area indicates the allowable location of the toilet paper dispenser. Dispensers should allow continuous paper flow and not control delivery.

## WATER CLOSETS

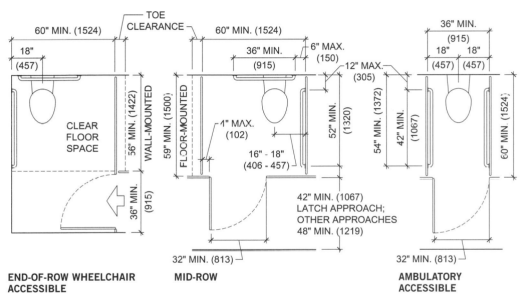

**END-OF-ROW WHEELCHAIR ACCESSIBLE**

**MID-ROW**

**AMBULATORY ACCESSIBLE**

Toe clearance 9 in. (230 mm) high and 6 in. (152 mm) deep is required at the front and at least one side of accessible toilet compartments. Toe clearance is not required when the compartment size exceeds the minimum dimension by 6 in. (152 mm) or more.

## TOILET COMPARTMENTS

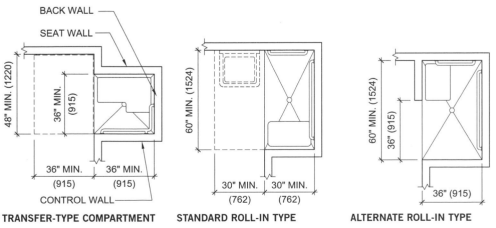

**TRANSFER-TYPE COMPARTMENT**

**STANDARD ROLL-IN TYPE**

**ALTERNATE ROLL-IN TYPE**

A fixed, folding, or removable seat is required in transfer-type compartments. Seats in roll-in showers, where provided, should be folding-type and located on the wall adjacent to the control wall.

Shower compartment thresholds are not permitted to exceed ½ in. (13 mm). A 59-in. (1,500-mm) minimum-length shower spray unit is required.

## SHOWERS

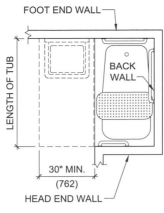

**WITHOUT PERMANENT SEAT**

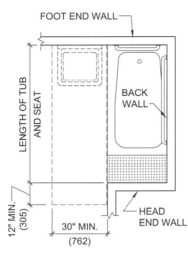

**WITH PERMANENT SEAT**

Bathtub controls, other than drain stoppers, must be located on an end wall between the tub rim and grab bar and between the open side of the tub and the midpoint of the tub width. A 59-in. (1,500-mm) minimum-length shower spray unit is required.

Tub enclosures must not obstruct controls, interfere with transfer from a wheelchair to the tub, or have tracks mounted on the tub rim.

## BATHTUBS

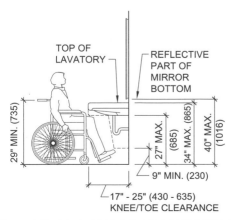

**LAVATORIES**

Exposed pipes and water supply pipes located beneath accessible lavatories must be insulated or located so as to protect users from contact.

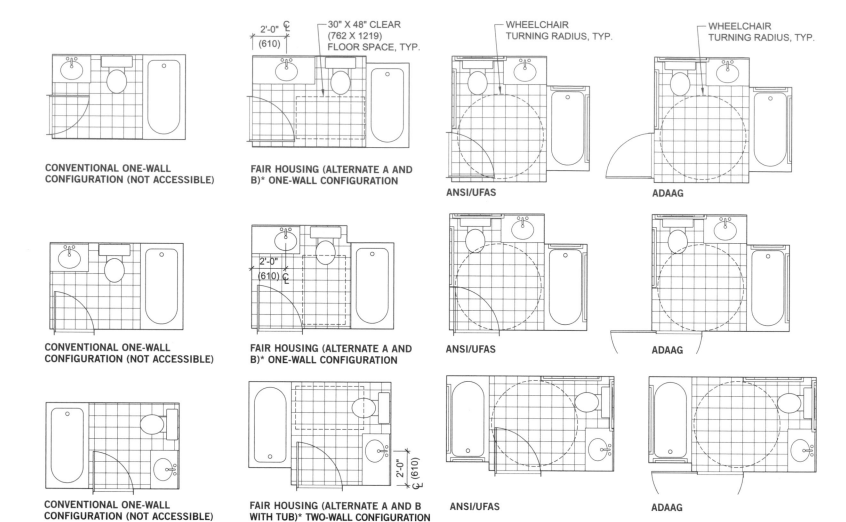

**BATHROOM LAYOUTS**
*For alternate B, reverse the plumbing at the tub.*

## ACCESSIBILITY STANDARDS FOR BATHROOMS

Residential bathrooms and single-use toilet rooms can be divided into two general categories: *private facilities* such as those located in single- or multifamily dwellings, and *public or institutional facilities* such as those located in nursing homes, hospitals, dormitories, or hotels.

Wheelchair bathroom standards for private dwellings were first included in the 1981 edition of ANSI A117.1. Four years later, the Uniform Federal Accessibility Standard (UFAS) published nearly identical bathroom standards for dwellings included in federal projects. In most multifamily projects, whether privately or publicly funded, between 1% and 5% of the total dwellings must meet the ANSI or UFAS standards for full wheelchair accessibility.

In 1988, the Fair Housing Amendments Act (FHAA), a federal civil rights law that addressed private multifamily housing design, was enacted. FHAA guidelines included new and different standards for residential bathrooms. The Fair Housing guidelines include two alternative bathroom design standards. In covered dwellings with two or more full bathrooms, the more strict standards can be used for one bath; more minimal standards can be applied to the second bathroom.

In 1991, the Americans with Disabilities Act (ADA) included new design standards called the Americans with Disabilities Act Accessibility Guidelines (ADAAG). ADAAG standards are not typically applied to private residential facilities because the previously issued Fair Housing standards already apply. However, bathrooms located in "transient lodging" facilities, such as hotels, or public institutional facilities, such as hospitals, may be required to meet both ADA and Fair Housing standards.

### Maneuvering Space

Bathrooms that comply with Fair Housing must be "usable" rather than "accessible" and therefore have lower maneuvering space standards. According to FHAA, if the entry door swings into the bathroom, there must be enough clear space to position a wheelchair clear of the door swing.

All of the standards permit required floor space for fixtures to overlap with required maneuvering space. Current ADAAG standards, however, do not permit the bathroom door (even in single-user facilities) to swing into any fixture clearance.

### Bathroom Entry Doors

Fair Housing permits a 2-ft-10-in. (864-mm) door to provide a "nominal" 32-in. (813-mm) clear opening. ANSI, UFAS, and ADAAG require installation of at least a 3-ft-0-in. (915-mm) door to provide the full 32-in. (813-mm) clear opening.

### Grab Bars

Grab bar arrangement can influence the floor plan of an accessible bathroom. FHAA grab bar standards are less strict, and this permits the design of smaller bathrooms.

### Adaptable Features

In residential bathroom design, *adaptability* was a new term when introduced in the 1980 ANSI edition. Adaptability in this case is defined as "the capability of certain elements to be altered or added so as to accommodate the needs of persons with or without disabilities, or to accommodate the needs of persons with different types or degrees of disabilities." Some codes and civil rights laws require provisions in certain bathrooms for "adaptable" features.

For single-family custom homes or remodeling projects, bathroom designs should be specially tailored to the individual homeowners. If a master bathroom is planned for a wheelchair user, for example, the design should reflect that person's individual capabilities and preferences.

*Kim A. Beasley, AIA, and Thomas D. Davies, Jr., AIA;*
  *Paralyzed Veterans of America Architecture; Washington,*
  *D.C.*

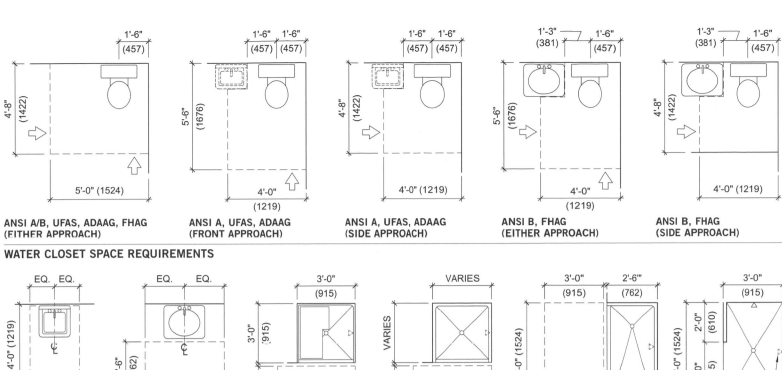

ANSI A/B, UFAS, ADAAG, FHAG
(EITHER APPROACH)

ANSI A, UFAS, ADAAG
(FRONT APPROACH)

ANSI A, UFAS, ADAAG
(SIDE APPROACH)

ANSI B, FHAG
(EITHER APPROACH)

ANSI B, FHAG
(SIDE APPROACH)

## WATER CLOSET SPACE REQUIREMENTS

ANSI A, UFAS, ADAAG
(WITH KNEE SPACE)

ANSI B
(NO KNEE SPACE)

ANSI A, UFAS, ADAAG
(STALL SHOWER)

ANSI B, FHAG
(STALL SHOWER)

ANSI A, UFAS, ADAAG
(ROLL-IN SHOWER)

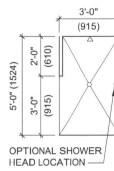

OPTIONAL SHOWER
HEAD LOCATION

ADAAG (ALTERNATE
ROLL-IN SHOWER)

## LAVATORY AND SHOWER SPACE REQUIREMENTS

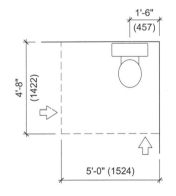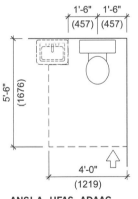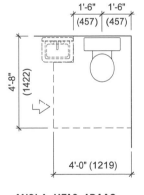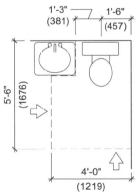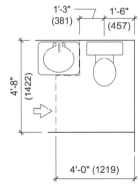

ANSI A, UFAS, ADAAG
(PARALLEL APPROACH)

ANSI A, UFAS, ADAAG
(PERPENDICULAR APPROACH)

ANSI A, UFAS, ADAAG
(TUB/SHOWER WITH SEAT)
For a tub/shower with seat, an
additional 1 ft (305 mm) of clear
space beyond the seat is required.

ANSI B, FHAG
(ALTERNATE A)

ANSI B, FHAG
(ALTERNATE B)

## BATHTUB SPACE REQUIREMENTS

## PLUMBING FIXTURE STANDARDS

### Water Closets

The major differences between FHAA and the other standards are the minimum space required behind the water closet and the configuration of the lavatory or vanity that may be located adjacent to the toilet. In order to meet FHAA standards, an adjacent lavatory does not have to include knee space, whereas knee space is an important ANSI/UFAS and ADAAG requirement.

### Lavatories and Vanities

FHAA does not require knee space, but the other standards do. In some instances, the knee space height

required by ADAAG is greater than that required by ANSI or UFAS. All accessibility standards except Fair Housing include requirements for a maximum sink depth. ADAAG, ANSI, and UFAS also include requirements for faucets, mirrors, and medicine cabinets.

### Bathtubs and Tub/Showers

The ADAAG, ANSI (pre-1998), and UFAS accessible bathtub standards also have subtle differences. The bathtub clear floor space requirements are similar to those for water closets in that an approach direction is indicated (either perpendicular or parallel).

FHAA offers two different clear space requirements; the designer may choose to comply with either. Of these alternatives, Alternate B is stricter because it requires clear space adjacent to the foot of the tub.

### Stall Showers and Roll-in Units

Accessible showers include both transfer stalls (where a bather moves from a wheelchair to a bench or portable seat) and roll-in stalls (where a bather remains seated in a special shower chair and is either pushed by an attendant or self-propelled into the stall). All accessibility standards require either wall reinforcing or grab bars inside a shower.

*Lawrence G. Perry, AIA; Silver Spring, Maryland*

## ACCESSIBILITY GUIDELINES FOR KITCHENS

The 1980 American National Standards Institute (ANSI) A117.1 and the 1984 Uniform Federal Accessibility Standards (UFAS) were the first to include kitchen design standards that focused on the needs of wheelchair users. The kitchen standards in the 1988 Fair Housing Amendments Act (FHAA), a federal civil rights law, include less specialized wheelchair design features for multifamily housing.

Designers should carefully verify which kitchen requirements are appropriate for their specific project because accessibility codes and civil rights laws have very different design standards.

Accessible kitchens should reflect conventional layout principles with regard to proper workflow and functional adjacencies.

### Fixture and Appliances

The three general types of wheelchair standards for residential kitchens are:

- General kitchen maneuvering space
- Individual fixture and appliance maneuvering space
- Other fixture specifications such as basin depths, switch locations, and faucet configurations

Sufficient clear floor space must be provided at fixtures and appliances to accommodate either a parallel or front approach, depending on the applicable design standard requirements.

The 1998 ANSI appliance clearances are more sophisticated than previous standards. For example, oven clearances depend on whether the unit is a self-cleaning model and the door is side- or bottom-hinged.

ANSI and UFAS require either adjustable height counters or fixed counters at a height of 34 in. (865 mm). FHAA does not address counter heights.

### Adaptable Features

The term *adaptability* is defined as "the capability of certain elements to be altered or added so as to accommodate the needs of persons with or without disabilities." For accessible kitchens, adaptable elements might include removable base cabinets that can be eliminated to provide knee space below countertops, or adjustable-height countertop sections that can be raised and lowered.

*Lawrence G. Perry, AIA; Silver Spring, Maryland*

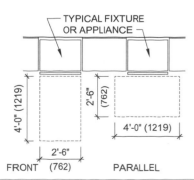

**APPROACH DIAGRAM FOR FIXTURES OR APPLIANCES**

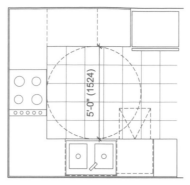

FHAA guidelines require a 5-ft-0-in. (1,524-mm) clearance if a sink, range, or cooktop is installed in the base leg of the U. If the base leg fixture includes a knee space or removable base cabinets, the 5-ft-0-in. (1,524-mm) clearance is not required.

**U-SHAPED KITCHEN PLAN**

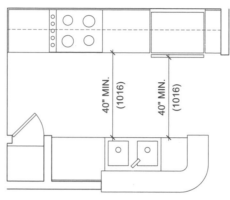

ANSI and UFAS require a 40-in. (1,016-mm) clearance between kitchen cabinets and opposing walls, cabinets, or appliances *where the counters provide knee space.* Otherwise, an accessible route is required. The FHAA guidelines, however, require a 40-in. (1,016-mm) clearance in all cases.

**GALLEY KITCHEN PLAN**

### FLOOR SPACE AND KNEE SPACE REQUIREMENTS FOR FIXTURES AND APPLIANCES

| APPLIANCE | REQUIRE-MENT | FAIR HOUSING | ANSI/ UFAS |
|---|---|---|---|
| Sink | Approach | Parallel | Parallel or front |
| | Knee space | No | Yes |
| Range/ cooktop | Approach | Parallel | Parallel or front |
| | Knee space | No | Optional |
| Workspace | Approach | Not required | Front |
| | Knee space | No | Yes |
| Refrigerator | Approach | Parallel or front | Parallel or front |
| | Knee space | No | No |
| Dishwasher | Approach | Parallel or front | Parallel or front |
| | Knee space | No | No |
| Oven (self-cleaning) | Approach | Parallel or front | Front |
| | Knee space | No | No |
| Oven (non-self-cleaning) | Approach | Parallel or front | Front |
| | Knee space | No | Yes (off-set) |
| Trash compactor | Approach | Parallel or front | Parallel or front |
| | Knee space | No | No |

*Note: HUD interpretations of FHAA guidelines require clear floor space to be centered on the appliance or fixture. In a kitchen plan, this can have significant design impact.*

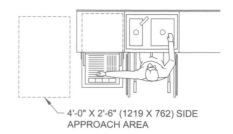

4'-0" X 2'-6" (1219 X 762) SIDE APPROACH AREA

The sink should be a shallow unit with easy-to-operate faucets. A tall spout and a pullout spray attachment are also recommended. Garbage disposals must be offset in order to provide full knee space under the sink.

**KITCHEN SINK AND DISHWASHER**

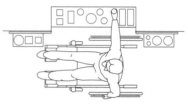

The design of kitchen storage space for wheelchair users should provide both visual and physical access to wall and base cabinets, drawers, and pantries. Base cabinets, for example, can be specified to include pull-out shelves or drawers that will provide easy access to items stored in the back of the cabinets.

**KITCHEN STORAGE**

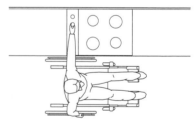

A range or cooktop should have front- or side-mounted controls so the seated user does not need to reach over the heated surfaces. A smooth cooktop surface allows pots to be slid rather than lifted on and off the burners.

**STOVES AND COOKTOPS**

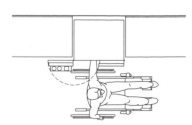

Side-by-side models offer the user both freezer and refrigerator storage at all height levels from the floor to the top shelf.

**REFRIGERATORS**

# WAYFINDING

Wayfinding refers to the way people orient themselves in a given environment and find their destination. The ability to orient oneself is based on many pieces of information—visual clues, memories, knowledge of a place—and the ability to reason. Environmental psychology terms the ability to acquire, code, store, recall, and decode information about the physical environment *cognitive mapping*. Successful wayfinding is the ability to naturally orient oneself in the environment and to easily locate a destination without experiencing stress.

## HIGHLY IMAGEABLE SPACES

The work of Kevin Lynch, presented in *The Image of the City* (1960), was based on studies that found three components for the analysis of environmental imaging.

IDENTITY, or objects in background

STRUCTURE, or objects in relationship to each other

MEANING, or personal, societal, or figurative belief

Lynch focused on the identity and structure of spaces to discern what makes cities imageable or known. He notes: "[Imageability is]… that quality of a physical object which gives it a high probability of evoking a strong image in any given observer. It is that shape, color, or arrangement which facilitates the making of a vividly identified, powerfully structured, highly useful mental image of the environment. It might also be called legibility."

A highly imageable space has components that relate in a well-structured manner. The way a space is mapped for an individual varies, depending on the person. Certain images and visual clues are perceived similarly by groups of people who share similar backgrounds, activities, or routines, and recurrent features in their environment. For example, a group of schoolchildren may be of a similar age, share the learning and play activities of a school, and be aware of the physical features of the school building.

## MAPPING ELEMENTS

Lynch's research resulted in the identification of five categories of elements that people use to map an environment:

PATHS: Channels of movement

EDGES: Boundaries that break, contain, or run parallel to the forms

DISTRICTS: Areas of recognizable identity

NODES: Places of intense activity

LANDMARKS: Points of reference that are visually distinguishable

## COGNITIVE MAPS

Cognitive maps are psychological impressions or representations of individuals' ability to understand space and the organizing elements by which they orient themselves. Cognitive maps usually combine several of the mapping elements. These elements are not formed simply in the floor plan, but the three-dimensional characteristics of a space, the material choices, the colors, and the lighting can all impact the formation of edges, districts, or nodes.

Where the boundaries of the districts meet, an edge may be formed, providing a sense of having exited one area and entered another. A node may occur at an intersection of activities or along paths where activity is concentrated. Landmarks may be used by the designer to mark entrances or points of interest.

## WAYFINDING AND AGE

The process of learning involves an increase in perception of detail as a person develops. The following reference systems, proposed by Gary Moore (1976), relates the phases of development to the progress of perception from early childhood to the adult years:

1. An egocentric reference system; that is, one organized around the child's own position and actions in space.
2. Several different possibilities of fixed reference systems organized around various fixed, concrete elements, or places in the environment.
3. An abstract or coordinated reference system organized in terms of abstract geometric patterns including—in special cases—the cardinal directions (north, south, east, and west).

As adults, people tend to rely on maps, diagrams, and more highly abstract information for orientation and finding their way within a new area. An adult who is visiting an unfamiliar city will use a city map to reach a destination (reference system 3 on the preceding list). Adults navigate wide-reaching, complex environments on a daily basis, whereas children's environments are more limited in overall range and tend to be perceived on the basis of reference points. The adolescent child's orientation system (reference system 2) may be based on a local hang-out, the path of travel between home and school, local landmarks within the community, and similar points of reference. The designer of environments for small children should be aware that children are naturally oriented in relation to their own positions (reference system 1).

Children see the world always in relation to themselves. For example, an especially enjoyable piece of equipment at the playground and its relationship to the toilet facility a child uses while at the playground may be the elements by which he or she organizes and understands that environment. A child's cognitive map will likely include detailed aspects of a space with which he or she is directly involved.

## SIGNAGE

Signage is an important part of directing people through a space. Building signage can include building identification, building layout illustration, directional signs, and place signs.

Signs should be designed and placed consistently throughout the facility. The overuse of signage and cluttered signage, which becomes ineffective, should be avoided. Signs should be placed strategically at decision-making areas.

## WAYFINDING CLUES

In addition to signage, visual clues can be utilized to help orient the user. Architectural elements like lobbies, stairs, elevators, and areas of special use can create a framework into which users can place themselves. The following interior treatments typically used for aesthetic effect can also assist the designer in creating a highly understandable environment:

- Change of wall color, type, or texture
- Change in flooring
- Use of lighting to highlight or minimize areas
- Change of ceiling treatments
- Furniture arrangement or type

The extent of wayfinding clues incorporated in the environment should vary from public to private spaces. Public areas require more information to be presented to aid visitors in locating their destinations. As the spaces become more private, fewer clues will be needed because of the occupants' knowledge of the environment.

*Source: Bradford Perkins (Stephen Kliment, Ed.),* Building Type Basics for Elementary and Secondary Schools, *(New York: John Wiley & Sons, Inc.), 2001, pp. 193-200.*
*Source: Kevin Lynch,* The Image of the City, *(Cambridge: MIT Press), 1960.*
*Source: Gary T. Moore, "The Development of Environmental Knowing: An Overview of an Interactional-Constructivist Theory and Some Data on Within-Individual Development Variations," In* Psychology and the Built Environment, *David Carter and Terrence Lee, Eds. (London: Architectural Press), 1976.*

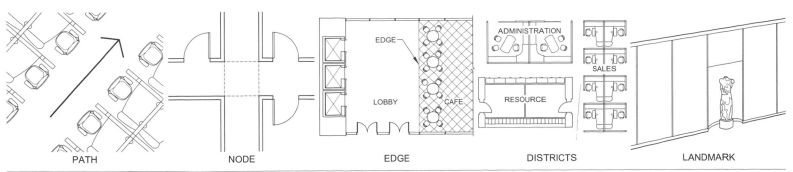

PATH    NODE    EDGE    DISTRICTS    LANDMARK

**MAPPING ELEMENTS**

# CLASSICAL ORDERS

## HISTORY

With a 2,500-year history, classical architecture and decoration is the primary architectural language in the West. After being developed by Greek architects over a 500-year period, the forms and rules for Classical architecture and decoration were reformulated by the Romans. This legacy was revived and further developed over another half-millennium, from the advent of the Renaissance to the Second World War. Classicism is currently being reinvestigated by a group of architects and designers who believe that contemporary design issues can be solved by using its formal vocabulary and theoretical principles.

Classical theoretical principles assist in achieving a sense of strength, function, and beauty in a structure or an interior. The designer's basic premise is that models from past productions can be imitated for development, and adapted with invention, to solve current problems. This belief is key to the paradigmatic method articulated in about 20 B.C. by the Roman architect, Vitruvius, in his *Ten Books on Architecture*. His work synthesized the ideas of Greek treatises for a revival of Greek-inspired architecture under the Emperor Augustus. Vitruvius's text was honored throughout the Middle Ages by being copied for intense revival and development from the Renaissance to the present. *The Ten Books on Architecture* was essential to Andrea Palladio, for example, who called Vitruvius his "master and guide."

Both today and historically, the application of classical elements and ideals are at once consistent with core principles, yet diverse. The variety of interpretation stems from different cultural perspectives, from access to diverse models for imitation, and from the effects of the varying temperaments of the individuals who have successively reestablished classicism over two millennia.

## COLUMN TYPES

Vitruvius considered columns and their entablatures, or beam structures, to be the fundamental concept of what classical architecture entails. Vitruvius did not refer to column "orders," as they came to be called in the Renaissance; instead he referred to them more generally as types, or kinds, because he considered columns and beam structures to be components of a large collection of elements, including doors, windows, and railings.

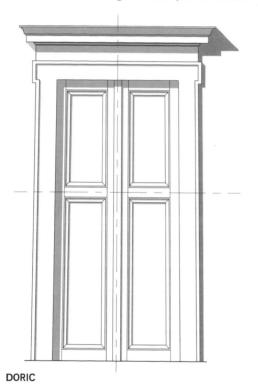

**DORIC**

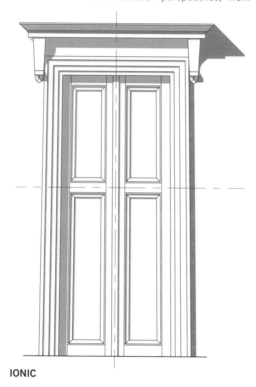

**IONIC**

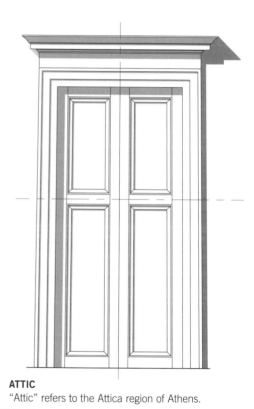

**ATTIC**
"Attic" refers to the Attica region of Athens.

**VITRUVIAN PORTALS** *Source: Mati Rosenshine; Mati Rosenshine Architect; Jerusalem, Israel*

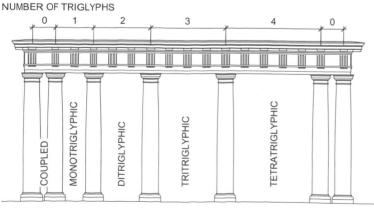

NUMBER OF TRIGLYPHS

0  1  2  3  4  0

COUPLED | MONOTRIGLYPHIC | DITRIGLYPHIC | TRITRIGLYPHIC | TETRATRIGLYPHIC

**ROMAN DORIC INTERCOLUMNIATION**

NUMBER OF MODULES

2  3  5  5  7  8

COUPLED | PYCNOSTYLOS (TIGHTLY COLUMNED) | SYSTYLOS (CLOSELY COLUMNED) | EUSTYLOS (CORRECTLY COLUMNED) | DIASTYLOS (OPENLY COLUMNED) | AEROSTYLOS (WIDELY COLUMNED)

**ROMAN IONIC INTERCOLUMNIATION**

## INTERCOLUMNIATION

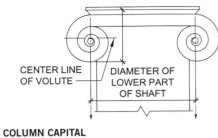

**COLUMN CAPITAL**

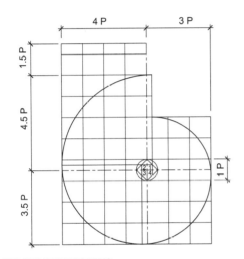

**VOLUTE**

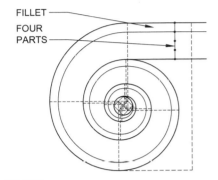

**VOLUTE PROPORTIONS**

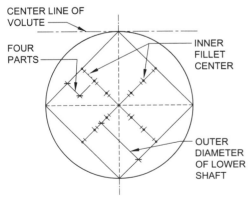

**VOLUTE CONSTRUCTION**

Below the centerline of the volute, draw a circle with a diameter of one-eighth the height of the volute. Inscribe a rotated, quartered square within this circle, or "eye." The six divisions of the centerline of this square give the centers for a series of diminishing arcs. From center 1 draw arc 1, from center 2, arc 2, and so on. Successive arcs meet at a line defined by their centers.

**VOLUTE PLACEMENT AND CONSTRUCTION**

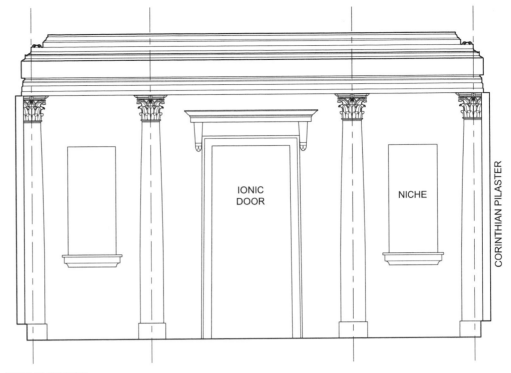

**IONIC ELEVATION**

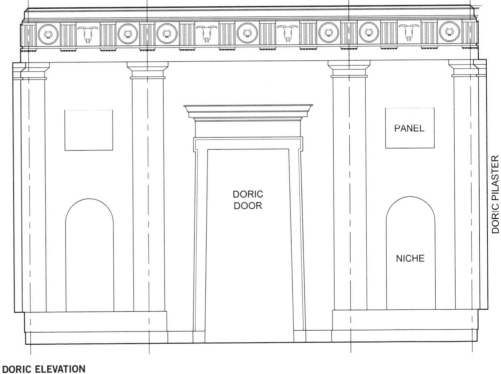

**DORIC ELEVATION**

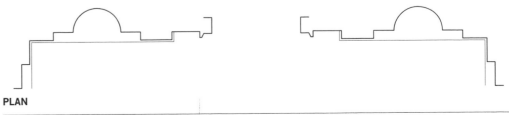

**PLAN**

**SALON ELEVATION WITH SUPERPOSED PILASTERS**

## CLASSICAL INTERIORS

Many systems of proportion for rooms have been proposed since ancient times. Vitruvius provided interrelated ratios for the width and length of atria and ratios for the height of their ceilings and the size of the roof opening. Andrea Palladio provided similar ratios for the principal rooms of a house.

### Room Proportions

One rule of thumb is to have a 2:3 ratio of width to length in plan. The ceiling height could be the same as the width, creating a square interior elevation, or the height could be achieved by dividing the width into four parts and multiplying the result by five. Thus, an ideal room of 20 by 30 ft (6 by 9 m) would have a ceiling height of 20 or 25 ft (6 or 7.5 m). It is rare to be able to work with such volumes today, but even when we do, other factors must often be accommodated. These include preexisting structural conditions, the functional requirements of adjacent rooms, or the modules of building systems.

### Classical Salon

The salon illustrated on the following two pages has a roughly 2:3 plan with a ceiling height of just over 2, similar to the width ratio. The ceiling is divided into three squares on each side with two rectangles flanking an open shaft for a skylight. On one of the short elevations, the equal ceiling coffers correspond to the central portal and adjacent cabinet doors. A Doric entablature surrounds the room at the height of the door lintel. The frieze has triglyphs and metopes with traditional cow skulls. The entablature is projected forward along with the door jambs. The adjacent friezes are adjusted to achieve two full-size triglyphs meeting at the corners. The proportions of the architrave, frieze, and cornice are different from the other model shown here. This demonstrates the variety of proportions that are possible. Working within the established geometries of Doric and Ionic architecture is one of the stimulating challenges of engaging the classical language in interior design. Making subtle and inventive variations in response to many constraints is one of the rewards of learning to "speak" and manipulate the classical vocabulary and its rules of "grammar."

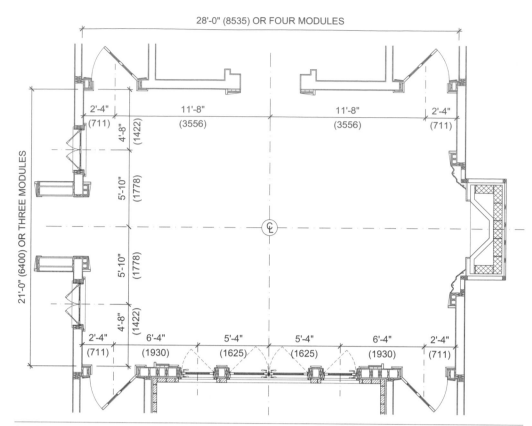

**CLASSICALLY PROPORTIONED SALON—PLAN**

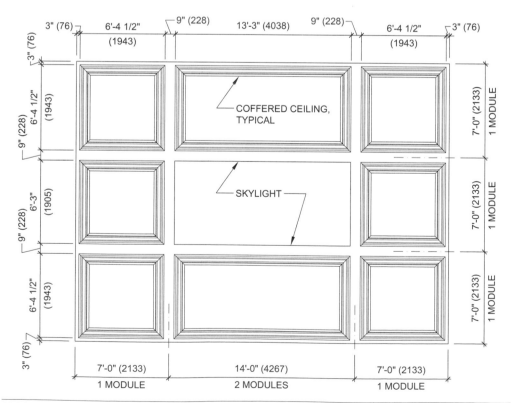

**CLASSICALLY PROPORTIONED SALON—REFLECTED CEILING PLAN**

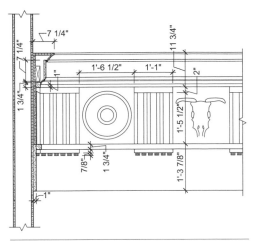

**DORIC ENTABLATURE**

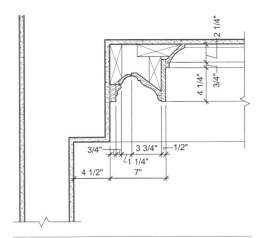

**CORNICE**

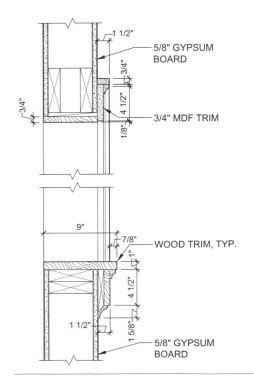

5/8" GYPSUM BOARD

3/4" MDF TRIM

9"

7/8"

WOOD TRIM, TYP.

4 1/2"

1 1/2"

1 5/8"

5/8" GYPSUM BOARD

**CABINET SECTION**

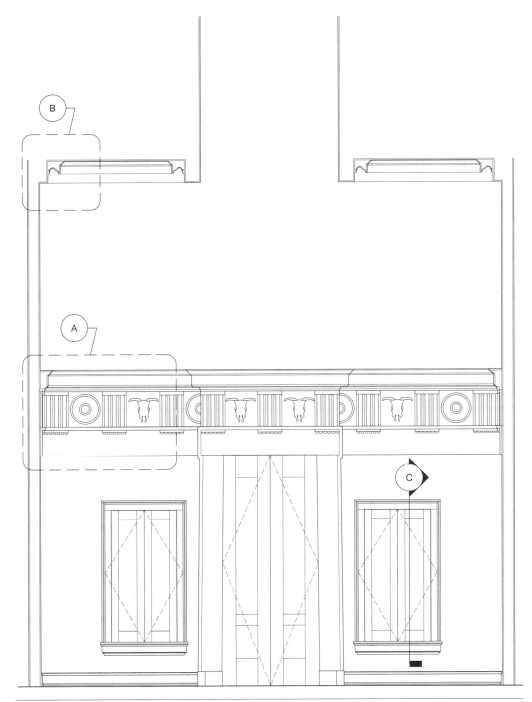

**CLASSICALLY PROPORTIONED SALON—ELEVATION**

This illustrates a parallel comparison based on Vignola proportions with a constant lower diameter. The proportional relationships of the column types and their entablatures are based on a modular system, usually based on the lower diameter of the column shaft. This module is multiplied or divided to obtain the measurements of both large and small components.

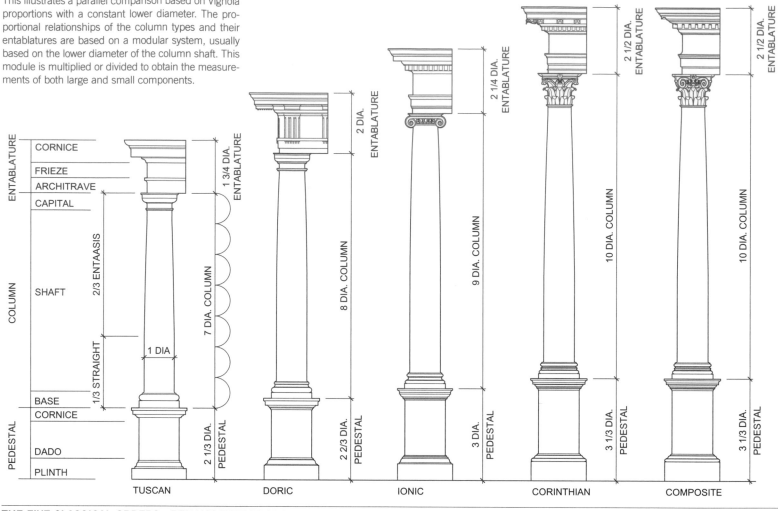

**THE FIVE CLASSICAL ORDERS—RENAISSANCE PROPORTIONS**

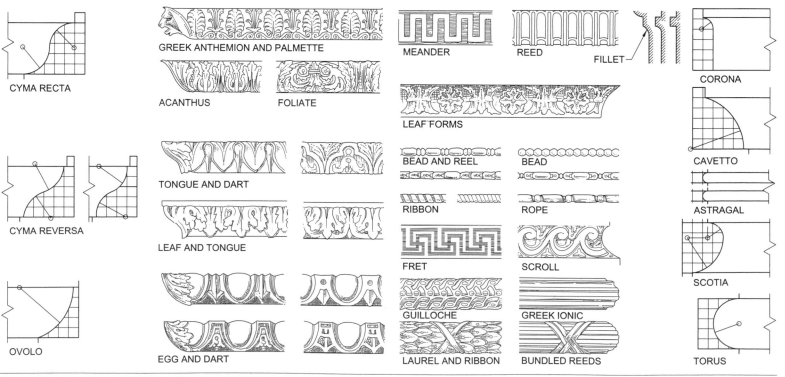

**MOLDINGS—TYPES, PATTERNS, AND DECORATION**

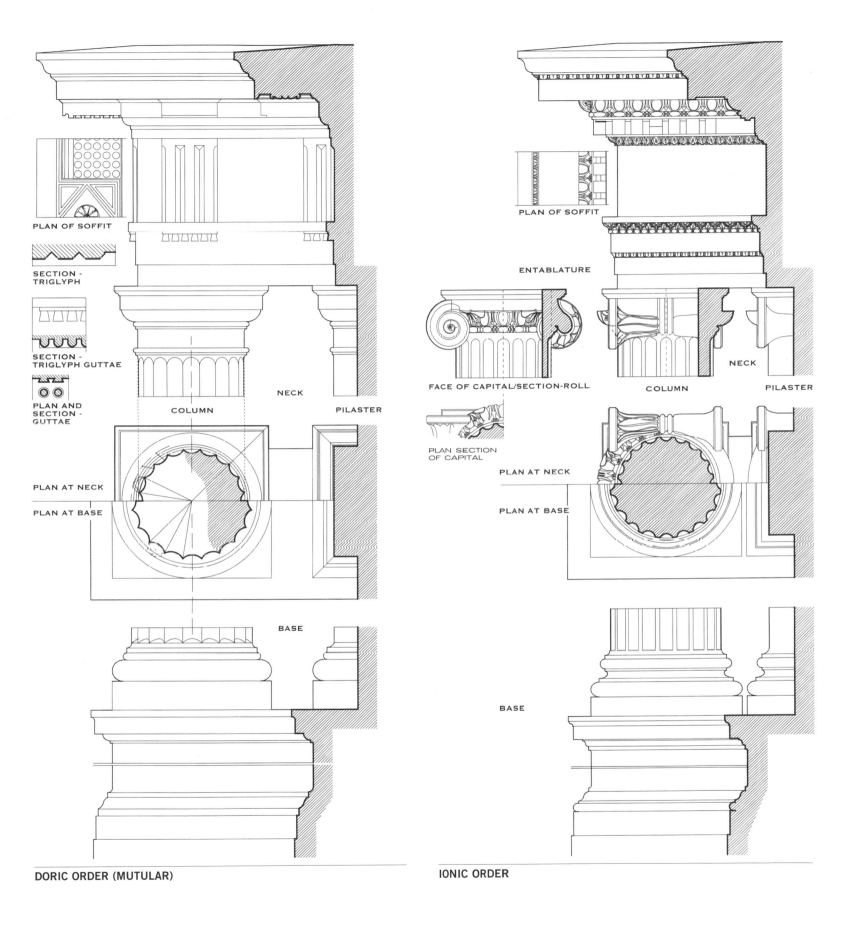

PLAN OF SOFFIT

SECTION - TRIGLYPH

SECTION - TRIGLYPH GUTTAE

PLAN AND SECTION - GUTTAE

PLAN OF SOFFIT

ENTABLATURE

FACE OF CAPITAL/SECTION-ROLL

COLUMN

NECK

PILASTER

PLAN SECTION OF CAPITAL

NECK

COLUMN

PILASTER

PLAN AT NECK

PLAN AT BASE

PLAN AT NECK

PLAN AT BASE

BASE

BASE

**DORIC ORDER (MUTULAR)**

**IONIC ORDER**

## APPROPRIATE CHOICE OF COLUMN TYPES

The tradition of classical interiors is as diverse as the parallel architectural developments. The concept that Vitruvius called *decor* describes the need to make appropriate choices of which column type to use to convey the correct meaning for the function of an interior. The selected architectural armature must then be deliberately interpreted in a spectrum from the most articulate detail through successive levels of abstraction. These choices can convey different nuances of meaning even within one kind, such as Doric. These decisions also respond to varying levels of expenditure. Since the "language of architecture" is relatively mute by nature, sculpture, painting, and decorative embellishment can be incorporated within rooms to convey specific ideas through iconographic programs.

*Thomas Gordon Smith, AIA; Thomas Gordon Smith Architects; South Bend, Indiana*
*Scot C. McBroom, AIA; Alexandria, Virginia*

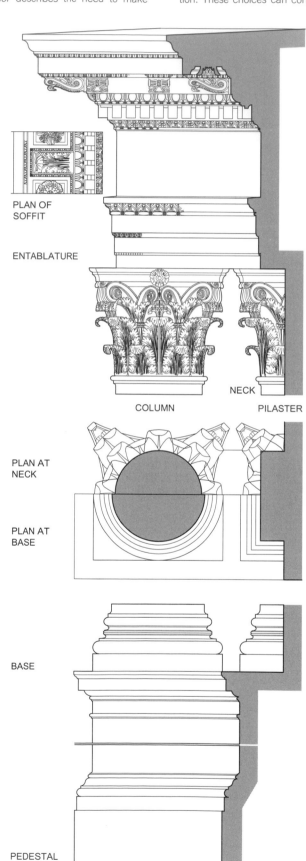

PLAN OF SOFFIT

ENTABLATURE

COLUMN          PILASTER

NECK

PLAN AT NECK

PLAN AT BASE

BASE

PEDESTAL

**CORINTHIAN ORDER**

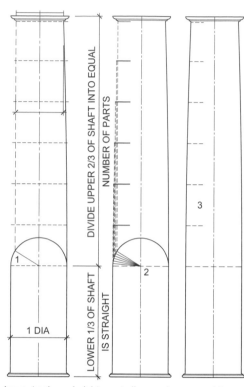

DIVIDE UPPER 2/3 OF SHAFT INTO EQUAL NUMBER OF PARTS

LOWER 1/3 OF SHAFT IS STRAIGHT

1 DIA

Lay out column height, centerline, and upper and lower diameters at one-third point on column; draw a half circle equal to lower diameter. Drop a line from the upper diameter to the semicircle (1). Divide the resulting minor arc and upper two-thirds of the shaft into an equal number of equal parts. Draw vertical lines from the arc divisions to the horizontal shaft divisions (2). The resulting points define the curved profile of the column shaft (3).

**ENTASIS**

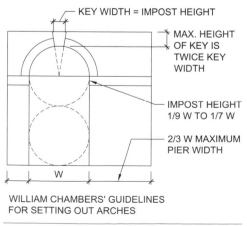

KEY WIDTH = IMPOST HEIGHT

MAX. HEIGHT OF KEY IS TWICE KEY WIDTH

IMPOST HEIGHT 1/9 W TO 1/7 W

2/3 W MAXIMUM PIER WIDTH

W

WILLIAM CHAMBERS' GUIDELINES FOR SETTING OUT ARCHES

**ARCHED DOORWAY CONSTRUCTION**

# PROPORTIONING SYSTEMS

## IDEAL PROPORTIONS

Geometric methods have been developed to determine the ideal proportions. These systems attempt to establish an aesthetic rationale for design.

## GENERATIVE GEOMETRY

The archetypal circle and square can geometrically generate many forms. Ancient cultures recognized these forms and relationships as essential and sacred, a metaphor of universal order. The circle and square in the act of self-division gives three generative roots: the square roots of 2, 3, and 5 (Figures 1A and 1B). These root relationships are all that are necessary to form the five regular (Platonic) solids that are the basis for all volumetric forms (Figure 1C). Also, 2, 3, and 5 are the only numbers required to divide the octave into musical scales.

## THE SQUARE ROOT OF 2

In seeming paradox, the half of a square produces its double; this is analogous to biological growth from cell division and the generation of musical tone. In Figure 2A, the diagonal of square ABCD (square 1, Figure 2A) is exactly equal to the side of square ACFG (square 2). The area of square 2 is exactly twice that of square 1. The side of a square is called its *root*. The side of square 1 equals 1; the side of square 2 equals the square root of 2. The diagonal of square 2 equals 2, exactly twice the side of the primary square. The division of the square by the diagonal yields three seemingly contradictory, yet geometrically true, relationships:

$$\frac{root}{diag} : \frac{root}{diag} :: \frac{1}{\sqrt{2}} : \frac{\sqrt{2}}{2} \quad \frac{root}{diag} : \frac{diag}{root} :: \frac{1}{\sqrt{2}} : \frac{\sqrt{2}}{2}$$

The square root of 2 represents the power of multiplicity through the geometric progression a:b::b:c (Figure 2B). The relationship of the side to the diagonal may be written:

$$\frac{1}{\sqrt{2}} : \frac{\sqrt{2}}{2} : \frac{2}{2\sqrt{2}} : \frac{2\sqrt{2}}{4} : \frac{4}{4\sqrt{2}}, \text{ and so on}$$

## THE VESICA PISCIS AND THE SQUARE ROOT OF 3

The Vesica Piscis is a form generator of the triangle, square, and pentagon—the basic planar elements of the five Platonic solids. The overlapping circles are an excellent representation of a cell or any unity in the midst of becoming dual. Medieval churches and cathedrals incorporated the fish-shaped geometry as a symbol of Christ.

To construct the Vesica Piscis, draw a circle of any radius about center A; at any chosen point on the circumference, draw another circle of equal radius (B). The area and shape defined by the two centers and the overlap of the two circumferences is known as the Vesica Piscis (Figure 3A).

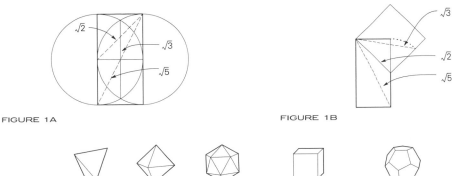

FIGURE 1A                     FIGURE 1B

TETRAHEDRON  OCTAHEDRON  ICOSA-HEDRON     CUBE     DODECAHEDRON

FIGURE 1C

## GENERATIVE GEOMETRY

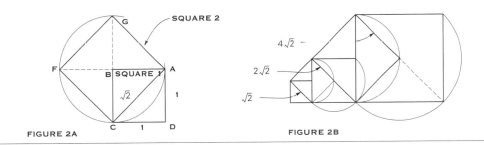

FIGURE 2A                          FIGURE 2B

## THE SQUARE ROOT OF 2

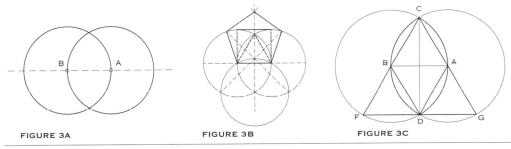

FIGURE 3A                    FIGURE 3B                    FIGURE 3C

## THE SQUARE ROOT OF 3

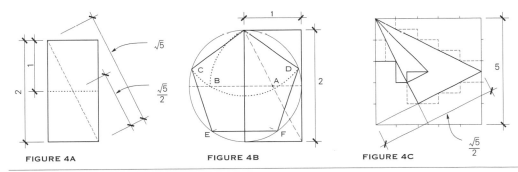

FIGURE 4A                    FIGURE 4B                    FIGURE 4C

## THE SQUARE ROOT OF 5

Figure 3B shows the generation of equilateral triangles.

In Figure 3C, we see that if AB=1, then DG=1, CG=2, and, by the Pythagorean Theorem ($a^2 + b^2 = c^2$), the major axis:

$$CD = \sqrt{(CG^2 - DG^2)} = \sqrt{3}$$

## THE SQUARE ROOT OF 5

The square root of 5 may be generated from a 1:2 rectangle (a double square); see Figure 4A. Figure 4B demonstrates the relationship of the square root of 5, both with the number 5 (as the square of its root) and with the fivefold symmetry of the pentagon. The 3, 4, 5 "Pythagorean" triangle (Figure 4C) is derived from the crossing of three semidiagonals (square root of 5 divided by 2). The square root of 5 is the proportion that opens the way for the family of relationships called the Golden Proportion.

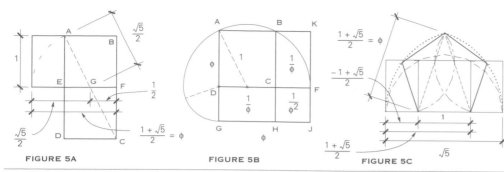

FIGURE 5A          FIGURE 5B          FIGURE 5C

## THE GOLDEN PROPORTION

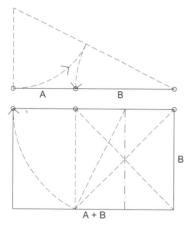

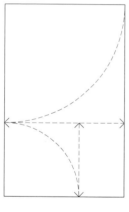

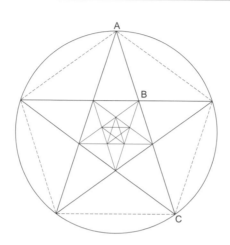

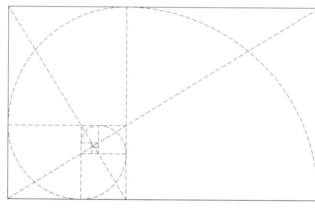

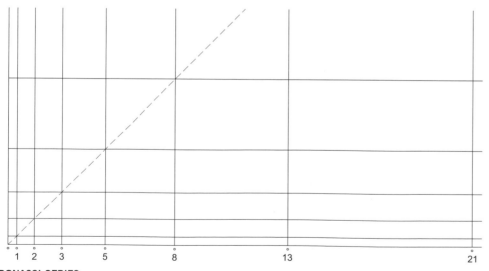

**FIBONACCI SERIES**
The Fibonacci Series is a sequence of numbers where the first two terms are 1 and 1, and each subsequent term is the sum of the two preceding numbers; 1, 1, 2, 3, 5, 8, 13, 21, and so on. The ratio between consecutive terms approximates the Golden Proportion.

## GOLDEN PROPORTION CONSTRUCTION METHODS

## RATIO AND PROPORTION

Ratio is the relation in magnitude, quantity, or degree between two or more similar things.

A:B                                        A/B

Proportion is the comparative, harmonious relation of one part to another or to the whole with respect to magnitude, quantity, or degree.

A:B:C                                      A/B=B/C

## THE GOLDEN PROPORTION

The Golden Proportion can be found in nature, where it governs plant growth patterns and human proportions. Its presence can be found in the sacred art and architecture of Egypt, India, China, Greece, Islamic countries, and other traditional cultures. It was hidden in Gothic cathedrals, celebrated in Renaissance art, and used by modernist architects such as Le Corbusier (pseudonym of Charles-Edward Jeanneret) and Frank Lloyd Wright.

Discontinuous proportions contain four terms (a:b::c:d). Geometric relationships are of a three-term proportional type (a:b::b:c). There is only one proportional division that is possible with two terms; this is written a:b::b:(a + b). The unique two-term proportion (designated by the Greek letter ø was called "golden" by the ancients because the original unity is always represented in its division, written

$$\frac{1}{\text{ø}^3} : \frac{1}{\text{ø}^2} : \frac{1}{\text{ø}^2} : \frac{1}{\text{ø}} : \frac{1}{\text{ø}} : 1 :: 1 : \text{ø} :: \text{ø} : \text{ø}2 :: \text{ø}2 : \text{ø}3,$$ and so on

Figure 5A shows the construction of the Golden Proportion from the 1:2 rectangle. Figure 5B demonstrates the relationship of three squares related by f. Figure 5C reveals an important pentagonal relationship: the side of a pentagon is in relation to its diagonal as:

$$(1 + \sqrt{5}) \text{ ø } 2 \quad \text{or} \quad 1 : \text{ø},$$ the golden section

where ø represents a coinciding of the processes of addition and multiplication called the Fibonacci Series, which manifests itself in some biological growth patterns.

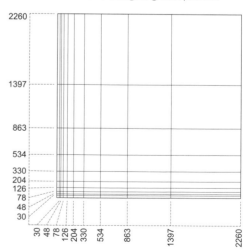

**LE MODULOR**
Le Corbusier developed Le Modulor proportioning system based on a standard human height of 1,829 mm (6 ft). (Dimensions shown are millimeters.)

Scott C. McBroom, AIA; Alexandria, Virginia

# HISTORIC PRESERVATION

## DEFINITIONS

*Historic preservation* is a term used to describe the act or process of maintaining the historic materials and historic character of a *historic property*. Historic properties may be buildings, structures, sites, objects, or landscapes. When there is a collection of historic properties within a close geographic area, the collection is sometimes designated a *historic district*.

## HISTORIC PRESERVATION MOVEMENT

The historic preservation movement in the United States came into its own in the final three decades of the twentieth century. Historic preservation efforts typically integrate many interests, the greatest of which are economic, environmental, aesthetic, and cultural. Historic properties enhance the character of our communities by providing a tangible connection to the past and variety in the built environment. Historic preservation has changed the way we plan, modify, and create communities. Preservationists commonly believe that preserving the historic character of our communities improves our quality of life.

The historic preservation movement in the United States began two centuries ago as an effort to preserve nationally significant buildings, battlegrounds, and cemeteries. Today, it has become a more broadly encompassing effort to preserve buildings (exteriors and the interiors), objects, sites, structures, districts, communities, and cultural landscapes that have local, state, or national significance.

Historic preservation efforts in the United States involve individual building owners, nonprofit organizations, and government at local, state, and federal levels. The primary efforts of historic preservation are as follows:

- *Identification* of historic properties worthy of preservation
- *Documentation* of the historical significance of these properties
- *Recordation* of the physical characteristics of historically significant properties
- *Designation* of historically significant properties by placement on a local, state, or national list of historic properties worthy of protection
- *Protection* of designated properties through education and regulation.

## GOVERNMENT EFFORTS IN HISTORIC PRESERVATION

A significant portion of the federal historic preservation effort is accomplished through the National Park Service (NPS), which is under the Secretary of the Interior. Federal statutes give the Secretary of the Interior and the National Park Service the authority to work with state and local governments to foster historic preservation efforts. Among the many ways that the NPS assists states and local governments is by the administration of federal matching grants to states. These grants are used to implement historic preservation programs. A portion of each state's federal matching grant is passed through to Certified Local Governments for the implementation of historic preservation programs.

The federal government has also established several incentive programs to encourage historic preservation. Among the most popular of these programs is the Federal Historic Preservation Tax Incentives.

### Historic American Buildings Survey

In 1935, the federal Historic Sites Act was passed. Among other actions, it created the Historic American Buildings Survey (HABS) to record historic buildings. This program, which began during the Depression as a way to employ architects and draftsmen, now has two sister programs: the Historic American Engineering Record (HAER), for recordation of works of engineering, and the Historic American Landscape Survey (HALS), for recordation of historic landscapes. The documentation of properties created under HABS, HAER, and HALS is preserved in the Library of Congress.

### Historic Preservation Act

The demolitions required by federal interstate highway and urban renewal programs during the post–World War II years created a public backlash to the destruction of neighborhoods and historic buildings. This public sentiment to protect historic buildings resulted in passage by Congress of the Historic Preservation Act of 1966, and this proved to be a turning point for the historic preservation movement in the United States. Among the many significant changes this act created for historic preservation was the establishment of the Advisory Council on Historic Preservation. Through Section 106 of the Historic Preservation Act of 1966, the Advisory Council on Historic Preservation administers a process to protect historic properties from adverse effects as a result of federal actions or federally funded actions.

The Historic Preservation Act of 1966 also authorized grants to states to establish offices that would partner with the federal government to administer historic preservation programs. As a result of these grants, each state has a State Historic Preservation Office that implements a comprehensive preservation program. These state programs identify, document, record, designate, and protect historic properties. States also provide and/or administer financial incentives in the form of grants and tax incentives for historic preservation. State Historic Preservation Offices work with individuals, organizations, and governmental entities to preserve historic properties. Most states make it a priority to educate their citizens about the benefits, objectives, and techniques of historic preservation.

### Local Government Programs

Local governments throughout the United States have established programs that foster preservation in their communities. Many local governments have chosen to become Certified Local Governments under a program sponsored by the National Park Service and State Historic Preservation Offices. Historic preservation programs at the local level have been used across the country to provide economic and physical revitalization of historic properties, with an apparent emphasis on commercial areas and older neighborhoods. Local historic preservation programs typically include a process for local designation of historic buildings and historic districts. Local programs frequently provide financial incentives and technical assistance to encourage historic preservation.

## NONPROFIT EFFORTS IN HISTORIC PRESERVATION

The history of historic preservation in the United States has typically been based on the significant efforts of individuals and groups that have been, in many cases, organized as nonprofit entities. Therefore, in addition to the governmental entities with historic preservation responsibilities, there are numerous local, national, and international nonprofit organizations that implement historic preservation programs.

The most prominent national preservation organization is the National Trust for Historic Preservation. Although it was established by the U.S. Congress in 1949, it is both a public and a private organization because it is supported primarily through memberships and donations. Among its numerous activities are the ownership and preservation of historic properties, the sponsorship of an annual national preservation conference, and the publication of a journal entitled *Preservation*.

In addition to national and international nonprofit organizations, most states have statewide nonprofit preservation organizations that have been established to advocate for historic preservation. Local nonprofit organizations are also numerous and influential in preserving historic properties.

## NATIONAL REGISTER OF HISTORIC PLACES LISTING

The National Register of Historic Places is the official list of historic properties that are recognized as having local, state, or national significance in American history, architecture, archeology, engineering, and culture. These "listed" historic properties have been deemed worthy of preservation.

## National Register of Historic Places Description

The *National Register Bulletin 15: How to Apply the National Register Criteria for Evaluation*, published by the U.S. Department of the Interior, National Park Service, Interagency Resource Division, describes the National Register of Historic Places as follows:

*The National Register of Historic Places documents the appearance and importance of districts, sites, buildings, structures, and objects significant in our prehistory and history. These properties represent the major patterns of our shared local, state, and national experience. To guide the selection of properties included in the National Register, the National Park Service has developed the National Register Criteria for Evaluation. These criteria are standards by which every property that is nominated to the National Register is judged. In addition, the National Park Service has developed criteria for the recognition of nationally significant properties, which are designated National Historic Landmarks...*

To nominate a property in the National Register of Historic Places, individuals may contact their State Historic Preservation Office. Nominations that meet the criteria for listing are forwarded to the Keeper of the Register by the State Historic Preservation Officer. The Keeper of the Register, which is within the National Park Service, has the authority to add properties to the National Register of Historic Places. State and local historical designations are also common and usually follow a process similar to that used for listing in the National Register of Historic Places.

Historical designation of a property typically affords opportunities for financial assistance through grants and tax credits. National Register designation provides Section 106 protection from federal projects that adversely affect listed properties. Local and state regulation of projects adversely affecting listed properties is also common. Regulation of activities affecting historic properties usually follows the Secretary of the Interior's Standards for the Treatment of Historic Properties.

## Standards for the Treatment of Historic Properties

The Secretary of the Department of the Interior has developed Standards for the Treatment of Historic Properties. These standards are philosophical rather than prescriptive. The National Park Service has published guidelines to interpret the application of the standards. The Secretary of the Interior's standards address four treatment options, which are defined by *The Secretary of the Interior's Standards for the Treatment of Historic Properties with Guidelines for Preserving, Rehabilitating, Restoring & Reconstructing Historic Buildings*, U.S. Department of the Interior, National Park Service. They are:

• *Preservation*. The act or process of applying measures necessary to sustain the existing form, integrity, and materials of an historic property. Work, including preliminary measures to protect and stabilize the property, generally focuses upon the ongoing maintenance and repair of historic materials and features rather than extensive replacement and new construction.
• *Rehabilitation*. The act or process of making possi-

ble a compatible use for a property through repair, alterations, and additions, while preserving those portions or features that convey its historical, cultural, or architectural values.
• *Restoration*. The act or process of accurately depicting the form, features, and character of a property as it appeared at a particular period of time by means of the removal of features from other periods in its history and reconstruction of missing features from the restoration period.
• *Reconstruction*. The act or process of depicting, by means of new construction, the form, features, and detailing of a nonsurviving site, landscape, building, structure, or object for the purpose of replicating its appearance at a specific period of time and in its historic location.

Among these treatment options, rehabilitation is the most common approach because it provides for modifications of the property to meet contemporary user needs. The Secretary of the Interior's Standards for Rehabilitation are as follows:

• A property will be used as it was historically or be given a new use that requires minimal change to its distinctive materials, features, spaces, and spatial relationships.
• The historic character of a property will be retained and preserved. The removal of distinctive materials or alteration of features, spaces, and spatial relationships that characterize a property will be avoided.
• Each property will be recognized as a physical record of its time, place, and use. Changes that create a false sense of historical development, such as adding conjectural features or elements from other historic properties, will not be undertaken.
• Changes to a property that have acquired historic significance in their own right will be retained and preserved.
• Distinctive materials, features, finishes, and construction techniques or examples of craftsmanship that characterize a property will be preserved.
• Deteriorated historic features will be repaired rather than replaced. Where the severity of deterioration requires replacement of a distinctive feature, the new feature will match the old in design, color, texture, and, where possible, materials. Replacement of missing features will be substantiated by documentary and physical evidence.
• Chemical or physical treatments, if appropriate, will be undertaken using the gentlest means possible. Treatments that cause damage to historic materials will not be used.
• Archeological resources will be protected and preserved in place. If such resources must be disturbed, mitigation measures will be undertaken.
• New additions and adjacent or related new construction will be undertaken in such a manner that, if removed in the future, the essential form and integrity of the historic property and its environment would be unimpaired.
• New additions, exterior alterations, or related new construction will not destroy historic materials, features, and spatial relationships that characterize the property. The new work shall be differentiated from the old and will be compatible with the historic materials, features, size, scale and proportion, and massing to protect the integrity of the property and its environment.

The National Park Service produces many informative publications on historic preservation, including a series of

Preservation Briefs. Several of these briefs are especially helpful in planning and understanding the preservation of historic interiors. The briefs of greatest assistance for individuals working with historic interiors are listed here:

Preservation Brief 17, "Architectural Character: Identifying the Visual Aspects of Historic Buildings as an Aid to Preserving Their Character," by Lee H. Nelson, AIA

Preservation Brief 18, "Rehabilitating Interiors in Historic Buildings—Identifying Character-Defining Elements," by H. Ward Jandl

Preservation Brief 21, "Repairing Historic Flat Plaster Walls and Ceilings," by Marylee MacDonald

Preservation Brief 23, "Preserving Historic Ornamental Plaster," by David Flaharty

Preservation Brief 24, "Heating, Ventilating, and Cooling Historic Buildings: Problems and Recommended Approaches," by Sharon C. Park, AIA

Preservation Brief 28, "Painting Historic Interiors," by Sara B. Chase

Preservation Brief 31, "Mothballing Historic Buildings," by Sharon C. Park, AIA

Preservation Brief 32, "Making Historic Properties Accessible," by Thomas C. Jester and Sharon C. Park, AIA

Preservation Brief 33, "The Preservation and Repair of Historic Stained and Leaded Glass," by Neal A Vogel and Rolf Achilles

Preservation Brief 34, "Applied Decoration for Historic Interiors: Preserving Composition Ornament," by Jonathan Thornton and William Adair, FAAR

Preservation Brief 35, "Understanding Old Buildings: The Process of Architectural Investigation," by Travis. C. McDonald, Jr.

Preservation Brief 37, "Appropriate Methods of Reducing Lead-Paint Hazards in Historic Housing," by Sharon C. Park, AIA and Douglas C. Hicks

Preservation Brief 40, "Preserving Historic Tile Floors," by Anne E. Grimmer and Kimberly A. Konrad

## RESOURCES

Advisory Council on Historic Preservation
1100 Pennsylvania Avenue, NW, Suite 809
Old Post Office Building
Washington, DC 20004
www.achp.gov

National Main Street Center of the National Trust for Historic Preservation
1785 Massachusetts Avenue, NW
Washington, DC 20036
www.mainst.org/

Heritage Preservation Services
National Park Service
1849 C Street, NW (org. 2255)
Washington, DC 20240-0001
www2.cr.nps.gov

National Preservation Institute
P.O. Box 1702
Alexandria, VA 22313
www.npi.org

National Trust for Historic Preservation
1785 Massachusetts Avenue, NW
Washington, DC 20036
www.nationaltrust.org

*Barbara Anderson; Kansas State University; Manhattan, Kansas*

# COLOR

## DESCRIBING COLOR

The three universal, measurable characteristics of color are as follows:

- *Hue:* The spectral category to which the color belongs; hue is the basic name of a color, such as "red."
- *Value:* The lightness or darkness of the color; high-value samples are light, low-value samples are dark.
- *Saturation:* The brilliance or dullness of the color; the amount of hue in a color. For example, vermilion has a great deal of red, but pink has very little.

## INDETERMINATE ATTRIBUTES OF COLOR

More than 90% of what we know of the world comes to us through our vision. The eye's retina absorbs the light and sends a signal, or sensation, to the brain. This sensation makes us aware of a characteristic of light—color. The National Bureau of Standards estimates that the human eye can distinguish more than 10 million different colors.

Indeterminate attributes are assigned to our perceptions of colors—to the way they make us feel. They cannot be measured; rather, they arise from our intuitive experience of color. These indeterminate attributes provide the mystery of color and range from the poetic language we use to express our perceptions of color to the psychological effects of color on our mood.

## DETERMINATE ATTRIBUTES OF COLOR

Determinate attributes of color can be measured by various instruments. Optics is the branch of science that analyzes the mechanisms we use to perceive color—the rods and cones on the eye's retina. Colorimetry measures the color systems developed to precisely communicate color. The mystery and the mechanics of color are tightly entwined. We seldom see a single color in isolation, completely independent from the influence of other colors or other external factors, such as the light source, the surface of the object, and the surrounding objects. Neither do we perceive color without the modifying influences of psychological and symbolic factors. Our response to color depends on who we are and what our culture tells us certain colors should mean.

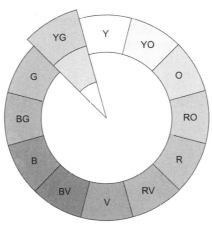

### THE COLOR WHEEL
The color wheel displays the visible hues. The color wheel acts as a synopsis of the basic spectrum available to the designer; there are too many hues in the range of human vision to include.

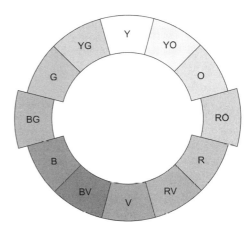

### MONOCHROMATIC COLOR SCHEMES
Monochromatic schemes use one hue with variations on its value; for example, beige, taupe, and mustard yellow, or white, black, and gray (silver). These schemes are often used in professional offices or high-end retail spaces, and suggest sophistication, even elegance.

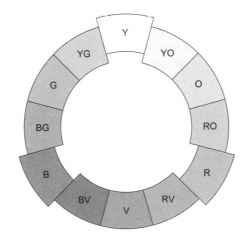

### COMPLEMENTARY COLOR SCHEMES
Complementary schemes use two hues that are situated opposite each other on the color wheel; for example, yellow and purple, or red-orange and blue-green. These energized schemes are the boldest and popular for use in sales offices and shopping malls.

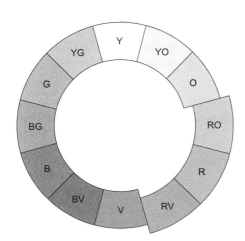

### ANALOGOUS COLOR SCHEMES
Analogous schemes use two or more hues that sit within a 90° arc of each other on the color wheel. These schemes can be energized when warm and cool colors are mixed, such as red-orange, red, and red-violet. Analogous schemes are popular choices for facilities supporting high-energy activity such as grade schools, child care centers, and sports facilities.

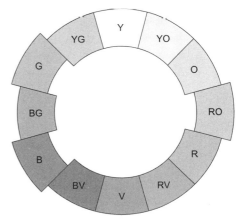

### CONTRASTING COLOR SCHEMES
Contrasting schemes use colors whose location on the color wheel create an equilateral triangle, such as red, blue, and yellow. These schemes are bold and are often used in large spaces such as sports arenas and entertainment facilities.

### SPLIT COMPLEMENTARY COLOR SCHEMES
Split complementary schemes use one hue from one side of the color wheel and the two hues adjacent to its complementary color; for example, red-orange, blue, and green. The complement contrasts vibrantly against the harmonious adjacent colors. These schemes are used to create impact and can often be seen in businesses specializing in innovation, bars, and dance clubs.

**THE COLOR WHEEL**

# VISUAL DEVICES

A visual illusion is a misperception; it is an interpretation of visual sensations that contradicts the reality of what a person sees. When the human eye receives electromagnetic energy, sensations are transmitted to the brain, and the brain translates these stimuli into meaningful images. This is vision. Visual perception is influenced by prior knowledge of the focal objects and the context of those objects. Since specific visual stimuli are understood in specific conditions, designers are able to devise a wide range of spatial configurations that simulate these conditions and create impressions that defy the physical character of space.

The human eye seeks order over chaos. Often, the brain will edit difficult visual information to clarify its understanding of the world around it, resulting in selective perception. Sometimes the brain is unable to distinguish elements due to ambiguity or camouflage, or it misunderstands what it sees because of intellectual expectations for conditions such as symmetry or constancy. By becoming familiar with these types of visual phenomena, the designer is able to manipulate a scene, intentionally altering the viewer's perception.

Commonly used visual devices include the manipulation of surfaces, light, form, and space.

## SURFACE MANIPULATION

### Color and Texture
Color and texture are two of the easiest-to-use and most powerful tools in the design of interior space. Surface coverings, material finishes, and furnishing selections are fundamental to creating the ambiance of a room or a space. Color can be used to compress a space or extend the perceived dimensions of a room. Texture can make a solid surface dematerialize or give a sense of stability to a lightweight object. Dark colors make spaces appear smaller, and light colors make spaces seem larger; but there are other applications of surface color and texture that can alter the appearance of an interior.

The muscles in the human eye respond differently to the various wavelengths of the visible spectrum, creating a relationship between color and the impression of spatial depth. These muscular reactions cause warm hues (red, orange, yellow) to appear as though they are advancing, and cool hues (blue, green, gray) to appear to be receding. In addition, distant objects appear cooler the farther they are from an individual because dust particles in the air obscure the purity of their color waves as they meet the human eye. These physical properties combine to create the illusion that objects identical in size, shape, and distance from the viewer, but differing in color and/or texture, will appear to be in different locations. Color *value*, the amount of lightness or darkness in a color, also impacts the perception of objects in space. High contract makes objects appear to advance and low contrast makes areas look as though they recede. A textured object lit to articulate high contrast will appear to have deep relief.

Using these principles, the vertical space of a room can appear taller if the ceiling is white or a light color, while a dark ceiling can lower the perceived height of a room. A ceiling height can appear even more compressed by lowering the crown molding from its typical position at the intersection of the wall and the ceiling to a height along the upper part of the wall. The illusion can be reinforced by painting the wall plane above the molding the same color as the ceiling. This phenomenon is achieved through the designer's combined understanding of the effects of using a continuous hue on adjacent surfaces and of defying the expectation that a crown molding marks the height of a room.

The horizontal dimensions of a room can be affected by color as well. By painting one wall of a room in contrast to the others, a room can grow deeper or shallower in perception and feel. A room will seem cozier with the introduction of warm tones, and will open up with cool tones.

### Faux Finishes
*Faux* finishes are surfaces painted to appear as though they were made from another material, such as a column painted to look like marble, a wainscot painted to look like wood, or a floor painted to look like mosaic tile.

The grand lobby of the USG Building in Chicago's Loop, designed by Skidmore, Owings, and Merrill, is a rich interior, with a dynamic floor pattern in marble tile, and walls faced with a white marble block—or so it appears. In actuality, only the lower portion of the wall is faced in marble tile; the upper portion of the wall is painted to appear as though it were.

Faux finishing can be brought into the third dimension, as well. In 1867, Baron Georges Haussmann designed *Parc des Buttes-Chaumont*, a romantic garden in northeast Paris. The then-new material portland concrete was used to imitate the look of rocks, unpolished stone, and even wood in the design of cliffs, a grotto, a classical colonnaded temple, handrails, and benches. Concrete's plasticity and ability to absorb color made it a perfect material for "fooling" the parkgoer.

Faux finishing techniques are often used in conjunction with *trompe l'oeil* perspectives to create both spatial and material deception.

### Trompe l'Oeil Perspective
The development of *trompe l'oeil* perspective during the Renaissance corresponded with the rediscovery of linear perspective. Literally meaning the "fooling of the eye," tromp l'oeil perspective employs mathematical principles and painting techniques to translate depth onto a two-dimensional surface, thereby altering the viewer's understanding of distance.

Leon Battisa Alberti (1404–1472) and Filippo Brunelleschi (1377–1446) are credited with making the techniques for creating linear perspective comprehensible. Brunelleschi gave public demonstrations of perspective in his "Peepshows," and Alberti described his discoveries in his 1435 treatise *Della Pitura (On Painting)*. Both explained the nature of visual depth perception and the mechanics of portraying what the eyes see: parallel lines, both horizontal and vertical, appear to converge at a vanishing point, and objects of equal size appear reduced in inverse proportion to their distance from the viewer. Since that time, Western artists and designers have used the principles of perspective to create the illusion of deep, proportionally correct space on a two-dimensional picture plane.

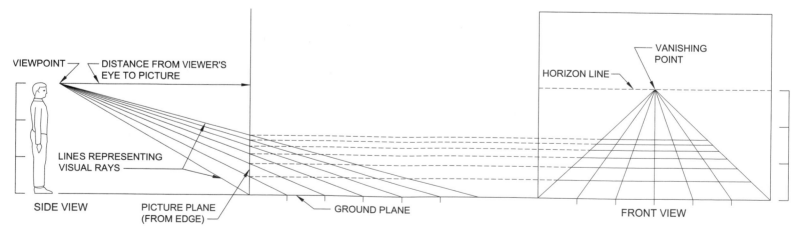

Depth perception and the mechanics of portraying what the eyes see: parallel lines, both horizontal and vertical, appear to converge at a vanishing point, and objects of equal size appear reduced in inverse proportion to their distance from the viewer.

**LINEAR PERSPECTIVE**

## TROMPE L'OEIL PAINTING

The great hall of the *Villa Farnesina* in Rome is an early example of trompe l'oeil. Appropriately named the *Salone delle Prospective,* it was painted in 1517 by Baldassare Peruzzi (1481–1526) who was an architect, painter, and stage-set designer. He drew on his theatrical expertise and his knowledge of classical wall painting to create the illusion that the *Salone* extended beyond the dimensions of its floor plate. He painted dramatic porticoes on all four sides of the salon, each leading to low "stone" balconies, which in turn overlooked beautiful imagined landscapes.

Trompe l'oeil continues to be a favorite device in the design of interiors. Architect Beverly Willis used the technique in her design for the Greenwich Apartment, situated on the steep eastern side of San Francisco's Telegraph Hill. With an exquisite view of the bay, Willis created an illusion by painting a scene on the living room wall that used the same horizon line as the exterior view, which terminates with a view of the exterior itself. The water level is the same inside and out, blurring the edges between the interior of the residence and the exterior.

Muralist Richard Haas has enhanced many urban settings with his masterly trompe l'oeil painting. His *112 Prince Street* façade in New York City depicts a masonry wall with punched windows on a surface previously blocked from view by an adjacent building. Complete with a cat sitting on a window sill, Haas's composition is a convincing continuation of the building's rhythm of pilasters and openings. Haas used his photorealistic painting art in interior space as well.

### Placement of Paintings

Mural paintings and frescos can greatly enhance an interior space, but careful planning must be used in the placement of these elements in order to achieve the best effect.

As part of the Iowa Art in State Buildings program, Richard Haas was commissioned to create paintings for the end walls of the long corridors of the Agronomy Building. Haas incorporated the hallway's existing architectural details, such as floor tiles, window moldings, and columns, into the ground floor corridor's composition. The mural plays with the illusionary effects of the horizon line and one-point perspective, depicting a view of Iowa's rolling landscape through a painted window. Included in the landscape are fields, farm buildings, livestock, and the skyline of Iowa's state buildings in the distance, a convincing view of what might be seen if there was fenestration at the end of the hall.

Arguably one of the world's most mysterious illusions, Leonardo da Vinci's *The Last Supper* (15 ft × 22 ft –10 in. (4.5 m × 6.9 m)) occupies the north wall of the refectory (monastic dining room) of the Convent of Santa Maria delle Grazie, Milan. The fresco sits high on the wall directly over the entrance to the refectory and is designed to look like a deep upper room overlooking the dining room. Da Vinci painted the scene's coffered ceiling in deep perspective, suggesting that the upper room is located adjacent to the dining room, behind the architectural cornice and the lunettes. The abbot and monks of the convent ate on the lower level at the other end of the refectory, perhaps imagining themselves to be sharing their meal with 13 others. The unusual perspective of *The Last Supper* lifts the viewer's eye from the floor to the correct viewpoint.

### Mirrors

Mirrors are commonly used in public places to give the illusion of space. Restaurants and hotel lobbies use reflective surfaces to imply greater patronage as well. Mirrors bring light into dark spaces and bring reflected views into a room. Mirrors set across from one another create an effect of infinite reflection.

The traditions of the Chinese art of placement, *feng shui,* include the use of mirrors for their illusionary properties as much as for their capabilities to bring good *ch'i* (life force) into a living space and deflect bad *feng shui* spatial configurations. For example, mirrors are used to create a healthy visual sense of distance when walls are too close together or a room is too crowded.

The Hall of Mirrors *(Gallerie des Glaces)* at Versailles is an extreme example of how mirrors can extend the perceived space of a room. In 1684, interior designer Charles Le Brun designed the grandiose hall in Louis XIV's country home, which included 17 arched windows opening out toward the great gardens of the chateau. On the wall opposite the fenestration, he designed a series of 17 arched recessed panels, each faced with a Venetian mirror, "mirroring" the size and shape of the windows, themselves. This dynamic composition succeeds in bringing the outside in as well as visually enlarging the space for the festivities of the kings of France.

At the other end of the scalar spectrum, mirrors have been incorporated in the design of furniture, as well. For example, pier tables were popular pieces of furniture in the American colonies of the late eighteenth and nineteenth centuries. Typically placed with their backs flat against a wall, these tables were curved in the front (both on the tabletop and the lower surface). The back panel between these surfaces is mirrored, and the reflections complete the curvilinear form of the table while subtly suggesting an extension of the volume of the room. Located below the tabletop, the viewer is less aware that the surface is reflective, making the discovery of the device that much more rewarding.

### Light

The ethereal quality of light makes it a wonderfully deceptive element for interior design. In its close connection to the properties of color, bright light can make a space expand, and the absence of light can make a space contract.

A more obscure characteristic of light is that shadows cast by light are the complementary color of the source of the light. Outdoors, shadows are black because the light from the sun is white; indoors, the possibilities differ. Architect Luis Barragon used this phenomenon in the Chapel for the *Capuchinas Sacramentarias del Purisimo Corazon de Maria* in Tlalplan, Mexico. He placed a cross in front of a yellow-tinted glass window. When direct sunlight shines through the window, it becomes a yellow light, and the shadow cast by the cross is purple.

The right eye of Jesus occupies both foreground and background simultaneously. In the foreground, the eye is part of the painting's story; in the background, it is the vanishing point. In both cases, that point is about 15 ft (4.5 m) above the floor level.

In order for the painting to appear like an extension of the refectory, the vanishing point should be lower, at the spectator's eye level; instead, the intensity of the perspective seems to lift the viewer from the floor to the correct viewing point, creating a spiritually uplifting phenomenon.

**LEONARDO DA VINCI'S *THE LAST SUPPER***

Standing at the entry to Borromini's garden colonnade, a figure's height is less than half that of the barrel vault above.

A false impression of depth is created by proportionally diminishing the architectural details toward the rear of the colonnade.

Standing at the rear of the colonnade, the same figure is much taller and wider compared to the surrounding barrel vault.

**FRANCESCO BORROMINI, PALAZZO SPADA: GARDEN PERSPECTIVE COLONNADE**

## FORM

Principles of scale and proportion are useful in creating visual illusions. Scale, the relationship of the size of objects to the size of people, can be easily manipulated to make individuals feel much smaller or much larger. Proportion, the internal relationship of one part of an object or collection of objects to itself, can be manipulated to deceive individuals into misunderstanding the dimensional qualities of space.

Michelangelo experimented with both concepts in the design of the vestibule to the Laurentian Library, in 1525, in Florence. By giving the entrance staircase a monumental scale, visitors to the library are made to feel small compared to the importance of the library they are about to enter. The extraordinary stair rises to the library door in three flights, although only the center flight has treads that are easy to climb. It is set in a small square space, potentially too small for such a staircase. In order to balance the composition, Michelangelo manipulated other details to open the space of the vestibule. He de-emphasized the double columns by placing them in niches and integrating their presence into the surface of the wall, and he proportionally enlarged the brackets to match the size of the stair instead of the columns. Through this play of scale, and by changing proportional relationships among the elements of the classical composition, patrons of the library are convinced that the monumental stair is suited for the space in which it sits.

Sir John Soane (1753–1837) was another proponent of visual manipulation. In his home at 13 Lincoln's Inn Fields in London, he played with scale to impact the impression his spaces convey. Visitors to the home's crypt are made to feel like Titans—eye level with the capitals of the space's columns. On the upper floors, Soane exaggerated the perceived monumentality of the rooms by narrowing their vertical features, such as the doors and cabinets. He used cast-iron to create thin columns in rooms, such as the dining room, to reinforce the vertical expression.

Japanese designs are detailed with small-scaled objects to provide a sense of space that is otherwise difficult to find on the densely populated island nation. Bonsai trees are strategically placed in gardens to suggest that they are at a great distance from the viewer, although they are a mere yard (meter) or two.

### Space

Forced perspective is based on the same principles of Renaissance perspective that are used in trompe l'oeil, but extended into the third dimension. Often accompanied with trompe l'oeil painting and faux finishes, the designer can achieve an artificial sense of dimension through the deliberate manipulation of objects in space. Since parallel lines converge, and objects in space appear smaller, actually converging parallel elements and reducing the size of the objects will deepen a shallow space or, in reverse, foreshorten a deep space, despite the actual dimensions of a place.

In designing the church of *Maria presso S. Satiro* in Milan, Donato Bramante (1482–1492) used forced perspective with trompe l'oeil to masterly affect. The site for the church was not long enough to include the choir required to complete the traditional cruciform plan. In a mere 6-ft- (2-m-) deep space, Bramante created the illusion of a full choir. He created the impression of deep space beneath a barrel vault by narrowing and slanting elements of the vault toward the vanishing point. The ceiling's coffers, the lines of columns, and the full suite of architectural details diminish in size and shape to imitate the effects of perspective, suggesting that the area beyond the altar is a full, deep choir. The visual device is not evident to a visitor to the church until he or she is close to the altar, delighting the visitor with an understanding of Bramante's clever design solution.

Francesco Borromini (1599–1667) created a false impression of great depth in the inner courtyard of Rome's *Palazzo Spada* in 1652. The elements of the apparently lengthy arcade mimic perspective effects; the columns literally get smaller the farther back they go, and they are thicker at the front than the back; the floor slopes upward, and the cornices downward; and the ceiling coffers and the squares on the pavement pattern are actually trapezoids. Despite appearances, the perspective arcade is only 28 ft- 2 in. (8.5 m) long.

Of course, when seen from the opposite end, the arcade foreshortens, suggesting that the arcade can be traversed in just a few paces.

Forced perspective and trompe l'oeil are popular techniques used in theatrical scenic design. In *Teatro Olimipco,* 1580, Andea Palladio (1508–1580) built a system combining both techniques into the architecture of the theatre. Built in Vicenza, Italy, Palladio designed five narrow tunnels at perspectival angles behind arched openings in the far wall (upstage) of the stage. Set designer Vincenzo Scamozzi created his vision of the "ideal city," a permanent series of urban street scenes built in accelerated perspective, visible to the audience through the openings. He painted the walls of the streets in a forced perspective along a narrow backstage area. He used trompe l'oeil to simulate the marble and stucco façades, and he incorporated the effects of light and color to reinforce the deep three-dimensionality of the image.

Landscape architects have incorporated forced perspective in their designs as well. Andre le Notre denies the great distance of a statue of Hercules in the garden of *Vaux le Viscomte* by lowering the topography below the horizon line in the expanse of the garden and by raising the focus of the statue high on a hill above the vanishing point. By contrast, the great lawn behind the Federalist-style mansion at Dumbarton Oaks in the Georgetown area of Washington, DC, appears longer than it is by the symmetrical trapezoidal shape leading to the wooded valley below.

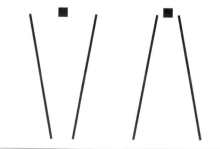

**FORCED PERSPECTIVE**

## Combining Effects

The Arthur M. Sackler Gallery at Harvard University, designed by James Sterling in 1987, combines two effects, forced perspective and a scale shift. The monumental, single-directional staircase narrows as it moves upward, exaggerating the visual phenomenon of a one-point perspective. The perceived distance is increased again by the placement of the torso of a Roman statue of Aphrodite, dating from the second century B.C. The viewer anticipates that the torso is a larger-than-life marble sculpture, appearing smaller because of its great distance from the bottom of the staircase. The deception is revealed when the visitor reaches the destination more quickly than anticipated and then discovers that the torso is a mere 38 in. (970 mm) high.

Venturi, Scott Brown and Associates used a number of illusionary principles in their 1981 design of the Sainsbury Wing addition to the National Gallery located in London's Trafalgar Square. Walking toward the new galleries, the viewer is confronted with a series of four arched entries. The arches recede in actual size, proportionally, the way they would appear in perspective, forcing the view to appear longer than its measured length. This distance is given even greater depth by the placement of a painting, the *Incredulity of Saint Thomas* by Cima (c. 1504): its arched top continues the visual rhythm created by the forced perspective and leads the eye beyond the back wall on which the painting is placed.

*Sally Levine, AIA; Cleveland, Ohio*

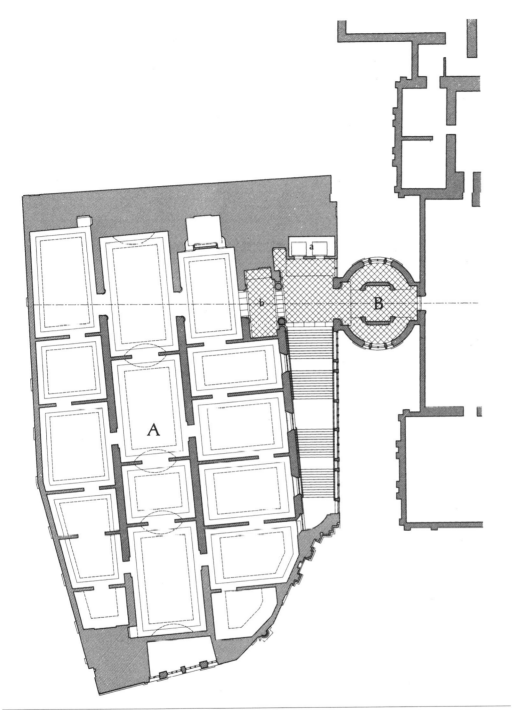

**SECTION THROUGH MAIN STAIR** *Sainsbury Wing, National Gallery, London; Venturi, Scott Brown and Associates*

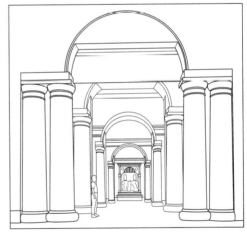

**VIEW FROM POINT "B"**

**LOCATION OF PAINTING, *THE INCREDULITY OF SAINT THOMAS*** *Sainsbury Wing, National Gallery, London; Venturi, Scott Brown and Associates*

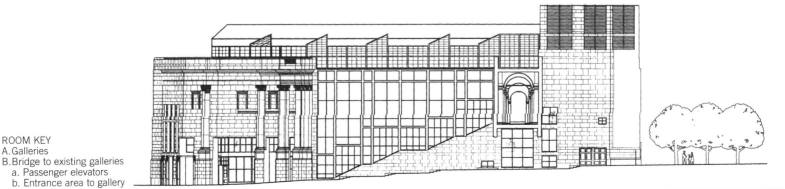

ROOM KEY
A. Galleries
B. Bridge to existing galleries
   a. Passenger elevators
   b. Entrance area to gallery

**PLAN** *Sainsbury Wing, National Gallery, London; Venturi, Scott Brown and Associates*

# PARALINE AND PERSPECTIVE DRAWINGS

## DRAWING METHODS

Perspective and paraline drawing methods are used to create three-dimensional drawings. Three-dimensional modeling software is available to generate such drawings. These computer programs are based on the basic principles of handdrawn perspectives. Paraline drawings differ from perspective drawings, in that the projection lines remain parallel instead of converging to a point on the horizon.

## PARALINE DRAWINGS

Paraline drawings are sometimes referred to as axonometric (Greek) or axiometric (English) drawings. These drawings are projected pictorial representations of an object, which portray a three-dimensional quality. They can be classified as *orthographic projections,* as the plan view is rotated and the side view is tilted. The resulting "front" view is projected at a 90° angle to the picture plane.

Paraline drawings are useful for interior spaces and objects, particularly for cabinet and furniture design drawings. Exploded drawings of this type are often used to convey how various components can be made into a whole. Manufacturer's product literature often uses exploded isometrics to illustrate how to assemble a product or to create a component list. Designers can use these drawings to convey a design idea or show a contractor how an intended installation should be assembled.

In paraline drawing, parallel lines are used to create three-dimensional drawings that have a true measured or proportional scale in three principal axes: width, depth, and height. These drawings are typically easier to construct than perspective drawings and can convey a proportional three-quarter view of an object or space.

## ORTHOGRAPHIC DRAWING

Two-dimensional, scaled orthographic drawings are used to develop three-dimensional paraline and perspective drawings. Orthographic drawings include:

- plan, or top view
- section, or crosssection, cutaway view
- elevation, facade, or side view

## OBLIQUE DRAWING

In an oblique drawing one face (either plan or elevation) of the object is drawn directly on the picture plane. Projected lines are drawn at a 30° or 45° angle to the picture plane. The length of the projecting lines varies according to the angle chosen.

## Plan Oblique

An axonometric drawing, also referred to as a *plan projection,* is projected and generated from plan. The plan remains in scale and perpendicular to the line of sight. The vertical components of an object or wall are projected vertically from the plan.

## Elevation Oblique

An elevation oblique, also referred to as an *elevation projection,* is an axonometric drawing projected and generated from the elevation or sides. The elevation remains in scale and perpendicular to the line of sight. The horizontal components of an object or wall are projected from the elevation.

## Planometric

A planometric is a combination of the plan oblique and the elevation oblique. The plan and elevation are both used in scale and in relationship to each other when constructing the drawing so that both the plan and elevation remain in scale.

## Dimetric

A dimetric drawing is similar to oblique, with one exception: the object is rotated so that only one of its corners touches the picture plane. In dimetric drawings, two different scales are used to draft an object. Two of the width:depth:height scale ratios remain equal, such as 1:1:⅝.

The most frequently used angle for the projecting lines is an equal division of 45° on either side of the leading edge. A 15° angle is sometimes used when it is less important to show the "roof view" of the object.

## Isometric

The isometric, a special type of dimetric drawing, is the easiest and most popular paraline drawing, and is generated from the dimensions of the object. All axes of the object are simultaneously rotated away from the picture plane and kept at the same angle of projection (30° from the picture plane). All legs are equally distorted in length at a given scale and therefore maintain an exact w:d:h proportion of 1:1:1.

## Trimetric

The trimetric drawing is similar to the dimetric, except that the plan of the object is rotated so that the two exposed sides of the object are not at equal angles to the picture plane. Three different w:d:h scale ratios are used, such as 1:¾:⅝. The plan is usually positioned at 30/60° angle to the ground plane. The height of the object is reduced proportionately as illustrated (similar to the 45° dimetric).

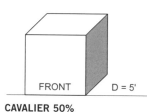 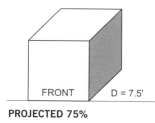 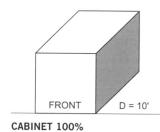

| CAVALIER 50% | PROJECTED 75% | CABINET 100% |
| --- | --- | --- |
| FRONT    D = 5' | FRONT    D = 7.5' | FRONT    D = 10' |

Given:
Width = 10 ft
Depth = 10 ft
Height = 10 ft

If front elevation is drawn at scale, ¼ in. = 1 ft 0 in.
Depth is ¾ × ¼ = ³⁄₁₆ in.
Use scale ³⁄₁₆ in. = 1 ft 0 in.

**OBLIQUE ELEVATION**

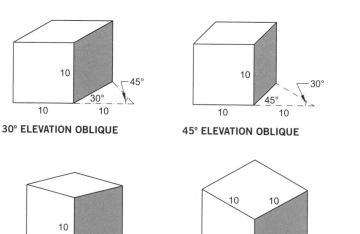 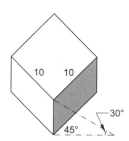

**30° ELEVATION OBLIQUE**   **45° ELEVATION OBLIQUE**   **45° DIMETRIC (PLAN OBLIQUE)**

**15° DIMETRIC**   **ISOMETRIC**   **TRIMETRIC**

**AXONOMETRIC—MEASURED METHOD**

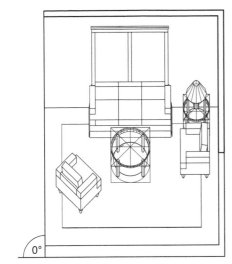

**0° PLANOMETRIC**

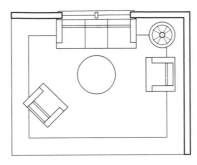

**PLAN**

**ELEVATION**

## ADJUSTING THE OBLIQUE DIMENSION TO REDUCE DISTORTION

Dimetric and trimetric adjustments can be made to correct distortions to the image caused by the optical illusion when an object is rotated from view. Adjusting the proportional factor in computer programs allows the adjustment of the angle of view to compensate for distortion.

**1:½:1**

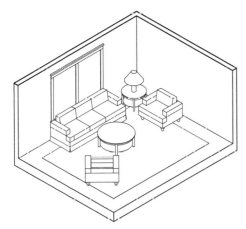

**ISOMETRIC 1:1:1**

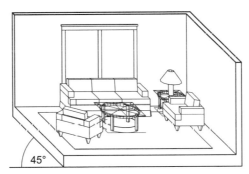

**ELEVATION OBLIQUE 1:½:1**

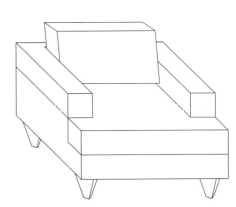

**1:¾:1**

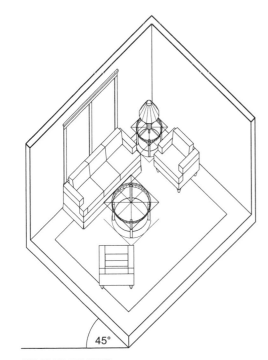

**45° PLAN OBLIQUE**

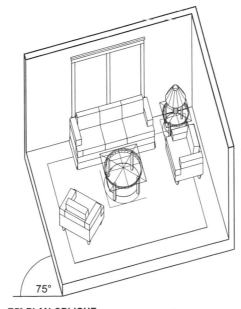

**75° PLAN OBLIQUE**

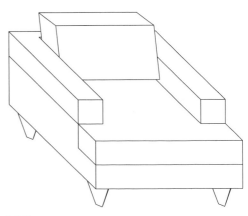

**1:1:1**

The width/depth/height ration has been adjusted in these illustrations by a factor of ½ and ¾, respectively. Adjusting the scale of the depth of an oblique drawing will result in a more believable proportion.

**ORTHOGRAPHIC DRAWINGS**

**DIMETRIC ADJUSTMENT OF DEPTH**

## PERSPECTIVE DRAWINGS

The major types of perspective drawings include:

- one-point perspectives
- two-point perspectives
- three-point perspectives
- multipoint perspectives

## ONE-POINT INTERIOR PERSPECTIVES

A one-point perspective typically presents one face of a room or space perpendicular to the viewer and parallel to the picture plane. The primary face of the room or object is turned fully toward the viewer. This will appear in plan as a 0° relationship to the picture plane. All objects that are oriented in this manner will appear to be in an orthographic, flat, or an end-on view relationship to the viewer. All of the perpendicular planes to this plane will appear to converge toward the central vanishing point, which can be either in front of or behind the picture plane. The vanishing point is usually located at the sitting or standing height of an average person within the space (eye level can be located at 5 ft 4 in (1,626 mm) from the floor). In most cases, the vanishing point is located within the confines of the enclosed space being represented in the drawing. In one-point perspectives, the true height line can coincide with the entire measured plane that is in scale. Therefore, horizontal as well as vertical scale measures can be used to project the proportions of an intended subject.

## CONSTRUCTION OF A ONE-POINT INTERIOR PERSPECTIVE

Construction of a one-point interior perspective is as follows:

1. Draw the primary elevation, or section, to scale. Locate the horizon line and vanishing point (VP) within the confines of the interior space. Locate the 45° measuring point (45° MP), which is also the station point (SP) in section. Strike an arc from the most remote corner of the room to a vertical line drawn from the VP. From this intersection draw a line upward at 60° (to the vertical) to meet the horizon. This intersection shall be the 45° MP.
2. Determine the room depth by starting at point 0 on the ground line and measuring to the right. Connect this point to the 45° MP on the horizon. The back wall is located where the line intersects the vertical base line drawn from the vanishing point to the ground line.
3. Complete the back wall as illustrated. Note that all lines occurring at a 45° angle in the elevation remain parallel in perspective. All surfaces that are parallel to the picture plane will remain parallel in perspective.

## TWO-POINT PERSPECTIVES

Two-point perspectives allow for a wide variety of drawing angles. They are more dynamic and more widely used to depict three-dimensional space and objects. Traditional hand-constructed projections as well as computer-generated images can be used to develop quick sketch models, which can be used to further refine design elements by freehand sketch overlay techniques.

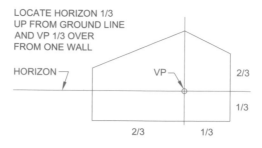

LOCATE HORIZON 1/3 UP FROM GROUND LINE AND VP 1/3 OVER FROM ONE WALL

DRAW FRONT ELEVATION TO DESIRED SCALE

**FRONT ELEVATION**

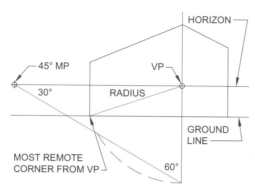

**LOCATE 45° MEASURING POINT**

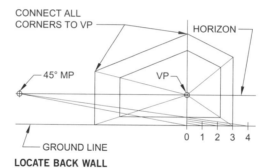

**LOCATE BACK WALL**

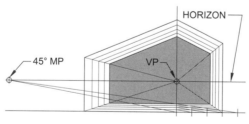

**COMPLETE**

**ONE-POINT DIRECT MEASURED INTERIOR PERSPECTIVE**

## TWO-POINT PERSPECTIVE USING THE MEASURING POINT METHOD

This is a simplified alternative to the conventional method of laying out the plan picture plane and projecting the vanishing lines. The measuring point method of drawing a two-point perspective eliminates the necessity of the preliminary layout of the plan. One of the obvious advantages of this method is the ease with which the size of the drawing can be adjusted. A perspective can be made larger by simply increasing the scale of the drawing.

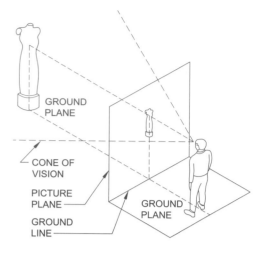

A linear perspective is created by using the basic principles of ground plane and picture plane. The perceived object, in this case a sculpture, is plotted on a plane (referred to as the *picture plane*) parallel to the stationary viewer. A scale image is produced this way.

## PERSPECTIVE PRINCIPLES

### PERSPECTIVE

**Terminology and Concepts**

HORIZON LINE: A line drawn on the picture plane to represent the horizon. It is usually located at the point where all parallel lines recede away from the viewer and finally converge.

PICTURE PLANE: An imaginary, transparent plane, onto or through which the object is perceived in a perspective rendering. The picture plane is a curved plane for a wide angle perspective view.

STATION POINT: The point from which the object is viewed. The location of this point will be the factor that determines the width of the drawing. A 30° cone of vision is drawn from the station point. A common way of determining the distance between the station point and the picture plane is by referring to the following parameters:

- Minimum – 1.73 times the width of the image
- Average – 2.00 times the width of the image
- Maximum – 2.5 times the width of the image

VANISHING POINT: A specific point or points located on the horizon line, where all parallel lines, drawn in perspective, converge or terminate. The location of the vanishing points varies with the type of perspective drawing. In the two-point perspective, the distance between the vanishing point left and the vanishing point right is estimated as being approximately four times the overall size of the object being rendered.

## TWO-POINT PERSPECTIVE USING 30°/60° DIRECT MEASURED SYSTEM

Two-point perspectives using the 30°/60° direct measured system are constructed as follows:

1. SETUP: Draw a horizon line and locate vanishing point right (VPR) and vanishing point left (VPL) separated at a distance that is approximately 4 to 4.5 times the maximum width of the image. Follow the illustration to locate the station point and leading corner of the image.
2. LENGTH: Measure, to scale, the length of the image along length line L. A perpendicular line is drawn from these designated points to the ground line. The vanishing perspective lines are then drawn directly from these points to the appropriate vanishing point (VPL). In this way the correct length of the line can be determined. Note what happens when equally spaced points are projected from the ground line to the vanishing point. The visual distance (length) between them, as they get closer to the vanishing point, is progressively foreshortened.
3. WIDTH: The width is measured along the width line at double scale. That is, if the perspective is drawn at a scale of ⅛ in = 1 ft, and a particular line is to be drawn at 5 ft, measure 5 ft at ¼ in. scale starting at the corner, and measure to the left of the corner horizontally. A line is drawn from each point on the width line to the appropriate vanishing point (VPR). The intersections of the length and width vanishing lines will define the "plan" in perspective.
4. HEIGHT: Since the leading corner of the image is placed directly on the picture plane, the height is measured, to scale, directly on the horizon line. It is then carried to VPL and VPR, as illustrated.

## TWO-POINT PERSPECTIVE USING 45° DIRECT MEASURED SYSTEM

Two-point perspectives using the 45° direct measured system are constructed as follows:

1. SETUP: Similar to the method used in the 30°/60° setup, the vanishing points are placed on the horizon line and separated by 3 times the diagonal width.
2. LENGTH: Measure, to scale, the length of the image along the length line L. Connect the points directly to VPL.
3. WIDTH: In this setup, the width is the same as the length scale. Measure the width of the image along the width line W. The length and width lines will form an outline of the "plan" in perspective.
4. HEIGHT: The height line is positioned at a 45° angle and marked off to scale. A line representing the leading corner of the image is drawn perpendicular to the ground line. Connect or draw a line from the measurement points along the height line horizontally to the vertical corner line. As in the 30°/60° setup, these points are then carried to VPR and VPL.

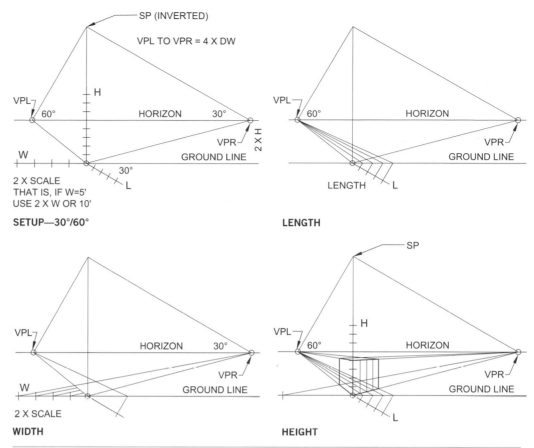

TWO-POINT PERSPECTIVE—30°/60° DIRECT MEASURED SYSTEM

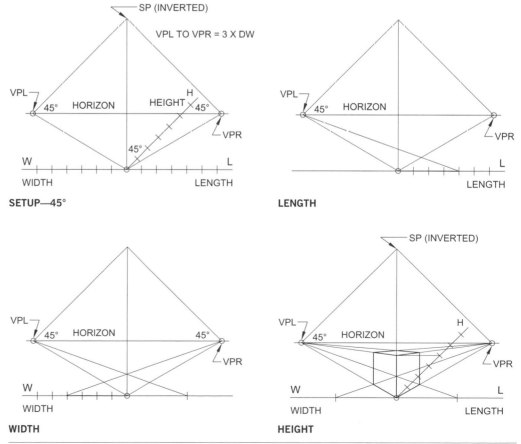

TWO-POINT PERSPECTIVE—45° DIRECT MEASURED SYSTEM

## THREE-POINT PERSPECTIVES

Three-point perspectives are used to develop a third orientation and vertical diminution of form. In one- and two-point perspectives, objects are shown to converge toward vanishing points that are located on the horizon line or at eye level. All vertical dimensions are drawn to scale relative to one another. Vertical lines do not become more diminutive in a one- or two-point perspective, since many interior spaces are one or few stories high and rarely does the dominant view exceed the normal cone of vision. In the perspective drawing of taller and larger interior spaces and buildings, a third vanishing point is introduced somewhere along the vertical visual axis of the center of vision located by the station point. In the three-point perspective, the picture plane, which is assumed to be perpendicular to the center of vision, is rotated vertically from the station point creating a vertical as well as a horizontal component of the picture plane.

Three-point perspectives are constructed as follows:

1. LENGTH: The length line is drawn at the same scale as the line connecting points 1 and 2 (which is four times the maximum length of the object). Measured points are projected perpendicularly from the length line L to the ground line. From the ground line, the measured points are connected to vanishing point left (VP1).

2. WIDTH: The width should be double the scale used for length. For example, if the length is at a ¼ in. scale, use ½ in. scale for the width. Locate the distances along the width line, and connect these points directly to the vanishing point right (VP2).

3. HEIGHT: Using the original scale, mark off the measuring points along the height line (H). These points are projected perpendicularly to the line labeled "vertical plane." From these points a line is drawn to VP2, thereby cutting the vertical lines vanishing to VP2.

4. 45° POINT: This point on the horizon is determined by projecting a line from the upside-down station point so that it will meet the horizon line at a 75° angle. All lines occurring at a 45° angle to the picture plane (in viewing) will converge to this point; it is, therefore, often convenient to use this as a reference point when converting exact width to length, or vice versa, in plan.

## MULTIPLE VANISHING POINT DRAWINGS

Multiple vanishing point perspectives are a combination of two or more perspectives in one space. When an object in the room depicted is rotated from the parallel planes of the room, that object or series of objects will have its-their own corresponding vanishing points on a common horizon line. Each orientation or parallel plane will have its own vanishing point. For example, in a one-point perspective, a chair that has been turned from view may have its own vanishing points.

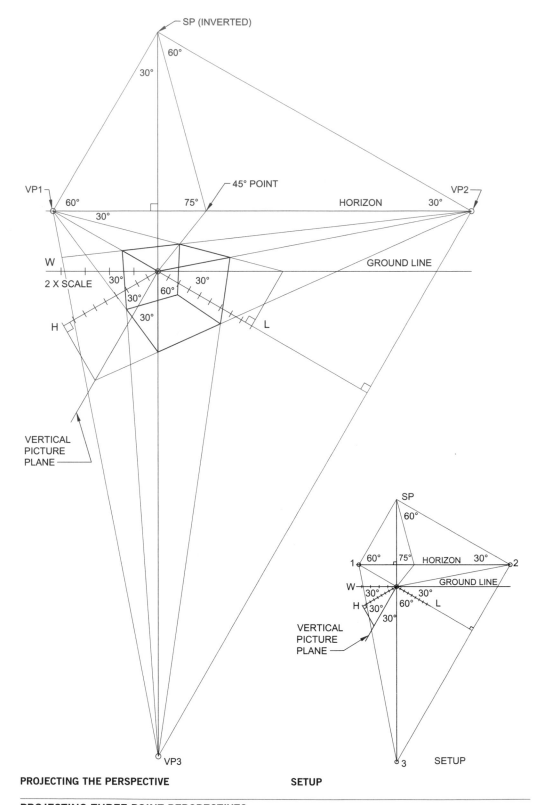

PROJECTING THE PERSPECTIVE                    SETUP

**PROJECTING THREE-POINT PERSPECTIVES**

## PLAN PROJECTION METHOD OF PERSPECTIVE CONSTRUCTION

Before the drawing can be laid out, the following information must be obtained:

1. An approximation of the overall dimensions of the interior space.
2. The location of the interior space in relation to the picture plane.
3. The orientation of the interior space, either in front of or behind the picture plane.

While the interior space can be located anywhere in the drawing—in front of, behind, or at any angle to the picture plane—the simplest approach is to place the interior space at the picture plane. The horizontal lines of the interior space would be parallel to the picture plane in a one-point perspective or placed at an angle to the picture plane. Usually this will be a 30°/60° or 45° angle in a two-point perspective.

**ONE-POINT PERSPECTIVE**

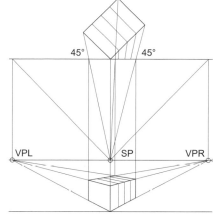

**45° TWO-POINT PERSPECTIVE**

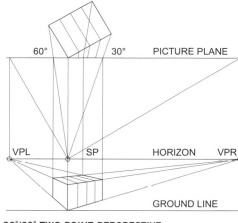

**30°/60° TWO-POINT PERSPECTIVE**

---

## PERSPECTIVE CONSTRUCTION—PROJECTION METHOD

## USING THE PLAN PROJECTION METHOD OF PERSPECTIVE CONSTRUCTION

The following steps are taken to construct a perspective using the plan projection method:

1. Consider the most important features of the room or object. Identify the location in plan from which the subject is viewed. This is the station point (SP).

2. Rotate and arrange the plan, slightly above where the perspective will be drawn. Conventional orientations could include a 30°/60° or 45° for two-point perspectives and 90° for one-point perspectives. Orientations such as a 15°/75° and others are possible. This allows the layout of two-point perspectives that have two vanishing points.

3. Establish a cone of vision (COV). The average person has an approximately 60° normal cone of vision, with additional peripheral vision. Typically, a maximum of 90° is used.

4. Establish the picture plane (PP). The picture plane is an imaginary plane, represented as a line in plan, onto which the intended subject will be drawn. Visual rays will be drawn from the viewer at the station point to the object. Where they intersect, the picture plane will determine their graphic position in the perspective layout. The picture plane should be drawn through some known and measurable point in the plan. Later, this point will be used as a scale measure line or true height line.

5. Establish the vanishing point locations on the picture plane. In a one-point perspective, there is only one vanishing point. When two or more vanishing points are used in one drawing they can be labeled with a subscript such as vanishing point left (VPL); vanishing point right (VPR). The vanishing points are determined by extend-

ing visual rays from the station point to the picture plane parallel to the object being drawn. In order to properly lay out and draft a perspective drawing, the drawing area should be arranged parallel to the picture plane.

6. Establish the direction of the angle of view. Once the direction of view is established, the SP should be at least 30° away from the furthest point of the intended subject. This will ensure the incorporation of a 60° cone of vision.

7. Identify the 60° cone of vision, which is an imaginary angle of view that closely approximates normal vision. The station point should be far enough away from the intended subject to view it within the normal cone of vision. Objects that are drawn outside of the normal cone of vision will become distorted in shape. Some computer programs will allow the adjustment of the cone of vision. In most interior perspectives a 90° maximum cone of vision is typical.

8. Establish the ground line (GL). The ground line ordinarily corresponds to either the floor level of the space or object being drawn.

9. Draw the horizon line at the appropriate eye level above the ground line. The eye level would be approximately 5 ft to 5 ft 6 in. (1,524 mm to 1,676 mm) above the ground level in a conventional perspective. If a higher view is desired, for example, from the top floor of an atrium space, the eye level would be 5 ft 6 in. (1,676 mm) plus the floor-to-floor height.

10. Locate the true height line (TH). The true height line is a line which begins at the ground line and extend upward and will serve as a point of reference or scale, from which all of the vertical elements and measurements in the perspective drawing will be derived. The true height line is usually a point of known scale that intersects the picture plane. It is helpful to place the picture plane within the interior space or touching

or intersecting an object being drawn. This primary true height line will be in the same scale as the plan.

11. Locate the lines of convergence that correspond to the major design elements in the plan. These will include the walls, large-scale planes and surfaces, including rugs or floor patterns as well as dominant architectural elements such as doors, window openings, or columns.

12. Locate the "leading edge" or nearest edge of the closest object to be drawn and its corresponding major coordinates (four corners, in the case of a rectangular object) by extending visual rays from the station point to the object and through or to the picture plane. These intersecting points will establish the vertical connection or relative position along the eye level of the perspective drawing.

13. Locate the major furnishings or other architectural elements in the plan by extending the vertical edges to the perspective drawing. Reduce complex forms to their simplest shapes prior to adding detail. Such shapes may include rectilinear and cubic solids.

14. Determine the depth of the drawing by extending the location of each object's footprint along the ground plane. Determine the height of the objects by lines from the vertical dimensions or the elevation to the true height line and following the perspective proportional height through the perspective space.

15. Extend the lines of a footprint, such as a sofa to the wall, to find the alignment of the sofa to that wall in perspective by extending the visual rays from the station point to the picture plane and back down to the perspective. By extending lines of convergence from the vanishing point forward into the room, the intersecting lines with the vertical extension lines will determine the four corners of the sofa.

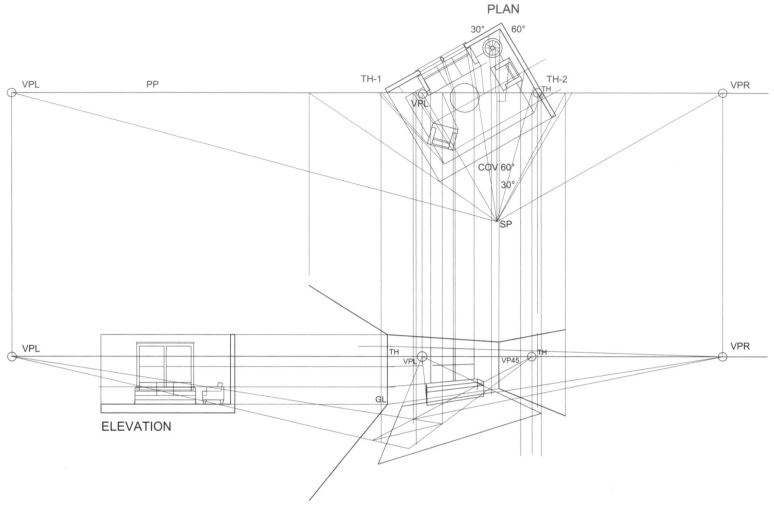

**PROJECTION SETUP**
Locate major floor and ceiling elements. Locate footprint of major furniture elements and sketch out basic volumes in perspective.

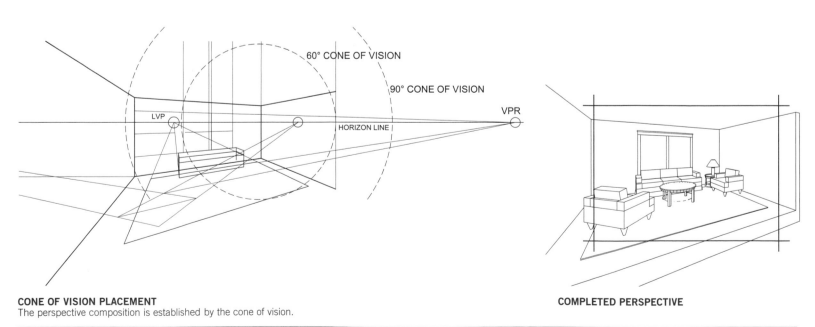

**CONE OF VISION PLACEMENT**
The perspective composition is established by the cone of vision.

**COMPLETED PERSPECTIVE**

**PLAN PROJECTION METHOD OF PERSPECTIVE CONSTRUCTION**

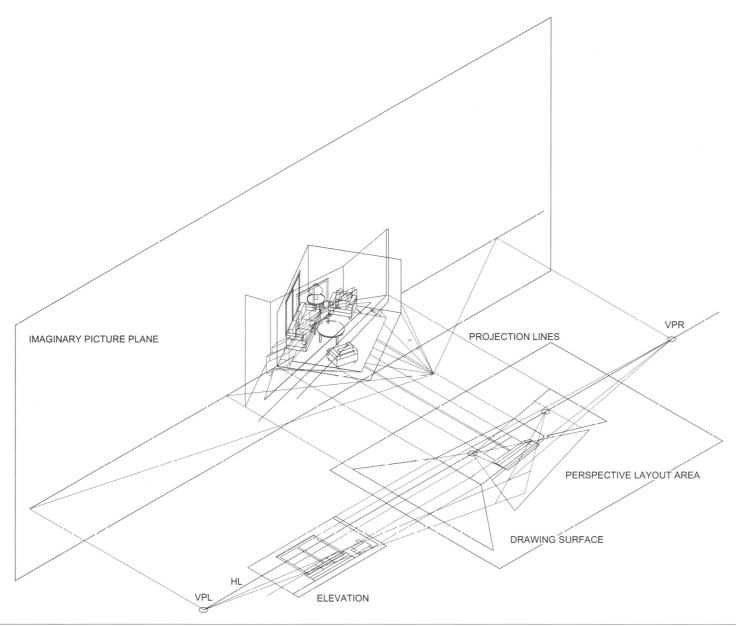

IMAGINARY PICTURE PLANE

PROJECTION LINES

VPR

PERSPECTIVE LAYOUT AREA

DRAWING SURFACE

HL

VPL

ELEVATION

## SCHEMATIC DIAGRAM OF PLAN PROJECTION METHOD OF PERSPECTIVE CONSTRUCTION

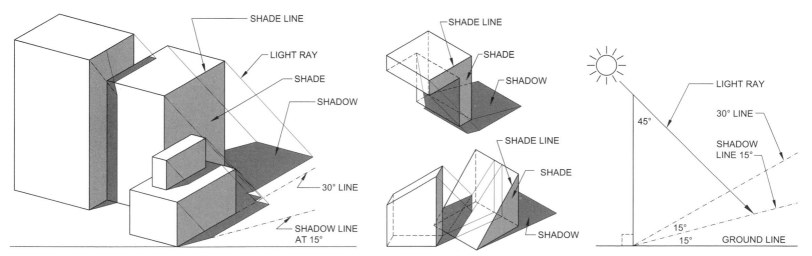

SHADE LINE

LIGHT RAY

SHADE

SHADOW

30° LINE

SHADOW LINE AT 15°

SHADE LINE

SHADE

SHADOW

SHADE LINE

SHADE

SHADOW

LIGHT RAY

30° LINE

SHADOW LINE 15°

45°

15°

15°

GROUND LINE

Shadows are constructed by drawing a line, representing a light ray, from a corner of the lighted surface at a 45° angle to the ground plane. The 45° light ray is extended until it meets the shadow line, and this point determines the length of the shadow for any given vertical height of the object. The shade line is the line (or the edge) that separates the light area from the shaded areas of the object. Shadow lines of all vertical edges of the object are drawn parallel to one another.

## AXONOMETRIC SHADES AND SHADOWS

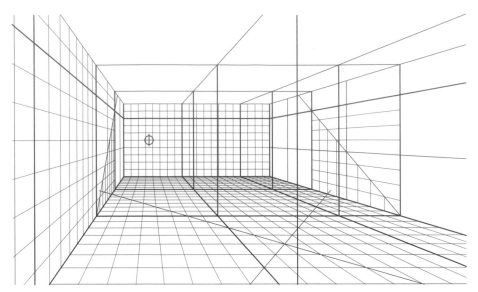

The one-point perspective grid tends to be more formal in appearance than a two-point perspective. This can be used to advantage in some presentation schemes. It is relatively easy to master the use of this grid.

**ONE-POINT PERSPECTIVE GRID**

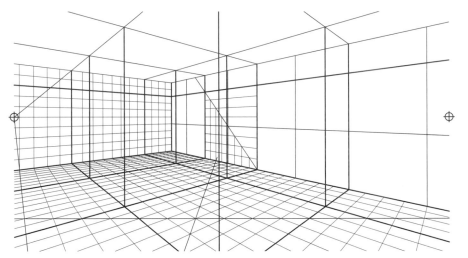

This spatial grid has been rotated 45° from the view and the imaginary picture plane. In this view two sides of a wall or object can be seen, depending upon its orientation to the viewer.

**45° TWO-POINT PERSPECTIVE GRID**

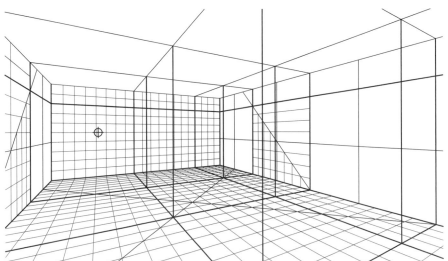

This spatial grid has been rotated 30°, allowing the viewer to see an entire room within a slightly expanded cone of vision. When extending the spatial grid in these drawings, ensure that unnecessary distortion is avoided at the extremes of the drawing layout.

**30°/60° TWO-POINT PERSPECTIVE GRID**

## PERSPECTIVE CHARTS

Perspective charts can be used for quick sketches of interior space and furnishings. The use of these charts requires a basic understanding of the concepts of convergence and vanishing points. The three basic charts shown can be extended, rotated, or mirrored to facilitate compositions and views that will more clearly convey design ideas.

## USING THE CHART METHOD OF PERSPECTIVE CONSTRUCTION

When using the chart method of generating perspectives, the projected perspective of the chart serves as a gridwork to locate and define architectural form and space. The following steps are taken to construct a perspective using a chart:

1. Determine the station point or point from which a viewer will be observing the space. A preliminary thumbnail sketch may be advantageous. Imagine what the space may look like from the preferred view.
2. After choosing an appropriate angle of view, choose the appropriate chart and chart orientation.
3. Identify the furthest distances from the viewer.
4. Determine the perimeter, enclosures, or wall elements on the chart.
5. Find and trace along the charted lines or grids the appropriate heights for ceilings, door, and windowsills and heads.
6. Along the gridded ground plane, locate the intended architectural objects, furnishings, and other items such as major accessories. Lesser accessories and details can be added later.
7. Using either the known dimensions or elevation drawings and other information, determine the major vertical dimensions of all the objects to be drawn. Most manufacturers publish product dimensions, including height, width, depth, and seat height and arm height of a piece of furniture.
8. Simplify complex shapes to the simplest geometric forms such as cubes, or cylinders, or intersecting patterns. A sofa or armchair can be reduced to a composition of several rectangular forms. A coffee table can be reduced to its simplest geometry.
9. Using reference photos, magazine cuts, catalog information, or repeat pattern dimensions, fill in and refine the layout.

## THREE-POINT PERSPECTIVE GRIDS

Three-point perspective grids can be used to produce drawings that have the appearance of looking up or down into a space. Since a three-point perspective may be difficult to layout using the plan projection method, an adequate perspective can be achieved by adding detail using the vanishing points that are established by the chart or a rough wire frame computer model.

*Robert Bernier, AIA; Somerset, Massachusetts*

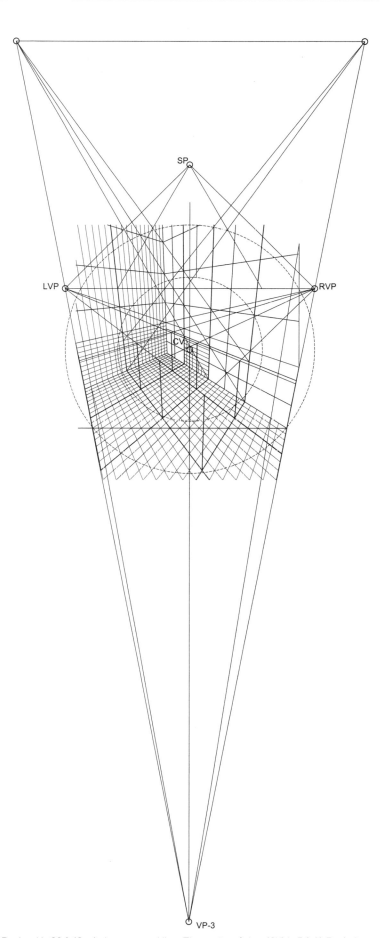

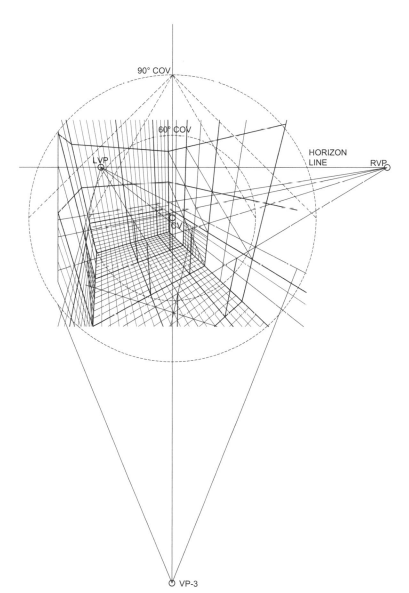

Eye level is 20 ft (6100 mm) above ground line. The center of view (CV) is 5 ft (1525 mm) above ground line.

**45° THREE-POINT PERSPECTIVE GRID**

Eye level is 20 ft (6 m) above ground line. The center of view (CV) is 5 ft (1.5 m) above ground line.

**30°/60° THREE-POINT PERSPECTIVE GRID**

# ACOUSTICS

## SOUND

Sound is energy produced by a vibrating object or surface and transmitted as a wave through an elastic medium. Such a medium may be air (airborne sound) or any solid common building material, such as steel, concrete, wood, piping, gypsum board, and so on (structure-borne sound). A sound wave has *amplitude* and *frequency*.

## AMPLITUDE (DECIBELS)

| Difference between sound levels (in dB) | 0–1 | 2–3 | 4–9 | >10 |
|---|---|---|---|---|
| Add this number to higher sound level | 3 | 2 | 1 | 0 |

For example, 90 dB + 20 dB = 90 dB; 60 dB + 60 dB = 63 dB.

The amplitude of sound waves is measured in decibels (dB). The decibel scale is a logarithmic scale based on the logarithm of the ratio of a sound pressure to a reference sound pressure (the threshold of audibility). The values of a logarithmic scale, such as the decibel levels of two noise sources, cannot be added directly. Instead, use the simplified method described in the table entitled "Decibels."

## FREQUENCY

The frequency of sound waves is measured in Hertz (Hz; also known as cycles per second) and grouped into octaves (an octave band is labeled by its geometric center frequency). An octave band covers the range from one frequency (Hz) to twice that frequency (f to 2f). The range of human hearing covers the frequencies from 20 to 16,000 Hz. Human hearing is most acute in the 1,000- to 4,000-Hz octave bands.

The human ear discriminates against low frequencies in a manner matched by the A-weighting filter of a sound-level meter, measured in dBA, or A-weighted decibels. This is the most universally accepted single-number rating for human response to sound.

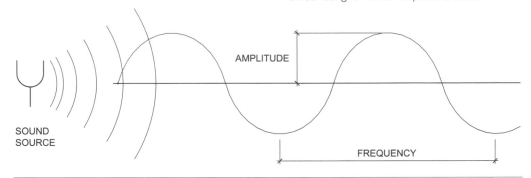

**SOUND AND FREQUENCY**

## TYPICAL SOUND LEVELS

| SOUND LEVEL (DBA) | SUBJECTIVE EVALUATIONS | ENVIRONMENT | |
|---|---|---|---|
| | | OUTDOOR | INDOOR |
| 140 | Deafening | Near jet engine and artillery fire | — |
| 130 | Threshold of pain | Jet aircraft departure (within 500 ft (152 m) | — |
| 120 | Threshold of feeling | Elevated train | Hard-rock band |
| 110 | | Jet flyover at 1,000 ft (305 m) | Inside propeller plane |
| 100 | Very loud | Power mower, motorcycle at 25 ft, auto horn at 10 ft | Crowd noise in arena |
| 90 | | Propeller plane flyover at 1,000 ft, noisy urban street | Full symphony or band, food blender, noisy factory |
| 80 | Moderately loud | Diesel truck at 40 mph (18 m/s) at 50 ft (15 m) | Inside auto at high speed, garbage, disposal, dishwasher |
| 70 | Loud | Heavy urban traffic | Face-to-face conversation, vacuum cleaner, electric typewriter |
| 60 | Moderate | Air-conditioning condenser at 15 ft (4.5 m), near freeway auto traffic | General office |
| 50 | Quiet | Large transformer at 100 ft (30 m) | Large public lobby, atrium |
| 40 | | Bird calls | Private office, soft radio music in apartment |
| 30 | Very quiet | Quiet residential neighborhood | Bedroom, average residence without stereo |
| 20 | | Rustling leaves | Quiet theater, whisper |
| 10 | Just audible | Still night in rural area | Recording studio |
| 0 | Threshold of hearing | — | — |

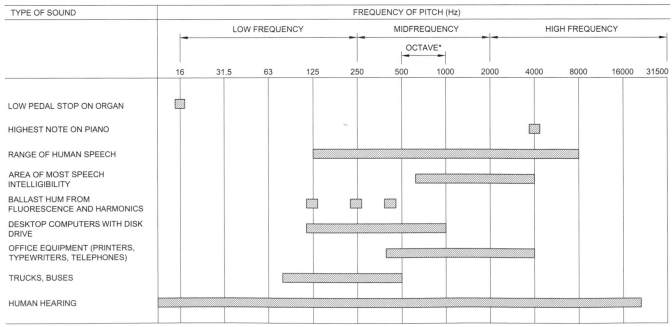

*OCTAVE - A FREQUENCY RATIO OF 2:1

**FREQUENCY OF COMMON SOUNDS**

# SOUND ABSORPTION PROPERTIES OF MATERIALS

All materials and surfaces absorb some sound greater than 0% and less than 100%. The percentage of incident sound energy that is absorbed by a material, divided by 100, equals the coefficient of absorption, designated $\alpha$, which ranges from 0 to .99. The coefficient varies as a function of frequency, Hz.

Any material can be tested in a proper laboratory to determine its $\alpha$ values, as per ASTM C423, *Standard Test Method for Sound Absorption and Sound Absorption Coefficients by the Reverberation Room Method*. Some tests give values greater than 1.0, but this is an anomaly caused by the testing procedure; such values should be corrected to be not more than 1.0, since no material can absorb more than 100% of the incident energy that strikes its surface.

## Sound Energy Absorption Mechanisms

There are three mechanisms by which sound energy is absorbed or dissipated as it strikes a surface. In all cases, sound energy is converted to heat, although never enough heat to be felt.

- *Porous absorption* entails the use of soft, porous, "fuzzy" materials such as glass fiber, mineral wool, and carpet. The pressure fluctuations of a sound wave in air cause the fibers of such materials to move, and the friction of the fibers dissipates the sound energy.
- *Panel absorption* involves installation of thin lightweight panels such as gypsum board, glass, and plywood. Sound waves cause panels to vibrate. Sound absorption for a panel is greatest at its natural or resonant frequency.
- *Cavity absorption* entails the movement of air pressure fluctuations across the narrow neck of an enclosed air cavity, such as the space behind a perforated panel or a slotted concrete masonry unit, also called a Helmholtz resonator. Friction of the resonating air molecules against the wall of the neck converts sound energy to heat. If there is also insulation within the cavity, additional energy is extracted via the porous absorption mechanism.

## Sound Absorption Average (SAA)

The method for determining the sound absorption average (SAA) is defined by ASTM C423. *Pink noise* is generated by a computer-controlled sound system and

### FREQUENCY

| RANGE OF OCTAVE (HZ) | OCTAVE BAND CENTER FREQUENCY (HZ) |
|---|---|
| 22-44 | 31.5 |
| 44-88 | 63 |
| 88-175 | 125 |
| 175-350 | 250 |
| 350-700 | 500 |
| 700-1,400 | 1,000 |
| 1,400-2,800 | 2,000 |
| 2,800-5,600 | 4,000 |
| 5,600-11,200 | 8,000 |

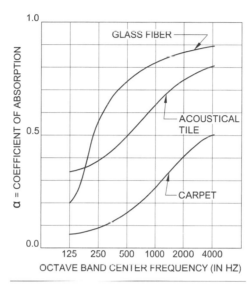

**TYPICAL VALUES FOR POROUS ABSORPTION**

it is emitted from two loudspeakers in the receiving room. While the sound is triggered on and off, 50 decay rates (from 80 to 500 Hz) are measured with (referred to as *full room*) and without (referred to as *empty room*) the test specimen installed in the chamber. The decay rate data is used to calculate the empty and full room absorption. The empty and full room absorption is used to calculate the SAA rating.

## Noise Reduction Coefficient (NRC)

Noise reduction coefficient (NRC) is obsolete; however, references to these values may continue to be made. Usually, the numerical value of NRC is almost the same as that for SAA.

### SUBJECTIVE REACTIONS TO CHANGE IN SOUND LEVEL

| CHANGE IN SOUND LEVEL* | CHANGE IN APPARENT LOUDNESS |
|---|---|
| 1 to 2 | Imperceptible |
| 3 | Barely perceptible |
| 5 or 6 | Clearly noticeable |
| 10 | Significant change—twice as loud (or half as loud) |
| 20 | Dramatic change—four times as loud (or a quarter as loud) |

*Measured in decibels (plus or minus)*

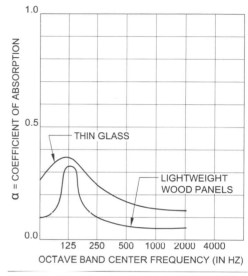

**TYPICAL VALUES FOR PANEL ABSORPTION**

## Sound-Absorbing Coefficients

The sound-absorbing coefficients for a given material may vary depending on the thickness of the material, how it is supported or mounted, the depth of the air space behind the material, and the facing in front of the material. In general, thicker, porous materials absorb more sound. The air space behind a material will increase the absorption efficiency, especially at low frequencies. Thin facings degrade high-frequency absorption.

## Mounting Assemblies

For consistency in comparing test results, standards have been set for the mounting assembly used in testing absorbent materials. These mounting conditions should be reported along with test data so that the data accurately reflect field conditions.

## SOUND-ABSORBING COEFFICIENTS FOR VARIOUS MATERIALS

| TYPICAL DATA/MATERIAL | 125 Hz | 250 Hz | 500 Hz | 1,000 Hz | 2,000 Hz | 40,000 Hz | NRC |
|---|---|---|---|---|---|---|---|
| Marble | .01 | .01 | .01 | .01 | .02 | .02 | .00 |
| Gypsum board, ½ in. | .29 | .10 | .05 | .04 | .07 | .09 | .05 |
| Wood, 1 in. thick, with air space behind | .19 | .14 | .09 | .06 | .06 | .05 | .10 |
| Heavy carpet on concrete | .02 | .06 | .14 | .37 | .60 | .65 | .30 |
| Acoustical tile, surface-mounted | .34 | .28 | .45 | .66 | .74 | .77 | .55 |
| Acoustical tile, suspended | .43 | .38 | .53 | .77 | .87 | .77 | .65 |
| Acoustical tile, painted (est.) | .35 | .35 | .45 | .50 | .50 | .45 | .45 |
| Audience area: empty, hard seats | .15 | .19 | .22 | .39 | .38 | .30 | .30 |
| Audience area: occupied, upholstered seats | .39 | .57 | .80 | .94 | .92 | .87 | .80 |
| Glass fiber, 1 in. | .04 | .21 | .73 | .99 | .99 | .90 | .75 |
| Glass fiber, 4 in. | .77 | .99 | .99 | .99 | .99 | .99 | .95 |
| Thin fabric, stretched tight to wall | .03 | .04 | .11 | .17 | .24 | .35 | .15 |
| Thick fabric, bunched 4 in. from wall | .14 | .35 | .55 | .72 | .70 | .65 | .60 |

Note: This table gives representative absorption coefficients at various frequencies for some typical materials. To determine values not provided here, refer to manufacturer's data or extrapolate from similar constructions. All materials have some absorption values that can be determined from proper test reports.

# TRANSMISSION LOSS PROPERTIES OF MATERIALS

The property of a material or construction system that blocks the transfer of sound energy from one side to another is transmission loss (TL), which is measured in decibels (dB). Specifically, TL is the attenuation of airborne sound transmission through a construction during laboratory testing, according to ASTM E90, *Method for Laboratory Measurements of Airborne-Sound Transmission Loss of Building Partitions.* Transmission loss values range from 0 to 70 or 80 (or higher). A high TL value indicates a better capability to block sound; that is, more sound energy is "lost" as the sound wave travels through the material.

Sound transmission class (STC) is a single-number rating system designed to combine TL values from many frequencies. STC values for site-built construction range from 10 (practically no isolation; e.g., an open doorway) to 65 or 70 (such high performance is only achieved with special construction techniques). Average construction might provide noise reduction in the range of STC 30 to 60.

It is very difficult to measure the STC performance of a single wall or door in the field because of the number of flanking paths and nonstandard conditions. Field performance is measured with Apparent Sound Transmission Class (ASTC) ratings, which cover effects from all sound transfer paths between rooms. ASTC ratings, previously referred to as the Noise Isolation Class (NIC), is derived by using the STC procedure (ASTM E413, *Standard Classification for Determining Sound Transmission Class*) to rate the uncorrected sound-level difference spectrum without correction or normalization factors.

## Derivation and Use of the STC Curve

To determine the STC rating for a particular construction, the STC curve shown in the accompanying figure is applied over the transmission loss (TL) curve for a laboratory test of the construction. The STC curve is then manipulated in accordance with prescribed rules to obtain the highest possible rating. The procedure states that the TL curve cannot be more than 8 dB less than the STC curve in any one-third octave band, nor can the TL curve be more than a total of 32 dB less than the STC curve (average of 2 dB for each of 16 one-third octave band frequencies). Any values from the TL curve that are above the STC curve are of no benefit in the rating. The object is to move the STC curve up as high as possible and to read the STC rating number from the point at which the STC curve at 500 Hz crosses the TL curve.

The STC curve has three segments: the first segment, from 125 to 400 Hz, rises at the rate of 9 dB per octave (3 dB per one-third octave); the second segment, from 400 to 1,250 Hz, rises at the rate of 2 dB per octave (1 dB per one-third octave); and the third segment, from 1,250 to 4,000 Hz, is flat.

## Transmission Loss

Design of construction and materials for high transmission loss builds on three principles:

- *Mass:* Lightweight materials do not block sound. Sound transmission through walls, floors, and ceilings varies with the frequency of sound, the weight (or mass) and stiffness of the construction, and the cavity absorption. Theoretically, the transmission

loss increases at the rate of 6 dB per doubling of the surface weight of the construction. A single solid panel behaves less well than the mass law would predict, since the mass law assumes a homogeneous, infinitely resilient material/wall.

- *Separation:* Improved TL performance without an undue increase in mass can be achieved by separation of materials. A true double wall with separate unconnected elements performs better than the mass law predicts for a single wall of the same weight. The transmission loss tends to increase about 5 dB for each doubling of the airspace

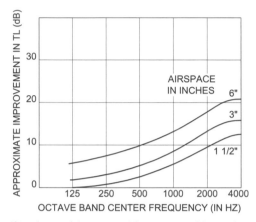

If two layers of dense material are separated by an airspace (rather than being continuous), they create two independent walls. The improvement in transmission loss depends on the size of the airspace and the frequency of sound. Avoid rigid ties between layers in all double wall construction. The accompanying graph indicates the approximate improvement in TL when a wall of a given weight is split into two separate walls.

**BENEFIT OF AIRSPACE IN IMPROVING TRANSMISSION LOSS (TL)**

between wythes (minimum effective space is approximately 2 in.). Resilient attachment of surface skins to studs or structural surfaces provides a similar benefit, as do separate wythes.

- *Absorption:* Use of soft, resilient, absorptive materials in the cavity between wythes, particularly for lightweight staggered or double stud construction, increases transmission loss significantly. Viscoelastic (somewhat resilient but not fully elastic) materials, such as certain insulation boards, dampen or restrict the vibration of rigid panels such as gypsum board and plywood, increasing transmission loss somewhat. Follow manufacturer-recommended installation details.

## NOISE REDUCTION

Noise reduction (NR) depends on the properties of a room and is the actual difference in sound pressure level between two spaces. It is the amount of sound blocked by all intervening sound paths between rooms, including the common wall, but also the floor, ceiling, outside path, doors, and so on.

Noise reduction also depends on the relative size of a room. If the noise source is in a small room next to a large receiving room (e.g., an office next to a gymnasium), the noise reduction will be greater than the TL performance of the wall alone because the sound radiating from the common wall between office and gym will be dissipated in such a large space. On the other hand, if the noise source is in a large room next to a small one (as from a gym to an office next door), the noise reduction will be far less than the TL of the wall alone because the common wall, which radiates sound, is such a large part of the surface of the smaller room. An adjustment for this ratio, plus the contribution of the absorptive finishes in the receiving room, enters into the calculation of actual noise reduction between adjacent spaces.

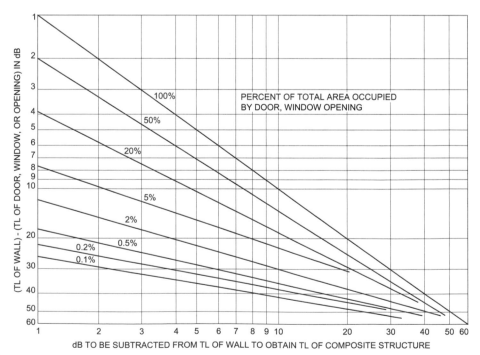

When a wall or surface of a room is made up of two or more different structures (e.g., a window in an outside wall or a door in an office), the TL performance (or STC) of the composite construction should be evaluated by combining the TL (or STC) values of the components, in accordance with the accompanying chart. Note that small gaps and cracks such as the perimeter of an ungasketed door can dramatically degrade the performance of a high TL construction.

**GRAPHIC TECHNIQUE TO DETERMINE COMPOSITE TRANSMISSION LOSS (COMBINING TWO DIFFERENT CONSTRUCTION ELEMENTS)**

# SOUND ISOLATION AND NOISE REDUCTION

One goal in the design of sound isolation construction is acoustical privacy. This privacy is a function of whether the signal from the neighbor is audible and above the ordinary background noise level.

Privacy index = noise reduction + background noise

Noise reduction is measured as a field performance, where it is evaluated and given an STC value.

Normal privacy, you are aware of a neighbor's activity but not distracted by it, can usually be requires a privacy index of 68 or higher. Confidential privacy, in which you are unaware of the neighbor, usually requires a privacy index of 75 or higher. A quiet environment with little natural background sound (from HVAC systems) requires a higher degree of sound-separation construction to achieve privacy.

## IMPACT NOISE RATING

Floors are subject to impact or structure-borne sound transmission noises such as footfalls, dropped objects, and scraping furniture. Parallel to development of laboratory STC ratings for partition constructions is the development of an impact insulation class (IIC). This is a single-number rating system used to evaluate the effectiveness of floor construction in preventing impact sound transmission to spaces beneath the floor. The current IIC rating method is similar to the STC rating.

Testing for IIC ratings is a complex procedure using a standard tapping machine. Because the machine is portable, it cannot simulate the weight of a person walking across a floor; therefore, the creak or boom that footsteps cause in a timber floor cannot be reflected in the impact rating. The correlation between tapping machine tests in the laboratory and field performance of floors under typical conditions may vary greatly, depending on the construction of the floor and the nature of the impact.

### Impact Noise Reduction Design

Often the greatest annoyance caused by footfall noise is the low-frequency sound energy it generates, which is beyond the frequency range of standardized tests. Sometimes this sound energy is near or at the resonant frequency of the building structure. Whenever possible, to stifle unwanted sounds, use carpet with padding on floors in residential buildings, and resilient, suspended ceilings with cavity insulation. For especially critical situations, such as pedestrian bridges or tunnels, hire an acoustical consultant.

Slamming doors or cabinet drawers are other sources of impact noise. If possible, bureaus should not be placed directly against a wall. Door closers or stops can be added to cushion the impact of energy from a door so it is not imparted directly into the structure. Common-sense arrangements can help minimize problems in multifamily dwellings. For example, kitchen cabinets should not be placed on the other side of a common wall from a neighbor's bedroom.

*Jim Johnson; Wrightson, Johnson, Haddon & Williams, Inc.; Dallas, Texas*
*Doug Sturz; Acentech, Inc.; Cambridge, Massachusetts*
*Carl Rosenberg, AIA; Acentech, Inc.; Cambridge, Massachusetts*

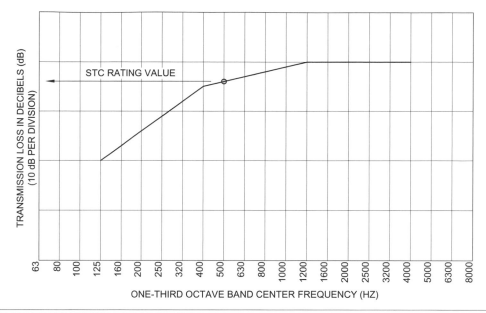

**SOUND TRANSMISSION CLASS (STC) RATING CURVE**

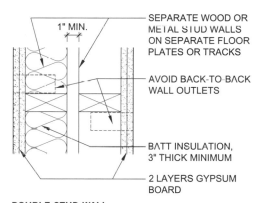

**DOUBLE STUD WALL**

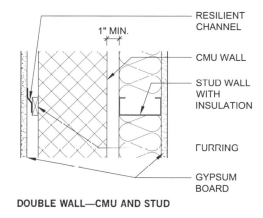

**DOUBLE WALL—CMU AND STUD**

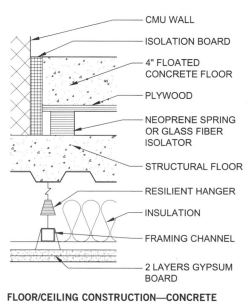

**FLOOR/CEILING CONSTRUCTION—CONCRETE**

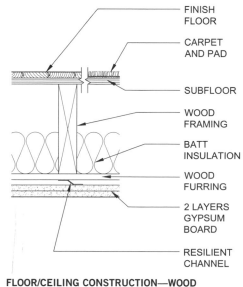

**FLOOR/CEILING CONSTRUCTION—WOOD**

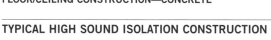

**TYPICAL HIGH SOUND ISOLATION CONSTRUCTION**

# INTERIOR LIGHTING

## FUNCTIONS OF LIGHTING

Light is one of many tools available to design a space. Considering the basic functions of lighting at the beginning of a project can help ensure the desired design effect:

- *Performance of tasks:* Lighting to perform work, whether it is reading, assembling parts, or seeing a blackboard, is referred to as task lighting. Visual work is a primary functional reason for providing lighting.
- *Enhancement of space and structure:* It is only through the presence of light that spatial volume, planes, ornament, and color are revealed. For centuries, structural systems evolved partly in response to aesthetic as well as functional desires for light of a certain quality. The progress from bearing wall to curtain wall was driven by the push of newly discovered technologies (both in materials and in technique), by evolving cultural desires for certain spatial characteristics, and by a desire to admit light of a particular quality. These developments are reflected in the Gothic church window, the baroque oculus, and the Bauhaus wall of glass. With the advent of electric lighting systems, this connection of structure to light was no longer entirely necessary, but most architects continue to pay homage to this historical tie.
- *Focusing attention:* The quality of light in a space profoundly affects people's perception of that space. The timing and the direction of an individual's gaze are often a function of the varying quality and distribution of light through the space. Lighting draws attention to points of interest and helps guide the user of a space.
- *Provision of safety and security:* Lighting can enhance visibility and thereby engender a sense of security. Lighting can also be used to illuminate hazards, such as a changing floor plane or moving objects.

## ILLUMINANCE

Most lighting standards discuss the quantity of light in terms of incident light or light that falls onto a surface. This light, called *illuminance*, is measured in footcandles (fc) or lux. Although convenient to calculate, illuminance is not, of course, what actually enters our eyes.

Light that reaches our eyes is usually reflected either off the details of the task (typed letters), the immediate background (e.g., paper), and the surround (e.g., desktop and room). Important exceptions are electronic visual displays using cathode ray tubes (CRTs) and light-emitting diodes (LEDs), which emit their own light. In these visual tasks, light reflected off their surfaces generally reduces their legibility, and much attention needs to be given to the lighting of the surround.

## LIGHT SOURCE SELECTION

When selecting a light source, the designer should consider several important issues including *color, size, efficiency, life,* and *maintenance*.

## Color

Each lamp family has its own inherent color characteristics. The different light sources render color qualities differently and create varying perceived color effects (see color plate C-11).

## Size

It is useful to think of sources and source/fixture combinations classified into *point, line,* or *area sources*. Point sources—for example, bare incandescent lamps, recessed incandescent, or high-intensity discharge (HID) fixtures with small apertures and specular reflectors—can be precisely controlled in terms of where light is and is not and can provide sparkle in a space by means of reflections off polished room surfaces. Line sources—bare fluorescent tubes and linear fluorescent fixtures—can be controlled in their transverse axis of output, but not longitudinally. This makes them useful for lighting large open areas where repetitive rows of fixtures are suitable. Area sources—for example, a window—are arrays of line sources covered by a diffusing element. These sources usually provide medium to high levels of light with little directional control.

## Efficiency

A source's inherent efficiency can be crucial to its acceptability for energy conservation. Some sources such as incandescent and tungsten halogen possess desirable color, size, and cost advantages, but are relatively inefficient. Most high-intensity discharge sources are very efficient but might require sacrifices of other attributes.

## ILLUMINANCE VALUES FOR VARIOUS INDOOR ACTIVITIES

| TYPES OF ACTIVITY | ILLUMINANCE CATEGORY | RANGES OF ILLUMINACE | | REFERENCE WORK PLANE |
|---|---|---|---|---|
| | | LUX | FOOTCANDLES | |
| Public spaces with dark surroundings | A | 20-30-50 | 2-3-5 | General lighting throughout spaces |
| Simple orientation for short, temporary visits | B | 50-75-100 | 5-7,5-10 | |
| Working spaces used only occasionally for visual tasks | C | 100-150-200 | 10-15-20 | |
| Performance of visual tasks of high contrast or large size | D | 200-300-500 | 20-30-50 | Illuminance on task |
| Performance of visual tasks of medium contrast or small size | E | 500-750-1,000 | 50-75-100 | |
| Performance of visual tasks of low contrast or small size | F | 1,000-1,500-2,000 | 100-150-200 | |
| Performance of visual tasks of low contrast and very small size over a prolonged period | G | 2,000-3,000-5,000 | 200-300-500 | Illuminance on task, provided by a combination of general and local (supplementary) lighting |
| Performance of very prolonged and exacting visual tasks | H | 5,000-7,500-10,000 | 500-750-1,000 | |
| Performance of very special visual tasks of extremely low contrast and small size | I | 10,000-15,000-20,000 | 1,000-1,500-2,000 | |

Note: Standards for lighting and illumination in North America are established by the Illumination Engineering Society of North America (IESNA). These recommendations are summarized in the IESNA Lighting Handbook, 8th edition, from which this table is taken.

## LIGHT SOURCE SELECTION GUIDE

| | APPLICATION |
|---|---|
| **LAMP CCT[1] (KELVINS OR K)** | |
| <2500 | Bulk industrial and security (HPS) lighting |
| 2,700–3,000 | Low light levels in most spaces (<10FC); general residential lighting; hotels, fine dining and family restaurants, theme parks |
| 2,950–3,200 | Display lighting for retail and galleries; feature lighting |
| 3,500–4,100 | General lighting in offices, schools, stores, industry, medicine; display lighting; sports lighting |
| 4,100–5,000 | Special application lighting when color discrimination is very important; not commonly used for general lighting |
| 5,000–7,500 | Special application lighting when color discrimination is critical; uncommon for general lighting |
| **MINIMUM LAMP CRI[2]** | |
| <50 | Noncritical industrial, storage, and security lighting |
| 50–70 | Industrial and general illumination when color is of minor important |
| 70–79 | Most office, retail, school, medical, and other work and recreational spaces |
| 80–89 | Retail, work, and residential spaces when color quality is important |
| 90–100 | Retail and work spaces when color rendering is critical |

[1]CCT: correlated color temperature
[2]CRI: color rendering index

## LIGHT SOURCE COMPARISON

| LIGHT SOURCE CHARACTERISTICS | INCANDESCENT | TUNGSTEN HALOGEN | FLUORESCENT | COMPACT FLUORESCENT | NEON/COLD CATHODE | DELUXE MERCURY | METAL HALIDE | HIGH-PRESSURE SODIUM | WHITE SODIUM | CERAMIC METAL HALIDE | LOW VOLTAGE HALOGEN |
|---|---|---|---|---|---|---|---|---|---|---|---|
| Ballast/transformer | No | No | Yes | Yes | Yes | Yes | Yes | Yes | Yes | Yes | Yes |
| Operating position Restrictions | None to few | None to few | None | None to few | None | None | Some | None | None | None to some | None |
| Color rendition | Very good | Good to very good | Fair to very good | Very good | N/A | Fair | Fair to good | Poor to fair | Good | Good | Good to very good |
| Efficacy (lm/W) | Low | Low | High to very high | High | Moderate | Moderate | High | High to very high | High | Moderate to high | Low |
| Life | 750–1,000 hours | 2,000–3,000 hours | 18,000–24,000 hours | 10,000–20,000 hours | 25,000+ hours | 24,000+ hours | 10,000–20,000 hours | 24,000+ hours | | 10,000–20,000 hours | 2,000–4,000 hours |
| Lumen maintenance | Good | Very good | Fair to good | Good | Good | Fair | Poor to fair | Fair to good | Good | Fair to good | Very good |
| Optical control | Good | Very good | Fair to good | Fair to good | Poor | Poor | Good | Good | Good | Good | Very good |
| Starting time (to full output) | Instant | Instant | Instant to fast | Fast | Fast | 7 to 9 minutes | 5 to 10 minutes | 3 to 5 minutes | 3 to 5 minutes | 5 to 7 minutes | Instant |

[1]CCT: correlated color temperature
[2]CRI: color rendering index

### Lamp Life

Lamp life varies significantly from source to source and is an important operational factor for most projects. Short-lived sources should be avoided whenever possible in hard to reach areas. Shorter life lamps may offer some first-cost advantages, but trade-offs in long-term maintenance must be explored.

### Lumen Maintenance

An electric light source degrades in output over its life. Some lamps, such as metal halide and mercury vapor, may lose 30% to 50% of their light prior to failing. Conversely, incandescent and most fluorescent sources maintain their light producing levels to with just a few percentage points of their original output. Lighting system designs must account for these losses to assure functional illuminance levels over time.

## ESTABLISHING LIGHTING DESIGN CRITERIA

Lighting design requires the definition of the following criteria for each application: *quantity of illumination, quality of illumination, color of light,* and *suitable luminaire styles.*

### Quantity of Illumination

Standards for illumination are set by the Illuminating Engineering Society of North America (IESNA). Illumination is generally measured in the horizontal plane 30 in (760 mm) above the floor. The units of illumination are footcandles (lumens per sq ft) and lux (lumens per sq m). IESNA-recommended levels are summarized on the following page (Lighting and Lighting Systems)—more detailed and specific information is given in the *IESNA Lighting Handbook* and in other IESNA publications.

Specific lighting levels are also established by codes, such as life safety and health codes. For instance, NFPA 101, *National Fire Protection Association Life Safety Standard,* recommends an average illumination of 1 fc (10 lux) along a path of emergency egress with an emergency power source. Some owners establish their own lighting level requirements for specific areas.

Choosing lighting levels involves thoughtful application of IESNA recommendations to meet the goals of the project. Too much light will lead to excessive energy use and failure to meet energy code limits.

The uniformity of interior lighting levels is also identified in IESNA recommendations. For interior lighting, IESNA generally recommends the following ratios of illumination for comfort:

*Task-to-immediate surround:* 1:3 to 3:1

*Task-to-distant surround:* 1:10 to 10:1

When light is designed to maintain these relationships, the human eye continually adapts to the light level and responds quickly to visual stimulus. However, visual interest is caused by contrast in which ratios between task and surround might be 100:1 or even greater. This is one of the greatest paradoxes of lighting design: The most appealing visual scenes are often uncomfortable.

### Guidelines for Illumination

- *Eliminate flicker.* Light sources should minimize or eliminate flicker caused by AC power or other influences.
- *Eliminate or minimize glare:* Shield lamps from view. Minimize very bright and very dark surfaces. Illuminate walls and ceilings.
- *Use light sources with good color rendering:* Halogen, high CRI (color rendering index) full-size and compact fluorescent, and high CRI metal halide and white high pressure sodium (HPS) lamps should be used whenever possible.

### Color of Light

Both the correlated color temperature (CCT) and color rendering index (CRI) for light sources should be used in choosing light sources. In general, try to match CCT when mixing sources, such as halogen and fluorescent.

### Suitable Luminaire Styles

Many design problems have reasonably obvious solutions determined by a combination of budget, energy code, and industry standards. For instance, most office lighting designs utilize recessed troffers because they are cost-effective and energy-efficient and they meet the standard expectations of owners and tenants.

Choices among troffers require further consideration, although at that point style is a lesser issue.

Some situations call for uncommon or creative designs. In these cases, the distribution of the luminaire and its physical appearance become critical. In particular, luminaires that enhance the architecture are desired for residences, hotels, restaurants, and other nonwork spaces. Decorative styles range from contemporary to very traditional; lamp options may permit a choice between incandescent and more energy-efficient light sources, such as compact fluorescent or low-watt high-intensity discharge (HID) luminaires. In fact, energy-efficient decorative lighting fixtures, both interior and exterior, are one of the fastest growing parts of the lighting fixture industry as the market expands for attractive luminaires that comply with energy codes.

### Lighting Terms

LUMINAIRE: A structure that holds an electric lamp and its socket, wiring, and auxiliaries, such as ballasts.

PORTABLE LUMINAIRE (LAMP): A luminaire equipped with a cord and plug and designed to be moved from space to space.

LIGHTING FIXTURE: A luminaire that is permanently attached ("hard wired") to a building.

LIGHTING SYSTEM: The lighting fixtures in a building, sometimes including portable lights, subdivided into smaller systems (e.g., the lighting system in a room or all luminaires of a particular type in a room or building).

ILLUMINANCE: The measure of light striking a surface, in footcandles (lumens per square meter). Illuminance can be measured and predicted using calculations; also illumination.

LAMP: The electric bulb or tube within a luminaire.

PHOTOMETRY: The measure of light, especially with respect to a luminaire.

PHOTOMETRIC REPORT: A report that describes the manner in which light is emitted from a luminaire, presented in an industry standard format.

## CONTRAST

Without contrast, the environment produced has the quality of a cloudy, overcast day. If all objects and surfaces in a room receive equal emphasis from light, contrast is lost. Patterns of luminance contrast evoke positive emotions in much the same way as background music. Lighting contrast can affect the performance of tasks, the behavior of people, and the degree of contentment and pleasure.

Over time, a lack of contrast can cause feelings of listlessness and even depression. To establish patterns of luminance contrast, the lighting designer must first evaluate the activities or tasks that will occur in the space. Some activities and tasks benefit from a high degree of contrast, to encourage participation and stimulate enjoyment. Other activities and tasks benefit from a minimum of contrast, to help a person feel contented, comfortable, and relaxed. Although individuals react differently to the same environment, there is a high degree of similarity in people's reactions to light.

After the activity or task has been identified, luminance contrast is established by developing patterns of light and shade. The relationship between foreground and background is determined by selecting specific surfaces and objects to receive lighting emphasis while leaving others in comparative darkness.

In addition to altering our perception of space, the direction and distribution of light affect the perception of surfaces and objects in a room.

## THREE-DIMENSIONAL FORMS

Three-dimensional forms are seen as a pattern of luminance contrasts, often consisting of highlights and shadows. A change in this pattern, caused by a change in the direction and distribution of light, alters visual impressions of form and surface.

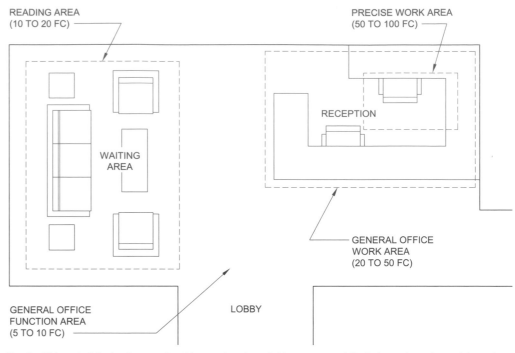

Use the high end of the level ranges for older people, where finishes are especially dark, or where the work is particularly important or requires great speed.

**LIGHTING LEVELS FOR TYPICAL RECEPTION AREA**

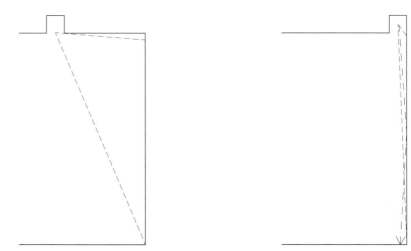

**DIFFUSE WASH LIGHT**
Diffuse wash light reduces the likelihood that surface flaws will be noticed, and strengthens an impression of surface smoothness. This is more suitable for a gypsum board wall or an acoustical tile ceiling. Diffuse wash light from the front is particularly successful in reducing or removing shadows and small luminance variations.

**GRAZING LIGHT**
Grazing light from luminaires located close to the lit surface strengthens highlights and shadows. It enhances the perception of depth by emphasizing the textures and sculptural relief of the surface. It is also used for inspection to detect surface blemishes and errors in workmanship. Grazing light is appropriate for lighting heavily textured surfaces such as rough plaster, masonry, or concrete. It is not appropriate for smooth surfaces because minor surface imperfections such as trowel marks, tape, and nail-head depressions are magnified by the shadows that result from grazing light.

**THE PERCEPTION OF TEXTURE** *Source: Gordon and Nuckolls,* Interior Lighting for Designers, *3rd Ed., John Wiley & Sons, Inc., 1995.*

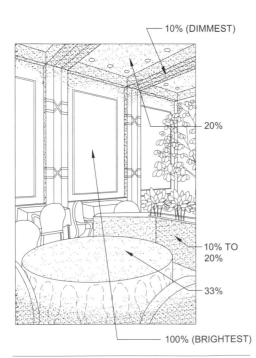

**LUMINANCE CONTRAST**

> **Design Guidelines for Material Transmission**
>
> Most direct transmission materials, such as clear or tinted glass, clear acrylics, and open mesh, maintain visual transparency, permitting a view through the apposite side.
>
> When attempting to rear-illuminate a semidiffuse material such as most fabrics, translucent acrylics, and frosted glass, pay special attention to the light source location and its intensity. Remove it from the normal line of sight to the material so that a fuzzy, intense image is not seen through it.
>
> The more diffuse a material is, the easier it is to softly backlight it.
>
> When working with light through perforated metals, it is often advisable to place a secondary translucent material as a backing.

# REFLECTION AND TRANSMISSION

## Design Guidelines for Material Reflectance

Materials of high gloss or mirror appearance reflect their surroundings. Be conscious of the influence of other light sources and surfaces in the space on the material's final rendition.

Light sources that have been mounted close to a polished or specular wall surface in an attempt to wash it with light are relatively ineffective. The extreme angle at which the light strikes the surface causes most of that light to reflect downward to the floor at the base of the wall.

Semispecular materials such as brushed metals, vinyl wall coverings, many woods, and some stones, will look different when lighted, depending on the angle from which they are viewed.

Diffuse materials, such as drywall, matte paints, rough stone, unfinished brick, and some wood finishes, can offer the softest and, sometimes, richest reflections (lighted uniformly from a distance) or very dramatic returns (highlighted by sources placed very close to the surface).

Diffuse materials may exhibit changes in their reflectance characteristics over time due to the wearing down of textures or finish. A surface's reflectance characteristics—specular, semispecular, or diffuse—are independent considerations from its reflectance value, or percentage. For example, a marble wall can be highly polished and specular, yet reflect vastly different quantities of light depending on whether it is predominantly dark- or light-colored.

Always select the materials using the light source under which it will normally be viewed. Conduct informal mock-ups of how the material is rendered when illuminated in different ways.

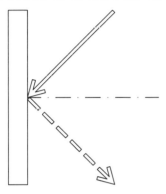

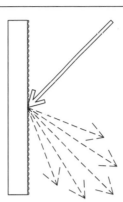

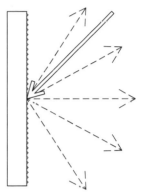

### SPECULAR REFLECTION
A smooth, highly polished surface like a mirror alters the direction of a beam of light without changing its form. The angle of reflection is equal to the angle of incidence, a property that makes specular materials ideal where precise beam control is desired. Because these surfaces are virtually mirrors, their own surfaces are almost invisible; they may appear dark or bright, depending on the observer's position and on the luminance of the reflected image.

### SEMISPECULAR (SPREAD) REFLECTION
Irregular surfaces, such as those that are corrugated, hammered, brushed, sandblasted, or etched, partially disperse the reflected beam. The greatest intensity, however, is still reflected at an angle near the angle of incidence. Semispecular materials appear with highlights or streaks of higher luminance on a background of lower luminance. In interiors, they are often used as elements of sparkle. In luminaires, semispecular materials produce a moderately controlled beam that is smooth and free from striations.

### DIFFUSE REFLECTION
Rough or matte surfaces neutralize the directional nature of the incident beam. Light is reflected from each point in all directions, with maximum intensity perpendicular to the surface. Sand on the beach is an example of a diffuse reflecting surface. There are no bright spots; the surface appears the same from all angles of view. In interiors, this quality is often desirable for walls, ceilings, and work surfaces. In luminaires, diffuse reflection materials are used to produce wide distributions of light.

Reflection is the return of light from a surface; it occurs when a portion of the light falling on a surface is thrown back by that surface, just as a ball bounces back from the floor. Three kinds of reflection are involved in the control of light: *specular, semispecular,* and *diffuse. Source: Gordon and Nuckolls,* Interior Lighting for Designers, *3rd Ed., John Wiley and Sons, Inc., 1995.*

## REFLECTION

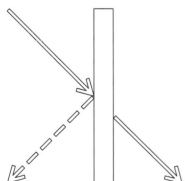

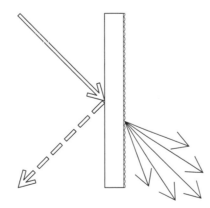

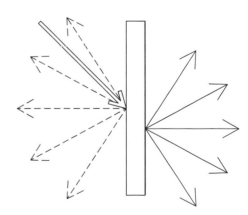

### DIRECT TRANSMISSION
Transparent materials leave the light distribution unchanged. They are used as protective covers for absorbing or reflecting infrared or ultraviolet radiation or where change in the color of light is desired while maintaining the light distribution produced by reflecting contours. Because the light remains visible, materials such as clear glass and plastic are ineffective for glare control.

### SEMIDIFFUSE (SPREAD) TRANSMISSION
Translucent materials emit light at wider angles because of configurations on at least one side of the material. A slight redirection of the transmitted beam is achieved by minor surface irregularities, such as shallow facets or flutes, which smooth out imperfections and striations. A greater degree of diffusion is achieved by etches, sandblasts, and matting aerosol sprays. Semidiffuse materials provide lamp concealment and glare control.

### DIFFUSE TRANSMISSION
Diffuse transmission disperses light in all directions and eliminates the directional quality of the beam. Full diffusion is achieved by using opal glasses and plastics that incorporate microscopic particles and remove all directionality from the transmitted beam.

Transmission is the propagation of light through a medium. The transmission of light is effected by two conditions: the reflections at each surface of the material and the absorption and reflection within the material. *Source: Gordon and Nuckolls,* Interior Lighting for Designers, *3rd Ed., John Wiley and Sons, Inc., 1995.*

## TRANSMISSION

# PSYCHOLOGICAL ASPECTS OF LIGHTING

Pioneering lighting research efforts in the early 1970's lead by the late professor John Flynn, demonstrated that as patterns of luminance contrast change in the environment, the strength of visual stimuli changes, altering our impressions of space. As a part of this important work, evidence was uncovered that lighting changes alone can elicit significantly different reactions from people. It was found that alterations in lighting cues could induce consistent and predictable responses in three areas: spaciousness, perceptual clarity, and pleasantness.

## Impressions of Spaciousness

An impression of largeness or smallness is affected by the intensity and uniformity of the room perimeter. Differences in the quantity of horizontal illuminance from overhead systems have negligible influence on impressions of pleasantness. Differences in quantity of illuminance significantly alter impressions of perceptual clarity and spaciousness. The higher illuminance values are often described as clear, bright, distinct, large, and more spacious.

## Impressions of Perceptual Clarity

The appearance of people's faces is of critical importance to the lasting impression made by an interior. Lighting schemes that are rated high in facial clarity are considered more public; schemes that are rated low in facial clarity are considered more private.

The importance of lighting as an influence on one's subjective impression of space should not be overlooked. From workplaces to restaurants, lighting can either enhance or detract from the designer's ultimate vision for the environment. By considering these influences during the lighting design process, it is possible to predict and control these effects for the betterment of the project.

Public space implies intermingling and bringing people together. The potential for visual contact improves as the intensity of general illuminance is increased. Increasing intensities reduce anonymity and bring people together because facial expressions and gestures are more clearly perceptible.

Private space suggests separating people and keeping them apart. Shadow and silhouette strengthen feelings of detachment and privacy because these lighting techniques inhibit the ability to perceive precise facial detail; even nearby individuals become more anonymous.

In a crowded space, when it is impossible to separate people physically by distance, it is possible to separate them visually by lighting. This technique is used in cocktail lounges, fine restaurants, and reception rooms.

## Impressions of Pleasantness

The nonuniform luminance produced by the downward-concentrating system rates more favorably than the uniform luminance produced by the diffuse system. The nonuniform luminance is often perceived as more friendly, pleasant, sociable, and interesting.

When wall lighting is added, ratings shift to the positive for all three categories of impression. Lighted vertical surfaces strengthen feelings of spaciousness, clarity, and pleasantness.

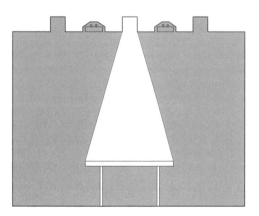

**OVERHEAD DOWNLIGHTING—LOW INTENSITY**

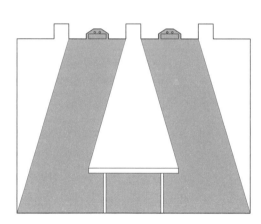

**OVERHEAD DOWNLIGHTING WITH LIGHTED END WALLS**

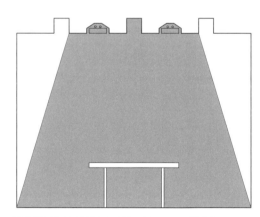

**PERIPHERAL WALL LIGHTING—ALL WALLS**

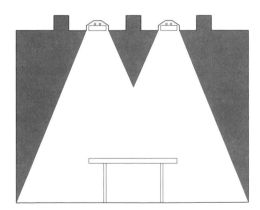

**OVERHEAD DIFFUSE—HIGH INTENSITY**

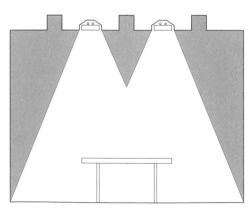

**OVERHEAD DIFFUSE—LOW INTENSITY**

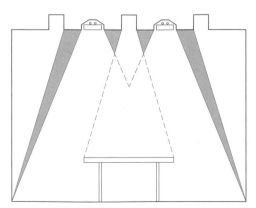

**OVERHEAD DOWNLIGHTING WITH OVERHEAD DIFFUSE**

**LIGHTING EFFECTS** *Source: Gordon and Nuckolls,* Interior Lighting for Designers, *3rd Ed., John Wiley & Sons, Inc., 1995.*

## CALCULATIONS: LUMEN METHOD

Lighting design involves determining how many luminaires are needed for a particular application and where to locate them. The most accurate means of determining illumination performance is by computer; a number of point-by-point lighting programs are available (see the annual computer issue of *Lighting Design and Application,* an IESNA publication, for a current list of commercially available programs). It is also possible to estimate illumination results from a proposed lighting design using the lumen method and photometric reports from candidate luminaires.

The lumen method, also known as the *zonal cavity system,* is a calculation method that can be used to determine the horizontal illuminance that will result from a proposed lighting fixture selection and layout or the number of fixtures required by a proposed fixture selection and its horizontal illuminance value.

The lumen method is based on the definition of average footcandles over an area. The method modifies the fundamental equation of 1 fc = 1 lumen/sq ft (10 lux/sq m) to account for room size and proportion; reflectance from walls, ceiling, and floors; fixture efficiency; and reduction in output over time due to dirt accumulation, deterioration of reflecting surfaces, and reduction of lamp lumen output.

The lumen method requires the following information:

- Room dimensions (to compute wall area and floor area)
- Height of fixtures above work plane
- Reflectance values of major surfaces (ceiling, walls, floor)
- An estimate of the light loss factor (LLF)
- Initial lamp lumens
- A target illuminance level
- Lighting manufacturer's photometric test report

## COEFFICIENT OF UTILIZATION

The coefficient of utilization (CU), found in the photometric test report, is the percentage of total lamp lumens generated within the fixture that actually reaches the work plane. As such, it has nothing to do with the intensity of the fixture but rather with the efficiency of the fixture (lumens emitted from the fixture divided by lamp lumens and the direction of the lamp output—this direction of output is graphically represented by the candlepower distribution curve). For purposes of this procedure, the plane of interest is invariably a horizontal plane (typically either the floor or desk level), therefore a fixture that distributes the greatest percentage of its lumens downward will have a higher CU (room cavity ratio and reflectance values being equal) than one that distributes light in any other direction. A higher CU is not necessarily a virtue; it only ranks fixtures according to their ability to provide horizontal illuminance.

The lumen method/zonal cavity system is limited by the following:

- It is based on a single number, average value.
- It assumes a uniform array of lighting fixtures.
- It assumes all room surfaces have a matte finish.
- It assumes the room is devoid of obstruction, at least down to the level of the work plane.

### Formulas for Average Lighting Calculations

$$\text{NUMBER OF LUMINAIRES} = \frac{\text{footcandles desired} \times \text{room area}}{\text{CU} \times \text{LLF} \times \text{lamps/luminaire} \times \text{lumens/lamp}}$$

$$\text{AVERAGE FOOTCANDLES} = \frac{\text{lumens/lamp} \times \text{lamps/luminaire} \times \text{CU} \times \text{LLF}}{\text{area of room (sq ft)}}$$

$$\text{POWER DENSITY (W/sq ft)} = \frac{\text{design watts (including ballast)}}{\text{area of room}}$$

Where:
CU = coefficient of utilization (percentage of light that actually reaches task)
LLF = light loss factor (time-dependent depreciation factors)

**Note:** *See the Illuminating Engineering Society's* Lighting Handbook *for manufacturer's photometric tables of values for CU, LLF, lumens/lamps, and others.*

$$\text{NUMBER OF FIXTURES} = \frac{50 \times 25 \times 40}{0.67 \times 0.7 \times 4 \times 2,850} = 9.35 \text{ luminaires (use 9 or 10)}$$

$$\text{POWER DENSITY (W/sq ft)} = \frac{9 \times 111}{25 \times 40} \text{ or } \frac{10 \times 111}{25 \times 40} = \begin{array}{l} 0.999 \text{ W/sq ft (9 luminaires) or} \\ 1.111 \text{ W/sq ft (10 luminaires)} \end{array}$$

**Typical Examples**
Room size 25 × 40 ft (7.6 × 12 m); ceiling height 9 ft; illumination level 50 fc (500 lux) (IESNA category 10); 2 × 4 ft (2.7 m) recessed troffers with four 32-watt T8 lamps (2,850 lm) each.

CU – 0.67 (plastic lens)
Electronic ballast input watts = 111
LLF = 0.7

## LIGHT LOSS FACTOR

The light loss factor (LLF), also known as the *maintenance factor,* is used to calculate the illuminance of a lighting system at a specific point in time under given conditions. It incorporates variations from test conditions in temperature and voltage, dirt accumulation on lighting fixtures and room surfaces, lamp lumen output depreciation, maintenance procedures (mainly frequency of cleaning and relamping), and atmospheric conditions.

To use a CU table, assumptions must first be made about the reflectance of major room surfaces. If surface finishes have been selected for the space, these assumptions can be made more reliably. Then the room cavity ratio (RCR) can be determined according to one of the following formulas:

For rectangular rooms: RCR = [5 × H(L + W)] / (L × W), in which H is the cavity height

For odd-shaped rooms: RCR = 2.5 wall area/floor area

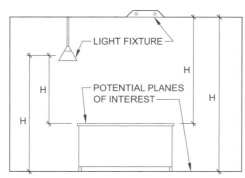

Any one of these dimensions may be the cavity height (H), which is the distance from the light fixture to the work plane of interest.

**CAVITY HEIGHT DIAGRAM**

## LIGHTING ENERGY CODES

Most codes presently calculate allowable lighting power based on building type and area. Codes generally determine allowed interior lighting watts in one of these three ways:

- ROOM BY ROOM: Determine the specific use of each room and its net area. Multiply the area of each room by the allowed power density (watts/sq ft) adjusted for the room cavity ratio (RCR). Add the wattage for all rooms together; for example, private office, open office, coffee room, copy room, and toilet rooms.
- AREA: Determine the use of major portions of a building or renovation and the gross lighted area of each. Multiply the gross lighted area by the allowed power density (watts/sq ft) for each group of rooms by type. Add the figures for all areas together; for example, all offices, all storage rooms, and general support areas.
- WHOLE BUILDING: Determine the building type and the gross lighted area for the entire building. Multiply the gross lighted area by the allowed power density (watts/ sq ft) for the entire building by type; for example, all habitable square footage within the building or project.

To find the total allowable lighting power for the interior of a building, start with the total wattage as determined by one of the three methods above. Then subtract "credit" watts for lighting controlled by advanced automatic devices, such as daylighting or motion sensing and add other allowed watts, if any.

An allowed lighting load can also be determined by using a building energy simulation program like DOE-2. However, because the program's algorithm is based on the same power density assumptions as the allowed amount given above, it is unlikely the value for lighting determined in this manner will be significantly different, only more accurate.

### Commonly Encountered Lighting Code Requirements

- Mandatory use of readily accessible switching in all enclosed spaces. (Exceptions are allowed for spaces in which this would be unsafe.)
- Use of multilamp or electronic fluorescent ballasts whenever possible.
- Separate switching for daylighted and nondaylighted spaces in building interiors.
- Ability through switching or dimming to adjust lighting levels in a space exceeding 100 sq ft (9 sq m) and 100 watts.
- Time-clock-activated shutoff controls for lights in spaces in larger buildings [usually larger than 5000 sq ft (464.5 sq m)].
- Time-clock-activated shutoff controls for exterior lights.
- Use of occupancy sensors to automatically shut off lights in spaces left unoccupied.
- Mandatory use of daylight-sensing photocells in spaces with skylights or clerestories.
- Available control credits for use of energy-efficient automatic control devices. These enable the designer to reduce overall energy use for code-compliance calculations.

## LIGHTING ENERGY CODE COMPLIANCE STRATEGY

To realize design compliance with local energy codes without significant redesign, observe the following guidelines:

- Choose a general lighting system that uses one of these sources predominantly: fluorescent T-8 or T-5 with electronic ballasts, compact fluorescent with electronic ballast, or metal halide or high-pressure sodium (HPS).
- Make certain the luminaire and room combination are reasonably efficient. Use localized direct lighting for tasks whenever possible, and make room finishes light, especially ceilings.
- Design to meet IESNA minimum recommendations for each space, unless it is absolutely necessary to use higher levels.
- For downlighting, wall-washing, and other traditional incandescent applications, use compact fluorescent or high-intensity discharge (HID) sources when possible.
- Use incandescent and halogen sources sparingly, confining them to applications where color, precise control, or the lighting's decorative characteristics are critical.
- Add advanced controls such as motion or occupancy sensors and daylight photocells with in-line dimming. These allow the reduction of actual lighting watts and can help bring a design into compliance with energy efficiency requirements.

## LIGHTING CONTROLS

Most energy codes require readily accessible switching for all electric lights. The National Electric Code requires switching at specific locations in residential settings. Traditional switches meet these requirements.

## TYPICAL APPLICATIONS FOR LIGHTING CONTROLS

| | |
|---|---|
| Office buildings schools | Motion sensors in private offices, classrooms, and conference rooms |
| | Time scheduling systems for open office areas, corridors, halls, and lobbies |
| | Motion sensors in toilet rooms and storage |
| | Daylighting in areas adjacent to windows, skylights or clerestories |
| | Combined systems (e.g., motion and daylighting) whenever logical |
| Retail | Time scheduling for store windows, general and display lighting |
| | Motion sensing for storage dressing rooms and restrooms |
| | Daylighting and lumen maintenance near skylights and clerestories |
| | Adaptation compensation for general lighting |
| Industrial, institutional | Time scheduling in most areas |
| | Daylighting near windows, skylights and clerestories |
| | Motion sensing in restrooms, little used storage areas |

## ENERGY-EFFICIENT LIGHTING CONTROLS

| DEVICE OR METHOD | OPERATION | TYPICAL CREDIT |
|---|---|---|
| Time, clock (with manual override readily accessible) | Turns lights on and off at scheduled times | 0–10% |
| Wallbox Dimmer | Reduces lighting power by manual adjustment | 0% |
| Motion (occupancy) sensor | Turns lights on and off based on space | 15% (>250 sq ft) to 30% (<250 sq ft) |
| Daylighting controls | Reduces interior lighting power based on amount of daylight in space | 20% (stepped) to 30% (continuous dimming) |
| Preset (scene) dimming | Reduces average power by dimming combinations of lighting systems | 10–20% |
| Tuning | Reduces lighting power by hidden adjustment | 10–15% |
| Lumen maintenance | Reduces interior lighting power based on age of lamps and cleanliness of space | 10–15% |
| Combined systems | Combinations of the above are not necessarily directly additive | Up to 45% |

*The credit offered varies from code to code and may not be available everywhere.*

Other lighting controls choices are discussed in the following subsections.

### Switching

Standard single-throw (toggle) switches are the most commonly used lighting controls. Three-way and four-way switches permit control from several locations. Examples include on/off "toggle" switches, electronic touch-switches, and so on.

### Wall Box Dimming

Manual dimming is popular in residential applications and commercial spaces where flexibility in illumination levels is desired. Incandescent dimming is inexpensive and simple to apply. The dimming of fluorescent lighting should make use of electronic high-frequency dimming ballasts and associated dimming controls. An energy credit may be available for using manual dimming under some conditions.

### Preset Dimming

Preset dimming or multichannel scene-dimming systems are increasingly being used for spaces with four or more independent dimming channels, such as restaurants, conferencing facilities, auditoriums, hotel lobbies, and custom-built homes. Preset dimming systems are similar in function to modern theatrical dimming in that there is a cross-fade between specific scenes, which are combinations of preset dimming levels for the channels controlled by the system. By establishing these scenes in advance, the user need only push a single button to bring all lighting in the space to the desired level for a specific function.

### Time Scheduling

Lighting controls that use clocks to operate lighting systems on predictable schedules are the most commonly used form of automatic lighting controls. Some energy codes require automatic controls of this type as a minimum standard. Controls may vary from individual time clock switches to electronic programmable timers and large-scale energy management systems.

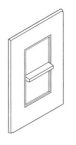  

| LINEAR SLIDE CONTROL | ROTARY OR PUSH ON/OFF CONTROL | TOUCH-PLATE CONTROL |
|---|---|---|

**DIMMING CONTROL DEVICES**

## Occupancy Sensing

Motion sensors can be used to control lights according to space occupancy. Passive infrared sensors are the most commonly used; ultrasonic sensors are also popular and work better in spaces with partitions. Sensors possess sensitivity and time-out adjustments to fine-tune the controller to the peculiarities of the space. For small rooms, choose wall box sensors with internal switches or dimmers; for larger rooms, choose ceiling-mounted sensors with remote relays. Multiple sensors are needed in larger spaces to ensure adequate area coverage and detection.

Energy credits for using motion sensor systems are fairly substantial, as these systems save significant energy in most applications. The payback on these devices is relatively short, especially in retrofit situations.

## Daylighting And Related Controls

Daylighting systems use dimming or switching to reduce interior lighting when adequate daylight of sufficient quality is present. In buildings with windows near the work area, savings can be significant, and most codes permit a substantial controls credit for daylighting.

## Lumen-Maintenance Controls

Lumen-maintenance controls allow lighting to be dimmed automatically when it is new and, through photoelectric sensing, to be increased gradually over time as lamps age and luminaires get dirty. The equipment for these controls is similar to that for daylighting, and most systems can be programmed to do both.

## Adaptation Compensation Controls

Adaptation compensation controls (the opposite of daylighting) increase interior light as exterior light increase levels. Tunnels are classic applications for adaptation compensation, but the same principles can be used to save energy in interior lighting situations where the daylight tends to overpower the electric light during the day, while at night this additional light intensity may not be necessary.

## Demand Management

Lighting can be gradually dimmed up to 20% with little effect on productivity but a profound impact on overall building load. By sensing incoming electric service for peaks, lighting can be dimmed when other building systems are peaking in load. The result is a "flattening" of the energy use curve, which lowers electric energy cost, normally computed using peak demand values.

# LUMINAIRE DESIGN

## Luminaires

A luminaire is any device that includes a lampholder, a means of electrification, and a support. Lighting fixtures are luminaires that are permanently attached to a building. Luminaires are characterized by the manner in which light is distributed.

## Luminaire Characteristics

*Direct luminaires* tend to be the most efficient because they distribute light directly onto the normal task areas. They generally result in darker ceilings and upper walls, which can be dramatic but may create discomfort from high-contrast conditions.

*Indirect luminaires* produce comfortable low-contrast soft light when appropriately spaced, which psychologically enlarges space. Though they tend to be less efficient for delivering light to a traditional horizontal task, the appealing nature of their light compensates for this deficiency .

*Diffuse luminaires* create broad general light that often is considered glaring due to the lack of shielding at the critical angles at which the luminaire is viewed. Their decorative architectural or ornamental appropriateness is often the principal reason for their selection.

## LUMINAIRE TYPES

| TYPE | LIGHT DISTRIBUTION |
|---|---|
| Direct | Emits over 90% light downward. Most recessed lighting types, including downlights and troffers, are direct luminaires. |
| Indirect | Emits over 90% light upward, so it bounces from a ceiling into the space below. Many styles of suspended luminaires, sconces, and some portable lamps provide indirect lighting. |
| Diffuse | Emits light in all directions uniformly. This type includes most bare lamps, globes, and chandeliers and some table and floor lamps. |

*Direct/Indirect luminaires* are often a good compromise between the efficiency of direct lighting and the comfort of indirect lighting.

# INDIRECT AND DIRECT/INDIRECT LIGHTING SYSTEMS

Most indirect and direct/indirect lighting systems are designed to illuminate offices and similar finished spaces. In most cases, the ceiling should be finished in white paint or white acoustical tile, as the reflectance of the ceiling plane is critical.

## Indirect Lighting Systems

Indirect lighting systems only produce uplight. Generally they should be mounted at least 15 to 18 in. (381 to 457 mm) below the ceiling; longer suspension lengths can improve uniformity but potentially will decrease efficiency. To maintain adequate clearance, ceilings should be at least 9 ft (2.7 m) high.

## Direct/Indirect Lighting Systems

Direct/indirect lighting systems are intended to produce some indirect lighting for its comfort and balance, and some direct lighting, for efficient production of task lighting. Similar suspension length and ceiling height considerations apply. The percentage of uplight to downlight varies; generally, the higher the ceiling, the greater the downlight percentage recommended.

| TYPE | LIGHT DISTRIBUTION |
|---|---|
| Direct/Indirect | Emits light upward and downward but little to the side. Many types of suspended luminaires, and some table and floor lamps, offer this type of lighting. These luminaires can offer mostly direct or mostly indirect lighting. |
| Asymmetric | For special applications. For instance, asymmetric uplights are indirect luminaires with a stronger distribution in one direction, such as away from a wall. Wall washers are a form of direct luminaire with stronger distribution to one side to light a wall. |
| Adjustable | Luminaires with inherent, usually flexible, adjustable mechanisms to permit the principal focus of the distribution to be altered for specific effects or functions. Examples are track lights, floodlights, and accent lights. |

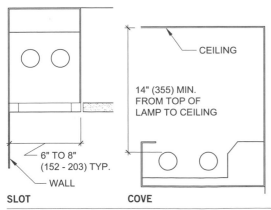

14" (355) MIN. FROM TOP OF LAMP TO CEILING

CEILING

6" TO 8" (152 - 203) TYP.

WALL

SLOT    COVE    DIRECT    INDIRECT    INDIRECT/DIRECT

**INDIRECT, DIRECT/INDIRECT, AND DIRECT LUMINAIRES**

# LIGHTING FIXTURES (LUMINAIRES)

## Troffers

Troffers are widely used in offices, stores, schools, and other commercial and institutional facilities for general lighting in work and sales areas. They are the most common type of fluorescent luminaire.

Most troffers are recessed and designed to be laid into acoustic tile ceilings, with the fixture face matching the size of the tile. The most common troffer sizes are 2 × 4 ft (610 × 1220 mm), although 2 × 2 ft (610 × 610 mm) and 1 × 4 ft (305 × 1220 mm) are also readily available. Other sizes exist, often to match a specific ceiling (such as 20 × 60 in. (508 × 1524 mm) fixtures for a 5-ft (1,524-mm) ceiling grid system). Different mounting types are made, including the following identified by the National Electrical Manufacturers Association (NEMA):

NEMA "G": For fixtures in a standard exposed inverted T-grid.

NEMA "F": For fixtures furnished with a flange and designed to be installed in an opening in plaster or gypsum board.

NEMA "SS": For fixtures in a screw-slot inverted T-grid.

NEMA "NFSG": For fixtures in a narrow face slot T-grid.

NEMA "Z": For fixtures in a concealed Z-spline ceiling.

NEMA "MT": For fixtures in a metal pan ceiling system.

Some recessed troffers are also designed to interface with the building HVAC system: *Heat extraction troffers* have vents in the top of the fixture to allow return air to be pulled into the troffer, past the lamps, and into the ceiling plenum. *Air-handling fixtures* have slots around the lens or louvers to supply air to a room (by means of a special boot that can transfer air to the supply air system) or to remove it (by connection to a return duct).

Troffers can also be equipped with emergency battery packs to power some or all of the lamps during a power outage or emergency condition.

## Lensed Troffers

Lensed troffers use an acrylic or polycarbonate lens to refract light and distribute it into useful zones. Lenses can contain internal Radio Frequency Interference (RFI) shields for use in hospital operating and laboratory rooms. Lens troffers equipped with highly polished internal reflectors can offer very high efficiency.

## Parabolic Troffers

Parabolic troffers have parabolically shaped aluminum or plastic louvers that shield the lamp from direct view to improve visual comfort. These troffers offer sharp cutoff, which makes some of them suitable for use in computer work spaces. "Parabolics" generally refer to deep-cell louvers 6 in. (152 mm) or larger across; "paracubes" are shallower louvers with smaller cells. Larger cells are more efficient, but smaller cells possess a more extreme cutoff angle.

## Troffer Ratings

Most troffers are rated for standard dry indoor applications and must not touch insulation. Some special types include

GASKETED: Can be damp or even wet-rated.

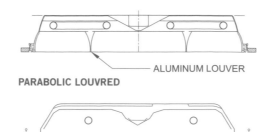

—— ALUMINUM LOUVER

**PARABOLIC LOUVRED**

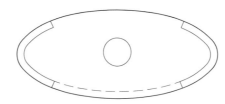

—— ACRYLIC LENS

**LENSED**

## TROFFERS

FIRE-RATED: Can maintain up to one-hour ceiling rating in certain rated ceilings.

VANDAL-RESISTANT: Equipped with vandal-resistant lens and latching hardware.

RFI: Lens troffers that are shielded from radio frequencies.

Troffers can be equipped with most fluorescent technologies, including dimming, magnetic or electronic ballasts, and T-12, T-8, or T-5 lamps. Special troffers are made for ceiling systems like the linear metal slat system (4 in. (100 mm) wide). Recessed troffer depth varies from 3½ in. (89 mm) to more than 7 in. (177 mm), so troffers must be coordinated with other elements above the ceiling.

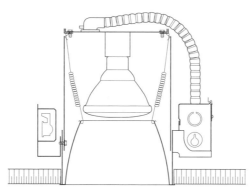

**PAR LAMP DOWNLIGHT**

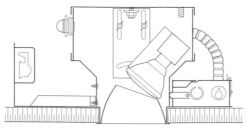

**PAR LAMP WALL WASHER**

**PAR LAMP ADJUSTABLE ACCENT**

## DOWNLIGHTS

## Downlights

Downlights are used principally for general illumination in a wide range of residential and commercial applications, especially in lobbies, halls, corridors, stores, and other finished spaces. Downlights can be equipped with incandescent, halogen, low-voltage, compact fluorescent, or high-intensity discharge (HID) lamps. There are several major types of downlights, which accommodate varying sources, ceiling heights, plenum heights, room types, and beam spreads. These include the following:

OPEN REFLECTOR: The reflector of this type of downlight shields the lamp from direct view and forms a beam pattern.

OPEN BAFFLE: Ridged baffles, usually black, shield the lamp from direct view and minimize glare.

OPEN ELLIPSOIDAL: An elliptical reflector allows a small aperture; this beam spread is highly efficient.

LENSED PRISMATIC, ARTICULATED, OR FRESNEL: Often used outdoors or in wet locations, the lens protects and seals the lamp compartment; some lens types are used to provide additional beam shaping.

DIFFUSER: A diffuser distributes light broadly, which is especially useful in closets and showers.

ADJUSTABLE: An adjustable downlight can be used as a downlight or as an accent light.

PULL-DOWN: This feature allows the light to be used as a downlight or an accent light, and permits higher aiming angles.

## Downlight Ratings

Choice of a downlight depends on the applications for which it is listed. The primary rating types are as follows:

THERMALLY PROTECTED (T): These downlights are suitable for all applications except direct concrete pour.

INSULATION PROTECTED (IP): These downlights are used when the fixture may come in contact with insulation. They are designed to prevent fixture overheating.

INSULATION CEILING (IC): These fixtures are used when the fixture is intended to be in contact with insulation.

AIRTIGHT INSULATION CEILING AIC): These downlights are for applications in which the fixture is in contact with insulation and air leaks in the ceiling must be prevented.

DAMP LOCATION FIXTURES: These fixtures can be exposed to moist air but not to direct water spray or rain.

WET LOCATION FIXTURES: These can be exposed to direct water spray or rain.

SPA OR SHOWER FIXTURES: These are designed to be used in a shower stall, over a spa, or in a locker room.

CONCRETE-POUR FIXTURES: These are designed to be installed in direct contact with concrete.

EMERGENCY FIXTURES: These are equipped with a backup battery to produce light for at least 90 minutes during a power outage (generally available only for compact fluorescent luminaires).

## Architectural and Decorative Lighting Fixtures

Wall washers come in several types. *Eyelid wall washers* essentially are downlights with an eyelid-shaped shield on the room side. *Recessed lens wall washers* resemble downlights but use an angled lens to throw light more to one side. *Surface and semi-recessed lens and open wall washers,* which throw light onto an adjacent wall, generally work best; they can also be mounted to track. *Downlight/wall washers* are designed to illuminate rather than scallop an adjacent wall, although the light they provide may not be intense enough for display purposes.

## Linear Wall Grazing Fixtures

Linear wall grazing fixtures, sometimes called *wall slots,* are used to illuminate walls in lobbies, corridors, and core areas. They are especially suited for textured or polished surfaces.

## Accent Fixtures

Accent fixtures focus light on specific targets such as art, retail displays, lecterns and building façade features. *Recessed accent lights* appear as downlights but internally permit rotation and elevation of the light beam. *Eyeballs and pull-down* accents resemble downlights, but can be adjusted. Track lighting systems are specifically designed for accent lighting of art and retail displays, with easy relocation of lamp holders along the track.

## Commercial Fluorescent Fixtures

Several types of fluorescent direct luminaires appropriate for general and utility lighting are employed as commercial fixtures. Most utilize wraparound lenses or diffusers in which the lamp is surrounded by the lens; the lamp is hidden from direct view while radiating light downward and to the sides. Commercial luminaires are among the lowest-cost lighting fixtures and are typically used for general and utility and back-of-house lighting in modest projects.

## Industrial Lighting Fixtures

These fixtures generally have a utilitarian or functional appearance. Fluorescent industrials incorporate strip lights in open fixtures, with simple reflectors that are designed to be surface-mounted or hung by chains or rods. HID industrials include high-bay and low-bay downlights. Industrial fixtures are generally used in factories and warehouses, and increasingly in schools and retail stores where a less finished appearance is desired.

## Linear Cove Lights

Linear cove lights provide asymmetric uplighting from coves or other architectural elements more efficiently than strip lights, and without socket shadows.

## Task Lights

Task lights are specifically designed to illuminate a task area while minimizing veiling reflections (reflected glare).

## Chandeliers

Chandeliers are ornate luminaires that generally comprise many small incandescent lamps to simulate the effect of candle flames. Chandeliers are hung from the ceiling and are used for decorative-only applications or, occasionally, general illumination in areas such as dining rooms, foyers, and other formal spaces where few demanding visual tasks are performed.

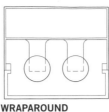
**WRAPAROUND FLUORESCENT WITH ACRYLIC DIFFUSER**

**FLUORESCENT STRIP**

**HIGH BAY HID LAMP**

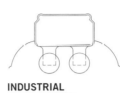
**INDUSTRIAL FLUORESCENT**

**COMMERCIAL AND INDUSTRIAL FIXTURES**

### Pendant Fixtures

Pendants are also ceiling-hung decorative fixtures. In general, the term is used for luminaires that are less formal than chandeliers, such as those used in offices or restaurants. Some pendant luminaires also use incandescent lamps, although most modern variations are available with HID or compact fluorescent sources.

### Close-to-Ceiling Fixtures

Close-to-ceiling luminaires are similar to pendants but are mounted close to the ceiling to allow use in rooms with lower ceiling heights.

**ROUND [4 TO 9 IN (101 TO 228 MM) DIAMETER]**
Up, down, or up/down

**OVOID**
Up, down, or up/down

**RACETRACK OVAL**
Up, down, or up/down

**ELONGATED OCTAGON**
Up, down, or up/down

**"V" OR WEDGE**
Up only

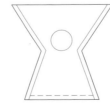
**OPTIMAL FOR USE WITH VIDEO TERMINAL**
Up/down

**SUSPENDED LIGHTING SHAPES**

## Sconces

Sconces are usually decorative wall-mounted luminaires. Often they are used in concert with an adjacent chandelier; in other cases, they are the sole decorative lighting element. Most commercial sconces use compact fluorescent sources, while in hospitality and residential applications, wide use of traditional incandescent continues.

## Lamps

Lamps are traditional portable luminaires generally used for table or floor mounting. *Torchères* are floor lamps designed for uplighting. Most portable lighting uses incandescent or halogen sources, although compact fluorescent options should be considered for commercial and hospitality applications.

## GENERAL LIGHTING SYSTEM ALTERNATIVES

FLUORESCENT STRIP LIGHTS AND LENSED TROFFERS provide adequate light for the lowest cost, are the easiest to install, and tend to be the most efficient. These systems also are accompanied by a significant amount of glare and may appear to the consumer as a budget-driven choice.

HID INDUSTRIAL-STYLE FIXTURES provide good basic light at relatively low cost, but also appear to be a budget-conscious choice and may be a glare source if not properly shielded. They can be used to help create a warehouse look and feel. Perimeter valances or display lighting may can enhance these systems.

PARABOLIC LOUVERED SYSTEMS produce inherently less offending glare and may suggest the presence of higher-quality merchandise. They should be used in conjunction with valances and/or other perimeter and display lighting to avoid the darker wall appearance that often accompanies parabolic systems.

SUSPENDED DIRECT, DIRECT/INDIRECT, AND INDIRECT SYSTEMS work best in ceilings greater than 8 ft (2.4 m). These lighting types play a major role in the appearance and style of a space and are generally chosen to reinforce a specific marketing motif.

TROFFER SYSTEMS, lensed or parabolic fluorescent, provide good, acceptable light at low cost; they are commonly used in schools. Recessed lighting minimizes vandalism and is efficient.

SUSPENDED DIRECT/INDIRECT AND INDIRECT SYSTEMS are favored for better visual comfort and are generally suited for spaces with ceilings higher than 9 ft (2.7 m).

INDUSTRIAL-STYLE HIGH-INTENSITY DISCHARGE (HID) LIGHTING SYSTEMS are often used in industrial education, arts, gymnasium, and other spaces requiring plentiful, relatively inexpensive, durable lighting. If using HID sources, provide quartz auxiliary lamps in some fixtures for emergency backup lighting during power loss.

SPECIAL APPLICATION LUMINAIRES come in hundreds of different types, each optimized for a specific job, workstation, environment, or hazard. Examples include explosion-proof, vapor tight, and paint-booth luminaires. Consult the IESNA *Lighting Handbook* for a comprehensive outline of industrial specialty luminaires.

## DAYLIGHT MEDIA GUIDELINES FOR WORKSPACES

| | ORIENTATION | CONTROL TECHNIQUES | SURFACE REFLECTANCE GUIDELINES | | MOST APPROPRIATE ELECTRICAL LIGHTING | APPLICATION NOTES |
| | | | WALLS | CEILINGS | | |
|---|---|---|---|---|---|---|
| Monitors | North East West South | Moderate transmission glass (30% to 50%) Architectural baffles or louvers (exterior) Architectural setbacks Overhangs Light shelves | Medium to light (30% to 50%) | Very light (90%) | Indirect Semi-indirect Direct/indirect | Avoid small, intermittent, punched openings. Assess time-of-day occupancy to establish best orientation(s). |
| Clerestories | North East West South | Moderate transmission glass (30% to 50%) Architectural baffles or louvers (exterior) Architectural setbacks Overhangs Light shelves | Medium to light (30% to 50%) | Very light (90%) | Indirect Semi-indirect Direct/indirect | Avoid small, intermittent, punched openings. Assess time-of-day occupancy to establish best orientation(s). |
| Skylights | (Controllable only on sloped roofs) North East West South | Very low transmission glass (2% to 10%) Architectural baffles or louvers (exterior) Deep skylight wells Frit patterns Solar shades, blinds | Medium (30% to 50%) | Very light (90%) | Indirect Semi-indirect Direct/indirect Direct | Avoid large-area, shallow openings. Assess time-of-day occupancy to establish best orientation(s). |
| Windows | North East West South | Low transmission glass (5% to 15%) Significant overhangs Architectural baffles or louvers (exterior) Frit patterns Solar shades, blinds | Light (30% to 50%) | Light to Very light (80% to 90%) | Indirect Semi-indirect Direct/indirect Direct | Avoid small, intermittent, punched openings. Assess time-of-day occupancy to establish best orientation(s). |

## DAYLIGHTING

### Health

Exposure to daylight offers significant health benefits, which include the physiological aspects of circadian rhythms that are important for minimizing seasonal affective disorder (SAD) and for the production of vitamin D.

### Illuminance

Daylight can provide much of the light needed to perform many home and work-related tasks. Because daylight is highly variable and has limited availability, designing the daylighting system in any building to meet illuminance targets requires an immense team effort and typically entails greater initial and maintenance costs. While this should certainly not eliminate daylighting from consideration, it indicates the degree of care, finesse, integration, and user education that is necessary a successful daylight-integrated installation. Illuminance from daylight, when correctly implemented, should result in reduced energy use.

### Luminance

Luminance balancing (from surface to surface) can be achieved with daylight. However, the variability and intensities of daylight will present a serious challenge for the design team. In effect, daylight is not a free energy source. Successfully implementing daylight raises the following issues: initial capital expenditures that are higher than most clients or users may be expecting, an ongoing maintenance requirement, sophisticated controls, and a team whose members all must be equally experienced with installing successful, effective electric lighting.

### Sustainabiltiy

The success of daylighting as a sustainable practice is very sensitive to the integration and interaction of the various building materials and systems. The sun (also called the solar disc) and the sky are the two most significant daylight sources readily available to designers. Reflected daylight from other surfaces is secondary. Any of these daylight sources can introduce lumi-

nances of such significance that one or several of the following may occur:

- Distraction
- Direct glare
- Reflected glare
- Veiling reflections
- Transient adaptation

The key to successful design using daylighting requires managing daylight to provide at the least a view, and at the most a view, illuminance, and luminance. To achieve cost and occupant effective sustainable daylighting, it is necessary to use such daylight media as monitors, clerestories, skylights, and windows with appropriate orientation, shading control, and room surface finishes along with proper electric lighting.

*Randy J. Burkett, FIALD, IES, LC; Burkett Lighting Design, Inc.; St. Louis, Missouri*
*James Robert Benya, PE, FIES, IALD; Pacific Lightworks; Portland, Oregon*
*Robert Sardinsky; Rising Sun Enterprises; Basalt, Colorado*

# PROGRAMMING

Architectural programming is the process of identifying and defining user requirements before proceeding with design development. The goal is to develop and document the client's business system and his or her needs. During the process, the analyst also gathers information on what is, and is not, currently working, and what exists, or needs to exist, for the client to carry out his or her purpose or mission. In the field of architecture, these needs are related to space requirements, which, when completely defined, are referred to as the *architectural program*.

Architectural programs have several fundamental components:

- Summary of the project scope and program results (answers who, what, why, where, and how,)
- Program support analysis, including projections for headcount, conference room utilization, cafeteria, and so on
- Business and building analysis, including adjacency diagrams and supporting analysis
- Program document, program summary reports, and interview notes
- Appendices, containing supporting information provided by the client or from related research

Architectural programming is the first step in the design process and is, perhaps, the most important phase. Meaningful communication is required to assess, review, refine, and document a client's space requirements. During the programming process, the client's problems are identified and clarified in order to develop a solution for today and for the future. Programming promotes an understanding of the whole problem, as opposed to symptoms or pieces or parts of the client's problem.

Unless the designer completely understands the needs and uses of a space, the resulting design will fall short of the needs of the client and the users of the space. Also, more often than not, an incomplete understanding of client needs results in project cost overruns, and unidentified or misunderstood needs result in design changes. Changes made late in the design process or during implementation are much more expensive than changes made early in the programming or schematic phase of the design. A thoughtful architectural program supports the designer and his or her design by fully capturing the needs of the client. The result is a more effective design that is implemented on time and within budget parameters.

## PROGRAMMING EFFECT ON COST

Changes made as a project design is being implemented increase the overall cost of the project. Effective programming—that is, fully identifying and defining client needs at the beginning of the project—enables design projects to better meet budget and schedule goals.

## ADDITIONAL PROGRAMMING SERVICES

Some clients may have needs that are more complex than simple space planning; for example, the need to move or lease more space Clients want to use space

**ARCHITECTURAL PROGRAMMING AND DESIGN**

more effectively; want to tailor workspace to their employees' needs; are dealing with space standards for the first time; feel the space they have is not being used effectively; are changing their culture; want to be more competitive; have staff recruitment and retention issues; or have any number of other business circumstances that impact space. For clients with these types of needs, additional services are often provided.

Typical additional services provided in support of developing a program are:

- *Work methods analysis,* to identify individual workspace requirements; for example, to support developing new space standards for a client.
- *Alternative office solutions analysis,* to identify nontraditional solutions to workspace needs; for example, to increase the utilization of real estate.
- *Benchmarking studies,* to identify how a client's competitors are meeting their workspace and environmental needs; for example, by comparing workspace standards.

## PROGRAMMING TRENDS

Driving current trends are client needs for space efficiency, flexibility, and economy. The goal of many real-estate-savvy firms is to reduce overall real estate costs as well as costs and time associated with *churn,* the movement of, or change in, people and groups of people. *Churn rate* is used as a measure of the level of dynamics of an organization. Churn costs have historically been high, and timeframes have been too long. As business product life cycles and development times become shorter and shorter, the need to shift and move people or whole organizations increases. Loss of time in today's business environment equates directly to loss of profit and leadership in competitive markets. The insightful programmer working to meet the client's real estate goals must keep abreast of current design solutions and thinking associated with client needs.

## PROGRAMMING PROCESS

Reducing the programming process to its most elementary level results in three steps, as follows:

1. *Information gathering,* which involves research, listening, and learning about the client's needs.
2. *Analyzing and synthesizing,* which involves consolidating the acquired information for a full understanding of the client's problems, needs, options, and potential costs, as well as proposing options and making recommendations.
3. *Documentation and validation,* which involves documenting the findings, reviewing the findings and recommendations with the client, then getting feedback, modifying the program, and reissuing the program document.

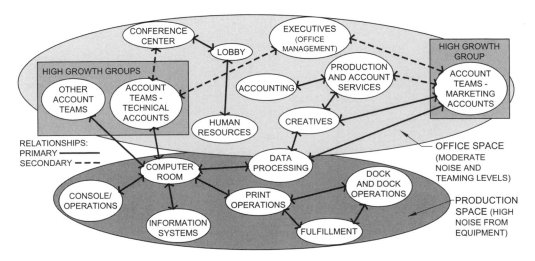

**ADJACENCY DIAGRAM FOR TYPICAL OFFICE WITH PRODUCTION FACILITY**

## Step 1: Information-Gathering Process

The first step in the programming process, information gathering, consists of three primary activities: the *initial meeting*, the *goal-setting session*, and the *needs and requirements interviews*.

### Active Listening

During this initial programming step, and throughout the process, active listening is critical to the success of the programmer. Active listening involves quieting the mind and focusing completely on the information being presented. If questions arise, they are quickly asked, then documented in your notes when the speaker has completed all his or her thoughts associated with the previous question. Repeating back to the speaker what was heard, using the listener's own words, is also a critical part of active listening. It accomplishes two primary goals: first, it gives the speaker confidence that he or she was heard and understood; second, it gives the speaker the opportunity to clarify ideas or points that may have been misunderstood.

Advance preparation of questions frees the mind to focus on the speaker and his or her comments. The program is only good if the gathered information is complete and accurate. If we listen well, we increase the probability of generating an effective program.

### Initial Meeting

The initial, or "kickoff," meeting is a forum for discussing the logistics of the project and for gaining an understanding of the timeline and the client's role. If not established prior to this meeting, the following are identified: the members of the project's decision-making team and the organization members to be interviewed. A tour of the site with the client enables a deeper understanding of the project and associated issues.

### Goal-Setting Session

The goal-setting, or "vision," session is held with the members of the project decision-making team. The programmer facilitates this meeting. During this session, the goals of the business, environment, and project—what the client wants to achieve and why—are discussed. The objective of the session is to identify, understand, and document the goals of the client for both the project and the new environment. It is important to devise questions in advance that will facilitate the brainstorming process and ensure that required issues are exposed and discussed.

### Needs and Requirements Interviews

The final activity in this step is to conduct the needs and requirements interviews. Interviews can take two forms: *face-to-face question-and-answer sessions* or *questionnaires*. The most effective means of gathering information is to hold either individual or focus group interviews. Information gained in interviews is less open to interpretation and can be clarified on the spot. That said, there are situations where interviewing personnel is neither feasible nor acceptable to the client, in which case questionnaires are in order. Regardless of the method by which the information is gathered, the programmer must prepare clear, well-bounded, nonleading questions. When developing the questions, the programmer considers how to construct the question so as to extract the required information, given the specifics of the project. Interviews are also useful for testing concepts proposed by management or the facility team. Questions are developed in advance and used for each interview to ensure that consistent information is gathered from each group. Ideally, interview sessions also include a walk-through of the spaces currently occupied by the department or group interviewed.

---

**Step 1: Information-Gathering Process: Activities and Products**

**Activities**
- Research client.
- Acquire floor plans, client organization chart, and current personnel report.
- Prepare questions for "vision-image" and interviews.
- Walk through site.
- Facilitate vision-image or goal-setting session.
- Develop mission statement.
- Conduct interviews.
- Gather space demand/utilization information for conference rooms, cafeterias, training rooms, and so on.

**Products**
- Client background and an understanding of who/what the client is today.
- Documented project goals and vision with mission statement.
- Interview notes.
- Marked-up floor plate drawings with notes and updates.
- Client data, including current personnel report and space utilization reports for conference rooms, cafeterias, training rooms, and so on.

---

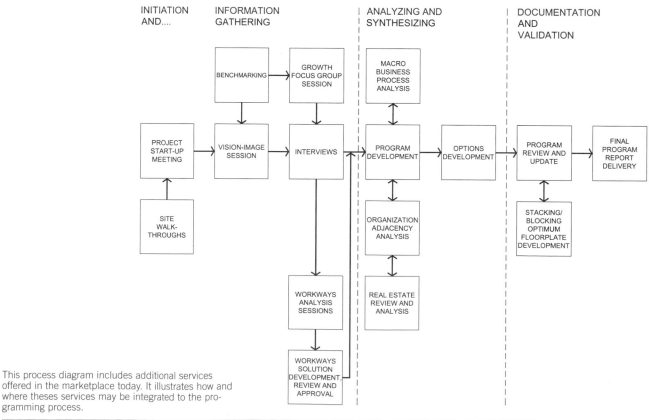

This process diagram includes additional services offered in the marketplace today. It illustrates how and where theses services may be integrated to the programming process.

**STRATEGIC PROGRAMMING PROCESS**

## Step 2: Analysis and Synthesis Process

After gathering and organizing a comprehensive review of the information, quantitative and qualitative specifics about each required space are extracted, to include the following:

- Space types
- Sizes
- Quantities
- Design characteristics

The result is a fundamental set of space types for both individual organizational groups and common or shared spaces. Space standards (standard workplace sizes to be applied throughout the program) that meet the needs of individual work processes and the building module are developed at this time. Space sizes for all of the various space types are also identified and documented. Generic space diagrams are included to illustrate how space sizes are developed and what they mean to the user in terms of functionality.

Space quantities are developed next. Analyzing headcount projections, support space utilization statistics, and any other quantifiable data available enables the programmer to understand the quantities required for specific spaces. The result of quantifying both the size and number of each space required by the client is the net square footage (NSF) of the space requirement. Circulation factors must be selected and applied at both micro and macro levels in the program to develop both initial total usable and total rentable square footage (RSF) results. Total usable square footage and total rentable square footage are two key products of the programming process. At this point, a draft program should be nearing completion.

---

### Step 2: Analysis and Synthesis Process: Activities and Products

**Activities**

- Analyze interview notes.
- Develop flow diagram of business process.
- Identify themes and potential conflicts in needs.
- Resolve conflicts or open issues with client.
- Analyze headcount and develop projections.
- Analyze space utilization reports for conference rooms, cafeterias, training rooms, and so on.
- Develop program, space list, and quantities.
- Analyze interactions and develop adjacency diagram.
- Acquire rentable square footage (RSF) and rentable factors for buildings being examined, or desired factors for potential shell designs.
- Develop stacking and blocking diagrams.
- Perform cost analysis.
- Develop options with associated costs.

**Products**

- Base program.
- Headcount projections.
- Conference rooms, cafeteria, and training room demand/utilization projections.
- Adjacency diagram and other potential diagrams.
- Process flow diagram (optional, based on client need).
- Stacking and blocking diagrams.
- Program options and costs.
- List of conflicts or issues requiring resolution.

---

## SECONDARY CIRCULATION FORMULA AND TABLES: RULES OF THUMB

Secondary Circulation Factor is used to calculate the Usable Square Footage from the programmed Net Square Footage.

The Secondary Circulation Factor is calculated using the following formula:

$$\text{CIRCULATION FACTOR} = \frac{1}{(1.0 - \% \text{ circulation})}$$

The Usable Square Footage (USF) is equal to the Net Square Footage (NSF) multiplied by the Secondary Circulation Factor.

USF written as an equation is:

$$\text{USF} = \text{NSF} \times \frac{1}{(1.0 - \% \text{ circulation})}$$

**Example:** Given the NSF is 50,000 square feet and the appropriate Secondary Circulation is identified as 35%, then:

$$\text{USF} = 50,000 \times \frac{1}{(1.0 - 0.35)}$$

$$\text{USF} = 50,000 \times 1.54$$
$$\text{USF} = 77,000 \text{ Usable Square Feet}$$

| % SECONDARY CIRCULATION | SECONDARY CIRCULATION FACTOR |
|---|---|
| 50% | 2.00 |
| 45% | 1.82 |
| 40% | 1.67 |
| 35% | 1.54 |
| 30% | 1.43 |
| 25% | 1.33 |
| 20% | 1.25 |
| 15% | 1.18 |
| 10% | 1.11 |

*Note: Typical circulation percentage assumed for typical office space is 35%.*

**DESIGN DEPARTMENT SECONDARY CIRCULATION**

| SPACE TYPES | DESIGN DEPENDENT PERCENTAGES |
|---|---|
| Break Spaces | 25%-40% |
| Executive Briefing Centers | 10%-25% |
| Copy Center | 25% |
| Fitness Spaces | 25% |
| Kitchen Spaces | 25%-40% |
| Large Meeting Spaces | 25% |
| Loading Dock | 10% |
| Mail Room | 25% |
| Site Amenities | 40% |
| Support Spaces | 35% |
| Training Spaces | 25% 40% |
| Visitor Reception | 25%-50% |
| Workspace – Open | 35%-40% |
| Workspace – Open – Call Centers | 50%-55% |
| Workspace – Closed Intermingled with Open | 35%-40% |
| Workspace – Closed – Traditional Layout (for example, law firm) | 25%-35% |

*Note: The Design Department Secondary Circulation Numbers in the above chart assume a standard rectangular building with good planning efficiencies.*

Circulation factors vary depending on type of business and other factors.

Statistics and other analytical tools are required to understand the meaning and implications of some of the data gathered. Data projection is required during this process. It is typical, for example, to project headcounts at least three years into the future for a program. Clients do not always have the information required to program future needs, especially those beyond three years. Statistics can provide information that enables the programmer to project data into the future when the data available from the client is incomplete.

The program is the synthesis of the client information and the specification of the client's needs. Outcomes of the synthesis of the information include the program document, adjacency diagrams, and stacking diagrams.

## Step 3: Documentation and Validation

The final step in the process is to document and validate the program. Once the program is complete, a program review meeting is scheduled. The program review may be held at various levels of detail, depending on the client's personality and project complexity. Each page may be examined in detail; or an overview of the results, assumptions, and key issues may be provided to the client. Regardless, all fundamental assumptions, such as projections of headcount, conference usage, and so on, must be reviewed in detail, agreed to, and signed off by the client.

Once the assumptions and draft program have been reviewed and signed off, the final program can be completed and the program report developed. The completed program report is a "stand-alone" document that communicates to the client all required information about the environment, its functions, and the space needs; it should not require additional explanation. A good-quality program fills the individual and unique needs, or answers the questions, of everyone in the process. When a program is well conceived and executed, it becomes a useful tool for the real estate broker, the design team, and the client.

### Acceptance Statement

The final step in the process is twofold: delivering the final program report and getting a signed program acceptance statement from the client. The acceptance statement is a critical, and often overlooked, part of the process. Sign-off is an important step, both to confirm that a client agrees with the fundamental assumptions and the resulting program as well as to provide documentation that reduces future liability to the design firm. The program is only as good as the information provided and gathered. Given economic ups and downs and other changes, tomorrow's headcount could be very different from the level projected. Programmers are given information by the client that is processed in order to identify the space implications. Those implications and solution options are reported to the client, who then selects the direction and desired solution.

---

**Step 3: Documentation and Validation: Activities and Products**

**Activities**

- Summarize findings.
- Document findings in report format.
- Review findings, program, and options with client.
- Identify program direction and document program changes.
- Update program and documentation.
- Get client sign-off on program and projections.

**Products**

- Draft of program report.
- Options analysis.
- Program review meeting notes.
- Revised and final program report.
- Signed program acceptance statement.

---

## SAMPLE PROGRAM WITH INTERVIEW NOTES FOR A SMALL DEPARTMENT

| AREA TYPE POSITION | SPACE/STD. | AREA | STAFF/QTY/AREA (SQ.FT.) | | | | | | | | |
|---|---|---|---|---|---|---|---|---|---|---|---|
| | | | YE 2003 | | | YE 2008 | | | YE 2012 | | |
| | | | STAFF | QTY | AREA | STAFF | QTY | AREA | STAFF | QTY | AREA |
| Workplaces | | | | | | | | | | | |
| 1 Shareholder | PO.01 | 225 | 2 | 2 | 450 | 2 | 2 | 450 | 2 | 2 | 450 |
| 2 Shareholder Growth | PO.01 | 225 | 1 | 1 | 225 | 2 | 2 | 450 | 2 | 2 | 450 |
| 3 Other LC Growth | PO.02 | 150 | 3 | 3 | 450 | 3 | 3 | 450 | 4 | 4 | 600 |
| 4 Paralegals | PO.03 | 100 | 1 | 1 | 100 | 1 | 1 | 100 | 1 | 1 | 100 |
| 5 Paralegal Growth | PO.03 | 100 | 2 | 2 | 200 | 3 | 3 | 300 | 3 | 3 | 300 |
| 6 Secretary | WS03 | 65 | 1 | 1 | 65 | 1 | 1 | 65 | 1 | 1 | 65 |
| 7 Secretary Growth | WS03 | 65 | 2 | 2 | 130 | 3 | 3 | 195 | 3 | 3 | 195 |
| SUBTOTAL NET (USF) Workplaces | | | | 12 | 1,620 | | 15 | 2,010 | | 16 | 2,160 |
| Secondary Circulation | | 43% | | | 697 | | | 864 | | | 929 |
| SUBTOTAL (USF) Work places | | | 12 | 12 | 2,317 | 15 | 15 | 2,874 | 16 | 16 | 3,089 |
| Support Areas | | | | | | | | | | | |
| 1. Local Files-Attorney | FILE 01 | 9 | 0 | 24 | 216 | 0 | 32 | 288 | 0 | 32 | 288 |
| 2. Secretarial file cabinets | FILE 01 | 9 | | 6 | 54 | | 8 | 72 | | 8 | 72 |
| SUBTOTAL NET (USF) Support Areas | | | | 30 | 270 | | 40 | 360 | | 40 | 360 |
| Secondary Circulation | | 43% | | | 166 | | | 155 | | | 155 |
| SUBTOTAL (USF) Support Areas | | | 0 | 30 | 386 | 0 | 40 | 515 | 0 | 40 | 515 |
| SUBTOTAL NET (USF) Area Types | | | | 42 | 1,890 | | 55 | 2,370 | | 56 | 2,520 |
| Total Secondary Circulation | | 43% | | | 813 | | | 1,019 | | | 1,084 |
| TOTAL (USF) Financial Institutions | | | 12 | 42 | 2,703 | 15 | 55 | 3,389 | 16 | 56 | 3,604 |

Space standards are developed in response to the program. Individual space requirements are developed from the needs defined by the client and what is known about the potential furniture solution.

# INFORMATION INDEX

| CONSIDERATIONS | GOALS | FACTS | CONCEPTS | NEEDS | PROBLEM |
|---|---|---|---|---|---|
| Function | Mission | Statistical data | | Space requirements | Unique and important |
| People | Maximum number | Area parameters | Service grouping | Parking requirements | Performance requirements |
| | Individual identity | Manpower/workloads | People grouping | Outdoor space | that will shape |
| | Interaction, privacy | User characteristics | Activity grouping | requirements | building design |
| | Ranking of values | Community characteristics | Priority | | |
| | Exercise of authority | Authority structure | Hierarchy | | |
| Activities | Security | Value of potential loss | Security controls | | |
| | Progression | Time-motion study | Sequential flow | | |
| | Segregation | Traffic analysis | Separated flow | | |
| | Encounters | Behavioral patterns | Mixed flow | | |
| | Efficiency | Space adequacy | Relationships | | |
| Relationships | Information exchange | Type/intensity | Communication | | |
| Form | Bias on site elements | Site analysis | Enhancement | Site development costs | Major form considerations |
| Site | Sound structure | Soil analysis | Special foundations | | that will affect building design |
| | Efficient land use | F.A.R. (floor area ratio) | Density | | |
| | Physical comfort | Climate analysis | Environmental controls | Environmental | |
| | Life safety | Code survey | Safety precautions | influences on costs | |
| Environment | Sociality | Surroundings | Neighbors | | |
| | Individuality | Psychological implications | Home base | | |
| | Encoded direction | Point of reference | Orientation | | |
| | Direct entry | Entry symbols | Accessibility | | |
| | Projected image | Generic nature | Character | | |
| Quality | Building quality level | Cost/sq ft | Quality control | | |
| | Spatial quality level | Building efficiency | | Building cost/sq ft | |
| | Technical quality level | Equipment costs | | Building efficiency | |
| | Functional quality level | Area per unit | | Equipment costs | |
| Economy | Extent of funds | Cost parameters | Cost control | Cost estimate analysis | Attitude toward the initial |
| Initial Budget | Cost-effectiveness | Maximum budget | Efficient allocation | | budget and its influence |
| | Maximum return | Time-use factors | Multifunction | | on the fabric and geometry |
| | Return on investment | Market analysis | Merchandising | | of the building |
| Operating Costs | Minimize operating costs | Energy source costs | Energy conservation | Energy budget (if req'd) | |
| | Maintenance and operating costs | Activities and climate factors | Cost control | Operating costs (if req'd) | |
| Life-Cycle Costs | Reduce life-cycle costs | Economic data | Cost control | Life-cycle costs (if req'd) | |
| Time | Historic preservation | Significance | Adaptability | | |
| Past | Static dynamic activities | Space parameters | Tolerance | | |
| | Change | Activities | Convertibility | | |
| Present | Growth | Projections | Expansibility | | |
| | Occupancy date | Durations | Linear/concurrent scheduling | Time schedule | |
| Future | Cost-controlled growth | Escalation factors | Phasing | Time/cost scheduling | |

This matrix represents typical programmatic issues and provides an information index. The index can be used by the programmer as a reference tool to aid in collecting the information relevant to the project at hand. *Source:* Problem Seeking, *William Pena, John Wiley & Sons, Inc., New York, 2001.*

## INFORMATION INDEX

*Problem Seeking,* by William Pena, defines a five-step process for gathering and organizing programming information. The process provides a methodology for capturing, organizing, and processing information. The five steps of the process are:

- *Establish goals.* "What does the client want to achieve and why?"
- *Identify facts.* "What is it all about?"
- *Uncover concepts.* "How does the client want to achieve the goals?"
- *Determine needs.* "How much space, money, and quality?"
- *State the problem.* "What are the significant conditions and the general directions that the design should take?"

Information gleaned and developed during each step of the process is organized into the following categories:

- *Function,* which relates to people, activities, and relationships.
- *Form,* which relates to the site, the environment, and the quality of construction, finishes, and furnishings.
- *Economy,* which relates to the initial budget, operating costs, and life-cycle costs.
- *Time,* which relates to past, present, and future considerations.

*Anne Mott; lauckgroup; Dallas, Texas*

# LIFE-CYCLE COSTING

The selection of construction materials, finishes, or furniture is often based on four types of criteria:

- *Functional*. Will the product perform safely and effectively, meeting all relevant code requirements?
- *Aesthetic*. Does the product reflect the design intent for the project in terms of shape, color, or size?
- *Sustainability*. Will this product deplete natural resources or negatively impact the environment?
- *Financial*. Does the product cost correspond with the project budget?

Considerations should include financial criteria in the form of indirect costs associated with a product as well as the more familiar purchase and installation costs. To evaluate the true cost of a product, these indirect costs must be considered:

- *Maintenance costs*. How easy is the product to clean or repair? Will special techniques, equipment, or cleaning supplies be needed?
- *Operational costs*. Are there ongoing utility costs associated with the product, such as power?
- *Length of useful life*. How long will the product last, assuming regular maintenance and normal wear and tear?
- *Replacement costs*. How much will it cost to replace the product at the end of its useful life? Is it likely that an identical product will be available as a replacement, or will a new product need to be specified at some future date?
- *Residual value*. Is there any resale or recyclable value to the product when it is no longer useful to the project?
- *Disposal costs*. Are there special handling requirements and fees for disposing of the product at the end of its useful life?

All of these costs are of significant concern to the client long after the project is completed, and thus need to be considered by the designer when initial product selections are being made. These costs, together with the initial purchase and installation costs, are called *life-cycle costs*, and the process of quantifying these costs and accurately comparing them across multiple product choices is referred to as *life-cycle costing*. Performing a life-cycle cost analysis enables the designer to quantify the rationale behind specific choices using the objective measure of total cost over the life of the product. Clients may not be able to support design decisions made solely for functional or aesthetic reasons, but can readily understand and endorse a case for a specific product made on a financial basis.

## THE VALUE OF MONEY

A consideration in life-cycle cost analysis is the value of money, which changes over time due to inflation, investment potential, and interest rates. A common frame of reference is needed to compare costs incurred in one year with costs incurred at some other year in the future. For this reason, an effective life-cycle cost analysis converts all product costs to "today's dollars"—or the *present value*—to determine the true value of all expenditures from installation through eventual recycling or disposal.

The process for converting future values to the present value requires an understanding of the client's cost of capital, which is the current interest rate for borrowed funds. (In common practice, the term *discount rate* is used interchangeably with the term *interest rate*.) Once this interest rate is known, the formula to convert a given amount to its present value can be applied:

$$PV = Cost\ (1 + i)^{-n}$$

where $i$ is the interest rate and $n$ refers to the number of periods (or years) in the future that the cost is incurred. A standard business calculator typically includes this formula in its preprogramming, simplifying the calculations. Spreadsheet programs such as Microsoft Excel also have a present value calculation function, making it easy for designers to calculate these costs quickly and accurately.

An alternative way to determine present value is to consult a present value factor chart. This chart shows a factor for each combination of interest rate and number of periods that can be multiplied by the projected cost to determine that cost in today's dollars.

## LIFE-CYCLE COSTING PROCESS

To perform a life-cycle cost analysis, the following steps are required:

1. *Determine all costs associated with the product.* Contacting the product manufacturer or sales representative is often the best starting point for obtaining information about the cost of purchase, installation, maintenance, repair, and replacement, including any residual value for items that can be sold or recycled at the end of their useful life. Note, however, that some of these costs cannot be predicted with complete accuracy. Different installation conditions may affect length of product life, and the manufacturer's recommendations for care may not correspond to what really occurs in the field. Whenever possible, solicit information from a contractor or installation professional who is familiar with the advantages and disadvantages of the product over time. In addition, contacting end users who have had the product in their facilities may help determine realistic patterns of maintenance, durability, and repair.

2. *Identify the costs associated with the product in the year or years in which they occur.* Preparing a spreadsheet is useful in this step. The year the material or goods are installed is the first year in the spreadsheet (Year 0). Record both one-time and recurring costs associated with the life of the product. For each year, add up all of the costs to obtain a net cost for the entire year. Where there is positive cash flow from the residual value of a product from resale or recycling, deduct that amount from the costs for that year.

## IDENTIFYING COSTS ASSOCIATED WITH THE PRODUCT IN THE YEAR(S) THEY OCCUR (STEP 2)

| TYPE OF COST | YEAR 0 | YEAR 1 | YEAR 2 | YEAR 3 | YEAR 4 | YEAR 5 | YEAR 6 | YEAR 7 | YEAR 8 |
|---|---|---|---|---|---|---|---|---|---|
| Purchase | $ cost | | | | | | | | |
| Delivery | $ cost | | | | | | | | |
| Storage | $ cost | | | | | | | | |
| Installation | $ cost | | | | | | | | |
| Deep Cleaning (Yearly) | | $ cost | $ cost | $ cost | $ cost | $ cost | $ cost | $ cost | |
| Weekly Cleaning | | $ cost | $ cost | $ cost | $ cost | $ cost | $ cost | $ cost | $ cost |
| Reupholstery | | | | | $ cost | | | | |
| Resale Value or Disposal Cost | | | | | | | | | $ income or $ cost |
| NET ANNUAL COST | Year 0 $ | Year 1 $ | Year 2 $ | Year 3 $ | Year 4 $ | Year 5 $ | Year 6 $ | Year 7 $ | Year 8 $ |

In this example, the costs for an upholstered restaurant chair are analyzed.

3. *Identify the interest or discount rate.* Consult with your client or with a local bank to determine a suitable cost of capital, typically the interest rate your client could obtain for this kind of expenditure.

4. *Calculate the present value of each net annual cost.* Using a business calculator or a spreadsheet program, compute the present value of each net cost using the formula given above, plugging in the interest rate ($i$) and the number of years from Year 0 ($n$). Alternatively, consult the present factor chart in the Present Value table to identify the relevant present value factor for each year in the calculation. To organize the calculation process, it is helpful to set up a second table that identifies the present value factor applied, net annual costs from the first table, and the resulting present value.

5. *Compute the net present value for the product.* Add together all of the present values to determine the overall present value for the product, ensuring that all costs, as well as any income from resale or recycling, have been included.

Once a net present value has been calculated for two or more competing products, their life-cycle costs can be compared objectively, and this cost information can be used in the decision-making process. This generally occurs during the schematic design phase of a project.

When comparing life-cycle costs of products with differing lengths of life, it is practical to compare these costs over the number of years that the longest-lived product will be useful. For example, when comparing a product with a five-year life against a product with an eight-year life, compute the present value of all costs and incomes associated with each product over eight years, in order to fairly attribute the true costs of the shorter-lived product and compare them objectively to the more durable choice.

## CALCULATE THE PRESENT VALUE OF EACH NET ANNUAL COST (STEP 4)

| | PRESENT VALUE (PV) FACTOR* | NET COST FOR THE YEAR | PRESENT VALUE OF NET COST (NET COST × PV FACTOR) |
|---|---|---|---|
| Year 0 (Today) | 1.0000 | Year 0 $ | PV of Year 0 $ |
| Year 1 | 0.9259 | Year 1 $ | PV of Year 1 $ |
| Year 2 | 0.8573 | Year 2 $ | PV of Year 2 $ |
| Year 3 | 0.7938 | Year 3 $ | PV of Year 3 $ |
| Year 4 | 0.7350 | Year 4 $ | PV of Year 4 $ |
| Year 5 | 0.6806 | Year 5 $ | PV of Year 5 $ |
| Year 6 | 0.6302 | Year 6 $ | PV of Year 6 $ |
| Year 7 | 0.5835 | Year 7 $ | PV of Year 7 $ |
| Year 8 | 0.5403 | Year 8 $ | PV of Year 8 $ |

*From Present Value Table

This spreadsheet assumes an 8% discount rate and identifies the present value factor applied, net annual costs (see Step 2), and the resulting present value.

## PRESENT VALUE TABLE

| | | | | | | DISCOUNT RATE | | | | | | |
|---|---|---|---|---|---|---|---|---|---|---|---|---|
| YEAR | 4.5% | 5.0% | 6.0% | 7.0% | 8.0% | 9.0% | 10.0% | 11.0% | 12.0% | 13.0% | 14.0% | 15.0% |
| 1 | 0.9569 | 0.9524 | 0.9434 | 0.9346 | 0.9259 | 0.9174 | 0.9091 | 0.9009 | 0.8929 | 0.8850 | 0.8772 | 0.8696 |
| 2 | 0.9157 | 0.9070 | 0.8900 | 0.8734 | 0.8573 | 0.8417 | 0.8264 | 0.8116 | 0.7972 | 0.7831 | 0.7695 | 0.7561 |
| 3 | 0.8763 | 0.8638 | 0.8396 | 0.8163 | 0.7938 | 0.7722 | 0.7513 | 0.7312 | 0.7118 | 0.6931 | 0.6750 | 0.6575 |
| 4 | 0.8386 | 0.8227 | 0.7921 | 0.7629 | 0.7350 | 0.7084 | 0.6830 | 0.6587 | 0.6355 | 0.6133 | 0.5921 | 0.5718 |
| 5 | 0.8025 | 0.7835 | 0.7473 | 0.7130 | 0.6806 | 0.6499 | 0.6209 | 0.5935 | 0.5674 | 0.5428 | 0.5194 | 0.4972 |
| 6 | 0.7679 | 0.7462 | 0.7050 | 0.6663 | 0.6302 | 0.5963 | 0.5645 | 0.5346 | 0.5066 | 0.4803 | 0.4556 | 0.4323 |
| 7 | 0.7348 | 0.7107 | 0.6651 | 0.6227 | 0.5835 | 0.5470 | 0.5132 | 0.4817 | 0.4523 | 0.4251 | 0.3996 | 0.3759 |
| 8 | 0.7032 | 0.6768 | 0.6274 | 0.5820 | 0.5403 | 0.5019 | 0.4665 | 0.4339 | 0.4039 | 0.3762 | 0.3506 | 0.3269 |
| 9 | 0.6729 | 0.6446 | 0.5919 | 0.5439 | 0.5002 | 0.4604 | 0.4241 | 0.3909 | 0.3606 | 0.3329 | 0.3075 | 0.2843 |
| 10 | 0.6439 | 0.6139 | 0.5584 | 0.5083 | 0.4632 | 0.4224 | 0.3855 | 0.3522 | 0.3220 | 0.2946 | 0.2697 | 0.2472 |
| 11 | 0.6162 | 0.5847 | 0.5268 | 0.4751 | 0.4289 | 0.3875 | 0.3505 | 0.3173 | 0.2875 | 0.2607 | 0.2366 | 0.2149 |
| 12 | 0.5897 | 0.5568 | 0.4970 | 0.4440 | 0.3971 | 0.3555 | 0.3186 | 0.2858 | 0.2567 | 0.2307 | 0.2076 | 0.1869 |
| 13 | 0.5643 | 0.5303 | 0.4688 | 0.4150 | 0.3677 | 0.3262 | 0.2897 | 0.2575 | 0.2292 | 0.2042 | 0.1821 | 0.1625 |
| 14 | 0.5400 | 0.5051 | 0.4423 | 0.3878 | 0.3405 | 0.2992 | 0.2633 | 0.2320 | 0.2046 | 0.1807 | 0.1597 | 0.1413 |
| 15 | 0.5167 | 0.4810 | 0.4173 | 0.3624 | 0.3152 | 0.2745 | 0.2394 | 0.2090 | 0.1827 | 0.1599 | 0.1401 | 0.1229 |
| 16 | 0.4945 | 0.4581 | 0.3936 | 0.3387 | 0.2919 | 0.2519 | 0.2176 | 0.1883 | 0.1631 | 0.1415 | 0.1229 | 0.1069 |
| 17 | 0.4732 | 0.4363 | 0.3714 | 0.3166 | 0.2703 | 0.2311 | 0.1978 | 0.1696 | 0.1456 | 0.1252 | 0.1078 | 0.0929 |
| 18 | 0.4528 | 0.4155 | 0.3503 | 0.2959 | 0.2502 | 0.2120 | 0.1799 | 0.1528 | 0.1300 | 0.1108 | 0.0946 | 0.0808 |
| 19 | 0.4333 | 0.3957 | 0.3305 | 0.2765 | 0.2317 | 0.1945 | 0.1635 | 0.1377 | 0.1161 | 0.0981 | 0.0829 | 0.0703 |
| 20 | 0.4146 | 0.3769 | 0.3118 | 0.2584 | 0.2145 | 0.1784 | 0.1486 | 0.1240 | 0.1037 | 0.0868 | 0.0728 | 0.0611 |

## APPLYING LIFE-CYCLE COSTING: A CASE STUDY

The following example of a life-cycle cost analysis compares the financial ramifications of selecting one of two solid-surface flooring materials:

In a 12 × 100 ft (3.6 × 30 m) hospital corridor that receives high pedestrian traffic and heavy rolling loads, the choice to use a hard, solid-surface flooring material complies with the following two

- Functional criteria: code-compliant, slip-resistant, antibacterial
- Aesthetic criteria: conceptually sound color and pattern

The designer decides to analyze two products—vinyl sheet flooring and linoleum—both of which meet the functional and aesthetic needs for this hospital corridor. The initial product cost of the linoleum is somewhat higher than the sheet flooring, but the designer wants to see if these higher initial costs will be mitigated as all costs over the life of the product are factored into the analysis.

The two flooring selections are similar in many ways. Installation costs are the same for each, and include a three-coat sealant application after installation. Disposal costs are the same as well, as there is currently no residual value to these products, nor can they be recycled. Both have a 10-year warranty, and can be expected to perform well for those 10 years and be due for replacement at the end of the tenth year.

However, the differences between these two products are the initial purchase price and the maintenance schedule. The purchase price is $2.50 per square foot for vinyl sheet flooring versus $4.75 per square foot for linoleum. To maintain vinyl sheet flooring, additional steps must be taken to ensure the quality of finish of the material in this high-traffic corridor, and include a semiannual stripping and sealant application, followed by weekly buffing. Linoleum, in comparison, does not require stripping and resealing, nor does it need repeated buffing. Routine damp mopping is all that is required.

## CONCLUSION

In this example, linoleum costs $5,352.12 less than vinyl sheet flooring over a 10-year period. The linoleum is the less expensive choice over the life of both of the flooring materials, despite its higher initial cost.

*Rhonda Gilmore and Stephani Robson; Cornell University; Ithaca, New York*

### COSTS ASSOCIATED WITH VINYL SHEET FLOORING

| | YEAR 0 | YEAR 1 | YEAR 2 | YEAR 3 | YEAR 4 | YEAR 5 | YEAR 6 | YEAR 7 | YEAR 8 | YEAR 9 | YEAR 10 |
|---|---|---|---|---|---|---|---|---|---|---|---|
| Purchase | $2.50/SF | | | | | | | | | | |
| Installation | $7.00/SF | | | | | | | | | | |
| Maintenance | | $1,800 | $1,800 | $1,800 | $1,800 | $1,800 | $1,800 | $1,800 | $1,800 | $1,800 | $1,800 |
| Disposal | | | | | | | | | | | $75 |
| TOTAL ANNUAL COST | $11,400 | $1,800 | $1,800 | $1,800 | $1,800 | $1,800 | $1,800 | $1,800 | $1,800 | $1,800 | $1,875 |

### COSTS ASSOCIATED WITH LINOLEUM

| | YEAR 0 | YEAR 1 | YEAR 2 | YEAR 3 | YEAR 4 | YEAR 5 | YEAR 6 | YEAR 7 | YEAR 8 | YEAR 9 | YEAR 10 |
|---|---|---|---|---|---|---|---|---|---|---|---|
| Purchase | $4.75/SF | | | | | | | | | | |
| Installation | $7.00/SF | | | | | | | | | | |
| Maintenance | | $600 | $600 | $600 | $600 | $600 | $600 | $600 | $600 | $600 | $600 |
| Disposal | | | | | | | | | | | $75 |
| TOTAL ANNUAL COST | $14,100 | $600 | $600 | $600 | $600 | $600 | $600 | $600 | $600 | $600 | $675 |

These two charts break down all costs for installing 1,200 sq ft of these two products on a year-by-year basis over their 10-year lives.

### LIFE-CYCLE COST COMPARISON OF VINYL SHEET FLOORING AND LINOLEUM

| | | VINYL SHEET FLOORING | | LINOLEUM | |
|---|---|---|---|---|---|
| | PV FACTOR (FROM CHART) | NET COST FOR THE YEAR | PRESENT VALUE OF NET COST (NET COST × PV FACTOR) | NET COST FOR THE YEAR | PRESENT VALUE OF NET COST (NET COST × PV FACTOR) |
| Year 0 (Today) | 1.0000 | $11,400 | $11,400.00 | $14,100 | $14,100.00 |
| Year 1 | 0.9259 | $1,800 | $1,666.62 | $600 | $555.54 |
| Year 2 | 0.8573 | $1,800 | $1,543.14 | $600 | $514.38 |
| Year 3 | 0.7938 | $1,800 | $1,428.84 | $600 | $476.28 |
| Year 4 | 0.7350 | $1,800 | $1,323.00 | $600 | $441.00 |
| Year 5 | 0.6806 | $1,800 | $1,225.08 | $600 | $408.36 |
| Year 6 | 0.6302 | $1,800 | $1,134.36 | $600 | $378.12 |
| Year 7 | 0.5835 | $1,800 | $1,050.30 | $600 | $350.10 |
| Year 8 | 0.5403 | $1,800 | $972.54 | $600 | $324.18 |
| Year 9 | 0.5002 | $1,800 | $900.54 | $600 | $300.18 |
| Year 10 | 0.4632 | $1,875 | $868.50 | $675 | $312.66 |
| LIFE-CYCLE COST | | | $23,512.92 | | $18,160.80 |

This table demonstrates the calculation of the true life-cycle costs for each flooring choice, using present value factors at an 8% discount rate from the Present Value table.

# CONTRACT DOCUMENTS

Contract documents describe the proposed construction of furniture, furnishings, and equipment installation. They include written specifications and graphic documentation, such as drawings, which communicate the design of the project. The two sets of contract documents that a designer must prepare for a complete commercial interiors project are the *construction contract documents*, and the *furniture, furnishings, and equipment (FF&E) contract documents*

## THE CONTRACT FOR CONSTRUCTION

The agreement between the owner and the construction contractor is the contract for construction. The construction contractor's responsibilities are described in AIA A201, *The General Conditions of the Contract for Construction*. The construction contractor is responsible for supervising and directing the construction of the project. This includes providing labor, materials, equipment, tools, water, heat, utilities, and other facilities and safety features. The *construction contractor* employs the various trades required to accomplish the work of the contract, or makes agreements with subcontractors. The *general contractor* coordinates the work of these specialty contractors, such as electricians, plumbers, painters, carpenters, and carpet installers.

In addition to orchestrating various construction activities, construction contractors perform a variety of administrative tasks. The general contractor is usually responsible for securing and paying for the building permit and other permits required for completion of the project. The general contractor is also generally responsible for the preparation of a construction schedule, and must prepare and submit shop drawings and samples for the architect's approval.

Shop drawings illustrate specific situations or details of a project. They are prepared by the construction contractor, one of the subcontractors, the product manufacturer, or the supplier. These drawings are then submitted to the designer for approval (for example, samples of the materials or workmanship); these are used to verify selections and to establish standards by which the completed work will be judged. Shop drawings and samples are not contract documents. They are submitted to demonstrate the way in which the construction contractor intends to accomplish the design expressed by the contract documents.

## CONSTRUCTION PROJECT TYPES

The traditional approach to a construction project is the design-award-build sequence of events. The designer fully documents the project in the contract documents, which include the construction drawings and specifications. Proposals to build the project are requested from construction contractors. These bids are evaluated, a contractor is selected, and a construction contract between the successful bidder and the owner is signed. The "owner" in most cases is the tenant, but, depending on the terms of the lease and work letter, the owner may also be the landlord. The architect is usually retained to administer the contract for construction between the owner and the construction contractor.

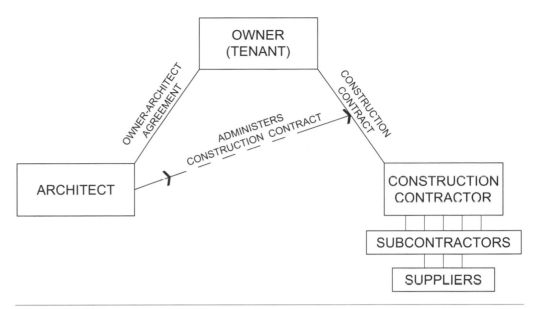

**CONSTRUCTION CONTRACT**

It is often necessary to begin construction as soon as possible because of accelerated occupancy schedules or the high cost of financing a project. In the fast-track approach to construction, building begins before the project design is complete. Separate construction contracts are defined, and contract documents are prepared for each phase. Items that are last to be installed or constructed, such as custom casework, will be the last to be fully designed and bid. The design schedule extends into the construction schedule, reducing the duration of the project. Fast-tracking often increases construction costs due to decreased labor efficiency.

In design/build projects, one party is responsible for both the design and the construction of the interior. The design/build firm may be a construction company with in-house designers or one that has hired a design firm consultant. The advantage of this method of con-

struction contracting is that the contractor is involved with the project from the initial stages. Costs, material availability, and scheduling can be estimated much more accurately.

Construction for commercial interiors on leased properties is referred to by various names, including *tenant build-out work, tenant fit-up,* or *tenant improvements.* Lease provisions often require that the landlord approve the prime, or general, contractor and the subcontractors. In some cases, landlords retain contractors to build all tenant spaces in their buildings.

## FURNITURE, FURNISHINGS, AND EQUIPMENT (FF&E) CONTRACTS

The FF&E contractor is responsible for procuring, delivering, and installing the goods described in the FF&E contract. The designer typically administers the agreement between the owner and the FF&E contractor. The FF&E contractor is often a furniture dealer but may also be a furniture manufacturer or a design professional.

### FF&E Contractors

The furniture dealer is the local or regional presence of the manufacturer. The dealer processes the sale and provides various support and follow-up services to the owner. In this way, the manufacturer concentrates on product development and production, and the dealer focuses on sales and service. One of the services a dealer typically offers is warehousing the goods between the time manufacturing has been completed and the point at which the project site is ready to receive them for installation.

A direct sales force represents the manufacturer, not the manufacturer's dealer. Equipment is commonly procured directly from the manufacturer through a direct sales force. For example, a hospital bed manufacturer may not require a showroom to market a relatively expensive product with a limited user base. The sale may be effectively accomplished by sending a sample bed to the hospital on a trial basis or by arranging a tour of the factory showroom.

**DESIGN/BUILD CONTRACT**

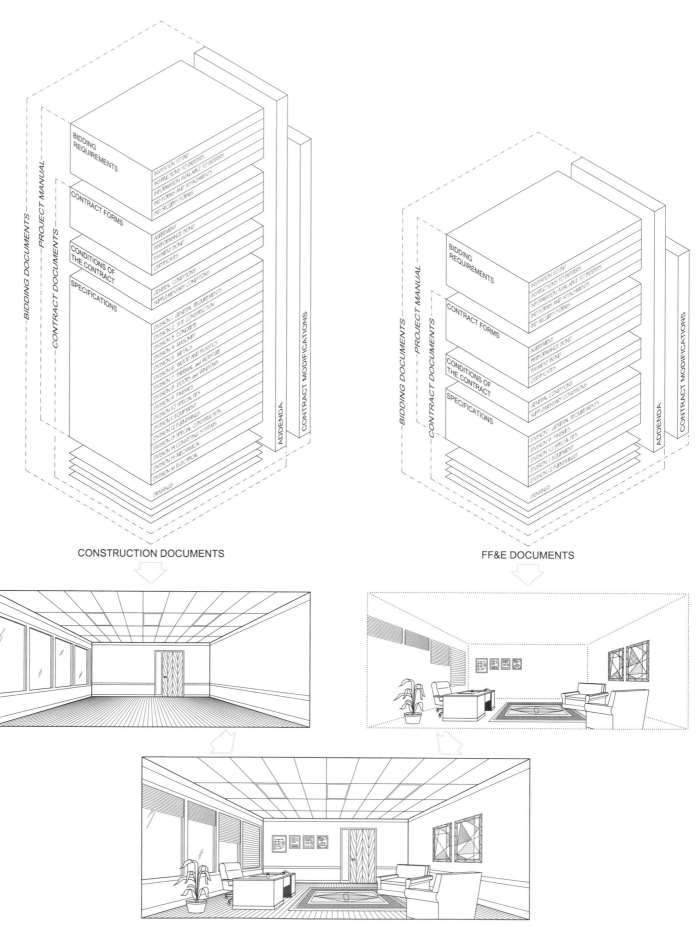

Construction documents diagram, reprinted from the Construction Specifications Institute's *Manual of Practice*.

**COMPLETE CONTRACT DOCUMENTS FOR A COMMERCIAL INTERIORS PROJECT**

## COMPARISON OF CONSTRUCTION CONTRACT AND FF&E CONTRACT BY PROJECT PHASE

| CONSTRUCTION CONTRACT FOR INTERIORS | FF&E CONTRACT | DESIGNER | TENANT | FF&E OR CONSTRUCTION CONTRACTOR |
|---|---|---|---|---|
| **PREDESIGN** | | | | |
| Programming | | P | A | |
| Select Building | N/A | R | P | |
| Work Letter/Lease Negotiation | Space Planning or Test Layouts | P | R, A | |
| Site Survey | FF&E Inventory | P | | |
| Building Standards | Work Station Standards | | R | |
| **SCHEMATIC DESIGN** | | | | |
| Conceptual Design | | P | A | |
| Initial Plans | | P | A | |
| Conceptual Elevations | | P | A | |
| Outline Specifications | | P | A | |
| Consultant Coordination<br>  Acoustical<br>  Electrical<br>  Mechanical<br>  Structural | Consultant Coordination<br>  Planting (Indoor Landscaping)<br>  Signage<br>  Furniture Project Manager | P | | |
| Preliminary Pricing | | P | R, A | |
| Meetings/Presentation | | P | R, A | |
| **DESIGN DEVELOPMENT** | | | | |
| N/A | Research FF&E | P | R, A | |
| Construct Mockups | Install Mockups/Manufacturer Presentation | R, A | A | P |
| Definitive Construction Documents | Definitive FF&E Documents | P | R, A | |
| Definitive Construction Specifications | Definitive FF&E Specifications | P | R, A | |
| Develop Budget for Construction | Develop Budget for FF&E | R | P | |
| **CONTRACT DOCUMENTS** | | | | |
| Final Construction Drawings | Final FF&E Drawings | P | R, A | |
| Final Construction Specifications | Final FF&E Specifications | P | R, A | |
| Prepare Bid Documents<br>UNIT PRICES (adjustment to contract made by change order during contract administration). These prices are determined by bidder.<br>ALTERNATES (options are priced separately): Alternates are accepted by tenant.<br><br>ALLOWANCES (monies reserved in contract): Tenant allows for work not determined at time of bid. | Prepare Bid Documents<br>UNIT PRICES: Bids are itemized as unit prices. Cost per item is determined by contractor's discount price.<br>ALTERNATES: Less commonly used. Costs are known during design phase and are factored in item selection.<br>ALLOWANCES: Less commonly used. Tenant can use allowances for budgeting purposes. | P | R, A | R |
| **BIDDING OR NEGOTIATION** | | | | |
| Prequalification of Bidders | | A | | |
| Issue Addenda | | P | A | R |
| Receive Bids | | R | P, A | |
| Bid Review/Analysis | | P | R | |
| Confirm Performance Bond | | | P | |
| Confirm Insurance | | | P | |
| Award Contracts | | R | P | |
| Submit Construction Schedule | Submit P.O. Tracking Report | R | | P |
| **CONTRACT ADMINISTRATION** | | | | |
| **CONSTRUCTION** | **INSTALLATION** | | | |
| Determine Deposits/Orders for Long Lead Items | Determine Deposits for FF&E Orders | R | P | |
| Set up Temporary Facilities | Determine Staging Area | | A | P |
| Project Coordination Contractor responsible for subcontractors. | Project Coordination: Tenant coordinates FF&E contractors and their work with construction contractor. | R | | P |
| Construction Meetings | Job Progress Meetings | R, A | A | P |
| Submittal Review | | R, A | | P |
| Review Project Progress | | P | A | |
| Product Substitutions; proposed by contractor | Typically not permitted. Contractor points out reason why substitution must be made. Designer proposes substitute to tenant. | R, A | A | P |
| Authorize Payments | P.O.s may not be submitted to designer for approval. | R, A | | P |
| Issue Certificate of Payments | Tenant pays P.O. invoice. | R, A | | P |
| Contract Document Revision | | P | A | |
| Issue Change Orders | Issue, revise, or cancel P.O.s | R, A | A | P |
| Determine Substantial Completion | Tenant pays P.O. invoice. | A | | P |
| Not Applicable | P.O. Coordination | R, A | | P |
| Prepare Punchlist | | P | A | R |
| Not Applicable | Move Coordination | P | A | |
| Determine Final Completion | Tenant pays final P.O. invoice. | A | | P |

*P = Performs task*

*R = Reviews*

*A = Approves*

*American Institute of Architects; Washington, D.C.*

## FF&E Contractor Roles

The FF&E contractor prepares purchase orders based on the FF&E contract. A purchase order is the form used to obtain the required goods for the project. It contains a description of the goods, the supplier's catalog number, the number of items required, and the price. Separate purchase orders are prepared for each supplier involved in the project.

An *acknowledgment*, also referred to as a *purchase order acknowledgment*, is prepared by the supplier as confirmation of the purchase order. The acknowledgment must be verified by the FF&E contractor to make sure it is an accurate interpretation of the purchase order. If the purchase order acknowledgment is correct, the order is placed and the manufacturing process begins.

The FF&E contractor coordinates the requirements for customer's own material (C.O.M.), material that is not supplied by the product manufacturer. C.O.M. is purchased separately from the product and supplied to the product manufacturer for application. "Customer" in this case does not refer to the designer's customer, the owner, but to the manufacturer's customer, the party placing the order, which is the FF&E contractor. It is the FF&E contractor who is responsible for the acquisition and coordination of C.O.M.

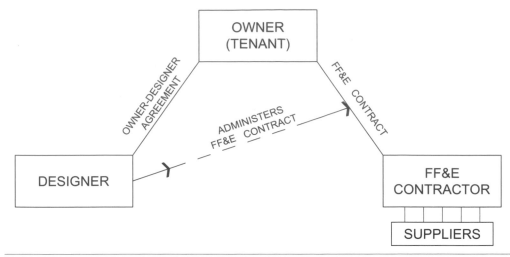

**FF&E CONTRACT FOR INTERIORS PROJECT**

The owner can also procure the required goods through their in-house purchasing departments. Large corporations can purchase products—for example, carpet, furniture, fabric, and light fixtures—and supply them to the contractor for installation. This allows a business to establish national accounts with vendors and to reduce costs by buying in volume.

After the goods have been manufactured, they are packaged for delivery. An invoice, a bill requesting payment for the goods, is prepared by the manufacturer and sent to the FF&E contractor, typically at the same time the goods are shipped.

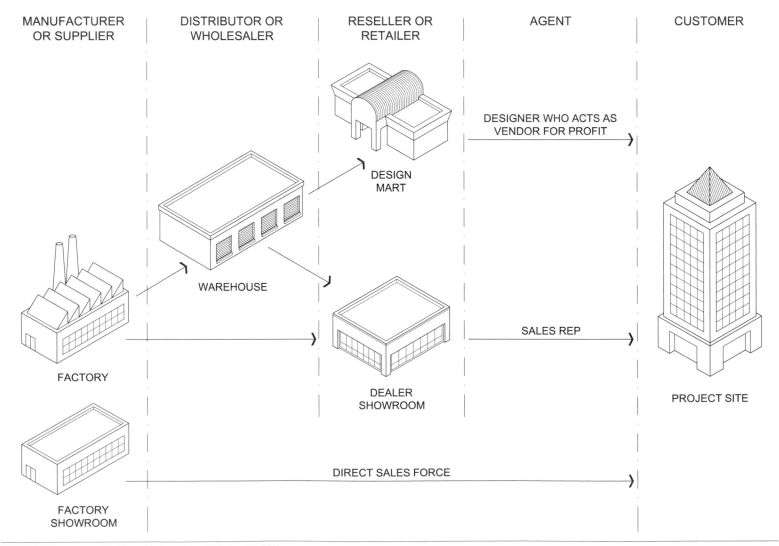

**THREE COMMON METHODS OF FF&E DISTRIBUTION**

## DELIVERY AND INSTALLATION OF FF&E

The Uniform Commercial Code (UCC) defines many of the terms, and sets forth the procedures, used in the delivery of goods. Delivery is defined by the UCC as voluntary transfer of possession (UCC 1-201). Delivery does not necessarily indicate ownership. Title means ownership. If you have title to goods, you own them. For example, a manufacturer delivers furniture to a carrier for transportation to its destination. The manufacturer is not transferring title to the goods; therefore the carrier does not own the furniture. Receipt is defined as taking physical possession of goods (UCC 2-103).

A carrier is a transportation company. Carriers that operate in interstate commerce are regulated by the Interstate Commerce Commission (ICC). Common carriers offer transportation services to the general public. They are usually responsible for the goods they are shipping, whether or not they have been negligent. Contract carriers provide transportation only to those with whom they choose to do business. They do not insure the goods they transport unless they are contracted to do so. Private carriers are not in the transportation business. They own and operate trucks to transport their own goods. The ICC does not regulate private carriers.

With few exceptions, such as when goods are picked up by the buyer (see UCC 2-509), whoever has title to the goods bears the risk of their being lost, stolen, damaged, or destroyed. The risk of loss is commonly indicated by the abbreviation F.O.B., defined by the UCC as "free on board" (UCC 2-319).

F.O.B. at a named place indicates where title to the goods and risk of their loss or damage pass from the seller to the buyer, which is typically the FF&E contractor. The buyer pays the transportation costs from the point named in the F.O.B. "place."

### F.O.B. Designations

When goods are sent *F.O.B. place of shipment*, the buyer owns the goods at the place of shipment (typically, the manufacturer's factory loading dock). The goods are given to the carrier (typically, a truck), and the seller is no longer responsible for the delivery of the goods or their condition upon arrival. The buyer pays for shipping. If the goods are stolen, damaged, or destroyed in transit, it is the buyer's responsibility to recover damages from the carrier. When the terms of shipment do not specify shipping point or destination, it is assumed to be F.O.B. place of shipment.

*F.O.B. place of destination* means the seller is responsible for delivering the goods. The cost of the goods includes shipping charges. If the goods are stolen, damaged, or destroyed in transit, it is the seller's responsibility to recover damages from the carrier (UCC 2-319).

*F.O.B. factory—freight prepaid* means that the buyer has title to the goods during transit but that the supplier pays the transportation charges to the destination. In this way, the buyer has the convenience of not having to arrange for transportation, and the supplier reduces its liability.

### Shipment Tracking

A *drop shipment* means the goods will be shipped to a destination different from that of the party who ordered and paid for them. A *bill of lading* is defined

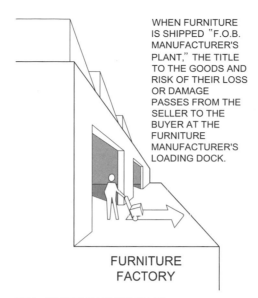

WHEN FURNITURE IS SHIPPED "F.O.B. MANUFACTURER'S PLANT," THE TITLE TO THE GOODS AND RISK OF THEIR LOSS OR DAMAGE PASSES FROM THE SELLER TO THE BUYER AT THE FURNITURE MANUFACTURER'S LOADING DOCK.

**FURNITURE FACTORY**

**F.O.B. MANUFACTURER'S PLANT**

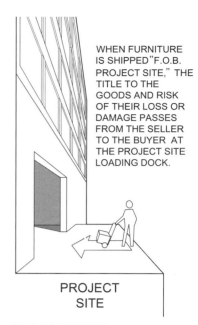

WHEN FURNITURE IS SHIPPED "F.O.B. PROJECT SITE," THE TITLE TO THE GOODS AND RISK OF THEIR LOSS OR DAMAGE PASSES FROM THE SELLER TO THE BUYER AT THE PROJECT SITE LOADING DOCK.

**PROJECT SITE**

**F.O.B. PROJECT SITE**

**F.O.B. "FREE ON BOARD"**

### PASSAGE OF TITLE

| | SELLER ASSUMES EXPENSE AND RISK OF... | PASSAGE OF TITLE OCCURS AT... | PRICE OF GOODS... |
|---|---|---|---|
| F.O.B.: Place of shipment | Putting goods into the possession of the carrier place of shipment | Place of shipment (typically manufacturer's factory loading dock) | Does not include shipping charges |
| F.O.B.: Place of destination | Transporting the goods to the destination | Destination (typically the project site's loading dock) | Includes shipping charges |

by the UCC as a document confirming the receipt of goods for shipment issued by a person engaged in the business of transporting (UCC 1-201).

The supplier prepares the bill of lading. The carrier verifies that the goods loaded on its vehicle match those listed on the bill of lading. The bill of lading lists the number of boxes, crates, or packages. It is not intended to verify that the goods being transported are the goods that were ordered. A packing list is a detailed list of quantities and descriptions of the goods being delivered. It is used to check the items, and it cross-references the bill of lading. The packing list is typically attached to the outside of the shipping package in a clear plastic envelope.

## LAWS GOVERNING CONTRACTS FOR INTERIORS PROJECTS

A contract is an agreement between two or more parties that is based on mutual promises to do (or refrain from doing) something that is neither illegal nor impossible. A contract is basically a promise that the law will enforce. U.S. laws must conform to the U.S. Constitution and can originate from any of the three branches of government: executive, legislative, or judicial. Laws governing interiors projects stem from a variety of sources. These sources include *constitutional law*, *statutory law*, *common law*, and *administrative law*, as well as *contract and commercial law*.

### Constitutional Law

A constitution is the basic law of a nation or state. Constitutional law is the supreme law of a nation. All forms of law must conform to the constitution. The

U.S. Constitution establishes the organization of the federal government.

### Statutory Law

Laws passed by a legislature are known as *statutes*. At the federal level, these are the laws that are passed by Congress and signed by the president. At the state level, statutes are enacted by state legislative bodies. Statutory law also includes ordinances passed at the local level by cities and counties.

Because many different statutes are passed each year by each state's legislative body, there are significant differences in statutory law throughout the United States. This may present problems when parties from different states and subject to different laws try to do business. The most important development in uniform legislation among the states has been the Uniform Commercial Code (UCC), the group of statutory laws governing sales transactions in the United States. The UCC governs contracts for FF&E.

### Common Law

Common law is based on the outcome of previous court cases under comparable circumstances. The tradition of common law dates back to the early English kings' attempts at establishing a fair system of rules that all courts in the kingdom could hold in common. Consistency was maintained by relying on previous legal decisions. These previous decisions, known as *precedents*, became model cases for the courts to follow when facing similar situations. Common law, as modified by statute, governs contracts for construction.

## Administrative Law

Contemporary society often presents problems so complex that neither legislators nor judges have the expertise to provide adequate counsel. To assist in this effort, legislators commonly delegate their power to others by creating administrative agencies, boards, and commissions. The rules made by administrative agencies comprise administrative law.

## Contract Law and Commercial Law

All contracts contain agreements, but not all agreements are contracts. An agreement may or may not be legally enforceable. To be enforceable, an agreement must conform to the law of contracts. Contract law is the framework for all commercial law. It serves as the basis for much of the law described in more specialized areas, such as the sale of goods.

## SALES CONTRACTS AND SERVICES CONTRACTS

If the subject of a contract is real estate or services, common law and certain statutory provisions govern. If the subject of a contract is goods, then the UCC applies. Goods are defined as all things (except money, stocks, and bonds) that are movable. When a contract includes both goods and services, the dominant element of the contract determines whether it is a sales contract or a services contract.

A contract for construction, which is between the owner and the construction contractor, is essentially an agreement to provide expertise and service, and includes the purchase of construction materials. It is regulated by common law as modified by statute. A contract for FF&E, which is between the owner and the FF&E contractor, includes services such as warehousing, delivery, and installation, but it is primarily a sale-of-goods contract. A contract for FF&E is regulated by the UCC.

## Uniform Commercial Code

The Uniform Commercial Code (UCC) is the set of statutes that governs the commercial transactions of all 50 states (except Louisiana, which has adopted only Articles 1, 3, 4, and 5, and the District of Columbia and the Virgin Islands). For practical purposes, the rules governing commercial transactions are consistent throughout the country because of the UCC.

In cases in which the UCC is silent, the common law of contracts and applicable state statutes govern. Common law rules and UCC provisions are quite often the same. The UCC simplifies the law governing commercial transactions by making the fundamental rules of contract law less rigid. UCC provisions are more appropriate than common law for a variety of circumstances typical of sales transactions. Although many common law rules and UCC provisions are the same, there are some significant differences.

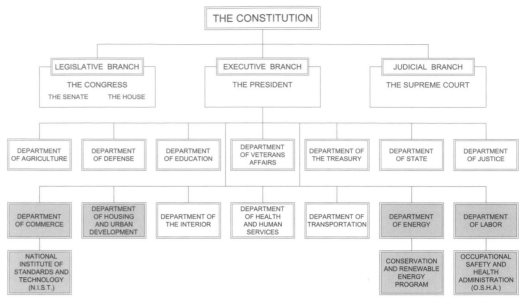

Shaded departments are involved in building regulations.

**THE U.S. GOVERNMENT**

### Differences between Contract Law and Commercial Law: Warranties

#### Offer and Acceptance in Formation of Contract (UCC 2-206)

Rules of commercial law regarding the way an offer is made and accepted are not as strict as those of contract law. In many cases, an enforceable sales contract can be made in any way—written, oral, or by conduct that shows an agreement has been reached. Unless the original agreement is in writing with a stipulation that it may not be modified except by a signed contract, mutual promises are not required to modify a contract for the sale of goods. In a sale-of-goods contract, the purchase price may be omitted and the amount of goods to be sold need not always be defined.

#### UCC Warranty Definitions

The UCC is the primary source for rules regarding warranties in commercial transactions. It defines two important types of warranties: *express* and *implied*.

**An express warranty** is a representation about the quality of a product. There are three different ways to make an express warranty: by a statement of fact or promise, by a description of the goods, or by a sample or model (UCC 2-313).

**An implied warranty** is inferred from the nature of the transaction. The seller does not offer an implied warranty; it is imposed by law. Implied warranties are designed to promote fairness and honesty. There are two types of implied warranties: an *implied warranty of merchantability* and an *implied warranty of fitness* for a particular purpose.

An implied warranty of merchantability assures the buyer that the goods are fit for the ordinary purpose for which they are to be used. This warranty type applies only to sales made by merchants who deal in goods of the kind sold (UCC 2-314). For example, a furniture dealer makes an implied warranty of merchantability every time it sells a desk, but a neighbor selling the same desk at a yard sale does not. For a claim to be made for a breach of this type of warranty, a defect must exist at the time the goods are purchased.

When a buyer relies on a seller's judgment to select the goods, it is implied that the seller warrants that the goods will be fit for the purpose for which they are to be used. This creates the implied warranty of fitness for a particular purpose. This warranty type applies to both merchants and nonmerchants. If the seller knows how the buyer will use the goods and knows the buyer is relying on the seller's skill in selecting the goods, there is an implied warranty of fitness (UCC 2-315).

### DIFFERENCES BETWEEN THE UCC AND CONTRACT LAW

| UCC | CONTRACT LAW |
| --- | --- |
| Not all terms have to be included in the contract (UCC 2-204). | An offer must be definite enough for the parties (and the courts) to ascertain its essential terms when the contract is accepted. |
| Firm written offers by merchants for three months or less cannot be revoked (UCC 2-205). | An offer can be revoked any time before acceptance. |
| The price does not have to be included to have a contract (UCC 2-305). | Price must be included. |
| Variation in terms between the offer and the acceptance may not be a rejection (UCC 2-207). | Variation in terms between the offer and the acceptance act as a rejection of, and a counteroffer to, the offer. |
| A modification for the sale-of-goods contract does not require mutual agreement (UCC 2-209). | Modification of common law contract requires mutual agreement. |

# CONSTRUCTION SPECIFICATIONS

## TYPES OF SPECIFICATIONS

There are four basic types of specifications: *proprietary, descriptive, performance,* and *reference standard.* Most specifications incorporate features from more than one of the four types. For example, a proprietary specification for a particular fabric might also include reference standards for flammability and abrasion resistance.

### Proprietary Specifications

Proprietary specifications require a specific product from a specific manufacturer indicated by a brand name or model number. The specifier has complete control over what will be incorporated in the project when a proprietary specification is used. FF&E specifications are commonly proprietary. For example, "Knoll Group, Studio Line, Barcelona Chair, with black leather upholstery," is a proprietary specification.

### Descriptive Specifications

Descriptive specifications detail the requirements for material properties and workmanship. Manufacturers and products are not named. Descriptive specifications are the most difficult to write, because every aspect of the topic must be considered. For example, an acoustical ceiling tile would be specified by describing the tile material, pattern, finish, color, edge detail, thickness, and size.

### Performance Specifications

Performance specifications describe the required results. They describe how a product or material is to perform, not necessarily what it is. The construction contractor or FF&E contractor has a choice of products, materials, and processes that will be used to achieve these results. Performance specifications typically make reference to industry standards. It is helpful to include standard test methods to ensure that performance requirements are met objectively. For example, an acoustical wall panel could be specified by describing its fire-test-performance characteristics, acoustical properties expressed by a noise reduction coefficient (NRC) value, and the abrasion resistance of its fabric covering. This specification type is relatively rare, because designers are most often concerned with a product's appearance as well as its performance.

### Reference Standard Specifications

Reference standard specifications are based on requirements set by an accepted authority. For example, by specifying compliance with ANSI A108, *Specifications for Installation of Ceramic Tile,* the requirements of the standard are included in the specification by reference. Reference standard specifications tend to be the briefest type of specifications. When referencing a standard, it is important that the specifier understand the standard and verify that all provisions of the standard apply to the project.

## SPECIFICATION INFORMATION CLASSIFICATION

In 1963, CSI introduced *MasterFormat* in an effort to standardize language, project manual organization, and data filing systems. MasterFormat is a list of numbers and titles that classify the materials and requirements of construction and FF&E projects. It is used to organize project specifications and file product information in the United States and Canada. MasterFormat is composed of 16 divisions, each identified by a five-digit numbering system. The first two digits indicate the division number; the last three denote the section location within the division.

The topics of Divisions 2 through 16 are included in a project specification only if they are relevant to the project. However, every project specification includes a Division 1–General Requirements. The specification sections of Division 1 govern the execution of sections in Divisions 2 through 16. Division 1 contains the administrative and procedural requirements pertaining to all the specification sections and is the key to administering a construction or FF&E contract.

## DIVISION 1—GENERAL REQUIREMENTS

The Division 1 sections cover those aspects of the topic that apply to all specification sections in the project manual; the section articles cover those aspects that are peculiar to that section. For example, the Division 1 section titled "Submittal," describes information for use with all submittals: the transmittal form, how the submittals are to be numbered and identified, and the number of copies required. The section article "Submittals" describes which materials, finishes, or products discussed in that section should be submitted and what information the shop drawings or product data must contain.

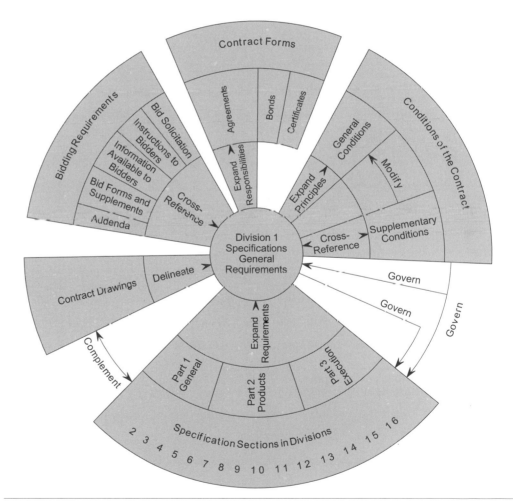

**DIVISION 1 RELATIONSHIP TO OTHER DOCUMENTS**
*Source: Construction Specifications Institute; Alexandria, Virginia*

| PART 1—GENERAL | PART 2—PRODUCTS | PART 3—EXECUTION |
|---|---|---|
| **SUMMARY** | **MANUFACTURERS** | **INSTALLERS** |
| Section Includes: | **EXISTING PRODUCTS** | **EXAMINATION** |
| Products Supplied But Not Installed | **MATERIALS** | Site Verification of Conditions |
| Under This Section | **MANUFACTURED UNITS** | **PREPARATION** |
| Products Installed But Not Supplied | **EQUIPMENT** | Protection |
| Under This Section | **COMPONENTS** | Surface Preparation |
| Related Sections | **ACCESSORIES** | **ERECTION** |
| Allowances | **MIXES** | **INSTALLATION** |
| Unit Prices | **FABRICATION** | **APPLICATION** |
| Measurement Procedures | Shop Assembly | **CONSTRUCTION** |
| Payment Procedures | Fabrication Tolerances | Special Techniques |
| Alternates | **FINISHES** | Interface with Other Work |
| **REFERENCES** | Shop Priming, Shop Finishing | Sequences of Operation |
| **DEFINITIONS** | **SOURCE QUALITY CONTROL** | Site Tolerances |
| **SYSTEM DESCRIPTION** | Tests, Inspection | **REPAIR/RESTORATION** |
| Design Requirements | Verification of Performance | **REINSTALLATION** |
| Performance Requirements | | **FIELD QUALITY CONTROL** |
| **SUBMITTALS** | | Site Tests, Inspection |
| Product Data | | Manufacturers' Field Services |
| Shop Drawings | | **ADJUSTING** |
| Samples | | **CLEANING** |
| Quality Assurance/Control Submittals | | **DEMONSTRATION** |
| Design Data, Test Reports | | **PROTECTION** |
| Certificates | | **SCHEDULES** |
| Manufacturers' Instructions | | |
| Manufacturers' Field Reports | | |
| Qualification Statements | | |
| Closeout Submittals | | |
| **QUALITY ASSURANCE** | | |
| Qualifications | | |
| Regulatory Requirements | | |
| Certifications | | |
| Field Samples | | |
| Mockups | | |
| Preinstallation Meetings | | |
| **DELIVERY, STORAGE, AND HANDLING** | | |
| Packing, Shipping, Handling, and | | |
| Unloading | | |
| Acceptance at Site | | |
| Storage and Protection | | |
| Waste Management and Disposal | | |
| **PROJECT/SITE CONDITIONS*** | | |
| Project/Site* Environmental | | |
| Requirements | | |
| Existing Conditions | | |
| **SEQUENCING** | | |
| **SCHEDULING** | | |
| **WARRANTY** | | |
| Special Warranty | | |
| **SYSTEM STARTUP** | | |
| **OWNER'S INSTRUCTIONS** | | |
| **COMMISSIONING** | | |
| **MAINTENANCE** | | |
| Extra Materials | | *"Project Conditions" is the preferred term in the United States; "Site Conditions" is the preferred term in Canada.* |
| Maintenance Service | | |

**SECTIONFORMAT OUTLINE**
*Source: Construction Specifications Institute; Alexandria, Virginia*

## SPECIFICATION FORMATS

The Construction Specifications Institute (CSI) has established formats for specification information classifications (MasterFormat; see Appendix), sections (SectionFormat), and pages (PageFormat). These three formats provide the basis for a complete, concise, and coordinated project manual in which information can be reliably and easily located.

### Specification Section Organization

*SectionFormat* organizes the information presented in each specification section into three parts: Part 1—General; Part 2—Products; and Part 3—Execution. Part 1—General describes the administrative and procedural requirements specific to the section. Part 2—Products contains the requirements for the appearance and performance attributes of the items included in the section. Part 3—Execution describes the preparation for and the construction or installation of items included in the section. Each part of the section is divided into articles. Article titles should be selected for inclusion based on their applicability.

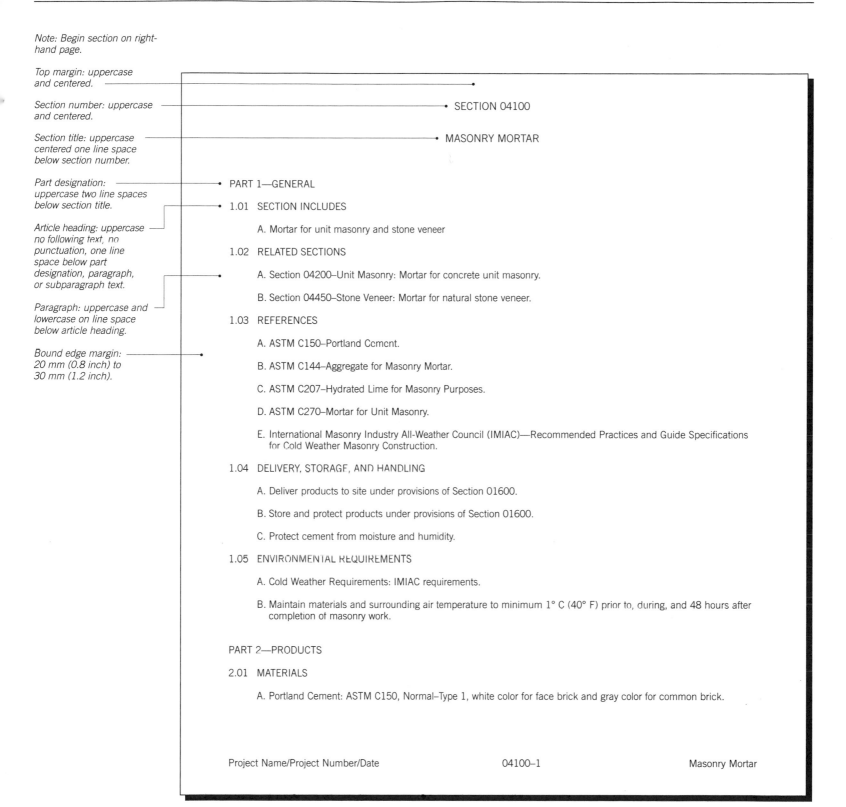

Note: Begin section on right-hand page.

Top margin: uppercase and centered.

Section number: uppercase and centered.

Section title: uppercase centered one line space below section number.

Part designation: uppercase two line spaces below section title.

Article heading: uppercase no following text, no punctuation, one line space below part designation, paragraph, or subparagraph text.

Paragraph: uppercase and lowercase on line space below article heading.

Bound edge margin: 20 mm (0.8 inch) to 30 mm (1.2 inch).

SECTION 04100

MASONRY MORTAR

PART 1—GENERAL

1.01  SECTION INCLUDES

A. Mortar for unit masonry and stone veneer

1.02  RELATED SECTIONS

A. Section 04200–Unit Masonry: Mortar for concrete unit masonry.

B. Section 04450–Stone Veneer: Mortar for natural stone veneer.

1.03  REFERENCES

A. ASTM C150–Portland Cement.

B. ASTM C144–Aggregate for Masonry Mortar.

C. ASTM C207–Hydrated Lime for Masonry Purposes.

D. ASTM C270–Mortar for Unit Masonry.

E. International Masonry Industry All-Weather Council (IMIAC)—Recommended Practices and Guide Specifications for Cold Weather Masonry Construction.

1.04  DELIVERY, STORAGE, AND HANDLING

A. Deliver products to site under provisions of Section 01600.

B. Store and protect products under provisions of Section 01600.

C. Protect cement from moisture and humidity.

1.05  ENVIRONMENTAL REQUIREMENTS

A. Cold Weather Requirements: IMIAC requirements.

B. Maintain materials and surrounding air temperature to minimum 1° C (40° F) prior to, during, and 48 hours after completion of masonry work.

PART 2—PRODUCTS

2.01  MATERIALS

A. Portland Cement: ASTM C150, Normal–Type 1, white color for face brick and gray color for common brick.

Project Name/Project Number/Date          04100–1          Masonry Mortar

**SAMPLE CSI SECTION TEXT**
*Source: Construction Specifications Institute; Alexandria, Virginia*

## Specification Page Organization

*PageFormat* organizes each page of the project manual. PageFormat includes recommendations for headers, footers, and part, article, and paragraph designations. Part and article titles are presented in capital letters. For ease in referencing information—for example, in correspondence or during contract administration—articles are numerically labeled with a designation consisting of the part number, a decimal point, and a two-digit number starting with 01. Paragraphs are outlined using the traditional alphanumeric system (e.g., A.1.a.1).

Mortar aggregate: ASTM C144, standard masonry type; clean, dry; protected from dampness, freezing, or foreign matter.

B. Hydrated Lime: ASTM C207, Type S.

C. Water: Clean and potable.

D. Mortar Color: Mineral oxide pigment; chocolate brown color; "Great Stuff," manufactured by Acme Manufacturing Co. Ltd.

2.02   MIXES

A. Mortar for Load-Bearing Walls and Partitions: ASTM C270, Type S, using proportion method.

B. Mortar for Nonload-Bearing Walls and Partitions: ASTM C270, Type N, using proportion method.

2.03   MORTAR MIXING

A. Thoroughly mix mortar ingredients in quantities needed for immediate use in accordance with ASTM C270.

B. Add mortar color in accordance with manufacturer's instructions. Provide uniformity of mix and coloration.

C. Do not use antifreeze compounds to lower the freezing point of mortar.


PART 3—EXECUTION

3.01   INSTALLATION

A. Install mortar in conjunction with Sections 04200 and 04450.

3.02   FIELD QUALITY CONTROL

A. Field testing will be preformed under provisions of Section 01400.


END OF SECTION


Project Name/Project Number/Date                     04100–2                     Masonry Mortar


**SAMPLE CSI SECTION TEXT** *(continued)*
*Source: Construction Specifications Institute; Alexandria, Virginia*

## RESOURCE

The figures used in this section are published by the Construction Specifications Institute (CSI) and are used with permission from CSI, 2003. For those interested in a more in-depth explanation of these documents and their use in the construction industry, contact:

Construction Specifications Institute (CSI)
99 Canal Center Plaza, Suite 300
Alexandria, Virginia 22314
(800) 689–2900; (703) 684–0300
CSINet: www.csinet.org

# PROJECT MANAGEMENT CHECKLIST FOR COMMERCIAL INTERIORS

## PROJECT MANAGEMENT CHECKLIST FOR COMMERCIAL INTERIORS

| REQUIREMENTS AND COMMENTS | NAME | NAME | NAME | NAME | NAME | NAME | CONSTRUCTION CONTRACT | FF&E CONTRACT | NAME | NAME | NAME | NAME | NAME | NAME |
|---|---|---|---|---|---|---|---|---|---|---|---|---|---|---|

P—Performs Task: Verification, Determination, or Calculation
R—Reviews
A—Approves
S—Support

**Predesign**

| | Programming | |
|---|---|---|
| | Work Letter/Lease Negotiation | Space Planning or Test Layouts |
| | Site Survey | FF&E Inventory |
| | Building Standards | Work Station Standards |

**Schematic Design**

| | CONSTRUCTION CONTRACT | FF&E CONTRACT |
|---|---|---|
| | Conceptual Design | |
| | Initial Plans | |
| | Conceptual Elevations | |
| | Outline Specifications | |
| | Consultant Coordination | Consultant Coordination |
| | • Acoustical | • Furniture Project Manager |
| | • Electrical | • Signage |
| | • Mechanical | • Interior Landscaping |
| | • Structural | • Specialized Equipment |
| | • Other | • Other |
| | Preliminary Pricing | |
| | Present Schematic Design to Owner | |
| | Written Approval from Owner of Schematic Design | |

**Design Development**

| | CONSTRUCTION CONTRACT | FF&E CONTRACT |
|---|---|---|
| | Review Schematic Design | |
| | • Project Budget | • Furniture Budget |
| | • Scope of work, so that additional services can be established | • Scope of work, so that additional services can be established |
| | • Regulatory Analysis, including: | |
| |   • Fire marshall | |
| |   • Zoning Commission | |
| |   • Planning Commission | |
| |   • Department of Health, Department of Education, etc., if applicable | |
| | Establish Project Documentation | |
| | • Project file | |
| | • Directory of in-house and out-of-house team members | |
| | • Finish sample binders | • Cut sheet binders |
| | • Product information binders | • FF&E information binders |
| | • Outline specifications (coordinate format with consultants) | • Equipment specifications |
| | • List of drawings | • List of drawings |
| | • Cartoon set of drawings | • Cartoon set of drawings |
| | Mock-ups | |
| | • Construct mock-ups for Owner verification. | • Install mock-ups/manufacturer presentation for Owner verification. |
| | • Approval of construction assembly mock-ups | • Approval of furniture mock-ups |
| | Prepare Definitive Contract Documents | |
| | Design Development Closeout | |
| | • Confirm construction budget. | • Confirm furniture budget. |
| | • Provide cost estimate to Owner, if in Scope of Work. | • Provide cost estimate to Owner, if in Scope of Work. |
| | • Confirm Owner's signed approval of DD drawings, product data, and finishes manual. | • Confirm Owner's signed approval of DD drawings and furniture selections. |
| | • Provide consultants with DD drawings for coordination. | • Provide consultants with equipment specifications and requirements. |
| | • Archive DD construction drawings in preparation for Contract Documents phase. | • Archive DD FF&E drawings in preparation for Contract Documents phase. |

CONTRACT ADMINISTRATION  ☐  1

## PROJECT MANAGEMENT CHECKLIST FOR COMMERCIAL INTERIORS *(continued)*

| REQUIREMENTS AND COMMENTS | P—Performs Task: Verification, Determination, or Calculation / R—Reviews / A—Approves / S—Support | | | | | | CONSTRUCTION CONTRACT | FF&E CONTRACT | P—Performs Task: Verification, Determination, or Calculation / R—Reviews / A—Approves / S—Support | | | | | |
|---|---|---|---|---|---|---|---|---|---|---|---|---|---|---|
| | NAME | NAME | NAME | NAME | NAME | NAME | | | NAME | NAME | NAME | NAME | NAME | NAME |
| **Contract Documents** | | | | | | | | | | | | | | |
| | | | | | | | Final Construction Drawings | Final FF&E Drawings | | | | | | |
| | | | | | | | Final Construction Specification | Final FF&E Specifications | | | | | | |
| | | | | | | | Prepare Bid Documents | | | | | | | |
| | | | | | | | • Unit Prices (adjustment to contract made by change order during contract administration)—These prices are determined by bidder. | • Unit Prices—Bids are itemized as unit prices. Cost per item is determined by Contractor's discounted price. | | | | | | |
| | | | | | | | • Alternates (options that are prices separately)—Alternates are accepted by tenant. | • Alternates—Less commonly used. Costs are known during the design phase and are a factor in item selection. | | | | | | |
| | | | | | | | • Allowances (monies reserved in contract)—Tenant allows for work not determined at time of bid. | • Allowances—Less commonly used. Owner can use allowances for budgeting purposes. | | | | | | |
| **Bidding or Negotiation** | | | | | | | | | | | | | | |
| | | | | | | | Prequalification of Bidders | | | | | | | |
| | | | | | | | Issue Addenda | | | | | | | |
| | | | | | | | Receive Bids | | | | | | | |
| | | | | | | | Bid Review and Analysis | | | | | | | |
| | | | | | | | Confirm Performance Bond | | | | | | | |
| | | | | | | | Confirm Insurance | | | | | | | |
| | | | | | | | Award Contracts | | | | | | | |
| | | | | | | | Review construction schedule. | Review Purchase Order Tracking Reports. | | | | | | |
| **Contract Administration** | | | | | | | | | | | | | | |
| | | | | | | | CONSTRUCTION | INSTALLATION | | | | | | |
| | | | | | | | Verify deposits. | Verify deposits. | | | | | | |
| | | | | | | | Verify orders for long lead times. | Determine orders for long lead items. | | | | | | |
| | | | | | | | Review submittals | | | | | | | |
| | | | | | | | Review project progress | | | | | | | |
| | | | | | | | Review substitutions | | | | | | | |
| | | | | | | | Review payment requests. | Review purchase orders, if in Scope of Work | | | | | | |
| | | | | | | | Review change orders. | Review, revise, or cancel purchase orders, if in Scope of Work. | | | | | | |
| | | | | | | | Respond to Requests for Information (RFIs) | | | | | | | |
| | | | | | | | Initiate bulletins | | | | | | | |
| | | | | | | | Review payment applications and compare with schedule of values. Request subcontractor lien waivers with each application and make sure that they are notarized. | Review purchase orders, if in Scope of Work. | | | | | | |
| | | | | | | | Prepare Punchlist | | | | | | | |
| | | | | | | | Determine Substantial Completion Initiate certificate of substantial completion when work is sufficiently complete in accordance with the Contract Documents, to the extent that the Owner can occupy the project for the use for which it was intended. Attach punchlists to the application if any items are outstanding. | | | | | | | |
| | | | | | | | Move Coordination | | | | | | | |
| | | | | | | | Determine Final Completion | | | | | | | |
| | | | | | | | Project Closeout | | | | | | | |
| | | | | | | | Review Contractor's Punchlist | | | | | | | |
| | | | | | | | Ensure Owner receives as-built drawings; review as-built drawings, if in Scope of Work. | | | | | | | |
| | | | | | | | Submit record drawings to Owner, if in Scope of Work. | | | | | | | |
| | | | | | | | Review final application for payment. | | | | | | | |
| | | | | | | | Request subcontractor lien waivers with application. | | | | | | | |
| | | | | | | | Ensure Owner receives warranty and O&M (owner and maintenance manuals) | | | | | | | |
| | | | | | | | Ensure Owner receives spare parts and materials, as well as keys and keying schedule. | | | | | | | |
| | | | | | | | Archive CAD files, specifications, etc. | | | | | | | |

1 　□　 **CONTRACT ADMINISTRATION**

# COORDINATION CHECKLIST FOR CONSTRUCTION DRAWINGS AND SPECIFICATIONS

This checklist can be used to verify that all aspects of the project are described either in the Specifications or on the construction documents. It is organized by engineering and other disciplines that are often assigned to consultants. By locating relevant information in one place only, modifications and project coordination can be simplified.

Modify this checklist to suit the specific requirements of your practice or of a project.

## COORDINATION CHECKLIST FOR CONSTRUCTION DRAWINGS AND SPECIFICATIONS

### MECHANICAL COORDINATION

| General | CONFIRMED |
|---|---|
| What type of heating and cooling system is specified, and which devices will be visible? | |
| Coordinate space requirements or ceiling devices, shafts, duct runs, and connections. | |
| Consider requirements for supplemental air (e.g., equipment rooms, after-hours work). | |
| Provide equipment specifications to engineer. | |

| **Ductwork and Piping** | |
|---|---|
| Verify that ductwork is sized logically. | |
| Verify that mechanical ducts and pipes do not conflict with architectural features, light fixtures, or structural members. | |
| Verify that adequate ceiling height exists at worst-case duct intersection or largest beam. | |
| Provide ventilation at stairwells, elevator/dumbwaiter, shafts, and at all toilet rooms. | |

| **Ventilation** | |
|---|---|
| Indicate structural supports for mechanical equipment on structural drawings. | |
| Verify that only required ductwork penetrates special acoustical partitions. | |
| Provide sound liners as required. | |
| Verify that air transfer ducts are included and occur above door. | |
| Indicate dampers at smoke partitions and fire walls. | |
| Provide exhaust fans as required: | |
|   • Toilet rooms | |
|   • Smoking rooms | |
|   • Copy centers | |
|   • Kitchen areas | |

| **Diffusers and Grilles** | |
|---|---|
| Confirm specification trim and finish of diffusers. | |
| Design supply and return grilles, considering the following: | |
|   • Coordinate location with mechanical engineer's drawings. | |
|   • Review specifications to assure mechanical engineer has specified desired grille type. | |
|   • Long-term maintenance of interior finishes, art, and so on: verify that air diffuser location will not accumulate dirt/soot that will be visible on or damaging to an adjacent surface. | |
| Locate Young's regulators (a sort of "keyhole" for manually adjusting dampers in gypsum wallboard ceilings) and specify if concealed or exposed. | |

| **Equipment** | |
|---|---|
| Verify that equipment is located at accessible ceiling locations to avoid or minimize access panels in gypsum wallboard ceilings. Where required, access panels are frameless type. | |
| Verify working space around equipment required for use and servicing. | |
| Verify that mechanical equipment will fit in spaces allocated and that there is room for maintenance such as for removing filters or replacing parts. | |
| Verify that supplemental 24-hour air-handling units are located in computer rooms and rooms used after hours and on weekends. | |
| Verify that horsepower ratings, phases, and voltages of major items of equipment shown on drawings match that which is specified. | |
| Verify that cutsheets of all visible mechanical equipment have been received from consultants and have been reviewed (baseboard heat, fan coil units). | |
| Coordinate outdoor equipment on rooftop units with roof design, areas served, and views to buildings. Locate pads as required and coordinate with building design. | |
| Coordinate with mechanical engineer for items that require wall access panels, such as plumbing in an adjacent room. | |
| Coordinate wall heaters with mechanical engineer's drawings. Show them on interior elevations. | |

| **Thermostats** | |
|---|---|
| *Note:* Generally, thermostats operate better when located in the center of the room, away from direct sunlight, and out of the path of air movement. If the thermostat is located on a column in open office space, assure it will not conflict with furniture panels or be subject to damage if facing into a high-traffic corridor. | |
| Specify finishes for thermostat and provide instruction to Owner for HVAC controls. | |
| Review thermostat options with mechanical engineer and review again on shop drawings. | |
| Verify that thermostat type reinforces the design concept of the space. *Note:* The type of thermostat may be determined by the Owner's prescribed system for HVAC controls. | |
| Discuss with the mechanical engineer and the Owner whether the occupants of the space should have access to adjust the thermostat. If not, select a thermostat that prevents user access. Avoid the use of locking plastic covers over thermostats, applied after the fact, to prevent thermostat adjustment by room occupants. | |

### ELECTRICAL COORDINATION

| General | CONFIRMED |
|---|---|
| Verify that the finishes of cover plates, switchplates, and so on are specified or that architectural color has been modified to match backsplash, fabric panel, and wall paint. | |
| Power receptacles: Coordinate locations with electrical engineer's drawings and others whose work requires electrical outlets (e.g., A/V equipment, coffeepots, copiers, microwaves, fax machines, printers, other equipment, outlets required within casework, etc.). | |
| Data and phone jacks: Coordinate locations with electrical engineer's drawings, A/V designer's drawings, and others for jacks for phones, computers, other computer network devices, fax machines, and so on. | |
| What is the Owner standard regarding power/data provisions? Refer to the approved program. | |
| Are emergency power provisions required? | |
| Define and coordinate furniture systems requirements. How many circuits? How many wires? How are they fed? | |
| Determine "clean" and "dirty" power requirements. | |

**COORDINATION CHECKLIST FOR CONSTRUCTION DRAWINGS AND SPECIFICATIONS** *(continued)*        **CONFIRMED**

Is a conduit required for data or security?

Has Owner provided specifications for all Owner-provided equipment?

Establish size allowances for all equipment.

Is a public address system required? Coordinate device locations.

What are the audiovisual requirements?

Is CATV required?

Are lighting controls systems (dimmers) required? Who will provide systems? Coordinate switch locations.

Coordinate with electrical engineer and/or lighting designer for energy code, emergency lighting, and other technical requirements for lighting.

If the fixture is located in rated ceiling, determine if it requires rated construction around it (e.g., above ceiling).

Verify that emergency light fixtures are indicated.

Verify that occupancy sensors are provided, if required.

Verify that dimming systems have been provided where required.

Verify that engineer has been provided with the latest architectural background.

**Power Supply**

Verify that all equipment power has been provided and that dedicated circuits have been provided as required.

Verify that systems furniture power requirements are provided and coordinated with manufacturers' requirement. Verify that whips are not concealed behind panels if not allowed by jurisdiction.

Address clean/dirty power requirements with Owner.

Verify that electrical circuits are appropriate for:

  • Computers

  • Printers

  • Copiers

  • Other equipment

Verify that electrical shades and motorized projection screens are powered and that their switch locations are logical.

Verify that electrical power is provided for high-density storage systems.

**Light Fixtures**

*Location*

  Coordinate with electrical engineer's or lighting designer's drawings.

  Coordinate with other ceiling items on mechanical engineer's and architectural drawings.

  Determine that pendant fixtures do not conflict with operable items such as door swings, projection screens, and so on, and will not obstruct views (e.g., view to signage or projection screen beyond, view of art on wall beyond) or increase "clutter" in small spaces.

  Verify that mounting heights are coordinated with architectural drawings

  Verify that task lighting is provided at workstations and that override switches are provided.

*Fixture Type*

  Determine who selects and specifies fixtures and whether lamps need to be energy-efficient. Verify that trim colors, other accessories, and color of lamp are specified.

  Determine whether maintenance will be done from above or below the fixture. Account for servicing the fixture (cleaning, lamp replacement, access to ballasts).

  Assure that fixture location does not prohibit access for lamp replacement.

  Review specifications for coordination with drawings of fixture type, size, finish, housing, voltage, lamp, lamp color (temperature), and so on.

  Meet with electrical engineer and/or lighting designer to review catalogue cuts and specifications.

  Verify that light fixtures are scheduled to mount in scheduled ceiling finish (suitable to gypsum wallboard, acoustical ceiling tile, or exposed regular edge).

*Lighting Controls*

  Determine if dimming or multilevel switching is required.

  Locate lighting controls and coordinate with electrical engineer's and lighting designer's drawings.

**Other Electrical Equipment**

Verify that equipment has electrical connections and that horsepower ratings, phases, and voltages are consistent with other discipline schedules.

Verify that the equipment layout matches other discipline floor plans and that there are no conflicts with columns.

Verify that equipment is connected to utility systems.

Verify that outdoor equipment is coordinated with building design and views and that the required pads are provided.

Verify that cable tray locations are coordinated with other trades.

**Pantry Equipment**

Verify that pantry equipment matches architectural equipment list.

Indicate outlet mounting heights above millwork, counters, and backsplashes.

Locate ventilating fans.

Verify if garbage disposal is required.

Verify if coffeepot timer is required.

**Data and Telephone**

Verify that data/telephone locations are designated to ring and string to ceiling above.

Verify data/telephone locations in floor.

Verify if A/V equipment is required.

Verify that junction boxes are provided in ceiling for AV or other equipment.

Verify if ATM is required.

**Panels**

Verify that locations of panel boards are consistent with architectural, mechanical, and plumbing floor plans, and that panel boards are indicated on the electrical riser diagram.

Verify that there is sufficient space for electrical panels to fit.

Verify that electrical panels are not recessed in fire-rated walls; provide plywood backboard if required.

Verify that locations of electrical conduit, runs, floor trenches, and openings are coordinated with structural plans.

**Security Systems**

Security systems, such as switches to disable the system when opening for business: Coordinate with Owner's security staff and hardware consultant.

Switches for "panic alarms"

Switches for autolocking of doors

Switches to disarm card reader door locks for patient/customer entry, and so on.

1  ☐  **CONTRACT ADMINISTRATION**

## COORDINATION CHECKLIST FOR CONSTRUCTION DRAWINGS AND SPECIFICATIONS *(continued)*

| Automatic Door Operators | CONFIRMED |
|---|---|
| Require push buttons on the wall or on separate bollards, and sometimes require bulky equipment located at the door head. | |
| Coordinate with hardware consultant for type, size, style, and with ADA requirements for push button height and proximity to door, and so on. | ☐ |
| Controlled entry devices | |
| Intercoms | |
| Door chime buttons | |
| Door chime speakers | |
| Cameras | |
| Motion detectors | |
| Occupancy sensors (for energy management of lighting) | |
| Card reader doors (if required as "request to exit" device) | |
| Theft detection or metal detection devices (floor- or wall-mounted) | |

| Life Safety | |
|---|---|
| Fire pull stations: Locate according to fire code and ADA-compliant heights. | |
| Coordinate with other wall-mounted devices (switches, thermostats, etc.) for attractive grouping of items. | |
| Fire extinguishers: Locate according to fire code. | |
| Select type appropriate to design, such as wall-mounted or in a cabinet (cabinet type includes wall mount, semi-recessed, fully recessed, and fire-rated for recessed installation in fire-rated walls). | |
| Locate for ADA-compliant height. Review Owner's policy for signage; some require signage on the wall above the cabinet for distant viewing over furniture and people. | |
| Fire horn/strobes: Locate per ADA and fire code. | |

| Other Concerns | |
|---|---|
| Review locations with art or other wall features (refer to discussion above about thermostats). | |
| Switches for lighted signage | |
| Locations of electrical signage | |
| "White noise" or other continuous audio systems (includes volume controls) | |
| Switches for operation of Owner's equipment | |

### PLUMBING COORDINATION

| General | CONFIRMED |
|---|---|
| Plumbing fixtures match plumbing schedules, cutsheets, and architectural locations; verify color and finish. | |
| Pantry equipment is plumbed, including refrigerators with icemakers, dishwashers, and coffeemakers; include drain lines at icemakers. | |
| Sanitary drain system pipes have been sized and connect all fixtures. | |
| Verify floor penetrations required by plumbing lines do not conflict with structural member locations. | |

| Sprinklers | |
|---|---|
| *Note:* Sprinklers are appropriate in rooms including closets under 50 sq ft (4.6 sq m), under stairs, soffits, where required, computer/equipment rooms, kitchens, and atria. | |
| Specify if heads are to be in the center of the tile, centered on corridor, or other. | |
| Verify that run does not conflict with other plenum elements. Provide cutouts at structural members. | |
| Coordinate with other ceiling items and consider conflicts with sprinkler pipe. | |
| Specify recessed, concealed, or exposed. | |
| Verify finishes. | |
| Review specifications to assure mechanical engineer has specified type desired (be aware that there are often requirements by the Owner's insurance coverage that dictate sprinkler head type). | |

| Fire Hose Valves | |
|---|---|
| Verify that requirements for locations of fire hose valves (lengths of hose) and fire extinguisher cabinets are met. | |
| Verify that valves and cabinets are not located in rated partitions, where possible (provide rated cabinet if required), and coordinate with architectural drawings. | |
| Verify that cabinets are recessed type. | |

| Water Heaters | |
|---|---|
| Identify concealed water heaters. | |
| Provide plastic drip pan at overhead water heater. | |
| Provide access to water heater in lower cabinets as required. | |

| Waterlines and Filters | |
|---|---|
| Provide filters as needed for: | |
| • Tap water | |
| • Ice machines | |
| • Coffee lines | |
| Provide waterline for equipment as required: | |
| • Ice machines in refrigerators | |
| • Freestanding coffee stations | |
| • Mechanical equipment | |
| • Dishwashers | |
| • Clothes-washing machines | |

| Toilet Room Fixtures | |
|---|---|
| Coordinate sinks, lavatories, restrooms, and shower doors with wall depth and fire rating, if recessed. | |
| Consider method of trimming out recessed items, if not self-trimming. | |
| Verify that plumbing ducts and pipes do not conflict with architectural features, light fixtures, or structural members. | |

### STRUCTURAL COORDINATION

| General | CONFIRMED |
|---|---|
| Verify expansion joint locations. | |
| Fireproofing is coordinated with architectural drawings per code requirements. | |
| Slab openings, sizes, and locations; reframing around existing conditions is indicated on drawings. | |
| Reinforcing for heavy equipment (including mechanical) or furniture is provided. | |

**COORDINATION CHECKLIST FOR CONSTRUCTION DRAWINGS AND SPECIFICATIONS** *(continued)*       CONFIRMED

| | CONFIRMED |
|---|---|
| Equipment pads are provided if required. | |
| Structural supports for mechanical equipment are provided. | |
| Depressed or raised slabs are indicated and match architectural drawings. | |
| Note location, size, and configuration of lateral bracing that may impact openings in walls. | |
| **Columns** | |
| Columns, floor beams, and roof beams are listed in column and beam schedules. | |
| Roof framing plan column lines and column locations match foundation plan column lines and column locations. | |
| Length of columns in column schedule match the length shown in section and the elevation on drawings. | |
| Verify if ATM is required. Existing floor loading may be inadequate. | |

| **OTHER COORDINATION ISSUES** | |
|---|---|
| Verify acoustic ratings and requirements of partition types. | |
| Do certain areas require special acoustic consideration? Sound attenuation? | |
| Will floor penetrations affect spaces below? Is there exposed structure below? | |
| Audiovisual | |
| Food service | |
| Furniture | |
| Graphics | |
| Lighting | |
| Security | |
| Specialized equipment | |
| Telecommunications | |

## CONSTRUCTION DRAWING CHECKLIST

This checklist lists items that should appear in construction documents if they occur in a project. The checklist is organized by drawing type to help ensure that each sheet of the construction documents is complete. Modify this checklist to suit the specific requirements of your practice or of a project.

### CONSTRUCTION DRAWING CHECKLIST

**FLOOR PLAN, SMALL SCALE**

**ARCHITECTURAL ISSUES**

| **Area of Work** | CONFIRMED |
|---|---|
| Differentiation between new and existing construction | |
| Structural grid | |
| Elevator shafts for new elevator sizes per manufacturer | |
| Doors with swing | |
| Fire extinguisher, hose, and valve locations | |
| Casework location (show hatched) | |
| Partition height; that is, ceiling height or extend to structure above | |
| Partition rating indication | |
| Partitions drawn accurately with nominal (not actual) thickness; that is, 5 in. for steel stud, 8 in. for CMU | |
| Room names and numbers | |
| Penetrations coordinated with floor/ceiling below | |
| Systems furniture requirements and layout | |
| Communications room and LAN room requirements (including raised flooring and ramps) | |
| Verify toilet rooms have required fixture count and ADA clearances. | |
| **Mechanical Issues** | |
| Verify mechanical floor plans match architectural floor plans. | |
| Coordinate thermostat locations with architectural drawings (e.g., at doors, above outlets, away from dimmers, away from accent walls). | |
| **Electrical Issues** | |
| Verify that electrical floor plans match the latest architectural and mechanical drawings. Check that the location of the floor-mounted equipment is consistent between the disciplines. | |
| Power and telecommunications plans | |
| Equipment location, including copier and fax machines | |
| Pantry equipment locations: Verify ADA requirements. | |
| Electric water cooler locations: Verify ADA requirements. | |
| Confirm clearances and power requirements for Owner equipment. | |
| Determine space requirements for electrical closets and equipment rooms. | |
| **Life Safety** | |
| Verify that exit signs have been installed and do not conflict with door swings. | |
| Verify that strobes/pull stations are provided, meet ADA requirements, and do not conflict with architectural and furniture elements. | |
| **Plumbing Issues** | |
| Plumbing floor plans match architectural floor plans. | |
| Plumbing fixtures match architectural floor plans. | |
| Wall chases are provided to conceal vertical piping. | |
| Dimension fittings and chases accommodate carriers for wall-hung toilets. | |
| Sanitary drain system pipes have been sized and connect all fixtures. | |
| Verify that fire hose valves and cabinets are not located in rated partitions, where possible (provide rated cabinet if required), and coordinate with architectural drawings. | |
| Verify that plumbing ducts and pipes do not conflict with architectural features, light fixtures, or structural members. | |

## CONSTRUCTION DRAWING CHECKLIST *(continued)*

**Structural Issues**

| | |
|---|---|
| Structural grid | |
| Size of existing structural columns | |
| Locations of columns, bearing walls, and overall building dimensions | |

## FLOOR PLAN, LARGE-SCALE

**Architectural Issues**

| | |
|---|---|
| Dimensioned building core | |
| Dimensioned elevator shafts, stairs | |
| Exit corridors, life safety, ADA-required clearances marked | |
| Dimensioned toilet rooms | |
| Entry lobby | |
| Other special, unusual, or complex areas | |

## FINISH PLANS

**Architectural Issues**

| | |
|---|---|
| Floor patterns | |
| Floor transition accessories | |
| Wall finishes | |
| Finish schedules | |

## MILLWORK AND CASEWORK PLANS AND DETAILS

**Architectural Issues**

| | |
|---|---|
| Plans | |
| Elevations | |
| Sections | |
| Edge profiles | |
| Joinery methods | |
| Veneer grain pattern | |
| Veneer matching | |
| Operating hardware | |

**Electrical Issues**

| | |
|---|---|
| Outlets in casework | |
| Under-cabinet light fixtures in casework | |

**Plumbing Issue**

| | |
|---|---|
| Sinks in casework | |

## INTERIOR ELEVATIONS

**Architectural Issues**

| | |
|---|---|
| Special or complex areas, such as a lobby | |
| Walls with finishes | |
| Walls requiring coordination information | |
| Toilet room fixture heights: | |

- Mirrors
- Soap dispensers
- Lotion dispensers
- Paper towel dispensers (for folded towels or on a roll)
- Waste receptacles
- Shower soap dispensers
- Shower curtains
- Grab bars
- Towel bars
- Towel heaters
- Feminine product dispensers and disposal
- Seat cover dispensers
- Toilet paper dispensers
- Automatic air freshener dispensers
- Hooks
- Shelves
- Baby changing tables
- Hair dryers
- Hand dryers

| | |
|---|---|
| Toilet rooms showing generic wall finishes, partition mounting (overhead or floor mount) | |
| Verify that wall-mounted diffuser locations match mechanical drawings and are located exactly in gypsum wallboard ceilings. | |

**Mechanical Issues**

| | |
|---|---|
| Show wall heater locations. | |
| Coordinate thermostat locations with architectural drawings (e.g., at doors, above outlets, away from dimmers, away from accent walls). | |
| Verify that mounting height of thermostat is ADA-compliant, especially if operable by room occupants. | |

## CONSTRUCTION DRAWING CHECKLIST *(continued)*

### Electrical Issues

| | |
|---|---|
| Verify that mounting heights for wall-mounted light fixtures are shown and coordinated with electrical drawings. | |
| Power receptacles: | |
|    • A/V equipment | |
|    • Coffeepots | |
|    • Copiers | |
|    • Microwaves | |
|    • Fax machines | |
|    • Printers | |
|    • Outlets required within casework | |
| Phone jacks | |
| Data jacks | |
| Switches, general: | |
|    • Light fixtures | |
|    • Electrical shades | |
|    • Motorized projection screens | |
|    • Task lighting | |
|    • Switches for operation of Owner's equipment | |
|    • Switches for lighted signage | |
| Security: | |
|    • Security systems disable switch | |
|    • "Panic alarm" switch | |
|    • Switches for automatic locking of doors | |
|    • Switches to disarm card reader door locks for patient/customer entry, and so on | |
| Automatic door operator push buttons<br>*Note:* Coordinate with hardware consultant for type, size, style, and with ADA requirements for push button height and proximity to door, and so on. | |
| Controlled entry devices | |
| Intercoms | |
| Door chime buttons | |
| Door chime speakers | |
| Cameras | |
| Motion detectors | |
| Occupancy sensors (for energy management of lighting) | |
| Card reader doors (if required as "request to exit" device) | |
| Theft detection or metal detection devices (floor- or wall-mounted) | |

### Life Safety

| | |
|---|---|
| Fire pull stations: Locate according to fire code and ADA-compliant heights. | |
| Fire horn/strobes: Locate per ADA and fire code. | |

### Other Concerns

| | |
|---|---|
| Review locations with art or other wall features. | |

## REFLECTED CEILING PLANS

### Architectural Issues

| | |
|---|---|
| Acoustic ceiling grids, with set-out points | |
| Ceiling materials | |
| Lighting fixtures: Coordinate with depth of ceiling plenum and with door and cabinet door swings. | |
| HVAC register and diffusers | |
| Sprinklers | |
| Exposed structure locations | |
| Ceiling heights | |
| Soffits, coves, drapery pockets | |

### Mechanical Issues

| | |
|---|---|
| Verify that diffuser locations match mechanical reflected ceiling plans and are located exactly in gypsum wallboard ceilings. | |
| Show ceiling access doors and panels. | |

### Electrical Issues

| | |
|---|---|
| Show light fixtures to scale and verify that there is adequate space above ceiling for fixture. | |
| Show junction boxes if required in ceiling for AV or other equipment. | |

### Plumbing Issues

| | |
|---|---|
| Show sprinkler heads in design-sensitive spaces. | |
| Position sprinkler heads in center of tile, located exactly in gypsum wallboard ceilings. | |

## CONSTRUCTION DETAILS

### Architectural Issues

| | |
|---|---|
| Typical door head, sill, jamb | |
| Blind door and other atypical head, sill, jamb conditions | |
| Typical partition types, keyed to plan | |
| Casework and millwork | |
| Stair details, including tread, stringers, and railings | |
| Special ceiling conditions, keyed to Reflected Ceiling Plan | |
| Transitions between elements | |
| Transitions between planes | |
| Special, unusual, or complex conditions | |

**1** ☐ **CONTRACT ADMINISTRATION**

# INTERIOR LANDSCAPING

## CONSIDERATIONS

Thriving indoor plants are dependent on the successful integration of the requirements of the plant material and the interior environmental conditions. Typically, plant materials tolerant to existing interior conditions must be selected. However, in projects in which plants are a significant part of the design statement, or when an interior landscape designer is involved early in the design process, the environmental conditions can be adjusted to accommodate the needs of plants. The primary considerations for supporting plant growth indoors are light, temperature, humidity, and irrigation.

## Light

The intensity, duration, and quality of both natural and artificial light affect plant life. These three attributes must be addressed for plants to thrive.

### Light Intensity

It is a popular misconception that some plant species thrive on low light; in fact, they merely tolerate low light better than other species. Very few species can be successfully sustained for an extended period of time under less than 50 foot candles (fc) (500 lx) of light.

### LIGHT INTENSITY FOR PLANTS

| SPECIMENS | WILL TOLERATE |
|---|---|
| "Low-light" plants | 35–100 fc (350–1,000 lx) |
| "Medium-light" plants | 90-400 fc (900–4,000 lx) |
| "High-light" plants | More than 300 fc (3,000 lx) |

Direct sunlight outdoors during the summer may vary from 8,000 to 12,000 fc (80,000 to 120,000 lx).

### Light Duration

Like outdoor plants, indoor plants benefit from light available during daylight hours, or from approximately 8 hours a day during the winter to 16 hours a day during the summer in temperate climates. Skylights alone rarely provide high levels of light for more than a few hours a day. Lack of intensity can be somewhat compensated for by increasing duration, but a well-defined day/night cycle (or *photoperiod*) is essential to plant health. Plants lighted 24 hours a day will be placed under stress and will experience shorter life spans. A maximum of 16 hours a day of available light year round is recommended.

### Light Quality

Daylight provides outdoor plants with a full range of light, from infrared through the entire visible light spectrum to ultraviolet. Indoor plants are lighted either from electric sources whose light spectrum is limited or from daylight that has been altered as it passes through glazing. Neither artificial light nor natural light through glazing provides the full spectrum of light. Optimal spectral energy for plants occurs at two peak frequencies for both chlorophyll synthesis and photosynthesis. Ideal lighting for indoor plants will utilize either electric lamps or glazing that offers peaks in those frequencies.

**Electric Light.** Metal halide is generally considered the best electric light source for plant growth. Because it is a high-intensity discharge (HID) source, its beam can be altered by the shape of its reflector to focus on a wide or narrow target and it can effectively light plants from a distance. Many fluorescent lamps are similarly capable of providing acceptable spectral quality for plant growth, but the characteristics of fluo-

rescent lights and their fixtures require the lamps to be within 18 in. to 8 ft (457 mm to 2,438 mm) from the foliage. Halogen can also be used successfully for plant growth, though its spectral quality is not as ideal as metal halide or fluorescent.

**Daylight.** Clear, single-pane glass is optimal for plant growth; however, it is not used in commercial buildings because of the associated heat gain and heat loss. Interior landscape designers must ascertain the percentage of light transmittance of glazing systems used to provide plant growth lighting or obtain a daylighting analysis of the space to determine anticipated lighting levels.

## TEMPERATURE

Plants available for indoor use thrive in room-temperature conditions (68°F to 72°F (20°C to 22°C). Temperatures may vary substantially within a room, most notably near windows or exterior doors, where nighttime lows during winter in a northern temperate climate could reach as low as the mid-50s°F (10s°C), and daytime highs in summer could exceed 100°F (37°C). Such temperature extremes will damage, and even kill, plants. Locating plants close to air supplies should also be avoided or otherwise addressed. Forced-air movement can cause plants to desiccate (dry out). This can occur even when room-temperature air is discharged.

## HUMIDITY

Virtually all plants prefer higher humidity than will be found in a typical interior environment. It is not unusual for an interior space in a northern temperate climate during the winter to have a relative humidity as low as 10% to 15%. Most subtropical and tropical plants used indoors prefer a relative humidity of 50% or more. Because of potential problems in introducing higher humidities to interior spaces (generation of molds and mildew, condensation, rust, human discomfort, etc.), successful indoor plants are those that can adapt to lower humidity levels.

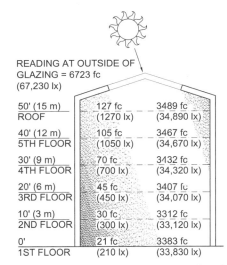

READING AT OUTSIDE OF GLAZING = 6723 fc (67,230 lx)

| | | |
|---|---|---|
| 50' (15 m) ROOF | 127 fc (1270 lx) | 3489 fc (34,890 lx) |
| 40' (12 m) 5TH FLOOR | 105 fc (1050 lx) | 3467 fc (34,670 lx) |
| 30' (9 m) 4TH FLOOR | 70 fc (700 lx) | 3432 fc (34,320 lx) |
| 20' (6 m) 3RD FLOOR | 45 fc (450 lx) | 3407 fc (34,070 lx) |
| 10' (3 m) 2ND FLOOR | 30 fc (300 lx) | 3312 fc (33,120 lx) |
| 0' 1ST FLOOR | 21 fc (210 lx) | 3383 fc (33,830 lx) |

This computer model indicates light level readings for direct sunlight passing through glazing into an atrium space at the latitude of Detroit, Michigan (42°–20' N), at noon on March 21. Direct sunlight loses only 3% of its intensity from skylight to the atrium floor, while indirect light loses 83%.

### LIGHT LEVELS IN ATRIUM SPACE

## THE GREENHOUSE EFFECT

Multistory atrium spaces that are skylighted or sidewall glazed can experience an unusual environmental condition called the *greenhouse effect* that can be extremely dangerous to plants. Solar gain in a well-lighted multistory space will cause the air temperature at upper levels of the space to heat more quickly than at lower levels. Tall plants located on the ground floor of skylighted atria can be badly damaged by high temperatures, unless the warmer air can be recirculated into the lower portions or vented outside the building. *See also* Interior Plantings, for irrigation methods.

*Nelson Hammer; Hammer Design, Landscape Architecture; Boston, Massachusetts*

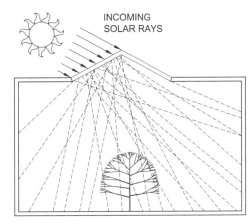

INCOMING SOLAR RAYS

**TRANSLUCENT GLAZING**
Translucent glazing has the capability to disperse even low-angle, early-morning, and late-afternoon sunlight into useful plant growth lighting.

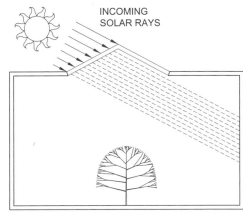

INCOMING SOLAR RAYS

**TRANSPARENT GLAZING**
In winter, midday, the low angles of the sun may preclude direct sunlight passing through clear glazing from reaching an atrium floor.

Glazing systems incorporating fiberglass or other similarly translucent materials can be highly advantageous for plants because the dispersion of light will result in a net increase in brightness without increasing heat gain.

**DISPERSED SUNLIGHT**

# SUSTAINABLE DESIGN CRITERIA

## CONTEXT

For thousands of years people have been creating structures that, out of necessity, have been specific to a given region and its climate. These structures were, by nature, "sustainable" within their local landscapes. Design strategies had to work with climate conditions as well as within the limitations of local materials.

Since the late nineteenth century, advances in technology have enabled a shift from this model, allowing nature to be simply overpowered. But as widespread concern is raised over the limitations of natural resources, as well as the planet's finite ability to absorb pollutants, the role of technology is being reconsidered. Today, technology is increasingly being employed to augment natural processes rather than outdo them, and materials are being utilized with greater efficiency and more in harmony with the Earth's ecology.

In 1987, the World Commission on Environment and Development described sustainable development as that "which meets the needs of the present without compromising the ability of future generations to meet their own needs." Many viable sustainable design models provide guidance in implementing this overarching goal. The four primary areas of investigation required for sustainable design are *energy*, *resources*, *water*, and *health*. Energy, water, and resources revolve primarily around efficiency and pollution prevention; health deals primarily with maintaining the environment.

## ENERGY

The Worldwatch Institute, a nonprofit public policy research organization, estimates that buildings are responsible for 40% of total energy use worldwide. Thus energy consumption accounts for a majority of the environmental impacts associated with buildings. Energy generation and use has been linked to air pollution, acid rain, reduced water quality, ozone depletion, risk of global warming, and depletion of nonrenewable resources. Energy conservation is a high priority and serves to improve a building's overall environmental performance while reducing operating costs.

### Systems Approach

When designing with environmental and health impacts in mind, all elements of a project necessarily become interrelated. For example, energy systems design should not be isolated from site selection or building design; both have an effect on energy efficiency and conservation. This systems approach is most effective when begun early in the design process.

### Renewable and Alternative Energy

Renewable energy systems provide nonpolluting power for building-scale applications without depleting nonrenewable natural resources. Alternative energy systems, which provide cleaner, less polluting options for power generation, can be implemented as follows:

- Incorporate wind, photovoltaic (solar), and/or hydro-generation systems.
- Incorporate net metering, which eliminates battery systems and allows direct offset of utility costs

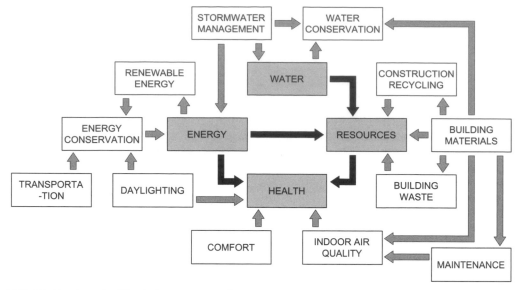

Links between elements of the design process are shown.

### SYSTEMS THINKING MODEL

- Choose "green power" from utility company.
- Supplement with fuel cells and desiccant cooling systems.

### Energy Conservation and Efficiency

Reduction in energy use associated with buildings involves many interrelated actions. Passive techniques involve simple design choices integrated during schematic design, and are achieved through building orientation, form, and layout. Energy efficiency focuses on minimizing overall heating, cooling, and electrical loads, and may be implemented as follows:

- Align building with solar orientation.
- Utilize shading devices to reduce heat gain.
- Provide passive ventilation.
- Incorporate vestibules at main entrances.
- Install vegetated roofs to reduce energy flow through roof envelope and reduce urban heat island effect.
- Superinsulate the building envelope and eliminate thermal bridging.
- Use high-performance glazing (such as low-e).
- Specify Energy Star appliances (see "Programs," below).
- Reduce energy for hot water with solar or tankless "on demand" water heaters, or utilize waste heat from air conditioning systems.
- Use energy-modeling software.
- Install energy-efficient mechanical systems, such as geothermal with heat recovery ventilators (HRVs).
- Specify mechanical systems that are free of chemicals with ozone-depleting potential such as fluorocarbons.

### Lighting and Daylighting

Electrical lighting not only requires energy, but also generates unwanted heat, which subsequently increases the load on cooling systems. Utilizing available sunlight as an additional resource reduces energy consumption while providing high-quality light. The U.S. Department of Energy (DOE) estimates that total lighting costs in commercial buildings can be cut by 30% to 60% through efficient lighting and daylighting strategies. Additionally, sunlight produces positive physiological and psychological effects for occupants, thus improving overall indoor environmental quality. The following lighting strategies are commonly employed in lighting design:

- Design glazing to capture available daylighting.
- Utilize window treatments to control glare and heat gain without eliminating views.
- Utilize automatic daylight-dimming sensors.
- Specify energy-efficient, low-mercury lighting.
- Provide occupant-controlled task lighting.
- Ensure that all exterior lights focus downward.
- Enroll in a fluorescent light recycling program.
- Specify LED exit signs.

## ECOSYSTEM RESOURCES

The construction and operation of buildings accounts for an estimated 40% of the Earth's extracted raw materials and half of all waste generated, according to the Worldwatch Institute. The result is destruction of landscapes, air and water pollution, deforestation, depletion of nonrenewable resources, and overburdened landfills. By reducing the total resource burden through preservation and conservation strategies, the health and balance of the Earth's ecosystems can be preserved.

### Building Reuse

Existing buildings are themselves a resource, with aesthetic, historical, and cultural value. Reusing an existing building promotes resource efficiency in two ways: demolition materials are not sent to landfills, and fewer virgin materials are used in construction. Consider building reuse in site selection, salvaging and recycling demolition waste, and retrofitting the existing thermal envelope to increase energy efficiency.

## Building Materials

Often the most visible element of sustainable design is the selection of finish materials. Materials frequently are removed and discarded before their useful life is over. Dealing with such high rates of renovation magnifies the overall environmental and health impacts of materials selection. It also creates a unique opportunity to promote healthy and sustainable building materials in a visible setting.

Healthy resources are those that do not:
• Threaten human health
• Negatively impact natural ecosystems

Sustainable resources can be defined as:
• Renewable or regenerative
• Acquisitioned without ecological damage
• Used at a rate that does not exceed the natural rate of replenishment

Resource conservation can ultimately result in "closed-loop" acquisition streams, where existing "waste" is viewed as valuable raw material for new products. Closed-loop models are economically sustainable, as they do not rely on nonrenewable resources. Specifying environmentally preferable building materials involves establishing the following eight health and sustainability criteria:

REDUCED: lower total burden
• Create smaller compact plans.
• Use structural elements as finishes.
• Optimize material use.
REUSED: longer life span
• Incorporate salvaged materials.
• Design for dismantling and reuse.
• Create flexible designs (that don't need to be redesigned as often).
RENEWABLE: replenished by natural systems
• Specify agriculture-based products.
• Specify certified sustainably harvested wood.
RECYCLED: waste becomes a resource
• Specify products with a minimum of 25% post-consumer or 40% postindustrial waste.
HEALTHY: nontoxic
• Avoid products with ozone-depleting or global-warming potential.
• Avoid toxic chemicals or minerals.
• Avoid products that support pathogens or bio-contaminants (such as mold/mildew, fungi, bacteria).
• Create details that protect materials from water damage.
• Select materials that are easy to maintain.
LOCAL: less transportation energy
• Give preference to locally manufactured materials.
DURABLE: longer life span
• Specify high-quality, long-lasting products.
• Specify materials that can be partially replaced as needed (such as carpet tiles).
• Create details that protect materials from premature damage.
POSTUSE: avoid disposal
• Select materials that can be salvaged, reused, or recycled (with no downgrading).
• Select materials that are biodegradable.

## Building Waste Management

Commercial operations realize savings on disposal expenses by maximizing waste recycling efforts. In a typical office, wastepaper is the predominant component of the waste stream, representing an average of 70% of total waste. Categories of recyclable building waste include white paper, mixed paper, cardboard; mixed containers of metal, glass, or plastic; food; and landscaping. The remaining 30% of waste includes glass, metal, plastics, food, and miscellaneous trash. To conserve building waste, consider the following:

• Outline items to be separated for recycling.
• Identify local haulers or recycling facilities for each waste category.
• Provide convenient, centralized recycling containers and/or chutes.
• Participate in programs that assist in educating all building occupants on reducing and recycling waste.

### Construction Waste Recycling

Recyclable waste materials are generated during demolition, construction, and remodeling. The key element of successful construction waste recycling is on-site separation. Categories of recyclable construction waste include: land-clearing debris, concrete and masonry, metals (steel, aluminum, copper, iron), untreated wood, gypsum board, insulation, paints, cardboard, paper goods, plastic, glass, and salvaged goods. Once separation methods are established, recycling can be accomplished with little effort. Most job sites experience increased materials-use efficiency with the act of separation, ultimately resulting in increased profits. Consider the following:

• Include a construction waste recycling specification with construction documents.
• Outline separation, salvage, and recycling strategies.
• Identify categories of recyclable and salvageable waste.
• List local recycling purchasers and salvage organizations.

### Product Labeling

Several organizations and agencies provide product labeling to help identify environmentally preferable choices:

**Green Seal:** Nonprofit organization that evaluates material categories and awards a "Green Seal of Approval" to products.

**Energy Star:** Federal energy-efficient product labeling program through the EPA and DOE.

**Certified Forest Products Council (CFPC):** Nonprofit organization that promotes use of responsible forest products through an online database listing suppliers of certified wood products.

**Forest Stewardship Council (FSC):** Member of CFPC that certifies wood for sustainable forest management and chain-of-custody.

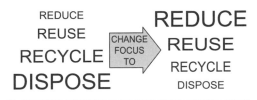

**RECYCLING MODEL**

## WATER

The Worldwatch Institute estimates that U.S. buildings alone use 17% of all freshwater flows. Growth in development has been linked to lower water tables worldwide. Rainwater is diverted along impervious surfaces and prevented from replenishing groundwater tables and aquifers. Increased runoff flows promote erosion and contribute to nonpoint source pollution. Water treatment facilities are responsible for introducing environmental pollutants such as chlorine and phosphorous into natural bodies of water in unnatural quantities. Sustainable sites encourage natural water filtration processes and reduce overall use of potable water.

### Stormwater Management

The primary goal of stormwater management initiatives is to promote the absorption of normal rainwater flows. Consider the following:

• Reduce impervious surfaces with pervious paving and vegetated roof systems.
• Place vegetated swales and infiltration strips to absorb excess stormwater runoff (especially from parking areas).
• Utilize native plant species that are appropriate to climatic conditions for all landscaping.
• Collect rainwater in cisterns for irrigation or toilet flushing.

### Water Conservation

Water conservation results in savings in operating costs while reducing the burden on local water processing facilities. Potable water resources are most efficiently used when limited to applications where it is reasonable that a person may ingest water, such as drinking fountains, sink faucets, and showers. Nonpotable uses of water, such as irrigation and toilet flushing, can utilize site-processed graywater or collected rainwater. Consider the following:

• Specify ultralow-flow faucets with aerators and automatic shutoff sensors.
• Specify toilets that meet or exceed *Energy Policy Act of 1992* (EPACT) specifications. Specify waterless urinals.
• Specify water-efficient appliances.
• Do not use potable water for irrigation.

## SUSTAINABLE BUILDING MATERIALS

The standard product selection process involves weighing a variety of criteria, including aesthetics, performance, and cost. Environmental and health impacts present additional criteria when specifying green materials.

### Evaluation Tools

Two primary methods are used to evaluate building materials for environmental impacts: *embodied energy* and *life-cycle analysis* (LCA). Embodied energy calculations establish energy expenditures; LCA assesses environmental and health impacts.

### Embodied Energy

Embodied energy calculations quantify the total energy consumption embedded in a particular material, from raw material acquisition and manufacturing processes through transportation to point-of-use. The more processing associated with a given material, the greater its embodied energy. The total energy associated with all materials in a typical building is estimated to equal 20 years of operating energy. Selecting materials with lower embodied energy values saves energy costs and reduces environmental impacts related to the use of fossil fuels.

### EMBODIED ENERGY

| PROS | CONS |
|---|---|
| Quantitative results are easily compared (if calculated by single source). | Limited available data. |
| | Calculation assumptions vary. |
| Provides a useful relative indicator. | No consideration of health or nonenergy impacts. |
| | No differentiation between sources of energy (natural gas vs. coal vs. solar). |
| | Evaluation ends with delivery to site. |

### Life-Cycle Analysis (LCA)

LCA is a qualitative evaluation tool that provides context for material selection. LCA examines environmental and health impacts from "cradle to grave": from acquisition of raw materials through end-of-use recovery. (A cradle-to-cradle approach closes the acquisition loop.) Analyzing the entire life cycle provides a complete, transparent assessment of impacts on health and the environment.

### LIFE-CYCLE ANALYSIS

| PROS | CONS |
|---|---|
| Reflects total impacts through entire life cycle. | Evaluation is subjective. |
| | Involves educating the end user. |
| Evaluation is "transparent." | |
| Allows prioritization. | |
| Can be updated. | |
| Embodied energy data can be included. | |

### Evaluation Process

In order to specify healthy and sustainable materials, it is necessary to define pertinent criteria. Rarely are there products that meet all green criteria as well as requirements for suitability and cost. Therefore, the relative importance of each issue is prioritized depending on the client, region, and project goals. For example, indoor air quality might be of primary concern where sensitivity to air pollutants is an issue; energy conservation might be prioritized if long-term energy costs are an issue.

Embodied energy is a useful indicator of one aspect of environmental impact; that is, the total energy required to produce and deliver a material. Calculation methods are, however, complicated, and require data that is often difficult to quantify. Resulting values are useful primarily on a relative basis. For example, one can say that "wood has lower embodied energy than steel" or "a product imported from overseas has higher embodied energy than a local equivalent." When using embodied energy values, it is recommended to note the source and date that the calculations were developed, as well as the margin of error.

LCA is a more broadly applicable tool for evaluating building materials. Since the entire life cycle of the material is evaluated, results present a more global picture of environmental and health impacts. LCA also allows for differences between products and lends itself to prioritization of issues. Embodied energy data can be included in LCA evaluations.

### Performing Analysis

Analyzing a material throughout its life cycle involves gathering research data. The entirety of this research comprises the LCA for that material. Data can include embodied energy values, other published LCA evaluations, and supporting data on health and environmental issues. Specific product data is acquired by questioning manufacturers.

A product questionnaire can provide useful information from manufacturers on life-cycle impacts of their products. Ask for substantiation of all test results (through independent labs) and for a material safety data sheet (an MSDS) to support claims regarding safety and toxicity. Life-cycle categories include:

Raw Material Acquisition

Manufacturing Process

Packaging

Shipping

Installation

Indoor Air Quality

Durability

Resource Recovery

Recovery of materials at end-of-use provides raw material for new products.

**LIFE-CYCLE ANALYSIS—CLOSED LOOP MODEL**

The results of LCA are typically in the form of a report or a comparative matrix. Information is transparent and therefore easily updated to reflect changes in environmental and health priorities, as well as innovations in manufacturing.

### Interpreting Results

Determining the health and sustainability of a material involves subjective evaluation. Ultimately, materials are judged relative to the typical application and through the weighted priorities for a given project.

### MATERIALS GOALS

| MATERIAL ATTRIBUTE | GOAL |
|---|---|
| Raw Materials | Safe, low-impact |
| Manufacturing Process | Safe, closed-loop, and nonpolluting systems |
| Packaging | Minimal waste |
| Shipping | Minimal transportation |
| Installation | Safe; minimal waste |
| Indoor Air Quality | No negative health impacts |
| Durability | Suited to use; long-lasting |
| Resource Recovery | Reusable, recyclable, biodegradable |

---

### Environmental Quality Glossary

**carcinogen**   A substance identified as causing cancer. A carcinogen is classified as "known," "probable," "presumed," or "suspected," depending on test study data.

**downcycling**   Recycling into a product that has less value or is considered more disposable than the original.

**EPA 33/50 Program**   Voluntary EPA program targeting 17 priority chemicals for reduction.

**EPACT (Energy Policy Act of 1992)**   Comprehensive legislation to improve conservation and efficiency in energy and water use.

**NIOSH (National Institute for Occupational Safety and Health)**   Part of the U.S. Department of Health and Human Services that conducts research and makes recommendations on health and safety standards.

**ODP (ozone-depleting potential)**   A relative measure of the ability of a substance to break down the stratospheric ozone layer.

**off-gassing**   The vaporization of chemical compounds into surrounding air.

**postconsumer**   Waste material that has served an intended use.

**postindustrial**   Waste material from manufacturing processes.

**teratogenic**   A substance that has been directly linked to birth defects during human fetus development.

**toxicity**   The degree to which a material causes or threatens to cause adverse health effects to living organisms. Expressed in exposure limits.

**VOC (volatile organic compound)**   Chemical compounds that contain carbon and that partially vaporize at normal room temperature. VOCs are a group of chemicals that have varying degrees of toxicity and effects.

## PRODUCT QUESTIONNAIRE

| LIFE CYCLE | QUESTIONS TO ASK MANUFACTURERS | CRITERIA FOR EVALUATION |
|---|---|---|
| RAW MATERIALS ACQUISITION | Is the product made up of salvaged materials? | Material is reused with minimal processing/refinishing. |
| | Does the product contain rapidly renewable resources or agricultural waste? | Materials such as straw, soy, cornhusks, bagasse (sugar cane husks), etc. |
| | If the product contains wood, is the wood certified as being sustainably harvested? | Certified by the Forest Stewardship Council or equivalent. |
| | Does the product contain significant recycled content? | Minimum of 30% postconsumer or 50% postindustrial content. |
| | Are there toxic constituents in the product? | Products contain noVOCs and chemicals targeted for reduction by the EPA; verify information with an MSDS. |
| | Are highly energy-intensive raw materials avoided? | Materials such asrecycled aluminum are used instead of virgin aluminum made from mined bauxite. |
| | Does raw material acquisition for this product negatively impact the ecosystem? | Materials should not be acquired using methods such as strip mining, dredging, clear cutting, and so on. |
| MANUFACTURING PROCESS | Is the manufacturing facility local to raw material acquisition? | Facility should be wthin 200 miles of the job site. |
| | Does the manufacturing process recycle all in-plant waste back into product? | Manufacturing process uses a closed-loop material (no scrap is generated in manufacture). |
| | Is the manufacturing process highly energy-intensive? | Manufacturer should be able to quantify energy use without unusual difficulty |
| | Is power for manufacturing generated with renewable sources? | A percentage of power for manufacturing is generated by a source such as wind, solar orhydroelectric. |
| | Is all water used in manufacturing a closed-loop system? | All water is filtered and reused on-site or water use is minimized by verifiable water-reduction strategies. |
| | Has manufacturing eliminated environmentally harmful emissions? | Harmful emissions include greenhouse gases, chemicals that have ozone-depleting potential, or chemicals that contribute to acid rain (such as $CO_2$, SOX, and NOX, CFCs, HCFCs, HFCs) |
| PACKAGING AND SHIPPING | Is packaging for this product eliminated or minimized? | Items bundled for shipping instead of wrapping individually. |
| | Is packaging reusable? (Reuse strategy must be plausible.) | Packaging is accepted bythe manufacturer for reuse? |
| | Does packaging contain 100% postconsumer recycled materials? (Does it contain any recycled content?) | Recycled packaging materials include cardboard, plastics, peanuts |
| | Is packaging easily recyclable? | Standard local facilities exist for recycling |
| | Are manufacturing facilities local to the project? | Facility or regional distributor should be wthin 200 miles of the job site. |
| | Are products shipped using energy-efficient methods? | Shipping methods should be full loads only and direct delivery.; |
| INSTALLATION | Does installation pose any health risk to installers? | Verify with the MSDS if protective clothing or equipment isrequired for installation |
| | Does installation require any materials that emit VOCs (such as adhesives)? (Are there nontoxic alternatives, such as mechanical fasteners or nontoxic products?) | Installation materials should be zero –VOC and nontoxic |
| | Does installation involve large amounts of waste material? | Materials such as tile produce less waste material than sheet goods. |
| | Can installation waste be readily recycled locally? | Installation waste should be accepted for recycling by the manufacturer or at standard local facilities. |
| | Are any special tools or methods required for installation? | Materials should be able to be installed with conventional tools and methods. |
| INDOOR AIR QUALITY | Does this product or any material required to install it contain or emit VOCs? | VOC Emission can be verified with the MSDS, and/or third-party IAQ testing data (such as ASTM, or CA or WA state IAQ testing). |
| | Does this product or any material required to install it contain any toxic compounds? | Verify with the MSDS that VOCs and chemicals should not be targeted for reduction by the EPA (see list) |
| | Is this type of product known to support microbial growth? | Materials should not be used in an application that will encourage the growth of mold, mildew or other microbes. |
| | Can this product be cleaned and maintained with non-toxic cleaning methods and materials? | Verify that the use of nontoxic cleaning materials and methods will not affect warranty coverage. |
| DURABILITY AND PERFORMANCE | Is this product suitable in the intended application? | Verify product limitations in specific used such as wet applications or structural requirements |
| | Is the product as long- or longer-lasting as industry standards? | Support product durability with warranty information and/or product testing data. |
| | Is the product line available in patterns and colors that outlast style fads? | Faddish styles or colors would potentially cause replacement before the product's useful life is over. |
| | Can elements of the product be replaced individually? | Materials such as carpet tile can be individually replaced, whereas products such as broadloom cannot. |
| | Does the product facilitate some other aspect of sustainability? | Such as energy or water efficiency, natural daylighting, recycling, etc. |
| RESOURCE RECOVERY | Do recommended installation techniques allow this product to be easily removed without damage? | The product be reasonably removed with the intention of reusing it (for example solid surface goods attached with mechanical fasteners are removable whereas laminates cannot be removed) |
| | Is product inherently reusable? | The product is long-lasting and durable |
| | Is product biodegradable after its useful life? | Theroduct shouldcompletely breakdown into benign, organic components |
| | Is product recyclable (with no downcycling)? | The product should be recyclable into a similar product. |
| | Does disposal pose an environmental health risk? | Disposal should not harm the environment with any disposal technique, including landfill, incineration and so on. |
| COMPANY PROFILE | Does company have any overall environmental policy? | A copy of the company's written environmental policy should be available on request. |
| | Does company meet ISO 14000 criteria "Environmental Management System Standard Certification?" | Verify that the company has participated in ISO 14000 in the past |
| | Are products third-party-certified as being environmental? | Environmental certification comes from organizations such as Green Seal, Forest Stewardship Council, Energy Star, etc. |
| | Do company facilities have recycling program for all waste? | Companies should recycle office paper, cans and so on. |
| | Are company facilities constructed such that they are themselves examples of sustainable design? | Facilities should be energy- and water-efficient; using such techniques as filtering and absorbing stormwater and providing easy ways for employees to commute via mass transit or bicycle |

*Sigi Koko; Down to Earth; Arlington, Virginia*

## ROLE OF THE U.S. GREEN BUILDING COUNCIL (USGBC)

The U.S. Green Building Council (USGBC) was established in 1993 as a national nonprofit organization, with a voluntary, diverse membership that operates on consensus principles. The heart of the USGBC are committees that provide a forum for members to resolve differences, build alliances, and find solutions that add value to the existing membership.

USGBC works with members to incorporate their ideas into the overall organization. The consensus of USGBC members is to work together to promote green building and help to foster greater economic vitality and environmental health. USGBC accomplishes this by working with the industry to help bridge ideological gaps, thus providing benefits for the entire construction commuinity.

### Leadership in Energy and Environmental Design (LEED) Rating System

One of the many achievements of USGBC is the establishment of the Leadership in Energy and Environmental Design (LEED) rating system. Launched in 1995, LEED is a voluntary point-based rating guideline that establishes consistent criteria for sustainable design projects. LEED serves as a tool to aid integrated sustainable design and to help owners and design teams obtain the benefits in the overall health and efficiency of building design. LEED is based on accepted energy and environmental principles, and strikes a balance between known effective practices and emerging concepts.

During the development of LEED, committee members carefully reviewed existing green building rating systems such as Building Research Establishment Environmental Assessment Method (BREEAM) and Building Environment Performance Assessment Criteria (BEPAC). The committee determined that these existing systems involved a costly infrastructure for which the U.S. market was not ready to follow.

### LEED Rating System Categories

LEED has five categories:

Sustainable Sites

Water Efficiency

Energy and Atmosphere

Indoor Environmental Quality

Materials and Resources

Each category is composed of individual points and prerequisites that, in aggregate, allows a participant to achieve one of four levels of certification of sustainability as defined by USGBC.

Of the five LEED categories, Materials and Resource (MR) specifically addresses interior finishes and specifications. This category has one prerequisite that must be met before any points can be obtained: for each building, an area specifically located on a ground floor must be dedicated to the separation, collection, and storage of materials for recycling paper, glass, plastic, and metals.

In addition to the recycling prerequisite, the following specifically address interior finishes and specifications:

*MR Credit 3—Resource Reuse:* Specifically addresses the percentage of salvaged or refurbished materials that are required for building materials. One point is available for using 5% of building materials; another point is available for using salvaged or refurbished materials for 10% of the total building materials. The intent of this credit is to divert material from the solid waste stream and avoid environmental impacts of producing new construction and product materials.

*MR Credit 4—Recycled Content:* Specifies the percentage of postconsumer recycled content and postindustrial recycled content in building materials. Recycled content in a product has a significant effect on reducing the solid waste stream by recycling material rather than disposing of it in a landfill. USGBC provides one point for providing 25% of the building materials that contain in aggregate a minimum weighted average of 20% postconsumer recycled content material or 40% postindustrial recycled content. An additional point can be earned by improving from 25 to 50% of the building materials. Through the voluntary LEED rating system, USGBC has managed to alter the way in which many manufacturers produce products, providing both financial and environmental benefits.

*MR Credit 5—Local/Regional/Materials:* Sets a radius of 500 miles from a project site for the purchase of building materials. The intent of this credit is to support the local economy and reduce transportation costs and environmental impacts on moving goods across the country.

*MR Credit 6—Rapidly Renewable Materials:* Requires the specification of alternative materials that substantially replenish themselves faster than traditional extraction. In addition, the materials must not result in significant biodiversity loss, increased erosion, or air quality changes. One point is available for specifying rapidly renewable building materials for 5% of the total building materials. Such materials include cork, linoleum, and bamboo.

*MR Credit 7—Certified Wood:* Encourages the use of forest products that are certified as sustainably harvested building materials; specifically, they must be in compliance with the Forest Stewardship Council Guidelines (FSC). One point is available for specifying 50% or more of the wood-based materials compliant with FSC guidelines.

In aggregate, 8 out of 13 points are dedicated to interior finishes in the Materials and Resources category. By selecting materials carefully and reducing waste, the result is the use of materials with less environmental impact, which creates a healthier environment for the end user and future generations.

### LEED RATING SYSTEM

| LEVEL | POINTS PERCENTILE |
|---|---|
| LEED Certified | 32–38 (50–60%) |
| Silver Level | 39–45 (61–70%) |
| Gold Level | 46–51 (71–80%) |
| Platinum Level | 52+ (81% or better) |

## MATERIAL SAFETY DATA SHEETS (MSDS)

A material safety data sheet (MSDS) provides information about the physical and health hazards of a chemical product. The United States Occupational Safety and Health Administration (OSHA) requires all manufacturers to issue an MSDS with the first shipment of any hazardous (or even potentially hazardous) chemical product. OSHA also requires that MSDSs must be accessible to employees.

### Limitations

MSDSs are an important source of health and safety information, but they should not be the only source of information used to evaluate chemical hazards. While MSDSs discuss short-term chemical exposure, they do not describe possible effects from low levels of carcinogens or toxins that may affect a chemically sensitive person. They also do not consider the effects of materials on the environment.

### MSDS Content

An MSDS lists the manufacturer's information and identification of the substance. This includes the name, address, and contact numbers of the company that produced the material. The MSDS's date of issue or most recent revision and the name of the material are also given. The latter must be spelled exactly as it is seen on the container; if it is not, it may be the wrong MSDS, as many chemical names appear to be similar. If one generic MSDS is used to cover various grades of a material, all grades must be listed, as well as any known synonyms.

*Source: "Material Safety Data Sheets"; Washington, DC,
   U.S. Department of Labor, OSHA, 1977.*
*Source: "Preparing, Understanding, and Using Material
   Safety Data Sheets," Lab Safety Supply, 1988.*
*Source: The MSDS Pocket Dictionary, 3rd Ed.;
   Schenectady, NY, Genium Publishing Corp., 1999. (This
   pamphlet explains how to read an MSDS and defines
   commonly used terms.)*
*Source: Spiegel, R., and Meadows, D., Green Building
   Materials: A Guide to Product Selection and
   Specification; John Wiley & Sons, Inc., 1999, pp. 67–70.
   Michelle Scurfield, AIA; Scurfield Architects, LLC;
   Washington, D.C.*

*Margery Morgan; Symmes Maini & McKee Associates;
   Cambridge, Massachusetts*
*Heidi Rhodes; Rhode Island School of Design; Providence,
   Rhode Island.*

# INDOOR AIR QUALITY

## INDOOR AIR POLLUTION

Over the past few decades, office building construction has increasingly focused on meeting both the demands of climate control and the need for energy efficiency. As a result, the nearly across-the-board adoption of central heating and cooling systems has also prompted the development of airtight buildings that reduce energy consumption by minimizing air loss. Though energy efficiency has increased markedly, such sealed environments can at times pose serious health risks, which are aggravated by the simultaneous use of more complex chemicals and compounds in the furniture, clothing, cleaners, detergents, and other products that fill them. Combined, these trends have created workplaces where exposure to harmful particles and gases has created indoor air pollution.

According to the World Health Organization (WHO), 40% of all buildings pose significant health hazards from indoor pollution; and according to the Environmental Protection Agency (EPA), indoor air in the United States is now on average 2 to 10 times more contaminated than the air outside. As a result, a reported 20% of all workers suffer from related irritations or illnesses. Poor indoor air quality—and its role in Sick Building Syndrome (SBS) and Building-Related Illness (BRI) has been declared by the EPA as the country's number-one environmental health problem.

### Indoor Air Quality (IAQ) Defined

Indoor air quality, or IAQ, refers to the quality of air inside buildings where people work or live. Air quality is essential for comfort and productivity, but, most importantly, good air promotes good health. IAQ can be compromised under the following four conditions:

- Inadequate ventilation doesn't provide enough outside air.
- Chemicals used in cleaning and office products get trapped inside a building.
- Outdoor pollutants enter and are trapped inside.
- Mold or other microorganisms grow, multiply, and disperse particles through heating, air conditioning, and ventilation systems.

### Sick Building Syndrome (SBS)

When IAQ is poor, often what results is SBS and BRI. SBS describes a wide range of physical afflictions, often similar to mild allergic reactions, that usually result from exposure to contaminants in indoor air (although noises and other environmental factors can contribute, as well). The specific causes are not identified, but the symptoms coincide with time spent in a particular building and disappear once the sufferer leaves. A BRI describes the same range of ailments, from mild allergic reactions to more serious infections such as pneumonia, except it applies in cases where the specific cause is known. Both SBS and BRI are largely the result of poor indoor air quality.

## PARTICULATE IRRITANTS

### Microorganisms

The most prevalent particles in the air that can cause problems are microorganisms, dust, and pollen. Though bacteria and fungi are present everywhere, in both outdoor and indoor environments, office buildings are especially vulnerable, as they provide areas of high humidity and standing water in circulation and air conditioning ducts, ceiling tiles, insulation, and even ice machines. These intruders release what are called *bioaerosols,* which include the tiny spores from molds and other fungi that float through the air, causing skin and mucous membrane irritation and coughing. Such allergic reactions are also induced by dust, pollen, and endotoxins from certain bacteria that circulate throughout the air. Sensitive people, such as the elderly, very young, or those with weaker immune systems, can be at risk of serious infection.

### Respirable Particles

Respirable particles are defined as particles less than 10 microns in diameter (the diameter of a human hair is about 100 microns). In humans, larger particles are usually caught in the nose before they reach the lungs. Because of their minute size, however, respirable particles flow easily through the nasal passage and can be inhaled deeply into the lungs to cause coughing, wheezing, and even respiratory tract infection. In an office, respirable particles are given off by everything from human skin to the carbon from copy machines.

## GASEOUS IRRITANTS

### Volatile Organic Compounds (VOCs)

The use of strong office cleaning products, paints, glues, and photocopiers intensifies the IAQ problem. At room temperature, synthetic organic chemicals release vapors and gases that are known as volatile organic compounds (VOCs). Consistently found at higher levels indoors, VOCs come from many different sources including building materials, consumer products, and combustion sources such as car engines and heating systems. Many VOCs are toxic, including benzene and carbon tetracycline, and can induce a host of health problems, from eye irritation to fatigue and dizziness. Some VOCs have been determined to be carcinogens, so long-term exposure could possibly cause cancer. Though not all are as seriously harmful, many do cause discomfort and are found nearly everywhere in offices: one major VOC irritant is formaldehyde, a pungent gas that exists in nearly 3,000 different products, including certain floor adhesives, wallcoverings, particleboard, and furniture.

### Carbon Monoxide

Carbon monoxide (CO) is an odorless, colorless gas. It is a dangerous pollutant that is regulated outdoors, making it an even greater hazard if found indoors. Carbon monoxide is given off by fuel-burning engines such as those in cars, and though the highest interior concentrations are usually found in underground or indoor garages, adjacent buildings can be contaminated if not properly ventilated. In these cases, the gas seeps into the building and its offices, where the prolonged exposure of employees decreases the oxygen-carrying capacity of their blood, resulting in shortness of breath, fatigue, and nausea.

### Other Pollutants

Some office equipment releases ozone, which is a respiratory irritant that at high concentrations can cause serious harm to people. And despite the fact that smoking has been all but eliminated in office buildings over the past decade, it can still pose a threat to nonsmoking workers. It, for example, outside air vents are located in close proximity to smoking areas, the smoke—and its carbon monoxide and harmful particles—can get sucked inside.

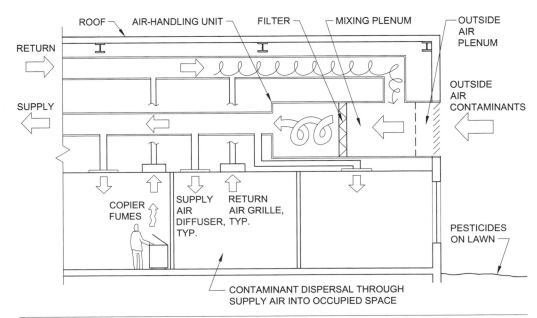

ROOF — AIR-HANDLING UNIT — FILTER — MIXING PLENUM — OUTSIDE AIR PLENUM

RETURN

SUPPLY

OUTSIDE AIR CONTAMINANTS

COPIER FUMES

SUPPLY AIR DIFFUSER, TYP.

RETURN AIR GRILLE, TYP.

PESTICIDES ON LAWN

CONTAMINANT DISPERSAL THROUGH SUPPLY AIR INTO OCCUPIED SPACE

**IRRITANT PARTICLE SIZES (IN MICRONS)**

## DETERMINING INDOOR AIR QUALITY

Currently, methods of air pollution detection are complicated, time-consuming, and costly. Air-quality consulting agencies may be brought in if a building's management suspects an air problem. These agencies start with a lengthy question-and-answer session to help occupants determine which health effects are being felt, how long they have persisted, and what, if any, preexisting issues may be causing them. The agency will then conduct a walk-through of the office to see if there are any obvious sources of contamination, and to check air temperature, humidity levels, and airflow. All these are factors in the spread of indoor pollutants and can give clues to their presence; for instance, if humidity is at a high level, it would be reasonable to suspect that bacterial contamination could be the problem. If a definitive cause still eludes these efforts, air sampling is usually the next step.

## FIGHTING POOR INDOOR AIR QUALITY

Once the pollutant has been identified, there are two primary ways of fighting it: *ventilation* and *air cleaning*. As both are usually components of integrated systems, they are not mutually exclusive.

### Ventilation

According to most experts, including the American Society of Heating, Refrigerating, and Air-Conditioning Engineers (ASHRAE), increasing ventilation and air distribution is the best and most cost-effective way of freshening the air inside most buildings. Air enters office buildings through both mechanical ventilation systems and natural circulation. The latter occurs, primarily in older buildings, largely by way of leaks around windows and doors and other openings. Newer, larger, and highly energy-efficient buildings with sealed windows and heavy insulation depend primarily on mechanical ventilation.

In a modern office building, the HVAC system is designed to keep occupants comfortable and healthy by controlling temperatures and bringing outside air into the internal environment, simultaneously filtering both incoming and recirculated air. Ventilation is thus an integral part of HVAC systems, and is accomplished by blowers and fans that move the air, ductwork that delivers it to the building's rooms, and vents that distribute it. A good ventilation design will distribute supply air uniformly—except in areas with heat- and vapor-producing office machines that require added airflow—and place supply and exhaust vents sufficiently apart to allow fresh air to circulate more freely. ASHRAE has established a general guideline of 20 cu ft (.56 cu m) of outside air per minute/per person for an office environment to sufficiently dilute building contaminants and maintain a healthy environment.

### Cleaning Air with Filtration

Following the energy crisis of the 1970s, the trend toward airtight buildings resulted in the widespread installation of HVAC systems that recirculate already-temperature-adjusted air rather than bringing in untreated air from the outside. Consequently, these buildings rely heavily on filtration to preserve air quality. The most widely used methods of filtering out gases and particles are lower-efficiency filters, High-Efficiency Particulate-Arresting (HEPA) filtration, and adsorption with activated carbon.

## MAJOR CONTAMINANTS, THEIR SOURCES, AND HEALTH EFFECTS

| TYPE OF CONTAMINANT | SOURCES | HEALTH EFFECTS |
|---|---|---|
| **PARTICLES** | | |
| Microorganisms, bioaerosols, and other biological contaminants:<br>Animal dander<br>Molds and fungi<br>Dust mites<br>Viruses<br>Bacteria<br>Pollen | Areas of high humidity or condensation<br>Damp organic materials<br>Porous wet surfaces<br>Humidifiers<br>Animals and insects<br>Food and food products<br>Plants<br>Human respiration | Exacerbation of asthma<br>Sneezing/runny nose<br>Recurrent fever<br>Malaise<br>Sore throat<br>Muscle aches<br>Tightness of chest<br>Cough<br>Eye irritation<br>Infectious diseases (rare) |
| Respirable particles (<10 microns):<br>Any particles or particle fragments less than 10 microns<br>Some molds<br>Viruses<br>Bacteria | *Same as above, and:*<br>Tobacco smoke<br>Unvented combustion appliances (e.g., gas stoves, kerosene heaters) | *Same as above* |
| **GASES** | | |
| Volatile organic compounds (VOCs):<br>Formaldehyde<br>Benzene<br>Carbon tetracycline<br>Trichloroethylene<br>Toluene<br>Methyl ethyl ketone<br>Alcohols<br>Methacrylates<br>Acrolein<br>Polycyclic aromatic hydrocarbons<br>Pesticides | Personal products (fragrances and hair sprays)<br>Cleaning products<br>Office equipment (photocopiers and printers)<br>Office products (permanent markers, correction fluids, carbonless copy paper)<br>Glues and adhesives (including those used in carpeting, textiles, furniture, wallcoverings, etc.)<br>Asphalt<br>Paints<br>Insecticides and herbicides<br>Gasoline vapors<br>Tobacco smoke<br>Combustion products | Nose, throat discomfort<br>Headache<br>Allergic skin reactions<br>Eye, respiratory tract, mucous membrane irritation<br>Nausea<br>Epistaxis (for formaldehyde)<br>Fatigue<br>Dizziness<br>Possibly cancer |
| Carbon monoxide | Tobacco smoke<br>Fossil-fuel engine exhausts<br>Improperly vented fossil-fuel appliances | Dizziness<br>Headache<br>Nausea<br>Cardiovascular effects<br>Death (in extreme cases) |

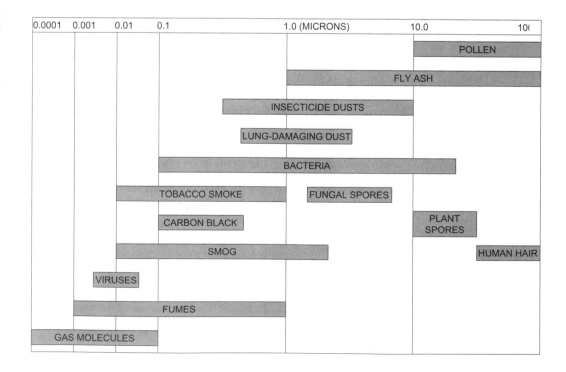

## Particle Filtration

When air is being circulated in an HVAC system, it passes through filters installed at various points to stop particles from passing through. Based on economic constraints, either lower-efficiency filters or HEPA filters are used. Most buildings use lower-efficiency filters that employ woven fiberglass strands to catch particles. These filters are less expensive; and with a lower density weave, air flows more freely through them so smaller fans and less energy are needed. However, they can trap only larger particles—and fewer of them. They tend to catch only between 10% and 60% of particulates.

On the other hand, HEPA filters are generally made from a single sheet of water-repellent fiber that is pleated to provide more surface area with which to catch particles, making them much more effective. HEPA filters are able to catch 99.97% of all particles, including those that are respirable. But because they are more densely woven, they require larger and more energy-intensive fans, making their greater expense economically undesirable in most buildings—not to mention the added noise from the bigger motors. Accordingly, HEPA filters are usually reserved for hospital operating rooms, manufacturing clean rooms (such as those for computer chips), and other spaces especially sensitive to contamination.

## Gas and Vapor Filtration

The most widely used and cost-effective vapor and gas removal technique is called *adsorption* (as opposed to absorption). Whereas absorption describes a process in which one substance mixes evenly into another, adsorption is the physical attraction and adherence of a gas to the surface of a solid, usually activated carbon in the case of filtration. Once the gas is on the activated carbon, it moves down into the carbon particle, eventually condensing into a liquid. Though effective,

these filters capture only a small percentage of certain gases and vapors.

## Independent Air Purification Units

### Personal Air Filters

Particle and gas filtration systems are not only used in HVAC systems, but are also employed in personal or room air purifiers; the small size of the units makes use of HEPA filters more economically feasible. Personal or room HEPA purifiers, specifically designed for respirable particle removal, are able to capture up to 99.97% of all particles larger than 0.3 microns in spaces up to 400 sq ft (11.3 sq m). Personal or desktop purifiers can be effective ways of cleaning the air in a limited workspace to at least create a "comfort zone" of clean air for the worker. In addition to the more traditional filtration methods discussed above, these machines can also use two to three different types of purification techniques not available in buildingwide systems, including negative ionization, ozone, and ultraviolet light.

### Negative Ionization

In personal air purifiers using negative ionization, air and any accompanying particles pass through an electrical field within the purifier, which charges the particles. These particles are then attracted to and trapped on oppositely charged collector plates within the unit, much like a magnet would attract metal dust. While personal air purifiers using this technology can have a beneficial effect on airborne particles, they may also require frequent maintenance and cleaning.

### Ozone

Although it is harmful in high concentrations, ozone may also help reduce pollutants. When oxygen ($O_2$) is broken down with an electrical discharge, the molecules end up coming back together in groups of three to form ozone ($O_3$) molecules. Once released into the air, ozone actively seeks out pollutants, attaching itself

to a wide range of contaminants—including chemical gases, bacteria, mold, and mildew—and destroying them by cracking their molecular membranes. Because ozone has a very short life span—between 20 and 30 minutes—it is easy to avoid achieving the high concentrations that can be detrimental to people's health.

### Ultraviolet Light

Personal air purifiers may also use ultraviolet (UV) light, which is believed to be one of nature's own methods of purifying the air. The light rays are germicidal and effectively destroy the DNA structure of viruses, bacteria, and fungi. UV has been used for years in hospitals to sanitize rooms and equipment, and is also effective in eliminating many odors and the spread of colds and flu viruses. However, it can be more expensive than other purification techniques.

---

**Strategies for Improving Indoor Air Quality**

1. ASSESSMENT. Determine which contaminants are in the air through inspection and testing by outside consulting firms or in-house facilities managers.
2. VENTILATION. Bring in sufficient air from the outside by opening windows and doors (where possible); using mechanical systems (HVAC); or passively, through cracks and leaks in exterior walls and windows (usually only possible in older buildings).
3. AIR CLEANING. Clean interior air through particle, gas, and vapor filters installed in HVAC systems and/or in freestanding personal units.
4. PRODUCT SPECIFICATION. Source low-emitting products that are certified to contribute minimal levels of pollutants into the air.

---

*Tom Revelle; Humanscale; New York*

# STAIR DESIGN

Stairways are an essential component in the circulation and egress systems of most buildings. In the United States, they are also the site of accidents that, annually, result in approximately 4,000 deaths and 1 million injuries requiring hospital treatment. For these reasons, stairway design is strictly controlled by building regulations.

The information contained in this section summarizes most International Building Code (IBC) and access regulation requirements. Check authorities having local jurisdiction for additional requirements.

## MINIMUM REQUIREMENTS

Consult the IBC for stairway requirements to determine dimensional limits for treads, risers, landings, and stair width. Verify that local codes are not more restrictive. Refer to the Americans with Disabilities Act (ADA) for accessibility requirements regarding stairs.

### Stair Details

Treads and risers within a flight must be uniform in size within close tolerances. Treads must be slip-resistant. Carpeting or other stair coverings should be applied securely and should not create a nosing radius greater than permitted. Handrails, guardrails, and stairways themselves must meet structural load requirements.

Access regulations in some localities require that floor material strips of contrasting color be located at the top approach to a stair and at the lowest tread. These markings are intended to aid the visually impaired in identifying the limits of the stair. The application of such markings may be appropriate even where not required, particularly where a high proportion of elderly or visually impaired users are anticipated.

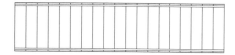

**DIRECT FLIGHT**

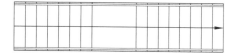

**STRAIGHT RUN**

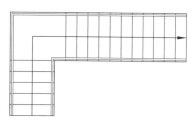

**L-SHAPED**

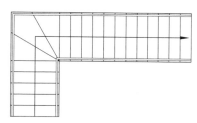

**WINDERS**

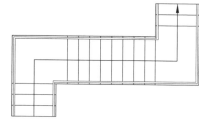

**Z-SHAPED**

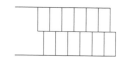

**ALTERNATIVE STEP**

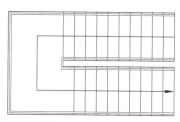

**DIVIDED RETURN**

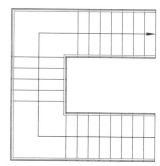

**WIDE-U, RETURN FLIGHT**

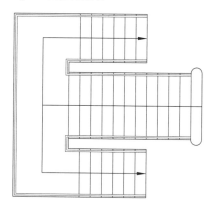

**SPLIT-U**

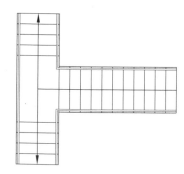

**T-SHAPED**

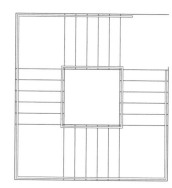

**O-SHAPED**

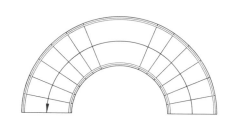

**CIRCULAR**

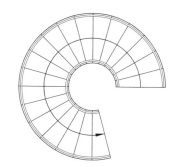

**SPIRAL**

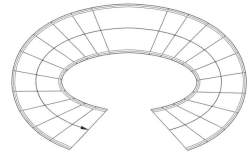

**CURVED OVAL**

**STAIR TYPES**

## Stair Types

Stair type refers to its design and plan layout. Stair types vary, and are subject to code requirements. Stair type selection depends on the space available, the starting and ending points required of the stair, and the appearance desired.

Egress stairs must be enclosed as required by building codes, but the designer can vary the openness of nonegress stairs.

Layout refers to the overall horizontal and vertical dimensions required to meet functional and building code requirements. This includes determining the width, total rise, and run of the stair, and space for landings.

Tread and riser dimensions are proportionally related to each other. The tread and riser proportion, or pitch, affect safety as well as the comfort of using the stair. Code requirements are minimums.

Minimum stair widths are defined by building and accessibility codes, based on occupancy, tread and riser dimensions, handrail dimensions and positions, headroom requirements, and distance between landings.

Details of construction include how the treads and risers are supported, handrail profiles and construction, materials used, and other finish considerations, including slip resistance.

## Stair Layout

Maintain minimum headroom of 6 ft 8 in. (2,032 mm) for nonresidential, and 6 ft 6 in. (1,981 mm) for residential stairs.

Avoid flights with fewer than three risers, to minimize tripping hazards. If one or two risers are used, increase tread depth and clearly mark the level changes.

The use of door alcoves is recommended to prevent stairway doors from obstructing the egress travel path.

### Stair Width

The minimum width of any straight stair is 36 in. (914 mm) when the occupant load is 50 or fewer. The minimum width is 44 in. (1,118 mm) when the occupant load is more than 50. Handrails may encroach no more than 4½ in. (114 mm) on each side. For large occupancies, calculate the minimum width according to the exit width provisions of the IBC. When the stair serves an area of evacuation assistance, the minimum clear width between handrails must be 48 in. (1,219 mm).

In residential occupancies, wider stairways allow for easier movement of furniture. For commercial occupancies, wider stairways allow for more comfortable circulation when two people are passing or carrying objects.

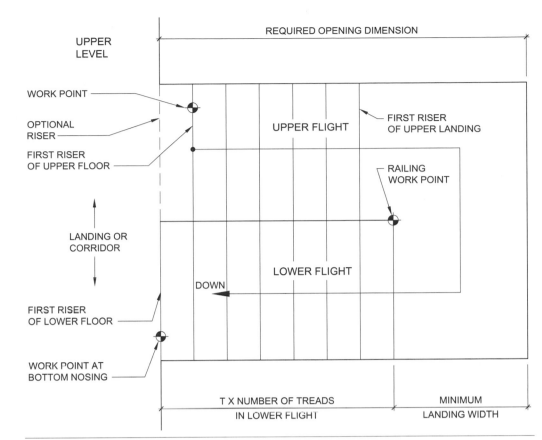

**RETURN STAIR PLAN LAYOUT**

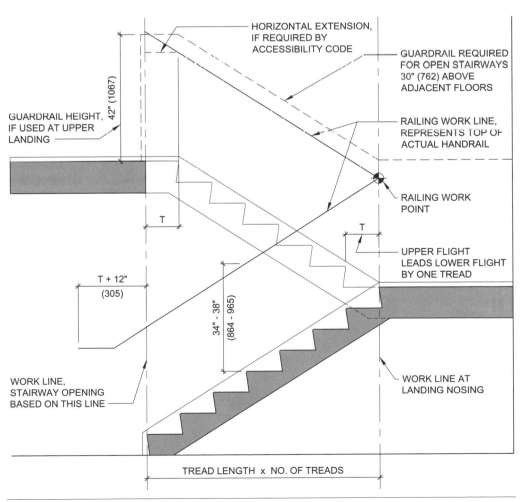

**RETURN STAIR SECTION LAYOUT**

## Horizontal Stair Layout

Steps involved in sizing the horizontal layout of the stair are as follows:

1.  **Determine riser height.** The number of risers required determines the number of treads required. For standard straight stairs, begin the calculation by taking the total rise of the stairway, in inches, and dividing by 7 in. (179 mm). This is a comfortable riser height and is the maximum allowed for most commercial stairways. If the result is not an even number, select the next-highest even number and divide that number into the total rise. This establishes a riser height of less than 7 in., which is a whole number and is the number of risers required. The number of treads is one less than this number for a straight-run stair and two less for a return or L-shaped stair (the landing takes the place of one tread). For straight-run residential stairways where allowed by code, divide by 7.75 in. (197 mm). This is the maximum allowable riser height for Group R-3 occupancies and within dwelling units in Group R-2 occupancies.

2.  **Determine the proportion between the riser and tread dimensions.** Stair dimensions are based on the normal stride of a person while ascending and descending a stair. Several formulas relating rise and tread have been proposed through the years, but one of the most common is:

$$2R = T = 25 \text{ or } T = 25 - 2R$$

where R is the riser height and T is the tread depth. The IBC identifies the minimum tread depth of 11 in. (279 mm) for commercial stairs and 10 in. (254 mm) for residential stairs. For straight-run, L-shaped, T-shaped, and wide-U stairs, the total run is the number of treads multiplied by the tread depth. For return stairs, an unequal number of risers and treads in the lower and upper flight is recommended, to allow the first riser of the upper landing to lead the last riser of the lower landing by one tread depth. The handrail can then make a clean switchback without having to offset vertically.

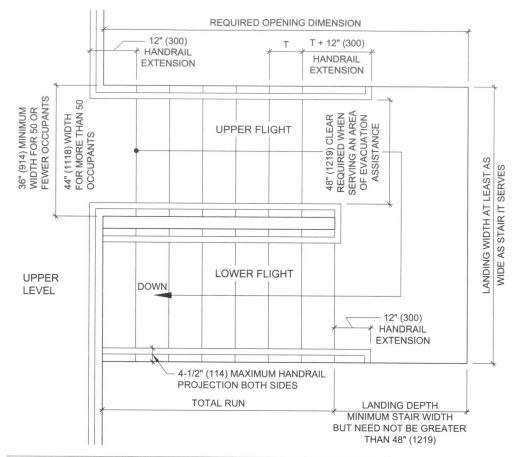

**HORIZONTAL LAYOUT**

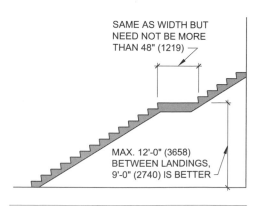

**LANDINGS**

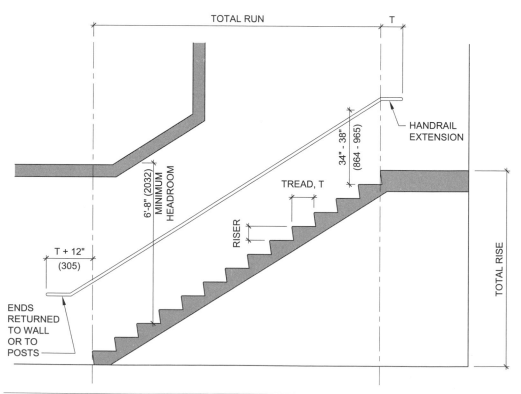

**HANDRAIL DIMENSIONS**

## HANDRAILS

Handrail requirements are governed by building and accessibility codes. Typically, handrails are required on both sides of stairs. Exceptions include dwelling units and private dwellings where there is a change of only one step at an entrance or egress door. In these cases, only one handrail is required. Handrail gripping surfaces must be continuous, without interruption by newel posts or other obstructions. Handrails in dwelling units are allowed to have newel posts at landings and volutes at the lowest tread.

For wide stairways used as a means of egress, intermediate handrails are required so that all portions of the stairway width are within 30 in. (762 mm) of a handrail. On monumental stairs, handrails must be located along the most direct path of egress travel.

### Handrail Mounting Height

Handrails must be mounted with their top surface from 34 to 38 in. (864 to 965 mm) above the nosings. Some research studies have shown that the higher end of the range is best for safety, especially when descending a stair. For open stairways more than 30 in. (762 mm) above the floor, the IBC also requires a guard 42 in. (1,067 mm) above the nosing in addition to a handrail.

### Handrail Extensions

Handrails must extend beyond the top and bottom treads as required by codes. At the inside turn of return stairs, the handrail must be continuous. The ends of the handrail must return to the wall or a guard, or the floor or must be continuous to the next handrail of an adjacent stair flight.

## AREA OF RESCUE ASSISTANCE

The ADA and building codes identify requirements for Areas of Rescue Assistance. Areas of Rescue Assistance are stairway clear widths that allow for easier maneuverability of rescue personnel and physically challenged persons, as well as the clear dimensions at specified areas on landings provided as waiting areas for a person in a wheelchair.

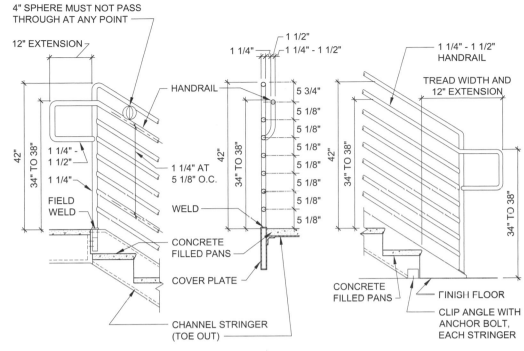

**STEEL STAIR HANDRAILS**   **STEEL STAIR HANDRAIL AT FLOOR**

### HANDRAILS

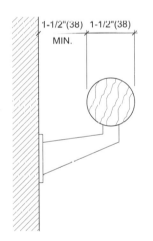 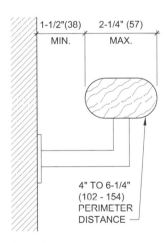 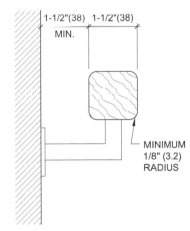

IBC and ADA require handrails to be a circular cross-section, with a dimension between 1½ in. (32 mm) and 2 in. (51 mm).

Other shapes are allowed if the perimeter dimension is between 4 and 6½ in. (102 and 159 mm) and the maximum cross-sectional dimension does not exceed 2½ in. (57 mm).

Edges must have a minimum radius of ⅛ in. (3.2 mm).

### HANDRAIL GRASPABILITY

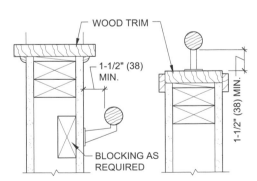

The IBC and ADA require a minimum clearance of 1½ in. (38 mm) between the inside of the handrail and the wall. Some studies have suggested that a better dimension is 2 in. (51 mm). This larger dimension is good for general graspability and works better for a person wearing gloves. For children, an additional handrail should be 1⅛ to 1½ in. (29 to 32 mm) in diameter and mounted 22 to 24 in. (559 to 610 mm) above the nosing line.

### RAILINGS AT WALLS

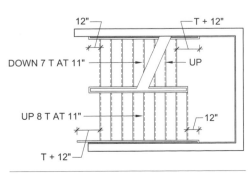

**PLAN SHOWING HANDRAIL EXTENSIONS**

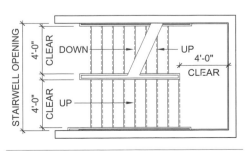

**PLAN DIMENSIONS REQUIRED FOR RESCUE ASSISTANCE (ADA)**

# TREADS, RISERS, AND NOSINGS

## Treads

The minimum dimensions for stair treads are indicated in the building codes. If space permits, research has shown that slightly deeper treads than the minimum are more comfortable and safer to use.

Tread material should be nonslip, but not so rough that feet may be caught on the nosing. Traditionally, a coefficient of friction of 0.5 or greater has been a widely accepted standard for slip resistance. In areas where slip resistance is a concern, it is recommended that tread materials be selected with a greater coefficient of friction than the minimum requirements.

## Risers

Straight, vertical risers are permitted by the IBC and the ADA; however, treads with nosings are more comfortable for the user. Treads must be designed to follow requirements that prevent sharp or abrupt edges, which may catch a person's foot and present a safety hazard.

Open risers may not be used in most situations. The IBC limits the amount of nosing overhang to 1¼ in. (32 mm), while the ADA limits the amount to 1½ in. (38 mm). A 1-in. (25-mm) overhang is usually sufficient.

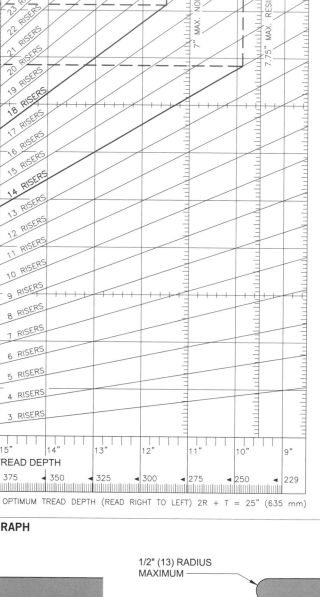

STAIR PROPORTIONING GRAPH

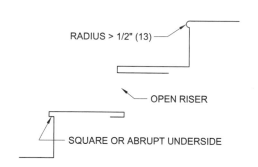

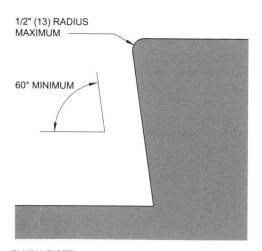

**UNACCEPTABLE NOSINGS AND RISERS**

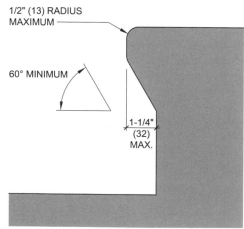

**FLUSH RISER**

**ANGLED NOSING**

**ROUNDED NOSING**

**NOSINGS**

# WOOD STAIRS

Wood stairs used in private, residential applications usually are not governed by the ADA; however, wood stairs in commercial facilities and places of public accommodation must conform to ADA Accessibility Guidelines (ADAAG).

Verify requirements that may differ from the general recommendations provided here. In general, a minimum interior stair width of 36 in. (914 mm) should be provided.

Minimum headroom is 6 ft 8 in. (2 m) as measured vertically from a diagonal line connecting tread nosings to the underside of the finished ceiling or stair landing directly above the stair run. Recommended headroom is 7 ft (2.1 m).

Only handrails and stair stringers may project into the required width of a stair. Use the following guidelines:

- The maximum handrail projection is 3½ in. (89 mm).
- The maximum stringer projection is 1½ in. (38 mm).
- For a stair to comply with ADAAG, no projections are allowed into the minimum required stair width.
- The width of a landing or platform should be at least as wide as the stair.
- The maximum vertical rise of a stair between landings is 12 ft (3.6 m).
- Riser height should be 4 in. (102 mm) minimum and 7 in. (178 mm) maximum.
- Tread depth should be 11 in. (279 mm) minimum, measured from riser to riser.
- Variation in adjacent treads or risers should not exceed ³⁄₁₆ in. (4.8 mm). The maximum variation allowed in the tread depth or riser height within a flight of stairs is ⅜ in. (9.5 mm). ADAAG requires uniform treads and risers.
- Nosings project 1½ in. (38 mm) max. Verify that building codes and ADAAG don't require other restrictions.

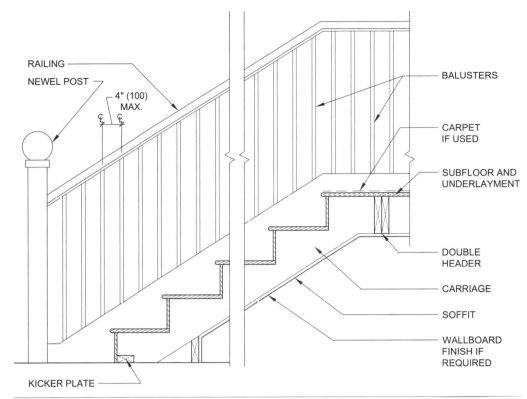

**WOOD STAIR SECTION**

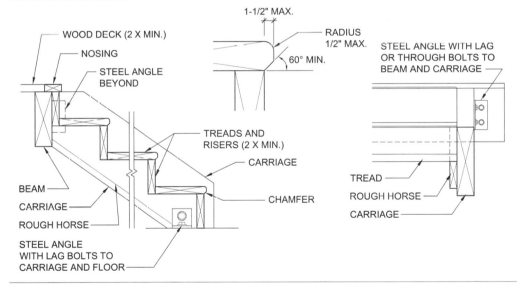

**HEAVY TIMBER STAIR**

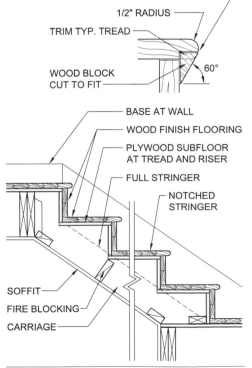

**CLOSED RISER STAIR/WOOD FINISH**

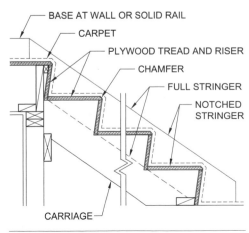

**CLOSED RISER STAIR/CARPET FINISH**

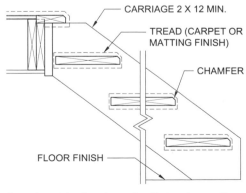

Open riser stairs do not comply with Americans with Disabilities Act Accessibility Guidelines.

**OPEN RISER STAIR**

## WOOD STAIR HANDRAILS

Per ADAAG, the height of a handrail above stair nosings should be 30 to 34 in. (762 to 864 mm) or 34 to 38 in. (864 to 965 mm). Guardrail height at landings should be 36 or 42 in. (914 or 1067 mm); check local code.

Design handrails that are easy to grip and fit the hand. Recommended diameter is 1¼ to 1½ in. (32 to 38 mm) for round handrails and a similar size for an elliptical or rounded square-edge section. Handrails should be structurally designed so that both downward (vertical) and lateral (horizontal) thrust loads are considered.

Extensions of handrail at top and bottom of stair may affect total length of required run. Verify extensions required by local codes or ADAAG when designing a stair.

## METAL STAIRS

Metal stairs are normally constructed of steel, and fabricated in the shop to fit the dimensions required by the opening in which they are used.

Treads and landings are typically filled with 1½ to 2 in. (38 to 51 mm) of concrete. Any finish material can then be applied over the concrete. Balusters are anchored by welding, bolting, or screwing to the stringers, as shown in the diagrams. Glass balusters are anchored into a special U-shaped channel, which is attached to the edge of the stringer. A similar detail can be used for glass railings.

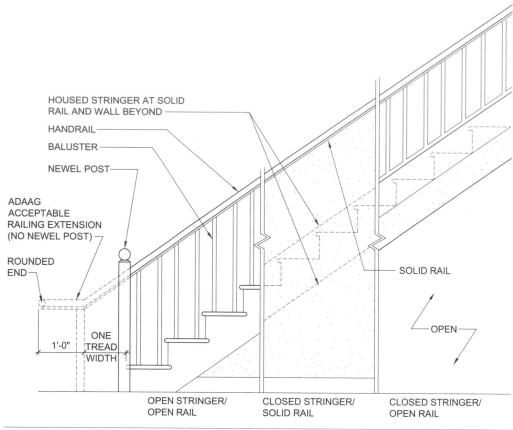

**ELEVATION OF FACE STRINGER**

---

**Design Guidelines for Metal Stairs**

1. Width of stair:
   a. Dwelling stairs: minimum 36 in. (914 mm) treads
   b. Public exit stairs: minimum 44 in. (1,118 mm) treads
   c. Rescue assistance area (ADA): 48 in. (1,219 mm) between handrails
2. Treads:
   a. Dwellings: 9 in. (229 mm) minimum (nosing to nosing)
   b. Other (ADA): 11 in. (279 mm) minimum (nosing to nosing)
   c. Uniform depth within one flight
3. Risers:
   a. Dwellings: 8¼ in. (206 mm) in maximum
   b. Other (ADA): minimum 4 in. (102 mm), maximum 7 in. (178 mm)
   c. Uniform height within one flight
4. Nosing: maximum 1½ in. (38 mm) with 60° under nosing; maximum ½ in. (13 mm) radius at edge.

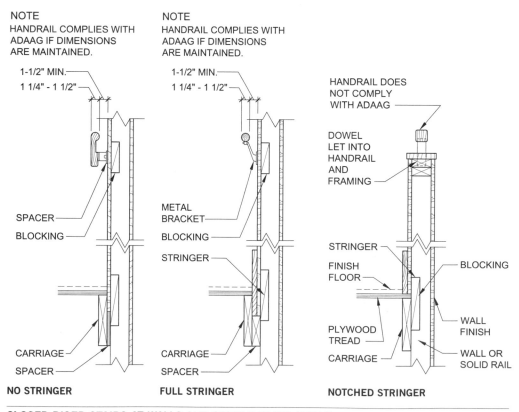

**CLOSED RISER STAIRS AT WALLS AND SOLID RAILING WALLS**

## Design Guidelines for Metal Stair Handrails

1. Stair rails:
   a. Height in dwellings: 36 in. (914 mm)
   b. Height in exit stairs: 42 in. (1,067 mm)
   c. Arrange rails so that a sphere 4 in. (102 mm) in diameter cannot be passed through.
   d. Arrange rails to discourage climbing.
   e. Concentrated load nonconcurrently applied at the top rail must be 200 lbf (1,156 N) in vertical downward and horizontal direction. The test loads are applicable for railings with supports not more than 8 ft (2.4 m) apart.

2. Handrails:
   a. Dwellings: on one side only, required
   b. Other (ADA): required on both sides
   c. Height: 34 to 38 in. (864 to 965 mm)
   d. Grip surface: 1¼ to 1½ in. (32 to 38 mm)
   e. Clearance at wall: 1½ in. (38 mm)
   f. Projecting or recessed
   g. Extension at top of run: 12 in. (305 mm)
   h. Extension at bottom of run: 12 in. (305 mm) plus depth of tread
   i. When a guardrail more than 38 in. (965 mm) high is used, a separate handrail should be installed.
   j. Nothing should interrupt the continuous sliding of hands.

3. Regulators and standards: building codes, ADA, ASTM, ANSI, NFPA, and OSHA

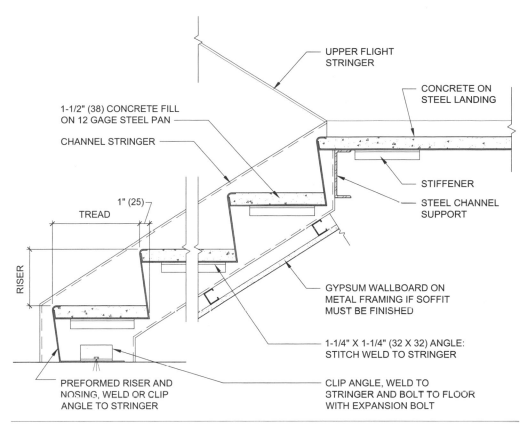

**METAL STAIR SECTION**

Labels: UPPER FLIGHT STRINGER; CONCRETE ON STEEL LANDING; 1-1/2" (38) CONCRETE FILL ON 12 GAGE STEEL PAN; CHANNEL STRINGER; TREAD; 1" (25); RISER; STIFFENER; STEEL CHANNEL SUPPORT; GYPSUM WALLBOARD ON METAL FRAMING IF SOFFIT MUST BE FINISHED; 1-1/4" X 1-1/4" (32 X 32) ANGLE: STITCH WELD TO STRINGER; PREFORMED RISER AND NOSING, WELD OR CLIP ANGLE TO STRINGER; CLIP ANGLE, WELD TO STRINGER AND BOLT TO FLOOR WITH EXPANSION BOLT

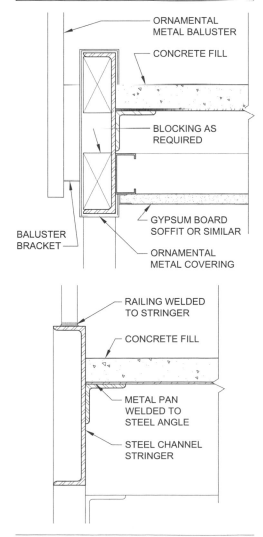

**STRINGER DETAILS**

Labels: ORNAMENTAL METAL BALUSTER; CONCRETE FILL; BLOCKING AS REQUIRED; BALUSTER BRACKET; GYPSUM BOARD SOFFIT OR SIMILAR; ORNAMENTAL METAL COVERING; RAILING WELDED TO STRINGER; CONCRETE FILL; METAL PAN WELDED TO STEEL ANGLE; STEEL CHANNEL STRINGER

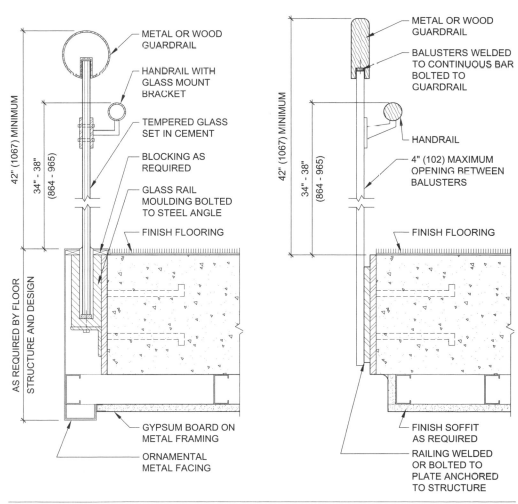

**RAILING DETAILS**

Labels: METAL OR WOOD GUARDRAIL; HANDRAIL WITH GLASS MOUNT BRACKET; TEMPERED GLASS SET IN CEMENT; BLOCKING AS REQUIRED; GLASS RAIL MOULDING BOLTED TO STEEL ANGLE; FINISH FLOORING; 42" (1067) MINIMUM; 34" – 38" (864 – 965); AS REQUIRED BY FLOOR STRUCTURE AND DESIGN; GYPSUM BOARD ON METAL FRAMING; ORNAMENTAL METAL FACING; METAL OR WOOD GUARDRAIL; BALUSTERS WELDED TO CONTINUOUS BAR BOLTED TO GUARDRAIL; HANDRAIL; 4" (102) MAXIMUM OPENING BETWEEN BALUSTERS; FINISH FLOORING; FINISH SOFFIT AS REQUIRED; RAILING WELDED OR BOLTED TO PLATE ANCHORED TO STRUCTURE

## ALTERNATE STAIR TYPES

Alternate stair types include *winding stairs*, *circular stairs*, and *spiral stairs*. Generally, the IBC does not allow these types of stairs to be used for egress except within private dwelling units. Spiral stairs may also be used as egress from a space not more than 250 sq ft (23 sq m) and serving not more than five occupants. When these alternate stair types are allowed, they must meet the minimum dimensional requirements of the codes. Riser heights for circular and winding stairs must meet the code maximums of 7 in. (178 mm) for commercial stairs and 7¾ in. (197 mm) for residential stairs. Riser heights for spiral stairs must be such that clear headroom of 78 in. (1,981 mm) is provided, but in no case can the riser height be greater than 9½ in. (241 mm).

### Spiral Stairs

Spiral stairs are composed of wedge-shaped treads supported from a central column, usually 4 in. (102 mm) in diameter. Prefabricated spiral stairs are commonly made from steel.

Spiral stairs are available in custom sizes. To meet building code requirements as a means of egress, stairs must be at least 5 ft (1.5 m) in diameter to meet the 26 in. (660 mm) clear width requirement, assuming a 4-in. (102-mm) center post. Larger diameters increase perceived comfort, ease of use, and safety. Treads are available with 22½°, 27°, and 30° angle treads. The most common are 27° and 30° tread angles because these can maintain at least a 7½ in. (190 mm) dimension 12 in. (305 mm) from the center pole. Tread selection depends on the riser height desired, the total rise, the headroom clearance requirements, and the top and bottom riser orientation.

Critical minimum headroom dimensions should be calculated based on a three-quarter turn of the stair, even if a full 360° turn is being used to travel the full rise.

David Ballast, AIA; Architectural Research Consulting; Denver, Colorado
Sukamorn Prasithrathsint; Rhode Island School of Design; Providence, Rhode Island
Yoko Matsuno; Rhode Island School of Design; Providence, Rhode Island
David W. Johnson; Washington, D.C.
The Bumgardner Architects; Seattle, Washington
Janet B. Rankin, AIA; Rippeteau Architects; Washington, D.C.
Charles A. Szoradi, AIA; Washington, D.C.

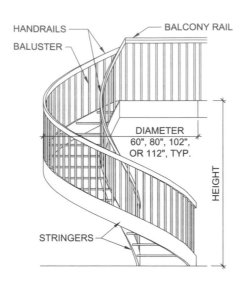

**ELEVATION**

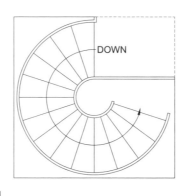

**PLAN**
Design considerations for circular stairs are similar to those for spiral stairs. A fabricated steel tube serves as a one-piece stringer to which treads are bolted or welded. Risers can be open or closed.

**CIRCULAR STAIRS**

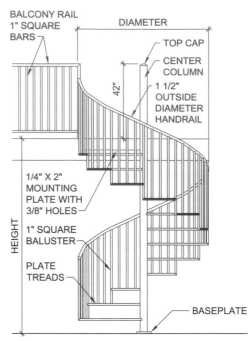

Note: For clarity, only one baluster per tread is shown.

**ELEVATION SPIRAL STAIR**

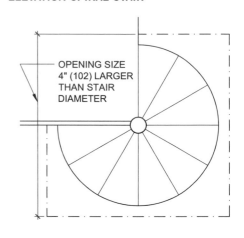

**PLAN VIEW SPIRAL STAIR**

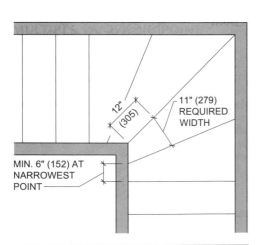

**WINDING STAIRWAY**

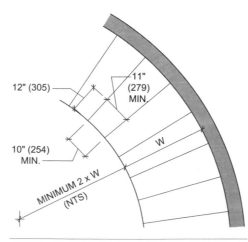

**CIRCULAR STAIR**

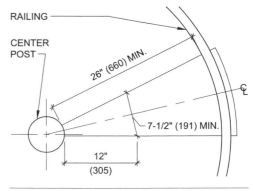

**SPIRAL STAIR**

# BUILDING CODES

## CODES AND REGULATIONS AFFECTING INTERIORS

There are many types of codes and regulations that affect interior design. These include requirements at the local, state, and national level. Building codes are usually adopted at the local level, either by a city or, in sparsely populated area, a county. Some states have adopted a statewide code. The legal entities that have adopted the code are commonly referred to as the *authorities having jurisdiction.*

Although some jurisdictions write their own codes, most adopt one of the model codes promulgated by code-writing organizations that write, update, and publish a code and related material. The local jurisdiction may add local amendments to the model code to account for regional differences.

Until 2000, there were three main model codes used in the United States: the Uniform Building Code (UBC), the Building Officials and Code Administrators (BOCA) National Building Code, and the Standard Building Code. The three organizations responsible for writing these codes worked together as the International Code Council (ICC) to create the International Building Code (IBC), which was first published in 2000. In addition, the ICC publishes other related international codes, including the International Mechanical Code, the International Plumbing Code, and others. Some jurisdictions have adopted the IBC while others are still using various versions of one of the other model codes.

The National Fire Protection Association (NFPA) is in the process of developing an alternate building code, which may be adopted by some authorities having jurisdiction. This section describes the IBC, as the NFPA code has yet to be published.

## OTHER REGULATIONS

In addition to the IBC (or whichever code is applicable in the jurisdiction of the project), the following regulations may also affect your project:

- *Local agency requirements such as municipal health department rules and regulations.* For example, a local health department may have rules governing finishes for restaurants.
- *State or federal agency requirements that govern specific building types.* These may include codes for schools, prisons, and health facilities, as well as regulations governing federal facilities built for the Department of Defense, General Services Agency, Federal Housing Authority, and the Department of Justice.
- *Energy codes.* These are usually adopted at the state level, but the authorities having jurisdiction may require energy conservation measures as part of the local amendments to the code used.
- *Flammability regulations.* In addition to model code requirements for interior finish flammability, cities or states may adopt standards regulating flammability for furniture, draperies, and finishes.

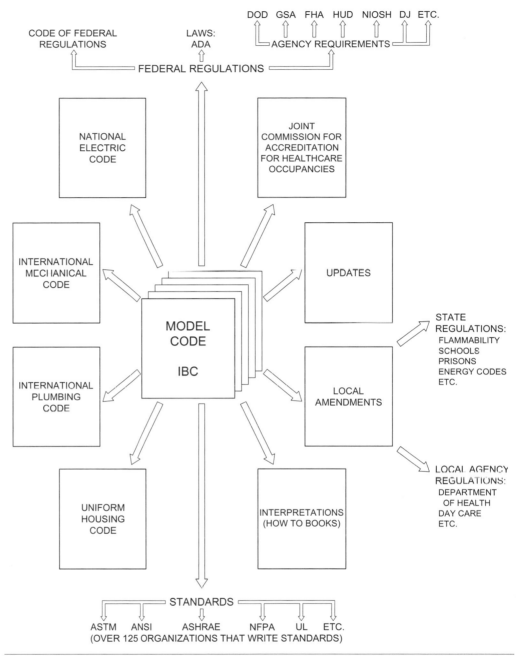

**REGULATIONS AFFECTING INTERIOR DESIGN**

- *Federal regulations.* These include federal laws, such as the Americans with Disabilities Act (ADA), as well as regulations published in the Code of Federal Regulations, such as the regulation for safety glazing.
- *Standards adopted by reference.* All model codes adopt, by reference, standards developed by hundreds of trade associations, testing agencies, and standards-writing groups. For example, the American Society for Testing and Materials (ASTM)

publishes thousands of standards and test methods for a wide variety of materials that are referred to by the IBC.
- *Indoor air quality.* Local or state agencies may adopt requirements for indoor air quality. These requirements may limit the amount of outgassing or certain materials, limit the use of materials with volatile organic compounds (VOCs), or require certain levels of ventilation.

## COMMERCIAL PROJECT CODE REVIEW CHECKLIST FOR INTERIOR DESIGN

| STEP | PROCEDURE | IRC SECTION |
|---|---|---|
| 1. | Determine occupancy group(s). Also determine incidental and accessory uses (Sections 302.1.1 and 302.2). | Sections 302–312 |
| 2. | Check specific requirements for certain occupancies. | Chapter 4 |
| 3. | Calculate occupant load(s). | 1003.2.2 and Table 1003.2.2.2 |
| 4. | Determine mixed-occupancy separations required, if applicable. (Fire separations between mixed occupancies are not required if the building is designed for the most restrictive occupancy (see Section 301.3.2). | 302.3 and Table 302.3.3 |
| 5. | Verify if construction-type information will be applicable (e.g., new column covers). If available, new interior construction must conform to fire-resistive requirements in Table 601. | Chapter 6 and Table 601 |
| 6. | Check for common path of egress travel. (If the common path of egress travel distance is exceeded in a space that would normally only require only one exit, additional exits may be required.) | 1004.2.5 |
| 7. | Determine number of exits required. | 1004.2; 1005.2.1 |
| 8. | Verify that maximum distance to exits has not been exceeded. | 1004.2.4 and Table 1004.2.4 |
| 9. | Determine arrangement of exits. (In odd-shaped spaces, be conservative and measure the distance that is greatest.) | 1004.2.2 |
| 10. | Determine width of exits. | 1003.2.3; Table 1003.2.3; 1004.3.2.2; 1005.3.3.1 |
| 11. | Check for dead-end corridors, exits through adjoining rooms, and special exiting requirements of Sections 402–415. | 1004.2.3; 1004.3.2.3; Chapter 4 |
| 12. | Verify special exiting requirements for A and R occupancies at the end of Chapter 10. | 1008; 1009 |
| 13. | Determine required extent and construction of corridors. | 1004.3.2.1 and Table 1004.3.2.1 |
| 14. | Verify exit door rating, size, hardware, and swing. | 1003.3.1 |
| 15. | Verify stairway requirements, if applicable. | 1003.3.3; 1005.3.2 |
| 16. | Check requirements for ramps, if applicable. | 1003.3.4 |
| 17. | Determine maximum flame spread requirements for interior finishes. | Chapter 8 and Table 803.4 |
| 18. | Check required light, ventilation, and sanitation requirements for occupancy, if applicable. (Chapter 12 also contains requirements for sound transmission in R occupancies, minimum interior space dimensions, and requirements for surrounding finish materials in toilet and bathing rooms.) | Chapter 12; Chapter 29 |
| 19. | Verify accessibility requirements for type of use. (The IBC adopts ICC/ANSI A1171.1, *Accessible and Usable Buildings and Facilities*, as the standard for accessibility. The ADA Accessibility Guidelines should also be consulted. | Chapter 11 and ADAAG |
| 20. | If glass is used, verify glazing requirements. | 714.3.6; 2406 |
| 21. | If guards are used, check requirements. ("Guards" is the new terminology for guardrails used in previous codes.) | 1003.2.12 |

See also *Regulatory Analysis Checklist for Commercial Interiors—Building Codes and Other Authorities Having Jurisdiction.*

## RESIDENTIAL PROJECT CODE REVIEW CHECKLIST FOR INTERIOR DESIGN

| STEP | PROCEDURE | IRC SECTION |
|---|---|---|
| 1. | Check minimum sizes and heights for rooms. | R304 and R305 |
| 2. | Check spacing of plumbing fixtures, if applicable. | R307 |
| 3. | If glass or glass block is used, check requirements. | R308 and R610 |
| 4. | If remodeling sleeping areas, verify requirements for emergency escape windows. | R310 |
| 5. | Verify requirements for stairs and other exit components. | R311; R312; R313; R314; R315; and R316 |
| 6. | Verify requirements for finish flame spread. | R319 |
| 7. | Verify requirements for interior wall finishes. | R702 |
| 8. | Check requirements for plumbing fixtures, if applicable. | Chapter 27 |
| 9. | Verify requirements for electrical outlets. Also verify requirements for alarm devices, e.g., smoke alarms. | E3801 and E3802 |
| 10. | Verify requirements for lighting. | E3803; E3903; and E3905 |

## OCCUPANCY (IBC CHAPTER 3)

*Occupancy* refers to the use of the building or interior space. Occupancies are based on occupant- and content-related hazards and the life-safety characteristics of the building. Occupant-related hazards include considerations such as the number, density, age, and mobility of the occupants. Buildings or portions of buildings may also consist of more than one occupancy, in which case the code may require fire separation between the occupancies.

Because many other requirements of building codes are based on occupancy, one of the first steps in code-conforming design is to determine the occupancy classification. If the classification of a project is unclear, consult the local building officials.

### Incidental and Accessory Uses (IBC 302.1.1; 302.2)

An incidental use area is a room or area that poses a risk not typically addressed by the provisions of the occupancy group under which the main building or space is classified but that does not qualify as a different occupancy, creating a mixed-use condition. Incidental use areas may apply to all occupancy groups. Incidental use areas require fire-rated separation from other areas. For example, a furnace room presents a special hazard, and will require a separation from other occupied areas.

An accessory use is a minor use necessary to the function of a building's major use, but that has few characteristics of the major occupancy. For example, a small office area (B occupancy) is required for the administration of a large warehouse (S-2 occupancy). In these cases (except for H-occupancies), where the accessory use does not exceed 10% percent of the floor area of the major use, no fire separation is required.

### Mixed Occupancies (IBC 302.3)

When a building or portion of a building contains two or more different occupancies, it is considered a mixed occupancy. The code requires that particular combinations of adjacent occupancies be separated with fire barrier walls or horizontal assemblies, or both, with an hourly rating defined by the code. Hourly ratings range from one hour to four hours.

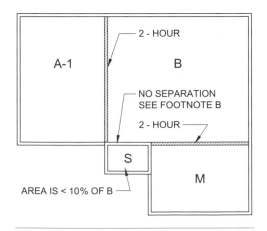

**OCCUPANCY SEPARATION**

## OCCUPANCY CLASSIFICATION. (IBC 303; 312)

| OCCUPANCY | DESCRIPTION | EXAMPLES |
|---|---|---|
| A-1 | Assembly with fixed seats for the viewing of performances or movies | Movie theaters, live performance theaters |
| A-2 | Assembly for food and drink consumption | Restaurants, bars, clubs, banquet halls |
| A-3 | Assembly for worship, recreation, and similar activities not classified elsewhere | Libraries, art museums, churches, conference rooms for more than 50 people, lecture halls |
| A-4 | Assembly for viewing of indoor sports | Arenas, swimming pools |
| A-5 | Assembly for outdoor sports | Stadiums, bleachers |
| B | Business for office or service transactions | Offices, educational functions above 12th grade, doctor's offices, banks, TV stations |
| E | Educational used by more than five people for grades 12 and lower | Grade, middle, and high schools, day care if >5 children and >2.5 years old |
| F-1 | Factory of moderate-hazard uses that is not classified as an H occupancy | Manufacturer of metals, photographic film, millwork, etc. |
| F-2 | Factory and industrial low-hazard uses, which include the use of noncombustible materials and uses which that do not cause a significant fire hazard. | Manufacturer of nonalcoholic beverages, ceramics, glass, and similar products |
| H | See code for groups and complete requirements | Flammable liquids, explosives, etc. |
| I-1 | Residential buildings housing more than 16 ambulatory people | Assisted living facilities, group homes, alcohol and drug centers, halfway houses |
| I-2 | Medical care facilities used on a 24-hour basis by people who are not capable of self-preservation | Hospitals, skilled care nursing homes |
| I-3 | Facilities of more than five people who are under restraint or security | Jails, prisons, reformatories |
| I-4 | Day care for five adults or infants under 2.5 years, for less than 24 hours per day | Day care for infants or adults |
| M | Mercantile for the display and sale of merchandise | Department stores, retail stores, sales rooms, markets |
| R-1 | Residential for transient lodging (<30 days) | Hotels and motels |
| R-2 | Residential with three or more units where residents are primarily permanent | Apartments, dormitories, convents |
| R-3 | One or two dwelling units with attached uses or child care for fewer than six on less than a 24-hour basis | Houses, duplexes, small child-care; see the International Residential Code |
| R-4 | Residential assisted living where the number of occupants exceeds 5, but is less than 16 | Small assisted living center |
| S-1 | Storage not otherwise classified as H occupancy | See IBC |
| S-2 | Low-hazard storage | See IBC |
| U | Buildings or structure of accessory character | Carports, private garages |

## CONSTRUCTION TYPES (IBC 602)

Every building is classified into one of five types of construction, based on the fire resistance of certain building components. Four of the types are further subdivided into two groups, using the suffixes A and B. The building components include the structural frame, interior and exterior bearing walls, floor and roof construction, and exterior walls.

- Type I and II buildings must be constructed of noncombustible materials.
- Types III, IV, and V are considered combustible.
- Type I buildings are the most fire-resistive.
- Type V buildings are the least fire-resistive.

Construction type can affect the required fire ratings of structural element coverings, floor and ceiling assemblies, and openings in rated walls. Generally, interior, nonbearing partitions require one-hour construction unless otherwise noted in the code. The fire-resistance rating of the building elements is governed by the type of construction as defined in IBC Chapter 6.

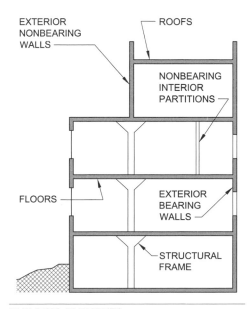

**BUILDING ELEMENTS**

## EGRESS (IBC CHAPTER 10)

Designing an egress system requires the following:

- Planning the spaces and components that allow an occupant to safely exit a building during an emergency.
- Detailing the individual parts of the system to meet the requirements of the code.

A means of egress is a continuous and unobstructed path of vertical and horizontal egress travel from any point in a building to a public way. Once the overall exiting plan is developed, the following must be done:

- Determine occupant load.
- Determine the number of exits required.
- Verify the length of the common path of egress travel.
- Verify the maximum travel distance.
- Determine the arrangement of exits.
- Calculate the width of exits.
- Check for dead-end corridors.

### Egress Components

#### Exit Access
The exit access is that portion of the means of egress that leads to the entrance to an exit. It is generally the most distant part of the building from safety. Exit access areas may or may not be protected, depending on the specific requirements of the code based on occupancy and construction type. They may include components such as rooms, spaces, aisles, intervening rooms, hallways, corridors, ramps, and doorways. In some cases in the IBC, the exit access is required to be a protected path of travel. The exit access is the portion of the building where travel distance is measured and regulated.

#### Exit
The exit is the portion of the egress system that provides a protected path of egress between the exit access and the exit discharge. Exits are fully enclosed and protected from all other interior spaces by fire-resistance-rated construction with protected openings (doors, glass, etc.). Exits may be as simple as an exterior exit door at ground level or may include exit enclosures for stairs, exit passageways, and horizontal exits. Exits may also include exterior exit stairways and ramps. Depending on building height, construction type, and passageway length, exits must have either a one- or two-hour rating.

#### Exit Discharge
The exit discharge is the portion of the egress system between the termination of an exit and a public way. It is usually not a consideration in the design of interiors. Exit discharge may also include building lobbies of multistory buildings if one of the exit stairways opens onto the lobby and certain conditions are met. The exit door in the lobby must be clearly visible, and the level of discharge must be sprinklered. The entire area of discharge must be separated from areas below by the same fire-resistance rating as for the exit enclosure that opens onto the area of discharge.

### Public Way

A public way is any street, alley, or similar parcel of land essentially unobstructed from the ground to the sky that is permanently appropriated to the public for public use and having a clear width of not less than 10 ft (3 m).

### Accessible Egress Route

If components of the egress system are part of an accessible route, they must conform to all the requirements of the ADA Accessibility Guidelines (ADAAG), which may be more stringent than the IBC requirements. For example, accessible egress stairways must be a minimum of 48 in. (1,219 mm) wide between handrails instead of 44 in. (1,117 mm).

## OCCUPANT LOAD (IBC 1003.2.2)

The occupant load is the number of people that the code assumes will occupy a building or portion of a building for egress purposes. Occupant load is dependent on the occupancy classification of the building or space and assumes that certain types of use will be more densely occupied than others, and that exiting provisions must respond accordingly.

Occupant load is determined by the largest number established by one of the following conditions:

- The number of occupants calculated using the occupant load factors given in the code based on the intended use and size of the space. (This is the method most commonly used.)
- The actual number of occupants a space is designed to serve.
- The number of occupants, by combination, used when occupants from adjoining spaces egress through an area.

The IBC provides Occupant Load Factor Tables to determine the maximum floor area allowed per occupant, based on building and occupancy type.

## OCCUPANT LOAD IN SEATING AREAS

For areas with fixed seating, the occupant load is the number of fixed seats installed. When the fixed seating does not have dividing arms (such as church pews), the occupant load is determined by dividing the length of the seating by 18 in. (457 mm). If there are multiple rows of such seating, the length should be multiplied by the number of rows before dividing by 18 to avoid rounding problems.

For areas with booths, the occupant load is calculated by taking the length of the booth measured at the backrest of the seat and dividing by 24 in. (610 mm). When a mezzanine is used in a room or space, the occupant load of the mezzanine must be added to the occupant load of the room or space.

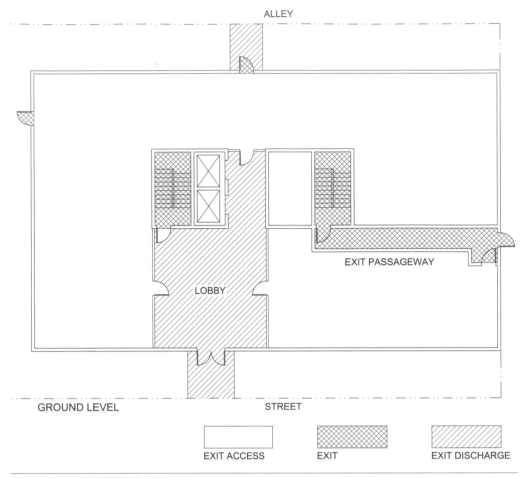

**GROUND-LEVEL EGRESS**

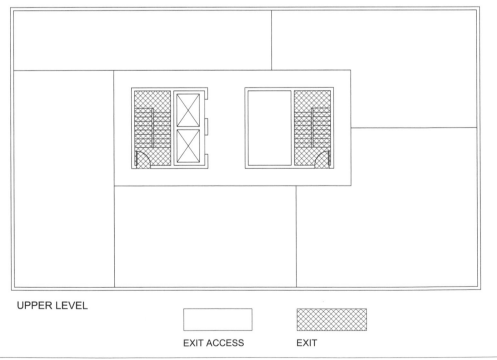

**UPPER-LEVEL EGRESS**

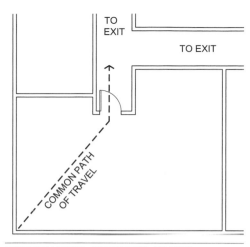

**COMMON PATH OF EGRESS TRAVEL**

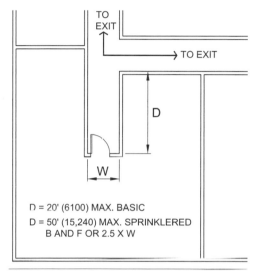

D = 20' (6100) MAX. BASIC
D = 50' (15,240) MAX. SPRINKLERED
   B AND F OR 2.5 X W

**DEAD-END CORRIDOR CONDITION**

**SPACES WITH ONE MEANS OF EGRESS**

| OCCUPANCY | MAXIMUM OCCUPANT LOAD |
|---|---|
| A, B, E, F, M, U | 50 |
| H-1, H-2, H-3 | 3 |
| H-4, H-5, I-1, I-3, I-4, R | 10 |
| S | 30 |

**MINIMUM NUMBER OF EXITS FOR OCCUPANT LOAD**

| OCCUPANT LOAD | MINIMUM NUMBER OF EXITS |
|---|---|
| 1–500 | 2 |
| 501–1,000 | 3 |
| More than 1,000 | 4 |

**COMMON PATH OF TRAVEL**

| OCCUPANCY | COMMON PATH OF TRAVEL | |
|---|---|---|
| | NONSPRINKLERED FT (M) | SPRINKLERED FT (M) |
| A, E, I-1, I-2, I-4, M, R, U | ≤ 75 (22.8) | ≤ 75 (22.8) |
| B, F, S | ≤ 75 (22.8) | ≤ 100 (30.4) |
| H-1, H-2, H-3 | — | ≤ 25 (7.6) |
| H-4, H-5 | — | ≤ 75 (22.8) |
| I-3 | ≤ 100 (30.4) | ≤ 100 (30.4) |

**COMMON PATH OF TRAVEL**

| OCCUPANCY | OCCUPANT LOAD | COMMON PATH OF TRAVEL | |
|---|---|---|---|
| | | NONSPRINKLERED FT (M) | SPRINKLERED FT (M) |
| B, S, U | ≤ 3075 | ≤ 100 (30.4) | ≤ 100 (30.4) |
| B, S, | > 30 | ≤ 75 (22.8) | ≤ 100 (30.4) |
| U | > 30 | ≤ 75 (22.8) | ≤ 75 (22.8) |

# NUMBER OF EXITS
## (IBC 1004.2; 1005.2.1)

The number of means of egress required from a room or area depends on the occupant load and the occupancy. Rooms or areas are permitted to have only one exit or exit access doorway until they exceed a certain occupant load. (Reference Table 1004.2.1 of the IBC.)

The reason for requiring two or more means of egress is to allow alternate means of egress in case one exit is blocked by fire. However, when there are small spaces or areas with limited occupant load, the code recognizes that two exits are not necessary. Factors that contribute to the different numbers include concentration and mobility of occupants and the presence of hazardous materials.

When the occupant load becomes very large, additional exits may be required in very large spaces. (Reference IBC Table 1005.)

# DEAD-END CORRIDORS
## (IBC 1004.3.2.3)

A dead end is a corridor or exit path that has only one way to exit. Generally, dead ends are limited to 20 ft (6 m). Exceptions for building occupancies may be granted if the building is entirely sprinklered, and dead-end corridors do not exceed prescribed lengths.

# COMMON PATH OF EGRESS TRAVEL
## (IBC 1004.2.5)

The common path of egress travel is the portion of an exit access that the occupants are required to traverse, before either there is a choice of exits, or two paths merge to become one. The length of the common path is measured from the most remote point of a room or area to the nearest point where more than one exit path is available. Common paths of egress travel must be included within the permitted travel distance.

If furniture or equipment is located in the area, it may be necessary to measure the common path of travel around the furniture instead of on a straight path.

Even if two exits are not required based on occupant load, if the common path of travel exceeds the allowable distances, then two exits from a space are required.

In most cases, the common path is limited to 75 ft (22.9 m). For B, F, and S occupancies, if the building is sprinklered, the distance may be increased to 100 ft (30.5 m). In tenant spaces in B, S, and U occupancies, when the occupant load is 30 or fewer, the distance may be increased to 100 ft (30.5 m).

# ARRANGEMENT OF EXITS
## (IBC 1004.2.2)

When two exits or exit access doorways are required, they must be separated enough so that if one becomes blocked, the other is available for use. In non-sprinklered buildings, two exits or exit access doorways must be placed a distance apart equal to not less than one-half of the length of the maximum overall diagonal dimension of the room or area to be served. In sprinklered buildings, the minimum distance is one-third the diagonal dimension of the room or area to be served. If the room or area is irregular in shape, the dimension that gives the greatest length should be used.

When exit enclosures are connected with a one-hour fire-resistance-rated corridor, the required exit separation is measured along a direct line of travel in the corridor. The walls of the exit enclosures must be a minimum of 30 ft (9.1 m) apart at any point in a direct line of measurement.

When three or more exits or exit access doorways are required, at least two must be placed a distance apart equal to not less than one-half of the length of the maximum overall diagonal dimension of the area served. Additional exits or exit access doorways must be arranged a reasonable distance apart so that if one becomes blocked, the others will be available.

The code requires that the exits be located so that they are obvious and unobstructed at all times. There is no definitive statement about where the measurement between doors should be made; different officials measure differently. Often, this distance is measured to the centerlines of the doors.

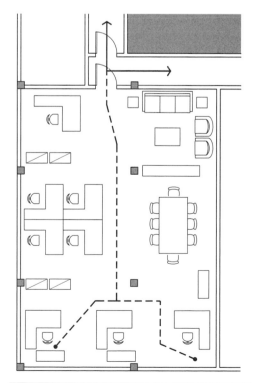

**COMMON PATH OF EGRESS TRAVEL WITH FURNITURE**

**LIFE SAFETY CONSIDERATIONS** ☐ 1

## EXITS THROUGH INTERVENING SPACES (IBC 1004.2.3)

Egress paths may pass through an adjoining room or area only if the adjoining room or area is accessory to the area served, is not a high-hazard occupancy, and provides a discernible path of travel to an exit.

Egress paths may not pass through kitchens, storerooms, closets, or spaces used for similar purposes, nor may they pass through rooms that can be locked to prevent egress.

Egress from dwelling units or sleeping areas may not pass through other sleeping areas, toilet rooms, or bathrooms. There are two exceptions:

- Egress path may pass through a kitchen area that serves adjoining rooms that are part of the same dwelling unit or guest room.
- Egress through high-hazard occupancies is permitted where the spaces involved are the same occupancy group.

## WIDTH OF EXITS (IBC 1003.2.3; 1004.3.2.2)

The minimum required width of exits is determined by multiplying the occupant load of the area served by a factor identified in IBC Table 1003.2.3. The factors vary depending on the exit component and whether the building is sprinklered. Stairways require slightly wider dimensions because people tend to slow down when descending a stair. However, in no case may exit width be less than the minimum requirements for corridors, as shown in the Minimum Exit Component listing.

When multiple exits are required, they must be sized so that the loss of one will not reduce the required exit width by more than 50%. Also, the maximum capacity from any area or floor must be maintained to the exit discharge or public way.

When exit widths are calculated for several areas, each area must be checked individually to determine the exit widths for that area; then the occupant load for all the areas must be added to calculate the widths for exits serving the combined areas.

## DOOR ENCROACHMENT (IBC 1003.2.3.1)

When doors open onto the path of egress, they cannot reduce the required width by more than one-half during the course of the swing and cannot project more than 7 in. (178 mm) when fully open. These restrictions do not apply to doors within a dwelling unit.

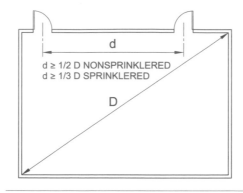

d ≥ 1/2 D NONSPRINKLERED
d ≥ 1/3 D SPRINKLERED

**EXIT SEPARATION IN A ROOM**

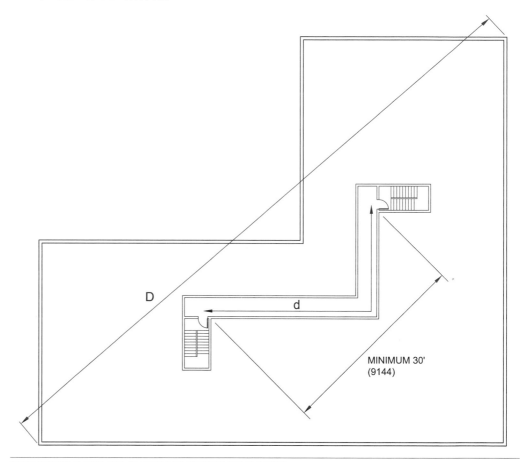

MINIMUM 30'
(9144)

**EXIT SEPARATION ON FLOOR OR GROUP OF ROOMS**

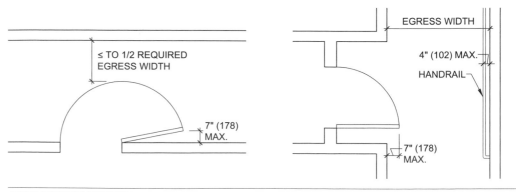

≤ TO 1/2 REQUIRED EGRESS WIDTH

7" (178) MAX.

EGRESS WIDTH

4" (102) MAX.

HANDRAIL

7" (178) MAX.

**DOOR ENCROACHMENT**

## EXIT ACCESS TRAVEL DISTANCE[1]

| OCCUPANCY | WITHOUT SPRINKLER SYSTEM FT (M) | WITH SPRINKLER SYSTEM FT (M) |
|---|---|---|
| A, E, F-1, I-1, M, R, S-1 | 200 (61) | 250 (76.2) |
| B | 200 (61) | 300 (91.4) |
| F-2, S-2, U | 300 (91.4) | 400 (121) |
| H-1 | Not permitted | 75 (22.8) |
| H-2 | Not permitted | 1100 (30.4) |
| H-3 | Not permitted | 150 (45.7) |
| H-4 | Not permitted | 175 (53.3) |
| H-5 | Not permitted | 200 (61) |
| I-2, I-3, I-4 | 150 (45.7) | 200 (61) |

*Source: International Building Code; International Code Council; Falls Church, Virginia, 2001*

*Note:*

*See the following sections for modifications to exit access travel distance requirements:*

*Section 402: For the distance limitation in malls*

*Section 404: For the distance limitation through an atrium space*

*Section 1004.2.4.1: For increased limitation in Groups F-1 and S-1*

*Section 1008.6: For increased limitation in assembly seating.*

*Section 1008.6: For increased limitation for assembly open-air seating*

*Section 1005.2.2: For buildings with one exit*

*Chapter 31: For the limitation in temporary structures*

*Buildings equipped throughout with an automatic sprinkler system in accordance with Section 903.3.1.1 or 903.3.1.2 See section 903 for occupancies where sprinkler systems according to Section 903.3.1.2 are permitted.*

*Buildings equipped throughout with an automatic sprinkler system, in accordance with Section 903.3.1.1*

## RESIDENTIAL EXITING (IBC 1009; IRC R310)

Both the IBC and the International Residential Code (IRC) require emergency escape and rescue openings in Group R occupancies. The IBC also requires such openings in Group I-1 occupancies. The IRC requires basements with habitable space and every sleeping room, as well as basements and sleeping rooms below the fourth story, to have at least one such opening. These openings must open directly into a public street, public alley, yard, or court. In the IBC, exceptions include:

- Fully sprinklered buildings except R-3.
- Sleeping rooms with a door to a fire-resistant-rated corridor having access to two remote exits in opposite directions, except R-3.

Openings may open onto a balcony within an atrium if the balcony provides access to an exit and the dwelling unit or sleeping room has a means of egress that is not open to the atrium. When the emergency escape opening is below grade level, both the IBC and IRC allow window wells, if minimum dimensional requirements are met.

## TRAVEL DISTANCE (IBC 1004.2.4)

Because exit access areas are not protected, the code limits how far someone must travel to safety. Exit access travel distance is the distance that an occupant must travel from the most remote point in the occupied portions of the exit access to the entrance of the nearest exit. Maximum travel distances are based on the occupancy of the building and whether the building is sprinklered.

Travel distance is measured in a straight line from the most remote point through doorways, unless furniture or equipment requires a measurement along an actual path of travel. When the path of travel includes unenclosed stairways, the distance is measured along a plane parallel and tangent to the stair tread nosings in the center of the stairway.

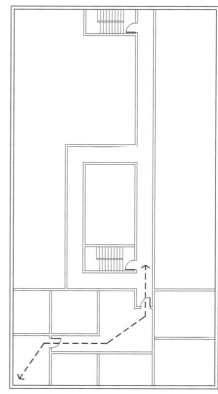

**MAXIMUM TRAVEL DISTANCE**

## EGRESS WIDTH PER OCCUPANT SERVED

| OCCUPANCY | WITHOUT SPRINKLER SYSTEM STAIRWAYS (INCHES (MM) PER OCCUPANT) | WITHOUT SPRINKLER SYSTEM OTHER EGRESS COMPONENTS (INCHES (MM) PER OCCUPANT) | WITH SPRINKLER SYSTEM STAIRWAYS (INCHES (MM) PER OCCUPANT) | WITH SPRINKLER SYSTEM OTHER EGRESS COMPONENTS (INCHES (MM) PER OCCUPANT) |
|---|---|---|---|---|
| Occupancies other than those listed below | 0.3 (7) | 0.2 (5) | 0.2 (5) | 0.15 (3) |
| Hazardous: H-1, H-2, H-3 | 0.7 (17) | 0.4 (10) | 0.3 (0.7) | 0.2 (5) |
| Institutional: I-2 | 0.4 (10) | 0.2 (5) | 0.3 (0.7) | 0.2 (5) |

*Source: International Building Code; International Code Council; Falls Church, Virginia, 2001*

*Note: 1 inch = 25.4 mm*

*Buildings equipped throughout with an automatic sprinkler system, in accordance with Section 903.3.1.1 or 903.3.1.2, where allowed.*

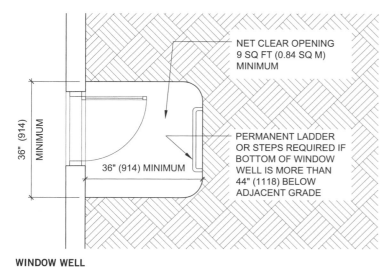

NET CLEAR OPENING 9 SQ FT (0.84 SQ M) MINIMUM

36" (914) MINIMUM

36" (914) MINIMUM

PERMANENT LADDER OR STEPS REQUIRED IF BOTTOM OF WINDOW WELL IS MORE THAN 44" (1118) BELOW ADJACENT GRADE

**WINDOW WELL**

**RESIDENTIAL EMERGENCY EXIT**

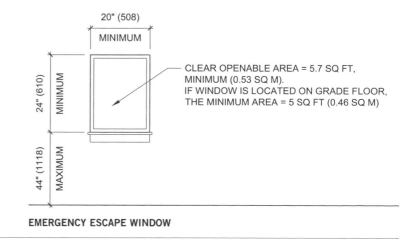

20" (508) MINIMUM

24" (610) MINIMUM

44" (1118) MAXIMUM

CLEAR OPENABLE AREA = 5.7 SQ FT, MINIMUM (0.53 SQ M). IF WINDOW IS LOCATED ON GRADE FLOOR, THE MINIMUM AREA = 5 SQ FT (0.46 SQ M)

**EMERGENCY ESCAPE WINDOW**

## FIRE DETECTION AND SUPPRESSION (IBC 903, 904, 907)

Fire detection and suppression refers to any fire alarm or fire-extinguishing system that is designed and installed to detect, control, or extinguish a fire, or to alert the occupants or the fire department that a fire has occurred. For dwelling units, the system may be limited to smoke detectors. In commercial buildings, the system may include many elements, such as smoke and heat detectors, sprinklers, portable fire extinguishers, standpipes, smoke control systems, manual alarms, and smoke and heat vents.

Chapter 9 of the IBC specifies under which conditions fire detection and suppression systems are required. The IBC also cites many instances where sprinklers may be used as equivalent protection to other code requirements. If installed, but not required, sprinkler systems are still required to conform to NFPA standards.

The design and installation of sprinkler systems is governed by NFPA 13, *Installation of Sprinkler Systems*, published by the National Fire Protection Association. Sprinkler systems for residential occupancies are governed by NFPA 13R or 13D.

The IBC also refers to the International Fire Code (IFC) for many provisions. For examples, portable fire extinguishers must be provided in occupancies and locations in accordance with the IFC. Refer to Section 907 of the IBC for those occupancies that require fire alarm and detection systems and how they must operate.

Although the design and layout of a sprinkler system is the responsibility of the mechanical engineer or fire protection contractor, the preferred location of the heads is often based on the designer's reflected ceiling plan.

## Types of Sprinkler Heads

Sprinkler heads are available in many styles, including recessed, pendant, upright, and sidewall.

- *Recessed heads* are completely or partially recessed above the level of the ceiling. Completely recessed heads have a metal cover, which conceals their appearance. When there is a fire, the cover falls away and the sprinkler activates.
- *Pendant sprinklers* are the traditional types for finished ceilings, where the head extends a few inches below the ceiling. The sprinkler heads are visible at the ceiling plane.
- *Upright heads* sit above exposed plumbing in rooms with high, unfinished ceilings.
- *Sidewall heads* are used for corridors and small rooms where one row of sprinklers will provide adequate coverage for narrow spaces, or where it is more practical to run pipe along the wall rather than in the ceiling.

### Locating Sprinkler Heads

For light-hazard occupancies such as offices, stores, and restaurants, one sprinkler head is required for each 225 sq ft (21 sq m) of floor area if the system is hydraulically designed.

If obstructions are present, such as beam enclosures, dropped ceilings, tall bookshelves, or high office system partitions, certain horizontal and vertical dimensions must be maintained.

Refer to NFPA 13, *Installation of Sprinkler Systems*, NFPA 13R, *Installation of Sprinkler Systems in Residential Occupancies up to and Including Four Stories in Height*, or NFPA 13D, *Installation of Sprinkler Systems in One- and Two-Family Dwellings and Manufactured Homes*, as required, for complete descriptions of all occupancy classifications and detailed design and installation requirements.

## INTERIOR FINISHES (IBC 803)

The IBC limits the use of interior finish materials based on their flammability, the occupancy group, and the areas of the building in which they are used. Materials and finishes are classified according to their flame spread and smoke-developed characteristics when tested according to ASTM E84, *Test Method for Surface-Burning Characteristics of Building Materials* (Steiner Tunnel Test).

Interior finish materials include the exposed surfaces of walls and ceilings including partitions, wainscoting, paneling, and other finishes applied structurally or for decoration, acoustical correction, surface insulation, or for similar purposes. However, it does not include trim such as baseboards, window and door casing, or similar materials used in fixed applications. Trim cannot exceed 10% of the area in which it is located.

Interior finish requirements also do not apply to finishes less than 0.036-in.- (0.9-mm-) thick applied directly to the surface of walls or ceilings or to the exposed portions of structural members complying with Type IV construction requirements.

When walls or ceilings are required to have a fire-resistance rating or to be noncombustible, finishes must be applied directly to the construction element or to furring strips not greater than 1¾-in.- (44-mm-) thick applied directly to the construction element. If the finishes project greater than this amount or are suspended from the structure above, then it must be a Class A material or have sprinklers on both sides.

Material less than or equal to ¼-in.- (6-mm-) thick must be applied directly against a noncombustible backing unless it is a Class A material or it has been tested in a suspended or furred out position.

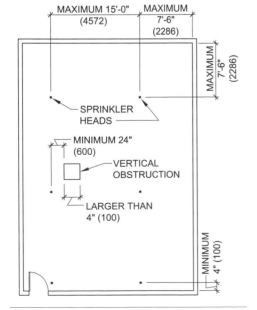

**SPRINKLER HEAD LOCATIONS**

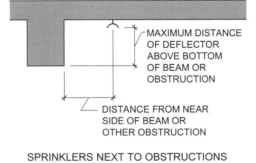

SPRINKLERS NEXT TO OBSTRUCTIONS

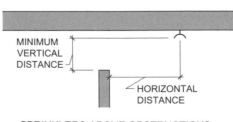

SPRINKLERS ABOVE OBSTRUCTIONS

**OBSTRUCTION CONDITIONS**

### Definitions

**Noncombustible:** A material that meets the requirements of ASTM E136, *Standard Test Method for Behavior of Materials in a Vertical Tube Furnace at 750°C*. This means that the material will not ignite or burn when subjected to fire. Noncombustible also includes composite materials, such as gypsum wallboard, that are composed of a surfacing not more than 0.125- in.- (3-mm-) thick that has a flame spread index not greater than 50, as long as the structural base is noncombustible.

**Flame-resistant:** A material that restricts the spread of flame in accordance with NFPA 701, *Standard Methods of Fire Tests for Flame-Resistant Textiles and Films*. This test is commonly referred to as the Vertical Ignition Test.

**Trim:** Picture molds, chair rails, baseboards, handrails, door and window frames, and similar decorative or protective materials used in fixed applications.

**Combustible:** A material that will ignite and burn, either as a flame or glow, and that undergoes this process in air at pressures and temperatures that might occur during a fire in a building.

## INTERIOR FINISHES

### Textile Wall and Ceiling Coverings (IBC 803.5)

Textiles include materials having woven or nonwoven, napped, tufted, looped, or similar surface. Textile wall coverings must meet either of the following conditions:

- They must have a Class A flame spread index and be protected by automatic sprinklers. When used to limit the spread of fire, sprinklers in this instance only have to be installed where the textile wall coverings are used.
- They must meet the criteria of NFPA 265, *Standard Methods for Evaluating Room Fire Growth Contribution of Textile Wall Coverings*, when tested in the manner intended for use, using the product mounting system, including adhesive. NFPA 265 is the Room Corner Test and simulates conditions of the contribution of wall coverings to room fire growth.
- Textile ceiling finishes must have a Class A flame spread index and be protected by sprinklers.

### Acoustical Ceilings

If an acoustical ceiling is part of a fire-resistance-rated construction, it must be installed in the same manner used in the assembly tested and comply with the requirements of IBC Chapter 7.

### Decorations and Trim (IBC 805)

Curtains, draperies,, and decorative materials suspended from walls or ceilings in Ooccupancies of Groups A, E, I, R-1, and dormitories in Group R-2 must be flame-resistant or noncombustible. In Groups I-1 and I-2, combustible decorations must be flame-retardant, unless they are of such limited quantities that a hazard of fire development or spread is not present. In Group I-3 occupancies, only noncombustible decorations are permitted.

Flame-resistant decorative material is limited to 10% of the aggregate area of walls and ceilings except for auditoriums in Group A, where the permissible amount is 50% and the building is sprinklered.

Flame-resistant material must conform to Tests 1 or 2 of NFPA 701, *Standard Methods of Fire Tests for Flame-Resistant Textiles and Films*.

### Floor Finish Requirements (IBC 804)

Floor finishes regulated by the IBC include carpet, combustible materials installed in or on floors of Type I or Type II buildings, and flooring in certain exit and exit access areas of particular occupancies. Floors of traditional materials including wood, vinyl, linoleum, terrazzo, and resilient floor covering are composed of fibers that are not regulated.

## FLAMMABILITY TESTS

### Steiner Tunnel Test

ASTM E84, *Standard Test Method for Surface-Burning Characteristics of Building Materials*, also known as the Steiner Tunnel Test, is used to rate the surface-burning characteristics of building materials and interior finishes and to provide data on smoke density. Materials are rated from 0 to 200 for flame spread and from 0 to 800 for smoke density. Materials with ratings from 0 to 25 are Class A; from 26 to 75 are Class B; and from 76 to 200 are Class C. Class A has the lowest flame spread. The test is also known as NFPA 255 and UL 723.

### Vertical Ignition Test

NFPA 701, *Standards Methods of Fire Tests for Flame-Resistant Textiles and Films*, commonly referred to as the Vertical Ignition Test, defines two test procedures that are used to assess the propagation of flame beyond the area exposed to an ignition source. The tests are appropriate for testing materials, such as draperies, curtains, or other window treatment, that are exposed to air on both sides. This test method also includes multiple layers of fabrics, for example, lined draperies. Test 1 provides a procedure for assessing the response of fabrics lighter than 21 oz/sq yd (712 g/sq m) individually and in multiple layer composites used as window treatments. Test 2 is for fabrics weighing more than 21 oz/sq yd (712 g/sq m). Rating is either pass or fail. The test is also known as ASTM D6413.

### Smoke Density Test

Smoke generated by fire inhibits vision and breathing, making escape more difficult. ASTM E622, *Standard Test Method for Specific Optical Density of Smoke Generated by Solid Materials*, the Smoke Density Test, measures the density of smoke that affects visibility during egress from a fire. It does not measure the effect of eye irritants, which can significantly limit the visual range. This test measures the transmission of light through smoke generated from a cube of solid material.

### Room Corner Test

NFPA 265, *Standard Methods of Fire Tests for Evaluating Room Fire Growth Contribution of Textile Wall Covering*, commonly referred to as the Room Corner Test, was developed exclusively for textile wall-coverings. It was designed to simulate more realistic circumstances than the Steiner Tunnel Test, which mounts materials on the ceiling of the test chamber. The wall substrate, adhesive, and textile wallcovering to be used are installed in a near full-scale room and tested. This test determines the contribution to a room fire made by a wall finished with a textile wallcovering.

## CLASSIFICATION OF FINISHES

| CLASS | FLAME SPREAD | SMOKE DEVELOPED |
|-------|--------------|-----------------|
| A | 0–25 | 0–450 |
| B | 26–75 | 0–450 |
| C | 76–200 | 0–450 |

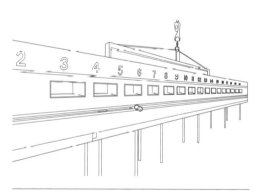

**STEINER TUNNEL TEST**

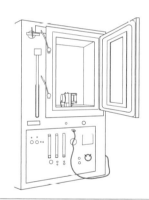

**SMOKE DENSITY TESTING DEVICE**

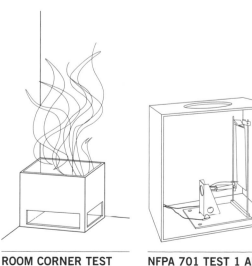

**ROOM CORNER TEST**     **NFPA 701 TEST 1 APPARATUS**

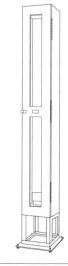

**NFPA 701 TEST 2 APPARATUS**

## FABRIC APPLICATION AND FLAMMABILITY REQUIREMENTS

| APPLICATION | APPLICABLE FLAMMABILITY TEST |
|---|---|
| **Attached to Wall** | |
| Stretched-fabric wall systems | Steiner Tunnel Test |
| Freestanding furniture panels | |
| Tackboards | |
| Acoustic panels | |
| Wallcoverings | Room Corner Test |
| **Free Hanging** | |
| Window treatments | Vertical Ignition Test |
| Banner and flags | |
| **Seating** | |
| Upholstery | Cigarette Ignition Resistance Test of Furniture Components |
| **Floor Covering** | |
| Carpet in corridors | Flooring Radiant Panel Test |
| Carpet tile in corridors | |
| Area rugs | Methenamine Pill Test |

### Methenamine Pill Test

ASTM D2859, *Standard Test Method for Flammability of Finished Textile Floor Covering Materials,* prescribes the standard for testing carpet flammability with a methenamine tablet for carpets larger than 6 ft (1,830 mm) in one dimension and greater than 24 sq ft (2.23 sq m) in area offered for sale in the United States. The test is also known as CPSC 16 CFR, Part 1630, *Standard for the Surface Flammability of Carpets and Rugs.*

### Flooring Radiant Panel Test

Floor coverings are not usually regarded as the primary cause of flame spread during a fire. However, flooring material in corridors has been observed to present problems in full-scale tests and actual building fires. In a fully developed fire, the combination of heat, flame, smoke, and gases emanating from burning rooms surrounding a corridor can make a substantial contribution to flame spread.

ASTM E648, *Standard Test Method for Critical Radiant Flux of Floor Covering Systems Using a Radiant Heat Energy Source,* known as the Flooring Radiant Panel Test, exposes the floor covering sample to radiant heat and igniting flames. This test was designed to simulate more realistic circumstances than the Steiner Tunnel Test, which mounts materials on the ceiling of the test chamber. The Flooring Radiant Panel Test is different from most other flammability test methods because it measures an actual property of the carpet system. It is not based on an arbitrary scale.

### Full Seating Test

ASTM E1537, *Test Method for Fire Testing of Real-Scale Upholstered Furniture Item,* evaluates the response to an open flame of an actual sample of furniture. During the test several measurements are made, including the rate of heat and smoke release, total amount of heat and smoke released, concentration of carbon oxides, and others. The most important measurement is the rate of heat release, which quantifies the intensity of the fire generated. It is one of the strictest tests for furniture and is required in several states. The test is also known as CAL Tech 133, NFPA 266, and BFD IX-10.

### Cigarette Ignition Resistance Test for Furniture Components

ASTM E1353, *Standard Test Method for Cigarette Ignition Resistance of Components of Upholstered Furniture,* evaluates individual components (fabric and fillings) of upholstered furniture to cigarette ignition as well as flame. Separate fill materials, such as expanded polystyrene beads, cellular materials, feathers, nonartificial filling, and artificial fiber filling are tested separately for a variety of characteristics. The test is essentially the same as the Fabric Standard Classification Test by the Upholstered Furniture Action Council. The test is also known as CAL Tech 117, NFPA 260, and UFAC FSCTM.

### Cigarette Ignition Resistance Test for Furniture Composites

ASTM E1352, *Standard Test Method for Cigarette Ignition Resistance of Mock-Up Upholstered Furniture Assemblies,* is used to evaluate the cigarette ignition resistance of upholstered furniture by using a mock-up. It determines how the composite material (padding and covering) reacts to a lighted cigarette. A mock-up includes vertical and horizontal surfaces meeting at a 90° angle. The cushion fails the test if the cushion breaks into flames or if a char develops more than 2 in. (50 mm) long. It is not intended to measure the performance of upholstered furniture under conditions of open flame exposure. The similar Business and Institutional Furniture Manufacturer's Association (BIFMA) test allows a 3 in. (76 mm) char length before the sample fails. The test is also known as CAL Tech 116, NAPA 261, and BIFMA X5.7.

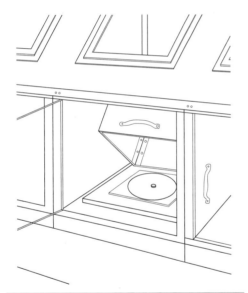

**METHENAMINE PILL TEST**

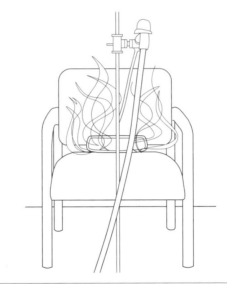

**FULL SEATING TEST**

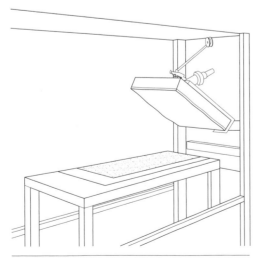

**FLOORING RADIANT PANEL TEST**

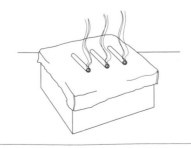

**THE CIGARETTE IGNITION TEST FOR FURNITURE COMPOSITES**

*David Kent Ballast, AIA; Architectural Research Consulting; Denver, Colorado*
*Bob Pielow; Pielow Fair Associates; Seattle, Washington*

**1  ☐  LIFE SAFETY CONSIDERATIONS**

# DETAILING CONCEPTS

Construction detailing originates from, and reinforces the design concept of, the space. When designing details for incorporation into the contract documents, designers should show the intent of the detail, not describe how the assembly is to be constructed. It is the general contractor's responsibility to decide how a detail can best be executed with the available fabrication methods and craftspeople.

Sufficient information must be shown on the drawings and described in the specifications to indicate the intent of the design. For details involving structural calculations (for example, handrails) or for complex assemblies involving skilled craftspeople (for example, for veneered wood panels), the fabricator prepares shop drawings so that the designer can verify the intent and effect.

There are six fundamental methods by which materials meet or change planes: applied overlay, butt joint, reveal, overlap, infill, and warp. The way a design is detailed reinforces the design concept.

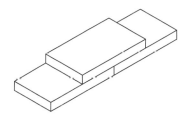

**APPLIED OVERLAY DETAILING MODEL**

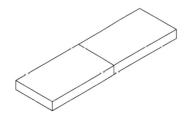

**BUTT JOINT DETAILING MODEL**

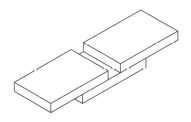

**REVEAL DETAILING MODEL**

## APPLIED OVERLAY DETAILING

### Characteristics

Applied overlay detailing is the traditional detailing method. Historically, applied overlay detailing has been used to conceal construction tolerances, which can be as much as ¼ in. (6 mm), and to add ornament to a space.

This method of detailing is typically the most cost-effective because it often requires less precision and craftsmanship. This detailing method can be used to highlight components or finishes by framing them with trim pieces. Applied overlay detailing is often used to give scale to a space by providing the traditional base and cap found in Classical architecture.

### Design Concept

The applied overlay detailing model explores the concept of applied ornament. It calls attention to a change in plane or material and the rendering of materials.

## BUTT JOINT DETAILING

### Characteristics

Butt joints often require tight construction tolerances and skilled craftspeople to implement, and thus are typically more expensive. Butt joints are often subtle, even precious. They invite closer inspection and appreciation of the machine-tooled precision.

Butt joints are appropriate where the craftsmanship of the construction is as much a part of the design statement as the space that is formed. Care must be taken not only in the construction of most butt joints, but often in their maintenance as well. For example, a gypsum board wall without an applied base is more susceptible to damage than a base protected by a vinyl or wood base.

### Design Concept

Butt joint detailing explores the concepts of continuity, contrast, and machine-precision craftsmanship.

## REVEAL DETAILING

### Characteristics

Reveal detailing provides relief to planar surfaces by introducing depth and shadows. Reveals can create the illusion of floating inspired by the lightness of many modern construction materials.

The integrity of the material is implied, however; veneer wood panels are often used in reveal detailing for affordability. In this case, the width of the reveal must be such that the panel edge condition cannot be seen.

### Design Concept

Reveal detailing explores the concepts of honesty and integration. When material thicknesses are exposed, the homogeneity of the material is implied, even though this is sometimes not the case; for example, as with wood veneer panels. Reveal details are multivalent—they deal with the complexity inherent in layering.

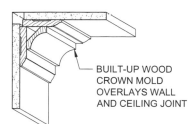

BUILT-UP WOOD CROWN MOLD OVERLAYS WALL AND CEILING JOINT

**BUILT-UP CROWN MOLD**

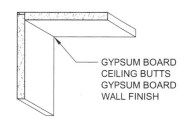

GYPSUM BOARD CEILING BUTTS GYPSUM BOARD WALL FINISH

**GYPSUM BOARD WALL AT CEILING**

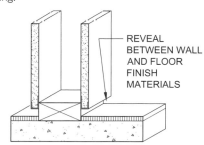

REVEAL BETWEEN WALL AND FLOOR FINISH MATERIALS

**REVEAL BASE AT GYPSUM BOARD WALL**

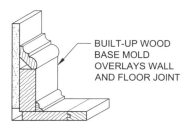

BUILT-UP WOOD BASE MOLD OVERLAYS WALL AND FLOOR JOINT

**BUILT-UP BASE MOLD**

Traditional built-up base and crown mold conceal construction tolerances, provide ornament, and draw attention to a change in plane.

**TYPICAL APPLIED OVERLAY DETAILS**

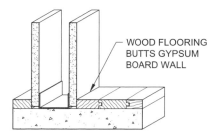

WOOD FLOORING BUTTS GYPSUM BOARD WALL

**GYPSUM BOARD WALL WITHOUT AN APPLIED BASE**

Butt joints often require construction tolerances of less than ⅛ inch (3 mm).

**TYPICAL BUTT JOINT DETAILS**

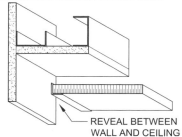

REVEAL BETWEEN WALL AND CEILING

**GYPSUM BOARD WALL AT SUSPENDED CEILING**

Reveal detailing is employed to create the impression of floating planes, so that the space is bounded by surfaces, not the corners of the room.

**TYPICAL REVEAL DETAILS**

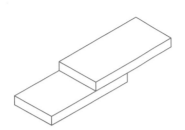

**OVERLAP DETAILING MODEL**

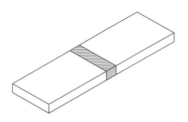

**INFILL DETAILING MODEL**

**WARP DETAILING MODEL**

## OVERLAP DETAILING

### Characteristics

Overlapping materials provide sequence and depth and can incorporate transparency. Transitions are highlighted. Overlap detailing can also allude to growth or evolution, as subsequent materials are revealed.

Overlap detailing represents a change of materials in parallel, not perpendicular, planes.

### Design Concept

Overlap details explore the concepts of transition, depth, and planar shifts.

## INFILL DETAILING

### Characteristics

Infill details highlight transitions. They are typically clean lines that can organize space or reduce it to a more approachable scale.

Infill detailing breaks up planar surfaces with a mixture of textures and sheens; for example, a brass inlay strip in a floor separating honed stone paving from carpet. It can also create a pattern or graphic image in, for example, a terrazzo floor.

### Design Concept

Infill detailing explores the concepts of separateness, compartmentalization, organization, and transition.

## WARP DETAILING

### Characteristics

Warp detailing often exploits modern materials and fabrication methods; for example, plastics, bent wood forms, or the "fish-scaling" of materials. Recent technical advances in material sciences have enabled designers to create with materials that can function equally well as a work surface, privacy partition, or overhead canopy.

Warped detailing can evoke the sense of weightlessness found in outer space, where the lines between floor, wall, and ceiling no longer exist. The popular image of a skateboarding tunnel, where the floor and wall form a continuous surface, is an example of a warp detail.

Warp detailing represents a change of planes, not of materials.

### Design Concept

Warp detailing explores the concepts of ambiguity, weightlessness, metamorphosis, continuity, and fluidity.

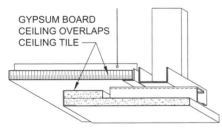

**GYPSUM BOARD CEILING SUSPENDED BELOW ACOUSTICAL TILE CEILING**

GYPSUM BOARD CEILING OVERLAPS CEILING TILE

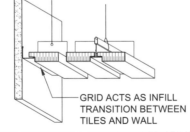

**GYPSUM BOARD WALL AT SUSPENDED CEILING**

GRID ACTS AS INFILL TRANSITION BETWEEN TILES AND WALL

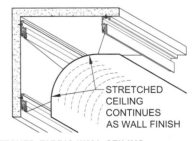

**STRETCHED FABRIC WALL CEILING**

STRETCHED CEILING CONTINUES AS WALL FINISH

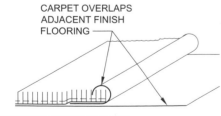

**CARPET TRANSITION STRIP**

CARPET OVERLAPS ADJACENT FINISH FLOORING

Overlap details can conceal unfinished edge conditions while creating depth in a space.

**TYPICAL OVERLAP DETAILS**

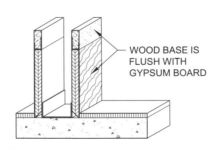

**FLUSH WALL BASE**

WOOD BASE IS FLUSH WITH GYPSUM BOARD

Infill detailing is often used to break up a surface by varying colors, textures, and sheens.

**TYPICAL INFILL DETAILS**

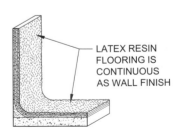

**POURED FLOORING**

LATEX RESIN FLOORING IS CONTINUOUS AS WALL FINISH

Warp details eliminate the line formed where planes intersect, often creating a surrealistic environment.

**TYPICAL WARP DETAILS**

*Faith Baum, AIA, IIDA; Faith Baum Architect; Lexington, Massachusetts*
*Jeffrey Meese, AIA; Cambridge, Massachusetts*

# WOOD ROOF TRUSS AND WOOD FLOOR TRUSS

**Legend**
A: Shingles and roofing felt with metal flashing
B: Wood roof truss and plywood sheathing
C: Acoustical tile
D: Wood frame
E: Batt insulation
F: Gypsum board
G: Wood floor truss and plywood subfloor
H: Ducts and diffusers
I: Lapped wood siding
J: Window assembly
K: Slab on grade, concrete masonry foundation wall, and concrete footing
L: Carpet
M: Below-slab perimeter ducts

## STRUCTURAL

In this example, a standard wood framing system is employed with prefabricated roof and floor trusses and exterior sheathing. The trusses are built at the factory to engineering specifications. The exterior panels act in concert with wall studs as a structural skin and weathering surface. The wood frame system unifies envelope and structure when this external skin acts as a diaphragm over the studs, joists, and rafters. Because trusses are made from commonly available dimension lumber, there is little chance that supply shortages will delay projects.

Bridging between floor trusses may be eliminated, depending on the depth of the truss and the application and rigidity of subflooring and ceiling finishes. When such bridging is used, it should not block possible transverse duct runs. Most floor truss systems allow for a continuous-edge ribbon at the truss ends in lieu of a header. Before truss units are lifted into place, it is wise to inspect them for uniformity of depth and camber and for general tightness. If substantial fieldwork is contemplated, it may be desirable to use plywood I-trusses, which can be cut to length and drilled to allow threading of pipes and wires.

## Envelope

Wood components treated with fire retardants can now be used in many applications for which untreated wood is unsuitable. Some fire-retarding treatments may discolor wood, accelerate corrosion of metal fasteners, or alter the structural properties of the wood. For example, plywood can become delaminated, a particularly difficult problem when the plywood sheathing itself acts as the exterior finish surface.

## Mechanical

Open web trusses allow threading of wiring, piping, and ductwork without on-site drilling or cutting, thus greatly speeding and easing the installation of heating, plumbing, and electrical systems.

## Interior

The open web wood trusses permit longer clear spans than conventional timber framing, leaving greater flexibility for the location of interior partition walls that need not be load-bearing.

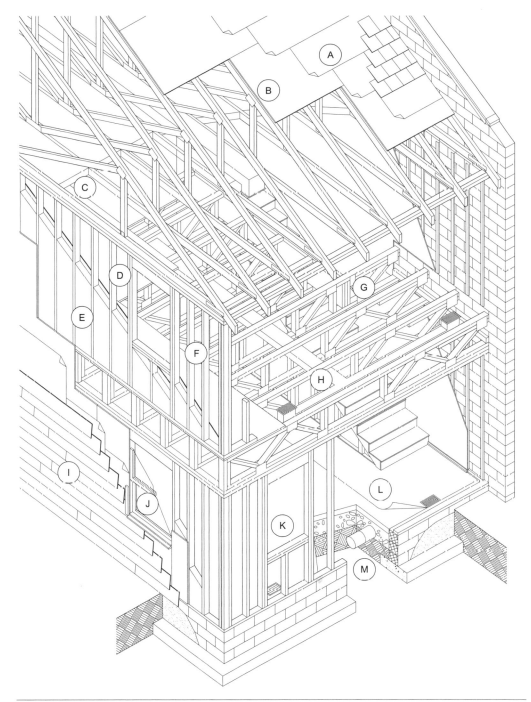

**WOOD ROOF TRUSS AND WOOD FLOOR TRUSS**

## SYSTEM SUMMARY

Prefabricated roof and floor trusses eliminate much field labor, thus speeding on-site construction; help ensure dimensional stability; and may eliminate the need for intermediate load-bearing partitions. Longer clear spans are possible with floor trusses than with generally available dimension lumber, and recent advances in manufacturing techniques make it possible to specify many special features. Open web trusses are lighter in weight than dimension lumber and can be lifted easily in gangs by a small crane or lift. Trusses are available in standard configurations 12 to 24 in. (305 to 610 mm) deep; they allow threading of mechanical systems without cutting the members, which speeds installation. The smaller wood components used in these trusses are more readily available, from sustainable forests, as opposed to the older-growth trees harvested for larger standard lumber sections.

*Richard J. Vitullo, AIA; Oak Leaf Studio; Crownsville, Maryland*
*Based on Richard D. Rush, AIA,* The Building Systems Integration Handbook *(John Wiley & Sons, 1986).*

# WOOD FRAME CONSTRUCTION

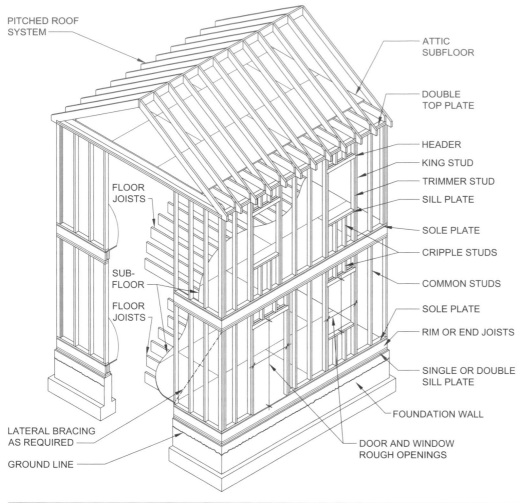

PITCHED ROOF SYSTEM

FLOOR JOISTS

SUB-FLOOR

FLOOR JOISTS

LATERAL BRACING AS REQUIRED

GROUND LINE

ATTIC SUBFLOOR

DOUBLE TOP PLATE

HEADER

KING STUD

TRIMMER STUD

SILL PLATE

SOLE PLATE

CRIPPLE STUDS

COMMON STUDS

SOLE PLATE

RIM OR END JOISTS

SINGLE OR DOUBLE SILL PLATE

FOUNDATION WALL

DOOR AND WINDOW ROUGH OPENINGS

**TYPICAL TWO-STORY WOOD FRAMING**

PITCHED ROOF SYSTEM

NAILER FOR CEILING FINISH

DOUBLE TOP OR ROOF PLATE

2 X WALL STUDS

SOLE PLATE

SUBFLOOR EXTENDS TO FACE OF WALL FRAMING AND SERVES AS WORK PLATFORM

FLOOR JOISTS BEAR ON TOP PLATE OR WALL BELOW

NAILER FOR CEILING FINISH

DOUBLE TOP PLATE

2 X WALL STUDS

SOLE PLATE

SUBFLOOR

FLOOR JOISTS BEAR ON FOUNDATION SINGLE OR DOUBLE SILL PLATE

FOUNDATION

**EXTERIOR WALL SECTION**

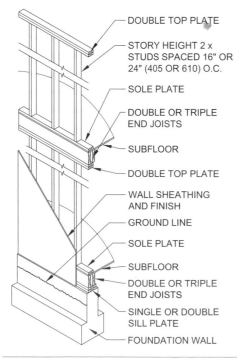

DOUBLE TOP PLATE

STORY HEIGHT 2 x STUDS SPACED 16" OR 24" (405 OR 610) O.C.

SOLE PLATE

DOUBLE OR TRIPLE END JOISTS

SUBFLOOR

DOUBLE TOP PLATE

WALL SHEATHING AND FINISH

GROUND LINE

SOLE PLATE

SUBFLOOR

DOUBLE OR TRIPLE END JOISTS

SINGLE OR DOUBLE SILL PLATE

FOUNDATION WALL

**EXTERIOR WALL ASSEMBLY**

## WOOD FRAMING

*Platform frame construction* is the standard wood frame system used in the U.S. for residential buildings. A floor, or platform, is built at each story and load-bearing walls are erected upon it. A platform frame is typically made entirely of nominal 2-in. wood studs (actual 1½ in. (38 mm)). Two-by-fours are commonly used for interior partitions and exterior walls. Two-by-sixes are also used for exterior walls to provide increased wall thickness for more insulation. All connections are made quickly with nails, which do not require predrilling as would a screw connection. Because of flammability, weight, and sawdust generation problems, wood studs are not typically used for commercial interior partitions.

### Joists

*Joists* are the primary structural members of a floor system. Joists span between structural supports, which are wood studs in platform frame construction. Joists are often nominal 2-in. (actual 1½ in. (38 mm)) wood studs of 6-, 8-, 10-, or 12-in. (152-, 203-, 254-, or 305-mm) depth. Solid timbers, built-up beams, and glue-laminated beams can also be used to form the basis of the floor support system.

### Stud Spacing

A maximum 24 in. (610 mm) on-center spacing of wood studs is required by most building codes; a wood stud spacing of 16 in. (406 mm) on center is often preferred. Wider stud spacings require thicker sheathing on the exterior and gypsum board on the interior to increase the stability of the wall and to span the studs without deformation or sagging.

### Sheathing

*Sheathing* is a facing layer applied to an exterior stud wall to stabilize the construction into an integral structural unit. The "stick" nature of stud construction does not provide adequate resistance to lateral forces, such as wind. Sheathing is typically a manufactured board product such as plywood. Diagonal bracing can also be used, but a panel provides a uniform surface for the attachment of air and vapor barriers and exterior finishes.

# LIGHT-GAUGE STEEL FRAME CONSTRUCTION

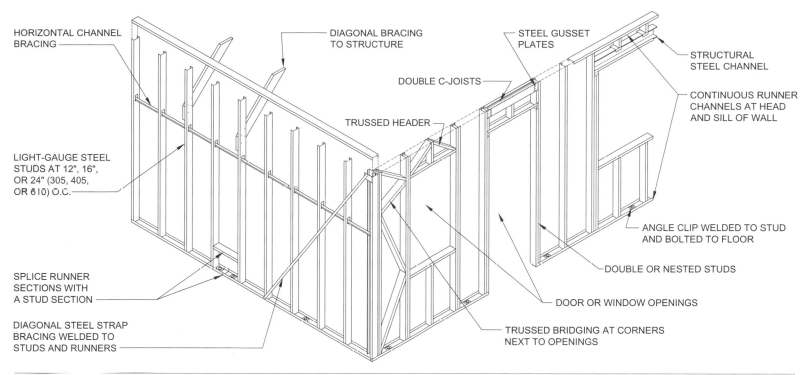

**TYPICAL INTERIOR PARTITION FRAMING**

## LIGHT-GAUGE STEEL FRAMING

Light-gauge steel studs are preferred for commercial interior construction because they are noncombustible and are quickly cut and installed with self-drilling screws. They are prepunched with holes at 2-ft (600-mm) intervals so that holes for wires, cables, and pipes do not have to be field-drilled in the stud.

### Steel Stud Strength

Unlike wood studs, both the depth of the stud and the thickness of the steel from which it is made determine a stud's stiffness and load-bearing capacity. Light-gauge steel framing members used as studs are cold-formed into the shape of a "C" for stiffness. Framing members used as runners and headers are "U" shaped.

Steel studs used for nonload-bearing interior partitions range in thickness from 20 to 25 gauge. These studs are not load-bearing and cannot support floor loads. Steel studs used in load-bearing walls are typically made of 18-gauge steel.

### Stud Spacing

Steel stud spacing is typically 24 in. (610 mm) on center for partitions. A spacing of 16 in. (406 mm) on center is used where improved flatness or greater impact resistance is required. For example, fluctuations in a very long or high wall surface painted with gloss paint could be easily detected, and in this application a 16 in. (406 mm) on-center stud spacing is appropriate.

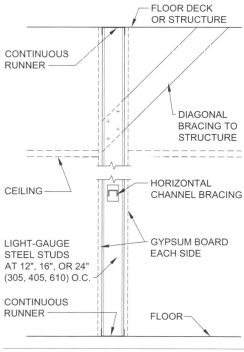

**INTERIOR WALL SECTION**

## STEEL FRAMING MEMBER THICKNESSES

| THICKNESS (MM) | CORRESPONDING GAUGE | COMMON USES |
|---|---|---|
| 68 | 14 | (Thick, heavy framing member; not commonly used) |
| 54 | 16 | Furring channels and suspended ceilings |
| 43 | 18 | Bearing walls |
| 33 | 20 | Interior partition walls and walls supporting cementitious backer units |
| 27 | 22 | Interior partition walls |

# LAMINATED WOOD POST AND BEAM

**Legend**

A: Rigid conduits run through decking
B: Standing seam roof, roofing felt, and rigid insulation
C: Plywood sheathing and wood roof, tongue-and-groove wood decking
D: Ducts, supply and return system
E: Incandescent light fixtures
F: Window assembly
G: Wood siding
H: Heavy glued laminated wood beams
I: Carpeting
J: Exposed wood frame and plywood sheathing
K: Wood stud framing
L: Drywall
M: Clay tile flooring
N: Slab on grade and concrete foundation
O: Vapor barrier under slab

## STRUCTURAL

Heavy glued and laminated beams and columns, which define the interior of the building, make up the frame in this example. The roof structure is laminated tongue-and-groove decking, nominally 2¼ in. (50 mm) thick, laid over the beams.

Considerable flexibility is available in selecting structural modules and bay sizes in heavy timber construction by varying the depth of beams and increasing the thickness of decking to span between beams. Columns are frequently overdesigned to give an appropriate appearance. If sized only to carry the loads transferred from above, they may appear too spindly in proportion to other framing elements.

Glued laminated beams, columns, and decking are generally preferred over dimensioned sawcut lumber because appearance is easier to specify and ensure. A variety of custom shapes, sizes, and presawn joints can be obtained in glued laminated pieces, and they are drier and more resistant to twisting, checking, and shrinkage. All pieces should remain factory-wrapped until in place and out of the weather, as rain and snow will stain them.

### Envelope

Lower portions of perimeter walls are framed conventionally with wood studs between main timber columns; a vapor barrier is placed toward the occupied side, and the voids are filled with batt or rigid insulation. The exterior is sheathed in plywood and finished with diagonal wood siding. The roof deck is covered with a moisture barrier and insulated on top with rigid insulation board between sleepers. A standing seam metal roof is applied over the sleepers, which also provide diagonal bracing.

### Mechanical

Space heating and cooling is provided by air supply-and-return ducts. Kitchens, lavatories, and other areas requiring both odor removal equipment and greater amounts of fresh air are separated by walls and covered by suspended or furred ceilings.

### Interior

The underside of the laminated tongue-and-groove decking is exposed to interior view and should be specified for appearance grade.

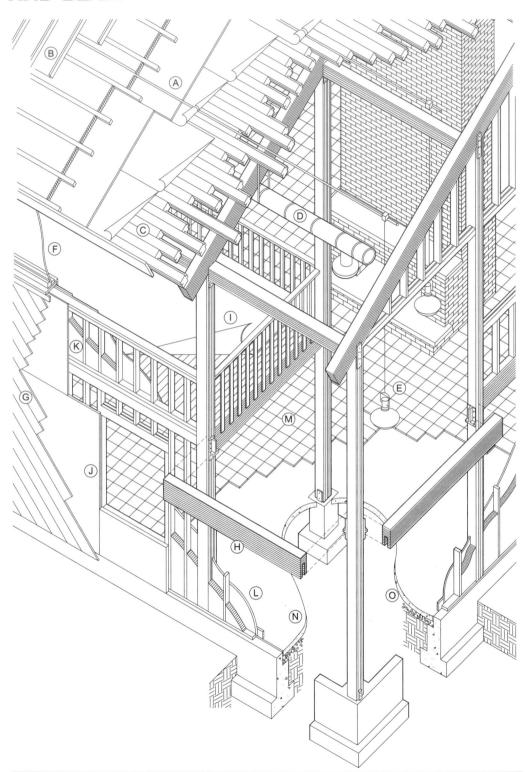

**LAMINATED WOOD POST AND BEAM**

## SYSTEM SUMMARY

Although used historically for larger buildings, post-and-beam construction is now generally confined to buildings of three stories or fewer. Its main advantages are simplicity of elements and details, combined with the potential for visual integration and bold structural and architectural forms.

Structure and interior are unified in post-and-beam construction. Because the structural elements in this system are exposed to view, as are portions of the mechanical system, care is required in the visual integration of these components and in the design and appearance of hardware used to join the wood members. Certain parts of the mechanical system can be concealed within interior partitions and exterior walls. The sizing of structural members and joinery details may be influenced more by considerations of visual proportion and appearance than strictly by the loading and stress conditions involved.

*Source: Based on Richard D. Rush, AIA,* The Building Systems Integration Handbook *(John Wiley & Sons, 1986).*

# LIGHT-GAUGE STEEL FRAME AND BRICK VENEER

**Legend**
A: Ridge flashing
B: Shingles and roofing felt
C: Metal roof frame (C-stud brace, C-rafter, C-channel, C-joist)
D: Ducts with diffusers
E: Suspended acoustical tile
F: Gypsum board
G: Brick veneer
H: Window assembly
I: Carpet
J: Ceramic floor tile
K: Batt insulation
L: Metal floor frame (C-joist), steel deck, and concrete topping
M: C-stud assembly, wiring threaded through wall assembly
N: Resilient floor tile
O: Dampproofing
P: Slab on grade with concrete foundation

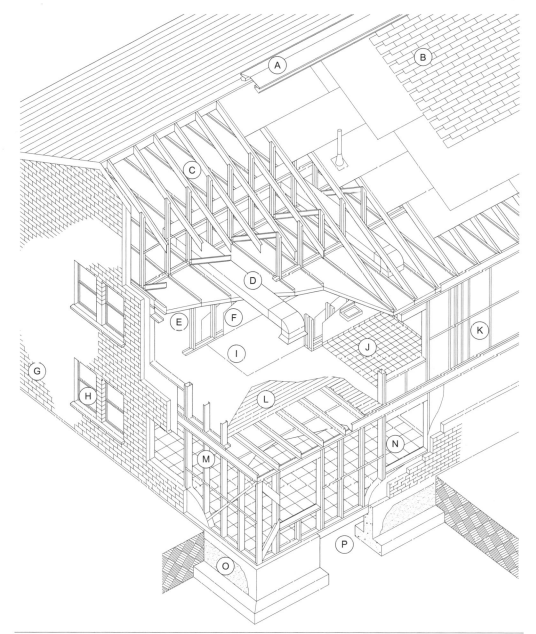

**LIGHT-GAUGE STEEL FRAME AND BRICK VENEER**

## STRUCTURAL

The light-gauge cold-formed steel members are load-bearing, and beams, columns, channels, headers, and other elements can be built up from standard steel shapes and sections. The frame's rigidity depends on crossbracing, the distance from exterior corner to exterior corner, and the type and layout of fasteners used. Sheathing both sides of the frame also provides some lateral stability. Steel studs used for masonry backup should be crossbraced with steel straps. Horizontal and diagonal bracing increase the frame's rigidity. Welded connections are stronger than self-tapping screws. The method of attachment can affect costs substantially. The positioning and types of fasteners for affixing both interior and exterior sheathing should be carefully specified, because these factors significantly affect lateral stability.

Cold-rolled steel framing is detailed and fastened quite differently from wood framing, so special noncarpentry tools and equipment are required. Advantages of cold-formed steel framing include its light weight, dimensional stability, speed and ease of assembly, resistance to moisture and decay, and, in some cases, readier availability than wood framing members. Also, steel framing members are frequently made from recycled scrap and can be endlessly recycled.

### Envelope

Deflection in light-gauge steel frame construction can be several times greater than deflection in exterior masonry veneer; such differentials must be accommodated in anchoring details, or overcome by adding structural rigidity to the wall frame. The masonry ties that anchor the veneer to the steel frame should permit free and independent movement of the two materials. Where the veneer depends on the steel frame for lateral stability, anchors should be flexible and should not resist shear; wire ties that allow independent movement are recommended. The framing design and method of fastening windows and doors should account for the differences in movement. In general, fenestration components should be attached to either the framing or the veneer, but not attached rigidly to both. When filled with batt insulation and fully sheathed, the lightweight steel frame wall is thermally isolated from the single wythe of masonry veneer. This results in greater differential thermal movement in the veneer than would occur with solid double-wythe masonry construction; the interior heat is not transferred as readily to the exterior masonry.

### Mechanical

Prepunched holes in the studs provide easy routing of plumbing and electrical lines. Most codes require the use of electrical conduit or sheathing of the prepunched stud opening to avoid stripping the insulation as wires are drawn through.

### Interior

Interior gypsum board, along with exterior sheathing, applied to steel studs provides additional lateral bracing.

## SYSTEM SUMMARY

Light-gauge steel frame-bearing wall construction is often used in low-rise commercial and residential buildings. The long-term performance of lightweight steel framing in structures over three stories is a concern. To date, its use in medium- and high-rise buildings has been mainly for exterior partitions or as nonbearing backup for exterior veneers.

Speed of construction, noncombustibility, and relative light weight are key advantages of this system. The space between studs eases insulation and accommodates piping and electrical distribution. Because the framing can be completed independent of the masonry veneer, the interior is out of the weather quickly and can be finished while the exterior brick veneer is laid. In nonresidential construction, which is likely to have fewer bracing walls and longer vertical spans and horizontal runs, added cold-formed bridging or bracing to the frame increases lateral stability. This can also be accomplished by decreasing the stud spacing or increasing the stud gauge.

*Richard J. Vitullo, AIA; Oak Leaf Studio; Crownsville, Maryland*
*Based on Richard D. Rush, AIA,* The Building Systems
Integration Handbook *(John Wiley & Sons, 1986).*

# STEEL BAR JOIST WITH BEARING WALL

**Legend**
A: Rooftop mechanical unit
B: Built-up roofing and rigid insulation
C: Steel decking and open-web steel joists
D: Exterior insulation and finish system (EIFS)
E: Suspended acoustical tile, sprinkler system suspended from structure in ceiling plenum
F: Fluorescent light fixture in ceiling
G: Ductwork
H: Concrete masonry bearing wall and concrete footing
I: Glazed interior face on concrete masonry unit (CMU)
K: Canopy assembly
J: Resilient tile
L: Vapor barrier and dampproofing
M: Slab on grade
N: Window assembly

## STRUCTURAL

Bearing wall and bar joist roof building systems employ masonry walls bearing on a turndown slab on grade or conventional spread footings. The walls support a roof structure of open-web steel bar joists, through which mechanical distribution systems are threaded. Spans for J- and H-series open-web joists generally may not exceed more than 20 times the joist depth, or more than 50 to 60 ft (15 to 18 m). Long-span joists are available, as are a wide variety of special shapes. By their nature, open-web joists spaced at even intervals are best suited to relatively light, uniform loads; joists may be doubled or tripled to accommodate heavier, concentrated loads or may be combined with other steel framing for roof openings and rooftop mechanical equipment. The roof deck may be precast concrete plank, tongue-and-groove wood decking, or, more commonly, steel decking. Small openings in the roof area can be framed between joists by means of specially designed headers.

In buildings with masonry bearing walls, each joist should be anchored to the masonry by means of a joist anchor embedded in the masonry. Steel joists can be designed to cantilever beyond the edges of the bearing walls. Continuous horizontal bracing of both top and bottom joist chords is possible with spot-welded connections at each joist and with the ends of the bracing members anchored to a bearing wall; this type of system is well suited to seismic risk zones.

### Envelope

The concrete masonry unit (CMU)-bearing walls are insulated on the exterior to take better advantage of the wall's thermal mass by placing it toward the occupied side. Long-span open-web steel joist roofs can deflect substantially, and the camber of the joists alone is often not sufficient to maintain the necessary slope to roof drains.

### Interior

Suspended interior ceilings are nearly always preferred to directly attached interior ceilings. Finished ceilings attached directly to the bottom joist chord are not only difficult to alter but must be designed to accommodate the high degree of deflection the roof assembly will experience.

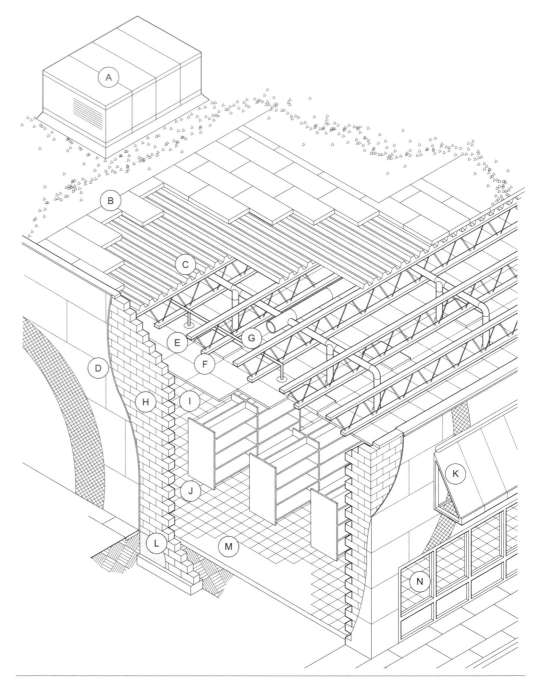

**STEEL BAR JOIST WITH BEARING WALL**

### Mechanical

If ductwork is to be housed within the depth of the joist, headers or branches must be fed through the joist webs, perpendicular to the spanning direction.

## SYSTEM SUMMARY

Steel open-web joist and bearing wall construction yields buildings that have relatively large interior clear spans and flexible interior layouts. The open webbing of the joist provides a lightweight structure that is easily penetrated by mechanical systems. The bottom chords of the joists are used for suspension of interior finishes, lighting fixtures, and air diffusers in finished areas, although they may be left uncovered. Masonry bearing walls and metal joist roofs are among the simplest and easiest to design and build. The relatively low cost of the system makes it attractive for speculative projects, as does the fact that contractors find this construction method familiar and easy to erect. Retail commercial facilities often require flexibility in lighting, partitioning, and mechanical systems and large expanses of column- and wall-free space; the envelope and structural systems chosen often reflect these demands.

The height to which masonry bearing walls can be built without resorting to lateral bracing is limited, so they are used most frequently in one-story structures. Roof spans up to 60 ft (18 m) can generally be accommodated. The spacing and depth of joists is related to the spanning capability of the roof decking material and the requirements for loads on the roof structure.

*Richard J. Vitullo, AIA; Oak Leaf Studio; Crownsville, Maryland
Based on Richard D. Rush, AIA, The Building Systems
Integration Handbook (John Wiley & Sons, 1986).*

# STEEL FRAME WITH CURTAIN WALL

**Legend**
A: Steel decking welded to frame
B: Built-up roofing or single-ply membrane on rigid insulation
C: Suspended acoustical tile
D: Ducts, with diffusers, either suspended from structure in ceiling plenum or placed in floor plenum beneath access floor
E: Curtain wall units
F: Steel with welded and bolted connections
G: Fluorescent light fixture in ceiling
H: Electrical wires and cables placed in structural/electrified floor
I: Insulated spandrel panels
J: Gypsum wallboard
K: Systems furniture
L: Carpeted access floor system
M: Steel decking welded to primary frame members, with cast-in-place concrete topping
N: Waterproofing and protective board with foundation drain
O: Slab on grade with concrete foundation
P: Vapor barrier under slab

## STRUCTURAL

Core shear walls add rigidity to frame; composite action of structural steel framing and a steel and concrete floor diaphragm result in relatively long, uninterrupted clear spans with smaller depth of construction. Heights can range from 1 to more than 100 stories. System allows for off-site fabrication of frame components, easy shipping to site, and rapid assembly. The corrugated steel deck becomes a working surface as soon as it is placed and provides formwork for concrete topping.

### Envelope

The envelope is structurally independent of the steel frame, providing flexibility in weight, size, and configuration of the envelope system. Curtain wall units preassembled at the factory must be designed with shipping, storage, installation, and general handling in mind, emphasizing protection from damage at all stages.

### Mechanical

Mechanical systems, hidden in floor or ceiling plenums or both, can be accessed through removable panels in ceiling or floor systems.

### Interior

Suspended ceiling provides space for distribution of internal services, but it tends to be used principally for overhead lighting and ductwork. Structural/electrified floors and access floor systems keep all wires and cables in the space below the finish floor, which are easily accessible by removing floor panels. This allows for a high degree of flexibility for the interior environment. Buildup of static electricity and the ensuing risk of equipment damage and shocks must be considered. Access floors are not suited to situations involving heavy point loads or shifting heavy equipment. Stringerless systems are among the most flexible and least costly varieties, but they lack the stability of fully gridded systems and depend on perimeter walls for restraint. Use of access floors to create an air plenum, requiring tight and uniform joints between access panels, may hinder access to wires, cables, and pipes; ductwork in floor plenums may

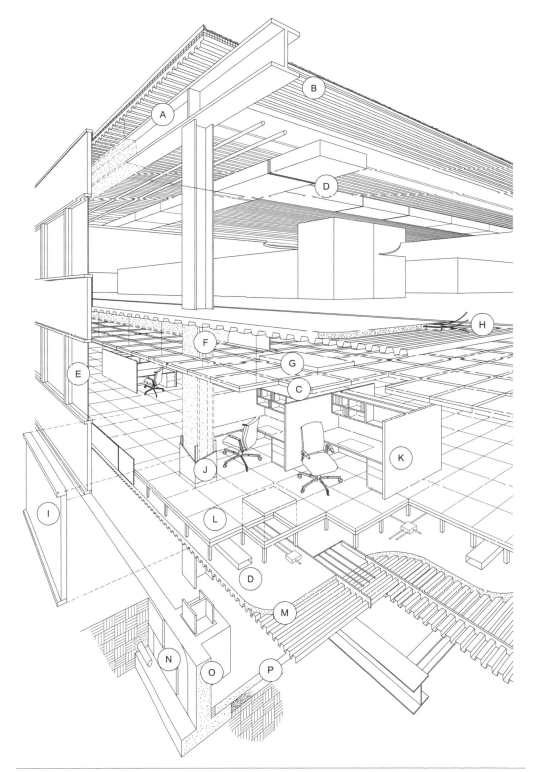

**STEEL FRAME WITH CURTAIN WALL AND ACCESS FLOOR**

eliminate the advantages of access floors by blocking the path for wiring, cables, and pipes.

## SYSTEM SUMMARY

Steel frame and curtain wall construction allows for off-site fabrication of frame and envelope components, easy shipping to the site, and rapid assembly at the site. The steel and concrete in the floors are designed to act as a composite diaphragm, providing a thin, lightweight structural element with or without an access floor. The access floor is advantageous in office environments that need especially flexible interior layouts. This system keeps all wires and cables in the space below the finish floor (generally not less than 4 in. (100 mm) deep) and out of wall cavities. Although access floors may add to overall floor-to-floor heights, the access floor conceals the most visually obtrusive distribution elements.

*Richard J. Vitullo, AIA; Oak Leaf Studio; Crownsville, Maryland Based on Richard D. Rush, AIA*, The Building Systems Integration Handbook *(John Wiley & Sons, 1986).*

# STAGGERED STEEL TRUSS

**Legend**

A: Rigid insulation under single-ply roofing and ballast

B: Ducts, with diffusers, and sprinkler system; underside of concrete planks, either painted or covered with acoustical ceiling tile

C: Precast hollow-core concrete plank deck

D: Staggered story-high steel trusses

E: Tile

F: Gypsum board

G: Window assembly

H: Precast shear panels

I: Steel columns

J: Conduit fed through vertical chases in outer walls

K: Joints at floor planks grouted; tops carpeted

L: Precast exterior wall panels that support floor slabs on both top and bottom chords

M: Slab on grade with concrete foundation

N: Vapor barrier and waterproofing with protective board

O: Precast stiffener beams

## STRUCTURAL

This system is best suited to multiunit residential or hotel buildings of 7 to 30 stories with repetitive floor plans. Floor-height Pratt trusses are placed atop every other column in a staggered pattern, strengthening the structural system while reducing overall weight; precast hollow-core concrete planks serve as the floor without a topping slab, allowing for bays of approximately 60 x 60 ft (18 x 18 m) (twice the truss spacing). A fire-resistant membrane, such as drywall, is usually added to each side of a truss to provide protection; these walls also serve to divide individual units. Lower floors in this system can be finished and trimmed while upper-level structural members are still being laid; the structure becomes rigid as soon as the precast exterior wall panels and the outer concrete deck elements have been installed.

### Envelope

Precast concrete wall members act as an envelope system as well as a structural system.

### Mechanical

Because the Pratt-type trusses extend from floor to ceiling, with openings for corridors and elevator doors only, horizontal running of pipes, wiring, and ductwork can be difficult. For this reason, separate unit-by-unit heating and air-conditioning systems are often preferable. Also, unitary HVAC systems offer economic and maintenance advantages in multifamily residential construction. Utilities are typically fed upward through chases and risers on outer walls, with service or supply units placed to either side on each floor; end-wall stair enclosures are also used for this purpose. Most sprinkler systems are laid out in this fashion as well.

### Interior

The smooth surface of concrete deck planks can provide interior ceiling finishes, if desired.

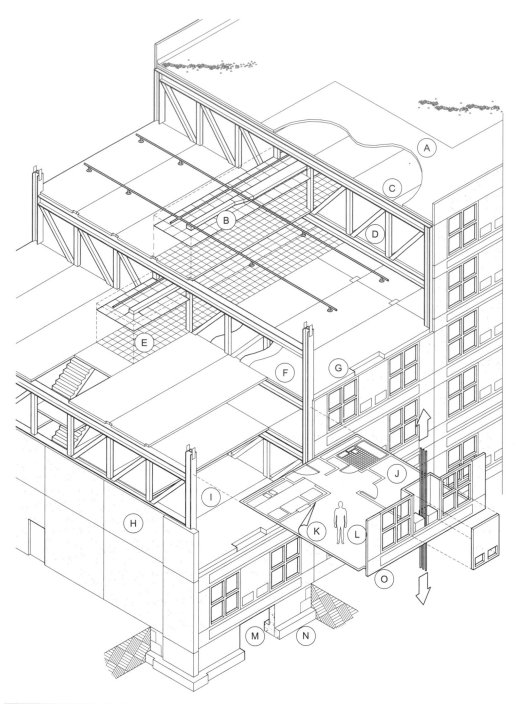

**STAGGERED STEEL TRUSS**

## SYSTEM SUMMARY

Staggered truss construction is most often used for double-loaded residential-type occupancies, including hotels, high-rise apartments, nursing homes, and hospitals. Such building types usually have highly repetitive floor plans and can benefit from systems that integrate objectives regarding structure, interior unit separations, fire compartmentalization, and acoustical privacy. The system is not generally considered economical for low-rise buildings due to the manufacturing costs of the jigs for the trusses and the forms for the spandrel precasting. The system easily allows for long structural bays, permitting a high degree of flexibility in unit interiors. The ground floor is free of trusses and interior columns and thus is suitable for parking or retail commercial use. The system's light weight reduces foundation size.

*Richard J. Vitullo, AIA; Oak Leaf Studio; Crownsville, Maryland*
*Based on Richard D. Rush, AIA, The Building Systems Integration Handbook (John Wiley & Sons, 1986).*

# SPACE FRAME

**Legend**
A: Built-up roofing and rigid insulation
B: Space frame and metal deck
C: Ducts suspended from hubs of the frame
D: Light fixtures
E: Glass block panel
F: Concrete masonry unit (CMU) bearing wall
G: Brick veneer and rigid insulation
H: Wood flooring
I: Slab on grade and concrete foundation
J: Vapor barrier

## STRUCTURAL

Space frames serve as both structural and interior systems, while providing a structure for envelope connections and space for meshing of mechanical distribution elements. A metal deck and built-up roof cover the space frame shown. Space frames may appear in horizontal, vertical, domed, vaulted, stepped, sloped, or tower configurations. In this example, the edges of the space frame are glazed to permit perimeter clerestory lighting of interior areas. Tubular high-strength extruded aluminum struts are joined by means of solid aluminum hubs, also designed to accommodate the hardware for fastening of clerestory glazing.

Space frames are commonly used as atrium covers; they have also been used as structures for entire building envelopes. In perimeter-supported applications, truss depth-to-span ratios of up to 1:30 are practical. In addition to their light weight and economy of materials, space frames have the quality-control advantages of factory production.

### Envelope

Structure and envelope are connected in this example, with the exposed nature of the space frame requiring a high degree of visible integration between the frame's structural components and parts of the mechanical system.

### Mechanical

Because the space frame is a highly regular structure and is exposed to view in most applications, the coordination of service systems with patterns in the frame is essential for visible integration. Piping can be suspended from the hubs of the frame and should correspond to the patterns of the frame. Fireproofing of space frames generally destroys their appearance, so sprinkling is usually a consideration unless the exposed frame is 20 ft (6 m) or more above floor level.

### Interior

The ceiling unifies interior and structural systems and meshes them with unified mechanical and interior systems. The solid hubs in the frame serve to join the struts and can also accommodate mountings for the envelope system and various types of interior equipment.

## SYSTEM SUMMARY

The triangulated space frame network is one of the strongest and most efficient structural configurations, permitting long column-free spans. Slender structural members make space frames advantageous where high light permeability is sought, yet where significant

**SPACE FRAME**

live structural loading may also occur. Typical applications include spans above entries, sports arenas, and convention centers.

*Based on Richard D. Rush, AIA,* The Building Systems Integration Handbook, *John Wiley & Sons, Inc., 1986.*

# STEEL FRAME SYSTEMS

The most commonly used framing systems for steel construction include open-web steel joists, rigid frames, framed tubes, braced cores, space frames, and moment-resisting frames.

## OPEN-WEB STEEL JOISTS

Open-web steel joists are usually covered by 2½ to 3 in. (60 to 75 mm) of concrete on steel decking. Concrete thickness may be increased to accommodate electrical conduit or electrical/communications raceways. Precast concrete, gypsum planks, or plywood can also be used for the floor system.

Ceiling supports can be suspended from or mounted directly to the bottom chords of joists, although suspended systems are recommended because of dimensional variations in actual joist depths.

## RIGID FRAME

Rigid frame construction combines columns and a beam or girder welded together to make a rigid connection. Such a frame can carry vertical loads and resist horizontal forces, either wind or seismic. Rigid frame buildings are usually single-story. The roofs are generally sloped, usually at least 1 in 12.

Because they span fairly long distances relatively cheaply (widths range between 30 and 130 ft (9 and 39 m)), rigid frame structures are used for recreational buildings; warehouses; light industrial buildings; and commercial buildings, such as supermarkets, automobile dealer showrooms, and garages. Bay sizes are usually 20 to 24 ft (6 to 7 m) but may be extended to 30 ft (9 m). The roof profile is most often configured as a symmetrical gable, but such a profile is not a structural necessity. Some manufacturers offer precast concrete and masonry siding. Preengineered buildings most often use rigid frames for roof and wall supports.

## FRAMED TUBE

In the framed tube system, structural steel members form the load-bearing exterior perimeter wall; this wall is designed so the entire building becomes, in effect, a structural steel tube. The tubular strength is achieved in two ways: the exterior columns are spaced closely together (perhaps 6 ft (2 m) on center) and connected to spandrel beams, and the structure is stiffened by the floors to form a torsionally rigid tube. The spandrel beams are generally very deep, in units of feet as opposed to inches. The columns and spandrel beams are welded together to create a moment-resisting connection. Often this system is referred to as a pierced tube, the pierced areas being the window openings.

The framed tube system is most economical for very tall buildings. The World Trade Center Towers in New York were framed tube construction. The Sears Tower in Chicago is the most conspicuous existing example of this construction system. Systems like that at the Sears Tower, a combination of nine framed tubes in a 3 × 3 array, are sometimes called *bundled tubes*.

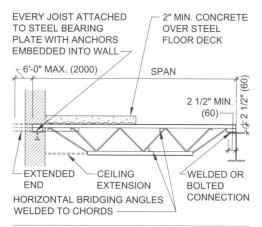

**SECTION THROUGH JOIST BEARING**

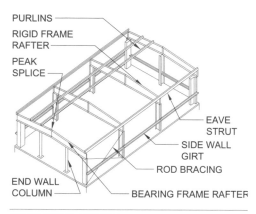

**RIGID STEEL FRAME**

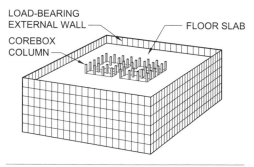

**FRAMED STEEL TUBE**

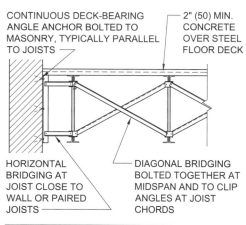

**SECTION THROUGH LONG-SPAN STEEL JOISTS**

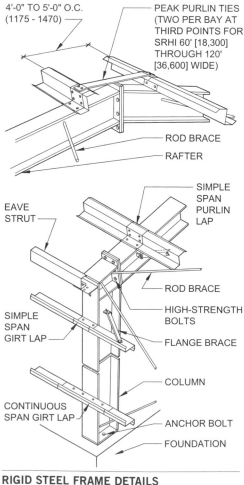

**RIGID STEEL FRAME DETAILS**

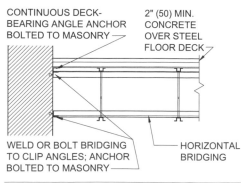

**SECTION THROUGH STEEL JOIST**

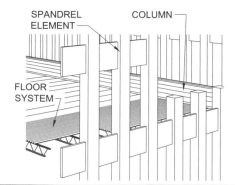

**PERIMETER FRAMED TUBE WALL DETAIL**

## BRACED CORE

In the braced core system, walls around elevator shafts and stairwells are designed to act as vertical trusses that cantilever up from the foundation. The chords of each truss are building columns; the floor beams act as ties. Diagonals placed in a K-pattern (occasionally in an X-pattern) complete the truss. A system employing knee braces is used in seismic areas because of its greater capability to dissipate earthquake energy. Braced core systems can be used efficiently in single-story buildings as well as in buildings over 50 stories.

## SPACE FRAMES

A space frame is a three-dimensional truss with linear members that form a series of triangulated polyhedrons. It can be seen as a plane of constant depth that can sustain fairly long spans and varied configurations of shape. The prime attributes of space frame structural systems are their light weight; inherent rigidity; their wide variety of form, size, and span; and compatible interaction with other building support systems,

primarily HVAC. Most systems are designed for specific applications, and a structural engineer with space frame experience should always be consulted. Manufacturers can provide the full range of capabilities—loading, spans, shapes, specific details—for their products. Standardized systems in 4- and 5-ft (1,220 and 1,525 mm) modules are available.

Metal space frames are classified as noncombustible construction and can usually be exposed when 20 ft (6 m) above the floor. However, an automatic fire-extinguishing system or a fire-rated ceiling may be required.

## Moment-Resisting Frame

A moment-resisting frame's lateral stability and resistance to wind and seismic forces depend on a fixed connection of beams and columns. A moment-resisting connection is achieved when the top and bottom flanges of each beam are welded to the flanges of the connecting columns with full-depth welds. By directly welding the beam web to the column flange, the beam's horizontal reaction to wind forces is transferred to the column. (A connection using web angles and

high-strength bolts is also permitted.) The building's floors are designed to act as diaphragms that connect all of the columns and beams, enabling the building to react as a unit.

Moment-resisting frames are uneconomical in tall steel buildings because the larger lateral forces in such buildings can be handled more efficiently by diagonal members, as found in braced frames. To save costs, often the upper stories of a braced frame building use moment-resisting beam-column connections to resist wind loads.

*Donald J. Neubauer, P.E.; Neubauer-Sohn, Consulting Engineers; Potomac, Maryland*
*Richard J. Vitullo, AIA; Oak Leaf Studio; Crownsville, Maryland*

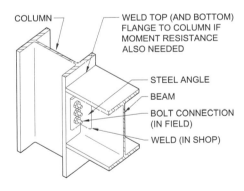

**BRACED CORE**

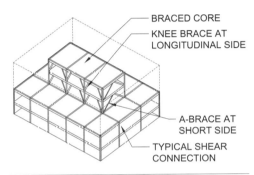

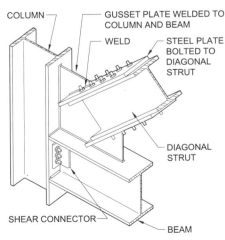

**BRACED CORE DETAILS**

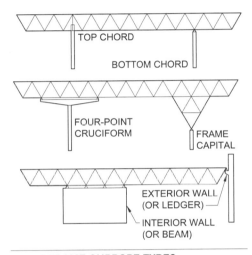

**SPACE FRAME SUPPORT TYPES**

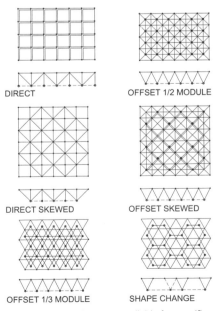

Many proprietary systems are available for specific applications and budgets.

**COMMON SPACE FRAME PATTERNS**

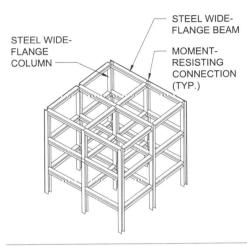

**MOMENT-RESISTING STEEL FRAME**

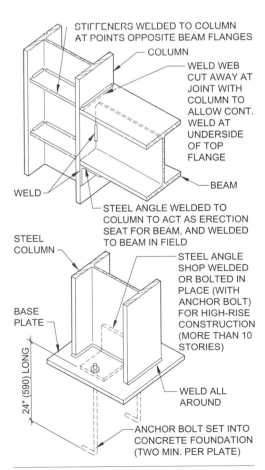

**MOMENT-RESISTING STEEL DETAILS**

# CONCRETE FLOOR SYSTEMS

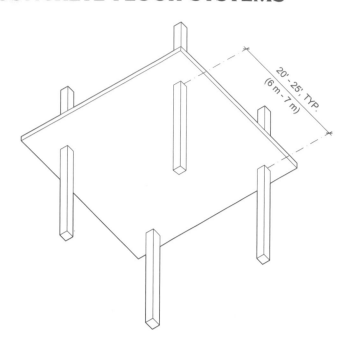

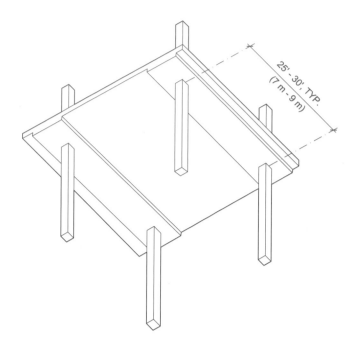

A flat plate is best for moderate spans because it is the most economical floor system and has the lowest structural thickness. Penetrations for piping and ductwork through the slab near columns must be avoided. Spandrel beams may be necessary.

*Advantages:* Inexpensive formwork; ceilings may be exposed; minimum slab thickness; fast erection; and flexible column location.

*Disadvantages:* Excess concrete for longer spans; low shear capacity; greater deflections.

*Appropriate Building Types:* Hotels, motels, dormitories, condominiums, and hospitals.

## FLAT PLATE

A banded slab has most of the advantages of a flat plate, but permits a longer span in one direction. It can resist greater lateral loads in the direction of the beams.

*Advantages:* Longer spans; typically posttensioned; minimum slab thickness.

*Disadvantages:* Must reuse formwork many times to be economical.

*Appropriate Building Types:* High-rise buildings; same use as flat plates if flying forms can be used more than 10 times.

## BANDED SLAB

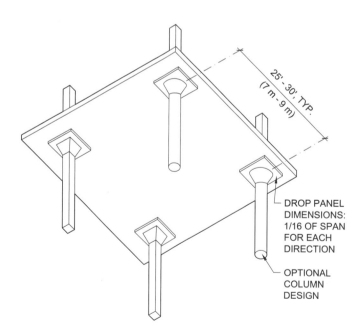

DROP PANEL DIMENSIONS: 1/16 OF SPAN FOR EACH DIRECTION

OPTIONAL COLUMN DESIGN

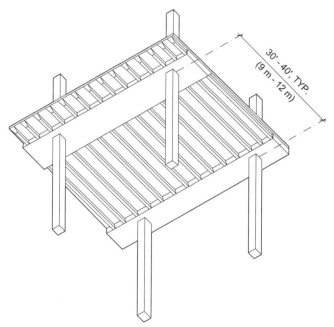

Flat slabs are most commonly used today for buildings supporting very heavy loads. When live loads exceed 150 psf (7,182 Pa), flat slabs are by far the most economical.

*Advantages:* Economical for design loads greater than 150 psf (7,182 Pa).

*Disadvantages:* Formwork is costly.

*Appropriate Building Types:* Warehouses, industrial structures, parking structures.

## FLAT SLAB

This is the best scheme if slabs are too long for a flat plate and the structure is not exposed. The slab thickness between joints is determined by the fire requirements. Joists are most economical if beams are the same depth as the joists.

*Advantages:* Minimum concrete and steel; minimum weight, thus reduced column and footing size; long spans in one direction; accommodates poke-through electrical systems.

*Disadvantages:* Unattractive for an exposed ceiling; formwork may cost more than flat plate.

*Appropriate Building Types:* Schools, offices, churches, hospitals, public and institutional buildings, buildings with moderate loadings and spans.

## JOIST SLAB

*Russell S. Fling, P.E.; Consulting Engineer; Columbus, Ohio Based on Richard D. Rush, AIA,* The Building Systems Integration Handbook, *John Wiley & Sons, Inc., 1986.*

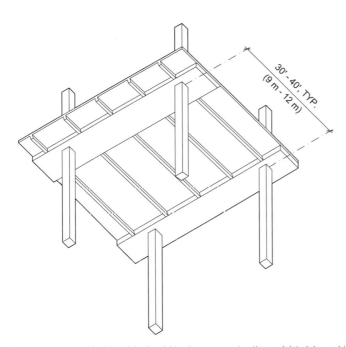

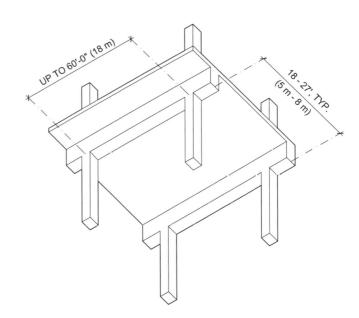

For large projects, a skip joist slab should be less expensive than a joist slab, and it permits lights and equipment to be recessed between joists.

*Advantages:* Uses less concrete than joist slab; incurs lower steel rebar placing costs; joist space is used for mechanical systems; permits lights and equipment to be recessed between joists.

*Disadvantages:* Similar to joist slab; joists must be designed as beams; forms may require special order.

*Appropriate Building Types:* Same as for joist slabs; especially for longer fire ratings.

## SKIP JOIST

This scheme is most favored for parking garages, but the long span of about 60 ft (18 m) must be prestressed unless beams are quite deep. Shallow beams will deflect excessively.

*Advantages:* Long span in one direction.

*Disadvantages:* Beams interfere with mechanical services; more expensive forms than flat plate.

*Appropriate Building Types:* Parking garages, especially with posttensioning.

## ONE-WAY BEAM AND SLAB

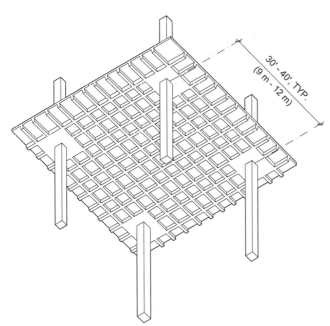

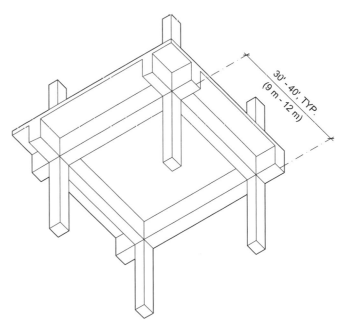

Column spacing should be multiples of pan spacing to ensure uniformity of drop panels at each column. Drop panels can be diamond-shaped, square, or rectangular.

*Advantages:* Longer two-way spans; exposed ceiling pattern; heavy load capacity.

*Disadvantages:* Formwork costs more and uses more concrete and steel than a joist slab.

*Appropriate Building Types:* Prominent buildings with exposed ceiling structure; same types as are suitable for flat slab, but with longer spans.

## WAFFLE SLAB

The high cost of formwork and structural interference with mechanical systems make this scheme unattractive unless heavy concentrated loads must be carried.

*Advantages:* Long span in two directions; small deflection; can carry concentrated loads.

*Disadvantages:* Same as for one-way beams, only more so.

*Appropriate Building Types:* Portions of buildings in which two-way beam framing is needed for other reasons; industrial buildings with heavy concentrated loads.

## TWO-WAY SLAB AND BEAM

*Russell S. Fling, P.E.; Consulting Engineer; Columbus, Ohio*
*Based on Richard D. Rush, AIA,* The Building Systems
  Integration Handbook, *John Wiley & Sons, Inc., 1986.*

# FLAT-PLATE CONCRETE

**Legend**

A: Elevator equipment in penthouse
B: Rigid insulation and ballast
C: Protected roof membrane
D: Window assembly
E: Cast-in-place concrete flat plate
F: Suspended acoustical tile
G: Ducts with diffusers suspended from structure in ceiling plenum
H: Power and communication supplied to furniture by overhead poles or under carpet flat cable
I: Batt insulation
J: Gypsum board and metal stud assembly
K: Cast-in-place concrete column
L: Carpeting
M: Precast concrete spandrel panels
N: Slab on grade and concrete pile foundation
O: Waterproofing and protective board at foundation, with vapor barrier under slab

## STRUCTURAL

Combines cast-in-place concrete columns with two-way concrete slab plates of uniform thickness. Two-way flat-plate concrete floors are among the simplest concrete structures for reinforcing, formwork, and detailing. Exterior precast concrete plates can be attached on lower floors, even with flat-plate shoring still in place, while concrete is being poured for upper-floor columns and plates. When crane hoists are used to lift concrete buckets or large equipment, a hole is generally left in a section of each plate to allow for passage of the hoist; this hole is filled later, when large components have been moved and concrete pouring is complete.

Flat-plate concrete construction permits more stories to be fitted into a given building height than any other system. This is because its floor structure has minimum thickness, especially when posttensioned. In addition, in many building types the underside of the floor plate can serve as the finish ceiling.

## Envelope

Exterior precast concrete panels can be attached on lower floors, even with flat-plate shoring still in place, while concrete is being poured for upper-floor columns and plates. Window-framing elements and glazing are installed after the spandrels have been set.

## Mechanical

Centralized core permits relatively uniform, short horizontal runs for power, plumbing, lighting, and other systems.

## Interior

Workstations in unpartitioned interior offices can be serviced unobtrusively by ceiling height power and communications poles, in furred-out areas around columns, and in corridor partition walls. Office workstations require daylight exposure and views. Because the central core is farthest from perimeter zones, usable floor area in the perimeter can be maximized. On constrained urban sites, the central core may be moved against an unfenestrated wall and still retain this advantage.

## SYSTEM SUMMARY

The drawing "Flat-Plate Concrete" combines cast-in-place columns and two-way concrete flat plates of uniform thickness, with precast concrete spandrel

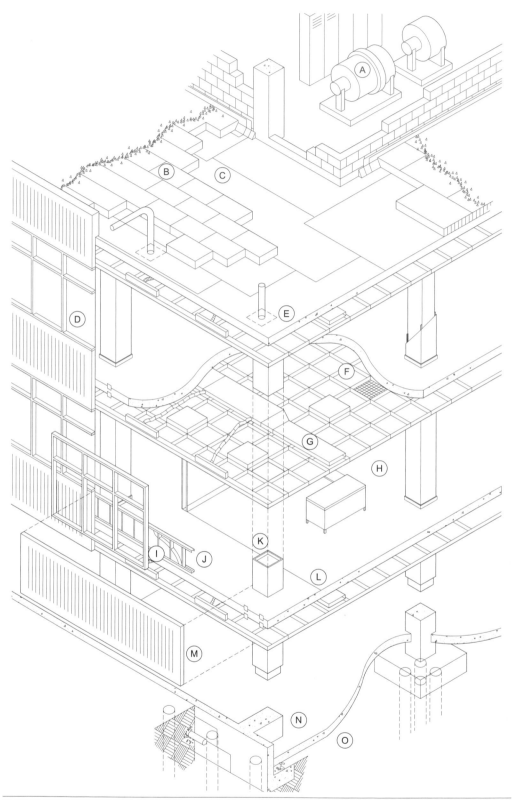

## FLAT-PLATE CONCRETE

panels. The system usually has a central core for vertical circulation and services, and it is typically employed for low- to medium-rise construction because of the costs and difficulties associated with placement of materials and labor in higher buildings. The central core also permits consolidation of vertical service risers, increasing fire protection by reducing or eliminating through-floor penetrations in office areas.

Flat-plate concrete construction is especially applicable to apartments, hotels, and dormitories, in which no suspended ceiling is required. Story height can be minimized in these applications by using the undersides of the slabs as finish ceiling.

*Richard J. Vitullo, AIA; Oak Leaf Studio; Crownsville, Maryland Based on Richard D. Rush, AIA, The Building Systems Integration Handbook (John Wiley & Sons, 1986).*

# POSTTENSIONED CONCRETE

**Legend**

A: Built-up roofing or single-ply membrane on rigid insulation
B: Concrete slab with reinforcing steel bars
C: Ducts, with diffusers, suspended from structure in ceiling plenum
D: Fluorescent light fixture in ceiling
E: Suspended acoustical tile ceilings
F: Resilient floor
G: Operable partitions
H: Metal stud and gypsum wallboard assembly
I: Window assembly
J: Concrete
K: Brick and concrete masonry with rigid insulation
L: Slab on grade and concrete foundation
M: Vapor barrier under slab
N: Waterproofing and protective board at foundation

## STRUCTURAL

Posttensioning is a highly sensitive integration of the compressive strength of concrete with the tensile strength of steel. Plastic-sheathed, high-strength steel tendons are cast in the slab and, after curing, are placed in the tubes, anchored, and jacked into tension from one end. After stresses are applied, the tendon channels may be grouted to bond the tendons to the slab. For lengths greater than 100 ft (30 m), stresses must be applied simultaneously from two ends. Integration of mechanical services is influenced greatly by the positioning of tendons, which controls the locations of through-slab penetrations. Posttensioning permits the use of shallower beams and slabs, reducing overall building height and permitting longer spans with thinner structural members. The structure is quite rigid and less subject to movement and creep, allowing use of masonry infill envelope. Alterations and demolition can be difficult due to potential forces latent in posttensioned tendons.

### Envelope

The building skin rests on the concrete frame by means of steel shelf angles attached to spandrel beams.

### Mechanical

Mechanical systems hidden in ceiling plenums can be accessed through removable panels. This system is optimal for additions to hospitals and other medical facilities, which often require floor-to-floor heights that match those of the existing structure. Although contemporary standards for servicing and mechanical equipment require deeper interstitial spaces than are found in many older buildings, the shallower slabs and beams of posttensioned concrete construction can conserve such space.

### Interior

A suspended ceiling provides space for distribution of internal services but tends to be used only for overhead lighting and ductwork.

## SYSTEM SUMMARY

Posttensioned concrete construction is virtually identical to flat-plate concrete construction. The major difference lies in the thickness of the concrete slab, which is slightly reduced in this type of construction.

Posttensioning is a method of reinforcing concrete by stretching steel-reinforcing tendons after placement and

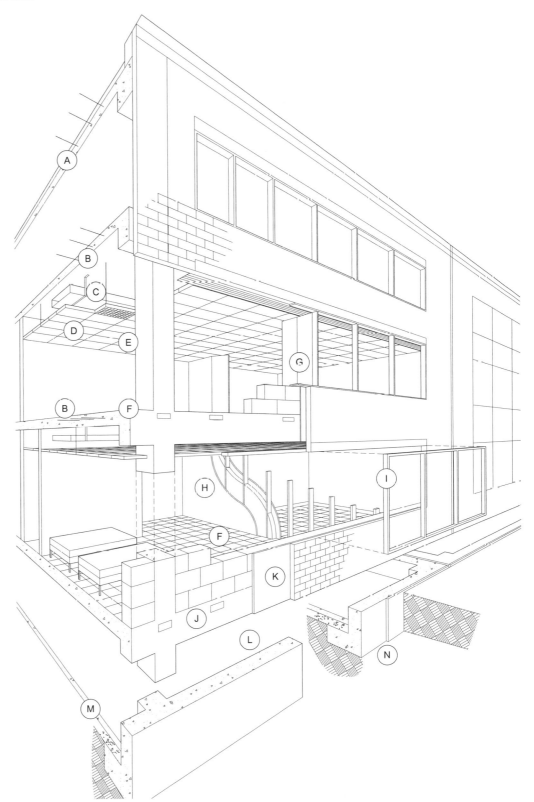

**POSTTENSIONED CONCRETE**

curing of the concrete structure. This prestressing reduces or eliminates tensile stresses on the concrete under use loading and strengthens the slab without increasing its thickness or adding the dead loads introduced by additional steel-reinforcing rods. Posttensioning is useful when slab thickness is important to economical or functional design aspects or when concentrated live loads are high and the building height must be kept to a minimum. It is also effective when project conditions require minimal floor-to-floor heights but maximum ceiling heights with generous space above the ceilings.

*Richard J. Vitullo, AIA; Oak Leaf Studio; Crownsville, Maryland
Based on Richard D. Rush, AIA, The Building Systems
Integration Handbook (John Wiley & Sons, 1986).*

# PRECAST CONCRETE FRAME

**Legend**
A: Concrete topping as floor finish
B: Prestressed precast concrete double-T
C: Fluorescent light fixtures attached to structure
D: Prestressed precast concrete columns and spandrel beams
E: Cast-in-place concrete vertical circulation
F: Slab on grade, with cast-in-place concrete piles
G: Elevator equipment for hydraulic elevator

## STRUCTURAL

This system is most commonly used for parking garages. Double-T joists are generally 8 or 12 ft (2 or 3.5 m) wide, at a depth of 18 to 36 in. (460 to 915 mm), depending on the spanning requirements. Spans of 60 ft (18 m) are considered maximum, due to the constraints of shipping and lifting the pieces, but longer spans and deeper sections are possible. It is advantageous to use as many similar elements as possible; that is, floors, inverted T-girders, and columns should all be of the same length and design. Off-site precasting can conserve time and materials for concrete forming, and on-site erection time is considerably faster than for cast-in-place construction. Cast-in-place core provides lateral stability to the frame. Adding final finishes and installation hardware to prestressed components before erection helps reduce on-site construction time. Temporary shoring and bracing may be required during construction, particularly until the toppings have cured to service strength (if the structure is composite). Lifting loops are generally embedded in the precast pieces and then covered with the topping or cut off after installation.

### Envelope

For parking garages, the most common application of precast concrete frame, a weathertight condition is not needed; therefore, structural components can be directly exposed to the elements. Some aesthetic treatments can be cast in or applied to surfaces, but are not needed for moisture protection.

### Mechanical

In parking structures, the requirements for through-floor penetrations are minimal. However, holes or sleeves can be cast in the stems and flanges of the Ts, to allow for passage of conduit and piping. These holes and openings can be as great as one-third of the stem's total depth but must avoid the reinforcing tendons; openings toward the top of the stem in midspan and toward the bottom at the ends are most common. Preplanning of all openings is essential to minimize sitework and to realize the inherent economies of the system. Ts may be notched at the ends to permit passage of conduit along girders or bearing walls. Also, channels can be formed by chamfering mated edges of adjacent Ts at the upper surface, setting the conduit, then pouring a concrete topping slab.

### Interior

Most typical interior elements are not needed because of the open-air nature of the building type; however, all elements provided are attached directly to the exposed structure. In parking garages, the depth of the structural Ts and concerns for minimizing floor-to-ceiling height present special challenges for the integration of lighting and signs.

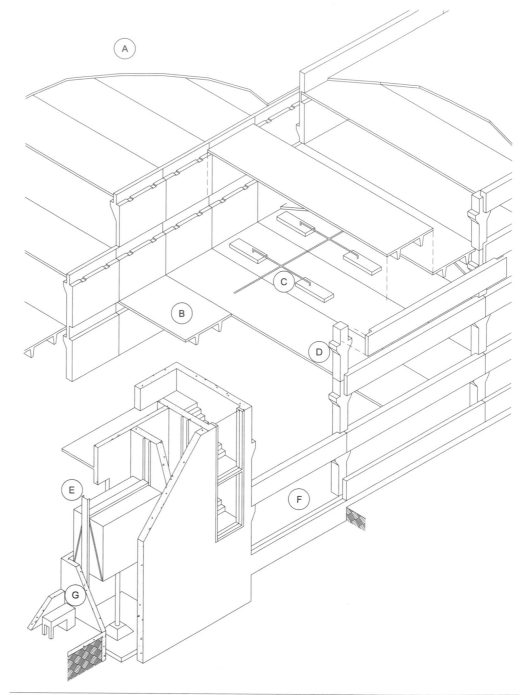

**PRECAST CONCRETE FRAME**

## SYSTEM SUMMARY

Precast concrete components are usually pretensioned. Pretensioning is a method of prestressing concrete in which steel tendons are stretched prior to placement of concrete and maintained in tension until the concrete is cured. The external tension on the tendons is then released to compress the concrete. This example employs prestressed columns, inverted T-girders, ledger girders, and double-T joists, all of the same length and design. Once the floor and roof Ts are set, the surface is covered with a thin concrete topping that provides the finished, weather-exposed surface and a horizontal structural diaphragm. The precast components are fabricated off-site and lifted into place by crane. Various finished surfaces are possible, and the unity of materials presents an opportunity for natural visible integration of elements. Thin brick or tile can also be used as a surface material.

*Richard J. Vitullo, AIA; Oak Leaf Studio; Crownsville, Maryland*
*Based on Richard D. Rush, AIA,* The Building Systems
Integration Handbook *(John Wiley & Sons, 1986).*

# FLYING FORM

**Legend**
A: Concrete masonry parapet backup
B: Built-up roofing and rigid insulation
C: Concrete
D: Ducts and diffusers
E: Suspended acoustical tile ceiling
F: Fluorescent light fixture
G: Window assembly
H: Metal stud and drywall assembly
I: Carpet tile
J: Under-carpet flat cable
K: Flat plate
L: Precast concrete spandrel panels
M: Slab on grade and concrete
N: Vapor barrier

## STRUCTURAL

Flying-form construction requires almost total regularity in structural bay widths. Flying forms can be used to construct flat slabs, pan-joist slabs, waffle slabs, and various types of beams-in-slabs. They are also used to form spandrels of varying configuration. Flat-plate or flat-slab construction is preferred, as this eases movement of the flying-form "table" and minimizes special additional forming. For flying forms to be economical, the building structural layout must be uniform, and the beams and spandrels should be very shallow.

There are three principal types of flying forms: *adjustable postshoring, manufactured truss forms, and column-supported forms.* Adjustable postshoring uses scaffolding that rests on a wood sill and blocking, which is raised by jacks. The forms are moved horizontally, usually by means of rollers, and are generally suitable for pours of up to 40 ft (12 m) in length.

### Envelope

As in the case of conventionally cast-in-place flat-plate concrete construction, the structural and mechanical systems are concealed from view, with the precast concrete envelope spandrel and glazing units connected to the structural frame. Flying-form construction, which requires relatively uniform bay widths, can have an effect on visible integration because it produces regularity in the rhythm of structural elements.

### Mechanical

In office applications, the high quality of the slab's finished surface lends itself readily to the use of flat wiring for power, lighting, electronics, and communications. Extra fire protection measures are unnecessary, as there are no through-slab penetrations to be sealed.

### Interior

Flying-form construction permits great flexibility in interior layouts and furniture arrangements. The use of flat wiring frees the electrical system from restraints imposed by the structure, permitting the furniture layout and power needs to remain variable until very late in the construction process.

## SYSTEM SUMMARY

Speed of construction, the economies realized through reuses of the forms, and the high quality of finished surfaces are among the most attractive features of this construction method. The systems employed with flying-form construction do not differ substantially from those found in other types of reinforced concrete con-

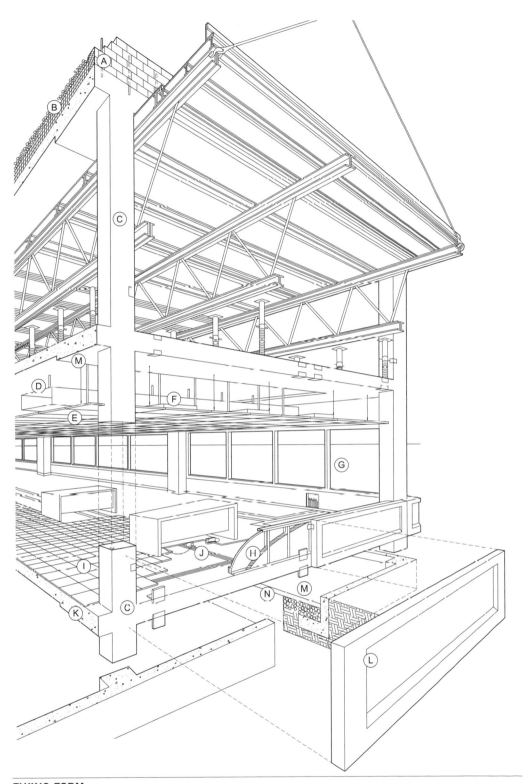

## FLYING FORM

struction; the difference lies in the method of forming slabs and spandrels and in the sequencing of pours. A disadvantage of the flat-plate construction system is the relative difficulty of punching through the slab or plate. An important consideration with the use of flying forms is the regularity of bay spacing and the absence of deep beams or spandrels.

During construction, the forms are placed and removed in a sequence of related operations, with temporary shoring used after form removal under the slabs until they have cured. The repetitive use of the forms can lead to conservation of both time and, of course, the materials used in forming. Mechanical and interior systems are meshed in the suspended ceiling assembly. The use of flat wiring atop the floor slabs for internal distribution of power, lighting, electronics, and communications dictates the use of removable carpet tiles and yields a set of requirements for interfaces with furnishings and equipment.

*Source: Based on Richard D. Rush, AIA,* The Building Systems Integration Handbook *(John Wiley & Sons, 1986).*

# TILT-UP CONCRETE

**Legend**
A: Skylights
B: Built-up roofing and rigid insulation
C: Steel deck and open-web steel joists
D: Ductwork in open-web bar joists
E: Radiant heat panels in suspended ceiling
F: Fluorescent light fixture
G: Window assembly
H: Precast concrete panels
I:  Resilient tile flooring
J:  Slab on grade and concrete footing
K: Rigid insulation

## STRUCTURAL

Load-bearing tilt-up wall panels provide a unified vertical envelope, structure, and interior. The panels are precast on-site, generally using the floor slab or grade as the casting surface, and tilted or lifted into position. The floor slab used as a form must be level, smoothly finished, and treated with a bond-breaking agent to permit easy separation of the cast pieces. The wall panels, usually 6 in. (150 mm) in nominal thickness, may extend from one to several stories in height, and must be designed to withstand the bending loads involved in tilting and lifting, as well as loads that will be encountered once in place. They may be plain, reinforced, or prestressed, and are often provided with temporary timber or steel "strongbacks" for tilting, particularly when there are large window openings.

The panels must be braced during construction until all wall and roof structural members are in place. Columns are usually cast in place following installation of the panels. In load-bearing tilt-up wall systems, the roof and floor members are bolted or welded to plates, and angles are cast into a continuous ledge beam. Roofing systems may be steel open-web joists, precast concrete Ts, or hollow-core planks. Flashing reglets and other roofing connection details can be cast with the panels.

### Envelope

Joints between panels should be designed to be concealed. This is easily accomplished where cast-in-place columns are designed to lap the panel edges or where the panels insert into a precast column channel.

### Mechanical

Because the slab on which the panels are cast must be smooth, utility raceways, pipes, and conduits that will penetrate the slabs must be stubbed below the finish slab level, covered during wall panel casting, and then uncovered for final connections.

### Interior

The site-cast panels are the load-bearing elements for the roof members and provide both interior and exterior finish. The building shell can be erected quickly, permitting interior work to proceed along with final joining and sealing of the envelope panels.

The clear spans produced by the bar joist roof structure and option for hung ceiling allow interior partitions to be placed virtually anywhere.

## SYSTEM SUMMARY

Tilt-up walls have been used routinely in a variety of building types and heights, especially for single-story buildings with large, uncomplicated exteriors. The sys-

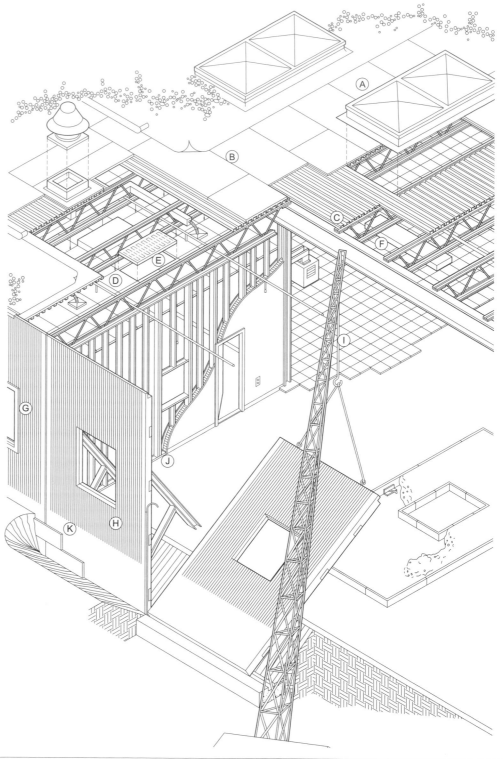

**TILT-UP CONCRETE**

tem is also increasingly used for multistory low-rise projects. Significant savings in time and formwork costs can be achieved, and long lead times required for precast or structural steel components are often averted. Because most of the forming and erection work is done within the floor slab area, tilt-up systems work well in confined construction sites.

Conservation of time and forming material is realized when there is uniformity in panel design and when the

floor surface can be used for forming. Careful planning of the forming, storage, and lifting sequence is essential, and early consultation with manufacturers and contractors is advisable. Regular inspection of casting and lifting operations is essential.

*Based on Richard D. Rush, AIA,* The Building Systems Integration Handbook, *John Wiley & Sons, Inc., 1986.*

# PART 2

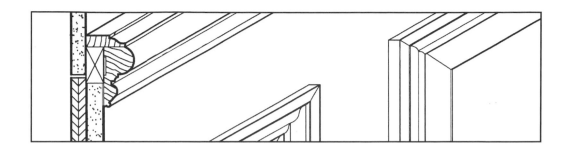

# INTERIOR BUILDING COMPONENTS

Vitruvius' second principle of architectural design is *firmness,* or durability. The building materials and assemblies commonly used in commercial interiors — and their successful application and installation — are described in Part 2.

The sequence and organization of the information in this section is based on MasterFormat™. MasterFormat is a master list of titles developed to organize information about construction requirements, products, and activities into a standard sequence. Effective communication among the variety of professionals required to design and construct is essential to the successful execution of a design MasterFormat is the organizational system used to sequence information in construction and furniture contract documentation, filing product information, and identifying drawing objects in the United States and Canada. MasterFormat was developed and is promulgated by the Construction Specifications Institute (CSI) and Construction Specifications Canada (CSC). MasterFormat, including the associated five-digit numbering system, is reprinted in its entirety in the Appendix.

| | |
|---|---|
| Masonry | Ceilings |
| Metals | Flooring |
| Wood | Wall Finishes |
| Plastics | Paints and Coatings |
| Finish Carpentry | Access Floors |
| Custom Casework | Fabrics |
| Countertops | Task Lighting |
| Architectural Woodwork | Window Treatments |
| Doors | Furniture |
| Windows | Conveying Systems |
| Plaster and Gypsum Board | Mechanical Systems |
| Tile | Electrical Systems |
| Terrazzo | |

# CONCRETE MASONRY ASSEMBLIES

## CHARACTERISTICS

Concrete masonry units (CMU) are modular building units composed of aggregate particles embedded in a cementitious matrix. Concrete masonry units, with high compressive strength, conform to ASTM C90, *Specifications for Loadbearing Concrete Masonry Units*. Load-bearing units and concrete brick are commonly used in building core and shell construction. Nonload-bearing units may be specified for partitions and are commonly used for fire protection of steel columns and fire-rated partitions.

## CONCRETE MASONRY UNIT TYPES

Type I, or moisture-controlled units, are specified to obtain a uniform degree of volume change due to moisture loss in a particular climate. The specification of Type I units facilitates the location of control joints. Type II, or nonmoisture-controlled units, may be more economical but will typically require closer spacing of control joints.

In addition to type, concrete bricks are specified by grade. Grade N is intended for use as architectural veneer and facing units in exterior walls and where high strength and resistance to moisture penetration and severe frost action are desired. Grade S is intended for general masonry where moderate strength and resistance to frost action and moisture penetration are required. Grade S is appropriate for use in interior construction.

Concrete masonry units are available in a variety of colors, sizes, textures, configurations, and weights, to accommodate design, detailing, and construction. Colors are now provided with lightfast metallic oxide pigments conforming to ASTM C979, *Standard Specification for Pigments for Integrally Colored Concrete*. The textures may be smooth, ground, split, ribbed, or otherwise prepared to maximize design versatility. Smooth finishes and more color options are available with prefaced, "integral glazed" concrete masonry units.

## SIZES AND WEIGHTS

Concrete masonry units are specified as width by height by length. They are manufactured in both English and metric modular sizes. English-size CMU is nominally 8 × 8 × 16 in., and actually 7⅝ × 7⅝ × 15⅝ in. with a ⅜-in. grout joint. Metric size CMU is nominally 200 × 200 × 400 mm, and actually 190 × 190 × 390 mm with a 10-mm grout joint.

The weight of the units also varies. Depending on the aggregate used, concrete masonry units are typically made using concrete with densities ranging from 85 to 140 pcf (1,362 to 2,243 kg/m³). The lighter units tend to provide more fire resistance and have an improved noise reduction coefficient; they often are more economical to place in the wall. Heavier units tend to provide increased compressive strength, better resistance to sound penetration, higher water penetration resistance, and greater thermal storage capabilities.

Concrete masonry walls should be designed and constructed with modular coordination, to maximize efficiency. Concrete masonry unit sizes should be considered when building a wall; the use of full- or half-length masonry units is desirable when constructing a concrete masonry wall.

## SINGLE WYTHE MASONRY

Single wythe masonry wall construction is common for many applications, both load-bearing and nonload-bearing and interior and exterior walls. These single wythe masonry systems are frequently used as interior partitions for fire protection.

Single wythe walls may be insulated on the interior or exterior. The insulation may be adhered or mechanically fastened directly to the masonry, or it may be installed in conjunction with conventional furring or studding systems.

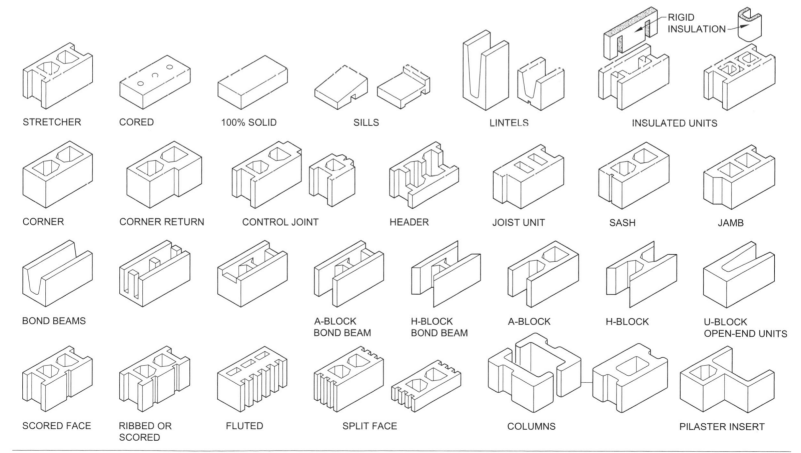

STRETCHER    CORED    100% SOLID    SILLS    LINTELS    RIGID INSULATION    INSULATED UNITS

CORNER    CORNER RETURN    CONTROL JOINT    HEADER    JOIST UNIT    SASH    JAMB

BOND BEAMS    A-BLOCK BOND BEAM    H-BLOCK BOND BEAM    A-BLOCK    H-BLOCK    U-BLOCK OPEN-END UNITS

SCORED FACE    RIBBED OR SCORED    FLUTED    SPLIT FACE    COLUMNS    PILASTER INSERT

**TYPICAL CONCRETE MASONRY UNIT SHAPES**

## DIMENSIONING CMU WALLS

Concrete masonry unit construction should be dimensioned and detailed to minimize cutting and fitting on the site. The module established for concrete masonry design is 4 in. (100 mm) vertically and horizontally. Maintaining this module reduces waste and provides ready coordination with other masonry products, as well as window and door openings.

Standard dimensions for concrete masonry units are equal to the nominal dimension less the thickness of one mortar joint of ⅜ in. (English) or 10 mm (metric). The nominal 8-in.- (200-mm-) high, 16-in.- (400-mm-) long concrete masonry unit has an actual height of 7⅝ in. (190 mm) and an actual length of 15⅝ in. (390 mm). When laid into a wall with a ⅜ -in. (10-mm) mortar joint, the unit always occupies an area of 8 by 16 in. (200 by 400 mm).

### Outside Corner to Outside Corner Measurement

From the outside corner to the outside corner, a CMU wall has one fewer mortar joint than it has blocks. To calculate the actual length of the wall, the width of a mortar joint (⅜ in. (10 mm)) must be deducted from the nominal length of the wall.

### Outside Corner to Inside Corner Measurement

Between an outside corner and an inside corner, a CMU wall has the same number of mortar joints and blocks. The length of the wall will be an exact multiple of 8 in. (200 mm) and the actual length is the same as the nominal length of the wall.

### Inside Corner to Inside Corner and Opening Measurements

From inside corner to inside corner, a CMU wall has one more mortar joint than it has blocks. The actual dimension is ⅜ in. (10 mm) more than the nominal dimension.

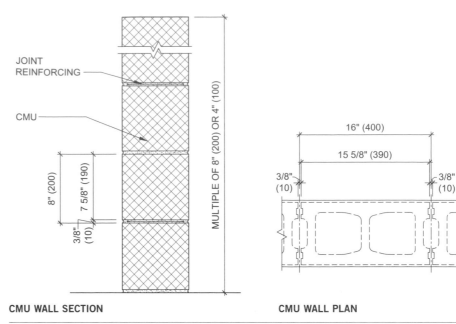

**CMU WALL SECTION**                **CMU WALL PLAN**

**SINGLE WYTHE CONCRETE MASONRY UNIT WALL**

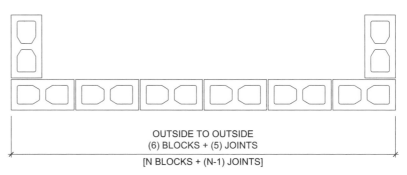

OUTSIDE TO OUTSIDE
(6) BLOCKS + (5) JOINTS

[N BLOCKS + (N-1) JOINTS]

**OUTSIDE CORNER TO OUTSIDE CORNER MEASUREMENT**

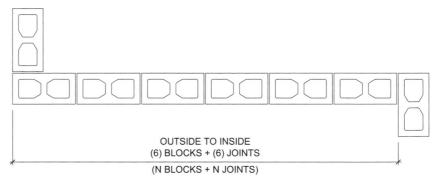

OUTSIDE TO INSIDE
(6) BLOCKS + (6) JOINTS

(N BLOCKS + N JOINTS)

**OUTSIDE CORNER TO INSIDE CORNER MEASUREMENT**

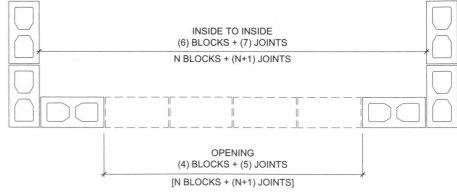

INSIDE TO INSIDE
(6) BLOCKS + (7) JOINTS

N BLOCKS + (N+1) JOINTS

OPENING
(4) BLOCKS + (5) JOINTS

[N BLOCKS + (N+1) JOINTS]

**INSIDE CORNER TO INSIDE CORNER MEASUREMENT**

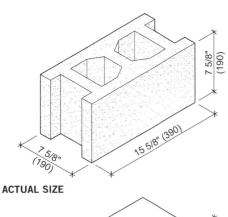

**ACTUAL SIZE**

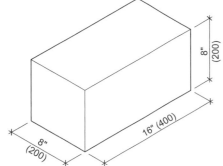

**NOMINAL SIZE**

**CONCRETE MASONRY UNITS (CMU)**                **CALCULATING CMU WALL LENGTHS**

## REINFORCEMENT

In many applications, single wythe walls are reinforced. The term *partially reinforced* is erroneous. Reinforcement schedules are designed for a particular application, and all the required reinforcement is necessary. Nonreinforced single wythe walls are used in interior construction where no loads, including lateral loads, or other forces are anticipated. Consult with the National Concrete Masonry Association and engineers to determine wall construction requirements.

Concrete masonry unit walls are often partially grouted; that is, only the cells or cavities of the wall containing reinforcement are grouted. When walls are partially grouted, special units or construction fabric are used for vertical containment of the grout. Horizontal containment is usually provided by mortaring the webs of the masonry units. When steel placement is frequent, it may become economical or necessary to fully grout the walls.

Structural components of a building using reinforced masonry combine the tensile strength of reinforcement with the compressive strength of the masonry to resist design loads. The benefits of incorporating reinforcement are improved ductility, structural integrity, and resistance to flexural and shear stresses. Reinforced masonry provides economical construction, especially when a high degree of resistance to lateral loads is necessary.

Seismic performance categories A and B require no special provisions. In many instances, the wind loads will govern the minimum reinforcing levels in seismic performance category C and above. For designs in seismic performance category C, vertical reinforcement of at least 0.20 in. (5 mm) in cross-sectional areas must be provided continuously from support to support at each corner, at each side of each opening, and at the ends of walls. Horizontal reinforcement of not less than 0.20 in. (5 mm) must be provided at the bottom and top of all openings and extend not less than 24 in. (610 mm) nor less than 40 bar diameters past the opening. Horizontal reinforcement should be installed continuously at structurally connected roof and floor levels, at the tops of walls, and at the bottom of the wall or at the top of the foundation; maximum spacing is 10 ft (3 m), unless uniformly distributed joint reinforcement is provided.

For designs in seismic performance categories D and E, walls must be reinforced both vertically and horizontally. Requirements in addition to those for seismic performance category C include that spacing cannot exceed 4 ft (1,219 mm), except for designs using moment-resisting space frames, where the spacing of principal reinforcement must not exceed 2 ft (6 m). Also, the diameter of the reinforcement cannot be less than ⅜ in. (10 mm), except for joint reinforcement. Consult with an engineer and the National Concrete Masonry Association for information on specific project requirements for reinforcing.

Grace S. Lee; Rippeteau Architects, PC; Washington, D.C.
Stephen S. Szoke, P.E.; National Concrete Masonry Association; Herndon, Virginia
Brian E. Trimble; Brick Institute of America; Reston, Virginia
MASTERSPEC®; published by ARCOM; Salt Lake City, Utah, and Alexandria, Virginia

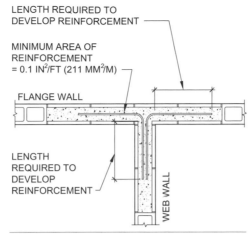

**INTERIOR BOND BEAM**
*Source: National Concrete Masonry Association; Herndon, Virginia*

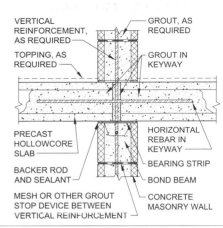

**CMU WALL/CEILING INTERSECTION**
*Source: National Concrete Masonry Association; Herndon, Virginia*

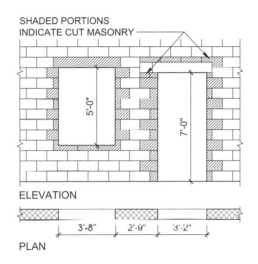

**INCORRECT**
Cut CMU units required.

**CORRECT**
No cut CMU units required.

**CMU WALL DESIGN AND CONSTRUCTION** *Source: National Concrete Masonry Association; Herndon, Virginia*

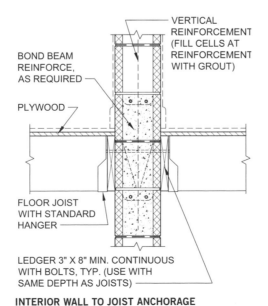

**INTERIOR WALL TO JOIST ANCHORAGE**

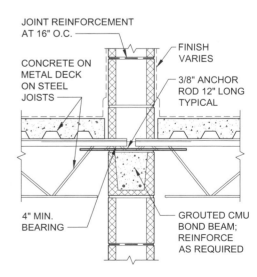

**CMU WALL TO STEEL JOIST ANCHORAGE**

**WALL ANCHORAGE DETAILS**

# GLASS UNIT MASONRY ASSEMBLIES

## CHARACTERISTICS

Glass unit masonry, commonly referred to as *glass block*, is a diverse building material whose many applications exhibit its multifaceted characteristics. The varying forms of glass block—type, thickness, size, shape, and patterns—along with the methods of installation can be combined to create unique design solutions.

Applications range from entire facades, windows, interior dividers, and partitions to skylights, floors, walkways, and stairways. In all applications, glass block units permit the control of light, both natural and artificial, for function or drama. Glass block also allows for control of thermal transmission, noise, dust, and drafts. With the use of thick-faced glass block or solid 3-in. (76-mm) bullet-resistant block, security can also be achieved.

An optimum mortar mix for installing glass block units is 1 part portland cement, ½ part lime, and 4 parts sand.

## GLASS BLOCK SUPPORT

When specifying supports and shelf angles, the installed weight and deflection limitation of the glass block should be considered. Local building codes should be consulted for limits on panel sizes or installation details.

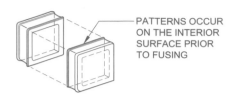

PATTERNS OCCUR ON THE INTERIOR SURFACE PRIOR TO FUSING

### GLASS BLOCK
The basic glass block unit is made of two halves fused together with a partial vacuum inside. Faces may be clear, figured, or with integral relief forms.

Glass block is available in thicknesses ranging from a minimum of 3 in. (75 mm) for solid units to a maximum of 4 in. (100 mm) nominal for hollow units. Metric thicknesses range from 76 to 98 mm.

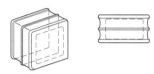

### SQUARE GLASS BLOCK
4½ in. × 4½ in.
6 in. × 6 in. (5½ in. × 5½ in. actual)
7½ in. × 7½ in.
8 in. × 8 in. (7¾ in. × 7¾ in. actual)
9½ in. × 9½ in.
12 in. × 12 in. (11¾ in. × 11¾ in. actual)
115 mm × 115 mm
190 mm × 190 mm
240 mm × 240 mm
300 mm × 300 mm
Metric sizes are available from foreign manufacturers through distributors in the United States.

### GLASS MASONRY UNIT TYPES

REGULAR        THICKSET

### THICK BLOCK
Some manufacturers provide thick blocks for critical applications where a thick-faced, heavier glass block is needed. These blocks have superior sound transmission rating properties. Their faces are three times as thick as regular glass block units.

INSERT OR EXTERIOR COATING

### SOLID AND COATED UNITS
Solid glass block units (glass bricks) are impact-resistant and allow through vision.

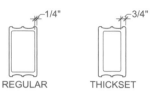

SURFACE DESIGN

### SURFACE DESIGN
Surface decoration may be achieved with fused-on ceramic, etching, or sandblasting. Glass block units may be split or shipped in halves if special decoration is to be applied to the interior of the unit. Blocks must then be resealed. Resealed blocks will not perform the same under various stresses as factory-sealed units. Placement in walls or panels should be limited to areas receiving minimum loading.

---

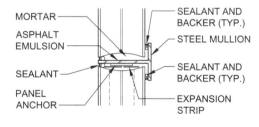

MORTAR — SEALANT AND BACKER (TYP.)
ASPHALT EMULSION — STEEL MULLION
SEALANT — SEALANT AND BACKER (TYP.)
PANEL ANCHOR — EXPANSION STRIP

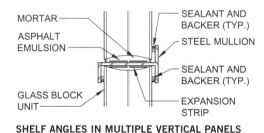

MORTAR — SEALANT AND BACKER (TYP.)
ASPHALT EMULSION — STEEL MULLION
GLASS BLOCK UNIT — SEALANT AND BACKER (TYP.)
— EXPANSION STRIP

**SHELF ANGLES IN MULTIPLE VERTICAL PANELS**

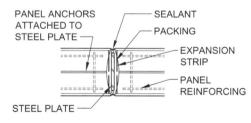

PANEL ANCHORS ATTACHED TO STEEL PLATE — SEALANT
— PACKING
— EXPANSION STRIP
— PANEL REINFORCING
STEEL PLATE

**SUPPORT IN MULTIPLE HORIZONTAL PANELS**

Panels with an expansion joint stiffener incorporating a concealed vertical plate should be limited to a 10 ft (3 m) maximum height.

## SECTIONS AT SUPPORTS

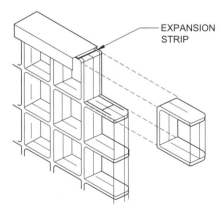

EXPANSION STRIP

End block units have a rounded, finished surface on one edge. These units may be used to terminate interior partitions or walls, or, when installed horizontally, as space dividers.

### END BLOCK

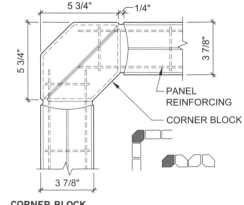

5 3/4"    1/4"
3 7/8"
5 3/4"
3 7/8"
PANEL REINFORCING
CORNER BLOCK
3 7/8"

### CORNER BLOCK
Selected manufacturers provide special shapes to execute corner designs. These units may also be placed together for varying patterns and forms.

3 7/8"
1 1/4"
PANEL REINFORCING
2 1/4"
2 1/4"
45° BLOCK

### SPECIAL CORNER SHAPES

Grace S. Lee; Rippeteau Architects, PC; Washington, D.C.

# STONE

## ORIGINS OF STONE

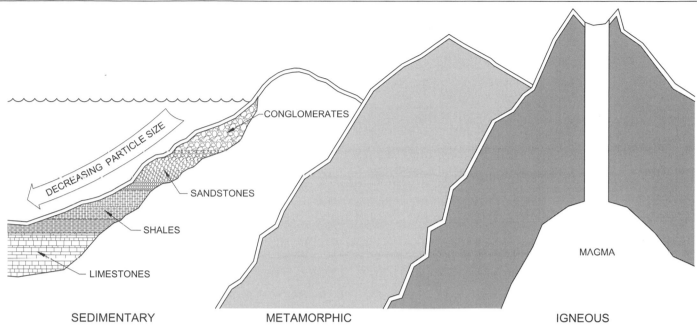

DECREASING PARTICLE SIZE

CONGLOMERATES

SANDSTONES

SHALES

LIMESTONES

MAGMA

SEDIMENTARY          METAMORPHIC          IGNEOUS

|  | SEDIMENTARY | METAMORPHIC | IGNEOUS |
|---|---|---|---|
| Origins | Erosion | Preexisting igneous or sedimentary rocks, which responded to pressure and temperature | Magma |
| Formed by | Accumulation of deteriorated igneous rock that was cemented, crystallized, and hardened with chemical solutions and biological deposits. | Sedimentary rocks that were subjected to heat, pressure, and sheer. For example, marble is a result of the crystallization of limestone or dolomite. Often more crystalline and dense than sedimentary stone. | The liquid of the forming earth's crust, which slowly cooled and hardened. Composed of quartz, feldspar, mica, and sometimes ferro magnesium minerals. |
| Appearance Characteristics | Sandy and uniform | Veined or cleft | Granular |
| Stone Types | Limestone | Marble | Granite |
|  | Travertine (actually a variety of limestone) | Travertine (sometimes classified with marble for polished surface finishes) | Gabbro (Plutonite) |
|  | Sandstone | Slate | Basalt |
|  | Bluestone | Serpentine | Porphyry |
|  | Brownstone | Onyx |  |
|  | Flagstone | Quartzite |  |
|  | Soapstone | Schist |  |
|  |  | Gneiss |  |

## TYPES OF STONE

Stone is classified in three categories, based on the manner in which it was formed: *igneous, sedimentary, metamorphic*. All stone originates with volcanic activity. Hot molten magma rises from the Earth's core and cools and hardens, forming igneous stone. Over the course of billions of years, igneous deposits are eroded by exposure to wind and rain. These eroded stone particles accumulate in lake bottoms and seabeds, forming sedimentary stone. As a result of extreme pressure, these accumulated eroded materials are consolidated to form sedimentary stone. Igneous and sedimentary deposits exposed to the shifting of the Earth's rocky crust or the pressure of the continual layering of material above can be transformed into metamorphic stone. Metamorphic stones often bear the evidence of these geologic shifts; for example, the swirling vein patterns in marble or the foliation of slate, the latter which gives slate its characteristic cleft face.

### Igneous Stone Types

*Granite* is a hard, durable, low-maintenance stone. It is a grainy rock that imparts a visual strength. Granites are composed primarily of feldspar and quartz. They

have a crystalline form and texture, appearing as aggregates in a uniform matrix.

*Gabbro*, referred to as *plutonite* in many European countries, is similar in texture to granite, but has a lower silica content, which yields more dark-colored stones. Black granites are often classified as gabbro.

*Basalt* is a fine-grained igneous stone that is uniform in appearance. Basalt colors are generally dark grays and blacks.

*Porphyry* stones are characterized by large aggregates or crystals within a finer-grain matrix. They are typically red, red-orange, or purple in color, and are often used in interiors as anchored or adhered veneer or as thickset pavers.

### Sedimentary Stone Types

*Limestone* varies in hardness, density, and porosity from one type to another. Their color range is limited to a neutral palette of buff and gray. More commonly used as exterior cladding for buildings, limestone is susceptible to staining and should not be exposed to excessive soil.

*Travertine* is distinguished by its natural cavities, formed by plants embedded during the rock's formation, which must be filled to achieve a smooth surface. Filling materials are typically portland cement, epoxy resins, or polyester resins. Although travertine is a type of limestone, some travertines that take a polish are classified as marble. It is popular for use as a flooring material because its grainy appearance conceals dirt much better than most other stones.

*Sandstone* is composed of quartz and is bonded with silica, calcium carbonate, or iron oxide. Iron oxides provide variation in colors ranging from yellow, buff and brown, to red. Some sandstones containing greater quantities of quartz are lighter in color. Related stone types include *bluestone, brownstone,* and *flagstone.*

*Soapstone* is very dense and very soft, which makes it easy to carve. The primary components of soapstone are talc and chlorite; talc gives soapstone its characteristic slippery feel. Soapstone is typically gray-green or gray-brown in color and is most commonly used as a countertop surface in interiors.

## Metamorphic Stone Types

*Marble* is identified by its variegated, veined surface, and is valued for its range of colors and luxurious surface. Marbles are comparatively soft, easily scratched stones that require dedicated maintenance, especially if a polished finish is selected. Marbles can be polished, honed, sawn, sandblasted, bush-hammered, split-faced, tumbled, and acid-washed.

*Slate* is formed from shale and clay. Historically used for roofing, slate is commonly used as an interior floor or wall finish. Slate splits easily into thin sheets. The finish resulting from the natural face is referred to as a *cleft finish*. Slate can also be sand-rubbed to a smooth finish, or honed.

*Serpentine* is similar to marble and is characterized by its green color and serpentlike swirls of color. It is dense, but not always hard, and is used in interiors for wall veneers, paving, casework, and furniture.

*Onyx* is a decorative stone, prized for its unique characteristics, including colored and banded patterns. Onyx is formed from quartz crystals, and the appearance can be enhanced by chemical treatment. There are many types of stone known as onyx, including chalcedony and agate. Onyx marble is a type of banded travertine, composed of calcium carbonate. Onyx is typically translucent, is relatively soft, and is brittle in its natural state. Treatment with resins can improve its performance and durability. Onyx is available in slab and tile forms. Applications for onyx include interior wall facing, flooring, tiles, decorative lighting, furniture, sculpture, and carvings.

*Quartzite* is formed from recrystallized sandstone, occasionally with slatelike planar characteristics. Quartzite contains silica, which contributes to this stone's density and durability and resistance to high traffic and selected caustic materials. Quartzite is available in honed, sandblasted, and split- or cleft-faced finishes. Due to its composition, quartzite is easily split; therefore, bullnose or ogee-type details may be difficult to fabricate.

*Schist* is essentially slate that has been subjected to further metamorphosis. It is often confused with granite because of its similar appearance; however, unlike granite, it is foliated, meaning it has a layered cleavage similar to slate. Schist is used as wall veneer, thinset and thickset paving, and in casework and furniture.

*Gneiss stones* are essentially schist stones that have been subjected to further metamorphosis. Gneiss stones differ from schist stones in their light- and dark-colored bands of mineral deposits and their mineral composition, which is primarily feldspar and quartz. It is used similarly to schist.

## Dimension Stone

Dimension stone is defined as quarried stone with usually one or more mechanically dressed surfaces. These are thick slabs of stone that are marked as they are cut for matched-pattern installations, such as book-match or end-match configurations.

Dimension stone tiles are less than ¾ in. (19 mm) thick. They provide the natural beauty of a stone surface without the weight, depth, and expense of dimension stone. However, their thinness makes stone floor tiles more prone to cracking from impact or normal floor deflection. Stone tiles are installed either by the thick-bed or the thinset installation methods.

North American and European dimension stones are cut to different thickness standards. North American stone is sawn to nominal inch thicknesses; European stone is sawn to nominal metric thicknesses measuring 20, 30, 50, 80, and 100 mm (approximately $1\frac{3}{16}$, $1\frac{3}{16}$, 2, $3\frac{3}{16}$, and $3\frac{15}{16}$ in.). If standard European thicknesses are used for stone wall facing, standard North American wraparound door hinges may not fit accurately and may require modification or shimming. If imported stone is required, final cuts and finish work are generally performed by local fabricators.

## STONE FINISHES

The stone finish affects the perception of the color, texture, and slip resistance of stone flooring. Common stone finishes are as follows:

- *Polished finishes* are the most reflective. They provide a mirror gloss with sharp reflections, which brings out the stone's full depth of color and pattern.
- *Honed finishes* have a satin or dull sheen with little or no gloss. These surfaces are often good choices for commercial floors because of their slip resistance; however, they are susceptible to stain absorption.
- *Sawn finishes* are textures that are not processed after the slab has been sawn from the block of stone. The texture is typically nondirectional, and consists of circular markings and grooved surfaces.
- *Sandblasted finishes* are achieved by blasting the stone surface with sand to create a coarse, nondirectional texture. Interior paving stone with a sandblasted finish is inherently slip-resistant, although the texture will be worn down to a honed finish under heavy pedestrian traffic.
- *Acid-washed finishes* are produced by the application of acidic solutions to the stone surface to create a rustic texture. This texture is applied to calcium-based stones, such as marbles and limestones.
- *Thermal—also known as flamed—finishes* are achieved by the application of intense flaming heat to the surface of the stone. The finish texture is coarse and irregular, following the crystal structure of the stone. A thermal finish is generally lighter in color, and the stone characteristics are less pronounced than in polished or honed finishes.
- *Waterjet, or hydro, finishes* are created by the use of high-pressure water forces, which texturize the surface and highlight the color of the stone. Waterjet finish textures are between honed and thermal finishes.
- *Cleft-face finishes* are natural textures produced from cleaved, naturally foliated stones, including slate and quartzite. Textures vary according to the density of the stone; very dense stones will cleave in flatter planes than less dense stones.
- *Tumbled finishes* impart an antique appearance to the stone. Typically used on small stone blocks, the tumbling process softens edges and corners and rusticates the surface of the stone.
- *Bush-hammered and tooled finishes* are created by striking the stone surface with tools to create surface texture.
- *Split-faced textures* are similar to cleft-faced stone, but are used on stones that are not naturally foliated. Split-faced textures are created using either a guillotine or wedges, the latter which are power-driven into the stone.

Resource: Mark A. Chacon, Architectural Stone: Fabrication, Installation, and Selection, *John Wiley & Sons, Inc.*, 1999.

## STONE FINISHES

| | STONE TYPES | | | | | | | | | | | | | | |
| | SEDIMENTARY | | | | METAMORPHIC | | | | | | | IGNEOUS | | | |
| FINISH | LIMESTONE | TRAVERTINE | SANDSTONE, BLUESTONE, BROWNSTONE, FLAGSTONE | SOAPSTONE | MARBLE | SLATE | SERPENTINE | ONYX | QUARTZITE | SCHIST | GNEISS | GRANITE | GABBRO, OR PLUTONITE | BASALT | PORPHYRY |
|---|---|---|---|---|---|---|---|---|---|---|---|---|---|---|---|
| Polished | • | • | | | • | | • | • | | | | • | • | • | • |
| Honed | • | • | • | • | • | • | • | | • | • | • | • | • | • | • |
| Sawn | • | • | • | | • | | • | | | • | • | • | • | • | • |
| Sandblasted | • | | | | • | • | • | | • | • | • | • | • | | |
| Acid-washed | | • | | | • | | • | | | | | • | • | | |
| Thermal (flamed) | • | | | | | | | | | • | • | • | • | | |
| Waterjet, or hydro | | | | | | | | | | • | • | | • | | |
| Cleft-face | | | • | | | • | | | • | | | | | | |
| Tumbled | • | • | | | • | | • | | | | | | • | | |
| Bush-hammered | • | | | | • | | • | | | • | • | • | • | • | • |
| Split-faced | | • | • | | • | • | | | • | | | | • | • | • |

The stone finish affects the perception of the color, texture, and slip resistance of stone flooring.

# METALS

## PROPERTIES OF METALS

Metals are generally categorized by iron content. Ferrous (from the Latin *ferrum*, meaning "iron") metals consist mostly of iron. Steel is a ferrous metal. Nonferrous metals contain little or no iron, generally have good corrosion resistance, and are nonmagnetic. Nonferrous metals include copper and aluminum. Desirable properties of different metals can often be combined by mixing metals together to form alloys.

### METALS

| FERROUS (CONTAIN IRON) | NONFERROUS (CONTAIN LITTLE OR NO IRON) |
|---|---|
| Steel | Copper |
| Stainless Steel | Aluminum |
| Iron | Tin |
| | Magnesium |

## FERROUS METALS

### Steel

Steel comprises the various alloys of iron and carbon. More than 90% of the steel manufactured into finished products is carbon steel.

*Carbon steel* is iron that contains low to medium quantities of carbon. A higher carbon content increases metal strength and hardness but reduces its ductility and weldability. It is reasonably strong but has poor resistance to corrosion. Galvanizing is the application of zinc to the surface of carbon steel or steel alloys to prevent corrosion. The coating can be applied in one of two ways: *hot-dipped* or *electroplated*. Carbon steel is used in structural shapes such as welded fabrications or castings, metal studs and joists, fasteners, wall grilles, and ceiling suspension systems.

*High-strength, low-alloy (HSLA) steels* have better corrosion resistance than carbon steels, and they are chosen when weight is a consideration and higher strength is specified.

Typical elements used to modify steel include:

- *Aluminum* for surface hardening.
- *Chromium* for corrosion resistance.
- *Copper* for atmospheric corrosion resistance.
- *Manganese* in small amounts for additional hardening, in larger amounts for better wear resistance.
- *Molybdenum*, combined with other metals such as chromium and nickel, to increase corrosion resistance and raise tensile strength without reducing ductility.
- *Nickel* to increase tensile strength without reducing ductility; in high concentrations, nickel improves corrosion resistance.
- *Silicon* to strengthen low-alloy steels and improve oxidation resistance; larger amounts produce hard, brittle castings that are resistant to corrosive chemicals.
- *Sulfur* for free machining.
- *Titanium* to prevent intergranular corrosion of stainless steels.
- *Tungsten, vanadium, and cobalt* for hardness and corrosion resistance.

### STAINLESS-STEEL ALLOYS

| SERIES DESIGNATION | STRUCTURE | ALLOYING ELEMENTS |
|---|---|---|
| 400 | Martensitic (hardenable by heat treatment; ferromagnetic) | 12–18% Chromium |
| | Ferritic (nonhardenable; ferromagnetic) | 12–27% Chromium |
| 300 | Austenitic (hardenable by cold-working; nonmagnetic) | 16–26% Chromium and 6–22% Nickel |
| 200 | Austenitic (hardenable by cold-working; nonmagnetic) | 16–19% Chromium, 3.5–6% Nickel, and 5.5–10% Manganese |

### STANDARD DESIGNATIONS FOR STAINLESS-STEEL FINISHES

| FINISH DESIGNATION | DEFINITION | TYPICAL USES |
|---|---|---|
| **Unpolished or Rolled Finishes** | | |
| No. 1 | A rough, dull surface that results from hot-rolling to the specified thickness, followed by annealing and descaling | Furnace stacks, kiln liners |
| No. 2D | A dull finish that results from cold-rolling, followed by annealing and descaling and perhaps a final light roll pass through unpolished rolls. A 2D finish is used where appearance is of no concern. | Institutional kitchen equipment, furnace parts |
| No. 2B | A bright, cold-rolled finish resulting from the same process used for a No. 2D finish, except that the annealed and descaled sheet receives a light final roll pass through polished rolls. This is the general-purpose cold-rolled finish that can be used as-is or as a preliminary step to polishing. | Cookware, flatware |
| **Polished Finishes** | | |
| No. 3 | An intermediate polished surface obtained by finishing with a 100-grit abrasive. Generally used where a semifinished polished surface is required. A No. E finish usually receives additional polishing during fabrication. | Institutional kitchen equipment |
| No. 4 | A polished surface obtained by finishing with a 120–150 mesh abrasive, following initial grinding with coarser abrasives. This is a general-purpose bright finish with a visible "grain" that prevents mirror reflection. | Column covers, wall panels, furniture, sinks, storefronts |
| No. 6 | A dull satin finish having lower reflectivity than a No. 4 finish. It is produced by Tampico brushing a No. 4 finish in a medium abrasive and oil. It is used for architectural applications and ornamentation where a high luster is undesirable, and to contrast with brighter finishes. | Furniture (finish not generally available from stainless-steel producers, but can be obtained from metal finishers and may be applied to a product after manufacturing.) |
| No. 7 | A highly reflective finish that is obtained by buffing finely ground surfaces, but not to the extent of completely removing the "grit" lines. It is used chiefly for architectural and ornamental purposes. | Furniture (finish not generally available from stainless-steel producers, but can be obtained from metal finishers and may be applied to a product after manufacturing.) |
| No. 8 | The most reflective surface, which is obtained by polishing with successively finer abrasives and buffing extensively until all grit lines from preliminary grinding operations are removed. It is used for applications such as mirrors and reflectors. | Furniture (finish not generally available from stainless-steel producers, but can be obtained from metal finishers and may be applied to a product after manufacturing.) |

Source: *Finishes for Stainless Steel*, AMP 503, National Association of Architectural Metal Manufacturers (NAAMM), Chicago, Illinois, 1988, p. 5.

### Stainless Steel

Stainless steel is an iron alloy that is inherently corrosion-resistant because of the addition of chromium. The self-healing chromium-oxide forms a transparent film on the surface of the steel, preventing oxidation (rust). Stainless steels contain at least 11.5% chromium. Nickel or molybdenum is added when maximum corrosion resistance is required. Stainless steel is used in construction of handrails, floorplates, wall panels, hardware, fasteners, and anchors. Decorative shapes and statuary can be cast in stainless steel.

Stainless steel is not affected by mortar or concrete and does not stain adjacent surfaces. It is popular for use in commercial interiors as column covers and railings, hardware, wall panels, and numerous other products. Its durability, finish retention, and other properties also make it useful for equipment used in food preparation and other commercial equipment, furniture, accessories, and fine eating utensils.

There are three series designations for stainless-steel alloys:

- *Series 200* alloys contain magnesium in addition to chromium and nickel.
- *Series 200 and 300* alloys are austenitic (normally nonmagnetic).
- *Series 300* is more corrosion-resistant and is easier to fabricate and weld than any other type of stainless steel.
- *Series 400* does not contain nickel and is therefore less corrosion-resistant.

Although stainless steel is available in approximately 60 different alloys, Types 302 and 304 are most frequently used for both interior and exterior architectural applications. Sometimes referred to as *18–8*, these alloys contain approximately 18% chromium and 8% nickel. Types 302 and 304 are very similar in performance and appearance. The specification of Type 302/304 indicates that either alloy is acceptable.

# IRON

Iron and steel, and their alloys, are usually the most cost-effective metal choices for structural applications.

Iron that contains no trace of carbon is soft, ductile, and easily worked, but it rusts in a relatively short time and is susceptible to corrosion by most acids. A higher carbon content increases metal strength and hardness but reduces its ductility and weldability.

*Gray irons* are high in carbon and silicon content and are rather brittle; however, they are excellent for damping (absorbing vibrations). Applications include decorative shapes, such as fences and posts, gratings, and stair components.

*Malleable iron,* which is more expensive than gray iron, has been used for decades in applications that require great toughness and high ductility. This low-carbon white iron is cast, reheated, and slowly cooled, or annealed, to improve its workability.

*Ductile iron* is made by adding magnesium to molten iron shortly before the metal is poured into molds. The magnesium alters the surface-tension mechanism of the molten iron and precipitates the carbon out as small spheres instead of flakes, which make the iron casting more ductile. Ductile iron is less brittle, stiffer, stronger, and more shock-resistant than gray iron. Ductile iron is the fastest-growing segment of the metal casting industry.

Ductile castings using a special austempering heat-treating process offer much higher tensile strengths. Called *ADI castings,* they rival or surpass certain alloy steel castings in tensile and yield strengths.

*White-iron castings,* which are extremely hard and brittle, are used primarily in industrial machinery parts that experience high wear and require abrasion resistance.

*Compacted graphite iron* characteristics fall between those of gray and ductile iron. The properties of this metal are so difficult to control during production that very few metal casters manufacture it.

*High-alloy irons* are gray, ductile, or white irons with an alloy content of 3% to more than 30%. Their properties are significantly different from those of unalloyed irons.

*Wrought iron* is made from iron ore that is heated until it is soft but not melted. Wrought iron or steel is relatively soft, corrosion- and fatigue-resistant, and machinable. It is easily worked, making it ideal for railings, grilles, fences, screens, and various types of ornamental work. It is commercially available in bars, rods, tubing, sheets, and plates.

*Cast iron* contains a large amount of carbon, making it so hard and brittle that it cannot be worked into the required shape but must be cast into molds. The characteristics of the many types of cast iron vary widely among six basic groups: gray, malleable, ductile, white, compacted graphite, and high-alloy iron. Cast iron is relatively corrosion-resistant. Plumbing drainage pipes and ornamental rails for exterior applications are often made from cast iron.

# NONFERROUS METALS

## Aluminum

About 8% of the Earth's crust is composed of aluminum, making it the world's most plentiful metal. Unlike the ores of gold and silver, aluminum ore is not found free in nature. It is always chemically combined with other elements and must therefore be extracted.

A unique combination of properties make aluminum the most versatile metal. Aluminum is soft and flexible, allowing it to be easily fabricated. It is light in weight yet remarkably strong. Some aluminum alloys have greater strength than structural steel. Unlike steel, it is highly resistant to corrosion. Aluminum is an excellent thermal and electrical conductor; electrical wiring is often made of aluminum. Aluminum is used for door frames and hardware, interior window frames, horizontal louver blind slats, and contemporary furniture.

## Aluminum Finishes

Because it is inherently corrosion-resistant, aluminum often requires no special finish. A protective oxide film forms rapidly and naturally on the surface when exposed to air. Aluminum is, however, susceptible to attack by alkaline chemicals such as those found in concrete and masonry mortar.

Finishes are frequently applied to aluminum for decorative purposes. Conversion coatings are generally used to prepare the metal for painting, but can also be used as final finishes. Because aluminum's natural oxide film does not always provide a good bonding surface for coatings, the surface is "converted" to one with improved adhesion if a coating is desired.

The most common finish that is applied principally to aluminum and its alloys is the anodic coating. Anodizing involves passing an electrical current across a solution (most commonly sulfuric acid) in which the aluminum is immersed. The resulting coating is much thicker than the naturally formed aluminum oxide coating—as thick as 0.0012 in. (0.030 mm)—providing increased corrosion resistance. Anodized coatings can be transparent, translucent, or opaque, and can increase surface abrasion resistance without changing the surface texture.

## SUMMARY OF STANDARD DESIGNATIONS* FOR ALUMINUM FINISHES

### MECHANICAL FINISHES (M)

| As Fabricated | Buffed | Directional Textured | Nondirectional Textured |
|---|---|---|---|
| M10–Unspecified | M20–Unspecified | M30–Unspecified | M40–Unspecified |
| M11–Specular as fabricated | M21–Smooth specular | M31–Fine satin | M41–Extra-fine matte |
| M12–Nonspecular as fabricated | M22–Specular | M32–Medium satin | **M42–Fine matte** |
| M1x–Other | M2x–Other | M33–Coarse satin | **M43–Medium Matte** |
| | | M34–Hand-rubbed | **M44–Coarse matte** |
| | | M35–Brushed | M45–Fine shot blast |
| | | M3x–Other | M46–Medium shot blast |
| | | | M47–Coarse shot blast |
| | | | M4x–Other |

### CHEMICAL FINISHES (C)

| Nonetched Cleaned | Etched | Brightened | Conversion Coatings |
|---|---|---|---|
| C10–Unspecified | C20–Unspecified | C30–Unspecified | C40–Unspecified |
| **C11–Degreased** | C21–Fine matte | C31–Highly specular | C41–Acid chromate-fluoride |
| **C12–Chemically cleaned** | C22–Medium matte | C32–Diffuse bright | C42–Acid chromate-fluoride-phosphate |
| C1x–Other | C23–Coarse matte | C3x–Other | C43–Alkaline chromate |
| | C2x–Other | | C44–Nonchromate |
| | | | C45–Nonrinsed chromate |
| | | | C4x–Other |

### COATINGS—ANODIC (A)

| General | Protective and Decorative | Architectural Class II | Architectural Class I |
|---|---|---|---|
| A10–Unspecified anodic coating | A21**–Clear (natural) | **A31–Clear (natural)** | **A41–Clear (natural)** |
| A11–Preparation for other applied coatings | A22**–Integral color | **A32–Integral color** | A42–Integral color |
| A12–Chromic acid anodic coating | A23**–Impregnated color | **A33–Impregnated color** | **A43–Impregnated color** |
| A13–Hard coating | A24**–Electrolytically deposited color | **A34–Electrolytically deposited color** | **A44–Electrolytically deposited color** |
| A1x–Other | A2x–Other | A3x–Other | A4x–Other |

*All designations are to be preceded by the letters AA, to identify them as Aluminum Association designations. For example, AA-M12C22A31 specifies a nonspecular mechanical finish as fabricated; an etched, medium matte, chemical finish, with a clear anodic coating 0.01 mm (0.4 mil) or thicker.

**Third digit (1, 2, or 3) added to designate minimum thickness in 1/10 mils.

Note: Finishes printed in boldface type are those most frequently used on architectural work.

Note: The Aluminum Association (AA) and NAAMM use the same designation system for aluminum and its alloys.

Source: Finishes for Aluminum, *AMP 501,* from the National Association of Architectural Metal Manufacturers (NAAMM), Chicago, Illinois, 1988, p.16.

## Copper

Copper is readily available, easily fabricated, and corrosion-resistant under a wide range of conditions. Copper is not affected by alkaline chemicals and so is often used where metal-to-masonry contact is required. In interior applications, the greatest use of copper is in electrical wiring; it has the second highest conductivity of any material (silver is only slightly higher). Copper is also popular for use in plumbing supply pipes and fittings. Copper can be made harder and stronger by adding small amounts of tin.

Prolonged exposure of an untreated copper surface results in a brown and, eventually, green patina. A patina is a thin layer of corrosion resulting from oxidation. Polishing the surface to remove the oxide film can restore copper's appearance. The metallic surface can also be preserved by the application of a transparent coating.

## Bronze and Brass

Bronze was originally a copper-tin alloy, but the term today is used to identify other alloys with a bronze color, including aluminum bronzes, silicon bronzes, and leaded phosphor bronzes. Phosphor bronze is a copper-tin- phosphorus alloy; and leaded phosphor bronze is composed of copper, lead, tin, and phosphorus.

Brass, a copper-zinc alloy, is commonly used for door hardware and upholstered furniture tacks. Good thermal and electrical conductivity, corrosion resistance, and easy forming and joining all make copper and its alloys useful in construction. Some brass alloys may be called bronzes even though they have little or no tin in them. Common nonbronze brass alloys are commercial bronze (90% copper, 10% zinc), naval brass (60% copper, 29% zinc, and 1% tin), muntz metal (60% copper, 40% zinc), and manganese bronze (58% copper, 39% zinc, and 1% tin and iron). When a metal is identified as bronze, the alloy cannot contain zinc or nickel; if it does, it is probably brass. Architectural brasses and bronzes are actually all brasses; they are used for doors, windows, door and window frames, railings, trim and grilles, and finish hardware. Muntz metal, also called malleable brass, is a bronze alloy resembling extruded architectural bronze in color. Available in sheet and strip, it is used in flat surfaces in architectural compositions in connection with extruded architectural bronze.

Copper-based alloys characteristically form adherent films that are relatively impervious to corrosion and protect the base metal from further attack. Lacquer coatings can help retain the original alloy color.

## Lead

An extremely dense metal, lead is corrosion-resistant and easily worked. Alloys are added to it to improve properties such as hardness and strength. Typical applications of lead include waterproofing, sound and vibration isolation, and radiation shielding. Lead can be combined with tin alloy to plate iron or steel, which is commonly called *terneplate*. Care should be taken as to how and where lead is used because lead vapors and lead dust are toxic if ingested.

## Zinc

Although it is corrosion-resistant in water and air, zinc is brittle and low in strength. Its major use is in galvanizing (dipping hot iron or steel in molten zinc), although zinc is also used to create sandcast or diecast components. Major building industry uses are roofing, flashing, nails, plumbing hardware, structural parts, and decorative shapes.

## Tin

Key properties of tin are its low melting point (450°F (232°C)), relative softness, good formability, and readiness to form alloys. Principal uses for tin are as a constituent of solder, a coating for steel (tinplate, terneplate), and an alloy with other metals that can be cast, rolled, extruded, or atomized. Tin is most popular as an alloy for copper, antimony, lead, bismuth, silver, and zinc. Pewter alloys contain 1% to 8% antimony and 0.5% to 3% copper. Alloy metal in tin solders ranges from 40% lead to no lead and 3.5% silver.

## SUMMARY OF STANDARD DESIGNATIONS FOR COPPER ALLOY FINISHES

### MECHANICAL FINISHES (M)

| As Fabricated | Buffed | Directional Textured | Nondirectional Textured |
|---|---|---|---|
| M10–Unspecified<br>M11–Specular as fabricated<br>M12–Matte finish as fabricated<br>M1x–Other (to be specified) | M20–Unspecified<br>M21–Smooth specular*<br>M22–Specular*<br>M2x–Other (to be specified) | M30–Unspecified<br>M31–Fine satin*<br>M32–Medium satin<br>**M33–Coarse satin**<br>**M34–Hand-rubbed**<br>M35–Brushed*<br>M36–Uniform<br>M3x–Other (to be specified) | M40–Unspecified<br>M41–(Unassigned)<br>M42–Fine matte*<br>M43–Medium matte<br>M44–Coarse matte<br>M45–Fine shot blast<br>M46–Medium shot blast<br>M47 Coarse shot blast<br>M4x–Other (to be specified) |

### CHEMICAL

| Nonetched Cleaned | Conversion Coatings |
|---|---|
| C10–Unspecified<br>C11–Degreased<br>C12–Cleaned<br>C1x–Other (to be specified) | **C50–Ammonium chloride** (patina)<br>**C51–Cuprous chloride-hydrochloric acid** (patina)<br>**C52–Ammonium sulfate** (patina)<br>C53–Carbonate (patina)<br>C54–Oxide (statuary)<br>**C55–Sulfide*** (statuary)<br>C56–Selenide (statuary)<br>C5x–Other (to be specified) |

### COATINGS—CLEAR ORGANIC (O)

| Air Dry (General Architectural Work) | Thermoset (Hardware) | Chemical Cure |
|---|---|---|
| 060–Unspecified<br>06x–Other (to be specified) | 070–Unspecified<br>07x–Other (to be specified) | 080–Unspecified<br>08x–Other (to be specified) |

### COATINGS—LAMINATED (L)

L90–Unspecified
L91–Clear polyvinyl fluoride
L9x–Other (to be specified)

### COATINGS—VITREOUS AND METALLIC

Since the use of these finishes in architectural work is rather infrequent, it is recommended that they be specified in full, rather than being identified by number.

### COATINGS—OILS AND WAXES

These applied coatings are primarily used for maintenance purposes on-site. Because of the broad range of materials in common use, it is recommended that, where desired, such coatings be specified in full.

*Note: In this listing, finishes printed in boldface type are those most frequently used for general architectural work; those marked with an asterisk (*) are commonly used for hardware items.*

The Copper Development Association (CDA) and NAAMM use the same designation system for copper and its alloys.

*Source: Finishes for the Copper Alloys, AMP 502. Reprinted with the permission of the National Association of the Architectural Metal Manufacturers (NAAMM); Chicago, Illinois, 1988.*

## Nickel

Whitish in color, nickel is used for plating other metals or as a base for chromium plating. Nickel polishes well and does not tarnish. It is also widely applied as an additive in iron and steel alloys as well as other metal alloys. Nickel-iron castings are more ductile and more resistant to corrosion than conventional cast iron. Adding nickel makes steel more resistant to impact.

## Chromium

A hard, steel-gray metal, chromium is commonly used to plate other metals, including iron, steel, brass, and bronze. Plated cast shapes can be brightly polished and do not tarnish. Several steel alloys, such as stainless plate, contain as much as 18% chromium. Chromium does not rust, which makes chromium alloys excellent for exterior uses.

## Magnesium

Lightest of all metals used in construction, pure magnesium is not strong enough for general structural functions. Combining other metals such as aluminum with magnesium results in lightweight alloy materials used in ladders, furniture, hospital equipment, and wheels for automobiles.

## DISSIMILAR METALS

When dissimilar metals are connected by an electrolyte, a current, called a *galvanic current,* flows from one to the other. An electrolyte is any liquid that conducts electricity, for example, water. The current causes one of the metals to deteriorate, and this reaction is called *galvanic corrosion.* The threat of galvanic corrosion is greatest in exterior applications where materials are exposed to rain or high humidity. However, even in interior applications, galvanic corrosion is of concern. Dissimilar metals in contact with each other, including nails, screws, and bolts, must be coated with or separated by a nonabsorbent, nonconductive material.

## GALVANIC SCALE

**CORRODED (ANODIC) END/MORE NOBLE**

Zinc
Aluminum
Galvanized Steel
Cadmium
Mild Steel, Wrought Iron
Cast Iron
Stainless Steel, Types 304 and 316 (active)
Lead-Tin Solder
Lead
Brass, Bronze
Copper
Stainless Steel, Types 304 and 316 (Passive)

*Source: Sheet Metal and Air Conditioning Contractors' National Association (SMACNA); Architectural Sheet Metal Manual, 5th ed.; Chantilly, Virginia, 1993.*

Metals that are higher on the galvanic scale will corrode when electrolytically connected to metals that are lower on the scale. The metal that is more anodic will corrode, or lose material to, the metal that is more cathodic. The farther apart metals are on the scale, the more rapid the corrosion.

In addition to the dissimilarity of metals, the amount of metal also plays a part in galvanic corrosion. The less "noble" (inactive or inert) metal will more likely corrode severely if its surface area is small in comparison with the more noble metal. For example, aluminum (more noble) screws used to fasten a sheet of stainless steel (less noble) to a wall would present a serious corrosion problem in the presence of an electrolyte. But stainless-steel screws in an aluminum sheet most likely would perform acceptably.

## METAL FINISHES

There are two primary references for metal finishes: one for metal sheets and shapes and one specifically for hardware. Metal finishing for aluminum, copper alloys, stainless steel, carbon steel, and iron is described in the *Metal Finishes Manual* published by the Architectural

Metal Products Division (AMP) of the National Association of Architectural Metal Manufacturers (NAAMM). The Builders Hardware Manufacturers Association (BHMA) sponsors ANSI A156.18, *American National Standard for Materials and Finishes*, which establishes finishes for metal hardware.

A third reference for metal finishes is still in use by some manufacturers. The Department of Commerce, Commercial Standard CS22-40, used the designation "US" to define metal finishes. However, this standard was discontinued after World War II. For easy comparison, ANSI A156.18 lists the nearest U.S. equivalents to the BHMA designation.

## FINISHING PROCESSES

AMP 500, *Introduction to Metal Finishing*, describes the three basic finish types—mechanical, chemical, and coating—for various metals. Application environments, service requirements, and aesthetics together determine which metal finish or coating is best to specify. Finishes are usually selected for both appearance and function. Chromium plating on metal bathroom water faucets and handles or baked enamel on sheet metal lighting fixtures, for example, must be attractive as well as functionally protective.

### Mechanical Finishes

Mechanical finishes are accomplished by buffing, grinding, polishing, or otherwise texturing the metal surface for a specific appearance.

*As-fabricated finishes* comprise the texture and surface appearance given to a metal by the fabrication process.

*Buffed finishes* are produced by successive polishing and buffing operations using fine abrasives, lubricants, and soft fabric wheels. Polishing and buffing improve edge and surface finishes and render many types of cast parts more durable, efficient, and safe.

*Patterned finishes* are available in various textures and designs. They are produced by passing an as-fabricated sheet between two matched-design rollers, embossing patterns on both sides of the sheet, or between a smooth roll and a design roll, embossing or coining on one side of the sheet only.

*Directional textured finishes* are produced by making tiny parallel scratches on the metal surface using a belt or wheel and fine abrasive or by hand-rubbing with steel wool. Metal treated this way has a smooth, satiny sheen.

*Peened finishes* are achieved by firing a stream of small steel shot at a metal surface at high velocity. The primary aim of shot peening is to increase the fatigue strength of the component; the decorative finish is a by-product. Other nondirectional, textured finishes are produced by blasting metal, under controlled conditions, with silica sand, glass beads, and aluminum oxide.

## GUIDELINES FOR SELECTION OF FASTENERS BASED ON GALVANIC ACTION

| FASTENER METAL<br><br>BASE METAL | ZINC AND GALVANIZED STEEL | ALUMINUM & ALUMINUM ALLOYS | STEEL AND CAST IRON | BRASSES, COPPER, BRONZES, MONEL | MARTENSITIC STAINLESS TYPE 410 | AUSTENITIC STAINLESS TYPES 302/304, 303, 305 |
|---|---|---|---|---|---|---|
| Zinc and Galvanized Steel | A | B | B | C | C | C |
| Aluminum and Aluminum Alloys | A | A | B | C | Not recommended | B |
| Steel and Cast Iron | AD | A | A | C | C | B |
| Terne- (Lead-Tin-) Plated Steel Sheets | ADE | AE | AE | C | C | B |
| Brasses, Copper, Bronzes, Monel | ADE | AE | AE | A | A | B |
| Ferritic Stainless Steel (Type 430) | ADE | AE | AE | A | A | A |
| Austenitic Stainless Steel (Type 302/304) | ADE | AE | AE | AE | A | A |

**KEY:**
A. The corrosion of the base metal is not increased by the fastener.
B. The corrosion of the base metal is marginally increased by the fastener.
C. The corrosion of the base metal may be markedly increased by the fastener material.
D. The plating on the fastener is rapidly consumed, leaving the bare fastener metal.
E. The corrosion of the fastener is increased by the base metal.
*Note: Surface treatment and environment can change activity.*
*Source: Nickel Development Institute; Design Guidelines for the Selection and Use of Stainless Steel; Toronto, Ontario, 1991.*

## Chemical Finishes

*Chemical cleaning* cleans the metal surface without affecting it in any other way. This finish is achieved with chlorinated and hydrocarbon solvents and inhibited chemical cleaners or solvents (for aluminum and copper) and pickling, chlorinated, and alkaline solutions (for iron and steel).

*Etched finishes* produce a matte, frosted surface with varying degrees of roughness by treating the metal with an acid (sulfuric and nitric acid) or alkali solution.

*The bright finish process,* not used widely, involves chemical or electrolytic brightening of a metal surface, typically aluminum.

*Conversion coating* is typically categorized as a chemical finish, but since a layer or coating is produced by a chemical reaction, it could be considered a coating as well. Conversion coatings typically prepare the surface of a metal for painting or for receiving another type of finish but are also used to produce a patina or statuary finish. They can be applied either by spray or immersion and provide temporary resistance to a mildly corrosive environment. They can be specified for gray, ductile, and malleable iron castings as well as for steel castings, forgings, or weldments, such as railings and outdoor furniture.

## Coatings

*Organic coatings* on metal can provide protection and serve decorative purposes. Protective coatings include primers or undercoats, pigmented topcoats in hidden areas, and clear finish protective coatings. General categories of organic coatings include paints, varnishes, enamels, lacquers, plastisols, organisols, and powders. Application techniques include dipping and spraying.

*Electrodeposition,* an increasingly popular alternative to spraying, is similar to electroplating, except that organic resins are deposited instead of metal. The coating builds up to a uniform thickness without runs or sags and can be deposited into the deeply recessed areas of a complex shape. The process of electrodeposition does not waste paint and emits low levels of volatile organic compounds (VOCs); however, it has limited coating thicknesses, and after the first coat, subsequent coats must be sprayed.

*Powder coating* is perhaps the best known, environmentally acceptable painting process. The paints are solventless, and therefore safer. Powdered paints are formulated in much the same way as solvent-based paints, with the same pigments, fillers, and extenders. Heat-reactive or "heat-latent" hardeners, catalysts, or cross-linkers are used as curing agents. Powder coatings are either thermoplastic or thermosetting. Thermoplastic coatings, which include vinyl, polyethylene, and certain polyesters, are melted by heat during application. Thermosetting paints undergo a chemical change; they cannot be remelted by heat. The thermosets do not require a primer. Coating powders include epoxies, polyurethanes, acrylics, and polyesters.

All three coating types are used extensively on aluminum. Carbon steel and iron require finishes to stabilize the metal surface. Copper alloys are commonly finished with both mechanical and chemical methods. Stainless steel is most frequently finished by mechanical means.

## METAL TUBING AND PIPES

Rectangular and square tubing is typically fabricated with from steel and aluminum. The metal tubing fabricated with sharp corners is typically used for miscellaneous architectural metalwork.

Round tubing is measured by the outside diameter and the wall thickness by gauge, fractions, or decimals of an inch. Round tubing is used where a high-grade finish is required and exact diameters are necessary. Round tubing is available in steel, aluminum, copper, stainless steel, and other metals. Consult manufacturer's data for availability of materials and sizes.

Round pipe is made primarily in three weights: standard, extra strong (or extra heavy), and double-extra strong (or double-extra heavy). Outside diameters of the three weights of pipe in each size are always the same: extra wall thickness is always on the inside and therefore reduces the inside diameter of the heavy pipe. All sizes are specified by "nominal inside diameter." Round pipe is available in steel, aluminum, and stainless steel. Consult manufacturer's data for availability of materials and sizes.

## METAL ANGLES, T'S, Z'S, AND CHANNELS

Miscellaneous metal angles, t's, z's, and channels are available in steel and aluminum. Consult manufacturer's data for availability of sizes and metal types for each shape.

*Betty Ng; Rhode Island School of Design; Providence, Rhode Island*
*Robert C. Rodgers, P.E.; Richmond Heights, Ohio*
*MASTERSPEC®; published by ARCOM; Salt Lake City, Utah, and Alexandria, Virginia*

## COMPARATIVE APPLICABILITY OF VARIOUS FINISHES FOR ARCHITECTURAL APPLICATIONS

| TYPE OF FINISH OR TREATMENT | ALUMINUM | COPPER ALLOYS | STAINLESS STEEL | CARBON STEEL AND IRON |
|---|---|---|---|---|
| **MECHANICAL FINISHES** | | | | |
| As-fabricated | Common to all of the metals (produced by hot-rolling, extruding, or casting) | | | |
| Bright-rolled | Commonly used (produced by cold-rolling) | | | |
| Directional grit textured | Commonly used (produced by polishing, buffing, hand-rubbing, brushing, or cold-rolling) | | | |
| Nondirectional matte textured | Commonly used (produced by sand- or shotblasting) | | | |
| Bright polished | Commonly used (produced by polishing and buffing) | | | |
| Patterned | Available in light sheet gauges of all metals | | | |
| **CHEMICAL FINISHES** | | | | |
| Nonetch cleaning | Commonly used on all of the metals | | | |
| Matte finish | Etched finishes; widely used | Seldom used | Not used | Not used |
| Bright finish | Limited uses | Rarely used | Not used | Not used |
| Conversion coatings | Widely used as a pretreatment for painting | Widely used to provide added color variation | Not used | Widely used as a pretreatment for painting |
| **COATINGS** | | | | |
| Organic | Widely used | Opaque types rarely used; transparent types common | Sometimes used | Most important type of finish |
| Anodic | Most important type of finish | Not used | Not used | Not used |
| Vitreous | Widely used | Limited use | Not used | Widely used |
| Metallic | Rarely used | Limited use | Limited use | Widely used |
| Laminated | Substantial uses | Limited use | Not used | Substantial uses |

*For more information, see the Metal Finishes Manual for Architectural and Metal Products, published by the Architectural Metal Products Division of the National Association of Architectural Metal Manufacturers.*

# WOOD

## WOOD CLASSIFICATION

Tree species are divided into two classes—softwood and hardwood—but these terms do not describe a wood's hardness or density. Basswood, for example, is classified as a hardwood but is actually relatively easy to cut or scratch. Softwoods are defined as coniferous trees, evergreens that have needles instead of leaves. Softwoods, by far the more widely used type of wood, are used as framing lumber and in decorative moldings. Hardwoods are from deciduous trees, which have broad leaves that are shed each winter; these include fruit and nut trees. Hardwoods are often used as flooring and furniture components.

## WOOD HARVESTING

In response to environmental and lumber availability concerns, wood harvesting of many tree species has undergone change. Some woods, such as teak, are grown on regulated tree farms. Pine trees have been specifically grown for lumber for decades. If wood sources are of concern, an investigation of the source and related lumber practices may be useful.

## SOLID WOOD AND WOOD COMPOSITE PANELS

Several different wood products are available for use in interior construction and furniture manufacturing. The traditional solid wood is giving way to the consistency and affordability of a variety of wood composite panels such as particleboard, plywood, medium-density fiberboard, and hardboard.

### Solid Wood

Solid wood is used where durability and strength are of concern, for example, in countertop or table edges and chair legs. Unlike veneers or plastic laminates, which must be replaced when damaged, solid wood can be sanded down and refinished. The method by which wood is sawed affects its appearance and usability.

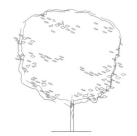

**CONIFEROUS TREE**      **DECIDUOUS TREE**

**CONIFEROUS NEEDLES**      **DECIDUOUS LEAF**

### CONIFEROUS (SOFTWOOD) AND DECIDUOUS (HARDWOOD) TREES

*Plain-sawn* is the most common type of sawn lumber. It produces the least waste and requires the least labor. The cuts are made tangentially to the annual growth rings, which, when viewed from the end of the board, are 30° or less to the face of the board.

*Quarter-sawn lumber,* available in certain species, is more costly to produce than plain sawn. The growth rings, when viewed from the end of the board, are 60° to 90° to the face of the board. Quarter-sawn lumber is often preferred for wood flooring; because of its uniform surface, it tends to wear more evenly.

*Rift-sawn lumber* is cut with the growth rings at 30 to 60 degrees to the face of the board. In certain species, primarily oak, rift sawing produces flecks on the surface of the board.

### Wood Composite Panels

Decreasing supplies of prime timber may continue to increase the popularity of wood composite panels. These boards are known not for their appearance, but for their performance and affordability.

### Particleboard

Particleboard is manufactured from wood particles or fibers, which are bonded under heat and pressure with an adhesive resin. The wood particles can be viewed easily by examining a piece of particleboard. Its surface is relatively smooth and hard and can hold a shaped edge fairly well. It is one of the most dimensionally stable of the cellulosic boards. Exposed particleboard edges are usually covered, often with a solid wood edging, to improve their appearance. The edges offer poor screw-holding capability.

Particleboard is the most commonly specified substrate for decorative laminates. It is also popular for use as kitchen cabinet shelving and as a flooring underlayment. ANSI A 208.1, *Wood Particleboard,* sponsored by the National Particleboard Association (NPA), establishes the minimum performance requirements for particleboard.

## HARDWOODS AND SOFTWOODS

| SPECIES | SOFT-WOOD | HARD-WOOD | HARD-NESS |
|---|---|---|---|
| Ash | | — | Hard |
| Basswood | | — | Soft |
| Beech | | — | Hard |
| Birch, Yellow | | — | Hard |
| Cedar, Western Red | — | | Soft |
| Cherry, American Black | | — | Hard |
| Fir, Douglas | — | | Medium |
| Hickory | | — | Very hard |
| Maple, Hard | | — | Very hard |
| Maple, Soft—"Natural" | | — | Medium |
| Oak, English Brown | | — | Hard |
| Oak, Red | | — | Hard |
| Oak, White | | — | Hard |
| Pecan | | — | Hard |
| Pine, Ponderosa | — | | Medium |
| Pine, Southern Yellow | — | | Medium |
| Redwood | — | | Soft |
| Teak | | — | Hard |
| Walnut, American Black | | — | Hard |

*Source: AWI, Architectural Woodwork Institute; Reston, Virginia*

## PARTICLEBOARD INTERIOR APPLICATIONS

| APPLICATION | GRADE (ANSI A208.1) | PRODUCT REFERENCES |
|---|---|---|
| Floor Underlayment | M-1 | ICBO, SBCCI, BOCA, One- and Two-Family Dwelling Code |
| Shelving | M-1 M-2 M-3 | |
| Countertops | M-2 M-3 | ANSI A161.1 |
| Kitchen Cabinets | M-S M-2 | ANSI A161.1 |
| Door Cores | LD-1 | MWWDA Industry Series IS 1 (*Wood Flush Doors*) |
| Stair Treads | M-3 | HUD/FHA UM 70a |
| Moldings | M-3 | WWMMP Standard WM 2 |

*Source: National Particleboard Association; Buyer's and Specifier's Guide to Particleboard and MDF, 1994–95.*

## PARTIAL LIST OF REQUIREMENTS IN ANSI A 208.1, *WOOD PARTICLEBOARD*

**REQUIREMENTS FOR GRADES OF TYPE 1 WOOD PARTICLEBOARD (FOR INTERIOR APPLICATIONS)**

| GRADE | HARDNESS | GENERAL USES |
|---|---|---|
| 1-H-1 | 500 | High-density industrial products |
| 1-H-2 | 1000 | |
| 1-H-3 | 1500 | |
| 1-M-1 | 500 | Underlayment, commercial |
| 1-M-2 | 500 | Industrial |
| 1-M-3 | 500 | Industrial |
| 1-M-S | 500 | Commercial, industrial |
| 1-LD-1 | NS | Door core |
| 1-LD-2 | NS | Door core |

*H—High nominal density (above 50 lbs/sq ft (240 kg/sq m ))*
*M—Medium nominal density (40 to 50 lbs/sq ft (200 to 240 kg/sq m ))*
*LD—Lower nominal density (less than 40 lbs/sq ft (200 kg/sq m ))*

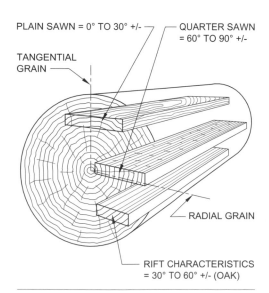

PLAIN SAWN = 0° TO 30° +/-      QUARTER SAWN = 60° TO 90° +/-

TANGENTIAL GRAIN

RADIAL GRAIN

RIFT CHARACTERISTICS = 30° TO 60° +/- (OAK)

## METHODS OF SAWING WOOD

*Source: Architectural Woodwork Institute; Reston, Virginia*

## Plywood

Plywood is a sandwich of wood or wood products between two layers of wood veneer, top and bottom. Particleboard and medium-density fiberboard (MDF) are commonly used as a core for plywood. Layers of wood veneer or solid lumber can also be used. There are generally two categories of plywood: that which is faced with hardwood and used for decorative purposes and that which is used for underlayment or other concealed construction applications.

Construction-grade plywood is graded and marked according to product standard PS 1, *Construction and Industrial Plywood,* promulgated by the U.S. Department of Commerce, National Institute of Standards and Technology (NIST), in cooperation with the American Plywood Association (APA). Construction-grade plywood is rated and marked according to application, exposure (whether appropriate for interior or exterior use), and thickness.

Hardwood veneer plywood is used extensively in the manufacturing of furniture and decorative wall paneling. The Hardwood Plywood Manufacturers Association (HPMA) sponsors ANSI HP-1, *Hardwood and Decorative Plywood.* This standard classifies hardwood veneer plywood by species, grade of veneers, type of plywood, composition of the plywood panel, and size and thickness.

### Medium-Density Fiberboard (MDF)

Medium-density fiberboard (MDF) is manufactured by breaking down wood particles into fibers through the use of steam pressure. The resulting fibers are mixed with an adhesive resin and pressed into MDF panels. The fineness of the fibers used in MDF determines its homogeneous appearance and very smooth surface. The panel edge allows intricate machining, and the face can be embossed to produce three-dimensional cabinet door fronts and moldings. MDF is also used as a substrate for decorative laminates.

## ANSI HP CLASSIFICATION CATEGORIES FOR HARDWOOD AND DECORATIVE PLYWOOD

### SPECIES

Seventy-one species are classified in four categories (A, B, C, and D), based primarily on their modulus of elasticity and specific gravity.

### GRADES OF VENEERS

| | |
|---|---|
| Face Grades (Grade AA permits the fewest number of natural characteristics; more and larger flaws are permitted in each successive grade.) | Grades AA, A, B, C, D, E |
| Specialty Grade | SP |
| Back Grades | 1, 2, 3, and 4 |
| Inner Ply Grades | J, K, L, and M |

### TYPES OF PLYWOOD

(Listed in descending order of the bond water-resistance.)

| |
|---|
| Technical (Exterior) |
| Type 1 (Exterior) |
| Type 2 (Interior) |

### CONSTRUCTIONS (BASED ON THE KIND OF CORE)

| |
|---|
| Hardwood veneer core |
| Softwood veneer core |
| Hardwood lumber core |
| Softwood lumber core |
| Particleboard core |
| Medium-density fiberboard (MDF) core |
| Hardboard core |
| Special core |

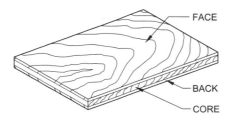

**THREE-PLY VENEER CORE CONSTRUCTION**

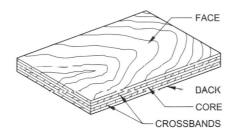

**FIVE-PLY VENEER CORE CONSTRUCTION**

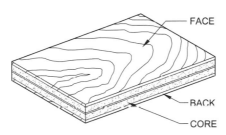

**THREE-PLY PARTICLEBOARD OR MDF CORE CONSTRUCTION**

## PLYWOOD TYPES

ANSI A 208.2, *Medium-Density Fiberboard,* sponsored by the NPA, describes the requirements for the strength and dimensional stability of MDF. MDF is available in different thicknesses and is classified by density and use (interior or exterior). There are four product grades: high-density; two medium densities, one for thicknesses greater than ⅞ in. (21 mm) and another for those of ⅞ in. (21 mm) or less; and low-density. As much as 95% of the MDF manufactured in the United States is medium-density grade.

### Hardboard

Hardboard is essentially a high-density fiberboard. It is made from the same type of fibers used in MDF but is bonded under higher pressure, often without an adhesive. Hardboard is commonly known by the trade name Masonite. The familiar pegboard is made of hardboard. Two types of hardboard are available: smooth on one side or smooth on both sides. ANSI A 135.4, *Basic Hardboard,* sponsored by the American Hardboard Association (AHA), defines five classes of hardboard. Class 4 Service panels are recommended as underlayment for resilient flooring.

## CLASSIFICATION AND MARKING OF HARDBOARD IN ANSI A135.4, *BASIC HARDBOARD*

| CLASS NUMBER | NAME | MARKING (NUMBER AND COLOR OF STRIPES ON BOARD'S EDGE) |
|---|---|---|
| 1 | Tempered | 1 red |
| 2 | Standard | 2 red |
| 3 | Service tempered | 1 green |
| 4 | Service | 2 green |
| 5 | Industrialite | 1 blue |

## WOOD FINISHING

Finishing operations include the application of stains and a protective topcoat. Finishing protects the wood surface from permanent staining by sealing the pores; it also guards against damage to the wood surface caused by heat, dirt, and spills, and enhances the beauty of the wood grain and color.

Concerns regarding volatile organic compounds (VOCs) have led to the development of water-based finishes. Recent improvements have increased the clarity and durability of the newer wood finishes.

### Stains

Stains are transparent or opaque coatings that penetrate and color a wood surface without masking its inherent grain. Stains can be used to change the color of a piece of wood. For example, mahogany is usually stained a deep red-brown to modify its natural light-orange color. Sometimes wood is stained to resemble a different species.

### Lacquers

Lacquers dry by the evaporation of their strong solvents. The solvents evaporate so fast that lacquers are typically spray-applied, rather than brushed on. Lacquers may or may not contain pigments and are the most popular commercial furniture and casework finishes. Acrylic and vinyl lacquers are available, which do not have a nitrocellulose base as do noncatalyzed and catalyzed lacquers.

Standard, or noncatalyzed, lacquers can be touched up easily or recoated, because the solvent in each coat slightly dissolves the previous coat, forming a monolithic finish. They are the most popular furniture finishes.

Catalyzed lacquers, like noncatalyzed lacquers, contain nitrocellulose. They dry faster than standard lacquers, so dust is even less likely to settle on the curing coat and contaminate the finish. Catalyzed lacquers are harder than standard lacquers and are moderately easy to touch up. They are very hard and brittle, and tend to splinter and spiderweb.

### Varnishes

Varnishes cure by evaporation of the solvents, oxidation of the oil, or both. Polyurethane, added to make varnish resistant to water and alcohol, is popular as a wood floor finish. Conversion varnishes, like the lacquers, are very durable and fast drying, forming thick coats. They have superb resistance to a variety of common chemicals.

### Polyester and Polyurethane Finishes

The contemporary, high-tech polyester and polyurethane coatings are known for their excellent chemical resistance and incredibly durable, dense, and smooth finishes. When pigmented, they resemble high-pressure decorative laminates. They require special skill and equipment for application and are expensive. Spectacularly shiny gloss levels can be achieved with these coatings. Polyesters are basically 100% solids when applied and are extremely difficult to touch up. Like polyesters, polyurethanes exhibit hardness and excellent resistance to chemicals but are much easier to apply.

# PLASTICS

Plastics comprise a widely diverse group of materials; worldwide, there are about 15,000 different plastic formulas available. Like metals, plastics can be alloyed (mixed) with other such materials to improve performance characteristics. Many plastics have long, multisyllable chemical titles, and manufacturers often devise trade names for better marketability. For example, polytetrafluoroethylene is best known by the trade name Teflon.

All plastics share three common traits:

- First, with few exceptions (silicone is one), plastics are based on the carbon atom.
- Second, plastics are derived from petrochemicals.
- Third, all plastics are *polymers,* which are giant molecules, composed of up to millions of relatively light, simple molecules. *Polymerization,* the formation of these giant chains, is basic to the formation of plastics. Polymers are characterized by high molecular weight, outstanding stability, and a strength of intermolecular force that prevents easy destruction.

## COMPONENTS OF PLASTICS

Resin (like polymer, an alternative term used for *plastic*) is the basic ingredient of plastic. Resins are combined with fillers, stabilizers, plasticizers, pigments, and other components to form plastics.

- *Fillers* are added to impart a certain characteristic property, such as durability or heat resistance. Some fillers, called *extenders,* may be added to decrease the amount of relatively expensive plastic required and to increase the mass of the product.
- *Stabilizers* lend protection against degradation of the plastic resulting from exposure to environmental conditions such as ultraviolet rays and even oxygen.
- *Plasticizers* are mixed with the resin to increase flexibility, resiliency, and impact resistance. The addition of plasticizers lends the required flexibility to sheet vinyl so that it can be rolled without cracking.

Plastics are commonly categorized as either thermoplastic or thermosetting materials.

- *Thermoplastics* become soft when heated and can be remolded repeatedly without affecting the properties of the plastic. Thermoplastics harden when cooled and require the addition of plasticizers to increase their flexibility.
- *Thermoset plastics* are permanently hardened after undergoing an irreversible chemical change during processing. Once they are set, they cannot be softened and remolded.

## THERMOPLASTICS

Thermoplastics generally offer higher impact strength, easier processing, and better adaptability to complex designs than thermosets. Thermoplastics commonly used in construction materials and furniture include acrylonitrile-butadiene-styrene, acrylics, cellulosics, fluoroplastics, nylons, polyolefins, polystyrenes, and vinyls.

### Acrylonitrile-Butadiene-Styrene (ABS)

Introduced in the late 1940s, acrylonitrile-butadiene-styrene (ABS) is very tough, but not brittle, and is resistant to chemicals and to impact. ABS is used in construction for plumbing drain, waste, and vent pipes. Outdoor furniture, drawer liners, and chair shells are common furniture applications for ABS.

### Acrylics

Acrylics have the clarity of glass, good weatherability, surface hardness, and chemical resistance. This material is lightweight and colorfast; it does not yellow with age. Acrylics are used for skylight glazing, safety glazing, and paint resins. Lucite and Plexiglas are popular trade names.

### Cellulosics

Developed in 1868, cellulose nitrate was the first synthetic plastic material. One of its early uses, in response to an ivory shortage, was in hair combs and billiard balls. Celluloid (photographic film) and cellophane (packaging material) are in the cellulosic family of plastics. The breakage resistance of cellulosics makes them ideal for table edging, venetian blind wands, signage, and store fixtures.

### Fluoroplastics

Common characteristics of fluoroplastics are outstanding chemical resistance, resistance to temperatures from 425°F (220°C) to 500°F (260°C), low coefficient of friction, and practically no moisture absorption. Polyvinyl fluoride (PVF) and polytetrafluoroethylene (commonly known by the trade name Teflon) are the most commonly used fluoroplastics in architectural applications.

### Nylon

Nylon was originally developed by DuPont in the 1930s and was first used as a high-strength fiber for women's stockings. Nylons offer high strength, toughness at low temperatures, and good wear and abrasion resistance. Nylon is probably best known as an extruded fiber in textiles and carpet. It is commonly used for chair caster rollers and drawer glides because of its low friction characteristic.

### Polyolefins

The family of polyolefins includes many popular plastics used in commercial interiors products, such as polybutylenes, polyethylenes, and polypropylenes.

- *Polybutylenes* (PB) exhibit good retention of mechanical properties at elevated temperatures and high tensile strength. The largest markets for PB are plumbing supply pipe, hot-melt adhesives, and sealants.
- *Polyethylenes* are known for their strength and flexibility. They are tough materials, have excellent chemical resistance, offer a low coefficient of friction, and are easy to process. Polyethylene is commonly used for electrical wire insulation. In clear sheet form, it is used as a vapor barrier. It is also used as molded seating, drawer glides, and door tracks.
- *Polypropylenes* are among the most versatile plastics and are employed in many fabrication methods. They are semitranslucent or milky white in color and have excellent colorability and chemical resistance, a high melting point, and are moderately priced. Fiber is a major market for polypropylenes. They are commonly used in upholstery fabric, carpet backing, and indoor/outdoor carpet fiber.

### Polystyrenes

Polystyrenes are inexpensive and easy to process. They are noted for their sparkling clarity, hardness, and extreme ease of processing. They have excellent colorability and are widely used for disposable fast-food packaging and cups. In the construction industry, polystyrenes are used for light fixture diffusers in sheet form and as the core material for doors in foamed, or expanded, form. For furniture, they are commonly used for wood-grain-patterned chair parts and mirror frames.

### Vinyls

Vinyls encompass a large group of plastics, including polyvinyl chloride (PVC) and polyvinyl butyral (PVB). PVC has good impact resistance and dimensional stability and may be best known for its application as plumbing pipe. PVCs constitute perhaps the largest volume of plastics consumed worldwide.

Since 1938, PVB has been used as an interlayer in safety glass; it is also popular for use as a textile coating. Within the interiors industry, materials such as floor coverings, window blinds, upholstery material, and wallcoverings are largely made of vinyl.

## THERMOSETS

Thermosets generally resist higher temperatures and provide greater dimensional stability than thermoplastics. Thermosets include alkyds, epoxies, furans, melamines, thermoset polyesters, and polyurethanes.

### Alkyds

Alkyds are classified as polyesters. Alkyd plastics are actually by-products of the alkyd coating industry. Offering moderately high heat resistance, alkyds have a rapid cure cycle and good mold flow characteristics, which allow them to be molded into relatively complicated shapes. Their most prevalent use in commercial interiors is as a paint coating.

### Epoxies

Epoxy resins react with curing agents or hardeners to form an exceptionally durable plastic. Epoxies have superior adhesion and excellent resistance to chemicals and corrosion. Their application in the construction industry is mainly as adhesives or protective coatings for floors and walls. Epoxy ester coatings are often used in floor and gymnasium finishes. Powder coatings, based on heat-cured epoxy resins, are increasingly popular as metal furniture finishes. Epoxies are an important component of solid surfacing materials such as Corian.

### Furans

Furan resins are naturally dark in color and turn black when catalyzed to cure. Their most common use is in corrosion-resistant cements and grouts. The floors and walls of such structures as manholes and processing tanks can be protected by furan cement.

### Melamines

Hardness, clarity, and stain resistance characterize the melamine family of plastics. Melamine surfaces are difficult to scratch or cut and they do not yellow with age. Most laminating resins for both low- and high-pressure laminates are melamines.

*Thermoset decorative laminates,* sometimes referred to as *low-pressure laminates,* are made by impregnating laminating paper with melamine resin and then applying it to a substrate (usually particleboard) under low pressure and low heat. The substrate is cut to the required size and shape, and the thermoset decorative laminate is applied, effectively sealing in the substrate. Polyester-impregnated paper is also used on thermoset decorative laminates. These panels are often used as interior panels and shelves in casework. They are not as durable as high-pressure decorative laminates, but they are far less expensive.

*High-pressure decorative laminates* (HPDLs) consist of a sandwich of melamine-impregnated overlay and decorative surface papers, over phenolic resin-impregnated

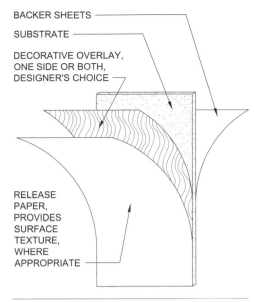

BACKER SHEETS

SUBSTRATE

DECORATIVE OVERLAY, ONE SIDE OR BOTH, DESIGNER'S CHOICE

RELEASE PAPER, PROVIDES SURFACE TEXTURE, WHERE APPROPRIATE

**LOW-PRESSURE LAMINATE**

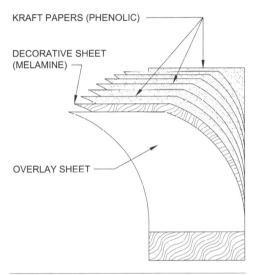

KRAFT PAPERS (PHENOLIC)

DECORATIVE SHEET (MELAMINE)

OVERLAY SHEET

**HIGH-PRESSURE DECORATIVE LAMINATE**

papers. These layers are pressed under temperatures exceeding 265°F (130°C) and high pressure. HPDLs are known by the common trade name Formica. Unlike thermoset decorative laminates, sheets of HPDLs are adhered to the surface of substrates, such as particleboard, which can then be trimmed and edge-banded.

The National Electrical Manufacturers Association (NEMA) publishes the standard for HPDLs—NEMA LD 3 *High-Pressure Decorative Laminates.* Before World War II, laminates were produced primarily for

electrical insulation. Although HPDLs today are used in a much greater variety of decorative applications, NEMA still promulgates the standard.

The four most common types of HPDL sheets are:

*HGS, formerly GP (General Purpose).* Used for most horizontal surfaces, for example, countertops. This type can be bent to a radius of approximately 6 in. (152 mm).

*CLS, formerly CL (Cabinet Liner).* A thin sheet used for vertical applications, typically inside casework, that will not be required to withstand heavy wear. (The cabinet liner should not be used as a balancing/backer sheet for countertops.)

*BKL, formerly BK (Backer).* Economical, nondecorative sheets used on the side of the substrate hidden from view to prevent warping as a result of changes in temperature or humidity.

*HGP, formerly PF (Postforming).* Used for tightly radiused curves, for example, at the edge of a formed countertop.

### Polyesters

Thermoset polyesters include a very large family of plastics. Polyester is commonly used with glass fibers to form *fiberglass. Alkyds,* used in paints and other coatings, are oil-modified polyesters. A *gel coat* is a pigmented polyester coating that is applied to the inside surface of a mold and becomes an integral part of the finished piece. Cultured marble countertops are fabricated with a polyester gel coat.

### Polyurethanes

Polyurethanes are available in a multitude of forms with an extensive variety of physical properties. Rigid polyurethane foam is widely used as a building insulation material. However, the most common application of polyurethane is for cushioning in seating and mattresses. Polyurethane foam can be molded for a preformed chair seat or back, or foam slabs can be cut into the desired shape.

### Silicones

Silicones are unique among plastics because they are based on the silicon atom, rather than the carbon atom. The raw material for silicone is one of the most abundant on the Earth's surface—sand (quartzite). Silicone is still obtained by a process developed by General Electric in the 1940s. Similar to the way in which iron is reduced from iron ore, silicone is obtained by the reduction of silicon dioxide in a furnace. Silicones are known for their stability through a wide range of temperatures, ultraviolet radiation, and harsh weather. They are used in commercial interior applications as water-repellent fabric finishes and joint sealants.

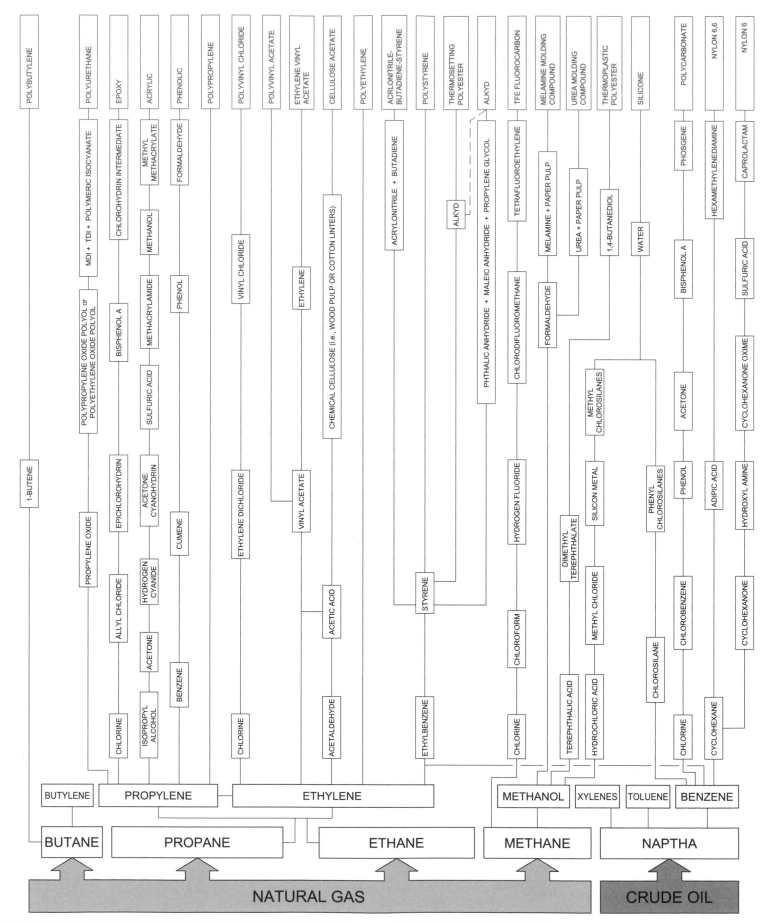

**DERIVATION OF MAJOR PLASTIC RESINS**

# UTILITY WOOD SHELVING

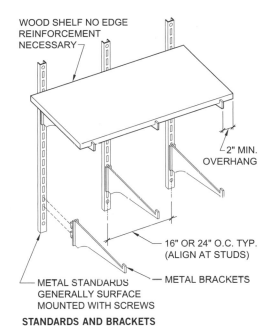

WOOD SHELF NO EDGE REINFORCEMENT NECESSARY

2" MIN. OVERHANG

16" OR 24" O.C. TYP. (ALIGN AT STUDS)

METAL BRACKETS

METAL STANDARDS GENERALLY SURFACE MOUNTED WITH SCREWS

**STANDARDS AND BRACKETS**

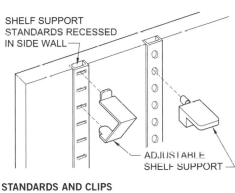

SHELF SUPPORT STANDARDS RECESSED IN SIDE WALL

ADJUSTABLE SHELF SUPPORT

**STANDARDS AND CLIPS**

**STANDARDS SHELVING SYSTEM**

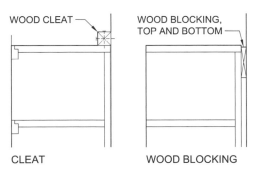

WOOD CLEAT

CLEAT

WOOD BLOCKING, TOP AND BOTTOM

WOOD BLOCKING

All details except hanging bracket and rail must also be floor-supported.

**BOOKSHELF WALL ATTACHMENT METHODS**

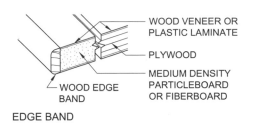

WOOD VENEER OR PLASTIC LAMINATE

PLYWOOD

MEDIUM DENSITY PARTICLEBOARD OR FIBERBOARD

WOOD EDGE BAND

EDGE BAND

**SHELF EDGE DETAILS**

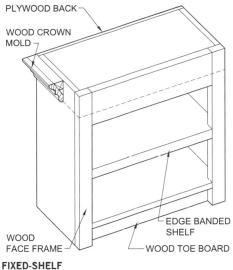

PLYWOOD BACK

WOOD CROWN MOLD

WOOD FACE FRAME

EDGE BANDED SHELF

WOOD TOE BOARD

**FIXED-SHELF**

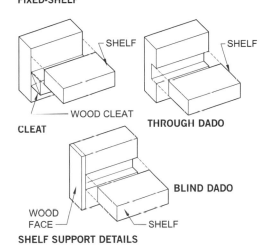

SHELF

WOOD CLEAT

**CLEAT**

SHELF

**THROUGH DADO**

WOOD FACE

SHELF

**BLIND DADO**

**SHELF SUPPORT DETAILS**

**FIXED-SHELF SYSTEM**

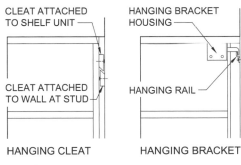

CLEAT ATTACHED TO SHELF UNIT

CLEAT ATTACHED TO WALL AT STUD

HANGING CLEAT

HANGING BRACKET HOUSING

HANGING RAIL

HANGING BRACKET

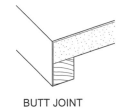

BUTT JOINT

SOLID WOOD

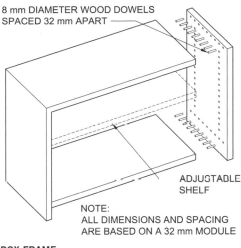

8 mm DIAMETER WOOD DOWELS SPACED 32 mm APART

ADJUSTABLE SHELF

NOTE:
ALL DIMENSIONS AND SPACING ARE BASED ON A 32 mm MODULE

**BOX FRAME**

PLASTIC OR METAL HOUSING SET INTO BOTTOM OF SHELF; HOUSING FITS OVER FIXING SCREW

8 mm DIAMETER HOLES FOR BOX FRAME CONSTRUCTION

32 mm O.C.

32 mm O.C.

SHELF SUPPORT PINS

FIXING SCREW

5 mm DIAMETER HOLES FOR REMOVABLE SHELF PINS

**32-MM SHELF SUPPORT SYSTEM**

METAL CAM INSERTED INTO FRAME WALL

METAL EXPANSION SUPPORT PIN SCREWED INTO SHELF

CAM SCREW

WOOD SHELF

**SEMIFIXED SHELF DETAIL**

**BOX FRAME SHELF SYSTEM**

BULLNOSE

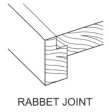

RABBET JOINT

*Helmut Guenschel, Inc.; Baltimore, Maryland*

**FINISH CARPENTRY**  □  **2**

# STANDARD CASEWORK AND CLOSET SHELVING DIMENSIONS

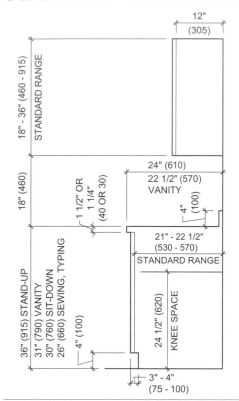

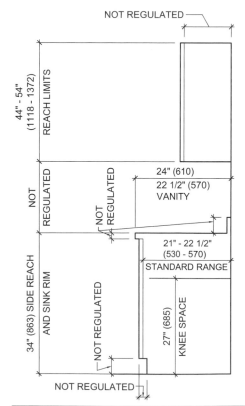

**WALL-HUNG AND BASE CABINETS**

**ADA-COMPLIANT WALL-HUNG AND BASE CABINETS**

*Source: Architectural Woodwork Institute;* Architectural Quality Standards, *7th Ed. (Version 1.2); Reston, Virginia, 1999*

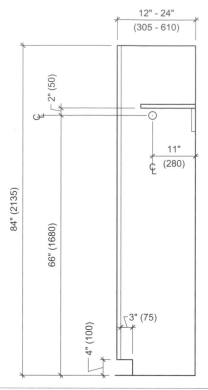

**CLOTHES CABINET**

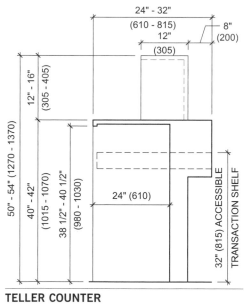

**TELLER COUNTER**

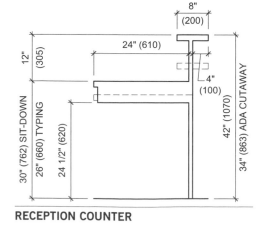

**RECEPTION COUNTER**

## CLOSET AND UTILITY SHELVING

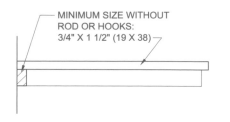

MINIMUM SIZE WITHOUT ROD OR HOOKS:
3/4" X 1 1/2" (19 X 38)

**SHELF**

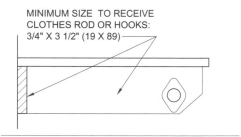

MINIMUM SIZE TO RECEIVE CLOTHES ROD OR HOOKS:
3/4" X 3 1/2" (19 X 89)

**SHELF WITH CLOTHES ROD**

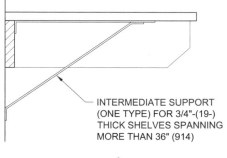

INTERMEDIATE SUPPORT (ONE TYPE) FOR 3/4"-(19-) THICK SHELVES SPANNING MORE THAN 36" (914)

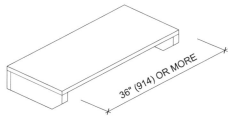

36" (914) OR MORE

**SHELF WITH INTERMEDIATE SUPPORT**

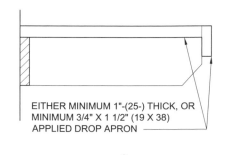

EITHER MINIMUM 1"-(25-) THICK, OR MINIMUM 3/4" X 1 1/2" (19 X 38) APPLIED DROP APRON

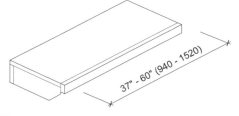

37" - 60" (940 - 1520)

**SHELF WITH APPLIED DROP APRON**

*Kelsey Kruse, AIA; George Vaeth Associates, Inc.; Columbia, Maryland*

# CABINET CONSTRUCTION

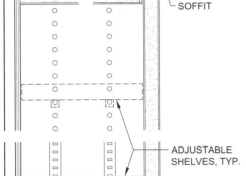

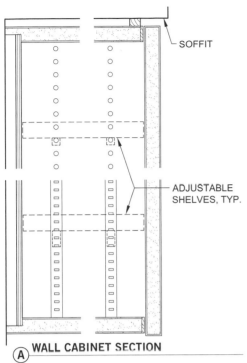

(A) **WALL CABINET SECTION**

- SOFFIT
- ADJUSTABLE SHELVES, TYP.

- PLASTIC LAMINATE COUNTERTOP ON MDF OR INDUSTRIAL PARTICLEBOARD
- DRAWER
- HARDBOARD BACKING, TYP.
- KILN-DRIED SOLID LUMBER OR PANEL PRODUCT

(B) **BASE CABINET SECTION**

## FLUSH OVERLAY CONSTRUCTION

Flush overlay construction offers a clean, contemporary look because only the doors and drawer fronts are visible in elevation. When specified, grain matching between doors and drawer fronts can be achieved by having all pieces cut from the same panel. This style lends itself well to the use of plastic laminate for exposed surfaces. Conventional as well as concealed hinges are available for a variety of door thicknesses.

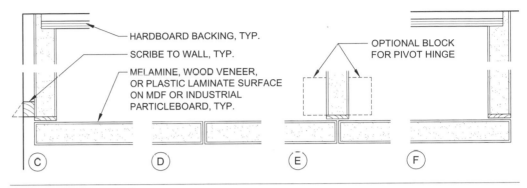

- HARDBOARD BACKING, TYP.
- SCRIBE TO WALL, TYP.
- MELAMINE, WOOD VENEER, OR PLASTIC LAMINATE SURFACE ON MDF OR INDUSTRIAL PARTICLEBOARD, TYP.
- OPTIONAL BLOCK FOR PIVOT HINGE

(C)    (D)    (E)    (F)

**WALL CABINET DETAILS**

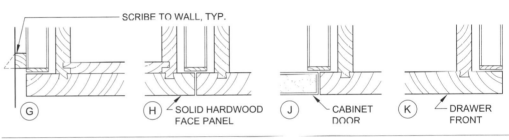

- SCRIBE TO WALL, TYP.
- SOLID HARDWOOD FACE PANEL
- CABINET DOOR
- DRAWER FRONT

(G)    (H)    (J)    (K)

**DRAWER DETAILS AT BASE CABINETS**

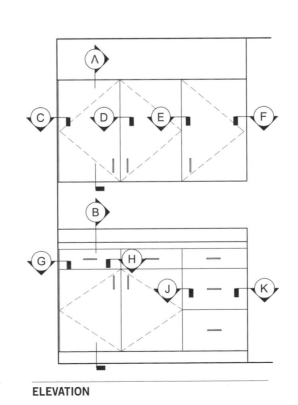

**ELEVATION**

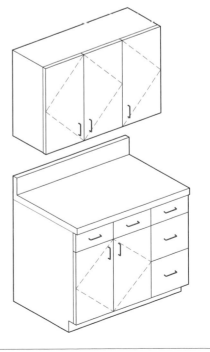

**AXONOMETRIC**

*Source: Architectural Woodwork Institute; Architectural Quality Standards, 7th ed. (Version 1.2), Reston, Virginia, 1999.*

**FINISH CARPENTRY** ☐ 2

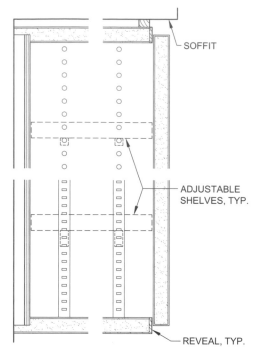

SOFFIT

ADJUSTABLE SHELVES, TYP.

REVEAL, TYP.

Ⓐ **WALL CABINET SECTION**

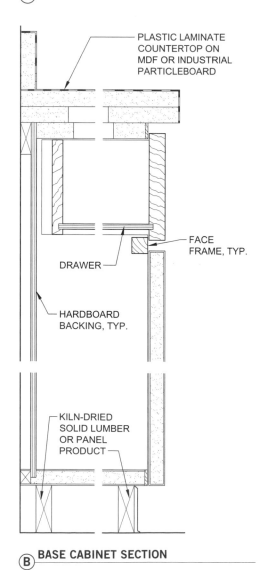

PLASTIC LAMINATE COUNTERTOP ON MDF OR INDUSTRIAL PARTICLEBOARD

FACE FRAME, TYP.

DRAWER

HARDBOARD BACKING, TYP.

KILN-DRIED SOLID LUMBER OR PANEL PRODUCT

Ⓑ **BASE CABINET SECTION**

## REVEAL OVERLAY CONSTRUCTION

Reveal overlay construction accents the separation between doors and drawer fronts by a reveal. This style is equally suited to either wood or plastic laminate construction. Although the detail shown here incorporates a reveal at all horizontal and vertical joints, this can be varied by the designer. A reveal of more than ½ in. (13 mm) requires the addition of a face frame, which will change the hinge requirements. With or without a face frame, this style allows the use of conventional or concealed hinges.

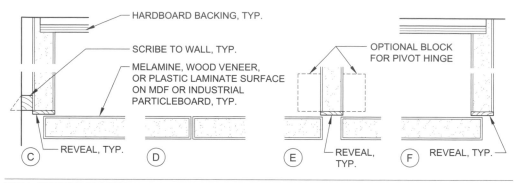

HARDBOARD BACKING, TYP.

SCRIBE TO WALL, TYP.

MELAMINE, WOOD VENEER, OR PLASTIC LAMINATE SURFACE ON MDF OR INDUSTRIAL PARTICLEBOARD, TYP.

OPTIONAL BLOCK FOR PIVOT HINGE

Ⓒ   REVEAL, TYP.   Ⓓ        Ⓔ   REVEAL, TYP.   Ⓕ   REVEAL, TYP.

**WALL CABINET DETAILS**

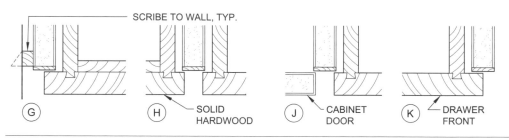

SCRIBE TO WALL, TYP.

Ⓖ        Ⓗ   SOLID HARDWOOD   Ⓙ   CABINET DOOR   Ⓚ   DRAWER FRONT

**DRAWER DETAILS AT BASE CABINETS**

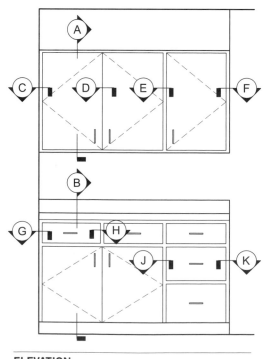

**ELEVATION**

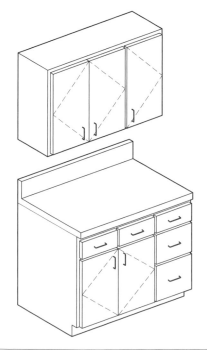

**AXONOMETRIC**

*Source: Architectural Woodwork Institute; Architectural Quality Standards, 7th ed. (Version 1.2), Reston, Virginia, 1999.*

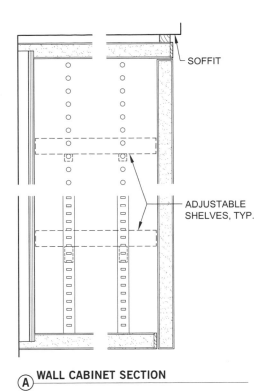

SOFFIT

ADJUSTABLE SHELVES, TYP.

**A** **WALL CABINET SECTION**

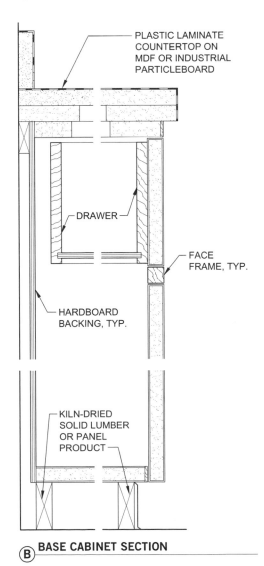

PLASTIC LAMINATE COUNTERTOP ON MDF OR INDUSTRIAL PARTICLEBOARD

DRAWER

FACE FRAME, TYP.

HARDBOARD BACKING, TYP.

KILN-DRIED SOLID LUMBER OR PANEL PRODUCT

**B** **BASE CABINET SECTION**

# FLUSH INSET CONSTRUCTION WITHOUT FACE FRAME

Flush inset construction without a face frame is a highly functional style that allows the use of different thicknesses of door and drawer fronts. Door and drawer faces are flush with the face of the cabinet. This is generally an expensive style due to the increased care required in fitting and aligning the doors and drawers. This style does not lend itself to the economical use of plastic laminate covering finishes.

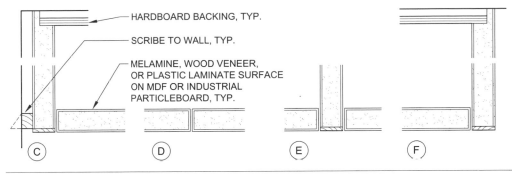

HARDBOARD BACKING, TYP.

SCRIBE TO WALL, TYP.

MELAMINE, WOOD VENEER, OR PLASTIC LAMINATE SURFACE ON MDF OR INDUSTRIAL PARTICLEBOARD, TYP.

C D E F

**WALL CABINET DETAILS**

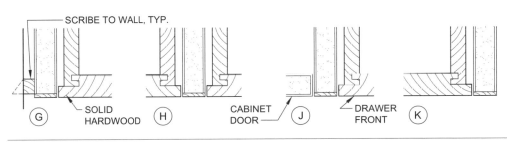

SCRIBE TO WALL, TYP.

G SOLID HARDWOOD H CABINET DOOR J DRAWER FRONT K

**DRAWER DETAILS AT BASE CABINETS**

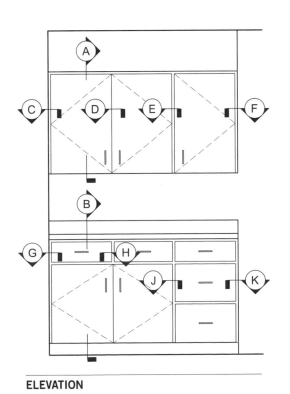

**ELEVATION**

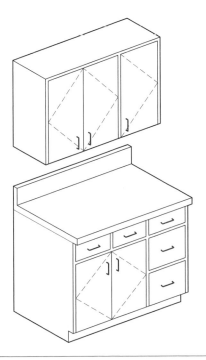

**AXONOMETRIC**

*Source: Architectural Woodwork Institute; Architectural Quality Standards, 7th ed. (Version 1.2), Reston, Virginia, 1999.*

**FINISH CARPENTRY** ☐ **2**

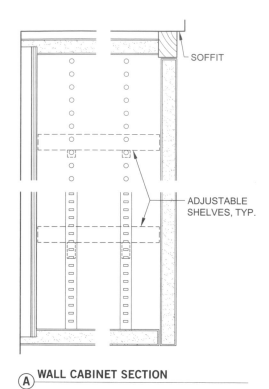

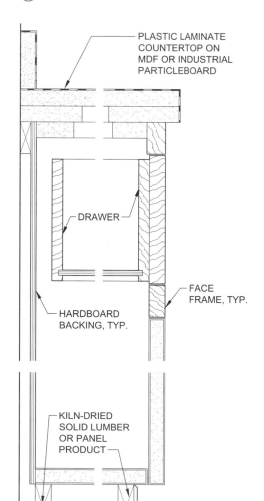

(A) **WALL CABINET SECTION**

- SOFFIT
- ADJUSTABLE SHELVES, TYP.
- PLASTIC LAMINATE COUNTERTOP ON MDF OR INDUSTRIAL PARTICLEBOARD
- DRAWER
- FACE FRAME, TYP.
- HARDBOARD BACKING, TYP.
- KILN-DRIED SOLID LUMBER OR PANEL PRODUCT

(B) **BASE CABINET SECTION**

## FLUSH INSET CONSTRUCTION WITH FACE FRAME

Flush inset construction with a face frame is a highly functional style that allows the use of different thicknesses of door and drawer fronts. Door and drawer faces are flush with the face of the cabinet. This is generally the most expensive of the four styles due to the increased care required in fitting and aligning the doors and drawers, in addition to the cost of providing the face frame. Conventional butt hinges should be avoided where hinge screws are attached to the edge-grain of panel products. This style does not lend itself to the economical use of plastic laminate covering finishes.

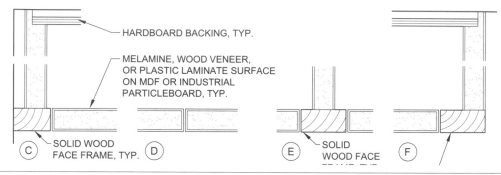

- HARDBOARD BACKING, TYP.
- MELAMINE, WOOD VENEER, OR PLASTIC LAMINATE SURFACE ON MDF OR INDUSTRIAL PARTICLEBOARD, TYP.
- (C) SOLID WOOD FACE FRAME, TYP. (D)
- (E) SOLID WOOD FACE (F)

**WALL CABINET DETAILS**

- (G) SOLID WOOD FACE FRAME, TYP. (H)
- CABINET DOOR (J)
- DRAWER FRONT (K)

**DRAWER DETAILS AT BASE CABINETS**

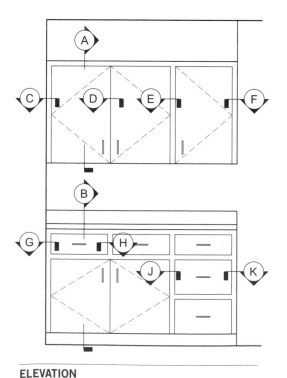

**ELEVATION**

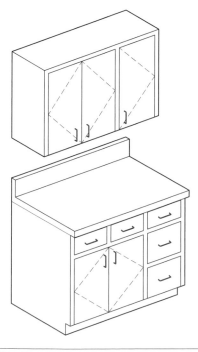

**AXONOMETRIC**

*Source: Architectural Woodwork Institute; Architectural Quality Standards, 7th ed. (Version 1.2), Reston, Virginia, 1999.*

# CABINET JOINERY

Spline joints are used to strengthen and align faces when gluing panels in width or length, including items requiring site assembly.

## SPLINE JOINT

Stub tenant joints are commonly used for assembling stile and rail frames that require additional supports, such as web or skeleton case frames.

## STUB TENON

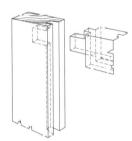

Haunch mortise and tenon joints are commonly used for assembling paneled doors or stile and rail-type paneling.

## HAUNCH MORTISE AND TENON JOINTS

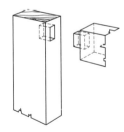

Conventional mortise and tenon joints are commonly used for assembling square-edged surfaces such as case face frames.

## CONVENTIONAL MORTISE AND TENON JOINT

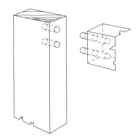

Dowel joints are an alternative joinery method serving the same function as the conventional mortise and tenon joint.

## DOWEL JOINT

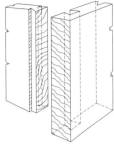

French dovetail joints are used to join drawer sides to fronts when fronts conceal metal extension slides or overlay the case faces.

## FRENCH DOVETAIL JOINT

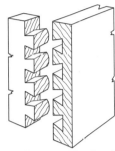

Dovetail joints are the conventional method for joining drawer sides to fronts or backs. Usually limited to flush- or lipped-type drawers.

## CONVENTIONAL DOVETAIL JOINT

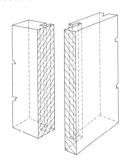

Drawer lock joints are another joinery method for joining drawer sides to fronts. It is usually used for flush-type installations but can be adapted to lip- or overlay-type drawers.

## DRAWER LOCK JOINT

Butt joints can be used at exposed finished ends for an economical treatment.

## BUTT JOINT

Lock miter joints can be used at exposed finished ends.

## LOCK MITERED JOINT

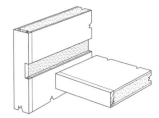

Through dado joints are conventionally used for the assembly of case body members. The dado is usually concealed by application of the case face frame.

## THROUGH DADO

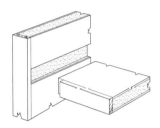

Blind dado joints are a variation of conventional dado joints, with applied edge "stopping" or concealed dado groove. They are often used when the case body edge is exposed.

## BLIND DADO

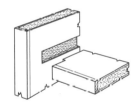

Stop dado joints are another method of concealing dado exposure. They are applicable when veneer edging or solid lumber is used.

## STOP DADO

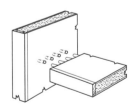

Dowel joints are fast becoming an industry standard assembly method. This joint is often based on a 32 mm (1¼ in) spacing of dowels.

## DOWEL JOINT

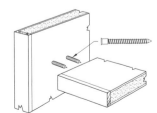

Screwed joints can be used where exposed fasteners are appropriate.

## SCREWED JOINT

*Architectural Woodwork Institute; Reston, Virginia*

**FINISH CARPENTRY** ☐ 2

*Source: Architectural Woodwork Institute; Architectural Quality Standards, 7th Ed. (Version 1.2), Reston, Virginia, 1999.*

# CABINET DOOR HINGES AND CATCHES

## CABINET HINGES

| Hinge Type | BUTT | WRAPAROUND | PIVOT (KNIFE) | EUROPEAN (CONCEALED) | FACE-MOUNT |
|---|---|---|---|---|---|
| Elevation of Cabinet Face | | | | | |
| Door Swing | 180° | 180° | 180° | 95°, 125°, or 170° | 180° |
| Easily Adjusted after Installation | No | No | No | Yes | Yes |
| Strength | High | Very High | Moderate | High-Moderate | Moderate |
| Requires Mortising | Yes | Occasionally | Usually | Yes | No |
| Cost of Hinge | Low | Moderate | Low | High | Low |
| Ease of Installation | Moderate | Easy | Moderate | Very Easy | Easy |
| Adjustability | No | One-Way | Two-Way | Three-Way | No |
| Easily Adjusted after Installation | No | No | No | Yes | No |

Self-closing hinges spring-close the cabinet door when it is within 28° from being closed. When it is opened beyond 30°, the self-closer does not function, allowing the door to be left open. The self-closing feature eliminates the need for catches. Butt hinges are the only listed hinges not available with the self-closing feature.

*After: Architectural Woodwork Institute; Reston, Virginia*

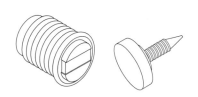

**BUTTON CATCH WITH STRIKE**

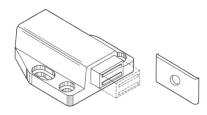

**TOUCH LATCH CATCH WITH STRIKE**

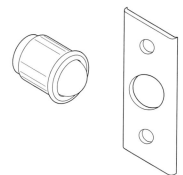

**BALL CATCH**

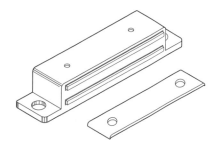

**BAR CATCH WITH STRIKE**

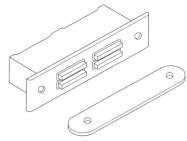

**BAR CATCH WITH STRIKE**

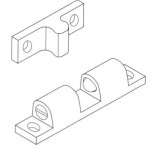

**DOUBLE ROLLER CATCH WITH C-CLIP STRIKE**

**MAGNETIC CATCHES**

**FRICTION CATCHES**

# CABINET DRAWER GLIDES

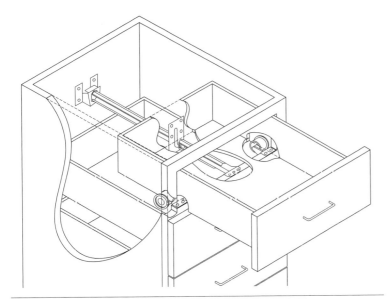

**TRI-ROLLER GLIDE**

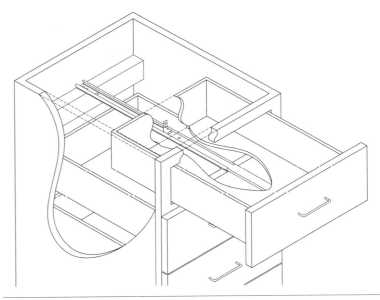

**CENTER-MOUNT GLIDE**

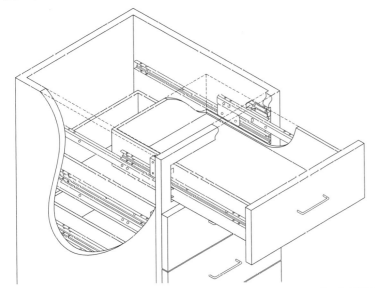

**SIDE-MOUNT GLIDE WITH THREE-FOURTHS EXTENSION**

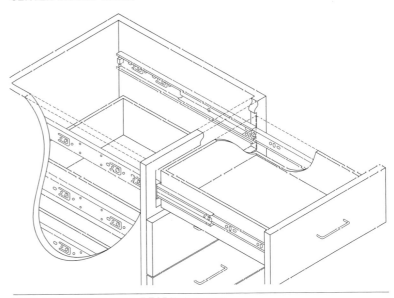

**FULL-EXTENSION BALL BEARING GLIDE**

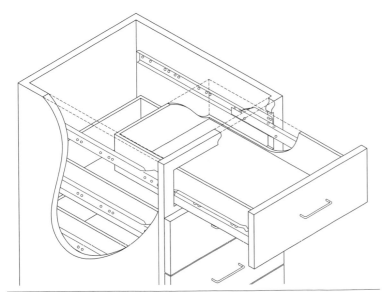

**EUROPEAN SIDE-MOUNT GLIDE WITH THREE-FOURTHS EXTENSION**

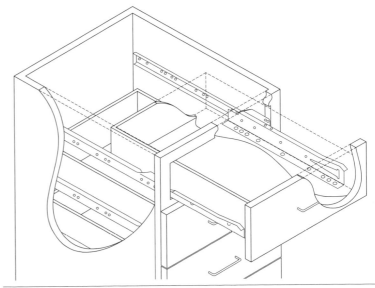

**EUROPEAN BOTTOM-MOUNT GLIDE WITH THREE-FOURTHS EXTENSION**

# STANDARD BASE CABINETS

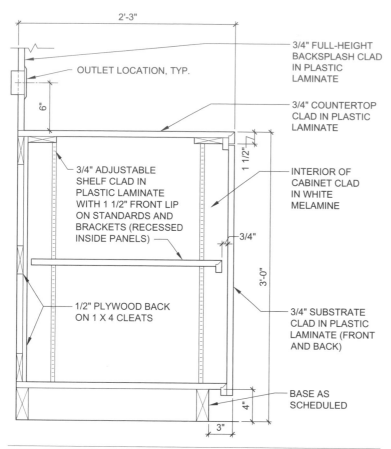

2'-3"

OUTLET LOCATION, TYP.

6"

1 1/2"

3/4" FULL-HEIGHT BACKSPLASH CLAD IN PLASTIC LAMINATE

3/4" COUNTERTOP CLAD IN PLASTIC LAMINATE

3/4" ADJUSTABLE SHELF CLAD IN PLASTIC LAMINATE WITH 1 1/2" FRONT LIP ON STANDARDS AND BRACKETS (RECESSED INSIDE PANELS)

INTERIOR OF CABINET CLAD IN WHITE MELAMINE

3/4"

3'-0"

1/2" PLYWOOD BACK ON 1 X 4 CLEATS

3/4" SUBSTRATE CLAD IN PLASTIC LAMINATE (FRONT AND BACK)

BASE AS SCHEDULED

4"

3"

**BASE CABINET WITH SINGLE DOOR**

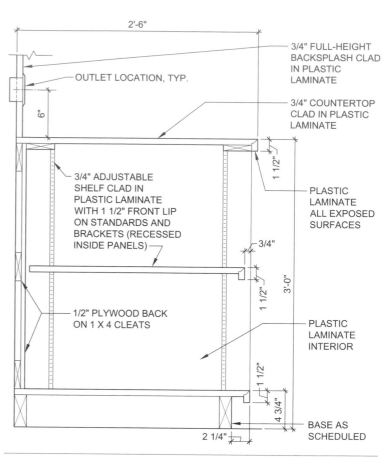

2'-6"

OUTLET LOCATION, TYP.

6"

1 1/2"

3/4" FULL-HEIGHT BACKSPLASH CLAD IN PLASTIC LAMINATE

3/4" COUNTERTOP CLAD IN PLASTIC LAMINATE

3/4" ADJUSTABLE SHELF CLAD IN PLASTIC LAMINATE WITH 1 1/2" FRONT LIP ON STANDARDS AND BRACKETS (RECESSED INSIDE PANELS)

PLASTIC LAMINATE ALL EXPOSED SURFACES

3/4"

1 1/2"

3'-0"

1/2" PLYWOOD BACK ON 1 X 4 CLEATS

PLASTIC LAMINATE INTERIOR

1 1/2"

4 3/4"

2 1/4"

BASE AS SCHEDULED

**OPEN BASE CABINET WITH SHELF**

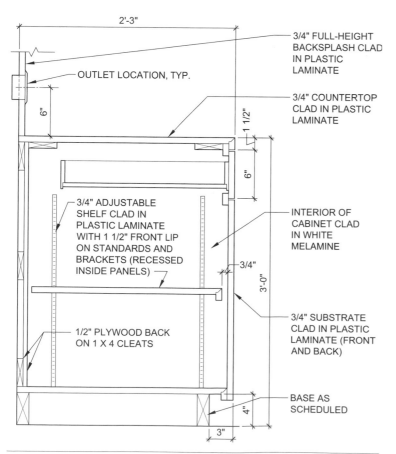

2'-3"

OUTLET LOCATION, TYP.

6"

1 1/2"

3/4" FULL-HEIGHT BACKSPLASH CLAD IN PLASTIC LAMINATE

3/4" COUNTERTOP CLAD IN PLASTIC LAMINATE

6"

3/4" ADJUSTABLE SHELF CLAD IN PLASTIC LAMINATE WITH 1 1/2" FRONT LIP ON STANDARDS AND BRACKETS (RECESSED INSIDE PANELS)

INTERIOR OF CABINET CLAD IN WHITE MELAMINE

3/4"

3'-0"

1/2" PLYWOOD BACK ON 1 X 4 CLEATS

3/4" SUBSTRATE CLAD IN PLASTIC LAMINATE (FRONT AND BACK)

BASE AS SCHEDULED

4"

3"

**BASE CABINET WITH PENCIL DRAWER AND SHELF**

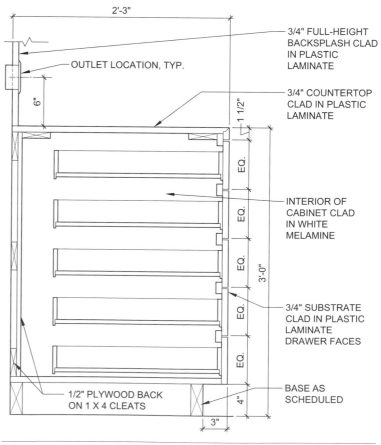

2'-3"

OUTLET LOCATION, TYP.

6"

1 1/2"

3/4" FULL-HEIGHT BACKSPLASH CLAD IN PLASTIC LAMINATE

3/4" COUNTERTOP CLAD IN PLASTIC LAMINATE

EQ.

EQ.

EQ.

EQ.

EQ.

3'-0"

INTERIOR OF CABINET CLAD IN WHITE MELAMINE

3/4" SUBSTRATE CLAD IN PLASTIC LAMINATE DRAWER FACES

1/2" PLYWOOD BACK ON 1 X 4 CLEATS

BASE AS SCHEDULED

4"

3"

**BASE CABINET WITH DRAWERS**

# STANDARD BASE AND WALL-HUNG CABINETS

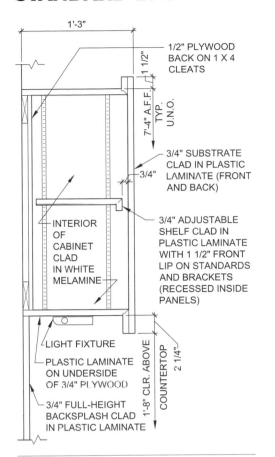

1'-3"

1/2" PLYWOOD BACK ON 1 X 4 CLEATS

1 1/2"

7'-4" A.F.F. TYP. U.N.O.

3/4" SUBSTRATE CLAD IN PLASTIC LAMINATE (FRONT AND BACK)

3/4"

INTERIOR OF CABINET CLAD IN WHITE MELAMINE

3/4" ADJUSTABLE SHELF CLAD IN PLASTIC LAMINATE WITH 1 1/2" FRONT LIP ON STANDARDS AND BRACKETS (RECESSED INSIDE PANELS)

LIGHT FIXTURE

PLASTIC LAMINATE ON UNDERSIDE OF 3/4" PLYWOOD

3/4" FULL-HEIGHT BACKSPLASH CLAD IN PLASTIC LAMINATE

1'-8" CLR. ABOVE COUNTERTOP

2 1/4"

**WALL-HUNG CABINET WITH SINGLE DOOR**

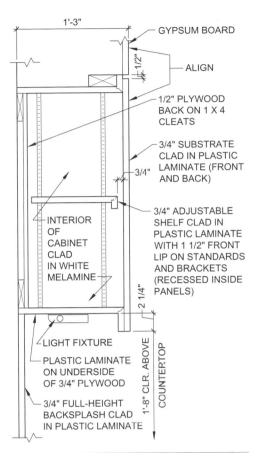

1'-3"

GYPSUM BOARD

1/2"

ALIGN

1/2" PLYWOOD BACK ON 1 X 4 CLEATS

3/4" SUBSTRATE CLAD IN PLASTIC LAMINATE (FRONT AND BACK)

3/4"

INTERIOR OF CABINET CLAD IN WHITE MELAMINE

3/4" ADJUSTABLE SHELF CLAD IN PLASTIC LAMINATE WITH 1 1/2" FRONT LIP ON STANDARDS AND BRACKETS (RECESSED INSIDE PANELS)

2 1/4"

LIGHT FIXTURE

PLASTIC LAMINATE ON UNDERSIDE OF 3/4" PLYWOOD

3/4" FULL-HEIGHT BACKSPLASH CLAD IN PLASTIC LAMINATE

1'-8" CLR. ABOVE COUNTERTOP

**WALL-HUNG CABINET WITH TOP PANEL**

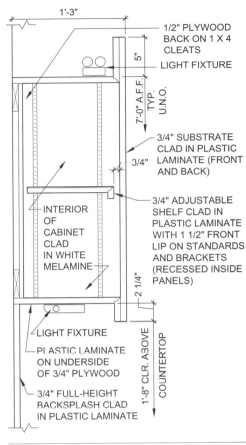

1'-3"

1/2" PLYWOOD BACK ON 1 X 4 CLEATS

5"

LIGHT FIXTURE

7'-0" A.F.F. TYP. U.N.O.

3/4" SUBSTRATE CLAD IN PLASTIC LAMINATE (FRONT AND BACK)

3/4"

INTERIOR OF CABINET CLAD IN WHITE MELAMINE

3/4" ADJUSTABLE SHELF CLAD IN PLASTIC LAMINATE WITH 1 1/2" FRONT LIP ON STANDARDS AND BRACKETS (RECESSED INSIDE PANELS)

2 1/4"

LIGHT FIXTURE

PLASTIC LAMINATE ON UNDERSIDE OF 3/4" PLYWOOD

3/4" FULL-HEIGHT BACKSPLASH CLAD IN PLASTIC LAMINATE

1'-8" CLR. ABOVE COUNTERTOP

**WALL-HUNG CABINET WITH COVE LIGHTING**

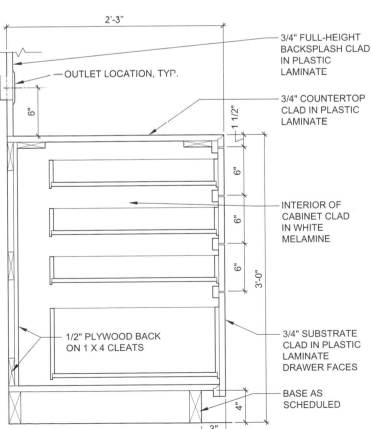

2'-3"

OUTLET LOCATION, TYP.

6"

3/4" FULL-HEIGHT BACKSPLASH CLAD IN PLASTIC LAMINATE

3/4" COUNTERTOP CLAD IN PLASTIC LAMINATE

1 1/2"

6"

6"

6"

3'-0"

INTERIOR OF CABINET CLAD IN WHITE MELAMINE

1/2" PLYWOOD BACK ON 1 X 4 CLEATS

3/4" SUBSTRATE CLAD IN PLASTIC LAMINATE DRAWER FACES

BASE AS SCHEDULED

4"

3"

**BASE CABINET WITH PENCIL AND FILE DRAWERS**

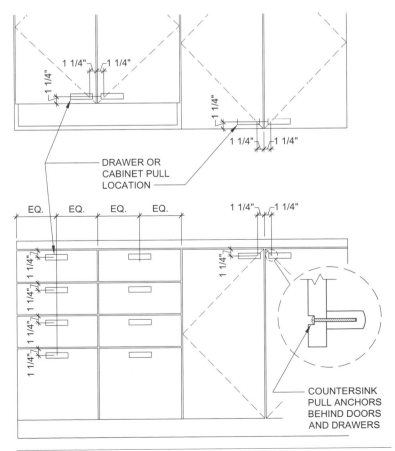

1 1/4"    1 1/4"

1 1/4"

1 1/4"

1 1/4"    1 1/4"

DRAWER OR CABINET PULL LOCATION

EQ.    EQ.    EQ.    EQ.

1 1/4"    1 1/4"

1 1/4"

1 1/4"

1 1/4"

1 1/4"

1 1/4"

1 1/4"

COUNTERSINK PULL ANCHORS BEHIND DOORS AND DRAWERS

**CABINET PULL LOCATIONS**

*Ted Kollaja, AIA; lauckgroup; Dallas, Texas*

# RECEPTION DESK

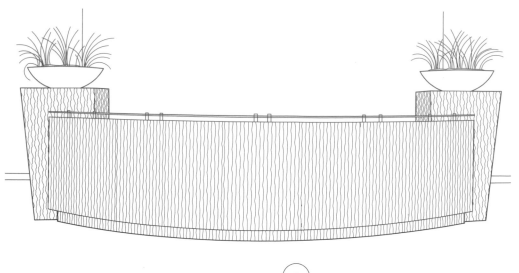

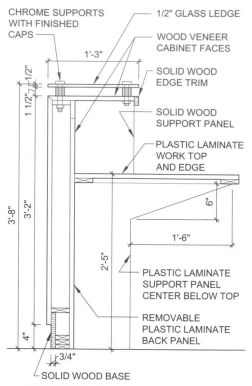

**CHROME SUPPORTS WITH FINISHED CAPS**
**1/2" GLASS LEDGE**
**WOOD VENEER CABINET FACES**
**SOLID WOOD EDGE TRIM**
**SOLID WOOD SUPPORT PANEL**
**PLASTIC LAMINATE WORK TOP AND EDGE**
1'-3"
1 1/2"   1/2"
3'-8"
3'-2"
6"
1'-6"
2'-5"
**PLASTIC LAMINATE SUPPORT PANEL CENTER BELOW TOP**
**REMOVABLE PLASTIC LAMINATE BACK PANEL**
4"
3/4"
**SOLID WOOD BASE**

Ⓒ **SECTION AT COUNTER**

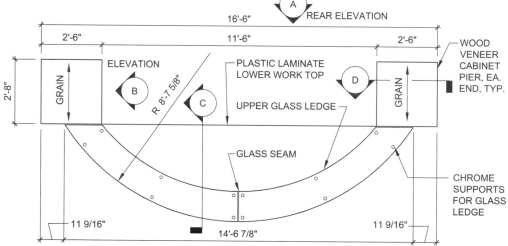

Ⓐ REAR ELEVATION

16'-6"
2'-6"    11'-6"    2'-6"
ELEVATION
Ⓑ
R 8'-7 5/8"
Ⓒ
2'-8"
GRAIN
**PLASTIC LAMINATE LOWER WORK TOP**
Ⓓ
GRAIN
**WOOD VENEER CABINET PIER, EA. END, TYP.**
**UPPER GLASS LEDGE**
**GLASS SEAM**
**CHROME SUPPORTS FOR GLASS LEDGE**
11 9/16"    14'-6 7/8"    11 9/16"

**PLAN**

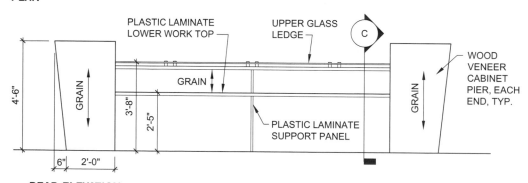

**PLASTIC LAMINATE LOWER WORK TOP**
**UPPER GLASS LEDGE**
Ⓒ
4'-6"
GRAIN
3'-8"
2'-5"
GRAIN
**PLASTIC LAMINATE SUPPORT PANEL**
**WOOD VENEER CABINET PIER, EACH END, TYP.**
6"   2'-0"

Ⓐ **REAR ELEVATION**

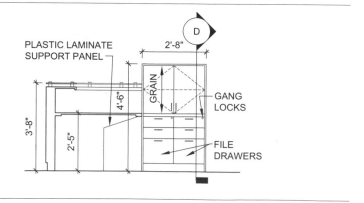

**PLASTIC LAMINATE SUPPORT PANEL**
2'-8"
Ⓓ
GRAIN
4'-6"
3'-8"
2'-5"
**GANG LOCKS**
**FILE DRAWERS**

Ⓑ **ELEVATION AT CABINET**

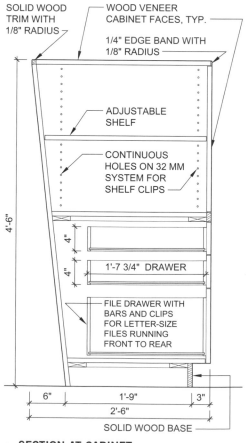

**SOLID WOOD TRIM WITH 1/8" RADIUS**
**WOOD VENEER CABINET FACES, TYP.**
**1/4" EDGE BAND WITH 1/8" RADIUS**
**ADJUSTABLE SHELF**
**CONTINUOUS HOLES ON 32 MM SYSTEM FOR SHELF CLIPS**
4'-6"
4"
4"
1'-7 3/4"  DRAWER
**FILE DRAWER WITH BARS AND CLIPS FOR LETTER-SIZE FILES RUNNING FRONT TO REAR**
6"   1'-9"   3"
2'-6"
**SOLID WOOD BASE**

Ⓓ **SECTION AT CABINET**

*Project: St. Louis Rams Training and Administration Complex; Earth City, Missouri*
*Designer: O'Toole Design Associates; St. Louis, Missouri*
*Woodworker: Classic Woodworking; St. Louis, Missouri*
*Source: Design Solutions, Winter 2000*

# LECTERN

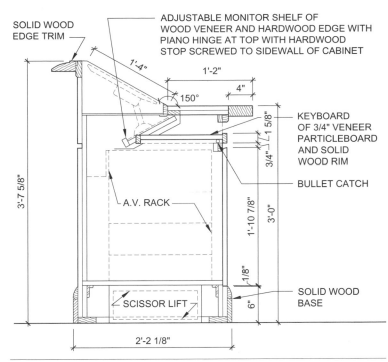

SOLID WOOD
EDGE TRIM

ADJUSTABLE MONITOR SHELF OF
WOOD VENEER AND HARDWOOD EDGE WITH
PIANO HINGE AT TOP WITH HARDWOOD
STOP SCREWED TO SIDEWALL OF CABINET

1'-4"

1'-2"

4"

150°

1 5/8"

3/4"

KEYBOARD
OF 3/4" VENEER
PARTICLEBOARD
AND SOLID
WOOD RIM

BULLET CATCH

A.V. RACK

3'-7 5/8"

1'-10 7/8"

3'-0"

1/8"

6"

SOLID WOOD
BASE

SCISSOR LIFT

2'-2 1/8"

**SECTION AT A/V RACK**

*Project: Pentair Corporate Offices; Minneapolis, Minnesota*
*Designer: BWBR Architects; St. Paul, Minnesota*
*Woodworker: Wilkie Sanderson; Sauk Rapids, Minnesota*
*Source: Design Solutions, Spring 2001*

# JEWELRY DISPLAY CASE

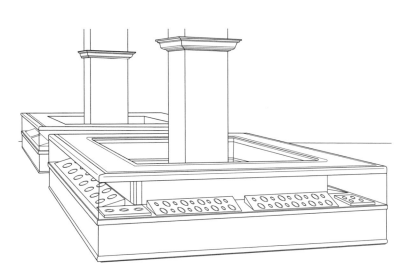

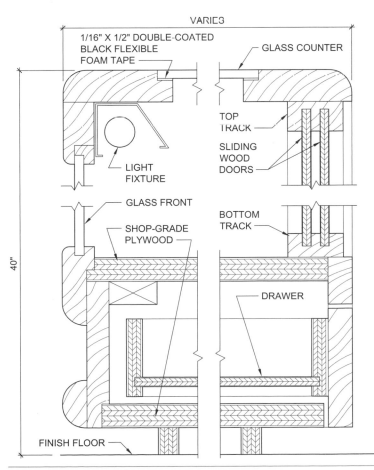

VARIES

1/16" X 1/2" DOUBLE-COATED
BLACK FLEXIBLE
FOAM TAPE

GLASS COUNTER

TOP
TRACK

SLIDING
WOOD
DOORS

LIGHT
FIXTURE

GLASS FRONT

BOTTOM
TRACK

SHOP-GRADE
PLYWOOD

DRAWER

40"

FINISH FLOOR

*Project: Carleton Varney; White Sulphur Springs, West Virginia*
*Designer: Dorothy Draper Co.; New York, New York*
*Woodworker: Architectural Wood; Roanoke, Virginia*
*Source: Design Solutions, Spring 1997*

**JEWELRY CASE SECTION**

# COUNTERTOPS

## COUNTERTOPS

Countertops for commercial and residential applications are fabricated from a number of different materials and finishes, ranging from high-pressure plastic laminate to stone, tile, wood, stainless steel, and manufactured materials. Function, appropriateness for the application, economy, and aesthetics should be considered when selecting a countertop material. Countertops are commonly supported by base cabinets, but can be installed as freestanding or supported units.

## CONSTRUCTION

Countertop construction varies with the type of surface material selected and the type of support required. Some surface materials such as stone rest directly on a support system, while other finish surfaces require lamination to a substrate. All countertops require support, either on an architectural woodwork base cabinet or other undercounter support such as wall brackets or steel outriggers when no base cabinet is provided, or the countertop can be mounted on legs. When the countertop is not supported by a base cabinet or other similar unit, a careful review of the countertop support system is recommended. Anticipated loads should be reviewed, including the possibility of the countertop being used as a seat if it is mounted at a lower height.

## SUBSTRATES

For laminated countertops such as HPDL, substrates include particleboard or medium density fiberboard (MDF), usually ¾ in. (19 mm) thick, as the surfaces are smooth and consistent. When moisture is a concern, exterior grade plywood is used, although the surface is not as fine as the particleboard or MDF. Plywood is not commonly used as an HPDL substrate, as the imperfections may telegraph through to the surface. Exterior grade plywood is used as a substrate under stone, tile, and other materials requiring a rigid substrate with resistance to moisture.

## COUNTERTOP MATERIALS

Some of the most prevalent countertop types are laminated countertops, which include high-pressure decorative laminates (HPDL), wood veneers, linoleum, and some metal sheets such as zinc, with or without edging of different materials. Stainless steel, stone, tile, concrete, solid wood, and other finish surfaces may be used for countertop units.

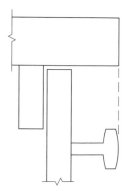

Countertop should extend to or beyond the cabinet's pulls.

**COUNTERTOP CLEARANCE**

### COUNTERTOP MATERIALS COMPARISON

| MATERIAL | FEATURES | CONCERNS |
|---|---|---|
| Concrete | Durable<br>Custom colors possible<br>Objects can be recessed<br>Tactile surface<br>Acquires patina from use | Qualified installers required<br>Sealer recommended<br>Subject to staining and cracking<br>Hot elements will damage sealer |
| Engineered Composite Stone (Silestone®, Zodiaq™) | Requires no sealing<br>Nonporous<br>Abrasion, stain and impact resistant | Not as heat-resistant as natural stone<br>Resinous feel and appearance |
| Epoxy resin | Used for laboratory countertops<br>Extremely durable<br>Resistant to chemicals | Costly<br>Qualified installers required |
| Granite (polished, honed, flamed) | Durable<br>Stain resistant when sealed<br>Water and heat resistant<br>Natural stone features | Expensive to install<br>Qualified installers required<br>Avoid ammonia products |
| Laminates, Plastic (HDPL) | Moderate cost<br>Dark edge on standard laminate<br>Color through laminates offer less visible scratch marks<br>Waterproof, stain resistant<br>Easily cleaned | Not heat resistant<br>Seam lines<br>Joints susceptible to damage, delamination<br>Scratches cannot be repaired |
| Lavastone, glazed (Pyrolave) | Water and heat resistant | Costly<br>Easily scratched |
| Limestone | Dolomitic limestone preferred<br>Heat resistant<br>Neutral and soft colors | As porous as marble<br>Sealer required<br>Qualified installers required |
| Linoleum | Inexpensive<br>"Green" product<br>Water, stain, and heat resistant<br>Antibacterial surface | Edge trim required |
| Marble (polished or honed) | Heat resistant<br>Natural stone features<br>Tactile feel on honed finish | Costly<br>Qualified installers required<br>Sealer required<br>Susceptible to staining |
| Quartzite | Iridescent, crystalline appearance<br>Cool, pale colors<br>Water and heat resistant | Sealer required<br>Qualified installers required |
| Slate | Available in honed finish<br>Water and heat resistant<br>Stainproof and antibacterial | Costly<br>Qualified installers required<br>Avoid ammonia products |
| Soapstone | Soft, satiny, tactile feel<br>Water, heat, and stain resistant | Bimonthly oil treatment required to prevent chipping<br>Qualified installers required<br>Costly |
| Solid Surface (DuPont Corian, Wilsonart Gibraltar, Nevamar Fountainhead) | Water and stain resistant<br>Light stains, scratches, and scorch marks can be buffed out<br>Integral sinks available | Not heatproof<br>Costly to fabricate and install<br>Avoid acetone |
| Stainless Steel | Water, heat, and stain resistant<br>Used in commercial food service<br>Integral sinks available | Subject to water spots<br>Qualified installers required<br>Plywood backup recommended to reduce noise |
| Tile, Ceramic | Heat and stain resistant<br>Water resistant when properly grouted<br>Durable | Costly to install<br>Glaze may be damaged by grit<br>Grout requires maintenance<br>Tile can be chipped from impact |
| Tile, Stone | Less costly than dimension stone<br>Water, heat, and stain resistant<br>Natural stone features in tile form | Labor-intensive to install<br>Grout requires maintenance |
| Travertine | Heat resistant | Qualified installers required<br>Natural stone features<br>Filled travertine recommended<br>Sealer required |
| Wood (Veneer and Solid Laminated) | Forgiving surface; does not dull knives | Susceptible to water damage<br>Monthly application of mineral oil required<br>Scorch marks and light stains can be sanded |
| Zinc | Warm metal appearance<br>Zinc surface laminated similar to plastic laminate<br>Many surface finishes available | Qualified installers required<br>Easily maintained<br>Protect from corrosive materials<br>Large sheet sizes |

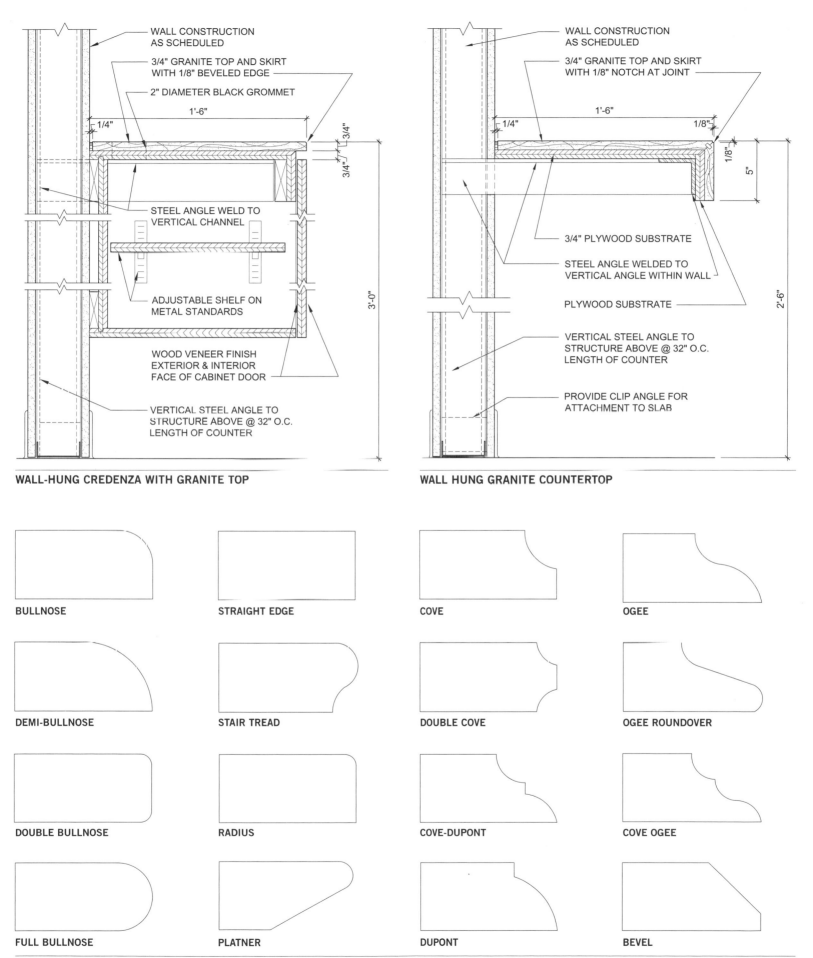

WALL CONSTRUCTION AS SCHEDULED

3/4" GRANITE TOP AND SKIRT WITH 1/8" BEVELED EDGE

2" DIAMETER BLACK GROMMET

1'-6"

1/4"

3/4"

3/4"

STEEL ANGLE WELD TO VERTICAL CHANNEL

ADJUSTABLE SHELF ON METAL STANDARDS

WOOD VENEER FINISH EXTERIOR & INTERIOR FACE OF CABINET DOOR

VERTICAL STEEL ANGLE TO STRUCTURE ABOVE @ 32" O.C. LENGTH OF COUNTER

3'-0"

**WALL-HUNG CREDENZA WITH GRANITE TOP**

WALL CONSTRUCTION AS SCHEDULED

3/4" GRANITE TOP AND SKIRT WITH 1/8" NOTCH AT JOINT

1'-6"

1/4"

1/8"

1/8"

5"

3/4" PLYWOOD SUBSTRATE

STEEL ANGLE WELDED TO VERTICAL ANGLE WITHIN WALL

PLYWOOD SUBSTRATE

VERTICAL STEEL ANGLE TO STRUCTURE ABOVE @ 32" O.C. LENGTH OF COUNTER

PROVIDE CLIP ANGLE FOR ATTACHMENT TO SLAB

2'-6"

**WALL HUNG GRANITE COUNTERTOP**

BULLNOSE

STRAIGHT EDGE

COVE

OGEE

DEMI-BULLNOSE

STAIR TREAD

DOUBLE COVE

OGEE ROUNDOVER

DOUBLE BULLNOSE

RADIUS

COVE-DUPONT

COVE OGEE

FULL BULLNOSE

PLATNER

DUPONT

BEVEL

**COMMON COUNTERTOP EDGE PROFILES**

## WOOD AND PLASTIC LAMINATE COUNTERTOP WORKMANSHIP CRITERIA

| CRITERIA | PREMIUM | CUSTOM | ECONOMY |
|---|---|---|---|
| Selection at field joints on exposed surfaces | Selected for uniformity of grain, color, and/or pattern | Selected for pleasing blend of grain or pattern | No selection required |
| Selection for solid laminated (butcher block) components | Selected for pleasing blend of grain or pattern | No selection required | No selection required |
| End joints for solid (butcher block) components | Shall meet joint tolerances for exposed components, and no more than 1 per 4 sq ft (.4 sq m) | Shall meet joint tolerances for exposed components, and no more than 1 per 2 sq ft (.2 sq m) | Shall meet joint tolerances for exposed components, and no more than 1 per 1 sq ft (.1 sq m) |
| End matching of veneers on exposed surfaces | Leaves individually book matched and end matched | Selected for pleasing blend of grain or pattern | No selection required |
| Balancing sheet requirements for HPDL overlay | Standard .020" phenolic backer minimum required in all cases | Paper backer required wherever unsupported area exceeds 6 sq ft (.6 sq m) and core is ¾" (19 mm) thick; 8 sq ft (8 sq m) and core is 1" (25 mm) thick; 10sq ft (1sq m) and core is 1⅛: (28 mm) or thicker | No backer required |
| Edge application for HPDL | Edge laminated before top | Edge laminated before top | Edge laminated after top |
| Flatness (after installation) is a defect when maximum deviation exceeds | ¹⁄₁₆" (1.6 mm) in any 4" × 8" (1,220 mm × 2,440 mm) segment | ⅛" (3 mm) in any 4" × 8" (1,220 mm × 2,440 mm) segment | ¼" (6 mm) in any 4" × 8" (1,220 mm × 2,440 mm) segment |
| Field joints | More than 48" (1,220 mm) apart, and shall not occur within 48" (1,220 mm) of the end of any top | More than 36" (914 mm) apart, and shall not occur within 36" (914 mm) of the end of any top | No requirement |
| Sealing of substrate at sink cuts | Required | Required | Not required |
| Maximum allowable separation between factory assembled splash and top components | ¹⁄₆₄" (.4 mm) x 3" (76 mm) and no more than 1 per 4' (1,220 mm) section of top | ³⁄₃₂" (.8mm) x 5" (127 mm) and no more than 1 per 4' (1,220 mm) section of top | ¹⁄₁₆" (1.6 mm) × 8" (203 mm) and no more than 1 per 4' (1,220 mm) section of top |
| Application of silicone sealant to factory assembled joint between HDPL top and splash | Required | Not required | Not required |
| Use of thermoset decorative overlay as backer material | Not allowed | Allowed | Allowed |
| Joint in HDPL or substrate at factory sink cut | Not allowed | Not allowed | Not allowed |

The Architectural Woodwork Institute's Quality Standards identify three levels of construction: premium, custom, and economy grades. It is recommended that both the countertops and base cabinets be fabricated with the same grade of construction for functional compatibility.
*Source: Architectural Woodwork Institute; Reston, Virginia*

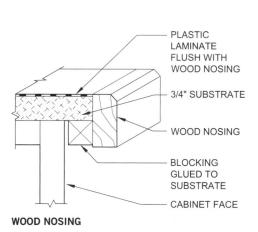

PLASTIC LAMINATE FLUSH WITH WOOD NOSING

3/4" SUBSTRATE

WOOD NOSING

BLOCKING GLUED TO SUBSTRATE

CABINET FACE

**WOOD NOSING**

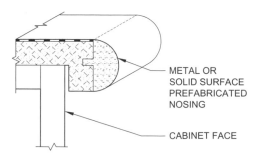

METAL OR SOLID SURFACE PREFABRICATED NOSING

CABINET FACE

**METAL OR SOLID SURFACE NOSING**

Applied nosings can be wood, metal, or solid surface, adhered to the countertop substrate. Depending on the nosing detail, the applied edge can protect the plastic laminate surface from damage.

**APPLIED NOSINGS**

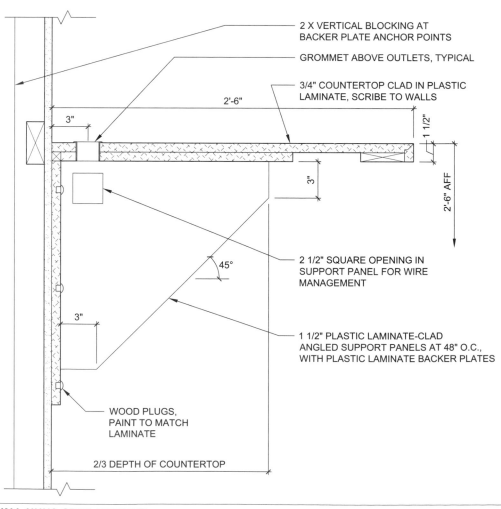

2 X VERTICAL BLOCKING AT BACKER PLATE ANCHOR POINTS

GROMMET ABOVE OUTLETS, TYPICAL

3/4" COUNTERTOP CLAD IN PLASTIC LAMINATE, SCRIBE TO WALLS

2'-6"

3"

1 1/2"

3"

45°

2'-6" AFF

2 1/2" SQUARE OPENING IN SUPPORT PANEL FOR WIRE MANAGEMENT

1 1/2" PLASTIC LAMINATE-CLAD ANGLED SUPPORT PANELS AT 48" O.C., WITH PLASTIC LAMINATE BACKER PLATES

WOOD PLUGS, PAINT TO MATCH LAMINATE

2/3 DEPTH OF COUNTERTOP

**WALL-HUNG OPEN COUNTER**

# PLASTIC LAMINATE

High-pressure decorative laminate (HPDL), commonly known as *plastic laminate,* is one of the most economical countertop materials. It is available in numerous colors and textures, performs well, and is easily fabricated, installed and maintained. ANSI A162.2 *Performance Standard for Fabricated High Pressure Decorative Laminate Countertops,* defines the standards for performance of HPDL countertops. HPDL is formed from a sandwich of a melamine-impregnated overlay sheet, and decorative or colored surface paper over phenolic resin-impregnated kraft papers bonded together under high pressure and heat.

The four most common types of HPDL sheets are as follows:

HGS, formerly GP–General Purpose: Used for most horizontal surfaces, for example, countertops. This type can be bent to a radius of approximately 6 in. (152 mm).

CLS, formerly CL–Cabinet Liner: A thin sheet used for vertical applications, typically inside casework that will not need to withstand heavy wear. (The cabinet liner should not be used as a balancing or backer sheet for countertops.)

BKL, formerly BK–Backer: Economical, nondecorative sheets used on the side of the substrate hidden from view to prevent warping as a result of changes in temperature or humidity.

HGP, formerly PF Postforming: Used for lightly radiused curves, for example, at the edge of a formed countertop.

## COLORTHROUGH LAMINATES

Colorthrough laminates are a solid color through the thickness of the sheet. This eliminates the problem of the HPDL's brown kraft paper core showing when the cut edge is exposed. Colorthrough HPDL is manufactured in thicknesses from 0.050 in. to 0.060 in.(1.3 mm to 1.5 mm) and must be carefully adhered to the substrate. Because of their high melamine resin content, colorthrough HPDLs can buckle when temperature or humidity shifts.

## PLASTIC LAMINATE COUNTERTOP FABRICATION

HPDL countertops are fabricated by adhering plastic laminate to a substrate. Particleboard is often preferred as a substrate because it has a fine, smooth face without imperfections that could telegraph through the plastic laminate. Exterior grade plywood is preferred for

countertops exposed to liquids or high humidity because of its increased resistance to moisture. A backer sheet is applied to the unexposed, underside of the substrate to prevent warping and dimensional instability in changing temperature or humidity.

HPDL countertops are fabricated with three edge, or nosing, types: *self-edge, postformed edge,* and *applied*

edge. Plastic laminate is adhered to the counter substrate under uniform pressure and is trimmed flush with a router. Because seams are susceptible to water penetration, if possible, do not locate seams where water will be present, such as at a sink area. Plastic laminate countertops should be fabricated using balanced construction (backer sheet applied to underside of countertop) to minimize possibility of warping.

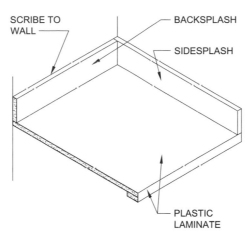

**COUNTERTOP WITH BACKSPLASH AND SIDESPLASH**

**HPDL HGS COUNTERTOP**

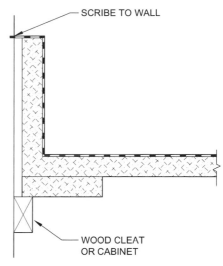

**BACKSPLASH**

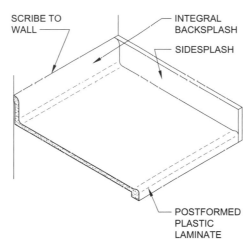

**COUNTERTOP WITH BACKSPLASH AND SIDESPLASH**

**HPDL HGP COUNTERTOPS**

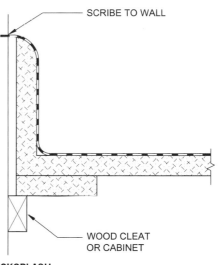

**BACKSPLASH**

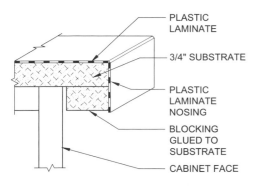

**SELF-EDGE NOSING**

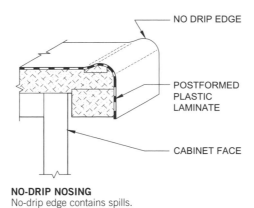

**NO-DRIP NOSING**
No-drip edge contains spills.

**HPDL POSTFORMED NOSING TYPES**

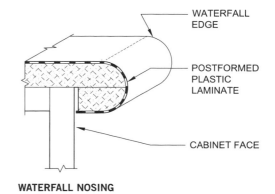

**WATERFALL NOSING**

## SOLID LAMINATE WOOD COUNTERTOPS

Solid laminated wood tops are constructed of narrow strips of wood that are face-glued together. The appearance is similar to "butcher block." The wood species preferred for this type of countertop is maple, due to the density of the wood. Expansion and contraction of wood countertops is to be expected, so the installation must allow for movement of the top. Solid wood tops are constructed of boards that are edge-glued to a desired width. Typically there is no matching of wood grain or color.

## WOOD VENEER COUNTERTOPS

Wood veneer countertops require maintenance to preserve their appearance. Veneered countertops can be used where moisture is not present. Wood veneer is installed over a stable substrate and is edged with wood or other materials.

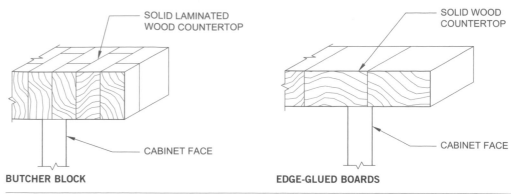

**BUTCHER BLOCK**    **EDGE-GLUED BOARDS**

**SOLID WOOD LAMINATED COUNTERTOPS**

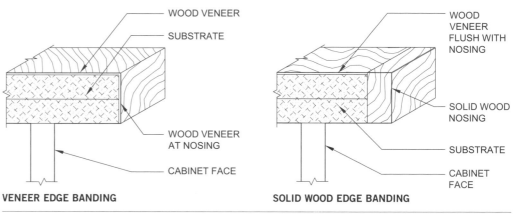

**VENEER EDGE BANDING**    **SOLID WOOD EDGE BANDING**

**WOOD VENEER COUNTERTOPS**

## MATERIAL GRADES AND SIZE REQUIREMENTS FOR WOOD AND HPDL COUNTERTOPS

| TYPE | PREMIUM | CUSTOM | ECONOMY |
|---|---|---|---|
| Solid wood | Grade I | Grade II | Mill option |
| Solid laminated | Grade I | Grade II | Mill option |
| Panel products | "AA" Face veneer | "A" Face veneer | Mill option |
| HPDL overlay | HGS - .048" nominal | HGS - .048" nominal | HGS - .048" nominal |
| **WIDTH AND MATCH** | | | |
| Solid wood—max width of individual boards in glue-up: Hardwood: 4¼" (108 mm) Softwood: 7¼" (185 mm) | Well matched for grain and color | Compatible for color | No match required |
| Solid wood, face laminated | Well matched for grain and color | Compatible for color | No match required |
| Solid wood & Veneer combined and/or adjacent.* | Well matched for grain and color | Compatible for color | No match required |
| Panel products—If width exceeds 48" (1,220 mm), shall have shop assembled joint | Sequence matched | Compatible for color | No match required |
| HPDL overlay—If width exceeds 60" (1,524 mm), shall have shop assembled joint (some limited to 48", determined by pattern selected or specified) | No match required | No match required | No match required |

*It is recognized that the grain and color of solid lumber and the same species and cut of veneer will appear different. The cutting and pressing of the veneer often modifies the surface cells. These natural differences are acceptable in any grade.

| **MINIMUM THICKNESS** | | | |
|---|---|---|---|
| Solid wood | 1" (25 mm) | 1" (25 mm) | ¾" (19 mm) |
| Solid laminated | 1⅛" (28 mm) | 1⅛" (28 mm) | ¾" (19 mm) |
| Panel products | ¾" (19 mm) | ¾" (19 mm) | ¾" (19 mm) |
| HDPL overlay | ¾" (19 mm) | ¾" (19 mm) | ¾" (19 mm) |
| **CARE AND SUBSTRATE** | | | |
| Panel product for HDPL | Industrial grade medium density particleboard or medium density fiberboard | | |
| Premium and custom grade tops and backsplashes in which sinks occur | Shop sanded exterior grade veneer core plywood: or industrial grade particleboard or fiberboard with a 24 hr. thickness swell factor of 5% or less and a 24 hr. water absorption factor of 10% or less. | | Industrial grade medium density particleboard or medium density fiberboard. |

*Source: Architectural Woodwork Institute; Reston, Virginia*

## SOLID SURFACE COUNTERTOPS

Solid surface countertops are formed from a polymer composition material that is easily shaped and molded into numerous edge profiles. Their integral uniform color and texture provide visual concealment of slight imperfections such as scratches. Each proprietary type of solid surface material is susceptible to different staining agents. Solid surface countertops can be fabricated with integral sinks.

## CERAMIC AND STONE TILE COUNTERTOP INSTALLATION

Tile modules provide strength, abrasion, heat and water resistance, and are available in ceramic tile and stone tile units. Both types are installed with ceramic tile installation methods. Cement grout is most commonly used for countertops. Epoxy grout is stain-resistant, expensive, and difficult to work with. Colored grouts are available, but may be susceptible to bleeding and staining adjacent tiles.

There are three types of setting methods for ceramic tile countertops: the traditional *thickset cement mortar method*, the more common *thinset method*, and *adhering to a plywood substrate*.

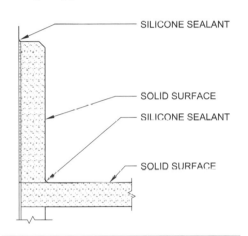

**SOLID SURFACE BACKSPLASH**

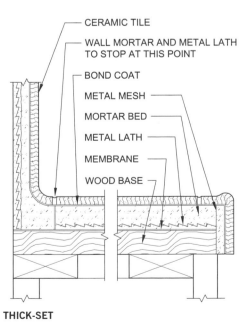

**CERAMIC TILE COUNTERTOPS**

### Thickset Method

A portland cement mortar bed [¾-in.- to 1-in.- (19-mm- to 25-mm-)] thick is applied over a substrate, typically ¾ in. exterior-grade plywood. The thick-set method is highly durable, labor intensive, and expensive. The tile is set in a thick bed of mortar and the joints grouted.

### Thinset Method

Cementitious backer board ¼-in.- to ¾-in.- (6- mm- to 19-mm) thick is adhered to a ¾ inch (19 mm) plywood substrate. The tile is adhered to the substrate and the joints grouted.

### Adhering Method

The tile is adhered to a substrate and the joints are grouted. This method is appropriate for use in low-moisture, low-wear applications.

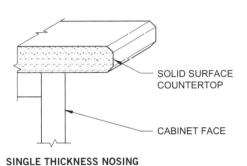

**SINGLE THICKNESS NOSING**

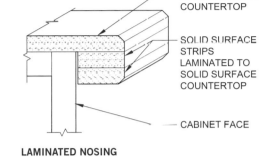

**LAMINATED NOSING**

**SOLID SURFACE COUNTERTOP NOSINGS**

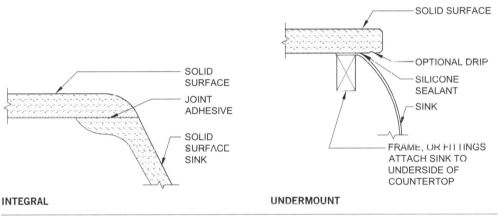

**INTEGRAL**

**UNDERMOUNT**

**SOLID SURFACE SINKS**

## STONE COUNTERTOPS

Stone countertops are elegant, durable, and resistant to heat and water. Other properties vary with the type of stone selected, such as scratch resistance. Stone countertops are fabricated from dimension stone, ranging from ¾-in. (2 cm) to 1¼-in. (3 cm) thick, in large slabs which vary in size. Stone is one of the heaviest countertop materials.

Stone counters require substantial, rigid substrates to minimize the possibility of cracking. Very thick stone slabs may be installed without a substrate. Consult with the stone supplier or fabricator for information on specific installation recommendations for a particular stone. Stone can be set on a substrate with a thin-set epoxy or a silicone adhesive, based on the installer's recommendations for the stone. Stone seams are typically butt joints, bonded with colored epoxy adhesives, which match the stone. Built-up front nosings are also fabricated with colored epoxy, which minimizes the appearance of any joints. Stone countertops should be sealed to protect the surfaces.

## GRANITE COUNTERTOPS

Granite is one of the most popular stones for countertops, due to its strength, numerous varieties, and hardness. Granite countertops are typically highly polished, but smooth-honed and flamed finishes perform well.

## MARBLE COUNTERTOPS

Marble is a porous stone, and typically is not as strong as granite. It is easily damaged by acids, and chips easily due to the structure of the stone. However, the aesthetic qualities of marble make it a popular choice, and marble can be successfully used in countertop applications if properly prepared and supported with an appropriate substrate. Marble finishes are typically honed or highly polished and the colors and textures vary widely.

## LIMESTONE COUNTERTOPS

Limestone is available in two basic types: *dolomitic* and *oolitic*. While dolomitic limestone is generally preferred for interior flooring and wall surfacing, both types can be used for countertops, if hard wear is not anticipated. Limestone is a sedimentary stone and is porous, so it is susceptible to damage and staining. Limestone is generally honed and is available in light and neutral colors.

## SLATE COUNTERTOPS

Slate is a split finish stone that appears rougher than other stone countertop materials and is fairly porous. Slate is available in a range of colors. Slate countertops should be sealed.

## ENGINEERED COMPOSITE STONE COUNTERTOPS

Engineered composite stone is a recent development; it typically consists of finely crushed stone aggregate, usually quartz. The stone is bound together by a resin and is formed into large sheets of specified thicknesses. Thinner sheets of engineered stone are installed similar to thin-bed ceramic tile.

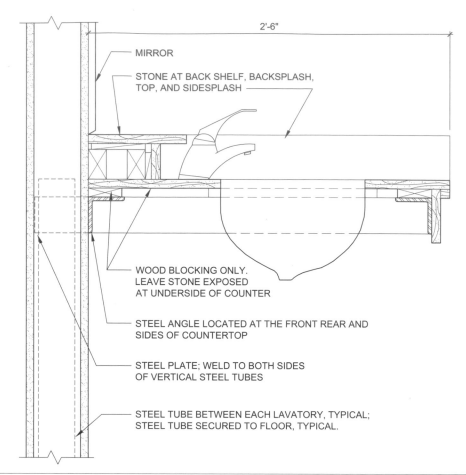

MIRROR

STONE AT BACK SHELF, BACKSPLASH, TOP, AND SIDESPLASH

2'-6"

WOOD BLOCKING ONLY. LEAVE STONE EXPOSED AT UNDERSIDE OF COUNTER

STEEL ANGLE LOCATED AT THE FRONT REAR AND SIDES OF COUNTERTOP

STEEL PLATE; WELD TO BOTH SIDES OF VERTICAL STEEL TUBES

STEEL TUBE BETWEEN EACH LAVATORY, TYPICAL; STEEL TUBE SECURED TO FLOOR, TYPICAL.

**WALL HUNG STONE COUNTERTOP WITH LAVATORY**

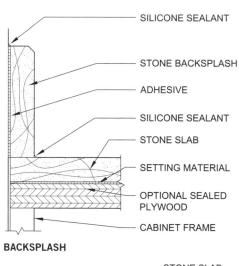

SILICONE SEALANT

STONE BACKSPLASH

ADHESIVE

SILICONE SEALANT

STONE SLAB

SETTING MATERIAL

OPTIONAL SEALED PLYWOOD

CABINET FRAME

**BACKSPLASH**

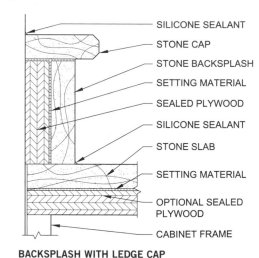

SILICONE SEALANT

STONE CAP

STONE BACKSPLASH

SETTING MATERIAL

SEALED PLYWOOD

SILICONE SEALANT

STONE SLAB

SETTING MATERIAL

OPTIONAL SEALED PLYWOOD

CABINET FRAME

**BACKSPLASH WITH LEDGE CAP**

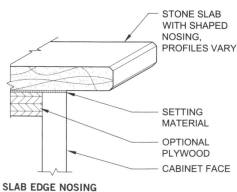

STONE SLAB WITH SHAPED NOSING, PROFILES VARY

SETTING MATERIAL

OPTIONAL PLYWOOD

CABINET FACE

**SLAB EDGE NOSING**

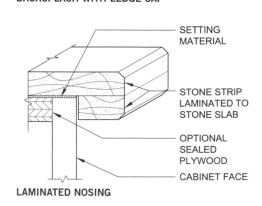

SETTING MATERIAL

STONE STRIP LAMINATED TO STONE SLAB

OPTIONAL SEALED PLYWOOD

CABINET FACE

**LAMINATED NOSING**

**STONE SLAB COUNTERTOPS**

## SHEET METAL COUNTERTOPS

Galvanized steel, zinc, copper, and other metals can be used for countertops, but are not suitable for contact with food. Stainless steel countertops are used in food service areas and in locations where sanitation, stain, water, and heat resistance are critical. Stainless steel countertops provide strength and functionality in a durable surface. Fabrication and installation of stainless steel countertops by qualified companies is critical.

Stainless steel should be 16 gage or thicker to avoid denting. Substrates are typically ¾ in. (19 mm) plywood, but MDF is also used if no water will be present during use. Metal tops are shop-fabricated, and are bent and welded or soldered together and ground smooth. A No. 3 satin polished finish is commonly used on stainless steel countertops, although the finish may vary based on the intended use of the countertop. The materials used in the countertop surface must be nontoxic to avoid contamination, especially in food service areas. Nosings and backsplashes are formed by bending the metal, and integral sinks, if used, are welded to the counter surface. The metal top is attached to the substrate with a setting material, similar to a ceramic tile setting bed. Fabrication of stainless steel countertops is generally not done by architectural woodworkers, but by sheet metal and specialty metal shops.

## CONCRETE COUNTERTOPS

Concrete countertops are durable and inexpensive units, and are fairly heat, stain, and abrasion resistant. They are monolithic, cast-in-place, or precast units.

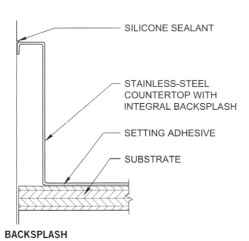

**BACKSPLASH**

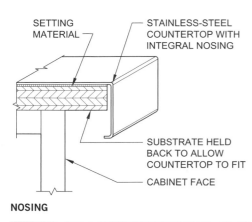

**NOSING**

**STAINLESS STEEL COUNTERTOP**

Appearance varies, due to the variety of colored pigments and aggregate types that may be added to the concrete mixture.

### Cast-in-Place Countertops

Cast-in-place countertops are fabricated from cement, sand, aggregate, additives, and water, and are cast in place over a moisture resistant substrate, such as exterior grade plywood. A sheet moisture barrier should be placed on top of the substrate prior to casting the countertop. To shape the countertop, formwork must be installed and reinforcing placed where stresses will be greatest. The concrete is poured into the formwork and the surface texture is applied to finish the concrete. The concrete must be cured for the appropriate length of time to develop its strength, and should be sealed to protect the concrete upon completion. When installing cast-in-place concrete, care should be taken to not damage adjacent work.

### Pre-cast Concrete Countertops

Precast concrete is typically factory-fabricated. However, large countertops may need to be formed

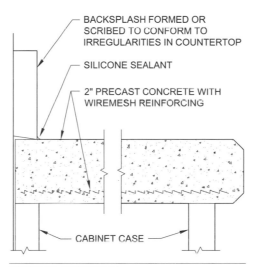

**PRECAST CONCRETE**

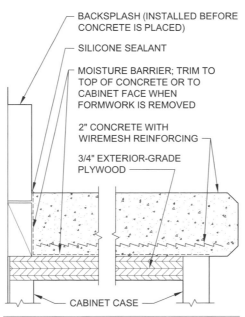

**CAST-IN-PLACE CONCRETE COUNTERTOP**

from more than one precast section, due to manufacturing limitations, and seams may be quite visible.

Coordination of cutouts for sinks and other openings in countertops is critical to ensure proper placement and to allow adequate support for the units mounted within or on the countertop.

## ACCESSIBLE COUNTERTOPS

Other concerns regarding countertops include coordination with adjacent architectural woodwork, such as base cabinets. Compliance is mandatory with Americans with Disabilities Act (ADA) requirements for accessible counters, when applicable. Partition construction, such as a gypsum board alcove that receives a countertop, may affect the final size of the countertop. Field verification of such conditions is recommended, as may be the use of reveals, which are scribed to fit the opening.

The ADA also establishes overall heights of accessible counters from 28 to 34 in. (711 mm to 864 mm) above the finish floor. A minimum clear height of 29 in. (737 mm) must be maintained for accessible lavatory countertops. The need for accessible countertops may affect the counter nosing dimension, undercounter support, and the installed height of the unit in areas under the accessibility requirements.

### Food Service

Where food or drink is served at counters exceeding 34 in. (865 mm) in height for consumption by customers seated on stools or standing at the counter, a portion of the main counter which is 60 in. (1,525 mm) in length minimum shall have at least one accessible route or service shall be available at accessible tables within the same area.

### Sales, Service, and Information Counters

In areas used for transactions where counters have cash registers, at least one of each type shall have a portion of the counter which is at least 36 in. (915 mm) in length with a maximum height of 36 in. (915 mm) above the finish floor. It shall be on an accessible route.

In areas used for transactions that may not have a cash register but at which goods or services are sold or distributed, for example, ticketing counters, teller stations, registration counters in transient lodging facilities, information counters, box office counters, and library checkout areas, there are three options:

- A portion of the main counter, which is a minimum of 36 in. (915 mm) in length, shall be provided with a maximum height of 36 in. (915 mm).
- An auxiliary counter with a maximum height of 36 in (915 mm) in close proximity to the main counter be provided.
- If a separate counter can't be provided, an equivalent facility must be provided for use by persons with disabilities. For example at a hotel registration counter, equivalent facilitation might consist of either a folding shelf attached to the main counter on which an individual with a disability can write, and use of the space on the side of the counter or at the concierge desk, for handing materials back and forth.

*Ted Kollaja, AIA; lauckgroup; Dallas, Texas*
*Sarah Bader; Gensler; Chicago, Illinois*

# WOOD VENEERS

Monumental woodwork projects encompass widespread application of custom-selected wood veneers, either throughout a contiguous space or across broad elevations. In order to create large areas of matching wood panels, *flitches* are matched and applied to an appropriate substrate. A flitch is a part of a log created by slicing the trunk longitudinally, while keeping the sequence of individual leaves in the order they were created. When spliced together, flitches cut from the same log offer a uniform and continuous appearance of wood grain and character. No waste is generated in this process because the logs are sliced with long blades, not sawn, and so no sawdust is generated.

Of the more than 15,000 species of trees, only about 150 are normally sliced into veneer, and only about 25 are of suitable use for monumental woodworking. No more than 10% of any individual species cut and sliced for veneer yields material that meets even the minimum standards of the Architectural Woodwork Institute (AWI) for premium grade.

## SELECTION CRITERIA

Environmental, market, and political factors affect the availability, cost, log size, and other factors that determine the suitability of a veneer to be used for large-scale interior architecture. There are four principal factors: availability, size of log, appearance, and physical properties.

The following species are currently readily available for use as "architectural" veneers:

Anegre
Ash, European
Avodire
Beech (steamed and unsteamed), European
Bubinga
Douglas fir
Etimoe
Eucalyptus
Mahogany (African and Honduras)
Makore
Moabi
Movinque
Oak, American red (various cuts)
Oak, American white (various cuts)
Oak, European white
Okoume
Pommele (Makore, Sapele, Moabi)
Sapele
Sycamore, American
Sycamore, English
Teak
Tigerwood
Walnut, American
Wenge
Zebrawood

Commonly specified veneers such as American cherry and maple are omitted because of their wide inconsistencies within the species and relative scarcity of high-grade flitches.

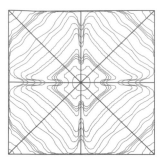
EIGHT-PIECE SUNBURST

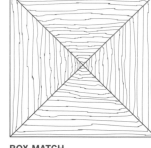
BOX MATCH

PARQUET MATCH

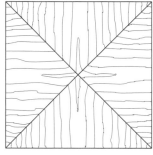
REVERSE OR END GRAIN BOX

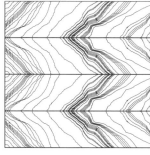
HERRINGBONE

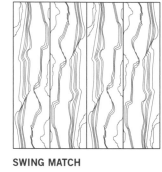
SWING MATCH

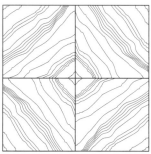
DIAMOND

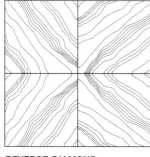
REVERSE DIAMOND

SKETCH FACE

SPECIAL WOOD VENEER MATCHING OPTIONS

## COMMON FACE VENEER PATTERNS OF SELECTED COMMERCIAL SPECIES

| PRIMARY COMMERCIAL HARDWOOD SPECIES | FACE VENEER PATTERNS[1] | | | |
|---|---|---|---|---|
| | PLAIN-SLICED (FLAT-CUT) | QUARTER-CUT | RIFT-CUT AND COMB GRAIN | ROTARY-CUT |
| Ash | Yes | Yes | — | Yes |
| Birch | Yes | — | — | Yes |
| Cherry | Yes | Yes | — | Yes |
| Hickory | Yes | — | — | Yes |
| Lauan | — | Yes | — | Yes |
| Mahogany (African) | Yes | Yes | — | Yes |
| Mahogany (Honduras) | Yes | Yes | — | Yes |
| Maple | Yes | Yes | — | Yes |
| Meranti | — | Yes | — | Yes |
| Oak (red) | Yes | Yes | Yes | Yes |
| Oak (white) | Yes | Yes | Yes | Yes |
| Pecan | Yes | — | — | Yes |
| Walnut (black) | Yes | Yes | — | Yes |
| Yellow poplar | Yes | — | — | Yes |
| Typical methods of cutting[2] | Plain slicing or half-round on rotary lathe | Quarter-slicing | Offset quarter on rotary lathe | Rotary lathe |

[1] The headings below refer to the face veneer pattern, not to the method of cutting. Face veneer patterns other than those listed are obtainable by special order.

[2] The method of cutting for a given face veneer pattern must be at mill option unless otherwise specified by the buyer in an explicit manner to avoid the possibility of misunderstanding. For example, plain-sliced veneer cut on a vertical slicer, or plain-sliced veneer cut on a half-round rotary lathe, could be specified.

Source: Hardwood, Plywood, and Veneer Association

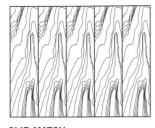

**SLIP MATCH**

**BOOK MATCH**

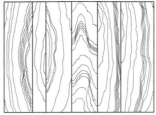

**RANDOM MATCH**

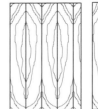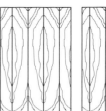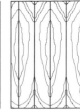

**RUNNING MATCH**

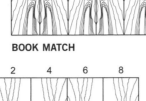

8    7    6    5

1    2    3    4

**PANEL END MATCH**

2    4    6    8

1    3    5    7

**ARCHITECTURAL END MATCH**

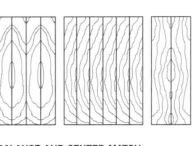

**BALANCE AND CENTER MATCH**

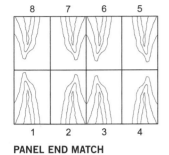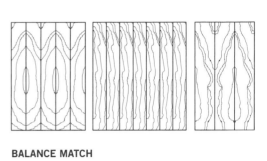

**BALANCE MATCH**

**WOOD VENEER MATCHING**

## CHARACTERISTICS OF WOOD VENEER SPECIES

| SPECIES | TYPE OF CUT | WIDTH (FROM–TO) IN. (MM) | LENGTH (FROM–TO) FT (M) | LOG SIZE | COST | AVAILABILITY |
|---|---|---|---|---|---|---|
| Anegre | Quartered—nonfigured | 6–14 (150–355) | 9–12 (2.7–3.6) | Large | Low | Good |
| | Quartered—figured | 4–20 (100–510) | 9–12 (2.7–3.6) | Medium/large | Moderate/high | Good |
| | Quartered—fiddleback figure | 4–16 (100–405) | 9–12 (2.7–3.6) | Medium/large | High | Limited |
| | Plain-sliced—nonfigured | 9–24 (230–610) | 9–12 (2.7–3.6) | Medium | Low | Good |
| | Plain-sliced—figured | 9–24 (230–610) | 9–12 (2.7–3.6) | Medium | Moderate/high | Limited |
| Avodire | Quartered | 4–8 (100–200) | 9–12 (2.7–3.6) | Medium | Moderate | Good |
| Ash, European | Quartered/plain-sliced—figured | 4–10/10–26 (100–255/255–660) | 9–14 (2.7–4.2) | Medium | Moderate | Good |
| European beech (steamed) | Quartered/plain-sliced | 4–10/10–26 (100–255/255–660) | 9–12 (2.7–3.6) | Small/medium | Low | Good |
| European beech (unsteamed) | Quartered/plain-sliced | 4–8/8–22 (100–200/200–560) | 9–12 (2.7–3.6) | Small/medium | Low | Limited |
| Bubinga | Quartered/plain-sliced | 6–12/12–30 (150–305/305–760) | 9–12 (2.7–3.6) | Large | Moderate | Good |
| Douglas fir | Quartered | 5–12 (130–305) | 9–13 | Medium/large | Moderate | Good |
| Etimoe | Quartered—figured | 6–14 (150–355) | 8–11 | Large | Moderate | Good |
| Eucalyptus | Quartered—figured | 6–12 (150–305) | 9–14 (2.7–4.2) | Medium/large | Moderate | Good |
| Mahogany | Quartered | 6–24 (150–610) | 9–15 (2.7–4.5) | Large | Low | Good |
| (African; aka Khaya) | Quartered—figured | 4–12 (100–305) | 9–12 (2.7–3.6) | Medium/large | Moderate | Limited |
| | Plain-sliced | 8–26 (200–660) | 8–11 (2.4–3.3) | Small/medium | Low | Good |
| Mahogany (Honduras) | Quartered/plain-sliced | 6–10/9–20 (150–250/230–510) | 9–12 (2.7–3.6) | Small/medium | Low | Good |
| Makore | Quartered—nonfigured | 6–18 (150–460) | 9–14 (2.7–4.2) | Large | Low | Good |
| | Quartered—figured | 6–24 (150–610) | 9–14 (2.7–4.2) | Large | Moderate | Good |
| | Quartered—fiddleback figure | 6–18 (150–460) | 9–14 (2.7–4.2) | Large | Very high | Very limited |
| | Plain-sliced—nonfigured | 9–24 (230–610) | 9–14 (2.7–4.2) | Medium | Low | Limited |
| | Plain-sliced—figured | 9–24 (230–610) | 9–14 (2.7–4.2) | Medium | Moderate | Limited |
| Moabi | Quartered | 4–14 (100–355) | 9–12 (2.7–3.6) | Large | Low | Good |
| | Quartered—figured | 4–12 (100–305) | 9–12 (2.7–3.6) | Large | Moderate | Good |
| Movinque | Quartered—figured | 6–16 (150–405) | 9–12 (2.7–3.6) | Large | Moderate | Good |
| Oak, American white | Quartered | 5–10 (130–250) | 9–12 (2.7–3.6) | Small | Low | Good |
| | Plain-sliced | 8–20 (200–510) | 9–12 (2.7–3.6) | Small | Low | Good |
| | Rift-cut | 4–9 (100–230) | 9–12 (2.7–3.6) | Small | Moderate | Limited |
| Oak, American red | Quartered | 5–10 (130–250) | 9–12 (2.7–3.6) | Small | Low | Good |
| | Plain-sliced | 8–24 (200–610) | 9–12 (2.7–3.6) | Small | Low | Good |
| | Rift-cut | 6–12 (150–305) | 9–12 (2.7–3.6) | Small | Moderate | Limited |
| Oak, European white | Quartered | 4–9 (100–230) | 9–11 (3.3–3.3) | Small/medium | Moderate | Good |
| Okoume | Quartered—figured | 7–14 (180–355) | 9–12 (2.7–3.6) | Large | Moderate | Good |
| Pommele (Makore, Sapele, Moabi) | Rotary-cut | 6–30 (150–760) | 9–12 2.7–3.6) | Large | High | Good |
| Sapele | Quartered | 5–14 (130–355) | 9–14 (2.7–4.2) | Large | Low | Good |
| | Quartered—figured | 5–14 (130–355) | 9–14 (2.7–4.2) | Large | Moderate | Good |
| | Plain-sliced | 10–22 (250–560) | 9–14 (2.7–4.2) | Medium/large | Low | Good |
| Sycamore, American | Quartered | 3–9 (75–230) | 9–12 (2.7–3.6) | Medium | Moderate | Limited |
| Sycamore, English | Quartered/plain-sliced—figured | 4–10/8–22 (100–250/200–560) | 9–14 (2.7–4.2) | Medium | High | Limited |
| Teak | Quartered/plain-sliced | 4–8/8–22 (100–200/200–560) | 9–14 (2.7–4.2) | Small/medium | Moderate/high | Limited |

## Size of Log

The diameter and length of the log determine two key aspects of the veneer produced from it. The diameter directly determines the width of the veneer leaves. It is important to determine if a flitch will yield the square footage, leaf width, and length that a project requires.

Tropical species such as Anegre, Makore, and Sapele can provide very large quantities of wide veneer from a single log, often enough to complete a substantial project. Temperate species, on the other hand, are generally not available in such large flitches and leaf widths. In order to execute a very large project using these species, it is necessary to match up many flitches, "marrying" appearances including grain structure, natural color, and degree and type of figure.

## Appearance

The appearance of wood is determined by naturally occurring characteristics that include grain, figure, color, heartwood or sapwood, knots and pin knots, and mineral and sap deposits. *Grain* is an expression of the annual growth ring structure of the tree that is revealed upon the cutting of the wood. *Figure* is caused by the convoluted growth of the wood fiber in the tree at a cellular level. Some trees grow quite regularly and therefore have an even orientation of wood fiber; once revealed, this wood shows a *nonfigured* appearance. When an irregular or aberrant growth pattern is established in the tree, the resulting wood shows figure. Bird's-eye maple and fiddleback Anegre are two such woods.

There are many figure types, but it is important to know that they are not found universally in all woods;

and in many cases, they occur rarely or on a one-of-a-kind basis. The natural color of a particular species can vary greatly depending on various factors, including the growing area of the tree, the time of year the log was cut, and the length of time the log was steamed prior to slicing. Knots, pin knots, and mineral and sap deposits are all naturally occurring features that either diminish or enhance one's appreciation of the wood depending on the aesthetic at hand.

## Physical Properties

All commercially available veneer is sliced, not sawn. A veneer-slicing machine uses a very sharp knife that contacts the flitch and cleanly slices off one piece of veneer without the waste inherent in sawdust. The log must first be "steamed." Steaming is a process whereby the log, after debarking, is soaked in large tanks of very hot water for up to three days. How much time a log is steamed, and at what temperature, depends on the species and size of the log. Steaming softens the wood within the log and allows the knife to slice through cleanly.

Combined, steaming and slicing affect the wood in several ways. First, the raw wood color is affected by steaming, and the veneer manufacturer must control this to provide a uniform wood color. In addition, slicing affects the very nature of the wood fiber. As the knife enters the wood, it puts the leading edge of the cut in compression, and the trailing surface (the back of the leaf being created) in tension. Thus, the two sides of every leaf of wood veneer created by a veneer slicer have opposite wood fiber properties, called *tight face* and *loose face*.

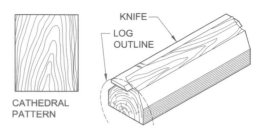

This is the slicing method most often used to produce veneers for high-quality architectural woodworking. Slicing is done parallel to a line through the center of the log. A combination of cathedral and straight-grain patterns results, with a natural progression of pattern from leaf to leaf.

**PLAIN-SLICED (FLAT-SLICED) VENEER**

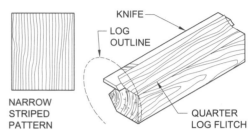

Quarter slicing, roughly parallel to a radius line through the log segment, simulates the quarter-sawing process used with solid lumber. In many species the individual leaves are narrow as a result. A series of stripes is produced, varying in density and thickness among species. "Flake" is a characteristic of this slicing method in red and white oak.

**QUARTER-SLICED VENEER**

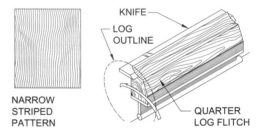

Rift veneers are produced most often in red and white oak, rarely in other species. Note that rift veneers and rift-sawn solid lumber are produced so differently that a "match" between them is highly unlikely. In both cases the cutting is done slightly off the radius lines, minimizing the "flake" associated with quarter slicing.

**RIFT-SLICED (RIFT-CUT) VENEER**

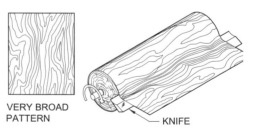

To create rotary-cut veneers, the log is center mounted on a lathe and "peeled" along the path of the growth rings, like unwinding a roll of paper. This provides a bold, random appearance. Rotary-cut veneers vary in width, and matching at veneer joints is extremely difficult. Almost all softwood veneers are cut this way. Rotary-cut veneers are the least useful in fine architectural woodwork.

**ROTARY-CUT VENEER**

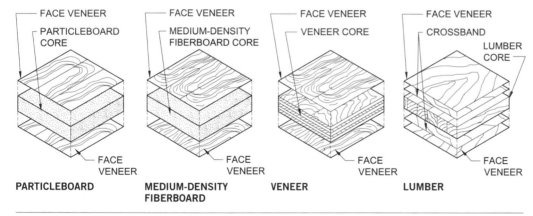

**HARDWOOD PLYWOOD CORE TYPES**

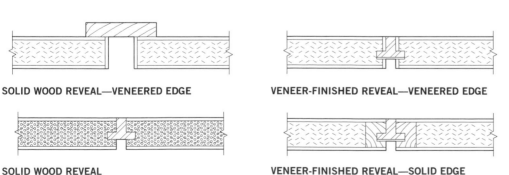

MDF core recommended for incised reveals. MDF not readily available as fire-rated panels.

**VENEER PANEL JOINTS**
*Source: Architectural Woodwork Institute; Architectural Quality Standards, 7th Ed. (Version 1.2), Reston, Virginia, 1999.*

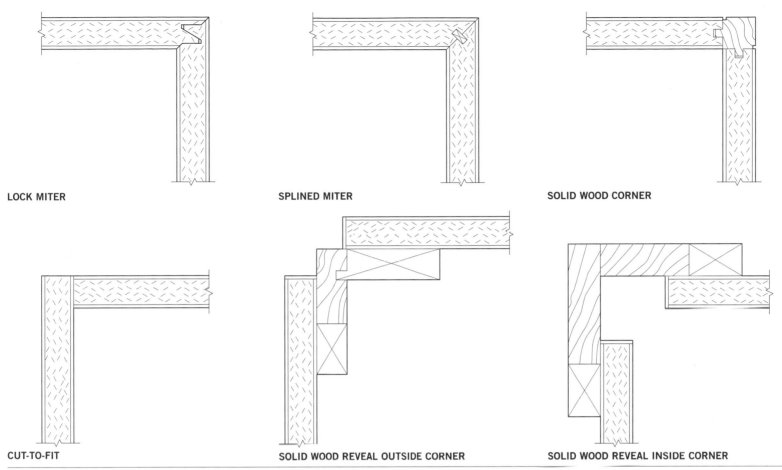

LOCK MITER     SPLINED MITER     SOLID WOOD CORNER

CUT-TO-FIT     SOLID WOOD REVEAL OUTSIDE CORNER     SOLID WOOD REVEAL INSIDE CORNER

**VENEER PANEL CORNER JOINTS AND TRANSITIONS** *Source: Architectural Woodwork Institute; Architectural Quality Standards, 7th Ed. (Version 1.2), Reston, Virginia, 1999.*

## CHARACTERISTICS* OF CORE MATERIAL PERFORMANCE

| PANEL TYPE | FLATNESS | VISUAL EDGE QUALITY | SURFACE UNIFORMITY | DIMENSIONAL STABILITY | SCREW-HOLDING STRENGTH | BENDING STRENGTH | AVAILABILITY |
|---|---|---|---|---|---|---|---|
| Industrial particleboard core (medium density) | Excellent | Good | Excellent | Fair | Fair | Good | Ready |
| Medium-density fiberboard core (MDF) | Excellent | Excellent | Excellent | Fair | Good | Good | Ready |
| Veneer core—all hardwood | Fair | Good | Good | Excellent | Excellent | Excellent | Ready |
| Veneer core—all softwood | Fair | Good | Fair | Excellent | Excellent | Excellent | Ready |
| Lumber core—hardwood or softwood | Good | Good | Good | Good | Excellent | Excellent | Limited |
| Standard hardboard core | Excellent | Excellent | Excellent | Fair | Good | Good | Ready |
| Tempered hardboard core | Excellent | Good | Good | Good | Good | Good | Limited |
| Moisture-resistant particleboard core | Excellent | Good | Good | Fair | Fair | Good | Limited |
| Moisture-resistant MDF core | Excellent | Excellent | Good | Fair | Good | Good | Limited |
| Fire-resistant particleboard core | Excellent | Fair | Good | Fair | Fair | Good | Limited |

*Characteristics of core material performance are influenced by the grade and thickness of the core and specific gravity of the core species. Visual edge quality is rated before treatment with edge bands or fillers and, for lumber core, assumes the use of "clear edge" grade. Surface uniformity is directly related to the performance of fine veneers placed over the surface. Dimensional stability is usually related to exposure to wide variations in relative humidity. Screw-holding and bending strength are influenced by proper design and engineering.

## FLITCH SELECTIONS

Veneer companies specializing in architectural veneer inventory their flitches for the designer's selection and specification. Every flitch of veneer carries a flitch number that identifies it, and this number can be included in the construction documents. Because there are so many variables to getting the desired results, flitches are identified and secured at the time a job is being specified.

*Dan Meyerson; R.S. Bacon Veneer Company; New York, New York*

# INTERIOR ARCHITECTURAL WOODWORK

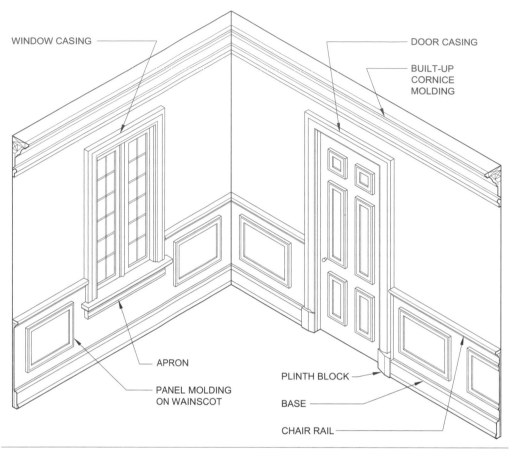

WINDOW CASING

DOOR CASING

BUILT-UP CORNICE MOLDING

APRON

PANEL MOLDING ON WAINSCOT

PLINTH BLOCK

BASE

CHAIR RAIL

**TYPICAL WOOD TRIM**

BASE CAPS

SHINGLES

BASE CAP

MULLION

ASTRAGAL

CASING

S4S

COVES

S4S

BASE CAPS

COVE

WAINSCOT CAP

BASE

S4S

HALF-ROUND

COVE

**CHAIR RAILS**

Interior trim is generally a decorative treatment applied after wall, floor, and ceiling finishes have been installed. It can be made of flat or molded wood, from single pieces of wood, or from built-up pieces that give a more complex and decorative appearance. Interior trim conceals joints between different materials and blocks air infiltration through walls, which typically is greatest at material joints. Interior trim also frames wall and ceiling openings (for example, door, window, and skylight trim), defines planar edges (for example, crown and base molding), and acts as a visual divider between dissimilar materials (for example, a chair rail).

## STANDING AND RUNNING WOOD

The Architectural Woodwork Institute differentiates wood trim according to its length. *Standing wood trim* is trim that can be accommodated easily with single lengths of wood (depending on species), such as crown moldings, fascias, soffits, chair rails, baseboards, and shoe moldings. *Running trim* is usually made up of finger-jointed wood to achieve the lengths customarily needed for this type of trim. Most flat trim like baseboards and casing have a ploughed or relieved back, which gives wide trim a degree of flexibility, allowing it to fit snugly against a wall surface.

## INSTALLATION

Woodwork should be stored in a dry, ventilated space. Moldings should be at optimum moisture content at the time of installation and should be allowed to acclimate to project conditions before installation. Joints in adjacent and related members should be staggered.

Inside corners should be coped, and outside corners should be mitered to produce tight-fitting joints with full surface contact throughout the length of the joint. Scarf joints (face-mitered joints) should be used for end-to-end joints in trim. Blind nailing with finishing nails in exposed areas should be required. Predrilling trim can eliminate splitting.

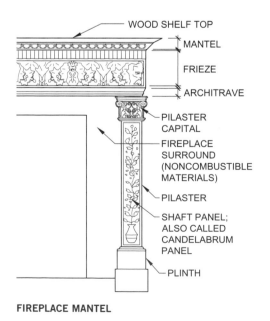

WOOD SHELF TOP

MANTEL

FRIEZE

ARCHITRAVE

PILASTER CAPITAL

FIREPLACE SURROUND (NONCOMBUSTIBLE MATERIALS)

PILASTER

SHAFT PANEL; ALSO CALLED CANDELABRUM PANEL

PLINTH

**FIREPLACE MANTEL**

**MANTELS**

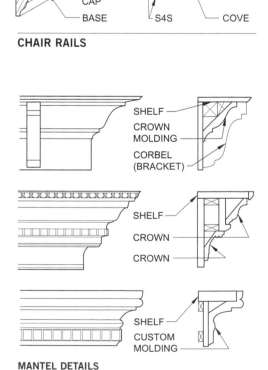

SHELF

CROWN MOLDING

CORBEL (BRACKET)

SHELF

CROWN

CROWN

SHELF

CUSTOM MOLDING

**MANTEL DETAILS**

*Source: Architectural Woodwork Institute; Architectural Quality Standards, 7th ed. (Version 1.2), Reston, Virginia, 1999.*

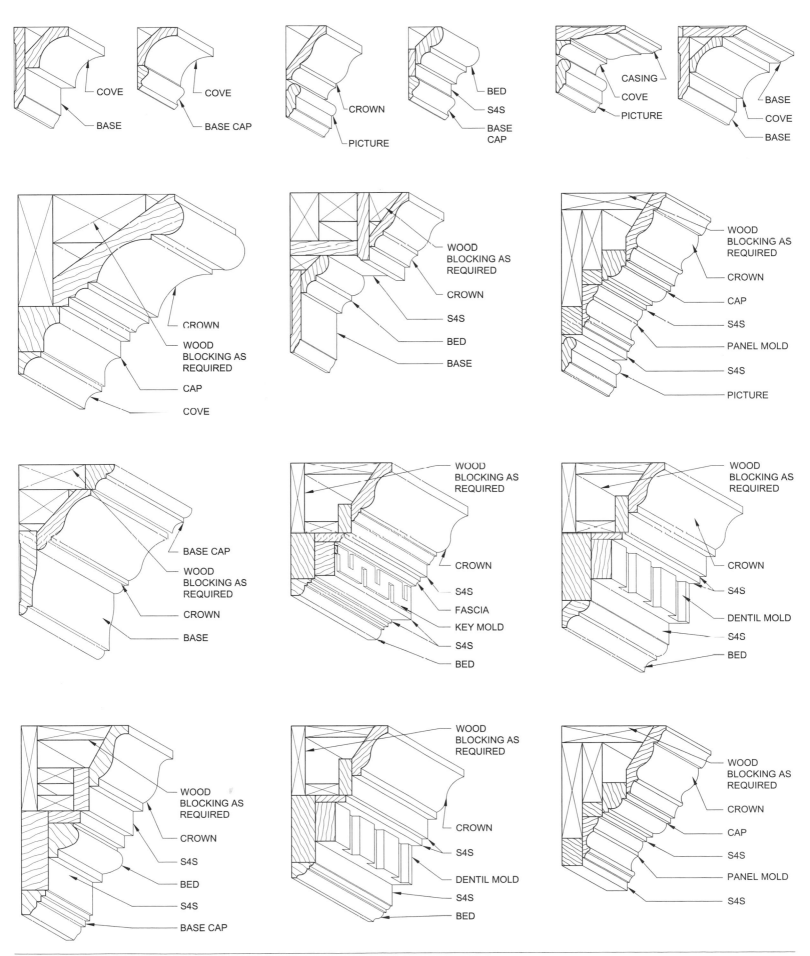

**BUILT-UP CORNICES**

*Source: Architectural Woodwork Institute; Architectural Quality Standards, 7th ed. (Version 1.2), Reston, Virginia, 1999.*

## PANELED WAINSCOT DETAILS

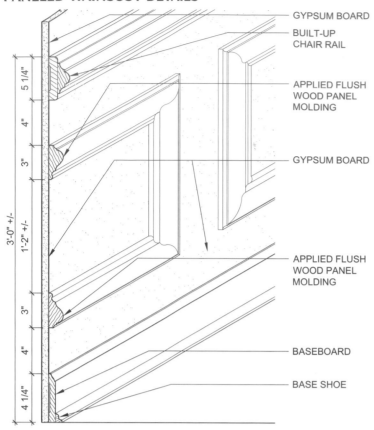

GYPSUM BOARD

BUILT-UP CHAIR RAIL

APPLIED FLUSH WOOD PANEL MOLDING

GYPSUM BOARD

APPLIED FLUSH WOOD PANEL MOLDING

BASEBOARD

BASE SHOE

5 1/4"
4"
3"
3'-0" +/-
1'-2" +/-
3"
4"
4 1/4"

Wainscot must be painted to conceal variety of materials. This is the least expensive wainscot option.

**WOOD MOLD APPLIED TO GYPSUM BOARD**

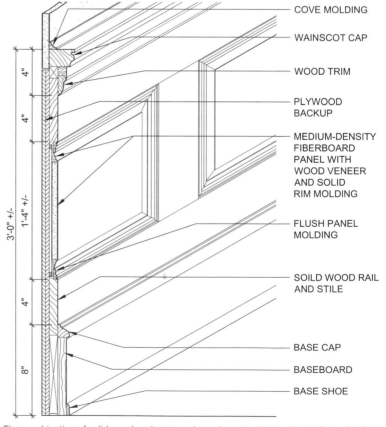

GYPSUM BOARD

CHAIR RAIL

WOOD TRIM

APPLIED FLUSH WOOD PANEL MOLDING

FLAT PLYWOOD PANEL WITH WOOD VENEER

APPLIED FLUSH WOOD PANEL MOLDING

BASE CAP

BASEBOARD

BASE SHOE

4 3/4"
4"
3"
3'-0" +/-
1'-1" +/-
3"
4"
4 1/4"

Wainscot must be painted to conceal variety of materials. This is a less expensive wainscot option.

**WOOD MOLD APPLIED TO PLYWOOD PANEL WITH VENEER**

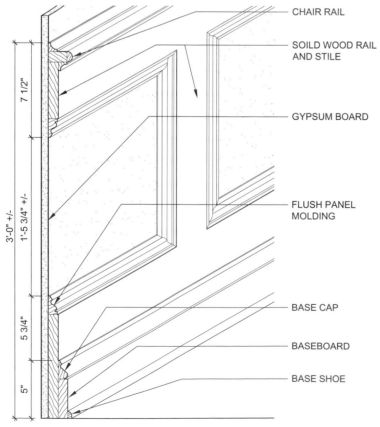

CHAIR RAIL

SOILD WOOD RAIL AND STILE

GYPSUM BOARD

FLUSH PANEL MOLDING

BASE CAP

BASEBOARD

BASE SHOE

7 1/2"
3'-0" +/-
1'-5 3/4" +/-
5 3/4"
5"

Wainscot must be painted to conceal variety of materials. This is a less expensive wainscot option.

**WOOD MOLD, STILE, AND RAIL APPLIED TO GYPSUM BOARD**

COVE MOLDING

WAINSCOT CAP

WOOD TRIM

PLYWOOD BACKUP

MEDIUM-DENSITY FIBERBOARD PANEL WITH WOOD VENEER AND SOLID RIM MOLDING

FLUSH PANEL MOLDING

SOILD WOOD RAIL AND STILE

BASE CAP

BASEBOARD

BASE SHOE

4"
4"
3'-0" +/-
1'-4" +/-
4"
8"

The combination of solid wood and veneered wood composite panels can be stained. This is an expensive wainscot option.

**APPLIED WAINSCOT WITH GYPSUM BOARD WALL ABOVE**

## PANELED WAINSCOT DETAILS

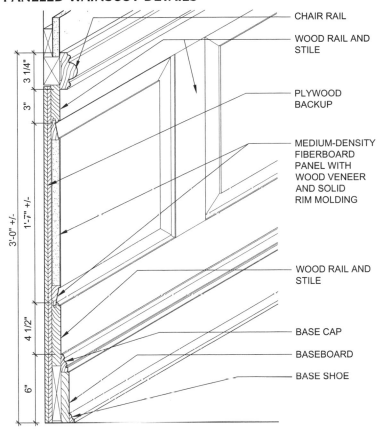

CHAIR RAIL

WOOD RAIL AND STILE

PLYWOOD BACKUP

MEDIUM-DENSITY FIBERBOARD PANEL WITH WOOD VENEER AND SOLID RIM MOLDING

WOOD RAIL AND STILE

BASE CAP

BASEBOARD

BASE SHOE

3 1/4"
3"
1'-7" +/-
3'-0" +/-
4 1/2"
6"

The combination of solid wood and veneered wood composite panels can be stained. This is an expensive wainscot option.

**WAINSCOT FLUSH WITH GYPSUM BOARD WALL ABOVE**

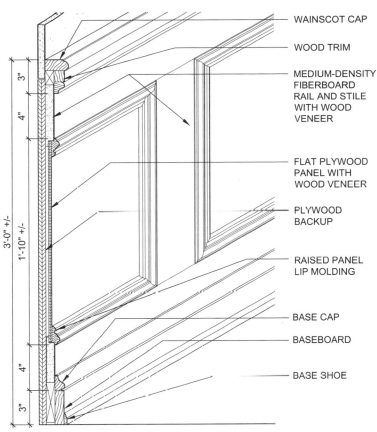

WAINSCOT CAP

WOOD TRIM

MEDIUM-DENSITY FIBERBOARD RAIL AND STILE WITH WOOD VENEER

FLAT PLYWOOD PANEL WITH WOOD VENEER

PLYWOOD BACKUP

RAISED PANEL LIP MOLDING

BASE CAP

BASEBOARD

BASE SHOE

3"
4"
1'-10" +/-
3'-0" +/-
4"
3"

The combination of solid wood and veneered wood composite panels can be stained. This is an expensive wainscot option.

**APPLIED WAINSCOT WITH GYPSUM BOARD WALL ABOVE**

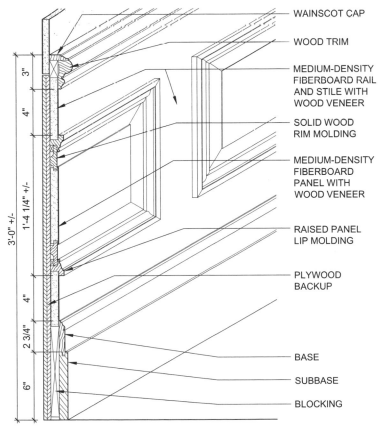

WAINSCOT CAP

WOOD TRIM

MEDIUM-DENSITY FIBERBOARD RAIL AND STILE WITH WOOD VENEER

SOLID WOOD RIM MOLDING

MEDIUM-DENSITY FIBERBOARD PANEL WITH WOOD VENEER

RAISED PANEL LIP MOLDING

PLYWOOD BACKUP

BASE

SUBBASE

BLOCKING

3"
4"
1'-4 1/4" +/-
3'-0" +/-
4"
2 3/4"
6"

The combination of solid wood and veneered wood composite panels can be stained. This is an expensive wainscot option.

**APPLIED WAINSCOT WITH GYPSUM BOARD WALL ABOVE**

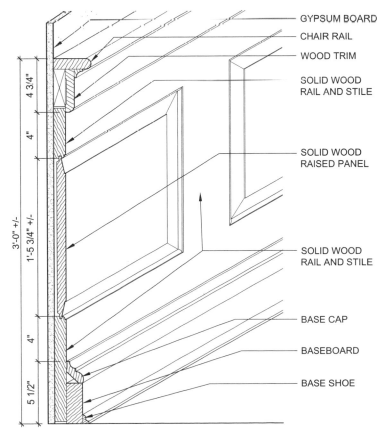

GYPSUM BOARD

CHAIR RAIL

WOOD TRIM

SOLID WOOD RAIL AND STILE

SOLID WOOD RAISED PANEL

SOLID WOOD RAIL AND STILE

BASE CAP

BASEBOARD

BASE SHOE

4 3/4"
4"
1'-5 3/4" +/-
3'-0" +/-
4"
5 1/2"

Solid wood panels can be stained. This is a more expensive wainscot option.

**APPLIED WAINSCOT WITH GYPSUM BOARD WALL ABOVE**

## BASE TRIM

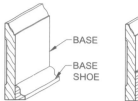 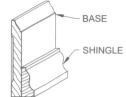

**TWO-PIECE BASE TRIM WITH PROFILED BASE** — BASE, BASE SHOE

**TWO-PIECE BASE TRIM WITH PROFILED BASE** — BASE, SHINGLE

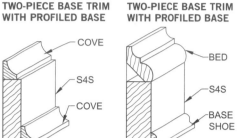

**THREE-PIECE BASE TRIM** — COVE, S4S, COVE

**THREE-PIECE BASE TRIM** — BED, S4S, BASE SHOE

### BUILT-UP WOOD BASE TRIM

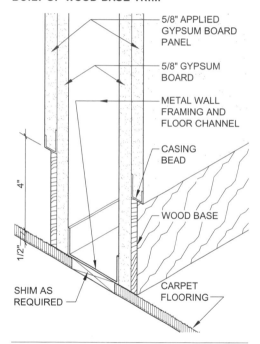

- 5/8" APPLIED GYPSUM BOARD PANEL
- 5/8" GYPSUM BOARD
- METAL WALL FRAMING AND FLOOR CHANNEL
- CASING BEAD
- WOOD BASE
- 4"
- 1/2"
- SHIM AS REQUIRED
- CARPET FLOORING

### RECESSED WOOD BASE

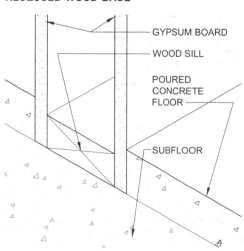

- GYPSUM BOARD
- WOOD SILL
- POURED CONCRETE FLOOR
- SUBFLOOR

Base of gypsum board wall surface is susceptible to damage. This detail requires skill to execute properly.

**NO BASE WITH POURED CONCRETE FLOOR**

---

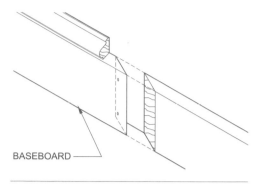

- BASEBOARD

### SCARF JOINT

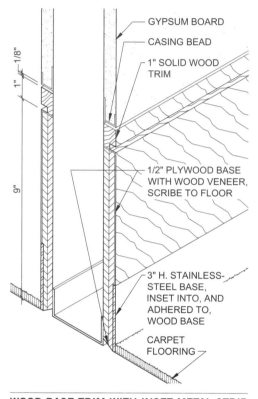

- GYPSUM BOARD
- CASING BEAD
- 1" SOLID WOOD TRIM
- 1/8"
- 1"
- 9"
- 1/2" PLYWOOD BASE WITH WOOD VENEER, SCRIBE TO FLOOR
- 3" H. STAINLESS-STEEL BASE, INSET INTO, AND ADHERED TO, WOOD BASE
- CARPET FLOORING

**WOOD BASE TRIM WITH INSET METAL STRIP**
*Source: Zimmer Gunsul Frasca Partnership; Seattle, Washington*

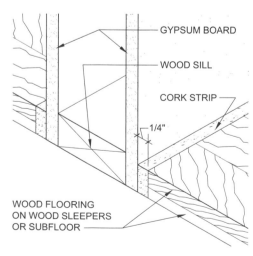

- GYPSUM BOARD
- WOOD SILL
- CORK STRIP
- 1/4"
- WOOD FLOORING ON WOOD SLEEPERS OR SUBFLOOR

Base of gypsum board wall surface is susceptible to damage.

**NO BASE WITH WOOD FLOOR**

---

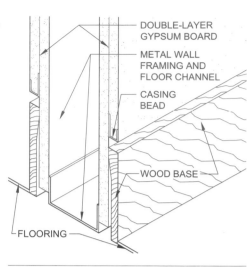

- DOUBLE-LAYER GYPSUM BOARD
- METAL WALL FRAMING AND FLOOR CHANNEL
- CASING BEAD
- WOOD BASE
- FLOORING

### WOOD BASE WITH GYPSUM BOARD REVEAL

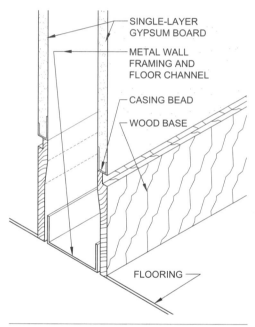

- SINGLE-LAYER GYPSUM BOARD
- METAL WALL FRAMING AND FLOOR CHANNEL
- CASING BEAD
- WOOD BASE
- FLOORING

**WOOD BASE WITH WOOD REVEAL**

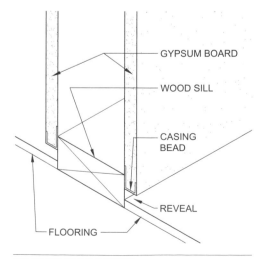

- GYPSUM BOARD
- WOOD SILL
- CASING BEAD
- REVEAL
- FLOORING

**NO BASE WITH REVEAL**

# PANELED PORTAL WITH ACCESS DOORS

Project: *National Gallery of Art; Washington, D.C.*
Designer: *Vitetta Group/Studio Four; Philadelphia, Pennsylvania*
Woodworker: *Washington Woodworking Company, Inc.; Landover, Maryland*
Design Solutions, *Summer 1990*

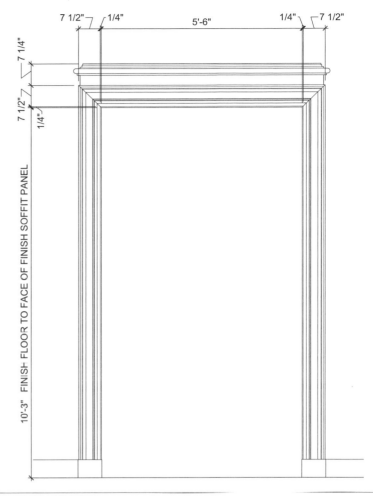

**DOOR ELEVATION**

10'-3"  FINISH- FLOOR TO FACE OF FINISH SOFFIT PANEL

7 1/2"    1/4"       5'-6"       1/4"    7 1/2"
7 1/4"
7 1/2"
1/4"

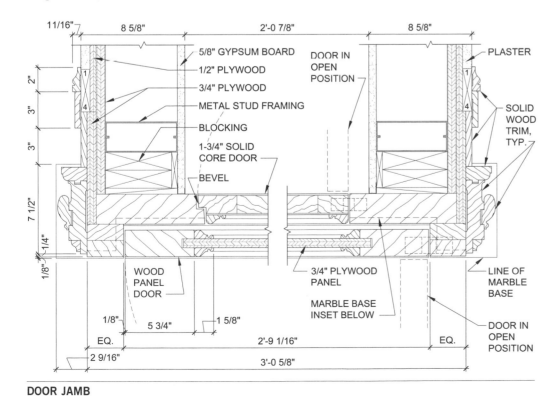

**DOOR JAMB**

5/8" GYPSUM BOARD
1/2" PLYWOOD
3/4" PLYWOOD
METAL STUD FRAMING
BLOCKING
1-3/4" SOLID CORE DOOR
BEVEL
DOOR IN OPEN POSITION
PLASTER
SOLID WOOD TRIM, TYP.
WOOD PANEL DOOR
3/4" PLYWOOD PANEL
MARBLE BASE INSET BELOW
LINE OF MARBLE BASE
DOOR IN OPEN POSITION

11/16"    8 5/8"       2'-0 7/8"        8 5/8"
2"
3"
3"
7 1/2"
1/4"
1/8"
1/8"    5 3/4"    1 5/8"
EQ.        2'-9 1/16"        EQ.
2 9/16"
3'-0 5/8"

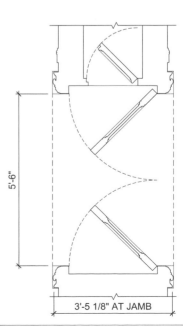

**PLAN AT DOOR**

5'-6"

3'-5 1/8" AT JAMB

# CURVED PANELED WALL

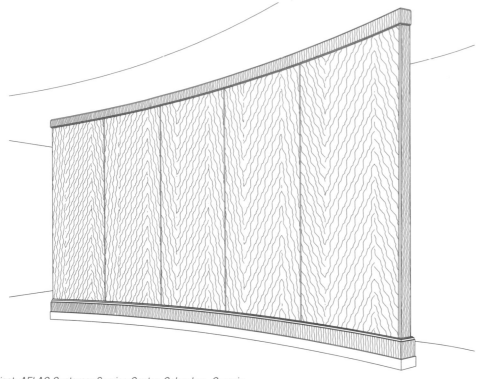

Project: AFLAC Customer Service Center; Columbus, Georgia
Designer: Hecht, Burdeshaw, Johnson, Kidd & Clark; Columbus, Georgia
Woodworker: Columbus Cabinet Company; Columbus, Georgia
Design Solutions, Winter 2000

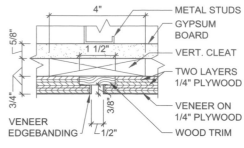

**(A) DETAIL AT REVEAL**

METAL STUDS
GYPSUM BOARD
VERT. CLEAT
TWO LAYERS 1/4" PLYWOOD
VENEER ON 1/4" PLYWOOD
WOOD TRIM
VENEER EDGEBANDING

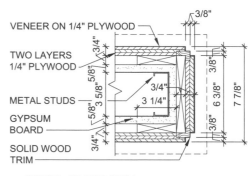

**(B) DETAIL AT END WALL**

VENEER ON 1/4" PLYWOOD
TWO LAYERS 1/4" PLYWOOD
METAL STUDS
GYPSUM BOARD
SOLID WOOD TRIM

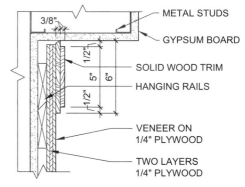

**(C) DETAIL AT CEILING**

METAL STUDS
GYPSUM BOARD
SOLID WOOD TRIM
HANGING RAILS
VENEER ON 1/4" PLYWOOD
TWO LAYERS 1/4" PLYWOOD

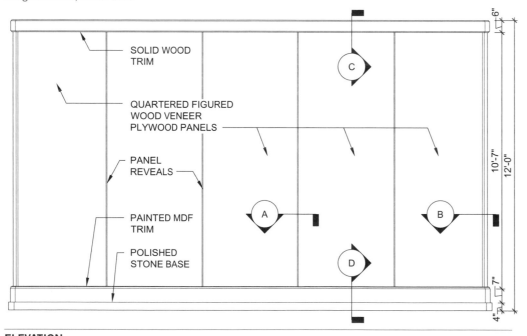

**ELEVATION**

SOLID WOOD TRIM
QUARTERED FIGURED WOOD VENEER PLYWOOD PANELS
PANEL REVEALS
PAINTED MDF TRIM
POLISHED STONE BASE

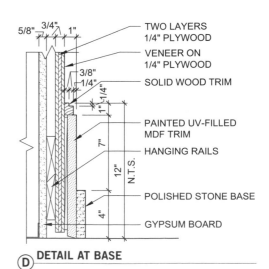

**(D) DETAIL AT BASE**

TWO LAYERS 1/4" PLYWOOD
VENEER ON 1/4" PLYWOOD
SOLID WOOD TRIM
PAINTED UV-FILLED MDF TRIM
HANGING RAILS
POLISHED STONE BASE
GYPSUM BOARD

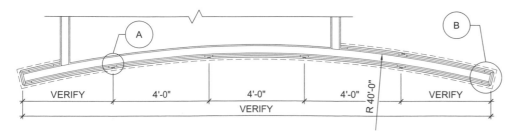

VERIFY   4'-0"   4'-0"   4'-0"   VERIFY
VERIFY
R 40'-0"

**PLAN**

# PANELED LOBBY WITH CONCEALED DOOR JAMB

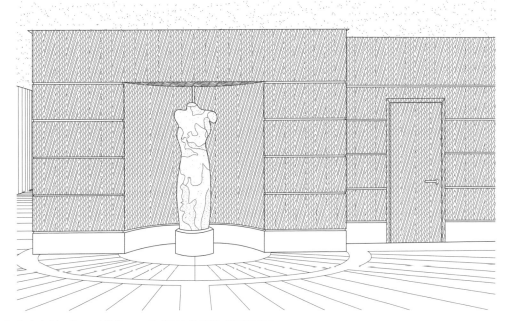

Project: Lobby, Second & Seneca Building; Seattle, Washington
Designer: Zimmer Gunsul Frasca Partnership; Seattle, Washington

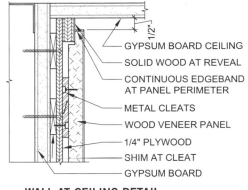

- GYPSUM BOARD CEILING
- SOLID WOOD AT REVEAL
- CONTINUOUS EDGEBAND AT PANEL PERIMETER
- METAL CLEATS
- WOOD VENEER PANEL
- 1/4" PLYWOOD
- SHIM AT CLEAT
- GYPSUM BOARD

Ⓓ **WALL AT CEILING DETAIL**

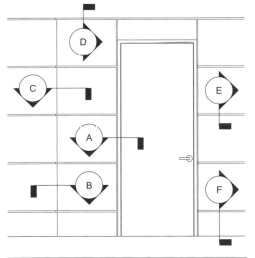

**DOOR ELEVATION**

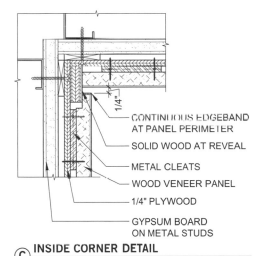

1 3/8"
1/4"   5/8"

- CONTINUOUS EDGEBAND AT PANEL PERIMETER
- SOLID WOOD AT REVEAL
- METAL CLEATS
- WOOD VENEER PANEL
- 1/4" PLYWOOD
- GYPSUM BOARD ON METAL STUDS

Ⓒ **INSIDE CORNER DETAIL**

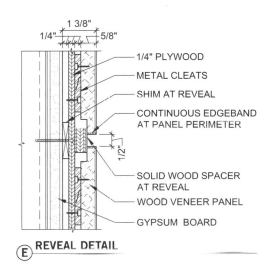

1 3/8"
1/4"   5/8"

- 1/4" PLYWOOD
- METAL CLEATS
- SHIM AT REVEAL
- CONTINUOUS EDGEBAND AT PANEL PERIMETER
- SOLID WOOD SPACER AT REVEAL
- WOOD VENEER PANEL
- GYPSUM BOARD

Ⓔ **REVEAL DETAIL**

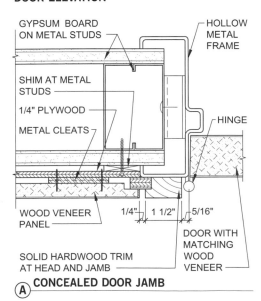

- GYPSUM BOARD ON METAL STUDS
- HOLLOW METAL FRAME
- SHIM AT METAL STUDS
- 1/4" PLYWOOD
- METAL CLEATS
- HINGE
- WOOD VENEER PANEL
- 1/4"   1 1/2"   5/16"
- DOOR WITH MATCHING WOOD VENEER
- SOLID HARDWOOD TRIM AT HEAD AND JAMB

Ⓐ **CONCEALED DOOR JAMB**

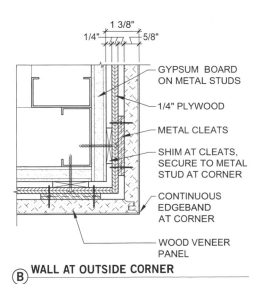

1 3/8"
1/4"   5/8"

- GYPSUM BOARD ON METAL STUDS
- 1/4" PLYWOOD
- METAL CLEATS
- SHIM AT CLEATS, SECURE TO METAL STUD AT CORNER
- CONTINUOUS EDGEBAND AT CORNER
- WOOD VENEER PANEL

Ⓑ **WALL AT OUTSIDE CORNER**

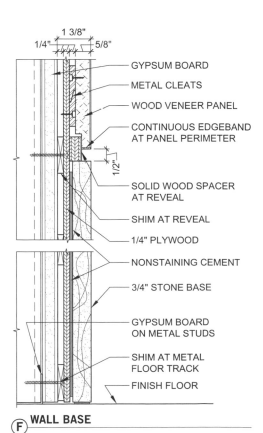

1 3/8"
1/4"   5/8"

- GYPSUM BOARD
- METAL CLEATS
- WOOD VENEER PANEL
- CONTINUOUS EDGEBAND AT PANEL PERIMETER
- SOLID WOOD SPACER AT REVEAL
- SHIM AT REVEAL
- 1/4" PLYWOOD
- NONSTAINING CEMENT
- 3/4" STONE BASE
- GYPSUM BOARD ON METAL STUDS
- SHIM AT METAL FLOOR TRACK
- FINISH FLOOR

Ⓕ **WALL BASE**

**ARCHITECTURAL WOODWORK** ☐ **2**

# DOORS AND FRAMES

## INTERIOR DOOR TYPES AND MATERIALS

Basic interior door types include hinged swinging, sliding pocket, folding, pivoted, bipass, and accordion doors. Standard materials for interior doors include solid core and hollow wood, hollow metal (steel), aluminum, and glass.

## Special-Purpose Doors

There are many types of special-purpose doors. Performance-based interior door types that are integrated into openings of compatible performance include fire-rated, acoustic, security, and ballistic threat-resisting doors. Other types of special-purpose doors include heavy insulated cold storage doors; radio-frequency-shielded doors, which are lined with copper foil; and X-ray shielding doors, which are lead-lined.

## Door Systems

Storefront, automatic opening, and overhead coiling doors are commonly provided as complete systems that are integrated into the design.

## Selection and Specification of Interior Doors

Interior doors can be sophisticated, complicated pieces of equipment. For example, automatic doors require power mechanisms and controls; acoustic doors often use automatic door bottoms that seal the door undercut as the door is closed; a coordinator may be required to ensure that the inactive leaf of a pair of doors closes before the active leaf. Consultants are often required to ensure the proper selection and specification of interior doors.

## Other Types

Other door types include overhead coiling, sound-retardant, blast-resistant, security, revolving, and radiation-shielding. Refer to manufacturers' catalogs for specific door types and details of construction and installation.

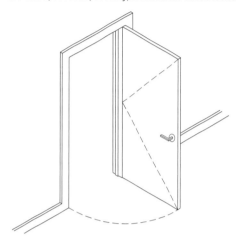

**HINGED SWINGING DOOR**
- Most common type of door; easy to install and most convenient to use. Requires space for swing.
- Fire rating available.
- Edges easily sealed to prevent passage of smoke, light, or sound.
- Available in wide range of materials and finishes, with multiple hardware options.

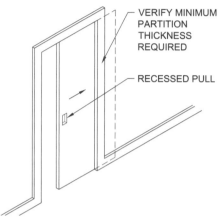

VERIFY MINIMUM PARTITION THICKNESS REQUIRED

RECESSED PULL

**SLIDING POCKET DOOR**
- Door is hung on track and slides into space within width of partition.
- No operating space is required.
- Relatively inexpensive.
- Awkward for frequent use.
- Difficult to seal against light or sound.
- Cannot be used as an exit door.

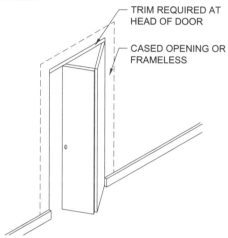

TRIM REQUIRED AT HEAD OF DOOR

CASED OPENING OR FRAMELESS

**FOLDING DOOR**
- Consists of hinged door panels that slide on overhead track.
- Uses minimum operating space.
- Often used as closet doors or as visual screen to other spaces.
- Awkward to use.
- Cannot be used as an exit door.

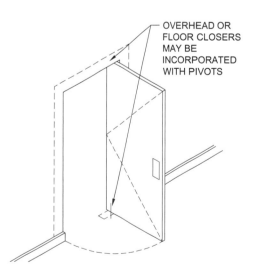

OVERHEAD OR FLOOR CLOSERS MAY BE INCORPORATED WITH PIVOTS

**PIVOTED DOOR**
- Center- or offset-hung; or balanced pivot hardware required.
- Center-hung pivots allow door to swing in both directions.
- Minimizes appearance of hardware, especially if center-hung pivots are used.
- Large, heavy door capacity.
- Balanced doors require less space to operate and take less effort to open.
- May be used for concealed doors.

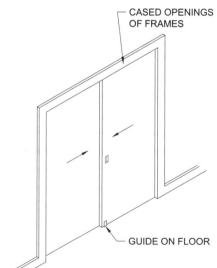

CASED OPENINGS OF FRAMES

GUIDE ON FLOOR

**BIPASS DOORS**
- Doors are hung on track; heavy doors may slide on track in floor.
- No operating space required.
- Generally used for closet doors.
- Difficult to seal.
- Awkward for frequent use.
- Cannot be used as an exit door.
- Surface sliding doors, like barn doors, slide on surface of partition; not often used but may be applied for special effect.

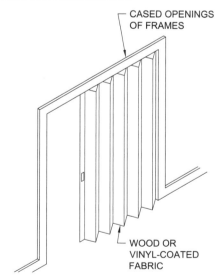

CASED OPENINGS OF FRAMES

WOOD OR VINYL-COATED FABRIC

**ACCORDION DOOR**
- Used for subdividing space or as a visual screen.
- Is poor sound barrier.
- Cannot be used as an exit door.

**TYPICAL INTERIOR DOOR TYPES**

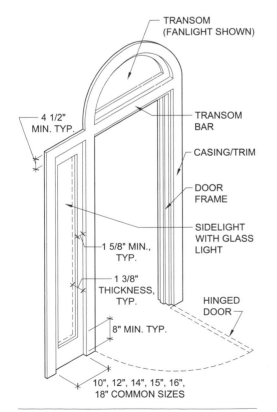

**DOOR-OPENING COMPONENTS**

CRIPPLE STUD
HEADER
DOUBLE STUD, WOOD OR METAL
KING STUD
TRIMMER STUD
WALL FINISH MATERIAL
HEAD
JAMB
STOP
CAP
ROUGH OPENING
6'-10 1/2" FOR 6'-8" DOOR, TYP.
BUCK
ROUGH OPENING
ROUGH OPENING
SUBCASING
SILL
TRIM OR CASING
PLINTH
TRIM
BASEBOARD

TRANSOM (FANLIGHT SHOWN)
4 1/2" MIN. TYP.
TRANSOM BAR
CASING/TRIM
DOOR FRAME
SIDELIGHT WITH GLASS LIGHT
1 5/8" MIN., TYP.
1 3/8" THICKNESS, TYP.
HINGED DOOR
8" MIN. TYP.
10", 12", 14", 15", 16", 18" COMMON SIZES

**DOOR NOMENCLATURE**

PLANTED STOP (OR DOUBLE-RABBETED STOP)     RABBETED STOP

**FRAME AND STOP TYPES**

FRAME WITHOUT STOPS FOR DOOR, OR FOR WINDOW

SPLAY     REVEAL     CASED

**OPENING TYPES**

PARALLEL BEVEL     RABBETED

BEVEL     T-ASTRAGAL

STRAIGHT     ASTRAGAL

**MEETING EDGE TYPE FOR DOUBLE-DOOR LEAVES**

## DOOR HANDING

The *hand*, or the *handing*, of a door refers to the standard method of describing the way a door swings. Handing is used in the industry to communicate how a door swings and the kind of hardware that must be supplied for a specific opening. Some hardware is specific to the hand of the door due to the bevel on the strike side of the door. Hardware that works on any hand of door is called *reversible* or *nonhanded*.

Handing is determined by standing on the outside of the door looking at the door. If the door hinges on the left and swings away, it is a left-hand door.

The corridor side is considered the outside of a room door, as is the lobby side of a door opening into a room or the room side of a closet door. When the distinction between outside and inside is not clear, the outside is considered the side of the door where the hinge is located.

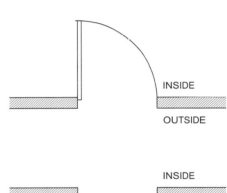

INSIDE
OUTSIDE
INSIDE
OUTSIDE

**LEFT-HAND DOOR**

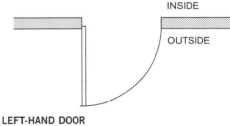

INSIDE
OUTSIDE
INSIDE
OUTSIDE

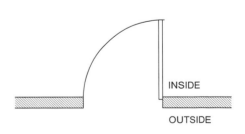

**RIGHT-HAND DOOR**

**DOOR HANDING**

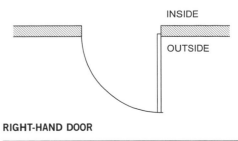

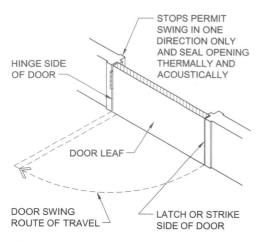

**SINGLE-ACTING DOOR**

The single-acting door, the most common door type, has a leaf that operates in a swinging or sliding motion in only one direction.

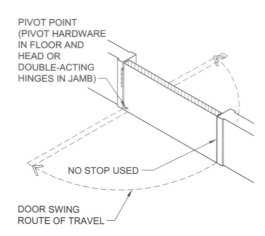

**DOUBLE-ACTING DOOR**

Double-acting doors have a leaf that operates in two directions. There is usually no stop present to restrict the motion of the door, but when the door can be stopped, it can be released mechanically to permit access in an emergency.

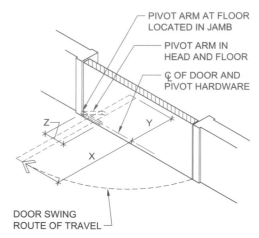

**BALANCED DOOR**

A balanced door is a single-action swinging door mounted on offset pivots. The leaf operates independently of the jamb, and the elliptical trajectory of the leaf requires less clear floor space than a conventional swinging door.

## SINGLE-DOOR LEAF TYPES

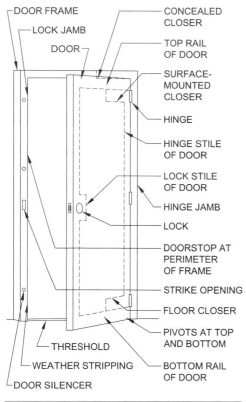

**PARTS OF A DOOR**

### Definitions

*Active leaf:* The primary operating leaf of a door pair.

*Air curtain:* A mechanically produced downward stream of air across a door opening intended to prevent transmission of heat and weather.

*Automatic closing:* A door that is normally open but that closes without the necessity for human intervention and is activated as a result of a predetermined temperature rise, rate of temperature rise, or combustion products.

*Automatic door bottom:* A device applied to the back side of a door at the bottom or mortised into the bottom edge of a door, which seals the undercut of a door as it is closed.

*Balanced door:* A door equipped with double-pivoted hardware designed to cause a semicounterbalanced swing action when opening.

*Buck:* A subframe of wood or metal set in a wall or partition to support the finish frame of a door.

*Casing:* The finished, often decorative framework around a door opening, especially that which is parallel to the surrounding surface and at right angles to the jamb.

*Coordinator:* A device used on a pair of doors to ensure that the inactive leaf is permitted to close before the active leaf.

*Door bevel:* The slight angle given to the lock stile (vertical edge) of a door, which prevents the door from touching the lock jamb as it swings. Typical bevels are: 1⅜ in. (35 mm) door—none; 1¾ in. (44 mm) door—⅛ in. (3 mm); 2¼ in. (6 mm) door—9/64 in. (3.5 mm).

*Double-egress door:* A pair of doors within a single special frame that swing in opposite directions to allow emergency egress from either side. Typically used where a fire or smoke partition crosses a corridor.

*Flush bolt:* A door bolt set flush with the face or edge of the door.

*Fire-door assembly:* Any combination of a fire door, frame, hardware, and other accessories that together provide a specific degree of fire protection.

*Fire exit hardware:* Panic hardware that is listed for use on fire-door assemblies.

*Head:* The horizontal portion of a door frame above the door opening.

*Jamb:* The vertical members at the sides of a door opening.

*Labeled:* Equipment, products, or materials marked with the label, symbol, or other identifying mark of an approved testing organization that indicates compliance with standards for manufacture and testing.

*Listed:* Equipment, devices, materials, or services included in a list published by a testing agency that have been shown to meet applicable standards for use in fire-rated assemblies or that have been tested and found suitable for use for a specified purpose.

*Panic hardware:* A door-latching assembly incorporating a device that releases the latch upon the application of a force in the direction of egress travel.

*Power-assisted door:* A door with a mechanism that helps to open the door or to relieve the opening resistance of the door.

*Prehung door:* Door and frame combination fabricated and assembled by the manufacturer and shipped to the site.

*Sill:* The horizontal members at the bottom of a door opening.

*Subcasing:* The finish frame components that support and guide the door.

*Undercut:* The space between the bottom edge of a door and the sill or threshold.

## ACCESSIBILITY REQUIREMENTS

Door accessibility requirements are outlined below. For more information, consult the ADA Guidelines and ICC/ANSI A117.1, *Accessible and Usable Buildings and Facilities,* for additional requirements

- For opening width compliance, use doors 3 ft (914 mm) wide.
- Kickplates are recommended outdoors along accessible routes.
- Maximum opening force for interior hinged doors, sliding, and folding doors is 5.0 lb (22.2N). Minimum opening force for fire doors is regulated by the local authority having jurisdiction.
- Door closing speed must be a minimum of five seconds from an open position of 90° to an open position of 12°.

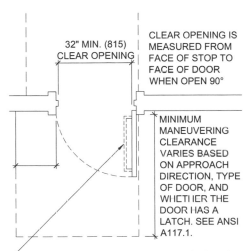

32" MIN. (815) CLEAR OPENING

CLEAR OPENING IS MEASURED FROM FACE OF STOP TO FACE OF DOOR WHEN OPEN 90°

MINIMUM MANEUVERING CLEARANCE VARIES BASED ON APPROACH DIRECTION, TYPE OF DOOR, AND WHETHER THE DOOR HAS A LATCH. SEE ANSI A117.1.

NO PROJECTIONS INTO THE CLEAR OPENING WIDTH ARE ALLOWED BELOW 34" (865) ABOVE FLOOR LINE. PROJECTIONS INTO THE CLEAR OPENING WIDTH FROM 34" - 80" (865 - 2020) MAY BE A MAXIMUM OF 4" (102)

**CLEAR WIDTH OF ACCESSIBLE DOORWAYS**

## DOOR AND FRAME DETAILING

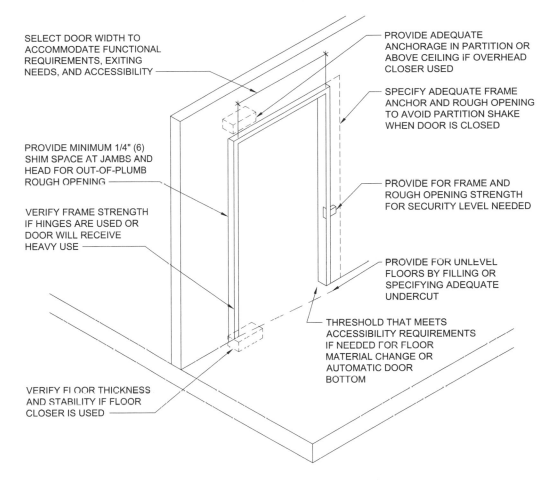

SELECT DOOR WIDTH TO ACCOMMODATE FUNCTIONAL REQUIREMENTS, EXITING NEEDS, AND ACCESSIBILITY

PROVIDE MINIMUM 1/4" (6) SHIM SPACE AT JAMBS AND HEAD FOR OUT-OF-PLUMB ROUGH OPENING

VERIFY FRAME STRENGTH IF HINGES ARE USED OR DOOR WILL RECEIVE HEAVY USE

VERIFY FLOOR THICKNESS AND STABILITY IF FLOOR CLOSER IS USED

PROVIDE ADEQUATE ANCHORAGE IN PARTITION OR ABOVE CEILING IF OVERHEAD CLOSER USED

SPECIFY ADEQUATE FRAME ANCHOR AND ROUGH OPENING TO AVOID PARTITION SHAKE WHEN DOOR IS CLOSED

PROVIDE FOR FRAME AND ROUGH OPENING STRENGTH FOR SECURITY LEVEL NEEDED

PROVIDE FOR UNLEVEL FLOORS BY FILLING OR SPECIFYING ADEQUATE UNDERCUT

THRESHOLD THAT MEETS ACCESSIBILITY REQUIREMENTS IF NEEDED FOR FLOOR MATERIAL CHANGE OR AUTOMATIC DOOR BOTTOM

These detailing considerations for frames and partitions apply to the design of openings for doors of all types and materials.

**DOOR DESIGN AND DETAILING CONSIDERATIONS**

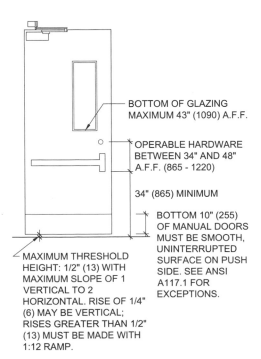

BOTTOM OF GLAZING MAXIMUM 43" (1090) A.F.F.

OPERABLE HARDWARE BETWEEN 34" AND 48" A.F.F. (865 - 1220)

34" (865) MINIMUM

BOTTOM 10" (255) OF MANUAL DOORS MUST BE SMOOTH, UNINTERRUPTED SURFACE ON PUSH SIDE. SEE ANSI A117.1 FOR EXCEPTIONS.

MAXIMUM THRESHOLD HEIGHT: 1/2" (13) WITH MAXIMUM SLOPE OF 1 VERTICAL TO 2 HORIZONTAL. RISE OF 1/4" (6) MAY BE VERTICAL; RISES GREATER THAN 1/2" (13) MUST BE MADE WITH 1:12 RAMP.

**ACCESSIBLE DOOR FEATURES**

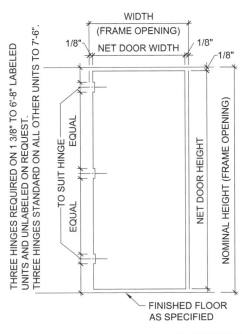

WIDTH (FRAME OPENING)

NET DOOR WIDTH

1/8"      1/8"

1/8"

THREE HINGES REQUIRED ON 1 3/8" TO 6'-8" LABELED UNITS AND UNLABELED ON REQUEST. THREE HINGES STANDARD ON ALL OTHER UNITS TO 7'-6".

TO SUIT HINGE

EQUAL

EQUAL

NET DOOR HEIGHT

NOMINAL HEIGHT (FRAME OPENING)

FINISHED FLOOR AS SPECIFIED

**STANDARD DOOR AND DOOR CLEARANCE**

### Door Design Checklist

- For doors in corners, the hinge jamb must allow at least a 90° opening (with space for hardware).
- For doors serving a large number of people, use doors (and hardware) that will open at least 110°.
- Recess doors so they do not interfere with traffic or obstruct the required exit width.
- Verify that the door will swing clear of carpeting, uneven floors, and other obstructions.
- Verify the required maneuvering space and the maximum force requirements for accessibility.
- Include vision panels in double-acting and double-egress doors.
- Include required protection on the door such as armor plates, kickplates, edge guards, and so on.
- If used, verify that gaskets and sound seals are readjusted after a period of use.
- For wood doors, verify design compatibility with adjacent wood trim, woodwork, and furniture.
- For concealed doors, verify that the doors will operate after the application of finish material.
- Verify whether door tolerances need to be specified differently from industry standards.

## WOOD DOORS

### Face Material

Wood doors are available with face materials of wood veneer, composite veneer, high-density plastic laminate, medium-density overlay, and hardboard. Wood veneer on manufactured doors is available in the species offered by the manufacturer. Custom doors may be faced with any veneer available on the world market. Both reference standards listed below require face veneers of at least 1/50 in. (0.5 mm), but thicker veneers may be specified. Veneers may be rotary-cut, plain-sliced, quarter-sliced, or rift-cut, and may be matched with random, slip, and bookmatched methods.

- *Composite veneers* are manufactured by slicing sustainably grown hardwoods, then vat-dying and pressing them into new, composite "logs." The composite logs are then sliced to form new veneers that replicate other natural woods. By using various colors of natural veneers and slicing angles of the composite log, a nearly unlimited number of simulated wood species and veneer patterns can be created. These veneers can be applied to doors in the same way as natural veneers.
- *Plastic laminate veneers* provide a durable surface with hundreds of available colors and patterns.
- *Medium-density overlay (MDO) faces* are used to provide a smooth, paintable surface that resists grain raising and moisture. For this reason, they are often used for exterior doors.
- *Hardboard* is used with three-ply construction for interior doors that are to be painted and as a lower-cost option for MDO.

### Wood Door Standards

The two main wood door standards are WDMA, I.S. 1-A, *Architectural Wood Flush Doors,* published by the Window and Door Manufacturers Association, and the *AWI Architectural Woodwork Quality Standards,* published by the Architectural Woodwork Institute. Generally, the WDMA standard is used to specify standard manufacturers' doors, while the AWI standards are used to specify custom doors. The Woodwork Institute of California also publishes standards in its *Manual of Millwork.*

### Wood Door Grades

Both WDMA and AWI standards classify doors into three grades: Premium, Custom, and Economy. There are, however, some differences between the WDMA and AWI standards, and these should be verified before specifying.

- *Premium grade* is specified when the highest level of materials, workmanship, and installation is required.
- *Custom grade* is suitable for most installations and is intended for high-quality work.
- *Economy* is the lowest grade and is intended for work where price is a primary factor.

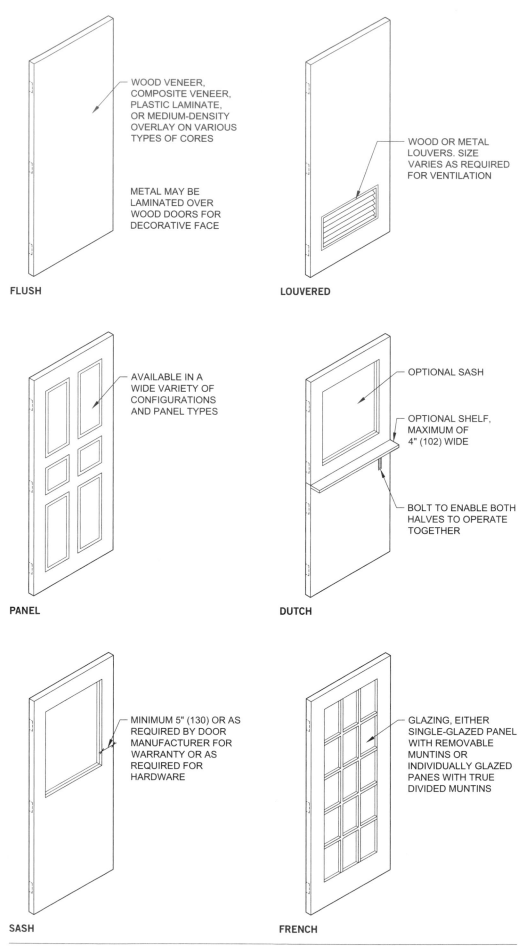

FLUSH — WOOD VENEER, COMPOSITE VENEER, PLASTIC LAMINATE, OR MEDIUM-DENSITY OVERLAY ON VARIOUS TYPES OF CORES / METAL MAY BE LAMINATED OVER WOOD DOORS FOR DECORATIVE FACE

LOUVERED — WOOD OR METAL LOUVERS. SIZE VARIES AS REQUIRED FOR VENTILATION

PANEL — AVAILABLE IN A WIDE VARIETY OF CONFIGURATIONS AND PANEL TYPES

DUTCH — OPTIONAL SASH / OPTIONAL SHELF, MAXIMUM OF 4" (102) WIDE / BOLT TO ENABLE BOTH HALVES TO OPERATE TOGETHER

SASH — MINIMUM 5" (130) OR AS REQUIRED BY DOOR MANUFACTURER FOR WARRANTY OR AS REQUIRED FOR HARDWARE

FRENCH — GLAZING, EITHER SINGLE-GLAZED PANEL WITH REMOVABLE MUNTINS OR INDIVIDUALLY GLAZED PANES WITH TRUE DIVIDED MUNTINS

**WOOD DOOR TYPES**

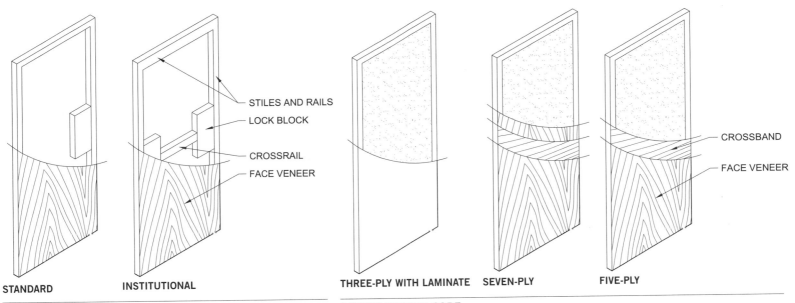

STILES AND RAILS
LOCK BLOCK
CROSSRAIL
FACE VENEER

**STANDARD**   **INSTITUTIONAL**

**HOLLOW CORE**

CROSSBAND
FACE VENEER

**THREE-PLY WITH LAMINATE**   **SEVEN-PLY**   **FIVE-PLY**

**PARTICLEBOARD CORE**

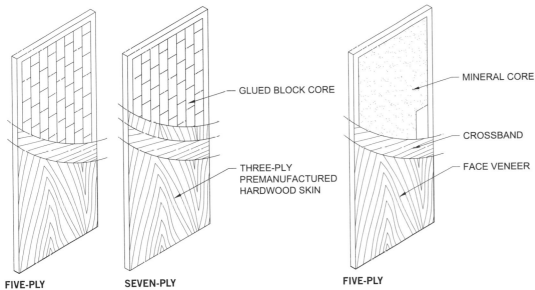

GLUED BLOCK CORE

THREE-PLY
PREMANUFACTURED
HARDWOOD SKIN

**FIVE-PLY**   **SEVEN-PLY**

**STAVED LUMBER CORE**

MINERAL CORE
CROSSBAND
FACE VENEER

**FIVE-PLY**

**MINERAL COMPOSITION CORE**

These are the most common core types. Other options are available, including structural composite lumber (or laminated strand lumber). These alternate types of cores are replacing the traditional staved lumber core doors:

*Sound insulating core:* A special core available in thicknesses of 1¾ in. (44 mm) and 2¼ in. (57 mm). The 1¾-in. (44-mm) core can provide a Sound Transmission Class (STC) rating of 36; the 2¼-in. (57-mm) core can achieve an STC of 42. Barrier faces are separated by a void or damping compound to keep the faces from vibrating in unison. Special stops, gaskets, and threshold devices are also required.

*Lead-lined core:* A special core consisting of ⅟₃₂-in. (.8-mm) to ½-in. (13-mm) continuous lead sheeting edge to edge inside the door construction. This material may be reinforced with lead bolts or glued. See Underwriters Laboratory requirements.

## CORE TYPES

### Hollow Core versus Solid Core Doors

Hollow core doors are typically used in residential construction and for commercial doors subject only to light use. Institutional hollow core doors, with heavier stiles and rails and with additional blocking, have increased strength and resistance to warping, but may cost as much as some solid core doors.

Solid core doors are more secure, more durable, more resistant to warping, and allow less acoustical transmission. They are used in most institutional and commercial projects.

### Door Bevel

Doors are beveled to allow the door to open past the jamb without binding. The standard bevel is ⅛ in. in 2 in. (3 mm in 51 mm) (3½°). Generally, unit locksets are only available with the standard bevel; cylindrical locksets are available with either flat or standard bevel, and mortise locksets are available with bevels adjustable from flat to standard.

### Bonded versus Nonbonded Cores

Solid core doors can either be bonded or nonbonded. With a bonded core, the stiles and rails are glued to the core material and the whole assembly is sanded as a unit before the faces are applied. This reduces the likelihood of telegraphing. With a nonbonded core, the elements can vary slightly in thickness and can telegraph through the faces noticeably. Five-ply doors are typically made with a bonded core, while seven-ply doors are made with a nonbonded core.

## DOOR SIZES

Both wood and hollow metal doors are available in a variety of standard widths. Custom doors can be made in any size, but in general it is best to specify standard width doors and vary the height when ordering custom sizes.

Most door manufacturers do not offer a warranty if maximum heights are exceeded.

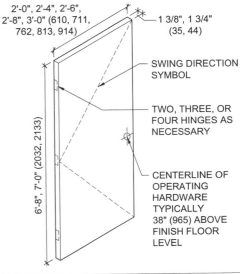

2'-0", 2'-4", 2'-6", 2'-8", 3'-0" (610, 711, 762, 813, 914)

1 3/8", 1 3/4" (35, 44)

6'-8", 7'-0" (2032, 2133)

SWING DIRECTION SYMBOL

TWO, THREE, OR FOUR HINGES AS NECESSARY

CENTERLINE OF OPERATING HARDWARE TYPICALLY 38" (965) ABOVE FINISH FLOOR LEVEL

**STANDARD DOOR SIZES**

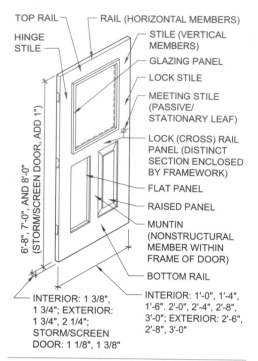

TOP RAIL
HINGE STILE
RAIL (HORIZONTAL MEMBERS)
STILE (VERTICAL MEMBERS)
GLAZING PANEL
LOCK STILE
MEETING STILE (PASSIVE/STATIONARY LEAF)
LOCK (CROSS) RAIL PANEL (DISTINCT SECTION ENCLOSED BY FRAMEWORK)
FLAT PANEL
RAISED PANEL
MUNTIN (NONSTRUCTURAL MEMBER WITHIN FRAME OF DOOR)
BOTTOM RAIL
6'-8", 7'-0", AND 8'-0" (STORM/SCREEN DOOR, ADD 1")
INTERIOR: 1 3/8", 1 3/4"; EXTERIOR: 1 3/4", 2 1/4"; STORM/SCREEN DOOR: 1 1/8", 1 3/8"
INTERIOR: 1'-0", 1'-4", 1'-6". 2'-0", 2'-4", 2'-8", 3'-0"; EXTERIOR: 2'-6", 2'-8", 3'-0"

**STILE AND RAIL TERMINOLOGY**

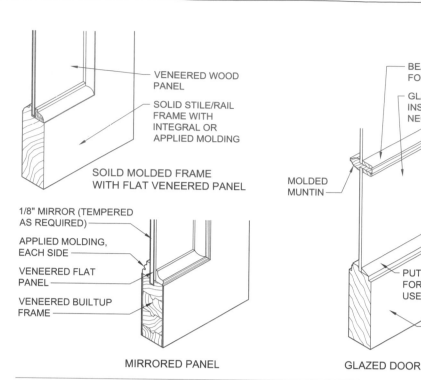

VENEERED WOOD PANEL
SOLID STILE/RAIL FRAME WITH INTEGRAL OR APPLIED MOLDING

**SOILD MOLDED FRAME WITH FLAT VENEERED PANEL**

1/8" MIRROR (TEMPERED AS REQUIRED)
APPLIED MOLDING, EACH SIDE
VENEERED FLAT PANEL
VENEERED BUILTUP FRAME

**MIRRORED PANEL**

BEAD STOP MOLDING FOR INTERIOR USE
GLAZING (TEMPERED, INSULATING, ETC., AS NECESSARY)
MOLDED MUNTIN
PUTTY STOP FOR EXTERIOR USE
SOLID FRAME WITH INTEGRAL MOLDING STOP

**GLAZED DOOR**

**STILE AND RAIL DOOR DETAILS**

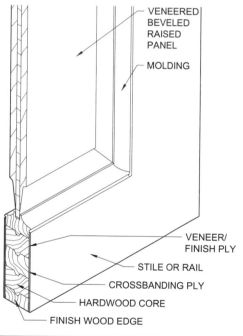

VENEERED BEVELED RAISED PANEL
MOLDING
VENEER/FINISH PLY
STILE OR RAIL
CROSSBANDING PLY
HARDWOOD CORE
FINISH WOOD EDGE

**STILE AND RAIL—RAISED PANEL**

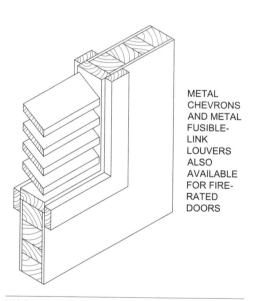

METAL CHEVRONS AND METAL FUSIBLE-LINK LOUVERS ALSO AVAILABLE FOR FIRE-RATED DOORS

**WOOD SLATS**

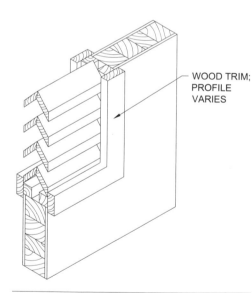

WOOD TRIM; PROFILE VARIES

**WOOD CHEVRONS**

## STILE AND RAIL DOORS

Panel doors consist of a framework of vertical (stile) and horizontal (rail) members that hold solid wood or plywood panels, glass lights, or louvers in place.

The doors are made of solid or built-up stiles, rails, and vertical members (*muntins*), typically doweled per applicable standards. Stock material includes ponderosa pine, fir, hemlock, or spruce and hardwood veneers. Hardboard, metal, and plastic facings are available in various patterns.

## GLAZING

Most building codes require all glass in doors to be safety glazed. Insulated safety glazing is available for increased thermal or acoustical performance.

## BUILT-UP MEMBERS

The core and edge strip materials are similar to those used in flush doors. Face veneer is typically hardwood at ⅛ in. (3 mm) minimum thickness.

## GLASS STOPS AND MUNTINS

Typical profiles used for trim work include cove, bead, or ovolo.

## PANELS

Flat panels are typically three-ply hardwood or softwood. Raised panels are constructed of solid hardwood or softwood built up of two or more plies. Doors 1 ft 6 in. (457 mm) wide or less are one panel wide.

## WOOD DOOR FRAMING

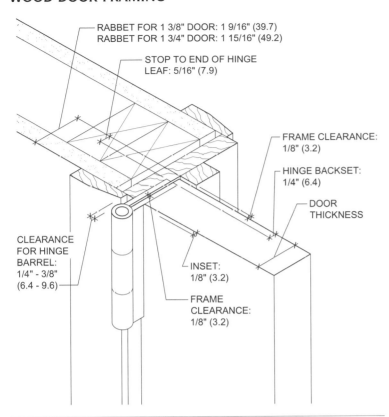

RABBET FOR 1 3/8" DOOR: 1 9/16" (39.7)
RABBET FOR 1 3/4" DOOR: 1 15/16" (49.2)

STOP TO END OF HINGE LEAF: 5/16" (7.9)

FRAME CLEARANCE: 1/8" (3.2)

HINGE BACKSET: 1/4" (6.4)

DOOR THICKNESS

CLEARANCE FOR HINGE BARREL: 1/4" - 3/8" (6.4 - 9.6)

INSET: 1/8" (3.2)

FRAME CLEARANCE: 1/8" (3.2)

**STANDARD DOOR FRAME AND HINGE-SETTING DIMENSIONS**

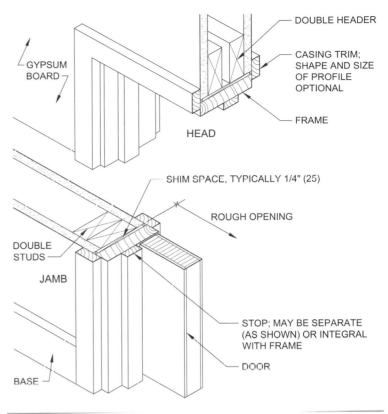

DOUBLE HEADER

CASING TRIM; SHAPE AND SIZE OF PROFILE OPTIONAL

FRAME

GYPSUM BOARD

HEAD

SHIM SPACE, TYPICALLY 1/4" (25)

ROUGH OPENING

DOUBLE STUDS

JAMB

STOP; MAY BE SEPARATE (AS SHOWN) OR INTEGRAL WITH FRAME

DOOR

BASE

**TYPICAL DOOR AND FRAME IN WOOD STUD PARTITION**

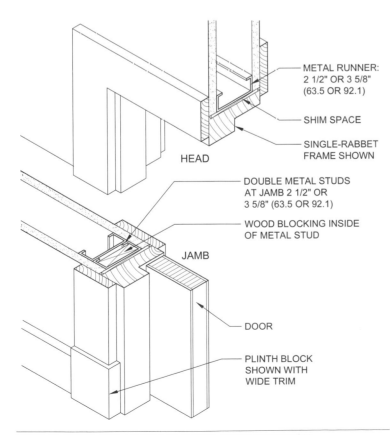

METAL RUNNER: 2 1/2" OR 3 5/8" (63.5 OR 92.1)

SHIM SPACE

SINGLE-RABBET FRAME SHOWN

HEAD

DOUBLE METAL STUDS AT JAMB 2 1/2" OR 3 5/8" (63.5 OR 92.1)

WOOD BLOCKING INSIDE OF METAL STUD

JAMB

DOOR

PLINTH BLOCK SHOWN WITH WIDE TRIM

**TYPICAL DOOR AND FRAME IN METAL STUD PARTITION**

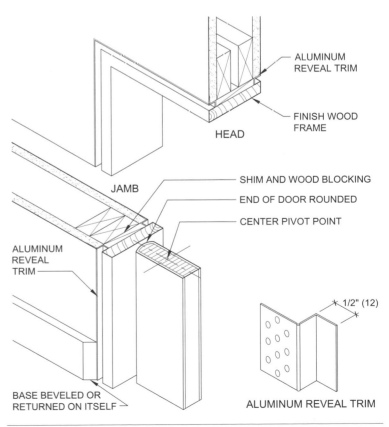

ALUMINUM REVEAL TRIM

FINISH WOOD FRAME

HEAD

JAMB

SHIM AND WOOD BLOCKING

END OF DOOR ROUNDED

CENTER PIVOT POINT

ALUMINUM REVEAL TRIM

BASE BEVELED OR RETURNED ON ITSELF

1/2" (12)

ALUMINUM REVEAL TRIM

**WOOD FRAME WITHOUT CASING FOR DOUBLE-ACTING DOOR**

## WOOD DOOR FRAMING

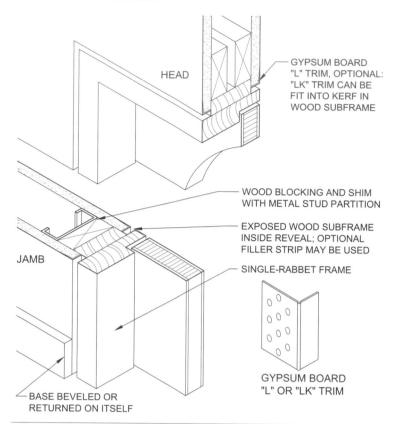

HEAD

GYPSUM BOARD
"L" TRIM, OPTIONAL:
"LK" TRIM CAN BE
FIT INTO KERF IN
WOOD SUBFRAME

WOOD BLOCKING AND SHIM
WITH METAL STUD PARTITION

EXPOSED WOOD SUBFRAME
INSIDE REVEAL; OPTIONAL
FILLER STRIP MAY BE USED

JAMB

SINGLE-RABBET FRAME

GYPSUM BOARD
"L" OR "LK" TRIM

BASE BEVELED OR
RETURNED ON ITSELF

**SINGLE-RABBET FRAME WITHOUT CASING**

HEAD

CONTINUOUS
WOOD STOP
(SHOWN) OR
METAL ANGLE
STOP IN HEAD

JAMB

ROLLER LATCH USED ON
STRIKE SIDE OF DOOR

RECESSED PULL
OR EDGE PULL

KERF CUT IN EDGE
OF DOOR TO ACCEPT
WALLCOVERING

DOOR AND WALL
COVERED IN VINYL OR
FABRIC WALLCOVERING

BASE
CONTINUES
ON DOOR

DOOR SWINGS OUT

CENTER-HUNG PIVOT
USED ON HINGE JAMB

**HIDDEN DOOR**

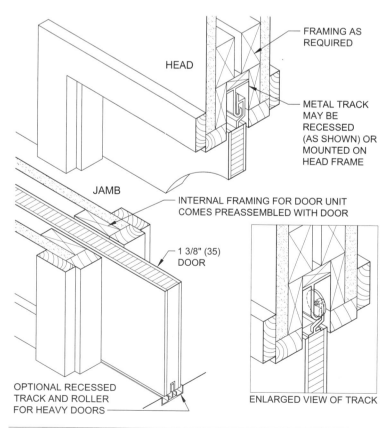

FRAMING AS
REQUIRED

HEAD

METAL TRACK
MAY BE
RECESSED
(AS SHOWN) OR
MOUNTED ON
HEAD FRAME

JAMB

INTERNAL FRAMING FOR DOOR UNIT
COMES PREASSEMBLED WITH DOOR

1 3/8" (35)
DOOR

ENLARGED VIEW OF TRACK

OPTIONAL RECESSED
TRACK AND ROLLER
FOR HEAVY DOORS

**SLIDING POCKET DOOR**

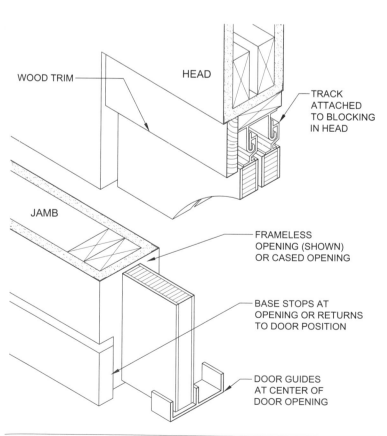

WOOD TRIM

HEAD

TRACK
ATTACHED
TO BLOCKING
IN HEAD

JAMB

FRAMELESS
OPENING (SHOWN)
OR CASED OPENING

BASE STOPS AT
OPENING OR RETURNS
TO DOOR POSITION

DOOR GUIDES
AT CENTER OF
DOOR OPENING

**BIPASS DOORS**

# HOLLOW METAL DOORS

## Door Types

Hollow metal doors are doors constructed from sheet steel attached to various types of cores. They are used in steel frames, also constructed of sheet steel bent into various profiles.

There are several types of steel doors. The Steel Door Institute uses a standard door design nomenclature to identity each type. Many of these are shown in the diagrams below. Refer to SDI 106, *Recommended Standard Door Type Nomenclature,* for a complete listing and for more information on door nomenclature.

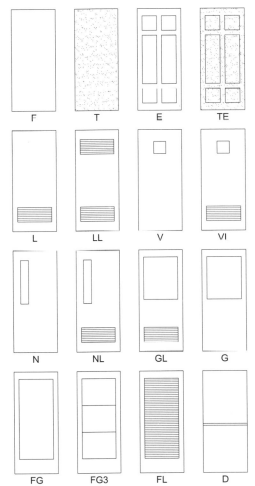

**DOOR TYPES**

### Nomenclature Letter Symbols

| | |
|---|---|
| F | Flush |
| T | Textured |
| E | Embossed |
| TE | Textured and embossed |
| L | Louvered (top or bottom) |
| LL | Louvered (top and bottom) |
| V | Vision lite |
| VL | Vision lite and louvered |
| N | Narrow lite |
| NL | Narrow lite and louvered |
| GL | Half glass and louvered |
| G | Half glass (several options available) |
| FG | Full glass |
| FG3 | Full glass, three panes |
| FL | Full louver |
| D | Dutch door |

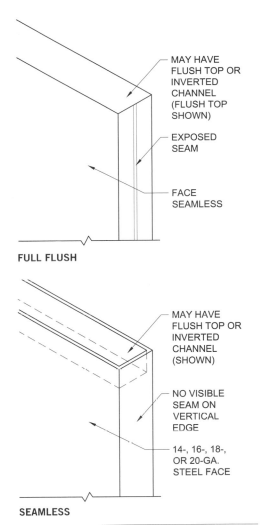

Custom doors can be manufactured to nearly any practical size; however, standard widths should be used whenever possible.

**Standard Widths**

| | |
|---|---|
| 2 ft 0 in. (610 mm) | 3 ft 4 in. (1,016 mm) |
| 2 ft 4 in. (711 mm) | 3 ft 6 in. (1,067 mm) |
| 2 ft 6 in. (762 mm) | 3 ft 8 in. (1,118 mm) |
| 2 ft 8 in. (813 mm) | 3 ft 10 in. (1,168 mm) |
| 2 ft 10 in. (864 mm) | 4 ft 0 in. (1,219 mm) |
| 3 ft 0 in. (914 mm) | |

**Standard Heights**

| 1¾-in.-doors | 1⅜-in.-doors |
|---|---|
| 6 ft 8 in. (2,032 mm) | 6 ft 8 in. (2,032 mm) |
| 7 ft 0 in. (2,134 mm) | 7 ft 0 in. (2,134 mm) |
| 7 ft 2 in. (2,184 mm) | 7 ft 2 in. (2,184 mm) |
| 7 ft 10 in. (2,388 mm) | |
| 8 ft 0 in. (2,438 mm) | |

**STANDARD HOLLOW METAL DOOR SIZES**

**HOLLOW METAL DOOR CONSTRUCTION**

## STANDARD STEEL DOOR GRADES AND MODELS

| LEVEL | | MODEL | FULL FLUSH OR SEAMLESS | | | CONSTRUCTION |
|---|---|---|---|---|---|---|
| | | | GAGE | IN. | MM | |
| I | Standard Duty | 1 | 20 | 0.032 | 0.8 | Full Flush |
| | | 2 | | | | Seamless |
| II | Heavy-Duty | 1 | 18 | 0.042 | 1.0 | Full Flush |
| | | 2 | | | | Seamless |
| III | Extra Heavy-Duty | 1 | 16 | 0.053 | 1.3 | Full Flush |
| | | 2 | | | | Seamless |
| | | 3 | | | | Stile and Rail* |
| IV | Maximum Duty | 1 | 14 | 0.067 | 1.6 | Full Flush |
| | | 2 | | | | Seamless |

*Stiles and rails are 16-gage; flush panels, when specified, are 18-gage.

Source: Steel Door Institute, SDI-108; Cleveland, Ohio

## SDI DOOR LEVELS

SDI 108, *Recommended Selection and Usage Guide for Standard Steel Doors,* provides recommendations for levels of doors within a variety of building types and usages. In general, the following levels should be used:

*Level 1:* Doors for interior use in residences, dormitories, and hotels, except for entrances; individual office doors in office buildings and other commercial structures; and closets in most buildings.

*Level 2:* Doors for entrances to apartments, dormitories, and hotels, stairways, toilet rooms, hospital patient and operating rooms, and school classrooms.

*Level 3:* Entrance and stairwell doors in most buildings; in commercial and industrial buildings and schools, except closets; and in hospital kitchens.

*Level 4:* Doors for high-traffic entrances and stairwells in commercial and industrial buildings and entrances requiring increased security. Entrance and gymnasium doors in schools.

If doors are used in severe, humid environments or in humid areas such as pools or kitchens, a galvanized coating should be specified using either the hot-dip or electrolytic process.

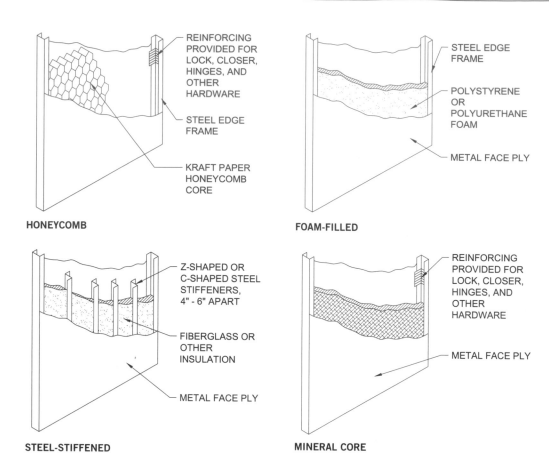

**HONEYCOMB**

- REINFORCING PROVIDED FOR LOCK, CLOSER, HINGES, AND OTHER HARDWARE
- STEEL EDGE FRAME
- KRAFT PAPER HONEYCOMB CORE

**FOAM-FILLED**

- STEEL EDGE FRAME
- POLYSTYRENE OR POLYURETHANE FOAM
- METAL FACE PLY

**STEEL-STIFFENED**

- Z-SHAPED OR C-SHAPED STEEL STIFFENERS, 4" - 6" APART
- FIBERGLASS OR OTHER INSULATION
- METAL FACE PLY

**MINERAL CORE**

- REINFORCING PROVIDED FOR LOCK, CLOSER, HINGES, AND OTHER HARDWARE
- METAL FACE PLY

**CORE TYPES**

## Core Construction

Four types of cores are commonly used for hollow metal doors: honeycomb, steel stiffeners, foam plastic, and mineral board:

*Honeycomb cores:* These cores are made from heavy kraft paper formed into hexagonal cells ranging from ½ in. (13 mm) to about 1 in. (25 mm) in size. The core is impregnated with phenolic resin to resist moisture, mildew, and vermin.

*Steel-stiffened cores:* These doors use vertical stiffeners spaced between 4 in. (102 mm) and 6 in. (152 mm). The cavities in between are usually filled with fiberglass insulation. These types of cores are used primarily for exterior doors, where high rigidity is important.

*Foam plastic cores:* These may be filled with either polystyrene or polyurethane, materials used for their high insulative values. Polystyrene is used for typical exterior doors, and polyurethane is used where extreme protection from frigid cold is important. Both of these insulation types melt at relatively low temperatures, which may prevent using a hot baked-on paint system applied in the factory.

*Mineral cores:* These cores are constructed with a fire-resistive material similar to gypsum board. They are used on labeled doors where a temperature-rise limit is required.

## HOLLOW METAL FRAMES

### Frame Material Thickness

The thickness for frames is governed by the level of door installed, as shown in the table below. For each of the levels, except level 2, two options are provided. The option selected depends on security needs, width of opening, whether the door is for interior or exterior use, expected frequency of use, severity of service, availability, and cost.

Frames may be welded, knockdown, or gypsum board slip-on.

Hollow metal door frames are available in various steel gages according to where and how they will be used. Local codes and governing authorities establish minimum gages, which should always be consulted. Some manufacturers make custom moldings for a specific design, as long as a sufficient quantity is required.

For security, the exterior moldings on exterior doors should be welded into the frame, and exposed fasteners should be tamperproof.

### RECOMMENDED THICKNESS FOR STEEL FRAMES BASED ON DOOR LEVEL

| LEVEL | GAGE | THICKNESS IN. (MM) |
|---|---|---|
| 1 | 18 or 16 | 0.042 (1) or 0.053 (1.3) |
| 2 | 16 | 0.053 (1.3) |
| 3 | 16 or 14 | 0.053 (1.3) or 0.067 (1.6) |
| 4 | 14 or 12 | 0.067 (1.6) or 0.093 (2.3) |

*Source: Steel Door Institute, SDI-100; Cleveland, Ohio*

## Frame Types

Door frames can be factory- or field-assembled. All frames must be adequately anchored at the jambs and floor according to the manufacturer's specifications.

*Light-gage metal frames* are constructed of head and jamb members, with or without a transom panel, of aluminum (45-minute maximum rating) or light-gage steel (1.5-hour maximum rating). They consist of a single frame that slips over the partition. Separate casing trim pieces are then snapped onto the edges of the frames. These frames are available in 18-, 20-, and 22-gage thicknesses.

*Pressed steel (hollow metal) frames* have head and jamb members, with or without solid or glazed transoms or sidelights, of 18-gage or heavier steel (3-hour maximum rating). This frame is required for most metal doors.

*Steel frames* are generally made from one piece of sheet steel bent into the required profile in either a double-rabbet or single-rabbet configuration. These frames are available in 12-, 14-, 16-, and 18-gage thicknesses.

### FRAME GAGES

| GRADE | DUTY | MINIMUM GAGE |
|---|---|---|
| I | Standard | 18 |
| II | Heavy | 16 |
| III | Extra heavy | 14 |

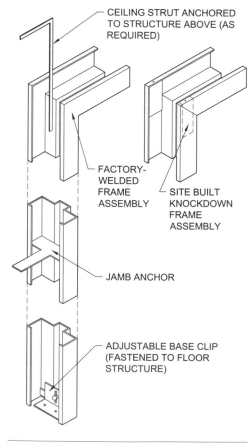

- CEILING STRUT ANCHORED TO STRUCTURE ABOVE (AS REQUIRED)
- FACTORY-WELDED FRAME ASSEMBLY
- SITE BUILT KNOCKDOWN FRAME ASSEMBLY
- JAMB ANCHOR
- ADJUSTABLE BASE CLIP (FASTENED TO FLOOR STRUCTURE)

**HOLLOW METAL FRAME COMPONENTS**

## Hollow Metal Frame Finishes

Hollow metal frames should receive at least one shop coat of rust-inhibitive primer before delivery to the job site. In very corrosive atmospheres, such as saltwater beach locations, is it advisable to have doors and frames hot-dipped-galvanized for additional protection.

Frames with factory-applied paint finishes in various colors are available from several manufacturers.

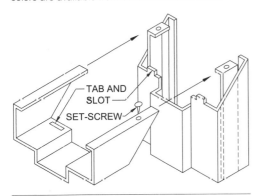

### KNOCKDOWN FRAME CORNER CONSTRUCTION

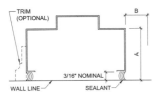

Use anchors appropriate for the type of wall construction; a minimum of three per jamb is required.

Grout frame with mortar or plaster as used in wall.

Caulk frame at wall.

Dimension A is minimum 3 in. in area of pull or knob hardware.

Trim may be used to cover joint at wall line.

Check dimension B on hinge side for door swing greater than 90°.

### BUTT FRAME/FLUSH FRAME

Basic wall dimension is less than throat opening dimension.

Use anchors appropriate for the type of wall construction; a minimum of three per jamb is required.

Fill frame with mortar or plaster as used in the wall.

Grout frame at masonry wall.

### WRAPAROUND FRAME

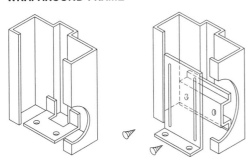

### FLOOR KNEES

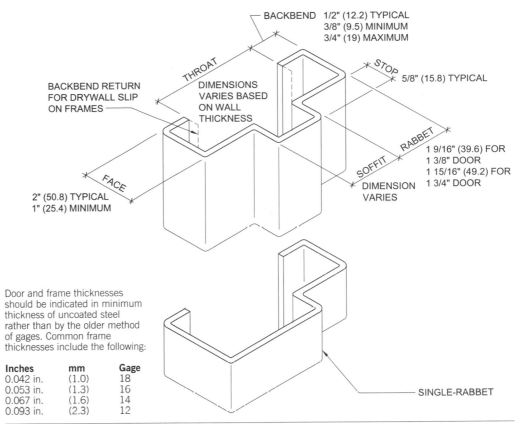

Door and frame thicknesses should be indicated in minimum thickness of uncoated steel rather than by the older method of gages. Common frame thicknesses include the following:

| Inches | mm | Gage |
|---|---|---|
| 0.042 in. | (1.0) | 18 |
| 0.053 in. | (1.3) | 16 |
| 0.067 in. | (1.6) | 14 |
| 0.093 in. | (2.3) | 12 |

### STANDARD HOLLOW METAL FRAMES

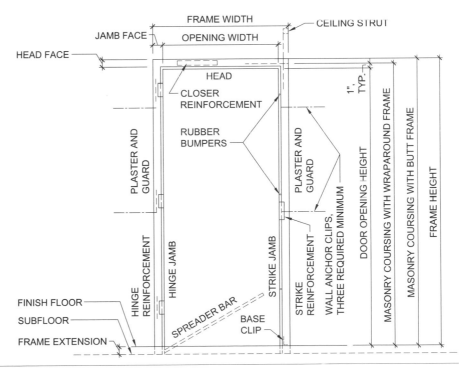

### STANDARD STEEL FRAME

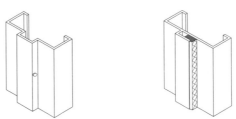

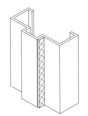

### HOLLOW METAL FRAME STOPS AND SEALS

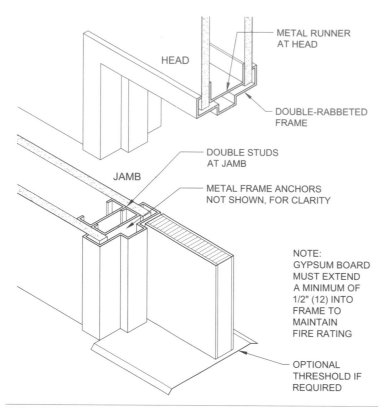

METAL RUNNER
AT HEAD

HEAD

DOUBLE-RABBETED
FRAME

DOUBLE STUDS
AT JAMB

JAMB

METAL FRAME ANCHORS
NOT SHOWN, FOR CLARITY

NOTE:
GYPSUM BOARD
MUST EXTEND
A MINIMUM OF
1/2" (12) INTO
FRAME TO
MAINTAIN
FIRE RATING

OPTIONAL
THRESHOLD IF
REQUIRED

**HOLLOW METAL FRAME IN METAL STUD PARTITION**

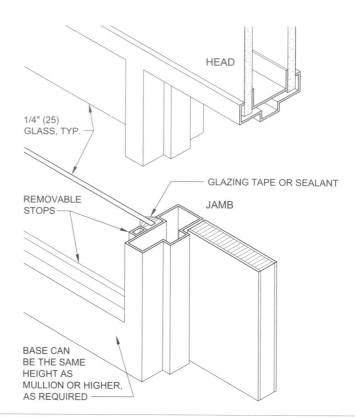

HEAD

1/4" (25)
GLASS, TYP.

GLAZING TAPE OR SEALANT

REMOVABLE
STOPS

JAMB

BASE CAN
BE THE SAME
HEIGHT AS
MULLION OR HIGHER,
AS REQUIRED

**HOLLOW METAL FRAME WITH SIDELITE**

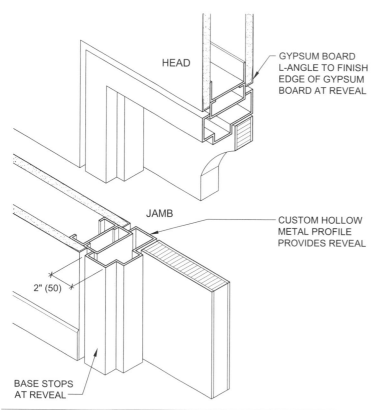

HEAD

GYPSUM BOARD
L-ANGLE TO FINISH
EDGE OF GYPSUM
BOARD AT REVEAL

JAMB

CUSTOM HOLLOW
METAL PROFILE
PROVIDES REVEAL

2" (50)

BASE STOPS
AT REVEAL

**HOLLOW METAL FRAME FLUSH WITH PARTITION**

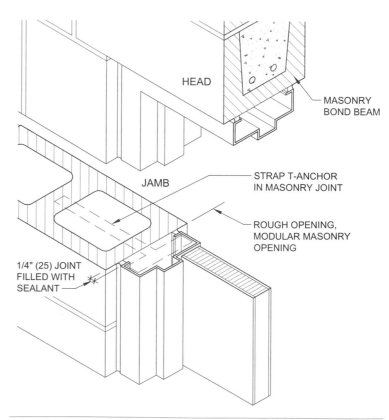

HEAD

MASONRY
BOND BEAM

STRAP T-ANCHOR
IN MASONRY JOINT

JAMB

ROUGH OPENING,
MODULAR MASONRY
OPENING

1/4" (25) JOINT
FILLED WITH
SEALANT

**HOLLOW METAL FRAME IN MASONRY WALL**

# GLASS DOORS

Glass doors are constructed primarily of glass, with fittings to hold the pivots and other hardware. Their strength depends on the glass rather than the framing. Glass doors are generally constructed of ½-in. (13-mm) or ¾-in. (19-mm) tempered glass.

Glass doors may be installed within an opening or as part of an all-glass entrance system. If used alone, glass doors may be set within a wall opening with or without a frame, or they can be installed between glass sidelights. The same type of fitting used on the door is generally used for sidelights. Although jamb frames of aluminum, wood, or ornamental metal can be used, they are not necessary and the glass sidelights can be butted directly to the partition.

The minimum configuration for a glass door requires some type of door pull and a corner fitting at the top and bottom (sometimes called the *shoe*) to hold the pivots. Some manufacturers provide hinge fittings that clamp on the glass and support the door in much the same way as a standard hinged door.

If the door is used for egress, the local building code may require the use of special hardware that allows the door to be locked from the outside, but still allows the door to be unlatched and opened from the inside with a single push on a push bar. Glass doors are heavy and may require a power operator or a balanced door system.

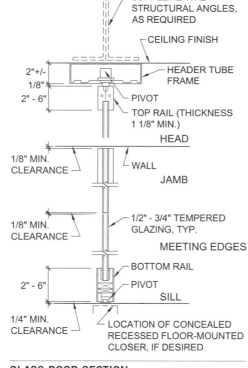

GLASS DOOR SECTION

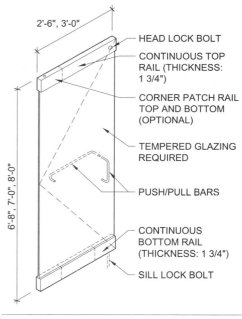

GLASS DOOR PARTS

## All-Glass Entrances

All-glass entrances, commonly used for interior storefronts, include glass doors and surrounding glazing that does not use visible framing members. Instead, special fittings are used to clamp adjacent glass pieces together and to support the glass doors. The glass, typically ½-in.- (13-mm-) or ¾-in.- (19-mm-) thick, is installed in channels set in the floor and above the ceiling. Glass fins, for additional lateral support, may be placed perpendicular to the main glass plane and attached with silicone sealant.

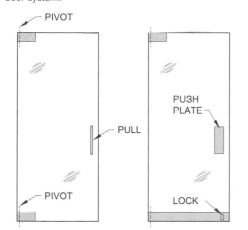
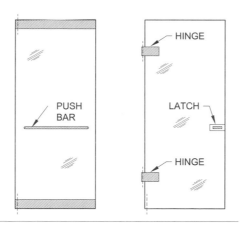

GLASS DOOR CONFIGURATIONS

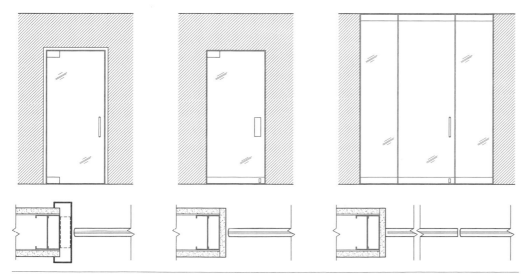

GLASS DOOR INSTALLATIONS

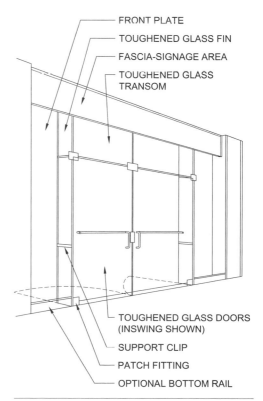

TYPICAL ALL-GLASS ENTRANCE

# FIRE-RATED OPENINGS

## Code Requirements

Building code requirements apply to any door that occurs at any location in the means-of-egress system. These requirements include criteria for size, swing, opening force, and hardware, among others.

In addition to these requirements, when an egress door serves as an opening in a rated partition, it is an *opening protective,* also called a *fire door assembly,* or *fire-rated assembly.* An opening protective is a rated assembly that prevents the spread of fire or smoke through an opening in a rated wall. For doors, this assembly includes the door, the frame, hardware, and accessories, including gasketing. Each component is crucial to the overall performance of the assembly as a fire barrier. Choices to be made regarding the enclosure of openings in fire-rated walls include the following:

1. Fire-rated wall requirements
2. Size of opening
3. Means of egress
   a. Required size per occupancy
   b. Quantity and location
   c. Direction of egress flow and operation of enclosure
   d. Hardware requirements
   e. Window egress requirements
4. Materials and finishes
5. Security
6. Visibility and glazing

## Fire Protection Criteria

National Fire Protection Association (NFPA) 80, *Standard for Fire Doors and Fire Windows,* is a consensus standard that establishes minimum criteria for installing and maintaining assemblies and devices used to protect openings in walls, ceilings, and floors from the spread of fire and smoke. The degree of fire protection (in hours) required for a given opening is referenced in the model building codes and the *Life Safety Code* (NFPA 101). Fire doors are classified by hourly references determined by testing done in accordance with NFPA 252, *Standard Method of Fire Tests of Door Assemblies* (also known as UL 10B). Further information is available in Chapter 6, Section 6 of the NFPA's *Fire Protection Handbook.*

## Positive Pressure Testing

The IBC requires that fire door assemblies be tested under conditions that simulate actual fire situations. For positive pressure testing, the IBC references UL 10C, *Standard for Positive Pressure Fire Tests of Door Assemblies,* and NFPA 252, *Standard Methods of Fire Tests of Door Assemblies,* but local jurisdictions may have their own requirements.

When a door is required to meet the requirements of positive pressure fire testing, it must have approved gasketing or intumescent material along the edge of the door or frame.

Doors in corridors and smoke barriers must meet the requirements for a smoke- and draft-control door assembly tested in accordance with UL 1784. Local jurisdictions may require that they carry an S-label.

---

## Definitions

*Automatic:* Providing a function without the necessity of human intervention.

*Fire barrier:* A continuous membrane, either vertical or horizontal (for example, a wall, floor, or ceiling assembly), that is designed and constructed with a specified fire-resistance rating to limit the spread of fire and restrict the movement of smoke.

*Fire resistance:* The property of materials or their assemblies that prevents or retards the passage of excessive heat, hot gas, or flames under conditions of use.

*Fire-resistance rating:* The time, in minutes or hours, that materials or assemblies have withstood fire exposure in accordance with the test procedure of NFPA 252, *Standard Methods of Fire Tests of Door Assemblies.*

*Labeled:* Equipment or materials marked with the label, symbol, or other identifying mark of an organization concerned with product evaluation that is acceptable to the local jurisdiction. This organization must periodically inspect production of labeled equipment, and the manufacturer, by labeling the product to indicate compliance in a specified manner with appropriate standards or performance.

*Noncombustible:* A material that, in the form in which it is used and under the conditions anticipated, will not aid combustion or add appreciable heat to an ambient fire.

*Self-closing:* As applied to a fire door or other protective opening, self-closing means the door is normally closed and is equipped with an approved device that will ensure closure after the door has been opened.

*Smoke barrier:* A continuous membrane, either vertical or horizontal, such as a wall, floor, or ceiling assembly, that is designed and constructed to restrict the movement of smoke. A smoke barrier may or may not have a fire-resistance rating.

---

## Types of Openings

The hourly protection rating for openings depends on the use of the barrier, as in exit enclosures, vertical openings in buildings, building separation walls, corridor walls, smoke barriers, and hazardous locations. In most codes, class designations have been replaced by hour classifications:

**4-hour and 3-hour openings:** Located in fire walls or in walls that divide a single building into fire areas.

**1½-hour and 1-hour openings:** Located in multistory vertical communication enclosures and in two-hour-rated partitions providing horizontal fire separations.

**¾-hour and 20-minute openings:** Located in walls or partitions between rooms and corridors with a fire-resistance rating of one hour or less.

---

**FRAME LABEL**

**DOOR LABEL**

**TESTING LABELS**

## RATINGS OF DOORS BASED ON PARTITION TYPE

| TYPE OF PARTITION | RATING OF PARTITION | REQUIRED DOOR ASSEMBLY RATING |
|---|---|---|
| Corridors Smoke barriers | 1 hour or less | 20 minutes |
| Fire partitions Exit passageways | 1 hour | ¾ hour |
| Exit stairs Occupancy Separation Vertical shafts | 1 hour | 1 hour |
| Exit stairs Fire separations | 2 hours | 1½ hour |

## TYPES OF FIRE-RATED FRAMES

Fire-rated door frames can be assembled at the factory or in the field. Frames must be adequately anchored at the jambs and floor according to the manufacturer's specifications. Codes require doors to be installed in accordance with NFPA 80. Section 2-5, *Frames,* indicates that only labeled frames are to be used.

*Light-gage metal frames* have head and jamb members with or without transom panel made from aluminum (45-minute maximum rating) or light-gage steel (1½-hour maximum rating) and are installed over a finished wall.

*Pressed steel (hollow metal) frames* have head and jamb members with or without solid or glazed transoms or sidelights made from 18-gage or heavier steel (3-hour maximum rating). They are required for most metal doors.

*Wood frames* may be used if they meet the testing standards used by the code. Some manufacturers supply wood frames that have fire ratings of 20, 45, 60, and 90 minutes. Verify availability with individual manufacturers.

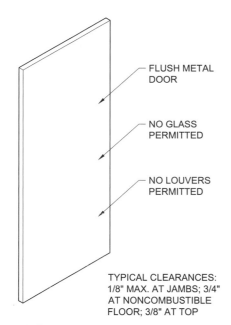

FLUSH METAL DOOR

NO GLASS PERMITTED

NO LOUVERS PERMITTED

TYPICAL CLEARANCES: 1/8" MAX. AT JAMBS; 3/4" AT NONCOMBUSTIBLE FLOOR; 3/8" AT TOP

**4-HOUR/3-HOUR CLASSIFICATION**

All hinges or pivots must be fabricated from steel. Two hinges are required on doors up to 5 ft (1,524 mm) in height; an additional hinge is required for each additional 2 ft 6 in. (762 mm) of door height or fraction thereof. The same requirement applies to pivots.

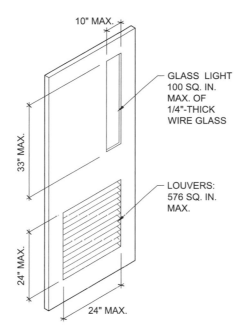

10" MAX.

33" MAX.

24" MAX.

24" MAX.

GLASS LIGHT 100 SQ. IN. MAX. OF 1/4"-THICK WIRE GLASS

LOUVERS: 576 SQ. IN. MAX.

**1½-HOUR/1-HOUR CLASSIFICATION**

While wired glass ¼-in.- (6-mm-) thick is the most common material used for glass lights, other materials have been listed and approved for installation. Refer to the UL fire protection directory.

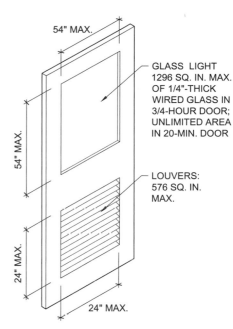

54" MAX.

54" MAX.

24" MAX.

24" MAX.

GLASS LIGHT 1296 SQ. IN. MAX. OF 1/4"-THICK WIRED GLASS IN 3/4-HOUR DOOR; UNLIMITED AREA IN 20-MIN. DOOR

LOUVERS: 576 SQ. IN. MAX.

**¾-HOUR/20-MINUTE CLASSIFICATION**

Consult all authorities with jurisdiction before installing glass lights and louvers.

Fusible-link/automatic closing louvers are permitted in fire-rated doors with restrictions, but they are not permitted in smoke-barrier doors.

## FIRE-RATED DOOR CLASSIFICATIONS

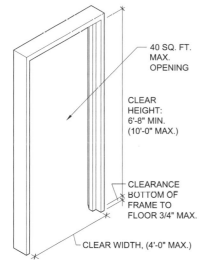

40 SQ. FT. MAX. OPENING

CLEAR HEIGHT: 6'-8" MIN. (10'-0" MAX.)

CLEARANCE BOTTOM OF FRAME TO FLOOR 3/4" MAX.

CLEAR WIDTH, (4'-0" MAX.)

The minimum width of each door opening must be sufficient for the occupant load it serves. Consult applicable building codes.

### DOOR OPENINGS FOR MEANS OF EGRESS

#### MAXIMUM DOOR SIZES (HOLLOW METAL, ALL CLASSES*)

| Single door | 4 × 10 ft (1,219 × 3,048 mm) with labeled single-point or three-point latching device |
| | 4 × 8 ft (1,219 × 2,438 mm) with fire exit hardware |
| Pair of doors | 8 × 10 ft (2,438 × 3,048 mm) active leaf with labeled single-point or three-point latching device |
| | 8 × 10 ft (2,438 × 3,048 mm) inactive leaf with labeled two-point latching device or top and bottom bolts |
| | 8 × 8 ft (2,438 × 2,438 mm) with fire exit hardware |

*Wood door size requirements are similar.*

## SWINGING FIRE DOORS

Types of swinging fire doors include:

*Composite fire doors:* Wood, steel, or plastic sheets bonded to and supported by a solid core material.

*Hollow metal fire doors:* Flush or panel design with a steel face of not less than 20-gage steel.

*Metal-clad fire doors:* Flush or panel design consisting of metal-covered wood cores or stiles and rails and insulated panels that are covered with steel of 24-gage or lighter.

*Sheet metal fire doors:* Steel of 22-gage or lighter of corrugated, flush sheet, or panel design.

*Tin-clad fire doors:* Wood core with a terne metal plate or galvanized steel facing (30- or 24-gage).

*Wood core doors:* Wood, hardboard, or plastic face sheets bonded to a woodblock or wood particleboard core material with untreated wood edges. Wood doors are available in fire ratings up to 90 minutes from some manufacturers, while hollow metal doors are required for ratings higher than 90 minutes.

### Door Operation

Doors that swing in the direction of egress are preferred for fire-rated doors. Horizontal sliding and revolving doors are permitted with restrictions.

### Hardware

Door hardware is provided by the builder, independent of the assembly, or furnished by the manufacturer with the door assembly. In either case, the manufacturer prepares the door and frame to receive hardware to ensure the integrity of the fire-rated assembly.

Fire doors are hung on steel ball-bearing hinges and must be self-closing. Labeled automatic latches and door closers can be self-operated or controlled by fail-safe devices that activate in a fire.

Pairs of doors require coordinators with astragals to ensure that both doors close. Heads and jambs should be sealed with gaskets when smoke control is required. Panic hardware may be required when space occupancy is greater than 100 people.

## SPECIAL DOORS USED AS EGRESS DOORS

Doors which can be used as a means of egress include the following:

*Revolving doors:* May be used if they do not supply more than 50% of the egress capacity and if the leaves collapse under opposing pressures with a resulting exit path of at least 36 in. (914 mm). At least one exit door must be located in close proximity.

*Power-operated doors:* May be used if they can be opened manually in the event of a power failure with a maximum force of 50 lb (222 N).

*Horizontal sliding doors:* May be used if they comply with eight criteria, including the capability to be operated manually in the event of a power failure with no special effort or knowledge.

*Access-controlled doors:* May be used if they comply with six criteria. Refer to the IBC for additional information.

*Security grilles:* May be used if they do not provide more than 50% of the required egress and if they remain open during the time the space is occupied.

# GLASS

Glass is a hard, brittle amorphous substance made by melting silica (sometimes combined with oxides of boron or phosphorus) with certain basic oxides (notably sodium, potassium, calcium, magnesium, and lead) to produce annealed flat glass by a controlled cooling process. Most glasses soften at 932 to 2,012°F (500 to 1,100°C). Minute surface scratches in manufacturing greatly reduce glass strength.

Glass is considered a liquid, even though it is rigid and behaves like a solid. As is characteristic of a liquid, the atoms in a sheet of glass are randomly arranged. They are frozen in place by rapid cooling during manufacturing. In most other mineral solids, the atoms are arranged in a recognizable geometric pattern and have a crystalline structure.

## FLOAT GLASS

Generally accepted as the successor to polished plate glass, float glass has become the quality standard of the glass industry. More than 95% of the glass manufactured in the United States is float glass. It is manufactured by floating molten glass on a surface of molten tin. Because the molten metal is denser than the glass, the two liquids do not mix together. This process produces a glass with very uniform thickness and flatness. After forming, the glass is cooled by a controlled process known as *annealing*.

Annealing relieves internal strains that may have developed during the manufacturing process. It ensures that the glass does not cool and contract at different rates across its surface. If glass is not annealed, it may fracture from differential stresses throughout the sheet when it reaches room temperature. The requirements for float glass are defined in ASTM C1036, *Specification for Flat Glass*. It is available in thicknesses ranging from 3 to 22 mm (⅛ to ⅞ in.).

## STRENGTHENED GLASS

There are several types of glass with increased strength: *fully tempered*, *heat-strengthened*, *laminated*, and *wire glass*.

### Fully Tempered Glass

Fully tempered glass is produced by heating float glass and then suddenly cooling it with special blowers. The outer surface cools quickly and contracts, constraining the hot inner core as it continues to cool. The surface and edges of fully tempered glass are in compression, while the inner core is in tension. Fully tempered glass is three to five times more resistant to impact, applied pressure, and bending stresses than annealed glass, because the surface tension must be overcome before the glass can be broken. The tempering process is defined by ASTM C1048, *Specification for Heat-Treated Flat Glass—Kind HS, Kind FT, Coated, and Uncoated Glass.*

Cutting or drilling fully tempered glass will destroy the integrity of the skin's compressive strength and will likely cause breakage, therefore, fully tempered glass cannot be field-cut. Fully tempered glass must be fabricated with the required holes or cutouts. It is available in thicknesses from 3 to 25 mm (⅛ to 1 in.).

## BASIC GLASS TYPES

|  | ANNEALED (REGULAR FLOAT GLASS) | FULLY TEMPERED | HEAT-STRENGTHENED | LAMINATED | WIRED |
|---|---|---|---|---|---|
| Safety glass | No | Yes | No | Yes | No |
| Can be field-cut or drilled | Yes | No | No | Depends on glass type laminated | Yes |
| Shatter pattern | Shards | Small cubes | Shards | Pieces adhere to interlayer | Pieces held in place by wire |
| For use in fire-rated assemblies | No | No | No | No | Yes |

### Heat-Strengthened Glass

The heat-strengthened glass manufacturing process is similar to that of fully tempered, except that the glass is only partially tempered. Annealed glass is heated and cooled in a manner similar to that for fully tempered glass; however, lower surface stresses are produced. Heat-strengthened glass is about twice as resistant to breakage as float glass.

### Laminated Glass

Laminated glass consists of two or more layers of glass and an interlayer material sandwiched together to form a single sheet. There are two types of interlayers: *polyvinyl butyral* (PVB) sheets, which are bonded under heat and pressure, and *urethane acrylate resin*, a liquid that is cured under ultraviolet light. PVB interlayers can be colored or patterned and can be combined for a decorative effect. The interlayer blocks a portion of ultraviolet rays, and is a sound barrier, which dampens vibrations between the two pieces of glass. Rice paper and other ornamental sheets can also be used in the lamination process. Cast resin interlayers are clear or custom-colored, and allow more heavily textured glass to be laminated.

Annealed, fully tempered, heat-strengthened, and wire glass types can be laminated. Security glass (bullet- or burglar-resistant) and acoustical glass are types of laminated glass using thicker interlayers. If laminated glass is broken, the glass remains bonded to the interlayer, offering protection from injury, which makes it popular for use in skylights. Laminated glass with an interlayer of .030 in. (.76 mm) minimum thickness meets the Federal Safety Glazing requirements of ANSI Z97.1, *Glazing Materials Used in Buildings—Safety Performance Specifications and Method of Test,* and Consumer Product Safety Commission (CPSC) 16 CFR Part 1201, *Safety Standard for Architectural Glazing Materials,* Category II, similar to tempered glass. Laminated glass with an interlayer thickness of .38 mm (.015 in.) meets the requirements of Category I glass. The standard for laminated glass is ASTM C1172, *Specification for Laminated Architectural Flat Glass.*

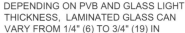

DEPENDING ON PVB AND GLASS LIGHT THICKNESS, LAMINATED GLASS CAN VARY FROM 1/4" (6) TO 3/4" (19) IN THICKNESS

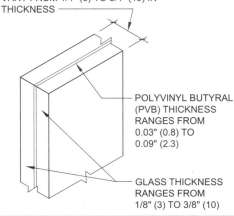

POLYVINYL BUTYRAL (PVB) THICKNESS RANGES FROM 0.03" (0.8) TO 0.09" (2.3)

GLASS THICKNESS RANGES FROM 1/8" (3) TO 3/8" (10)

**LAMINATED GLASS**

### Wire Glass

Wire glass has wire mesh or parallel wires rolled into the center of the glass sheet; it is available in various patterns and pattern sizes such as square-welded mesh, diamond-welded mesh, and linear parallel wire. Pattern sizes range from 13 to 25 mm (½ to 1 in.), depending on pattern type. Some distortion, wire discoloration, and misalignment are inherent. If breakage occurs, the wire helps to hold the glass fragments in the opening, thus preventing personal injuries. This is the standard glass type used for fire-rated doors or partition assemblies.

## SAFETY GLASS

Safety glass is glazing material that, if shattered, breaks in a way that reduces the likelihood of cutting and piercing injuries. Fully tempered and laminated glass qualifies as safety glass. Fully tempered glass breaks into small cubical pieces. If laminated glass is shattered, the broken glass adheres to the interlayer.

The requirements for safety glass are defined by two very similar standards: CPSC 16 CFR Part 1201, and ANSI Z97.1. These standards use the same test procedures, with the exception that the CPSC standard uses a greater impact load. Although wired glass does not pass the tests for safety glass described in CPSC 16 CFR Part 1201, it is granted an exemption because it is the only glass type that performs successfully in fire tests.

## SECURITY GLASS

Security glass is composed of multilayers of glass and/or polycarbonate plastic laminated together (under heat and pressure) with a polyvinyl butyral (for glass) or polyurethane plastic (for polycarbonate) film. It is available in multilayer laminated glass, insulating, laminated insulating, and double-laminated insulating or spaced configurations. Thicknesses range from 9 to 63 mm (⅜ to 2½ in.) as a laminated product and up to about 120 mm (4¾ in.) for insulating and spaced construction products.

Bullet-resistant glass should meet the requirements of UL 752, *Standard for Bullet-Resisting Equipment* and burglar-resistant UL 972, *Standard for Burglary Resisting Glazing Material*. Consult manufacturers for blast-resistant glass. Security glass products, depending on type, are subject to size limitations; consult with the manufacturer for glazing requirements and restrictions on use.

## TINTED GLASS

Tinted glass was developed to control solar heat gain and glare. Float glass is tinted, and is available in green, bronze, gray, and blue, in thicknesses ranging from 3 to 13 mm (⅛ to ½ in.). The glass absorbs a portion of the sun's energy due to its admixture content and thickness; it then dissipates the heat to both the exterior and interior. The thicker the glass, the greater the solar energy absorption. Newer tinted glass types allow more visible light transmission, while blocking a higher percentage of infrared energy than standard tinted glass.

Heat-absorbing tinted glass has a higher temperature when exposed to the sun than clear glass; the central area expands more than the cooler shaded edges, causing tensile stress buildup.

Indoor shading devices such as blinds and draperies reflect energy back through the glass, thus increasing the temperature of the glass. Spaces between indoor shading devices and the glass, including ceiling pockets, should be vented adequately. Heating elements should be located on the interior side of shading devices, directing warm air away from the glass. Consider tilt-limit devices on horizontal blinds to allow for ventilation.

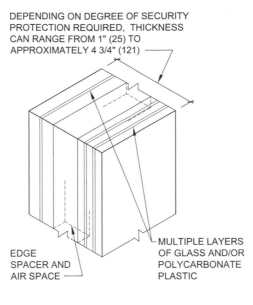

DEPENDING ON DEGREE OF SECURITY PROTECTION REQUIRED, THICKNESS CAN RANGE FROM 1" (25) TO APPROXIMATELY 4 3/4" (121)

MULTIPLE LAYERS OF GLASS AND/OR POLYCARBONATE PLASTIC

EDGE SPACER AND AIR SPACE

**INSULATING OR SPACED CONSTRUCTION SECURITY GLASS**

## REFLECTIVE GLASS

Reflective glass reduces the amount of transmitted, absorbed, and reflective portions of the incident light and energy spectrum, thus improving the energy balance within a building. Typically, pyrolitic or "hard coat" coatings are used on exposed glass surfaces, which are more scratch-resistant than sputtered "soft coat" coatings. Reflective coatings are derived from metals, and are applied to glass, based on the glazing system requirements. Pyrolitic reflective coatings on side 1 (the outside surface) are susceptible to exterior environmental factors. Reflective coatings on sides 2 or 3 are protected from damage, if used in a double-glazed unit.

Reflective glass can be used in interior applications such as shower doors and enclosures, countertops, wall cladding, and furniture.

## LOW-EMISSIVITY GLASS

Low-emissivity (Low-E) glass was developed to address energy efficiency concerns for glazing. Hard or soft metallic coatings are applied to the glass, based on application type. Low-E coatings provide more reflectivity for the shortwave solar energy that strikes the glass at a high angle of incidence during the summer, while permitting this warmth to enter during the winter when the angle of incidence is lower. Low-E coatings are applied to side 2 on the first pane of glass in a double-glazed unit. The overall light transmission rate is higher than in tinted and reflective glass types.

## INSULATING GLASS

Insulating glass acts as a barrier to conductive heat loss. Insulated glass units are created by sealing an air pocket between two lights of glass, separated by a spacer. The energy efficiency of insulated glass can be increased by adding more lights of glass, or by the use of thin heat-reflecting films suspended between the spacers. New spacer types have been developed that provide a thermal break between the two lights of

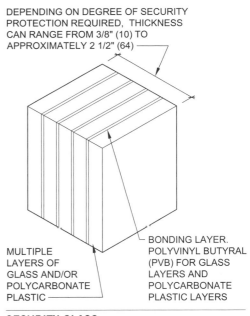

DEPENDING ON DEGREE OF SECURITY PROTECTION REQUIRED, THICKNESS CAN RANGE FROM 3/8" (10) TO APPROXIMATELY 2 1/2" (64)

MULTIPLE LAYERS OF GLASS AND/OR POLYCARBONATE PLASTIC

BONDING LAYER. POLYVINYL BUTYRAL (PVB) FOR GLASS LAYERS AND POLYCARBONATE PLASTIC LAYERS

**SECURITY GLASS**

glass, for conditions in which there is a large temperature differential between the edges and the center of the glass. Stresses on the seal may cause the eventual deterioration of the sealant, and moisture may appear as condensation between the glass lights. Insulated glass dampens vibrations and sound. Insulated glass units may be created to protect and seal specially treated glass, such as sandblasted glass surfaces.

## SPECIALTY GLASS TYPES

### Low-Iron Glass

Low-iron glass, or *ultraclear glass*, has high clarity and high visible light transmittance, without the marked greenish tint visible on the edge of standard glass. The clarity in the glass is achieved by the reduction of the iron content by approximately 10%. Thicknesses range from 3 to 19 mm (⅛ to ¾ in.). Low-iron glass can be heat-strengthened, tempered, sandblasted, etched, or assembled into laminated glass. Low-iron glass is used in areas where color rendition is critical, and for furniture, mirrors, museum display cases, signage, and where glass is to be back-coated with light-colored pigments. Trade names for the major manufacturers producing low iron glass are PPG Starphire, Pilkington Opti-White, and Saint Gobain Diamante.

### Textured Glass

Textured patterned glass is also known as *rolled* or *figured glass*. It is made by passing molten glass through rollers that are etched to produce the design. Designs include flutes, ribs, grids, and other regular and random patterns, which provide translucency and a degree of obscurity. Usually only one side of the glass is imprinted with a pattern. Patterned glass can be silvered, sandblasted, or have applied colored coatings. A form of textured glass is *impression glass*, in which a clear resin, applied to the glass, is impressed with a pattern. Tempering and sheet size limitations for patterned glass must be verified. Patterning a glass surface may make tempering impossible. Sheet sizes and thicknesses can vary greatly, depending on the type of pattern desired.

## FORMED GLASS

### Cast Glass

Cast glass, also known as *molded glass*, is formed in molds, using combinations of colors and textures to form the desired product. Cast glass may be molded to precise dimensions and tolerances or it may be formed into art glass units. The casting process allows an unlimited number of glass forms, colors, and textures to be created. Thicknesses and overall sizes are dependent on the design and intended use for the cast glass. Forms of cast glass include glass tiles, stair treads, countertops, artwork, and glass panels.

### Translucent Linear Glazing System

Pilkington Profilit manufactures a channel-shaped translucent cast glass product that can be used as an interior wall system. Its most common face dimension is about 10 in. (255 mm) wide, and its structural capabilities allow it to be used in interior application heights of 20 ft (6 m) or more, providing a dramatic linear effect. It is nearly always installed "double-glazed," creating an air space that offers a smooth appearance on both surfaces, and STC reduction of up to 42 dB. It is installed in a system of aluminum channels that can be finished to complement the surrounding conditions, or recessed into the perimeters for a flush appearance. The system can be curved, and glass-to-glass angled corners also can be easily installed, eliminating the necessity of any vertical metal framing at the interior glass area.

### Fused Glass

Multiple-layer glass units are formed by fusing compatible glass together under controlled heating. Various glass colors, textures, and compatible three-dimensional materials such as wire, stainless steel, and copper screen can be incorporated into the fused unit. A t*exture* or *tack* fuse maintains a degree of separation between the individual pieces of glass. A *full* fuse melts the various elements and layers into a uniform homogenous form with a smooth surface and rounded edges. Different colors used in a full-fused piece will blend more than in a tack-fused piece. Coated and reflective glass may be fused onto glass substrates. Fused glass is typically used for furniture and decorative accents, glass borders, tiles, panels, light fixtures, and other interior elements.

### Slumped Glass

Glass can be molded into various shapes when heated to provide the proper viscosity in a semimolten state. Slumped glass with thicknesses up to 10 mm (⅜ in.) will have the impression of the mold translated to the back side, while thicker glass units will be relatively smooth on the opposite side. Tinted or reflective glass types can be slumped, and processes such as gold leafing, silvering, and airbrushed coloring can be incorporated into the slumped glass texture. Panels up to 4 by 8 ft (1,219 by 2,438 mm) are possible, and the slumped glass can be tempered if required. Molds may be made of materials that can withstand the kiln-slumping temperature of approximately 1,350°F (732°C). Tabletops, shower enclosures, wall panels, and signage can be created from slumped glass.

### Bent Glass

A precise, strict tolerance form of slumped glass is known as bent glass. Bent glass is often laminated to meet safety glazing requirements, and may be tempered. Some visual distortion may occur when the radius of the bent glass is tight. Curved shower enclosures, wall partitions, and automobile windshields are applications for bent glass.

## PRIVACY GLASS

### Blind Glass

Blind glass is float glass that is acid-etched on both sides in a linear, offset pattern, obscuring visibility when viewed perpendicular to the glass. Visibility through the glass is possible when viewing at a 45° angle. Produced in 5-mm (³⁄₁₆-in.) and 8-mm (⁵⁄₁₆-in.) thicknesses, the thicker glass is more effective for a "see-through" effect, while the thinner glass is suited to areas requiring more privacy, such as in doors and in furniture applications.

### Electrochromic Glass

Electrochromic glass switchable privacy glazings, identified as polymer dispersed liquid crystal (PDLC), consists of liquid crystals that are enclosed in transparent polymer capsules. The capsules are sandwiched between two sheets of transparent electroconductive film. When voltage is applied, the liquid crystals line up in rows, allowing light to pass freely through the transparent film and glass. Without voltage, the liquid crystals do not line up in rows. This diffuses the light, making the glass appear opaque or obscure.

## SURFACE TEXTURING

Surface textures on glass soften transmitted light, add decorative designs, increase obscurity for privacy, or lightly fracture the glass surface for a frosted effect. Surface-texturing processes can be applied to clear, tinted, or reflective glass, prior to tempering.

### Sandblasting

Sandblasting is used to create a translucent frosted effect of a desired design on the glass surface. The glass is blasted with small abrasive particles of sand and high-pressure air projected through a nozzle. Different degrees of coarseness are used to achieve varying levels of smoothness. The resulting granular textured surface is susceptible to the absorption of oils. Fingerprints and dirt are typically visible on sandblasted surfaces unless treated with an applied sealer. The sandblasted surface may be protected by enclosing it within an insulated double-glazing unit.

Sandblasting is also the first treatment applied to glass, prior to additional treatments. A sandblasted surface provides improved adhesion for applied sprayed coatings. Laminated glass may be sandblasted, but care should be taken so that the interlayer is not compromised.

### Acid Etching

Sandblasted glass is submerged in a bath of hydrofluoric and hydrochloric acids to create a hardened, sealed surface. The glass appears matte, with a soft, light-diffusing quality. Depending on the coarseness of the sandblasting grit, the etched texture may be relatively smooth or grainy. Acid-etched glass may be coated or silvered. It does not show dust, dirt, or fingerprints, and is used in retail residential, and commercial applications for tabletops, counters, shelving, wall cladding, stair treads, and other interior architectural elements. Stencils and etching creams are available to etch smaller areas of glass for signage, mirrors, and windows.

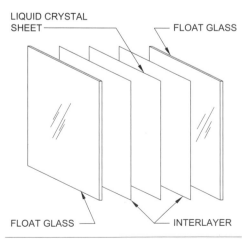

POLYMER DISPERSED LIQUID CRYSTAL PRIVACY GLASS

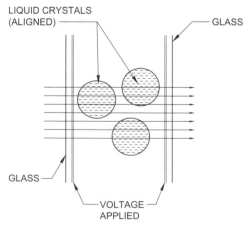

**VOLTAGE APPLIED**
When voltage is applied (switch is on), the liquid crystals line up in rows, allowing light to pass through.

POLYMER DISPERSED LIQUID CRYSTAL DISPLAY

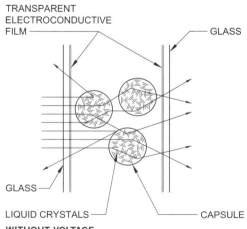

**WITHOUT VOLTAGE**
Without voltage (switch is off), the liquid crystals scatter, making the glass appear opaque or obscure.

## Glue Chip Glass

To create a fractured, ice-crystal-like frosted effect, hot glue is applied to sandblasted glass, and as it cools, the glue dries and shrinks, removing flakes of glass from the surface. Traditionally, horsehide glue was used for this process, but it has been replaced by synthetic glues. Greater pattern density can be created by a second application of the glue, resulting in a more obscure, frosted appearance. Clear or tinted glass may be glue-chipped, and the glass may be tempered for added strength.

## Decorative Silk-Screened (or Frit) Glass

Annealed clear or tinted glass is washed, and ceramic frit paint (in standard or custom colors) is silk-screened on its surface in a standard or custom pattern or design (such as dots, holes, lines, or a logo), then dried in an oven. The frit-coated glass is then subjected to very high temperatures in a tempering furnace to fire the ceramic frit permanently to the glass surface. As a result, silk-screened glass will be either heat-strengthened or tempered after firing. Reflective and low-emissivity coatings can also be applied to the glass surface. Silk-screened glass can be used monolithically or for insulating or laminated glass products. A newer coating process for silk-screened glass uses water-based polymers. This material can be custom-colored or is available in metallic, crackle, frosted, and other custom finishes. This process is much more environmentally friendly than solvent-based coatings. The finish is cured in a low-temperature oven, and the glass may be tempered. Using this process, the glass may be cut, drilled, polished, and postfabricated to suit project needs.

## Miscellaneous Coatings

Epoxy coatings are typically applied to the back of glass units. Special printing techniques provide numerous design options on the glass. Coatings may contain glass beads and mica chips, which add a more reflective or metallic appearance. Special metallic coatings can be applied to increase glass reflectivity to light and heat and to carry an electric current.

A form of metallic coating is the dichroic coating, consisting of molecularly thin layers of titanium or zirconium that are highly reflective of one color wavelength of light, while transmitting an entirely different color. Dichroic coatings can be applied to clear or textured glass substrates. Size restrictions may apply due to the dichroic application process limitations. It is used in furniture, accent glass pieces, and art glass. Silicone coatings have been used for decades as a color backing for spandrel glass.

## APPLIED MATERIALS

Applied films can be used to modify the appearance or performance of glass. Mylar films can be permanently bonded to the glass with nonyellowing adhesives to create special designs. Tinted films are used as a low-cost alternative to tinted glass in retrofits of existing glass in commercial, residential, and automotive applications. Clear, tough films are available with a Category II safety glazing alternative for glass that is too thin, textured, or shaped so that it cannot be tempered. Applied films are used in jewelry store windows and display cases, where additional protection is needed without affecting the visual quality of the glass. Nylon-fiber-reinforced adhesive-backed films are used on the backs of mirrors for wardrobe doors and wall cladding where safety is a concern but where tempering would cause unacceptable visual distortion.

## MIRRORS

Mirrors are created by coating a piece of glass with a reflective coating of silver, with a backing of copper, protected by an epoxy paint top coat. Tinted and clear glass may be silvered with the pyrolitic process to produce mirrors.

One-way mirrors are used for discreet observation, such as in lineup rooms in law enforcement facilities. These mirrors are created by the use of a special reflective coating, which allows approximately 12% transmission and is reflective to the side with the highest light intensity. Light on the observation side is reduced by a 10:1 ratio, which maintains the reflective differential. One-way mirrors should be installed according to the manufacturer's instructions, and the lighting should be coordinated to provide secure one-way visibility.

## FIRE-RATED GLASS

Fire-rated glass is a transparent ceramic product. It can be used in fire-rated partitions, in larger areas than typical wire glass locations. Consult local codes and manufacturer's information for limitations. All fire-rated glass is listed and labeled by Underwriter's Laboratories (UL). Fire ratings vary by type of fire-rated glass and thickness, but range from 20 minutes to 2 hours. Three-hour ratings are available with some insulated glass units. Thicknesses range from 5 mm ($\frac{3}{16}$ in.) for nonimpact locations, such as transoms, to 8 mm ($\frac{5}{16}$ in.) for laminated, impact-safety-rated fire-rated glass used in doors. Fire-rated glass may be polished, unpolished, or patterned (obscure).

Fire-rated or fire/impact safety-rated insulated glass units (IGU) are composed of fire-rated glass and either tempered or annealed float glass. These units are available in tinted, low-E, reflective, one-way mirror, and art glass units. Consult manufacturers for specific unit types and applications.

Fire-rated and impact-safety-rated glazing is available that has an intumescent gel layer between two panes of glass. When exposed to heat and light, the gel layer turns opaque and blocks the transfer of radiant heat through the glass for a short period of time.

Special framing is required for fire-rated glazing installations, which must be compatible with the fire rating of the glass. Approved glazing compounds and fire-rated glazing tapes are required to maintain the rating of the installation.

## SPECIAL GLASS TYPES

X-ray shielding lead glass, super heat-resistant glass for industrial uses, and other special-use glass types are available for custom applications. Consult manufacturers for information.

## WATERJET CUTTING

Waterjet cutting is a precise computer-controlled glass-cutting method. High-velocity water is forced through a small ceramic nozzle, combined with a fine abrasive used as a cutting medium. It is capable of cutting through multiple layers of glass and is useful when dissimilar materials are nested together with the glass, such as metals. Tolerances are .001 in. (.025 mm). Shapes too intricate to be cut by hand or traditional glass-cutting techniques can be waterjet cut.

## EDGE TREATMENTS

### Polished Edges

Polished edges are created either by machine or by hand, using progressively finer sanding grits with a final polishing with a cork belt, impregnated with a polishing compound. If the glass is to be tempered, the sharp shoulders of the edge are sanded, or "seamed," to remove small cutting nicks, chips, and sharpness. This treatment is necessary to minimize thermal stresses that may occur with small edge fractures. Edge finishing of laminated glass is typically done by hand to protect the soft interlayer, and is typically limited to flat or pencil polishing. If a glass edge is flat-polished, the shoulders are accentuated with a slight polished chamfer known as an *arris* on both sides of the glass.

### Beveled Edges

Beveled edges on glass surfaces change the reflection angle of the light and create a framed appearance to the glass. Bevels are ground onto the face of the glass with a succession of diamond-grinding and -polishing wheels. Beveled glass is tempered with the bevel side down toward the horizontal rollers. Thick glass with bevels more than 1 in. (25 mm) wide may slump and warp at the edges, due to the heat required for the glass thickness during the tempering process. Some inconsistencies can be polished out after the tempering process is complete.

Robert Thompson, AIA; Creative Central; Tigard, Oregon
Jana Gunsul, AIA; DES Architects/Engineers; Redwood City, California

# GLAZING

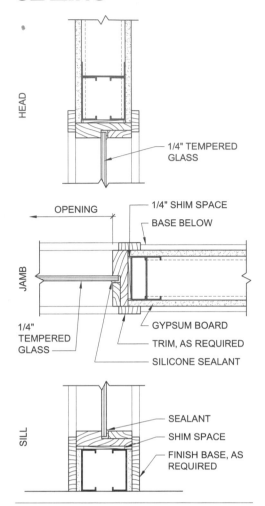

**FRAMED GLAZING DETAILS**

HEAD

1/4" TEMPERED GLASS

OPENING

1/4" SHIM SPACE

BASE BELOW

JAMB

1/4" TEMPERED GLASS

GYPSUM BOARD

TRIM, AS REQUIRED

SILICONE SEALANT

SILL

SEALANT

SHIM SPACE

FINISH BASE, AS REQUIRED

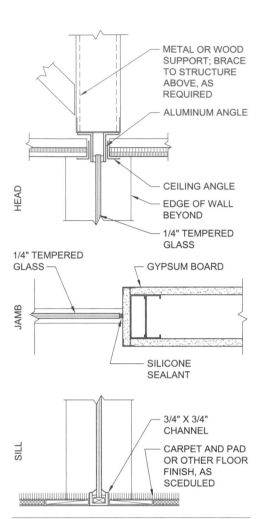

**FRAMELESS GLAZING DETAILS**

HEAD

METAL OR WOOD SUPPORT; BRACE TO STRUCTURE ABOVE, AS REQUIRED

ALUMINUM ANGLE

CEILING ANGLE

EDGE OF WALL BEYOND

1/4" TEMPERED GLASS

JAMB

1/4" TEMPERED GLASS

GYPSUM BOARD

SILICONE SEALANT

SILL

3/4" X 3/4" CHANNEL

CARPET AND PAD OR OTHER FLOOR FINISH, AS SCEDULED

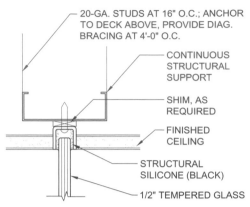

20-GA. STUDS AT 16" O.C.; ANCHOR TO DECK ABOVE, PROVIDE DIAG. BRACING AT 4'-0" O.C.

CONTINUOUS STRUCTURAL SUPPORT

SHIM, AS REQUIRED

FINISHED CEILING

STRUCTURAL SILICONE (BLACK)

1/2" TEMPERED GLASS

NOTE:
GLASS WILL BE END-BUTTED AT JAMBS AND CAULKED TO GYPSUM BOARD.

**HEAD**

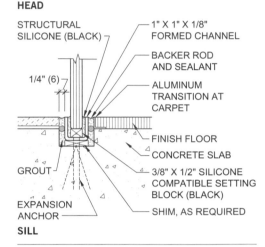

STRUCTURAL SILICONE (BLACK)

1" X 1" X 1/8" FORMED CHANNEL

BACKER ROD AND SEALANT

1/4" (6)

ALUMINUM TRANSITION AT CARPET

FINISH FLOOR

CONCRETE SLAB

GROUT

3/8" X 1/2" SILICONE COMPATIBLE SETTING BLOCK (BLACK)

EXPANSION ANCHOR

SHIM, AS REQUIRED

**SILL**

**CONCEALED FRAME GLASS PARTITION**

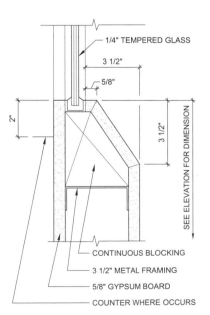

1/4" TEMPERED GLASS

3 1/2"

5/8"

2"

3 1/2"

SEE ELEVATION FOR DIMENSION

CONTINUOUS BLOCKING

3 1/2" METAL FRAMING

5/8" GYPSUM BOARD

COUNTER WHERE OCCURS

Sloped sill prevents sitting and the accumulation of debris.

**GLASS VISION PANEL WITH SLOPED SILL**

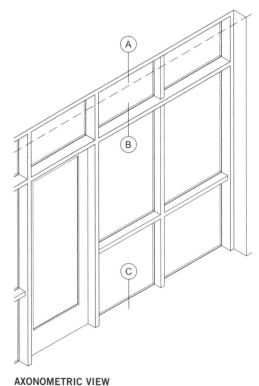

A

B

C

**AXONOMETRIC VIEW**

**INTERIOR STOREFRONT**

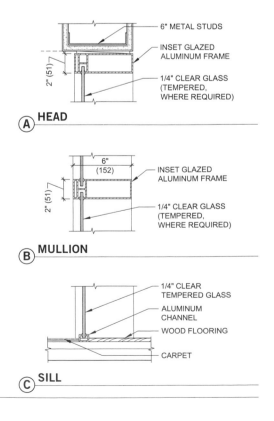

6" METAL STUDS

INSET GLAZED ALUMINUM FRAME

1/4" CLEAR GLASS (TEMPERED, WHERE REQUIRED)

2" (51)

Ⓐ **HEAD**

6" (152)

INSET GLAZED ALUMINUM FRAME

1/4" CLEAR GLASS (TEMPERED, WHERE REQUIRED)

2" (51)

Ⓑ **MULLION**

1/4" CLEAR TEMPERED GLASS

ALUMINUM CHANNEL

WOOD FLOORING

CARPET

Ⓒ **SILL**

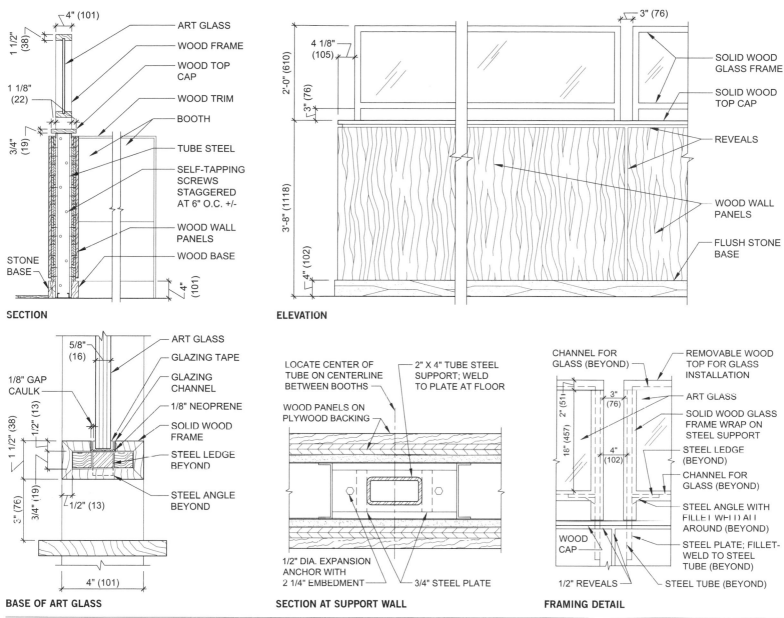

**SECTION**

- 4" (101)
- 1 1/2" (38)
- 1 1/8" (22)
- 3/4" (19)
- ART GLASS
- WOOD FRAME
- WOOD TOP CAP
- WOOD TRIM
- BOOTH
- TUBE STEEL
- SELF-TAPPING SCREWS STAGGERED AT 6" O.C. +/-
- WOOD WALL PANELS
- WOOD BASE
- STONE BASE
- 4" (101)

**ELEVATION**

- 3" (76)
- 4 1/8" (105)
- 2'-0" (610)
- 3" (76)
- 3'-8" (1118)
- 4" (102)
- SOLID WOOD GLASS FRAME
- SOLID WOOD TOP CAP
- REVEALS
- WOOD WALL PANELS
- FLUSH STONE BASE

**BASE OF ART GLASS**

- 5/8" (16)
- 1/8" GAP CAULK
- 1/2" (13)
- 1 1/2" (38)
- 3" (76)
- 3/4" (19)
- 1/2" (13)
- 4" (101)
- ART GLASS
- GLAZING TAPE
- GLAZING CHANNEL
- 1/8" NEOPRENE
- SOLID WOOD FRAME
- STEEL LEDGE BEYOND
- STEEL ANGLE BEYOND

**SECTION AT SUPPORT WALL**

- LOCATE CENTER OF TUBE ON CENTERLINE BETWEEN BOOTHS
- 2" X 4" TUBE STEEL SUPPORT; WELD TO PLATE AT FLOOR
- WOOD PANELS ON PLYWOOD BACKING
- 1/2" DIA. EXPANSION ANCHOR WITH 2 1/4" EMBEDMENT
- 3/4" STEEL PLATE

**FRAMING DETAIL**

- CHANNEL FOR GLASS (BEYOND)
- 2" (51)
- 18" (457)
- 3" (76)
- 4" (102)
- REMOVABLE WOOD TOP FOR GLASS INSTALLATION
- ART GLASS
- SOLID WOOD GLASS FRAME WRAP ON STEEL SUPPORT
- STEEL LEDGE (BEYOND)
- CHANNEL FOR GLASS (BEYOND)
- STEEL ANGLE WITH FILLET WELD ALL AROUND (BEYOND)
- STEEL PLATE; FILLET-WELD TO STEEL TUBE (BEYOND)
- WOOD CAP
- 1/2" REVEALS
- STEEL TUBE (BEYOND)

## ART GLASS WALL

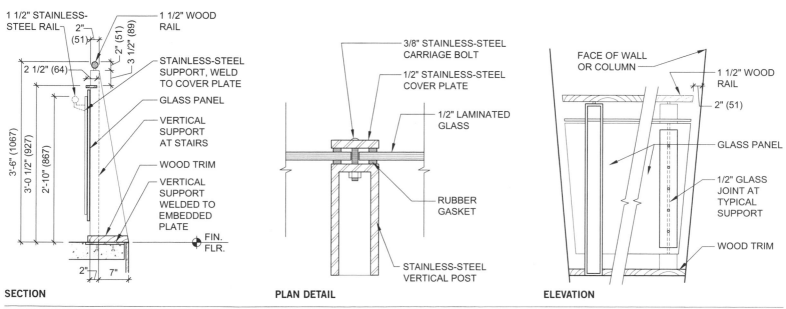

**SECTION**

- 1 1/2" STAINLESS-STEEL RAIL
- 1 1/2" WOOD RAIL
- 2" (51)
- 2" (51)
- 3 1/2" (89)
- 2 1/2" (64)
- 3'-6" (1067)
- 3'-0 1/2" (927)
- 2'-10" (867)
- 2"    7"
- STAINLESS-STEEL SUPPORT, WELD TO COVER PLATE
- GLASS PANEL
- VERTICAL SUPPORT AT STAIRS
- WOOD TRIM
- VERTICAL SUPPORT WELDED TO EMBEDDED PLATE
- FIN. FLR.

**PLAN DETAIL**

- 3/8" STAINLESS-STEEL CARRIAGE BOLT
- 1/2" STAINLESS-STEEL COVER PLATE
- 1/2" LAMINATED GLASS
- RUBBER GASKET
- STAINLESS-STEEL VERTICAL POST

**ELEVATION**

- FACE OF WALL OR COLUMN
- 1 1/2" WOOD RAIL
- 2" (51)
- GLASS PANEL
- 1/2" GLASS JOINT AT TYPICAL SUPPORT
- WOOD TRIM

## GLASS GUARDRAIL

*Jana Gunsul, AIA; DES Architects/Engineers; Redwood City, California*

# PLASTER

For centuries, prior to the advent of gypsum board manufacturing, plaster was the primary interior wall and ceiling finish. Conventional plaster provides superior wear resistance to taped gypsum board assemblies. Though it is preferred to attain a uniform, monolithic surface, plaster finishes are more labor-intensive than taped gypsum board assemblies, require greater skill, and can take as long as two days to cure. For these reasons, today, plaster finishes are most commonly used in restoration to match existing conditions and in high-end installations.

Three-coat plaster applications are required on all metal lath and on edge-supported gypsum lath used in ceilings. Three-coat applications are preferred on gypsum lath assemblies, but two-coat applications are acceptable where gypsum lath is properly supported and on masonry plaster bases such as porous brick, clay tiles, and rough concrete masonry units.

Keene's cement plaster is a specialty finish coat of gypsum plaster primarily used where a smooth, dense, vandal-resistant, white finish is desired.

Thickness, proportions of mixes of various plastering materials, and finishes vary. Systems and methods of application also vary widely, depending on local traditions and innovations promoted by the industry.

## ORNAMENTAL PLASTER

Molding plaster is used for ornamental trim, running cornices, and other cast plaster pieces. This specialty plaster has a very fine grain and is ideal for sharp detail when used for cast work. Higher-strength molding plaster may be required for ornamental work having thin sections or intricate detail.

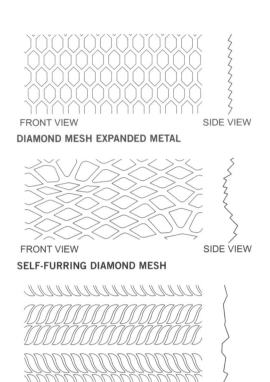

FRONT VIEW                SIDE VIEW
**DIAMOND MESH EXPANDED METAL**

FRONT VIEW                SIDE VIEW
**SELF-FURRING DIAMOND MESH**

FRONT VIEW                SIDE VIEW
**RIB-EXPANDED METAL**

**METAL LATH TYPES**

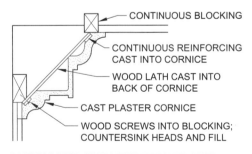

- CONTINUOUS BLOCKING
- CONTINUOUS REINFORCING CAST INTO CORNICE
- WOOD LATH CAST INTO BACK OF CORNICE
- CAST PLASTER CORNICE
- WOOD SCREWS INTO BLOCKING; COUNTERSINK HEADS AND FILL

**CAST PLASTER ORNAMENT ATTACHED WITH SCREWS**

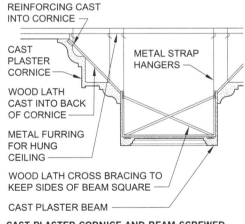

- CONTINUOUS REINFORCING CAST INTO CORNICE
- CAST PLASTER CORNICE
- WOOD LATH CAST INTO BACK OF CORNICE
- METAL FURRING FOR HUNG CEILING
- METAL STRAP HANGERS
- WOOD LATH CROSS BRACING TO KEEP SIDES OF BEAM SQUARE
- CAST PLASTER BEAM

**CAST PLASTER CORNICE AND BEAM SCREWED AND HUNG**

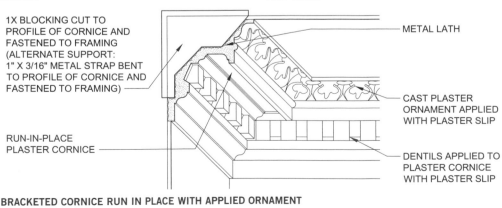

- 1X BLOCKING CUT TO PROFILE OF CORNICE AND FASTENED TO FRAMING (ALTERNATE SUPPORT: 1" X 3/16" METAL STRAP BENT TO PROFILE OF CORNICE AND FASTENED TO FRAMING)
- RUN-IN-PLACE PLASTER CORNICE
- METAL LATH
- CAST PLASTER ORNAMENT APPLIED WITH PLASTER SLIP
- DENTILS APPLIED TO PLASTER CORNICE WITH PLASTER SLIP

**BRACKETED CORNICE RUN IN PLACE WITH APPLIED ORNAMENT**

**TRADITIONAL CAST PLASTER**

## Definitions

*Basecoat:* A plaster coat applied before finish coat, scratch coat, and blow coats in three-coat plaster.

*Brown coat:* In three-coat plaster, the second coat; in two-coat plaster, the first coat.

*Fibered plaster:* Gypsum plaster containing fibers of hair, glass, nylon, or sisal.

*Finish coat:* The final coat of plaster, which provides the decorative surface.

*Furring:* Generally, channels or Z-shapes attached to the underlying wall (or structure for ceilings) for attaching gypsum or metal lath while allowing an air space. Often used on cementitious substrate, resilient furring is used to reduce sound transmission.

*Gypsum:* Hydrous calcium sulphate, a natural mineral in crystalline form.

*Gypsum lath:* A base for plaster; a sheet having a gypsum core, faced with paper. Also perforated for interior use.

*Hydrated lime:* Quicklime mixed with water, on the job, to form a lime putty.

*Lime:* Obtained by burning various types of limestone, consisting of oxides or hydroxides of calcium and magnesium.

*Lime plaster:* Basecoat plaster of hydrated lime and an aggregate.

*Neat plaster:* Basecoat plaster, fibered or unfibered, used for job-mixing with aggregates.

*Perlite:* Siliceious volcanic glass containing silica and alumina expanded by heat for use as a lightweight plaster aggregate.

*Plaster:* Cementitious material or combination of cementitious materials and aggregate that, when mixed with water, forms a plastic mass that sets and hardens when applied to a surface.

*Portland cement:* Manufactured combination of limestone and an argillaceous substance for exterior or wet-atmosphere applications.

*Scratch coat:* In three-coat plastering, the first coat, which is then scratched to provide a bond for the second, or brown, coat.

*Stucco portland cement:* Plaster used in exterior application. This plaster requires a waterset; it must not be applied to smooth dense surface or gypsum lath, requires control joints, and cannot have a Keene's cement-lime putty finish.

*Three-coat plaster:* Preferred application for all substrates; required over metal lath.

*Two-coat plaster:* Acceptable on lath and on interior face of rough concrete block, clay tile, or porous brick.

*Vermiculite:* Micaceous mineral of silica, magnesium, and alumina oxides made up in a series of parallel plates or laminae and expanded by heat for use as a lightweight plaster aggregate.

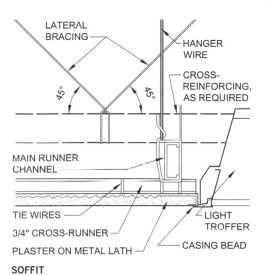

METAL LATH

PLASTER COATS EACH SIDE

SCRATCH-BROWN FINISH

## METAL STUD PARTITION WITH PLASTER AND LATH

LATERAL BRACING

HANGER WIRE

45°    45°

CROSS-REINFORCING, AS REQUIRED

MAIN RUNNER CHANNEL

TIE WIRES

3/4" CROSS-RUNNER

PLASTER ON METAL LATH

LIGHT TROFFER

CASING BEAD

### SOFFIT

HANGER WIRE

MAIN RUNNER

CROSS-RUNNER

PLASTER ON METAL LATH

PLASTER WALL

EXTERIOR MASONRY WALL

STIFFENER AND FURRING BRACKET

FURRING CHANNEL

INSULATION

### CEILING AT FURRED EXTERIOR MASONRY WALL

When interior walls are furred from an exterior masonry wall and insulated, the ceiling should stop short of the furred space. This allows wall insulation to continue above the ceiling line to ceiling or roof insulation, thus forming a complete insulation envelope. In a suspension system that abuts masonry walls, provide 1-in. (25-mm) clearance between ends of main runners or furring channels and wall face.

### SUSPENDED PLASTER CEILING DETAILS

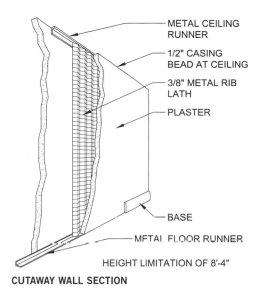

METAL CEILING RUNNER

1/2" CASING BEAD AT CEILING

3/8" METAL RIB LATH

PLASTER

BASE

METAL FLOOR RUNNER

HEIGHT LIMITATION OF 8'-4"

**CUTAWAY WALL SECTION**

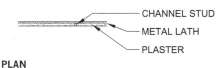

PLASTER

3/8" METAL RIB LATH

**PLAN**

### SOLID METAL LATH

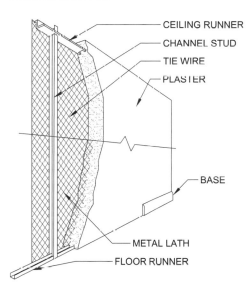

CEILING RUNNER

CHANNEL STUD

TIE WIRE

PLASTER

BASE

METAL LATH

FLOOR RUNNER

**CUTAWAY WALL SECTION**

CHANNEL STUD

METAL LATH

PLASTER

**PLAN**

### METAL LATH WITH CHANNEL STUD— ONE-HOUR FIRE-RATED

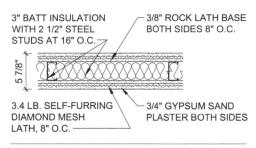

3" BATT INSULATION WITH 2 1/2" STEEL STUDS AT 16" O.C.

3/8" ROCK LATH BASE BOTH SIDES 8" O.C.

5 7/8"

3.4 LB. SELF-FURRING DIAMOND MESH LATH, 8" O.C.

3/4" GYPSUM SAND PLASTER BOTH SIDES

### GYPSUM AND PLASTER LATH—TWO-HOUR FIRE-RATED PARTITION

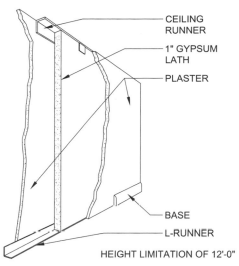

CEILING RUNNER

1" GYPSUM LATH

PLASTER

BASE

L-RUNNER

HEIGHT LIMITATION OF 12'-0"

**CUTAWAY WALL SECTION**

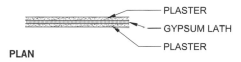

PLASTER

GYPSUM LATH

PLASTER

**PLAN**

### SOLID GYPSUM LATH

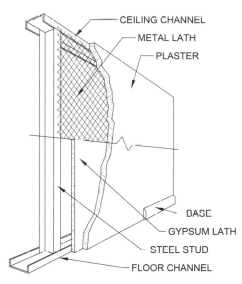

CEILING CHANNEL

METAL LATH

PLASTER

BASE

GYPSUM LATH

STEEL STUD

FLOOR CHANNEL

**CUTAWAY WALL SECTION**

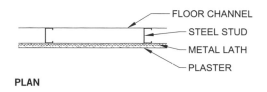

FLOOR CHANNEL

STEEL STUD

METAL LATH

PLASTER

**PLAN**

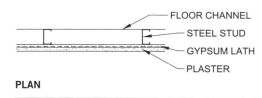

FLOOR CHANNEL

STEEL STUD

GYPSUM LATH

PLASTER

**PLAN**

### METAL STUD

# GLASS-REINFORCED GYPSUM (GRG)

## CHARACTERISTICS

One of the most important advances in modern plaster technique was the development of glass-reinforced gypsum (GRG), also referred to as *fiberglass-reinforced gypsum* (FRG) or *glass-fiber-reinforced gypsum* (GFRG). GRG is a remarkably lightweight, nontoxic, noncombustible composite of gypsum slurry and glass fiber. It is cast in molds at a manufacturing plant and shipped to the project site.

Since its conception in 1977, GRG has continued to grow in popularity in applications such as column covers, decorative domes, coffered ceilings, and other architectural elements previously available only in plaster. GRG manufacturing techniques can produce thin, high-strength shapes that are inherently flame-resistant.

GRG is suitably lightweight for ceilings or other applications in which weight is a concern. Standard gypsum wallboard finishing techniques are required for the installation of GRG. GRG products can be field-cut for plumbing, electrical, mechanical, or other penetrations with the use of conventional gypsum board tools.

## FABRICATION PROCESS

GRG products are cast in polyurethane or latex molds either by hand-laying or spraying. Hand-laying involves layering continuous glass-fiber mats and gypsum slurry in a mold. The spraying process utilizes a nozzle that mixes chopped glass-fiber strands into the gypsum slurry as it is sprayed into a mold. Molds are typically customized for particular projects; however, many proprietary GRG products are available.

The finish face of GRG is smooth and resembles a plaster surface. The back-side appearance is bumpy and irregular, resembling the inside of a fiberglass boat hull, with glass fibers and structural members often visible. When complete, each GRG product is carefully crated and stored to prevent warping or bowing.

Shorter stacking components are used where a smaller mold is needed for producing a series of identical elements. For example, tall columns are often broken into more manageable segments, or "lifts," to reduce installation costs. When pricing columns over 9 ft (3 m) in height, fabricators may propose shorter components. Producing and shipping shorter components may be less expensive, but the installation costs will likely be higher. Fabricators may be required to identify how many lifts will be used when bidding a project.

## FINISHING GRG

Because most GRG installations are designed to simulate monolithic plaster systems, a smooth, level finish is of particular concern. In order to ensure the required level of finish, designers should familiarize themselves with the fabrication process and recognize some of the difficulties the fabricator faces. Important questions to ask to determine the cost of fabricating GRG include:

- How can the detail be developed to simplify the installation process?
- Will the fabrication method contribute to simplifying installation?
- Which fastening details does the fabricator offer as standard?
- Which method will offer the required level of finish in the least time?

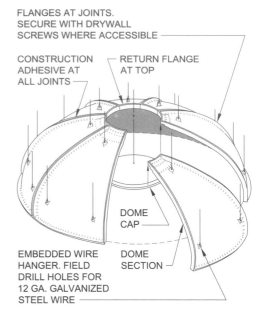

FLANGES AT JOINTS. SECURE WITH DRYWALL SCREWS WHERE ACCESSIBLE

CONSTRUCTION ADHESIVE AT ALL JOINTS — RETURN FLANGE AT TOP

DOME CAP

EMBEDDED WIRE HANGER. FIELD DRILL HOLES FOR 12 GA. GALVANIZED STEEL WIRE — DOME SECTION

Due to its light weight, GRG is popular for use in the fabrication of domed, coffered, and vaulted ceilings. GRG ceilings are suspended from integral fastening points inserted during the casting process. Larger ceiling areas may exploit the casting process by utilizing repeated forms from a limited number of molds.

**DOMED CEILING INSTALLATION**
*Source: Casting Designs, Inc.; Fort Worth, Texas*

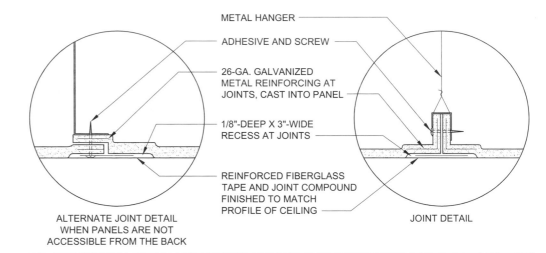

METAL HANGER

ADHESIVE AND SCREW

26-GA. GALVANIZED METAL REINFORCING AT JOINTS, CAST INTO PANEL

1/8"-DEEP X 3"-WIDE RECESS AT JOINTS

REINFORCED FIBERGLASS TAPE AND JOINT COMPOUND FINISHED TO MATCH PROFILE OF CEILING

ALTERNATE JOINT DETAIL WHEN PANELS ARE NOT ACCESSIBLE FROM THE BACK

JOINT DETAIL

**JOINT FINISHING**

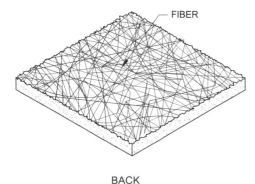

FIBER

BACK

**BACK SIDE OF SPRAYED GRG**

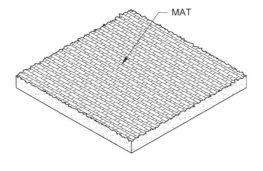

MAT

BACK

**BACK SIDE OF HAND-LAID GLASS-FIBER MAT GRG**

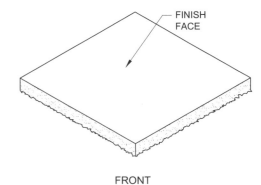

FINISH FACE

FRONT

**FINISH FACE**

**GLASS-REINFORCED GYPSUM FABRICATION**

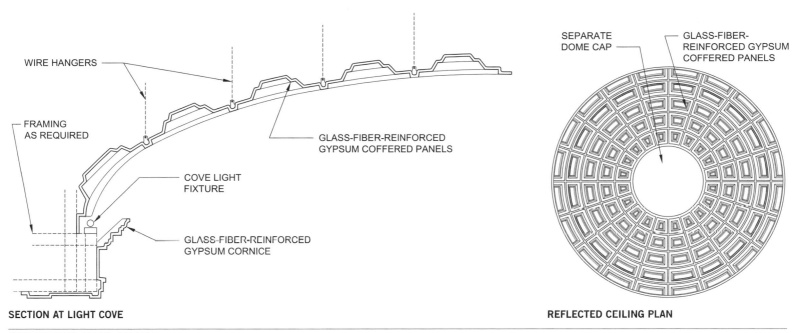

**SECTION AT LIGHT COVE**

WIRE HANGERS

FRAMING AS REQUIRED

COVE LIGHT FIXTURE

GLASS-FIBER-REINFORCED GYPSUM COFFERED PANELS

GLASS-FIBER-REINFORCED GYPSUM CORNICE

**REFLECTED CEILING PLAN**

SEPARATE DOME CAP

GLASS-FIBER-REINFORCED GYPSUM COFFERED PANELS

**COFFERED CEILING DETAILS**

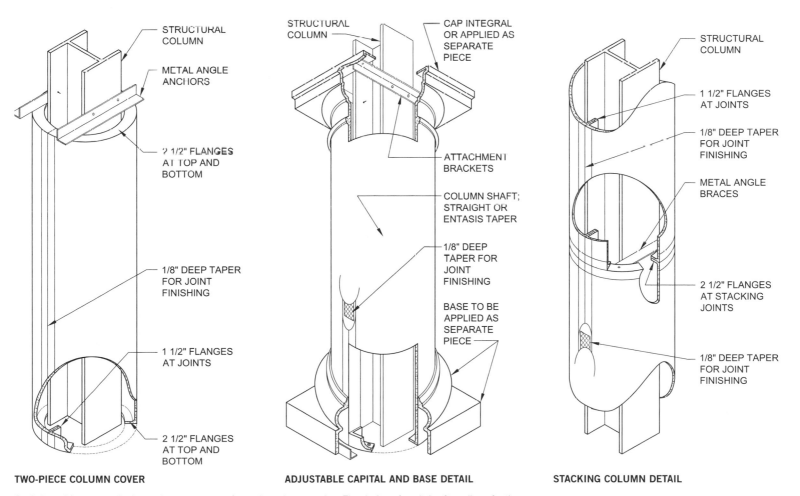

**TWO-PIECE COLUMN COVER**

STRUCTURAL COLUMN

METAL ANGLE ANCHORS

2 1/2" FLANGES AT TOP AND BOTTOM

1/8" DEEP TAPER FOR JOINT FINISHING

1 1/2" FLANGES AT JOINTS

2 1/2" FLANGES AT TOP AND BOTTOM

**ADJUSTABLE CAPITAL AND BASE DETAIL**

STRUCTURAL COLUMN

CAP INTEGRAL OR APPLIED AS SEPARATE PIECE

ATTACHMENT BRACKETS

COLUMN SHAFT; STRAIGHT OR ENTASIS TAPER

1/8" DEEP TAPER FOR JOINT FINISHING

BASE TO BE APPLIED AS SEPARATE PIECE

**STACKING COLUMN DETAIL**

STRUCTURAL COLUMN

1 1/2" FLANGES AT JOINTS

1/8" DEEP TAPER FOR JOINT FINISHING

METAL ANGLE BRACES

2 1/2" FLANGES AT STACKING JOINTS

1/8" DEEP TAPER FOR JOINT FINISHING

Capitals and bases may be integral to, or separate from, the column casting. The design of capitals often allows for the height to be adjusted, depending on the final ceiling level.

**GRG COLUMN COVERS**
*Source: Casting Designs, Inc.; Fort Worth, Texas*

*Yon-Hwa Jang; Rhode Island School of Design; Providence, Rhode Island*

# GYPSUM BOARD ASSEMBLIES

## ASSEMBLIES

Gypsum board assemblies are composed of gypsum board panels and the metal support systems to which they are attached. These systems include structural and nonstructural interior partitions, tile backer partitions, and shaft walls.

## GYPSUM BOARD PANELS

Gypsum board panels consist of a noncombustible gypsum core, faced with a paper surface. The panels are installed over steel or wood framing, including wall and ceiling assemblies. Certain gypsum board assemblies provide fire resistance of varying degrees and sound transmission reduction. The gypsum board may be finished with paint or other applied finish materials such as wallcovering or tile.

Gypsum board is installed by screwing (and sometimes nailing) it to studs or furring channels. The edges of the gypsum board are tapered to accept a paper-reinforcing tape or a self-adhering fiberglass tape and joint compound.

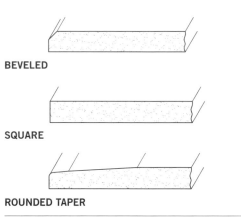

**BEVELED**

**SQUARE**

**ROUNDED TAPER**

**GYPSUM BOARD EDGE TYPES**

## GYPSUM BOARD TYPES

Gypsum board standard panel size is 4 × 8 ft (1,220 × 2,440 mm). Metric panel size is 1,200 × 3,600 mm. Gypsum board is available for a wide variety of specialty applications, including the following:

- *Type X* is manufactured to achieve fire-resistance ratings.
- *Moisture-resistant* (sometimes called *green board* because of its pale lime green color) has a water-repellant paper face and a moisture-resistant core. Moisture-resistant gypsum board is used as a backing for ceramic tile and in wet areas. It is available with a Type X core.
- *Foil-backed* has a layer of aluminum foil laminated to its backside. The foil surface provides an effective vapor retarder.
- *Gypsum board plaster base* is used as a substrate for veneer plaster and is erected in the same manner as regular gypsum board. It is often referred to as *blue board,* because of the color of its absorptive paper face, designed for a strong bond with plaster materials.
- *Prefinished* is covered with decorative vinyl- or textile-surfaced faces. It is often used in prefabricated demountable partition systems.

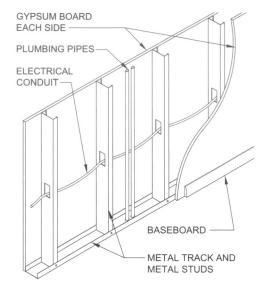

**METAL STUD PARTITION**

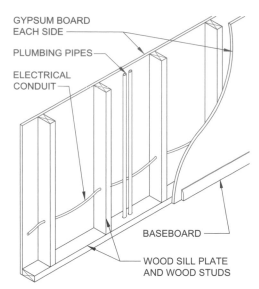

**WOOD STUD PARTITION**

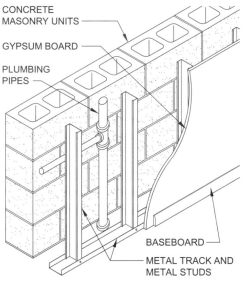

**CMU WALL WITH PLUMBING CHASE AND METAL STUD PARTITION**

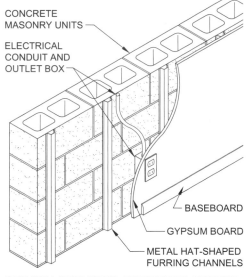

**CMU WALL WITH METAL HAT CHANNEL FURRING**

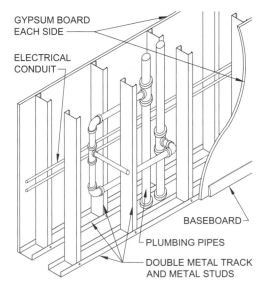

**DOUBLE-STUD PLUMBING CHASE**

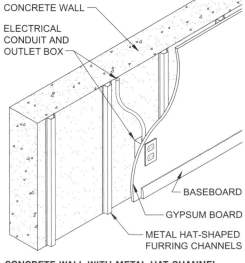

**CONCRETE WALL WITH METAL HAT CHANNEL FURRING**

**GYPSUM BOARD ASSEMBLIES**

## METAL FRAMING

Light-gage steel framing used in interior partitions is cold-formed, meaning that it is fed at room temperature from continuous coils through machines that fold it into stiff shapes. (Much heavier hot-rolled steel shapes are used in structural steel framing.)

### Thicknesses

There are three common steel stud thicknesses for nonstructural partitions: 25-, 22-, and 20-gage. These steel studs are nonload-bearing, and cannot support floor loads, but are able to support selected transverse loads, such as wall-mounted shelving, with proper blocking and support. ASTM C645, *Specification for Nonstructural Steel Framing Members,* and ASTM C754, *Specification for Installation of Steel Framing Members to Receive Screw Attached Gypsum Panel Products,* are helpful in specifying the proper steel stud gage for a given application.

Steel studs are commonly 0.0188-in. (0.48-mm) thick (25-gage) for typical interior partitions. To support cementitious backer units, 0.0346 in. (0.88-mm-) thick (20-gage) steel studs are recommended; 0.0451 in. (1.115 mm) (18-gage) steel studs are typically used for structural interior partitions.

### Steel Stud Spacing and Height

Steel stud spacing and stud height for single- and double-layer gypsum board partitions are identified in ASTM C754, *Standard Specification for Installation of Steel Framing Members to Receive Screw-Attached Gypsum Panel Products,* according to maximum deflection and minimum lateral loading requirements. The *Gypsum Construction Handbook,* published by United States Gypsum, recommends that the deflection limit for gypsum board assemblies be L/240. The maximum allowable deflection is L/120, since greater deflection could cause damage to the gypsum board. Applications of tile or other rigid finish materials to gypsum board partitions may require a deflection limit of L/360 or less. Consult with the applied finish product manufacturer for recommended partition deflection limits.

Steel framing is typically installed at 24 in. (610 mm) on center for partitions. Spacing of 16 in. (406 mm) on center improves the flatness and impact resistance of the partition.

Gypsum board ceilings and soffits are suspended from furring channels. Special profile steel studs are used for interior shaft-wall construction.

## GYPSUM BOARD ACCESSORIES

A variety of metal and plastic framing and furring accessories are available, including:

- *Metal angles* are made of 24-gage galvanized steel and are used to secure 1-in. (25-mm) coreboard or liner panels at floor and ceiling in laminated gypsum board partitions.
- *Cold-rolled channels* are made of 16-gage steel and used in furred walls and suspended ceilings.
- *Z-furring channels* are made of 24-gage steel and are used to mechanically fasten insulation blankets, rigid insulation, and gypsum board panels to concrete or masonry walls.

## TYPES OF GYPSUM PANEL PRODUCTS

| DESCRIPTION | THICKNESS IN. (MM) | WIDTH/EDGE FT (M) | STOCK LENGTH FT (M) |
|---|---|---|---|
| Regular gypsum board used as a base layer for improving sound control; repair and remodeling with double-layer application. | ¼ (6) | 4 (1.2), square or tapered | 8–10 (2.4–3) |
| Regular gypsum board used in a double wall system over wood framing repair and remodeling. | ⅜ (9) | 4 (1.2), square or tapered | 8–14 (2.4–4.3) |
| Regular gypsum board for use in single-layer construction. | ½, ⅝ (13, 16) | 4 (1.2), square or tapered | 8–16 (2.4–4.9) |
| Rounded taper edge system offers maximum joint strength and minimizes joint deformity problems. | ⅜ (9.5) ½, ⅝ (13, 16) | 4 (1.2), rounded taper | 8–16 (2.4–4.9) |
| Type X gypsum board with core containing special additives to increase fire-resistance ratings. Consult manufacturer for approved assemblies. | ½, ⅝ (13, 16) | 4 (1.2), tapered, rounded taper, or rounded | 8–16 (2.4–4.9) |
| Aluminum foil-backed board effective as a vapor barrier for exterior walls and ceilings and as a thermal insulator when foil faces ¾ in. (19.1 mm) minimum air space. Not for use as a tile base or in air conditioned buildings in hot, humid climates (Southern Atlantic and Gulf Coasts). | ⅜ (9.5 ) ½, ⅝ (13, 16) | 4 (1.2), square or tapered | 8–16 (2.4–4.9) |
| Water-resistant board for use as a base for ceramic tile and other nonabsorbent wall tiles in bath and shower areas. Type X core is available. | ½, ⅝ (13, 16) | 4 (1.2), tapered | 8, 10, 12 (2.4, 3, 3.7) |
| Prefinished vinyl surface gypsum board in standard and special colors. Type X core is available. | ½, ⅝ (13, 16) | 2, 2½, 4 (.6, .76, 1.2), square and beveled | 8, 9, 10 (2.4, 2.7, 3) |
| Prefinished board available in many colors and textures. See manufacturer's literature. | ⁵⁄₁₆ (8) | 4 (1.2), square | 8 (2.4) |
| Coreboard for use to enclose vent shafts and laminated gypsum partitions. | 1 (25) | 2 (.6), tongue and groove or square | 8–12 (2.4–3.7) |
| Shaft-wall liner core board Type X with gypsum core used to enclose elevator shafts and other vertical chases. | 1, 2 (25, 50) | 2 (.6), square or beveled | 6–16 (1.8–4.9) |
| Sound underlayment gypsum board attached to plywood subfloor acts as a base for any durable floor covering. When used with resiliently attached gypsum panel ceiling, the assembly meets HUD requirements for sound control in multifamily dwellings. | ¾ (19) | 4 (1.2), square | 6–8 (1.8–2.4) |

A large range of adhesives, sealants, joint treatments, and texture products are available from the manufacturers of most gypsum board products.

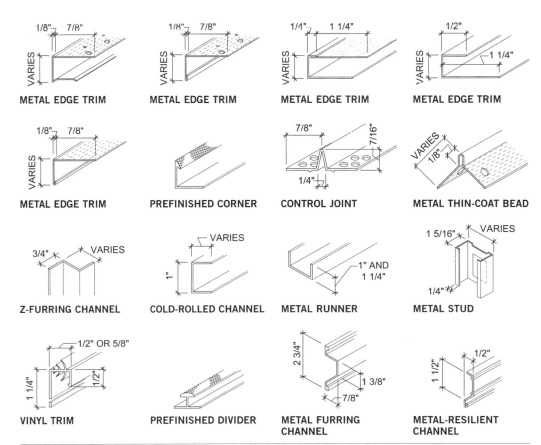

GYPSUM BOARD ACCESSORIES

## TYPICAL NONFIRE-RATED PARTITIONS AND CHASES

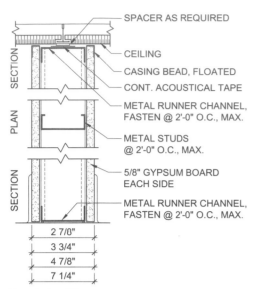

- SPACER AS REQUIRED
- CEILING
- CASING BEAD, FLOATED
- CONT. ACOUSTICAL TAPE
- METAL RUNNER CHANNEL, FASTEN @ 2'-0" O.C., MAX.
- METAL STUDS @ 2'-0" O.C., MAX.
- 5/8" GYPSUM BOARD EACH SIDE
- METAL RUNNER CHANNEL, FASTEN @ 2'-0" O.C., MAX.

2 7/0"
3 3/4"
4 7/8"
7 1/4"

Nonrated partition.

Ceiling is installed prior to installation of partition.

2½-in. (63-mm) metal stud is adequate for most commercial ceiling height partitions.

3¾-in. (95-mm) partition type may not accommodate back-to-back devices, such as junction boxes.

Sounds such as normal conversation, telephones, and some equipment may be audible.

STC range 35 to 39.

### CEILING HEIGHT PARTITION

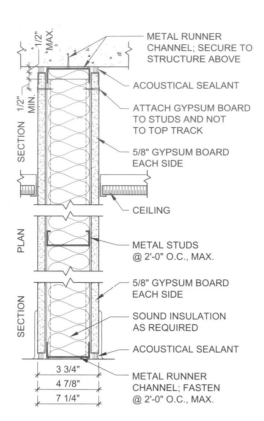

- 1/2" MAX.
- 1/2" MIN.
- METAL RUNNER CHANNEL; SECURE TO STRUCTURE ABOVE
- ACOUSTICAL SEALANT
- ATTACH GYPSUM BOARD TO STUDS AND NOT TO TOP TRACK
- 5/8" GYPSUM BOARD EACH SIDE
- CEILING
- METAL STUDS @ 2'-0" O.C., MAX.
- 5/8" GYPSUM BOARD EACH SIDE
- SOUND INSULATION AS REQUIRED
- ACOUSTICAL SEALANT
- METAL RUNNER CHANNEL; FASTEN @ 2'-0" O.C., MAX.

3 3/4"
4 7/8"
7 1/4"

Nonrated partition. Used where flexibility in the partition is desired to minimize cracking of the gypsum board.

### SLIP JOINT AT STRUCTURE ABOVE

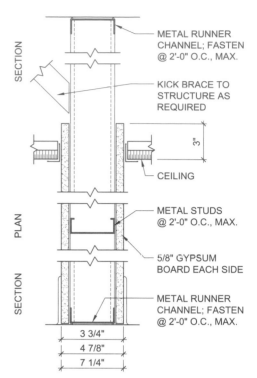

- METAL RUNNER CHANNEL; FASTEN @ 2'-0" O.C., MAX.
- KICK BRACE TO STRUCTURE AS REQUIRED
- 3"
- CEILING
- METAL STUDS @ 2'-0" O.C., MAX.
- 5/8" GYPSUM BOARD EACH SIDE
- METAL RUNNER CHANNEL; FASTEN @ 2'-0" O.C., MAX.

3 3/4"
4 7/8"
7 1/4"

Nonrated partition.

Ceilings installed within partitioned space.

Full-height metal studs provide a stable partition. Consult manufacturer's literature for information on allowable heights and transverse loading; for example, shelving.

STC 35.

### FULL-HEIGHT STUD PARTITION

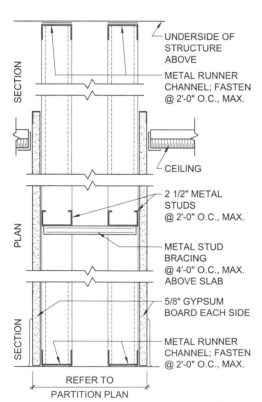

- UNDERSIDE OF STRUCTURE ABOVE
- METAL RUNNER CHANNEL; FASTEN @ 2'-0" O.C., MAX.
- CEILING
- 2 1/2" METAL STUDS @ 2'-0" O.C., MAX.
- METAL STUD BRACING @ 4'-0" O.C., MAX. ABOVE SLAB
- 5/8" GYPSUM BOARD EACH SIDE
- METAL RUNNER CHANNEL; FASTEN @ 2'-0" O.C., MAX.

REFER TO PARTITION PLAN

Can be used where additional nonfire-rated partition depth is desired.

Lateral bracing must be provided. Above-ceiling space may be used as a plenum.

### FULL-HEIGHT DOUBLE-STUD PARTITION

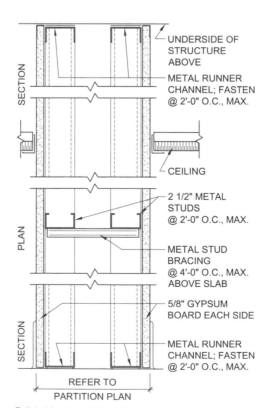

- UNDERSIDE OF STRUCTURE ABOVE
- METAL RUNNER CHANNEL; FASTEN @ 2'-0" O.C., MAX.
- CEILING
- 2 1/2" METAL STUDS @ 2'-0" O.C., MAX.
- METAL STUD BRACING @ 4'-0" O.C., MAX. ABOVE SLAB
- 5/8" GYPSUM BOARD EACH SIDE
- METAL RUNNER CHANNEL; FASTEN @ 2'-0" O.C., MAX.

REFER TO PARTITION PLAN

Full-height gypsum board provides moderate above-ceiling security and improved sound attenuation properties.

More stable than ceiling-height double-stud partitions.

### FULL-HEIGHT DOUBLE-STUD PARTITION, FULL-HEIGHT GYPSUM BOARD

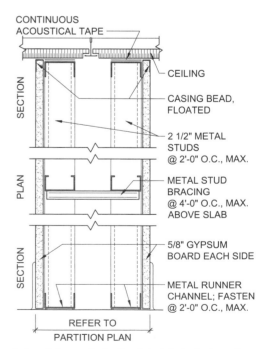

- CONTINUOUS ACOUSTICAL TAPE
- CEILING
- CASING BEAD, FLOATED
- 2 1/2" METAL STUDS @ 2'-0" O.C., MAX.
- METAL STUD BRACING @ 4'-0" O.C., MAX. ABOVE SLAB
- 5/8" GYPSUM BOARD EACH SIDE
- METAL RUNNER CHANNEL; FASTEN @ 2'-0" O.C., MAX.

REFER TO PARTITION PLAN

Suspended acoustical ceiling is installed prior to partition. Fasten head of partition to ceiling suspension system for stability.

Provides lateral bracing.

### CEILING-HEIGHT DOUBLE-STUD PARTITION

# FIRE-RESISTANCE-RATED ASSEMBLIES

A *fire-resistance rating* denotes the length of time a construction assembly can withstand fire and still serve as a barrier to fire and confine its spread to the area of origin. Fire spreads from one area to another when the barrier collapses, there are openings in the barrier, or sufficient heat is conducted through the barrier to exceed specified temperature limitations. Fire-resistive rating tests are conducted under controlled laboratory conditions by the procedures described in ASTM E119, *Standard Fire Tests of Building Construction Materials*. This test applies to floor- and roof-ceiling assemblies, beams, and columns, as well as partitions. The ratings are expressed in hours.

Fire-rated partitions with hourly ratings are identified in building codes for specific uses. The Underwriter's Laboratory (UL) *Fire Resistance Directory* and other publications are referenced for fire-resistance ratings. Fire-resistance-rated partition types are as follows:

- *Nonrated:* Includes ceiling-height (constructed from floor to ceiling) and full-height partitions (from floor to underside of structure above), not requiring fire-resistance rating. Full-height partitions may have gypsum board facing up to or extending above the ceiling, or fully enclosing the full-height studs.
- *One-Hour:* Separates different uses or occupancies, such as partitions between tenant spaces and public corridors in office buildings, or as indicated by building codes. One-hour partitions are used for smoke separation within a building.
- *Two-Hour:* Encloses vertical openings within a building, including elevator and mechanical shafts, exit stairwells, and mechanical and electrical rooms. Two-hour partitions are used for fire separation and smoke or fire separation within a building.
- *Three-Hour:* Separates and encloses higher-hazard areas.
- *Four-Hour:* Encloses very high-hazard spaces.

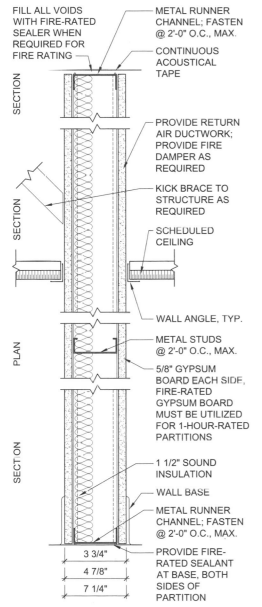

Typically used to separate different occupancy types. Consult authorities having jurisdiction for use and restrictions.

Seal all joints, penetrations, and openings with fire-rated sealant when used as a rated partition.

Provide fire dampers where ducts penetrate partitions.

3¾-in. (95-mm) partition type may not accommodate back-to-back devices, such as junction boxes.

Sound attenuation insulation provides improved acoustical properties. STC 45.

## FULL-HEIGHT PARTITION—ONE-HOUR FIRE-RATED

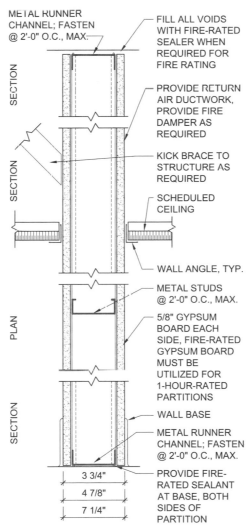

Typically used to separate different occupancy types. Consult authorities having jurisdiction for use and restrictions.

Seal all joints, penetrations, and openings with fire-rated sealant when used as a rated partition.

Provide fire dampers where ducts penetrate partitions.

Can be used as a nonrated partition when moderate security and slightly improved acoustical properties are desired.

This partition type may not accommodate back-to-back devices, such as junction boxes.

STC range 35 to 39.

## FULL-HEIGHT PARTITION—ONE-HOUR FIRE-RATED

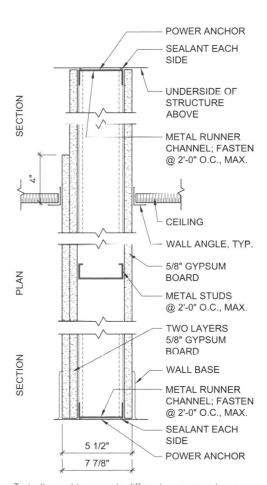

Typically used to separate different occupancy types. Consult authorities having jurisdiction for use and restrictions.

Seal all joints, penetrations, and openings with fire-rated sealant when used as a rated partition.

Provide fire dampers where ducts penetrate partitions.

Two layers of gypsum board on one side provide additional sound attenuation.

## FULL-HEIGHT PARTITION—ONE-HOUR FIRE-RATED

**PLASTER AND GYPSUM BOARD** □ **2**

## ACOUSTICAL PARTITIONS

The reduction of airborne sound transmission, such as normal conversation and other office noise, is identified by Sound Transmission Class (STC) ratings. The STC does not identify reductions of impact or vibration noise, which are classified in the impact insulation class (IIC). Impact and vibration noises may require isolation and sound dampening through means other than the partition.

Partition STC ratings are dependent on the partition mass, resiliency (or isolation), dampening, and sound absorption. Multilayer partitions have more mass than single-layer partitions. Wood studs are less resilient than steel studs and transmit more sound. Isolating wood studs by staggering their placement or using resilient channels improves the resistance to sound transmission. Sound attenuation insulation provides sound dampening and absorption.

Acoustical partitions require sealant at the perimeter edges of the partition assembly, as well as at openings in the gypsum board panel, such as junction boxes and other wall penetrations.

Published sound-rating assembly performance is developed under controlled laboratory conditions. Actual performance may vary from the published STC rating.

### RECOMMENDED STC VALUES

| RECEIVING ROOM | SOURCE ROOM | STC |
|---|---|---|
| Offices Requiring Privacy (e.g., doctor, executive) | Lobby or corridor | 50 |
| | General office | 45 |
| | Adjacent office | 50 |
| | Toilet room | 55 |
| Office Areas | Lobby or corridor | 45 |
| | Kitchen or dining room | 45 |
| Conference and Training Rooms | Other conference room | 50 |
| | Adjacent office | 50 |
| | General office | 50 |
| | Lobby or corridor | 50 |
| | Toilet room | 55 |
| Hotel Bedrooms | Adjacent bedroom, living room, or bathroom | 55 |
| | Lobby or corridor | 55 |
| Classrooms (K–12) | Adjacent classroom | 45 |
| | Laboratory | 50 |
| | Lobby or corridor | 50 |
| | Kitchen or dining room | 50 |
| | Vocational shop | 55 |
| | Music room | 55+ |
| | Toilet room | 50 |
| All Areas | Mechanical room | 60 |

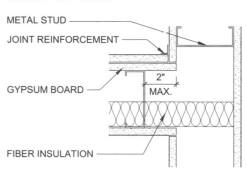

**INTERRUPTED CEILING**

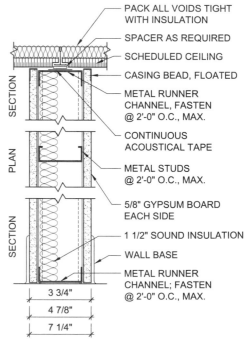

**PARTITION INTERSECTION**

### SOUND-ISOLATED ASSEMBLIES

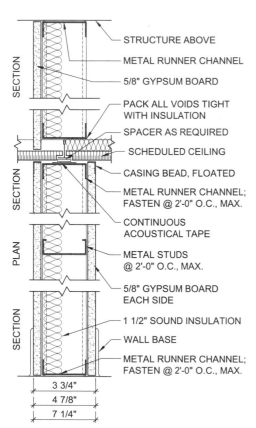

Ceiling is installed prior to installation of partition.

Used when improved acoustical qualities are desired and economy of installation is required.

Not as stable as a full-height partition with studs continuous to the structure above.

STC range 40 to 44.

### MODIFIED FULL-HEIGHT PARTITION

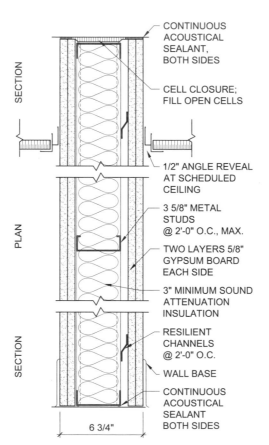

Acoustic sealant required for STC rating.

Nonrated or two-hour-rated with Type X gypsum board. Provides additional security due to double-layer gypsum board.

Resilient channel provides higher performance sound control.

STC range 55 to 60.

### DOUBLE-LAYER GYPSUM BOARD PARTITION

Nonrated partition.

Ceiling is installed prior to installation of partition.

Commonly used in commercial and high-quality residential construction.

Normal conversation is not audible, but loud sounds may be transmitted through the partition.

STC range 40 to 44.

### CEILING-HEIGHT PARTITION WITH SOUND ATTENUATION

## MOISTURE-RESISTANT PARTITIONS

*Water-resistant gypsum backing board,* known as *green board,* consists of a treated core and facings to increase water resistance. The core may soften over time when exposed to moisture. This product is intended for use as a substrate for wall tile or other finish material with a fused, impervious finish, set in adhesive, where wetting of the finish surface is intermittent. This backing board should not be exposed to a direct water flow or excessive moisture, and should not be applied over a vapor retarder. Water-resistant panels tend to sag; do not specify for ceiling installations.

*Glass-mat and cementitious backer units* are also used as backing panels for areas exposed to moisture. Glass-mat panels contain a gypsum core, covered by a coated glass-fiber mat, which protects the core from moisture. The gypsum core may soften over time when exposed to moisture. Cementitious backer units have a portland cement core, and glass-fiber mesh mats are applied to each face of the units. This product may be used in areas where moisture and direct water flow are present.

## VAPOR CONTROL PARTITIONS

Vapor retardation is difficult to control due to the number of penetrations within partitions. Installed more often in colder climates or where air conditioning is used in warmer climates, the vapor retarders are typically installed on the interior side of the exterior wall. Review the installation parameters of a vapor retarder with a mechanical engineer to determine the type and use. Foil-backed gypsum board may be used for vapor control.

## GYPSUM BOARD SHAFT-WALL ASSEMBLIES

Gypsum shaft-wall systems are lighter in weight and easier to install than traditional masonry shaft walls. Shaft walls surround multistory vertical chases for elevator or mechanical enclosures. To prevent a fire from quickly spreading to other floors, shaft walls are required to be fire-resistance-rated. Gypsum shaft-wall systems typically consist of floor and ceiling tracks, special studs, special gypsum panels, and Type X gypsum panels.

Gypsum board shaft-wall assemblies are used for elevator hoistway enclosures, return air shafts, chases, and stair enclosures. They are rapidly installed, fire-resistant, and lightweight. Many shaft-wall assemblies are two-hour fire-rated, as required by authorities having jurisdiction.

Shaft-wall assemblies are installed from the exterior of the shaft and utilize proprietary gypsum board liner panels, installed within special profile steel studs. Gypsum board is applied to the studs on the room side of the shaft wall. In stair enclosures, finish panels are also installed on the shaft side of the wall.

Manufactures of shaft walls can provide test data for their assemblies, including fire-resistive, structural, and acoustical characteristics. Not all assemblies have the same test results, so it is recommended that the manufacturer's data be reviewed and compared for a project's specific requirements. Metal stud profiles are specific to a particular proprietary assembly, and therefore cannot be used in an assembly in which it was not tested. Metal stud types from various manu-

facturers include C-T, I, and C-H profiles, which hold the liner panels in place in the shaft-wall assembly. E-studs are used at corners and termination conditions.

### Shaft-Wall Fire Resistance

Fire-resistance requirements and hourly ratings for shaft-wall assemblies are established by building codes based on the construction type and building use group. Consult authorities having jurisdiction for specific code requirements for these assemblies.

### Sound Transmission Class

STC ratings of shaft-wall assemblies are developed in laboratory conditions. Field conditions may differ from the manufacturer's published STC data. Acoustical sealant should be included in the assembly construction when subject to positive or negative air pressures. Sealant is installed at the perimeter of the assembly and at voids in which noise, dust, or smoke could pass.

### Construction Considerations

Considerations for shaft-wall assemblies include: limiting height and span support capabilities; allowable deflection limits; and intermittent air-pressure loads, which may cause the shaft wall to flex. All openings and devices within the shaft must not compromise the fire-resistance rating. This includes hoistway doors, elevator call buttons, indicator lights, and other items contained within the assembly.

Gypsum board shaft-wall assemblies may crack if subjected to excessive structural movement. Isolate the gypsum finish panels from the structural elements using sealant, installed according to the manufacturer's

assembly requirements. Install control joints in large areas of gypsum board panels. Corner reinforcing at openings may be required to minimize cracks in the finish panels.

## GYPSUM BOARD ASSEMBLY FINISHES

Gypsum board assemblies are finished with gypsum board tape and joint compounds. Joint compounds include a setting-type compound, formulated from a powder and mixed on-site, to drying-type joint compounds, available in ready-mixed or job-mixed formulations. Taping compounds produce a strong bond between the tape and gypsum board, but are harder to sand and finish than topping or all-purpose compounds. Topping compounds are not suitable for first coat or taping compounds. All-purpose joint compounds have good shrink resistance; however, they are softer than other joint compound types. Shrinkage of the joint compound is not desired, as cracking may result.

### Veneer Plaster Finishes

Although conventional plaster is the best system to attain a uniform, monolithic surface with excellent wear resistance, veneer plaster over gypsum board provides a similar performance in days less time. Veneer plaster systems use gypsum board panels (commonly referred to as *blue board*), which improve the speed of installation, while providing better abuse resistance than conventional gypsum board. Plaster thickness is reduced from the standard ½ in. (50 mm) associated with conventional plaster to ⁄₁₆ to ⅛ in. (1 to 3 mm), using high-strength gypsum in the formulation.

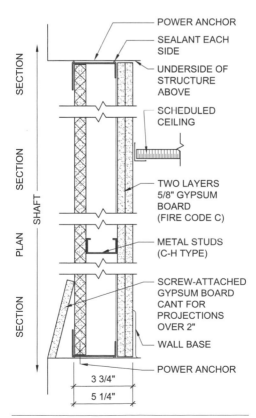

**TYPICAL SHAFT WALL**

Labels on diagram:
- POWER ANCHOR
- SEALANT EACH SIDE
- UNDERSIDE OF STRUCTURE ABOVE
- SCHEDULED CEILING
- TWO LAYERS 5/8" GYPSUM BOARD (FIRE CODE C)
- METAL STUDS (C-H TYPE)
- SCREW-ATTACHED GYPSUM BOARD CANT FOR PROJECTIONS OVER 2"
- WALL BASE
- POWER ANCHOR
- SECTION / SHAFT / PLAN / SECTION
- 3 3/4"
- 5 1/4"

### GYPSUM BOARD FINISH LEVELS

| LEVEL | DESCRIPTION |
|---|---|
| 0 | Taping, finishing, and corner beads are not required. |
| 1 | At joints and angles, embed tape in joint compound. Panel surfaces must be free of excess joint compound, but tool marks and ridges are acceptable. |
| 2 | At joints and angles, embed tape in joint compound and apply one separate coat of joint compound over tape, fastener heads, and flanges of trim accessories. Joint compound applied on the face of the tape when the tape is embedded is considered a separate coat. Panel surfaces must be free of excess joint compound, but tool marks and ridges are acceptable. |
| 3 | At joints and angles, embed tape in joint compound and apply two separate coats of joint compound over joints, angles, fastener heads, and flanges of trim accessories. Panel surfaces and joint compound must be free of tool marks and ridges. |
| 4 | At joints and angles, embed tape in joint compound and apply three separate coats of joint compound over joints, angles, fastener heads, and flanges of trim accessories. Panel surfaces and joint compound must be free of tool marks and ridges. |
| 5* | Finish must be equal to Level 4 (embedding coat and three finish coats) plus a skim coat over the entire gypsum board surface. Surfaces must be smooth and free of tool marks and ridges. |

*Level 5 is a high-quality gypsum board finish that is recommended for feature walls with strong lighting or for walls that will receive high-gloss paint. An alternative to the Level 5 finish is gypsum veneer plaster.*

*Source: MASTERSPEC®; published by ARCOM; Salt Lake City, Utah, and Alexandria, Virginia. Copyright ASTM INTERNATIONAL. Reprinted with permission.*

# GYPSUM BOARD REVEAL DETAILS

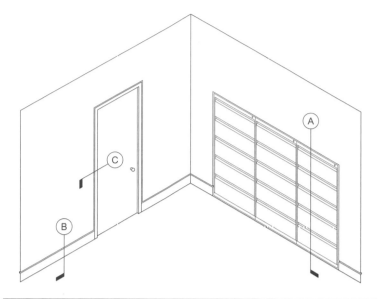

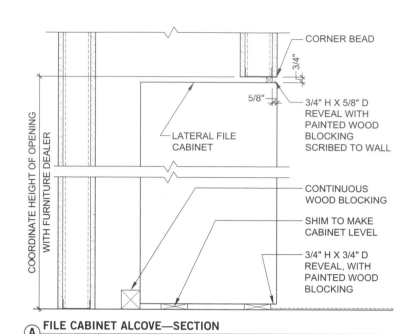

CORNER BEAD

3/4"

5/8"

3/4" H X 5/8" D REVEAL WITH PAINTED WOOD BLOCKING SCRIBED TO WALL

LATERAL FILE CABINET

COORDINATE HEIGHT OF OPENING WITH FURNITURE DEALER

CONTINUOUS WOOD BLOCKING

SHIM TO MAKE CABINET LEVEL

3/4" H X 3/4" D REVEAL, WITH PAINTED WOOD BLOCKING

**(A) FILE CABINET ALCOVE—SECTION**

**BASE, DOOR JAMB, AND FILE CABINET ALCOVE REVEAL DETAILS**

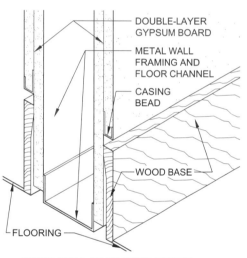

DOUBLE-LAYER GYPSUM BOARD

METAL WALL FRAMING AND FLOOR CHANNEL

CASING BEAD

WOOD BASE

FLOORING

**(B) WOOD WALL BASE WITH REVEAL**

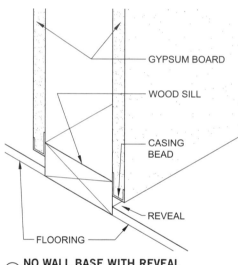

GYPSUM BOARD

WOOD SILL

CASING BEAD

REVEAL

FLOORING

**(B) NO WALL BASE WITH REVEAL**

**REVEAL WALL BASE DETAILS**

WIDTH OF FILE CABINETS PLUS 1 1/2" FOR REVEALS PLUS 1/8" MIN. TOLERANCE PER FILE CABINET

COORDINATE WIDTH OF OPENING WITH FURNITURE DEALER

SECTION THROUGH ALCOVE (A)

**FILE CABINET ALCOVE—ELEVATION**

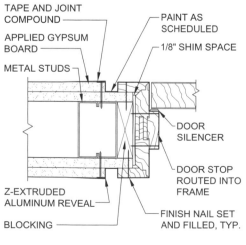

TAPE AND JOINT COMPOUND

APPLIED GYPSUM BOARD

METAL STUDS

PAINT AS SCHEDULED

1/8" SHIM SPACE

DOOR SILENCER

DOOR STOP ROUTED INTO FRAME

Z-EXTRUDED ALUMINUM REVEAL

BLOCKING

FINISH NAIL SET AND FILLED, TYP.

**(C) WOOD FRAME DETAIL**

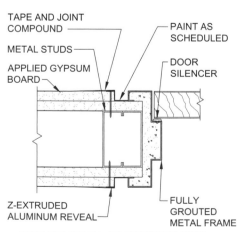

TAPE AND JOINT COMPOUND

METAL STUDS

APPLIED GYPSUM BOARD

PAINT AS SCHEDULED

DOOR SILENCER

Z-EXTRUDED ALUMINUM REVEAL

FULLY GROUTED METAL FRAME

**(C) HOLLOW METAL FRAME WITH TWO LAYERS OF GYPSUM BOARD DETAIL**

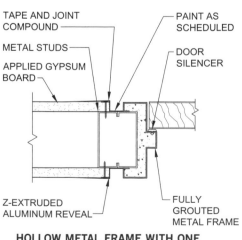

TAPE AND JOINT COMPOUND

METAL STUDS

APPLIED GYPSUM BOARD

PAINT AS SCHEDULED

DOOR SILENCER

Z-EXTRUDED ALUMINUM REVEAL

FULLY GROUTED METAL FRAME

**(C) HOLLOW METAL FRAME WITH ONE LAYER OF GYPSUM BOARD DETAIL**

**REVEAL DOOR JAMB DETAILS**

2  □  **PLASTER AND GYPSUM BOARD**

*Sarah Bader; Gensler; Chicago, Illinois*

# TILE-SETTING ACCESSORIES

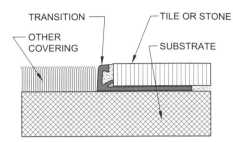

**EDGE PROTECTION**

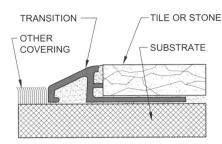

**TRANSITION BETWEEN FLOOR COVERINGS OF DIFFERENT HEIGHTS**

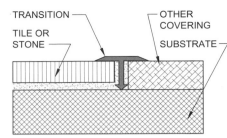

**TRANSITION BETWEEN FLOOR COVERINGS OF SAME HEIGHT**

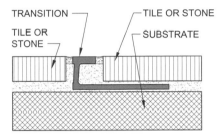

**DECORATIVE JOINT**

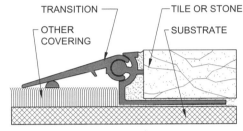

**VARIABLE TRANSITION BETWEEN FLOOR COVERINGS OF DIFFERENT HEIGHTS**

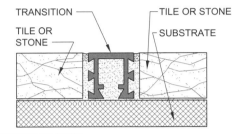

**DECORATIVE JOINT**

## EDGE PROTECTION AND TRANSITION PROFILES FOR FLOORS

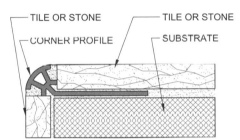

**OUTSIDE CORNER PROTECTION AND DECORATION**

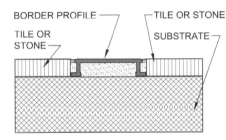

**DECORATIVE PROFILE**

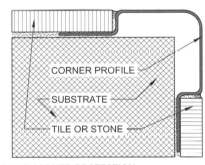

**OUTSIDE CORNER PROTECTION**

## FINISHING AND EDGE PROTECTION FOR WALLS

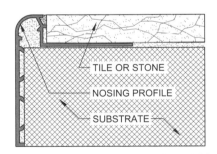

**EDGE PROFILE FOR COUNTERTOPS OR STAIRS**

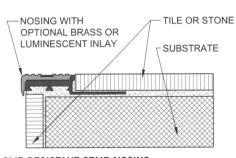

**SLIP-RESISTANT STAIR NOSING**

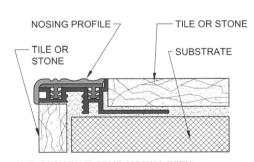

**SLIP-RESISTANT STAIR NOSING WITH REPLACEABLE THERMOPLASTIC TREAD**

## STAIR NOSING PROFILES

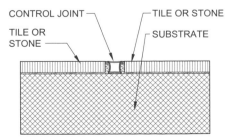

**CONTROL JOINT IN THINSET INSTALLATION**

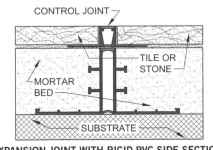

**EXPANSION JOINT WITH RIGID PVC SIDE SECTIONS**

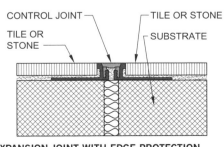

**EXPANSION JOINT WITH EDGE PROTECTION**

## EXPANSION AND CONTROL JOINT PROFILES

# CERAMIC TILE

Ceramic tile is fabricated from clay or a mixture of clay and ceramic materials. Natural clay is most commonly used, but porcelain is also available. Porcelain tile is fine-grained and smooth. It can be formed into sharply detailed designs. Tile dimensions are typically nominal. Refer to manufacturer's data for specific tile and trim piece dimensions.

## TILE COMPOSITION AND GLAZE

Ceramic tile is made from either natural clay or porcelain, and is glazed or unglazed.

- *Porcelain tile* is a ceramic mosaic or paver tile generally made by the dust-pressed method. It is dense, impervious, fine-grained, and smooth with a sharply formed face.
- *Natural clay tile* is a ceramic mosaic or paver tile with a distinctive, slightly textured appearance. It is made by the dust-pressed or plastic method from clays that have a dense body.
- *Glazed tile* has an impervious facial finish of ceramic materials that is fused to the body of the tile. The body may be nonvitreous, semivitreous, vitreous, or impervious.
- *Unglazed tile* is a hard, dense tile of uniform composition that derives color and texture from the materials used in its fabrication.

## TILE TYPES

There are a variety of tile types, including ceramic mosaic, quarry, paver, decorative, mounted, and conductive tile.

### Ceramic Mosaic Tile

Ceramic mosaic tile is formed either by the dust-pressed or the plastic method. Usually ¼- to ⅜-in. (6- to 9.5-mm) thick with a facial area of less than 6 sq in. (39 sq cm), it may be made of either porcelain or natural clay and may be plain or have an abrasive mixture throughout.

### Quarry Tile

Quarry tile is glazed or unglazed tile made by the extrusion process from natural clay or shale. It usually has a facial area of 6 sq in. (39 sq cm) or more. Quarry tile may be specified with an abrasive grit embedded in the surface for use in areas where slip resistance is a concern.

### Paver Tile

Paver tile is glazed or unglazed porcelain or natural clay tile formed by the dust-pressed method with a facial area of 6 sq in. (39 sq cm) or more.

### Decorative Thin-Wall Tile

Decorative thin-wall tile is a glazed tile with a thin body that is usually nonvitreous. It is suitable for interior decorative residential use when breaking strength is not a requirement.

### Mounted Tile

Mounted tile is assembled into units or sheets to facilitate handling and installation. Tile may be face-mounted, back-mounted, or edge-mounted. Material applied to the face of the tile is usually easily removed, but material bonded to the back is integrated to the tile installation.

### Conductive Tile

Conductive tile has specific properties of electrical conductivity but retains other normal physical properties of tile.

### WATER ABSORPTION OF CERAMIC TILE

| TYPE | WATER ABSORPTION | CERAMIC MATERIAL | USE |
|---|---|---|---|
| Nonvitreous | More than 7.0% | Natural clay | Not for use in continually wet locations |
| Semivitreous | More than 3.9%, but not more than 7.0% | Natural clay | Not for use in continually wet locations |
| Vitreous | 0.5%–3.0% | Natural clay | For use in continually wet locations |
| Impervious | 0.5% or less | Porcelain | For use in continually wet locations; superior wear resistance |

*ANSI A 137.1, Specification for Ceramic Tile, quantifies the four levels of water absorption for tile. The density and porosity of the tile determine its capability to absorb moisture. In general, the lower the water absorption level, the better the stain resistance of the tile.*

## WALL TILE TRIM SHAPES

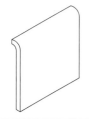

**BULLNOSES FOR THICKSET INSTALLATIONS**

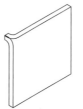

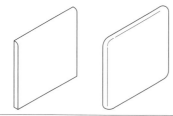

**BULLNOSES FOR THINSET INSTALLATIONS**

**COVE BASE**

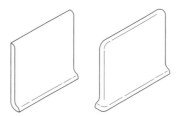

**SANITARY COVE BASES (ROUND TOP)**

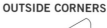

**BEADS**

## CERAMIC MOSAIC TILE TRIM SHAPES

**STRETCHER**

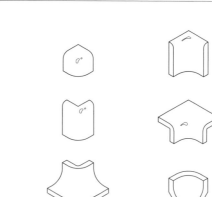

**OUTSIDE CORNERS**

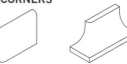

**INSIDE CORNERS**

## TILE INSTALLATION

There are two basic steps in tile installation: setting and grouting. Setting fixes the tile to the substrate with mortar or adhesive. Grouting fills in the spaces between the tiles, binding them into a continuous surface. Tile, mortar, and grout selection are interdependent.

### Thickset Installation

Thickset installations use portland cement. A mortar bed, ¾- to 2-in. (19- to 51-mm) thick, is laid. Accurate floor slopes to drains can be installed, and reinforcement with metal mesh or waterproof membranes is possible. Waterproof membranes are flexible sheets or liquids that cure to a seamless membrane and are used in applications that are regularly or continually exposed to water. Both thickset and thinset installations can incorporate waterproof membranes.

### Thinset Installation

Thinset installations are most popular (accounting for approximately 90% of installations in the United States) and can be as thin as ³⁄₃₂ in. (2 mm). All methods other than conventional portland cement applications are considered thinset. Bonding materials include dryset mortar, latex portland cement mortar, organic adhesive, epoxy mortar or adhesive, and modified epoxy emulsion mortar. Thinset application requires a continuous, stable, and undamaged surface.

Cementitious backerboards are sometimes used as an underlayment for thinset installations. Cementitious backerboards are made of portland cement or treated gypsum and lightweight aggregate, and are designed to provide a water-resistant base for ceramic tile installations regularly exposed to water; for example, a shower surround.

## MORTAR

Mortars are categorized as cementitious and noncementitious. Adhesives are also popular for use in fixing tiles to the substrate.

### Cementitious Mortars

*Portland cement mortar* is a mixture of portland cement and sand (for floors) or lime (for walls) used for thick-bed installation.

*Dryset mortar* is a mixture of portland cement with sand and additives, imparting water retention that eliminates the need to soak tiles.

*Latex portland cement mortar* is a mixture similar to dryset, but with latex (an emulsion of polymer particles in water) added to replace all or part of the water in the mortar. It provides better adhesion, density, and impact strength than dryset mortar and is more flexible and resistant to frost damage.

## SETTING MATERIALS

| TYPE | DESCRIPTION | FEATURES |
|---|---|---|
| **Cementitious** | | |
| Portland Cement Mortar | Portland cement and sand, in proportions of 1:5 for floors; portland cement, sand, and lime, in proportions of 1:5:½ to 1:7:1 for walls | Most surfaces, ordinary installations |
| Dryset Mortar | Portland cement with sand and additives imparting water retentivity, which is used as a bond coat for setting tile | Thinset installations |
| Latex-Portland Cement Mortar | Portland cement, sand, and special latex additive, which is used as a bond coat for setting tile | Latex additives improve adhesion, reduce water absorption, and provide greater bond strength and resistance to shock and impact. Required for large-unit porcelain-bodied tile. |
| **Noncementitious** | | |
| Epoxy Mortar | Epoxy resin and epoxy hardeners | Chemical-resistant |
| Modified Epoxy Emulsion Mortars | Emulsified epoxy resins and hardeners with portland cement and silica sand | High bond strength; little or no shrinkage; not chemical resistant |
| Furan Resin Mortar | Furan resin and furan hardeners | Chemical-resistant |
| Epoxy Adhesives | Epoxy resin and epoxy hardeners | High bond strength and ease of application; not optimal chemical resistance |
| Organic Adhesive | For interior use only; ready to use (no addition of liquid); cures by evaporation | Not suitable for continuously wet applications or temperatures exceeding 140°F |

### Noncementitious Mortars

*Epoxy mortar* is a two-part mixture (resin and hardener with silica filler) used where chemical resistance is important. It has high bond strength and high resistance to impact. This mortar and furan mortar are the only two types that can be recommended for use over steel plates.

*Modified epoxy emulsion mortars* are similar to epoxy mortars. This mixture contains a resin and hardener along with portland cement and sand. Although it is not as chemically resistant as epoxy mortar, it binds well. Compared with mortar created from portland cement exclusively, it allows little or no shrinkage.

*Furan mortars* are two-part mixtures, composed of furan resin and hardener. Excellent for chemical-resistant uses, they tolerate high temperatures up to 350°F (177°C). *Epoxy adhesive* is a mixture similar to epoxy mortar in bonding capability, but it is not as chemical- or solvent-resistant.

### Adhesives

*Organic adhesives* are one-part mastic mixtures that require no mixing. They remain somewhat flexible (as compared with portland cement mortar) and have good bond strength, but should not be used for exterior or wet applications.

### Grout

Grout is used to fill joints between tiles and is selected with a compatible mortar. Grout is either a portland-cement-based mixture or a mixture of other compounds to enhance its performance or ease its installation. The type and size of tile, service level, climatic conditions, tile spacing, and individual manufacturer's recommendations are factors that should be considered when selecting grout.

*Portland-cement-based grout* is a mixture of portland cement and sand (for floors) or lime (for walls) and is used for thickset installations. Portland-cement-based grouts include commercial portland cement grout, sand-portland, cement grout, dryset grout, and latex portland cement grout.

*Nonportland-cement-based grouts* include solid epoxy, furan, silicone, and mastic grouts. Mastic grout eliminates the need for mixing on-site.

- *Epoxy grout* is a two- or three-part mixture (epoxy resin hardener with silica sand filler) that is highly resistant to chemicals and has great bond strength. This grout and furan grout are made for different chemical and solvent resistance.
- *Furan resin grout* is two-part furan mixture (similar to furan mortar) that resists high temperatures and solvents.
- *Silicone rubber grout* is an elastomeric mixture of silicone rubber. It has high bond strength, is resistant to water and staining, and remains flexible under freezing conditions.

## GROUT GUIDE

| | GROUTS CONTAINING PORTLAND CEMENT | | | | | OTHERS | | | |
|---|---|---|---|---|---|---|---|---|---|
| | COMMERCIAL (SANDED) | JOB-SITE MIX (SANDED) | DRYSET (UNSANDED) | COMMERCIAL OR SET WITH LATEX (POLYMER) | MODIFIED EPOXY EMULSION | 100% SOLID EPOXY | FURAN | SILICONE OR URETHANE | MASTIC GROUT |
| W = wall use<br>F = floor use | 4 | | 4 | 4, 9 | 4 | 1, 3, 4, 6 | 1, 3, 4, 6 | 2, 4 | 3, 4 |
| **TILE TYPE** | | | | | | | | | |
| Glazed Wall Tile[7] | W | | W | W | | W | | W | W |
| Glazed Floor Tile[7] | W, F | W, F | W, F | W, F | W, F | W, F | | | W, F |
| Ceramic Mosaics | W, F | W, F | W, F | W, F | W, F | W, F | | W | W, F |
| Quarry, Paver, and Packing House Tiles[8] | W, F | W, F | | W, F | W, F | W, F | W, F | | |
| Large-Unit Porcelain or Vitreous Tile[8] | W, F | W, F | W, F | W, F | W, F | W, F | F | W | W, F |
| Dimension Stone[7, 8] including agglomerates | W, F | W, F | W, F | W, F | W, F | | | | |
| **USE** | | | | | | | | | |
| Dry/Limited Water Exposure | W, F | W, F | W, F | W, F | W, F | W, F | W, F | W, F | W, F |
| Wet Areas[10] | W, F | W, F | W, F | W, F | W, F | W, F | W, F | W, F | |
| Exteriors[8, 9, 10] | W, F | W, F | W, F | W, F | W, F | W, F 4 | W, F 4 | W, F | |
| **PERFORMANCE*** | | | | | | | | | |
| Suggested Joint Widths[5] | ⅛ to ⅝ in. (3 to 15 mm) | ⅛ to ⅝ in. (3 to 15 mm) | ⅛ to ⅝ in. (3 to 15 mm) | ⅛ to ⅝ in. (3 to 15 mm) | ⅛ to ⅝ in. (3 to 15 mm) | ⅛ to ⅝ in. (3 to 15 mm) | ⅜ to ⅝ in. (9 to 15 mm) | 1/16 to ¼ in. (1 to 6 mm) | 1/16 to ¼ in. (1 to 6 mm) |
| Stain Resistance | D | E | D | C | C | A | A | A | B |
| Crack Resistance | D | E | D | C | C | B | C | A | C |
| Color Availability | B | D | B | B | B | B | Black only | B | B |

*There are five performance ratings, from Best (A) to Minimal (E).

[1] Mainly used for chemical-resistant properties.

[2] Special tools needed for proper application. Silicon, urethane, and modified polyvinyl chloride used in pregrouted ceramic tile sheets. Silicone grout should not be used on kitchen countertops or other food preparation surfaces unless it meets the requirements of FDA Regulation No. 21, CFE 177.2600.

[3] Special cleaning procedures and materials are recommended.

[4] Follow manufacturer's directions.

[5] Joint widths are only guidelines. Individual grout manufacturer's products may vary. Consult manufacturer's instructions.

[6] Epoxies are recommended for prolonged temperatures up to 140°F, high-temperature-resistant epoxies and furans up to 350°F.

[7] Some types of glazed ceramic tiles, polished marble, marble agglomerates, and granite can be permanently scratched or damaged when grouted with sanded grout formulas. Do not use sanded grout or add sand to grout when grouting polished marble, marbled agglomerates, and ceramic wall tiles with soft glazes. Check the tile or marble manufacturer's literature and test grout on a separate sample area prior to grouting.

[8] Some types of ceramic tiles and dimensions stone may be permanently stained when grouted with pigmented grout of a contrasting color. WHITE GROUT IS BEST SUITED FOR GROUTING WHITE OR LIGHT-COLORED MARBLE OR GRANITE.

[9] Latex modification may be required in areas subject to freezing temperatures. Consult grout manufacturer for recommended products and methods.

[10] Colored cementitious grouts may darken when wet.

Source: Tile Council of America; Anderson, South Carolina

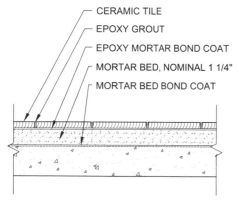

**EPOXY MORTAR AND GROUT**
Epoxy mortar and grout are used where leveling of subfloor is required and where moderate chemical exposure and severe cleaning methods are used, such as in food processing plants.

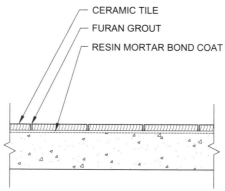

**FURAN RESIN MORTAR AND GROUT**
Furan resin mortar and grout are used in kitchens and chemical plants.

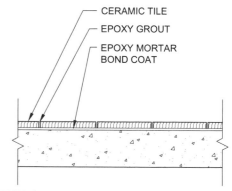

**EPOXY MORTAR AND GROUT**
Epoxy mortar and grout are for use where moderate chemical exposure and severe cleaning methods are used, such as in food processing plants.

## CHEMICAL-RESISTANT TILE INSTALLATIONS

## MOVEMENT JOINTS

Movement in the structure and the substrate must be accommodated by the ceramic tile installation. For quarry tile and paver tile, a movement joint width should be the same as a grout joint, but not less than ¼ in. (6 mm); for ceramic mosaic tile and glazed wall tile, a movement joint should be not less than ¼ in. (6 mm), but never less than ⅛ in. (3 mm). In addition to expansion joints, there are several types of movement joints, as follows:

- *Control joints or contraction joints* are formed, sawed, or tooled grooves in the concrete substrate, used to create a weakened location where the controlled cracking of the concrete can occur.
- *Construction joints* are located where two separate placements of concrete meet and where reinforcement may be continuous.

- *Isolation joints* are installed where adjoining areas of a concrete substrate may move in three directions and where the formation of cracks is to be avoided.
- *Cold joints* are formed when the size of a concrete slab is too large for one pour, and successive pours are required. Cold joints may crack with movement of the slab. Some slabs are saw-cut at regular intervals to provide controlled cracking locations.

### Movement Joint Materials

Backup strips are flexible and compressible types of closed-cell foam polyethylene, butyl rubber, or open-cell and closed-cell polyurethane. These strips should be rounded at the surface that contacts the sealant.

Sealants used are silicone, urethane, or polysulfide. Silicone sealants are used on interior vertical tile surfaces. Mildew-resistant silicone sealants are useful in wet areas. Urethane sealants are used in interior hori-

zontal tile installations. Sealants should comply with ASTM C920, *Standard Specification for Elastomeric Joint Sealants.*

### Movement Joint Locations

All expansion, control, construction, cold, and seismic joints in the structure should continue through the tile work, including such joints in vertical surfaces. Joints through tile work directly over structural joints must never be narrower than the structural joint. Expansion joints should be installed in the following circumstances:

- 24 to 36 ft (7.3 to 11 m) in each direction
- Tile work exposed to direct sunlight or moisture, 12 to 16 ft (3.7 to 4.9 m) in each direction
- Where tile work abuts restraining surfaces such as perimeter walls, dissimilar floors, curbs, columns, pipes, ceilings, and where changes occur in backing materials

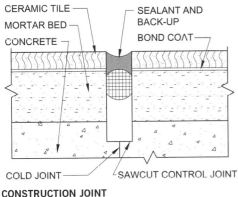
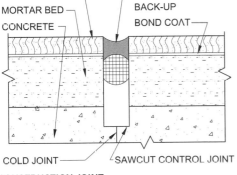

**CONSTRUCTION JOINT**

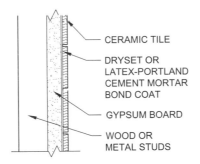

**ISOLATION/EXPANSION JOINT**

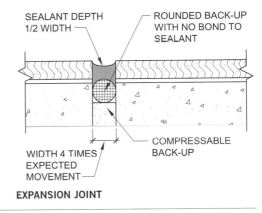

**EXPANSION JOINT**

**MOVEMENT JOINTS**
*Source: Tile Council of America, Inc.; Anderson, South Carolina*

## WALL TILE

Wall tile is a glazed tile with a body suitable for interior use. Usually nonvitreous, it is not required or expected to withstand excessive impact or freezing and thawing conditions.

Many tile manufacturers can accommodate custom designs and colors. Minimum orders typically are required.

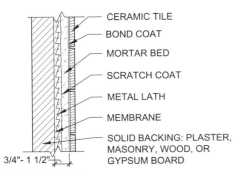

**CEMENT MORTAR**
Use cement mortar over masonry, plaster, or other solid backing, to provide firm anchorage for metal lath. This is the preferred method for showers and tub enclosures, and is used in remodeling.

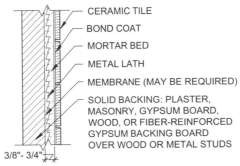

**LATEX PORTLAND CEMENT MORTAR**
Latex portland cement mortar is used in dry areas in schools, institutions, and commercial buildings. Do not use in areas where temperatures exceed 125°F (52°C).

**ONE-COAT METHOD**
The one-coat method is used for remodeling or on surfaces that present bonding problems. It is the preferred method of applying tile over gypsum plaster or gypsum board in showers and tub enclosures.

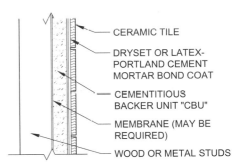

**DRYSET MORTAR (CEMENTITIOUS BACKER)**
Use dryset mortar in wet areas over well-braced wood or metal studs. Stud spacing should not to exceed 16 in. (405 mm) o.c., and metal studs must be 20-gage or heavier.

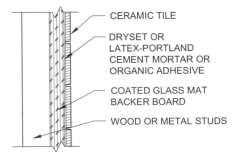

**COATED GLASS-MAT BACKERBOARD**
Coated glass-mat backerboard is used in wet areas over dry, well-braced wood or metal studs. Stud spacing should not exceed 16 in. (405 mm) o.c., and metal studs must be 20-gage or heavier.

**WALL DETAILS**
*Source: Tile Council of America, Inc.; Anderson, South Carolina*

# CERAMIC TILE DETAILS

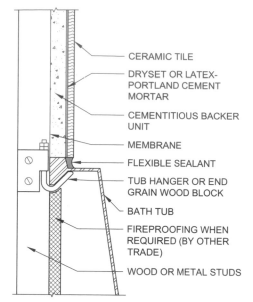

- CERAMIC TILE
- DRYSET OR LATEX-PORTLAND CEMENT MORTAR
- CEMENTITIOUS BACKER UNIT
- MEMBRANE
- FLEXIBLE SEALANT
- TUB HANGER OR END GRAIN WOOD BLOCK
- BATH TUB
- FIREPROOFING WHEN REQUIRED (BY OTHER TRADE)
- WOOD OR METAL STUDS

**CERAMIC TILE TUB ENCLOSURE**

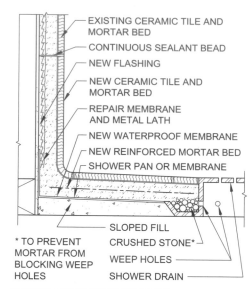

- EXISTING CERAMIC TILE AND MORTAR BED
- CONTINUOUS SEALANT BEAD
- NEW FLASHING
- NEW CERAMIC TILE AND MORTAR BED
- REPAIR MEMBRANE AND METAL LATH
- NEW WATERPROOF MEMBRANE
- NEW REINFORCED MORTAR BED
- SHOWER PAN OR MEMBRANE
- SLOPED FILL
- CRUSHED STONE*
- WEEP HOLES
- SHOWER DRAIN

\* TO PREVENT MORTAR FROM BLOCKING WEEP HOLES

**SHOWER RECEPTOR RENOVATION**

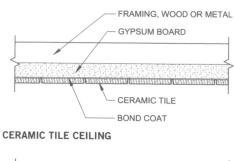

- FRAMING, WOOD OR METAL
- GYPSUM BOARD
- CERAMIC TILE
- BOND COAT

**CERAMIC TILE CEILING**

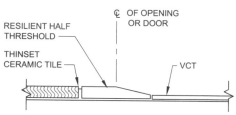

- CERAMIC TILE
- BOND COAT
- MORTAR BED ON SUSPENDED METAL LATH AND SCRATCH COAT, CONCRETE, OR TILE BACKER BOARD

**CERAMIC TILE CEILING**

## CEILINGS AND SOFFITS

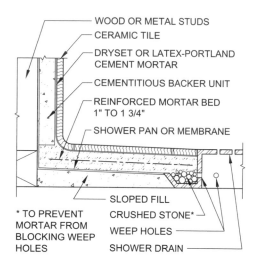

- WOOD OR METAL STUDS
- CERAMIC TILE
- DRYSET OR LATEX-PORTLAND CEMENT MORTAR
- CEMENTITIOUS BACKER UNIT
- REINFORCED MORTAR BED 1" TO 1 3/4"
- SHOWER PAN OR MEMBRANE
- SLOPED FILL
- CRUSHED STONE*
- WEEP HOLES
- SHOWER DRAIN

\* TO PREVENT MORTAR FROM BLOCKING WEEP HOLES

**BACKERBOARD WEEP HOLE CONDITION AT SHOWER**

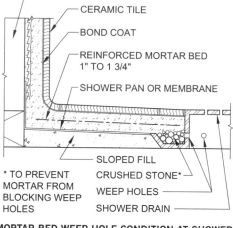

- WOOD OR METAL STUDS
- CERAMIC TILE
- BOND COAT
- REINFORCED MORTAR BED 1" TO 1 3/4"
- SHOWER PAN OR MEMBRANE
- SLOPED FILL
- CRUSHED STONE*
- WEEP HOLES
- SHOWER DRAIN

\* TO PREVENT MORTAR FROM BLOCKING WEEP HOLES

**MORTAR BED WEEP HOLE CONDITION AT SHOWER**

## TUBS AND SHOWERS

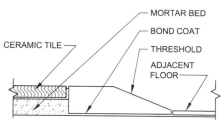

- RESILIENT HALF THRESHOLD
- ℄ OF OPENING OR DOOR
- THINSET CERAMIC TILE
- VCT

**THINSET THRESHOLD CONDITION**

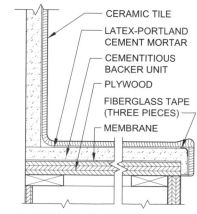

- MORTAR BED
- BOND COAT
- THRESHOLD
- ADJACENT FLOOR
- CERAMIC TILE

**THICKSET THRESHOLD CONDITION**

## THRESHOLDS

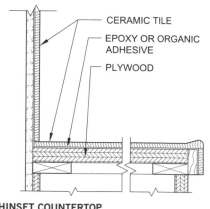

- CERAMIC TILE
- EPOXY OR ORGANIC ADHESIVE
- PLYWOOD

**THINSET COUNTERTOP**

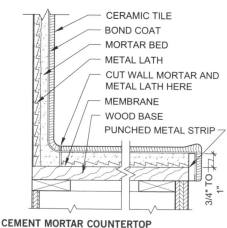

- CERAMIC TILE
- BOND COAT
- MORTAR BED
- METAL LATH
- CUT WALL MORTAR AND METAL LATH HERE
- MEMBRANE
- WOOD BASE
- PUNCHED METAL STRIP
- 3/4" TO 1"

**CEMENT MORTAR COUNTERTOP**

- CERAMIC TILE
- LATEX-PORTLAND CEMENT MORTAR
- CEMENTITIOUS BACKER UNIT
- PLYWOOD
- FIBERGLASS TAPE (THREE PIECES)
- MEMBRANE

**CEMENT BACKERBOARD COUNTERTOP**

## COUNTERTOPS

Tile Council of America, Inc.; Anderson, South Carolina
Winnie Cheng; Rhode Island School of Design; Providence, Rhode Island
Jess McIlvain, AIA, CCS, CSI; Jess McIlvain and Associates; Bethesda, Maryland

# TERRAZZO

Terrazzo is a very low-maintenance, seamless floor finish with the luxurious look of stone mosaic and durability comparable to that of concrete. Often selected for its decorative possibilities, terrazzo artistry can produce striking medallions or intricate inlaid patterns.

Terrazzo is a mixture of a binder and crushed aggregate, typically marble. Other aggregate types, such as glass, are available to vary the appearance of the terrazzo. Divider strips of brass, white alloy of zinc, or plastic, are used functionally as control joints, and aesthetically as design elements, to separate fields of color.

## AGGREGATE

Aggregate, or stone chips used in terrazzo, includes all calcareous serpentine and other rocks capable of taking a good polish. Marble and onyx are the preferred materials. Quartz, granite, quartzite, and silica pebbles are used for rustic terrazzo and textured mosaics not requiring polishing.

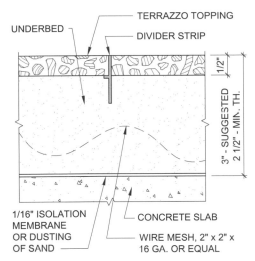

**SAND CUSHION TERRAZZO**

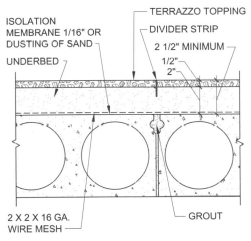

**SAND CUSHION TERRAZZO OVER PRECAST CONCRETE-TYPE DECK**

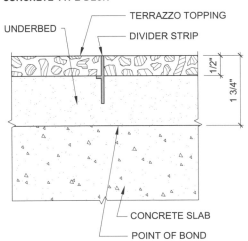

**BONDED TERRAZZO**

## TERRAZZO SYSTEMS

| SYSTEM | DESCRIPTION | ADVANTAGES | TOTAL THICKNESS | WEIGHT PSF (kPa) |
|---|---|---|---|---|
| Sand Cushion | ½ in. (13 mm) terrazzo topping over 2½ in. (63 mm) underbed, reinforced with wire mesh, over an isolation membrane over 1/16 in. (1 mm) of sand, on a concrete slab. For interior use only. | The best available cement terrazzo system, because it is the only system that completely separates the finish from the subfloor. This protects against minor substrate defects telegraphing through to the finish surface. | 3 in. (76 mm) including ½ in. (13 mm) terrazzo topping | 30 (206) |
| Bonded | ½ in. (13 mm) terrazzo topping over 1¼ in. (32 mm) underbed, on a concrete slab. Interior use only. | Requires less thickness than sand cushion. Can be used for walls. | 1¾ to 2¼ in. (44 to 57 mm) including ½ in. (13 mm) terrazzo topping | 18 (124) |
| Monolithic | ½ in. (13 mm) terrazzo topping on concrete slab. Performance dependent on the quality of the substrate. A level concrete slab must be provided. | Most economical system. Ideal for large areas such as shopping malls, schools, and stores. | ½ in. (13 mm) terrazzo topping | 7 (48) |
| Thinset | ¼ to ⅜ in. (4 to 9 mm) terrazzo topping over concrete slab. Thinnest and, typically, most expensive system. Considered to be a resinous flooring type. Epoxy or polyester matrix is used. | Good for renovation work. Both epoxy and polyester resist many types of chemicals, making them suitable for labs, hospitals, and manufacturing facilities. | ¼ to ⅜ in. (4 to 9 mm) | 4 (27.5) |
| Precast | Prefabricated custom units for steps, bases, planters, benches, and wall panels. | Variety of uses. | Custom | Varies |

*Source: Reprinted courtesy of NTMA*

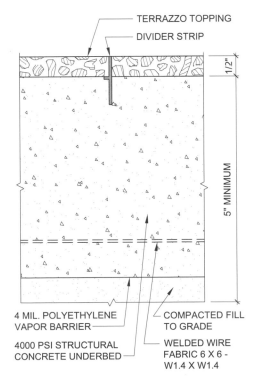

**STRUCTURAL TERRAZZO SYSTEM**

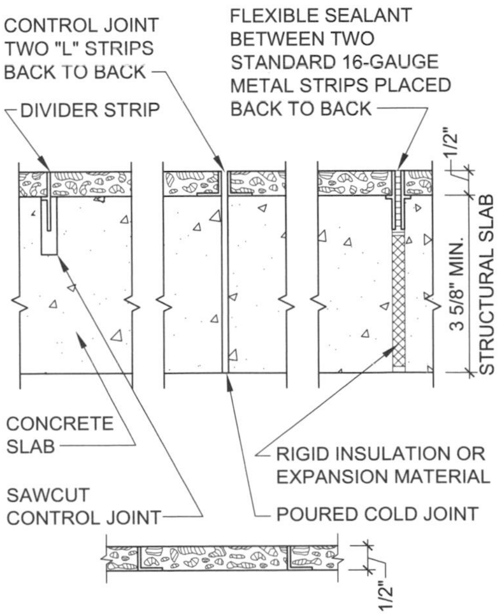

**MONOLITHIC TERRAZZO**

The National Terrazzo and Mosaic Association (NTMA), an association of terrazzo contractors, material suppliers, and distributors, publishes the *NTMA Technical Manual*, which contains complete specifications for all terrazzo systems.

## TERRAZZO SYSTEMS

*National Terrazzo and Mosaic Association, Inc.; Terrazzo Specification and Design Guide; Leesburg, Virginia*

## MATRICES

There are two basic types of matrices, or binders: portland cement and resinous chemical binders. Color pigments are added to create special effects. Limeproof mineral pigments or synthetic mineral pigments compatible with portland cement are required. Both white and gray portland cement are used, depending on final color.

Resinous binders are used to install the thinnest possible finish of terrazzo, as thin as ¼ in. (6 mm). Epoxy and polyester binders are two-part formulations, consisting of a resin and a catalyst, to which a dry mix is added. Resinous binders offer increased chemical and abrasion resistance and good impact strength. Resin-based terrazzo requires significantly less maintenance than its cement-based counterpart, and is commonly used in installations where economy and overall weight of the terrazzo system is a concern.

All five types of chemical binders provide excellent chemical and abrasion resistance, except for latex, which is rated good:

- *Epoxy matrix*: Two-component resinous matrix.
- *Polyester matrix*: Two-component resinous matrix.
- *Polyacrylate matrix*: Composite resinous matrix.
- *Latex matrix*: Synthetic latex matrix.
- *Conductive matrix*: Special formulated matrix to conduct electricity with regulated resistance; used in surgical areas and where explosive gases are a hazard.

### Divider Strips

White alloy of zinc, brass, or plastic strips are used to control shrinkage of the terrazzo. They vary in width from ⅛ to ½ in. (3 to 13 mm); ⅛ in. (3 mm) is standard.

For systems that adhere to the concrete subfloor, divider strips must also be used precisely above all concrete control joints. The structural engineer must locate control joints in accordance with "ACI Concrete Joint Placement" to prevent random cracking in the slab and terrazzo. Some of the standard requirements include:

- Joints should occur a maximum of three times in feet the depth of the concrete in inches. For example: 4-in. (100 mm) slabs should have concrete joints at a maximum spacing of 12 ft (3.6 m).
- Joints should occur at all corridor intersections and corners.
- Joints should not be spaced more than 1½ times the width of the concrete pour. For example: 6-ft-(2-m-) wide corridors should have joints at a maximum spacing of 9 ft (3 m). In addition, divider strips are typically used to separate colors or designs within the terrazzo.

### Control Joints

Plastic zip strips or double-angle strips are used to control cracking due to anticipated shrinkage in the subfloor at construction joints. These are not required in a sand cushion system due to the use of an isolation membrane.

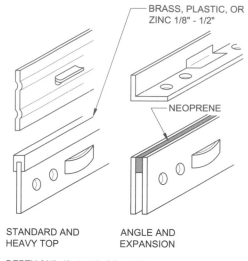

BRASS, PLASTIC, OR ZINC 1/8" - 1/2"

NEOPRENE

STANDARD AND HEAVY TOP

ANGLE AND EXPANSION

DEPTH 3/4", 1", 1 1/4", OR 1 1/2"

**DIVIDER STRIPS**

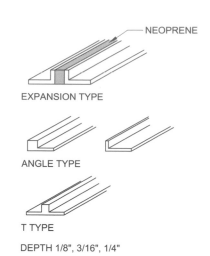

NEOPRENE

EXPANSION TYPE

ANGLE TYPE

T TYPE

DEPTH 1/8", 3/16", 1/4"

**DIVIDER STRIPS FOR THINSET TERRAZZO**

**DIVIDER STRIPS**

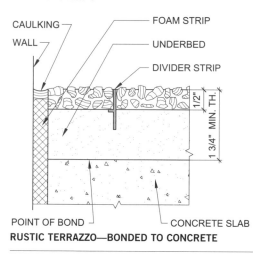

CAULKING
WALL
FOAM STRIP
UNDERBED
DIVIDER STRIP
1/2"
1 3/4" MIN. TH.
POINT OF BOND
CONCRETE SLAB

**RUSTIC TERRAZZO—BONDED TO CONCRETE**

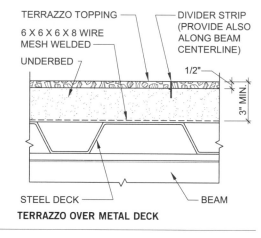

TERRAZZO TOPPING
6 X 6 X 6 X 8 WIRE MESH WELDED
UNDERBED
DIVIDER STRIP (PROVIDE ALSO ALONG BEAM CENTERLINE)
1/2"
3" MIN.
STEEL DECK
BEAM

**TERRAZZO OVER METAL DECK**

**INSTALLED DIVIDER STRIPS**

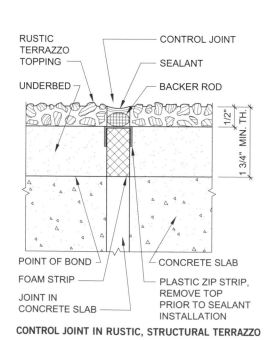

RUSTIC TERRAZZO TOPPING
CONTROL JOINT
SEALANT
UNDERBED
BACKER ROD
1/2"
1 3/4" MIN. TH.
POINT OF BOND
CONCRETE SLAB
FOAM STRIP
JOINT IN CONCRETE SLAB
PLASTIC ZIP STRIP, REMOVE TOP PRIOR TO SEALANT INSTALLATION

**CONTROL JOINT IN RUSTIC, STRUCTURAL TERRAZZO**

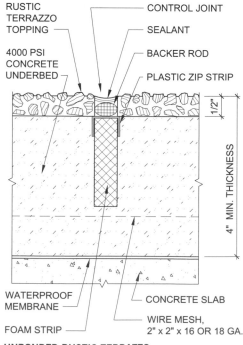

RUSTIC TERRAZZO TOPPING
CONTROL JOINT
SEALANT
4000 PSI CONCRETE UNDERBED
BACKER ROD
PLASTIC ZIP STRIP
1/2"
4" MIN. THICKNESS
WATERPROOF MEMBRANE
CONCRETE SLAB
FOAM STRIP
WIRE MESH, 2" x 2" x 16 OR 18 GA.

**UNBONDED RUSTIC TERRAZZO**

**CONTROL JOINTS**

## INSTALLATION

In a terrazzo installation, the binder and aggregate mixture are set in place on the prepared floor surface. After the terrazzo surface has cured, it is ground down to a smooth finish. The floor is then grouted to fill any voids, and sealed. A terrazzo floor consists of at least 70% stone. Because porosity can vary among stone types, the pores of both the stone and the binder require the protection of a sealer. For renovation work, terrazzo can be installed over practically any type of existing, stable hard-surface flooring.

## SURFACE TREATMENT

Terrazzo systems must be given an application of penetrating type sealer, which fills the pores of the surface to prevent absorption of traffic dirt and stains. Sealers will also highlight the natural colors of the aggregate.

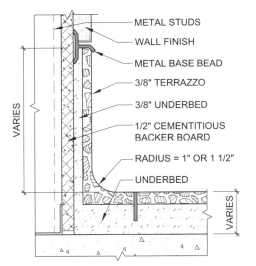

**FLUSH BASE**

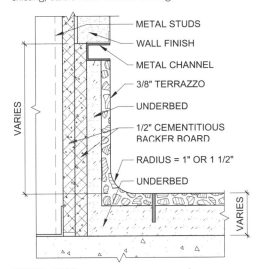

**REVEAL BASE**

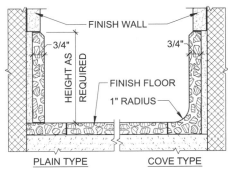

**PRECAST TERRAZZO BASE**
Precast terrazzo units are routinely available, and almost any shape can be produced. Examples include: straight, coved, and splayed bases; windowsills; stair treads and risers; shower receptors; floor tiles; and wall facings.

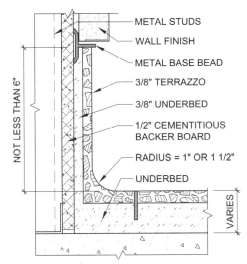

**RECESSED BASE**

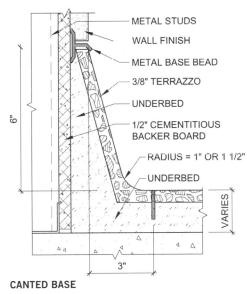

**CANTED BASE**

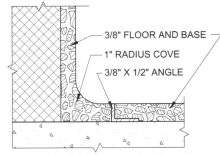

**POLYACRYLATE TERRAZZO FLOOR AND BASE**

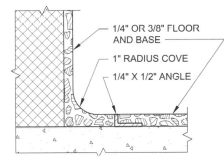

**EPOXY OR POLYESTER TERRAZZO FLOOR AND BASE**

### POURED-IN-PLACE TERRAZZO BASES

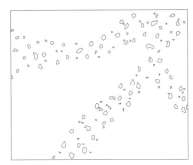

**PALLADIANA TERRAZZO**
Random fractured slabs of marble up to approximately 15 in. (380 mm) greatest dimension, ⅜ to 1 in. (9 to 25 mm) thick, with smaller chips filling spaces between.

**RUSTIC TERRAZZO**
Uniformly textured terrazzo in which matrix is depressed to expose chips; not ground or only slightly ground.

**VENETIAN TERRAZZO**
Larger chips (sizes #3 through #8), with smaller chips filling the spaces between.

**STANDARD TERRAZZO**
The most common type; relatively small chip sizes (#1- and #2-size chips).

### TYPES OF TERRAZZO CLASSIFIED BY APPEARANCE

*Trey Klein, AIA; crayfish design; Belmont, Massachusetts*
*Jason Dickerson; Rhode Island School of Design; Providence, Rhode Island*
*John C. Lunsford, AIA; Varney, Sexton Syndor Architects; Phoenix, Arizona*

# STRETCHED CEILING SYSTEMS

## CHARACTERISTICS

Stretched ceiling systems utilize lightweight, long-span, continuous sheets of prefinished material to create a large, smooth ceiling plane or a warped, curved ceiling. The maximum span of a stretched ceiling system is dictated by the material. Spans of up to 16 × 40 ft (5 × 12 m) are typical.

Stretched ceiling systems consist of three basic components: a flexible ceiling material, a perimeter rail, and a fitting that attaches the material to the rail. The material is either a polyvinyl chloride (PVC) membrane or a woven fabric, typically made of fire-resistant polyester. The rail is mounted around the perimeter of the space, in either straight or curved configurations. Intermediate supports are not commonly required because of the long spans that are possible with stretched ceiling systems. Rails can be either visible or fully concealed.

## CEILING MATERIALS

Translucent and perforated PVC membranes are available. Translucent PVC material can be backlit, creating a luminous appearance. Care should be taken to ensure that the frame profile is not projected onto the backlit surface, creating a shadow.

Photographic-quality artwork can be printed on PVC membranes. PVC systems are available in more than 100 colors. Custom colors are also available, but typically with a large order. Matte, satin, suede, metallic, and reflective finishes are available.

The PVC is recyclable, virtually impermeable to air and moisture (water-staining problems are eliminated), and can easily be cleaned with a soft cloth and liquid cleaner. Polyester-stretched ceiling systems can resemble plaster or gypsum board ceilings.

## ANTIMICROBIAL APPLICATIONS

Antimicrobial and antifungal treatments can be integrated into the ceiling material for applications such as hospital operating rooms, cleanrooms, laboratories, and food preparation spaces.

## INSTALLATION

Stretched ceiling systems offer a quick, dust-free installation without odors or fumes. These systems are installed relatively quickly; however, experienced installers are required. All forms of penetrations and recessed or surface-mounted fixtures, including lighting, alarms, sprinklers, and ventilation equipment, can be accommodated. Penetrations are all cut in the field to ensure a proper fit. The ceiling material is demountable, providing access to mechanical equipment behind. These systems can be installed over existing ceilings, commonly gypsum board or acoustical tile suspension systems, either with or without acoustical tile installed, depending on the sound characteristics required. For curved installations, wood or metal frames can be used at the perimeter.

Access to mechanical space behind the ceiling is achieved by temporarily removing the flexible material. Lights, sprinklers, and HVAC registers and grills can be incorporated in the ceiling. Penetrations are field-cut.

*Andy Adams; Anshen + Allen Architects; San Francisco, California*
*Brian Tan; Rhode Island School of Design; Providence, Rhode Island*

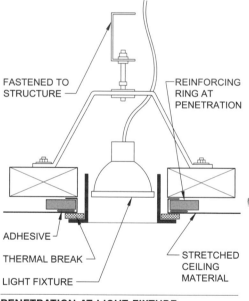

**PENETRATION AT LIGHT FIXTURE**

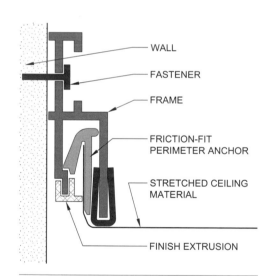

**FRICTION-FIT PERIMETER ASSEMBLY**

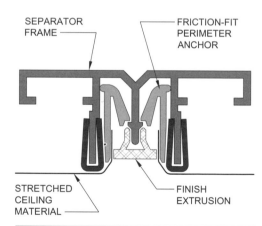

**INTERMEDIATE SUPPORT**

# ACOUSTICAL TILE CEILINGS

Acoustical tile ceilings are composed of prefabricated ceiling units, which are installed in a concealed or semiexposed metal suspension system. Acoustical tiles are typically 12 × 12 in. (305 × 305 mm); however, larger sizes are available. Thicknesses range from ½ in. (13 mm) to ⅝ in. (16 mm) to ¾ in. (19 mm). Acoustical panels are generally larger than 12-×-12-in. (305-×-305-mm) ceiling tiles, and are installed in exposed or semiconcealed grids.

Concealed spline ceiling installations provide the appearance of a monolithic ceiling surface because the metal suspension system is not exposed. Installation can be more costly, and maintenance of the tile ceiling is more difficult than that of exposed suspension system installations. Moreover, a concealed spline ceiling is not as easily accessible to above-ceiling areas as lay-in unit ceilings.

Fire-resistant acoustical tile assemblies are available when used with applicable UL design criteria.

## CEILING TILE COMPOSITION

Composition of the various acoustical tile types used in commercial construction include *mineral fiber base*

and *glass fiber base*. *Cellulose base* is used primarily in residential construction and is not as durable as the commercial-grade panel construction. Construction of the mineral fiber base acoustical panels is cast, wet-felted, or nodular, and is available in a number of textures and acoustical properties.

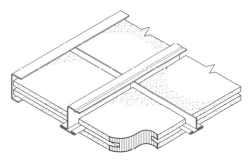

Kerfed-edge acoustical ceiling tile slides into a T- or Z-shaped grid.

**KERFED-EDGE ACOUSTICAL CEILING TILE**

## Water- or Wet-Felted Tiles

Water- or wet-felted tiles are fabricated from mineral wool, perlite, fillers, and binders, then mixed into a loose slurry that is formed into sheets by draining, compressing, drying, and cutting to size. Fissured, perforated, or stippled textures are added to the tiles prior to painting the units.

## Cast or Molded Tiles

Cast or molded tiles are fabricated from mineral fibers, fillers, and binders, then mixed into a pulp and poured into paper or foil-lined molds of the desired size. Surface textures are created by the manipulation of the surface of the molds. Integral colors can be added for a through-color product. The tiles are oven-dried, trimmed, and then painted.

## Nodular Tiles

Nodular tiles are fabricated from mineral fibers wound into balls, combined with perlite, fillers, and binders, then mixed into a slurry. The mixture is formed into sheets, oven-dried, and cut to size. The tiles, which are inherently porous, are then textured with fissures and are painted.

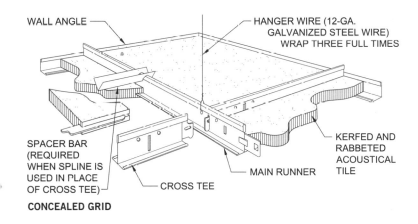

**CONCEALED GRID**

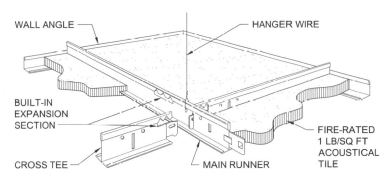

**FIRE-RATED GRID (CONCEALED GRID SHOWN)**

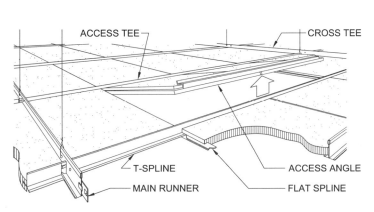

**CONCEALED GRID—UPWARD ACCESS (SIDE PIVOT SHOWN; END PIVOT AVAILABLE)**

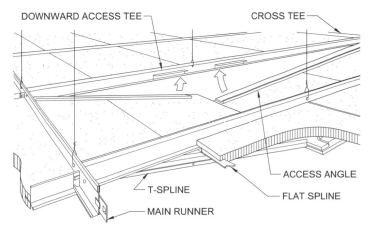

**FIRE-RATED CONCEALED GRID—DOWNWARD ACCESS (END PIVOT SHOWN; SIDE PIVOT AVAILABLE)**

**ACOUSTICAL CEILING TILE SUSPENSION SYSTEMS**

# ACOUSTICAL PANEL CEILINGS

Acoustical panel ceilings are composed of prefabricated ceiling units, installed in a metal suspension system. They are used where sound attenuation and accessibility to the above ceiling interstitial or plenum space are desired. Acoustical ceilings are large visual elements within a space, and are design elements as well as acoustical features. Partitions, light fixtures, ceiling diffusers, sprinklers, and other devices are attached to or installed within these ceilings, so coordination with the ceiling layout is critical.

Acoustical panels are installed on an exposed metal grid system suspended from the underside of the structure above. In contrast, acoustical tiles are inserted into a concealed suspension system and are generally 12 × 12 in. (305 × 305 mm) or 24 × 24 in. (610 × 610 mm). Common acoustical panel sizes typically range from 24 × 24 in. (610 × 610 mm) to 24 × 48 in. (610 × 1,220 mm) up to 60 × 60 in. (1,524 × 1,524 mm), and are available in rectangular shapes as well as square. Thicknesses range from ⅝ in. (16 mm) to ¾ in.

(19 mm) to 1 in. (25 mm), with other thicknesses available for special applications.

Acoustical panel ceiling products are available to meet special project requirements, including the need for greater durability, light reflectance, and humidity. Fire-resistant acoustical ceiling assemblies are available, when used with applicable UL designs.

## Ceiling Types

ASTM E1264, *Classification for Acoustical Ceiling Products,* provides a classification system for ceiling panels, which describes various types of panel faces; however, this system is not typically used by designers to specify ceiling panels.

Fiberglass panels are processed from a molten state into fibrous glass strands. A separate dimensionally stable facing material is laminated to the fiberglass core to provide texture and pattern. Backings are available as well.

## Edge Details

Common edge details are square or tegular (reveal) shapes. Acoustical panels with these edge details are easily dropped in place within the suspension system and are pushed up to access the ceiling plenum.

### Square Edge

Square-edge acoustical panels are economical and are installed on the exposed ceiling suspension grid flanges. Square-edge panels do not conceal the suspension grid.

### Tegular Edge

Tegular-edge acoustical panels have a reveal edge that allows the panels to extend below the suspension system, partially concealing the metal grid. Tegular edges can be square, angled, beveled, stepped, or other special shapes, and are generally selected for their aesthetic appearance. When installed within an exposed tee suspension system, the acoustical panels read as modular elements, due to the reveals between the panels. Other suspension system profiles fill the tegular-edge reveal, providing a more flush, monolithic appearance to the ceiling.

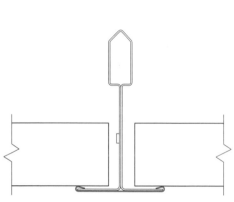

**SQUARE-EDGE LAY-IN PANEL FOR ¹⁵⁄₁₆-IN. (24-MM) EXPOSED TEE SYSTEM**

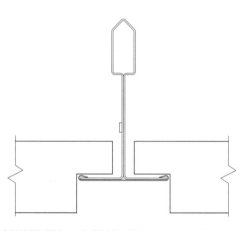

**SQUARE TEGULAR EDGE FOR ¹⁵⁄₁₆-IN. (24-MM) EXPOSED TEE SYSTEM**

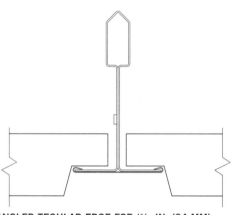

**ANGLED TEGULAR EDGE FOR ¹⁵⁄₁₆-IN. (24-MM) EXPOSED TEE SYSTEM**

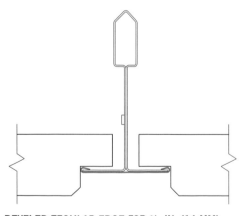

**BEVELED TEGULAR EDGE FOR ⁹⁄₁₆-IN. (14-MM) EXPOSED TEE SYSTEM**

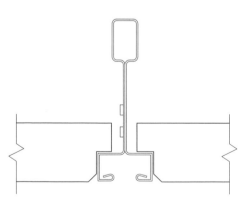

**BEVELED TEGULAR EDGE FOR ⁹⁄₁₆-IN. (14-MM) BOLT-SLOT TEE SYSTEM**

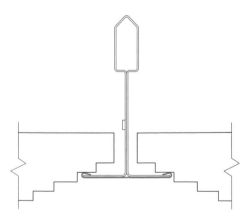

**SPECIAL TEGULAR EDGE**

**PANEL EDGE CONDITIONS**

# ACOUSTICAL CEILING DETAILS

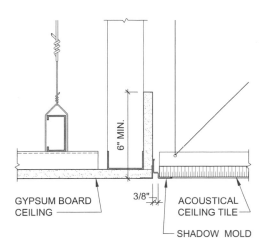

**FLUSH ACOUSTICAL CEILING TILE AT GYPSUM BOARD CEILING**

GYPSUM BOARD CEILING

6" MIN.

3/8"

ACOUSTICAL CEILING TILE

SHADOW MOLD

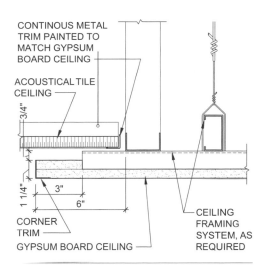

CONTINOUS METAL TRIM PAINTED TO MATCH GYPSUM BOARD CEILING

ACOUSTICAL TILE CEILING

3/4"

1 1/4"

3"

6"

CORNER TRIM

GYPSUM BOARD CEILING

CEILING FRAMING SYSTEM, AS REQUIRED

**RECESSED ACOUSTICAL CEILING TILE AT GYPSUM BOARD CEILING**

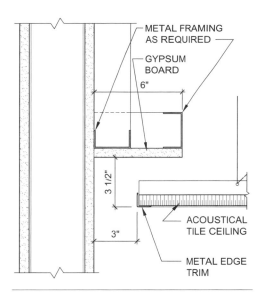

METAL FRAMING AS REQUIRED

GYPSUM BOARD

6"

3 1/2"

3"

ACOUSTICAL TILE CEILING

METAL EDGE TRIM

**PERIMETER SLOT AIR RETURN**

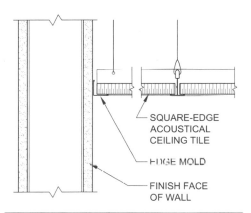

SQUARE-EDGE ACOUSTICAL CEILING TILE

EDGE MOLD

FINISH FACE OF WALL

**L-MOLD WITH SQUARE-EDGE ACOUSTICAL TILE**

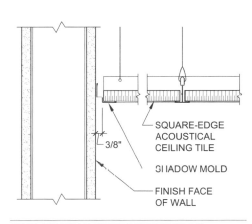

3/8"

SQUARE-EDGE ACOUSTICAL CEILING TILE

SHADOW MOLD

FINISH FACE OF WALL

**SHADOW MOLD WITH SQUARE-EDGE ACOUSTICAL TILE**

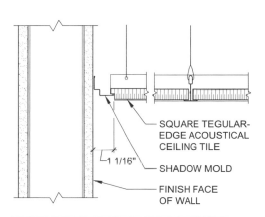

SQUARE TEGULAR-EDGE ACOUSTICAL CEILING TILE

1 1/16"

SHADOW MOLD

FINISH FACE OF WALL

**SHADOW MOLD WITH TEGULAR-EDGE ACOUSTICAL TILE**

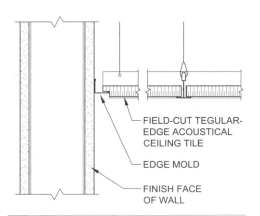

FIELD-CUT TEGULAR-EDGE ACOUSTICAL CEILING TILE

EDGE MOLD

FINISH FACE OF WALL

**L-MOLD WITH FIELD-CUT TEGULAR-EDGE ACOUSTICAL TILE**

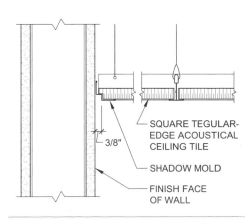

3/8"

SQUARE TEGULAR-EDGE ACOUSTICAL CEILING TILE

SHADOW MOLD

FINISH FACE OF WALL

**SHADOW MOLD WITH TEGULAR-EDGE ACOUSTICAL TILE**

*Richard Riveire, AIA; DMJM/Rottet; Los Angeles, California*

**CEILINGS** □ 2

# BRICK FLOORING

## APPLICATIONS

Brick is a homogenous clay and shale masonry unit, fired at extreme temperatures for a long duration to produce an abrasion-resistant surface material with very high compressive strength. Brick flooring does not require extensive maintenance when properly treated for the application. Interior brick pavers are available in varying sizes and thicknesses to meet the needs of varying installations; they can be specified to meet durability requirements, which range from exterior freeze/thaw exposure to typical indoor environment conditions, including chemical-resistant flooring.

Brick pavers are available in varying sizes and are known by many names. Bricks are available in standard and modular sizes. Nominal dimensions of pavers typically range from (width × length): 4 × 8 in. (102 × 203 mm) to 4 × 12 in. (102 × 305 mm); thickness from 1¼ to 2¼ in. (32 to 57 mm), although the 1¼-in.-thick brick is less commonly used since thin brick has become available. Thin brick pavers, of ⅜ to ½ in. thick (10 to 13 mm), also known as *brick tiles*, can be installed when material cost and setting depth are of concern. They have been installed in large-scale commercial brick paving projects in lieu of standard brick pavers. Additional brick trim pieces for special conditions such as copings and stair treads are available.

Interior brick paver appearance varies due to manufacturing and firing techniques. Colors range from buff, terra cotta, and darker natural tones to ironspot brick, in smooth to rough textures. Flashed brick is available in a color range featuring black, blue, and brown. Brick pavers are typically available in smooth or wire-cut (also known as *velour*) finishes and are available with chamfered and rounded edges; and special bricks can be fabricated with handicapped-detectable warning features. To add visual interest, brick pavers can be laid up in varying patterns and colors.

## SELECTION OF BRICK PAVERS

Brick paver durability is identified by Weathering Classes, defined by ASTM C902, *Pedestrian and Light Traffic Paving Brick*, and ASTM C1272, *Heavy Vehicular Paving Brick*. These standards measure the durability of brick in relation to its compressive strength, 24-hour cold-water absorption, and the saturation coefficient of the brick. Classes SX and MX are suitable for use in exterior installations. Class NX brick pavers are suitable for interior applications, and must be protected from freezing when wet. Most typical interior brick paving installations will not be subjected to freeze/thaw cycles.

The use of salvaged brick is generally not recommended for interior paving, as the durability of the brick is unknown.

Abrasion resistance of paving brick is measured by traffic type classifications, which identify the abrasion index and volume of abrasion loss on the brick, as identified by ASTM C902. Pedestrian traffic, especially from the impact of high-heeled shoes, is typically more abrasive than vehicular traffic.

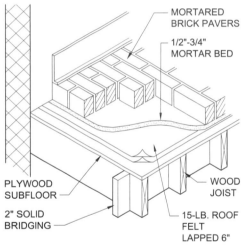

**MORTARED BRICK PAVERS ON WOOD FRAMING**

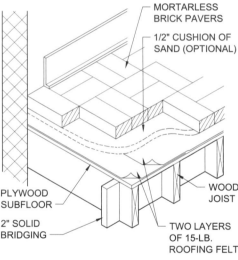

**MORTARLESS BRICK PAVERS ON WOOD FRAMING**

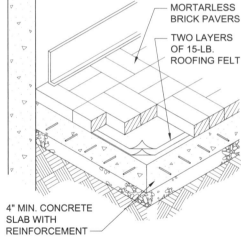

**MORTARLESS BRICK PAVERS ON CONCRETE SLAB**

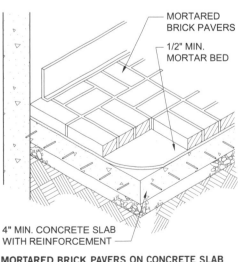

**MORTARED BRICK PAVERS ON CONCRETE SLAB**

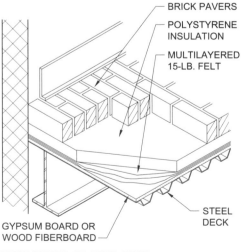

**BRICK PAVERS ON STEEL DECK**

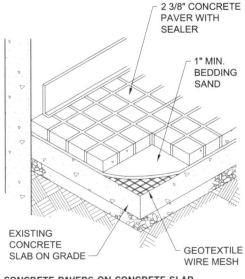

**CONCRETE PAVERS ON CONCRETE SLAB**

**BRICK FLOORING INSTALLATION**

## INSTALLATION

Mortar for interior setting beds is typically Type S, which is formulated from 1 part portland cement, ½ part hydrated lime, and 4½ parts sand; or 1 part Type S masonry cement and 3 parts sand. Mortar bed thicknesses vary from ⅜ to 1 in. (10 to 25 mm) thick. Thickset setting beds should be limited to installations where the substrate is a slab on grade or a slab where deflection is minimal to reduce cracking.

Joints between brick pavers may be filled with mortar, sand, or grout. The mortar in joints should be the same as used in the setting bed. For mortarless installations, the joints are hand-tight and filled with mason's sand. Grout composed of cement, lime, sand, and pigment for color is worked into the joints after the pavers have set in the mortar.

Thin brick pavers of ⅜ to ½ in. (10 to 13 mm) thickness may be installed using a thin mortar bed over a rigid substrate, such as concrete. A bond coat is applied to the substrate, prior to the installation of the mortar setting bed. The thin pavers are installed directly on the setting bed.

## SEALERS AND PROTECTIVE COATINGS

Sealers and protective coatings, usually in the form of wax, or a combination sealer/finish material, may be applied to interior brick paving to prevent staining. Brick surfaces should be clean and dry prior to the application of any coatings on the flooring. The slip resistance of the brick paving may be affected by the application of the coating.

## CHEMICAL-RESISTANT BRICK FLOORING

Chemical-resistant brick flooring has a very low water absorption rate and is fired at higher temperatures than typical interior brick pavers. It is used for industrial, food service, and sanitary areas, which require a chemical- and grease-resistant flooring surface. Chemical-resistant brick is available in varying types, based on the requirements of ASTM C279, *Standard Specification for Chemical-Resistant Masonry Units,* and ASTM C410, *Standard Specification for Industrial Floor Brick.*

Sizes of chemical-resistant brick are similar in length and width to standard brick sizes; however, thicknesses vary based on anticipated use. Bricks range in depth from 1, 1³⁄₁₆, 1⅜, or 1½ in. (25, 30, 35, or 38 mm) where foot and forklift traffic is anticipated. For heavy traffic areas, brick thickness is 2¼ in. (57 mm); and where severe abuse is anticipated, thickness of 3¾ or 4½ in. (95 or 114 mm) is recommended.

Surfaces of the chemical-resistant brick flooring range from smooth to textured and abrasive surfaces intended to improve slip resistance when wet. Textured surfaces make cleaning more difficult, and chipping/wear on many slip-resistant surfaces may occur. The bottom surface of the bricks is important to consider; use wire-cut or shallow-scored bottoms to minimize the possibility of trapping liquids and bacteria under the brick.

Chemical-resistant brick flooring is typically installed over a reinforced concrete slab. Grouts and resin mortars are usually furan- and epoxy-based. Floor drains are generally installed in chemical-resistant brick floors, and must be compatible with the entire flooring assembly to properly drain any caustic materials. Floors require a minimum slope of ¼ in. per foot (1:50) to drains. Membranes are commonly applied under chemical-resistant brick flooring to provide a barrier to liquids and to act as a cushion between the concrete subfloor and the mortar setting bed.

Any expansion joints required within the installation should be sealed with chemical-resistant sealants. Compatibility with mortars and grouts should be checked.

For specialized industrial chemical-resistant brick flooring installations, such as meatpacking plants and dairies, additional precautions must be taken when installing the chemical-resistant waterproof membrane and the brick flooring, to ensure that local and state health code requirements are met.

*Min Kyeny Kang; Rhode Island School of Design; Providence, Rhode Island*
*Mark Forma; Leo A. Daley Company; Washington, D.C.*
*MASTERSPEC®; published by ARCOM; Salt Lake City, Utah and Alexandria, Virginia*

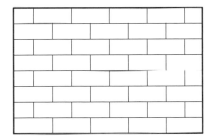

**RUNNING BOND**

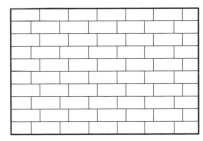

**OFFSET BOND**

**OFFSET BOND**

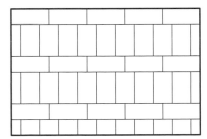

**MIXED RUNNING AND STACK BOND**

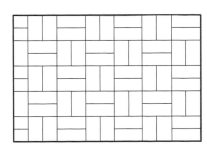

**BASKET WEAVE**

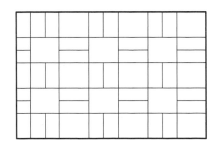

**BASKET WEAVE**

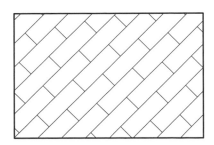

**DIAGONAL BOND**

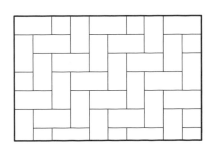

**HERRINGBONE**

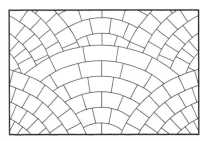

**ROMAN COBBLE**

**BRICK PATTERNS**

# STONE FLOORING

## STONE FLOORING TYPES

Stone flooring, or paving, in interior applications is a durable pedestrian traffic surface. Properly selected and installed, stone flooring wears well over time. Stone flooring can convey a sense of permanence and elegance, and is often used in lobbies and other public spaces.

Numerous types of stones can be used for flooring. The selection of a stone should be appropriate for the intended use. Not all stones are capable of withstanding the traffic of commercial installations, so a review of stone types with the stone fabricator or supplier is recommended.

Stone flooring is available in two basic types: *dimension stone*, which is installed in a thick mortar bed, and *dimension stone tiles,* which are installed in a thick mortar bed or in a thinset installation, similar to ceramic tile installations.

## STONE TILE AND PAVER INSTALLATION

Joint width should always be specified; $\frac{1}{16}$ to $\frac{1}{8}$ in. (1.6 to 3 mm) is considered standard. When installing stone flooring over a wood subfloor, the floor should be reinforced to ensure against deflection.

*Lippage* is a condition that occurs when tiles are installed with a thin bed over an uneven surface. Tiles may "lip" one edge higher than adjacent tiles, presenting a ragged appearance on the finished surface. In some conditions, a certain amount of lippage is unavoidable. As a general rule, the recommended maximum variation of the finished surface should be no more than $\frac{3}{16}$ in. (4.8 mm) cumulative over a 10 ft (3 m) lineal measurement, with no more than $\frac{1}{32}$ in. (.8 mm) variation between individual tiles.

## DIMENSION STONE

Dimension stone is defined as quarried stone with usually one or more mechanically dressed surfaces. These are thick slabs of stone that are marked as they are cut for matched-pattern installations, such as book-match or end-match configurations.

Dimension stone tiles are less than $\frac{3}{4}$ in. (19 mm) thick. They provide the natural beauty of a stone floor without the weight, depth, and expense of dimension stone. However, their thinness makes stone tiles more prone to cracking from impact or normal floor deflection. Stone tiles are installed by either the thick-bed or the thinset installation methods.

Stone flooring dimensions typically range from larger dimension stone paver units with face areas up to 48 sq in. × $\frac{3}{4}$, $1\frac{1}{4}$, or 2 in. (1,200 sq mm × 19 (2 cm), 32 (3 cm), or 50 mm) thick. Sizes and shapes are limited to the specific stone's characteristics. Stone tile modules are typically 12 to 24 sq in. × $\frac{1}{4}$, $\frac{3}{8}$, or $\frac{1}{2}$ in. (305 to 610 sq mm × 6, 10, and 13 mm) thick, and typically are furnished with a protective backing to improve the tile strength. Larger stone tile sizes may be available if appropriate for the stone type. Metric sizes for dimension stone and stone tiles are also available from selected manufacturers. Dimension stone for stair and threshold applications are typically custom-sized.

## STONE PAVER DURABILITY

Most typical interior stone paving installations will not be subjected to the freeze/thaw cycles of exterior stone paving. Most stones are adequately hard and sound to withstand the rigors of interior pedestrian and light vehicular traffic; however, each stone should be reviewed to determine its appropriateness for a particular paving application.

## STONE FINISHES

Stone finishes affect the perception of the color and the slip resistance of stone flooring. Common stone finishes are *polished, honed,* and *thermal.*

- *Polished finishes are the most reflective.* These high-maintenance finishes should be selected with care. For high-traffic public areas, such as lobbies, polished floor finishes are often eventually hidden under nonskid mats.
- *Honed finishes have a dull sheen.* These satin smooth surfaces are often good choices for commercial floors because of their slip resistance.
- *Thermal, sometimes called flamed, finishes are achieved by the application of intense flaming heat to the surface of the stone.* Thermal finishes are usually applied to granite.
- *Waterjet is a newer type of finish for granite, which is between honed and thermal finishes.* Created by high water pressure, the waterjet finish brings out the color of the stone, making it slightly darker than the thermal finish.

### TYPICAL FINISHES AND COMMON SIZES OF STONE TILES AND PAVERS

| STONE | FINISH | MINIMUM THICKNESS | | MAXIMUM FACE DIMENSION | | Ha[1] |
|---|---|---|---|---|---|---|
| | | IN | MM | IN | MM | |
| Granite | Polished Honed Thermal | $\frac{3}{8}$, $\frac{1}{2}$ (tiles) $1\frac{1}{4}$–4 (pavers) | 9.5, 13 (tiles) 32–102 (pavers) | 12 × 12 (tiles) 15 × 30 (pavers) | 305 × 305 (tiles) 381 × 762 (pavers) | N/A |
| Marble | Polished Honed | $\frac{1}{4}$–$\frac{1}{2}$ (tiles) $1\frac{1}{4}$ (pavers) | 6–13 (tiles) 32 (pavers) | 12 × 12 (tiles) 24 × 24 (pavers) | 305 × 305 (tiles) 610 × 610 (pavers) | 10 |
| Limestone | Smooth | $1\frac{3}{4}$ –$2\frac{1}{2}$ (pavers) | 44–64 (pavers) | 24 × 36 (pavers) | 610 × 915 (pavers) | 10 |
| Slate | Natural cleft Sand-rubbed | $\frac{1}{4}$–1 | 6–25 | 12 × 12 to 24 × 54 | 305 × 305 to 610 × 1,372 | 8 |
| Flagstone | Natural cleft Semirubbed | $\frac{1}{2}$–4 | 13–102 | 12 × 12 to 24 × 36 | 305 × 305 to 610 × 915 | 8 |

[1]Ha, the abrasive hardness value, is the reciprocal of the volume of the material abraded multiplied by 10. A minimum value of 10 is recommended for flooring. Stones with a difference of 5 or more in Ha should not be used together because they will wear differently.

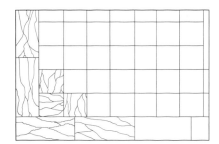

**SQUARES**

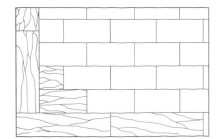

**COURSED**

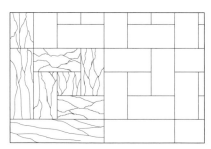

**GEOMETRIC**

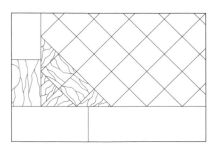

**DIAMOND**

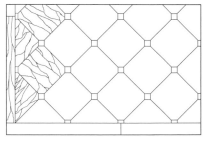

**OCTAGON SQUARE**

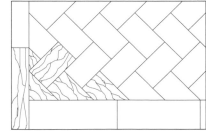

**HERRINGBONE**

**MARBLE AND GRANITE PATTERNS**

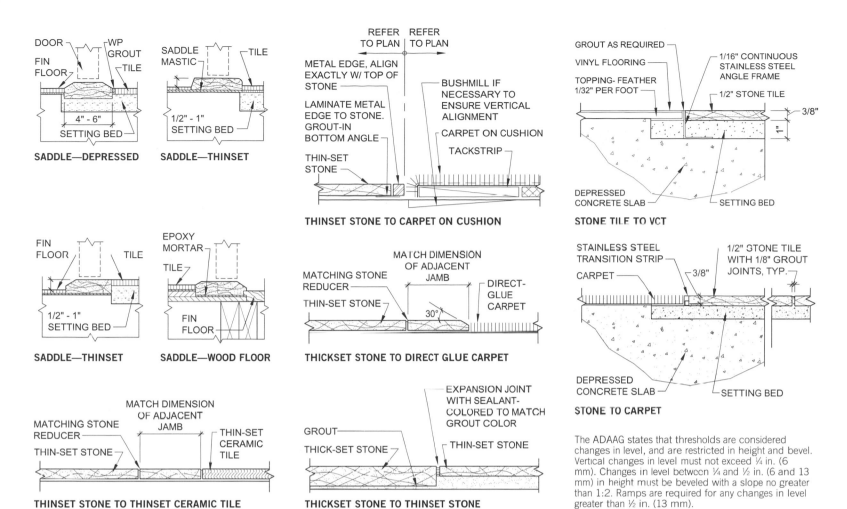

**STONE THRESHOLDS AND TRANSITIONS**

## SLIP RESISTANCE

Slip resistance for natural stone flooring is a controversial subject. Slip resistance is a relative measure of the frictional force required to prevent slipping on a paving surface. Various test methods are available to measure the static coefficient of friction (SCOF). ASTM C1028, *Standard Test Method for Determining the Static Coefficient of Friction of Ceramic Tile and Other Like Surfaces by the Horizontal Dynamometer Pull-Meter Method,* measures the static coefficient of friction for ceramic tile and similar surfaces (including stone), and is used under wet and dry conditions. ASTM D2047, *Standard Test Method of Friction of Polish-Coated Floor Surfaces as Measured by the James Machine,* the test for determining the static coefficient of friction for polish-coated floor surfaces, is used to measure slip resistance under dry conditions only. The greater the SCOF number, the less slippery the surface. Currently, there is no test specifically for the slip resistance of stone paving. The appendix to the Americans with Disabilities Act (ADA), *Accessibility Guidelines for Buildings and Facilities (ADAAG),* recommends, but does not require, that stone floors have a minimum static coefficient of friction of 0.6 for level

surfaces and 0.8 for ramped surfaces. The ADA does not specify a test method for the static coefficient of friction. These values differ from the Ceramic Tile Institute of America's recommendation of 0.5 or greater. Typically, only a thermal finish will provide the 0.8 SCOF.

When specifying a stone floor, consider the stone finish, application of any topical stone coatings, which may affect the slip resistance, and the type of traffic and use that is anticipated for the installation. Consult the stone fabricator or supplier's test data for SCOF information.

## STONE SEALERS

The use of sealers and coatings on interior stone flooring must be carefully considered, as many products are available and the results depend on many factors of the installation and ongoing maintenance of the floor. Sealers can reduce moisture absorption, but require reapplication periodically and may develop an unsightly buildup. Some sealers may change in color over time and may make the floor appear dingy from yellowing and from dirt buildup sticking to the sealer.

Coatings are available to improve slip resistance, conceal scratches, and protect the stone from moisture and tracked-in dirt. Consult the product's performance data; use—cautiously—sealers that have been successfully used in the past.

## ABRASION RESISTANCE

Abrasion resistance is the capability of the stone to resist wear and absorption, which affects staining and soiling of the stone. Abrasive hardness (Ha) is measured by ASTM C241, *Standard Test Method for Abrasion Resistance of Stone Subjected to Foot Traffic.* Recommended abrasive hardness is 10 for interior flooring. Consult with the stone fabricator or supplier for the selection of appropriate stone types for a particular installation and intended use.

The combination of different stones and different stone finishes may be of concern in interior installations, as the slip and abrasion resistance may differ. Marble and granite in combination will wear unevenly, and may produce additional hazards to pedestrians; moreover, maintenance and refinishing of the floor will be difficult.

## DIMENSION STONE INSTALLATION

Installation of interior dimension stone flooring typically uses a mortar setting bed over a structurally sound substrate, usually reinforced concrete. Substrates must support the flooring as well as the intended live and dead loads of the final occupancy. Steel decking systems and wood framing are acceptable if they are stiff enough to limit deflection. Stone can accommodate deflection of approximately 1/720 of the span. In cases where deflection may be a concern, stone tiles may be an option. Uneven substrates intended for thin-set stone tile can be leveled prior to installation. When moisture is a concern, a vapor-retardant membrane should be installed.

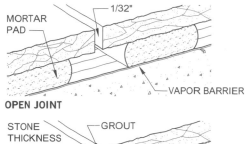

**OPEN JOINT**

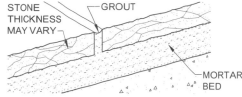

**THICK-SET–CLOSED JOINT STONE OVER WOOD FLOOR**

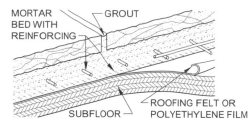

**STONE OVER WOOD FLOOR STONE SANDWICH FLOOR PANEL (PREFAB)**

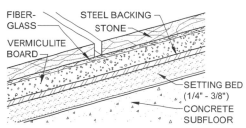

**STONE SANDWICH FLOOR PANEL (PREFAB)**

**STONE FLOORING**

## SETTING BEDS

Mortar beds are either bonded to the substrate or unbonded, allowing movement between the substrate and the mortar bed. A bonded bed is produced with a 1:3 or 1:4 cement-to-sand mortar mixture, 3/4- to 1-in. (19 to 25 mm) thick. Unbonded beds are composed of a semidry 1:3 cement-to-sand mortar mixture laid in thicknesses between 1 to 2½ in. (25 to 64 mm). Thickness of the mortar bed varies based on project conditions. When deflection of the floor is of concern, an isolating membrane should be installed between the substrate and the mortar bed. This bed should be a minimum of 1⅝ in. (40 mm) thick, with steel reinforcing mesh laid midbed for additional strength.

## ADHESIVE BEDS

Thinset adhesive beds are approximately ⅛ in. (3 mm) or less and are used for stone tile units. Thin adhesive beds follow the floor plane and cannot accommodate adjustments to the finished floor to become level. Thick adhesive beds range from ⅛ to ¼ in. (3 to 6 mm) in thickness and can accommodate greater adjustments in the level of the finished floor. Refer to the manufacturer's recommendations for suitability of the product to the application and for installation information.

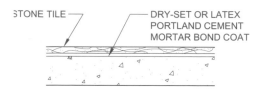

**LATEX-MODIFIED PORTLAND CEMENT MORTAR**
Use latex-modified portland cement mortar on level, clean slab-on-grade construction where no bending stresses occur and expansion joints are installed.

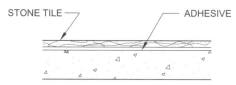

**EPOXY ADHESIVE**
Use epoxy adhesive in areas subject to moisture and certain chemicals. It is more costly and difficult to apply than latex portland cement mortar.

**THINSET FLOORING DETAILS**

## STONE STAIRS

Stone may be used on stairs as a finish material or can be supported by stringers to form structural treads. Fully supported treads are typically 3/4 to 1¼ in. (19 to 32 mm) thick. Stair substrates may be concrete or steel-framed treads and risers. Treads and risers are installed in a similar manner as stone flooring units, although the thin-set adhesive method is recommended. Based on project conditions, risers may require additional restraint, and treads may be detailed with recessed nonslip strip inserts.

The ADA has established requirements for the configuration and profile of stair elements. Consult the ADA for specific information on design requirements for stairs.

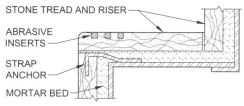

**METAL PAN WITH STONE SAFETY TREAD**

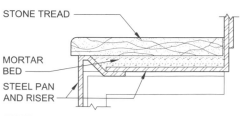

**STONE SUBTREAD AND RISER WITH STONE TREAD**

**STONE STAIRS WITH STEEL FRAME**

## JOINTS

Joints between stone flooring pavers are filled with grout. Latex additives in grout are commonly used to increase the flexural strength of the mortar and improve the curing process by retarding the evaporation of water. Dry-set unsanded grouts are used for joints up to ⅛ in. (3 mm) wide. Larger joints are typically filled with sanded grouts, such as portland cement grout, which are used because the sand reduces the shrinkage of the grout as it dries, thus minimizing cracking. Sanded grouts are not recommended for polished stone floors, due to the possibility of scratching by loose sand particles as the grout wears. Marble is more susceptible to scratching than granite.

*Control* or *expansion joints* are critical to the success of a large area stone floor installation. Dimensional changes in the floor may differ from one installed material to another, and may result from loading settlement and changes in temperature and humidity. Any movement at the substrate level must be reflected in the setting bed and the finish floor to minimize damage to the stone flooring.

*Min-Kyung Kang; Rhode Island School of Design; Providence, Rhode Island*
*Manami Nakabayashi; Rhode Island School of Design; Providence, Rhode Island*
*MASTERSPEC®, published by ARCOM; Salt Lake City, Utah, and Alexandria, Virginia*
*Mark Forma; Leo A. Daly Company; Washington, D.C.*
*Eric. K. Beach; Rippeteau Architects, PC; Washington, D.C.*
*Building Stone Institute; New York, New York*
*George M. Whiteside, III, AIA, and James D. Lloyd; Kennett Square, Pennsylvania*
*Tile Council of America, Inc.; Anderson, South Carolina*

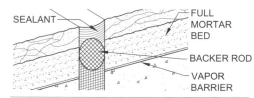

**CONTROL JOINT AND FULL MORTAR BED**

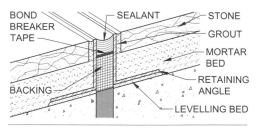

**FLEXIBLE JOINT OVER STRUCTURAL MOVEMENT JOINT—HEAVY TRAFFIC**

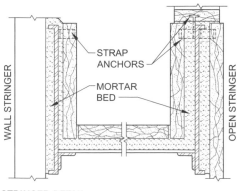

**STRINGER DETAIL**
Open risers are not allowed in areas under ADA jurisdiction.

# WOOD FLOORING

## SELECTION CRITERIA

Wood flooring consists of solid or engineered wood products, and is available in strip, plank, and parquet flooring. All wood floors require regular maintenance to maintain their appearance. Wood flooring industry organizations and suppliers provide detailed information on product specifications.

## SOLID WOOD FLOORING

Solid wood flooring is available in many hardwood and softwood species. It can be refinished multiple times. Solid wood flooring should not be installed below grade, due to the possibility of moisture damage to the wood floor.

## WOOD STRIP FLOORING

Wood strip flooring for normal use is typically a nominal ¾ in. (19 mm) thick, with actual thickness of $^{25}/_{32}$ in. (19.84 mm), in widths ranging from 1½ in. to 2¼ in. (38 to 57 mm). Lengths are random.

## WOOD PLANK FLOORING

Wood plank flooring is also typically a nominal ¾ in. (19 mm) thick, in widths ranging from 3 to 10 in. (76 to 250 mm) and is available in random lengths.

## WOOD PARQUET FLOORING

Wood parquet flooring consists of small wood strips, available in individual slats, or is formed into panels or tiles that are arranged to form a pattern. Thickness is typically $^{5}/_{16}$ in. (8 mm) for individual strips and square panels. Other thicknesses are available from some parquet flooring manufacturers. Sizes of panels vary according to pattern and availability.

## SELECTION OF WOOD FLOORING

Wood flooring should be selected after considering pedestrian and vehicular (cart) traffic, durability required, and potential damage to floors; typical usage, exposure to moisture and sunlight, maintenance, wood floor appearance expectations, and other criteria specific to the project.

The majority of woods specified for commercial flooring are hardwoods such as oak or maple. Best overall appearance, uniformity of color, limited amounts of character marks, and minimal sap marks indicate the most desirable wood flooring.

Flooring can be manufactured from practically every commercially available species of wood. For marketing purposes in the United States, wood flooring is roughly grouped according to species and region. Various grading systems are used with various species, and often specifications differ for boards of different sizes in a given species. For instance, recommended nail size and spacing vary among the several board sizes typically available in oak.

The table below shows typical grades and sizes of boards by species or regional group. Grade classifications vary, but in each case it can be assumed that the first grade listed is the highest quality and that the quality decreases with each succeeding grade. The best grade typically minimizes or excludes features such as knots, streaks, spots, checks, and torn grain, and will contain the highest percentage of longer boards. Grade standards have been reduced in recent years for most commercially produced flooring, hence a thorough review of exact grade specifications is in order when selecting wood flooring.

## ENGINEERED WOOD FLOORING

Engineered wood flooring is available in strip, plank, or parquet tiles. Hardwood face veneers are laminated to a dimensionally stable, multiple-ply substrate. Engineered wood floors are not as susceptible to moisture as solid wood flooring, and may be used in below-grade areas, with the proper installation techniques.

## TYPICAL GRADES AND SIZES OF BOARDS BY SPECIES OR REGIONAL GROUP

| GROUP | INDUSTRY ORGANIZATION | GRADE | THICKNESS IN. (MM) | WIDTH IN. (MM) | | NOTES |
|---|---|---|---|---|---|---|
| Oak, ash, black cherry, and walnut; also beech, birch, hard maple, pecan, and hickory | National Oak Flooring Manufacturers Association Memphis, Tennessee Tel: (901) 526-5016 www.nofma.org | Oak, ash, black cherry, and walnut: Clear<br><br>Select<br>Common (Nos. 1 and 2)<br>Beech, birch, and hard maple:<br>First (including red and white)<br>Second<br>Third<br>(See note for other species) | Strip<br>¾ (19)<br><br>½ (13)<br>Maple, beech, birch only<br>¾ (19), $^{25}/_{32}$ (20),<br>$^{33}/_{32}$ (26)<br>Plank<br>¾ (19) | Face<br>1½ (38), 2 (50),<br>2¼ (57), 3¼ (82)<br>1½ (38), 2 (50)<br><br>1½ (38), 2 (50),<br>2¼ (57), 3¼ (82)<br>3 (76), 4 (101), 5 (127),<br>6 (152), 7 (177),<br>8 (203) | | Factory-finished oak flooring is available in Prime, Standard, and Tavern grades ¾ in. (19) thick with a face width of 1½ or 2¼ in. (38 or 57 mm). NOFMA grades hickory/pecan as first grade, first grade red, first grade white, second grade, second grade red, and third grade. |
| Hard maple (*Acer saccharum*—not soft maple); also beech and birch | Maple Flooring Manufacturers Association Northbrook, Illinois Tel: (847) 480-9138 www.maplefloor.org | First<br>Second and Better<br>Third | $^{25}/_{32}$ (20), $^{33}/_{32}$ (26) | Face<br>1½ (38)<br>2¼ (57)<br>3¼ (82) | | The Maple Flooring Manufacturers Association states that beech and birch have physical properties that make them fully suitable as substitutes for hard maple. See manufacturer for available width and thickness combinations. |
| Southern pine | Southern Pine Inspection Bureau Pensacola, Florida Tel: (850) 434-2611 www.spib.org | B and B<br>C<br>C and Better<br>D<br>No. 2 | ⅜ (9), ½ (13), ⅝ (16),<br>1 (25), 1¼ (32), 1½ (38) | Nominal<br>2 (50)<br>3 (76)<br>4 (101)<br>5 (127)<br>6 (152) | Face<br>1⅛ (28)<br>2⅛ (54)<br>3⅛ (79)<br>4⅛ (104)<br>5⅛ (130) | Grain may be specified as edge (rift), near-rift, or flat. If not specified, manufacturer will ship flat or mixed-grain boards. Check with manufacturer for available width and thickness combinations. |
| Western woods (Douglas fir, hemlock, Englemann spruce, Idaho white pine, incense cedar; Lodgepole pine, Ponderosa pine, sugar pine, Western larch, Western red cedar) | Western Wood Products Association Portland, Oregon Tel: (503) 224-3930 www.wwpa.org | All but Idaho white pine:<br>B and Better Select<br>C Select<br>D Select<br>Idaho white pine:<br>Supreme<br>Choice<br>Quality | 2 in. (50) and thinner | Nominal<br>3 (76)<br>4 (101)<br>6 (152) | | Flooring is machined tongue and groove and may be furnished in any grade. Grain may be specified as vertical (VG), Flat (FG), or mixed (MG). Basic size for flooring is 1 in. × 4 in. × 12 ft (25 mm x 101 mm x 3.6 m); standard lengths are 4 ft (1.2 m) and longer. The moisture content of these grades is 15% MC, with 85% of the pieces less than 12% MC. |

*Source: National Oak Flooring Manufacturers Association; Memphis, Tennessee*

## WOOD CHARACTERISTICS

Annual growth rings are visible in the wood and vary in color and density. The inner part of the growth ring is known as *springwood,* and has relatively large cell cavities and thin cell walls. *Summerwood* has smaller cell cavities and thicker, denser cell walls than springwood. Growth rings, when exposed by sawing methods, provide the grain and pattern in the wood flooring.

In hardwoods, plain-sawn lumber generally contains mostly flat-grained wood, while quarter-sawn lumber is nearly all vertically grained.

*Figuring* is the pattern produced in a wood surface by annual growth rings, rays, knots, and deviations from regular growth.

*Medullary rays* extend radially from the core of the tree toward the exterior bark. They vary in height from a few cells in some species to 4 in. (100 mm) or more in the oaks; they are responsible for the flake effect common to the quarter-sawn lumber in certain species.

### Tangential Grain

Tangential grain is typically called *flat grain;* it is easily recognized by its parabolic (arched) effect. Lumber is considered flat-grained when the annual growth rings make an angle of less than 45° with the wide surface of the board.

### Radial Grain

Radial grain is known as *vertical* or *edge grain*. It is generally more stable than flat grain, and is less likely to expand or contract in width with changes in moisture. Lumber is considered vertical grained when the annual growth rings form an angle of 45° to 90° with the wide surface of the board.

### Durability

Durability of wood flooring varies with the wood species and the finish selected. Hardwoods such as oak and maple typically perform better than softwoods, such as pine. Not all hardwoods are suitable for wood flooring. The wood species hardness and the cut of the wood flooring affects its ability to resist indentation, wear, and marring.

Wood strip and plank flooring is quarter-sawn (edge grain) or plain-sawn (flat grain) and typically is milled into a tongue-and-groove shape. Quarter-sawn strip flooring is considered to be more durable, due to the exposure of the vertical grain of the wood. It is also more expensive than plain-sawn wood, as more waste wood is generated. Rift-sawn strips are generally associated with oak flooring; it is also costly, as there is more waste than from quarter-sawn wood strips. Jointed, or square-edged flooring is also available. End-grain wood blocks are durable flooring units, installed in a jointed fashion.

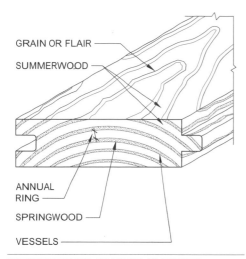

GRAIN OR FLAIR
SUMMERWOOD
ANNUAL RING
SPRINGWOOD
VESSELS

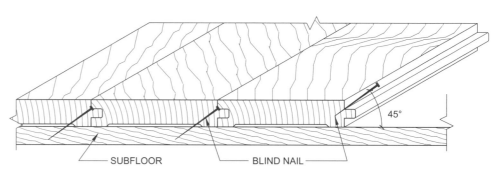

SUBFLOOR    BLIND NAIL    45°

Wood is a hygroscopic material that changes dimensionally with the absorption or release of moisture, causing swelling or shrinking. After manufacturing, wood flooring is kiln-dried at the factory to a 6% to 9% moisture content. At the project site, the flooring must be protected to maintain proper moisture content, and must acclimatize to the space, which should be of the manufacturer's recommended environmental conditions for installation. Prior to installation, provisions should be made for movement of the flooring at the perimeter of the wood floor. The relative humidity of the space and the moisture content of the wood are also factors, as is the moisture content of a concrete substrate.

**GROWTH RINGS IN WOOD FLOORING**
*Source: National Wood Flooring Association;*
*Manchester, Missouri*

**BLIND-NAILED TONGUE-AND-GROOVE WOOD FLOORING**
*Source: Maryrose McGowan;* Specifying Interiors; *John Wiley & Sons, Inc., 1996, p.171.*

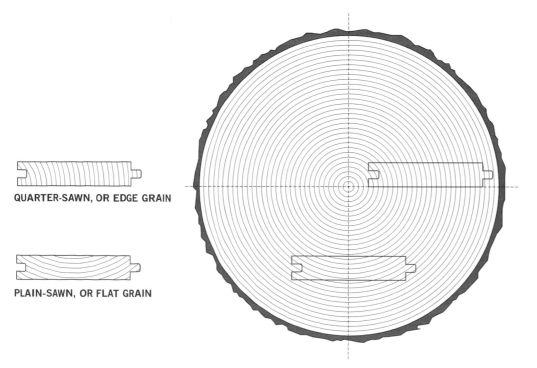

**QUARTER-SAWN, OR EDGE GRAIN**

**PLAIN-SAWN, OR FLAT GRAIN**

HOLLOW BACK
(EDGE GRAIN)

SCRATCH BACK
(FLAT GRAIN)

PLAIN
(EDGE GRAIN)

HOLLOW OR
SCRATCH BACK
(FLAT GRAIN)

The underside of flooring boards may be patterned, and it often contains more defects than are allowed in the top face. Grain is often mixed in any given run of boards. Edge grain is also called vertical grain.

**CROSS SECTION OF LOG**
*Source: Maryrose McGowan;* Specifying Interiors; *John Wiley & Sons, Inc., 1996, p.171.*

**BOARD CHARACTERISTICS**

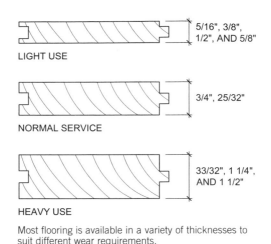

5/16", 3/8", 1/2", AND 5/8"

LIGHT USE

3/4", 25/32"

NORMAL SERVICE

33/32", 1 1/4", AND 1 1/2"

HEAVY USE

Most flooring is available in a variety of thicknesses to suit different wear requirements.

**VARIOUS THICKNESSES**

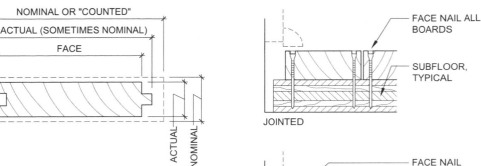

NOMINAL OR "COUNTED"

ACTUAL (SOMETIMES NOMINAL)

FACE

ACTUAL

NOMINAL

Cross-sectional dimensioning systems vary among species, patterns, and manufacturers. Trade organizations provide percentage multipliers for computing coverage.

**CROSS-SECTION DIMENSIONS**

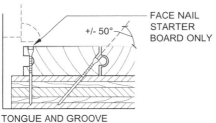

FACE NAIL ALL BOARDS

SUBFLOOR, TYPICAL

JOINTED

FACE NAIL STARTER BOARD ONLY

+/- 50°

TONGUE AND GROOVE

Jointed flooring must be face-nailed, usually with fully barbed flooring brads.

Tongue-and-groove boards are blind-nailed with spiral floor screws, cement-coated nails, cut nails, or machine-driven fasteners; follow the manufacturer's recommendations.

**FASTENING**

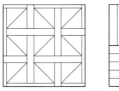  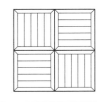  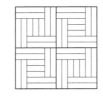

**PARQUET FLOOR PATTERNS**

## INSTALLATION

Wood flooring requires particular care in handling and installation. Prior to installation, the wood flooring should be allowed to acclimate to the space in which it is to be installed, at the humidity level of the final occupancy. Minimize moisture damage to wood floors by avoiding installation in close proximity to wet areas. In addition, to ensure constant temperature and humidity, install wood floors after all "wet" jobs have been completed and after the heating plant and all permanent lighting have been installed.

Wood flooring is subject to expansion and contraction; therefore, perimeter base details that allow for movement and ventilation are recommended. Wood structures require adequate ventilation in basements and crawl spaces. Under a slab on or below grade, moisture control can be further enhanced by use of a vapor barrier; this provision should be carefully considered for each installation.

Wearing properties of wood flooring vary from species to species and should be considered along with appearance when specifying wood floors. In addition, grain pattern affects the durability of a given species. For instance, industrial wood blocks are typically placed with the end grain exposed because it presents the toughest wearing surface. The thickness of the wood above the tongues in tongue-and-groove flooring may be increased for extra service.

Wood floors are installed over a plywood subfloor or over wood sleepers. Strips or planks are blind-nailed in tongue-and-groove installations and face-nailed in butt-jointed installations; parquet floors are commonly set in mastic. Vapor barriers are installed when the installation is slab on grade or below grade. Ventilation is required in certain installation conditions where moisture is a concern. Special conditions require additional detailing for proper installation.

## WOOD FLOOR FINISHES

Wood floors must be finished to protect the surface from wear. Applied finishes can be installed in the field or, in the case of engineered wood floors, they can be factory-finished. Floor finishes do not protect the wood from the effects of ultraviolet light, which can alter the appearance of the wood. Some species are more susceptible to change when exposed to sunlight; however, UV inhibitors are available to minimize fading. Color plates C-20 to C-27 illustrate the difference in appearance between water-base urethane and oil-modified polyurethane finishes applied to eight species of wood flooring.

### Field Finishes

Unfinished wood flooring can be stained to achieve an exact color match with other design elements or to mimic the appearance of a softer wood that might not have met the performance expectations of the installation.

Before the application of a field finish, wood floors are sanded so that they are level and smooth, then one of several finishes is applied. All of these finishes are subject to wear and must be touched up or removed and reapplied during the life of the floor.

There are basically three types of commercial finishes for wood floors: *acid curing, oil-modified polyurethanes,* and *water-based polyurethanes.*

### Acid Curing

Acid-curing finishes, sometimes called Swedish finishes, are hard and durable; they are thicker and less viscous than other types of finishes, making for heavier coats. Acid-curing finishes are solvent-based, two-part formulations requiring on-site mixing. They have a naturally high volatile organic compound (VOC) content, so masks are typically worn because of the noxious odor. These finishes tend to be less expensive than water-based polyurethanes, but more expensive than oil-modified polyurethanes.

### Oil-Modified Polyurethane

Oil-modified polyurethanes are easy to apply and the least expensive of the three finishes, but they also have a high VOC content. Oil-modified polyurethanes tend to turn amber-colored (slightly orange) as they age.

### Water-Based Polyurethane

Water-based polyurethanes have a low VOC content and do not yellow or change color over time. Because they are thinner, more coats are required to achieve the same depth as produced by an acid-curing finish. Water-based polyurethanes tend to be the most expensive type of wood floor finish.

*Tonn Lensment; Rhode Island School of Design; Providence, Rhode Island*
*Rippeteau Architects, P.C.; Washington, D.C.*
*Annica S. Emilsson; Rippeteau Architects, P.C.; Washington, D.C.*
*National Oak Flooring Manufacturers Association; Memphis, Tennessee*
*National Wood Flooring Association; Manchester, Missouri*
*MASTERSPEC®; published by ARCOM; Salt Lake City, Utah, and Alexandria, Virginia*

## Factory Finishes

Acrylic-impregnated (sometimes called *irradiated polymer*) wood flooring is extremely durable. This most recent advance in finishes imparts many of the qualities of resilient flooring to the wood, such as an increased resistance to abrasion and bacterial growth. The process involves removing the air from the pores of dried wood and forcing liquid acrylic into the voids. The plastic-filled wood is then irradiated (exposed to radiation), causing the acrylic to polymerize.

Prefinished wood flooring is also available with multiple coats of polyurethane or other proprietary finishes.

### Ecological Issues

The issue of tropical wood use and destruction of the tropical rainforests and other ecologically endangered areas is addressed by many manufacturers of imported wood flooring.  Studies have shown that land use changes have actually adversely affected the tropical rainforests more than the lumber industry. Check with wood flooring manufacturers to determine if they are using acceptable means of harvesting imported wood products.

## RESILIENT WOOD FLOORING

Resilient wood flooring is commonly used in athletic facilities. The typical wood flooring species for sports facilities is maple, which is preferred due to its density, fineness of grain, and nonsplintering qualities. Beech and birch are also used by some manufacturers for resilient wood floors. Finishes are typically transparent, and supplemental markings may be added with approved materials and techniques for floor striping and logos.

The Maple Flooring Manufacturers Association (MFMA) provides detailed information on the features, installation, and maintenance for maple flooring. Wood sports floor systems vary from one manufacturer to another, and some are engineered for specific purposes, such as aerobics use. Some systems are proprietary and are protected by patents. The information contained in this section refers to typical resilient wood flooring systems. Consult manufacturers for specific information.

Resilient wood flooring is commonly milled into tongue-and-groove-shaped strips of random length. Typical thickness is $^{25}/_{32}$ in. (20 mm ) for most general-purpose resilient wood flooring. A $1^{1}/_{32}$ in. (26 mm) thickness is available from selected manufacturers when additional loads are anticipated and where usage is expected to be more severe than normal. Widths range from $1^{1}/_{2}$ in. (38 mm) to $3^{1}/_{4}$ in. (83 mm).

The type of wood sports flooring chosen for a particular situation depends on the following criteria:

• Cost
• Performance of the floor
• Sport(s) to be played on the floor
• Other uses to which floor will be put
• Durability
• Environment in which the floor will be used

## Grades of Wood Sports Flooring

Maple, the wood most commonly used for sports flooring in the United States, is available in three grades, which designate only the appearance of the floor and not its performance or durability.

• *First grade:* Nearly free of defects; least color variation, with very little dark hardwood. First grade is used in premier sports venues where appearance is of primary concern.
• *Second and better:* May have tight, sound knots and other slight imperfections and some color variation. This grade of floor has a generally light appearance.
• *Third grade:* All defects and color variations are permitted. This grade of floor is mostly dark heartwood, and is used when cost is a consideration.

## Finishes and Game Lines

Wood sports floors are sanded, sealed, and finished with at least two coats of sealer and two coats of finish. Game lines are painted between the last coat of sealer and the first coat of finish. Game line paint must be compatible with sealer and finish.

*Karen K. Lindblad; Chicago, Illinois*
*Jim Swords; HOK Sports Facilities Group; Kansas City, Missouri*
*Connor/Aga Sports Flooring Corporation; Amasa, Michigan*
*Robbins Sports Surfaces; Cincinnati, Ohio*
*Exerflex; Indianapolis, Indiana*
*Maple Flooring Manufacturers Association; Northbrook, Illinois*

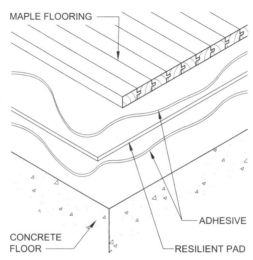

Lowest cost
Easy to install
Suitable for multipurpose applications
Use where floor performance is not critical

**MASTIC-APPLIED SYSTEM**

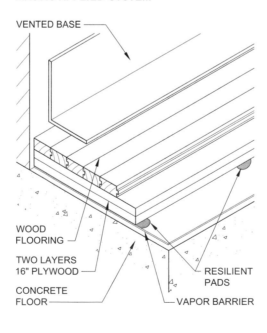

Good performance characteristics
Relatively low cost
Susceptible to moisture damage

**CUSHIONED SYSTEM**

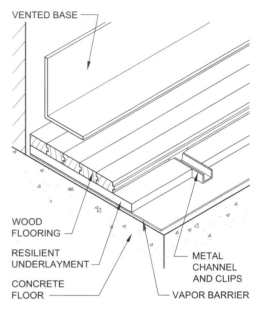

Dimensionally stable in all environments
Good multipurpose floor
Limited performance characteristics

**CHANNEL AND CLIP SYSTEM**

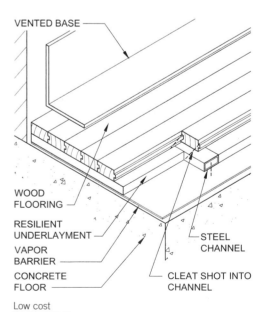

Low cost
Fast installation
Dimensionally stable in all environments
Good multipurpose floor
Limited performance characteristics

**NAIL-IN-CHANNEL SYSTEM**

# RESILIENT FLOORING

Resilient flooring provides a dense, nonabsorbent, pliant surface that is generally quiet, comfortable to walk on, and easy to maintain. Resilient flooring types include sheet vinyl, vinyl tile, rubber, linoleum, leather, and cork. Factors the designer may consider in choosing a resilient flooring type include cost, performance, durability, availability, energy and natural resource use, biodegradability, recycled content, recyclability, and toxicity.

## VINYL FLOORING

The five basic ingredients used in the manufacture of vinyl flooring are:

- *Polyvinylchloride* (PVC), which imparts wear resistance and durability. PVC is the basis of the binder, which constitutes most of the wear surface. The binder consists of PVC compounded with plasticizers and stabilizers.
- *Plasticizers,* which increase flexibility.
- *Stabilizers,* which provide color permanence and stabilize the pigments against heat and light deterioration.
- *Fillers,* which are added to supplement the bulk and thickness of the flooring. Mineral fillers, the most common, improve fire resistance. Natural fillers increase slip resistance.
- *Pigments,* for color.

### Sheet Vinyl

Sheet vinyl flooring, either solid vinyl or backed, forms a continuous finished floor covering. Because sheet vinyl flooring has fewer joints, it is used for applications where spills, dirt, or bacterial growth are of concern. It is commonly specified in hospital operating rooms or other areas where resistance to bacterial growth or water penetration is required.

### Sheet Vinyl Seams

There are two types of seams for sheet vinyl installations: *heat-welded* and *chemically welded.* Heat-welded seams are formed by melting a vinyl rod between sheets. Solid-color or patterned welding rods can either accent or camouflage seams. Heat welding requires special equipment and trained installers. Chemical welding is accomplished with the application of a one- or two-part solvent that is mixed on-site. This softens the edges of the vinyl, essentially melting them together. Chemical welding is more economical than heat welding.

## GRADES OF SHEET VINYL FLOOR COVERING WITH BACKING*

| TYPE | GRADE | WEAR LAYER THICKNESS, MINIMUM | |
|---|---|---|---|
| | | (IN.) | (MM) |
| 1 | 1 | 0.020 | 0.51 |
| | 2 | 0.014 | 0.36 |
| | 3 | 0.010 | 0.25 |
| 2 | 1 | 0.050 | 1.27 |
| | 2 | 0.030 | 0.76 |
| | 3 | 0.020 | 0.51 |

*According to ASTM F1303, Standard Specification for Sheet Vinyl Floor Covering with Backing

*Type I is defined by a wear layer binder content of not less than 90%. Type II is defined by a wear layer binder content of not less than 34%.*

## RESILIENT FLOORING SIZES

| TYPE | COMPONENTS | THICKNESS IN. (MM) | SIZES |
|---|---|---|---|
| Vinyl sheet | Vinyl resins with fiber back | 0.065–0.160 (1.6–4) | 6, 10, 12 ft (1.8, 3, 3.6 m) wide |
| Solid vinyl tile | Vinyl resins | 1/16–1/8 (1.5–3) | 9 × 9 in. (228 x 228 mm) 12 × 12 in. (305 x 305 mm) |
| Vinyl composition tile | Vinyl resins with filler | 0.050–0.095 (1.2–2.4) | 9 × 9 in. (228 x 228 mm) 12 × 12 in. (305 x 305 mm) |
| Rubber tile | Rubber compound | 3/32–3/16 (2.3–4.7) | 9 × 9 in. (228 x 228 mm) 12 × 12 in. (305 x 305 mm) |
| Cork tile | Raw cork and resins | 1/8–1/4 (3–6) | 6 × 6 in. (152 x 152 mm) 9 × 9 in. (228 x 228 mm) |
| Cork tile with vinyl coating | Raw cork with vinyl resins | 1/8–3/16 (3–4.7) | 9 × 9 in. (228 x 228 mm) 12 × 12 in. (305 x305 mm) |

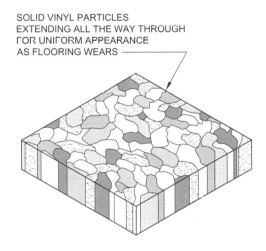

**HOMOGENEOUS, OR SOLID, SHEET VINYL**
Homogeneous, or solid, sheet vinyl floorings, have no backing. Homogeneous sheet vinyl has superior resistance to indentation, rolling loads, and chemicals, and is suitable for heavy-wear applications because its appearance remains consistent even when worn. It contains much more PVC than backed sheet vinyls, making it more resilient and more expensive.

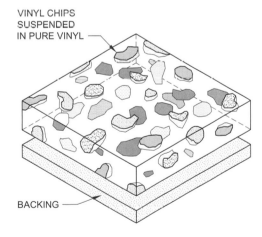

**BACKED SHEET VINYL**
Backed sheet vinyl consists of a vinyl wear layer that is bonded to a backing, with or without an interlayer between the two. Generally, the thicker the wear layer and the higher the binder content, the better the durability and the resistance to abrasion of the vinyl floor covering. The wear layer contains or protects the pattern and consists mainly of a vinyl binder, but may include pigments, fillers, and other ingredients.

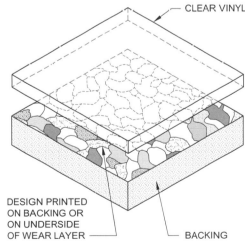

**TRANSPARENT WEAR LAYER SHEET VINYL**
Transparent, or translucent, wear layer sheet vinyl is produced by applying a clear vinyl film over a printed surface. The interlayer may include materials to impart a desired performance attribute.

**TYPES OF VINYL SHEET FLOORING**

## VINYL TILE

### Material

Two types of vinyl tile are *solid vinyl tile* and the less expensive *vinyl composition tile* (VCT). Solid vinyl tile, or homogeneous vinyl tile, contains much more PVC than VCT, making it more resilient and resistant to abrasion. Homogeneous vinyl tile has superior indentation and rolling/load resistance. Because the pattern is continuous through the thickness of the flooring, its appearance will remain consistent when worn. Three classes of VCT are defined by ASTM F1066, *Specification for Vinyl Composition Floor Tile:* Type 1, solid color tiles; Type 2, through-pattern tiles; Type 3, surface pattern tiles.

### Properties

Vinyl composition tile (VCT) is more brittle than vinyl sheet flooring because it contains much less PVC. VCT is composed mostly of fillers with comparatively small amounts of binder and pigments. Originally, the filler used in vinyl tile contained asbestos and was called *vinyl asbestos tile, VAT*.

### Installation

Vinyl tile is less expensive to install than sheet vinyl and easier to replace in damaged areas. Tile layout should consider the center of the room and the size of the last tile that falls at the perimeter. Typically, it is desirable for the perimeter tiles to be as large as possible, and no smaller than half a tile wide.

## RUBBER FLOORING

### Material

Rubber sheet or rubber tile flooring is composed of natural rubber or synthetic rubber (styrene butadiene), mineral fillers, and pigments.

### Types

Two types of rubber floor tile are *homogeneous* and *laminated*. Homogeneous rubber tile has coloring uniform throughout the tile thickness. Laminated rubber tile has coloring or patterning in the wear layer only.

### Properties

Durable, resilient, and resistant to a wide variety of harsh chemicals and solvents, rubber flooring is naturally resistant to cosmetic burns. Rubber flooring can tolerate high-traffic public areas.

The slip resistance of homogeneous rubber tile is enhanced by adding raised surface patterns. This material is popular for use as stair treads and nosings.

Rubber flooring is dimensionally stable, sound absorbent, and recyclable. It is resistant to heavy-impact loads, is puncture-resistant, and appropriate for use in indoor playgrounds, health clubs, or off-ice areas at ice skating rinks.

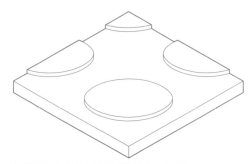

**RUBBER TILE WITH RAISED PATTERN**

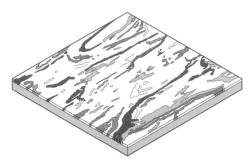

**LAMINATED RUBBER TILE**

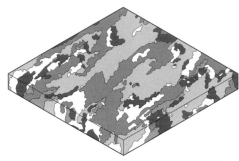

**LINOLEUM**

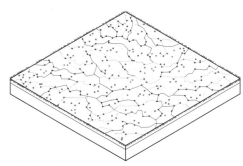

**LEATHER TILE**

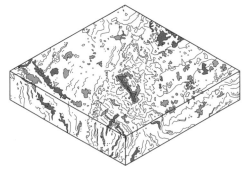

**COMPOSITION CORK**

**RESILIENT FLOOR TILES**

## LINOLEUM

### Material

Linoleum (derived from the Latin terms for "flax," *linum*, and "oil," *oleum*) is composed primarily of linseed oil, obtained from the flax plant. The oil is oxidized and mixed with a natural resin, such as rosin tapped from pine trees, and combined with powdered cork for flexibility and limestone for strength and hardness. Wood flour and pigments are added for color and colorfastness. For dimensional stability, this mixture is bonded to a fiber backing (typically burlap) for linoleum sheets or to a polyester backing for tile. Felt backings are used for linoleum countertop or tack surface sheets.

### Properties

Linoleum flooring is manufactured in Europe and imported to the United States. There is no American standard for linoleum at this time. Linoleum is biodegradable. Linoleum is a superior thermal and acoustic insulator because of the air pockets found naturally in cork (50% air). Linoleum thickness varies. It is used where superior resilience is required, such as the floors of dance rehearsal studios and health facilities. It is naturally bacteria-resistant and antimicrobial, preventing the growth of dust mites. The antistatic properties of linoleum prevent dust accumulation and reduce the potential for electric shock.

### Maintenance

A yellow film forms on the linoleum surface during the drying process when the linseed oil rises to the surface. The film should disappear when exposed to light within no more than six weeks. Linoleum flooring is maintained by damp-mopping. When sheet or tile linoleum is first laid, it is relatively porous, but the oxidization process continues over the life of the floor, during which it becomes progressively more nonporous.

### Installation

Linoleum seams can be heat-welded for water resistance, in areas over radiant floors and those exposed to direct sunlight. During the manufacturing process "stove bar marks" occur when the product is looped between suspended poles in the drying room. These deformations are either cut out in the field or eliminated with adhesive and weights during the installation process.

## LEATHER TILE

### Material

Leather tiles are typically cut from the center of a cowhide (usually a by-product of the food industry), where the fibers are tightest. The leather is vegetable-tanned and colored with penetrating aniline dyes. Leather tiles can be relatively expensive compared to other resilient flooring choices. Leather tiles will have natural grain and color variations. Leather tile flooring develops a patina over time as it wears and oxidizes in light and air.

### Maintenance and Installation

Waxing and buffing is required to maintain and protect leather flooring. It is often recommended that the floor be waxed with carnauba wax and buffed at least three times before using to ensure that the leather is properly protected. Plywood is the preferred subfloor for a leather tile installation.

# CORK FLOORING

## Material

Cork flooring is harvested from the outer layer of cork oak trees grown in Mediterranean regions. The bark becomes loose, approximately every nine years, and is cut away. Composition cork is the most common form of cork flooring. The bark material of the cork oak is granulated, pressed with binders such as synthetic resins, and then baked. The quality of composition cork varies according to the quality and size of granules, the type and quantity of the binder, and the density (compression) of the mix.

## Types

Unfinished tile is the standard product form. Also available is prefinished cork with a urethane top coating, vinyl-clad cork, or floating cork floors that either glue or mechanically snap together and float over a thin cork underlayment. Cork sheets and rolls are available with jute backing, but these are difficult to install. Cork is naturally honey-toned but is available in other colors.

## Properties

Cork flooring is inherently antistatic, hypoallergenic, and nonslip. Cork provides acoustic and thermal insulation. Cork is also used as an underlayment to increase the resiliency of other types of finish floors. It is temperature-sensitive and should not be used in combination with underfloor heating systems.

## Installation

Cork must be glued to a flat smooth surface, either plywood or a moisture-free concrete floor. Seams and depressions should be filled perfectly smooth with a portland-cement-based floor leveler.

## Maintenance

Compared to other types of resilient flooring, cork is difficult to maintain. Unless sealed, its appearance can deteriorate from water staining and ingrained dirt. Three to four coats of polyurethane or polymer sealant can prevent surface deterioration. Except for vinyl-finished cork, presealed cork should be sealed after installation to prevent moisture infiltration into the tile joints.

# RESILIENT FLOORING INSTALLATION

## Preparation

Subfloor preparation is critical to a successful resilient flooring installation. Joints and screw heads must be filled and sanded to prevent telegraphing to the finish floor surface. Also, paper felt can be used over plywood or hardboard (commonly known by the trade

name Masonite) to prevent nail or screw heads from showing. Subsurface-water migration and moisture vapor transmission through concrete slabs can cause resilient floor covering applications to fail. A dampproof membrane is required for moisture protection over slabs on grade.

## Adhesives

Adhesives, such as contact cement or mastic, are used to adhere resilient flooring to the substrate. Manufacturers and installers of adhesives are required to comply with the VOC requirements of authorities having jurisdiction. Water-based adhesives are available for many types of installations. Some manufacturers will warranty their flooring only if it is installed with their suggested adhesive.

*Faith Baum, AIA, IIDA; Faith Baum Architect; Lexington, Massachusetts*
*Mia Alwen; Rhode Island School of Design; Providence, Rhode Island*
*Lerlux Sophonpanich; Rhode Island School of Design; Providence, Rhode Island*
*MASTERSPEC®; published by ARCOM; Salt Lake City, Utah, and Alexandria, Virginia*

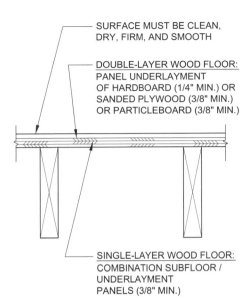

SURFACE MUST BE CLEAN, DRY, FIRM, AND SMOOTH

DOUBLE-LAYER WOOD FLOOR: PANEL UNDERLAYMENT OF HARDBOARD (1/4" MIN.) OR SANDED PLYWOOD (3/8" MIN.) OR PARTICLEBOARD (3/8" MIN.)

SINGLE-LAYER WOOD FLOOR: COMBINATION SUBFLOOR / UNDERLAYMENT PANELS (3/8" MIN.)

**WOOD SUBFLOORS**

SURFACE MUST BE CLEAN, DRY, FIRM, AND SMOOTH

2"-3" REINFORCED CONCRETE TOPPING OVER PRECAST SLABS

1" CONCRETE TOPPING OVER LIGHTWEIGHT CONCRETE SLABS

PROVIDE A VAPOR BARRIER AND A GRAVEL BASE UNDER SLABS ON GRADE.

FOR SLABS BELOW GRADE, PROVIDE A WATERPROOF MEMBRANE AND A 2" SUBSLAB.

**CONCRETE SUBFLOORS**

**SUBFLOOR PREPARATION FOR RESILIENT FLOORING**

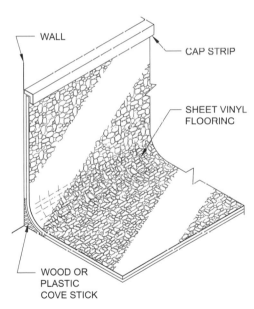

WALL

CAP STRIP

SHEET VINYL FLOORING

WOOD OR PLASTIC COVE STICK

Sheet goods, such as linoleum or sheet vinyl, can form an integral, monolithic cove base to simplify maintenance.

**COVE BASE**

## THERMAL CONDUCTIVITY OF FLOORING

| FLOORING | THICKNESS | | THERMAL CONDUCTIVITY (U VALUE) | |
|---|---|---|---|---|
| | IN. | MM | BTU/ft²h °F | W/m °K |
| Cork | 1/8 | 4 | 0.028 | 0.050 |
| Linoleum | 1/8 | 4 | 0.087 | 0.152 |
| Vinyl | 3/16 | 5 | 0.427 | 0.74 |
| Wood | 1/4 | 8 | 0.119 | 0.207 |
| Marble | 5/8 | 15 | 1.598 | 2.767 |

*Source: Arcobel; Houston, Texas*

## RESILIENT FLOORING PERFORMANCE ATTRIBUTES

| ATTRIBUTE | RESILIENT FLOORING TYPE |
|---|---|
| Resilience and quietness | Cork tile, rubber tile |
| Resistance to indentation | Solid vinyl tile |
| Stain resistance | Vinyl sheet and tile |
| Alkali resistance | Vinyl sheet and tile |
| Grease resistance | Vinyl sheet and tile, cork tile with vinyl coating |
| Durability | Vinyl sheet and tile |

# RESILIENT BASE AND ACCESSORIES

## MATERIALS

Resilient wall base and flooring accessories are available in three materials:

- *Vinyl* can be susceptible to shrinking when exposed to heat.
- *Thermoplastic rubber* is a vinyl compound with a comparatively small amount of rubber added for flexibility. Because of the high vinyl content, it performs similarly to vinyl, but is more flexible. It is commonly more expensive than vinyl but less expensive than vulcanized, thermoset rubber.
- *Thermoset rubber* is vulcanized natural rubber. It is the most flexible resilient base material and thus is easier to install and better at hiding surface imperfections in walls and floors. Thermoset rubber base is susceptible to color degradation due to UV exposure; however, it can be specially manufactured with UV inhibitors. White and dark-colored thermoset rubber base tends to hold color best. Lighter colors, especially gray, tend to be prone to color degradation. Thermoset rubber base also tends to be more vulnerable to scuffing than vinyl or thermoplastic rubber. Lighter colors tend not to show scuff marks as much as darker colors.

Although most building codes do not have flammability requirements for wall trim that constitutes less than 10% of the wall surface, the flame-spread ratings and the smoke generated from burning resilient flooring accessories differ among the three materials. Thermoset rubber, when burned, generates less smoke and toxic fumes than vinyl or thermoplastic rubber.

## WALL BASE

Wall base conceals the joint where the wall meets the floor. Premolded inside and outside corners are available from some manufacturers, but they may differ in texture and color from straight sections. Straight sections of resilient wall base are available in precut lengths (4 ft (1,219 mm) long) and coils (approximately 100 ft (30 m) long). Coils minimize the number of joints and may reduce installation costs.

There are three basic wall base profiles:

- *Straight base* is meant to be used with carpet.
- *Cove base* is meant to be used with resilient flooring.
- *Butt-to base*, sometimes referred to as *sanitary base*, is available from a limited number of manufacturers. It is installed prior to the finish floor covering. The finish floor covering must be of the same thickness as the butt-to base flange. The base is sealed to the floor and wall, creating an easy-to-clean, more sanitary joint that is popular for health care applications.

*Cove moldings* support sheet vinyl, sheet linoleum, or other flexible floor coverings when coved up the wall. *Cap moldings* help to finish the exposed edges of coved floor coverings, ceramic tile, or wood paneling.

*Ted Kollaja, AIA; lauckgroup; Dallas, Texas*

### RESILIENT BASE MATERIALS

|  | RESPONSE TO HEAT | FLEXI-BILITY | RESISTANCE TO GREASE AND OIL | RELATIVE COST |
|---|---|---|---|---|
| Vinyl | Shrinks | Good | Excellent | $ |
| Thermo-plastic Rubber | Expands | Better | Good | $$ |
| Thermoset Rubber | Expands | Best | Fair | $$$ |

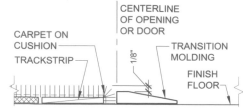

**CARPET ON CUSHION TO FINISH FLOOR**

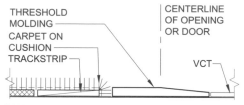

**CARPET ON CUSHION TO VCT**

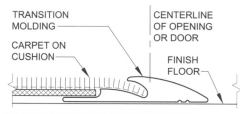

**CARPET ON CUSHION TO FINISH FLOOR**

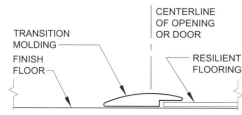

**FINISH FLOOR TO RESILIENT FLOORING**

Transition moldings create a smooth transition between different flooring materials or flooring heights and act to conceal seams.

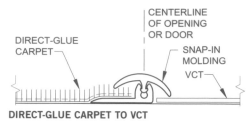

**DIRECT-GLUE CARPET TO VCT**

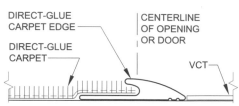

**DIRECT-GLUE CARPET TO VCT**

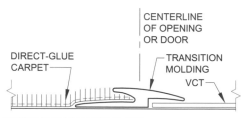

**DIRECT-GLUE CARPET TO VCT**

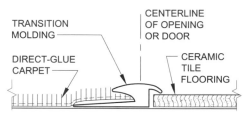

**DIRECT-GLUE CARPET TO CERAMIC TILE**

Snap-in moldings offer the advantage of wear-edge replacement without disrupting the flooring installation.

**RESILIENT TRANSITION MOLDINGS**

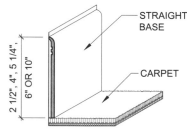

**STRAIGHT BASE**

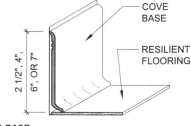

**COVE BASE**

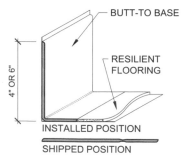

**BUTT-TO BASE**

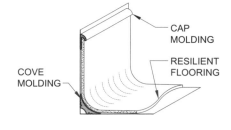

**CAP AND MOLDING**

**WALL BASE**

# CARPET

The specification of carpet and carpet tile requires evaluation of the following:

- Carpet construction, which includes tufted, fusion-bonded, woven, hand-tufted, knitted, and needle-punched processes
- Carpet fiber
- Carpet performance characteristics, including face and total weight, pile density, and appearance retention
- Density
- Thermal and acoustic considerations
- Installation
- Carpet cushion

## CARPET PERFORMANCE

| CHARACTERISTIC | REQUIREMENT (BASED ON FINISHED CARPET) | TEST METHOD |
|---|---|---|
| Average pile yarn weight (oz/sq yd) | No less than 6%, as specified | ASTM D418, *Method of Testing Pile Yarn Floor Covering Construction* |
| Tufts/sq in. | As specified | ASTM D418, *Method of Testing Pile Yarn Floor Covering Construction* |
| Pile height and/or pile height differential | As specified | ASTM D418, *Method of Testing Pile Yarn Floor Covering Construction* |
| Tuft bind | 10.0 lbf (44.5 N) for loop pile only (minimum average value) | ASTM D1335, *Test Method for Tuft Blind of Pile Floor Coverings* |
| Dry breaking strength | 100 lbf (44.5 N) for loop pile only (minimum average value) | ASTM D2646, *Standard Test Methods for Backing Fabric Characteristics of Pile Yarn Floor Coverings* |
| Delamination of secondary backing | 2.5 lbf per inch (11.1 N per 25.4 mm) (minimum average value) | ASTM D3936, *Standard Test Method for Resistance to Delamination of the Secondary Backing of Pile Yarn Floor Covering* |
| Resistance to insects (wool only) | "Resistant" | AATCC–24, *Resistance of Textiles to Insects* |
| Colorfastness to crocking | 4 minimum, wet and dry, using AATCC color transference scale | AATCC–165, *Colorfastness to Crocking: Carpets—AATCC Crockmeter Method* |
| Colorfastness to light | 4 minimum, after 40 AFU (AATCC facing units) using AATCC gray scale for color change | AATCC–16E, *Colorfastness to Light* |
| Electrostatic propensity | 3.5 KV (maximum value) for general commercial areas, 2.0 KV (maximum value) for critical environment | AATCC–134, *Electrostatic Propensity of Carpets* |
| Dimensional tolerance—width | Within 1% of specifications—physical measurements | — |

*Source: Carpet and Rug Institute; Dalton, Georgia*

## TESTING REQUIREMENTS FOR FINISHED COMMERCIAL CARPET

| CHARACTERISTIC | TEST METHOD/EXPLANATION | REQUIREMENT |
|---|---|---|
| Average pile yarn weight (oz/sq yd) | ASTM D418, *Method of Testing Pile Yarn Floor Covering Construction:* Chemically dissolves parts of the finished carpet sample to determine the pile mass or weight. Pile mass or weight includes the pile yarn, both above the primary backing and the amount hidden or buried below the backing. | As specified. |
| Tufts (per sq in.) | ASTM D418, *Method of Testing Pile Yarn Floor Covering Construction:* Determine the gauge and multiply by the stitches per inch (SPI). ASTM D418 offers instructions on counting the binding sites per unit length or width. | As specified. |
| Pile thickness or tuft height | ASTM D418, *Method of Testing Pile Yarn Floor Covering Construction:* Determine pile thickness for level loop carpet or tuft height for cut pile carpet. Accurate laboratory determination of height is important for the average pile yarn density determinations. | As specified. |
| Average pile yarn density | Calculation: Measures the amount of pile fiber by weight in a given area of carpet space. Typically calculated in ounces per cubic yard. Important element in equating quality of carpet to wearabilty, resilience, and appearance retention. | As specified. |
| Tuft bind | ASTM D1335, *Test Method for Tuft Blind of Pile Floor Coverings:* The amount of force required to pull a single carpet from its primary backing. Determines the capability of the tufted carpet to withstand zippering and snags. | The minimum average value is 10.0 lbf for loop pile. |
| Delamination strength of secondary backing | ASTM D 335, *Test Method for Delamination Strength of Secondary Backing of Pile Floor Coverings:* Measures the amount of force required to strip the secondary backing from the primary carpet structure. Measured in pounds of force per inch width. Its importance is to predict the secondary delaminating due to flexing caused by traffic or heavy rolling objects. | The minimum average value is 2.5 lbf per inch. |
| Colorfastness to crocking | Colorfastness to Crocking: Carpet—AATCC-165, Crockmeter Method: Transfer of colorant from the surface of a carpet to another surface by rubbing. The transference of color is graded against a standardized scale ranging from 5 (no color transference) to 1 (severe transference). | Rating of 4, minimum, wet and dry, using AATCC color transference scale. |
| Colorfastness to light | *Colorfastness to Light: Water-Cooled Xenon-Arc Lamp, Continuous Light,* AATCC-16, option E: Accelerated fading test using a xenon light source. After specified exposure, the specimen is graded for color loss using a 5 (no color change) to 1 (severe change) scale. | Rating of 4, minimum, after 40 AATCC fading units using AATCC gray scale for color change. |
| Electrostatic propensity | AATCC-34, *Electrostatic Propensity of Carpets:* Assesses the static-generating propensity of carpets developed when a person walks across them by laboratory simulation of conditions that may be met in practice. Static generation is dependent upon humidity condition; therefore, testing is performed at 20% relative humidity. Results are expressed as kilovolts (kV). The threshold of human sensitivity is 3.5 kV, but sensitive areas may require that a lower kV product be specified. | Less than 3.5 KV for general commercial areas. |
| Flammability | *Methenamine Pill Test;* FF 1–70 as found in 16 CFR 1630 and also ASTM D2859: Small-scale ignition test is required of all carpet for sale in the United States. | Seven passes from eight specimens tested. |
|  | Flooring Radiant Panel Test; ASTM E 648, *Test Method for Critical Radiant Flux of Floor Covering Systems Using a Radiant Heat Energy Source:* Depending upon occupancy use and local, state, or other building or fire codes, carpets for commercial use may require panel test classification (class I or II). Class I is considered to be a minimum rating of 0.45 watts per square centimeter; class II is considered to be 0.22 watts per square centimeter or greater. Most codes require only radiant panel testing for carpet to be installed in corridors and exit-way areas. | Per applicable local, state, and federal requirements. |
| Carpet tile size and thickness | Physical measurements | Typical tolerances are in the range of five thousandths of an inch (5 mils, 0.0005 in.) within 1/32 in. of dimensional specifications. |
| Carpet tile dimensional stability | *Machine-made Textile Floor Coverings—Determination of Dimensional Changes in Varying Moisture Conditions,* ISO 2551 (Aachen Test) | +/- 0.2% maximum. |

*Source: Carpet and Rug Institute; Dalton, Georgia*

# CARPET CONSTRUCTION

Carpet construction refers to the carpet manufacturing method. The three most popular construction methods for commercial carpet construction are tufting, weaving, and fusion bonding. Hand-tufted carpets are often specified for hospitality applications. Knitted and needlepunched carpets are available but less often specified.

- *Tufted carpets* account for as much as 95% of the carpet produced in the United States.
- *Woven carpets* are made on a loom using the original carpet construction method.
- *Fusion-bonded carpet tiles* dominate the carpet tile market in the United States.
- *Knitted carpets* use more face yarn than tufting.
- *Needlepunched carpets* are formed by hundreds of barbed needles punching through blankets of fiber.

# TUFTED CARPET

Since its introduction in the early 1950s, tufting has transformed the carpet industry. Compared to other carpet construction methods, tufting does not require skilled labor and requires less expensive equipment to manufacture. It is far less expensive and faster to produce than woven carpet. This process has enabled the mass production of an affordably priced, wide-width textile floor covering.

The tufted construction process is similar to sewing. Hundreds of needles stitch simultaneously through a backing material. To hold the tufted loops in place, the underside of the primary backing is coated with latex adhesive, a rubbery substance that dries hard but remains bendable. A secondary backing material is then applied.

*Primary backing materials* are the woven or nonwoven fabrics into which the tufts are inserted. They are typically olefin-based, either plain-woven or spunbonded. A thin polymer coating is often applied to bond the warp and weft threads and to minimize unraveling. Spunbonded olefin is inherently resistant to fraying or unraveling. During the tufting process, the olefin fibers are pushed aside, minimizing the distortion of the backing. This helps ensure a uniform pile height. Backings made of olefin are impervious to moisture and are mildew-resistant.

*Adhesives* used in tufted carpet are usually synthetic latex. Molten thermoplastic compounds are also used. Adhesives permanently anchor the tufts to the primary backing, preventing snags and unraveling.

*Secondary backing materials*, sometimes referred to as *scrims*, provide dimensional stability to the finished tufted carpet. A secondary backing is added for strength and stability. Secondary backing materials are often made of polypropylene, which is popular because it is moisture-resistant. Alternatives to secondary backings are attached carpet cushions, solid vinyl composites, and coatings referred to as *unitary backings*.

The standard dimension of most manufactured tufted carpet is a 12 ft (36 m) width, although some manufacturers provide 6 ft (1.8 m) and 15 ft (4.5 m) widths for special applications.

## CARPET BACKING SYSTEMS

| CONSTRUCTION METHOD | TYPICAL BACKING OR BACKING COMPONENTS | TYPICAL BACKCOATING CHEMICAL COMPOUNDS |
|---|---|---|
| Tufted | Primary<br>Woven polypropylene slit film<br>Nonwoven polypropylene or polyester | Synthetic SBR latex<br>Polyurethane<br>Polyvinyl acetate<br>Ethylene vinyl acetate<br>Polyvinyl chloride<br>Amorphous resins<br>Thermoplastic polyolefin |
| | Secondary:<br>Woven leno weave polypropylene<br>Nonwoven polypropylene or polyester<br>Woven jute<br>Fiberglass reinforcement | |
| Fusion-Bonded | Fiberglass matting | Polyvinyl chloride |
| Woven | Construction yarns may include:<br>Cotton<br>Jute<br>Polypropylene<br>Polyester<br>Viscose rayon<br>Blends or combinations | Similar materials to tufted, but usually thinner coatings |
| Hand-Tufted | Cotton canvas | Latex |
| Needlepunched | (None typically used.) | SBR latex<br>Acrylics<br>Ethylene vinyl acetate<br>SBR latex foam |

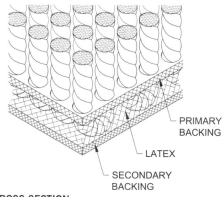

**MANUFACTURING PROCESS**

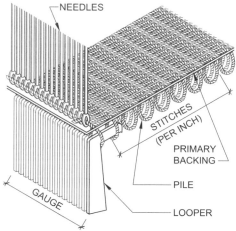

**CROSS SECTION**

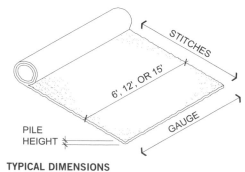

**TYPICAL DIMENSIONS**

**TUFTED CARPET**

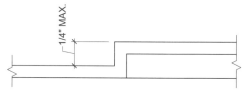

**ACCESSIBLE ROUTE CHANGES IN LEVEL UP TO ¼ IN. (6.5 MM)**

Changes in level up to ¼ in. (6.5 mm) may be vertical and without edge.

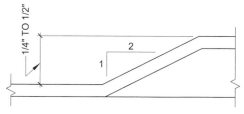

**ACCESSIBLE ROUTE CHANGES IN LEVEL BETWEEN ¼ IN. (6.5 MM) AND ½ IN. (13 MM)**

Changes in level between ¼ in. (6.5 mm) and ½ in. (13 mm) should be beveled with a slope no greater than 1:2. Changes in level greater than ½ in. (13 mm) should be accomplished by means of a ramp.

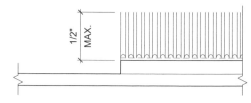

**ADA CARPET PILE THICKNESS**

Carpet having a pile height of ½ in. (13 mm) measured from the bottom of the tuft is allowed. Exposed edges should be secured and have a transition strip. Pile heights over ½ in. (13 mm) must have a transition ramp between the surfaces. Carpet should be securely attached, have a firm cushion or backing, or no cushion, and have a level loop, textured loop, level cut pile, or level cut/uncut pile.

**ADA REQUIREMENTS FOR CARPET**

## CARPET TILE

Carpet tiles provide ready access to a raised floor or easy replacement when soiled or worn. Carpet tile backing systems provide moisture barriers from the base of the pile yarn to the floor, preventing spills from penetrating to the subfloor. Backing materials include polyvinyl chloride (PVC), amorphous resins, and polyurethane cushion. The "hard backs" (PVC and amorphous resin) offer dimensional stability and seam and edge integrity for easy pattern matching. PVC backings are used most often for modular tiles.

*Fusion bonding* is the most common method of carpet tile construction. It is a thermoplastic process, whereby yarns are attached to a backing material by means of adhesion rather than stitching (as in tufted carpet) or weaving. The adhesive is applied to the backing material, and the yarns are implanted in it. Because the yarn is typically embedded between two parallel backings that must be sliced apart, fusion-bonded carpet is necessarily cut pile.

Fusion-bonded carpet has the greatest percentage of yarn available for wear, but is more expensive than tufted carpet. The cut pile construction of fusion bonding offers greater pile densities at comparable yarn weights than tufted constructions.

Carpet tiles are installed with standard adhesives, releasable adhesives, and mill-applied peel-and-stick adhesives. Carpet tile installation is easier and causes less downtime and productivity loss than traditional carpet installation. Systems furniture divider panels and office furniture do not have to be removed, but are simply lifted with a "jack" system. The tiles are then installed underneath the furniture while it remains in place.

## WOVEN CARPET

Weaving, the traditional carpet construction method, produces carpet on a loom, integrating the pile and backing yarns during the carpet construction. Most woven carpet is dimensionally stable as a result of the weaving process and does not require a secondary backing, as tufted carpet does. Weaving accounts for less than 2% of the carpet market in the United States. Its primary use is in the hospitality industry, where long-term durability and intricate pattern detail are primary considerations. There are three basic types of weaving processes: *velvet, Wilton,* and *Axminster.*

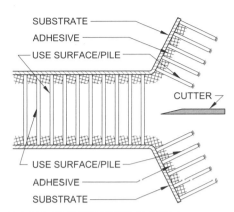

**I-METHOD MANUFACTURING PROCESS**

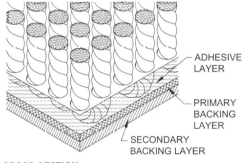

**CROSS SECTION**

**FUSION-BONDED CARPET**

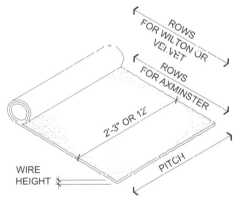

**TYPICAL DIMENSIONS**

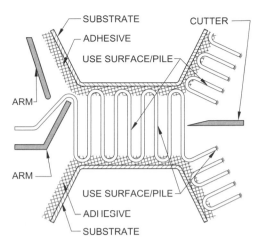

**U-METHOD MANUFACTURING PROCESS**

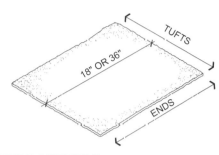

**TYPICAL DIMENSIONS**

### AXMINSTER SPECIFICATIONS

| APPLICATION | PITCH | ROW | WEIGHT OZ/SQ YD |
|---|---|---|---|
| Guest rooms | 7 | 6 | 28 |
| | 7 | 7 | 32 |
| Corridors | 8 | 7 | 37.75 |
| Ballrooms | 8 | 8 | 42 |
| Banks | 8 | 9 | 48 |
| Casino floors | 8 | 9 | 48 |
| Slot machine areas | 8 | 10 | 53.5 |

*Source: Soroush Custom Rugs; Kensington, Maryland*

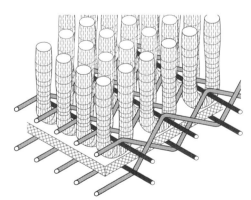

**VELVET CROSS SECTION**
Velvet carpets are made on looms similar to Wilton looms, but without the Jacquard mechanism, so intricate details and elaborate patterns are not available.

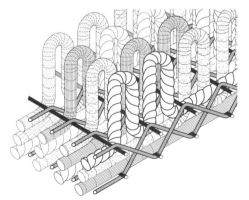

**WILTON CROSS SECTION**
Wilton carpets are limited to about five changes in yarn color. A Wilton carpet is thick and heavy because every color yarn used is carried beneath the pile surface.

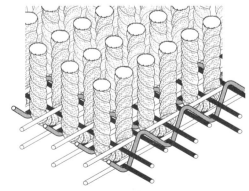

**AXMINSTER CROSS SECTION**
Patterns and colors for Axminster carpets are virtually limitless, because the colored yarns are inserted individually as they are required by the design. Axminsters are cut pile face construction.

**WOVEN CARPET**

## HAND-TUFTED CARPET

Hand-tufted rugs are most often custom-designed for a specific space. They are commonly made of wool and are popular for hospitality and high-end residential applications. Wool yarns are often dyed specifically for the hand-tufted rug. Hand-tufted rugs are made by inserting tufts one at a time by hand, with a tufting gun, into a backing, which is typically cotton canvas. The tufts are not in parallel rows as in machine tufting or weaving. The back of a completed, hand-tufted custom rug is coated with latex. The surface of the rug is finished by one of the following processes:

- *Tip-sheared rugs* are produced by cutting random loops that project beyond the surface of the rug. This process adds texture and visual interest to the level finished surface of the rug.
- *Cut-and-loop rugs* are continuously tufted like single-pile rugs. Those portions of the rug surface that will be cut pile are tufted in a deeper pile height and then cut down to the height of the loop surface.
- *Carved rugs* incorporate three-dimensional designs into the rug surface. After the tufting process is complete, electrically operated shears are used to cut patterns in the rug surface.

**Nonrectilinear hand-tufted shapes:** Unlike tufted or woven carpets, custom shapes and edge configurations are available in hand-tufted rugs. Hand-tufted rugs are often used in circular or other nonrectilinear applications and on spiral stair treads, where each tread carpet is different. An unlimited number of colors is possible, and intricate custom designs are often incorporated.

## KNITTED CARPET

As in the construction of woven carpet, the knitting process integrates pile and backing yarns in one operation. Needles are used to interlace yarns in a series of connecting loops, similar to the hand-knitting process. Knitted carpets are known for their plush piles, because there is more yarn in the wear surface than tufted carpets. Knitted carpet has a tendency to stretch, especially on the diagonal, and is difficult to seam during installation. Knitted carpet represents a very small percentage of the carpet produced in the United States.

## NEEDLEPUNCHED CARPET

Needlepunching is achieved by layering thick fiber batts, typically polypropylene, over a support fabric. Hundreds of barbed needles punch through the support fabric, compressing and entangling the fibers. Needlepunched carpets are permeable, which presents a problem when liquids are spilled on a wall-to-wall interior installation. The most common application of needlepunched carpet is outdoor carpet.

### HAND-TUFTED CARPET SPECIFICATIONS

| TYPICAL APPLICATIONS | PILE | |
|---|---|---|
| **HIGH-TRAFFIC PUBLIC SPACES AND RESIDENTIAL SPACES** | | |
| Standard traffic lobbies | Content | 100% semiworsted wool |
| Board rooms | Face weight | 56 oz/yd |
| Meeting rooms | Total weight | +/- 105 oz/yd |
| Bar areas | Pile height | 15/64 in. (6 mm) |
| Club rooms | Total thickness | 5/16 in. (8 mm) |
| Royal and presidential hotel suites | | |
| Grand staircases | | |
| **VERY HIGH-TRAFFIC PUBLIC SPACES** | | |
| Busy hotel lobbies | Content | 100% semiworsted wool |
| Casinos | Face weight | 72 oz/yd |
| Reception areas | Total weight | +/- 125 oz/yd |
| Lounge areas | Pile height | 18/64 in. (7 mm) |
| Ballrooms | Total thickness | 25/64 in. (10 mm) |
| Main corridors in luxury facilities | | |
| Business service areas in hospitality facilities | | |
| Grand staircases | | |
| **EXTREMELY HEAVY-TRAFFIC PUBLIC SPACES** | | |
| Hotel lobbies that also function as casino entrances | Content | 100% semiworsted wool |
| | Face weight | 88 oz/yd |
| Main promenade areas | Total weight | +/- 140 oz/yd |
| | Pile height | 18/64 in. (7 mm) |
| | Total thickness | 23/64 in. (9 mm) |

*Source: Soroush Custom Rugs; Kensington, Maryland*

### WOOL CARPET PILE WEIGHT DENSITY

| TYPE OF TRAFFIC | AMOUNT OF TRAFFIC | LOCATION | PILE WEIGHT DENSITY | PROJECTED LIFE EXPECTATION (IN YEARS) |
|---|---|---|---|---|
| Light | Up to 1,500 passages/week (250/day) | Hotel guest rooms, private offices, small meeting rooms | 80–114 | 5–7 |
| Medium | 1,500–5,000 passages/week (250–750/day) | Hotel guest corridors, conference rooms, small shops, larger offices | 115–149 | 5–7 |
| Heavy | 5,000–15,000 passages/week (750–2,500/day) | Restaurants, larger function rooms, open-plan offices, large shops, hotel main corridors | 150–199 | 5–7 |
| Very heavy | 15,000+ passages/week (2,500+/day) | Hotel lobbies, office entrance areas, department stores (ground floor), cash register counters, bars | 200+ | 5–7 |

*Source: Soroush Custom Rugs; Kensington, Maryland*

For specifying Axminster, Wilton, and hand-tufted wool carpets.

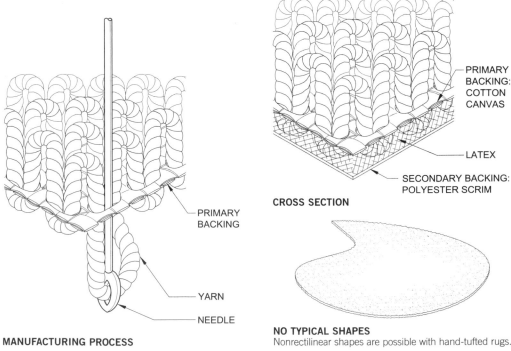

PRIMARY BACKING

YARN

NEEDLE

**MANUFACTURING PROCESS**

PRIMARY BACKING: COTTON CANVAS

LATEX

SECONDARY BACKING: POLYESTER SCRIM

**CROSS SECTION**

**NO TYPICAL SHAPES**
Nonrectilinear shapes are possible with hand-tufted rugs.

**HAND-TUFTED CARPET**

## CARPET FIBERS

A fiber is the fine, hairlike strand that forms the basis of a yarn. Fibers are found in nature or are manufactured (synthetic) and are categorized by their length as either staple or filament.

- *Staple fibers* are short, typically measured in centimeters or inches. All natural fibers except silk are staple fibers.
- *Filament fibers* are long and continuous. Because synthetic fibers are produced by extruding chemical solutions through a showerheadlike device called a *spinerette,* they are filament fibers. However, they can be cut to staple fiber lengths.

Yarns are formed by twisting fibers together to create a continuous strand. Yarns are classified in two types: *spun* and *filament.* Spun yarns are composed of staple fibers twisted together. Filament yarns are composed of continuous strands made from either a spinerette-generated synthetic fiber or from silk. *Bulked continuous filament* (BCF) yarns are continuous strands of synthetic fiber that are formed into yarn bundles without the need for spinning, which is required for all natural and staple synthetic fibers. BCF generally offers better wear, but staple fibers provide the much-sought-after "wool-like" appearance.

### Yarn Designations

Yarn designations express the relationship between length and weight. The denier system is used for filament yarns; the yarn count system is used for spun yarns.

#### Denier

Denier is a unit of yarn measurement equal to the weight in grams of 9,000 meters of the yarn. The higher the denier, the heavier the yarn and generally the better the strength, resiliency, and abrasion resistance. Heavier-filament yarns are designated by higher denier numbers. For example, a 15-denier yarn would be suitable for sheer hosiery; a 2,200-denier yarn would be suitable for carpet.

#### Yarn Count

The yarn count system is a relative gauge of a spun yarn's weight. Heavier yarns are designated by lower yarn count numbers. For example, a 70-count yarn is quite fine, whereas a 10-count yarn is thick and heavy.

## Carpet Fiber Types

### Acrylic

Acrylic was one of the first synthetic fibers to be used successfully in the production of carpet. However, because the color and texture of acrylic fiber can be glossy and harsh, and because acrylic carpet pile crushes easily, it is no longer recommended for use as a commercial carpet fiber.

### Nylon

Nylon is the most popular carpet fiber. Nylon has excellent wearability, abrasion resistance, and resilience; solution-dyed nylon is also resistant to harsh cleaning chemicals and sunlight fading. However, because of nylon's excellent durability, appearance retention is a concern. Long before a nylon carpet wears out, its appearance can be permanently ruined.

### Polypropylene

Polypropylene is the lightest commercial carpet fiber. Polypropylenes are known for their excellent stain and mildew resistance, low moisture absorbency, excellent colorfastness in sunlight, and high strength. They also minimize static electricity. Olefin is a polypropylene. Polypropylene is commonly used in outdoor carpeting.

### Polyester

Polyester fibers are known for their color clarity and their capability to retain color. More popular for residential carpet applications than for commercial uses, polyester has a luxurious feel.

### Wool

Used for centuries in the manufacturing of carpet, wool is still the standard against which other carpet fibers are judged. It is generally the most expensive carpet fiber and is commonly used in woven carpets. When exposed to flame, wool chars, rather than melting like most synthetic fibers, making it naturally flame-resistant. It dyes well and has good resistance to soil and wear.

### Sisal

Sisal is a strong, woody fiber produced from the leaves of the agave plant, which is found in Central America, the West Indies, and Africa. Used mostly in twine and rope, it has become a popular contemporary flooring fiber.

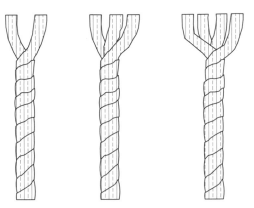

Ply is the number of single strands of spun yarn twisted together to form the yarn. Ply is not a measure of quality, but will affect the appearance of a carpet. Higher-ply counts give a coarser, nubbier texture.

**CARPET YARN PLIES**

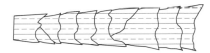

WOOL

NYLON

The outer layer of a wool fiber is scaly, which diffuses light, thus hiding soil. The inner core is composed of long, rounded cells that provide the elasticity essential for excellent appearance retention.

Nylon is extruded through a showerheadlike device called a *spinerette.* Nylon fibers are smooth and tend to be reflective or shiny.

**WOOL AND NYLON FIBER**

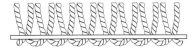

**CUT PILE**
Cut pile yarns are at the same height.

**LEVEL LOOP**
Uncut pile yarns are at the same height. Level loop has a pebbled surface texture that hides footprints and chair caster marks.

**CUT AND LOOP**
Sculptural effect is created.

**RANDOM TIP-SHEARED**
Tonal contrasts between cut and uncut loops of varying heights are produced in random tip-sheared yarn.

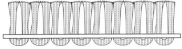

**VELVET OR PLUSH**
Velvet or plush has a smooth, cut pile. Yarn ends blend together for a consistent surface appearance. This pile type shows footprints and shading marks.

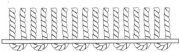

**SAXONY**
Saxony is similar to velvet pile but has twisted yarn, which gives definition to each tuft. The loops are cut during the construction process. Saxonies are made with heat-set yarn, usually in a dense, low-pile construction. This pile type shows footprints and shading marks.

**MULTILEVEL LOOP**
Uncut pile yarns are at varying heights.

**FRIEZE**
Frieze (pronounced *free-zay*) is a tightly twisted, heat-set yarn that hides dirt well.

Pile consists of yarns or fibers projecting from a substrate, acting as a wear surface. The selection of a pile type depends on the desired visual effect and performance expectations.

**PILE TYPES**

## CARPET DENSITY

Density, the amount of pile yarn in unit volume of carpet, is influenced by gauge—stitches per inch across the width—yarn size or thickness, and pile height. A larger yarn can be tufted at a wider gauge and receive the same density as a fine yarn at a small gauge. For areas where heavy foot traffic is likely, a density of 5,000 to 7,000 or more may be necessary. Office spaces with moderate traffic require a density of 4,000 to 6,000. Because of the fundamental differences in the manufacturing processes, different terms are used to describe carpet density for each type of carpet construction.

### Density Measurements for Tufted Carpet

**Widthwise Density Measurement**

*Gauge* is the measure of the spacing of the tufting needles, center to center, across the width of the carpet. Gauge is measured in fractions of an inch. For example, ⅛-gauge means that the tufting needles are spaced ⅛ in. (3 mm) apart, producing eight yarn ends per inch.

**Lengthwise Density Measurement**

*Stitches* define the number of ends tufted by the needles down the length of the carpet. Generally, the number of stitches per inch and the number of needles per inch are approximately the same. *Pile height* is the length of a tuft from the backing surface to the tip of the tuft. It is measured in fractions of an inch. Although a deep pile may provide a more luxurious feel underfoot, it also has a greater tendency to crush and show wear.

### Density Measurements for Woven Carpet

**Widthwise Density Measurement**

*Pitch* is the number of ends in a 27 in. (685 mm) width of carpet. A yarn loop in the surface of a carpet is referred to as an *end*. The pitch can be divided by 27 to compare widthwise density with that of a tufted carpet. For example, if the pitch is 216, it is divided by 27, which equals eight ends per inch, or ⅛-gauge in a tufted carpet.

**Lengthwise Density Measurement**

The terms *rows* in Axminster, and *wires* in Wilton and velvet carpets, refer to the number of ends per inch lengthwise. In woven carpet, the pile height is referred to as the *wire height*, referring to the height of the steel blades in the loom on which the tufts are formed. Wire height is stated in decimals of an inch.

## CARPET TRAFFIC CLASS RECOMMENDATIONS

| AREA | TRAFFIC CLASS |
|---|---|
| **Airports** | |
| Administrative offices | I |
| Corridors/all public and ticket areas | III |
| **Banks** | |
| Executive offices | I |
| Lobbies | II–III |
| Corridors | II–III |
| Teller windows | III |
| **Convention Centers** | |
| Auditoriums | II–III |
| Corridors and lobbies | III |
| **Places of Worship** | |
| Churches, synagogues, mosques, etc. | I–II |
| Meeting rooms | II |
| Lobbies | II–III |
| **Golf Clubs** | |
| Locker rooms/pro shops | III |
| Other Areas | II–III |
| **Health Care Areas** | |
| Executive/administrative offices | I–II |
| Patients rooms/lounges | II |
| Lobbies/corridors/nurses stations | III |
| **Hotels/Motels/Apartments** | |
| Rooms | I |
| Corridors | II |
| Lobbies | III |
| **Libraries/Museums/Art Galleries** | |
| Administrative offices | I |
| Public areas | II–III |
| **Office Buildings** | |
| Executive or private offices | I |
| Clerical areas | II |
| Corridors | II–III |
| Cafeteria | III |
| **Restaurants** | |
| Dining areas/lobbies | III |
| **Retail Stores** | |
| Windows and display areas | I |
| Minor aisles/boutiques/specialized departments | II |
| Major aisles/checkouts/ supermarkets, etc. | III |
| **Schools and Colleges** | |
| Administrative offices | I |
| Classrooms/dormitories | II |
| Corridors/cafeteria | III |

*Source: BASF; Dalton, Georgia*

## CARPET TRAFFIC CLASSIFICATION

| CLASS | TRAFFIC | WALK-ONS PER DAY | DESCRIPTION | EXAMPLES |
|---|---|---|---|---|
| I | Light | Up to 500 | Areas that undergo a limited amount of traffic and where there is some soiling | Executive offices, hotel bedrooms |
| II | Heavy | 500–1,000 | Areas that undergo frequent traffic flowing in the same direction and where there is heavy dirt, grit, twisting, turning, and spillage | Hotel corridors, auditoriums, school classrooms |
| III | Extra Heavy | More than 1,000 | Areas that are subject to extremely frequent and concentrated traffic flowing in the same direction and where there is severe dirt, grit, twisting, turning, heavy rolling, and spillage | Airports, bank teller window areas |

*Source: BASF; Dalton, Georgia*

## CARPET DENSITY GUIDELINES

| PILE TYPE | CLASS I | | CLASS II | | CLASS III | |
|---|---|---|---|---|---|---|
| | WEIGHT OZ/SQ YD | DENSITY OZ/CU YD | WEIGHT OZ/SQ YD | DENSITY OZ/CU YD | WEIGHT OZ/SQ YD | DENSITY OZ/CU YD |
| Level loop | 16 | 3,600 | 20 | 4,200 | 24 | 4,800 |
| Cut/loop | 20 | 3,600 | 24 | 4,200 | 28 | 4,800 |
| Cut pile, not heat-set | 28 | 3,800 | 33 | 4,500 | 38 | 5,000 |
| Cut pile, heat-set | 28 | 3,800 | 35 | 4,500 | 43 | 5,000 |

*Source: BASF; Dalton, Georgia*

Cut and loop pile type requires 100% latex penetration. Cut and loop with more than 50% cut surface should meet cut pile guidelines.

## GAUGE OR PITCH

| GAUGE | NEEDLES (ENDS) PER INCH | PITCH |
|---|---|---|
| ⅜ | 2.7 | 73 |
| ¼ | 4 | 108 |
| 3⁄16 | 5.3 | 144 |
| 5⁄32 | 6.4 | 173 |
| ⅛ | 8 | 216 |
| 1⁄10 | 10 | 270 |
| 5⁄64 | 12.8 | 346 |
| 1⁄16 | 16 | 432 |
| 1⁄20 | 20 | 540 |
| 1⁄25 | 25 | 675 |

To convert gauge to pitch, multiply needles (ends) per inch by 27; for example, 1⁄10-gauge is equivalent to 270 pitch, or 10 ends per inch × 27; ⅛-gauge is eight ends of yarn per inch × 27 = 216 pitch.

## CARPET PERFORMANCE

Wear resistance of a carpet, like that of other textiles, is affected by many factors, such as the face and total weight, pile density, type and length of the fiber, structure of the yarn, and the construction of the carpet.

*Face weight,* also referred to as *pile weight* or *yarn weight,* is the weight of the pile yarn in ounces per square yard of carpet. It does not include the weight of the backings or coating. The face weight describes the amount of yarn in the wear surface of the carpet.

*Total weight,* or *finished weight,* includes the face weight and the weight of backing materials, finishes, and coatings. It is expressed in ounces per square yard of carpet. Total weight is less an indication of quality than of face weight.

*Pile density* is the weight of pile yarn in a given volume of carpet face. It is determined by the number and size of the carpet tufts. Pile density is the most important selection factor in high-traffic installations. For example, nylon is a very durable fiber; however, if the pile density of a nylon carpet is too low, crushing can occur; and although the nylon may succeed in performance, it can fail in appearance. Average pile density is determined by the following formula:

$$D \text{ (oz/cu yd)} = \frac{36 \times W \text{ (oz/sq yd)}}{T \text{ (in)}}$$

[$D$ (oz/cu yd) ÷ 26,944.67 = g/cu cm], in which $D$ is the density, $W$ is the pile yarn weight, and $T$ is the pile height or thickness.

*Pile yarn* is the most expensive component in carpet manufacturing. For a given weight, a lower pile height and a higher pile density provide the greatest performance value. The industry standard for measuring average pile yarn weight, tufts per square inch, and average pile density is ASTM D418, *Standard Methods for Testing Pile Yarn Floor Covering Construction.*

*Abrasion resistance* is sometimes used as a relative measure of a carpet's durability. ASTM D3884, *Standard Test Method for Abrasion Resistance of Textile Fabrics (Rotary Platform, Double-Head Method),* describes the procedures for the Taber Abraser test, named after the company that manufactures the test equipment. In this test, a sample is abraded using a rotary rubbing action. As the sample rotates on a turntablelike platform, two emery wheels rub against the carpet, one rubbing outward and the other inward toward the center of the sample. The results of the test are typically reported in terms of number of cycles (revolutions of the turntable) required to expose the backing material. Because modern synthetic fibers are highly resistant to abrasive wear, wear resistance is not tested for as often as appearance retention.

*Appearance retention* tests aim to simulate floor traffic with mechanical devices. Pile appearance changes due to wear are commonly tested by either of two methods: the hexapod tumbler test or the Vettermann Drum Test. The Vettermann Drum Test is defined by ASTM D5417, *Standard Practice for Operation of the Vettermann Drum Tester.* A steel ball with 14 rubber studs rolls randomly over a carpet sample mounted inside a rotating drum. ASTM D5252, *Standard Practice for the Operation of the Hexapod Drum Tester,* describes the requirements for the hexapod (meaning six-legged) test. It is similar to the Vettermann Drum Test, except that a 1.97 in. (50 mm) metal cube, with a polyurethane stud screwed into each of its six faces, rolls over the carpet surface.

*Watermarking or pooling,* a phenomenon in the carpet industry associated primarily with cut pile carpet, is so called because a pool of water appears to be sitting on the carpet. It tends to be most noticeable with solid-color carpets installed in large open areas. Watermarking is not a manufacturer's defect. There is no known cause or remedy for watermarking. One of the theories of watermarking is that of subfloor irregularities, but various other theories exist. Where a cut pile carpet is preferred, the client should be notified in writing that watermarking may occur.

*Static control,* the electrostatic discharge properties of carpet, may need to be considered where sensitive electronic or computer equipment is in use. Static electricity is created by the friction of rubbing materials together—for example, the sole of a shoe and carpet fiber. Static electricity does not become apparent until the relative humidity drops below 40%. There are two methods for enhancing the electrostatic discharge properties of carpet: the incorporation of a conductive filament, typically carbon-loaded nylon, or the application of topical treatments.

Carpet with integral static-inhibiting fibers should comply with American Association of Textile Chemists and Colorists (AATCC) Test Method–134, *Electrostatic Propensity of Carpets.* This test is a laboratory simulation that assesses the static-generating tendency developed when a person walks across a carpet. Testing is performed at 20% ±2% relative humidity.

Carpet with static-resistant topical treatments do not generally provide reliable electrostatic discharge under all conditions. Topical finishes may be water-soluble and can lose effectiveness after repeated washings. They can also cause carpet to soil at an accelerated rate.

### CARPET STATIC GENERATION

| APPLICATION | MAXIMUM STATIC GENERATION |
|---|---|
| Residential | 5.0 KV |
| General commercial | 3.5 KV |
| Critical commercial | 2.0 KV |

### Carpet in Golf Club Houses and Athletic Facilities

- Specify cut pile rather than loop construction with a minimum pile height of 7/16 in.
- Dense carpet construction is important. Specify a minimum fiber weight of 45 ounces per square yard and a minimum density of 5,000 ounces of pile fiber per cubic yard.
- Contact manufacturers about the appropriateness of any product to be installed in areas where soft spike shoes are allowed. Specifically, always select engineered and tested products.
- Select solution-dyed fiber for colorfastness where there is a concern about fading from sunlight or color loss from chemicals.
- Carpet used outdoors should be designed to resist ultraviolet fading and degradation.

*Source: Carpet and Rug Institute; Dalton, Georgia*

## MINIMUM AVERAGE SPECIFICATIONS FOR CARPET IN SCHOOLS

| CARPET PROPERTY/ CHARACTERISTIC | MINIMUM SPECIFICATIONS | TEST METHOD |
|---|---|---|
| Type yarn | Solution or yarn-dyed | — |
| Color | Multicolored products (Select colors complementary to soil type/color in region) | — |
| Surface/style | Level loop, multilevel loop, textured loop, or cut and loop. Cut pile may be satisfactory for administrative areas. | — |
| Appearance-retention rating static | ≥3.5 (Vetterman 22K cycles or Hexapod 12K cycles) 3.5KV (maximum—not to exceed) | CRI TM–101 AATCC–134 Step Method |
| Indoor air quality (IAQ) | CRI IAQ Certification | CRI Test Program ASTM D5116 |

*Note:* In glue-down installation, include CRI IAQ Testing Program label for installation adhesives. For carpet over cushion, include CRI IAQ Testing Program label for carpet cushion.

| | | |
|---|---|---|
| Flammability–Radiant Panel Test | Class II (minimum) (Class I in some locations) (or per building code) | ASTM E648 |
| NBS smoke | <450 flaming mode | ASTM E662 |
| Tuft bind (dry) | 8 lbs, all products (16–20 lbs suggested for unitary backing) | ASTM D1335 |
| Delamination | Secondary backed products, 3.5 lbs | ASTM D3936 |
| Dimensional stability | Removable modular products, 0.2% or less | ISO 2551 |
| Colorfastness: light | 4 or better (60 AFU three cycles) | AATCC–16-E |
| Colorfastness: ozone | 4 or better after two cycles | AATCC–129 |
| Colorfastness: crocking | 4 or better (wet and dry) | AATCC–165 |
| Colorfastness: water | 4 or better, AATCC Transference Scale (only yarn-dyed carpets) | AATCC–107 (grade change in color and staining) |
| Soil-resistant treatment | Minimum average of 350 ppm fluorine on pile fiber of three separate tests | CRI TM-102 |

*Source: Carpet and Rug Institute; Dalton, Georgia*

## CARPET INSTALLATION

There are two types of carpet installation: *stretch-in* and *adhesive*. For broadloom carpet, there are three types of adhesive installation: *direct glue-down, double glue-down,* and the newest installation type, *self-stick.* Releasable adhesives can facilitate carpet repair or replacement.

### Stretch-In Installation

Stretch-in installation is the traditional method of carpet installation, whereby the carpet is stretched over a cushion and attached at the perimeter with a tack strip. This is the most common installation method for residential applications and is used commercially for woven wool carpets and in areas where underfoot comfort and luxury are required (for example, hotel lobbies and boardrooms). Stretch-in applications allow for easy removal and replacement of the carpet and cushion. Because stretch-in carpet is secured only around the perimeter, such installations can ripple, causing accessibility problems, hence they may not be appropriate for large areas and heavy commercial or rolling traffic.

Power stretchers are used to put the carpet in tension and stretch it drum-tight. The carpet should be stretched to its fullest to withstand changes in temperature and humidity and other stresses. Cushion selection should be coordinated with the carpet manufacturer to ensure that the carpet warranty is not voided.

### Adhesive Installation

#### Direct Glue-Down

The most common method of commercial installation, direct glue-down is economical and practical. The carpet is glued directly to the floor without a cushion. This is the most dimensionally stable installation method and is often required for stair or ramp applications, even if different installation methods are specified for other areas of the project. Proper substrate conditions are imperative for a successful glue-down installation. Uneven substrates can cause irregular wear patterns.

#### Double Glue-Down

This installation method combines the underfoot comfort of stretch-in installation with the stability of the direct glue-down method. The carpet cushion is adhered to the floor, then the carpet is glued to the cushion. With either the direct or the double glue-down method, admitting traffic before the adhesive has had time to cure can cause the installation to fail. Hardboard or plywood is typically recommended as protection for an adhesive installation, because covering a new adhesive installation with plastic sheeting may prevent proper curing and cause mold or mildew to develop.

#### Self-Stick

This is the latest development in carpet installation techniques. A flexible adhesive layer is applied to the carpet backing and is covered with a protective plastic film. The labor involved in adhesive application and the time required to ensure the proper tackiness are eliminated. This type of carpet type typically comes in smaller widths, about 6 ft (1.8 m), for ease of manipulation during layout and installation.

---

### Advantages of Stretch-in Carpet Installation

- Patterned carpet is easier to match.
- It is more resilient than direct glue-down.
- It extends carpet life.
- It is less crushing and packing of pile.
- It adds insulation value (R-value).
- It gives higher sound absorbency (NRC) values.
- It responds better to vacuuming.
- It can be used over floors that may be unacceptable for direct glue-down.
- Removal usually costs less than removal of a direct glue-down installation.
- Corrective measures, such as seam repair, are easier to perform.

---

### Advantages of Direct Glue-Down Carpet Installation

- Cushion cost is eliminated.
- Labor for direct glue-down is usually less expensive.
- It is suitable for rolling traffic and ramp areas.
- Seams are more durable because there is no vertical flex.
- Buckling is minimized in buildings that have heat and air conditioning turned off for extended periods, such as schools, churches, and theaters.
- There are no restretch situations.
- It facilitates access to electrical and telephone lines under the floor.
- Seam peaking is practically eliminated.
- It is unrestricted as to size of area.
- It has intricate border and inlay capabilities.

If carpet with an attached cushion is installed with the direct glue-down method, the following additional considerations apply:

- Improved appearance retention and foot comfort compared to direct glue-down (with no attached cushion) installations
- Increased delamination strength and improved edge ravel resistance
- Functionality as an effective moisture barrier
- Improved thermal and acoustical contribution
- Elimination of second adhesive requirement for double glue-down installation

---

### Advantages of Double Glue-Down Carpet Installation

- The stability of direct glue-down carpet is combined with the cushioning benefits of a separate cushion, stretch-in installation.
- Carpet appearance retention, comfort under foot, and overall performance is improved compared to direct glue-down installations.
- Carpet bordering and inlay is simplified.
- Double glue-down installations are suitabel for wheeled traffic area.
- Size of installation area is not restricted.

---

## CARPET TILE INSTALLATION

There are three methods of carpet tile installation: *free-lay, full-glue,* and with a *tile that has a preapplied pressure-sensitive adhesive coating.* In free-lay installations, a strip of adhesive is applied about every 15 ft (4.5 m) and around the room perimeter. Tiles in those areas are anchored in place, and surrounding tiles are

---

butted snugly against each other. Full-glue installations should be specified where heavy or wheeled traffic is anticipated. In this case, tiles are typically installed with a "stair-step" technique. The installation grows from the center of the room.

## COLORING METHODS

Carpet coloring is accomplished by predyeing the carpet fibers before the carpet is manufactured, or *postdyeing* the finished piece of carpet. Most carpet is postdyed, because this process allows manufacturers to respond quickly to the needs of the market.

### Predyeing Methods

*Solution dyeing* is commonly preferred in areas subject to sunlight fading or spills, because the color is integral to the fiber. The dye is combined with the fiber chemicals before the extrusion process. The color of solution-dyed yarn is consistent throughout the fiber. Solution-dyed yarns have excellent colorfastness qualities against both sunlight and crocking, and can withstand cleaning with harsh chemicals. Polyester and nylon are sometimes solution-dyed, but polypropylene is the fiber most commonly dyed in this manner. Solution-dyed yarn holds a large share of the commercial market but only a small portion of the residential market.

*Stock dyeing,* the oldest method of fiber coloring, is still popular for wool. Staple fibers are placed in large kettles, and the dye is circulated through the fiber. Stock dyeing applies the color to the staple fibers before they are spun into yarn. The color of stock-dyed yarns varies slightly from batch to batch. During the spinning operation, fibers from different dye lots are combined, providing a depth of color not achievable with solution-dyed fibers.

*Skein dyeing* is a coloring process that applies color after the fibers have been spun into yarn. Skein dyeing is labor-intensive and has limited dye lot capacities. These factors can result in higher dyeing costs than other methods. Skein dyeing is commonly used in dyeing yarn for woven carpets.

### Postdyeing Methods

The application of color to greige goods, or undyed carpet, immersed in a dye bath is called *piece dyeing.* After the carpet has been tufted onto its primary backing, and before a secondary backing has been attached, the carpet is dyed. Piece dyeing is generally used for solid-color carpets, but a limited range of patterns are possible by using fibers varying in their propensity to accept different dyes.

## PRINTING

Patterns can be applied to carpet (printed) after the finishing process. Printed carpet simulates the intricate patterns of woven carpet at a much lower cost. *Screen printing,* the most widely used printing methods for textiles, is generally faster and more accurate than other printing methods. Color is forced through a perforated plate onto the surface of the carpet as it rolls by. *Jet printing* utilizes rows of very closely spaced jets that spray the carpet with color as it passes by. The texture of jet-printed carpet is often preferred because, unlike screen printing, this process does not crush the carpet pile.

## ACOUSTICAL CONSIDERATIONS

Carpet is an important component of the contemporary open office space because of its sound-deadening properties. In office applications, noise created by discussions, office equipment, and furniture movement can effectively be absorbed by the proper selection of carpet and carpet cushion. In hotels, carpeted guest rooms significantly reduce the sound transmissions to the rooms below. In churches and theaters, the noise generated by latecomers can be lessened without altering the carefully engineered acoustics of the space.

One of carpet's most important contributions to the appeal of a space is its acoustical properties. These acoustical properties are measured in three ways:

- Noise Reduction Coefficient (NRC)
- Impact Noise Rating (INR)
- Impact Insulation Class (IIC)

### Sound Absorption

The Noise Reduction Coefficient (NRC) is the average of four absorption coefficients measured at frequencies from low- to high-pitched sounds and rounded off to the closest 5%. The NRC is determined by ASTM C423, *Standard Method of Sound Absorption and Sound Absorption Coefficients by the Reverberation Room Method*. The NRC is used in calculating the required amount of sound-absorbing material and can be used to compare the sound-absorption qualities of one material with another. The higher the NRC, the greater the sound absorption.

Cut pile carpets are somewhat more effective in absorbing sound than loop piles. The fiber content of the carpet has little effect on its capability to absorb sound.

### Noise Transmission

The Impact Noise Rating (INR) represents the sound insulation provided by a floor-ceiling assembly from an impact noise. Sound levels are measured in an isolated room below. The data are related to a minimum standard of 0 INR. Assembly ratings less than 0 are considered unsatisfactory. Assembly ratings more than 0 are deemed superior.

The Impact Insulation Class (IIC) also measures the sound insulation of a floor-ceiling assembly, but the IIC differs from the INR, not in the test procedure, but in the numerical scale applied. IIC rates floor-ceiling assemblies with positive numbers only in ascending order of efficiency. The higher the value, the less noise transmitted. An IIC value can be estimated by adding 51 to the INR value.

## THERMAL CONSIDERATIONS

Carpet contributes to the thermal insulation of a space. The total R-value of a carpet is more dependent on the total thickness of the carpet than the fiber content.

When the carpet R-value is not available, multiply the total carpet thickness measured in inches by a factor of 2.6 to approximate the carpet's R-value. R-values can be considered additive for any combination of materials. For example, a combination of carpet with an R-value of 1.3 and a prime polyurethane cushion with an R-value of 1.6 will yield an overall R-value of 2.9.

## INDOOR AIR QUALITY AND CARPET

Some people report allergy or flulike symptoms when exposed to emissions from new construction, including carpet, carpet cushion, and installation adhesives. Limited research to date has found no link between adverse health effects and the levels of chemicals emitted by the installation of new carpet.

To reduce the exposure of these pollutants, however, the Carpet and Rug Institute recommends that the ventilation system in public and commercial buildings be operated at maximum outdoor airflow before, during, and for 48 to 72 hours after new carpet installation. In homes, it is recommended that windows be left open, if possible, and that fans be used to increase the airflow. It is also recommended that carpet be installed when the area is not in use.

### CARPET R-VALUES

| FIBER TYPE | YARN TYPE | STYLE | PILE HEIGHT (IN.) | PILE WEIGHT (OZ/SQ YD) | GAUGE | STITCHES PER INCH (SPI) | TUFTS/ SQ IN. SPI X GA | R-VALUE |
|---|---|---|---|---|---|---|---|---|
| Nylon | CF | LL | .125 | 10 | $\frac{1}{10}$ | 8.0 | 80 | 0.68 |
| Nylon | CF | LL | .109 | 20 | $\frac{1}{8}$ | 6.0 | 48 | 0.65 |
| Nylon | CF | LL | .192 | 28 | $\frac{1}{8}$ | 8.4 | 67.2 | 0.67 |
| Nylon | CF | LL | .125 | 24 | $\frac{1}{10}$ | 8.6 | 86 | 0.55 |
| Nylon | S | Plush | .250 | 24 | $\frac{1}{8}$ | 11.0 | 88 | 1.12 |
| Nylon | CF | HLL | — | 24 | $\frac{5}{32}$ | 8.6 | 55 | 1.33 |
| Nylon | CF | Shag | 1.07 | 24 | $\frac{3}{16}$ | 5.2 | 27.7 | 1.51 |
| Acrylic | S | LL | .210 | 42 | $\frac{1}{10}$ | 8.0 | 80 | 0.78 |
| Acrylic | S | LL (FB) | .210 | 42 | $\frac{1}{10}$ | 8.0 | 80 | 1.03 |
| Polyester | S | Plush | .280 | 42 | $\frac{5}{32}$ | 8.5 | 54.4 | 0.95 |
| Polyester | S | HLL | — | 42 | $\frac{5}{32}$ | 8.5 | 54.4 | 1.66 |
| Nylon | S | Saxony | .552 | 40 | $\frac{3}{16}$ | 5.5 | 29.3 | 1.96 |
| Nylon | CF | Shag | 1.25 | 43 | $\frac{3}{16}$ | 4.2 | 22.4 | 2.46 |
| Wool | S | Plush | .487 | 43 | $\frac{5}{32}$ | 7.0 | 44.8 | 2.19 |
| Nylon | S | Plush | .812 | 58 | $\frac{1}{8}$ | 10.0 | 80 | 1.83 |
| Acrylic | S | Plush | .688 | 53 | $\frac{5}{32}$ | 9.0 | 57.6 | 1.90 |
| Acrylic | S | Plush | .530 | 44 | $\frac{3}{16}$ | 8.25 | 44 | 1.71 |
| Olefin | CF | LL | — | 20 | — | — | — | 0.70 |

*Legend: LL = Level Loop; HLL = High-Low Loop (tip-sheared); FB = Attached foam back; S = Spun Yarn; CF = Continuous Filament Yarn*
*Source: Carpet and Rug Institute; Dalton, Georgia*
*Study conducted by Georgia Institute of Technology, School of Textile Engineering*

### CARPET CUSHION R-VALUES

| MATERIAL | THICKNESS (IN.) | WEIGHT (OZ/SQ YD) | DENSITY (LBS/CU FT) | R-VALUE |
|---|---|---|---|---|
| Prime polyurethane | .40 | 10.3 | 2.2 | 1.61 |
| Slab rubber | .23 | 62.0 | — | 0.62 |
| Waffled sponge rubber | .43 | 49.2 | — | 0.78 |
| Hair- and jute-coated | .44 | 52.6 | — | 1.71 |
| Bonded polyurethane | .50 | — | 4.0 | 2.09 |

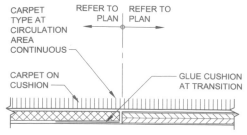

CARPET TYPE AT CIRCULATION AREA CONTINUOUS
REFER TO PLAN | REFER TO PLAN
CARPET ON CUSHION
GLUE CUSHION AT TRANSITION

**CARPET ON CUSHION TO CARPET ON PLYWOOD**

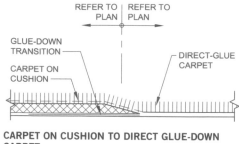

REFER TO PLAN | REFER TO PLAN
GLUE-DOWN TRANSITION
CARPET ON CUSHION
DIRECT-GLUE CARPET

**CARPET ON CUSHION TO DIRECT GLUE-DOWN CARPET**

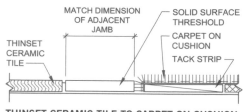

MATCH DIMENSION OF ADJACENT JAMB
SOLID SURFACE THRESHOLD
CARPET ON CUSHION
TACK STRIP
THINSET CERAMIC TILE

**THINSET CERAMIC TILE TO CARPET ON CUSHION**

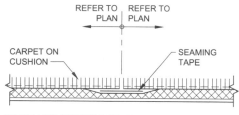

REFER TO PLAN | REFER TO PLAN
CARPET ON CUSHION
SEAMING TAPE

**CARPET ON CUSHION TO CARPET ON CUSHION**

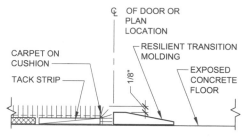

℄ OF DOOR OR PLAN LOCATION
RESILIENT TRANSITION MOLDING
EXPOSED CONCRETE FLOOR
CARPET ON CUSHION
TACK STRIP
1/8"

**CARPET ON CUSHION TO EXPOSED CONCRETE FLOOR**

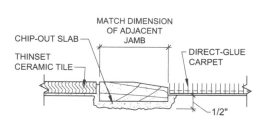

MATCH DIMENSION OF ADJACENT JAMB
CHIP-OUT SLAB
DIRECT-GLUE CARPET
THINSET CERAMIC TILE
1/2"

**THINSET CERAMIC TILE TO DIRECT GLUE-DOWN CARPET, STONE TRANSITION**

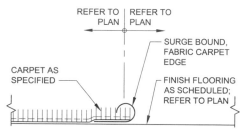

REFER TO PLAN | REFER TO PLAN
SURGE BOUND, FABRIC CARPET EDGE
FINISH FLOORING AS SCHEDULED; REFER TO PLAN
CARPET AS SPECIFIED

**CARPET TO FINISH FLOOR, SURGED EDGE**

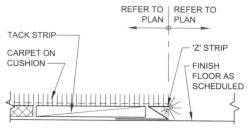

REFER TO PLAN | REFER TO PLAN
TACK STRIP
CARPET ON CUSHION
'Z' STRIP
FINISH FLOOR AS SCHEDULED

**CARPET ON CUSHION TO FINISH FLOOR**

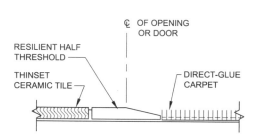

℄ OF OPENING OR DOOR
RESILIENT HALF THRESHOLD
DIRECT-GLUE CARPET
THINSET CERAMIC TILE

**THINSET CERAMIC TILE TO DIRECT GLUE-DOWN CARPET, RESILIENT TRANSITION**

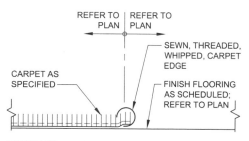

REFER TO PLAN | REFER TO PLAN
SEWN, THREADED, WHIPPED, CARPET EDGE
FINISH FLOORING AS SCHEDULED; REFER TO PLAN
CARPET AS SPECIFIED

**CARPET TO FINISH FLOOR, SEWN EDGE**

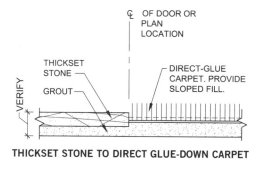

℄ OF DOOR OR PLAN LOCATION
THICKSET STONE
GROUT
DIRECT-GLUE CARPET. PROVIDE SLOPED FILL.
VERIFY

**THICKSET STONE TO DIRECT GLUE-DOWN CARPET**

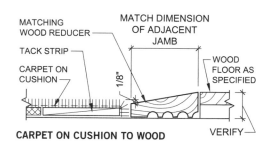

MATCH DIMENSION OF ADJACENT JAMB
MATCHING WOOD REDUCER
TACK STRIP
CARPET ON CUSHION
WOOD FLOOR AS SPECIFIED
1/8"
VERIFY

**CARPET ON CUSHION TO WOOD**

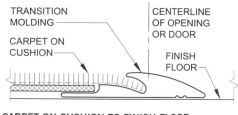

TRANSITION MOLDING
CENTERLINE OF OPENING OR DOOR
CARPET ON CUSHION
FINISH FLOOR

**CARPET ON CUSHION TO FINISH FLOOR**

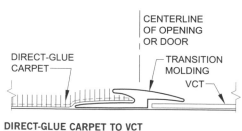

CENTERLINE OF OPENING OR DOOR
DIRECT-GLUE CARPET
TRANSITION MOLDING
VCT

**DIRECT-GLUE CARPET TO VCT**

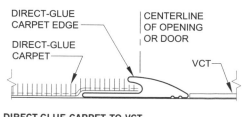

DIRECT-GLUE CARPET EDGE
DIRECT-GLUE CARPET
CENTERLINE OF OPENING OR DOOR
VCT

**DIRECT-GLUE CARPET TO VCT**

**CARPET TRANSITION DETAILS**

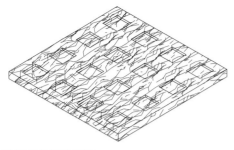

**HIGH-DENSITY JUTE**

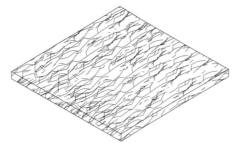

**SYNTHETIC**

**FIBER CARPET CUSHION**

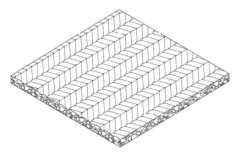

**TEXTURED FLAT RUBBER**

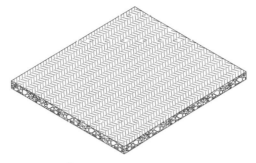

**FLAT RUBBER**

**SPONGE RUBBER CARPET CUSHION**

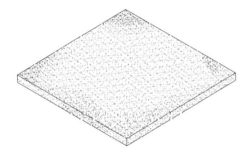

**DENSIFIED POLYURETHANE FOAM**

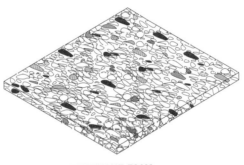

**BONDED POLYURETHANE FOAM**

**POLYURETHANE FOAM CARPET CUSHION**

## CARPET CUSHION

Carpet cushion can significantly extend the life of a carpet. Environmental conditions, anticipated traffic, and desired feel underfoot should be considered in the selection of a carpet cushion. Carpet cushions can be categorized by three types: *fiber, sponge rubber,* and *polyurethane foam.*

### Fiber Cushions

Fiber cushions are made by needlepunching natural fiber, synthetic fiber, or a combination of the two, into a feltlike pad. Antimicrobial treatments are recommended for natural fiber pads because they are susceptible to mold and mildew. Fiber cushions tend to have a firm feel underfoot. Over time, felted fiber cushions may be crushed under heavy wear.

### Sponge Rubber

Unlike felted fiber cushions, rubber cushions are highly compressible. Reinforced foam rubber has a smaller cell structure than sponge rubber, thus providing more uniform support. Sponge rubber cushions are generally open-cell foams, which are less resilient than closed-cell foams.

### Polyurethane Foam

The chemical compositions of polyurethane foam carpet cushions are similar, but their different cellular structures affect their performance. Bonded polyurethane foam (or *rebond,* as it is sometimes called) is manufactured from scraps of foam bonded together through an adhesive and heat fusion process. Modified prime polyurethane foam is manufactured in a continuous sheet and, unlike densified foam, may contain fillers. Densified foam is denser than modified prime foam and is highly resistant to bottoming out.

Ted Kollaja, AIA; lauckgroup, Dallas, Texas
Kim McGhee; Boston Architectural Center; Boston, Massachusetts
Lilliana Romerz; Boston Architectural Center; Boston, Massachusetts

## MINIMUM RECOMMENDATIONS FOR RESIDENTIAL CARPET CUSHION

| TYPE | KEY CHARACTERISTICS | CLASS 1[1] | | | CLASS 2[2] | | |
|---|---|---|---|---|---|---|---|
| | | WEIGHT OZ/SQ YD, MIN. | DENSITY LBS/CU FT, MIN. | THICKNESS[3] IN., MIN. | WEIGHT OZ/SQ YD, MIN. | DENSITY LBS./CU FT, MIN. | THICKNESS IN., MIN. |
| Urethane | Prime | | 2.2 | 0.3750 | Not recommended for class 2 | | |
| | Grafted prime | | 2.7 | 0.2500 | | 2.7 | 0.250 |
| | Densified prime | | 2.2 | 0.3130 | | 2.7 | 0.250 |
| | Bonded | | 5.0 | 0.3750 | | 6.5 | 0.375 |
| | Mechanically frothed | | 10.0 | 0.2500 | | 12.0 | 0.250 |
| Fiber | Rubberized hair jute | 40.0 | 12.3 | 0.2700 | 50.0 | 11.1 | 0.375 |
| | Rubberized jute | 32.0 | 8.5 | 0.3125 | 40.0 | 8.9 | 0.375 |
| | Synthetic fibers | 22.0 | 6.5 | 0.2500 | 28.0 | 6.5 | 0.300 |
| | Resinated recycled textile fiber | 24.0 | 7.3 | 0.2500 | 30.0 | 7.3 | 0.300 |
| Rubber | Flat rubber | 56.0 | 18.0 | 0.2200 | 64.0 | 21.0 | 0.220 |
| | Rippled rubber | 48.0 | 14.0 | 0.2850 | 64.0 | 16.0 | 0.330 |

[1] Class 1: Light and moderate traffic such as living and dining rooms, bedrooms, and recreational rooms. Class 2 cushions may be used in Class 1 applications.

[2] Class 2: Heavy-duty traffic, such as lobbies and corridors in multifamily facilities, and all stair applications.

[3] Maximum thickness for any product is 0.5 in.

*Source: Carpet Cushion Council; Riverside, Connecticut*

## CLASSIFICATION OF CARPET CUSHION

| TYPES OF CUSHION | CLASS I MODERATE TRAFFIC | CLASS II HEAVY TRAFFIC | CLASS III EXTRA-HEAVY TRAFFIC |
|---|---|---|---|
| Commercial Application | Office Buildings: Executive or private offices; conference rooms<br>Healthcare: Executive, administration<br>Schools: Administration<br>Airports: Administration<br>Retail: Windows and display areas<br>Banks: Executive areas<br>Hotels/Motels: Sleeping rooms<br>Libraries/Museums: Administration | Office Buildings: Clerical areas, corridors (moderate traffic)<br>Healthcare: Patient's rooms, lounges<br>Schools: Dormitories, classrooms<br>Retail: Minor aisles, boutiques, specialties<br>Banks: Lobbies, corridors (moderate traffic)<br>Hotels/Motels: Corridors<br>Libraries/Museums: Public areas (moderate traffic)<br>Convention Centers: Auditoriums | Office Buildings: Corridors (heavy traffic), cafeterias<br>Healthcare: Lobbies, corridors, nurses' stations<br>Schools: Corridors, cafeterias<br>Airports: Corridors, public areas, ticketing areas<br>Retail: Major aisles, checkouts, supermarkets<br>Banks: Corridors (heavy traffic), teller windows<br>Hotels/Motels: Lobbies and public areas<br>Libraries/Museums: Public areas<br>Convention Centers: Corridors and lobbies<br>Country Clubs: Locker rooms, pro shops, dining areas<br>Restaurants: Dining areas and lobbies |
| **FIBER** | | | |
| Rubberized Hair | Wt: 40 oz./sq. yd.<br>Th: .27"<br>D = 12.3 | Wt: 40 oz./sq. yd.<br>Th: .3125"<br>D = 12.3 | Wt: 50 oz./sq. yd.<br>Th: .375"<br>D = 11.1 |
| Rubberized Jute | Wt: 32 oz./sq. yd.<br>Th: .25"<br>D = 12.3 | Wt: 40 oz./sq. yd.<br>Th: .25"<br>D = 12.3 | Wt: 40 oz./sq. yd.<br>Th: .34"<br>D = 11.1 |
| Synthetic Fibers | Wt: 22 oz./sq. yd.<br>Th: .25"<br>D = 7.3 | Wt: 28 oz./sq. yd.<br>Th: .3125"<br>D = 7.3 | Wt: 36 oz./sq. yd.<br>Th: .35"<br>D = 8.0 |
| Resinated Recycled Textile Fiber | Wt: 24 oz./sq. yd.<br>Th: .25"<br>D = 7.3 | Wt: 30 oz./sq. yd.<br>Th: .30"<br>D = 7.3 | Wt: 40 oz./sq. yd.<br>Th: .375"<br>D = 8.0 |
| **SPONGE RUBBER** | | | |
| Flat Rubber | Wt: 62 oz./sq. yd.<br>Th: .150"<br>CR @ 25% = 3.0 psi min. D = 21 | Wt: 62 oz./sq. yd.<br>Th: .150"<br>CR @ 25% = 3.0 psi min. D = 21 | Wt: 62 oz./sq. yd.<br>Th: .150"<br>CR @ 25% = 4.0 psi min. D = 26 |
| Rippled Waffle | Wt: 56 oz./sq. yd.<br>Th: .270"<br>CR @ 25% = 0.7 psi min. D = 15 | Not recommended for use in this class | Not recommended for use in this class |
| Textured Flat Rubber | Wt: 56 oz./sq. yd.<br>Th: .220"<br>CR @ 25% = 1.0 psi min. D = 18 | Wt: 62 oz./sq. yd.<br>Th: .235"<br>CR @ 25% = 1.5 psi min. D = 22 | Wt: 80 oz./sq. yd.<br>Th: .250"<br>CR @ 25% = 1.75 psi min. D = 26 |
| Reinforced Rubber | Wt: 64 oz./sq. yd.<br>Th: .235"<br>CR @ 25% = 2.0 psi min. D = 22<br>CR @ 65% = 50.0 psi min | Wt: 64 oz./sq. yd.<br>Th: .235"<br>CR @ 25% = 2.0 psi min. D = 22<br>CR @ 65% = 50.0 psi min | Wt: 54 oz./sq. yd.<br>Th: .200"<br>CR @ 25% = 2.0 psi min. D = 22<br>CR @ 65% = 50.0 psi min |
| **POLYURETHANE FOAM** | | | |
| Grafted Prime | D = 2.7<br>Th: .25"<br>CFD @ 65% = 2.5 psi min. | D = 3.2<br>Th: .25"<br>CFD @ 65% = 3.5 psi min. | D = 4.0<br>Th: .25"<br>CFD @ 65% = 5.0 psi min. |
| Densified | D = 2.7<br>Th: .25"<br>CFD @ 65% = 2.4 psi min. | D = 3.5<br>Th: .25"<br>CFD @ 65% = 3.3 psi min. | D = 4.5<br>Th: .25"<br>CFD @ 65% = 4.8 psi min. |
| Bonded | D = 5.0<br>Th: .375"<br>CFD @ 65% = 2.5 psi min. | D = 6.5<br>Th: .25"<br>CFD @ 65% = 10.0 psi min. | D = 8.0<br>Th: .25"<br>CFD @ 65% = 8.0 psi min. |
| Mechanically Frothed | D = 13.0<br>Th: .30"<br>CFD @ 65% = 9.7 psi min. | D = 15.0<br>Th: .223"<br>CFD @ 65% = 49.9 psi min. | D = 19.0<br>Th: .183"<br>CFD @ 65% = 30.5 psi min. |

**LEGEND:**
CFD　Compression Force Deflection as measured by ASTM D 3574
CR　Compression Resistance in pounds per square inch as measured by ASTM D 3676
D　Density in pounds per cubic foot
min.　Minimum
Th　Thickness
Wt.　Weight

*Note: All thicknesses, weights, and densities allow a 5% manufacturing tolerance.*

*Reprinted, by permission, from the Carpet Cushion Council, Commercial Carpet Cushion Guidelines, 1997.*

# ORIENTAL RUGS

Oriental rugs are produced in a broad geographic region encompassing the Near East, Asia, India, and parts of Eastern Europe. True oriental rugs are handwoven of natural fibers, and are greatly prized for their artistry, patterns, and color. Motifs typically include geometric or floral designs, with striking field and border patterns.

## RUG PRODUCTION REGIONS

Sources for modern oriental rugs include the large rug production areas of India, Pakistan, and China. Other oriental rug-weaving centers are located in the countries or regions of Iran (Persia), Turkey (Anatolia), Georgia, Armenia, Azerbaijan (the Caucasus), and the Western and Eastern Turkestan (Afghanistan, Tibet, and Nepal) regions of central Asia. These comprise the seven major geographical groups involved in the production of oriental rugs, each of which has its own style and patterns. Other smaller rug-producing areas include Romania and Spain.

Historically, the Persian Empire (Iran) produced many of the finest rugs; however, the import of Iranian rugs into the United States was prohibited as part of an embargo during the 1970s.

## HISTORY

The earliest documented oriental rug dates from 400 to 500 B.C. Tribal nomadic groups were influential in the development of regional rug patterns. During the fifteenth and sixteenth centuries, the art of oriental rugmaking is considered to have reached a peak in Persia. And although popularity diminished in the eighteenth and nineteenth centuries due to the general decline in tribal nomadic groups, increased demand later in the nineteenth century from Western countries boosted production of rugs.

Modern production of oriental rugs continues for many nomadic tribal groups, as well as in the large rug production centers. Many traditional aspects of rugmaking are being revived, such as the use of natural dyes, motifs, and patterns.

## MATERIALS

Warp threads are typically made of cotton. Weft yarns are usually wool, but silk, camel wool, and goat hair are used in some rugs. Combinations of silk and wool are available. Historically, accent threads of silver and gold were sometimes used in high-quality rugs.

## CONSTRUCTION AND TYPES

Oriental rugmaking principles are consistent: a vertical foundation of threads, called *warps,* is stretched across a loom frame. Rows of horizontal threads, called *wefts,* are applied to the warp threads.

Two types of techniques can be used to develop the carpet pattern: *handknotting* or *flatweaving.*

## Handknotted Rugs

Handknotted rugs with face pile and smooth backs are created by wrapping warps with yarns, using specific knot types. The knots are stabilized by the weft threads, which are woven back and forth across the body of the rug.

## Flatwoven Rugs

Flatwoven, pileless rugs are created by weaving horizontal warp and vertical weft yarns together in a pattern. They are easier to produce than knotted pile and are less costly. Historically, they were popular due to the more compact size when transported.

## Kilims

Kilims are smooth-surfaced, flatwoven rugs found throughout the oriental carpet production area, typically of wool. Kilim patterns are predominately geometric in nature. They are usually reversible due to the nature of the weave.

## Soumaks

Soumaks are flatwoven carpets produced with the soumak weave, which produces a herringbone effect. The soumak weave produces many loose yarns on the back.

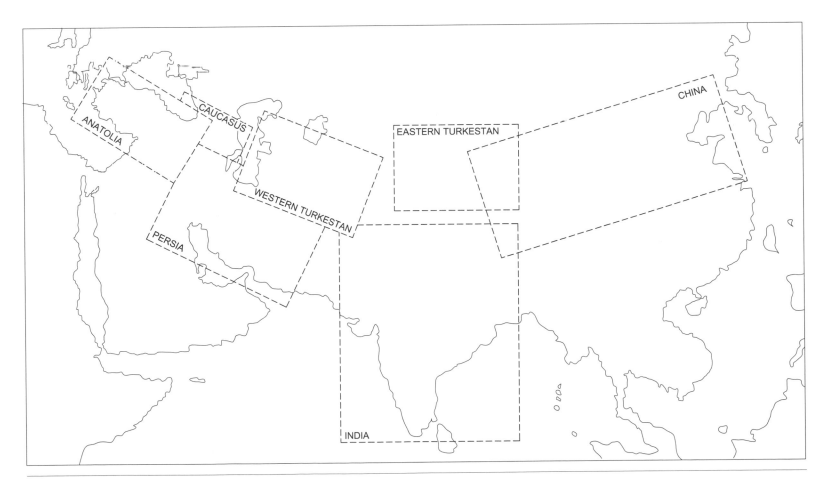

**MAP OF ORIENTAL RUG PRODUCTION AREAS**
*Source: Enza Milanesi,* The Bulfinch Guide to Carpets, *translated by Jay Hyams (Boston: Little, Brown and Company), 1993.*

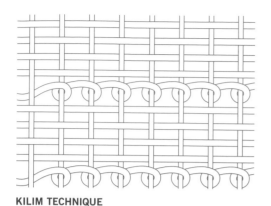

**KILIM TECHNIQUE**

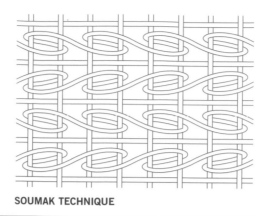

**SOUMAK TECHNIQUE**

**FLATWEAVE TECHNIQUES**

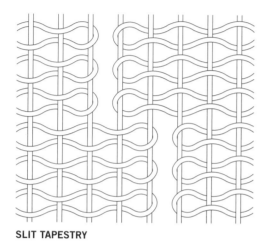

**SLIT TAPESTRY**

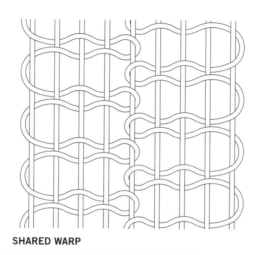

**SHARED WARP**

**FLATWEAVE COLOR CHANGE**

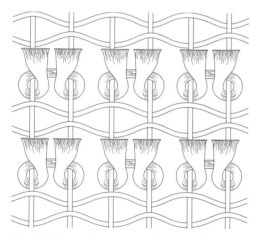

In the Turkish, or Ghiordes, knot, the ends of the yarn are pulled forward together between two adjacent warps. It is a symmetrical knot. The Turkish knot is primarily used in Turkey and the Caucasus, a mountain region in the former Soviet Union. This area includes Armenia, Azerbaijan, and Georgia.

**TURKISH KNOT**

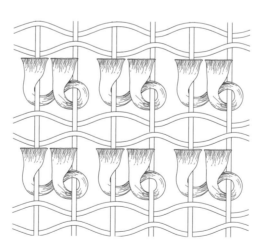

The Persian, or Senneh, knot is an asymmetrical knot, which encircles two warp threads, passing under one and around the other. The ends of the knot can face either left or right. The Persian knot primarily is used in Iran (Persia), India, Pakistan, and China.

**PERSIAN KNOT**

### Dhurries

Dhurries are typically cotton flatwoven rugs from northeastern India. Originally used as an underlayment for beds and carpets, dhurries were woven in vibrant designs and motifs.

*Wool dhurries* are produced in regions where the climate is severe, and camel hair is often used as the weft yarn.

### Druggets

Druggets are flatwoven rugs from India with a heavy weft-faced plain weave.

## TAPESTRY

Tapestry is the technique commonly used in the production of flatwoven rugs. Loose ends of weft yarn are buried in the rug construction, but this technique produces slits in the tapestry when vertical columns of color are woven. A technique used by Native American weavers to address this problem is to share a warp between adjacent colors.

## RUG KNOTS

Knotted oriental rugs are created by wrapping yarns around warp threads that have been strung on a loom. The two most common types of knots used in pile weaving are the Turkish, or Ghiordes, knot, and the Persian, or Senneh, knot. Knotting techniques vary within some regions, due to local preference. There is no apparent difference in the face appearance and performance of rugs between the two types of knots.

## RUG DYES

Traditionally, all natural dyes were used to color the weft yarn. Aniline dyes were introduced in the late nineteenth century, and while easier to produce and use, their colorfastness and color rendition were not as effective as the natural dyes. Currently, the use of natural dyes is increasingly popular in oriental rug production.

# RUG FEATURES

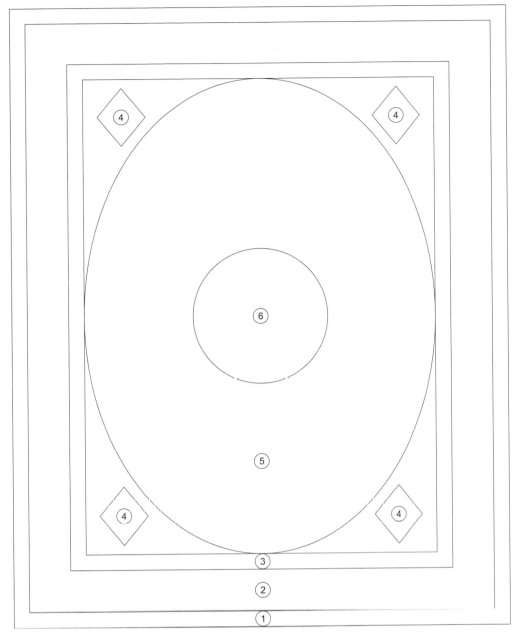

1. Outer guard stripe or border
2. Main border
3. Inner guard stripe or border
4. Spandrel
5. Field
6. Medallion

**ORIENTAL RUG COMPONENTS**

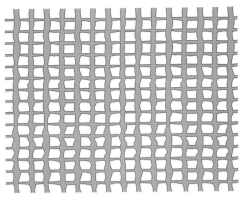

**FLAT RUG UNDERLAY**

**TEXTURED RUG UNDERLAY**

**OPEN-WEAVE FOAM RUG UNDERLAYS**

## IDENTIFICATION

Rugs can be identified by the style of weaving (Persian), for the tribe or group that produced the carpet (Afshar), the original area in which the rug was first developed (Belouchistan), for its design (tree of life), its use (*yastik,* which means pillow), or the period in which it was produced (Shah Abbas).

Oriental rugs imported into the United States must be labeled with a registration number, the country of origin, and fiber content. Rugs are considered semiantique if over 30 years old, antique if over 60 years old.

## INSTALLATION AND MAINTENANCE

The installation of an oriental rug is a function of the rug and flooring type. Hair and jute combination pads or solid sponge-rubber cushions are recommended under the rug to protect the rug and the floor and to stabilize the rug. Open-weave foam pads allow air to circulate under the rug and prevent it from slipping. They also allow dirt to fall through to the floor, reducing the abrasion of the back surface of the rug. Consult with a rug dealer to determine the proper type of pad or cushion, as well as for maintenance information.

*Resource: Oriental Rug Importers Association, Inc.; Secaucus, New Jersey*

## RUG PATTERNS

Rug patterns are commonly named after the town or region in which they are produced. A central medallion format is one of the most common; however, many carpets have a full-field pattern within the borders. There are many variations to the patterns, colors, and features of oriental rugs. Some rugs are asymmetrical in pattern, and are used as prayer rugs. The directional pattern may be more challenging to use in an installation.

Rug patterns and motifs often reflect tribal influences, such as the Turkoman "gul" emblems, which vary according to the tribal or nomadic group. Symbols were frequently used in oriental rugs with numerous variations.

## RUG DENSITY

Typically, the finer the warp, the denser the rug. The density of a pile rug is usually determined by the knots per square inch, or *knot count.* The first number is the number of horizontal knots and the second number is the number of vertical knots. Better-quality rugs have knot counts ranging from $^{19}\!/_{20}$ to $^{12}\!/_{24}$.

## RUG FINISHING

Upon completion of the weaving, the rug is removed from the loom and is finished by shearing and cleaning. Loose warp ends are usually braided or knotted to form a fringe end. The sides of the rug may be bound or have a selvage border added.

*Ted Milligan; Rhode Island School of Design; Providence, Rhode Island*

# ACOUSTICAL WALL PANELS

## PANEL CORE MATERIALS

Core materials can be combined in a panel to achieve the required performance. For example, a nailable surface can be achieved by inserting a plywood nailing strip into a panel with a fiberglass board core material. Common panel core materials:

- *Polyester batting* consists of fibers loosely inter-twined and is used to achieve a soft, upholstered appearance.
- *Fiberglass blanket* is a thick sheet of loosely inter-twined fiberglass strands. It is often used where acoustical absorption is a concern.
- *Fiberglass board* ranges in density from acousti-cally absorptive panels with fair tackability to acoustically reflective panels. Tackable, acoustic fiberglass board has a finish face of thin, rigid fiber-glass mesh. Fiberglass board heals well and is appropriate for tackable applications. Chemically hardened edges are applied to fiberglass board cores.
- *Mineral fiberboard* (for example, U.S.G. Micore) is a composite of inorganic mineral fibers. Unlike pressed, recycled paper products (for example, Homosote), mineral fiberboard is dimensionally stable. It is more durable and impact-resistant than fiberglass board and can be microperforated where an absorptive acoustic surface is required. The fin-ish face of mineral fiberboard is either sanded or coated. The sanded finish is gray and retains a tighter thickness tolerance. The white latex coating reduces read-through when used with light-colored or transparent fabrics.
- *Particleboard* is a nailable core material. Plywood can warp and is not recommended for use as a core material, but can be used as nailable strips in panels of other core materials.

## PANEL INSTALLATION

Common acoustical panel installation methods include:

- *Z-clips*, which are the preferred method for tempo-rary or movable panels. Z-clip panels require a reveal between the top of panel and the ceiling so that the panels can be lifted and lowered into place. The lower clip is fastened to the wall; the upper clip is fastened to the panel.
- *Hook and loop tape* is commonly known by the trade name Velcro. Mechanical fasteners should be used to secure the hook tape to the wall. This method is often used with adhesive to hold panels in place while the adhesive is setting.
- *Impaling clips* are fastened to the wall; the barbed projections of impaling clips are pressed into the panel back. This installation method is not com-monly used because of its inability to support substantial weight. It is also more prone to vandal-ism.
- *Adhesive*. Adhering an acoustical panel to a wall or ceiling is a permanent mounting method. Panels cannot be removed without damaging them and the substrate.

## PANEL CORE MATERIALS AND PERFORMANCE

| PANEL CORE MATERIAL | PANEL PERFORMANCE |
| --- | --- |
| Polyester batting | Acoustic absorption |
| Fiberglass blanket | Acoustic absorption |
| Mineral fiberboard | Acoustic absorption, tackable |
| Fiberglass board | Acoustic absorption, tackable |
| Plywood | Acoustic reflectivity, nailable |
| Particleboard | Acoustic reflectivity, nailable |
| Wood board | Acoustic reflectivity, nailable |

## PANEL TEXTILE SELECTION CONSIDERATIONS

| FABRIC ATTRIBUTE | SELECTION CONSIDERATION |
| --- | --- |
| Color | Light-colored textiles show soil more readily than dark-colored textiles. |
| Opacity | Core material should not read through the textile face. |
| Resilience | Nonbacked textiles ease stretching and do not impair acoustic transparency. |
| Self-healing | Tackable and nailable panel textiles must be snag-resistant. |

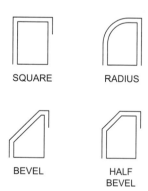

SQUARE    RADIUS

BEVEL    HALF BEVEL

Extruded panel frames are infilled with a core material. Fiberglass board edges can be chemically hardened to achieve a profile.

**PANEL EDGE PROFILES**

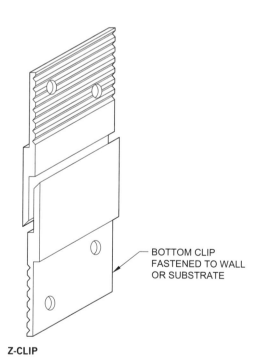

BOTTOM CLIP FASTENED TO WALL OR SUBSTRATE

Z-CLIP

**METHODS OF ATTACHMENT**

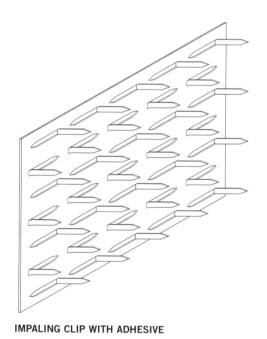

**IMPALING CLIP WITH ADHESIVE**

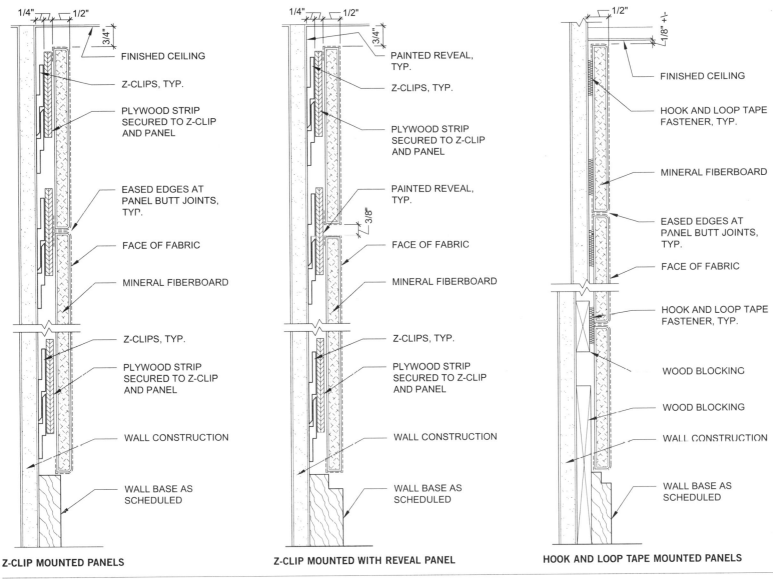

1/4" 1/2"
3/4"

FINISHED CEILING

Z-CLIPS, TYP.

PLYWOOD STRIP
SECURED TO Z-CLIP
AND PANEL

EASED EDGES AT
PANEL BUTT JOINTS,
TYP.

FACE OF FABRIC

MINERAL FIBERBOARD

Z-CLIPS, TYP.

PLYWOOD STRIP
SECURED TO Z-CLIP
AND PANEL

WALL CONSTRUCTION

WALL BASE AS
SCHEDULED

**Z-CLIP MOUNTED PANELS**

1/4" 1/2"
3/4"

PAINTED REVEAL,
TYP.

Z-CLIPS, TYP.

PLYWOOD STRIP
SECURED TO Z-CLIP
AND PANEL

PAINTED REVEAL,
TYP.

3/8"

FACE OF FABRIC

MINERAL FIBERBOARD

Z-CLIPS, TYP.

PLYWOOD STRIP
SECURED TO Z-CLIP
AND PANEL

WALL CONSTRUCTION

WALL BASE AS
SCHEDULED

**Z-CLIP MOUNTED WITH REVEAL PANEL**

1/2"
1/8" +/-

FINISHED CEILING

HOOK AND LOOP TAPE
FASTENER, TYP.

MINERAL FIBERBOARD

EASED EDGES AT
PANEL BUTT JOINTS,
TYP.

FACE OF FABRIC

HOOK AND LOOP TAPE
FASTENER, TYP.

WOOD BLOCKING

WOOD BLOCKING

WALL CONSTRUCTION

WALL BASE AS
SCHEDULED

**HOOK AND LOOP TAPE MOUNTED PANELS**

**SECTION DETAILS** *Source: StretchWall Installations, Inc.; Long Island City, New York*

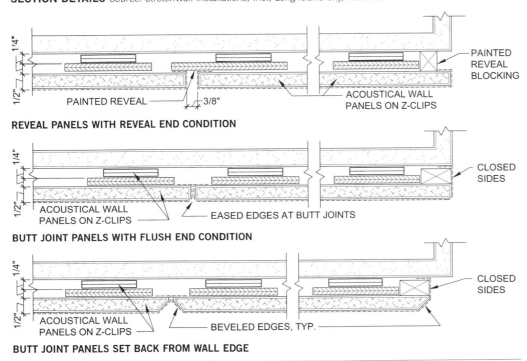

1/4"
1/2"

PAINTED
REVEAL
BLOCKING

PAINTED REVEAL        3/8"

ACOUSTICAL WALL
PANELS ON Z-CLIPS

**REVEAL PANELS WITH REVEAL END CONDITION**

1/4"
1/2"

CLOSED
SIDES

ACOUSTICAL WALL
PANELS ON Z-CLIPS

EASED EDGES AT BUTT JOINTS

**BUTT JOINT PANELS WITH FLUSH END CONDITION**

1/4"
1/2"

CLOSED
SIDES

ACOUSTICAL WALL
PANELS ON Z-CLIPS

BEVELED EDGES, TYP.

**BUTT JOINT PANELS SET BACK FROM WALL EDGE**

**PLAN DETAILS** *Source: StretchWall Installations, Inc.; Long Island City, New York*

*Merve Yoneyman; Rhode Island School of Design;*
*Providence, Rhode Island*
*Robin Staack; Boston Architectural Center; Boston,*
*Massachusetts*

# WALLCOVERINGS

Wallcoverings offer improved durability over paint finishes while providing texture and pattern to the wall surface. Wallcovering types include vinyl, textile, wallpapers, fiberglass, and wood veneer. The most popular wallcovering for commercial use is vinyl, favored for its affordability and durability.

## VINYL WALLCOVERINGS

The two vinyl wallcovering manufacturing processes are calendering and plastisol methods:

- *Calendering* squeezes liquid vinyl over a series of hot metal rollers, flattening the compound into a sheet. The vinyl is then laminated under heat and pressure to a backing material. Calendered vinyl wallcovering is harder, tougher, and usually much thicker than wallcovering manufactured by the plastisol method.
- The *plastisol* method spreads liquid vinyl onto a backing material, which are then fused together under high temperatures. Plastisol technology is used primarily for residential wallcoverings.

## TEXTILE WALLCOVERINGS

Not all textiles are suitable for use as wallcoverings. Textile wallcoverings are not appropriate in applications where wear resistance is a concern.

Textiles must be backcoated to be installed as wallcovering. The backing provides a barrier to prevent adhesives from bleeding through and ruining the finish face of the fabric. Backings also provide the dimensional stability required for a textile to withstand the stretching and smoothing operations of wallcovering installation.

Two types of backcoating treatments are paper backing and acrylic latex backing:

- *Paper backing* involves laminating paper to the reverse side of the textile. This process stiffens the textile for easier installation. The textile assumes properties similar to those of wallpaper.
- *Acrylic latex coating* involves stretching the textile in a frame and applying a latex compound. The textile retains some of its inherent flexibility and is much less dimensionally stable than paper-backed textiles. Latex backings can also improve ravel resistance and seam slippage. The use of latex-coated textile wallcoverings may increase installation costs. Often, this wallcovering's lack of rigidity requires that the adhesive be applied to the wall, rather than to the back of the wallcovering. This process is more labor-intensive and requires a higher degree of skill.

## FIBERGLASS WALLCOVERINGS

Fiberglass wallcovering is composed of fiberglass yarns adhered together. Fiberglass wallcovering is inherently flame-resistant and is suitable for use in reinforcing fragile or deteriorating wall surfaces. It is permeable, making it intrinsically mold- and mildew-resistant. Fiberglass wallcoverings must be painted after installation. This wallcovering type provides a textured pattern only, not a color. Typically, a latex paint is selected to maintain the breathability of the wall.

## WALLCOVERING DURABILITY CLASSIFICATIONS*

| PROPERTY | CATEGORY I: DECORATIVE ONLY | CATEGORY II: DECORATIVE WITH MEDIUM SERVICEABILITY | CATEGORY III: DECORATIVE WITH HIGH SERVICEABILITY | CATEGORY IV: TYPE I COMMERCIAL SERVICEABILITY | CATEGORY V: TYPE II COMMERCIAL SERVICEABILITY | CATEGORY VI: TYPE III COMMERCIAL SERVICEABILITY |
|---|---|---|---|---|---|---|
| Minimum colorfastness | | 23 h | 46 h | 200 h | 200 h | 200 h |
| Minimum washability | | 100 cycles | 100 cycles | 100 cycles | 100 cycles | 100 cycles |
| Minimum scrubbability | | | 50 cycles | 200 cycles | 300 cycles | 500 cycles |
| Minimum abrasion resistance | | | | 200 cycles (220 grit) | 300 cycles (220 grit) | 1,000 cycles (220 grit) |
| Minimum breaking strength | | | | | | |
| MD (machine direction) | | | | 40 lb (178 N) | 50 lb (222 N) | 100 lb (445 N) |
| CMD (cross machine direction) | | | | 30 lb (133 N) | 55 lb (245 N) | 95 lb (423 N) |
| Minimum crocking resistance | | | Good | Good | Good | Good |
| Minimum stain resistance* | | | Reagents 1 to 9 | Reagents 1 to 9 | Reagents 1 to 12 | Reagents 1 to 12 |
| Minimum tear resistance | | | | 12 | 25 | 50 |
| Maximum blocking resistance | | | | 2 | 2 | 2 |
| Minimum coating adhesion | | | | 2 lb/in. (17.8 N/5 cm) | 3 lb/in. (26.7 N/5 cm) | 3 lb/in. (26.7 N/5 cm) |
| Minimum cold cracking | | | | No change | No change | No change |
| Minimum heat aging resistance | | | | Pass | Pass | Pass |
| Maximum flame spread | 25 | 25 | 25 | 25 | 25 |
| Maximum smoke developed | 50 | 50 | 50 | 50 | 50 |
| Maximum shrinkage | | | | | | |

*Per ASTM F793, Standard Classification of Wallcoverings by Durability Characteristics, *Classification Criteria.*

**Reagents: (1) Distilled water, 65° to 75°F; (2) Distilled water, 115° to 125°F; (3) Ethyl alcohol ; (4) Vinegar, 3% acetic; (5) Alkali solution; (6) Hydrochloride, 5%; (7) Soup solution; (8) Detergent solution; (9) Pure orange juice; (10) Butter; (11) Catsup; (12) Tea

## THREE GRADES OF WALLCOVERING*

| TYPE | BACKING MATERIAL | COMMON COMPOSITION | TOTAL WEIGHT | COATING WEIGHT | USES |
|---|---|---|---|---|---|
| I—Light Duty | Scrim (very loose, open weave; similar to cheesecloth; lacks dimensional stability) | Polycotton | Between 7 and 13 oz/sq yd (0.237 and 0.442 kg/sq m) | Between 5 and 7 oz/sq yd (0.17 and 0.237 kg/sq m) | Ceilings, offices, hotel rooms, areas not subject to unusual abrasion or heavy traffic |
| | Nonwoven (paperlike) | Polyester cellulose | | | |
| II—Medium Duty | Osnaburg (loose, open weave) | Polycotton | Between 13 and 22 oz/sq yd (0.442 and 0.748 kg/sq m) | Between 7 and 12 oz/sq yd (0.237 and 0.407 kg/sq m) | Lounges, dining rooms, public corridors, and classrooms |
| | Nonwoven | Polyester cellulose | | | |
| III—Heavy Duty | Drill (denser, firmer weave similar to twill) | Polycotton | 22 oz/sq yd (0.748 kg/sq m) or more | 12 oz/sq yd (0.407 kg/sq m) | Hospital and food service corridors, wainscot or lower protection for areas of heavy traffic by movable equipment or rough abrasion |

*As defined by the Chemical Fabrics and Film Association CFFA-W-101-A, CFFA Quality Standard for Vinyl-Coated Fabric Wallcoverings, and FS CCCW-408C, Wallcovering, Vinyl-Coated.

# WOOD VENEER WALLCOVERINGS

Wood veneer wallcovering is made by bonding veneer slices, about 1/64 in. (0.39 mm) thick, to a woven backing material. The resulting wallcovering is thin enough to be pliable along the grain lines but too thick to be flexible in the horizontal direction (perpendicular to the wood grain). The inherent flexibility of wood veneer wallcovering allows easy installation around columns and other curved surfaces.

The thinness of wood veneer wallcovering raises three major concerns: finishing operations after installation, proper substrate preparation, and moisture. Wood veneer wallcovering is too thin to be sanded; therefore, care must be taken during installation so that the surface is not stained or damaged.

Wall surface imperfections tend to telegraph through the thin veneer. In areas where the substrate cannot be prepared to a smooth, level surface, veneered plywood panels are a better choice. Buckling and warpage caused by moisture can be a significant problem for this kind of wallcovering. It is not recommended that wood veneer wallcovering be applied to the interior surface of an exterior wall unless the finish face of the wall is furred out and dampproofed.

Wood veneer wallcoverings are available prefinished or unfinished. Unfinished veneers must be stained and finished after they are installed. Some finishes, for example, penetrating oils, can have an adverse effect on the wallcovering adhesive. Coatings applied to the surface of installed wood veneer should be approved by the wallcovering manufacturer.

The installation of wood veneer wallcovering is similar to the installation of other types of wallcovering; however, the sheets must be butted together and cannot be overlapped and trimmed.

# WALL PREPARATION

There are four traditional ways to prepare a wall surface for a wallcovering: prime, seal, size, or apply a wall liner.

- *Primers* assure proper adhesion and are the most commonly required wall preparation for commercial installations.
- *Sealers* are usually oil-based, made either of an alkyd or a shellac. They provide stain-sealing properties; for example, walls that have suffered water damage must typically be sealed before they can be finished with either paint or a wallcovering. Sealers also promote strippability without damage to the wall surface.
- *Sizing* a wall surface lowers the absorbency of the wall by reducing the penetration of the paste. However, sizing does not necessarily improve the bond between the adhesive and the wall surface.
- *Wall liners* are nonwoven sheets; their installation is similar to that of wallcovering. They are sometimes required where wall surfaces cannot be prepared by conventional means. Wall liners can be used to prevent cracks, holes, and gaps from telegraphing through the wallcovering. Wall liners may also be used in lieu of primer/sealers to mask contrasting colors or areas of light and dark on the substrate.

## DEFINITIONS OF SIX WALLCOVERING CATEGORIES BASED ON PERFORMANCE*

| CATEGORY | DESCRIPTION | USE | COMMENTS |
|---|---|---|---|
| I | Decorative only | For decorative purposes | Wallcoverings are not tested. Wallpaper and other primarily residential wallcoverings fall into this category. |
| II | Decorative with medium serviceability | Primarily decorative but more washable and colorfast than Category I wallcoverings | In addition to the testing required for minimum washability and colorfastness, wallcoverings are tested for maximum flame spread and smoke development. Primarily for residential use. |
| III | Decorative with high serviceability | For medium use, where abrasion resistance, stain resistance, scrubbability, and increased colorfastness are necessary | In addition to the testing required for Category II wallcoverings, wallcoverings are tested for minimum scrubbability, stain resistance, and cracking resistance. They meet more stringent requirements for colorfastness than Category II wallcoverings. Primarily for residential use. |
| IV | Type I Commercial serviceability | For use where higher abrasion resistance, stain resistance, and scrubbability are necessary in heavy consumer and light commercial use | In addition to the testing required for Category III wallcoverings, wallcoverings are tested for maximum shrinkage and minimum abrasion resistance, breaking strength, tear resistance, blocking resistance, coating adhesion, cold-cracking resistance, and heat-aging resistance. All test methods listed in the standard apply to Category III wallcoverings, but the wallcoverings meet more stringent requirements for colorfastness and scrubbability than Category III wallcoverings. Appropriate for private offices, hotel rooms, and areas not subject to unusual abrasion or heavy traffic. |
| V | Type II Commercial serviceability | For use where better wearing qualities are required and exposure to wear is greater than normal | Tested according to more stringent requirements for scrubbability, abrasion resistance, stain resistance, tear resistance, and coating adhesion than Category IV wallcoverings. Appropriate for public areas such as lounges, dining rooms, public corridors, and classrooms. |
| VI | Type III Commercial serviceability | For use in heavy-traffic areas | Category VI wallcoverings are tested for the highest scrubbability, abrasion resistance, breaking strength, tear resistance, coating adhesion, and maximum shrinkage. Category VI, Type III wallcoverings are commonly used in high-traffic service corridors where carts may bump into the walls. |

* Per ASTM F793, Standard Classification of Wallcoverings by Durability Characteristics.

The backing material, sometimes called the substrate, is the major component in determining the strength and dimensional stability of a wallcovering.

## Mildew Resistance

Impermeable wallcoverings such as vinyl can act as vapor barriers under specific climatic conditions. Mildew is a particular problem in warm, humid climates. Moisture migrating through a wall is trapped behind the wallcovering. Gypsum wallboard can become saturated with the condensation, fostering fungal growth. Perforated vinyl or woven fiberglass wallcoverings can be specified to increase the breathability of the wall. Mildew inhibitors can also be added to the vinyl.

Where mildew resistance is required, the wallcovering should have achieved a rating of 0 or 1 when tested according to ASTM G21, *Practice for Determining Resistance of Synthetic Polymeric Materials to Fungi.* A 0 rating means no fungal growth was observed on a wallcovering sample inoculated with spores and incubated for at least 21 days; a 1 rating means less than 10% of the sample surface area was covered with fungal growth.

## GUIDELINES FOR CALCULATING ONE LINEAL YARD OF WALLCOVERING

| WALLCOVERING WIDTH | SURFACE TO BE COVERED |
|---|---|
| 54 in. (1,370 mm) | 13 sq ft (1.2 sq m) |
| 36 in. (910 mm) | 9 sq ft (0.8 sq m) |

## WALLPAPERS

Wallpapers are composed of a paper face and a paper backing. They are not commonly used for commercial applications because of their fragility and poor wear resistance. However, the scratch, stain, and abrasion resistance of wallpaper can be improved by requiring that the finish face be coated with a clear vinyl film.

Typically, residential wallcoverings range from 20½ to 28 in. (521 to 711 mm) wide. A single roll yields 27 to 30 sq ft (2.5 to 2.8 sq m). Single rolls are packaged and sold in double-roll quantities. Double rolls have 56 to 58 sq ft (5.2 to 5.4 sq m) and are approximately 11 yards (10 m) long.

*Vinyl-coated papers,* consisting of a paper substrate coated with acrylic/vinyl or solid PVC with a total thickness of 2 to 5 mils (0.05 to 0.13 mm), are scrubbable and peelable or strippable. However, they are not suited for commercial applications; they are suitable for use in residential kitchens, bathrooms, and laundry rooms.

*Pattern and seam placement* may be critical. Large, complicated, dominant pattern repeats may need careful placement to establish a starting point. Dominant pattern repeats are often centered at eye level, with the pattern matching at 72 in. (1,830 mm) above the finish floor.

*Carl Henschel; Rhode Island School of Design; Providence, Rhode Island*
*MASTERSPEC®; published by ARCOM; Salt Lake City, Utah, and Alexandria, Virginia*

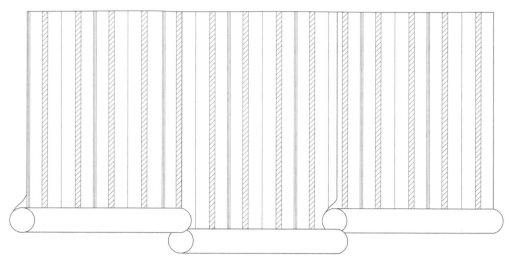

**RANDOM MATCH**
Random match is the least wasteful type of pattern matching. Panels do not align horizontally.

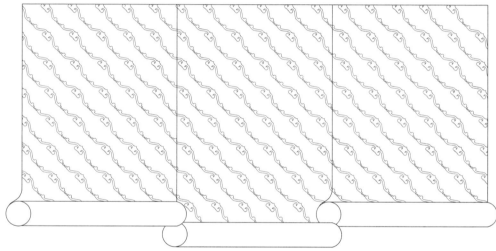

**DROP MATCH**
Drop match patterns do not repeat at the same distance from the ceiling line, creating the greatest potential for waste. Patterns that match every third or fourth panel are referred to as *multiple drop matches.*

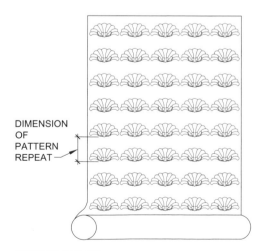

DIMENSION OF PATTERN REPEAT

**PATTERN REPEAT**

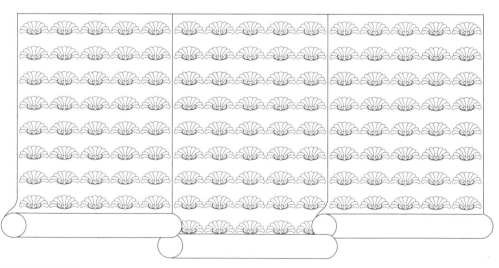

**STRAIGHT MATCH**
Straight match patterns match with the continuation of the pattern on the next panel. The pattern repeats at the same distance from the ceiling line.

**WALLCOVERING PATTERN MATCHING**

# UPHOLSTERED WALL SYSTEMS

Upholstered wall systems, also referred to as *stretched-fabric wall systems*, combine the luxuriousness of textile wallcoverings and the practicality of a tackable or acoustically absorptive wall surface. Upholstered wall systems are site-constructed coverings that stretch fabric taut over a frame and infill material. They can also be used in ceiling installations.

## FRAMING METHODS

The framing material is typically either a plastic extrusion or a wood frame. An extrusion system holds the fabric in place by friction or with concealed fasteners, sometimes aided by an adhesive. Concealed fasteners are used with a wood frame system.

## FABRIC SELECTION

Upholstered wall systems require the selection of a highly stable fabric. Upholstery-weight fabrics are good choices. The fabric should be hydrophobic (does not readily absorb moisture); otherwise, seasonal changes in relative humidity may cause sagging and rippling. A fabric that contains more than 30% rayon or viscose or 10% nylon fibers is typically not suitable for use in upholstered wall systems. If the wall system is to perform as a tackable or nailable surface, the selected fabric should be self healing and snag-resistant. For a seamless appearance, fabrics up to 120 in. (3,050 mm) wide can be specified and installed horizontally (sometimes referred to as *railroading*). Fabric selection considerations include the following:

- *Seams* can be emphasized or deemphasized, depending on fabric weave and color. Seams disappear in fabric that is vertically directional, yet tend to read as butt joints when the predominant direction of the grain is horizontal. In a nondirectional fabric, seams tend to be more apparent with light-colored fabrics, and less so with dark colors.

- *Joints* between square-edged panels with thin fabrics, tightly butted, tend to read as a monolithic, seamless installation. Wall panel joints are seen more clearly between panels with heavy or thick fabrics or with beveled frame edges.

- *Tackable and nailable surfaces* require fabric that will not easily snag. The heavier the yarn texture, the better for areas where pin-tacking or nailing is required. Linen works well in galleries because of its unobtrusive appearance behind artwork and because it is a hardy, natural fabric that maintains a good appearance through repeated use. Satin and sateen weaves are not recommended for tacking.

- *Weave types* and their dimensional stability must be considered. Taffetas and architectural silks, especially when treated with flame retardants, are subject to greater variance in expansion and contraction. They require limited fluctuation in temperature and humidity. Jacquards, damasks, and basket weaves—regardless of their yarn content—are more dimensionally stable

## CORE MATERIALS

| MATERIAL | APPLICATION |
|---|---|
| Acoustic batting (polyester or fiberglass) | Soft, upholstered appearance; acoustically absorptive |
| Plywood | Nailable; acoustically reflective surface |
| Mineral fiberboard | Tackable; acoustically absorptive |
| Fiberglass board | Durable; impact-resistant |

and can be used in areas where greater variances in temperature and humidity may occur.

- *Light-colored fabrics* (especially white) should be examined to verify that the wall construction will not "read through" the fabric and change its color. The fabric may need to be lined, and the lining may change the appearance of the upholstered wall. By placing the fabric under consideration over a light-colored surface and then over a dark-colored surface, the need for a lining can be determined.

## FIBER MOISTURE REGAIN VALUES

| FIBER | MOISTURE REGAIN @ 70°F (21°C) 65% RELATIVE HUMIDITY | ELASTIC RECOVERY FROM A 2–5% STRETCH | |
|---|---|---|---|
| Glass | 0% | 0% | Hydrophobic (doesn't absorb moisture readily) |
| Olefin | 0% | 90% | |
| Acrylic | 1.3–2.5% | 92% | |
| Poyester | .4–.8% | 97% | |
| Nylon | 4–4.5% | 100% | |
| Acetate | 6% | 58% | |
| Cotton | 7–11% | 75% | |
| Silk | 11% | 92% | |
| Rayon | 15% | 54% | |
| Wool | 13–18% | 99% | Hydrophilic (absorbs moisture readily) |

*Tanya Nachia; Rhode Island School of Design; Providence, Rhode Island*
*Robin Staack; Boston Architectural Center; Boston, Massachusetts*
*MASTERSPEC®; published by ARCOM; Salt Lake City, Utah, and Alexandria, Virginia*

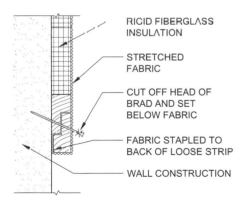

**STRETCHED FABRIC APPLIED ON SITE**
No size limitation.

Labels: RIGID FIBERGLASS INSULATION; STRETCHED FABRIC; CUT OFF HEAD OF BRAD AND SET BELOW FABRIC; FABRIC STAPLED TO BACK OF LOOSE STRIP; WALL CONSTRUCTION

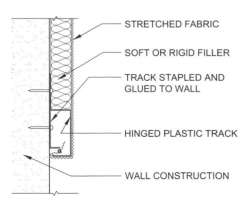

**PLASTIC TRACK SYSTEM WITH SITE-APPLIED FABRIC**
No size limitation.

Labels: STRETCHED FABRIC; SOFT OR RIGID FILLER; TRACK STAPLED AND GLUED TO WALL; HINGED PLASTIC TRACK; WALL CONSTRUCTION

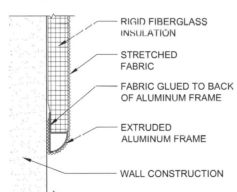

**WOOD- OR METAL-EDGED FABRIC-WRAPPED PANELS**
Limited in size to core and frame material and the ability to enter building, for example, door opening and elevator cab sizes.

Labels: RIGID FIBERGLASS INSULATION; STRETCHED FABRIC; FABRIC GLUED TO BACK OF ALUMINUM FRAME; EXTRUDED ALUMINUM FRAME; WALL CONSTRUCTION

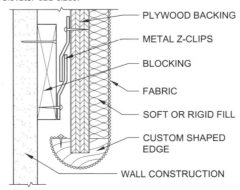

**CUSTOM-EDGED COMPOSITE PANEL**
Limited to size of core.

Labels: PLYWOOD BACKING; METAL Z-CLIPS; BLOCKING; FABRIC; SOFT OR RIGID FILL; CUSTOM SHAPED EDGE; WALL CONSTRUCTION

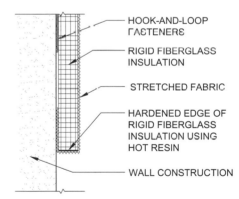

**LIGHTWEIGHT FABRIC PANELS AND FIBERGLASS FOAM CORE**
Limited to size of core.

Labels: HOOK-AND-LOOP FASTENERS; RIGID FIBERGLASS INSULATION; STRETCHED FABRIC; HARDENED EDGE OF RIGID FIBERGLASS INSULATION USING HOT RESIN; WALL CONSTRUCTION

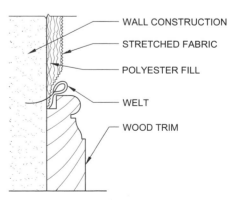

**UPHOLSTERED WALL—PADDED**
Usually stretched from floor to ceiling or between wood trim.

Labels: WALL CONSTRUCTION; STRETCHED FABRIC; POLYESTER FILL; WELT; WOOD TRIM

# STONE FACING

Numerous types of stones can be used for stone facing; however, consideration should be given to the selection of a stone that is appropriate for the intended use. Stone facing typically does not need to meet the rigorous performance criteria of stone flooring, but care should be taken to select a stone that can be cut and dressed to meet the project's design. A review with the stone fabricator or supplier is recommended to minimize the risk of incompatibility of the stone with the intended use.

## STONE FACING TYPES

Stone facing is available in two basic types: *dimension stone panels* and dimension *stone tiles*. Marbles and other stones that might be considered too soft for flooring can usually be used for stone facing, with the proper reinforcement and installation.

### Dimension Stone Panels

Dimension stone facing panel dimensions typically range from larger-dimension units with face areas up to 48 sq in. (1,200 sq mm) × ¾ in. (19 mm, also known as 2 cm), 1¼ in. to 2 in. (32 mm, also known as 3 cm, to 50 mm) thick. Sizes and shapes are limited to the specific stone's characteristics. A panel that is 2 ft 6 in. × 5 ft 0 in. (762 × 1,524 mm) is a size that stone fabricators can easily handle, and it conforms to the 5 ft (1,524 mm) module of many buildings.

### Dimension Stone Tiles

Stone tile modules are dimension stone units that do not exceed 4 sq ft (.37 sq m) and are less than ¾ in. (2 cm) thick. Stone tiles are typically 12 × 12 in. (305 × 305 mm) up to 24 × 24 in. (610 × 610 mm) × ¼, ⅜, and ½ in. (6, 10, and 13 mm) thick, and are usually furnished with a protective backing such as fiberglass to improve the tile strength. Larger stone tile sizes are offered by selected manufacturers.

## MARBLE WALL FACING PATTERNS

Stone with distinctive texture and markings, such as certain marbles, lends itself to specific pattern arrangements. The markings vary depending on whether the marble veneer is cut with or across its setting bed.

*Blend pattern.* Panels of the same variety of stone but not necessarily from the same block are arranged at random.

*Side-slip pattern.* Panels from the same block are placed side by side or end to end in sequence, to ensure a repetitive pattern and blended color.

*End-match pattern.* Adjacent panel faces are finished, and one panel is inverted and placed above the other.

*Book-match pattern.* Adjacent panel faces are finished, and one panel is next to the other.

## VENEER CUTTING

Quarry blocks are reduced to slabs by a gang saw. The gang saw consists of a series of parallel steel blades in a frame that moves forward and backward. The most productive and precise gang saws use diamond-tipped blades with individual hydraulic blade tensioners; others are fed a cutting abrasive in a stream of water.

Marble blocks can be sawn either parallel or perpendicular to the bedding plane. The perpendicular cut is referred to as an *across-the-bed* or *vein cut*. The parallel cut is a *with-the-bed* or *Fleuri cut*. Other marbles produce a pleasing surface only when sawn in one direction, and are generally available only in that variety.

## VENEER PATTERNS

Only certain marbles lend themselves to specific pattern arrangements, such as side-slip or end-slip, which require a constant natural marking trend throughout the marble block. Formal patterns require selectivity, which usually increases the installed cost of the marble veneer. Usually, material sawn for a vein cut can be matched. Fleuri cuts can only be blended.

Perfection in veneer matching is impossible because a portion of the marble block is lost during the sawing process and because the vein shifts. Ideally, jointing should be planned for groupings of four panels of equal size.

## WIRE-TIE ANCHORING SYSTEMS

Wire-tie anchoring systems with plaster or mortar spots are the traditional methods for installing interior stone facing. Wire ties are anchored to the gypsum board, masonry, or concrete wall. In gypsum board construction, wire ties are embedded in plaster-filled metal boxes or are inserted through the gypsum board and are fastened to the partition framing. In masonry walls, the wire ties are embedded in voids filled with mortar or plaster. The disadvantages of wire-tie anchoring systems are twofold: first, fire-rated gypsum board walls require another row of metal studs and another layer of gypsum board if the wire ties are not allowed to penetrate the fire-rated wall; second, seismic restraint for the stone panels is difficult to engineer.

A minimum of four anchors should be provided for stone panels up to 12 sq ft (1.1 sq m), with two additional anchors for each additional 8 sq ft (.74 sq m) of surface area. For stone facing panels over 96 in. (2,400 mm) high, the wire-tie method must be supplemented with intermediate horizontal supports for the vertical stone loads.

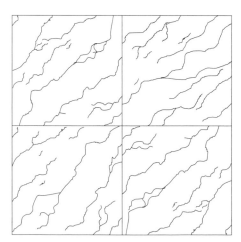

**BLEND PATTERN**

**SIDE-SLIP OR END PATTERN**

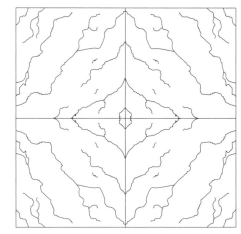

**END-MATCH, BOOK-MATCH, OR QUARTER-MATCH PATTERNS**

**MARBLE WALL FACING PATTERNS**

## TYPES OF STONE

### Granite

Granite can be used on interior walls in many finishes, ranging from highly polished to a rough thermal finish. A waterjet finish is a texture between honed and thermal, and brings out the color of the stone. It is slightly darker than the thermal finish appearance. Granite is much harder than marble, therefore it is more costly to fabricate and finish.

### Marble

Marble varieties that are not recommended for exterior use can be successfully used in interior wall panel applications, if properly prepared for vertical installations. Heavily veined marbles, prized for their aesthetic qualities, are examples. Dry seams can be glued together (sticking), voids can be filled (waxing), and weak areas can be reinforced with metal rods glued into the back of the stone panel (rodding). During fabrication, fragile marbles are frequently reinforced with a layer of fiberglass-reinforced plastic prior to final fabrication and polishing of the marble.

### Serpentine Marble

Green varieties, called serpentine marble, are sensitive to water and are prone to warping when wet. When installing serpentine stone, use setting materials that do not contain water, such as water-cleanable epoxy adhesives.

### Greenstone

Greenstone, a general term for metamorphosed igneous basaltic-type rock, is typically available in honed or cleft finishes, and is not suitable for a highly polished finish, due to the stone structure. Greenstone contains minerals that give it a green appearance: either actinolite, chlorite, or epidote. Sources are usually European, as it is no longer quarried in the United States.

### Dolomitic Limestone

Dolomitic limestone is more widely used for interior stone facing, as it is typically not as porous as oolitic limestone, and is often polished similar to marble. It is also available with a smooth-honed finish, a textured sandblasted finish, or a split-face finish.

### Slate

Slate is commonly used as a contemporary interior floor or wall finish. It is available in a palette of dark, rich colors including green, black, purple, and red. Slate splits easily into thin sheets. The finish resulting from the natural face is referred to as a cleft finish. Slate can also be sand-rubbed to a smooth or honed finish.

### Travertine

Travertine is distinguished by its natural cavities, formed by plants embedded during the rock's formation, which must be filled to achieve a smooth surface. Filling materials are typically portland cement, epoxy resins, or polyester resins. Travertine is actually a kind of limestone, but some types that take a polish are classified as marble. It is popular for use as a flooring because its visual texture conceals dirt much better than most other stones.

### Stone Tile

Stone tiles are fabricated under different conditions from dimension stone panels and are not typically matched to create patterns, such as book- or end-matching. The greater variation in stone color, pattern, and texture is common in stone tile, and should be factored into the project review prior to installation.

### Engineered Composite Stone

New technology has enabled the development of engineered composite stone products. Formulated from stone aggregate and synthetic resin matrix materials, these products are available in sizes ranging from tile units to large panel sheets for horizontal and vertical applications. Composite stone characteristics are strength, nonporosity, durability, and flexibility. Finishes are typically limited to polished; colors range from natural stone tones to vibrant colors. Thicknesses vary, and due to the strength of the composite units, can sometimes be thinner than natural dimension stone. Typical sheet sizes are ¾ in. (2 cm) or 1⅛ in. (3 cm). A manufacturer is currently introducing a ⅜-in.- (1-cm-) thick product for sheet panels. Installation for the sheet panels is similar to natural stone. Tile units are installed with the same thinset methods as for ceramic tile.

## STONE FINISHES

The finish of stone flooring affects the perception of its color and the slip resistance. Polished finishes are the most reflective. These high-maintenance finishes should be selected with care. For high-traffic public areas, such as lobbies, polished floor finishes are often eventually hidden under nonskid mats. Honed finishes have a dull sheen. These satin-smooth surfaces are often good choices for commercial floors because of their slip resistance. Thermal, sometimes called flamed, finishes are achieved by the application of intense flaming heat to the surface of the stone. Thermal finishes are usually applied to granite.

## ABRASION RESISTANCE

Abrasion resistance is the capability of the stone to resist wear and absorption, which affects staining and soiling of the stone. For interior stone facing, abrasion resistance is typically not a factor, unless the stone will be subjected to frequent bumping and scraping. Consult with the stone fabricator or supplier for the selection of appropriate stone types for a particular installation and intended use.

## TYPICAL FINISHES AND COMMON SIZES OF INTERIOR STONE WALL PANELS

| STONE | GRADE | FINISH | MINIMUM THICKNESS IN. (MM) | MAXIMUM FACE DIMENSION FT (MM) | NOTES |
|---|---|---|---|---|---|
| Granite | Building (exterior) Veneer Masonry | Polished Honed | ¾–1¼* (19–32) | 5 x 5 (1,525 × 1,525) | This very hard and durable surface is not likely to stain. Many colors and grains are available. |
| Marble | Group A (exterior) Group B Group C Group D | Polished Honed | ½–⅞* (13–22) | 4 x 7 (1,220 × 2,135) | The most colorful and interesting marbles are in Groups B, C, and D; however, some filling of natural voids may be required. Many colors and patterns are available. |
| Limestone | Select Standard Rustic Variegated | Smooth Tooled Polished | ⅞–3 (22–76) | 4 x 9 (1,220 × 2,745) | Soft and easy to shape, but shows wear and may discolor over time. Colors range in the buffs and grays. |
| Slate | Ribbon Clear | Natural Cleft Sand Rubbed Honed | 1–1½ (25–38) | 2 ft 6 in. x 5 ft (760 × 1,525) | Ribbon stock is distinguished by its ornamental integral bands, which are usually darker than the rest of the stone. Colors range in the pastel hues. |

* ¼ to ½ in. thick (6 to 13 mm) tiles (usually a face dimension of 12 × 12 in. (305 × 305 mm )) are available. Tiles can be directly applied to a wall with adhesive or thin set mortar, similar to flooring applications. Tiles are not recommended for walls over 8 ft (2.4 m) high.

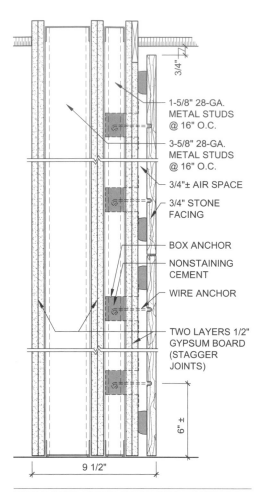

**1-5/8" 28-GA. METAL STUDS @ 16" O.C.**

**3-5/8" 28-GA. METAL STUDS @ 16" O.C.**

**3/4"± AIR SPACE**

**3/4" STONE FACING**

**BOX ANCHOR**

**NONSTAINING CEMENT**

**WIRE ANCHOR**

**TWO LAYERS 1/2" GYPSUM BOARD (STAGGER JOINTS)**

3/4"

6" ±

9 1/2"

**FIRE-RATED METAL STUD WALL—SECTION**

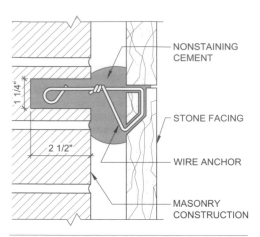

**NONSTAINING CEMENT**

**STONE FACING**

**WIRE ANCHOR**

**MASONRY CONSTRUCTION**

1 1/4"

2 1/2"

**WIRE LACE ANCHOR—SECTION**

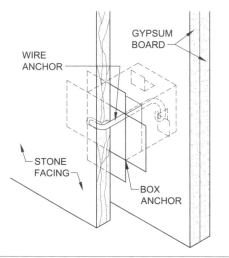

**GYPSUM BOARD**

**WIRE ANCHOR**

**STONE FACING**

**BOX ANCHOR**

**WIRE TIE AT FIRE-RATED METAL STUD WALL**

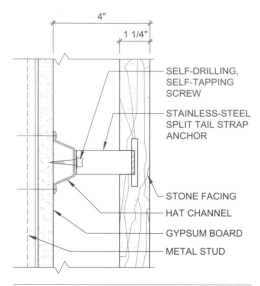

4"

1 1/4"

**SELF-DRILLING, SELF-TAPPING SCREW**

**STAINLESS-STEEL SPLIT TAIL STRAP ANCHOR**

**STONE FACING**

**HAT CHANNEL**

**GYPSUM BOARD**

**METAL STUD**

**STRAP-ANCHORED SECTION**

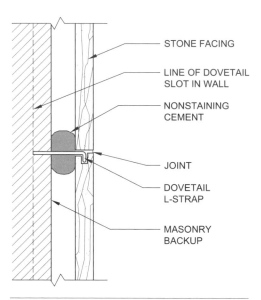

**STONE FACING**

**LINE OF DOVETAIL SLOT IN WALL**

**NONSTAINING CEMENT**

**JOINT**

**DOVETAIL L-STRAP**

**MASONRY BACKUP**

**DOVETAIL ANCHOR SECTION**

## MECHANICAL ANCHORING SYSTEMS

Mechanical anchoring systems fasten stone directly to the backup wall, eliminating the need for additional studding and gypsum board and providing verifiable seismic restraint. The stone is kerfed on the back side and is restrained by the use of straps or clips. Anchor systems, similar to those used for exterior work over masonry or metal framing, may be fastened to metal studs through gypsum board. Exterior anchors may also be used with metal channel struts, which eliminate the need to coordinate stud location with anchor locations. This type of anchor may still require plaster-setting spots.

## GROUT

Grout for interior stone facing is commonly mixed with latex additives, which produces a more flexible and durable joint installation. The stone industry is now referencing ANSI standards for ceramic tile-grouting materials. Dry-set grouts are mixtures of portland cement and water-retentive additives. Unsanded grouts are typically used in joints up to 1/8 in. (3 mm) wide. Wider grout joints are typically sanded, as the sand reduces grout shrinkage and minimizes cracking. When installing sanded grout on polished stone surfaces, protect the stone face to avoid scratching the surface finish.

## JOINT SIZES

Joint sizes vary depending on the type of stone and finish selected and whether joints are to be coordinated with exterior or floor joints. For polished stone installations, joints from 1/16 in. (1.5 mm) wide to 1/8 in. (3 mm) wide are used. Currently, the wider joint size is prevalent to allow for more latitude in fabrication dimensions and in backup construction dimensions. For highly textured stone finishes, such as a thermal or cleft finish, a joint width of 1/4 to 3/8 in. (6 to 10 mm) wide is common. The larger joint dimension minimizes the visibility of lipping of stone panels. When combining different stone textures, one size joint for the entire installation is recommended, usually the largest required for the different textures.

## LIPPAGE

Lippage is the condition where one panel is higher than adjacent panels; it is more common in thinset installations. The recommended maximum variation of the finished stone surface should be no greater than ⅛ in. (3 mm) cumulative over a 10 ft (3 m) lineal measurement, with no greater than a ¹⁄₃₂ in. (1 mm) variation between individual tiles or panels.

Each interior stone facing project should be reviewed to determine the best method of installation for the installation conditions. Setting space dimensions and project conditions may indicate the use of a particular installation method.

## INSTALLATION OF STONE TILE

Stone tile may be installed in a full mortar bed, a thinset mortar bed, or with an adhesive. Thin stone tiles are typically not restrained by ties or anchors, therefore their installation has limitations. Tiles that are installed above 8 ft (2.4 m) high must be additionally restrained with anchors.

Interior stone anchoring systems must be compatible with the stone and substrate. Stone facing may be installed on gypsum board construction, masonry, or concrete walls. Butt joints are not recommended due to potential spalling if movement occurs in the structure.

### Mortar Beds

Mortar beds can be used when installing thin stone tiles and thin panels in a thick portland cement mortar system consisting of metal lath, a scratch coat, and a float coat. The stone tile is set into the float coat.

### Thinset

Thinset installations are appropriate for vertical application of stone tiles and thin panels up to ½ in. (13 mm) thick. The stone is set in the same manner as ceramic tiles, directly on the substrate of gypsum board or cementitious backer units, using specific thin-bed setting systems. Adhesives should be non-staining, especially when installing light-colored stone.

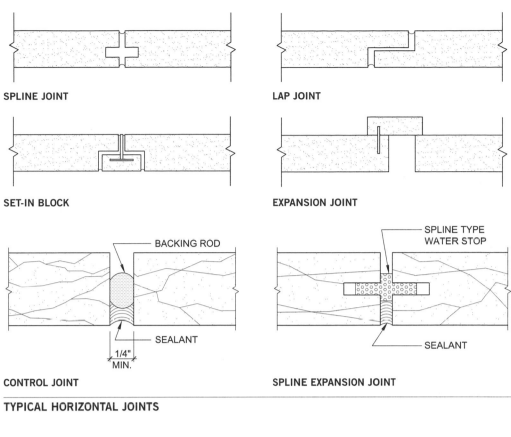

**SPLINE JOINT**

**LAP JOINT**

**SET-IN BLOCK**

**EXPANSION JOINT**

**CONTROL JOINT**

**SPLINE EXPANSION JOINT**

**TYPICAL HORIZONTAL JOINTS**

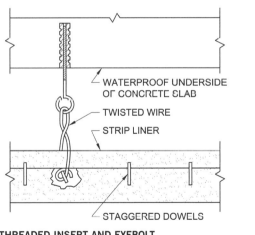

**THREADED INSERT AND EYEBOLT**

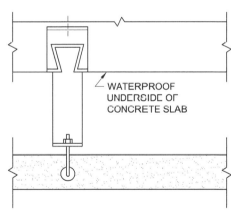

**DOVETAIL STRAP WITH HOOK ROD ANCHOR**

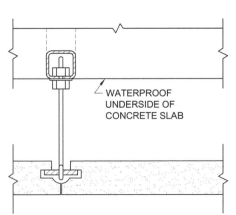

**EYEBOLT AND DOWEL BOLTED TO THREADED CONCRETE INSERT**

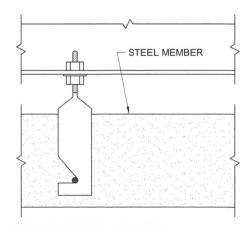

**FLAT HOOK ANCHOR AND DOWEL**

**TYPICAL SYSTEMS FOR HANGING INTERIOR VENEER STONE**

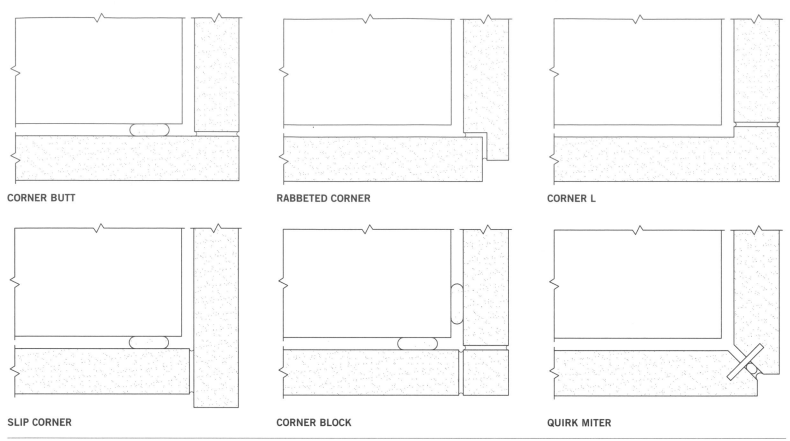

**CORNER BUTT**

**RABBETED CORNER**

**CORNER L**

**SLIP CORNER**

**CORNER BLOCK**

**QUIRK MITER**

**TYPICAL CORNER DETAILS**

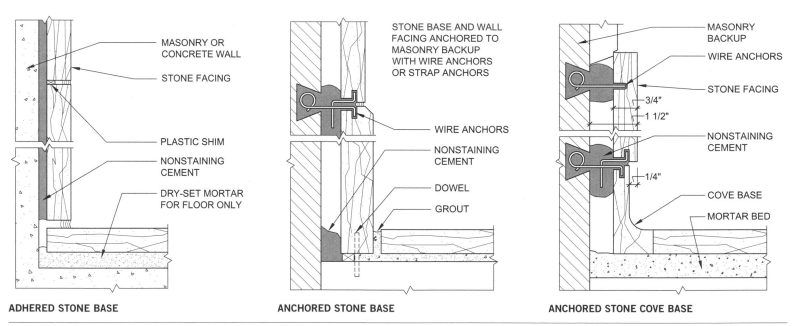

**ADHERED STONE BASE**

**ANCHORED STONE BASE**

**ANCHORED STONE COVE BASE**

**STONE BASES**

Mark Form; Leo Daly Company; Washington, D.C.
George M. Whiteside, III, AIA, and James D. Lloyd; Kennett Square, Pennsylvania
Alexander Keyes; Darrel Downing Rippeteau, Architect; Washington, D.C.
Elizabeth Aukamp; Rhode Island School of Design; Providence, Rhode Island
MASTERSPEC®; published by ARCOM; Salt Lake City, Utah, and Alexandria, Virginia

# PAINTS AND COATINGS

## COATING SELECTION CRITERIA

Paint has three basic functions: to decorate, to protect, or to modify the performance of the substrate to which it is applied. Paint ingredients, types, and applications all affect a coating's performance. The following criteria are considerations for selecting the appropriate coating for a given application:

Abrasion resistance
Adhesion
Impact resistance
Flexural qualities
Resistance to a given medium (e.g., chemicals)
Resistance to sunlight
Temperature resistance
Drying time (installation criteria)
Appearance
Wetting time
Emissive requirements (reflection and absorption)
Electrical insulation

## INGREDIENTS

There are four categories of paint ingredients: pigment, thinner, resin, and additives.

- *Pigment* provides color, hiding, and bulk.
- *Thinner* affects consistency and drying time and carries the pigment and resin to the substrate.
- *Resin* binds the pigment particles together and affects adhesion, durability, and level of protection of the paint film.
- *Additives* enhance the coating's performance with specific desirable characteristics.

The term *paint solids* refers to the resin. The thinner is called the *liquid*. A higher solids content provides a thick, durable, opaque coating. The solids content of paint can be specified by weight or by volume. Volume of solids is the better indicator of performance. Latex paints range from 25% to 40% volume of solids. Alkyd and oil-based paints can exceed 50% volume.

## PAINT FORMULATION

| Pigments | + | Resin | = | Solids |
|---|---|---|---|---|
| Solids | + | Liquid | = | Paint |
| Fused solids | − | Liquid | = | Final coating |

### Pigments

Pigments provide paints with color or whiteness, opacity, and bulk. Pigments are often the most expensive ingredients in paint. Pigment is added to paint either at the point of sale or in the factory. At the point of sale, colorants are mixed with tint bases or to white paints designed for tinting. Colorants are grounded color pigment particles dispersed in liquid. In the factory, dry powders or colorants are used to make prepackaged colored paints.

*Prime pigments* provide whiteness and color to paint. White pigment and whiteness in colored paint are predominantly supplied by titanium dioxide. Organic pigments and inorganic pigments supply paint with color. Organic pigments are brighter and not as highly durable as inorganic pigments.

*Extender pigments,* or inert pigments, impart bulk to coatings and enhance leveling and adhesion. They can negatively affect the final finish, the hiding capacity, and the scrub resistance of paint. Extenders are made from clay, silicates, talc, and zinc oxide.

### Thinners

Thinner, also referred to as the *solvent* or *liquid*, reduces coatings to the proper viscosity and provide the means of dispensing the coating from the container to the substrate. It allows the paint to flow and level itself on the substrate. The thinner determines whether paint hardens by oxidation, evaporation, chemical action, or by thermosetting at elevated temperatures. There are two types of thinners, water and solvent. Water is the thinning agent for water-based paints. Oil-based and alkyd paints are thinned by a combustible solvent made from mineral spirits.

### Resin

Resin, also referred to as the *binder* or *film former,* is the nonvolatile portion of the paint that binds the pigment particles together, forming the cured paint film. The resin determines the dried paint film's adhesion to the substrate. The resin provides continuity, flow, leveling, and gloss development. It enhances the hardness, toughness, and strength of the paint film.

There are two basic categories of resins: those that are solvent-thinned, such as oil-based and alkyd paints, and those that are water-thinned, such as latex paints. *Solvent-thinned resins* are made from natural or synthetic oils. When exposed to air, the thinner evaporates, leaving the resin oils to harden through the chemical process of oxidation. Oil-based and alkyd paints are made from a solvent, solvent-thinned oil resin, and pigments. Oil-based and alkyd paints have better adhesion and a smoother appearance, and dry much harder than latex paints that are water-thinned. Conversely, oil-based paints can harden to the point at which they become vulnerable to cracking, chipping, and yellowing. *Water-thinned resins* in latex paint are solid plasticlike materials dispersed as microscopic particles in water. This dispersion is a milky-white liquid that the paint industry calls *latex* or *emulsion*. (The *latex* used in the paint industry looks similar to but is not related to the natural latex extracted from rubber trees.) Water-thinned paint dries and hardens through evaporation. Coalescing agents in the paint ensure that the resin particles fuse together as they dry to form a continuous film.

Many types of synthetic polymer are used as resins in latex paint. They vary in terms of their particle size, flow and leveling, hardness, solids types, and price. One hundred percent acrylic and vinyl acrylic (PVA) are the two synthetic polymers most commonly used in North America. For interior applications, 100% acrylic binders are considered to be superior in terms of adhesion under wet conditions and resistance to waterborne stains, to sticking, and to alkaline cleaners. Acrylic latex binders perform well in interior wall paints as drywall primers and in satin and semigloss paints. Styrenated acrylic resins are used in masonry sealers, metal coatings, and in gloss paints.

### Additives

Additives are included as needed to enhance the properties of the solids or the liquid ingredients of paint. They can improve paint life within the container and paint application onto the substrate.

**PIGMENT VOLUME CONCENTRATION OF PAINT INGREDIENTS FOR INTERIOR COATINGS**
*Source: Guy Weismantel,* Paint Handbook, *McGraw-Hill, New York, 1981.*

# PAINT AND COATING TYPES

## Alkyd Paint

The solvent-thinned resin in alkyd paint is made from synthetic oils. Alkyd resins are oil-modified polyesters made primarily from alcohol and acid. They are the most common paint resin. Alkyd paints are faster drying, harder, and more durable, and have better color-retention properties than oil-based paints. They are easy to apply, are washable, and have less odor than other paints using solvent thinners. Alkyd paints have poor resistance to alkaline surfaces, such as masonry, and should not be used unless these substrates are properly primed.

## Latex Paint

Most water-based paints are referred to as latex paint. Latex paints have very little odor and a fast drying time. Their water-base thinner makes latex paints easy to apply, clean up, and discard. Latex paints are porous; when applied, a latex coating retains microscopic openings that allow it to breathe. Adhesion failure is prevented because moisture that might become trapped beneath the paint's surface can evaporate through these openings. Latex paints have a greater blistering tendency when high levels of tinting color are present.

## Oil-Based Paint

The solvent-thinned resin in oil-based paint is made from natural oils, such as linseed oil (from flax seed), soya oil (from soybeans), and tung oil (from china wood tree fruit).

## Primers

Primers make a surface more paintable by providing improved adhesion for coatings. Primers are selected in relation to the characteristics of the selected topcoat. Primers serve the following functions:

- Conceal the substrate surface so that the existing coating color does not read through.
- Provide a barrier to prevent moisture from destroying the paint bond.
- Bind substrate surface with the topcoat.
- Limit the paint absorption of a porous substrate, such as a skim coat of plaster.
- Recondition old paint to receive future paint coatings.
- Act as a rust inhibitor.

## COMMON PAINT ADDITIVES

| ADDITIVE | PURPOSE |
|---|---|
| Antiskinning Agent | Prevents skin from forming in can prior to use. |
| Biocide | Prevents spoilage resulting from bacterial growth. |
| Coalescent | Aids in formation of continuous film in latex paint. |
| Defoamer | Eliminates air from paint or reduces bubbling upon application. |
| Drier | Accelerates conversion of solvent paints from liquid to solid state. |
| Freeze-Thaw Stabilizer | Lowers latex paint freezing point. |
| Mildewcide | Resists growth of mildew. |
| Surfactant | Stabilizes mixtures of resins or pigments in solvents or water. |
| Thickener | Increases consistency of paint and prevents separation of pigment in oil- and water-based paints |

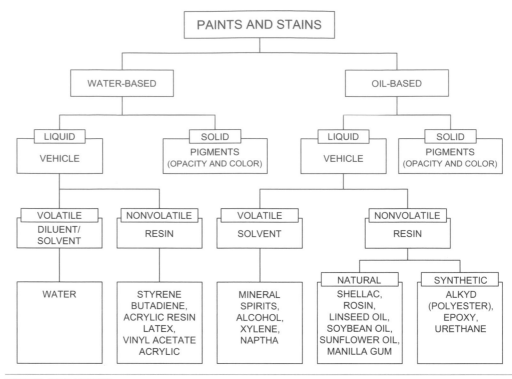

**PAINTS AND STAINS**

## Catalyzed Epoxy Paint

Catalyzed epoxy coatings resist chemicals, solvents, stains, physical abrasion, traffic, and cleaning materials. They have good adhesion and color retention. Catalyzed epoxies come in two parts, resin and catalyst. They have limited "pot life," hence are required to be mixed just prior to use. When applied to a substrate, a chemical action occurs that causes a dense hard film to form, similar to baked enamel. Adequate ventilation must be provided during and after application.

Three types of catalyzed epoxies are commonly used in commercial interiors:

- *Polyester epoxies* produce a tough glossy surface.
- *Polyamide epoxies* provide a flexible but durable film.
- *Urethane epoxies* are the most versatile of the epoxy coatings.

## Epoxy Ester Paint

Epoxy esters are similar to catalyzed epoxy but have no pot life restrictions and are packaged like conventional paint. The paint film occurs due to oxidation rather than a chemical reaction triggered by a catalyst. Epoxy esters are less durable than catalyzed epoxies.

## Flame-Retardant Paints

Flame-retardant paints slow the rate at which fire spreads by delaying the ignition of the surface that has been coated. They are used on combustible materials such as wood to achieve the required flame-spread ratings. These paints delay but do not prevent a fire from spreading. Flame-retardant paints are *intumescent* and protect the substrate from burning by swelling to form a charred layer of blisters when exposed to extremely high heat.

Flame-retardant paint is a foamlike material made with either a water-based thinner or a solvent-based thinner. Requisite fire ratings are achieved with this material based on the number of coatings applied to the substrate at a prescribed thickness. Intumescent paint manufacturers certify painters to ensure that their products are correctly applied.

## Fire-Resistant Paints

Fire-resistant paints resist the spread of fire by not contributing to the flame. They are less effective at controlling the spread of fire than intumescent coatings.

## Multicolor Coatings

Multicolor coatings are durable and scratch-resistant. They add a three-dimensional quality to a surface, similar to hand-sponge techniques. Multicolor coatings can be water-thinned or solvent-thinned. Traditional solvent-thinned multicolor coatings are composed of tiny bubbles of different sizes and colors suspended in a nonpigmented solution. The separated beads of pigment remain separate until they are spray-applied. They burst upon impact with the surface.

## Stains

Stains made from dyes dissolved in either drying oil or water provide translucent or transparent coatings for wood. Pigmented stains are opaque. Oil-based stains use drying oil made from various plants. The oil dries by absorbing oxygen from the surface, and the air creates a tough elastic film that protects a wood. Wood surfaces can be filled before staining in order to affect surface porousness and smoothness, but fillers may cause stains to be absorbed unevenly. Stain may be applied with a brush, spray, roller, or rag pad.

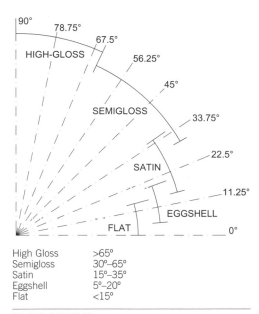

| High Gloss | >65° |
| Semigloss | 30°–65° |
| Satin | 15°–35° |
| Eggshell | 5°–20° |
| Flat | <15° |

**PAINT SHEENS**

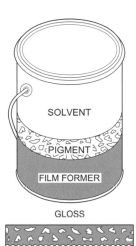
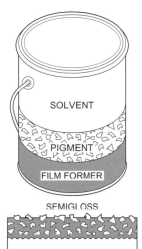
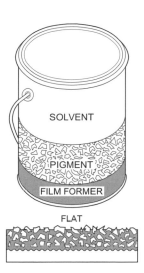

The ratio of the volume of pigment to the volume of resin in a paint is called the pigment volume concentration (PVC). Light reflects off a cured paint film with a low PVC for a glossy appearance. Light is diffused by a high PVC paint for a flat finish.

**PIGMENT VOLUME CONCENTRATION**

## DECORATIVE PAINT FINISHES

Decorative paint finishes are used for their aesthetic qualities and for masking minor surface defects. Generally, they provide a surface with a multitoned color and a texture. Decorative paint finishes can be achieved with oil- or water-based paints.

### Cobweb Finish
Cobweb finish is provided by a specialty paint that dries into a spiderweb pattern on the painted surface. It is applied with standard spray equipment.

### Crackle Finish
This paint technique gives an "alligator" texture to the painted surface. It requires a base coat over which a second specialty paint, crackle coat, is applied.

## SHEEN

The presence of pigment reduces the gloss of the cured paint film. By increasing the amount and dimension of the pigment particles in relationship to the amount of resin, the resin's level of gloss or the texture of the paint is reduced. The texture of cured paint is called sheen. Pigment color and sheen determine the light reflectivity of a painted surface, which affects the perception of the color. The more pigment that is

present relative to the resin, the rougher-textured, less reflective, and flatter is the paint's appearance. A glossy surface is achieved by a larger volume of resin that encases the pigment.

## APPLICATION

Because paint appearance varies depending on its sheen, the color, and the lighting, paint installations typically require mock-ups. Step samples on foam core boards showing progressive layers of coating systems are useful during contract administration. More often, a maximum of three 4 ft by 8 ft (2.1 m by 2.4 m) mock-ups are provided by a contractor for approval before final application is begun. The mock-ups should be applied directly to the substrate to be painted.

Paint adhesion failure appears as peeling, blistering, cracking, or flaking. Paint failure occurs for one or both of the following reasons:

- *The surfaces to be coated have not been properly prepared.* All substrates must be clean, dry, and smooth. All of the products to be coated must be compatible, including patching compounds, sealants, primers, sealers, paints, and other coat-

ings. The paint manufacturer should be consulted for recommendations regarding priming or sealing a substrate and for information describing the proper combination of products to be used.
- *Coatings have not been properly applied.* Optimal temperature application of most paints is crucial. Typically, interior installations require between 50°F (10°C) and 90°F (32°C). The manufacturer will specify. Paint manufacturers specify how much paint should be applied by giving an application rate or a dry film thickness.

$$Application\ Rate = Sq\ Ft/Gal$$

The application rate is the area of substrate in square feet covered by a gallon of paint.

$$Dry\ Film\ Thickness = DFT$$

The dry film thickness is the thickness of the cured paint finish measured in mils. One mil is equal to 0.00245 mm, which is equal to one one-thousandth of an inch.

*Faith Baum, AIA, IIDA; Faith Baum Architect; Lexington, Massachusetts*

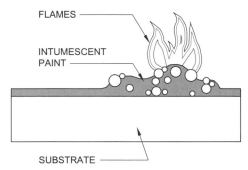

Intumescent paint bubbles and swells when exposed to high heat. The paint film forms a charred layer of blister, insulating the substrate from the fire.

**INTUMESCENT PAINT**

### Volatile Organic Compounds (VOCs)

During the curing process, solvent-thinned coatings (including latex and waterborne coatings) release volatile organic compounds (VOCs) into the atmosphere. The VOCs, in the presence of sunlight, mix with nitrogen oxide in the atmosphere and form the air-pollutant ozone, a component of smog. VOCs are measured in grams of organic solvent per liter of paint or lb/gal (g/l). Each jurisdiction has air pollution control agencies that determine the local VOC requirements. Due to rapidly changing regulations, the Environmental Protection Agency (EPA) should be contacted for current information on VOC regulation.

# ACCESS FLOORING

Access flooring creates a chase underneath the floor for wires, cables, and sometimes an air distribution plenum. Access flooring systems are often used in general offices, data centers, computer rooms, and cleanrooms. Multilevel access flooring systems are available that incorporate two or more continuous cavities beneath the floor panels to house wireways and an air distribution plenum. Access flooring consists of panels and an understructure system.

## UNDERSTRUCTURES

There are two types of access flooring understructures: low-profile systems and pedestal systems.

- *Low-profile systems* provide a low-height access floor (typically less than 4 in. (100 mm) high)) that does not significantly encroach on space height. In these systems, closely spaced plastic or metal supports incorporate cable management systems and provide support at regular intervals across the panel.
- *Pedestal systems* are composed of either a threaded rod or a telescoping tube, which support the panel at the corners (or at the edge at the floor perimeter). It is considered good practice to adhere pedestal bases to the subfloor to resist horizontal forces.

There are two basic types of pedestal systems: stringlerless and stringer systems.

### Stringerless Systems

Stringerless systems consist of pedestals located so that each pedestal head supports four panels at their corners. Stringerless systems provide maximum access to the underfloor cavity. Stringerless understructures can be less stable laterally than those with stringers and are less capable of withstanding lateral forces from earthquakes and other sources; consequently their use is limited to lower finished floor heights.

Two panel types are available for stringerless pedestal systems: *gravity-held* and *bolted-down panels.*

### Gravity-Held Panel Systems

Gravity-held panels are secured in place by nesting on an interlocking connection formed in both the panel

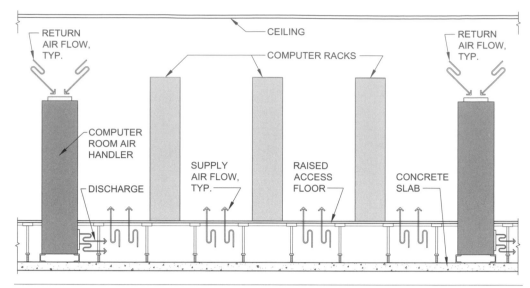

**TYPICAL ACCESS FLOORING COMPUTER SPACE AIRFLOW PATTERN**

and the pedestal head. This system provides the quickest access because no tools other than a panel lifter are required to remove panels.

### Bolted-Down Panels

Bolted-down panels are directly connected to pedestal heads by fasteners located in panel corners. Because the fasteners must be accessible to remove panels, floor coverings must be either removable or permanently attached to panels and of a type that can accommodate exposed countersunk fasteners. Carpet tile is generally selected for the former condition, and either high-pressure plastic laminate or resilient tile for the latter. Bolting panels to pedestals improves the entire system's lateral stability and adds resistance to rocking and overturning. The latter effect can result where partitions are fastened to panels and are subject to unbalanced loads that are not resisted by ceiling connections or other means.

### Stringer Systems

Stringer systems are offered with either bolted or snap-on (nonbolted) stringers. The purpose of stringers is to

provide additional lateral support, particularly where panels are frequently removed or where finished floor heights or earthquake loads exceed those that can be accommodated by stringerless systems.

Two panel types are available for stringer systems: *bolted* and *snap-on stringers.*

### Bolted Stringer

Bolted stringer systems consist of main stringers, usually two to three modules long, and cross stringers, one module long, which are bolted to pedestals. These stringers may or may not support panel edges.

### Snap-On Stringer

Snap-on stringer systems consist of stringers, each one module in length, located under the edge of each panel and interlocking with pedestal heads without using threaded fasteners; this makes the removal of grid members more convenient because no tools are needed. The disadvantage of snap-on stringers is that with frequent use they do not provide the same degree of restraint as bolted stringers.

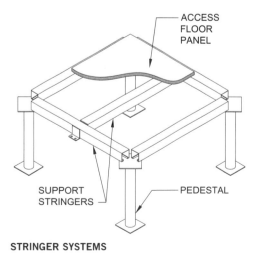

**STRINGER SYSTEMS**

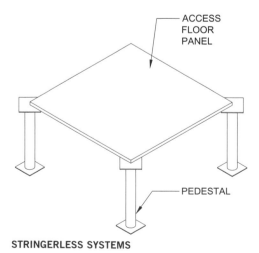

**STRINGERLESS SYSTEMS**

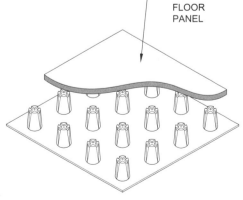

**LOW-PROFILE SYSTEMS**

**ACCESS FLOORING UNDERSTRUCTURE SYSTEMS**

Sarah Bader; Gensler; Chicago, Illinois
Tanya Nachia; Rhode Island School of Design; Providence, Rhode Island
MASTERSPEC®; published by ARCOM; Salt Lake City, Utah, and Alexandria, Virginia

# TEXTILES

## FABRIC IN INTERIORS

The immensity of the textile industry is reflected in the vast number of uses of textiles in commercial interior projects. Fabric is used on walls as wallcoverings, stretched-fabric wall and ceiling systems, wall-mounted panels, and systems furniture panels; as vertical hangings for draperies, banners, and vertical louver blinds; as upholstery for seating; and as floor coverings, including carpet and rugs. Leather, commonly used as a luxury upholstery material, can also be used as a floor tile.

## FIBERS

*Textiles* is the term given to any fabric composed of fibers, whether woven, knitted, felted, or manufactured by some other means. A fiber, the basic element of a textile, is a fine, hairlike strand that forms the basis of a yarn. Fibers are found in nature or are manufactured (synthetic). The characteristics that make a given fiber suitable for a particular end-use application are either inherent or engineered by production and processing techniques.

### Fiber Types

Fibers range in length from a fraction of an inch to several miles, and can be categorized as *staple* or *filament* fibers. Filament fibers are stronger than staples. Longer fibers typically provide greater strength than shorter ones. The strength of a fiber helps determine the abrasion resistance of the final textile. In addition, yarns made from filaments and longer staples generally seem smoother. All natural fibers except silk are staple fibers. Staple fibers are short and typically measured in centimeters or inches. Most cotton is just over 1 in. (3 cm) in length; wool, between 1 and 8 in. (3 and 20 cm). Filament fibers, such as silk, and synthetic fibers are long and continuous and measured in meters or yards. Silk filaments can approach 2 miles in length, and synthetic fibers can be produced to any continuous length desired. Filament fibers can also be cut to staple fiber lengths.

*Natural fibers* originate from animal, plant, or mineral sources, and as such are produced seasonally. They can be susceptible to the forces of nature, such as the level of rainfall and attack from insects.

*Synthetic, or manufactured, fibers* are also produced from natural substances, some of which are inherently fibrous. However, they are not referred to as natural fibers because the usable fiber form is produced through industrial processing. Synthetic fibers are produced by extruding chemical solutions through a showerheadlike device called a *spinneret*. Centuries ago, the silkworm's method of extruding silk was identified as a technique that could possibly be adopted for fiber production. However, commercial production of the first synthetic fiber—rayon—did not begin until 1939. Synthetic fibers are categorized under generic names that refer to their chemical composition. Most are thermoplastic, meaning that they soften and melt when heated.

### Natural Fibers

#### Cotton

Cotton is the most widely used plant fiber, and cotton fabric is used more in the apparel industry than in commercial interiors. Cotton fibers are fairly uniform in comparison with most other natural fibers and are relatively dimensionally stable. Like many cellulosic fibers, cotton has low elasticity and resiliency. It is one of the densest fibers, and wicks away moisture along the fiber and through the fabric. Cotton is, however, flammable and wrinkles easily.

Mercerized cotton is produced by treating cotton yarn under tension to increase its strength and reduce shrinkage. The process causes the fiber to swell slightly, making it appear rounder and smoother. The smoother surface increases the light reflection off the fiber surface, thus giving a more lustrous appearance.

#### Kapok

Kapok is derived from the seed pod of the Java kapok tree. It is too brittle to be spun into fiber but is soft enough to be used as cushioning material, and was once used for stuffing pillows and seat cushions. It is lightweight and nonabsorbent and can absorb about 30 times its weight in water.

#### Flax

Derived from the stalk of a plant, flax is referred to as a *bast fiber*. Flax provides a final fiber length of about 12 to 24 in. (300 to 600 mm). Probably the oldest fiber ever woven into fabric, flax was used for mummy wrappings in ancient Egypt.

#### Jute

Made from the stem and stalk of the jute plant, its fibers are harsh and brittle; it wrinkles easily and lints badly. These characteristics limit its use in interior finishes primarily to carpet and linoleum backing. Jute reacts to chemicals similarly to cotton and flax and has excellent resistance to microorganisms and insects.

#### Linen

Linen is derived from flax. It is extremely strong, provides virtually no elasticity, and tends to be brittle. It is not as soft or absorbent as cotton but is more resistant to mildew. Linen does not lint and resists fraying and seam slippage; it does, however, wrinkle and crease easily.

#### Ramie

Also referred to as *China grass*, ramie is produced from a perennial shrub. It is an exceptionally strong fiber and has a natural luster comparable to that of silk. Thin ramie fiber fabrics resemble fine linen, whereas coarse ramie fiber textiles can resemble canvas. Ramie tends to be stiff, nonelastic, and brittle, and is often blended with softer fibers such as cotton and rayon.

#### Sisal

Sisal is a leaf fiber named after a Mexican town in the Yucatan peninsula where it is grown. Sisal is also farmed in Africa and South America. It is a stiff and inflexible fiber that tends to stain and crush easily. Uses for sisal include floor mats and rugs.

## TEXTILE FIBERS

| GENERAL CHEMICAL TYPE | NATURAL | | | MAN-MADE | |
| --- | --- | --- | --- | --- | --- |
| | GENERIC TERM | SOURCE | | GENERIC TERM | SOURCE |
| Cellulose (Plant) | Cotton<br>Kapok | Seed | Cotton plant<br>Kapok tree | Rayon<br>Acetate<br>Triacetate | Wood and cotton |
| | Hemp<br>Jute<br>Flax (linen)<br>Ramie (China grass) | Stem | Hemp plant<br>Jute plant<br>Flax plant<br>Ramie shrub | | |
| | Sisal<br>Pina | Leaf | Agave plant<br>Pineapple plant | | |
| | Coir | Nut husk | Coconut | | |
| Protein (Animal) | Silk | Silkworm secretion | Moth larvae | | |
| | Wool<br>Mohair<br>Angora<br>Horsehair<br>Alpaca<br>Camel hair<br>Cashmere<br>Llama<br>Vicuna | Hair | Sheep<br>Angora goat<br>Angora rabbit<br>Horse mane and tail<br>Alpaca<br>Bactrian camel<br>Cashmere goat<br>Llama<br>Vicuna | | |
| Mineral | Asbestos | Asbestos rock fibers | | Glass<br>Metallic | Silica, sand, and limestone; various metals |
| Elastomers | Rubber | Rubber tree sap | | Synthetic rubber<br>Spandex | Chemicals |
| Synthesized | | | | Acrylic<br>Aramids<br>Modacrylic<br>Nylon<br>Olefin<br>Polyester<br>Saran<br>Vinyl<br>Vinyon | Petroleum (manufactured polymers) |

Source: D. Jackman and M. Dixon, The Guide to Textiles for Interior Designers; Winnipeg, MB, Canada, Peguis Publishers Limited, 1983.

## Silk

The strongest natural fiber, silk varies in length from 1,000 to 1,700 yd (900 to 1,550 m) or longer and is more wrinkle-resistant than the natural cellulosic fibers. Like wool, silk is not degraded by cleaning solvents; however, it does deteriorate under ultraviolet (UV) radiation (sunlight). Silk is comparatively more expensive than other fibers, due to the labor-intensive manufacturing process.

The growth of silk moths for silk production is known as *sericulture*. Liquid silk is excreted from the head of the silkworm to form a cocoon around its body. Cocoons are dried in an oven, killing the pupae inside while preserving the integrity of the cocoons. The silk is then carefully unwrapped and treated for use as a fiber.

**WOOL FIBER**

**WORSTED WOOL FIBER**

## WOOL

### Wool

Wool is sheared primarily from domesticated sheep. Its resiliency and elasticity are exceptional, making it an excellent fiber for use in carpets, upholstery, and apparel. Wool carpet remains the standard by which synthetic fiber carpets are judged. It has good flexibility and can be reshaped by steaming or pressing. Wool burns slowly and is self-extinguishing. Cigarette burns are quickly extinguished with minimal noticeable damage.

Though wool is susceptible to damage by insects, finishing treatments are available to make the fabric unpalatable to moths. Wool fiber has almost no resistance to alkalis (the ingredients found in most detergents); therefore wool must usually be dry-cleaned.

Fiber labeled "wool" may contain unused wool yarn that has been recovered and reconstructed into new yarns. The Wool Products Labeling Act of 1939 was enacted to assist the consumer in understanding the origin of the wool in a fiber or fabric. "Virgin wool" is the designation for wool made into yarn for the first time. "Lamb's wool" is sheared from animals under eight months of age.

### Asbestos

The only natural mineral found in fiber form, asbestos is completely fireproof and was used for many years in firefighters' apparel, hazardous industry applications, and domestic applications. Then it was discovered that, when inhaled, the insoluble, barbed-edge fibers become lodged in the lungs and cannot be expelled by coughing. Because lung cancer and other serious diseases have been associated with exposure to asbestos, its use in most applications is no longer legal.

## TEXTILE SELECTION CRITERIA

| CRITERIA | CHARACTERISTICS |
|---|---|
| **Performance and Safety** | |
| Functional Properties | Insulation, glare reduction, static reduction, fatigue reduction, acoustic control, mobility improvements, safety enhancement |
| Appearance Retention | Color retention, texture retention, resistance to pilling and snagging, soil hiding, soil repellency, soil shedding, soil release |
| Durability | Abrasion resistance, tear resistance, dimensional stability, fuzzy fiber loss, repairability, warranty availability |
| Structural Stability | Tuft bind strength, delamination strength, stability of yarn twist |
| Flame Resistance | Inherent or applied |
| Design and Performance Mandates | Flame resistance, indoor air quality, structural stability, colorfastness, wear resistance, functional properties, acoustical value, static reduction |
| **Maintenance** | |
| Cleanability | Washable, dry-cleanable, ease of stain removal, appearance after cleaning |
| Cleaning Location | On-site versus off-site cleaning |
| Level of Ironing Required | None, touch-up, extensive |
| Frequency of Cleaning | Daily, weekly, monthly |
| Cleaning Products Required | Toxic, biodegradable, readily available |
| **Environmental Product Selection Criteria** | |
| Manufacturing Issues | Effluents produced during manufacturing; products made of recycled materials |
| Product Issues | Potential for product recycling, potential impact of required cleaning agents |
| **Cost and Installation Product Selection Criteria** | |
| Initial Cost | Product price, accessories prices, fees for design professional, delivery charges, installation charges |
| Long-Term Costs | Maintenance costs, including equipment, cleaning agents, and labor; warranty costs; insurance costs; energy costs; interest charges |
| Installation Factors | Site preparation, labor, tools and level of skill needed, permanence: movable, removable, permanent |

*Source: Jan Yeager and Lura Teter-Justice,* Textiles for Residential and Commercial Interiors; *New York, Fairchild Publications, 2000, pp. 15–16.*

### Natural Rubber

In the 1920s, it was discovered that latex (liquid rubber) could be extruded into fiber. Its high elasticity, flexibility, and impermeability to water and air make it unique among natural fibers. Rubber fibers lose much of their strength through age, and deteriorate in sunlight, a trait also common to synthetic rubbers such as spandex.

## Synthetic Cellulosic Fibers

### Rayon

The first manufactured synthetic fiber—rayon—was originally referred to as "artificial silk." Rayon is fabricated principally from wood pulp. Two processes are used in the production of rayon: the *cuprammonium* and the *viscose* methods. The viscose is the major method used today.

The advantages of viscose rayon are that it blends well with other fibers; it is absorbent, and therefore dyes readily; it is economical to produce; and can be made to resemble cotton, linen, silk, or wool. Its disadvantages are that it is not particularly strong and loses strength when wet, has a low resiliency, and wrinkles easily.

### Acetate and Triacetate

Although acetate and triacetate have similar chemical compositions, they behave differently as fibers. Acetate has poor resiliency, whereas triacetate has good resiliency. Acetate fibers are flexible, resulting in fabric with excellent draping qualities. It is a thermoplastic fiber, which is easily damaged by heat and wrinkles easily. Triacetate is processed differently from acetate, resulting in a fiber of greater stability and abrasion resistance. It can be heat-treated to prevent the heat sensitivity inherent to acetate. Permanent pleats can be set in triacetate.

## Petroleum-Based Synthetic Fibers

### Acrylic

First introduced in 1950 under the trade name Orlon, acrylic fiber can be cut into staple lengths and then mechanically bulked for an insulative, fluffy, wool-like effect. It can also be made to simulate the look and feel of silk in filament form. It is exceptionally light, providing bulk without weight, and blends well with other fibers. Acrylic fibers accept dyes well, providing a good selection of colors. However, some acrylics pill easily.

### Modacrylics

Although similar to acrylics, modacrylics can withstand higher temperatures, a quality that has made them a popular choice in the manufacture of draperies and casements, as well as industrial products. Modacrylic fibers are also found in a number of specialty applications such as fake furs.

### Aramids

Among the various modern synthetic fibers, aramids have unique properties. Alkalis, acids, and solvents have virtually no effect on them. Aramids are marketed under the trade names Nomex and Kevlar. Nomex is a high-temperature-resistant fiber used mostly in apparel such as firefighters' clothing and space suits. Kevlar is also a high-temperature-resistant fiber and is stronger than comparably sized steel. It is also used in bullet-resistant vests. Aramids are difficult to dye, but because they are not used for decorative purposes, usually this is not considered a drawback.

## Nylon

Nylon, classified as a polymide, is one of the strongest synthetic fibers. It is highly elastic, with good elongation and recovery properties. Its great strength, high resiliency, and good abrasion resistance make it the most popular carpet fiber. Compared with the moisture absorbency of natural fibers, nylon's is low, so it dries quickly. However, this quality also makes it prone to the buildup of static electricity.

Nylon is available in many formulations. Nylon 6.6, the most widely used type for carpet fibers, has six carbon atoms per individual molecule in each of the two chemicals (hexamethylene diamine and adipic acid) used to make it.

## Olefin

Olefin (polypropylene and polyethylene) is relatively inexpensive and very popular for use as a carpet fiber and fabric-type wallcovering. Although today the most widely used olefin fiber is polypropylene, polyethylene was the first olefin fiber to reach commercial importance; for many years it was used as upholstery for airplane seats. Olefin is one of the lightest synthetic fibers and has excellent elastic recovery. Because of its outstanding resistance to stains and crushing and its lack of static generation, olefin continues to increase in popularity as a carpet fiber. Air barriers in buildings, such as Tyvek, are nonwoven olefin textiles.

## Vinyon

Vinyon, commonly called *vinyl* or *PVC*, is durable and easy to clean. The most popular application for vinyon in the contract market is as an upholstery fabric, to simulate leather or suede.

*Simulated leather* fabrics are produced by extruding or expanding polymer solutions. The most commonly used polymers are PVC and polyurethane. Because polymer films have little or no porosity, these fabrics may become uncomfortable in hot or humid weather. The synthetic sheet is bonded to a backing fabric, generally a knit, to give the textile the dimensional stability required for upholstery. Grain markings are embossed into the synthetic film to enhance its appearance as leather.

*Simulated suede's* surface texture is achieved by one of two processes:

- *Flocking* refers to an electrostatic process whereby charged flock fibers are deposited onto an adhesive coated substrate and then oven-dried.
- *Sueding* or *emerizing* roughens the surface and orients the flock in every direction, unlike brushing and smoothing finishes, which raise the fabric pile in a single direction. This is done by a series of sandpaper-covered disks, which revolve against the flocked surface.

## Saran

This relatively expensive fiber is often replaced by olefin fibers in the manufacture of fabric. Saran is, however, stronger and heavier, tough, and durable to maintain. Saran has applications in upholstery, draperies, and some outdoor textile products.

## Polyester

The initial research by Du Pont that led to the discovery of nylon also led to the invention of polyester. Among the many outstanding characteristics of polyester is its low moisture absorbency, wrinkle resistance, high strength and resiliency, abrasion resistance, and dimensional stability. Polyester also has excellent crease resistance and is easy to maintain. It is frequently blended with other fibers to enhance its performance.

## Mineral Fibers

### Glass

Although glass has been used for centuries, it was not until the mid 1800s that it was first produced in fiber form. Glass fiber is unaffected by fire and is sometimes used to stitch upholstery fabrics for seating that complies with California Technical Bulletin 133, a standard commonly used for evaluating the flammability of furniture. Sheer casements are popular applications for fabrics made of glass fibers. Glass fiber has a very low abrasion resistance. Owens-Corning's trade name for its glass fiber product is Fiberglas.

### Metallic Fibers

Gold, silver, and aluminum fibers are produced by splitting very thin sheets of metal into narrow ribbons. Because they are weak and soft, they are often combined around a stronger core fiber. The capability of aluminum to be colored makes it the most popular option in this category. In fibers such as Mylar, a polyester coating is applied to the aluminum fiber. In other products, both the polyester and aluminum may be finely ground and combined to produce tarnish-free, washable, but somewhat delicate fibers. Stainless-steel fibers provide strength, tear and abrasion resistance, and prevent static buildup. The fibers can also be used to transmit and radiate heat when connected to a power source.

### Elastomeric Fibers

Elastomers are rubberlike substances with fiber forms that offer exceptional elongation. The most common of these is spandex, which is composed of segmented polyurethane. Spandex fibers can be used in the filament form, as a wrapped or core yarn in collaboration with other fibers wrapped around it, or as a core spun yarn, where stable fibers are fed around the spandex core filament to produce a single yarn.

### Yarns

The term *yarn* refers to the twisting together of fibers to create a continuous strand. Yarns can have marked differences in their degrees of twist, textural characteristics, complexity, and relative fineness. Simple yarn constructions are common in the structure of carpets and rugs. They are uniform in diameter along their length, and may be composed of a single yarn or a number of single yarns twisted or plied together in different ways.

More complex decorative yarns are applied in textile wallcoverings, upholstery curtains, and drapery fabrics. Complex yarns may contain loops, curls, or other irregular textural effects to add textural and visual interest to the textile. They may contain variations in the level of twist along their length, decorative three-dimensional features, or changes of fiber content.

### SYNTHETIC FIBER TRADE NAMES

| TRADE NAME | FIBER | MANUFACTURER | CHARACTERISTICS | USE |
|---|---|---|---|---|
| Anso | Nylon | Honeywell | Filament and staple form; soil-resistant | Carpet |
| Antron III | Nylon | Du Pont | Filament and staple form; trilobal nylon 6.6 | Carpet |
| Cordura | Nylon | Du Pont | High-tenacity; nylon 6.6 | Upholstery |
| Hollofil | Polyester | Du Pont | — | Filling |
| Kevlar | Aramid | Du Pont | Filament form; bullet-resistant | Upholstery liner (Cal-Tech 133) |
| Micromattique | Polyester | Du Pont | Microdenier | Draperies |
| Nomex | Aramid | Du Pont | Filament and staple form; flame-resistant, heat-resistant | Upholstery liner (Cal-Tech 133) |
| Trevira | Polyester | Treviva GmbH | Flame-resistant | Cubicle curtains |
| Ultron | Nylon | Monsanto | Nylon 6.6; antistatic | Carpet |
| Zefstat | Nylon | BASF | — | Carpet |
| Zeftron | Nylon | BASF | — | Carpet |

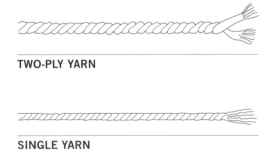

**TWO-PLY YARN**

**SINGLE YARN**

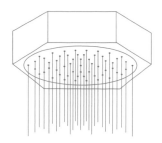

**SPINNERET**

Yarns are classified into two types: *spun* and *filament*. Spun yarns are composed of staple fibers twisted together. Filament yarns are composed of continuous strands made from either a spinneret-generated synthetic fiber or from silk.

Smooth, parallel filament yarns may be modified by the use of *throwing* or *texturing*. The great length of silk and filament yarns allow them to be directly twisted together, or "thrown," without the need for spinning. In the texturing process, yarn may be given a more natural appearance, greater elasticity, or a more attractive tactility. The texturing processes may also provide greater bulk or apparent volume in order to achieve greater covering power. Yarns modified in this way are referred to as *bulked continuous filament* (BCF).

Spinning is required for all natural and staple synthetic fibers. BCFs are typical of nylon and polypropylene fibers and generally offer better wear; that said, staple fibers provide the wool-like appearance that is desired in many textiles.

*Monofilament yarns,* unlike spun and filament yarns, are manufactured directly by the fiber producer. A single filament with a relatively large diameter is drawn and heat-set. Such yarns may be used in the production of lightweight transparent window coverings and as sewing thread for a number of interior textile products.

*Yarns are sold by weight, and yarn designations* express the relationship between length and weight. The *denier system* is used for filament yarns, and the *yarn count system* is used for spun yarns.

Denier is a unit of yarn measurement equal to the weight in grams of 9,000 meters of the yarn. The higher the denier, the heavier the yarn, and generally the better the strength, resiliency, and abrasion resistance. For example, a 15-denier yarn would be suitable for sheer hosiery; a 2,200-denier yarn would be suitable for carpet.

The yarn count system is a relative gauge of a spun yarn's weight. Heavier yarns are designated by lower yarn count numbers. For example, a 70-count yarn is quite fine, whereas a 10-count yarn is thick and heavy.

## PERFORMANCE OF YARNS IN FABRICS

| YARN TYPE | DURABILITY | COMFORT | APPEARANCE | CARE |
|---|---|---|---|---|
| Spun Yarns | Weaker than filament yarns.<br><br>Ply yarns stronger than simple yarns.<br><br>Fabrics tend to resist raveling and running. | Warmer, more absorbent. | Fabrics are cottonlike or wool-like in appearance.<br><br>Fabrics lint and pill. | Yarns do not snag readily. |
| Filament Yarns | Stronger than spun yarns.<br><br>Fabrics ravel and run readily. | Cooler; least absorbent. | Fabrics are smooth and lustrous.<br><br>Fabrics do not lint or pill readily. | Yarns may snag.<br><br>Resist soiling. |
| Textured Filament Yarns | Stronger than spun yarns.<br><br>Fabrics ravel and run less than those made with filament yarns, but more than those made with spun yarns. | Warmer than filament yarns.<br><br>More absorbent than filament yarns.<br><br>Stretch more than other yarns. | Fabrics are less lustrous; more similar to those made of spun yarns.<br><br>Fabrics do not lint, but may pill. | Yarns likely to snag.<br><br>Soil more readily than filament yarns. |
| Novelty Yarns | Weaker than filament yarns.<br><br>Most resist raveling. | Warmer.<br><br>More absorbent if part is spun. | Interesting texture.<br><br>Greater novelty effects show wear sooner than smaller novelty effects.<br><br>Fabrics lint and pill. | Yarns likely to snag.<br><br>Soil readily. |

*Source: Norma R. Hollen, Jane Sadler, Anna Langford,* Textiles; *New York, Macmillan, 1979, p. 303.*

### Yarnlike Structures

A number of elements employed in interior textiles are considered to be yarnlike structures. These components are composed of textile fibers that, although referred to as yarns, are produced with techniques other than throwing or spinning. Included in this group are chenille yarns, felted wool yarns, and metallic yarn. Natural rush, sea grass, and cane, used in handwoven seats and backs of chairs, can also be categorized as yarnlike in their structure.

### Woven Fabrics

The majority of textiles used in commercial interiors are woven. Woven fabrics are made by interlacing yarns at right angles to each other on a loom. Woven

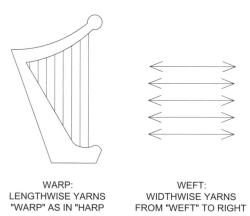

WARP:                           WEFT:
LENGTHWISE YARNS        WIDTHWISE YARNS
"WARP" AS IN "HARP       FROM "WEFT" TO RIGHT

**WARP AND WEFT**

fabrics commonly have one set of lengthwise yarns, referred to as *warps* or *ends*, and one set of crosswise yarns called *weft yarns, woof yarns,* or *filling yarns.*

The fabric count is employed to determine the closeness of the yarn in a material. The count refers to the number of warp and weft yarns in 1 sq in.(6 sq cm).

### Special Effects Weaves

Special effects weaves use one or more of the basic weaves for the purposes of creating cut or loop piles, multicolored designs, or particular textures.

*Dobby weaves* are popular for contract fabrics with small dots, geometric shapes, or florals woven in. They are produced on looms with dobby attachments that mechanically determine which warp threads will be raised or lowered. Piqué, waffle cloth, and huck toweling are dobby weaves.

*Matelassés* are double cloths in which extra sets of yarns are used to create a puffed or quilted effect.

*Crepes* are produced by plain or satin weaving. The yarn is twisted so tightly that it has a crinkled or pebbled appearance. Textured yarns are sometimes used to create crepes.

### Pile Weaves

Woven pile fabrics are constructed by weaving an additional set of warp or filling yarns into the ground, or basic, yarns. This produces a characteristic three-dimensional effect. The category includes velvet, velveteen, and corduroy fabrics.

## Jacquard Weaves

Detailed woven patterns are produced on more complex looms. The Jacquard loom employs a series of punched cards. Each hole in a jacquard card controls the action of one warp yarn. The method is used in tapestries, brocades, and damask. The jacquard process is time-consuming, making this one of the most costly weave types.

## Customer's Own Material (C.O.M.)

Seating manufacturers typically supply upholstery fabric options for their chairs. These fabric selections have been tested on their seating and have performed satisfactorily with regard to wear and flammability. Often, however, a designer will find the upholstery selection limiting and will instead select a fabric from a textile manufacturer. Fabric that is not supplied by the fabricator (seating manufacturer, drapery supplier, etc.) is referred to as the *customer's own material* (C.O.M.) or *customer's own leather* (C.O.L.). Written approval from the fabricator is usually required for the use of C.O.M. The fabricator must verify that the material is acceptable as an upholstery fabric. (Note that "customer" in these terms does not refer to the designer's customer; it refers to the manufacturer's customer—the party placing the order—which is the furniture, furnishings, and equipment (FF&E) contractor (furniture dealer, etc.). The material is purchased separately and supplied to the fabricator for application. The FF&F contractor is responsible for the acquisition and coordination of C.O.M.)

## APPEARANCE

The following performance factors influence the appearance of a fabric:

- *Luster* is the effect of light rays breaking and reflecting on the surface of a fabric. Silk has a relatively high luster, unlike cotton and wool, which have a low luster. Fabric construction and finishing will have an influence on the final luster of a fabric.
- *Fuzzing* refers to the accumulation of displaced fibers on the surface of a fabric. Pilling occurs as the fibers become tangled and rolled into balls, some of which, depending on the absorbency of the fibers, may be difficult to remove.
- *Electrical attraction of dust, thread, hair, and lint* to a fabric surface affects the appearance of the fabric. Hydrophobic, or nonabsorbent, materials will cling to the surface of a static-prone fabric.
- *Color change* of a fabric can be attributed to fading, crocking, and color loss. *Fading* occurs when dyestuffs are adversely affected by constant exposure to ultraviolet rays, effects of artificial light, or airborne pollutants. *Crocking* refers to the displacement of dyestuff through excessive rubbing or wear. *Color loss* may be attributed to the effects of cleaning agents. If the colorfastness of a particular fabric is unknown or is not guaranteed by the manufacturer, testing should be done on a sample before final selection.
- *Hand* refers to how a textile feels and drapes; it can be affected by the fiber type, yarn, and fabric construction. Hand is a crucial factor in the aesthetic appreciation of a textile. Additional modifications can also be achieved though finishing processes.

## BASIC WEAVES

| NAME | INTERLACING PATTER | GENERAL CHARACTERISTICS | TYPICAL FABRICS |
|---|---|---|---|
| Plain | Each warp interlaces with each filling. | Most interlacing per square inch. Balanced or unbalanced. Wrinkles most. Ravels most. Less absorbent. | Batiste Voile Percale Gingham Broadcloth Crash Cretonne |
| Basket | Two or more yarns in either warp or filling or both are woven as one in a plain weave. | Looks balanced. Fewer interlacing than plain weave. Flat looking. Wrinkles less. Ravels more. | Oxford Monk's cloth |
| Twill | Warp and filling yarns float over two or more yarns from the opposite direction in a regular progression to the right or left. | Diagonal lines. Fewer interlacing than plain weave. Wrinkles less. Ravels more. More pillable than plain weave. Can have higher count. | Serge Surah Denim Gabardine Herringbone |
| Satin | Warp and filling yarns float over two or more yarns from the opposite direction in a regular progression to the right or left. | Flat surface. Most are lustrous. Can have high count. Fewer interlacing. Long float; subject to slippage and snagging. | Satin Sateen |
| Crepe | An irregular interlacing of yarns. Floats of unequal lengths in no discernable pattern. | Rough-looking surface. Crepe-looking. | Granite cloth Moss crepe Sand crepe |
| Dobby | Special loom attachment allows up to 32 different interlacing. | Small figures. Cord-type fabrics. | Shirting madras Huck toweling Waffle cloth Pique |
| Jacquard | Each warp yarn controlled individually. An infinite number of interlacing is possible. | Large figures. | Damask Brocade Tapestry |
| Pile | Extra warp or filling yarns are woven in to give a cut or an uncut three-dimensional fabric. | Flush or looped surface. Warm. Wrinkles less. Pile may flatten. | Velvet Velveteen Corduroy Furlike fabrics Wilton rugs Terrycloth |
| Slack-tension | A type of pile weave. Some warp yarns can be released from tension to form raised areas in the cloth or a pile surface. | Crinkle stripes or pile surface. Absorbent. Nonwrinkling. | Seersucker Terrycloth Frieze |
| Leno | A doup attachment on the loom causes one of two yarns to be carried over the other on alternating passing of the filling yarns. | Meshlike fabric. Lower thread count fabrics that are resistant to slippage. | Marquisette Curtain fabrics |
| Swivel | An attachment to the loom. Small shuttles carrying extra filling yarns weave in small dots. | Dots on both sides of fabric as filling floats. | Dotted Swiss |

*Source: Norma R. Hollen, Jane Sadler, Anna Langford,* Textiles; *New York, Macmillan, 1979, p. 162.*

There are three basic weaves: plain, twill, and satin. Variations and combinations of these types form other weaves.

## PROPERTIES OF WOVEN FABRICS

| FABRIC TYPE | PROPERTIES |
|---|---|
| High-thread count | Firmness, strength, cover, body, compactness, stability, wind repellency, water repellency, fire retardancy, reduced raveling of seams. |
| Low-thread count | Flexibility, permeability, pliability, better drape, higher shrinkage potential, more seam raveling. |
| Balanced | Less seam slippage; warp and filling wear evenly, resulting in holes. |
| Unbalanced (usually more warp) | Seam slippage in low count; warp yarns wear out first, leaving strings (common in upholstery fabrics). In plain weave, crosswise ribs give interesting surface. |
| Floats | Luster, smoothness, flexibility, resiliency, tendency to ravel and snag; seam slippage in low count. |

*Source: Norma R. Hollen, Jane Sadler, Anna Langford,* Textiles; *New York, Macmillan, 1979, p. 161.*

# FABRIC CONSTRUCTION

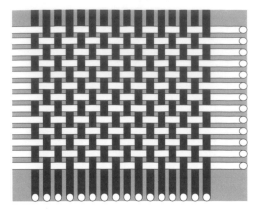

The plain weave process involves one warp yarn and one weft yarn alternately passing over one another. This results in no particular surface pattern or texture; this makes plain weave textiles ideal backgrounds for printed fabrics. Plain weaves wear well but tend to wrinkle.

**PLAIN WEAVE**

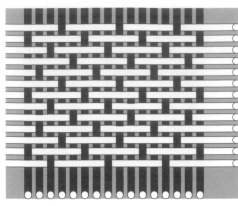

**FIVE-THREAD SATIN WEAVE**

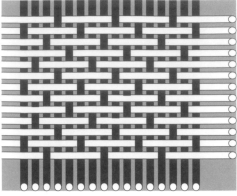

**FIVE-THREAD SATEEN WEAVE**

Each yarn floats over at least four yarns, resulting in a smooth, lustrous surface. Snagging may pose a problem with the textile because longer lengths of yarn appear on the surface of the textile. Sateen is commonly used in drapery linings.

**SATIN WEAVE**

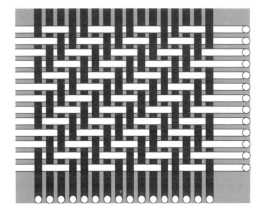

**TWO-TWO TWILL WEAVE**

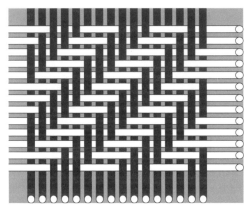

**THREE-THREE TWILL WEAVE**

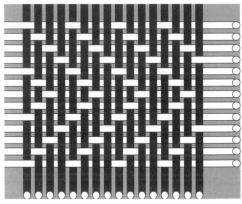

**HERRINGBONE WEAVE**

In twill weave, each warp yarn passes over and then under the weft yarns as in the plain weave, but the sequence is started slightly higher (or lower) on each successive yarn. A diagonal pattern is created. Herringbone, denim, and gabardine are twill weaves.

**TWILL WEAVE**

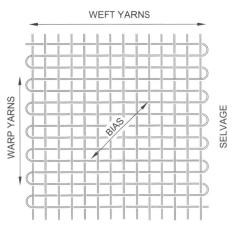

A fabric may also be assessed by the degree of elasticity along a 45° angle between warp and weft, known as the *true bias*. The lengthwise edges of the fabric are called *selvages*.

**SELVAGE AND BIAS**

**WEFT KNIT**
Weft knitting is based on the handknitting technique. The process produces flat or tubular goods classified as single or double knits.

**KNITTED FABRICS**

**WARP KNIT**
Warp knitting employs very fast machine techniques capable of producing varying weights of plain or tricot knit fabrics, including fine netting and fabrics intended for industrial use.

## PERFORMANCE

### Abrasion Resistance

Although abrasion resistance is associated with durability, the capability of a fabric to withstand deterioration varies with the application. Abrasion test results are helpful when they are used for purposes of comparison but are not a reliable prediction of actual wear-life.

Abrasion resistance for fabric is often stated in terms of the number of cycles it can endure on a specified machine. The Oscillatory Cylinder Method, commonly called the "Wyzenbeek test" after the man who developed the testing equipment, is the traditional test for abrasion resistance. The Taber Abraser test is sometimes used for fabric but is most often used for testing carpet.

### Wear Resistance

The wear resistance of fabric is affected by many factors, including the type and length of the fiber; the structure of the yarn; the construction of the fabric; and the type, kind, and amount of finishing material added to the fibers, yarns, or fabric.

### Absorbency

Absorbency refers to the fabric's capability to absorb moisture. Some fibers are stronger when wet, others weaken or show no change; this is an important factor in determining the cleaning methods to use to retain the look of a textile. Absorbency is an important factor in static buildup, stain removal, and dimensional stability should the fabric become wet. Fibers that absorb moisture easily are referred to as *hydrophilic*. Fibers that have difficulty absorbing moisture are known as *hydrophobic*.

### Elasticity, Elongation, and Recovery

Elasticity is the capability of the fabric to increase in length when under tension and to return to its original shape when the tension is released, an important factor in maintaining the appearance of upholstered furniture. Elongation addresses the point at which a fabric will break when stretched. Recovery refers to the capability of a fabric to regain its shape after periods of extended elongation, a crucial consideration in upholstery fabrics.

### Acoustical Transparency

Occasionally, a fabric will be used for the covering of a speaker or other sound-transmitting device. Hence, the fabric should be acoustically transparent, to minimize sound transmission blockage. Consult with an acoustical engineer and test the fabric to determine if it is suitable for use in this condition. Typically, an open-weave fabric allows sound to pass through more effectively than a more densely woven fabric.

### Fire Resistance

Fibers have varying degrees of resistance to heat and flame. In general, lighter, more open fabrics will burn more freely than denser material. Finishing also plays a crucial role in the resistance of a fabric to fire; effectiveness may decrease over time, and cleaning processes may reduce the amount of fire resistance.

## ESTIMATING FABRIC YARDAGE

| FABRIC WIDTH | PLAIN FABRIC | 2–14" (50–355 MM) REPEAT | 15"–24" (380–610 MM) REPEAT | 25"–27" (635–685 MM) REPEAT | 28"–36" (710–915 MM) REPEAT |
|---|---|---|---|---|---|
| 54" (1370 mm) | + 0% | + 10% | + 15% | + 20% | + 25% |
| 50" (1270 mm) | 10% | 20% | 25% | 30% | 35% |
| 48" (1220 mm) | 15% | 25% | 30% | 35% | 40% |
| 45" (1145 mm) | 40% | 50% | 55% | 60% | 65% |
| 36" (915 mm) | 50% | 60% | 65% | 70% | 75% |

Fabrics with a *repeat* (a repeated pattern) or narrower fabric will require more yardage than a standard 54-in.- (1,370-mm-) wide piece.

## PROPERTIES OF MAJOR TEXTILES

| PROPERTIES | COTTON | FLAX | WOOL | SILK | ACETATE | VISCOSE RAYON | TRIACETATE | ACRYLIC | GLASS | NYLON | OLEFIN | POLYESTER |
|---|---|---|---|---|---|---|---|---|---|---|---|---|
| Abrasion resistance | Good | Fair | Fair | Fair | Poor | Fair | Poor | Fair | Poor | Excellent | Excellent | Good |
| Absorbency (% M.R.) | 8.5 | 12 | 13.5 | 11 | 6.5 | 11 | 3.5 | 1.5 | 0 | 4.5 | 0.1 | 1 |
| Drapability | Fair | Poor | Good | Excellent | Excellent | Good | Excellent | Good | Poor | Good | Fair | Fair |
| Wash or dry clean | Either | Either | DC | Either | DC | Either | Either | Either | Hand Wash | Either | Either | Either |
| Sunlight Resistance | Fair | Good | Good | Poor | Good | Fair | Good | Excellent | Excellent | Poor | Good | Good |
| Hand | Good | Good | Fair–Excellent | Excellent | Excellent | Good | Excellent | Good | Poor | Fair | Fair | Fair |
| Pilling resistance | Good | Good | Fair | Good | Good | Good | Good | Fair | Excellent | Poor | Good | Very–poor |
| Resiliency | Poor | Poor | Good | Fair | Fair | Poor | Good | Good | Excellent | Good | Excellent | Excellent |
| Static resistance | Good | Good | Fair | Fair | Fair | Good | Fair | Poor | Excellent | Poor | Good | Very Poor |
| Strength (Grams/Denier) | 3.0/5.0 Good | 6.6/8.4 Excellent | 0.8/2.0 Poor | 3.9/4.5 Good | 0.8/1.5 Poor | 0.7/6.0 Poor–Good | 0.8/1.4 Poor | 1.8/3.5 Fair | 6.0/7.0 Excellent | 2.5/7.5 Excellent | 4.8/7.0 Good | 2.5/9.5 Excellent |
| Thermoplastic | No | No | No | No | Yes | No | Yes | Yes | Yes | Yes | Yes | Yes |

Source: A. Cohen; Beyond Basic Textiles; *New York, Fairchild Publications, 1982, p. 5.*

## Microorganism and Insect Resistance

Although some fibers have a natural resistance to mildew, fungi, and bacteria, others are susceptible in certain environmental conditions. Moisture and warmth and the buildup of soil on a fabric may promote microorganic growth. Bacteriostatic finishes are often used to protect vulnerable materials. Particular fibers may also attract insects such as moths, carpet beetles, and weevils. Treatments and finishes that inhibit insect activity should be considered.

## FABRIC FINISHING

Surface treatments can be applied to affect the performance of a fabric. Fabrics with applied treatments may stiffen from the resin, decrease in abrasion resistance and absorption, and change color. When considering fabric treatments, apply each to a sample to verify the desired effect.

### Water Resistance

A large number of silicone water-repellent finishes are available. Effective alternatives are fluorochemical finishes, which can be applied with other finishing treatments.

### Stain Resistance

Stain-resistant treatments make most fabrics resistant to oil- and water-based stains. These treatments are usually spray-applied and rarely have an effect on flame-resistant treatments applied to the same fabric. Fluids bead up on the surface of the treated fabric and do not spread, thus can be easily removed. These finishes are odorless, harmless, and do not alter the hand of the fabric.

### Flame Resistance

To comply with building and fire code requirements, fabrics must sometimes be treated with flame-resistant finishes. The type of fabric will determine which process is appropriate. The two types of flame-resistant treatments are polymers and salines.

- A *polymer flame-resistant treatment* is applied through an immersion and heat-setting process. Shrinkage can occur as a result of such a treatment. In some fabrics, there will be a noticeable change in color or stiffness. Although quite durable, most polymer flame-resistant treatments will eventually wash out if the fabric is dry-cleaned.
- *Saline flame-resistant treatments* are less expensive, but are not as durable as polymer solutions. The salt solution has a corrosive effect on metals, such as upholstery tacks and staples, and may leach out.

*Flame-resistant backings* provide far more protection against the spread of fire than flame-resistant treatments. Aramid fabrics, such as Du Pont's Kevlar, are laminated to the back of upholstery fabric. Lamination reduces the amount of labor involved in applying the barrier fabric between the seat cushion and the finish fabric. Instead of being upholstered twice, first with the aramid and then with the upholstery fabric, the seat is upholstered only once with the laminated fabric.

## REACTIONS OF UNMODIFIED FIBERS TO HEAT AND FLAME

| FIBER | HEAT RESISTANCE | NEAR FLAME | IN FLAME | REMOVED FROM FLAME | ODOR AND RESIDUE |
|---|---|---|---|---|---|
| Cotton | 150°C 300°F | No shrinkage; ignites on contact | Burns quickly | Continues burning | Burning paper odor; light fluffy ash |
| Flax | 260°C 500°F | No shrinkage; ignites on contact | Burns quickly | Continues burning | Burning paper odor; light fluffy ash |
| Wool | 132°C 275°F | Curls away from flame | Burns slowly | Self-extinguishing | Burning hair odor; small brittle bead |
| Silk | 135°C 275°F | Curls away from flame | Burns slowly, sputters | Usually self-extinguishing | Burning hair odor; crushable beadlike residue |
| Rayon | 177°C 350°F | No shrinkage; ignites on contact | Burns quickly | Continues burning | Burning paper odor; very little ash |
| Acetate | 177°C 350°F | Fuses and melts away from flame; ignites quickly | Burns quickly | Continues rapid burning | Acrid odor; irregular hard, black bead |
| Triacetate | 232°C 450°F | As acetate | As acetate | As acetate | As acetate |
| Acrylic | 150°C 300°F | Fuses and melts away from flame; ignites quickly | Burns rapidly with hot flame; sputters, melts | Continues burning and molten polymer drops off | Acrid odor; irregular hard, black bead |
| Modacrylic | 150°C 300°F | Fuses and melts away from flame | Burns slowly, if at all; melts | Self-extinguishing | Acrid odor; irregular hard, black bead |
| Nylon Nylon 6.6 | 150°C 300°F | Melts away from flame; shrinks, fuses | Burns slowly with melting | Self-extinguishing | Celerylike odor; hard, tough gray or brown bead |
| Olefin | 75°C 165°F | Fuses; shrinks from flame | Melts and burns | Continues burning and melting with sooty smoke | Paraffin wax odor; tough brownish bead |
| Polyester | 120°C 250°F | Fuses, melts, and shrinks from flame | Burns slowly with melting | Self-extinguishing | Chemical odor; dark, tough bead |
| Saran | 115°C 240°F | Fuses, melts, and shrinks from flame | Melts; yellow flame | Self-extinguishing | Chemical odor; crisp tough bead |
| Glass | 315°C 600°F | Will not burn | Softens; glows red | Hardens; may change shape | No odor; hard white bead |
| Metallic | Variable, dependent on coating, if any | Pure metal: no reaction; coated metal: melts, fuses, and shrinks | Glows red; burns as coating | Hardens as coating | No odor; skeleton outline as coating |
| Vinyon | 65°C 150°F | Fuses and melts away from flame | Burns, melts | Self-extinguishing | Acrid odor; irregular hard, irregular black bead |

*Source: D. Jackman and M. Dixon, The Guide to Textiles for Interior Designers; Winnipeg, MB, Canada, Peguis Publishers Limited, 1983, p. 116.*

## Antistatic Treatment

The complete removal of static buildup remains a challenge for textile chemists, especially in fabrics that will undergo regular laundering or dry-cleaning operations. Fabric softeners prove effective in reducing static by coating the fibers and restricting electrical conductivity. Finishes incorporated into the fabric fibers are also proving successful.

## Mothproofing

Soiled carpets and upholstery are particularly prone to attack by moth larvae. Treatment of the fibers ensures that protection remains despite regular cleaning. New mothproofing systems are being developed to reduce the attraction of the wool to the moth larvae.

## Bacterial Protection

Fibers that are exposed to moisture and that contain fungi, microbes, and bacteria lead to a buildup of mildew, mold, and rot. A wide range of materials are prone to bacterial buildup, which can lead to the spread of infection and produce unpleasant odors.

*Bacteriostatic and antimicrobial finishes* may be applied to the fabric yarn or be added to the fiber during manufacture. Many other finishes contain such repellents, and various products enable the user to maintain a sufficient level of protection.

## Insulating Finishes

Plastic and aluminum adhesive coatings are occasionally used to ensure thermal protection. The performance of closely hung drapery panels may be improved. Both may increase heat retention in the winter and reflect the heat of the sun in the summer.

## Minimum Care Finishing

Finishing resins provide crease resistance and make it easier to press fabrics. The resins react chemically with the molecular structure of the natural fibers to form a cross-linking system that holds the fabric in a particular configuration. This finishing process is most commonly used in cotton fabrics blended with polyester.

## COLORING AND PRINTING

Prior to the middle of the nineteenth century, all dyestuffs were derived from natural sources. With the 1858 discovery of mauve, a coal tar derivative, the development of man-made dyes has made it possible to employ a far greater palette of colored fabrics in interior spaces. A crucial factor in ensuring colorfast fabrics is to match the appropriate dyestuff to the fiber used. Synthetic fibers require very specific dyes, which are often developed with each new fiber type.

## Dyeing Methods

Dyeing methods include fiber, yarn, piece, and polychromatic dyeing:

- *Fiber dyeing* ensures greater colorfastness and excellent color penetration. The dye is applied to the natural fiber in its raw state or to the molten polymer or fiber solution. The result is an integrally colored fiber.
- *Yarn dyeing* is one of the oldest methods of fabric coloring. The fibers are spun into yarn prior to the dyeing process.
- *Piece dyeing* refers to the coloration of woven material. The process is the least expensive and easiest way to achieve solid-color fabrics; however, an even distribution of dyestuff can be achieved only if the fabric is made from one fiber type.
- *Polychromatic dyeing* enables random patterns to be dyed into the fabric. Dyestuffs are applied at varying speeds and in different directions through jets or rollers. Computer technology is providing greater options for pattern development.

## Printing Methods

In dye bath printing, also known as *resist*, a portion of the fabric is made resistant to the effects of the dye. Three printing techniques for commercial interior finish fabrics are direct, screen, and discharge printing.

## Direct Printing

Direct printing, also called *roller, calender,* or *cylinder printing,* is the most common printing method. Colors are deposited on the fabric in the same manner as printing wallpaper or a newspaper. One roller is required for each color. The fabric is passed between the etched color rollers. Most direct-printed fabrics have a white background. Direct-printing types are as follows:

- *Block prints* are produced by stamping the fabric with inked, carved blocks.
- *Flat-bed printing* is an outgrowth of block printing and has been used for more than 200 years. It is especially effective for small runs and large-pattern repeats.

## Screen Printing

Screen prints are made by forcing dye through a stencil. A different stencil is used for each color dye required. Screen-printing techniques are as follows:

- *Flat-bed screen printing* uses a squeegee to push dye through a stencil onto fabric that is stretched flat. The process is semiautomatic and can print about 7 yd (6.4 m) a minute.
- *Rotary screen printing* combines roller and screen printing and uses a perforated cylinder screen to apply color. It is a fast, frequently used process, capable of printing 110 yd (100 m) a minute.

## Discharge Printing

Discharge printing is a reverse procedure employed to remove dye from a colored fabric in a controlled pattern. A rotary screen-printing device, with bleach or a chemical dye remover, is used to make a design. Polka dot or small floral prints are usually discharge printed. This method can be combined with color printing to simultaneously remove color and print.

*Resources: D. Jackman and M. Dixon;* The Guide to Textiles for Interior Designers; *Winnipeg, MB, Canada, Peguis Publishers Limited, 1983.*
*Jan Yeager and Lura Teter-Justice;* Textiles for Residential and Commercial Interiors; *New York, Fairchild Publications, 2000.*

*MASTERSPEC®; published by ARCOM; Salt Lake City, Utah, and Alexandria, Virginia*

# LEATHER

## GENERAL

Leather is processed animal skin, primarily from cattle. Three factors contribute to the high cost of leather: the processes used are labor-intensive; the aniline dyes used to color leather are costly; and there is a high rejection rate of the finished hides.

Cattle hide, or cowhide, refers to the skin of a fully grown cow. Such skins are large hides, ranging from 50 to 60 sq ft (4.6 to 5.5 sq m). The center portion of the hide, called the bend, yields the best-quality hide.

Calfskin is the hide of a young animal and is considerably smaller, about 25 sq ft to 35 sq ft (2.3 sq m to 3.2 sq m) Calfskin is characterized by its softness, suppleness, and fine grain.

In calculating the yield of a hide, consider a waste factor of about 10% to 15%. Each yard (0.9 m) of 36-in.- (900-mm-) wide fabric requires about 16 sq ft (1.4 sq m) of leather. Each yard (0.9 m) of 54-in.- (1,370-mm-) wide fabric requires 18 sq ft (1.7 sq m) of leather.

## LEATHER PROCESSING

Four steps are required to transform leather hide into a suitable upholstery material: curing and cleaning, tanning, coloring, and finishing.

### Curing

Curing involves salting the raw hides to slow down bacterial action that results in the decomposition of the material. Hides are thoroughly cleaned, defleshed, and dehaired.

### Tanning

Tanning replaces the natural gelatinous materials found in the skin with tanning solutions; this puts life back into a leather, making it strong, supple, and enduring. There are three primary tanning agents: mineral, vegetable, and a combination of the two:

- *Mineral tanning.* Cured and cleaned hides are immersed in a solution comprising chromium-based salts and oils. About 90% of leather today is tanned by this method. Mineral-tanned hides accept dyes well, allowing rich, vibrant colors to be created.
- *Vegetable tanning.* Vegetable-tanned hides have a heavier feel. They are often left undyed. Vegetable-tanned hides become pliable when wet, yet retain their shape when dry. This tanning solution contains tree bark, typically oak, which provide tannins, which swell the hides. This also gives the leathers a distinct smell.
- *Combination tanning.* This tanning method produces a hide that is quite supple, with a limited acceptance of dyes.

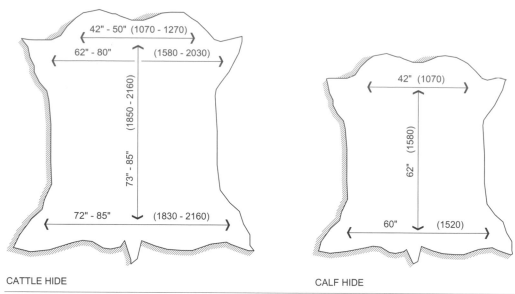

CATTLE HIDE

CALF HIDE

**HIDE SIZES** *Source:* Edelman Leather Handbook, *Teddy and Arthur Edelman, Ltd. Hawleyville, Connecticut*

## Hide Coloring

Coloring may be used to camouflage uneven natural color or provide an overall color to the leather.

*Aniline dyes* are translucent. They do not obscure the natural grain pattern and surface imperfections. The best-quality upholstery leathers are aniline-dyed. The dye penetrates the depth of the hide completely so that as the leather wears, the color remains the same.

*Semianiline dyes* contain some pigments. The normal variation from one dyed hide to another can be quite noticeable. The use of semianiline dyes helps to ensure uniformity in color among many hides.

## Finishing

Finishing refers to the final stages in leather processing. Lubricants and softening agents may be applied to increase suppleness. Imperfections in the hide surface may be removed by shaving or abrasion. Embossing techniques may be employed to increase or unify surface texture. Resins, waxes, and lacquer-based compounds may then be applied and polished to produce a glazed finish.

Leather is categorized by the surface imperfections and how it is processed, as described here:

- *Full-grain leather* (or full-top-grain leather, as it is sometimes called) possesses the genuine original grain of the hide. It has the fewest surface imperfections, hence constitutes the most expensive

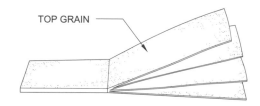

**SPLIT LEATHER**

type of hide. The surface is not embossed or altered in any way; it is the full, natural hide.
- In *top-grain leather,* the original surface pattern, including scars from barbed wire or brands, is removed by abrasion. This skinless surface is embossed with a pattern, typically resembling the grain of the skin that was removed.
- *Split leathers* are made by slicing the hide into two or three thin layers to give uniform thickness to the grain side of the hide. The inside layer is often finished as suede. Inexpensive leathers may be pigmented split leathers with an embossed imitation grain.
- *Suede* is leather with the flesh side exposed. It is rarely used in upholstery or other interior applications. Color may be easily removed by abrasion; this known as *crocking*.

# TASK LIGHTING

Task lighting can be defined as lighting that is controlled by the user or that has a specific purpose. Task lights consist of three components: a *light source*, a *reflector* or *diffuser*, and a *support structure*. Task lighting provides one of three types of lighting:

- *Uniform ambient lighting:* These include table and floor fixtures.
- *Local lighting:* These include pendant and portable fixtures.
- *Task-specific lighting:* These include under-shelf and desk fixtures.

## UNIFORM AMBIENT LIGHTING

Uniform ambient lighting creates a low-contrast perception. Fixtures should be nonglaring and provide indirect light. This type of lighting works well for senior citizens who have a low-contrast perception and are vulnerable to glare.

## LOCAL LIGHTING

Local lighting is specific lighting that requires a different light level than the surrounding space, such as art and object lighting. High-contrast lighting for a specific task, such as a cashier stand or bank transaction counter, is an example of local lighting.

## TASK-SPECIFIC LIGHTING

Task-specific lighting allows the users to have the highest level of individual control. The luminaires allow the user to control the optimum angular relationship between the view, task, and light source for specific task. This type of light is ideal when there are inadequate visual conditions or the users have weak eyes.

## TASK LIGHTING SELECTION CRITERIA

The quality of the ambient light, daylight, and other light sources in a space will affect the type of task lighting solutions required.

*Veiling reflections* are produced by light that is reflected off the task into the viewer's eyes. Veiling reflections reduce contrast. Task lights that redirect light to the sides will reduce or eliminate the veiling reflections. Mobile-arm task lights allow the user to position the light for best visibility. *Reflective glare* is caused by highly polished surfaces. Low or indirect light sources can be used when specular surfaces cannot be avoided. *Shadows* can be minimized by light from many directions.

To determine the type of task lighting, consider the following:

- *Activities that will occur in the space.* What light level ranges are required for anticipated tasks? Should they be adjustable by the user?
- *Age of user.* As the eye ages, color discrimination is less accurate. Also, the ability to discern or tolerate extremes of light intensity is reduced, and the aged eye is more sensitive to glare.
- *Control of the lighting system available to the user.* Does the user have individual dimming controls? Is multilevel switching available in the space?

## TYPE OF LUMINAIRES

*Under-shelf luminaires* are frequently supplied by furniture manufactures. Depending on the type of under-shelf luminaires, uniform illuminance and reflected glare may be a problem. *Bare fluorescent lamp strip lights* can produce direct glare if the direct view is not housed with an opaque covering or lip of shelf. *Luminaire strip lights* with an adjustable sleeve can be adjusted to partially block and redirect light. *Luminaires with optics* such as a batwing lens can reduce glare and veiling reflection. An opaque strip with a batwing lens can further reduce the glare of fluorescent lamps.

A portable task light is easy to relocate and allows great flexibility for the user. It can provide more light than an under-shelf product and the angle can maximize visibility. When reading, the portable task light should be positioned to the side rather than the back. The lamp should not be directly visible, to prevent direct glare. The unit should be placed to the left side for right-handed workers and to the right for left-handed workers, to avoid casting a shadow on the task from the person's hand. Some types of portable task lights clip on to the table or desk.

## TYPE OF LAMPS

Incandescent and halogen lamps are most commonly used in portable task lights. Incandescent and halogen lamps cover a small area, which makes it easy to direct light but can result in sharp shadows and bright reflections. Incandescent lamps are not as energy-efficient as fluorescent lamps and can become very hot to the touch.

Fluorescent lamps are cooler and more energy-efficient than incandescent. They produce a more diffused light with diffused shadows. The initial cost is higher than incandescent lamps, but the lamps last longer and are less expensive to operate. Approximately one-third less energy is required for fluorescent lamps than incandescent lamps.

*Tricia Moore; lauckgroup; Dallas, Texas*

**FRISBI**
*Flos; Huntington, New York*

**TABLE LAMP**
*Nessen Lamps, Inc.; Mamaroneck, New York*

**LOCAL LIGHTING**

**LUXO DESK LAMP**
*Luxo Corp.; Port Chester, New York*

**BERENICE**
*Artemide; Farmingdale, New York*

**TASK-SPECIFIC LIGHTING**

**DUOMO**
*Koch & Lowy; Avon, Massachusetts*

**TACCIA**
*Flos; Huntington, New York*

**UNIFORM AMBIENT LIGHTING**

---

### Task Lighting Glossary

*A-lamp:* The incandescent lamp is the most commonly used in North American households. The "A" designation refers to the lamp's bulbous shape.

*Compact fluorescent lamp:* Single-ended fluorescent discharge light sources with small-diameter tubes.

*Direct light:* Light emitted by a luminaire in the general direction of the task to be illuminated. The term usually refers to light emitted in a downward direction.

*Efficacy:* The ratio of light output (in lumens) to input of power (in watts), expressed as lumens per watt (LPW).

*Halogen lamp:* An incandescent lamp that uses a halogen-fill gas. Halogen lamps have higher-rated efficacies and longer lives than standard incandescent A-lamps.

*Illuminance:* The amount of light that reaches a surface. Illuminance is measured in footcandles (lux).

*Indirect lighting:* Light arriving at a surface after reflecting from one or more surfaces that are not part of the luminaire.

*Lamp:* A radiant light source that emits light.

*Luminaire:* A complete lighting unit consisting of a lamp or lamps and the parts designed to distribute the light, to position and protect the lamps and to connect the lamps to the power supply.

*Luminaire efficiency:* The ratio of light emitted by a luminaire to the light emitted by the lamp or lamps within it. Components of a luminaire, such as reflectors and diffusers, absorb some of the light from the lamp. A highly efficient luminaire emits most of the light that the lamp emits.

*Prismatic lens:* An optical component of a luminaire that is used to distribute the emitted light. It is usually a sheet of plastic with a pattern of pyramid-shaped refracting prisms on one side.

# WINDOW TREATMENTS

Window treatments control light and glare, provide privacy, act as acoustic buffers, and make design statements. Window treatments also play a significant role in the energy performance of a building and must be coordinated with heating and cooling load calculations. The energy efficiency of the building and the comfort of its inhabitants are heavily reliant on the proper selection of window treatments. They can be categorized according to two energy-saving functions: shading from solar heat gain in the summer and insulation from building heat loss in the winter.

## SHADING FROM SOLAR HEAT GAIN

Solar radiation is the primary heat source in a commercial building. When sunlight strikes a window, some of the heat energy is reflected and the rest is either absorbed by the glass or transmitted to the interior.

- *Reflected solar radiation* bounces off the surface and does not penetrate the glass.
- *Absorbed solar radiation* is soaked up by the glass and eventually is dissipated by convection or reradiation.
- *Transmitted heat energy* penetrates the glass and heats the building's interior.

*Shading coefficient* (SC), a term developed by ASHRAE in the 1960s, describes a window system's capability to reduce heat gain. The three solar heat gain factors—reflection, absorption, and transmission—determine a window system's SC. The shading coefficient is a function of the entire window system, including the window treatment. The SC is the ratio between the solar gain through a window system and the gain through ⅛-in.- (3-mm-) thick clear glass under the same conditions. An SC of .22 means that a window system allows 22% of the heat energy transmitted through ⅛-in.- (3-mm-) thick glass into the building's interior. The lower the shading coefficient, the better the window system's capability to reduce incoming solar radiation. Manufacturers typically provide SCs for window systems using blinds or shades.

The effectiveness of a window treatment to protect against solar heat gain depends on its capability to reflect incoming solar radiation back through the window before it can be converted into heat within the building. Because reflectance is the most important property of a window treatment in reducing heat gain,

color selection is an important factor. Dark colors tend to absorb heat, and light colors reflect it; thus, white and light-colored window treatments are the first choice for reducing heat gain.

## LOW EMISSIVITY GLAZING

Low emissivity can be thought of as the counterpart to high reflectivity. If a surface has high reflectivity, it has low emissivity (low-E). Low-E surfaces allow the visible spectrum of light through while reflecting back a large portion of the thermal radiation, which makes them popular for use as glass coatings. Light comes through, but most of the heat does not. Horizontal louver blind slats and roller shade fabrics are available with low-E coatings that increase the energy performance of a window system.

## INSULATION FROM HEAT LOSS

Heat energy moves from a warmer to a colder substance by conduction, convection, or radiation. Most window treatments do not effectively prevent heat loss, because they are inferior insulators.

- *Conduction* is the transfer of heat energy through a substance. Glass is an excellent conductor; heat or cold is quickly and efficiently conveyed through it.
- *Convection* is the transfer of heat energy through air. The human body loses and gains heat primarily through the air.
- *Radiation* is the transmission of energy by invisible light waves independent of a substance or air. For example, solar radiation travels through space (a vacuum) to reach the Earth in this manner.

## R-VALUE

Conduction, convection, and radiation determine a material's thermal resistance, referred to as its *R-value*. The R-value measures the insulating effect of a material, the material's resistance to the flow of heat. The larger the R-value, the greater the resistance and the better the insulating value. The effectiveness of a window treatment as an insulator depends on its capability to reduce the conductive transfer of heat to the interior. The R-values of window treatments such as blinds and shades may be quite low. However, in a fully lowered position, they form an insulating airspace next to the window, which somewhat improves the R-value of the window system.

## BLINDS

### Horizontal Blinds

Horizontal blinds are the traditional, cost-effective solution to controlling glare. Although microblinds have a narrower slat width than miniblinds, they are typically heavier because more slats are required for the same-size blind. This added weight can contribute to a shorter life span for the hardware of microblinds. Blind slats are commonly made of aluminum, PVC, or wood.

### Window Treatment Standards

The American Window Covering Manufacturers Association (AWCMA) standard for horizontal blinds calls for the uniform location of the cord lock on the right side of the head channel and the tilting mechanism (typically a wand) on the left side of the head channel. If other locations are required because of inaccessibility, specify the blind-operating hardware location or indicate it on the drawings.

### Selection Criteria

If tilt wand and lift cord lengths are not specified, manufacturers typically assume the window sill height to be 36 in. (915 mm) above the finish floor. In commercial applications where pets or children may be involved, accidental strangulation with the traditional end loop and cord equalizer is of concern. Break-through lift cord ends are available as a safety feature. The attached ends of the lift cord separate easily when force is applied.

Perforated slats preserve the view while reducing glare, conserving energy, and providing privacy. Evenly spaced tiny holes allow light through while protecting the interior from solar heat gain. The openness factor for horizontal blinds is typically limited to 6% of the area of the slat so that the strength of the slat is not diminished.

To maintain a uniform appearance in a building's exterior, the base building standard may require blinds with certain features. Top-locking cord locks offer only two blind positions: fully raised and fully lowered. Slat tilt limiters limit the slat angle position, allowing tilt only within a narrow range. A uniform blind color on the building exterior can be maintained, while using a variety of colors on the interior, by specifying slats with different finishes on the concave and convex sides. Where a dark-colored slat is required, the reflectance of the window system can be improved with a light-colored or low-E-coated concave slat side. The color and openness factor of blinds will affect the perception of the view. Perforated, dark window treatments minimize glare and appear to be more transparent.

In comparing horizontal blinds, an increased slat count (number of slats per given dimension) or decreased pitch (rung spacing) usually indicates a better-quality blind.

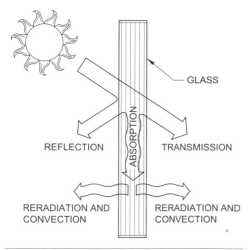

**SOLAR HEAT GAIN**

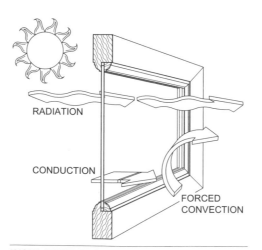

**INSULATION FROM HEAT LOSS**

### MAXIMUM RECOMMENDED SIZES FOR HORIZONTAL ALUMINUM SLAT BLINDS

| SLAT SIZE MM | MAXIMUM WIDTH FT (M) | MAXIMUM AREA SQ FT (SQ M) |
|---|---|---|
| 15–16 (nominally ½ in.) | 10 (3) | 70 (6.5) |
| 25 (nominally 1 in.) | 12 (3.6) | 100 (9.2) |
| 50 (nominally 2 in.) | 12 (3.6) | 135 (12.5) |

## Vertical Blinds

Vertical blinds are among the easiest window treatments to clean and repair. The vanes collect no more dust than walls or other vertical surfaces. Vertical blind vanes are also easier to replace than horizontal blind slats. Unlike horizontal blinds, vertical blinds can be specified where curved track applications are required. Similar to draperies, *stack-back dimensions* (the width of a window treatment in a fully open position at the side of the window) must be considered if the full window is to be exposed when the blinds are fully opened.

Vane materials for commercial use include fabric, polyvinyl chloride (PVC), and aluminum. The fiber content of fabric vanes is typically polyester; however, cotton, acrylic, fiberglass, and rayon are also available. The fabric can be woven or nonwoven. This vane type can be free-hanging, or the fabric can be inserted into an extruded PVC sleeve to add rigidity and durability. Fabric vanes can be treated with soil repellant or fire-retardant finishes. Sealed or sewn-in bottom weights, or bottom chains linking the vanes together, are often recommended to stabilize this relatively lightweight type of vane.

PVC can be extruded into a variety of vane profiles. These vanes typically contain titanium dioxide (a common light block found in some sunscreen lotions) for opaqueness. PVC vanes should be treated with an antistatic solution to prevent dirt attraction and static cling. Because of PVC's rigidity and weight, bottom chains linking the vanes together are not required. Because the structural integrity of a vane is not as crucial as that of a horizontal blind slat, a much larger openness factor (ranging from about 6% to 13%) is possible for vertical blinds than for horizontal blinds.

## ROLLER SHADES

The most effective type of interior protection against heat gain through a window is a light-colored, opaque roller shade. Flat roller shades are categorized by two methods of operation: those that are drawn up onto a roller at the top and those that roll up from the bottom. Bottom-up shades offer privacy while allowing light in. Bead-chain-operated shades are easier to keep clean, because the shades are not touched during operation. They are also ideal for applications where the bottom of a shade is difficult to reach.

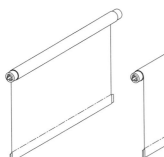

**REGULAR ROLL SHADE**
The roller is installed in front of the shade.

**REVERSE ROLL SHADE**
The roller is installed behind the shade. Reverse roll should be specified for print shade fabrics, because it allows only the finish face, not the back of the material, to be exposed to the interior.

**ROLLER SHADES**

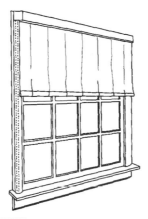

**ROLLER SHADE**
Roller shades can often be fabricated from the same material used for textile wallcoverings or upholstery. Blackout or translucent material is commonly laminated to the back of finish fabrics to change the appearance or performance of the shade. Room-darkening and blackout shades are typically made of fiberglass covered with a PVC film.

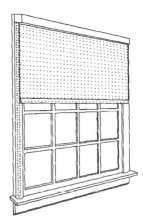

**PERFORATED ROLLER SHADE**
Perforated roller shades utilize a semitransparent shade cloth that permits sun penetration and a view to the outside, while providing heat and UV protection. Shade cloth openness factors range from 1% to 22%. Higher openness factors are achieved with vinyl-covered fiberglass (because of its dimensional stability), as opposed to vinyl-covered polyester.

**ROLLER SHADES** *Source: Knoll Textiles; East Greenville, Pennsylvania; and DFB Sales, Inc.; Long Island City, New York*

**DOUBLE ROMAN SHADE**
Double Roman shades require from 1½ to 2½ times the vertical fabric fullness of the flat Roman shade. Featuring overlapping folds that cascade down the full height of the shade, a double Roman shade includes horizontal supports at each backfold, which are attached to spacing tapes.

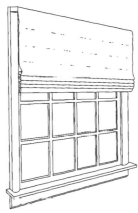

**FLAT ROMAN SHADE**
Flat Roman shades can be modified for a variety of design statements: for example, a shaped bottom hem, an extra fabric fold at the sill, chrome or brass rods attached to the face of the shade, inverted seams, or the use of horizontal seam spacing. This shade type requires the least amount of fabric.

**ROMAN SHADES** *Source: Knoll Textiles; East Greenville, Pennsylvania; and DFB Sales, Inc.; Long Island City, New York*

Austrian shades are unlined and designed to swoop between vertical shimming tapes. Increasing the number of swoops can create different visual effects, for example, one swoop as opposed to four swoops for the same opening. Austrian shades can be used as stationary top treatments or as valances.

**AUSTRIAN SHADE** *Source: Knoll Textiles; East Greenville, Pennsylvania; and DFB Sales, Inc.; Long Island City, New York*

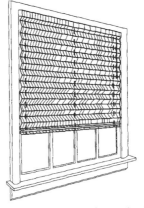

Pleated shades are typically made from polyester with an antistatic treatment. Pleated shades fabricated from C.O.M. are also available; however, the pleats may deform, sagging at the top and compressing at the bottom. Pleated shades are more commonly used in residential applications, rather than commercial.

**PLEATED SHADE** *Source: Knoll Textiles; East Greenville, Pennsylvania; and DFB Sales, Inc.; Long Island City, New York*

## DRAPERIES

Drapery fabric selection should include an evaluation of the drapeability, commonly referred to as the *hand*, of the fabric. By requesting a full-width sample at least 1 yard in length, the appropriateness of the fabric for a hanging application can be determined.

*Casements* are sheer or semisheer fabrics, often used with operable over-drapes or fixed side panels. Extra-wide fabrics, up to 118 in. (2,997 mm), are available to be "railroaded," thus eliminating the obvious seams inherent in sheer materials.

*Linings* are fabric backings that enhance the draping qualities of a fabric, increase the energy performance of the window system, or protect the drapery fabric from ultraviolet (UV) radiation. Linings can be sewn to the face fabric if they have compatible cleaning requirements, or they can hang on a separate track. *Metallic linings* in various weights can increase a window system's reflectivity, and *insulating linings* can boost the thermal performance. Ultraviolet inhibitors can be added to lining fabrics to help protect the drapery fabric against deterioration caused by sunlight. Water-repellant finishes protect linings from unsightly staining and streaking from condensation.

*Blackout linings* are used to darken a room completely. Such linings are popular in hospitality applications or in meeting rooms where the use of projection equipment is anticipated.

*Interlinings* enhance the performance or appearance of the drapery. For example, an acoustic interlining of heavy cotton flannel increases the sound-absorbing capability of a window treatment. An interlining for a stationary side panel can create more body, eliminating the necessity of a heavier, more expensive drapery fabric. Interlinings hang between the finish drapery fabric and the lining. They require the durability of a lining fabric for protection from UV radiation, moisture, and abrasion.

## DRAPERY OPERATION

*One-way draw operation* describes a drapery panel that opens entirely to one side. A one-way draw is designated as either *full left* or *full right*, indicating the direction in which the drapery stacks as you face it. For example, if you are looking at an open drapery stacked on the right, it is a right draw.

*Two-way* or *bipart draw* means that the drapery panels meet in the center and open to either side.

*Carriers* hold the drapery end that traverses the rod. *Butt master carriers* are often used in roll pleat and stack pleat draperies. *Overlap master carriers* are commonly the choice for conventional pleated drapes. Standard overlap for overlap master carriers is 3 in. (75 mm) per panel, and the right panel overlaps the left.

*Return* is the distance from the traversing rod to the wall or the depth of the projection. When casements and over-drapes are used in the same window opening, the depths of the returns should provide adequate clearance for unencumbered operation. The dimensions of the return and the overlap must be added to the dimension of the opening to determine the drapery panel width. The stack space dimension, or *stack back*, is the drapery width when fully opened. The

stack back must be considered when determining the traversing rod length and may determine the traversing direction.

*Manual track operation* options for manually operating draperies include wands or pull cords.

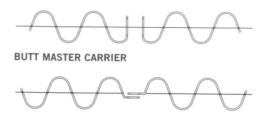

**BUTT MASTER CARRIER**

**OVERLAP MASTER CARRIER**

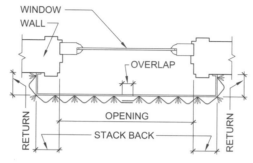

**DRAW DRAPERIES**
Finished drapery panel width for two-way draw draperies = return + stack-back width + one-half of the window opening width + drapery overlap.

**DRAPERY CARRIERS**

- *Wands* have no mechanized parts compared to other types of track operation hardware, making them the preferred choice for hard-use applications. The wand, also referred to as a baton, is used to drag the drapery into position on its track. Wands are suitable for lightweight draperies.
- *Pull cords* are either free-hanging or strung between a pulley and the drapery heading. The pulley system requires that the pulley be permanently mounted on the wall or floor. Free-hanging pull-cord ends should not be looped because of the strangulation hazard they pose.

*Electrical track operation* uses motor-operated drapery controls to drive individual or groups of draperies. Timing devices and temperature-sensing controls are available for automatic operation of draperies. Low-voltage motors can be attached to the track, hung below the track, or recessed into the ceiling above the track. Motorized tracks can be controlled remotely by infrared or radio waves or by a wall switch. Radio-controlled remote operation is often preferred because, unlike infrared remote controls, a line of sight is not required between the remote and the motor, and the receiver can be concealed behind the draperies.

*Drapery weight* affects track-carrying capacity. Carrying capacity decreases if the drapery track is curved. The minimum radius for inside and outside curved tracks varies with hardware type and track configuration.

*Fullness* is the ratio of the total fabric used, less allowances for side hems and seams, to the finished drapery width. For example, a drapery with 100% fullness is 100% wider than the width of the drapery in a closed position, or twice the finished drapery width.

### STACKING WIDTHS FOR PLEATED DRAPERY HEADINGS

| OPENING SIZE IN. (MM) | STACKING WIDTHS IN. (MM) | | | REQUIRED YARDAGE 150% FULLNESS 54-IN.- (137-CM-) WIDE FABRIC | |
|---|---|---|---|---|---|
| | PINCH PLEAT | BARREL AND BOX PLEAT | PENCIL PLEAT | FOR DRAPERY LENGTH TO SILL 72 IN. (1,828 MM) | FOR DRAPERY LENGTH TO FLOOR 102 IN. (2,590 MM) |
| 32 (812) | 14 (355) | 16 (406) | 13 (330) | 5 | 7 |
| 54 (1,371) | 20 (508) | 24 (609) | 18 (457) | 7.5 | 10.5 |
| 76 (1,930) | 25 (635) | 31 (787) | 23 (584) | 10 | 14 |
| 98 (2,489) | 30 (762) | 38 (965) | 27 (685) | 12.5 | 17.5 |
| 120 (3,048) | 36 (914) | 46 (1,168) | 32 (812) | 15 | 21 |
| 142 (3,606) | 41 (1,041) | 53 (1,346) | 37 (939) | 17.5 | 24 |
| 164 (4,165) | 47 (1,193) | 60 (1,524) | 42 (1,066) | 20 | 28 |
| 186 (4,724) | 52 (1,320) | 67 (1,701) | 47 (1,193) | 22.5 | 31.5 |
| 208 (5,283) | 58 (1,473) | 75 (1,905) | 52 (1,320) | 25 | 35 |

### PLEATED DRAPERY PANEL WIDTHS

| FULLNESS | MULTIPLIER TO DETERMINE DRAPERY PANEL WIDTH BEFORE PLEATING | CALCULATION (BASED ON 54-IN. (137-CM-) WIDE FABRIC) | PLEATED DRAPERY PANEL WIDTH |
|---|---|---|---|
| 100% | 2 | 54 in. ÷ 2 cm = 27 | 27 in. |
| 125% | 2.25 | 54 in. ÷ 2.25 cm = 24 | 24 in. |
| 150% | 2.5 | 54 in. ÷ 2.5 cm = 22 | 22 in. |
| 200% | 3 | 54 in. ÷ 3 cm = 18 | 18 in. |
| 225% | 3.25 | 54 in. ÷ 3.25 cm = 16.625 | 16⅝ in. |
| 300% | 4 | 54 in. ÷ 4 cm = 13.5 | 13½ in. |

### RECOMMENDED DRAPERY FULLNESSES

| | MINIMUM | AVERAGE | MAXIMUM |
|---|---|---|---|
| Unlined Traversing Drapery | 100% | 150% | 200% |
| Lined Traversing Drapery | 100% | 125% | 150% |
| Stationary Side Panels | 150% | 200% | 300% |

*Source: KnollTextiles East Greenville, Pennsylvania; and DFB Sales, Inc.; Long Island City, New York*

# TRADITIONAL PLEATED HEADING SYSTEMS

The *pleat to dimension* is the width of the drapery after it has been pleated. For example, if a 48 in. (1,220 mm) width of fabric is 19 in. (480 mm) after it has been pleated, it is specified as "pleat to 19 inches." Fullness for a conventional pleated drapery is typically 225% and can range up to 250%, making the stack-back dimension the largest among the drapery types. Pleated headings are reinforced with buckram or other stiffening materials, so special care must be taken in dry cleaning and pressing the pleats. Of all the drapery headings, these are the most readily adaptable at a project site. The required drapery fullness can be accommodated by adjusting the depth and the distance between the pleats.

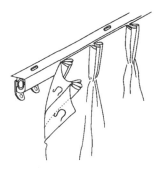

## PINCH, OR FRENCH, PLEATS

Pinch pleats, sometimes referred to as French pleats, are typically 4 in. (100 mm) high and spaced 4 in. (100 mm) apart. For large windows or a more dramatic appearance, pleats can be extended to 6 in. (150 mm) high. Each pleat has three folds. The amount of fabric in each pleat is determined by the fullness.

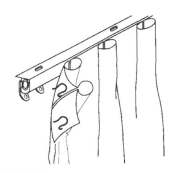

## BARREL PLEATS

Barrel pleats are fabricated into cylinder, or barrel, shapes. The pleats can range from small to large (1 to 3½ in. (25 to 90 mm) in diameter). Due to the construction, the stacking ratio is much greater for a given fullness.

## FESTOONS AND JABOTS

Festoons (A) are deep, horizontal folds with 200% fullness. Jabots (B) are usually self-lined or lined with a contrasting fabric because the back of the fabric is visible. Festoons and jabots are mounted to a valance board prior to installation.

## BOX PLEATS

Box pleats can be fabricated with heavy-duty buckram, which allows for the support of a great weight. Since the pleats are flat and can produce up to three times the fullness, this heading can be used for stationary side panels in a pocket where there is limited space.

## PENCIL PLEATS

Pencil pleats provide a soft heading while the uniformity of evenly spaced ⅜ in. (9 mm) pleats creates a structured appearance. This heading makes the drapery appear fuller than it is.

---

**TRADITIONAL PLEATED HEADING SYSTEMS**
*Source: KnollTextiles; East Greenville, Pennsylvania; and DFB Sales, Inc.; Long Island City, New York*

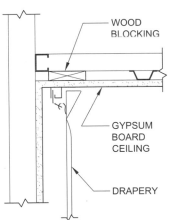

**CEILING-MOUNTED DRAPERY**

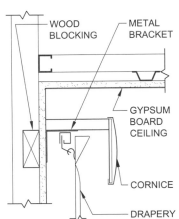

**WALL-MOUNTED DRAPERY WITH UPHOLSTERED CORNICE**

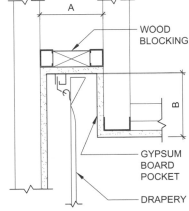

**SINGLE POCKET**

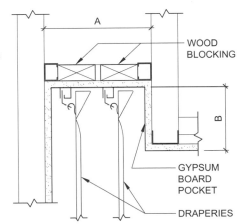

**DOUBLE POCKET**

### SINGLE-WINDOW TREATMENT POCKET DIMENSIONS*

|  | A IN. (MM) | B IN. (MM) |
|---|---|---|
| Drapery | 6 (152) | 6 (152) |
| Shade | 4 (101) | 4 (101) |
| Horizontal Blinds | 3 (76) | 2 (50) |
| Vertical Blinds | 2 (50) | 2 (50) |

*Add 20% to dimensions if track is motorized.*

### DOUBLE-WINDOW TREATMENT POCKET DIMENSIONS*

|  | A IN. (MM) | B IN. (MM) |
|---|---|---|
| Drapery with Drapery | 12 (304) | 12 (304) |
| Shade with Drapery | 10 (254) | 6 (152) |
| Horizontal Blinds with Drapery | 8.5 (215) | 6 (152) |
| Vertical Blinds with Drapery | 11 (279) | 6 (152) |

*Add 20% to dimensions if track is motorized.*

**WINDOW TREATMENT POCKET DETAILS**
*Source: KnollTextiles; East Greenville, Pennsylvania; and DFB Sales, Inc.; Long Island City, New York*

## LOW-PROFILE TRACK HEADING SYSTEMS

Low-profile track heading systems, sometimes referred to as *architectural heading systems,* appear the same from either side of the window and consequently do not need to be lined for the sake of appearance. These heading styles are popular in installations that require frequent cleaning, for example health care settings, because they can be machine-washed. When installed with a ceiling-mounted, low-profile track, these headings appear to be hanging directly from the ceiling.

## WINDOW TREATMENT CLEARANCES

Draperies and venetian blinds of other interior shading devices must be hung so as to provide space at the top and bottom, or on one side and bottom, to permit natural air movement over the room side of the glass. The following criteria must be met to avoid formation of a heat trap:

- Minimum clearance of 1½ in. (38 mm) is required on top and bottom, or on one side and bottom, between shading device and surrounding construction.
- Minimum clearance of 2 in. (50 mm) is required between glass and shading device. Heating/cooling outlets must be to room side of shading device.

If venetian blinds are being used, and these clearances cannot be provided, a two-direction positive stop or lockout that limits the movement of the blinds should be incorporated. For horizontal blinds, the lockout should limit the rotation of the blinds in both directions so that they are not in a position 60° off the horizontal when in the most closed position. For vertical blinds, the lockout should limit movement in both directions so that ½ in. (12 mm) of spacing exists between the blinds when in the closed position. If these guidelines cannot be followed, heat-strengthened glass should be specified in lieu of annealed glass.

Heat-strengthening or full tempering of the glass may be necessary for some installations to offset the effects of the glass size, solar absorption, exterior shading, interior shading, climactic conditions, lack of proper clearances noted above or improper placement, or directing of airflow.

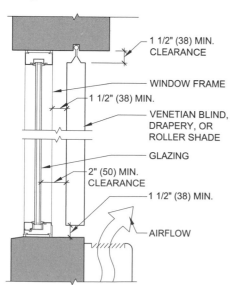

**WINDOW TREATMENT CLEARANCES**
*Source: Glass Association of North America; GANA Glazing Manual; Topeka, Kansas, 1997.*

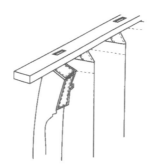

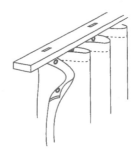

**STACK PLEATS**
Stack pleats are formed by sewing molded stiffeners to the top of the pleats. The effect at the heading is a well-defined V-shape, which requires a very small stacking width. Stack pleat draperies require the smallest stack-back dimension and can stack as tightly as one-sixth of the drapery width. Fullness and the depth of the pleat are interdependent, which is not the case with traditional pleated headings. The standard fullness for stack pleats is 100%, but fullnesses of 40%, 60%, 80%, and 120% are also available.

**ROLL PLEATS**
Roll pleats provide a soft, rounded pleating pattern. This drapery type is fabricated from flat panels of fabric. Because there is less fullness, there is also less stack back required for roll pleats than for conventional pleats. Fullness is achieved by varying the spacing between the snaps or grommets on the drapery heading. Standard fullness is 100%, but fullnesses of 60%, 80%, and 120% are also available.

**TACKED-ACCORDION PLEATS**
Tacked-accordion pleats are formed by sewing molded pleaters to the top of the pleat and then snapping them onto the carriers in the track. The tacked-accordion-pleat heading can be combined with a permanent-pleating process that is applied to the fabric, creating shape creases down the length of the drapery.

**ACCORDION PLEATS**
Accordion pleats provide the most efficient stacking ratio of the architectural heading systems, but this system produces the largest stacking depth, front to back. This is an excellent system for partitions. The heading can be fabricated with or without buckram, depending on the structure desired.

**LOW-PROFILE TRACK HEADING SYSTEMS**
*Source: KnollTextiles; East Greenville, Pennsylvania; and DFB Sales, Inc.; Long Island City, New York*

### STACKING WIDTHS FOR LOW-PROFILE DRAPERY HEADINGS

| OPENING SIZE IN. (MM) | STACKING WIDTHS IN. (MM) | | | REQUIRED YARDAGE 150% FULLNESS 54-IN.- (137-CM-) WIDE FABRIC | |
|---|---|---|---|---|---|
| | STACK PLEAT | ROLL AND TACKED-ACCORDION PLEAT | ACCORDION PLEAT | DRAPERY LENGTH TO SILL 72 IN. (1,828 MM) | DRAPERY LENGTH TO FLOOR 102 IN. (2,590 MM) |
| 32 (812) | 8 (203) | 8 (203) | 7 (177) | 5 | 7 |
| 54 (1,371) | 11 (279) | 13 (330) | 12 (304) | 7.5 | 10.5 |
| 76 (1,930) | 14 (355) | 17.5 (444) | 17 (431) | 10 | 14 |
| 98 (2,489) | 16 (406) | 23 (584) | 22 (558) | 12.5 | 17.5 |
| 120 (3,048) | 19 (482) | 27.5 (698) | 27 (685) | 15 | 21 |
| 142 (3,606) | 22 (558) | 32 (812) | 32 (812) | 17.5 | 24 |
| 164 (4,165) | 25 (635) | 38 (965) | 42 (1,066) | 20 | 28 |
| 186 (4,724) | 28 (711) | 43 (1,092) | 43 (1,092) | 22.5 | 31.5 |
| 208 (5,283) | 31 (787) | 46 (1,168) | 54 (1,371) | 25 | 35 |

*Source: KnollTextiles East Greenville, Pennsylvania; and DFB Sales, Inc.; Long Island City, New York*

# METAL FILE CABINETS

## FILE CABINET TYPES

File cabinets are either vertical, which can be used for front-to-back filing configurations only, or lateral, which are wider than they are deep and can be used for either side-to-side or front-to-back hanging file configurations.

Vertical file cabinets are one drawer wide and two to five drawers high. They can only be used for front-to-back hanging file configurations. Common cabinet widths are 15 in. (380 mm), letter size, and 18 in. (460 mm), legal size. Common cabinet depth is 29 in. (710 mm).

Lateral file cabinets are wider than they are deep and can be used for side-to-side and front-to-back hanging file configurations. Common cabinet widths are 30, 36, and 42 in. (760, 915, and 1,065 mm). A 48 in. (1,220 mm) width cabinet is also available and is often used as a systems furniture component. Common cabinet depth is 18 in. (460 mm). Overall cabinet depths and widths vary little among manufacturers, however, drawer height and internal configuration vary to accommodate a wide range of storage materials.

Lateral files require less pull and stand space than vertical files for the amount of material stored. Because lateral files are often a more efficient use of space and because their internal storage can be more easily reconfigured, they are more commonly used than vertical files. Two-drawer file cabinets can be used as credenzas and three-drawer units often serve as space dividers.

## SIZE AND CAPACITY

Sizes and capacities of metal file cabinets and components vary. Cabinets with the same nominal dimensions from different manufacturers do not always have the same actual sizes and interior capacities. Some manufacturers differentiate their products from those of other manufacturers by offering cabinets with dimensions that vary from industry standards and that provide increased storage space. Cabinets with shallow drawers can provide more storage space in less overall height. Verify exact dimensions; many manufacturers publish only nominal dimensions in their product literature.

## FEATURES

Exterior dimensions and interior capacities of file cabinets vary among manufacturers. Verify exact dimensions; some manufacturers publish nominal dimensions in their product literature.

Finish options provided by some manufacturers include acoustical panels for exposed file cabinet backs; wood drawer fronts; and stone, plastic laminate, and wood tops.

Leveling feet are used to ensure that the file cabinet is level and plumb. Structural damage to the file cabinet can result from twisting if the cabinet is not properly leveled. File cabinets should be leveled after they are fully loaded to compensate for floor deflection.

Enclosed base cabinets may have access to the space for wire and cable routing.

Stackable units offer the flexibility of changing the file cabinet's height in the field. A two-drawer cabinet can grow to three drawers by ordering and connecting another module. Also, the orientation of the drawers can vary in a freestanding group of file cabinets, with some drawers opening to the front and others opening to the back.

## PERFORMANCE STANDARDS

ANSI/BIFMA X5.2, *American National Standard for Office Furnishings—Lateral Files Tests,* for lateral file cabinets, and ANSI/BIFMA X5.3, *American National Standard for Office Furnishings—Vertical Files Tests,* for vertical file cabinets, are voluntary standards that include tests for conditions that, if present, may result in injury. The tests addresses static load, dynamic load, and endurance test cycles. Lateral files are tested for

**TWO-, THREE-, FOUR-, AND FIVE-DRAWER VERTICAL FILE CABINETS**

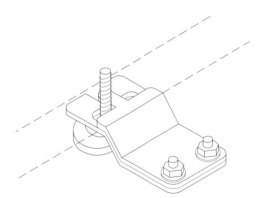

Anchor bracket attaches to the file cabinet's leveling glide and the floor. To reduce the risk of hazards during earthquakes, the California Office of Statewide Health Planning and Development (OSHPD) requires anchoring file cabinets that have the bottom of their top opening at 60 in. (1,524 mm) or higher.

**TIP-OVER PREVENTION METHODS**

interlock system performance (tip-over prevention) and retention of drawers or rollout shelves.

## FILE CABINET STABILITY

Interlock devices allow only one drawer to be opened at a time, ensuring that the cabinet will not accidentally tip over.

Anchoring file cabinets to the wall, floor, or adjacent cabinets (*ganging*) increases their stability. Seismic considerations may require that file cabinets be anchored. Cabinets that share a common countertop should be anchored to each other. If cabinets are anchored to each other, structural floor-loading limits should be verified; the weight of as few as four or five loaded, ganged cabinets can exceed floor-loading limits.

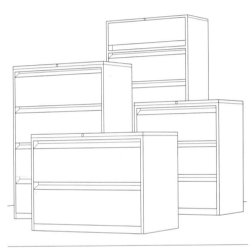

**TWO-, THREE-, FOUR-, AND FIVE-DRAWER LATERAL FILE CABINETS**

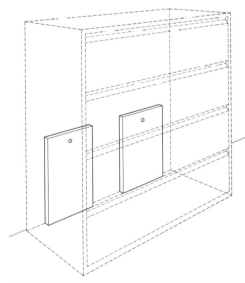

**COUNTERWEIGHTS PLACED IN THE BOTTOM OF THE FILE CABINET**

Consider counterweights for applications where top drawers may be used more frequently than bottom drawers, such as two-drawer lateral files adjacent to desks. Some cabinets come with counterweights; in others, they must be specified. If file cabinets are ganged, counterweights may not be necessary.

## LOCKS AND KEYS

Some manufacturers offer removable cylinders or locks that can be changed after the cabinets are installed. Two basic lock types are as follows:

- Plunger locks automatically secure themselves when pushed into engagement. They require key action only for unlocking.
- Cam locks require a rotary action for both locking and unlocking.

Three common keying methods are as follows:

- Random keying locks each cabinet with a different key.
- Alike keying locks each cabinet with the same key, providing no in-house security.
- Master keying locks each cabinet with its own key, but a single, master key can access all cabinets. Master keying is usually available for an extra charge. Grand-master and great-grand-master keying are also available.

## LOADING AND INSTALLATION

Manufacturers recommend loading file cabinets from the bottom to the top. Weight in the bottom drawer acts to balance the cabinet to prevent tipping.

For file cabinets installed in recesses or alcoves, opening dimensions must include required installation tolerances. Generally, at least an additional ⅛ in. (3 mm) in width per cabinet, for horizontal openings, and an additional ⅛ in. (3 mm) in height is required to allow for cabinet installation without damaging adjacent finishes.

*MASTERSPEC®; published by ARCOM; Salt Lake City, Utah and Alexandria, Virginia*

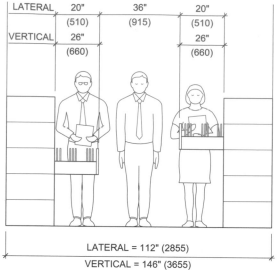

LATERAL 20" (510)  36" (915)  20" (510)
VERTICAL 26" (660)  26" (660)
LATERAL = 112" (2855)
VERTICAL = 146" (3655)
**DOUBLE SIDE ACCESS WITH CIRCULATION**

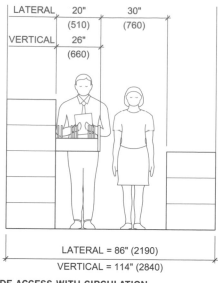

LATERAL 20" (510)  30" (760)
VERTICAL 26" (660)
LATERAL = 86" (2190)
VERTICAL = 114" (2840)
**SIDE ACCESS WITH CIRCULATION**

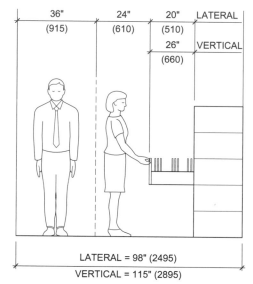

36" (915)  24" (610)  20" (510) LATERAL
26" (660) VERTICAL
LATERAL = 98" (2495)
VERTICAL = 115" (2895)
**FRONT ACCESS WITH CIRCULATION**

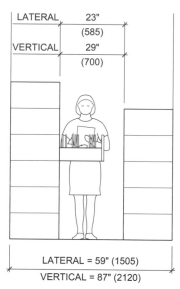

LATERAL 23" (585)
VERTICAL 29" (700)
LATERAL = 59" (1505)
VERTICAL = 87" (2120)
**SIDE ACCESS ONLY**

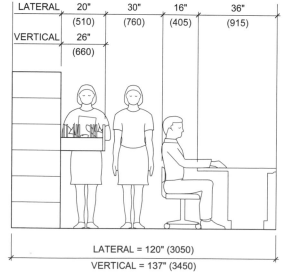

LATERAL 20" (510)  30" (760)  16" (405)  36" (915)
VERTICAL 26" (660)
LATERAL = 120" (3050)
VERTICAL = 137" (3450)
**SIDE ACCESS WITH CIRCULATION AND WORKSTATION**

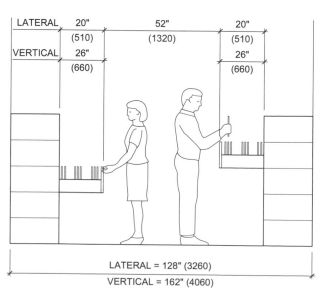

LATERAL 20" (510)  52" (1320)  20" (510)
VERTICAL 26" (660)  26" (660)
LATERAL = 128" (3260)
VERTICAL = 162" (4060)
**DOUBLE FRONT ACCESS WITH NO CIRCULATION**

**FILE CABINET ACCESS**

# SEATING

## SELECTION CONSIDERATIONS

Seating selection criteria include *function*—whether for task or lounge seating—and *construction*. Construction considerations include the type of frame, cushions, suspension systems, and whether casters or glides are used on the feet of the seating unit.

## SEATING FOR WORK

The chair has been singled out as the most critical comfort factor in the contemporary workplace. Back and arm aches, fatigue, and decreased productivity have all been associated with inadequately designed seating. No other piece of office furniture has been the subject of more lawsuits and insurance claims.

The contemporary office chair is a complicated piece of equipment. It accommodates the movement of its user in one of two ways: with a traditional swivel/tilt mechanism or a synchronized tilt mechanism. The standard swivel/tilt allows the seat to spin on its base and to tilt backward for comfort. In a synchronized tilt chair, the back and seat operate independently at different ratios of motion.

There is no single ideal posture for the performance of work. Each user has to find his or her own individual comfort level. Thus, the most important feature of any chair is adjustability. Separate seat and back assemblies are increasingly popular because they allow for maximum adjustability. There are four basic adjustments that allow the user to customize the fit of a chair: seat height, seat tilt, back height, and back tilt.

- *Seat height* adjustments are made either pneumatically or with a mechanical ratchet. Automatically adjusting chairs use the weight of the user to lower the seat once the pneumatic cylinder is engaged. The ease with which a pneumatic cylinder can be replaced should be considered in selecting this type of chair. Mechanically adjusted seats are twirled clockwise to lower them, and counterclockwise to raise them. An adjustable seat height ensures that the seat is the right height from the floor, the user has enough knee clearance, and the user's eyes and elbows are at the right heights for the work surface.
- *Seat tilt*, in conjunction with back tilt, works to maintain an angle of up to 135° between the torso and the thigh. This angle promotes the natural curvature of the lower spine in which the pressure is evenly distributed on the lumbar vertebrae. The use of a "waterfall" front seat edge helps promote circulation in the lower thigh and leg.
- *Back height* adjustments allow the user to position the backrest to properly and comfortably support the lumbar area. Some chairs allow for the adjustment of the seat depth by moving the backrest inward.
- *Back tilt* flexibility allows the user to lean back in the chair and stretch. The Human Factors Society recommends an adjustable back that ranges from 90° to 105°. The back tilt tension is often adjustable.

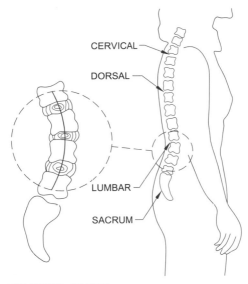

**THE SPINAL COLUMN**

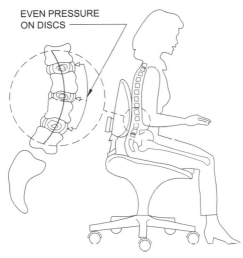

**CORRECT LUMBAR SUPPORT**
The natural curve of the lower spine is maintained with lumbar support.

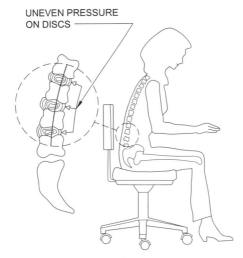

**INCORRECT LUMBAR SUPPORT**
The spine is flattened, exerting excessive pressure on the spinal discs.

**THE SITTING SPINE**

## TYPES OF OFFICE SEATING

Office seating lines are usually available in several design variations. The same visual characteristics are incorporated to a variety of styles that reflect different levels of management. The terms used to describe these differences vary among manufacturers, but the categories generally include a side or guest chair, task chair, one or two levels of seating for managers, and an executive chair.

- *A side chair* or *guest chair* is placed in an office for the use of visitors. It is designed with the expectation that the time a person is seated will be brief and that no tasks requiring posture support will be performed. A side chair does not have casters. A pedestal, four-legged, or glide base are the typical options for the chair base. Side chairs do not have adjustable features.
- *Task seating* (sometimes referred to as *secretarial* or *operational* seating) is designed to support typing and clerical tasks requiring extensive upper body movement, such as filing. A chair of this type usually has detachable arms and a low back.
- *A management chair* may have a low or high back and a wider, thicker seat than one used for task seating. Arms are almost always standard for a management chair. It is designed to support entry-through midlevel managers who spend part of a day working at their desks or keyboards and part of their day conferring.
- *An executive chair* is a larger-scale chair with arms. It has a wider, thicker seat and higher back, to impart an image of authority. Leather is a common upholstery option. Such chairs are not designed for the continuous, repetitive, movements of the average worker; they support computing, conferring, and telephoning. They are also appropriate for use in conference and boardrooms.

## PERFORMANCE AND DESIGN STANDARDS

BIFMA X5.1, *Test for General-Purpose Office Chairs*, evaluates the safety, durability, and structural adequacy of office seating. It tests the chair's capability to withstand the load of its user dropping into it, caster durability, swivel cycling, and tilt mechanism. It is a minimum standard: chairs either pass or fail. The standard does not grade or rank chairs.

The Human Factors Society sponsors ANSI 100, *Human Factors Engineering of Visual Display Terminal Workstations*. Among the seating features required by this standard are the following:

- Adjustable task arms to support the user's forearms and a distance between armrests of at least 18.2 in. (462 mm)
- Adjustable seat height range of 16 to 20½ in. (406 to 520 mm)
- Seat depth that permits contact with the seat back in the lumbar region
- Seat cushion at least 18.2 in. (462 mm) wide
- A fixed back angle of 90° or more, or an adjustable back that ranges from 90° to 105°

## UPHOLSTERED SEATING

An upholstered armchair, love seat, or sofa can warm a commercial interior with an invitation to sit, spend a moment, and relax. Commonly used in reception areas and executive offices, upholstered seating provides comfort and style. Four construction components must be considered when evaluating upholstered seating: the frame, the suspension system, the cushions, and the upholstery material.

### Upholstery Material

The seating frame, suspension system, and cushions form the foundation that is wrapped in an upholstery material. For fabrics with large patterns, the motif should be centered on each seat and back cushion, and should be continuous down the seat front and sides. Fabrics with a *repeat* (a repeated pattern), or narrower-width fabrics, will require more yardage than a standard 54-in.- (1,370-mm-) wide piece of upholstery material.

### Customer's Own Material (C.O.M.) and Customer's Own Leather (C.O.L.)

Seating manufacturers typically supply upholstery fabric options for their chairs. The fabric selections have been tested on their seating and have performed satisfactorily with regard to wear and flammability. Often a designer will find the upholstery selection limiting and will select a fabric from a textile manufacturer. Upholstery material that is not supplied by the seating manufacturer is referred to as C.O.M. or C.O.L. Written approval from the furniture manufacturer is usually required for its use. The furniture manufacturer must verify that the material is acceptable as an upholstery fabric.

"Customer" in this sense does not refer to the designer's customer, but to the manufacturer's customer—the party placing the order—which is the furniture, furnishings, and equipment (FF&E) contractor. The material is purchased separately from the seating and supplied to the furniture manufacturer for application. The FF&E contractor (usually the furniture dealer) is responsible for the acquisition and coordination of C.O.M.

### Frame

The frame gives an upholstered piece its structure and form. Kiln-dried hardwood provides a dimensionally stable frame foundation. The frame can be assembled with screws, nails, staples, and glue; however, a combination of mortise-and-tenon and double-doweled joints is often used in the most durable seating construction. Seat joints should be reinforced with corner blocks that are glued and screwed in place for added strength. For finer seating units, the portions of the frame that will be exposed are machine-sanded and then hand-sanded to ensure a smooth, scratch-free surface.

Some furniture manufacturers prestain the sanded wood frame to verify that there are no scratches. The prestain must be completely sanded off before the desired stain is applied by hand with either a rag or a brush. Sealer is applied after the wood is stained, preparing the surface to receive the finish coats. Catalyzed urethane is a popular choice for fine wood finishes, because it is extremely hard and resistant to water, alcohol, and scratches. Between each coat, the wood may be scuff-sanded to raise the grain of the wood and to ensure good adhesion.

**RUN-RIGHT OR UP-THE-BOLT APPLICATION**
This is the traditional method of upholstery application.

**"RAILROAD" APPLICATION**
This is usually the most efficient use of a fabric. The cushions are upholstered with the selvage edge of the fabric parallel to the seat cushion edge.

**UPHOLSTERY MATERIAL APPLICATION**

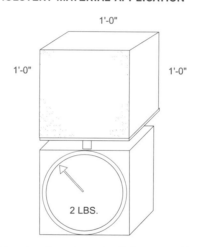

Flexible polyurethane foam density is measured in pounds per cubic foot.

**FOAM DENSITY CALCULATION**

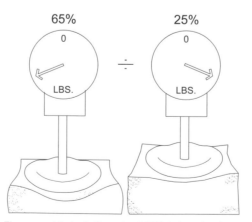

The support factor is the ratio of 65% indentation force deflection (IFD) divided by 25% IFD.

**FOAM COMPRESSION MODULUS (SUPPORT FACTOR)**

### Cushions

Polyurethane foam is the first choice for seating cushions. Multiple grades and densities of foam are usually bonded together to achieve the desired feel. For example, softer foams may be laminated to harder foams to provide surface softness along with firm support. Cushions can be preupholstered in muslin or bonded polyester to increase the life of the upholstery material.

Three basic properties affect the performance of a polyurethane foam: density, the Indentation Force Deflection, and the Compression Modulus.

- *Density* is a measurement of the mass per unit volume, expressed in lb/ft³ (kg/m³). Density is the most important foam property, as it determines the durability and support of the foam. The greater the foam density, the greater the support. Density is not a measurement of firmness; high-density foams can be quite soft. Water, for example, has a high density. Typically, higher-density foams are more expensive than low-density foams.

$$\text{Density} = \frac{\text{Weight (mass)}}{\text{Length} - \text{Width} - \text{Height (volume)}}$$

- *The Indentation Force Deflection (IFD)* is a measure of the foam firmness and is independent of density. It is determined by indenting the foam a percentage of its original height and noting the required force. IFD is an indication of comfort. A 25% IFD (indenting the foam 25% of its original height) is used to measure the surface feel of a foam. The less force required to compress the foam, the softer it is. *The Indentation Force Deflection (IFD)* is a measure of the foam firmness and is independent of density. It is determined by indenting the foam a percentage of its original height and noting the required force. IFD is an indication of comfort. A 25% IFD (indenting the foam 25% of its original height) is used to measure the surface feel of a foam. The less force required to compress the foam, the softer it is. For upholstery, 25% IFD can range from 5 to 50 lb (2.2 to 22 kg).

- *The Compression Modulus,* or support factor, is an indication of the foam's support and is primarily a function of the type of foam. The Compression Modulus is calculated by taking a second IFD measurement by indenting the foam 65% of its original height and dividing it by the 25% IFD. Typically, the greater the difference between the 25% IFD and the 65% IFD, the greater capability the foam has to support weight. To put it another way, the higher the support factor, the better the foam's capability to provide support. In most cases, the higher the foam density, the greater the Compression Modulus.

$$\text{Compression Modulus} = \frac{65\% \text{ IFD}}{25\% \text{ IFD}}$$

## SUSPENSION SYSTEMS

Much as a box spring is crucial to the proper support of a mattress, a chair's suspension system provides a firm foundation for the cushions. Several types of springing and webbing systems are combined to achieve the desired support in the seat and back.

Springing systems are used in conjunction with webbing to provide greater resilience and longer wear. There are two common springing systems—*coil spring* and *Marshall units*—each of which is supported by a webbing system. The eight-way hand-tied coil spring system is the most expensive, labor-intensive, and durable. The springs are held together with springing twine that is laced through the top of the spring and tied to adjacent springs in eight directions. This integrates the coils, forming a uniform surface of support. Marshall, or innerspring, units are springs that are contained inside individual pockets of muslin or burlap. Marshall units are purchased joined together, ready to be used as a springing system.

Five webbing systems are commonly used for commercial seating: *woven decking, webbing tape, corrugated steel, wire mesh,* and *sinuous spring.* Rubberized, woven decking is stretched taut across the frame and stapled in place, providing a firm but resilient base for cushions. Interwoven webbing tape, made of jute, cotton, or rubber, provides support directly for cushions or for coil springs. Corrugated steel bands are often used to support coil springs in an eight-way hand-tied suspension system. Plastic-covered wire mesh grids can be stretched across the seating frame for a more affordable suspension system. One of the most popular webbing systems is sagless, or sinuous, springs. This "wiggle wire" is linked together by small helical springs.

## CASTER AND GLIDE SELECTION

Two types of casters are popular for use on chair bases: *dual wheel* and *hooded.* The caster wheel is made of either hard or soft plastic, typically nylon. The selection of caster material is based in part on the type of flooring that will be used under the chair.

Hard casters are used on soft floorings such as carpet or carpet tile. The use of a rigid caster increases the chair's mobility on a carpeted surface. When selecting casters that will be used only on carpet floors, keep the following guidelines in mind:

- Hard casters with slightly rounded-wheel edge profiles tend to have better carpet wear characteristics than those with square edges.
- Hard rubber casters tend to mark a carpet more than plastic casters.
- Soft casters are used on hard or resilient floorings to help control the roll of the chair.

Glides are typically specified for chairs that will not be moved repeatedly or are required to remain stationary. Wide-based glides help distribute the weight of the chair and prevent the permanent indentation of a floor finish. Glides may reduce the height of the chair.

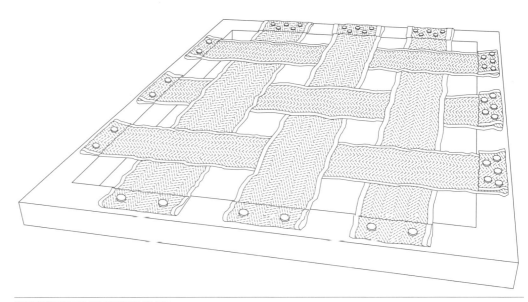

**INTERWOVEN WEBBING TAPE**

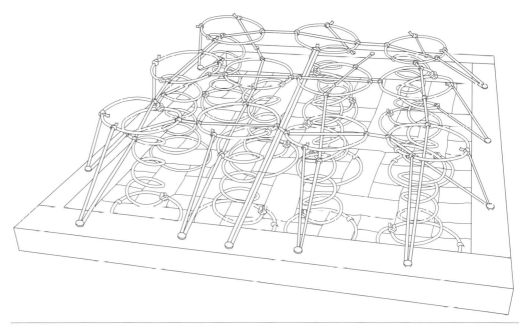

**EIGHT-WAY HAND-TIED COIL SPRINGS**

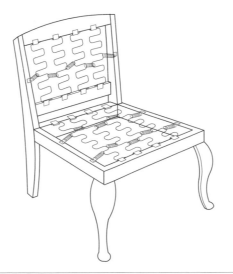

**SAGLESS, OR SINUOUS, SPRINGS**

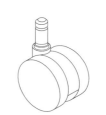 

**DUAL WHEEL CASTER**    **HOODED CASTER**

**CASTERS**

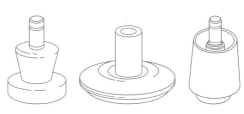

**GLIDES**

# WOOD-FRAME FURNITURE

## CONSTRUCTION

Solid wood is the most commonly used material for structural components of commercial furniture because it is durable, lightweight, and workable. Construction details can determine the useful life and affect the cost of the furniture. When evaluating a piece of wood furniture for the quality of its construction, consider the joinery methods, wood species, and finish.

### Joinery Methods

Joinery methods commonly used for wood commercial furniture include *interlocking* and *mechanical* joints. Glue may be used with one of these positive-joint methods; however, glue alone is not adequate to secure commercial furniture joints. In high-quality wood furniture, wood end grain, laminated board edges, and mechanical fasteners (such as screws or nails and joinery methods) are generally not exposed to view.

### Interlocking Joints

Interlocking joints include doweled, mortise-and-tenon, dovetail, and dado joints. Dowels are beveled on each end and can be grooved to carry excess glue and allow air to escape as the joint dries. Dowel joints are not as strong or stable as rabbet or mortise-and-tenon joints. Mortise-and-tenon joints are used in high-quality furniture construction to join components such as rails to the legs of tables. Interlocking joints, such as dovetail and dado joints, are used in residential furniture more than in high-quality commercial furniture. Dovetail joints are used to join drawer sides to drawer fronts and backs. Dado joints are used to hold the ends of fixed shelves.

### Mechanical Joints

Concealed mechanical fasteners are used to strengthen other carpentry joints. Miter joints are reinforced with corner blocks that are glued and mechanically fastened with screws. Mechanical joints can also permit controlled movement, such as collapsible table legs. Exposed mechanical fasteners are the most contemporary; they are commonly used for affordable furniture that has a limited life span and are popular for use with manufactured board products. Staples, crimped metal fasteners, or clamp nails are not durable enough to be used as commercial furniture fasteners.

## WOOD FINISHES

Staining, filling, and sealing, although not required, are often used to improve the appearance or performance of finishes.

### Stains

Stains are colorants, not protectants, that are used to make the wood grain more noticeable, change the color of the wood, or imitate a different wood species. After staining, the wood can be filled and sealed.

Stains contain soluble dyes or insoluble pigments as coloring agents that also keep the stains in liquid form.

### Water Stains

Water stains are powders that are mixed in water. They provide a fade-resistant, clear, permanent color and are the most difficult stains to apply properly. They raise the grain and usually require light sanding.

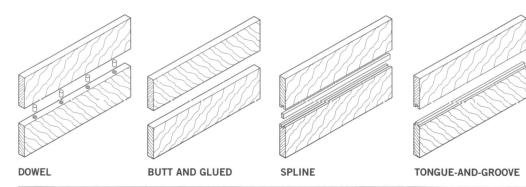

**DOWEL**    **BUTT AND GLUED**    **SPLINE**    **TONGUE-AND-GROOVE**

**METHODS OF JOINING BOARDS**

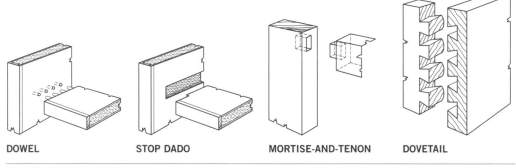

**DOWEL**    **STOP DADO**    **MORTISE-AND-TENON**    **DOVETAIL**

**INTERLOCKING JOINTS**

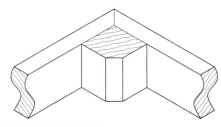
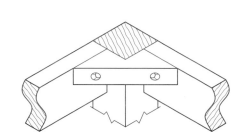

**GLUED CORNER BLOCK**    **SCREWED CORNER BLOCK**

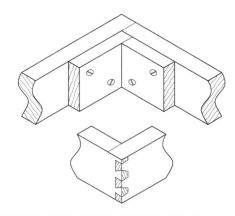
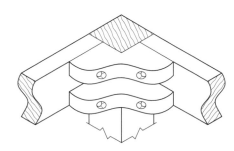

**DOVETAIL WITH CORNER REINFORCEMENT**    **DOUBLE-SCREWED CORNER BLOCK**

**CORNER REINFORCEMENT METHODS**

### Penetrating Oil Stains

Penetrating oil stains are premixed and are available in a variety of colors. They are likely to fade and bleed into other coats of the finish and are not recommended for most applications.

### Pigmented Oil Stains

Pigmented oil stains are the easiest to apply and will not raise the wood grain. Like the penetrating oil stains, they are sold premixed and are available in a variety of colors.

### Nongrain-Raising Stains

Nongrain-raising stains are known for their rapid drying time and transparent colors. They are spray-applied.

## Fillers

Fillers close the wood grain and pores and are used to produce smooth surfaces on woods with open grains or large pores.

Filler colors can match or contrast with the wood colors. Filler colors and stains can be used together to obtain several appearances.

- *Paste wood fillers* are often used with open-grained woods such as oak, walnut, and mahogany. They differ from wood putty, which is used to fill recesses and defects.
- *Liquid fillers* are used for woods with small pores, such as beech, maple, and cherry.

## Sealers

Sealers permeate the wood pores so topcoats are not absorbed into the wood, but adhere to its surface. Sealers are usually applied immediately before the topcoat. They secure the stain and filler and saturate the wood surface. Sealer selection is based on the type of topcoat to be applied. Polyesters, polyurethanes, and other synthetic finishes require specialized sealers.

## Topcoats

Topcoats protect the wood from moisture and wear. To prevent the topcoat from yellowing with age, ultraviolet (UV) inhibitors can be added. A clear finish is called *water white* in the furniture-manufacturing industry. Penetrating finishes, like oils and waxes that are often used for residential furniture, soak into the wood and do not build up a protective layer on the wood surface. They are also less durable than topcoats.

## Polyesters

Polyesters are the hardest type of topcoat. They are nearly 100% solids when applied and are almost as durable as high-pressure plastic laminates when cured. They also have good filling and leveling characteristics. Polyesters typically have a high gloss but are also available in matte finishes and have characteristics of plastics, such as good resistance to temperature extremes and crazing. Clear and opaque polyester film applications are available. The application of polyesters requires special equipment and skills. These finishes cannot be touched up on-site.

## Catalyzed Polyurethanes

Catalyzed polyurethanes are among the most durable finishes and are easier to apply than polyesters. Many consider them the first choice for commercial wood furniture finishing, and they are popular for applications that may be exposed to temperature extremes or UV radiation. Catalyzed polyurethane finishes do not water stain.

## Standard Lacquers

Standard lacquers, also called *noncatalyzed lacquers,* are most often used as a residential furniture topcoat. They are easy to apply, polish, and repair; have an unlimited shelf life; and dry quickly for dustproof coats. These lacquers have a high resistance to heat, water, and alcohol, and are available in a full range of sheens. Standard lacquers amalgamate successive coats; each coat partially dissolves previous coats as it is applied to produce a solid, monolithic finish.

## CHARACTERISTICS OF WOOD FURNITURE STAINS

| STAIN TYPE | CHARACTERISTICS | APPLICATION METHODS | DRYING TIME |
|---|---|---|---|
| Water | Clearest coat, nonbleeding, raises grain; requires light sanding | Wiping, sanding | 12 hours |
| Penetrating oil | Nongrain-raising, likely to bleed, fades | Wiping, brushing | 24 hours |
| Pigmented oil | Easiest to apply, nongrain-raising, hides grain | Wiping, brushing, spraying | 3–12 hours |
| Nongrain-raising | Dries rapidly, nonbleeding, nongrain-raising, clear colors, streaks easily | Spraying | 15 minutes–3 hours |

*Source: William P. Spence and L. Duane Griffiths, Furnituremaking: Design and Construction; Englewood Cliffs, NJ: Prentice Hall, 1991.*

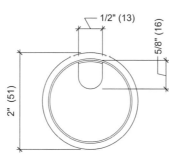

**ROUND GROMMET**
Round grommets are often selected for desks and work surfaces.

**RECTANGULAR GROMMET**
Rectangular grommets are often selected for credenzas and desk returns.

Grommets are used to organize and conceal electrical and phone line connections beneath the table surface. Dimensions vary among manufacturers.

**GROMMETS**

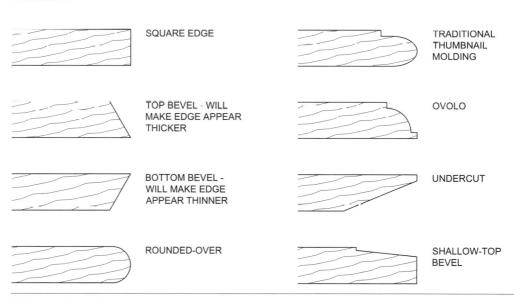

SQUARE EDGE

TOP BEVEL - WILL MAKE EDGE APPEAR THICKER

BOTTOM BEVEL - WILL MAKE EDGE APPEAR THINNER

ROUNDED-OVER

TRADITIONAL THUMBNAIL MOLDING

OVOLO

UNDERCUT

SHALLOW-TOP BEVEL

**TABLE EDGE PROFILES**
*Source: Vecta; Grand Prairie, Texas*

## Catalyzed Lacquers

Catalyzed lacquers have a limited shelf life and are difficult to repair if the finish is damaged. Types of catalyzed lacquers are vinyl, acrylic, and opaque. Vinyl lacquers have a plastic, rather than a nitrocellulose, base. Acrylic lacquers provide a good-quality clear finish. Opaque lacquers are pigmented, alkyd, nitrocellulose lacquers, and dry almost instantly.

## Conversion Varnishes

Conversion varnishes provide durable, quick-drying surfaces that resist most common chemicals, but they tend to yellow with age. Opaque conversion varnishes are also available.

## Water-Reducible Acrylic Lacquer

Water-reducible acrylic lacquer is not commonly recommended as a finish but may be required to comply with the VOC emission-control standards of authorities having jurisdiction.

*MASTERSPEC®; published by ARCOM; Salt Lake City, Utah, and Alexandria, Virginia*

# CONFERENCE TABLES

## SELECTION CRITERIA

Conference room table size and configuration influence the room size as well as the comfort of the occupants. A typical standard table size, which can be used in most conference rooms, improves efficiency in room layout and in furniture storage and retrieval. Accessibility issues for tables are addressed by manufacturers; review for conformance to codes.

Tables in trapezoidal or other shapes permit flexibility in nonstandard table arrangements, which may be useful for situations such as videoconferencing. Modular tables provide greater flexibility in room layout than one large table. Consider room usage and quality level in determining table types and styles. Large tables should be broken into smaller modules for ease of installation.

Table materials and finishes should reflect the function and quality level of the intended conference or training function. High-end quality rooms may be appropriate for custom tables of wood, stone, and glass. Midlevel conference room and training tables should be durable and comfortable, offer the appropriate features, and be cost-effective and easy to store. Tabletop finishes can include plastic laminate, linoleum, wood veneer, and other materials. Edge materials including wood, rubber, and leather provide additional protection and/or comfort. Beveled and eased table edges provide greater comfort than squared edges, and are less subject to edge damage. Table edges that are beveled on the underside provide more room for chair arms.

Guidelines for conference and training table design:

- The optimum dimension for each occupant is 30 in. (762 mm), which allows for an average-size chair and space between occupants, without straddling table legs.
- A common table length for two persons is 60 in. (1,524 mm).
- Typical training table size is 30 in. (762 mm) wide, 60 in. (1,324 mm) long, and 29 in. (737 mm) high.
- Table height should allow the armrest to fit under the table without impact. Accessible table heights must accommodate wheelchairs.
- Accessible tables may require special bases for clearance of a wheelchair.
- Table width should allow occupants to work comfortably and have reference space. A common minimum width is 24 in. (610 mm). A 30-in. (762-mm) or greater width can be used if space and function permits and if people are seated across from one another.
- Table bases should be stable, preferably with bearer bars.
- Folding or flip-top tables offer flexibility in room layout and usage.
- Tabletop or recessed power options include plug-in or hardwired capabilities with wire management for LAN, power, and telephone.
- For computer usage, consider recessed computer monitors in special tables to improve sight lines.

## SEATING CAPACITY GUIDELINES

### ROUND TOPS

| DIAMETER IN (MM) | APPROXIMATE CAPACITY | |
|---|---|---|
| 42 (1,067) | 4 | |
| 48 (1,219) | 5 | |
| 54 (1,372) | 5 | |
| 60 (1,524) | 6 | |
| 66 (1,981) | 6 | |
| 72 (1,829) | 7 | |
| 84 (2,134) | 8 | |
| 96 (2,438) | 10 | |
| 108 (2,743) | 11 | |
| 120 (3,048) | 12 | |

### SQUARE TOPS

| DEPTH IN (MM) | WIDTH IN. (MM) | APPROXIMATE CAPACITY | |
|---|---|---|---|
| 30 (762) | 30 (762) | 4 | |
| 36 (914) | 36 (914) | 4 | |
| 42 (1,067) | 42 (1,067) | 4 | |
| 48 (1,219) | 48 (1,219) | 4 | |
| 54 (1,372) | 54 (1,372) | 4 | |
| 60 (1,524) | 60 (1,524) | 8 | |

### RECTANGULAR TOPS

| DEPTH IN. (MM) | WIDTH IN. (MM) | APPROXIMATE CAPACITY | |
|---|---|---|---|
| 48 (1,219) | 24 (610) | 1 | |
| 60 (1,524) | 24 (610) | 4 | |
| 72 (1,829) | 24 (610) | 4 | |
| 84 (2,134) | 24 (610) | 3 | |
| 36 (914) | 30 (762) | 4 | |
| 48 (1,219) | 30 (762) | 4 | |
| 60 (1,524) | 30 (762) | 6 | |
| 72 (1,829) | 30 (762) | 6 | |
| 84 (2,134) | 30 (762) | 6 | |
| 96 (2,438) | 30 (762) | 8 | |
| 48 (1,219) | 36 (914) | 4 | |
| 60 (1,524) | 36 (914) | 6 | |
| 72 (1,829) | 36 (914) | 6 | |
| 84 (2,134) | 36 (914) | 6 | |
| 96 (2,438) | 36 (914) | 8 | |
| 72 (1,829) | 42 (1,067) | 6 | |
| 84 (2,134) | 42 (1,067) | 6 | |
| 96 (2,438) | 42 (1,067) | 8 | |
| 108 (2,743) | 42 (1,067) | 8 | |
| 120 (3,048) | 42 (1,067) | 10 | |
| 72 (1,829) | 48 (1,219) | 6 | |
| 84 (2,134) | 48 (1,219) | 8 | |
| 96 (2,438) | 48 (1,219) | 8 | |
| 108 (2,743) | 48 (1,219) | 10 | |
| 120 (3,048) | 48 (1,219) | 12 | |

### RACETRACK TOPS

| DEPTH IN. (MM) | WIDTH IN. (MM) | APPROXIMATE CAPACITY | |
|---|---|---|---|
| 72 (1,829) | 36 (914) | 6 | |
| 96 (2,438) | 48 (1,219) | 6 | |
| 120 (3,048) | 48 (1,219) | 8 | |
| 144 (3,658) | 48 (1,219) | 10 | |
| 120 (3,048) | 60 (1,524) | 10 | |
| 144 (3,658) | 60 (1,524) | 10 | |
| 180 (4,572) | 60 (1,524) | 12 | |
| 216 (5,486) | 60 (1,524) | 14 | |
| 240 (6,096) | 60 (1,524) | 16 | |

### BOAT TOPS

| DEPTH IN. (MM) | WIDTH—CENTER | WIDTH—END | APPROXIMATE CAPACITY |
|---|---|---|---|
| 72 (1,829) | 36 (914) | 30 (762) | 6 |
| 84 (2,134) | 38 (965) | 31 (787) | 6 |
| 96 (2,438) | 40 (1,016) | 32 (813) | 8 |
| 120 (3,048) | 44 (1,118) | 33 (838) | 10 |
| 144 (3,658) | 48 (1,219) | 34 (864) | 10 |
| 168 (4,267) | 52 (1,321) | 35 (889) | 12 |
| 192 (4,877) | 56 (1,422) | 36 (914) | 14 |
| 216 (5,487) | 60 (1,524) | 37 (940) | 16 |
| 240 (6,096) | 60 (1,524) | 38 (965) | 18 |
| 264 (6,706) | 60 (1,524) | 39 (991) | 20 |
| 288 (7,315) | 60 (1,524) | 40 (1,016) | 20 |

*Source: Vecta; Grand Prairie, Texas*

Approximate seating estimates are based on 30 in. (762 mm) per person. Chair widths are assumed to be 25 in. (635 mm), plus 5 in. (127 mm) space between chairs. Adjust these guidelines to accommodate the width of the chair.

# BOOTHS AND TABLES

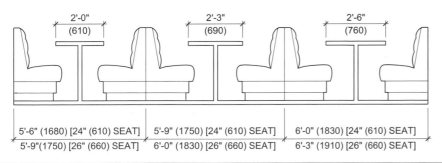

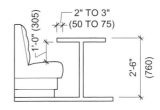

5'-6" (1680) [24" (610) SEAT]    5'-9" (1750) [24" (610) SEAT]    6'-0" (1830) [24" (610) SEAT]
5'-9"(1750) [26" (660) SEAT]    6'-0" (1830) [26" (660) SEAT]    6'-3" (1910) [26" (660) SEAT]

**BOOTH CENTERS**

**CLEARANCES**

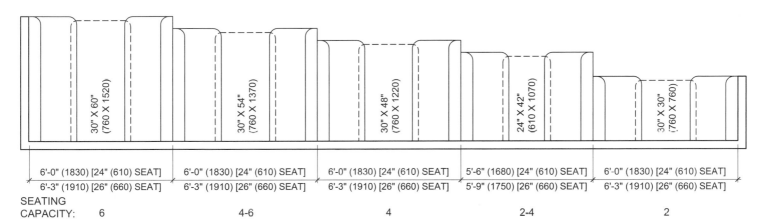

6'-0" (1830) [24" (610) SEAT]    6'-0" (1830) [24" (610) SEAT]    6'-0" (1830) [24" (610) SEAT]    5'-6" (1680) [24" (610) SEAT]    6'-0" (1830) [24" (610) SEAT]
6'-3" (1910) [26" (660) SEAT]    6'-3" (1910) [26" (660) SEAT]    6'-3" (1910) [26" (660) SEAT]    5'-9" (1750) [26" (660) SEAT]    6'-3" (1910) [26" (660) SEAT]

SEATING
CAPACITY:    6            4-6            4            2-4            2

TABLES SHOULD HAVE ROUNDED ENDS.
TABLES ARE OFTEN 2" (50) SHORTER THAN BOOTH.

Tables should have rounded ends. Tables are often 2 in. (50 mm) shorter than booth.

**SEATING CAPACITY**

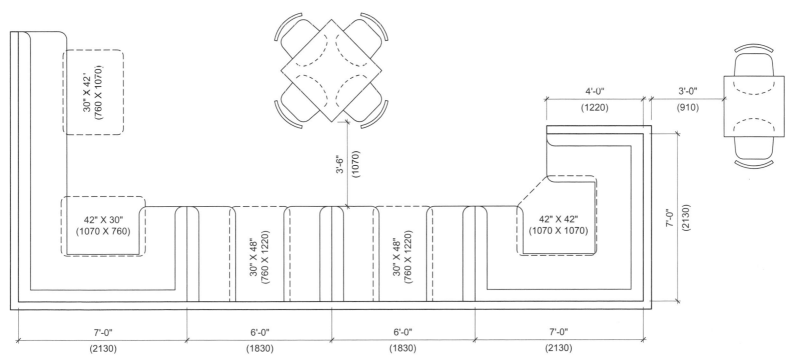

Booth sizes may be determined by local building codes.

**BOOTH LAYOUT**

# BANQUETTE SEATING

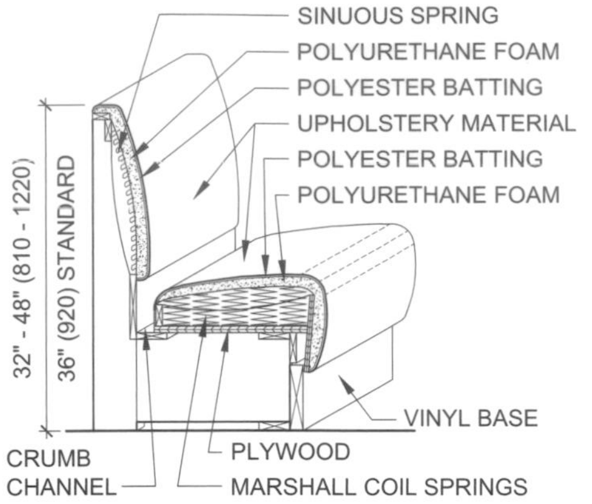
SINUOUS SPRING
POLYURETHANE FOAM
POLYESTER BATTING
UPHOLSTERY MATERIAL
POLYESTER BATTING
POLYURETHANE FOAM
32" - 48" (810 - 1220)
36" (920) STANDARD
VINYL BASE
CRUMB CHANNEL
PLYWOOD
MARSHALL COIL SPRINGS

**COIL SPRING**

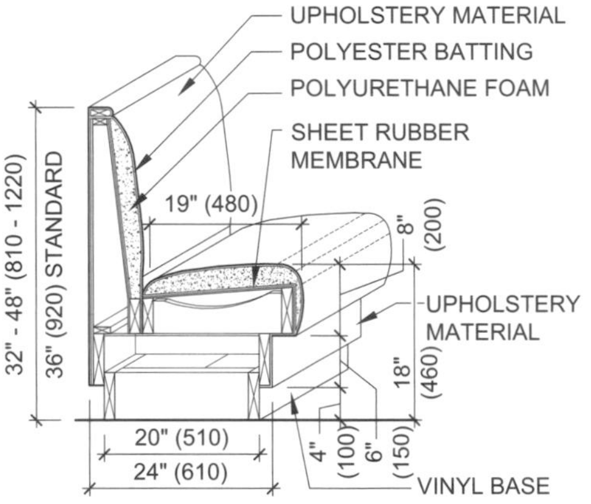
UPHOLSTERY MATERIAL
POLYESTER BATTING
POLYURETHANE FOAM
SHEET RUBBER MEMBRANE
19" (480)
8" (200)
UPHOLSTERY MATERIAL
18" (460)
32" - 48" (810 - 1220)
36" (920) STANDARD
20" (510)
24" (610)
4" (100)
6" (150)
VINYL BASE

**RUBBER MEMBRANE**

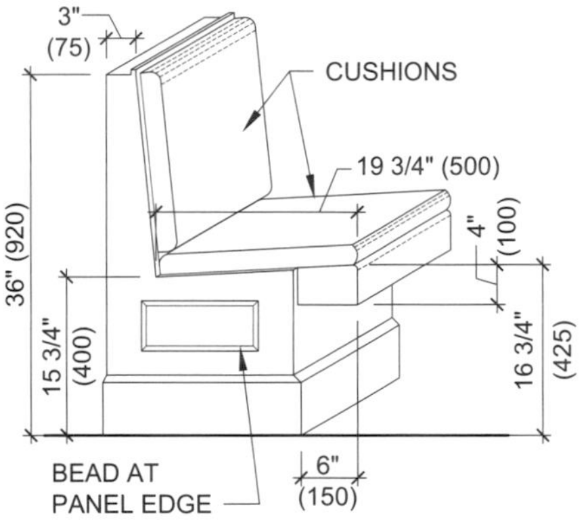
3" (75)
CUSHIONS
19 3/4" (500)
4" (100)
36" (920)
15 3/4" (400)
16 3/4" (425)
BEAD AT PANEL EDGE
6" (150)

**SLOPED SEAT**

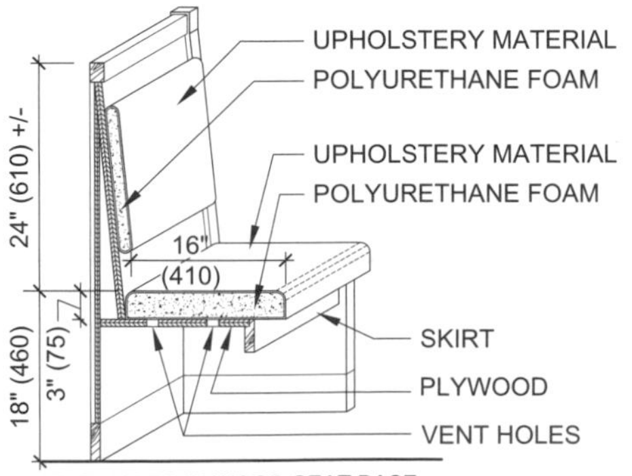
UPHOLSTERY MATERIAL
POLYURETHANE FOAM
UPHOLSTERY MATERIAL
POLYURETHANE FOAM
24" (610) +/-
16" (410)
18" (460)
3" (75)
SKIRT
PLYWOOD
VENT HOLES

VENT HOLES IN WOOD SEAT BASE ARE RECOMMENDED TO VENTILATE CUSHIONS WITH NO SPRING SYSTEM.

**CUSHION ON WOOD**

**BANQUETTE SEATING CONSTRUCTION**

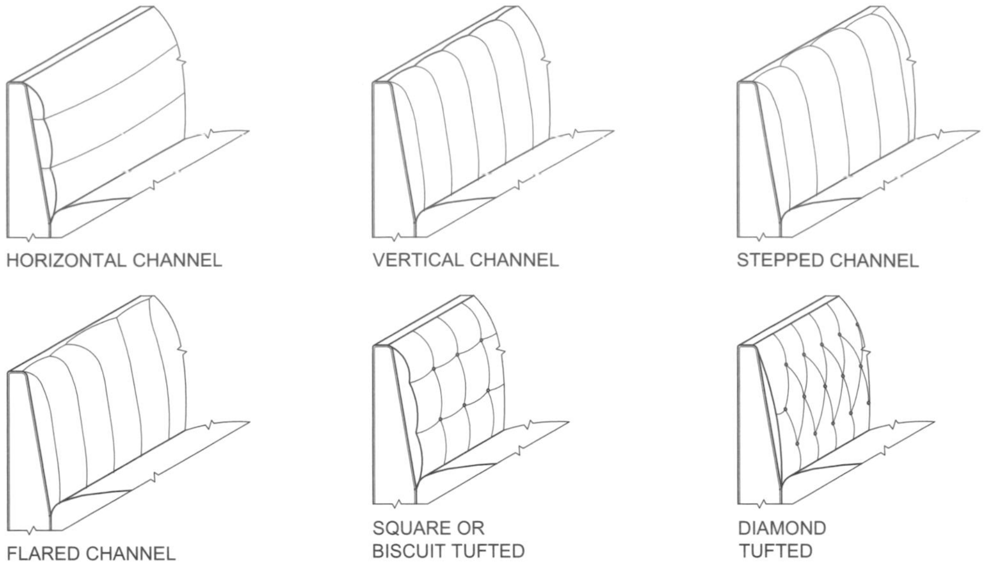
HORIZONTAL CHANNEL
VERTICAL CHANNEL
STEPPED CHANNEL
FLARED CHANNEL
SQUARE OR BISCUIT TUFTED
DIAMOND TUFTED

**SEAT BACKS**

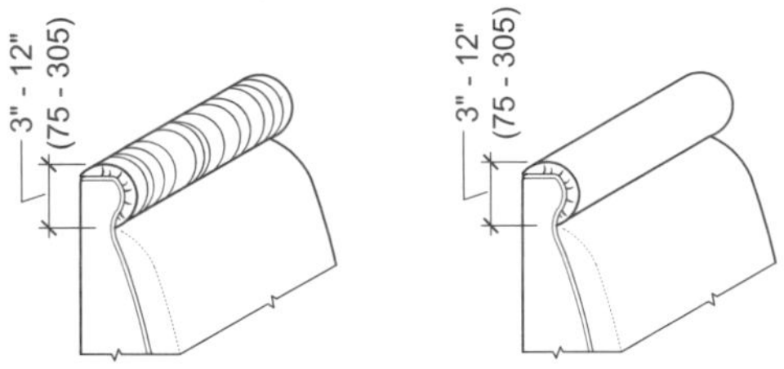
3" - 12" (75 - 305)
3" - 12" (75 - 305)

**SHIRRED** **PLAIN**

**HEAD ROLLS**

**BANQUETTE SEAT CRITERIA**

| | DINING | LOUNGE |
|---|---|---|
| Seat Depth | 19 in. (482 mm) | 18 in. (457 mm) |
| Pitch (Slope to Inside Back) | More pitch | Less pitch |
| Seat Cushion | Firmer | Softer |

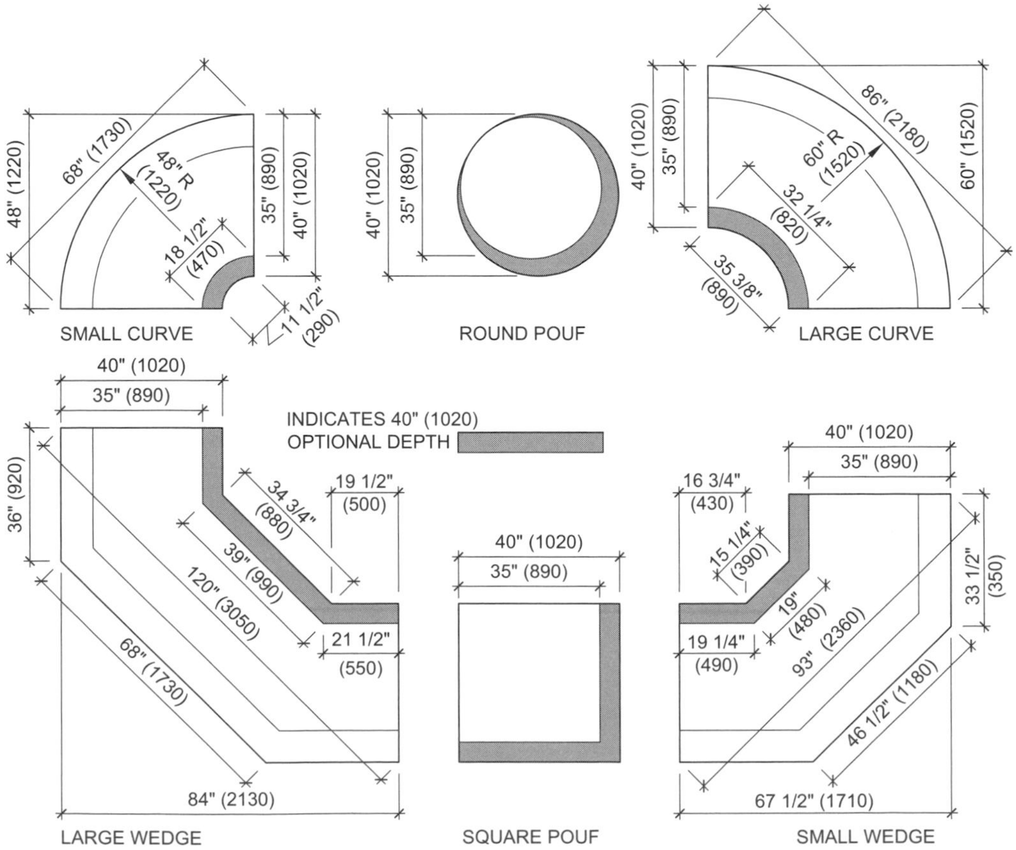
68" (1730)
48" R (1220)
18 1/2" (470)
48" (1220)
35" (890)
40" (1020)
11 1/2" (290)
SMALL CURVE
40" (1020)
35" (890)
ROUND POUF
40" (1020)
35" (890)
86" (2180)
60" R (1520)
32 1/4" (820)
35 3/8" (890)
60" (1520)
LARGE CURVE
40" (1020)
35" (890)
INDICATES 40" (1020) OPTIONAL DEPTH
36" (920)
34 3/4" (880)
19 1/2" (500)
39" (990)
120" (3050)
21 1/2" (550)
68" (1730)
84" (2130)
LARGE WEDGE
40" (1020)
35" (890)
SQUARE POUF
40" (1020)
35" (890)
16 3/4" (430)
15 1/4" (390)
19" (480)
33 1/2" (350)
19 1/4" (490)
93" (2360)
46 1/2" (1180)
67 1/2" (1710)
SMALL WEDGE

**OVERALL MINIMUM DIMENSIONS FOR SPECIAL SEATING SHAPES**



*Kisabeth Furniture; Fort Worth, Texas*

# SYSTEMS FURNITURE

## TYPES

There are two basic types of systems furniture: *panel-supported* and *freestanding* systems. Many manufacturers offer systems that combine freestanding components with traditional panel-supported units. These systems provide flexibility and function for workplace tasks. High-tech designs, as well as more conservative systems, are available.

Systems furniture is available that addresses the total workplace environment, using walls, panels, post-and-beam construction, work surfaces, filing, storage, raised-floor platforms for wiring and cabling, and other flexible elements. Many systems furniture products are compatible with others from the same manufacturer, allowing greater flexibility and applications.

## Panel-Supported Systems

Panel-supported systems, the most popular type of systems furniture, support the work surfaces, accessories, and other furniture components from panels that form the boundaries of the workstation. Wall-mounted slotted standards are also available so that these systems can be hung on a traditional gypsum wallboard wall. BIFMA has authored a standard for panel-based systems furniture; ANSI X5.6, *Standard for Office Furnishings Panel Systems*, tests the safety of panels and panel-mounted components.

## Freestanding Systems

Freestanding systems are independent of surrounding panels, and function like floor-supported desks. Furniture components can be attached to the work surface or may be freestanding mobile units. Freestanding systems can be surrounded by panels or installed in a space with constructed walls. New systems furniture types are being developed that integrate technology to the design of the furniture.

## PANELS

Panels are used to create workstations, divide work areas, and allow the attachment of work surfaces, storage units, and accessories. Panels must be supported, either by configuration, to create a stable unit, or with freestanding panel support feet. Panel sizes vary by manufacturer and are often described in nominal dimensions. Generic panel widths from major manufacturers are typically based on a 6 in. (152 mm) module: 12-, 18-, 24-, 30-, 36-, 42-, 48-, and 60-in.- (305-, 457-, 610-, 762-, 914-, 1,067-, 1,219-, and 1,524-mm-) wide panel. Common panel heights are 30, 36, 39, 42, 45, 47, 50, 53, 64, 72, 78, and 85 in. (762, 914, 991, 1,067, 1,143, 1,194, 1,270, 1,346, 1,626, 1,829, 1,981, and 2,159 mm). Some panel systems are also based on a 5 in. (127 mm) module: 20- to 60-in.- (508- to 1,524-mm-) wide panel.

Because panel thickness varies with each specific line of systems furniture, from 2 to 6 in. (51 to 153 mm), it should be factored into the overall dimensional footprint when space planning with systems furniture.

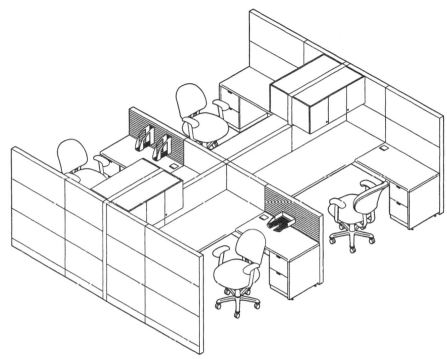

Panels are available in acoustical and nonacoustical versions. Other options include tackable surfaces, perforated metal, markerboard panels, and vision panels.

**TRADITIONAL PANEL-SUPPORTED SYSTEM**
*Source: Steelcase Inc., Grand Rapids, Michigan*

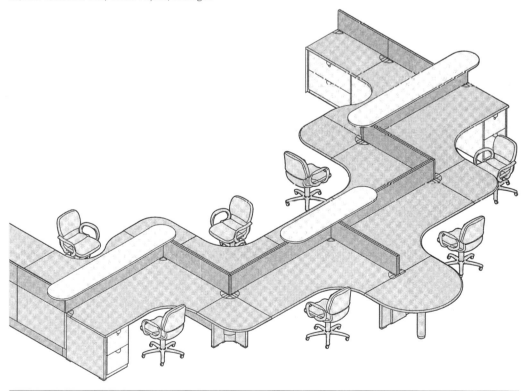

**FREESTANDING SYSTEM**
*Source: Steelcase Inc., Grand Rapids, Michigan*

## PLANNING CONSIDERATIONS

Panel widths and heights vary greatly among manufacturers and even among individual lines of furniture provided by the same manufacturer. Allowing for panel progression, if applicable, and careful consideration of a furniture system's capacity for reconfiguration allows the designer to make intelligent decisions in the initial phases of a project.

### Low Panels

Lower panel heights, in the 30 to 36 in. (762 to 915 mm) range can be used for desk height panel surrounds, where higher panels would create an obstruction and where communication and supervision may be required. Panels in the 40-in.- (1,016-mm-) high range can be used for transaction height configurations, often supplemented with a countercap transaction work surface. This is useful for reception desks and where an obscured sight line to the interior of the workstation is desired. Panel heights in the 54 to 63 in. (1,371 to 1,600 mm) range provide seated privacy for occupants of the work area, whereas panel heights in the 68 to 80 in. (1,727 to 2,032 mm) range provide standing privacy for the occupants.

Some panels are available with acoustical properties and some offer acoustical and tackable combination panels. Some panels are of perforated metal, to allow ventilation at the backs of equipment or at the base of a station for airflow. Metal and hard-surface panels are also available for ease of maintenance and cleanability and to address static control issues. Many manufacturers also offer open, or *vision,* panels to allow interaction or line of sight between workstations.

Other specialty panels or panel attachments can include markerboards and tool rails, on which to hang essential work tools such as the telephone, paper sorters, calendars, and other supplies, to free up work surface space.

## PANEL FABRICS AND FINISHES

Each manufacturer offers a multitude of panel fabrics and frame and component finishes. Confirm the availability of fabric and finishes for each furniture system, especially when combining two or more systems, to allow for finish coordination and compatibility.

Panel heights and widths vary among manufacturers. Shown are typical heights and widths.

**TYPICAL PANEL HEIGHTS AND WIDTHS**

## PANEL CONSTRUCTION

Most panels are constructed with a steel frame and various types of infill materials, a base, and top cap. Power and data raceways are located at various locations within the panel, most commonly at the base, but also at the belt line, commonly located at desk height. Some manufacturers offer additional horizontal raceways. Panels are typically furnished with slotted standards on the vertical edges, which allow attachment of components at 1 in. (25 mm) increments.

## MODULAR PANELS

There are four basic types of panels: *monolithic, tiled, beltway,* and *stackable.*

### Monolithic Panels

Monolithic panels provide one finish surface and one raceway location. This panel type is the most affordable and the least flexible.

### Tiled Panels

Tile panels incorporate stacked insert tiles within metal frames. This panel type provides flexibility in tile insert types, finishes, and heights. Different tile types can be combined; for example, a solid panel for modesty at the base and a vision panel above the work surface. Insert tile heights are typically 14 to 16 in. (356 to 406 mm). Other sizes are available to meet installation requirements.

Tiled panels offer the same versatility of material and finish transitions as the stackable panel but without the versatility of height changes, since the frame is integral to the whole panel height. The panel must be removed and replaced with a new height panel in order to achieve height differential. If height flexibility is not an issue for the client, then the tiled panel is a cost-effective way to achieve the look of the stacking panel.

### Beltway Panels

Beltway panels offer the convenience of having power, data, and phone receptacles at workstation height. This allows for a more ergonomic approach to equipment changes at the desktop and controls some of the clutter of wires at the base of panel.

### Stackable Panels

Some manufacturers offer stackable panels that offer greater versatility in varying the height of panels within a run of workstations, to create a functional and aesthetically pleasing office landscape. The materials and finishes can be changed at each height for function or design purposes, and the final product height can be added to or subtracted from without disruption to each panel or workstation.

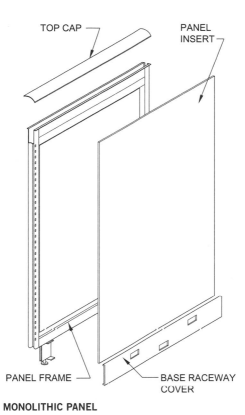

**MONOLITHIC PANEL**

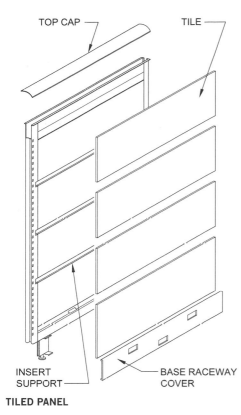

**TILED PANEL**

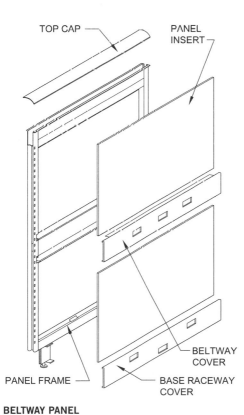

**BELTWAY PANEL**

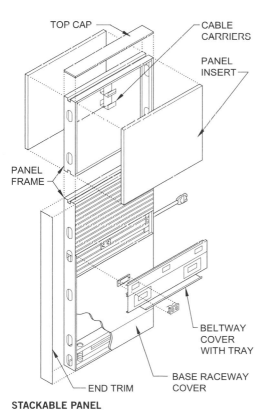

**STACKABLE PANEL**

Panel finishes, acoustical ratings, and general performance vary by manufacturer.

**PANEL CONSTRUCTION**
*Source: Knoll, Inc.; East Greenville, Pennsylvania*

## PANEL CONNECTIONS AND HARDWARE

Each manufacturer provides connecting hardware for panel attachment. Straight-line connectors, or hinges, align and secure straight panels in a row or where a straight panel is attached to a curved panel. Where panels are connected at right angles, hinge connectors are used. Some manufacturers provide special hinge connectors, capable of varying angle connections. T-connectors allow the attachment of the panels to the face of another panel or to a wall. Special connectors allow the attachment of panels of varying height. Off-module connectors are available from selected manufacturers for flexible placement of components independent of the systems furniture module. Consult manufacturers for descriptions of panel connection hardware.

## PANEL LOAD CONSIDERATIONS

Special consideration should be given to panel run lengths and panel load restrictions. Each manufacturer has recommended allowances for maximum panel run lengths and panel load tolerances within each system offered. Follow the manufacturer's recommendations to ensure safety within configurations.

## DOORS

Most manufacturers offer two types of doors that function in workstations with higher panel heights for privacy: *sliding* and *panel* (sometimes referred to as a *hinge*).

### Sliding Doors

Sliding doors are either outside-mounted or inside-mounted, depending on the manufacturer. Most systems provide a sliding door at a 54 to 60 in. (1,372 to 1,524 mm) panel height range, which allows the flexibility of an office atmosphere without sacrificing light or airflow to the general area.

### Panel, or Hinge, Doors

Panel doors are usually offered in higher panel heights, in the 72 to 90 in. (1,829 to 2,286 mm) panel height range. They offer the closest approximation to a gypsum board wall office without the cost of such construction. Higher panels should be treated like a gypsum-board-constructed wall in planning considerations since they can block some of the light and airflow to the general area.

## COMPONENTS

Most components are panel-hung or work-surface-supported. Balanced loads, such as binder bin storage hung on both sides of a panel, are more stable than a one-sided load.

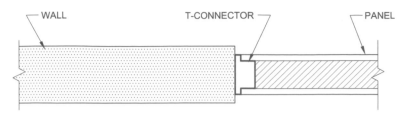

**T-WALL CONNECTOR OR WALL ATTACHMENT BRACKET**

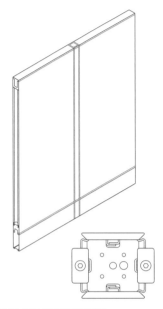

**STRAIGHT-LINE CONNECTION**

**L-CONNECTOR, HIGH/LOW PANEL CONDITION**

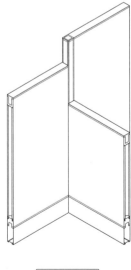

**T-CONNECTOR, HIGH/LOW PANEL CONDITION**

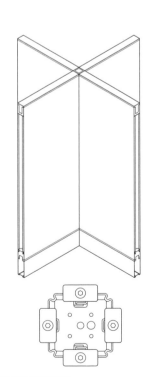

**FOUR-WAY CONNECTOR**

**PANEL CONNECTIONS**
*Source: Herman Miller; Zeeland, Michigan*

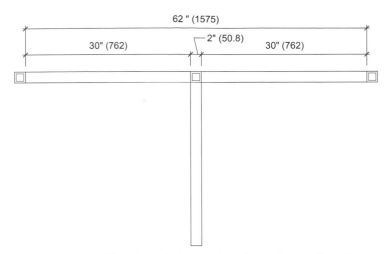

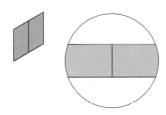

Progressive systems shift, or "creep," when panels are inserted perpendicular to a row of panels.

Nonprogressive systems are measured from centerline to centerline of the connector posts. Changes can be made without moving existing panels.

**PROGRESSIVE PANEL SYSTEM**

**NONPROGRESSIVE PANEL SYSTEM**

## PROGRESSIVE AND NONPROGRESSIVE PANEL SYSTEMS

The connection methods for panel-supported systems have ramifications in the design and future modification of workstations. Panel-supported systems furniture is considered either *progressive* or *nonprogressive* with regard to the panel-to-panel attachment method.

### Progressive Panel Systems

Progressive systems shift, or "creep," when additional panels are added. Panel thicknesses must be accounted for at each connection. Typical panel thickness is a nominal 2 in. (51 mm), although thicker panels are available from various manufacturers. Perpendicular panel connections require the insertion of a connector, resulting in a shift of all subsequent adjacent panels.

### Nonprogressive Panel Systems

Changes to the configuration of nonprogressive systems can be made without moving existing panels. Because every panel connection requires a connector post, perpendicular panels can be added or removed without disturbing adjacent workstations. Panel widths in nonprogressive systems are measured from centerline to centerline of the connector posts.

Nonprogressive panel systems are typically powered only at the central spine of a panel run to allow ease of reconfiguration of connecting panels without interruption and additional cost to power and data lines. This should be taken into account when configuring work surface placement, to allow maximum power and data feed from the spine and ensure proper placement of equipment to this proximity.

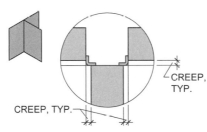

**STRAIGHT CONNECTIONS**
No creep occurs when panels of the same or varying heights are joined with hinges.

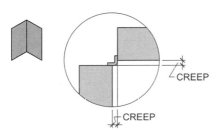

**L-CONNECTIONS**
A ³⁄₃₂ in. (2 mm) creep occurs at the intersection when panels are joined in an L-configuration.

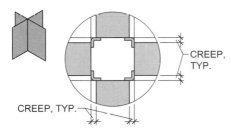

**T-CONNECTIONS**
A ³⁄₁₆ in. (4 mm) creep occurs when panels are joined in a T-configuration.

**X-CONNECTIONS**
A ³⁄₁₆ in. (4 mm) creep occurs in both directions of an X-configuration.

**PANEL CREEP CONSIDERATIONS**
*Source: Steelcase, Inc.; Grand Rapids, Michigan*

## WORK SURFACES

Horizontal work surfaces are available in various sizes and shapes. They can be attached to panels in panel-hung systems or can be supported by freestanding components, such as file cabinets. Depths are typically 24, 30, or 36 in. (610, 762, or 914 mm); lengths are 24, 30, 36, 45, 60, and 72 in. (610, 762, 914, 1,143, 1,524, and 1,829 mm). Straight, corner, curved, and peninsula-shaped work surfaces are available. Work surface edge profiles vary with each manufacturer but are typically offered in eased, bull-nose, radius, and square edges.

### Construction

Construction of work surfaces vary, but many are constructed in a box and cross-member fashion, with a honeycomb core to reduce weight. Finish materials vary, but are commonly plastic laminate or wood veneer. Work surfaces can be provided with grommets for wiring or inserts for attachment of components, such as brackets and pedestals. Custom sizes are available.

### Workstation Typicals

When designing workstation *typicals,* or *standards,* for each job function, consider the client's space allocation with regard to footprint dimension allowed for each job title. The requirements of a particular job function—for example, those of a telephone or traveling salesperson—may be minimal with regard to work surface but more extensive with regard to storage capacity for retrieval of, for example, specification and product brochures and client files. In contrast, when planning for a marketing or executive workspace, consider a more expansive work surface, along with additional storage, since these job functions typically require an abundance of both.

Other positions, such as that of administrative assistant, will usually require both ample work surface and storage to accommodate additional equipment. They might also require a transaction top so that workers can be approached without having their workspace invaded by their associates.

### Mock-up Workstations

When time and budget allow, a mock-up workstation should be erected by each competing manufacturer to show the client the inherent differences in product lines and to give a realistic sense of spatial relationships. A mock-up also allows for any last-minute revisions to further customize the workstation based on end-user feedback.

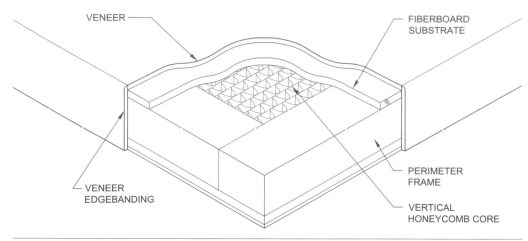

**WORK SURFACE CONSTRUCTION—WOOD**
*Source: Knoll, Inc.; East Greenville, Pennsylvania*

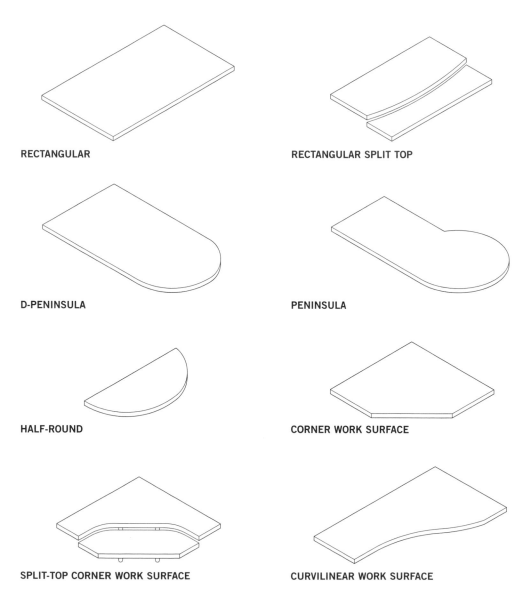

The sizes, shapes, and edge details of work surfaces vary greatly with each line of furniture and each manufacturer.

**WORK SURFACE TYPES**
*Source: Knoll, Inc.; East Greenville, Pennsylvania*

## OVERHEAD STORAGE

Panel-supported open shelves and closed binder bins with flipper doors are typically 12 in. (305 mm) deep, and are available in widths corresponding to most panel widths. Various other storage units and cabinets, both panel-hung and freestanding, are also available.

When selecting closed overhead storage or binder bins, consider ease of door operation. Overhead storage units should have lightweight doors that are easily opened from a seated position, since this is how most operators use their furniture. Some manufacturers offer special bins that enable the user to lightly touch the door to activate an operating mechanism.

## KEYING AND LOCKING

Keying and locking functions should also be specified with storage components since some job functions may require maintenance of confidential materials. Refer to specific manufacturer's product guides when making these selections.

## FILE CABINETS

Systems furniture file pedestals may be suspended from the work surface or be freestanding fixed or mobile units. They are available in various configurations of file and box drawer combinations, with optional locks. Many systems furniture companies offer separate file cabinet lines that are compatible with the systems furniture.

Some fixed-pedestal file units are mounted to the underside of work surfaces and are part of the support system for that work surface. Usually, these cabinets do not have a file top and are not easy to relocate. Other fixed-pedestal units are freestanding and not attached to the underside of work surfaces. They allow for easy reconfiguration since they are not specifically tied to any one workstation. Most furniture lines offer a few options for drawer pulls to allow for customer preferences.

Many manufacturers offer mobile pedestals with integral cushion tops to act as a guest seat when the workstation footprint is tight and will not allow for the more traditional side chair.

Other storage components include wardrobe and closed freestanding shelving units that add much needed storage space, as well as form, to the interior of a workstation without sacrificing the footprint of the space.

Less traditional components offer an even greater level of storage and flexibility, and should be considered when the application presents itself, such as for group interaction spaces that allow for sharing of components and mobility of these units within a given space. Some of these components include *slip surfaces*, which are small tables on casters that fit easily under fixed work surfaces and can be pulled out when

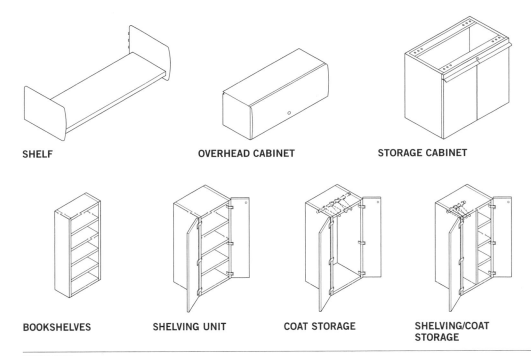

**SHELF**  **OVERHEAD CABINET**  **STORAGE CABINET**

**BOOKSHELVES**  **SHELVING UNIT**  **COAT STORAGE**  **SHELVING/COAT STORAGE**

**STORAGE**
*Source: Knoll, Inc.; East Greenville, Pennsylvania*

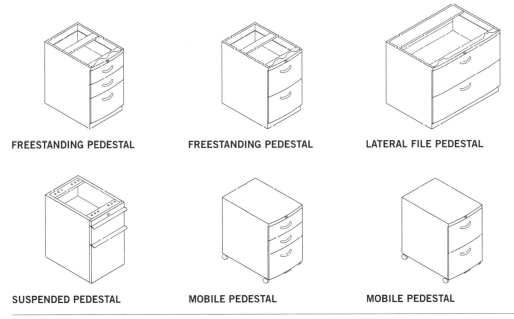

**FREESTANDING PEDESTAL**  **FREESTANDING PEDESTAL**  **LATERAL FILE PEDESTAL**

**SUSPENDED PEDESTAL**  **MOBILE PEDESTAL**  **MOBILE PEDESTAL**

**FILE CABINETS**
*Source: Knoll, Inc.; East Greenville, Pennsylvania*

needed; special storage taborettes; and flat files that function as both additional storage and work surface space. Tackboards, markerboards, CPU holders, wire managers, pencil drawers, and paper flow and divider units are also available. Check availability of these specialty components with each manufacturer.

## KEYBOARD AND MOUSE TRAYS

Keyboard and mouse trays should also be considered for specific end users, to resolve ergonomic issues with regard to repetitive stress injuries. Many types of trays are offered by each manufacturer, from simple adjustable trays to fully articulating tray types.

## TASK LIGHTING

Most systems furniture manufacturers offer task-lighting units, which are attached to overhead storage units. Task lights are used in tandem with general office area lighting.

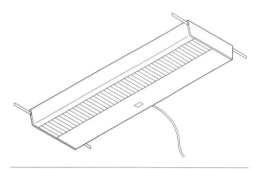

**TASK LIGHT**
*Source: Knoll, Inc; East Greenville, Pennsylvania*

## POWER AND COMMUNICATIONS

### Wire and Cable

Two types of conductors that carry signals are accommodated by systems furniture raceways: *electrical wiring* and *communications cabling*. Electrical wiring and communications cabling are typically separated within the raceway. Wire and cable are distributed from the base building source through the systems furniture to the workstation equipment. This can be accomplished through connections at walls, the floor, or from the ceiling.

### Electrical Wiring

Systems furniture manufacturers provide power in assemblies for the hookup of the panel's electrical wiring conduit, commonly called a "pigtail," to the building's electrical supply. Connections between panels are snapped together, making them easy to install and reconfigure. Electrical units are UL-listed. Certain jurisdictions do not accept prewired systems, so an electrician must install the wiring and make the connections from the main building electrical service source.

Systems furniture panels have a capacity of two to four electrical circuits, which vary according to manufacturer and intended use. Some systems furniture manufacturers offer up to six circuits. Panels typically have base raceway capacity for electrical and communications services. Some manufacturers provide *belt-line* power raceways. Others provide even greater flexibility in electrical wiring, dedicated circuits for equipment, and communications cabling placement.

### Electrical Disturbances

Some electrical equipment is vulnerable to disturbances or interferences from other electrical sources. Dedicated or designated circuits can be used to help ensure that equipment will not malfunction or be damaged.

### Dedicated Circuits

Dedicated circuits are used to keep power "clean," or free from electrical interferences, which can cause problems with sensitive equipment. Although "dedicated" is not defined by the National Electrical Code (NEC), the expression is widely used to describe a circuit that does not share a neutral wire, as many three-phase wiring systems do. The use of common *neutrals* in commercial and industrial situations is standard practice. The neutral return wire carries unbalanced current back to the power source, which can generate interference. These electromagnet fields generate an electric current that flows through wiring, creating electrical "noise."

### Designated Circuits

Designated circuits are circuits reserved for use by specific equipment. These circuits are often used for important equipment that requires a heavy electrical load or that is best isolated from other equipment in case of a power outage.

### Communications Cabling

Clear communication is an important part of success in the business arena. While phone lines are typically stranded wire, computer systems use a variety of other cable types, including twisted-pair, four-pair, coaxial, fiber-optic, and shielded cable.

### Twisted-Pair Cable

Twisted-pair is the traditional, economical type of cable for voice and lower-speed data communication. Each pair of insulated copper wires connects a single signal from one point to another. Twisted-pair cables are not suitable for high-speed and video transmissions.

### Four-Pair Cable

Four-pair cable has four sets of copper wire, twisted together and covered with an insulating material. It is inexpensive and is commonly used for voice and data cabling.

### Coaxial Cable

Coaxial cable consists of a single copper wire surrounded by an insulator encased in a metal shell, which acts as a ground return. The insulated return is surrounded by a braided wire or foil shield. This shielding makes coaxial cable relatively immune to interference. Coaxial cable transmits a large amount of data at very high speeds with relatively little signal loss. Broadband coaxial cable systems are used by the cable television industry.

### Fiber-Optic Cable

Fiber-optic cable consists of a thin glass wire filament, which is used for signal transmission. It is used more commonly in areas with high-tech requirements.

### Shielded Cable

Shielded cable is covered with metal foil to keep out electromagnetic interference. Twisted-pair cables are often shielded for improved performance.

## LOCAL AREA NETWORK (LAN)

A local area network is a telecommunications network that eliminates the possibility of signal interruption, offering reliable, linked transmission.

Technology continues to evolve, and new developments in communications include wireless networks for radio and infrared transmissions.

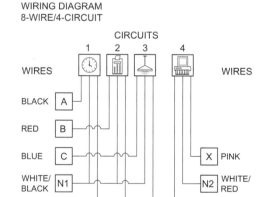

This circuit is used in areas where power usage is significant and a single isolated circuit is required for sensitive equipment.

**WIRING DIAGRAM—EIGHT-WIRE/ FOUR-CIRCUIT**
*Source: Knoll, Inc.; East Greenville, Pennsylvania*

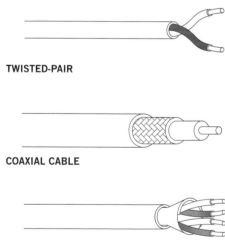

TWISTED-PAIR

COAXIAL CABLE

SHIELDED CABLE

**DATA AND COMMUNICATION CABLE TYPES**

# WIRE AND CABLE CONNECTIONS TO SYSTEMS FURNITURE

Wire and cable connections from the base building source to the equipment at the workstation can be made in a variety of ways, depending on the structure of the base building. Systems furniture panels are typically powered from a base feed, which is connected to the building's electrical and communications systems from a floor monument ("tombstone") or other floor power sources. Modular raised floors provide flexibility in power source locations. Wall connections are used when panels abut building partitions. Power poles provide service from the ceiling.

## Wall Receptacles

Wall receptacles connect wire and cable services from the building to the panel raceway. This connection type severely restricts the system's flexibility. Workstation location relies on proximity to power and data supplies. Relocating wall-mounted junction boxes is labor-intensive and generates a comparatively large amount of construction debris.

## Cellular Floor System

Cellular floor systems separate wire and cable to protect against electromagnetic interference. Outlets are typically concealed, and the floor finish is level, without the interruption of floor monuments.

## Access Floor System

Access flooring is a structural system of removable floor panels above the structural floor. These floor systems, commonly used for computer rooms, can handle the largest capacities. This is the most flexible distribution system, because virtually every inch of wire and cable can be accessed by the removal of a floor panel. However, it requires adequate ceiling heights to allow for a raised floor.

## Poke-Through System

Poke-through systems access wire and cable sources in the ceiling cavity below the floor. Modifying a poke-through system requires the disruption of activities on both floors. Fire-rated assemblies and floor monuments must be used to maintain the fire-resistance rating of the floor.

## Flat Wire

Flat wire is flexible conductor cable that is so thin it can be placed directly under the finish flooring. It can be folded or easily joined and there is virtually no disruption to the workplace. Carpet tile is the only finish flooring permitted by the National Electric Code (NEC) for use over flat wire.

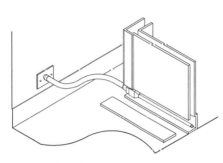

**WALL RECEPTACLE**
Underfloor steel ducts are separate, continuous steel channels cast in the concrete floor slab.

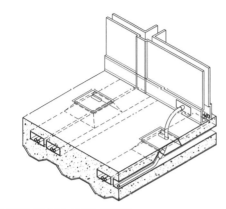

**UNDERFLOOR STEEL DUCTS**

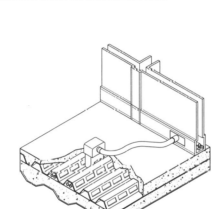

**CELLULAR FLOOR**
Cellular floor systems incorporate raceways in the structural metal deck.

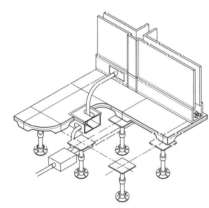

**ACCESS FLOOR**
Access floors offer direct access for easy reconfiguration of power and communication system connections.

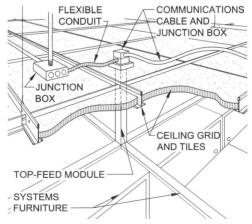

FLEXIBLE CONDUIT
COMMUNICATIONS CABLE AND JUNCTION BOX
JUNCTION BOX
CEILING GRID AND TILES
TOP-FEED MODULE
SYSTEMS FURNITURE

**TOP FEED WITH POWER POLE**
*Source: Haworth, Inc.; Holland, Michigan Illustration from* Designing Commercial Interiors, *by Christine Piotrowski and Elizabeth Rogers; John Wiley & Sons, Inc., 1999, p. 68.*

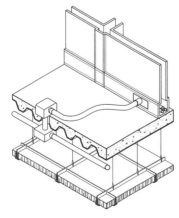

**POKE-THROUGH SYSTEM**
Poke-through systems access wire and cable in the ceiling below the floor.

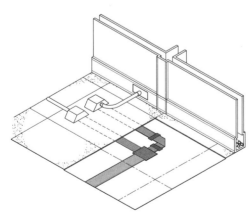

**FLAT WIRE**
Flat-wire power distribution is installed directly under carpet tile.

**WIRE AND CABLE CONNECTIONS TO SYSTEMS FURNITURE**

## DESIGN CONSIDERATIONS FOR SYSTEMS FURNITURE

When designing a space using systems furniture, consider the following:

- *Building code restrictions.* Local building codes should be reviewed to determine whether the use of systems furniture will impact the code requirements for the space. The requirements for exits will vary according to the type of use, occupancy, and other factors. Panels exceeding a certain height may be considered walls, and therefore will be subject to the minimum width requirements for aisles or corridors formed from these panels. Large areas with open office spaces composed of systems furniture may need to have full-height, rated partitions to meet local codes.

- *Materials* used in systems furniture should meet or exceed minimum code requirements. Vertical surface finishes on panels should have a flame spread index of 25 or less.

- *Lighting* is critical to the success of a systems furniture installation, particularly in an open office area. Systems furniture manufacturers offer task lighting for the immediate work area. General area lighting quality is important to the well-being and comfort of the office worker. The use of computers and the issue of glare has contributed to the development of alternative lighting concepts. Ambient light, which bounces off the ceiling, provides a softer, glare-free overall light in comparison to typical recessed fluorescent or incandescent light fixtures. If using recessed fluorescent fixtures, consider the type of lamp and lens to minimize glare.

- *Acoustics* in open systems furniture installations present unique challenges. Sound travels in all directions and may be difficult to contain. The use of acoustical panels improves sound absorption, but the noise from telephones, conversation, equipment, and other sources may be audible. An acoustical ceiling and carpet on the floor will absorb some of the sound. An acoustical engineer can offer suggestions on how to contain and control noise. Sound-masking systems, utilizing white noise, may be a consideration.

*Karen K. Lindblad; Chicago, Illinois*
*Susan Hardiman; Dorchester, Massachusetts*

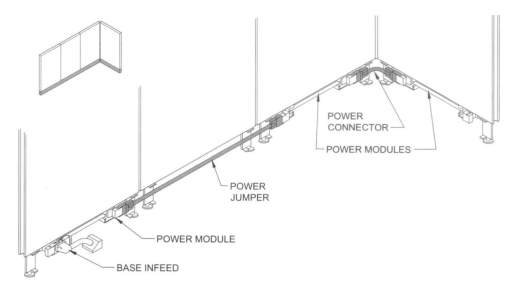

**BASE RACEWAY ELECTRICAL**

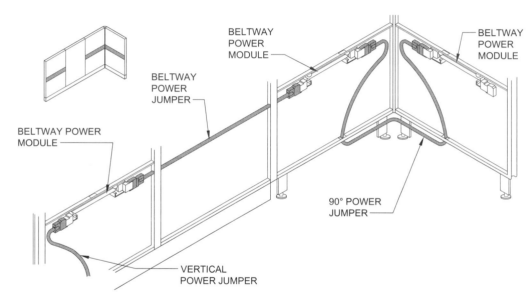

**BELTWAY ELECTRICAL**

**DUPLEX RECEPTACLE**        **SURGE SUPPRESSOR**

**ELECTRICAL RACEWAY COMPONENTS**
*Source: Knoll, Inc.; East Greenville, Pennsylvania*

# ELEVATORS

## SELECTION CRITERIA

An elevator system is a major building component, and as such must be carefully considered throughout the design process. Decisions about the number, size, speed, and type of elevators for an installation are based on a number of factors, including the handling capacity and quality of service desired. Proper selection also depends on the type of tenancy, number of occupants, and building design (number of floors, floor heights, building circulation, and other factors). In addition, passenger elevators on accessible routes should comply with the requirements of the *Americans with Disabilities Act Accessibility Guidelines* (ADAAG).

Consult representatives of the elevator industry, or elevator engineers, during the decision-making process to ensure selection of the most suitable elevator system for an application. And because elevator installation is highly regulated, it is also advisable to consult local code officials.

Elevators should be located where they can provide efficient and accessible service. As well, the operational systems (hoistway pit and machine room) and passenger spaces (lobby and elevator car) must be accommodated.

## ELEVATOR SYSTEMS

An elevator system includes a *hoistway, machine room, elevator car,* and *waiting lobbies.*

### Hoistway

The hoistway is a vertical shaft for the travel of one or more elevators. It includes a pit and usually terminates at the underside of the machine room in a traction system, and at the underside of the roof over the hoistway in a hydraulic system. Access to the elevator car and hoistway is normally through hoistway doors at each floor serviced by the elevator system. Hoistway design is determined by the characteristics of the elevator system selected and by applicable code requirements for fire separation, ventilation, soundproofing, and nonstructural elements.

### Machine Room for Traction Elevator

The machine room for a traction elevator is usually located directly above the hoistway, but it may also be situated below, to the side, or to the rear of it. The machine room contains elevator hoisting machinery and electronic control equipment. Adequate ventilation, soundproofing, and structural support for the elevator must be supplied. Also, the machine room must have a self-closing, self-locking access door. Local codes may forbid placement of electrical or mechanical equipment not associated with the elevator in the machine room.

## ELEVATOR TYPES BY USE

| NEED/USE | PRIVATE RESIDENTIAL | HYDRAULIC | GEARED TRACTION | GEARLESS TRACTION |
|---|---|---|---|---|
| Private houses | X | | | |
| Low-rise, low-speed | | X | | |
| Medium-rise, moderate-speed | | | X | |
| High-rise, high-speed | | | | X |
| Low initial cost | | X | | |
| No penthouse, lightweight construction | | X | | |
| Freight, low-rise | | X | X | |
| Freight, high-rise | | | X | |

### Machine Room for Hydraulic Elevator

Normally located near the base of the hoistway, a machine room for hydraulic elevators contains a hydraulic pump unit and electronic controls. Provisions should be made for adequate ventilation and soundproofing, and the room must have a self-closing, self-locking access door. Local codes may forbid placement of electrical or mechanical equipment not associated with the elevator in the machine room.

### Elevator Car

Guided by vertical rails on each side, the elevator car conveys passengers or freight between floors. It is constructed within a supporting platform and frame. Design of the car focuses on ceiling, wall, floor, and door finishes, and accompanying lighting, ventilation, and elevator signal equipment.

The car and frame of a *hydraulic elevator system* are supported by a piston or cylinder. The car and frame of a *traction elevator system* are supported by the hoist machine. The elevator and its counterweight are connected with steel ropes.

### Waiting Lobbies

Elevator waiting areas are designed to allow free circulation of passengers, rapid access to elevator cars, and clearly visible elevator signals. All elevator lobbies must be enclosed, with the exception of those at the entry level of main buildings.

## ELEVATOR TYPES

*Hydraulic elevators* use an oil hydraulic driving machine to raise and lower the elevator car and its load. Lower speeds and the piston length restrict the

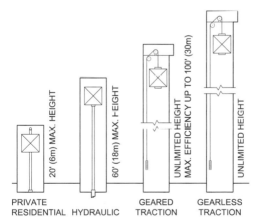

PRIVATE RESIDENTIAL — 20' (6m) MAX. HEIGHT
HYDRAULIC — 60' (18m) MAX. HEIGHT
GEARED TRACTION — UNLIMITED HEIGHT MAX. EFFICIENCY UP TO 100' (30m)
GEARLESS TRACTION — UNLIMITED HEIGHT

These dimensions are general guidelines for selecting an elevator type, using height as a criterion.

**ELEVATOR TYPES**

use of this system to heights of approximately 55 ft (16 m). Although it generally requires the least initial installation expense, this elevator type requires more power to operate.

*Traction elevators* are power elevators in which the energy is applied by means of an electric driving machine. Medium to high speeds and virtually limitless rise allow this elevator type to serve high-rise, medium-rise, and low-rise buildings.

*Geared traction elevator systems* are designed to operate within the range of 100 to 450 ft (30 to 137 m) per minute, restricting their use to medium-rise buildings.

*Gearless traction elevator systems* are available in preengineered units with speeds of 500 to 1,200 ft (150 to 365 m) per minute. They offer the advantages of a long life and a smooth ride.

*Service elevators* in industrial, residential, and commercial buildings are often standard passenger elevator packages modified for service use.

*Freight elevators* are usually classed as general freight loading, motor vehicle loading, industrial truck, or concentrated loading elevators. General freight loading elevators may be electric drum type or traction or hydraulic elevators.

*Private residential elevators* may be installed only in a private residence or to serve a single unit in a building with multiple dwelling units. By code, elevators in private residences are limited in size, capacity, rise, and speed.

## BUILDING CHARACTERISTICS

Physical building characteristics (such as building height and hoistway location) are considered in conjunction with population characteristics to determine the size, speed, type, and location of elevator systems. Characteristics that particularly affect the elevator systems are:

- *Height:* Determine the distance of elevator travel from lowest terminal to top terminal, the number of floors, and the floor height.
- *Building use:* Identify the location of heavily used building entrance areas, such as those leading to cafeterias, restaurants, auditoriums, and service areas. Typically, plan a building so that no prospective passengers must walk more than 200 ft (610 m) to reach an elevator.

The elevator selection process must begin with a thorough analysis of how people will occupy the building. Four issues are pertinent:

- *Total population and density:* Determine this figure for each floor.
- *Peak loading:* Identify the periods when elevators will carry the highest traffic loads.
- *Waiting time:* Determine the length of time a passenger is expected to wait for the next elevator to arrive.
- *Demand for quality:* Recognize that smooth operation may be as important as fancy finishes.

## RESIDENTIAL ELEVATORS

### Selection Criteria

Guidelines for selecting an elevator for a private residence can be simplified to a few parameters. By code, residential elevators are limited in size, capacity, rise, and speed, and can be installed only in a private residence or in a multiple dwelling as a means of access to a single residence. Preengineered systems generally offer only a few options for speed, capacity, aesthetic design, and electronic controls.

### Elevator Systems for Private Residential Use

Two types of elevator systems are commonly used in private residences: winding-drum machine and hydraulic elevators.

- *Winding-drum machine:* This type of traction elevator employs a grooved drum around which the hoisting cable wraps as it operates. This elevator type does not require a counterweight or a machine room above the hoistway, making it more practical for small places than a standard traction system.
- *Hydraulic elevator:* Hydraulic elevators in private

residences employ either a standard holeless arrangement or a roped hydraulic machine. Both types eliminate major construction and drilling, making the system economical and an excellent selection for retrofit applications.

The dimensions given here are appropriate for most applications. For exact dimensions required in specific circumstances, consult manufacturers.

### Load Capacity

The load capacity of drum-type machines is 500 lb (226 kg); speed is 30 ft (9 m) per minute. The load capacity of traction and hydraulic machines is 750 lb (340 kg); speed is 36 ft (11 m) per minute.

### Guide Rails

Manufacturers usually provide guide rails in 5 ft (1,525 mm) sections, although some manufacturers offer rails that can span the distance from floor structure to floor structure. If an existing structure cannot support guide rails, manufacturers can provide a self-supporting elevator tower that transmits the load to its base. This tower requires increased horizontal clearance in the hoistway.

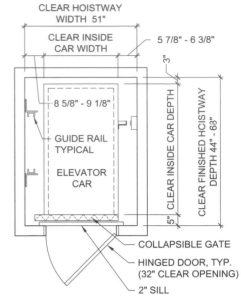

**SINGLE DOOR**

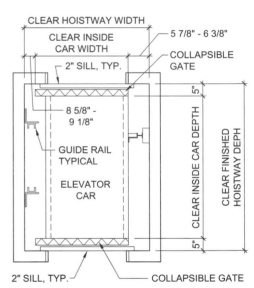

**TWO DOORS—OPPOSITE SIDES**

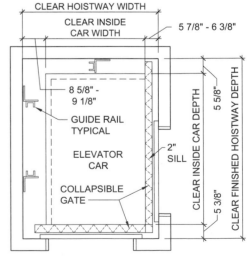

**TWO DOORS—ADJACENT SIDES**

Standard car size is 36 in. (915 mm) wide × 48 in. (1,220 mm) deep × 80 in. (2,030 mm) high. Other available car depths are 36 in. (915 mm) and 60 in. (1,525 mm).

**RESIDENTIAL ELEVATOR PLANS**

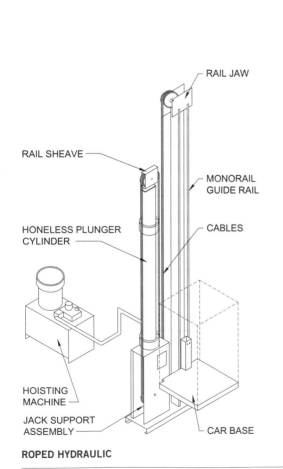

**ROPED HYDRAULIC**

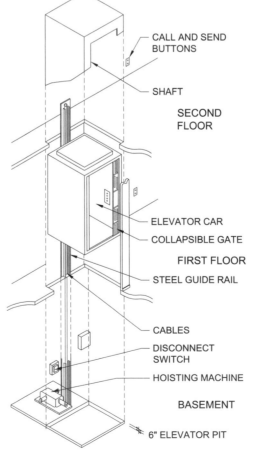

**WINDING-DRUM**

**ELEVATOR TYPES**

# TRACTION ELEVATORS

Medium- and high-rise buildings require geared traction and gearless traction elevator systems. The main difference between the two systems is in travel speed. General design considerations involving hoistway, machine room, and elevator planning are similar.

Both geared and gearless drive units are governed by electronic controls, which coordinate car leveling, passenger calls, collective operation of elevators, door operation, car acceleration and deceleration, and safety applications. A broad range of control systems are available to meet individual building requirements.

Structural requirements call for the total weight of the elevator system to be supported by the machine beams and transmitted to the building (or hoistway) structure. Consult with elevator consultants and structural engineers.

## Traction Elevator Design Considerations

- Pit depths, overhead clearances, and penthouse sizes should be in accordance with ASME requirements. Local codes may vary from these requirements.
- All overhead dimensions for passenger elevators are based on standard 8-ft- (2.4-m-) high cabs.
- Layout dimensions of the passenger elevator are based on center-opening entrances. Other types are available.
- The machine room for traction elevators is usually located directly above the hoistway. Provide space for the elevator drive, electronic control equipment, and governor; provide sufficient clearance for equipment installation, repair, and removal. Adequate lighting and ventilation (temperature maintained between 65°F and 100°F (18°C and 38°C)) are required by codes, and sound insulation should be provided. Machine room sizes may vary depending on number of cars, type of control, and so on. Check with elevator consultant for requirements.
- Check local codes for required fire enclosures.

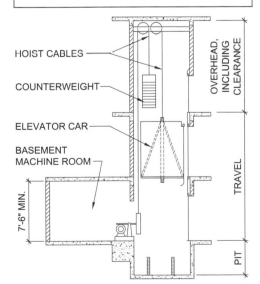

HOIST CABLES

COUNTERWEIGHT

ELEVATOR CAR

BASEMENT MACHINE ROOM

OVERHEAD, INCLUDING CLEARANCE

TRAVEL

7'-6" MIN.

PIT

This is a very specialized application, so consultation with experts is advised. Traction elevators with basement machine rooms are used in new and existing buildings where overhead clearance is limited.

## TRACTION ELEVATOR WITH BASEMENT MACHINE ROOM

*Rippeteau Rollins Architecture + Design; Washington, D.C.*

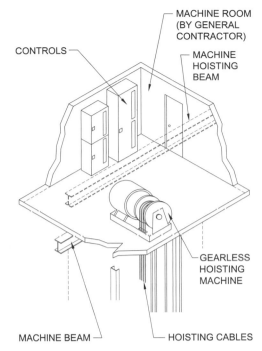

CONTROLS

MACHINE ROOM (BY GENERAL CONTRACTOR)

MACHINE HOISTING BEAM

GEARLESS HOISTING MACHINE

MACHINE BEAM

HOISTING CABLES

### GEARLESS ELEVATOR MACHINE ROOM

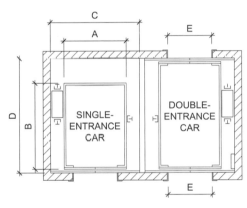

C

A

E

D

B

SINGLE-ENTRANCE CAR

DOUBLE-ENTRANCE CAR

E

### SIDE-MOUNTED COUNTERWEIGHT
Side-mounted counterweights allow an optional rear entrance door.

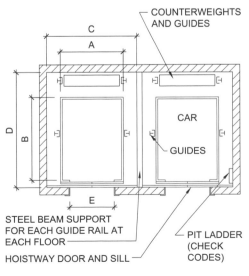

COUNTERWEIGHTS AND GUIDES

C

A

D

B

CAR

GUIDES

STEEL BEAM SUPPORT FOR EACH GUIDE RAIL AT EACH FLOOR

HOISTWAY DOOR AND SILL

E

PIT LADDER (CHECK CODES)

### REAR-MOUNTED COUNTERWEIGHT

## ELEVATOR HOISTWAY TYPES

## TRACTION ELEVATOR DIMENSIONS IN FT-IN. (MM)

| RATED LOAD LB (KG) | A | B | C | D | E |
|---|---|---|---|---|---|
| 2,000 (967) | 5-8 (1,727) | 4-3 (1,295) | 7-4 (2,235) | 6-11 (2,108) | 3-0 (914) |
| 2,500 (1,134) | 6-8 (1,828) | 4-3 (1,295) | 8-4 (2,540) | 6-11 (2,108) | 3-6 (1,066) |
| 3,000 (1,360) | 6-8 (1,828) | 4-7 (1,397) | 8-4 (2,540) | 7-5 (2,260) | 3-6 (1,066) |
| 3,500 (1,587) | 6-8 (1,828) | 5-3 (1,600) | 8-4 (2,540) | 8-1 (2,463) | 3-6 (1,066) |
| 4,500 (2,041) | 5-8 (1,727) | 7-10 (2,387) | 8-2 (2,489) | 10-5 (3,175) | 4-0 (1,219) |

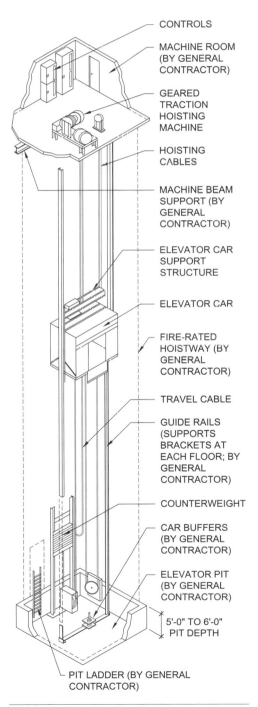

CONTROLS

MACHINE ROOM (BY GENERAL CONTRACTOR)

GEARED TRACTION HOISTING MACHINE

HOISTING CABLES

MACHINE BEAM SUPPORT (BY GENERAL CONTRACTOR)

ELEVATOR CAR SUPPORT STRUCTURE

ELEVATOR CAR

FIRE-RATED HOISTWAY (BY GENERAL CONTRACTOR)

TRAVEL CABLE

GUIDE RAILS (SUPPORTS BRACKETS AT EACH FLOOR; BY GENERAL CONTRACTOR)

COUNTERWEIGHT

CAR BUFFERS (BY GENERAL CONTRACTOR)

ELEVATOR PIT (BY GENERAL CONTRACTOR)

5'-0" TO 6'-0" PIT DEPTH

PIT LADDER (BY GENERAL CONTRACTOR)

## TRACTION ELEVATOR (GEARED)

# ESCALATORS AND MOVING WALKS

Escalators are a very efficient form of vertical transportation for very heavy traffic where the number of floors served is limited, normally a maximum of five to six floors. Escalators are not usually accepted as a required exit.

Dimensions are general and will vary somewhat with the manufacturer. Consult manufacturers for structural support, electrical supply, and specific dimensional requirements.

Moving passenger conveyors are particularly useful in transportation terminals, sports arenas, and exposition centers where large numbers of people must move long distances horizontally. The conveyors may be arranged in any combination of horizontal runs and inclines with a practical maximum of 12°.

It is generally not economical to provide moving sidewalks for distances of less than 100 ft (3 m); for distances greater than 300 ft (9 m), their slow operating speed invokes passenger frustration. Narrower units (26 in.; 660 mm) accommodate one adult; 40 in. (1,016 mm) widths allow for both walking and standing passengers.

*Alan H. Rider, AIA; DMJM; Washington, D.C.*

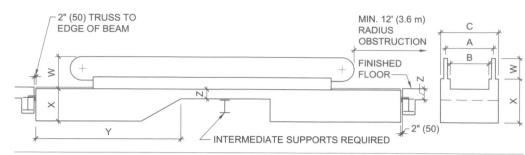

**MOVING PASSENGER CONVEYOR ELEVATION**

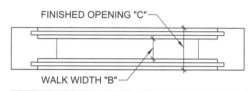

**MOVING PASSENGER CONVEYOR PLAN**

## MOVING PASSENGER CONVEYORS

| SYMBOL | DESCRIPTION | PLANNING DIMENSIONS SCHINDLER IN. (MM) | |
|---|---|---|---|
| A | Nominal width | 32 (812) | 48 (1219) |
| B | Width of walk | 26 (660) | 40 (1016) |
| C | Overall deck width | 4 ft–4½ in. (1333) | 5 ft–8½ in. (1740) |
| W | Top of handrail | 2 ft–11⁷⁄₁₆ in. (900) | |
| X | Depth of truss | 3 ft—6½ in. (1079) | |
| Y | Length of pit | 18 ft—10 in. (5740) | |
| Z | Maximum depth of truss | 3 ft–4⁷⁄₁₆ in. (1027) | |

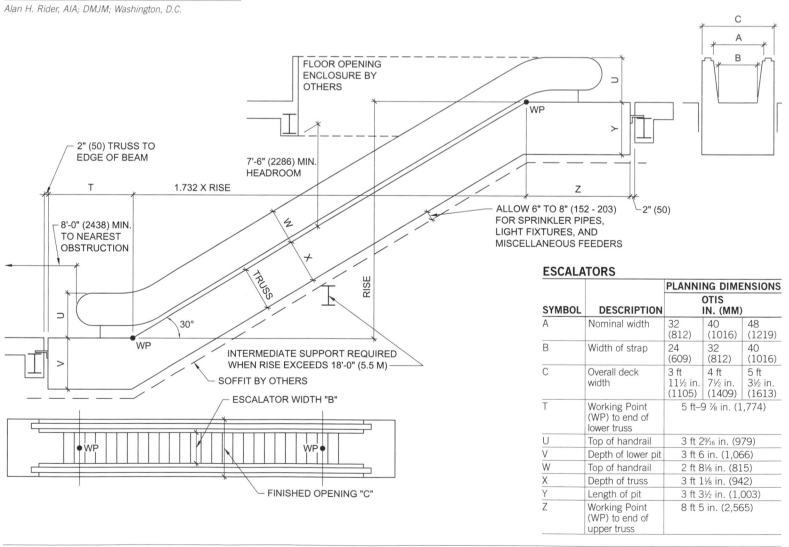

**ESCALATOR PROFILE**

## ESCALATORS

| SYMBOL | DESCRIPTION | PLANNING DIMENSIONS OTIS IN. (MM) | | |
|---|---|---|---|---|
| A | Nominal width | 32 (812) | 40 (1016) | 48 (1219) |
| B | Width of strap | 24 (609) | 32 (812) | 40 (1016) |
| C | Overall deck width | 3 ft 11½ in. (1105) | 4 ft 7½ in. (1409) | 5 ft 3½ in. (1613) |
| T | Working Point (WP) to end of lower truss | 5 ft–9 ⅞ in. (1,774) | | |
| U | Top of handrail | 3 ft 2⁹⁄₁₆ in. (979) | | |
| V | Depth of lower pit | 3 ft 6 in. (1,066) | | |
| W | Top of handrail | 2 ft 8⅛ in. (815) | | |
| X | Depth of truss | 3 ft 1⅛ in. (942) | | |
| Y | Length of pit | 3 ft 3½ in. (1,003) | | |
| Z | Working Point (WP) to end of upper truss | 8 ft 5 in. (2,565) | | |

# BASIC MECHANICAL SYSTEMS

## SYSTEM TYPES

The two major considerations in the design of a commercial heating, ventilating, and air conditioning (HVAC) system are the *source of energy* (fuel) to be used and the *method of distribution* within the building. Heat can be distributed in a building by air, water (hydronic systems), or electricity.

## AIR SYSTEMS

There are dozens of different all-air comfort conditioning systems, each addressing the complex requirements of larger commercial buildings. In large buildings there is often a simultaneous demand for heating, cooling, and ventilation. Rooms on the sunny side of a building need cooling, rooms on the shaded side need heating, and rooms in the building core require ventilation. Of the many year-round all-air systems in use, the most common are:

- Single-zone
- Multizone
- Single-duct or terminal reheat
- Single-duct variable air volume (VAV)
- Dual-duct

## HEATING DISTRIBUTION SYSTEMS

| SYSTEM | ADVANTAGES | DISADVANTAGES |
|---|---|---|
| Air | Can also perform other functions, such as ventilation, cooling, humidity control, and filtering. | Very bulky ducts require careful planning and space allocation. |
| | Prevents stratification and uneven temperatures by mixing air. | Can be noisy if not designed properly. |
| | Very quick response to changes of temperature. | Very difficult to use in renovations. |
| | No equipment required in rooms being heated. | Zones are not easy to create. |
| | | Cold floors result if air outlets are high in the room. |
| Hydronic | Compact pipes are easily hidden within walls and floor. | For the most part, can only heat, not cool (exceptions: fan-coil units and valance units). |
| | Can be combined with domestic hot water system. | No ventilation. |
| | Good for radiant floor heating. | No humidity control. |
| | | No air filtering. |
| | | Leaks can be a problem. |
| | | Slightly bulky equipment in spaces being heated (baseboard and cabinet convectors). |
| | | Radiant floors are slow to respond to temperature changes. |
| Electricity | Most compact. | Very expensive to operate (except heat pump). |
| | Quick response to temperature changes. | Wasteful. |
| | Very easily zoned. | Cannot cool (except heat pump). |
| | Low initial cost. | |

*Source: Norbert Lechner,* Heating, Cooling, Lighting: Design Methods for Architects, *2nd Ed.; New York, John Wiley & Sons, Inc., 2001.*

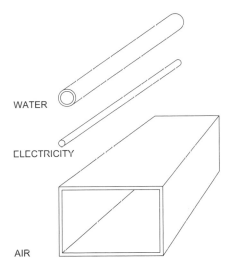

Because of their large size, air ducts require the most forethought in design and planning, while electrical heat requires the least. An air heating system requires 1% to 5% of the building's volume for ducts and air-handling equipment.

### THREE METHODS OF HEAT DISTRIBUTION

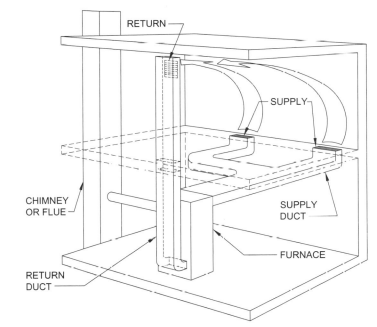

Air circulates through ducts with the aid of a blower.

### AIR SYSTEM

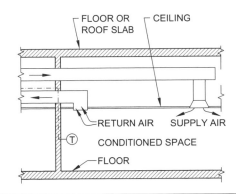

### SINGLE-ZONE SYSTEM

Single-zone systems are best applied to small residential and commercial buildings. The entire building is treated as a single zone, controlled by a single thermostat and served by a single air-handling unit, which supplies fixed quantities of air to the building spaces. If a change in air volume is required for seasonal changeover (heating to cooling, or vice versa), the duct volume dampers must be reset.

Multiple subzones can be established by thermostatic control of volume dampers in branch ducts feeding different areas. All these zones, however, are in the same mode—heating or cooling. This system has low first cost, simple maintenance, and a long life. However, because it is designed to handle a building as a single zone, often it is not sufficiently flexible to maintain comfort conditions in all rooms. As a result, larger buildings often use multizone systems.

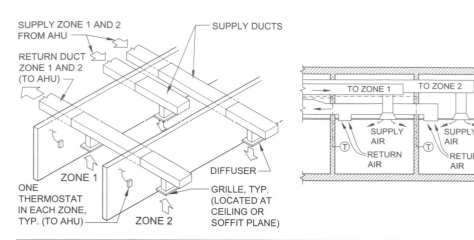

Multizone systems are used for medium-sized buildings where different zones have different conditioned air requirements. Hot and cold air are produced centrally and provided to each zone. Therefore, heating and cooling can be provided simultaneously to different zones. Limiting factors include the number of zones and energy costs.

The principal disadvantage of a multizone system is that the ductwork can become enormous. Other disadvantages are that the initial cost of the system is high, it can be difficult to control, and the operation costs can be high because the return air from all the different zones is mixed since there is only one air handler. As a result, warm air is mixed with cold air, resulting in a large waste of energy.

## MULTIZONE SYSTEMS

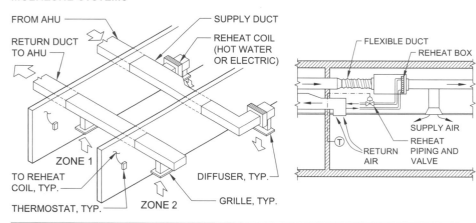

Single-duct reheat systems are not commonly used because of their energy inefficiency. This system uses a single duct that provides air (typically very cold) to the entire building. At each zone, a small reheat coil heats the cold air to the temperature required for that zone. The central system must provide air cold enough (as cold as 40°F (4.4°C)) to meet the maximum cooling load of the building's warmest zone. Though this system has a high first cost and high energy costs, it provides excellent control and constant air volume and does not require a changeover to switch from heating to cooling, or vice versa. This system is often used for laboratories, hospitals, and other facilities requiring accurate temperature control and constant volume for ventilation requirements.

## SINGLE-DUCT REHEAT SYSTEMS

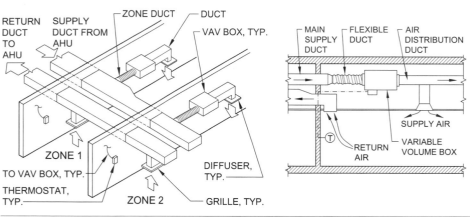

VAV systems compensate for variable loads by varying the volume of air supplied, rather than its temperature. The air volume variation is accomplished by a thermostatically controlled variable air-volume box. This box takes main duct air from the single-supply duct and modulates the air quantity supplied to a space to match its load. The central supply will furnish either cold air or warm air depending on outdoor conditions and prevailing indoor needs. This system is better suited for buildings that always need cooling (large interior zones) than to buildings with perimeters requiring constant air changes, such as labs or medical facilities. This system has become the most popular for medium-sized and large buildings because of its low first cost, low energy cost, and small ductwork. These systems cannot, however, simultaneously provide both heating and cooling.

## SINGLE-DUCT VARIABLE AIR VOLUME (VAV) SYSTEMS

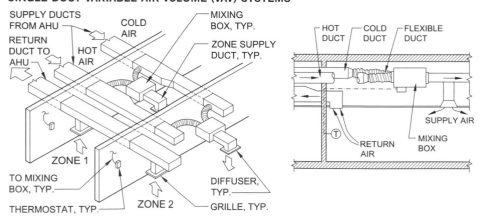

Dual-duct systems can either be variable-volume or constant-volume. The constant-volume system consists of two complete duct distribution systems—one with hot air and one with cold air. A mixing box at each zone location provides air at the temperature required for the load. Control is excellent with this system. The disadvantages are a high first cost, a high energy cost, and a large volume of building space occupied by a two-duct system.

The variable-volume dual-duct system uses one duct to supply primary air in accordance with the major demand (heating or cooling). This air has variable temperature but constant volume. The second air duct has a fixed temperature but variable volume. The two streams of air are mixed at each zone. This system uses smaller ductwork than the constant-volume system, is cheaper to install, and uses less energy. Control, however, is not as rapid and accurate as with the constant-volume system.

## DUAL-DUCT SYSTEMS

## DIFFUSERS, REGISTERS, AND GRILLES

The air supply and return devices are often the only element of an HVAC system seen by building occupants. They have a direct impact on thermal and acoustical comfort, and have an indirect impact on indoor air quality. Selection and specification of these devices are important parts of the design process.

Three types of devices are used to supply and return air:

- *Diffusers* are generally intended for ceiling-mounted supply air applications and are designed to provide good mixing of supply air with room air.
- *Registers* are used for supply or return air applications and may be appropriate for ceiling, sidewall, or floor installations.
- *Grilles* are less sophisticated devices primarily intended for return air applications.

Diffusers and registers are selected to deliver a specified airflow with appropriate throw (in terms of both distance and direction) and acceptable noise generation. Diffusers, manufactured of steel or aluminum, are available in a wide range of shapes, sizes, surface appearances, finishes, and installation detailing. Registers come in a more restricted range of shapes and sizes. Grilles are generally square or rectangular in shape.

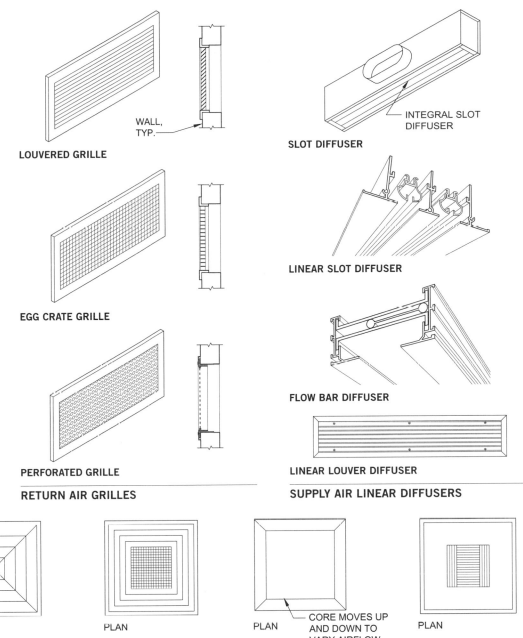

WALL, TYP.

**LOUVERED GRILLE**

**EGG CRATE GRILLE**

**PERFORATED GRILLE**

**RETURN AIR GRILLES**

INTEGRAL SLOT DIFFUSER

**SLOT DIFFUSER**

**LINEAR SLOT DIFFUSER**

**FLOW BAR DIFFUSER**

**LINEAR LOUVER DIFFUSER**

**SUPPLY AIR LINEAR DIFFUSERS**

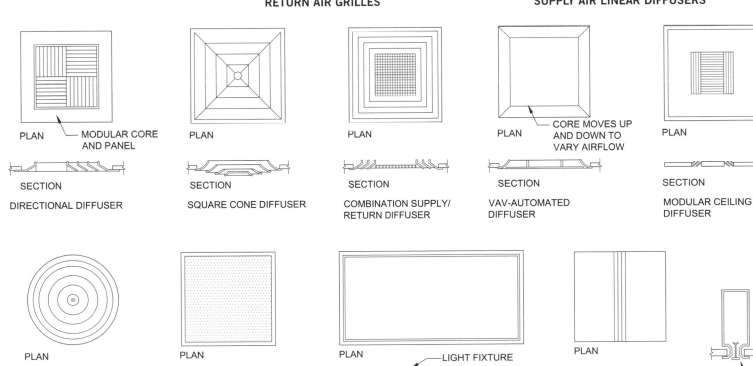

PLAN — MODULAR CORE AND PANEL

SECTION

**DIRECTIONAL DIFFUSER**

PLAN

SECTION

**SQUARE CONE DIFFUSER**

PLAN

SECTION

**COMBINATION SUPPLY/RETURN DIFFUSER**

PLAN — CORE MOVES UP AND DOWN TO VARY AIRFLOW

SECTION

**VAV-AUTOMATED DIFFUSER**

PLAN

SECTION

**MODULAR CEILING DIFFUSER**

PLAN

SECTION

**ROUND CONE DIFFUSER**

PLAN

SECTION

**PERFORATED FACE DIFFUSER**

PLAN — LIGHT FIXTURE

SECTION — AIR SLOT

**AIR SUPPLY LIGHTING TROFFER**

PLAN

SECTION

TWO-WAY SLOT

**T-BAR LAY-IN DIFFUSER**

**SUPPLY AIR DIFFUSERS**

## HYDRONIC SYSTEMS

Active heating and cooling systems for buildings use either air or water as the heat transfer medium. Heating systems that use water are referred to as *hydronic systems*. Cooling systems that use water are often referred to as *chilled-water systems*. Water is a very efficient means of transmitting heat to different areas of a building. Hot water carries almost 3,500 times more heat than the same volume of air. This is the principal advantage of a hydronic system—compactness. Although varied in design, all hydronic heating systems contain the following basic components:

• Hot water boiler and its controls and safety devices
• Expansion tank, also referred to as a compression tank
• Water pump, also called a circulator
• Terminal devices that transfer heat from the circulating water to the various building spaces
• Piping
• Controls that regulate the system

Three types of hydronic heating systems are often commonly referred to by their terminal units, which include the following:

• Fin-tube radiation
• Convectors
• Fan-coil units
• Radiant panels
• Cast-iron radiators
• Steel-panel radiators

### Fin-Tube Radiation

Fin-tube radiation units typically consist of a copper pipe on which are mounted square aluminum or copper fins. Hot water passes through the pipe, heating the pipe and, in turn, the fins. This "finned-tube" assembly is installed in a metal enclosure designed to encourage convective air current over the hot pipe and fins. Cool air enters the baseboard enclosure at the bottom, is heated as it passes over the hot-finned pipe assembly, and exits the top of the enclosure to heat the space. The heated air rises, is cooled by the room's heat loss, drops to the floor, and reenters the finned-tube radiator to be reheated.

### Convectors

Convectors consist of one or more vertical tiers of finned-tube radiation. They differ from the finned-tube radiators only in that convectors have a much larger capacity. Convector units installed on outside walls should have rear insulation to prevent significant heat loss through the wall. This is especially important for recessed convector units, because the R-value of the wall may be reduced by the recess.

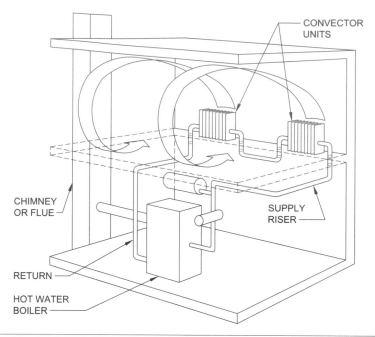

**HYDRONIC SYSTEM**

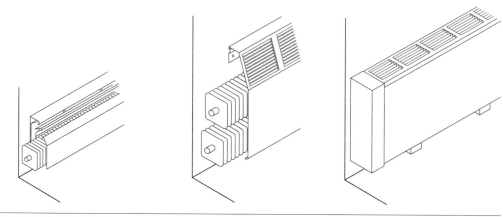

**FIN-TUBE RADIATORS**

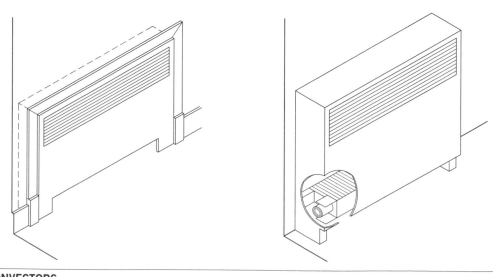

**CONVECTORS**

## Fan-Coil Units

Fan-coil units can provide heating, cooling, or both. A fan-coil unit is essentially a cabinet containing a hydronic coil assembly and a motor-driven blower. Hot or cold water is piped to the unit. Control of the blower is often given to the user. Fan-coil units do not usually provide dehumidification. Dehumidification occurs when the room air is cooled below its dew point as it passes over the cooling coil. A condensate pan and drain line is often provided to collect and remove the condensate. Recirculated room air can be filtered as it passes through the return air filter at the base of the unit.

## Radiant Panels

Radiant heating systems transfer heat from hot water tubing (or electric cables) embedded in the floor or ceiling to a medium that will distribute heat to the specified space. Hydronic radiant heating is expensive because of the large amount of pipes and valves involved. These systems are more popular in residential projects than in commercial projects.

Radiant floors induce convective air currents in the room because of the natural tendency of heated air to rise. Finish floors should not be made of a thermal insulating material; ceramic tile and wood flooring are suitable. Radiant ceiling installations are less common in commercial interiors because a blanket of heated air forms at the ceiling and remains there, which leads to a condition of stagnant air in a closed room. Overhead radiant panels are often used to heat loading docks and other partially exterior spaces that do not require a fine temperature control.

## Cast-Iron Radiators

The classic rib-type cast-iron radiator was originally developed for use in steam systems and later adapted to hydronic hot water systems. Each unit is connected to a water supply and return branch and is normally equipped with an air vent. Hot water passes through the unit and heats the cast-iron ribs, which then heat the room by a combination of radiation and convection. The thermal mass of the radiator itself, plus the contained water, provide a thermal lag that acts to smooth out rapid temperature variations.

## Steel-Panel Radiators

The size and unsightliness of the classic ribbed radiator and the hazard of an exposed high heat source were two of the factors that led to the development of flat steel radiators. The "ribs" of these units are flat steel tubes of rectangular cross section, arranged either vertically or horizontally. These units have a smaller thermal mass than cast-iron radiation.

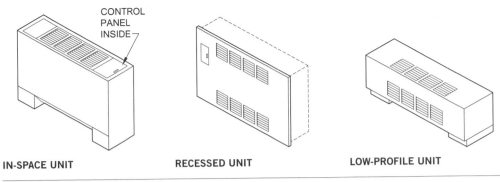

**IN-SPACE UNIT**    **RECESSED UNIT**    **LOW-PROFILE UNIT**

**FAN-COIL UNITS**

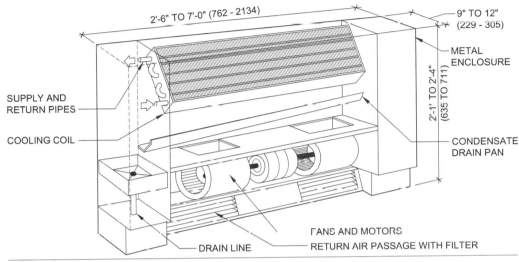

**COMPONENTS OF A FAN-COIL UNIT**

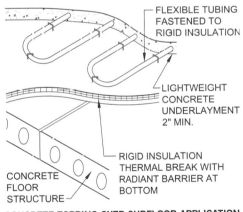

**CONCRETE TOPPING OVER SUBFLOOR APPLICATION**

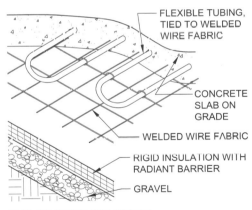

**SLAB-ON-GRADE APPLICATION**

**RADIANT FLOOR SYSTEMS**

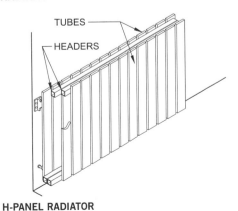

**H-PANEL RADIATOR**

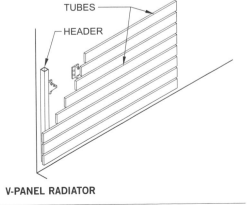

**V-PANEL RADIATOR**

**RADIATORS**

## ELECTRIC HEATING SYSTEMS

Electric heating systems for commercial use most commonly produce heat at the point of use. These systems, sometimes referred to as *space heating systems*, have a number of advantages. Installation costs are low because there is no need for a boiler or furnace, and expensive piping or ductwork is not required. Electric heat is also clean and quiet. However, electric heat is expensive in most parts of the United States, and a separate cooling system is required.

Electric energy is ideally suited for local space heating because it is simple to distribute and control. Electric heating systems are widely used in residences, schools, and commercial and industrial facilities. Heating units are placed in individual rooms or spaces and may be combined into zones with automatic temperature controls. Electric in-space heating systems may utilize natural convection, radiant, or forced-air units.

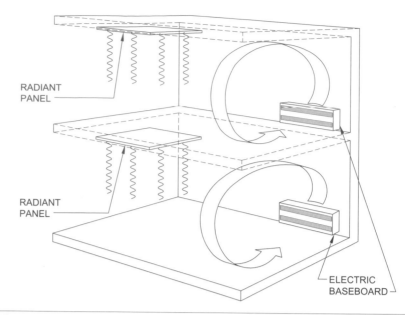

RADIANT PANEL

RADIANT PANEL

ELECTRIC BASEBOARD

**ELECTRIC HEATING SYSTEM**

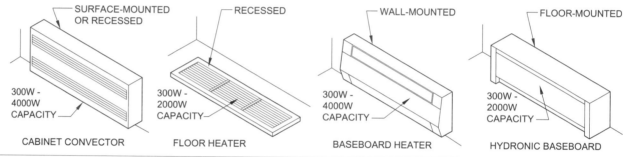

SURFACE-MOUNTED OR RECESSED

RECESSED

WALL-MOUNTED

FLOOR-MOUNTED

Natural convection units must be installed so that airflow across the resistor will not be impeded.

300W - 4000W CAPACITY

300W - 2000W CAPACITY

300W - 4000W CAPACITY

300W - 2000W CAPACITY

CABINET CONVECTOR

FLOOR HEATER

BASEBOARD HEATER

HYDRONIC BASEBOARD

**NATURAL CONVECTION UNITS**

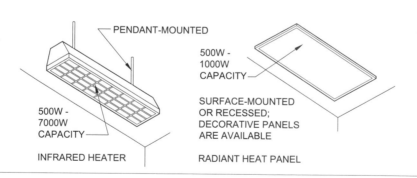

Radiant heaters are designed primarily to heat objects rather than space. Current flowing through a high-resistance wire heats up the element or surface of the unit. Heat is transferred from the unit to surfaces or occupants primarily by radiation. For an effective system, it is important to locate radiant heating units carefully in relation to the objects being heated.

PENDANT-MOUNTED

500W - 7000W CAPACITY

INFRARED HEATER

500W - 1000W CAPACITY

SURFACE-MOUNTED OR RECESSED; DECORATIVE PANELS ARE AVAILABLE

RADIANT HEAT PANEL

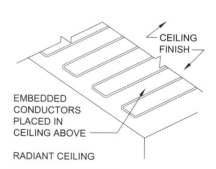

CEILING FINISH

EMBEDDED CONDUCTORS PLACED IN CEILING ABOVE

RADIANT CEILING

**RADIANT HEATING UNITS**

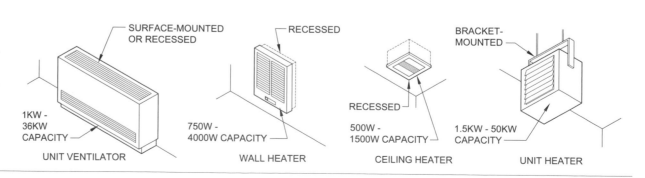

Forced-air units combine convection heating with fan-powered air circulation. Such units are available in a wide range of capacities to suit a variety of heating loads and occupancy types. Unit ventilations are commonly used on an outside wall, where they have access to outdoor air intake and can prevent cold air downdrafts from window areas.

SURFACE-MOUNTED OR RECESSED

1KW - 36KW CAPACITY

UNIT VENTILATOR

RECESSED

750W - 4000W CAPACITY

WALL HEATER

RECESSED

500W - 1500W CAPACITY

CEILING HEATER

BRACKET-MOUNTED

1.5KW - 50KW CAPACITY

UNIT HEATER

**FORCED-AIR UNITS**

# COMPUTER ROOM AIR CONDITIONING

Computers generate great quantities of heat in concentrated areas. To ensure proper operation, a precise temperature and humidity environment is required. The range of control may be as narrow as 72°F, ±2°F (22° C, ±1° C) temperature and 50% humidity, ±5%.

The air conditioning equipment should be able to meet the changing conditions created by relocation of equipment, facility expansion, and changes in heat output. Hotspots can result if flexibility is not built into the system.

## Downflow and Upflow Systems

Computer room air conditioning systems are either downflow or upflow.

- *Downflow systems* are more commonly used for a number of reasons. Air is returned through the top of the unit and supplied out through the bottom into a raised floor, thereby permitting large quantities of air without disturbing the occupants. Perforated floor outlets can easily be moved, providing flexibility in room layout. The units themselves also form part of the floor grid and can easily be moved.
- *Upflow systems* are used in areas where there is no raised floor (often the case in retrofit situations). They are also used in large rooms when the air is distributed by a ductwork system. Upflow systems are not as flexible as downflow systems for reorganizing equipment in a room.

## Redundancy

All systems should be designed with redundancy to provide full, continuous cooling. The degree of redundancy should be weighted against the consequences of downtime of the equipment. A minimum of 25% redundancy is recommended, but 100% may be warranted, depending on future expansion and the degree of backup required.

## Vapor Barriers

It is difficult and costly to maintain a computer room at a relative humidity of 50%, ±5%, throughout the year without a vapor barrier. In addition, room partitions should extend beyond the false ceiling to help prevent migration of moisture to and from adjoining areas.

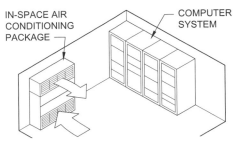

**IN-SPACE LOCAL UNIT APPLICATION**

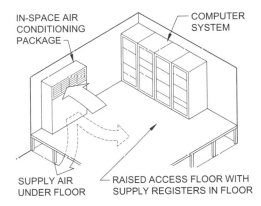

**DOWNFLOW (OR UPFLOW) SYSTEM WITH RAISED FLOOR**

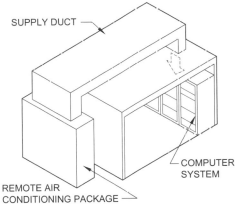

**LARGE REMOTE DUCTED SYSTEM**

**COMPUTER ROOM AIR CONDITIONING TYPES**

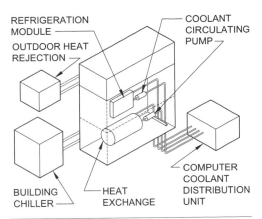

**COMBINED HEAT REJECTION IN MAINFRAME COOLING SYSTEM**

## Methods of Heat Rejection

Common methods of heat rejection include:

- *Self-contained air cooled:* Uses air within building return air plenum; limited to small-capacity units.
- *External air-cooled:* Uses outdoor condenser unit; refrigerant lines generally are limited to 100 ft (30 m) above, 30 ft (9 m) below, or 200 total ft (61 m) from computer room to outdoor unit.
- *Water-cooled:* Uses closed-loop condenser water pumped to an external cooling tower to remove heat from condenser within computer room fan-coil unit. Distance from cooling tower to computer room can be longer than that in an external air-cooled system.
- *Glycol-cooled:* Uses closed-loop glycol to carry rejected heat to external dry cooler or cooling tower, which allows greater separation of computer room from outside air. With additional coils, the system can provide "free cooling" during colder weather. This system is preferred in areas where ambient temperature is below –0°F.
- *Chilled water:* Chilled water is pumped from a remote chilled water plant to local fan-coil unit.
- *Combination unit:* May use two or more means of heat rejection to service the system during certain hours of operation or as a backup in case of primary system failure.

---

### Planning Issues

- Evaluate availability of building services and systems, mechanical chases, and electrical power capacities.
- Determine the overall heat load and plan size of system with client and engineer. Design for built-in redundancy with multiple circuits.
- Use qualified engineers to design and engineer the systems and to supervise testing and certification.
- Detail the construction of walls, ceiling, and floors to provide a complete vapor seal and adequate airflow.
- Evaluate energy-efficiency ratios of various kinds of proposed equipment.
- Select a system with high reliability and low noise level.
- Do not ventilate the space when unoccupied.

---

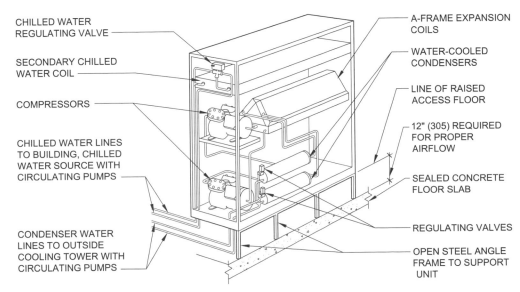

Large forced-air system is shown with combined heat-rejection systems.

**COMPUTER ROOM COOLING UNIT**

*William R. Arnquist, AIA; Donna Vaughan & Associates, Inc.; Dallas, Texas*
*Larry O. Degelman, P.E.; Texas A&M University; College Station, Texas*
*Walter T. Grondzik, P.E.; Florida A&M University; Tallahassee, Florida*

# PLUMBING

## WATER CLOSETS, URINALS, AND BIDETS

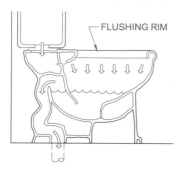

**REVERSE TRAP**
Water is introduced to the fixture only through the rim by a gravity flush tank. This action is low cost and used mostly for residential projects. Reverse traps may be used with flush tanks or valves.

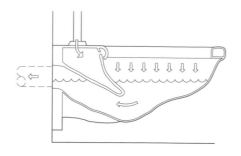

**BLOWOUT**
Water is introduced at high velocity through jets at the bottom of the waterway in a *blowout action*. This action is used for public facilities and industrial projects because of its capability to remove larger objects thrown into the fixture. Blowouts are used with flush valve water supplies only.

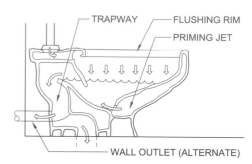

**SIPHON JET**
Water is introduced to the fixture both through the rim and by a jet at the bottom of the waterway. Quiet flushing and moderate cost make this the most commonly used flushing action. Less costly variations include *washout* and *washdown* actions that do not use the jet. The siphon jet can be used with flush valves or tanks.

### FIXTURE FLUSHING ACTION TYPES

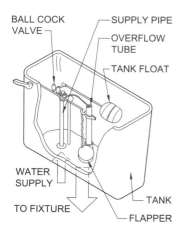

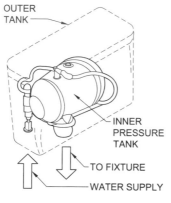

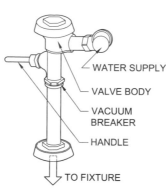

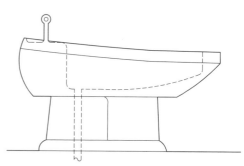

This low, basinlike plumbing fixture is designed to be straddled, for bathing the posterior of the body.

### BIDETS

**GRAVITY FLUSH TANK**
Water enters the tank through a ball cock and is stopped when the float valve reaches a predetermined level. The handle raises the flapper to release all the water in the tank into the fixture; it stops when the flapper closes. Gravity flush tanks require 10 psi water pressure.

**PRESSURE-ASSISTED FLUSH TANK**
Water enters a pressure tank installed inside the outer tank, partially filling the tank and compressing the air inside. When flushing is started, the air pressure causes the quick release of water into the fixture. Pressure-assisted flush tanks require 30 psi (2.1 kgf/sq cm) water pressure.

**FLUSH VALVE**
Flush valves are available in a wide variety of manual and automatic operation fixtures, some with infrared and other proximity sensors. Once flushing has started, a measured quantity of water is quickly introduced to the fixture. Flush valves require 25 psi (1.7 kgf/sq cm) water pressure.

### FIXTURE WATER SUPPLY TYPES

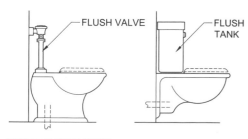

**WATER CLOSET TYPES**

Flush valves and tanks can be installed on either floor-mounted or wall-mounted water closets.

ADA 4.16, *Water Closets,* describes grab bar requirements for water closets. ADA 4.17, *Toilet Stalls,* describes approach, floor space, and grab bar requirements for water closets within toilet stalls. Water closet height should be 17 to 19 in. (430 to 480 mm) to the top of the toilet seat. Seats should not spring up. Mount controls on the wide side of the toilet no more than 44 in. (1,120 mm) above the floor.

For rough-in dimensions, refer to manufacturers' manuals.

Special toilet types are sometimes used, such as vacuum-vented, composting, and chemical toilets.

Current code requires that water closet flush valves and tanks be limited to 1.6 gallon, maximum, per flush of water.

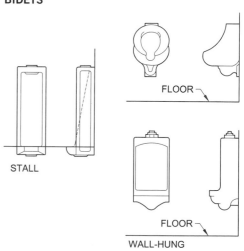

Urinals require flush valves as source of water supply. ADA 4.18, *Urinals,* requires 30 × 48 in. (760 × 1,220 mm) clear floor space in front of urinals to allow a forward approach. Urinals should be wall-hung, with an elongated rim a maximum of 17 in. (430 mm) above the floor. Shields, if provided, should not extend beyond the front of the urinal rim and must have a clearance of 29 in. (740 mm). Flush controls should be accessible and be no more than 44 in. (1,120 mm) above the floor.

If used, urinal tanks should be 92 to 94 in. (2,340 to 2,390 mm) above the floor.

Battery stalls, except accessible ones, should be installed 21 to 24 in. (530 to 610 mm), on center.

### WATER CLOSET MOUNTING TYPES AND CLEARANCES

### URINALS

# BATHTUBS AND SHOWERS: MATERIALS AND FINISHES

Bathtubs are available in many shapes and installation types, and are available in the following materials:

- *Fiberglass:* An economical and common choice, gel-coated fiberglass (also known as FRP) is lightweight and easy to install. Because the material can be molded, fiberglass tubs are available in a variety of shapes. Although not as durable as cast iron or acrylic, fiberglass can easily be repaired.
- *Acrylic:* Acrylic bath fixtures are more readily available than fiberglass, with which it is usually reinforced. Because acrylic is light and easily formed into different shapes, it is a good choice for whirlpools and other large tubs that would be too heavy in cast iron. Acrylic also is a good insulator, thus keeps the water warmer longer.
- *Cast iron:* Very heavy and extremely durable, traditional enamel-coated cast iron resists staining and scratching. It cannot be molded as freely as acrylic or fiberglass, so there are fewer shapes and styles from which to choose.
- *Enameled steel:* This is a lighter-weight, less-expensive alternative to cast iron.

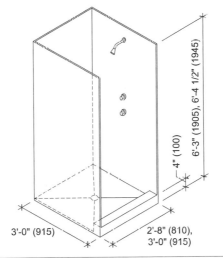

**BUILT-IN SHOWER UNITS**

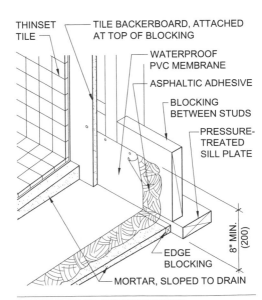

**SHOWER BASE CONSTRUCTION**

*American Society of Plumbing Engineers; Westlake, California
Michael Frankel, CIPE; Utility Systems Consultants;
Somerset, New Jersey*

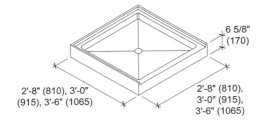

**SQUARE**

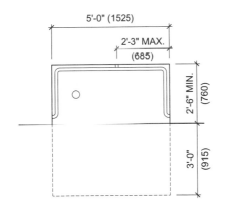

**RECTANGULAR**

**CORNER**

Materials for bases include acrylic with fiberglass reinforcement, enameled steel, and terrazzo.

**SHOWER BASES**

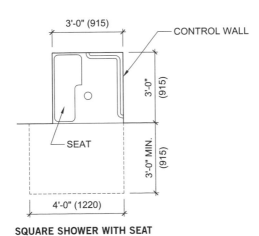

**RECTILINEAR SHOWER**

**SQUARE SHOWER WITH SEAT**

**SITE-BUILT SHOWER PANS**

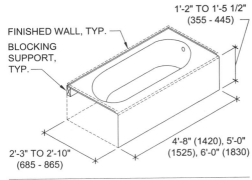

**BUILT-IN RECESSED BATHTUB**

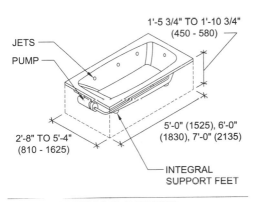

**DROP-IN WHIRLPOOL BATHTUB**

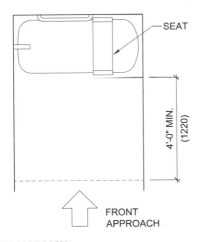

**FRONT APPROACH**

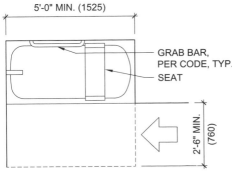

**SIDE APPROACH**

For tubs with a built-in seat at the head of the tub, the seat must be 15 in. (380 mm) wide, and clear floor space must be provided in front of the seat.

**CLEAR FLOOR SPACE FOR ACCESSIBLE BATHTUBS**

# BASIC ELECTRICAL AND CABLE SYSTEMS

## ELECTRICAL POWER

The two important concepts in understanding electricity—voltage and current (amps)—can be understood in terms of an analogy to water. The more water in a reservoir (voltage), the greater the flow (current) through the pipe (conductor). Voltage (a "reservoir" of electrons) and current flow (amps) create electrical power. By increasing the size of the pipe, the rate of flow can be increased.

Voltage can be thought of as a reservoir of electrons. The pressure (voltage) in the reservoir causes the electrons to move through the conductor. Voltage is a measure of the electrical "pressure" used to produce a flow of current through a circuit. Current is the amount of electrons flowing through an electrical current. Just as the size of the water pipe restricts how much water will flow, the conductor, typically an electrical wire, offers a specific resistance to the flow of current. The size of the conductor is one factor that determines how much electrical power will be available. The rate of flow of electrons is measured in units called *amperes*, or amps. The conductor carrying that current offers resistance. For example, "20-amp service" means that 20 amps of electrical power are available to that circuit. The term *ohms* describes electrical resistance. If the electrical conductor is too small (high ohms resistance), problems will occur.

## VA RATING

*Volt/amps*, or V/A, is the term used to describe available electrical power. The voltage rating divided by the supply voltage equals amps. For example:

$$\frac{2,400 \text{ (VA rating)}}{120 \text{ (Supply Voltage)}} = 20 \text{ Amps}$$

VA rating is a measure of how much power is available. *Watts* is a measure of how much power an electrical device uses.

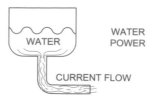

**WATER POWER**
Electrical power can be simply understood as an analogy to water power.

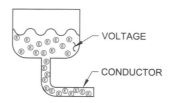

**VOLTAGE**
Voltage is the potential of electrical power, similar to a reservoir of electrons.

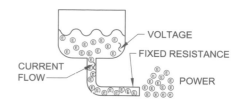

**CURRENT**
Current can be thought of as the amount of electrons flowing through an electrical conductor.

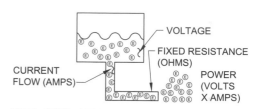

**AMPS, OHMS, AND V/A RATING**
The rate of flow of electrons is measured in units called amperes, or amps. Ohms describes electrical resistance. V/A describes available electrical power.

**ELECTRICAL POWER**

### ELECTRICAL AND TELECOMMUNICATIONS SYSTEMS

| TYPE | APPEARANCE | DESCRIPTION | USE | RELATIVE CAPACITY |
|---|---|---|---|---|
| Category 5 (high-capacity telephone/data wire) | | Four twisted pairs of high-capacity wire enclosed in an insulated sheath | Telephones, faxes, modems, Video, Data | Garden hose |
| RG 6 (coaxial cable) | | Heavily shielded and insulated copper core, which carries signal | Video, Data | Fire hose |
| Fiber-optic cable | | Glass-lined cable passing laser light pulses, which transmit voice data and image signals at the speed of light | All digital signals | Culvert |

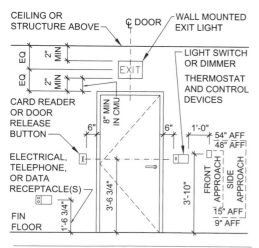

**STANDARD MOUNTING HEIGHTS FOR ELECTRICAL DEVICES**

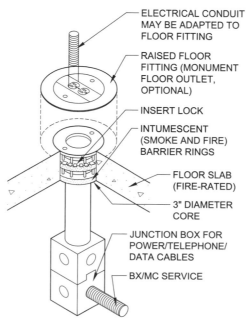

**POKE-THROUGH ELECTRICAL BOX**

**FLOOR-MOUNTED ELECTRICAL OUTLETS**

MONUMENT FLOOR OUTLET

# DISTRIBUTION SYSTEMS

## Poke-Through Systems

Poke-through systems are used in conjunction with overhead branch distribution systems that run in accessible suspended ceiling cavities to outlets in full-height partitions. When services are required at floor locations without adjacent partitions or columns, as in open office planning, they must either be brought down from a wireway assembly (known as a *power pole*) or up through a floor penetration containing a fire-rated insert fitting and flush or above-floor outlet assembly. To install a poke-through assembly, the floor slab must either be core-drilled or contain preset sleeves arranged in a modular grid. Poke-through assemblies are used in conjunction with cellular deck and underfloor duct systems when the service location required does not fall directly above its associated system raceway.

With one-floor penetration, the single poke-through assembly can serve all the power, communications, and computer requirements of a workstation. Distribution wiring in the ceiling cavity can be run in raceways. The more cost-effective method is to use armored cable (BX) for power and approved plenum-rated cable for communications and data when the ceiling cavity is used for return air. To minimize disturbance to the office space below when a poke-through assembly must be relocated or added, a modular system of prewired junction boxes for each service can be provided, although it is more common to elect this option for power only. A different type of working system must be selected for a floor slab on grade, above a lobby or retail space, above mechanical equipment space, or above space exposed to the atmosphere.

## Cellular Deck Systems

The low initial cost of a poke-through system makes it both viable and attractive for investor-owned buildings when tenants are responsible for future changes, and for corporate buildings with limited construction budgets. Poke-through systems are effective when office planning includes interconnecting workstation panels containing provisions (base raceways) to extend wiring above the floor, reducing the number of floor penetrations needed for services.

Based on the projected frequency of changes in office furniture layouts, a corporate or government organization may elect to invest in a permanent raceway system to minimize cost and disturbance to occupants when changes or additions are made. When structural design dictates the use of metal decking, a cellular floor raceway system utilizing trench header ducts is the most likely choice.

Cellular raceways come in a variety of sizes and configurations ranging from ½ to 3 in. (13 to 76 mm) high, with cells 8 or 12 in. (203 or 304 mm) on center, and 2 or 3 cells per section. An overall floor deck can be full cellular, where bottom plates are provided throughout, or blended, as shown.

Trench header ducts come in various sizes and configurations. The height is adjustable for slab depths above cells of 2½ to 4 in. (63 to 101 mm); widths vary from 9 to 36 in. (228 to 914 mm). Cover plates are ¼ in. (6 mm) thick, with lengths from 6 to 36 in. (152 to 914 mm), and can be secured either with spring clips or flush, flathead bolts.

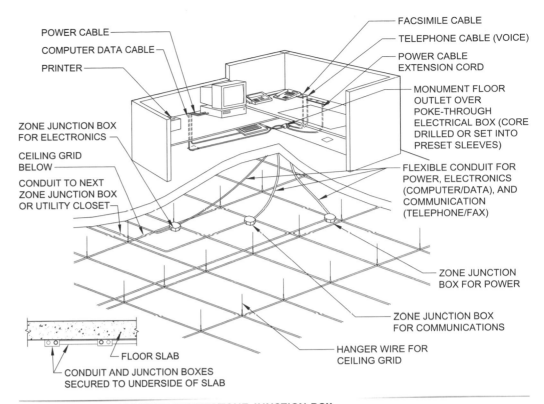

**POKE-THROUGH HARDWARE SYSTEM/ZONE JUNCTION BOX**

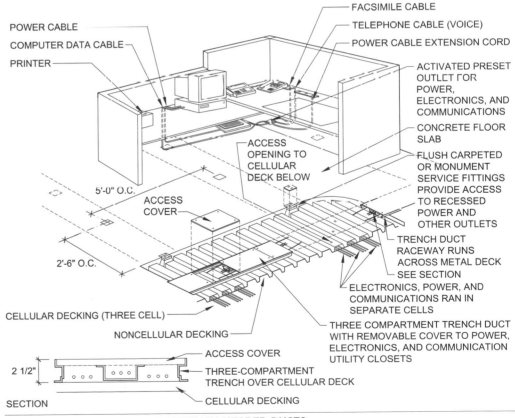

**CELLULAR DECK SYSTEM WITH TRENCH HEADER DUCTS**

## Raised Access Floor System

A raised access floor system provides maximum flexibility and lowest cost to relocate or add service. When used in conjunction with a modular system of power, communication and data wiring plug-in receptacles, and cable connector sets, changes can be made without an electrician or wiring technician. Access flooring systems have the highest initial cost of distribution systems.

Access floors can be provided with or without stringers, which are use to minimize the "creep" effect. For a custom installation without ramps or steps, the base floor is depressed.

Access floors do not necessarily require an increase in floor-to-floor height, and if so, the height added is at a much lower per-unit cost than for the rest of the building. When special attention is given to coordinating lighting with other elements in the suspended ceiling, or when lighting is provided below as from the workstations, the cavity can be compressed to compensate for the raised floor.

## Flat Cable Wiring System

Flat cable originates at transition boxes located at various intervals along core corridor walls and columns that are individually served from distribution centers in utility closets. Boxes can also be cast in the floor or atop a poke-through insert. Cables are not permitted to pass under fixed partitions and must be carefully mapped out to minimize crossovers and clutter.

To install a service fitting, an interface base assembly must first be secured directly to the concrete floor at the flat cable location. The base assembly stabs into conductors of the flat cable and converts them to round wire. When the service fitting is attached, it is activated and ready for use.

Careful consideration must be given to the application of this system based on limitations that may or may not be acceptable under different conditions. For example, it may be ideal for small areas or renovation of existing buildings where the poke-through or power pole systems are unacceptable or cannot be used. In new construction where poke-through has been chosen as the base building standard system, the flat cable system is a viable solution in areas where poke-through outlets cannot be installed, such as slab on grade.

Carpet tiles are required by most building codes as the floor covering to be used over flat cable installations to facilitate access to the flat cable. Where frequent changes and additions are anticipated, the resulting wear and tear on expensive, glued-down carpet tile may be a disadvantage.

Flat cable systems are labor-intensive to install. Actual installed initial costs and outlet relocation costs are comparable to cellular deck with trench header ducts.

*Richard F. Humenn, P.E.; Joseph R. Loring & Associates, Inc.; Consulting Engineers; New York, New York*
*Gary A. Hall; Hammel Green and Abrahamson; Minneapolis, Minnesota*

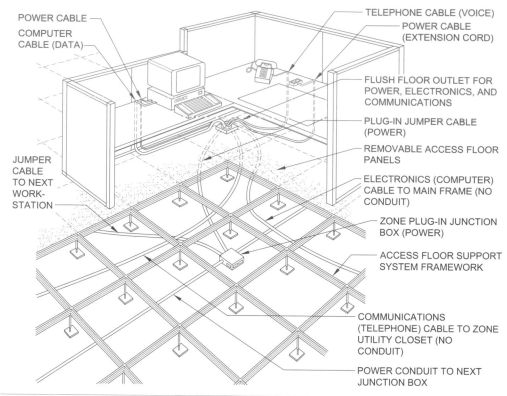

**RAISED-ACCESS FLOOR SYSTEM WITH MODULAR PLUG-IN DISTRIBUTION**

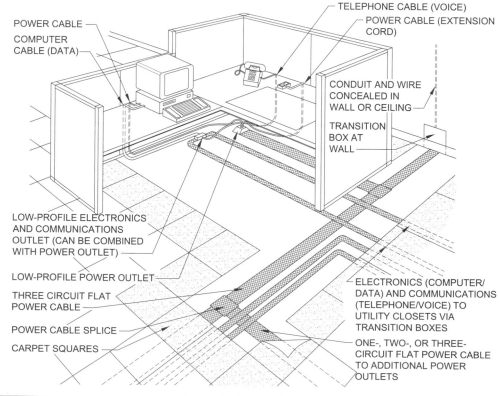

**FLAT CABLE WIRING SYSTEM**

# CABLES, BOXES, AND RACEWAYS

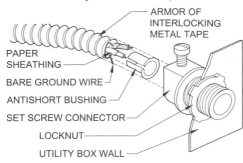

## ARMORED (BX)
Armored cable is manufactured with two-, three-, and four-conductor insulated wire. Its internal bonds help the armor itself serve as a bonding conductor.

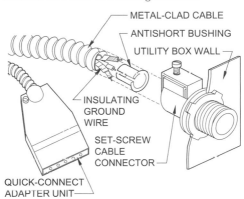

## METAL-CLAD (MC)
Manufactured in sizes and specifications similar to armored cable, metal-clad cable is available with a separate insulated ground conductor and in larger sizes.

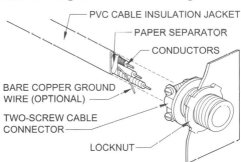

## NONMETALLIC SHEATHED (NM, ROMEX)
Manufactured in two- and three-conductor PVC insulated wire with or without ground wire, nonmetallic sheathed cable is permitted in residential and many other building types up to three stories.

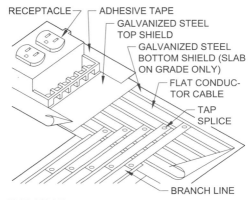

## FLAT CABLE
Flat cable has combinations of three, four, and five conductors for easy access under carpet squares. Data, communications, and TV flat cable are available.

## CABLES

---

## OCTAGONAL
Commonly used for flush ceiling outlets, octagonal boxes may also be used as floor boxes for monument receptacles.

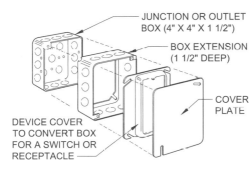

## SQUARE

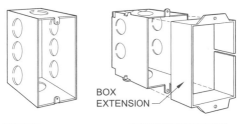

## FLUSH FLOOR
Boxes are mounted to wood floor structures (nonadjustable) or cast-in-place concrete with leveling screws. Concrete boxes include cast-iron, stamped-steel, or nonmetallic materials.

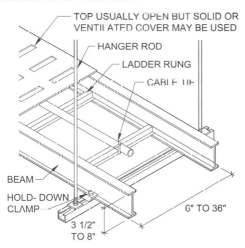

## UTILITY                SWITCH/RECEPTACLE
Metallic and nonmetallic boxes are available. Flush mounting in concrete requires a concrete tight box and rigid conduit and tubing. In CMU construction, a raceway tubing is threaded through the cavities.

## ELECTRICAL BOXES

---

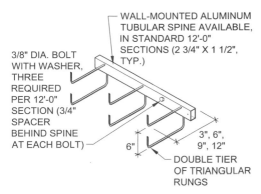

## WALL-MOUNT CABLE RACK

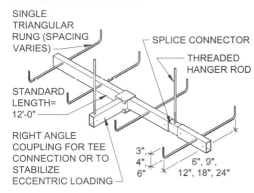

## CENTER-HUNG CABLE RACK

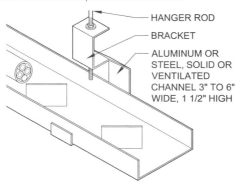

## CABLE TRAY SYSTEM
Cable trays protect and carry a large number of insulated cables in a limited space. For more protection or where heat buildup is not a problem, perforated or solid bottoms and top covers are available.

## CABLE CHANNEL
Cable channel can be used as a branch cable tray to carry a single large cable or conduit or several small ones.

## CONDUIT AND CABLE SUPPORTING DEVICES

# PART 3

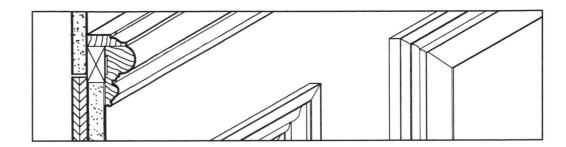

# INTERIOR TYPOLOGIES

Vitruvius' final principle of architectural design is *delight,* or beauty. By representing both the essence of and society's current posture on a human endeavor, an interior design serves as the physical manifestation of image, time, and purpose. Part 3, "Interior Typologies" presents historical background and design criteria specific to a variety of enterprises. Both the origins of an institution and its relationship to other endeavors in contemporary society must be realized to support the activities of that institution.

Commerce

Exhibition

Entertainment

Presentation Technology

Health Care Facilities

Hospitality

Education

# SPACE MEASUREMENT SYSTEMS

Space measurement of commercial property plays a crucial role in establishing rental rates and space assignment records. These rates are sometimes used to set designer's fees as well.

Several space measurement systems are in use in North America, many of which use identical or similar terms but interpret them in different ways; and sometimes their language is not precise. All systems strive to ensure the utmost fairness to occupants and building owners, but their rules are quite complex, particularly if they must be translated from one system to another. Although several additional regional variations are in use in major North American urban centers, here, six measurement systems are discussed:

- Building Owners and Managers Association (BOMA)—new standard
- Building Owners and Managers Association (BOMA)—former standard
- Real Estate Board of New York, Inc. (REBNY)
- Washington, DC, Association of Realtors (WDCAR)
- General Services Administration (GSA)—former system
- International Facility Management Association (IFMA)

Before 1992, little attempt was made to compare the systems; now, the trend is more toward reconciliation than standardization.

The most recent development in this field has been the promulgation of a major revision by BOMA to its standard. The U.S. General Services Administration has recently decided to classify all future space assignments, including lease actions, in terms compatible with BOMA's new system. The BOMA system is the most widely accepted in commercial real estate transactions, such as leasing. It is also used for tenants' space assignment allocation in many buildings.

## NEW BOMA SYSTEM

The BOMA system is tailored to the needs of the commercial office building lessor. It is the oldest and most widely used system. In June 1996, BOMA completed a major revision of its measurement standard ANSI Z65.1, *Standard Method for Measuring Floor Area in Office Buildings*.

As with the previous standard, HVAC convectors, columns, and interior building projections are included in the measurements. Another aspect that remains the same is that the usable area exclusive to one tenant is still measured from the office (tenant) side of walls separating tenant space from public corridors.

Unlike the old standard, the new standard defines *floor usable area* to include *buildingwide common areas* on that floor. Such areas are prorated to all building tenants on all floors. Areas such as public toilets and electrical and janitorial closets are considered *floor common areas*.

The 1996 standard represents a major departure from the previous edition in the following areas:

- It measures space on a buildingwide basis, rather than exclusively floor by floor.
- Most areas that were formerly amortized or absorbed in the base building cost (and therefore covered in the base rent) are now measured and prorated to all tenants.
- The new standard is much more explicit in naming many of the new building features designed to support all tenants in a building.
- Calculations are more complex, but the results provide a more rational approach to actual contemporary situations.
- Several new definitions have been introduced. Familiar terms like *rentable* and *usable* have been revised to reflect required changes in how they are calculated. The definition of *rentable area* includes office, store, portions of building common areas, and floor common areas prorated to each tenant. Building rentable area almost always remains constant for the life of the building. Usable area changes over the life of the building as tenant space changes. Basement storage and loading dock areas within the building line are considered part of rentable area; parking areas are not.

## FORMER BOMA SYSTEM

The former BOMA standard is described here for comparison, as it remains the baseline for rentable areas stated in thousands of leases. Moreover, of the six systems discussed here, it is the most generic, has the simplest set of definitions, and is the easiest to administer—as long as its few categories are specific enough for the intended application. Its major features include:

- Space is measured floor by floor, rather than by the building as a whole.

- Rentable space is constant for the life of the building; usable area changes over the life of the building.
- HVAC convectors are included in measurements.
- Amenities shared by several tenants—such as fitness centers, conference centers, lounges, and vending areas—are not considered rentable. Landlords are expected to factor the costs of such facilities into their basic rental rates. Basement storage and parking areas are not included as part of rentable area.

Except for mechanical penthouses, minimal definition is provided for the allocation of space for central building support operations, such as HVAC, electrical, telephone switch, and UPS systems for the entire building. Common practice is to exclude them all from rentable area, but the standard is not definitive.

Because the old BOMA system measures floor by floor, main lobbies and atrium areas are considered rentable. And because core factors tend to be very high on these floors, BOMA suggests renting usable area in this case.

Usable area exclusive to one tenant is measured from the office (tenant) side of walls separating tenant space and public corridors. Usable space excludes such support areas as public toilets, mechanical rooms, and electrical and janitorial closets.

---

**Three Categories of Commercial Office Space**

- *Space rented by measurement.* Represents space in each system that is measured and becomes the basis of the space allocated to a particular tenant and the rent calculation.
- *Space allocated pro rata.* Represents space in each system that is measured, tallied, and allocated pro rata to each tenant, in proportion to its share of space in the building. This share of space, often called the *core*, or *loss factor*, is added to the measured space described above to calculate the total rentable area written into a tenant's lease.
- *Space amortized into the base building cost.* Includes areas that are neither measured nor allocated pro rata in the tenant's lease. Therefore, the costs of such space must be recovered in the base rent charged in relation to measured space in the previous two categories.

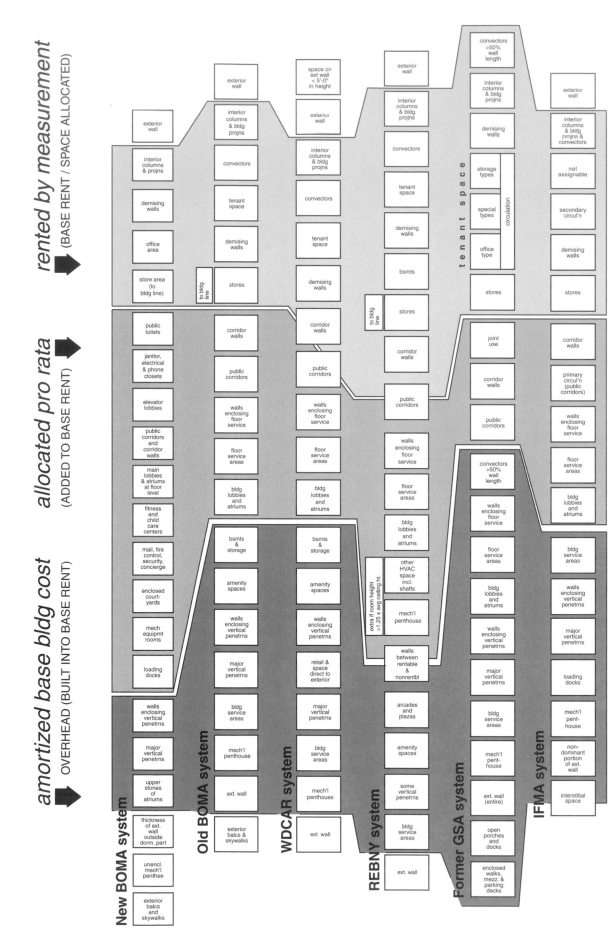

*rented by measurement* (BASE RENT / SPACE ALLOCATED) ➤

*allocated pro rata* (ADDED TO BASE RENT) ➤

*amortized base bldg cost* OVERHEAD (BUILT INTO BASE RENT) ➤

**New BOMA system**

| |
| --- |
| exterior wall |
| interior columns & projns |
| demising walls |
| office area |
| store area (to bldg line) |
| public toilets |
| janitor, electrical & phone closets |
| elevator lobbies |
| public corridors and corridor walls |
| main lobbies & atriums at floor level |
| fitness and child care centers |
| mail, fire control, security, concierge |
| enclosed court-yards |
| mech equipmt rooms |
| loading docks |
| walls enclosing vertical penetrns |
| major vertical penetrns |
| upper stories of atriums |
| thickness of ext. wall outside dorm. part |
| unencl. mech'l penthse |
| exterior balcs and skywalks |

**Old BOMA system**

| |
| --- |
| interior columns & bldg projns |
| convectors |
| tenant space |
| demising walls |
| to bldg line |
| stores |
| corridor walls |
| public corridors |
| walls enclosing floor service |
| floor service areas |
| bldg lobbies and atriums |
| bsmts & storage |
| amenity spaces |
| walls enclosing vertical penetrns |
| major vertical penetrns |
| bldg service areas |
| mech'l penthouse |
| ext. wall |
| exterior balcs & skywalks |

**WDCAR system**

| |
| --- |
| space on ext wall < 5'-0" in height |
| exterior wall |
| interior columns & bldg projns |
| convectors |
| tenant space |
| demising walls |
| corridor walls |
| public corridors |
| walls enclosing floor service |
| floor service areas |
| bldg lobbies and atriums |
| bsmts & storage |
| amenity spaces |
| walls enclosing vertical penetrns |
| retail & space direct to exterior |
| major vertical penetrns |
| bldg service areas |
| mech'l penthouse |
| ext. wall |

**REBNY system**

| |
| --- |
| exterior wall |
| interior columns & bldg projns |
| convectors |
| tenant space |
| tenant space |
| demising walls |
| bsmts |
| stores |
| to bldg line |
| corridor walls |
| public corridors |
| walls enclosing floor service |
| floor service areas |
| bldg lobbies and atriums |
| extra if room height >1.25 x avg ceiling ht. |
| other HVAC space incl. shafts |
| mech'l penthouse |
| walls between rentable & nonrentbl |
| arcades and plazas |
| amenity spaces |
| some vertical penetrns |
| bldg service areas |
| ext. wall |

**Former GSA system**

| |
| --- |
| convectors >50% wall length |
| interior columns & bldg projns |
| demising walls |
| storage types |
| special types |
| circulation |
| office type |
| stores |
| joint use |
| corridor walls |
| public corridors |
| convectors >50% wall length |
| walls enclosing floor service |
| floor service areas |
| bldg lobbies and atriums |
| walls enclosing vertical penetrns |
| major vertical penetrns |
| bldg service areas |
| mech'l pent-house |
| ext. wall (entire) |
| open porches and docks |
| enclosed walks, mezz. & parking decks |

tenant space

**IFMA system**

| |
| --- |
| exterior wall |
| interior columns & bldg projns & convectors |
| net assignable |
| secondary circul'n |
| demising walls |
| stores |
| corridor walls |
| primary circul'n (public corridors) |
| walls enclosing floor service |
| floor service areas |
| bldg lobbies and atriums |
| bldg service areas |
| walls enclosing vertical penetrns |
| major vertical penetrns |
| loading docks |
| mech'l pent-house |
| non-dominant portion of ext. wall |
| interstitial space |

This shows a general comparison among the six commercial office space measurement systems.

**COMPARISON OF SPACE MEASUREMENT SYSTEMS**
*Source: BOMI Institute;* Facilities Planning and Project Management, *1999; Arnold, Maryland.*

## REBNY SYSTEM

The REBNY space measurement system is the most landlord-oriented of the six systems described here because it includes the most nonusable space in the rentable area billed to a tenant. From a landlord's viewpoint, this approach has an advantage over the others: the total rentable area of the floor remains constant. In addition, unless space is actually added to or deleted from a tenant's holdings, the tenant's percentage of rentable area of the floor and of the entire building remains constant. This facilitates uniform, consistent allocation of tax increases and operating costs, thereby simplifying administrative procedures.

## WDCAR SYSTEM

The WDCAR system was adopted in 1989 by the Washington, DC, Association of Realtors, and supersedes an earlier system used by the Washington, DC, Board of Realtors. It is generally complementary to BOMA's old system, but is more specific. By explicitly excluding more general building support areas, it narrows the range of core factors on unusual floors and simplifies negotiations. Its features closely parallel those of the new BOMA system.

## FORMER GSA SYSTEM

GSA is undergoing the most profound change in its relationship with its tenant agencies since its founding in 1949. As a result, the Federal Property Management Regulation (FPMR) 101-17, Temporary Regulation D-76, which included the language of GSA's space measurement system, has expired, leaving no official space measurement system of record.

GSA has also decided to endorse the new BOMA standard as the method referenced in all future leases with private-sector building owners. To embrace this new standard and reconcile it with thousands of existing agency space assignments and leases, GSA has determined that what is called *occupiable space* in its old system equates almost exactly with *floor usable area* in the new BOMA system. The only significant discrepancy concerns HVAC convectors, which are excluded from GSA's *occupiable space* definition but are included in BOMA's *floor usable area*.

## IFMA SYSTEM

The IFMA system is the most recently developed. It has been adopted as a standard of the American Society for Testing and Materials (ASTM). It is based on and complements the old BOMA system, but differs in its detail of measurement categories of particular interest to the tenant and to space planners laying out actual furniture and equipment. It is positioned to align with efforts in other countries, particularly through the International Standards Organization (ISO), where the emphasis on space measurement tends to be more tenant-oriented.

*Lawrence W. Vanderburgh, RPA, FMA, CFM, RA; BOMI Institute; Arnold, Maryland.*

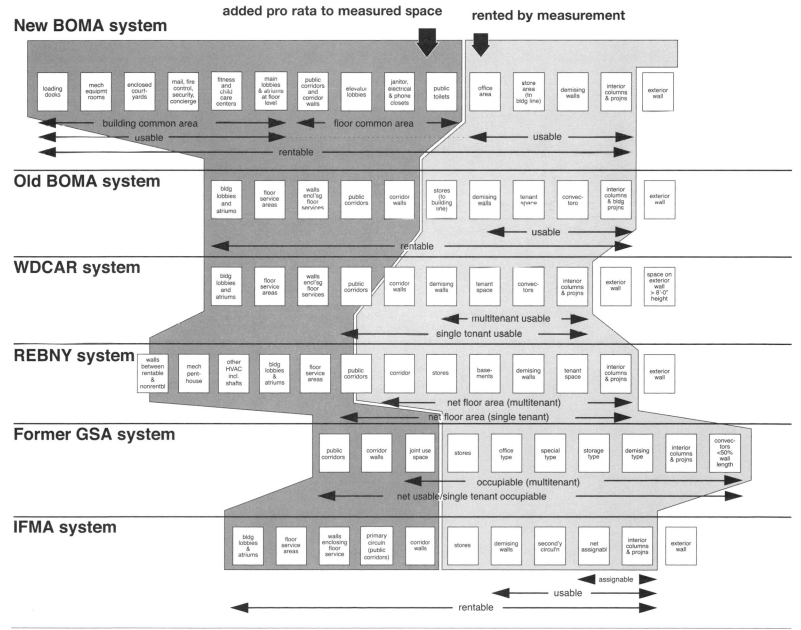

## KEY SPACE MEASUREMENT TERMS
*Source: BOMI Institute;* Facilities Planning and Project Management; *1999, Arnold, Maryland.*

# COMMERCIAL OFFICE SPACE

The design of commercial office space serves to function appropriately, extend human capability, and enhance productivity. Office space also serves as an aesthetic image of the company's mission.

## SPACE SUPPORT FOR WORK PATTERNS

Interaction and autonomy are the two key factors that must be considered together when understanding an organization's work processes. Space plans have a powerful effect on work processes. Performance is enhanced when space layouts support appropriate levels of interaction and autonomy.

## ALTERNATIVE OFFICING STRATEGIES

In response to changing business practices and the manner in which different generations work best, a variety of nontraditional strategies have evolved that limit the amount of dedicated office space assigned to each employee. These alternative strategies provide significant benefits to many businesses, including reduced office space rents, higher occupancy ratios, and reduced overhead costs. The term *alternative officing* emerged in the early 1990s to describe the ways businesses are addressing a variety of new work styles and the spaces that support them. *Telecommuting, virtual offices,* and *hoteling* are some of the terms used to describe these alternative officing strategies.

## Telecommuting

Telecommuting, which refers to employees who work from home using computers, telephones, and fax machines, has increased in popularity due to reduced overhead costs for employers, increasing demand by employees for flexible schedules, and the expense and inconvenience of commuting. Telecommuting may also be offered as an option for recruiting or retaining employees.

## Hoteling

Hoteling is a system of unassigned workspaces that are available to workers by reservation, similar to a hotel. A support person, referred to as a *concierge,* takes reservations and ensures that spaces are equipped when the employee "guest" arrives.

The Chicago office of Ernst & Young is credited with the first application of the term *hoteling,* an alternative officing concept wherein most employees do not have a permanent, assigned desk. Also referred to as *non-territorial space,* hoteling is appropriate for consulting operations where employees spend much of their time on-site at client offices.

## Virtual Officing

*Virtual officing* is an alternative work strategy that describes employees working anywhere at anytime. The use of laptop computers, cell phones, and other portable high-tech tools make the virtual office achievable for the knowledge-based worker.

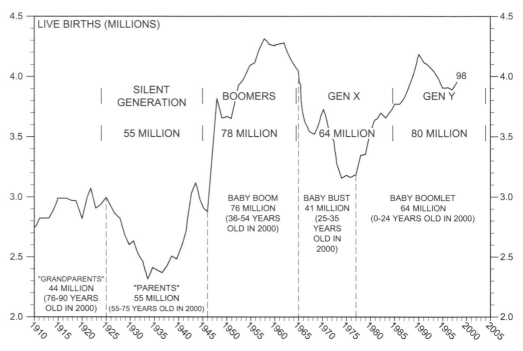

Numbers in parentheses represent the ages of the youngest and the oldest group members in 2000.

**U.S. WORKFORCE DEMOGRAPHICS**
*Source: Steelcase, Inc.; Grand Rapids, Michigan*

## WORK STYLES OF AMERICANS

|  | BOOMERS | GEN X | GEN Y |
|---|---|---|---|
| Schooling style/work style | Work alone<br>Structured<br>Unstructured, unsupervised; play with others | Group projects<br>Discussion<br>Team sports for women<br>Mothers worked<br>Computer as a tool | Care-free<br>Need it now<br>Have to be stimulated<br>Can't amuse themselves<br>Multitask |
| Thought process | Pen and paper | Personal digital assistant (PDA) | Computer |
| How they get information | Individual research | Internet | Internet; inquiry |
| What they do with information | "Power is knowledge"; can be knowledge hoarders | Share info across team and individuals | Team comes first; knowledge resides with the team |
| What they do if they don't like something | Protest, whine | Drop out, withdraw | Circumvent the rules |
| How they handle interruptions or noise | Close the door | Put on headset | Not bothered by interruptions—"just one more thing" |
| Expectations for their work environment | Office is a status symbol; need desk credenza, conference table, view | Quick access; not isolated; comfort<br><br>Community space; like to change environments, people, locations | Do not need to own space; need stimulation |
| Work hours | 8- to 12-hour days | Leave when the job is done | Flexible 24 hours |

## PATTERN OF WORK: GROUP PROCESS
*PROCESS TEAMS* TACKLE STRAIGHTFORWARD GROUP WORK THAT REQUIRES A CHANGING BALANCE OF DIFFERENT, INDEPENDENT SKILLS.

### TYPE OF SPACE LAYOUT: DEN
*OPEN AND SHARED.* GROUP SPACES WITH A MEDIUM AMOUNT OF STORAGE. COMPLEX AND CONTINUOUS SPACES INCORPORATE MEETING SPACES AND WORKSPACES.

### USE OF IT
PERSONAL COMPUTERS AND SOME SHARED SPECIALIZED GROUP EQUIPMENT.

## PATTERN OF WORK: TRANSACTIONAL KNOWLEDGE
*HIGH-PERFORMANCE TEAMS* MADE UP OF SELF-DIRECTED INDIVIDUALS WORK BOTH COLLABORATIVELY AND INDEPENDENTLY AS WORK PROCESSES ARE CONSTANTLY BEING REDESIGNED.

### TYPE OF SPACE LAYOUT: CLUB
*OPEN, CLOSED, AND SHARED.* DIVERSE, COMPLEX, AND MANIPUTABLE SPACES WITH A RANGE OF SETTINGS THAT SUPPORT A WIDE VARIETY OF TASKS.

### USE OF IT
VARIETY OF INDIVIDUAL PERSONAL COMPUTERS ON NETWORKS AND WIDESPREAD USE OF LAPTOPS.

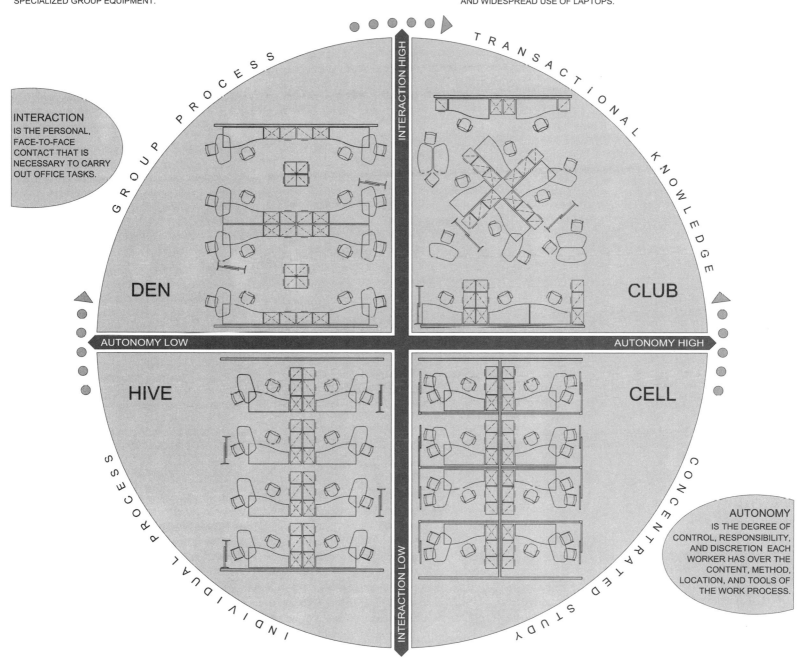

## PATTERN OF WORK: INDIVIDUAL PROCESS
*DIRECTED CONTRIBUTORS* PROCESS WORK THAT HAS BEEN BROKEN DOWN INTO DISCRETE TASKS USING INSTRUCTIONS WITH LITTLE DISCRETION.

### TYPE OF SPACE LAYOUT: HIVE
*OPEN.* CLUSTERED WORK SETTINGS WITH MINIMAL PARTITIONS, MAXIMUM FILING AND IMPOSED SIMPLE SPACE STANDARDS.

### USE OF IT
SIMPLE, "DUMB" TERMINALS OR NETWORKED PERSONAL COMPUTERS.

## PATTERN OF WORK: CONCENTRATED STUDY
*INDEPENDENT AGENTS* PERFORM ISOLATED, SELF-DIRECTED WORK.

### TYPE OF SPACE LAYOUT: CELL
*CLOSED.* PRIVATE WORKSPACES, SUCH AS ENCLOSED OFFICES OR INDIVIDUALLY USED, OPEN WORKSTATIONS WITH SCREENS OR PARTITIONS.

### USE OF IT
VARIETY OF INDIVIDUAL PERSONAL COMPUTERS ON NETWORKS AND WIDESPREAD USE OF LAPTOPS.

**SPACE SUPPORT FOR WORK PATTERNS**
*Steelcase, Inc.; Grand Rapids, Michigan; and Frank Duffy; DEGW Worldwide; New York, New York*

## SPACE USAGE IN A HOTELING ENVIRONMENT

Hoteling and other alternative workplace strategies involve the provision of spaces at ratios other than 1:5 for the occupants. This can also be referred to as the *deconstructed workplace,* in which the occupants circulate to a more tailored work environment that is appropriate to the task at hand, instead of providing an exclusive, personal space for each employee. Space is designed to accommodate multiple functions such as meetings, focused work, or equipment-centered tasks. This strategy requires a nonterritorial approach to the

usage of workspaces, and depends on successful sharing of the environment by the occupants, who are not considered permanent residents. By providing tailored work environments and implementing management techniques that support the sharing of such an environment, space efficiencies are realized through maximizing scheduling and usage of each workspace. The occupants go to the space that suits the task at hand, utilizing fewer work settings, hence requiring less leased area.

When studying potential hoteling candidates, the workforce is broken down into general job/type cate-

gories based on the tasks performed by the occupants. The population is divided into three groups: *permanent residents, semipermanent residents,* and *periodic residents.* For the semipermanent and periodic categories, the related work patterns and time spent in the office are surveyed and analyzed to develop the profile of space usage. Based on that information, ratios of the space types for each job type are developed. Usage times are averaged to provide the guidelines for reduced space quantities. Additional workspace can be provided by considering the areas traditionally considered support space, such as break rooms, conference rooms, or other workrooms.

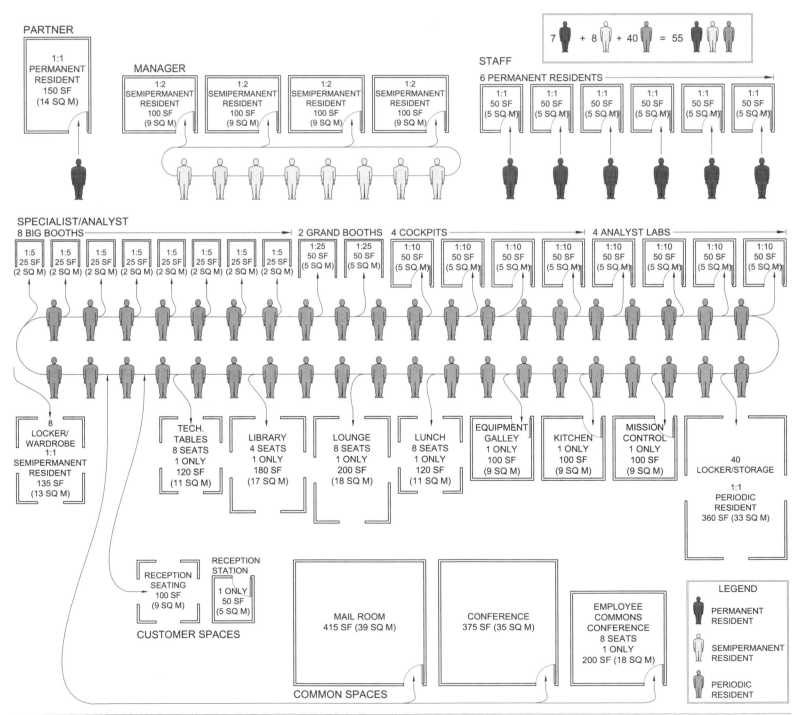

**ALTERNATIVE OFFICING STRATEGY**

## HOTELING

HOTELING MARKETPLACE

TEAM LEADER
TEAM LEADER
CORRIDOR
SERVICE COORDINATORS
TEAM LEADER
TEAM LEADER

DROP-IN DROP- DROP- DROP-IN
DROP-IN
SOLO
SOLO
SOLO
SOLO
SOLO
SOLO
SOLO

SERVICE COORDINATORS

SERVICE COORDINATORS

TEAM LEADER

TEAM LEADER

DROP- DROP-IN
IN
SOLO
SOLO
SOLO
SOLO
SOLO

PRINT / FAX

DROP- DROP-IN
IN
SOLO
SOLO

FILES

RESOURCE
RESOURCE

MAILBOX

MARKETPLACE EXCHANGE

SERVICE CENTER

COFFEE/COPY
FILES

SOLO
SOLO
SOLO
SOLO
COLLABORATIVE
SOLO
COLLABORATIVE

SOLO
DROP-IN
DROP-IN
SOLO
SOLO
COLLABORATIVE
COLLABORATIVE
COLLABORATIVE

DROP-IN
SOLO
COLLA-BORATIVE
DROP-IN
DROP-IN
DROP-IN

TEAM LEADER
TEAM LEADER
SOLO
COLLABORATIVE
COLLABORATIVE

CORRIDOR

LOCKERS
LOCKERS
LOCKERS
LOCKERS
LOCKERS
LOCKERS

CORRIDOR

CORRIDOR

### LEGEND

| | SOLO |
| | COLLABORATIVE |
| | DROP-IN |
| | TEAM LEADERS |

Hoteling applications provide one space for more than one employee. Space types are designed to support types of activities, such as solo and collaborative efforts. Spaces are not designed for individual employees; instead, lockers are provided to store employees' materials. The *marketplace exchange* is a communal casual meeting and brainstorming area.

## HOTELING STRATEGY

## WORKSTATIONS

Office planning frequently uses freestanding, less than full-height, movable system furniture panels. Both traditional and alternative officing strategies can be accommodated by systems furniture workstations. Workstations save space, provide flexibility, and generate less dust and debris than constructed walls when relocated. Although workstation panels often function as walls for visual, acoustic, and wiring purposes, they are considered furniture—not construction—and as such can be depreciated.

## CONSIDERATIONS FOR DEVELOPMENT OF WORKSTATION STANDARDS

| CONSIDERATION | STANDARD |
|---|---|
| Job Classification or Function | Workstation user and job function: executive, manager, supervisor, professional or technical, clerical |
| Work Surface Area | Number and size of work surfaces: primary, secondary, tertiary |
| Machine Use | Amount, types, and sizes of electronic equipment: VDT, PC, printer |
| Workstation Area | Amount of space to be allocated for the individual task |
| Conference Requirements | Number of guest chairs required |
| Storage Requirements | Amount and type or unit size of the material to be stored, and storage locations (under counter or overhead): letter or legal files, computer printouts, binders, bulk |
| Configuration | Configuration of work surfaces, primary orientation, and opening for the workstation |
| Wire Management | Type and location of wire management components: baseline wireway, beltline wireway, grommet locations, clips or trays |
| Accessories | Type and number of accessories: tack surfaces, pencil drawers |

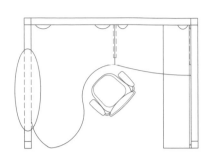

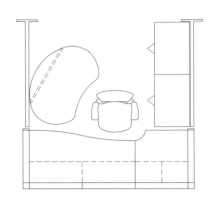

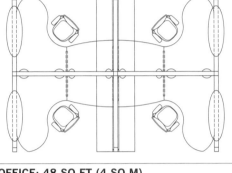

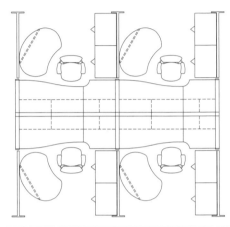

**OFFICE: 48 SQ FT (4 SQ M)**

**OFFICE: 64 SQ FT (6 SQ M)**

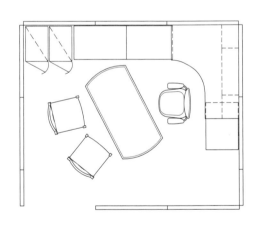

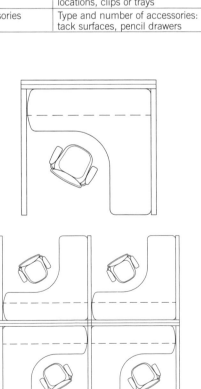

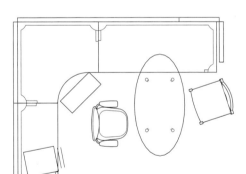

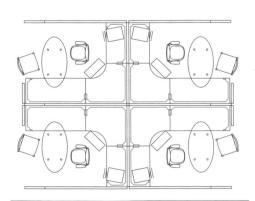

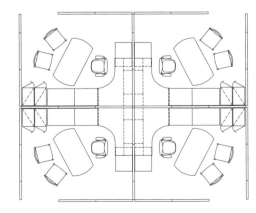

**OFFICE: 36 SQ FT (3 SQ M)**

**OFFICE: 80 SQ FT (7 SQ M)**

**OFFICE: 120 SQ FT (11 SQ M)**

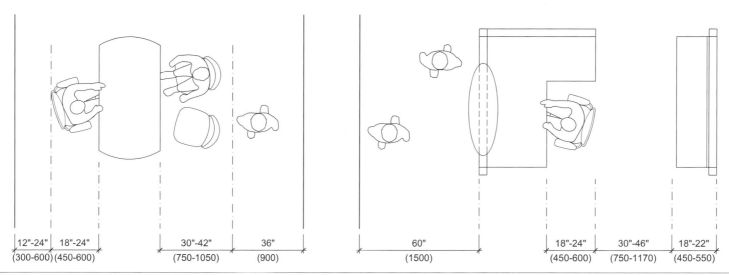

**CIRCULATION AND LAYOUT GUIDELINES**

## LIGHTING FOR OFFICE SPACES

### Lighting Levels within Workstations

The illumination that reaches a desktop in a direct lighting system is a combination of light arriving directly from the lighting fixture and indirectly via reflectance from various room surfaces. A partition not only interferes with this indirect component of light but can drastically reduce the potential direct component.

A rough approximation of the magnitude of the effect of partition height on lighting levels can be calculated using the following technique. (Note: Do not use this technique for total direct lighting systems unless several luminaires directly contribute light to the cubicle.)

1. Use the coefficient of utilization (CU) table for the fixture to calculate the average illuminance at the top of the partitions. Use the distance from the luminaires to the top of the partitions as the cavity height, and use actual reflectance values, except for the floor; use 0 for the floor cavity reflectance.
2. Determine the transfer coefficient of a virtual ceiling luminaire ("Transfer Coefficients" table). Use the distance from the top of the partition to the desktop as the cavity height. Use the cubicle's partition reflectance as the wall reflectance, and use the effective ceiling cavity reflectance of the actual ceiling cavity above the top of the partitions.
3. Multiply the illuminance from the first step (at the top of the partitions) by the transfer coefficient to find the approximate average illuminance at the desktop.

### Illumination Criteria

The lighting levels given are average figures, and assume an empty room.

- *Offices (low to moderate computer use):* 40 to 60 fc (400 to 600 lux), with task lighting as required.
- *Offices (moderate to high computer use):* 20 to 40 fc (200 to 400 lux), with task lighting as required.
- *Offices (paper-based tasks only):* 50 to 75 fc (500 to 750 lux), with task lighting at work locations to

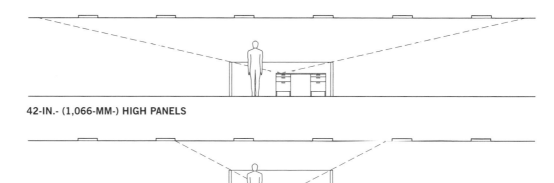

**42-IN.- (1,066-MM-) HIGH PANELS**

**60-IN.- (1,524-MM-) HIGH PANELS**

**PANEL HEIGHT COMPARISON**

provide higher lighting levels as required for specific tasks of high difficulty.
- *Conference and meeting rooms:* 30 to 50 fc (300 to 500 lux), with dimming control capabilities when appropriate.
- *Lobbies and hallways:* 10 to 20 fc (100 to 200 lux).Visual Comfort Probability (VCP) is only useful for comparing direct (lensed troffer) lighting systems. A minimum of 70 fc (700 lux) is recommended. (Note that high VCP does not guarantee visual comfort.)

## LIGHTING SYSTEM ALTERNATIVES

The following lighting systems, which are appropriate for use in office spaces, use fluorescent sources:

- *Lensed systems* provide adequate basic lighting at the lowest cost, are the easiest to install, and tend to be the most efficient. Many lensed systems exhibit higher-angle (greater than 55°) glare and prove problematic for computer-based offices.
- *Parabolic louvered systems* are low brightness and better for larger rooms where computer work is

undertaken. Supplemental lighting for walls is important when using parabolic systems to avoid an overly dim perimeter appearance.
- *Indirect lighting systems,* which provide a comfortable light, must be appropriately spaced to avoid excessively nonuniform brightness on the ceiling. They generally require ceilings of at least 8 ft (2,440 mm) to be feasible, and the use of supplemental task and/or accent lighting. *Direct/indirect lighting systems* must be appropriately spaced and offer a good balance between comfort and efficiency. They require ceilings of at least 8 ft (2,440 mm) to be feasible, and can be more costly than other lighting systems.

*Ted Kollaja, AIA; lauckgroup; Dallas, Texas*
*Shawn Parks; Rhode Island School of Design; Providence, Rhode Island*
*Randy J. Burkett, FIALD, IES, LC; Burkett Lighting Design, Inc.; St. Louis, Missouri*
*Jim Johnson; Wrightson, Johnson, Haddon & Williams, Inc.; Dallas, Texas*

# RETAIL

## DESIGN CRITERIA

Retail design distinguishes itself from other types of interiors because design decisions are made primarily on the basis of generating sales. Successful merchandising creates a cohesive design statement that complements the merchandise and the brand image of the retailer. Presenting merchandise in an appealing manner is imperative.

Understanding the buying behavior and demographics of the targeted shopper, the merchandise category (for example, fashion as opposed to commodity items), and the requirements of the different types of retail space and retail lighting—both general space lighting and display lighting—are key components in successful retail design.

## BUYING BEHAVIORS

Buying behaviors are essentially planned or impulse:

- Most impulse purchases can be categorized as emotion-based or a form of entertainment. Impulse buyers enjoy the experience of shopping perhaps as much as they do the goods they purchase. Goods appropriate for impulse buying must be exposed to potential customers and be within easy reach for examination and selection.
- Shoppers who plan purchases may not even enjoy shopping. Because planned-purchase shoppers are often in a hurry, goods appropriate for planned purchases must be easy to find. Efficient circulation, signage, and adequate lighting are important for the shoppers who plan their purchases.

## TYPES OF RETAIL SPACES

The three dominant types of retail spaces in the United States are *shopping malls* or *centers, department stores,* and *boutique* and *specialty retail stores.*

### Shopping Malls or Centers

Visiting shopping malls has become an American pastime. They are centers of relaxation and entertainment, as well as the most successful sites of sales in the country. Shopping centers rely on excitement, often theatrics, to attract regular and seasonal consumers. Malls often incorporate services and entertainment venues to encourage a more leisurely—and prolonged—stay.

### Department Stores

Department stores rely on circulation patterns and signage to draw customers through their store. Hard-flooring aisles, referred to as "hard aisles," provide a primary circulation path. Displays are typically located on carpeted areas to invite the customer to linger and browse, while enjoying the comfort underfoot. Continuity is required throughout the department store, even though each department may be designed separately to give the appearance of a series of boutiques.

The entry floor in department stores is often leased to vendors with high-markup products, such as cosmetics and jewelry. These salespeople receive a commission on each sale made.

### Boutiques and Specialty Retail Stores

Specialty stores require an up-to-date design image to attract consumers. Their renovation cycles and budgets are commonly far greater than those of shopping malls or department stores. These spaces rely heavily on window displays, interior finishes, lighting, and acoustics (typically, background music) to entice customers to enter the space. Salespeople are often on commission in boutiques and specialty retail stores.

## FIXTURE PLACEMENT

In order to effectively design a merchandising fixture layout, the designer must understand the retailer's merchandise capacity and volume requirements. Fixtures that are placed too close together can make it difficult to for the shopper to review the merchandise and may not comply with ADA requirements. Aisles between or around fixtures should be not less than 36 in. (1,100 mm), including hanger width.

## GENERAL SPACE LIGHTING

The lighting levels given here are average figures, and assume an empty room:

- *Grocery store, general light:* 70 to 90 fc (700 to 900 lux), which will result in average center-of-aisle illumination of 50 fc (500 lux), assuming 72 in. (1,830 mm) shelf heights.
- *Wholesale merchandise:* 30 to 50 fc (300 to 500 lux), with display lighting added as needed. For spaces with warehouse-style shelving, empty-room assumptions are not valid; and the 30 to 50 fc (300 to 500 lux) in aisles must account for shadows created by high shelving.
- *General merchandise:* 40 to 60 fc (400 to 600 lux), with display lighting added at key locations to provide 80 to 120 fc (800 to 1,200 lux) for secondary merchandise displays and 200 to 300 fc (2,000 to 3,000 lux) for primary displays.
- *Boutique and specialty retail stores:* 20 to 30 fc (200 to 300 lux) for general lighting. Display lighting is added throughout to provide 60 to 90 fc (600 to 900 lux) for most merchandise and 150 to 300 fc (1,500 to 3,000 lux) for primary displays.
- *Back-of-house storage and stock areas:* 10 to 20 fc (100 to 200 lux), with shadowing impact of high shelving taken into account.

## COLOR RENDERING INDEX (CRI) FOR DISPLAY LIGHTING

| | |
|---|---|
| Wholesale and grocery | 3,500 or 4,100K > 70 CRI |
| Boutique/specialty | 3,000 or 3,500K > 80 CRI |
| General merchandise | 3,500 or 4,100K > 70 CRI |
| Jewelry, art | 3,000 or 5,000K > 90 CRI |

CRI characteristics are used in the selection of retail light fixtures. See Color Plate C-11 for CRI characteristics for light, to use in the selection of light fixtures.

## LIGHTING POWER DENSITY

| | |
|---|---|
| Grocery | 1.4–2.0 watts/sq ft (15–21.5 watts/sq m) |
| Wholesale | 1.0–1.4 watts/sq ft (10.7–15 watts/sq m) |
| General merchandise | 1.2–1.7 watts/sq ft (12.9–18.2 watts/sq m) |
| Department store | 2.0–2.8 watts/sq ft (21.5–30 watts/sq m) |
| Specialty retail | 1.8–3.5 watts/sq ft (19.3–37.6 watts/sq m) |
| Jewelry, china | 2.0–4.5 watts/sq ft (21.5–48.4 watts/sq m) |

Listed are approximate design targets for whole stores, including back-of-house. These targets are based on HID (high-intensity discharge) systems and/or T-8/compact fluorescent lamps with electronic high-frequency ballasts, including display lights.

## DISPLAY LIGHTING

*Track lighting* is popular because of its adjustablility and commonly used display lighting system. Use halogen, compact fluorescent, or low-wattage high-intensity discharge (HID) display luminaires.

*Recessed display lights* are not as flexible as track lights but are concealed from view and generally possess better glare control. This category includes adjustable accent lights and wallwashers. Sources include halogen, low-wattage high-intensity discharge (HID), and compact fluorescent.

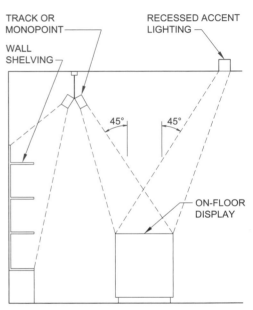

**CEILING LIGHT FIXTURES**
The maximum angle of elevation for lighting is 45°, except when walls are being lighted.

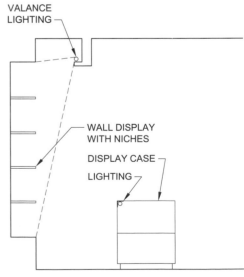

**CEILING AND DISPLAY CASE LIGHT FIXTURES**
Use wallwashers or accent lighting for walls and shelves; track lights or monopoints for floor displays; and valances in wall niches. Display case lighting is suitable for many applications, from jewelry cases to meat and produce counters.

**TYPICAL DISPLAY LIGHTING**

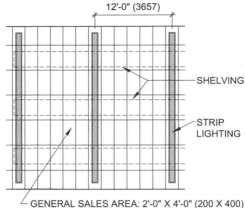

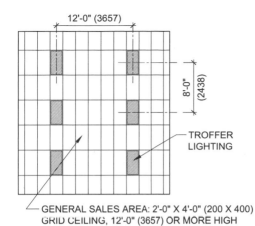

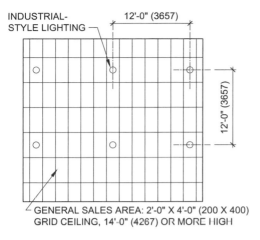

**STRIP LIGHTS/STRIP TROUGH LIGHTS**
Strip lights and strip trough lights are common in large retail grocery stores and many mass merchandise stores. This layout produces 60 to 80 fc (600 to 800 lux) in an empty room using F96T8 lamps in a strip light or open trough in continuous rows at 1.15 watts/sq ft (12.3 watts/sq m). Lights usually run perpendicular to shelving to allow rearrangement, but parallel lighting is preferable when shelves are fixed.

**TROFFER LIGHTING**
Troffers in lay-in ceilings are common in the discount retail industry and serve as general-purpose lighting for hardware and general merchandise. The layout above produces 60 to 70 fc (600 to 700 lux) in an empty room using four F32T8 lamps in a lensed or parabolic luminaire at 1.15 watts/sq ft. With high-light-level ballasts, this arrangement produces 80 to 100 fc (800 to 1,000 lux) at 1.58 watts/sq ft.

**INDUSTRIAL-STYLE LIGHTING**
Industrial-style lights are commonly used for lighting warehouse-style discount stores. The layout shown at left produces 30 to 40 fc (300 to 400 lux) in an empty room using one 100-watt metal halide lamp in an industrial-style luminaire at 0.85 watts/sq ft. Using a 150-watt metal halide lamp, the lighting level is about 40 to 60 fc (400 to 600 lux) at 1.27 watts/sq ft (13.6 watts/sq m).

**REFLECTED CEILING PLANS FOR WHOLESALE, GROCERY, AND MERCHANDISE STORES**

## OTHER DISPLAY LIGHTING TYPES

*Monopoint or canopy-mounted accent lights* are adjustable lights installed at fixed locations.

*Valance lighting* is used for merchandise displays along a store's perimeter or confined niche. Linear T-8 and T-5 fluorescent lamps work best for the application from both a color and efficiency standpoint.

*Display case lighting* is similar to valance lighting except the light is built into the display cases to illuminate the task. Linear fluorescent, compact fluorescent, or low-voltage incandescent or tungsten halogen lamps are used. Fiber-optic end-lighting systems may be useful in certain situations, especially where heat and space are primary considerations. Display case lighting is suitable for many applications, from jewelry cases to meat and produce counters.

### Dressing Rooms

Good lighting helps sell clothing. For higher-quality stores, provide attractive light with diffuse illumination of the customer; avoid downlights and track lighting without supplemental wallwashing. In lower-cost and trendy stores, place the emphasis on fixture style and durability.

### Store Windows

Use high-wattage track lighting and/or low-voltage accent lighting. Run track vertically along the window sides, across the top of the window, and possibly along the bottom of the window as well. Halogen, compact fluorescent, and HID are all acceptable source types for window display.

### Other Specific Applications

Use high-color-rendering or special-purpose fluorescent lamps for meat cases, fabrics, and similar merchandise with special color or visual discrimination needs. For fine jewelry, consider a high CRI, high-color-temperature compact fluorescent lamps, high-color-rendering metal halide lamps, and/or blue-filtered halogen lamps to achieve a flattering 4,100 to 5,000K.

*Janis Berglas; White Plains, New York*
*Randy J. Burkett, FIALD, IES, LC; Burkett Lighting Design, Inc.; St. Louis, Missouri*

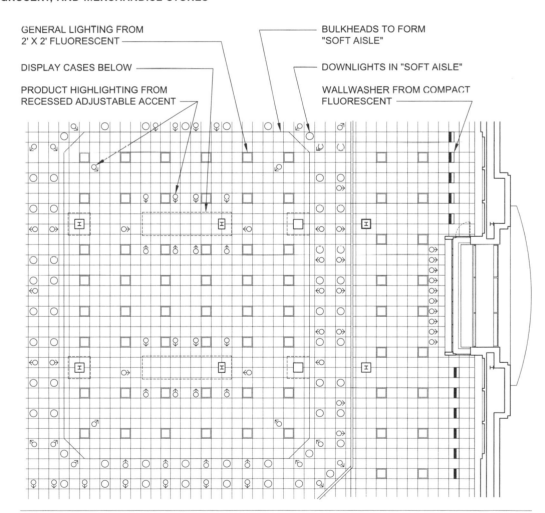

**TYPICAL DEPARTMENT STORE LIGHTING—REFLECTED CEILING PLAN**

# CONFERENCE AND TRAINING CENTERS

Today's corporate conference centers offer dedicated meeting facilities, which foster the quick exchange of information and ideas, either in person or by video-conferencing or teleconferencing. Conference centers provide spaces for meetings, presentations, and training functions in a distraction-free environment. Facilities range from nonresidential conference centers to residential conference centers, which include guest rooms and amenities, as well as conference and meeting spaces.

Training centers are designed for the dissemination and presentation of information and may more closely resemble classroom and learning facilities. Corporate training was developed in the United States in the latter half of the twentieth century. As service-oriented businesses became increasingly competitive, corporate training emerged as a way of attracting and maintaining talented employees. Today, many businesses are reliant on skilled workers, and corporate training is seen as an essential component of remaining competitive in business.

Conference center trends include:
• Rapidly changing business requirements
• Increasing workplace diversity
• Technology advancements
• Globalization and overseas competition

Conference and training center facilities have evolved to address current business strategies and programs. Technology has impacted conference and training programs and facility requirements. Videoconferencing, teleconferencing, wireless communications, and computer usage and programs will continue to develop in the near future; therefore, flexibility and planning for future needs should be incorporated into the conference center facility.

## CONFERENCE CENTER TYPES

Information contained within this section is for general guideline purposes; each facility is unique and may have different programs and fit-up requirements.

### Executive Conference Centers

Executive conference centers typically combine conference and lodging facilities in an independent or hotel-based center. This type of facility is geared toward mid- and upper-level management attendees. Various meeting room sizes accommodate small or large groups for training or management programs. High-end food service and other services support conference and guest needs. Guest rooms are typically larger than standard and are usually provided with work areas and technologically advanced facilities, including computer access, fax, and multiple telephone lines. Amenities such as fitness centers may be included in the facility.

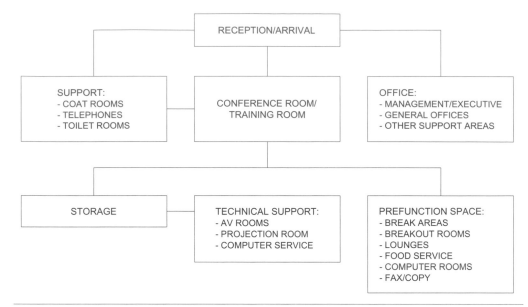

**CONFERENCE AND TRAINING CENTERS**

Resort conference centers combine executive-level services and facilities with additional recreation or special interest programs. Facilities are similar to executive conference centers.

### Corporate Conference and Training Centers

Corporate conference and training centers feature conferencing facilities, as well as employee training areas, for corporate use. Conference and training room types and sizes vary with the individual program requirements.

Corporate conference centers generally provide guest rooms to accommodate extended stays for conference attendees and trainees. Typically, corporate education center guest rooms are furnished with work areas and technologically advanced facilities, including computer access, fax, multiple telephone lines and features, closed-circuit television, and other amenities to support conference and training programs. Amenities such as fitness or recreation areas may be included in the facility.

### University Education Centers

University education centers serve a growing market of programs sponsored by universities. Many university education centers offer guest rooms and hotel-like support services.

Executive education centers are often physically connected to the educational facilities that they serve. Executive education centers are similar to conference centers, but are typically smaller in scale and include fewer amenities than executive conference centers.

Conference and executive education rooms average 25% to 35% of a residential university education center.

Ancillary areas include computer rooms for training and as resource areas; office areas for academic use; business center with computer, fax, copier, and other equipment; research areas; and other spaces required to support the university's programs.

Food service facilities may include faculty dining, conference dining, cafeteria-style student dining, and catering services. Conference dining may be incorporated into the classroom area.

Guest rooms for university education centers are typically slightly smaller than corporate conference center guest rooms, depending on the facility type. Levels of amenities vary, but typically include a private bathroom, work area and computer space, good lighting, lounge seating, and other selected appointments.

Continuing education centers provide teaching facilities for in-house and long-distance learning programs. These centers may offer guest rooms, which are typically less luxurious than their executive or corporate center counterparts. The majority of the space is dedicated to conference and classroom space.

University hotel and conference centers serve university-related conference and lodging needs, and may be available for rental for private functions. Facilities are similar to hotels and corporate conference centers.

## Nonresidential Conference Centers

Nonresidential conference centers, generally located in metropolitan areas, serve corporate and noncorporate users. Nonresidential conference center facilities are similar to corporate conference centers, but do not include guest rooms for overnight stays. These centers are used for day and evening functions.

Food service is typically limited to refreshments and catered food. Warming kitchens and pantries are preferred in lieu of major preparation kitchens. Conveniently located local lodging, parking, dining, and other amenities are desirable.

For nonresidential conference centers, the ratio of conference and assembly space is approximately half of the total gross area for the facility.

## CONFERENCE CENTER PROGRAM

A facility program should be developed in conjunction with the user/owner to determine the proposed requirements for the conference center. The program should identify all room types, sizes, uses, and fit-up requirements, including special construction, mechanical systems, electrical systems, plumbing systems, structural, life safety, acoustical, and other specialty requirements affecting interior design and construction.

## CONFERENCE CENTER PLANNING CRITERIA

A conference center program should be developed to determine all facility requirements for the project. An analysis of room types, capacity, layout, usage, and proposed function of each room will assist in the development of an efficient plan.

Issues to review when developing a program for a conference center include, but are not limited to:

- Type of conference center and image proposed
- Adjacencies required
- Traffic flow/circulation
- Lobby/reception area
- Conference and training programs and room types required
- Conference room requirements
- Training room requirements
- Audiovisual and other presentation requirements
- Technology requirements
- Lounge/breakout areas
- Food service types and scope
- Guest room quantity and type
- Fitness and recreation
- Administrative requirements
- Storage needs
- Office area requirements
- Laundry

All rooms and areas should be defined within the conference center program. Conference, amphitheater, and auditorium spaces should be easy to reach from the lobby. Review adjacencies to determine the best means of circulation and layout when planning the conference center.

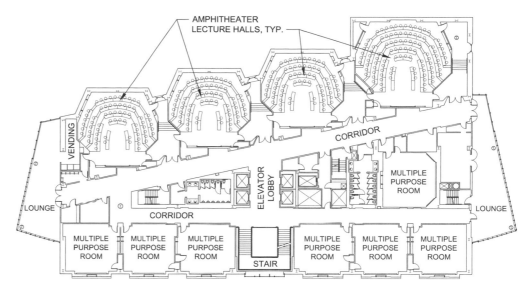

**MULTIPURPOSE ROOMS AND AMPHITHEATERS**

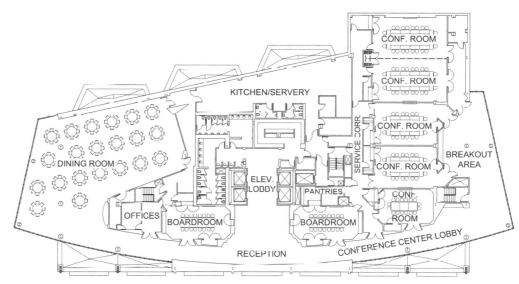

**CONFERENCE CENTER**

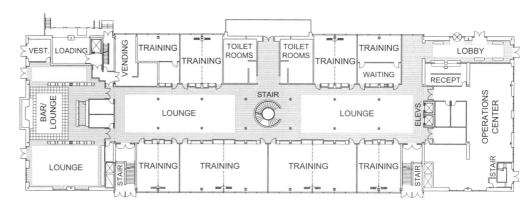

**TRAINING CENTER**

**PROTOTYPICAL CONFERENCE CENTERS AND TRAINING FACILITIES**
*Source: Lohan Caprile Goettsch Architects; Chicago, Illinois*

## CONFERENCE ROOM DESIGN

Considerations for conference room design include room usage, room size and shape, accessibility, capacity, furniture configuration, privacy and sound attenuation, need for windows/vision panels in doors, movable partitions, HVAC requirements, lighting and controls, accessories, and equipment.

Furniture, materials, and finishes should be appropriate to the quality level of the facility and should be durable and easy to maintain. Casework, such as credenzas, should be adequate to store products frequently used in the conference room.

## CONFERENCE ROOM TYPES

Most conference rooms are planned for sophisticated audiovisual presentations, as well as for teleconferencing capabilities. Room size and configuration are critical for the success of certain types of presentations. Consult with equipment manufacturers regarding critical dimensions.

- *Auditorium:* Large capacity of 150 or more, used for formal presentations, theater-type seating arrangement, sloped floor.
- *Amphitheater:* Tiered floor, built-in work surfaces, rounded, horseshoelike seating arrangement.
- *Ballroom:* Large-capacity meeting room and banquet room. Locate prefunction areas adjacent.
- *Boardroom:* Upgraded conference room, seating capacity between 16 and 24, 40 sq ft (4 sq m) per seat, high levels of finishes and furniture. Used by corporate board members; favored by businesses where status is important.
- *Large conference room:* Used for more formal presentations requiring little audience participation. Greater than 1,500 sq ft (139 sq m); room depth generally exceeds 50 ft (15m). May be divided with movable partitions.
- *Medium conference room:* Typically, 1,000 to 1,500 sq ft (93 to 139 sq m), and used for interactive group programs. This is one of the most popular sized conference rooms, and may be divided with movable partitions.
- *Small conference room:* Typically, 300 to 1,000 sq ft (28 to 93 sq m), and used for interactive group programs and small discussion groups. Informal conference areas are generally furnished with flexible, mobile furniture, ranging from modular tables and chairs to lounge-type seating.
- *Breakout room:* Small discussion area or informal meeting space.
- *Classroom/training room:* Varies in size, but generally between 300 and 800 sq ft (28 and 74 sq m).
- *Computer training room:* Workstation configuration requires 30 to 40 sq ft (3 to 4 sq m) per person.
- *Intensive strategy rooms:* Smaller, specialty-use rooms, with high-technology requirements and computer capability.

## EXECUTIVE CONFERENCE CENTER CONCEPTUAL REQUIREMENTS

| PROJECT ASPECT | AIMS AND REQUIREMENTS |
| --- | --- |
| Guest Rooms | Design the rooms for single occupancy during the week. Plan for some double occupancy for the weekend recreational market. Rooms should be similar in feel to first-class hotel rooms, but with special attention to the work area and such work amenities as phone and computer capability; consider the need for common areas. |
| Lobby | Create character that reinforces the image of the business meeting setting; clearly organize circulation so that visitors can easily locate conference wing, dining, and banquet areas. |
| Restaurants | Design the conference dining room to allow for expected meeting capacity plus 10%; include a specialty restaurant oriented to the local business community; add a small gourmet restaurant only if a market niche is available locally; lobby lounge should have capability to divide for small private receptions. |
| Conference Rooms | Provide a multipurpose conference room (flat-floored auditorium or junior ballroom) for full capacity; ballroom or banquet room for special meal functions; amphitheater. Principal focus is 1,000 sq ft (93 sq m) and larger conference rooms and large number of breakout rooms. |
| Conference Support | Include a large prefunction room near the principal conference room and smaller break areas near each group of meeting rooms; provide access to outdoor terraces, if possible; locate conference services at the conference core; determine need for high-level audiovisual, graphics, and other systems. |
| Recreation | Provide an indoor pool (outdoor if weather permits), racquetball courts, exercise and aerobics rooms, lockers, and a sauna. |

*Source: Richard H. Penner; Conference Center Planning and Design; New York: Watson-Guptill Publications; 1991.*

## CORPORATE CONFERENCE CENTER CONCEPTUAL REQUIREMENTS

| PROJECT ASPECT | AIMS AND REQUIREMENTS |
| --- | --- |
| Guest Rooms | Design the rooms primarily for single occupancy, except in entry-level training centers, where double rooms may be anticipated; rooms require moderate- to high-level furnishings and amenities; minimum per-room area of 250 sq ft (23.2 sq m); provide common area among the guest rooms. |
| Lobby | Create residential-scale space with the potential to establish image for the center; front desk should be understated; provide only limited seating, as most lounge and social spaces are located elsewhere. |
| Restaurants | Provide conference dining room for full capacity; consider a second restaurant if center has more than 300 rooms; provide social lounge, game room, library, or reading room, and if corporate policy permits, pub or entertainment lounge. |
| Conference Rooms | Provide auditorium or banquet room for full capacity; amphitheaters for management development centers should seat up to 100; provide multiple rear-projection conference rooms, breakouts, and specialized training to meet corporate requirements (computers, telecommunications, etc.). |
| Conference Support | Provide relatively large prefunction room, coffee break room, and flow areas to promote corporate image and opportunities for informal interchange; provide high amounts of audiovisual support, including rear-screen projection; decide whether trainers will be housed at the property, which might add 5,000 sq ft (465 sq m) or more. |
| Recreation | Provide an indoor pool (outdoor if climate allows), racquetball courts, exercise/aerobics areas, game room and lounge; include team sports facilities such as a gym. |

*Source: Richard H. Penner; Conference Center Planning and Design; New York: Watson-Guptill Publications; 1991.*

## UNIVERSITY CONFERENCE CENTER CONCEPTUAL REQUIREMENTS

| PROJECT ASPECT | AIMS AND REQUIREMENTS |
| --- | --- |
| Guest Rooms | Provide designs for single occupancy (double occupancy at campus hotels and continuing education centers); rooms should be of average size; include case discussion room on every floor. |
| Lobby | Create special space to reinforce image of university; separate circulation to faculty club or other nonconference functions; provide seating area for informal gathering. |
| Restaurants | Provide single conference dining room with buffet or servery design and with private dining alcoves; design discrete bar areas if required; include additional seating areas for spontaneous meetings. |
| Conference Rooms | Include 50 person-capacity amphitheaters for case study curricula; provide additional generic classrooms and numerous breakout rooms; add computer classroom if required. |
| Conference Support | Provide single conference foyer convenient to all rooms; include additional seating; equip with standard audio/visual systems. |
| Recreation | Provide small fitness center; other sports facilities are elsewhere on campus. |

*Source: Richard H. Penner; Conference Center Planning and Design; New York: Watson-Guptill Publications; 1991.*

## CONFERENCE ROOM LAYOUTS

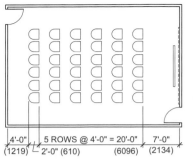

**THEATER-STYLE SEATING**

4'-0" (1219)   2'-0" (610)   5 ROWS @ 4'-0" = 20'-0" (6096)   7'-0" (2134)

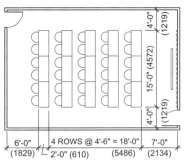

**CLASSROOM LAYOUT**

6'-0" (1829)   2'-0" (610)   4 ROWS @ 4'-6" = 18'-0" (5486)   7'-0" (2134)

15'-0" (4572)   4'-0" (1219)   4'-0" (1219)

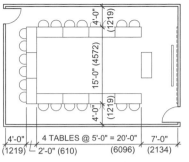

**U-SHAPED TABLE ARRANGEMENT**

4'-0" (1219)   2'-0" (610)   4 TABLES @ 5'-0" = 20'-0" (6096)   7'-0" (2134)

15'-0" (4572)   4'-0" (1219)   4'-0" (1219)

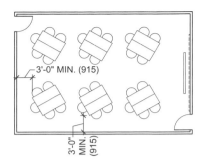

**CLUSTER TABLE ARRANGEMENT**

3'-0" MIN. (915)   3'-0" MIN. (915)

Theater-style seating offers the maximum seating capacity. Classroom, U-shaped, and cluster layouts with tables provide similar seating capacity, but are used for various presentation and teaching programs. Seating capacities vary with room dimensions and layout.

## CONFERENCE ROOM LAYOUTS
*Source: Richard H. Penner, Conference Center Planning and Design; New York: Watson-Guptill Publications, 1991.*

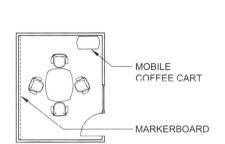

MOBILE COFFEE CART

MARKERBOARD

**CONFERENCE ROOM FOR 4: 150 SQ FT (14 SQ M)**

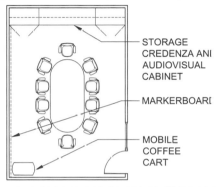

STORAGE CREDENZA ANI AUDIOVISUAL CABINET

MARKERBOARI

MOBILE COFFEE CART

**CONFERENCE ROOM FOR 10: 350 SQ FT (33 SQ M)**

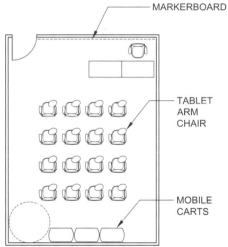

MARKERBOARD

TABLET ARM CHAIR

MOBILE CARTS

**TRAINING ROOM: 675 SQ FT (63 SQ M)**

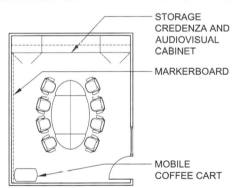

STORAGE CREDENZA AND AUDIOVISUAL CABINET

MARKERBOARD

MOBILE COFFEE CART

**CONFERENCE ROOM FOR 8: 300 SQ FT (28 SQ M)**

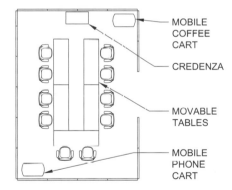

MOBILE COFFEE CART

CREDENZA

MOVABLE TABLES

MOBILE PHONE CART

**U-SHAPED TABLE; CONFERENCE ROOM FOR 10: 350 SQ FT (33 SQ M)**

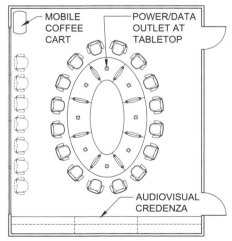

MOBILE COFFEE CART

POWER/DATA OUTLET AT TABLETOP

AUDIOVISUAL CREDENZA

**CONFERENCE ROOM FOR 16: 750 SQ FT (70 SQ M)**

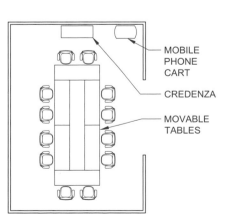

MOBILE PHONE CART

CREDENZA

MOVABLE TABLES

**CONFERENCE ROOM FOR 12: 450 SQ FT (42 SQ M)**

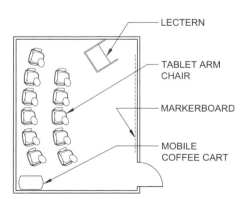

LECTERN

TABLET ARM CHAIR

MARKERBOARD

MOBILE COFFEE CART

**TRAINING ROOM: 275 SQ FT (26 SQ M)**

**CONFERENCE ROOM LAYOUT OPTIONS** *Source: lauckgroup; Dallas, Texas*

**TRAINING ROOM LAYOUT OPTIONS**
*Source: lauckgroup; Dallas, Texas*

## COMPUTER TRAINING ROOM LAYOUTS

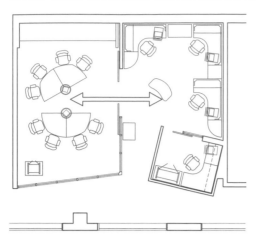

Plan demonstrates a combination of a flexible teaming environment that integrates conferencing and workspace for cross-functional teams.

### TEAMING AND CONFERENCE ENVIRONMENT
*Source: lauckgroup; Dallas, Texas*

## CONFERENCE ROOM SEATING STANDARDS*

| | THEATER STYLE EXECUTIVE SETUP[1] | THEATER STYLE MAXIMUM SETUP[2] | CLASSROOM STYLE EXECUTIVE SETUP | MAXIMUM SETUP | HOLLOW SQUARE SETUP | U-SHAPED SETUP | CONFERENCE SETUP | BANQUET SETUP |
|---|---|---|---|---|---|---|---|---|
| Ballroom | 14 (1.3) | 11 (1.0) | 22 (2.0) | 18 (1.7) | N/A | N/A | N/A | 14 (1.3) |
| Large Conference | 16 (1.5) | 13 (1.2) | 24 (2.2) | 20 (1.9) | 40–45 (3.7–4.2) | 50–55 (4.7–5.1) | N/A | 14 (1.3) |
| Medium Conference | 18 (1.7) | 15 (1.4) | 26 (2.4) | 22 (2.0) | 34 (3.2) | 42 (3.9) | 40 (3.7) | N/A |
| Small Conference | 20 (1.9) | 15 (1.4) | 30 (2.8) | 24 (2.2) | 32 (3.0) | 38 (3.5) | 35 (3.3) | N/A |
| Breakout Room | N/A | N/A | N/A | N/A | N/A | N/A | 25 (2.3) | N/A |
| Boardroom | N/A | N/A | N/A | N/A | 32 (3.0) | N/A | 40 (3.7) | N/A |
| Amphitheater | N/A | N/A | 25 (2.3) | N/A | N/A | N/A | N/A | N/A |

*Figures represent optimum square feet (square meters) per person.
[1]Executive setup includes executive conference chairs and 24- to 30-in.- (610- to 760-mm-) wide tables.
[2]Maximum setup includes stacking banquet chairs and 18-in.- (457-mm-) wide tables.
*Source: Richard H. Penner,* Conference Center Planning and Design; *New York: Watson-Guptill Publications, 1991, p 213.*

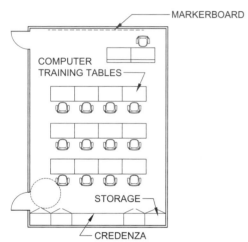

COMPUTER TRAINING: 725 SQ FT (67 SQ M)

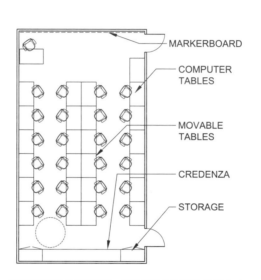

COMPUTER TRAINING—PERIMETER WORK AREAS: 800 SQ FT (74 SQ M)

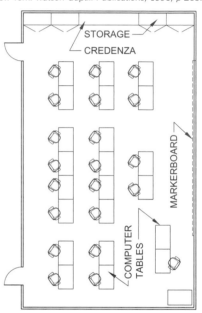

COMPUTER TRAINING FOR 20: 1,410 SQ FT (131 SQ M)

**COMPUTER TRAINING ROOM LAYOUT OPTIONS** *Source: lauckgroup; Dallas, Texas*

## VIDEOCONFERENCE ROOM LAYOUTS

### VIDEO CONFERENCE ROOM SIZES

| CAPACITY | ROOM SIZE FT (MM) | APPLICATIONS |
|---|---|---|
| 1–2 | Workstation or desk | Informal meetings |
| | | Interviews |
| | | Research |
| | | Development |
| 2–3 | 9 × 12 (2,745 × 3,660) | General business meetings |
| | | Interviews |
| | | Progress meetings |
| 3–5 | 11 × 16 (3,350 × 4,880) | General business meetings |
| | | New business development |
| | | Group sales meetings |
| | | Product demonstrations |
| 6–8 | 15 × 17 (4,570 × 5,180) | General business meetings |
| | | Branch site meetings |
| | | Capabilities demonstrations |

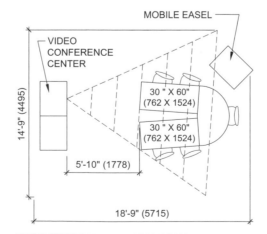

SMALL VIDEOCONFERENCING ROOM
*Source: Bretford Manufacturing, Inc.; Franklin Park, Illinois*

VIDEOCONFERENCING FOR 18: 600 SQ FT (56 SQ M)
*Source: lauckgroup; Dallas, Texas*

**VIDEOCONFERENCE ROOMS**

## FURNITURE AND CASE GOODS

Conference and training room furniture types range from traditional tables and chairs to more informal arrangements. Current trends in informal meeting rooms have influenced furniture types, including modular tables for flexible arrangements, special table sizes and shapes, lounge seating with attached tablet arms for use with laptop computers, and mobile accessories such as presentation boards and easels. Some manufacturers have developed conference modules within their systems furniture products, integrating conference spaces to open office areas.

## CONFERENCE ROOM SEATING

Seating comfort for meetings of long duration is critical. Conference room seating types may differ depending on the type of room and function. A related or compatible series of seating will unify the image of the conference facility. Consider the following when selecting seating for conferences:

- *Ergonomics* should be considered when selecting seating for a conference center. Adjustments for seat height, seat tilt, back height and positions, tilt posture controls, and arms are desirable, depending on the type of chair under consideration.
- *Upholstered seat and back cushions* should be firm and comfortable.
- *Chair shape and adjustment features* should accommodate the contours of the body.
- *Streamlined, lightweight chairs* allow for easier movement.
- *Five casters,* minimum, on a chair are desirable for stability. Caster type should be appropriate for the floor material used.
- *Upholstery selection* should reflect chair usage: leather is a high-end material; wool and wool/natural fiber blends wear well and reduce static electricity; polyester and other synthetic fiber blends are suitable for frequent use and durability. Some chairs have an open-weave upholstery fabric, which allows air circulation and provides a streamlined appearance.

Executive or corporate conference rooms may have mid- or high-back upholstered executive chairs on casters; training rooms may have task chairs or tablet armchairs; and typical conference rooms may have low-back upholstered swivel/tilt chairs on casters. Lounge-type seating with tablet arms may be used for informal meetings, facilitating laptop computer usage. Four-leg guest chairs are not as flexible as chairs on casters, but can be a cost-effective alternative. Many four-leg chairs are available as stacking chairs, which may be acceptable for banquet functions and short-term meetings. Stacking chairs are more easily and compactly stored than conventional seating.

## BUILT-IN CASEWORK

A built-in credenza or shelf complements the meeting or training room by providing additional storage or serving space. Built-in casework enhances the visual unity of the room and can be used to frame windows and enclose convector covers.

## CONFERENCE ROOM ACCESSORIES

Conference room accessories and equipment should be planned into the room design. Permanent equipment includes whiteboards, projection screens, hanging-rail systems, shelving, clocks, and other devices fastened to the partitions or ceiling. Movable fixtures and equipment include easels, lecterns, carts, equipment cabinets, and portable screens.

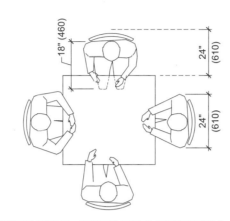

**SITTING ZONES—SQUARE TABLE, FOUR PEOPLE**

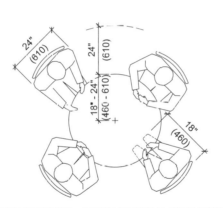

**SITTING ZONES—CIRCULAR TABLE, FOUR PEOPLE**

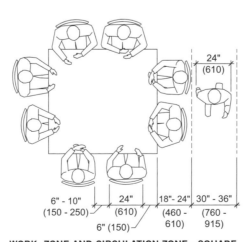

**WORK ZONE AND CIRCULATION ZONE—SQUARE TABLE**

## ANTHROPOMETRICS

Anthropometrics should be considered when designing conference and training areas. Sitting and working zones, as well as comfortable sight lines in various configurations, enhance the comfort of the users.

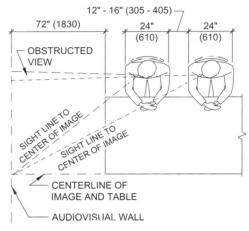

**AUDIOVISUAL CONFERENCE TABLE SIGHT LINES**

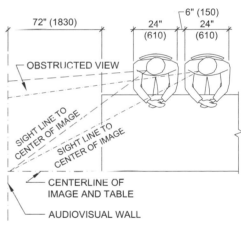

**AUDIOVISUAL CONFERENCE TABLE SIGHT LINES**

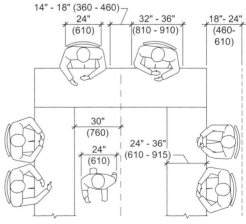

**U-SHAPED TABLE**

**CONFERENCE TABLE ANTHROPOMETRICS**
*Source: Julius Panero and Martin Zelnik,* Human Dimension and Interior Space; *New York: Whitney Library of Design; 1979.*

## LIGHTING FOR CONFERENCE AND MEETING ROOMS

Conferencing facilities have become a vital part of the modern office environment, and appropriate lighting to support their function is critical. A lighting system must provide general illumination, task lighting, perimeter wallwashing or accent lighting, and, often, audiovisual presentation support lighting. Additionally, decorative or architectural enhancement lighting may be appropriate.

A combination of lighting types is generally best in meeting rooms. Uplights from sconces or pendants produce ambient light, while recessed downlights illuminate the table. Wallwashers can light presentation or art walls, with adjustable accent lights providing flexibility in highlighting podiums and lecterns. Lighting controls should be employed to orchestrate the various lighting conditions through preset dimming, whenever possible.

## CONFERENCE CENTER AUDIOVISUAL PRESENTATION ROOMS

The construction of conference center audiovisual presentation rooms requires special consideration.

Locations of the rooms, privacy, acoustics, and other concerns should be addressed.

Exterior light and noise should not interfere with presentations. If walls are glazed, provide blackout shades to eliminate glare. Noise from the exterior should be reduced to less than 35 dBA to minimize distractions.

Reverberation should be maintained at less than 0.8 seconds for improved acoustics. A gypsum board ceiling in the front half of the space may be a useful sound reflector, amplifying sound to the audience. Nonrectilinear room shapes, especially circular and elliptical forms, may affect acoustics; consult with an acoustical engineer.

The HVAC NC/RC range should be kept as low as possible for greater speech intelligibility: 20 to 25 is a desirable range, 30 is acceptable if the project faces budget constraints.

Allow sufficient space above ceilings for ductwork to be in round or nearly square cross sections. Flat, wide ductwork may be noisy if the wide sections of sheet metal vibrate.

## CONFERENCE CENTER COMMUNICATIONS

Conference center communications, including long-distance learning, videoconferencing, television distribution, telephone, and Internet connections are commonly employed. Special features are required for functions such as videoconferencing, and future needs should be considered when designing for future technology. A control room may be required for receiving outside signals, recording, and transmitting programs throughout the facility and to other locations.

*Source: Richard H. Penner, Conference Center Planning and Design: A Guide for Architects, Designers, Meeting Planners, and Facility Managers; New York: Watson-Guptill Publications, 1991.*

*Ted Kollaja, AIA; lauckgroup; Dallas, Texas*
*Ted Milligan; Rhode Island School of Design; Providence, Rhode Island*

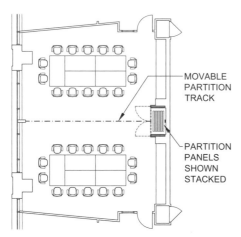

Plan illustrates the operable partition track (shown dotted) and panel stacking position in wall pocket with swing door closure. Panels are hung from overhead tracks. Fasten tracks to structure above for stability.

**CONFERENCE ROOM WITH OPERABLE PARTITION** *Source: lauckgroup; Dallas, Texas*

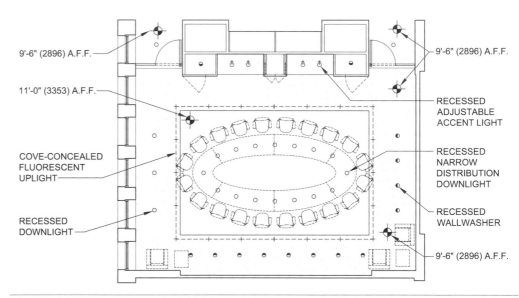

**TYPICAL CONFERENCE ROOM LIGHTING PLAN** *Source: Randy J. Burkett, FIALD, IES, LC; Burkett Lighting Design, Inc.; St. Louis, Missouri*

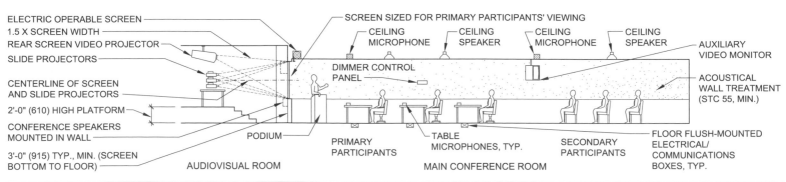

**SECTION—MULTIMEDIA CONFERENCE ROOM**

# MUSEUMS AND EXHIBIT SPACES

## MUSEUM TYPES

The defining characteristic of any modern museum is its collection. Each museum has its own special character and requirements. The more common types of museums include:

- Art museums
- Children's museums
- College and university museums
- History museums
- Nature centers
- Park museums and visitor centers
- Science and natural history museums
- Specialized museums: aeronautics and space, agriculture, architecture, forestry, and military

## MUSEUM SPACE RELATIONSHIPS AND SPACE TYPES

Museums consist of discrete blocks of space that must be kept separate for secure and efficient operations. Typically, the main departments include: public services, galleries, educational facilities, temporary exhibition support facilities, general staff services, collections management, collections storage, and curatorial and administrative offices.

## PROGRAMMING

The development of a thorough program for museum planning is critical. Museums are composed of many different spaces, each accommodating a particular function. Each anticipated function must be analyzed and accommodated individually. In addition, the future growth of museum collections and facilities must be addressed.

## ACCESSIBILITY

Compliance with the principles of the Americans with Disabilities Act (ADA) enhances the museum experience for disabled visitors and staff. Accommodation for special needs include:

- Ramps and elevators
- Large-print labeling and signage with good contrast and lighting
- Captioned film, video, and audio

Ramps and elevators may reduce accidents, and are preferred by persons in wheelchairs, families with strollers, the elderly, and those with limited mobility.

Place exhibit objects in positions that are visible from both seated and standing positions.

Large-print labeling and captioning encourages the visitor to read the informative text, while aiding those with some sight restrictions. Audio narration also assists visitors with sight impairment.

## PUBLIC SERVICE SPACES

Public nongallery spaces should be located together near the public entrance. They include vestibules, public lobby, information desk, coat and parcel checkroom, museum shop, auditorium, meeting rooms, A/V presentation/orientation room, public toilets, drinking fountains, and telephones.

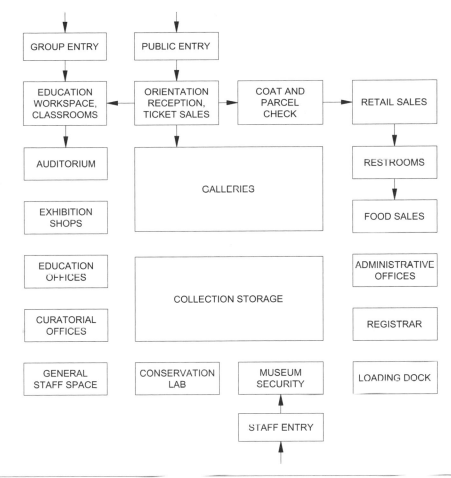

**SPACE RELATIONSHIPS**

### Public Lobby

The lobby has many practical functions: orientation and access to all public service functions within the museum and a setting for social functions. Size is often governed by the capacity needed for banquet dinners and/or receptions. During receptions, visitors may be dispersed throughout the galleries, depending on the kinds of events taking place in the museum's public spaces.

### Meeting Rooms and Auditoriums

These will vary widely according to the particular events program. Smaller museums usually have either a sloped-floor auditorium or a multipurpose room. Larger museums may have both. Rooms may be used for museum events or be rented to other public and private groups, depending on museum policy. For security and operating economy, auditoriums and meeting rooms must be accessible when the galleries are closed.

### Museum Shop and Bookstore

The retail shop should open to the lobby where it will be visible and attractive as visitors leave the museum. An adjacent office and inventory space are required.

### Public Restrooms

Restrooms should be sized to accommodate the largest anticipated exhibition openings or auditorium audiences. Plumbing fixture counts should be at least the code minimum, but greater if large groups are anticipated on a regular basis. Interpretations in plumbing fixture counts should be clarified with appropriate building code officials.

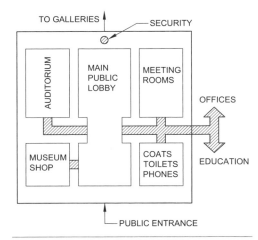

**PUBLIC SERVICE RELATIONSHIPS**

## VIEWING AND BEHAVIOR

Exhibit viewing heights are influenced by the average standing person's eye level and comfortable viewing range. Some displays are visible from a seated position, which enables persons of smaller stature and those in wheelchairs to view the objects on display.

## SITTING AND LEANING BEHAVIOR

People naturally gravitate toward surfaces at comfortable heights to lean against, perch, or sit. Galleries may be provided with some seating for visitors. Seating may affect the duration of the rest period. Hard benches provide places for short rest periods; comfortable chairs encourage longer periods of sitting.

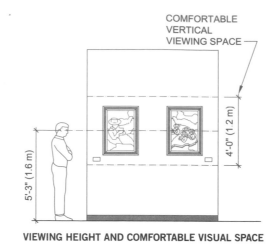
**VIEWING HEIGHT AND COMFORTABLE VISUAL SPACE**

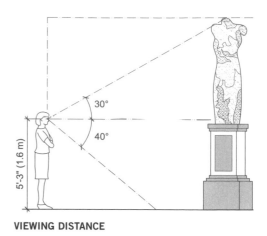
**VIEWING DISTANCE**

**VIEWING HEIGHT AND COMFORTABLE VISUAL SPACE**

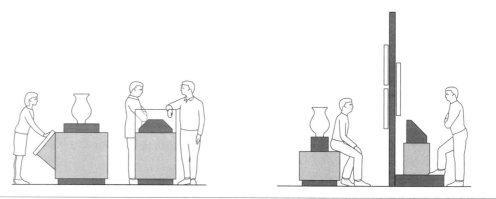

**SITTING AND LEANING BEHAVIOR**

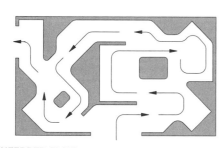
**INFERRED FLOW**

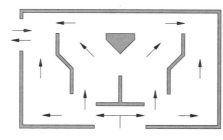
**UNSTRUCTURED FLOW**

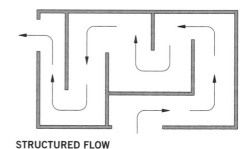
**STRUCTURED FLOW**

**EXHIBIT CIRCULATION**

# EXHIBIT GALLERY TYPES

Museum gallery types include:

- Art galleries
- Interpretive galleries
- Science center galleries
- Visible storage galleries
- Changing exhibition galleries

## GALLERY CHARACTERISTICS

Galleries should be isolated spaces conducive to concentrating on the objects exhibited. When the museum is closed, the galleries should become secure, dark vaults.

### Gallery Flexibility

Galleries must provide flexibility to house various exhibit types. This is achieved in traditional art museums by providing a variety of well designed, proportioned, and organized gallery rooms of different sizes and characters. Flexibility within gallery spaces is maintained with open floor space, a modular ceiling system, and movable exhibition walls, so the space can be reconfigured based on exhibition requirements. A level of physical changeability provides flexibility within the context of fixed gallery rooms.

### Proportions

A rectangular floor plan is generally desirable for gallery spaces. Ceiling heights should be proportional to the plan size of the room and to the objects to be exhibited: 11 to 14 ft (3.4 to 4.3 m) is appropriate. Lower ceilings may be acceptable in certain intimate galleries such as those exhibiting old master prints, photographs, or other very small objects. Very high ceilings may be desirable in feature areas of galleries, when exhibiting large artifacts.

### Finish Materials

Floors, walls, and (ideally) ceilings should be capable of supporting considerable weight through the use of fasteners. Floors and walls should have securely attached ¾ in. (19 mm) tongue-and-groove plywood substrates. Suitable flooring materials are tongue-and-groove hardwood strip flooring, stone, terrazzo, or carpet. Suitable wall materials are thin (¼ or ⅜ in.; 6 or 10 mm) drywall or stretched fabric. Ceilings may be painted drywall or acoustical ceiling panels. If the flooring is a hard-surface material, an acoustical ceiling is desirable.

# EXHIBIT CASEWORK AND DISPLAY UNITS

Most museum artifacts are exhibited in protective display cases. The artifacts are secured, while allowing visitors to view the objects within a sealed display environment. Temperature, relative humidity, contamination, and outside chemical pollutants are controlled within the sealed case.

## Case Construction

Cases may be constructed of wood or metal. Wood construction is less stable than metal, and should be treated with vapor barrier products to seal the wood surfaces. Metal cases provide dimensional stability. They may be fabricated from steel, which requires a protective coating to prevent corrosion, or aluminum. Case construction materials or finishes should be composed of conservation-appropriate materials that do not outgas any chemical substances.

Display cases may require ventilation and air filtration to remove contaminants from the air within the case. Provide power to cases as required; freestanding cases may require power feeds from the floor.

## Case Security and Seals

Display case security should be discussed with a security consultant before selecting secure construction type, case materials, glazing, and locking systems. Locking options include: pneumatic, electronic, and manual locking devices. Specify tamper-resistant screws that are exposed. Consider electronic detection sensors in high-security areas.

Cases may require seals to contain the internal environment within the unit. Gaskets are typically employed to seal the display case glazing in place.

## Case Lighting

Incandescent, fluorescent, or fiber-optic illuminator sources may be used for integral display case lighting. Provide ventilation to dissipate heat generated from lamps; fans may be required to evacuate hot air.

# INDIVIDUAL GALLERY SIZES AND CEILING HEIGHTS

| GALLERY TYPE | FLOOR AREA SQ FT (SQ M) | CEILING HEIGHT FT (M) |
|---|---|---|
| **Intimate Galleries** | | |
| Old master prints and drawings | 300–900 (28–84) | 9–11 (2.7–3.4) |
| Archival documents | | |
| Jewelry | | |
| Small decorative arts | | |
| Miniature dioramas | | |
| Gems and minerals | | |
| Insects, small animals | | |
| **Medium Galleries** | | |
| Fourteenth- to nineteenth-century paintings | 1,000–2,000 (93–186) | 11–14 (3.4–4.3) |
| Traditional sculpture | | |
| Furniture | | |
| Decorative arts | | |
| Small historical exhibits | | |
| Medium-sized artifacts | | |
| Most scientific exhibits | | |
| Interactive galleries | | |
| Most temporary exhibits | | |
| **Large Galleries** | | |
| Central gallery among smaller galleries | 2,000–5,000 (186–465) | 14–20 (4.3–6.1) |
| Large Baroque paintings | | |
| Twentieth-century paintings and sculpture | | |
| Temporary exhibitions | | |
| Industrial history | | |
| Architectural reconstructions | | |
| Historical reconstructions | | |
| Large dioramas | | |
| Large natural history exhibits (dinosaurs, etc.) | | |

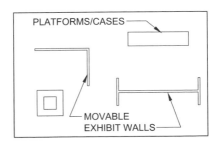

**FLEXIBLE OPEN-PLAN GALLERY**

PLATFORMS/CASES

MOVABLE EXHIBIT WALLS

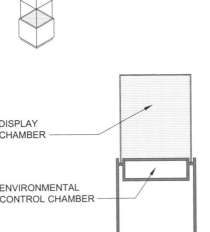
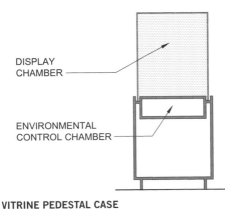

DISPLAY CHAMBER

ENVIRONMENTAL CONTROL CHAMBER

**VITRINE PEDESTAL CASE**

LIGHT ATTIC

DISPLAY CHAMBER

ENVIRONMENTAL CONTROL CHAMBER

**BACK WALL CASE**

**DISPLAY CASE CONSTRUCTION**
*Source: National Park Service, "Exhibit Conservation Guidelines," Division of Conservation, 1999.*

## MUSEUM LIGHTING

### Public Areas

Lighting in museum public areas differs from lighting in gallery areas. The hours of operation may affect lighting types; evening functions may require lighting effects and levels not utilized during daylight hours. Public areas generally do not contain exhibits, so the use of natural light is acceptable if the galleries are distinctly separate from these spaces.

### Lighting for Art

The two principal methods for lighting art are uniform illumination and nonuniform illumination.

- *Uniform lighting* for all vertical surfaces that will receive art allows viewers to select their own focus. It is possible to change objects without readjusting the lighting equipment.
- *Nonuniform lighting* focuses light on individual objects while leaving the surround in comparative darkness, creating a dramatic environment. Every time the art changes, the lighting equipment requires readjustment.

In a space that will have frequently changing exhibits and nonuniform illumination, a flexible lighting system is appropriate. Track systems are often used due to the ease of locating and aiming the track luminaries.

Excellent color rendering is essential for the proper appreciation of the objects. Continuous-spectrum, high-color-rendering sources allow the art to be viewed under spectral distribution conditions similar to those under which it was created.

The artwork medium, surface texture, type of frame, and enclosure (glass or plastic) of an object are considered in artwork lighting. For flat works mounted on a horizontal surface, the optimum placement for a light source is usually at an angle of 30° from nadir (straight down) to eye level (5 ft 6 in. [1,676 mm] above the finished floor, on average.

An aiming angle of less than 30° (more nearly vertical) causes shadows from the frame and distortion of the object due to exaggeration of the texture. An aiming angle greater than 30° (more nearly horizontal) results in reflected glare from the surface of the object, washing out the detail. This greater angle will also cause viewers to be standing in their own shadow and will cause the luminaire to be a source of glare to others.

The way three-dimensional objects are lighted also affects the viewer's perception of the piece. Concentrated beams create higher contrast and deeper shadows, emphasizing form and texture. Frontal lighting between 30° and 45° from horizontal, and between 30° and 45° from vertical, models objects in a manner that best replicates sunlight.

Lighting a vertical surface behind an object provides a luminous backdrop that serves to separate the object visually from its background. Lighting the object from the side as well as from above provides added dimension to the piece.

Reversing the expected relationship of highlight and shadow, and lighting an object from a less conventional angle, disturbs perception. Uplighting creates an ominously ghoulish impression; backlighting leaves an object in silhouette.

## CONSERVATION OF MATERIALS

Conservation of materials is a fundamental concern in the lighting of art. All organic material is susceptible to pigment change and weakening of strength from exposure to light and heat. These materials include paper, cotton, linen, parchment, leather, silk, wool, feathers, hair, dyes, oils, glues, gums, and resins; and because of similarities in chemical structure, most synthetic dyes and plastics.

Damage is related to wavelength. Ultraviolet (UV) radiation causes more damage, but more visible radiation is present in all light sources, including daylight. A material that is fairly "fast" (more stable), such as the oil in paintings, will be changed mainly by UV radiation. More sensitive dyes and pigments, which are damaged either by UV or visible radiation, will be changed mainly by the visible radiation, since it is more plentiful.

Design tips for artwork conservation include:

- Minimize daylight exposure and apply UV filter films to windows where necessary.
- Ensure that all electric sources are fitted with UV filters, especially those other than incandescent.
- Maintain general display lighting levels for moderately sensitive materials, such as oil and tempera paintings, lacquers, undyed leathers, ivory, and bone, at 15 fc (150 lux) or less.
- Maintain general display lighting levels for extremely sensitive materials such as pen-and-ink

drawings, prints, watercolors, tapestries, textiles, costumes, and manuscripts, at 5 fc (50 lux) or less.
- Minimize display exposure time whenever practical to lessen any potential degradation.
- Carefully control the intensity of all forms of light. Discuss lighting intensities with a qualified conservator.

### Lighting in Collections Storerooms

Lighting in collections storerooms should provide adequate illumination for handling and examination of objects, while protecting them from unnecessary exposure to ultraviolet light and visible radiation. Lighting may be switched so that general light is provided for safe passage in aisles; additional light can be switched on when required.

Fluorescent lighting must be provided with UV shielding. Indirect systems that reflect light from a painted white ceiling containing titanium dioxide will greatly reduce the UV component and result in even light distribution. Light from high-pressure sodium bulbs contains almost no ultraviolet light; however, color discrimination is difficult in this light.

## MUSEUM EXHIBIT OBJECT MAXIMUM LIGHTING LEVELS

| OBJECTS SENSITIVE TO LIGHT MAXIMUM 5 FC (50 LUX*) | OBJECTS LESS SENSITIVE TO LIGHT MAXIMUM 20 FC (200 LUX) | OBJECTS INSENSITIVE TO LIGHT MAXIMUM 30 FC (300 LUX) |
|---|---|---|
| Textiles | Oil and tempera | Metal |
| Tapestries | paintings | Stone |
| Costumes | Undyed leather | Glass |
| Watercolors | Horn | Ceramics |
| Gouache | Bone | Jewelry |
| Prints | Ivory | Enamel |
| Drawings | Oriental lacquer | |
| Manuscripts | | |
| Miniatures | | |
| Paintings in distemper media | | |
| Wallpapers | | |
| Dyed leather | | |
| Most natural history exhibits, including botanical specimens, fur, and feathers | | |

*Lumen: Measured light striking a display surface; 1 foot-candle = 1 lumen = 10.76 lux.

Source: Gary R. Steffy, Architectural Lighting Design, 2nd Ed.; New York: John Wiley & Sons, Inc., 2001.

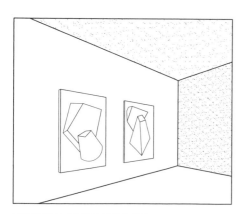

**UNIFORM WALLWASHING FOR ARTWORK**

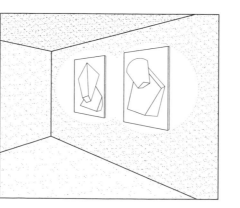

**NONUNIFORM ACCENT LIGHTING FOR ARTWORK**

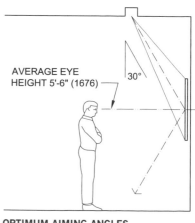

AVERAGE EYE HEIGHT 5'-6" (1676)    30°

**OPTIMUM AIMING ANGLES**

## GALLERY LIGHTING

Source: Gary Gordon, and James L. Nuckolls, Interior Lighting for Designers, 3rd Ed.; New York: John Wiley & Sons, Inc., 1995.

## MUSEUM ACOUSTICS

Museum acoustics vary within the different space types. Acoustics in museums may be less of a consideration than light control, flexibility, and ease of maintenance. Isolate noisy back-of-the-house spaces from the public areas of the museum. Isolate areas that are susceptible to vibration as well as noise.

The HVAC NC/RC range for mechanical equipment noise should be 25 in small to medium-sized spaces, and up to 30 in large galleries. Reverberation is generally well tolerated, unless the space is to be used for seminars or meetings. For auditorium spaces, reverberation time should be 0.8 seconds or less.

## MUSEUM SECURITY

Effective museum security is the result of thorough museum planning, quality lock and alarm systems, and vigilant professional and security staff practices. A specialized museum security consultant can assist the museum staff and the designer with these issues.

Security for the museum building and exhibit space should be achieved by:

• Physically resistant construction
• Electronic systems to deter and detect theft and vandalism
• Constant human presence or a rapid human response if alarms are triggered

Planning for security involves understanding the zones that must be kept separate, and how public, staff, and objects will move through the museum. When entering and leaving the galleries, the public should be required to pass through one easy-to-monitor checkpoint. Nongallery public functions (such as auditoriums, museum shops, or toilets) should not be accessible through the galleries. When closed, galleries should function as secure vaults. Emergency fire exits from galleries should be minimal, alarmed, and easy to locate.

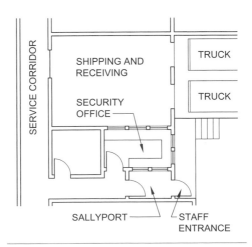

**SECURITY STATION AT SHIPPING AND STAFF ENTRANCE**

Staff areas should be clearly separated from galleries and public services. Shipping and receiving and staff entrances must be tightly monitored and easily controlled by the security staff. Collections storerooms should be treated as vaults and should not contain any mechanical or electrical equipment that might require access for maintenance or in emergencies. Mechanical ductwork and grilles must be designed to prevent access by burglars to locked galleries and collection storerooms.

### Alarm Systems

Electronic alarm systems should be designed by professionals who specialize in museum security systems. Such specialized professionals also should be consulted with regard to locking systems. Often, alarm system work is not part of the general construction contract for reasons of confidentiality. A source of backup power may be desirable. The issue of security should be reviewed with appropriate museum authorities.

### Public and Staff Access

Public and staff movement through the museum must be carefully separated. There should be only one public and one staff/shipping entrance to the museum. Public and staff areas will be open at different times, and each should be securable when not open. Public service areas, such as the lobby, museum store, restrooms, and food service areas, should be easily accessible during open hours.

Ideally, there should be only one point of access to the galleries from the public services area. Access from public to staff areas should be strictly limited and easily monitored. Staff should not need to move through galleries when they are closed. The staff entrance and shipping and receiving dock should be together and be easy to monitor and control by security personnel.

### Ancillary Spaces

Auditoriums, theaters, and food service facilities present special service access problems because they operate on different schedules from other museum functions, and these operations may conflict with the museum's needs for security and cleanliness. Separate service access for these facilities may be appropriate.

### Security Station

In most small and medium-sized museums, the central security station should be located at the service entrance with secure windows opening to the outdoors, to the shipping and receiving room, and to a staff entrance sallyport. In large museums, the central station may be in a more secure location away from all entrances, with a shipping clerk's station at the service entrance.

## CLIMATE CONTROL

Determine whether the entire building or only areas containing collections items (galleries and collections storerooms) will be maintained at conservation standards. If the conservation-standard areas are limited, the rest of the building can be treated like any other public building. Adequate physical separations, including vapor barriers, must be provided between conservation and human comfort zones.

### Humidity Control

Control of relative humidity (RH) is the single most critical factor in museum environments. Although ideal conditions vary for different kinds of collections, desirable RH for most museum objects is approximately 50%. This level must be held constant at all times. However, maintenance of 50% relative humidity throughout the winter months in cold climates tends to produce severe condensation on windows and within the exterior wall construction. Prevention of condensation requires installation of vapor barriers and insulation systems. A completely continuous *zero perm* vapor barrier system is essential. In this context, zero perm means a permeability rating of less than .01 grains of water per square foot per hour per inch of mercury vapor pressure, in accordance with ASTM E96, *Standard Test Methods for Water Vapor Transmission of Materials,* test procedure A, B, or BW.

In cold-climate situations, it may be determined that installation of zero perm vapor barriers and required mechanical equipment is impossible or impractical. The alternate approach is to design the wall and roof systems to permit one slow, controlled cycle per year, varying from about 25% RH in winter to about 50% in summer. Hourly, daily, or weekly fluctuations must be avoided under any circumstances.

### Air Filtration

Requirements for air filtration vary depending on the quality of the outside air and the conservation demands of the museum objects to be housed. Generally, an acceptable choice would be bag filters with disposable prefilters, UL Rating Class 1; that is, particulates removed to 95% efficiency on ASHRAE 52/76. Electrostatic filters must not be used because they produce destructive ozone. Activate carbon filters are effective in removing gaseous pollutants, but they are expensive and require active maintenance.

### Operating Cycles

Heating and cooling loads vary greatly between occupied galleries (with lights and people) and unoccupied ones (closed and dark). When unoccupied, systems should be designed to operate at a low maintenance level.

### Location of Piping, Outlets, Switches, and Controls

All piping containing liquids should be kept out of areas containing museum objects. Plumbing should not be located above galleries and collections storerooms.

All convenience outlets, switches, HVAC thermostats, humidistats, and other control devices must be kept off gallery walls. Outlets should be in the base and in the floor. Switches should be remote. Thermostats and humidistats can be located in return air ducts.

*Tim Shea, AIA; Richard Meier & Partners; Los Angeles, California*
*Douglas Flandro; Rhode Island School of Design; Providence, Rhode Island*
*Tam Youngcharoen; Rhode Island School of Design; Providence, Rhode Island*
*John D. Hilberry, AIA; John D. Hilberry & Associates, Inc., Architects and Museum Planners; Detroit, Michigan*

# PERFORMANCE THEATERS AND REHEARSAL HALLS

## PLANNING CRITERIA

The term *theater* originates from the Greek verb *theatai*, meaning to see or behold. Originally places of social ceremony as well as entertainment, modern theaters are designed to support the type of performances presented within the space. Some theaters are used for one purpose, but more commonly, multiple presentation styles must be accommodated within one space.

Theaters for music and dramatic performances are among the most complex building types, particularly with regard to the interior functions and acoustics. Audience sight lines, layout, seating capacity, aisles, exiting, size and type of performance areas, and acoustical volume guidelines determine interior design constraints.

Acoustics and lighting are of primary importance, and accommodation must be made for audiences that may be seated for several hours. Acoustical and lighting consultants are typically involved in theater projects. Testing of the acoustical design properties of the theater is critical to ensure that the acoustical calculations are appropriate to the actual space.

The circulation flow in a theater must be obvious and easy to navigate. Public spaces, including the lobby and auditorium, are separate from performance/back-of-house areas.

## Life Safety

Theaters are considered assembly spaces, therefore emergency exiting and general life safety issues are critical in theaters. Consult applicable building codes for local jurisdiction requirements.

## Interior Construction

Box-in-a-box construction may be used for the most critical spaces, with lobbies, galleries, promenades, and so on, acting as buffer zones between the interior envelope and the exterior building skin. Interior construction should attempt to reach STC 60-plus if the exterior construction is at least STC 50.

Heavy concrete and masonry construction tends to be more forgiving of noise and vibration transmission problems than lightweight, long-span steel construction. A more successful acoustically isolated theater is generally a result of a more substantial structure and partitioning system.

The circulation flow in a theater must be obvious and easy to navigate. Public spaces, including the lobby and auditorium, are separate from performance/back-of-house areas.

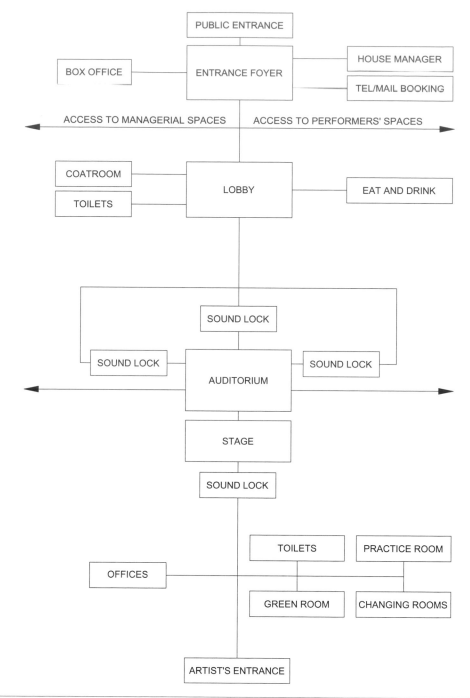

**THEATER ADJACENCY DIAGRAM**

## PRINCIPAL WESTERN THEATER FORMS AND CHRONOLOGY

### ANCIENT

PRIMITIVE

GREEK ARCHAIC
(IKRIA)

GREEK CLASSICAL

GRECO-HELLENISTIC

ROMAN

GRECO-ROMAN
ODEUM

**CLASSICAL: UP TO 400 AD**

### MODERN

SINGLE-VISTA STAGE
(SERLIO)

MULTIPLE-VISTA
STAGE (PALLADIO)

PROSCENIUM STAGE
(ALLIOTTI)

THEATER OF
SHAKESPEARE

GRANDE SALLE

AUDITORIUM

ORCHESTRA

STAGE

**LATE RENAISSANCE: 1550 TO 1650**

HORSESHOE-SHAPED
AUDITORIUM
PROSCENIUM STAGE

THEATER OF THE
RESTORATION

FAN-SHAPED
AUDITORIUM
PROSCENIUM STAGE

FAN-SHAPED AUDITORIUM
PROSCENIUM, APRON,
CALIPER STAGE

PARTIALLY ENVELOPING
AUDITORIUM
THRUST STAGE

FULLY ENVELOPING
AUDITORIUM
IN-THE-ROUND STAGE

**BAROQUE, NEO-BAROQUE: 1650 TO 1870**      **CONTEMPORARY: 1870 TO 1970**

Source: George C. Izenour, Theatre Design, 2nd Ed.; New Haven, CT: Yale University Press; 1996, p. 33.

## THEATER VIEWING ANGLE

### Orientation of Seated Spectator

Orienting chairs or rows of chairs so that the spectators face the center of action of the performing area minimizes head strain.

### Angle of Vision of Spectator

The human eye has a peripheral spread of vision of about 130°. This angle of view from chairs in the front rows will define the outer limits of the maximum-sized performing area.

### Angle of Encounter

The angle of encounter is defined by the 130° peripheral spread of vision of a single performer standing at the "point of command." Patrons seated outside the spread of this angle will not have eye contact with the performer.

### Distance between Performance and Last Row of Spectators

Minimizing this distance while satisfying the preceding parameters enhances achievement of visual and sound communication.

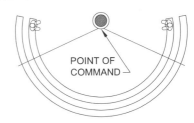
130°

**ANGLE OF ENCOUNTER**

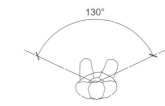
POINT OF
COMMAND

**ANGLE OF ENCOUNTER**

**VIEWING ANGLE**

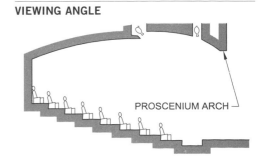
PROSCENIUM ARCH

**PROSCENIUM THEATER SECTION**

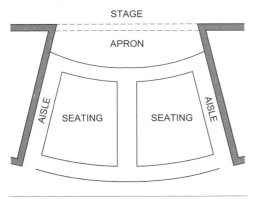
STAGE
APRON
AISLE
SEATING
SEATING
AISLE

**AMERICAN SEATING**

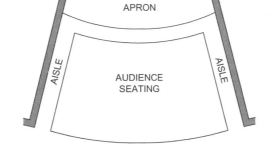
STAGE
APRON
AISLE
AUDIENCE
SEATING
AISLE

**CONTINENTAL SEATING**

Source: J. Michael Gillette, Theatrical Design and Production; Mountain View, CA: Mayfield Publishing Company, 1992.

## THEATER CONFIGURATIONS

The plan configuration of a theater should respond to the type of performances anticipated. The basic types of theater configurations include those planned for projected images, a proscenium stage (zero encirclement), 90° to 130° encirclement, 180° to 270° encirclement, and 360° encirclement. The same seating area is shown for each of the theater configurations on this page.

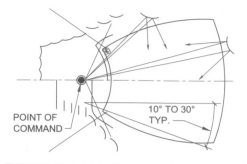

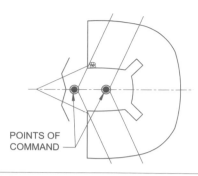

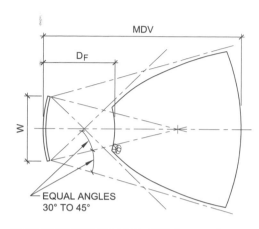

**SCREEN PROJECTION**

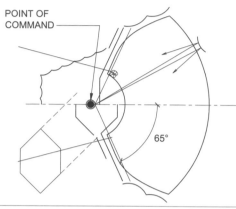

**ZERO ENCIRCLEMENT**

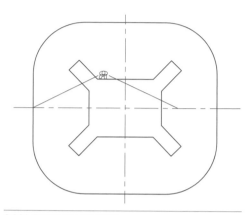

**180° TO 270° ENCIRCLEMENT**

**90° TO 130° ENCIRCLEMENT**

**360° ENCIRCLEMENT**

### Screen Projection

The following design considerations apply to a theater configured for images projected on a screen:

- The minimum distance between the first row and the screen (D$_F$) is determined by the maximum allowable angle between the sight line from the first row to the top of the screen and the perpendicular to the screen at that point. A maximum angle of 30° to 35° is recommended.
- The maximum distance between the screen and the most distant viewer (MDV) should not exceed eight times the height of the screen image. An MDV two to three times the screen width is preferred.
- Screen width (W) is determined by the use of the appropriate aspect ratio between the screen image width and height.
- Curvature of screens may reduce the amount of apparent distortion for a larger audience area. Curvature of larger screens may help to keep the whole of the image in focus and may provide a more uniform distribution of luminance.

### Zero Encirclement (Proscenium Stage, Picture Frame Stage, End Stage)

The following design considerations apply to a theater configured for zero encirclement:

- The angle of audience spread in front of a masking frame is determined by the maximum size of the corner cutoff from a rectangular-shaped performing area that can be tolerated by seats at the side.
- Audience may not fill angle of encounter from point of command.
- Audience is farthest from performing area.
- There is a large range in size of performing area.
- Provides for a large amount of scenic wall surfaces without masking sight lines.
- Horizontal movement of scenery is possible, perpendicular and parallel to centerline.
- Possibility exists of short differences in arrival time between direct and reflected sound at the spectator, which may be beneficial to music performances.

### 90° to 130° Encirclement (Pictorial Open Stage, Wide Fan, Hybrid, Thrust Stage)

The following design considerations apply to a theater configured for 90° to 130° encirclement:

- Audience spread is defined and limited by angle of encounter from point of command.
- Performing area shape is trapezoidal, rhombic, or circular.
- Audience is closer to performing area than with zero encirclement.
- Picture frame is less dominant.
- There is a range in choice of size of performing area.
- Provision for an amount of scenic wall surfaces is possible without obscuring the performing area.
- Horizontal movement of scenery is possible in directions at 45° to and parallel to centerline.
- Shape of seating area places maximum number of seats within the directional limits of the sound of the unaided voice, which is beneficial for speech performance.

### 180° to 270° Encirclement (Greek Theater, Peninsular, Three-Sided, Thrust Stage, Three-Fourths Arena Stage, Elizabethan Stage)

The following design considerations apply to a theater configured for 180° to 270° encirclement:

- Audience spread is well beyond angle of encounter from point of command in order to bring audience closer to performing area.
- Simultaneous eye contact between performer and all spectators is not possible.
- There is a minimum range of choice in size of performing area.
- Provision of small amount of scenic wall surfaces is possible without masking sight lines.
- Horizontal movement of scenery is only possible parallel to centerline.
- Large encirclement by audience usually demands actor vomitory entrance through or under audience.

### 360° Encirclement (Arena Stage, Theater-in-the Round, Island Stage, Center Stage)

The following design considerations apply to a theater configured for 360° encirclement:

- Performer is always seen from rear by some spectators.
- Simultaneous eye contact between performer and all spectators is not possible.
- Audience is closest to performance.
- No range of choice is available in size of performing area.
- No scenic wall surfaces are possible without obscuring the view of the performing area.
- Horizontal movement of scenery is not readily possible.
- Encirclement by audience demands actor vomitory entrance through audience area.

# LIVE PERFORMANCE THEATERS

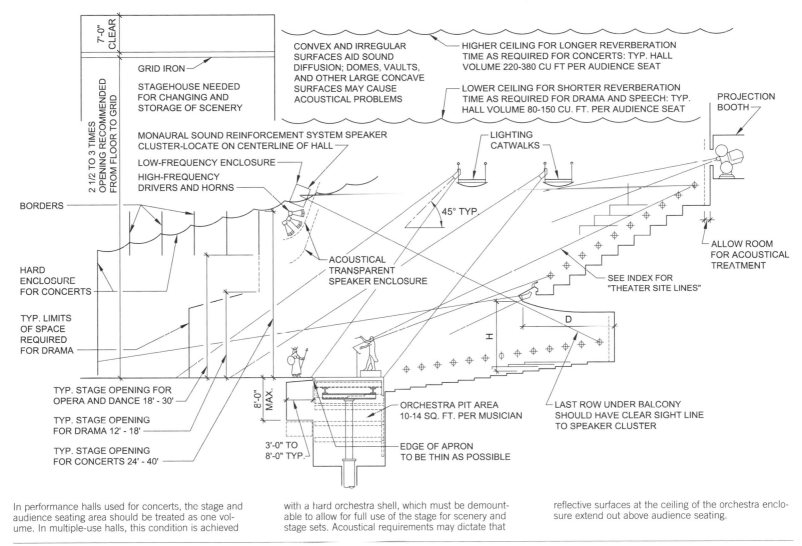

In performance halls used for concerts, the stage and audience seating area should be treated as one volume. In multiple-use halls, this condition is achieved with a hard orchestra shell, which must be demountable to allow for full use of the stage for scenery and stage sets. Acoustical requirements may dictate that reflective surfaces at the ceiling of the orchestra enclosure extend out above audience seating.

## CONFIGURATIONS FOR LIVE PERFORMANCES

# PROSCENIUM STAGES

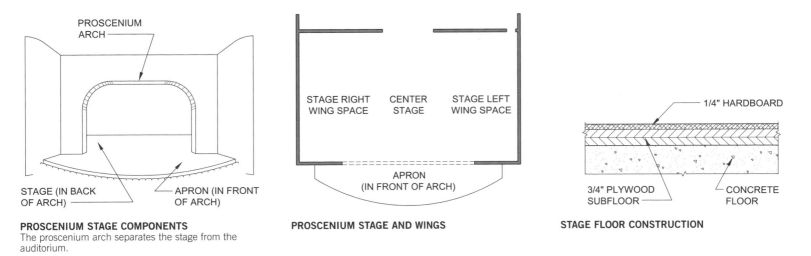

**PROSCENIUM STAGE COMPONENTS**
The proscenium arch separates the stage from the auditorium.

**PROSCENIUM STAGE AND WINGS**

**STAGE FLOOR CONSTRUCTION**

## PROSCENIUM STAGE

## THEATER SEATING

### Standard Seating Materials

Standard seating frame types include cast iron or steel, riser-mounted, or floor-mounted standards. Pedestal-mounted standards using continuous beam support or cantilevered standards are also available, and a folding tablet arm is usually available.

Chair arms may be of upholstered fabric, wood, plastic, or metal. Chair backs may be constructed of plastic, molded plywood, or rolled-stamped metal, or be upholstered front and rear. Higher backs and bottom extensions for scuff protection are also available. Chair seats may be upholstered, or of plywood, plastic, metal pan, coil or serpentine springs, or polyurethane foam.

### Row to Row Spacing Criteria

Consult local codes for required minimum row spacing. Codes typically stipulate a minimum clear plumb line distance measured between the unoccupied chair and the rear of the back of the chair in front, as follows:

- 32 to 33 in. (813 to 838 mm): Typical minimum for multiple-aisle seating.
- 34 to 37 in. (864 to 940 mm): Typical minimum for modified continental seating.
- 38 to 42 in. (965 to 1,067 mm): Typical minimum for continental seating.

### Comfort for the Seated Person

Guidelines for enough leg room to provide seated comfort are as follows:

- 32 in. (813 mm): Knees will touch chair back; uncomfortable
- 34 in. (864 mm): Minimum spacing for comfort.
- 36 in. (914 mm): Ideal spacing for maximum comfort.
- 38 in. (965 mm) and up: Audience cohesiveness may suffer.

### Ease of Passage in Front of Seated Persons

Guidelines for spacing seats to provide comfortable passage in front of seated patrons are as follows:

- 32 to 34 in. (813 to 864 mm): Seated person must rise to allow passage.
- 36 to 38 in. (914 to 965 mm): Some seated persons will rise.
- 40 in. (1,016 mm) and up: Passage in front of seated persons possible

### Safety

Excessive plumb line distance may entice exiting persons to squeeze ahead and cause a jam. Consult applicable codes for aisle and exit path widths.

### Efficiency

Minimum seat row spacing reduces maximum distance to stage.

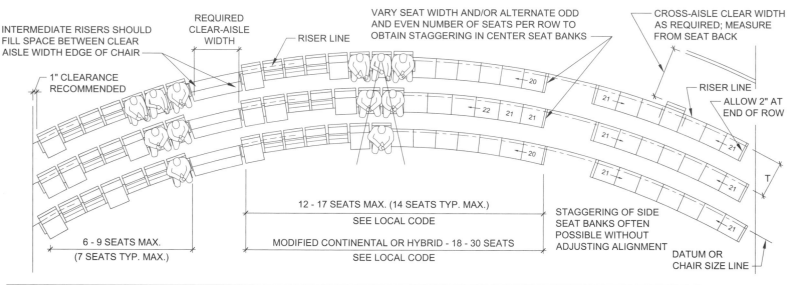

**MULTIPLE-AISLE SEATING**

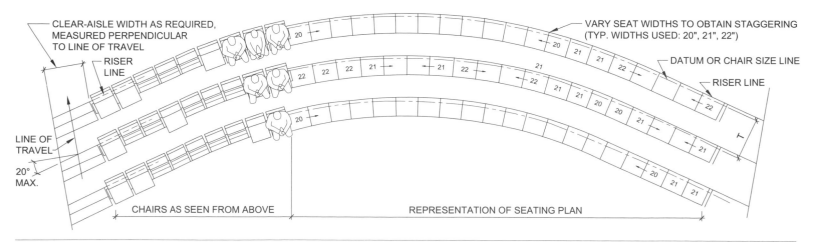

**CONTINENTAL SEATING**

# THEATER ACOUSTICS

## Acoustical Considerations

Theaters and performance spaces are rooms in which good hearing conditions are critical to the use of the space and exchange of aural information. The design of a performance space generally requires input from an acoustical consultant.

## Loudness

Sound generated by speakers or musicians should be projected efficiently to the audience and captured within the space. The *sending end* of the room (i.e., the stage) should be acoustically hard. Walls near the performer should be angled or splayed to enhance projection and prevent *flutter echoes* at the stage. Walls and ceilings in the audience area should be hard so they can reflect sound, unless absorptive treatment is needed to eliminate problematic reflections or focusing or to reduce reverberation time (RT) for particular program needs.

## Quiet

Good hearing environments should maximize the signal-to-noise ratio. In addition to the desired signal being well projected, unwanted noise should be eliminated. To accomplish this requires very low background sound levels (NC-20 range) from mechanical equipment. Sound-lock vestibules eliminate intrusive noise from a lobby and allow latecomers to enter without acoustical interference to the show. Carpeted aisles help reduce footfall noise. Noise from exterior environmental sources should also be considered. Avoid lightweight roofs, which will transmit rain noise.

## Spaciousness

Because of the lateral configuration of the human ear, sound signals that are slightly different in each ear allow the listener to hear an acoustical quality called *spaciousness*, which is usually highly desired, especially for classical music. This sense of spaciousness can be enhanced if the distribution of sound through a large hall is diffused, enabling the ear to literally hear reflections from many facets of the side and rear walls. This diffusion can be enhanced by protrusions and angled surfaces on the sidewalls.

## Reverberation Time (RT)

Refer to the accompanying tables on optimum reverberation times and preferred volume/seat ratios. Room volume and area of absorption can be calculated to predict RT. The design factor affecting RT the most is ceiling height. The relationship between the volume of a hall and the number of seats is often a good approximation of sound quality in the room.

In wide halls with high ceilings, seats in the center of the orchestra often suffer from lack of early reflections. Reflecting canopies or arrays over the front rows can bring reflected sound to these seating areas, which

otherwise may suffer from poor articulation. Often, seating at the rear of the balcony does not experience this problem, and these seats have excellent acoustics.

## Articulation

Much of the clarity of sound that audiences need for speech intelligibility and clear musical attacks comes from the sound reflected off hard surfaces that reaches listeners within 50 to 80 milliseconds of the direct sound (which always reaches the listener first). To enhance articulation of acoustics in a hall, the design must ensure there are enough surfaces to reduce the time gap between the initial (direct) sound and these early reflections; the initial time delay gap should be less than 50 milliseconds. Sound travels 1,120 ft/second (333 m/second), so the initial time delay gap for prime seating locations should not exceed 50 ft (13 m).

*Tim Shea, AIA; Richard Meier & Partners; Los Angeles, California*
*Leonor de Lope Friedeberg; Rhode Island School of Design; Providence, Rhode Island*
*Peter H. Frink; Frink and Beuchat; Architects; Philadelphia, Pennsylvania*

## PREFERRED VOLUME/SEAT RATIOS

| VOLUME/SEAT | | |
| --- | --- | --- |
| CU FT | CU M | SOUND QUALITY OF SPACE |
| Less than 200 | Less than 6 | Quite "dead"; suitable for speech and cinema |
| 300 to 350 | 8–10 | Good for music |
| Greater than 500 | Greater than 14 | Good for organ music only; too reverberant for speech |

## OPTIMUM REVERBERATION TIMES AT MIDFREQUENCIES (500–1000 Hz) FOR PERFORMANCE SPACES

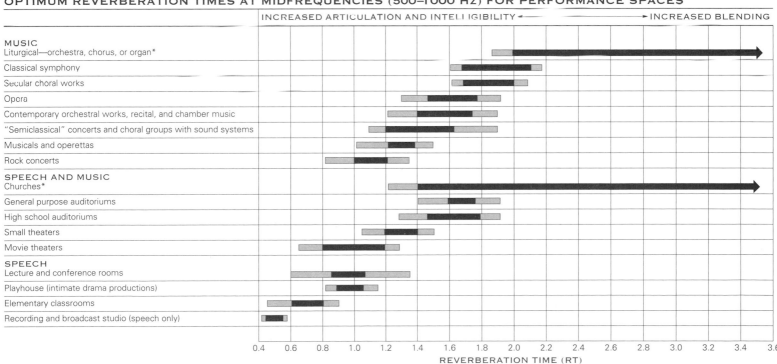

The breadth of RT range for each room type is a function of the room volume: the larger the room volume, the closer to the longer end of the range. The smaller the room volume, the closer to the shorter end of the range.

## PERFORMANCE SPACE ACOUSTICS

### Focusing

Focusing concentrates sound waves in one area, causing hotspots where the sound is louder or unnatural in quality. Concave surfaces either in plan or section can present major focusing problems if they are not identified and treated.

### Seats

The largest area of sound-absorbing surface in a performance hall is the seating. Absorptive properties will change dramatically when they are occupied, since a person introduces about 5 sabins for each seat, which significantly affects reverberation time. Use of upholstered seats makes the RT similar whether the seats are empty or fully occupied.

### Balconies

Balconies bring additional persons into the performance space and create more intimacy between audience and performer. But if the balcony overhang is too great, seating under a balcony can be cut off from the main volume of sound. A reasonable rule of thumb is that the overhang depth should not exceed the height of the opening (greater ratios are acceptable where live music is not part of the program).

### Orchestra Pit

The surface over the orchestra pit should be angled to project sound out to the audience, but diffuse so that some energy is reflected back to the performers onstage. The front wall of the orchestra pit should be a hard surface so the front rows of the audience do not hear direct sound and so that more energy is reflected back to the performers onstage. Front and back walls may require drapery to vary and control the degree of sound reflected off these surfaces.

### Sound System

Electronic sound systems may be used for amplification or for playback or recorded material. Depending on the source, the loudspeakers used to distribute the sound should be located at the center slightly in front of the speaker (for speech amplification) or on the left and right sides (for musical stereo playback or amplification of the orchestra pit). Additional loudspeakers may be needed under a balcony or at the rear of the hall to cover the upper balconies. The sound control location must be well placed within the audience area covered by the loudspeakers. Additional transmitters using infrared signals or FM radio signals can be used to meet ADA requirements.

## STAGE LIGHTING SYSTEMS

### System Design

A stage lighting system provides a flexible arrangement of dimmers, lighting positions, and outlet devices. Stage lighting fixtures may be placed where needed and controlled individually or in groups, according to the differing requirements of each production.

---

### Stage Lighting System Terms

*Dimmer.* A device that controls the intensity of stage lighting fixtures; a remotely controlled electronic device in current practice. Standard sizes are 1.2 kW, 2.4 kW, 6.0 kW, 12.0 kW, and 120V.

*Circuit.* A grounded stage lighting circuit; usually no common neutrals are permitted. Load sizes depend in part on local codes—20 A is average, 15 A is maximum in some areas; some 50 A are often also provided. Circuits are distributed throughout the theater for fixture plug-in; they terminate at a dimmer rack, patch panel, or transfer panel.

*Dimmer-per-circuit.* A configuration whereby every stage lighting circuit home-runs to an independent dimmer.

*Patch panel.* A custom-made device for interconnecting a large number of stage lighting circuits to a small number of dimmers.

*Transfer panel.* A custom-made device enabling permanent circuits to be disconnected from the theater's dimming system and connected to a show's touring dimming system. Front-of-house circuits are generally made "transferable" in this way in large multipurpose theaters that must accommodate tours.

*Front-of-house (FOH).* In a proscenium theater, the audience side of the proscenium.

*Followspot.* A very bright manually operated spotlight used to "follow" a performer around the stage. Light source can be incandescent, carbon arc, xenon, or HMI.

*Leko, fresnel, ellipsoidal, parcan, scoop, floodlights.* Theatrical lighting fixtures.

*Striplight.* A continuous fixture containing a number of lamps and used for downlight, backlight, footlight, and cyclorama lighting—usually 6 or 8 ft long (1.8 or 2.4 m) with 12 lamps in three or four circuits.

*Control console.* Often called the *light board,* a computerized, manual, or hybrid control device for stage lighting dimmers. Generic types include 2-, 5-, or 10-scene *preset consoles* (manual) and *memory consoles* (computerized).

*Connector strip.* A type of outlet device for stage lighting circuits; essentially, a continuous wireway with outlets or "pigtails."

---

*Cyclorama (cyc, for short).* A large seamless white or pale-blue backdrop, used scenically to represent the sky or provide a surface on which abstract colors and patterns can be projected with stage lighting fixtures. Usually cloth; plaster is difficult to repair, and is not recommended.

*Outlet box.* An outlet device for stage lighting circuits. Box size and circuit quantities vary. Surface-mounted or recessed styles are available. Circuit numbers must appear on the faceplate (with adhesive labels or engraved).

*Box boom.* An important front-of-house sidewall lighting position in a proscenium theater.

*Cove, beam, slot, truss.* A front-of-house lighting position located at the auditorium ceiling.

*Followspot booth.* Houses the followspots. Enclosed, if possible, and ventilated per code. Usually at or near the rear of the house and quite high; 30° to 45° to the edge of the stage is preferred. Four spots require a booth, nominally 24 ft (7.3 m) wide × 10 ft (3 m) deep; two spots require one, 12 ft (3.6 m) wide × 10 ft (3 m) deep.

*Control booth.* Primary location for control console. Good view of stage preferred. Often located on the main level at the rear of the house. Houselighting controls should be duplicated here as well as backstage.

*Dimmer room.* Location for dimmer racks. Can be remote from the stage. Locate for efficiency of load and feed-wire conduit runs. Ventilate to accommodate heat load (approximately 5% connected load). Control humidity to protect equipment.

*Booms, ladders, tormentors* (side pieces such as flats or drapes placed just upstage of the proscenium to adjust the width of the opening). Onstage sidelighting positions. Nonarchitectural; located temporarily for each production, as required.

*Pipes, battens, electrics.* Onstage overhead lighting positions. Usually rigging pipes or pipe grid members. In a proscenium theater, often one or more rigging pipes will be permanently designated as "electrics" and served with connector strips attached directly to the pipe.

---

The planning of a stage lighting system should address the following considerations:

- Type of use
- Size of performing area
- Size of theater, location of stage lighting positions
- Budget

Determine requirements for the following subjects:

- Dimmer-per-circuit or patched circuit system
- Quantity of dimmers
- Quantity of distribution of stage lighting circuits
- Electrical feed size
- Type of stage lighting outlet devices
- Type of control console
- Type and quantity of stage lighting fixtures and accessories

*Joshua Dachs; Jules Fisher Associates Inc., Theater Consultants; New York, New York*
*Carl Rosenberg, AIA; Acentech, Inc.; Cambridge, Massachusetts*

# AUDIOVISUAL PRESENTATION FACILITIES

## DESIGN DETERMINANTS

Audiovisual (A/V) presentation facilities include training rooms, lecture halls, classrooms, boardrooms, and auditoriums. The size, type, and location of displayed images must be determined so that the space supports the presentation for the intended audience. For instructional material, legibility of displayed characters and symbols is of critical importance.

## A/V EQUIPMENT

Presentation furnishings include easels, lecterns, and portable sound systems. An audiovisual presentation system often includes the following equipment:

- Video display (video projector, "flat-screen" plasma display, or video monitor)
- Loudspeakers and amplifier
- Routing switcher
- Remote control system
- A computer, for presentations or to browse the Internet
- Hookup for a portable notebook computer
- Document/object camera, for use with printed documents or small objects
- Video equipment, including TV monitors, plasma/flat/data monitors, VCRs, DVD players, TV/VCR combo units, professional camcorders

Typically, each of these components is provided by a different manufacturer. A/V dealers, referred to as *integrators,* combine these various components and ensure that they are properly installed.

## LARGE-SCREEN DISPLAYS

For large-screen display of video images, LCD, DLP, and D-ILA projectors are commonly used. Flat-panel displays (plasma displays) are available in limited sizes, with the largest current models limited to about 61 in. (1,549 mm) diagonal. For the legible display of instructional material where the viewing distance exceeds 15 to 20 ft (4.5 to 6 m), video projection technology is required to produce an adequate size image. For instructional uses, video display technology is supplanting film-based display technology (slides, motion fixture film, and overhead transparencies) because the newest film-to-video transfer devices preserve the resolution of the film media.

Digital echo cancellers are used with the microphones and loudspeaker system to help provide an echo-free and nonreverberant sound quality. In distance learning applications, a camera that can automatically track the movements of the instructor is often employed.

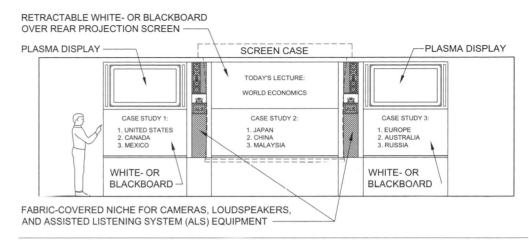

RETRACTABLE WHITE- OR BLACKBOARD OVER REAR PROJECTION SCREEN

PLASMA DISPLAY

SCREEN CASE

PLASMA DISPLAY

WHITE- OR BLACKBOARD

WHITE- OR BLACKBOARD

FABRIC-COVERED NICHE FOR CAMERAS, LOUDSPEAKERS, AND ASSISTED LISTENING SYSTEM (ALS) EQUIPMENT

**FRONT- AND REAR-PROJECTED IMAGES AND MARKING SURFACES**

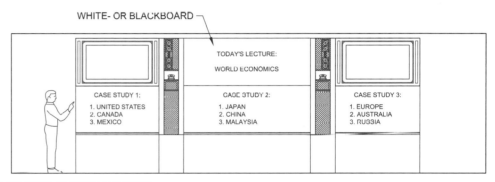

WHITE- OR BLACKBOARD

**TRADITIONAL BLACKBOARD MODE**

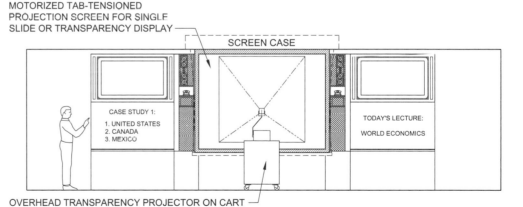

MOTORIZED TAB-TENSIONED PROJECTION SCREEN FOR SINGLE SLIDE OR TRANSPARENCY DISPLAY

SCREEN CASE

OVERHEAD TRANSPARENCY PROJECTOR ON CART

**TRANSPARENCY OVERHEAD MODE**

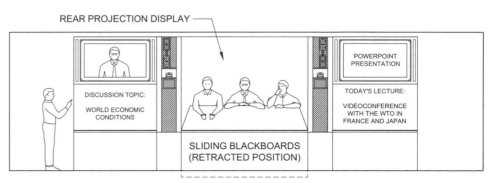

REAR PROJECTION DISPLAY

POWERPOINT PRESENTATION

SLIDING BLACKBOARDS (RETRACTED POSITION)

**VIDEOCONFERENCE MODE**

**DIFFERENT PRESENTATION MODES**

## VIDEOCONFERENCE AND DISTANCE LEARNING FACILITIES

Videoconference and distance learning systems are typically designed for the audiovisual presentation to the local audience. Common industries and applications include the following:

- *Education:* Distance learning classes, links with other schools, access to remotely located experts, preliminary employment interviews
- *Offices:* Staff, project, marketing and board meetings, employee
- *Health care:* Evaluation of X rays, charts, and other data; remote consultations; staff meetings
- *Government and military:* Strategic and network meetings, command center communications, training
- *Manufacturing:* Production meetings, product quality analysis, process review, collaboration, remote supplier meetings, training
- *Legal:* Remote depositions and arraignments, judicial proceedings

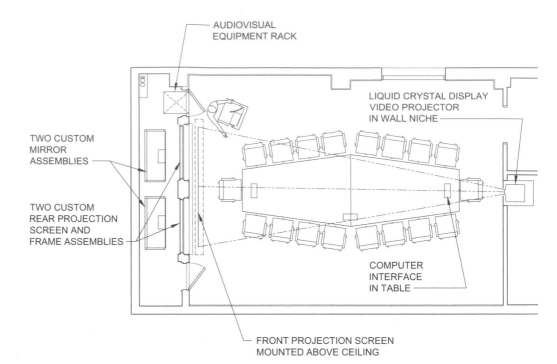

PLAN

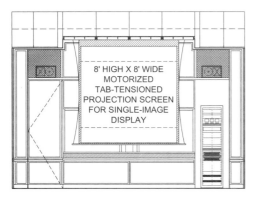

ELEVATION—FRONT PROJECTION MODE

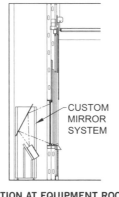

SECTION AT EQUIPMENT ROOM

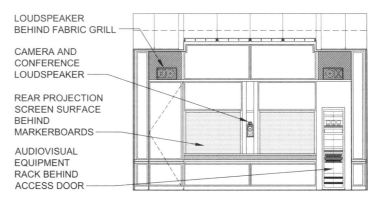

ELEVATION—VIDEOCONFERENCE MODE

**CONFERENCE ROOM FOR A/V PRESENTATIONS AND VIDEOCONFERENCES**

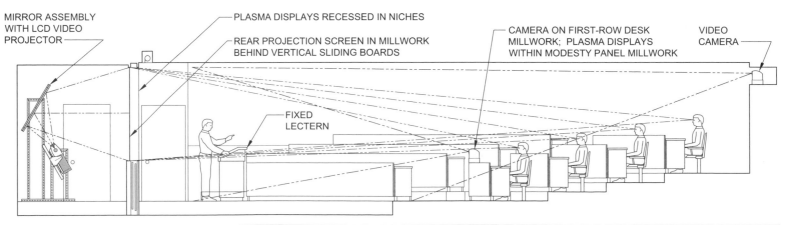

**TIER-STYLE CLASSROOM FOR DISTANCE LEARNING**

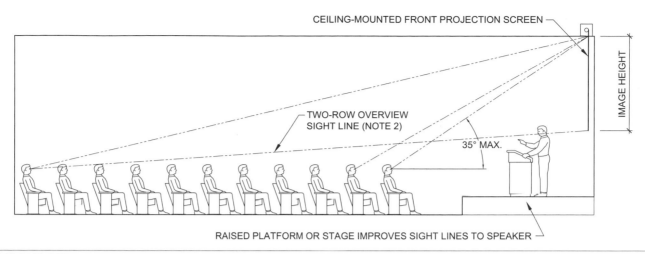

CEILING-MOUNTED FRONT PROJECTION SCREEN

IMAGE HEIGHT

TWO-ROW OVERVIEW SIGHT LINE (NOTE 2)

35° MAX.

RAISED PLATFORM OR STAGE IMPROVES SIGHT LINES TO SPEAKER

## SIGHT LINES WITH FLAT FLOOR

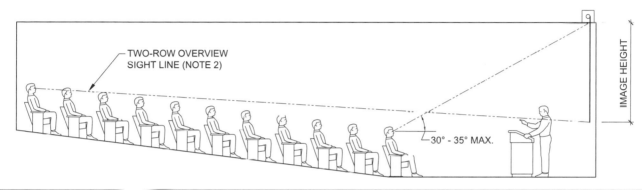

TWO-ROW OVERVIEW SIGHT LINE (NOTE 2)

IMAGE HEIGHT

30° - 35° MAX.

## SIGHT LINES WITH SLOPED FLOOR

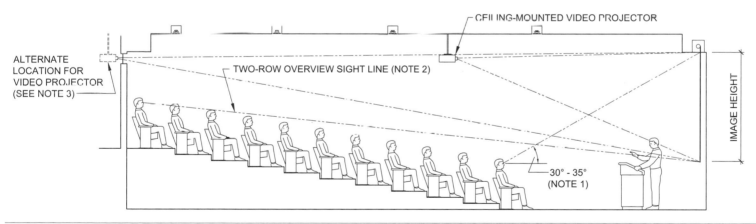

CEILING-MOUNTED VIDEO PROJECTOR

ALTERNATE LOCATION FOR VIDEO PROJECTOR (SEE NOTE 3)

TWO-ROW OVERVIEW SIGHT LINE (NOTE 2)

IMAGE HEIGHT

30° - 35° (NOTE 1)

## SIGHT LINES WITH STEPPED FLOOR

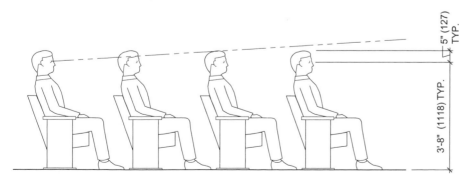

5" (127) TYP.

3'-8" (1118) TYP.

Minimum sight lines should be based on a two-row overview. This assumes that viewers can see between the heads of the people seated in the row directly in front of them.

## SIGHT LINES FOR TWO-ROW OVERVIEW

## SIGHT LINES

The vertical viewing angle is the angle from the viewer's eyes to the top of the image. For optimum sight line, it should not exceed 30° to 35° above the horizontal.

Many video projectors are available with optional lenses that allow placement toward the front or at the center or rear of the room. The majority of video projectors are designed to be elevated so that the lens is approximately aligned with the top or bottom of the image. For rear projection, the lenses are often designed to allow the projector to be on the axis of the screen center.

*Jeffrey E. Bollinger and Jason Martinez; Acentech, Inc.;*
*Cambridge, Massachusetts*

**PRESENTATION TECHNOLOGY**  □  **3**

# HEALTH CARE FACILITIES

## HISTORY OF HEALTH CARE

The practice of Western medicine predates the life of Hippocrates, an influential Greek physician during the fifth century BC. To this day, individuals entering the field of medicine are required to honor the Hippocratic Oath, which embodies the code of medical ethics.

During the early Roman Empire, facilities designed to serve the needs of the Roman military were commonly found. However, health care for the general public was very limited; the temple and the home were the principal places of healing. These Roman facilities were required to be compact and efficient in terms of their layout of functional spaces.

### Open Nursing Wards

Monasteries were typically arranged with guesthouse functions for the rich and infirmaries for the poor. The nursing ward in the infirmary was usually aisled with patient beds on each side; it also had a chapel at the end so that the sick could see the altar and hear the services. During the Middle Ages, medical treatment was so inadequate that these wards were essentially places where patients waited to die, hopefully in closer communication with God. Efficient layout of functional spaces continued to be an important part of the design.

In her book *Notes on Nursing* (written in 1859) and in a paper, "Notes on Hospitals," Florence Nightingale described the importance to the health of patients of adequate ventilation, noise control, light, cleanliness, and variety. The single greatest influence upon hospital architecture for more than 100 years was the Nightingale Pavilion, which consisted of open, cross-ventilated nursing wards connected by corridors.

### Private Rooms

In the twentieth century, with the advent of advanced pharmaceuticals, new diagnostic technologies, and the erection of high-rise hospitals, health care became more patient-focused. While the importance of Nightingale's basic concepts of nursing care are still relevant, the open nursing wards have given way to patient rooms that afford more privacy.

### U.S. Health Care Delivery

The U.S. health care delivery system has changed radically since the early 1980s. The federal government now attempts to control health care costs for patients receiving Medicare and Medicaid benefits by assigning fixed costs to hundreds of standard diagnoses (called *diagnostic related groups,* or DGRs) and reimbursing health care facilities only this amount for each patient stay. The result has been a substantial shift to outpatient treatment for many diagnoses, including surgery. Consequently, hospitals now face a surplus of inpatient beds and great pressures to revise physical plants to accommodate many more outpatients. At the same time, health insurance companies have cut benefits for inpatient care. All of this has changed the way hospitals are planned and has stimulated new conceptual responses to the new functional challenges. In addition, hospitals are no longer the only building types responding to health care needs.

### Codes and Regulations

Hospitals are also reviewed periodically by national organizations. The Joint Commission on Accreditation

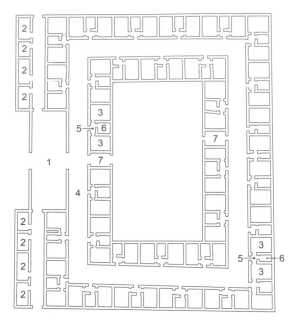

1. ENTRANCE HALL
2. ROOMS FOR NURSES AND ADMINISTRATORS
3. PATIENT ROOMS (TYP.)
4. CORRIDOR
5. ANTEROOM
6. SUPPORT ROOMS
7. PASSAGEWAYS

This Roman military hospital was constructed in the first century AD in Switzerland.

**ROMAN MILITARY HOSPITAL: VINDONISSA**

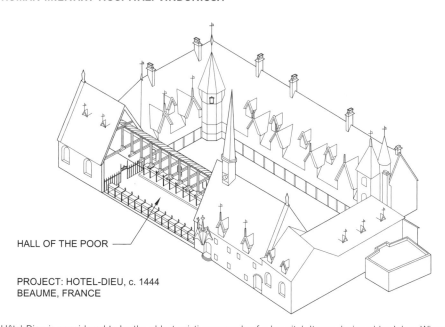

HALL OF THE POOR

PROJECT: HOTEL-DIEU, c. 1444
BEAUME, FRANCE

Hôtel-Dieu is considered to be the oldest existing example of a hospital. It was designed by Jehan Wisecrere and constructed in 1443, in Beaune, France.

**HALL OF THE POOR, HÔTEL-DIEU**

of Healthcare Organizations (JCAHO) is responsible for review of compliance with environment of care regulations and currently reviews hospitals based on the 1997 Life Safety Code. The Centers for Medicare and Medicaid Services (CMS), formerly known as the Health Care Financing Administration (HCFA), reviews hospitals for compliance with Medicare/Medicaid regulations and conditions of participation. It currently reviews under the 1985 Life Safety Code.

### Defend in Place

Hospital patients may have limited or no ability to seek safety without assistance in the case of fire or smoke. In the Defend in Place life safety approach, patients are not completely evacuated from the building but are moved to an adjacent smoke compartment or through a *horizontal exit,* which is an adjacent compartment separated by a partition of two-hour fire resistance. In this concept, the hospital is divided into compartments to limit fire spread.

Another life safety measure used in the modern hospital is the engineered smoke removal system. The primary cause of death in building fires is smoke, either through inhalation or through disorientation due to poor visibility. The engineered smoke removal system reduces injury and death by utilizing the hospital ventilating system to remove the products of combustion.

# HOSPITAL BUILDING TYPES

## Primary Care/Community

Like the family doctor, for many people, the community hospital is the first contact with the health care system. Hospital primary care provides general treatment and diagnostic services within a limited, well-defined geographic area. Such services usually include general surgery, standard radiography, and fluoroscopic imaging, routine laboratory tests, and emergency care, as well as general medicine, maternity, and pediatrics. A small unit usually serves as a combined intensive care unit (ICU) and cardiac care unit (CCU). The number of inpatient beds can range from 25 to 50 for small rural hospitals to 100 to 150 for facilities in developed areas.

## Regional Referral Hospitals

Compared to primary care hospitals, referral hospitals serve larger, less well-defined areas and provide not only basic care but also more specialized care, including orthopedics; eye, ear, nose, and throat (EENT); urology; cardiology; oncology; and neurology. Computerized tomography (CT), scanning, magnetic resonance imaging (MRI), ultrasonography, and nuclear medicine imaging are also present to support these specialties. Cardiac catheterization, open-heart surgery, and cancer treatment programs are sometimes available. The emergency department has a heavier workload because of the specialty capabilities available. The number of inpatient beds can range from 150 to 200 to 300 to 350 or more.

## Tertiary Care/Teaching

Because many tertiary care teaching hospitals have world-class reputations and provide extremely specialized services, they may attract patients from all over the world. Such facilities seek to provide not just health care but also a setting (and patients) for medical research and education. Balancing these objectives is an important consideration in the design of such hospitals. All the specialties are represented, as well as some state-of-the-art diagnostic and treatment modalities, which frequently are still in development. Imaging devices such as positron emission tomography (PET) scan, procedures such as "gamma knife" treatment for cancer, and "cleanrooms" for patients recovering from bone marrow transplants must all be housed in specially designed facilities. Tertiary care hospitals may be physically linked to a medical school's basic science and clinical research laboratories, academic offices, classrooms, and very large outpatient facilities. The number of inpatient beds can vary from 400 to 450 to 800 to 900 or more.

## Specialty Hospitals

Specialty hospitals, such as rehabilitation, psychiatric, and pediatric hospitals, treat only one kind of patient. Other specialty hospitals include those devoted to women's and children's health. While they contain most of the treatment and diagnostic areas of a standard hospital, they also have special design needs: patient privacy, appropriate scale, and nonthreatening environments.

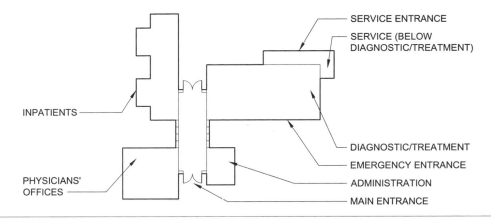

**PRIMARY CARE/COMMUNITY HOSPITAL**

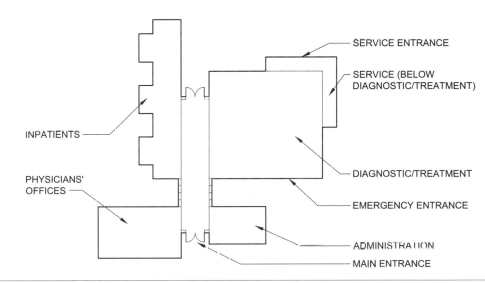

**REGIONAL REFERRAL HOSPITAL**

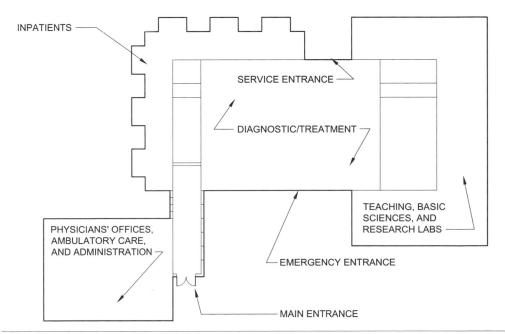

**TERTIARY CARE/TEACHING HOSPITAL**

# INPATIENT HOSPITALS

The modern inpatient hospital is a city in microcosm. The basic activities found in the city—birth, work, sleep, eating, and dying—all occur in the hospital. Consequently, even a small hospital is a complex organizational structure. Complicating the organizational structure are the systems required in the hospital. This complexity can be made easier to understand by dividing the hospital into its hierarchical component parts, just as a city can be understood through the hierarchy of its neighborhoods.

The most basic division in the hospital organization is between the *patient tower* and the *diagnostic/treatment and support chassis*.

## Patient Tower

The patient tower is composed of nursing units in which a group of patients receive care from a nursing team. In days of old, multibed wards were standard; these were replaced by two-patient semiprivate rooms. More recently, the private room has become the norm. Present-day surgery techniques, improvements in pharmacology, limits on cost imposed by HMOs, together with the recognition that patients may more comfortably convalesce at home have reduced the length of and need for inpatient hospital stays. This has resulted in a smaller but sicker inpatient population and a blurring of the difference between "regular" inpatients and ICU patients.

The future trend is toward the *universal room,* a private room large enough to accommodate the equipment normally seen in an intensive care unit and therefore capable of accommodating patients of all acuities. The use of computerized bedside charting improves the observation capabilities of the nursing staff, helping to make this possible. A typical nursing unit comprises approximately 32 beds, the nursing station, and support space. Each patient floor of a large hospital may have two such units, or about 64 beds.

## Diagnostic/Treatment and Support Chassis

The other major component in the hospital organization is the diagnostic/treatment and support chassis. If the nursing units form a tower, then this component is commonly referred to as a *pancake*. The requirement for windows in patient rooms limits the size of a patient floor. However, the relatively large diagnostic and treatment departments and their desired adjacencies result in a somewhat larger floorplate, hence the analogy to a pancake. As the term *diagnostic/treatment and support chassis* suggests, there are two principle divisions: the medical servicese and the ancillary services.

Diagnostics consists primarily of radiology and laboratories. The treatment component is composed of: surgery, cardiac catheterization, physical therapy, respiration therapy, labor and delivery, the pharmacy, and the emergency department. The ancillary support component consists broadly of: administration, admissions, medical records, dietary, material management, central sterile supply, morgue, housekeeping, and the energy plant.

Each department can be thought of as a neighborhood within the hospital "city."

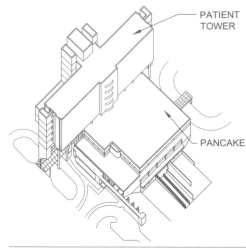

**INPATIENT HOSPITAL PATIENT TOWER AND DIAGNOSTIC/TREATMENT CHASSIS (THE "PANCAKE")**
*Perkins and Will; Atlanta, Georgia*

# OUTPATIENT HOSPITALS

Outpatient hospitals provide a simplified and less costly environment to deliver diagnostics and treatment to ambulatory patients. Compared to an inpatient hospital, an outpatient hospital is relatively simple, as there are neither patient nursing floors nor food preparation areas. Since long-term recovery and convalescence cannot be provided, the level of surgery that can be performed is limited. Recent developments in minimally invasive surgery, however, allow increasing numbers of procedures to be safely performed on an outpatient basis. A patient coming in for such surgery is prepped, undergoes surgery, recovers, and is sent home the same day. The outpatient hospital can offer several benefits to the patient: ease of access, streamlined registration, increased family member access, and a less institutional feel, especially compared to a large urban hospital.

Conceptually the outpatient hospital may be considered as similar to the diagnostic and treatment component of an inpatient hospital. Typically, surgery, noninvasive treatments such as lithotripsy (kidney stone treatment), physical therapy, and pain management may be provided, as well as diagnostic modalities such as radiography, fluoroscopy, computerized tomography, and magnetic resonance imaging. Because there are no patient sleeping rooms, a number of preop/postop patient holding rooms or cubicles are provided adjacent to the surgery suite. Depending on the level of recovery, they may be equipped with either a stretcher or recliner.

Specialized outpatient care may be provided, such as cancer care or orthopedics/sports medicine. A cancer center will offer radiation therapy and chemotherapy to the cancer patient. An orthopedics and sports medicine center will focus on problems of, and injury to, bones and muscles. Radiographic diagnostics and treatment through surgery, physical therapy, and hydrotherapy would be accommodated.

An outpatient center may be attached to an inpatient hospital and provide all the benefits of a stand-alone facility, but also allow for operational efficiency. A surgery suite can be laid out such that the inpatient and outpatient points of entrance are separated. The outpatient side can be designed much as it might be for a freestanding facility, but the operating rooms would be used for both inpatient and outpatient cases. The fact that OR staff, equipment, instruments, and central sterile supply are not duplicated enables greater efficiency, yet remains "invisible" to the patient and family.

*Project: Joan Glancy-Howell Station Outpatient Facility, Lawrenceville, Georgia*
*Designer: Perkins and Will; Atlanta, Georgia*

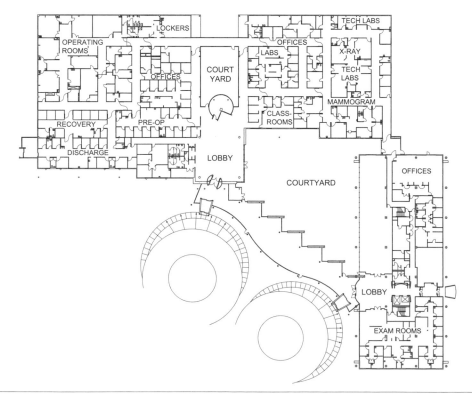

**OUTPATIENT HOSPITAL**

## MEDICAL OFFICE BUILDINGS: GENERAL

Medical office buildings (MOBs) fall under the general health care heading of "Outpatient" or "Ambulatory Care." MOBs are most commonly constructed to support the need for physician office space of one of the following health care providers: hospitals, health maintenance organizations, and private physician practices.

The typical MOB provides office space for individual physicians, physician groups, and ambulatory ancillary services that either complement the services provided by the hospital or that are not normally provided within the hospital itself.

While MOBs accommodate the spatial needs of the providers of ambulatory health care services, they are not considered as health care or institutional occupancies. MOBs are considered to be business occupancies by the various model codes.

## MEDICAL OFFICE BUILDINGS: HEALTH MAINTENANCE ORGANIZATION (HMO)-AFFILIATED

Health maintenance organizations (HMOs) fall under the general health care heading of "Managed Care." Most HMOs consist of a collection of health care professionals and business administrators who together, in an effort to manage the escalating costs of health care, provide health care insurance coverage to individuals and groups. HMOs provide low-cost, ongoing health care services to individuals and groups that become members of the HMO by paying regular, fixed monthly installments to the HMO system. Once enrolled as members, individuals may take advantage of the HMO's services, including its staff of nurses, general practitioners, specialists, and the HMO's buying power relative to prescription drug purchases. Members are encouraged to maintain their health by visiting the doctor on a regular basis, thus, the term "health maintenance."

HMOs deliver health care services through a variety of building types, which include hospitals, clinics, pharmacies, urgent care centers, and medical office buildings (MOBs).

Typically, HMO MOBs differ from hospital/developer-affiliated MOBs because most HMOs have their MOBs custom-designed based on a previously established clinical space and functional program, which depend on the particular medical services being offered. The design of each clinical space is typically based on previously established design standards for size and configuration of each particular space, HVAC requirements, lighting levels, quality of finishes, and so on.

A typical HMO MOB would include a typical general practice/internal medicine suite, ancillary departments, and an administrative area. Typical general practice/internal medicine suites include a waiting room/reception area, height/weight stations, exam room, procedure room, holding room, nurse station, patient toilets, physicians' offices, clean supply, and soiled utility. Administrative and support areas include an administration/business office, medical records, technical support, imaging, urgent care, laboratory, pharmacy, and central supply.

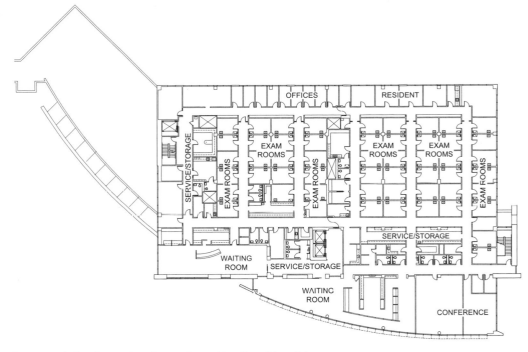

Programmatic functions and services are housed in adjacent hospital.

**EXAMINATION FUNCTION AND SERVICES**
*Project: Cannaday Building, Mayo Clinic; Jacksonville, Florida*
*Perkins and Will; Atlanta, Georgia*

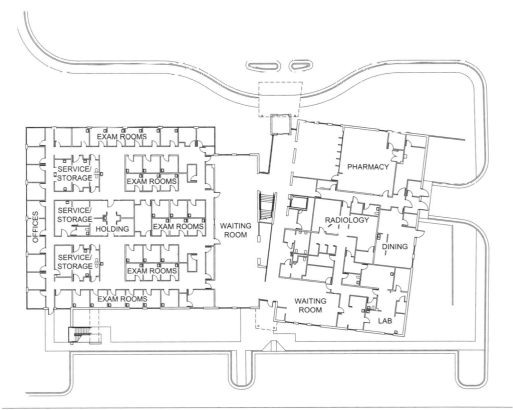

**MEDICAL OFFICE BUILDING—HMO-AFFILIATED**
*Project: Henry Towne Center, Kaiser Permanente; McDonough, Georgia*
*Perkins and Will; Atlanta, Georgia*

## MEDICAL OFFICE BUILDINGS: HOSPITAL/DEVELOPER-AFFILIATED

Historically, both new and existing hospital facilities have been faced with limited project budgets and limited land availability within the hospital campus. Therefore, most hospitals are restricted to project budgets that will accommodate only the essential clinical, diagnostic, and support functions and equipment required to provide the much-needed inpatient health care services. In many cases, project budgets are not adequate to accommodate physician office space or space for various ancillary support services.

As a result, the hospitals themselves or medical real estate developers may eventually construct one or more medical office buildings (MOBs) near the campus to supplement the office space needs and services provided by the hospital.

MOBs are generally very similar to a typical commercial speculative office building in their architectural layout:

- Efficient "skin" or building envelope
- Common building core elements (entrance lobby; elevators; exit stairs; toilets; mechanical, electrical, and plumbing; fire protection; and so on)
- "Racetrack" public corridor, which wraps the building core and provides access to potential medical office suites
- Common parking and loading facilities based on code minimum requirements

But where MOBs differ from commercial speculative office buildings most notably is in the manipulation of their architectural components. Size of the building floorplate, structural bay spacing, core-to-glass depths, space planning module, use of stretcher elevators, and so on are all dependent on the programmatic intent of the hospital/developer. Multiple small medical suites (800 to 1,500 sq ft (74 to 139 sq m)), multiple large medical suites (3,000 to 6,000 sq ft (278 to 557 sq m)), or a mixture of small and large medical suites, all will, in their own ways, influence the final architectural layout.

### Layout Parameters for MOBs

Typical architectural layout parameters for planning new or evaluating existing MOBs are as follows:

*Building floorplate:* 12,000 net sq ft (1,114 sq m) minimum

*Structural bay spacing:* 24 by 25 ft (7.3 by 7.6 m) and 30 by 32 ft (9.1 by 9.7 sq m)

*Core-to-glass depth varies:*

- 33 ft (10 m) nominal (for small medical suites)
- 37 ft (11.2 m) nominal (most common)
- 49 to 85 ft (14.9 to 25.9 m) nominal (for large medical suites)

*Space planning module:* 4 ft (1,229 mm), 4 ft 6 in. (1,370 mm) or 5 ft (1,525 mm)

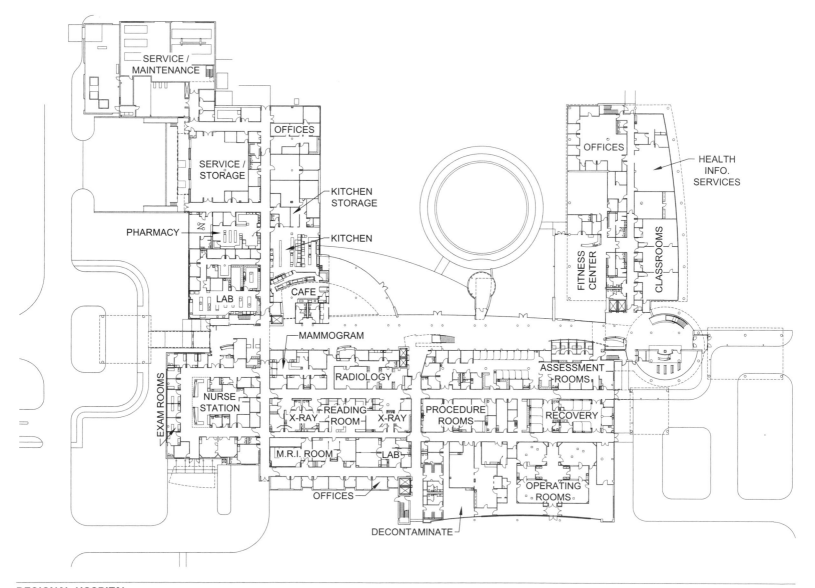

**REGIONAL HOSPITAL**
*Project: Florida Hospital—Heartland Medical Center; Sebring, Florida*
*Perkins and Will; Atlanta, Georgia*

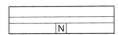

1900s: DOUBLE-LOADED CORRIDOR

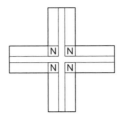

1930s TO 1950s: CROSS SHAPE

1940s: RACETRACK

1950s: COMPACT CIRCLE

1950s: COMPACT SQUARE

1970s: COMPACT TRIANGLE

N = NURSING STATION

---

**COMMON NURSING UNIT FORMS**
*Source: Stephen Kliment (ed.),* Building Type Basics for
Healthcare Facilities; *New York: John Wiley & Sons,
Inc., 2000, pp. 139–141.*

## NURSING UNIT PLANS AND ORGANIZATION

A clear recognition of each nursing unit's organizational pattern is required to ensure a floor plan that will support the unit. One of the most critical aspects is the variation in size, location, and makeup of the staff during shifts. A scheme with support space fully dispersed, with a close patient-nurse link during the day shift, may be very inefficient with reduced staffing at night and a consequent repositioning of the nurses to a location accessible to a larger number of beds.

Maximum and minimum travel distances from the center of the activity are as important as the average distance. With great distance variations, some patients may receive closer observation by nurses than others. Analysis of the maximum distance between patient rooms is an indicator of the inefficiency generated during lower staffing hours.

Current trends have eliminated inpatient care for patients who, 10 years ago, would have been admitted to the hospital. This means that patients who are admitted are in far greater need of observation. Therefore, the primary goal is to minimize distance— the average distance of travel, the range of distance between the nearest and the farthest patient rooms and the nurse work core, and the distances between all patient rooms. These distance calculations must be tempered by the number of beds per unit.

## NURSING UNIT PLAN TYPES

Having evolved from the open ward model of the Nightingale Pavilion, nursing units have continued to strive for improved nursing operational efficiencies, improved patient care, and the integration of technological advancements. Reducing travel distances for nursing staff is the primary planning objective for architects and designers. Reduced travel distances results in an increase in nurse/patient contact. The *distance-to-bed factor* is a summation of the distance from the nursing work center (nurse station) to the patient bed divided by the number of patient beds.

### Double-Loaded Corridor

The double-loaded corridor model was the standard design for many years because of the need for cross-ventilation and natural lighting. However, it made for very long distances between the nurse station and the end rooms of the unit. The core still contains space unrelated to nursing (elevator space, for example) and is thus less compact than it could be.

### Cross Shape

The cross shape unit is an early attempt at creating operational efficiencies by modifying the basic elements of the double-loaded model. Nurse stations and support areas remain at the center of the plan. Travel distances between the nurse stations and the most remote patient rooms are kept to a minimum; however, the round-trip travel distance remains similar to that of the double-loaded unit.

### Racetrack

This design demonstrated a far more efficient unit than the single, double-loaded corridor plan: it placed the nursing support core between two corridors in what has been called the *double corridor* plan. This unit shows a combination of one central work core with dispersal of support functions in the form of a pass-through "nurse server" adjacent to the door of each room to provide patient supplies for the convenience of the staff. Although this design was highly efficient during the day, the distances from the ends of the floor created problems when staffing was limited at night. The support core also contains space unrelated to nursing (elevators, stairs, HVAC) and is thus less compact than it could be.

### Compact Circle

This circular unit removed elevators, stairs, and HVAC components from the support core and located them where they could also serve additional nursing towers in the future. All patient beds are arrayed around the nursing support core, and travel distances are minimal. Another means of reducing nurse travel results from providing "redundant" circulation; that is, by providing more than one route from point to point.

Working within a circle has a number of built-in problems, however. The number and sizes of patient rooms dictated by program requirements control the diameter of the circle. It is strictly a coincidence when the resulting space in the center provides the required area to accommodate the program for nursing support.

Constructability issues associated with curved and angled partitions, odd-shaped spaces, and so on usually result in an increase in overall construction costs.

### Compact Square

This model is conceptually identical to the compact circle. However, the compact square, or rectangular, unit is much more flexible than the circular unit in terms of the ratio of patient rooms to the amount of support space, thanks to the ease of changing the exterior dimensions on each side while maintaining the same bed count. Most compact rectilinear plans have an efficiency rating close to that of the circular plans and provide a higher degree of flexibility in planning the units.

Due to the efficiency of the rectilinear plan, constructability issues are limited and economical construction costs are more easily achieved.

### Compact Triangle

This model is conceptually identical to the compact square.

---

*John L. Hogshead, AIA; John Elledge, AIA; Leisa Hardage, AIA; Marcia Knight, RID; Debbie Heitzman; Katrina Evans; Rey Perez; Joseph Fain; Perkins & Will; Atlanta, Georgia*

# HOTELS

### THE HOTEL GUEST

The words "hotel," "hospital," and "hospice" all are derived from the same Latin root, *hospitalitas,* meaning "of a guest." In the Middle Ages, monasteries provided food and lodging for travelers and pilgrims; the infirm would be kept comfortable, which was all that could be offered them due to inadequate medical care. Today, the business traveler and technology define the contemporary hotel guest's expectations of amenities in every area. Communication technologies such as fax, high-speed Internet accesses, and teleconferencing facilities are widely used in hotel guest rooms.

### DESIGN CONSIDERATIONS

The primary design considerations for hotel spaces include the following:

• Main lobby
• Circulation
• Guest rooms, including standard rooms and suites
• Guest room bathrooms
• Guest room corridors
• Food and beverage outlets
• Function rooms, including ballrooms, meeting rooms, and exhibition spaces
• Structural bay determinants

### HOTEL CLASSIFICATION

Hotels are often classified by a symbol or "star" system to distinguish their level of service, space, and facilities available, but the system varies in different countries and by hospitality association standards. Therefore, it is advisable to first establish the desired grade of the hotel with the operator before doing a detailed program. The required grade of the hotel will give a good indication of the required number of rooms, room sizes, number of public spaces and functions, staff-to-guests ratio, and the respective back-of-house spaces and sizes.

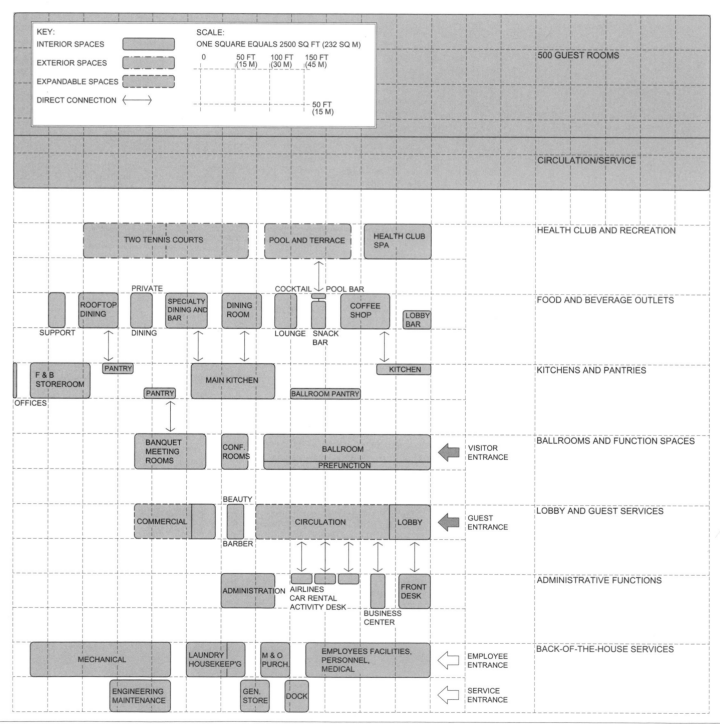

**HOTEL SPACES AND RELATIONSHIPS DIAGRAM**

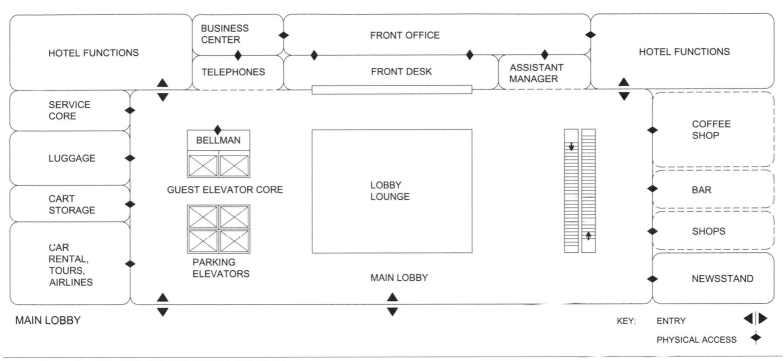

**MAIN LOBBY SPACES AND RELATIONSHIPS DIAGRAM**

## MAIN LOBBY: PLANNING AND DESIGN

The main lobby is the principal space around which the hotel is formed; it is the "heart" of the hotel. Functionally, it serves as the guest's point of orientation; all hotel functions radiate from the lobby; guest and visitor circulation begin and end here. This central space is the focus of many hotel operations and guest activities and conceptually serves as the organizing principle for the entire design.

### Circulation

The general circulation layout should facilitate movement and provide for the separation of guests, staff, and maintenance personnel, to avoid disturbing the guests and to enable efficient service. The designer should separate the circulation of resident and nonresident guests by providing direct access to, for instance, restaurants and banquet halls, to avoid congestion in the main reception area and provide better control and supervision. The quality of the design and practicality of the layout must satisfy four diverse functions:

• Guest services
• Social activities
• Guest Circulation
• Visitor Circulation

The arriving hotel guest's first concern is registration, therefore, the front desk should be accessible and highly visible from the entrance, along with the telephones, assistant manager's desk, concierge station, and the bell captain's station. The following facilities are often required in the registration area: standing-height counter, for guests to write on; house telephone; space for public transit timetables and tourist brochures; U.S. Postal Service mailbox and stamp dispenser; clocks and calendars, visible by staff and guests; a safe for guests' use; and luggage storage.

Other guest services that should be near, but not necessarily in, the lobby are the information desk; newsstand; luggage room; and airlines, car rental, and theater ticket concessions.

### Social Activities

The lobby is often the site of a lounge, bar, tea service, or restaurant. Even without food and beverage service as the focal point, however, groupings of furniture are typically arranged to facilitate conversation. A successful lobby design accommodates waiting, relaxing, and meeting both for residential and nonresidential guests.

### Guest Circulation

Guest arriving with baggage should receive assistance at the main entrance of the hotel by the doorman. Registration occurs at the front desk, with two excep-

tions: VIP guests may register on a special VIP floor, and large groups that have preregistered may use a meeting room to receive room keys and instructions. Direct access must be possible for all guests from the main entrance to the point of registration and to their individual guest rooms without passing through any ancillary spaces. Parking access to the hotel should connect to the main registration level and, for security reasons, be completely separate from guest floor circulation.

### Visitor Circulation

Visitors arriving at the hotel to browse, dine, or attend a scheduled function should be encouraged to pass through the main lobby. Certain hotel functions may, however, have separate entrances depending on the hotel's location and specific programmatic objectives. Frequently, a separate ballroom entrance is used where large-scale events may occur.

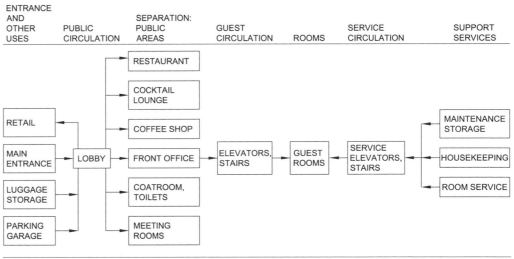

**HOTEL CIRCULATION AND RELATIONSHIP DIAGRAM**

## GUEST ROOMS

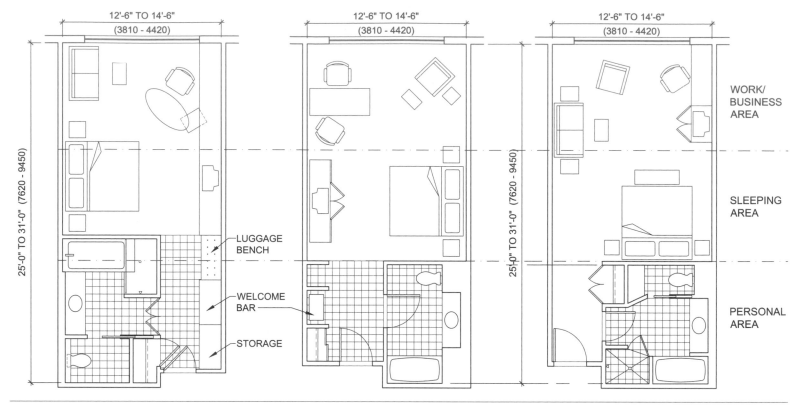

12'-6" TO 14'-6" (3810 - 4420)

12'-6" TO 14'-6" (3810 - 4420)

12'-6" TO 14'-6" (3810 - 4420)

25'-0" TO 31'-0" (7620 - 9450)

25'-0" TO 31'-0" (7620 - 9450)

WORK/ BUSINESS AREA

SLEEPING AREA

PERSONAL AREA

LUGGAGE BENCH

WELCOME BAR

STORAGE

**ROOM CONFIGURATIONS FOR STANDARD ROOM SIZE**

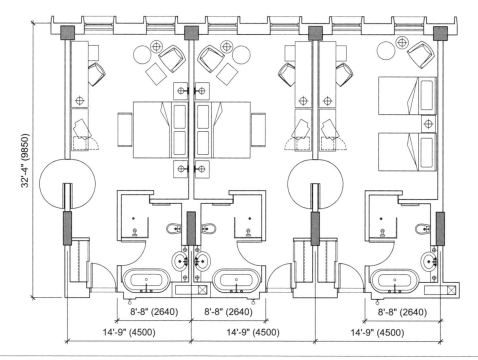

32'-4" (9850)

8'-8" (2640)    8'-8" (2640)    8'-8" (2640)

14'-9" (4500)    14'-9" (4500)    14'-9" (4500)

**STANDARD ROOM COMBINATIONS**

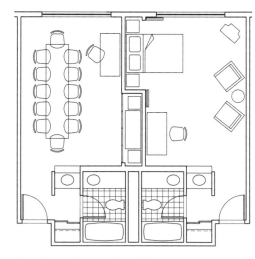

**GUEST ROOM ADAPTED AS MEETING ROOM**

## STANDARD SUITES

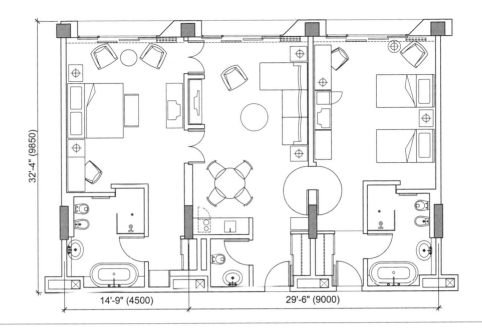

32'-4" (9850)

14'-9" (4500)   29'-6" (9000)

## TWO-BEDROOM SUITE

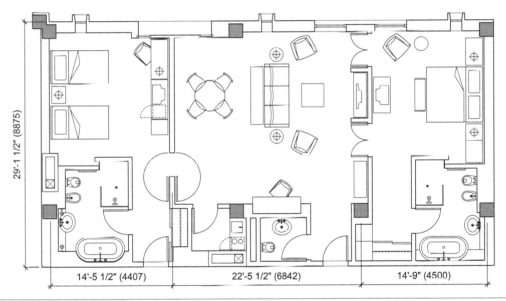

29'-1 1/2" (8875)

14'-5 1/2" (4407)   22'-5 1/2" (6842)   14'-9" (4500)

## TWO-BEDROOM LUXURY SUITE

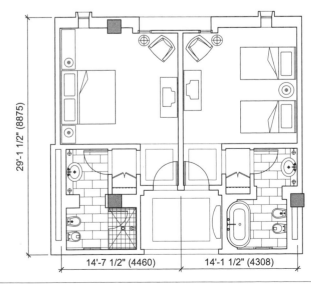

29'-1 1/2" (8875)

14'-7 1/2" (4460)   14'-1 1/2" (4308)

**PAIR ROOMS WITH ENTRY VESTIBULE**

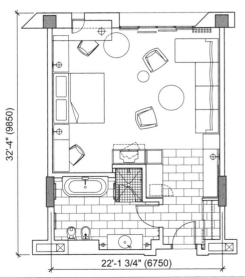

32'-4" (9850)

22'-1 3/4" (6750)

**SUITE WITH FIVE-FIXTURE BATHROOM**

## GUEST ROOM BATHROOMS

### Design Considerations

For many hotels, the guest room bathrooms are an important element in defining the level of luxury for the hotel. For high-end hotels, bathrooms may feature the separation of wet and dry areas and the compartmentalization of toilets and bidets. Consider the following for incorporation into the bathroom design:

- Durable hardware and finishes
- Adequate vanity lighting and a large mirror
- Sufficient counter/shelf area for cosmetics
- Adequate overhead lighting to allow reading in tub
- Number of fixtures

Typical U.S. guest room baths have three fixtures: toilet, sink, and tub. Luxury U.S. baths have four fixtures: toilet, sink, shower stall, and tub.  European and Middle-Eastern suites generally have four fixtures; toilet, bidet, sink, and tub. Deluxe suites will have large bathrooms with custom-designed tubs and two sinks. Occasionally, separate showers, sauna, or steam-rooms are provided.

Bathtubs are usually 5 ft (1.5 m) in length, although the 5 ft 6 in. (1.65 m) tub is popular in first-class hotels. All bathroom fixtures should have individual shut-off valves accessible within bathroom for easy maintenance. Countertops should be a minimum of 4 ft (1,220 mm) in length, with backsplashes against all adjacent walls.  Bathroom hardware usually includes the following:

- Shower rod 1¼ in. (30 mm) in diameter and 6 ft 2 in. (1.85 m) above the floor
- Towel shelf for clean towels
- Towel bar near sink
- Towel bar near tub
- Grab bar in tub
- Dual toilet paper holder
- Recessed soap dishes beside tub
- Robe hooks
- Facial tissue container, which may be built in
- Convenience outlet for shavers and hair dryers near sink

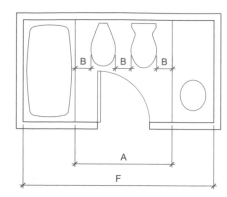

**FOUR-FIXTURE BATHROOM**

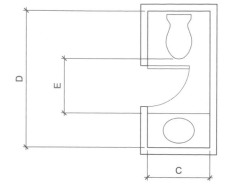

**TOILET ROOM**

**BATHROOM DIMENSIONS**

### BATHROOM DIMENSIONS

| | MINIMUM | COMFORTABLE | IDEAL |
|---|---|---|---|
| A | 4'-1" (1.25 m) | 4'-4" (1.32 m) | 4'-7" (1.40 m) |
| B | 7" (0.18 m) | 8" (0.2 m) | 10" (0.25 m) |
| C | 2'-8" (0.81 m) | 3'-0" (0.91 m) | 3'-0" (0.91 m) |
| D | 5'-10" (1.78 m) | 6'-6" (1.98 m) | 6'-8" (2.03 m) |
| E | 1'-6" (0.46 m) | 1'-10" (0.56 m) | 2'-0" (0.61 m) |
| F | 8'-7" (2.62 m) | 8'-10" (2.69 m) | 9'-1" (2.77 m) |

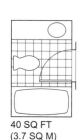

40 SQ FT
(3.7 SQ M)

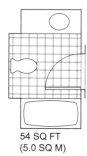

54 SQ FT
(5.0 SQ M)

72 SQ FT
(6.7 SQ M)

**THREE-FIXTURE BATHROOMS**

56 SQ FT
(5.2 SQ M)

78 SQ FT
(7.2 SQ M)

96 SQ FT
(8.9 SQ M)

110 SQ FT
(10.2 SQ M)

**FOUR-FIXTURE BATHROOMS**

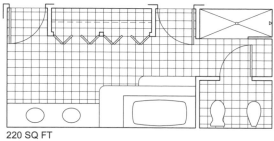

220 SQ FT
(20.4 SQ M)

**FIVE-FIXTURE BATHROOM**

# GUEST ROOM CORRIDOR DESIGN

Public corridor design should be a continuation of the quality, style, and ambiance established in both the public space and the guest rooms. The guest room corridor bridges the transition from the public space to the private space. Confluence of design can be achieved through imaginative repetition of basic design elements.

Long double-loaded corridors are typical for hotel guest room floors. The corridor is usually restricted to the minimum width and height. Large mechanical ducts typically run in the ceiling space of the public corridor and limit the ceiling height to the minimum of 7 ft (2,130 mm). The minimum corridor width is usually 8 ft (2,440 mm) for a double-loaded corridor.

A variety of design elements can be employed to break down the homogeneity of a long corridor. Door groupings and locations can be varied to create varying rhythms. Repetitive door recesses, altered ceiling heights, pilasters, repetitive light fixtures, and variations in carpet patterns, wall finishes, and color schemes can be used to add interest to a long, double-loaded corridor.

A maid's closet should be located in the corridor near the service elevator. Plan for one maid's closet for every 15 to 30 rooms, depending upon the level of service the hotel intends to provide.

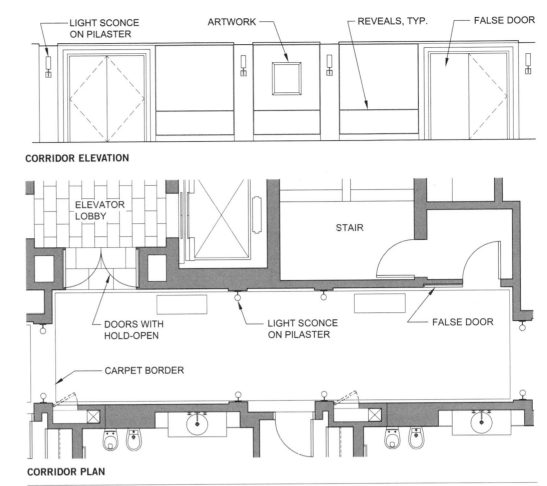

**CORRIDOR ELEVATION**

**CORRIDOR PLAN**

**OFFSET GUEST ROOM ENTRIES**

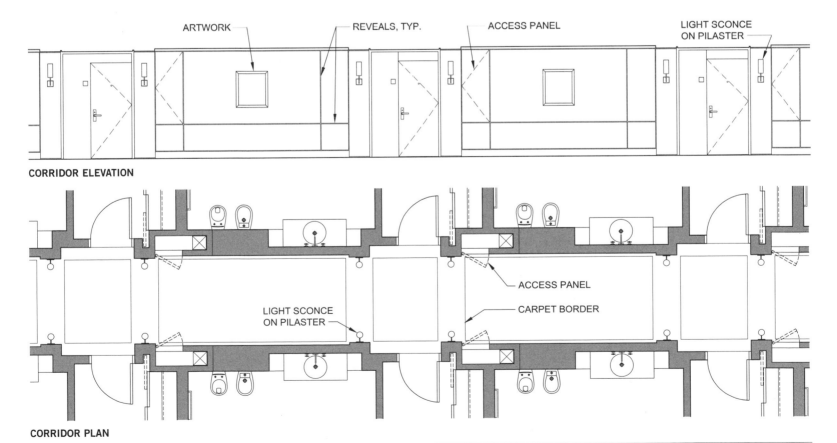

**CORRIDOR ELEVATION**

**CORRIDOR PLAN**

**ALIGNED GUEST ROOM ENTRIES AT REGULAR INTERVALS, FORMING NODAL POINTS**

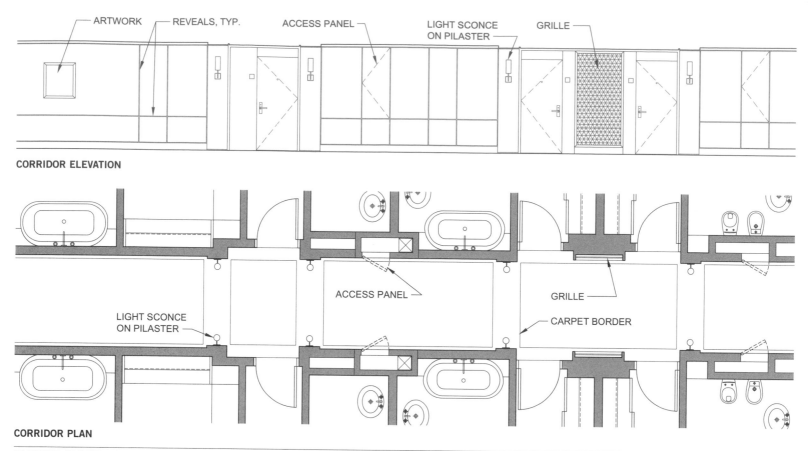

CORRIDOR ELEVATION

CORRIDOR PLAN

**ALIGNED GUEST ROOM ENTRIES AT ALTERNATING INTERVALS**

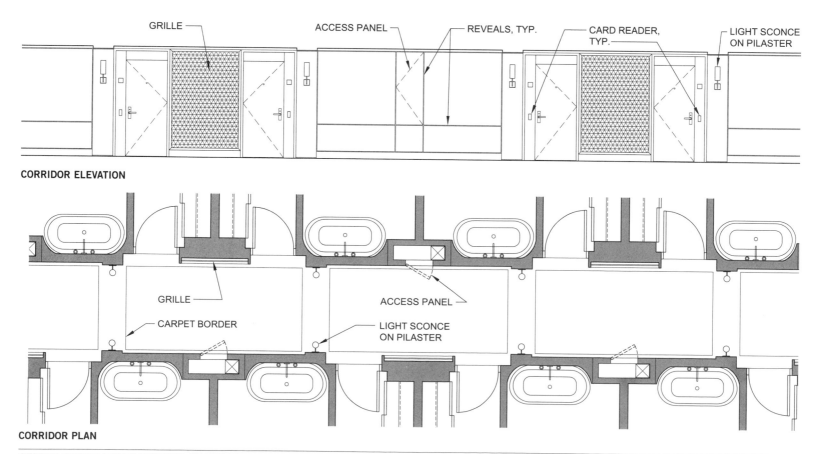

CORRIDOR ELEVATION

CORRIDOR PLAN

**OFFSET GUEST ROOM ENTRIES AT REGULAR INTERVALS**

# FUNCTION ROOMS

## Ballrooms

Ballrooms are used for formal entertainment and as banquet and meeting spaces. The décor is typically formal with quality finishes, carpeting, and decorative lighting. The adjacent prefunction space complements the ballroom décor and serves as a place to gather to have cocktails or to register for meetings.

Because ballrooms attract guests sometimes in evening attire, separation of circulation from exhibition traffic and more casual areas of the hotel is desirable. Direct and formal access from the main lobby is important because ballrooms are often used for community functions. Under certain circumstances, separate access to the street may be desirable. Ballrooms require expansive column-free space, which readily subdivides into two or three rooms, often in the proportion of one-third or two-thirds.

## Meeting Rooms

Meeting rooms are semiformal spaces used for lectures, conferences, meetings, and an occasional cocktail party. Direct access from the main lobby and guest rooms is desirable. An internal connection with the ballroom is important as well, to increase the flexibility in programming meetings and breakout sessions.

Meeting rooms should be planned as flexibly as possible to accommodate various size groups between 30 and 200 persons. Large meeting rooms need prefunction corridors to allow guests to congregate prior to meeting. Boardrooms and private dining rooms may function better when designed as fixed rather than as flexible space.

## Exhibition Spaces

Exhibition areas provide display space for various trade shows attended by guests, community members in the trade, and, on occasion, the general public. Direct access from the street is practical because of the number of visitors expected. Guest access, however, should be through the main lobby, for security reasons. Exhibition area finishes may be considered "serviceable," as these spaces must be designed for heavy traffic and constantly changing exhibits. Exhibition space is rarely provided in smaller or upscale properties.

Exhibition areas have columns located on a grid to accommodate display booths that are, maximum, 8 × 10 ft (2.4 × 3 m) and/or 10 × 10 ft (3 × 3 m), and aisles that are 8 to 10 ft (2.4 to 3 m) in width. Ceilings heights should be in comfortable proportion to the overall space. Division of the exhibition space is sometimes desirable to allow for different-size shows.

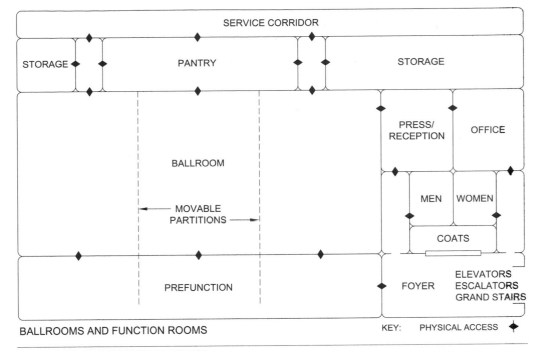

BALLROOMS AND FUNCTION ROOMS    KEY: PHYSICAL ACCESS ◆

**BALLROOM ADJACENCIES DIAGRAM**

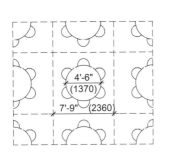 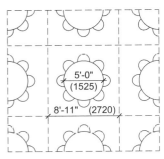 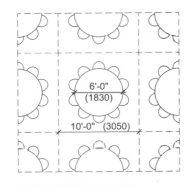

**TABLE SEATING FOR SIX**
Banquet module: 7 ft 9 in. by 7 ft 9 in. (2,360 by 2,360 mm)
Area: 60 sq ft (5.5 sq m)

**TABLE SEATING FOR EIGHT**
Banquet module: 8 ft 11 in. by 8 ft 11 in. (2,720 by 2,720 mm)
Area: 80 sq ft (7.4 sq m)

**TABLE SEATING FOR TEN**
Banquet module: 10 ft by 10 ft (3,050 by 3,050 mm)
Area: 100 sq ft (9.2 sq m)

**BANQUET SEATING—10 SQ FT (.9 SQ M) PER PERSON**

### Food and Service Considerations

Ballrooms, if not backed up to a main kitchen, require a full service pantry. Meeting rooms require small pantries or coffee service, while boardrooms and private dining rooms need adjacent pantries. Exhibition areas may occasionally have in-house food and beverage service. In general, vending machines are provided and operated by an independent company.

### Dock and Elevator Considerations

Exhibition areas and ballrooms may be used to exhibit large bulky items, even automobiles. Direct, same-level access with the loading dock is both efficient and economical, especially for exhibition areas. Having at least one major function on the dock level eliminates the need for additional large-freight elevators.

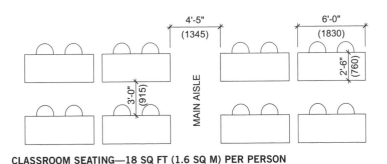 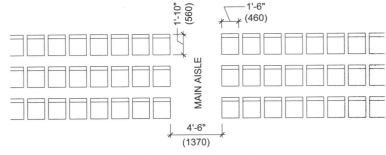

**CLASSROOM SEATING—18 SQ FT (1.6 SQ M) PER PERSON**

**THEATER SEATING—9 SQ FT (.8 SQ M) PER PERSON**

**MEETING SEATING**

## STRUCTURAL BAY DETERMINANTS

Guest rooms and ballrooms are the primary areas to be considered in establishing the structural span requirements for a hotel. Other hotel areas that require large spans (for example, recreational areas or nightclubs) may be located either on the roof level or within the ballroom's structural bay. Atrium and lobby spaces are generally located outside the guest tower footprint and have a separate framing system. Parking, when introduced to the building, should not determine, but rather be adjusted to fit within, the overall structural system.

Ballrooms and other areas requiring long spans or special structures should be located outside the footprint of the guest tower to alleviate major and expensive structural design problems required in transferring loads. Often these elements are placed adjacent to the guest tower, in the crux of an L- or between the legs of the H- and U-shaped guest towers.

Ballrooms must have column-free interiors, which necessitates long-span structural bays. Clear width requirements vary between 35 and 95 ft (10 and 28 m), depending on the programmed area specified by the hotel operator. Ballrooms spans are based on ballroom areas established from banquet seating requirements of 12 sq ft per person (1 sq m per person). The clear ceiling height for ballrooms is between 16 and 34 ft (1.5 and 3.1 m).

## ACOUSTICS

Isolate guest rooms from elevator shafts, ice and beverage dispenser rooms, and major duct chases. "Buffer spaces" such as janitorial services, storage, and stair towers can be placed between guest rooms and sources of noise. Avoid locating guest rooms over bars and live (amplified) entertainment spaces. Minimize glazing on exterior walls facing freeways, airports, rail lines, and other major sources of noise. Locate laundries, pool equipment, central plant equipment, and outdoor equipment, such as cooling towers, where noise is least likely to cause conflicts with guest activities or neighboring properties (local noise zoning ordinances may need to be reviewed).

### Guest Rooms

An STC of 50 or greater should be used for guest rooms. Place TVs in cabinets for better sound isolation from the adjacent wall. Insulate corridor doors to at least B-label standards. Use solid-core doors at bath. Locations near freeways, rail lines, airports, and racetracks may require special exterior skin design noise assistance from a consultant. Carpet floors for impact noise control. Use flat-slab construction for economy and ease of sealing demising partitions to overhead structure. Air conditioning background noise levels should be limited to NC 35.

### Meeting Rooms and Ballrooms

Enclose meeting rooms and ballrooms with STC 55 to 60 partitions. Use heavy doors with frame seals. Use corridors to buffer meeting rooms from kitchen noise. Movable partitions should provide STC 52 to 55; avoid accordion-style partitions if speech privacy is required. Specify carpet, especially if meeting room or ballroom is over occupied spaces. Portable dance floors can be set up on carpet when required. Mixes of drywall, wood, fiberglass-reinforced gypsum elements, and acoustical panels are acceptable for ceilings, if sound-absorbing area can be at least 50% of ceiling area.

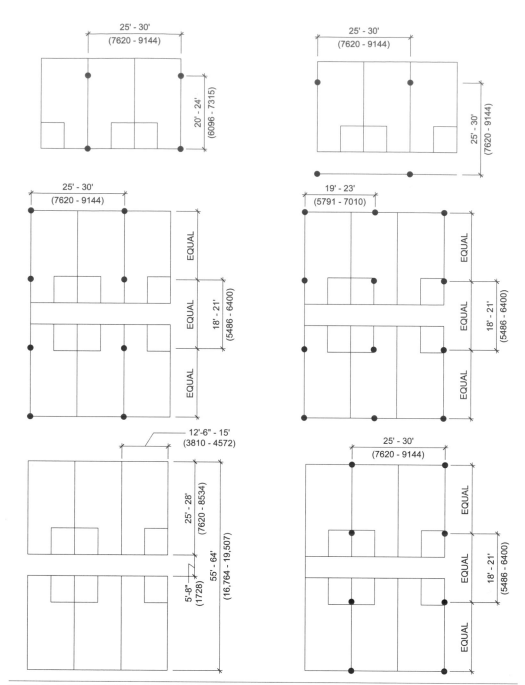

**TYPICAL STRUCTURAL BAYS AND COLUMN LOCATIONS FOR GUEST TOWERS**

### BALLROOM DIMENSIONS*

| OCCUPANCY | AREA SQ FT (SQ M) | LENGTH FT (M) | × | WIDTH FT (M) |
|---|---|---|---|---|
| 200 persons | 2,400 (216) | 70 (21) | × | 35 (10) |
| 400 persons | 4,800 (432) | 100 (30) | × | 48 (14) |
| 600 persons | 7,200 (648) | 120 (36) | × | 60 (18) |
| 800 persons | 9,600 (864 ) | 138 (41) | × | 70 (21) |
| 1,000 persons | 12,000 (1,080) | 150 (45) | × | 80 (24) |
| 1,500 persons | 18,000 (1,620) | 190 (57) | × | 95 (29) |

*Based on a proportion of 2:1 (width being clear span).

The minimum recommended ceiling NRC is 0.60. Sound-absorbing fabric-wrapped fiberglass panels on walls with an NRC of 0.80 are useful at reducing reverberant noise buildup during events. Treat 20% to 50% of available wall surface area with acoustical panels. Panels can be spaced up to a few feet apart for aesthetic purposes. For panels that are below door-head height, specify an impact-resistant construction, available from most panel manufacturers. HVAC rating should not exceed NC 35.

SOM; New York, New York
Michael L. Blankenship; Rhode Island School of Design; Providence, Rhode Island
May Sophonpanich; Rhode Island School of Design; Providence, Rhode Island

# RESTAURANTS

Restaurant interiors offer designers the opportunity to create a distinctive environment, which reinforces the restaurant concept. For restaurants, an inviting interior space is as desirable as a reputation for good food and service. A strong restaurant concept is essential for the design and operation of the restaurant to attract diners. The well-designed restaurant transcends restaurant type; an appealing fast-food café may be as successful as an upscale establishment.

## RESTAURANT TYPES

### Fast-Food Restaurants

Fast-food restaurants provide a limited menu that is inexpensive, cooked quickly, and served with little or no waiting. There is no table service in fast-food restaurants, and beverage, condiment, and trash receptacles may be located in the dining area. Often, eating utensils, such as spoons or forks, are not required to consume the food. Seating in fast-food restaurants, often molded fiberglass or other nonupholstered selections, is designed for ease of cleaning and maintenance. The seating is also limited in comfort, to encourage brief stays. The comfort of the seating arrangement is often related to the amount of money spent on a meal.

### Full-Service Restaurants

In a full-service restaurant, a wait staff serves seated patrons. Full-service restaurants range from casual dining establishments to upscale, fine dining restaurants. The level of comfort, refinement, and service reflects the type of restaurant. Full-service restaurants may include bars, private dining areas, banquet facilities, and possibly live entertainment areas. An upscale restaurant may contain higher-maintenance materials and finishes, and tables may be larger and more widely spaced than in a casual family restaurant. Comfortable chairs with arms might be used in a restaurant that anticipates a diner's stay to be over an hour.

## PLANNING AND DESIGN

Restaurant planning and design commences with the development of a restaurant program. The restaurant concept determines the type of design and the operation of the restaurant. The concept or dining experience desired, menu, type of clientele, hours of operation, and operations concerns all contribute to the success of the restaurant design.

A restaurant program incorporates subjective design criteria, which affect space allocation and design. For example, many restaurants prefer to have a small waiting area, which, when full, promotes the impression that the restaurant is popular. If a general dining room is planned to be a noisy, energetic space, then secluded or private dining areas might be incorporated as a bal-

ance. The number of dining seats is an important consideration in determining waiting area and kitchen space requirements. Each restaurant presents unique challenges, which must be addressed by the owner and operations staff, designer, and food service consultant.

### Front of House and Back of House

The *front-of-the-house* operations (areas the patron utilizes, such as entry area, waiting room, dining room, and bar) must be carefully coordinated with the *back-of-the-house* facilities (kitchen, food and beverage storage, offices, trash removal). Typically, the back of the house is designed by food equipment consultants. The design of the patron area must support the functions of the service areas; the service areas must carry out the concept of the patron area.

### Acoustic Considerations

Acoustic privacy is generally not an issue in large public dining spaces. Secluded banquettes and private dining rooms can be set apart for better acoustic and visual separation. Food preparation noise can be isolated by careful placement of kitchen entries or the use of a vestibule, double-entry doors, or serpentine staging areas.

Some restaurants are intentionally designed to be noisy to hasten departures and increase table turnaround, thus increasing profitability. The NC/RC range can be up to 40 for a noisy, quick turnaround restaurant. An NC/RC of 35 is more appropriate for a general-purpose service restaurant. For a quiet conversational environment, an NC/RC of 30 is desirable.

### Adjacencies

Restaurant adjacencies typically follow a prescribed flow, with public front-of-the-house spaces separated from the functional back-of-the-house areas. Consider waiting area, traffic to the dining and bar spaces, restroom locations, and service staff flow throughout the restaurant.

In the back of the house, separate the food preparation from the soiled dish and trash pickup. Traffic should not cross between the preparation food line and the soiled food/dishwashing areas. Consider adjacencies and circulation from the receiving area into the back-of-the-house spaces; food and supply deliveries, staging, and storage should not impede the flow of staff.

### RELATIONSHIP BETWEEN TIME AND MONEY SPENT ON MEALS

| TIME SPENT IN RESTAURANT | AMOUNT SPENT ON MEAL |
|---|---|
| < 45 minutes | Less than $15 |
| 45–90 minutes | Between $15 and $25 |
| > 60 minutes | More than $25 |

*Source: National Restaurant Association; Washington, D.C., 1993*

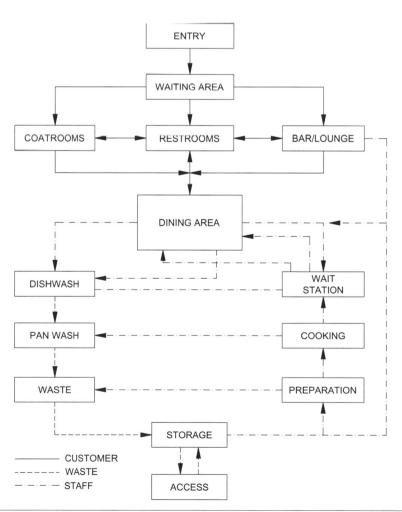

**RESTAURANT ADJACENCY DIAGRAM**

## SPACE ALLOCATION

The dining room and bar must be efficiently planned to ensure revenue potential. However, having more tables does not necessarily lead to increased revenue. Upscale restaurants generally require more space between tables for privacy. The restaurant concept, menu, and operation style influences space allocation. Depending on the type of restaurant and menu, kitchen areas range from 30% to 45% of the total restaurant area.

### PRELIMINARY GUIDE FOR FRONT-OF-HOUSE AREAS

| FOOD SERVICE VENUE | SUGGESTED AREA PER PATRON SQ FT (SQ M) |
|---|---|
| Banquet Facility | 10–11 (.9–1.0) |
| Fast-Food | 11–14 (1–1.3) |
| Full-Service | 15–18 (1.4–1.7) |
| Cafeteria | 6–18 (1.5–1.7) |
| Upscale Gourmet | 17–22 (1.6–2.0) |

## CODE REQUIREMENTS

Building codes identify restaurants as assembly spaces. Comply with local code requirements for construction, including plumbing fixture counts.

The *Americans with Disabilities Accessibility Guidelines* (ADAAG) defines requirements for accessible construction and furniture. These include handicapped accommodations in restrooms; counter, bar, and food service line-critical dimensions; furniture clearance requirements; and minimum dimensions for access aisles.

The local Department of Health reviews restaurants for compliance with regulations for general sanitation in food handling and proper food storage. Construction that is easily and readily cleanable, such as floor, wall, and ceiling surfaces, and equipment that is sanitary and cleanable is required. A food service consultant designs and specifies back-of-the-house stainless-steel equipment and installation methods.

## INTERIOR FINISHES

Restaurant interior finishes and materials vary from the front of the house to the back of the house. The public area interior finishes and materials should support the quality level and maintenance effort desired for the restaurant concept.

Interior materials are typically required to be flame-retardant. The selection of interior finishes and materials durability is dependent on the restaurant concept and desired life of the products. Restaurant interiors are often scheduled to be redesigned or refurbished on a five-year cycle, as not only do concepts become stale, but finishes become worn and stained.

The food-handling area finishes must be sanitary, easily cleaned, and durable. Flooring should be impervious and slip-resistant; bases should be coved or as defined by the local health department; wall surfaces should be FDA-approved fiberglass-reinforced plastic (FRP) panels or other acceptable material, such as tile or other impervious product; ceilings should be cleanable, such as Mylar-faced panels.

## LIGHTING

Lighting in restaurants establishes mood and ambiance. Lighting levels may vary based on hours of operation; a restaurant that is open only during the day may have different lighting requirements from an establishment open for evening dinner service. Restaurants typically utilize incandescent lighting, which provides a warm-quality light. Incandescent lamps are less energy-efficient than fluorescent lamps. The quality of fluorescent light is generally not desirable in restaurant public spaces; however, it is acceptable for back-of-the-house areas. Light fixtures located in food preparation areas should be equipped with a cleanable prismatic or other lens that covers the unit.

Consider the dramatic effect of local lighting or ambient lighting, which provides soft illumination. Multiple light source types may be appropriate.

Review the materials and finishes proposed for a restaurant, under conditions that replicate the space and under day and evening lighting conditions.

## RESTAURANT PATRON AREAS

### Dining and Bar Area

Restaurant patrons typically develop their first impressions of the restaurant from the main dining room and bar areas. The interior design and overall ambiance of the restaurant signal the type of dining experience for the patron. The restaurant concept may offer a variety of space types, including open or multilevel dining areas, secluded alcoves, private dining rooms, or features such as display cooking areas. A mix of seating and table types, adequate aisle and serving areas, and well-chosen materials and lighting combine to create a comfortable, inviting dining environment.

Flexibility in dining spaces is an asset. Private dining and compartmentalization of the main dining areas provide a means of accommodating large or small groups of diners without disrupting the general dining area.

Bar areas may be open to the dining area or separate, possibly with a different design aesthetic from the main dining area. Consider the hours of use, smoking areas (if allowed), and other elements that may influence the location and adjacency of the bar to the dining area, such as the noise generated with the use of televisions.

### Restrooms

Restrooms should be placed in a convenient location for restaurant patrons. Due to odors and noise, it may be prudent to locate the restrooms away from the entrance and waiting areas. Consider screening the restroom entrance from the dining area.

The design of the restrooms is as important as that for the dining areas. Patrons should be confident that the restrooms are clean, well maintained, and adequate for peak-time needs. Building codes identify minimum plumbing fixture counts; however, it may be advantageous to increase the fixture count to accommodate the patrons at peak occupancy times. Refer to the ADAAG for accessible restroom requirements.

## WAIT STAFF SERVICE STATIONS

Wait staff service stations are located between the front of the house and the back of the house. Service stations should be fabricated from stainless steel or other cleanable materials, and are typically furnished with equipment, supplies, and selected beverages. Many service stations include a point-of-service (POS) terminal to calculate patron bills and process credit card receipts, depending on the operations preference of the restaurant owner.

The size and configuration of the space may determine the number of wait staff stations/POS terminals.

## FURNITURE AND FURNISHINGS

Different table sizes and shapes offer variety in seating arrangements. Table sizes are known as *tops*—two-top, four-top—and reflect the number of seats at that table type. The mix of table sizes is dependent on the target clientele, menu, and general operational goals. Two-top tables are popular in urban areas for efficiency in seating; 36-in. (915-mm) square tables may be more desirable for two diners, but this table size occupies more area.

Table options include flip-up corners or edges to increase table size or to change shape (square table to a round table).

Chair selections reflect the type of comfort level desired; a fast-food restaurant may provide hard-surface chairs and nonupholstered seats to discourage lingering, while a full-service restaurant may provide comfortable, upholstered dining chairs. Chair arms assist diners in standing, and may be used more frequently in higher-end restaurants. Arms may not be desired in a casual dining area with tighter aisle clearances.

Banquettes can be used to provide comfortable, flexible seating arrangements and midheight privacy screens. The table size mix can vary at banquette areas by locating tables next to one another or separately. Two-tops, for instance, can be combined to create a table for four or more diners. Booths are desirable for comfort, privacy, and intimacy.

# RESTAURANT FURNITURE DESIGN CRITERIA

## SERVICE AISLES

- For square seating, allow 72 in. (1,830 mm) minimum between tables (30 in. (760 mm) aisle plus two chairs back to back).
- For diagonal seating, allow 36 in. (915 mm) minimum between corners of tables.
- For wall seating, allow 30 in. (760 mm) minimum between wall and seat back.
- Allow a minimum of 30 in. (760 mm) for bus cart and service cart access.

## PATRON AISLES

- Refer to local codes for restrictions on requirements.
- For wheelchair access, allow 36 to 44 in. (915 to 1,120 mm) in aisles.
- For wall seating, allow 30 in. (760 mm) minimum between walls and table.
- Provide clear floor space for table access. Such clear floor space cannot overlap knee space by more than 19 in. (485 mm).

## TABLE PLACEMENT

- Allow circulation space adjacent to doors and food service areas.
- Provide an adequate number of table types for seating flexibility.
- Consider restaurant type when designing table layouts; generally, upscale restaurants have a more generous table spacing than casual full-service restaurants.

## TABLE AND COUNTER CRITERIA

- The tops of accessible tables and counters should be 28 to 34 in. (711 to 864 mm) high. A portable raised leaf may be provided to adapt lower tables.
- If seating for people in wheelchairs is provided at tables or counters, knee space at least 27 in. (685 mm) high, 30 in. (760 mm) wide, and 19 in. (485 mm) deep must be provided.
- Where food and drink are served at counters exceeding 34 in. (864 mm) in height, a portion of the main counter, 60 in. (1,524 mm) in length, should be made accessible; or accessible tables must be located in the same area.
- Corners and edges of table and countertops should be rounded for safety.

## SEATING CRITERIA

- Chair seat height is usually 18 in. (457 mm). Seat heights should be slightly higher at wheelchair-accessible tables.
- Seats should be a minimum of 16 in. (406 mm) deep and 16 in. (406 mm) wide.
- Padding and cushions should be firm.
- Armrests aid diners in rising from the seat.
- Table or counter supports should not interfere with seat knee space so the feet can be positioned for rising.

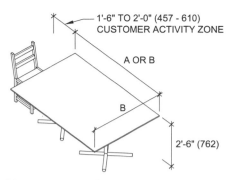

1'-6" TO 2'-0" (457 - 610) CUSTOMER ACTIVITY ZONE

A OR B

B

2'-6" (762)

**RECTANGULAR TABLE**

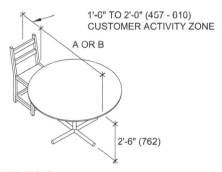

1'-6" TO 2'-0" (457 - 610) CUSTOMER ACTIVITY ZONE

A OR B

2'-6" (762)

**ROUND TABLE**

## STANDARD TABLE DIMENSIONS

### SQUARE TABLES

| PERSONS | A OR B |
|---|---|
| Two | 2 ft–2 ft 6 in. (610–760 mm) |
| Four | 3 ft–3 ft 6 in. (915–1,065 mm) |

### RECTANGULAR TABLES

| PERSONS | A | B |
|---|---|---|
| Two (on one side) | 3 ft 6 in.–4 ft (1,065–1,220 mm) | |
| Six (three on each side) | 5 ft 10 in.–7 ft (1,778–2134 mm) | 2 ft 6 in.–3 ft (760–915 m) |
| Eight (four on each side) | 7 ft 6 in.–9 ft (2,285–2,745 mm) | |

1'-6" TO 2'-0" (457 - 610) CUSTOMER ACTIVITY ZONE

A OR B

2'-6" (762)

**SQUARE TABLE**

Round tables are usually recommended for seating four or more persons.

Dimension "A" depends on the perimeter length required per seat (1 to 2 ft; 560 to 610 mm) per person. For cocktails, 1 ft 6 in. (460 mm) is sufficient.

Tables 3 ft (915 mm) and wider will seat at least one person at each end.

Smaller table sizes are satisfactory for drink service; larger sizes are needed for dining. Tables with center bases accommodate ganged table arrangements better than four-legged tables.

The type and style of service affects tables and arrangements. Consider the use of service carts and high chairs, as well as accessibility for the disabled.

### ROUND TABLES

| PERSONS | A |
|---|---|
| Four to five | 3 ft–3 ft 6 in. (915–1,065 mm) |
| Six to seven | 3 ft 6 in.–4 ft 6 in. (1,065–1,370 mm) |
| Seven to eight | 4 ft 6 in.–5 ft (1,370–1,525 mm) |
| Eight to ten | 5 ft–6 ft (1,525–1,830 mm) |

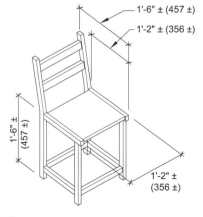

1'-6" ± (457 ±)

1'-2" ± (356 ±)

1'-6" ± (457 ±)

1'-2" ± (356 ±)

**CHAIR**

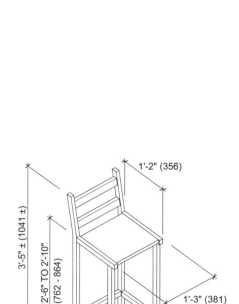

1'-2" (356)

3'-5" ± (1041 ±)

2'-6" TO 2'-10" (762 - 864)

1'-3" (381)

**STOOL**

**TYPICAL DIMENSIONS**

## ACOUSTICS

Acoustical requirements vary within a restaurant. The level of noise can be controlled with the use of sound-absorptive materials and finishes and by compartmentalization of areas. Certain restaurant types may desire noisier dining and bar areas. In these cases, a noisy, bustling, energetic environment is part of the restaurant concept.

### Privacy

Privacy is not an issue in large public dining areas. Secluded banquettes and private dining rooms can be set apart for more privacy, if desired.

Isolate kitchen noise through judicious placement of entrances and use of vestibules or serpentine staging areas to buffer against kitchen noise when doors are open.

### Reverberation and Reflection

Avoid creating areas that are too quiet, or "dead," to avoid connotation of little traffic or unpopularity. Many restaurants are designed to be loud and reverberant to create a vibrant atmosphere, discourage lingering, and increase "table turns" and, thus, profitability. Hard surfaces promote this philosophy.

Adding carpet, acoustical ceiling areas, and upholstered walls gives a plush, quiet atmosphere that is conducive to conversation, if that is the goal of the restaurant. High-backed, semienclosed banquettes can promote a sense of privacy even in a relatively noisy establishment.

### HVAC NC/RC Range

The NC/RC range may reach 40 or even 45 if a noisy, quick-turnaround atmosphere is desired. In general:

- 30 for a quiet, conversation-friendly and upscale environment.
- 40 for bars associated with restaurants.
- 35 for restaurants with quiet live music or piano bars; with amplified groups, 40 to 45.

### Exterior Noise Insulation

This is seldom an issue unless the restaurant is located in an extremely high noise environment. Vestibule entries and a central waiting area can buffer dining areas from exterior noise intrusion. Minimize glass area or increase its sound isolation rating, if required to reduce outdoor noise.

**BAR DIMENSIONS**

A = 8'-4" TO 11'-7" (2.5 m - 3.5 m)
B = 1'-6" TO 2'-0" (457 - 610)
C = 2'-4" TO 3'-2" (711 - 965)
D = 2'-6" TO 3'-0" (762 - 914)
E = 2'-0" TO 2'-6" (610 - 762)
F = 6" - 7" (152 - 178)
G = 1'-10" TO 2'-2" (559 - 660)
H = 2'-6" TO 2'-10" (762 - 864)
I = 11" TO 1'-10" (279 - 559)
J = 7" - 9" (178 - 229)
K = 6" - 9" (152 - 229)
L = 2'-6" (762)
M = 3'-6" TO 3'-9" (1067 - 1143)
N = 3'-0" TO 3'-6" (914 - 1067)
O = 5'-0" TO 5'-9" (1524 - 1753)

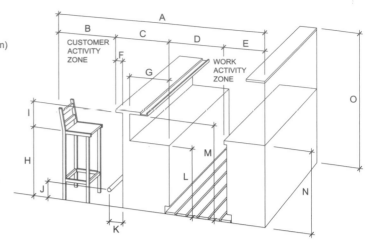

**BAR DIMENSIONS**
Ratio of counter seating to servers is 10:1 to 12:1.

**LOW COUNTER DIMENSIONS**

A = 4'-11" TO 5'-6" (1499 - 1676)
B = 3'-1" TO 3'-3" (940 - 991)
C = 1'-10" TO 2'-0" (559 - 610)
D = 1'-7" MINIMUM (483)
E = 1'-6" TO 2'-0" (457 - 610)
F = 2'-4" TO 2'-8" (711 - 813)
G = 2'-3" MINIMUM (686)
H = 4" - 8" (102 - 203)
I = 5'-0" MINIMUM (1524)

**LOW COUNTER DIMENSIONS**
A continental bar with low seating is one means of achieving accessibility. The bartender's area can be lowered or the seating area can be on a raised platform accessed by a ramp.

**BARS AND COUNTERS**

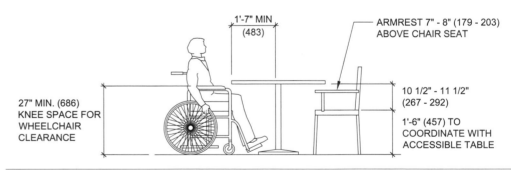

1'-7" MIN (483)

ARMREST 7" - 8" (179 - 203) ABOVE CHAIR SEAT

27" MIN. (686) KNEE SPACE FOR WHEELCHAIR CLEARANCE

10 1/2" - 11 1/2" (267 - 292)

1'-6" (457) TO COORDINATE WITH ACCESSIBLE TABLE

**ACCESSIBLE FURNITURE**

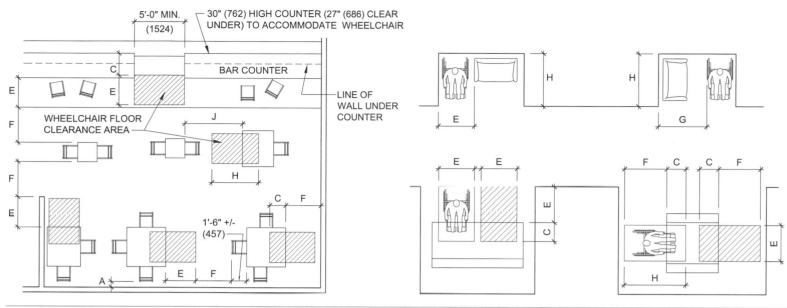

**SEATING ARRANGEMENTS FOR PERSONS USING WHEELCHAIRS**

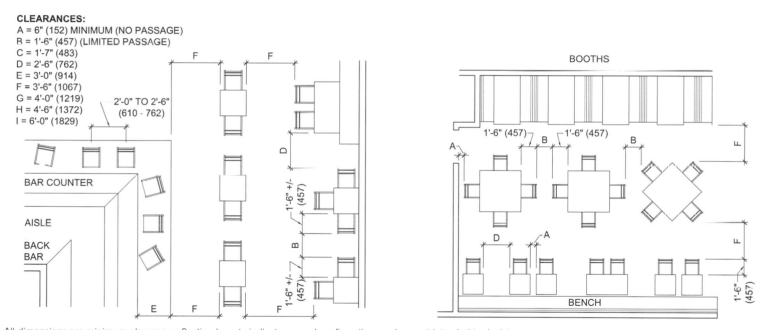

**CLEARANCES:**
A = 6" (152) MINIMUM (NO PASSAGE)
B = 1'-6" (457) (LIMITED PASSAGE)
C = 1'-7" (483)
D = 2'-6" (762)
E = 3'-0" (914)
F = 3'-6" (1067)
G = 4'-0" (1219)
H = 4'-6" (1372)
I = 6'-0" (1829)

All dimensions are minimum clearances. Seating layouts indicate general configurations and are not intended to depict any specific type of operation. Tables may be converted from square to round to enlarge seating capacity. Booth seating makes effective use of corner space. A wheelchair-accessible route, at least 36 in. (914 mm) wide, is required to connect the entrance, accessible fixed seating, and restrooms.

**TYPICAL SEATING ARRANGEMENTS**

# RESTAURANT SYSTEMS

## Mechanical

The mechanical system in a restaurant must function consistently to provide a comfortable environment for patrons. In the dining and bar areas, the heating and air conditioning needs may fluctuate with different occupancy levels and according to the changing seasons. Smoking areas (where allowed) in restaurants and bars are difficult to ventilate and may need to be in a different zone from other dining areas.

In kitchen, dishwashing, and other back-of-the-house areas, the heat and humidity generated will affect the overall mechanical system. Cooking areas require hoods to draw smoke and odors out of the kitchen area, and may tie into black-iron ducts. Certain cooking fuels, such as mesquite wood, can generate tarry substances, which may adhere to the inside of the ductwork. All grease-laden exhausts require cleanouts for access.

Some restaurants operate on a negative-pressure system, which helps in drawing heat, odors, and smoke out of the food service area. Consultation with mechanical engineers, code officials, and food service consultants is of utmost importance when designing exhaust hoods.

## Plumbing

Efficient, trouble-free plumbing is required for a restaurant operation. Dining area wait staff stations, bar areas, restrooms, food preparation areas, and dishwashing are all dependent on plumbing. Grease traps are required in kitchen/dishwashing areas.

## Coordination

Coordination of the food service equipment and the kitchen service supplies is critical. Rough-ins for plumbing, electrical, and gas service must be precisely located to ensure proper placement at equipment locations and coordination with finish materials.

## FOOD SERVICE EQUIPMENT

Food service equipment is typically specified by the food service consultant. All food service equipment must meet the sanitation and construction standards of the National Sanitation Foundation. Most equipment is located in the back of the house; however, some food serving display units are located in the public dining areas, in areas such as salad bars. Sneeze guards are required at open food displays, and refrigeration is required to store and serve perishable food.

Exhaust hoods remove air, water vapor, grease, and food odors from the kitchen area, and air and water vapor from dishwashing areas. Ovens and steam-jacketed kettles only require hoods that remove air, heat, and water vapor; but if large amounts of grease from a broiler, charbroiler, fryer, or grill are present, the hood system must extract this pollutant before the air is drawn outside by fans. This is done with grease "cartridges" or with stainless-steel extractors, both of which violently blow the exhausted air around. The grease particles are collected in a trough for easy removal, or are run out a drain.

- The length of the hood and the equipment types underneath determines CFM requirements for exhaust hoods. Typical requirements range from 150 to 450 CFM (4.2 to 12.7 cu m per minute) per linear foot (305 mm) of hood.
- Some codes may require a higher exhaust rate. To make up this air differential and to prevent more air from being drawn from surrounding areas, introduce air through a supply duct. The supplied air should make up 50% to 85% of the total exhaust.

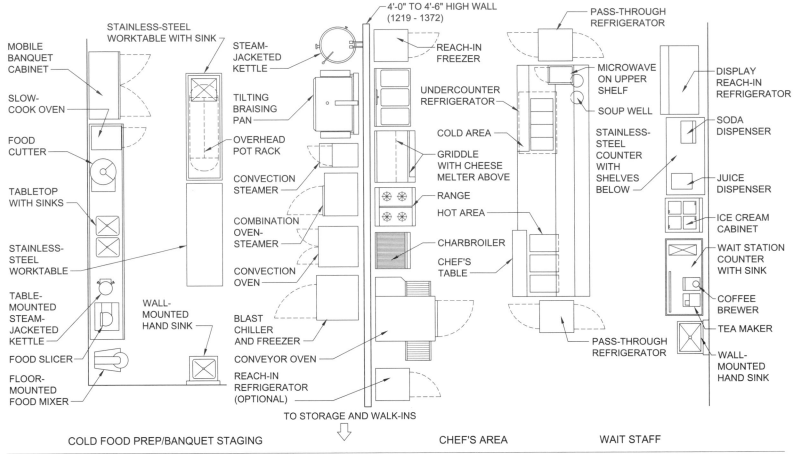

**TYPICAL KITCHEN PLAN**

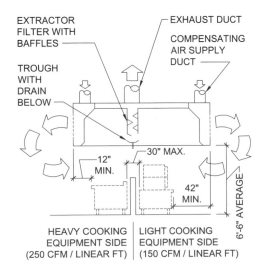

Single exhaust hoods are available for single cooking lines. Dimensions and capacities of exhaust hoods vary with particular kitchen cooking requirements.

**TYPICAL EXHAUST HOOD REQUIREMENTS**

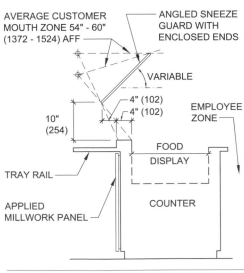

**COUNTER WITH SNEEZE GUARD**

*Source: Cini-Little International, Inc.; Schaumburg, Illinois*

Tim Shea, AIA; Richard Meier & Partners; Los Angeles, California
Ji-Seong Yun; Rhode Island School of Design; Providence, Rhode Island
Jim Johnson; Wrightson, Johnson, Haddon & Williams, Inc.; Dallas, Texas
Janet B. Rankin, AIA; Rippeteau Architects; Washington, D.C.
Cini-Little International, Inc., Food Service Consultants; Washington, D.C.

# LIBRARIES

## HISTORY

The word "library" is derived from the Latin word *liber*, for book. The earliest libraries were privately owned collections of books and scrolls, to be viewed only by the wealthy and the religious or political elite. As societies developed and economies expanded, centers of learning shifted from monasteries to schools and universities, where library collections were made available to scholars and students. With the invention of the printing press, the expansion of economic development, and, later, the establishment of more democratic governments, libraries began to open their doors to the public.

Early libraries housed their collections in simple cabinets. Books were opened upon lecterns for viewing and, often, were chained to the lectern to prevent thefts. Modern libraries today contain many different media and provide space for widely varying activities, from public lectures to private study, and from viewing film, video, DVDs, or other visual media to listening to audio collections on records, tapes, or CDs. With the advent of electronic information technologies, libraries are no longer simply repositories for physical collections of information, but are also portals of access to the enormous network of information on the Internet.

## CONCEPTUAL PLANNING

Conceptual planning for libraries begins with an assessment of the intended users of the facility. For example, a community or public library should respond to the wide range of ages and interests of the expected user groups. In contrast, an academic library designed only for upper-level collegiate work or private research will focus on the needs of a more specialized user group and inventory of library materials. In the programming phase, a set of spatial requirements is generated. This design program is written to reflect the specific needs of the facility and the materials that will be stored, accessed, and checked out.

Area calculations are made for these spatial requirements with a projected growth for the future. These calculations are based on formulas that differ for library types. The library staff and administration will contribute greatly to the design parameters that are outlined during the programming phase, since each library has unique operational procedures. If the facility will be a public library, often the design team will lead public meetings in order to understand the needs and goals of the community and to help the library board garner public support for the project. For larger libraries and academic libraries, often a library consultant is retained for this part of the design process.

## PROGRAM SPACES FOR LIBRARIES

The program for every library will differ in the content and layout of spaces. The diagram on this page is an example of interior spaces that may be included in the program for a small to medium-sized public library. A brief description of each of the major components is given in the following subsections.

### Auditorium

Some library boards desire an auditorium space in their program, for use in public presentations, readings, or other community events. This kind of space is generally adjacent to the public lobby, but is separate from the rest of the spaces that house the library's inventory of materials, to allow after-hours or separate use of the auditorium. The designer should determine early in the programming phase whether food or beverage vending is desired, and plan accordingly.

### Checkout

This is the central point in the flow of library materials and visitor traffic into and out of the facility. In addition to providing a desk where patrons check out materials, this area serves as a focal point for visitor inquiries and a source of initial wayfinding information for the facility. The library staff will have important input on the function and details for the design of this area, since the number of staff members and their duties will determine much of the programmatic direction for the space. Larger libraries may separate the checkout area from the control or inquiry functions for smoother traffic flow.

### Children's Area

For a community library, including a children's area will build enthusiasm for reading among children and for support of the library's reading programs. The children's area should be near the checkout desk to provide a visual connection between library staff and the area. Restrooms nearby are a basic requirement. Ideally, library visitors will be able to see the children's area from the lobby. Colorful signage and wall or ceiling materials will attract children's attention and provide a good signpost to guide them directly to the place designed just for them.

### Catalogue

Most libraries today have their collections catalogued on a database that is viewed from computer terminals. Some libraries, however, still utilize a paper card catalogue system, so the designer should confirm which system the library staff intends to use. Generally, this area should be located near the checkout desk so that staff members are available for inquiries, but it could be located separately if a staff desk is nearby so that patrons can conveniently seek assistance. Some libraries provide catalogue terminals within the stacks.

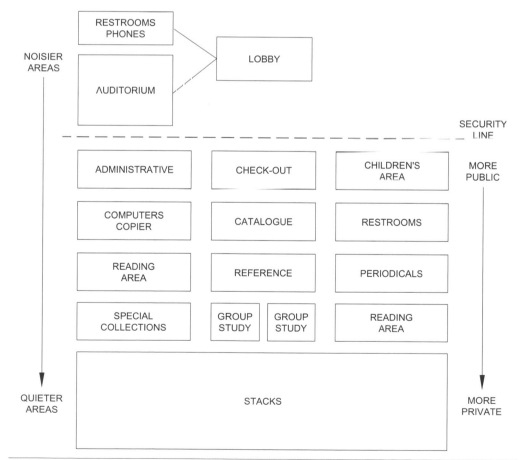

**CONCEPTUAL DIAGRAM FOR A SMALL PUBLIC LIBRARY**

## DESIGN CONSIDERATIONS

### Aisles

The aisles parallel to the stacks are called *range aisles;* those perpendicular to the stacks are called *cross aisles.* The minimum aisle width at accessible stacks is 36 in. (914 mm), to meet the requirements of the *Americans with Disabilities Act Accessibility Guidelines* (ADAAG); but 42 in. (1,066 mm) is preferred, to allow wheelchair access and enough space for an ambulatory person to pass. In some instances, the Building Code requires 44 in. (1,117 mm) aisles for adequate exiting, depending on whether the aisles are open to the public and the occupant load expected. The designer should review with the library staff where the more popular or frequently used collections will be positioned among the stacks, so that additional range aisle width can be provided to accommodate higher traffic in those areas. Range aisles are generally designed for the minimum required width in order to achieve maximum efficiency for the stack layout, with greater cross aisle width to handle the tributary loads of the range aisles. In all cases, the designer should review with the local code authority the minimum aisle and exit clearances at the stacks.

### Shelving

The shelving chosen for the stacks will depend on the size of materials in the library's collection. Standards in the United States for shelf depths are generally 7, 9, and 11 in. (177, 228, and 279 mm) actual dimension, or 8, 10, and 12 in. (203, 254, and 304 mm) nominal dimension, with deeper shelves available for oversize collections. Manufactured metal shelving is the most common product specified for new libraries because of its modularity, ease of adjustability, and cost-effectiveness. A variety of accessories are available, such as solid or wire bookends, slanted display shelves for periodicals, and placard holders. In regions where seismic concerns are important, shelving should be braced to the building structure to prevent overturning in an earthquake.

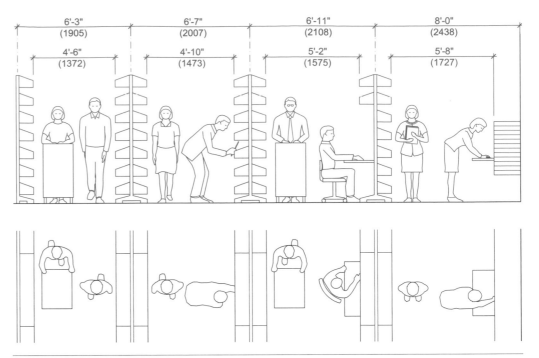

**STANDARD AISLE WIDTH**

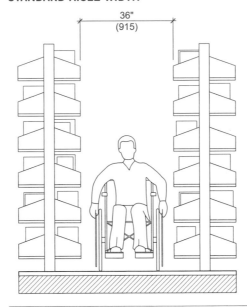

**AISLE WIDTH AT SHELVING**

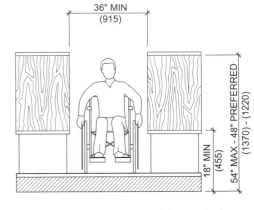

Human dimensions in very large aisles are clearly intended for very heavy use. The figure at the far right assumes a file cabinet that is 17½ in. (444 mm) deep, which is shallower than most. Even the typical card catalog cabinet is about 20 in. (508 mm) deep, including the handles.

**AISLE WIDTH AT CARD CATALOG**

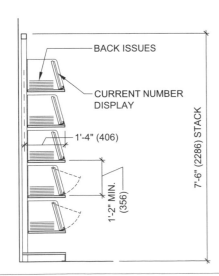

**PERIODICAL DISPLAY SHELVING**

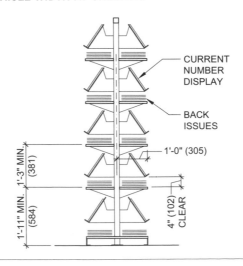

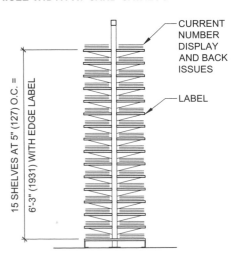

## Lighting

Adequate lighting, without glare, is the goal for most interior spaces in a library. Some collections may contain light-sensitive pieces, and these should be located in designated areas with lighting designed specifically for the parameters of the materials being stored and viewed.

Lighting at reading areas can be from overhead ambient sources, as well as from floor lamps or task lights on tabletops. Design of task lighting should be detailed to reduce glare on the table surface and to prohibit a direct view of the lamp source. Fixtures should be selected without a wide range of flexibility for the angle of the shade, to prevent users from inadvertently shining the fixture directly at those seated opposite.

### Ambient Lighting

Ambient lighting at the stacks can be provided with overhead fixtures, positioned in rows parallel to the shelving. This offers good light quality at the shelving, since the light shines directly on the face of the shelves. However, this limits flexibility in changing stack locations later, since the new stack location could be positioned directly below a fixture, resulting in shadows and dimly lit shelving.

### Overhead Lighting

Overhead fixtures positioned perpendicular to the stacks provide an even light quality in the space, but will result in slightly less direct light onto the shelving than if positioned parallel to the stacks. However, a perpendicular arrangement offers greater flexibility for layout or repositioning the stacks in the future than is possible with the parallel lighting arrangement.

### Indirect Lighting

The use of indirect fixtures provides an effective ambient light source, while reducing glare and shadows. These fixtures direct the light to the ceiling instead of the floor, which results in bounce-light off the surface of the ceiling for general illumination. The designer may choose to have the shelf units at the stacks outfitted with indirect fixtures on top that point up to the ceiling; an alternative is to select fixtures that are separate from the stacks, either ceiling-suspended above the stacks or mounted on the columns or walls. This type of lighting will require a ceiling surface that is light-colored for good reflectivity and that is near enough to the stacks to be feasible as a reflective surface for the light.

### Mounted Lighting

For spaces with very high ceilings, where ceiling-mounted light fixtures would be too far above the stacks, another option is to affix lighting to the shelving unit itself or to a system of struts that span between the shelf units. This offers the benefits of lighting parallel to the stacks, with flexibility for moving the stacks later.

### Daylighting

Designing for natural light in libraries creates inviting spaces that encourage people to come to the library and settle in with a good book. Skylights that are posi-

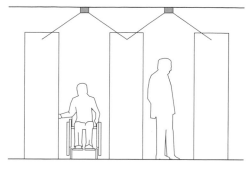

**LIGHTING PARALLEL TO STACKS**

**LIGHTING PERPENDICULAR TO STACKS**

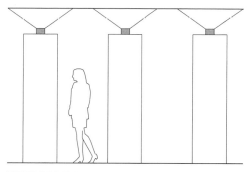

**INDIRECT LIGHTING AFFIXED TO STACKS**

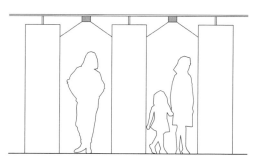

**STRUTS AFFIXED TO STACKS WITH PARALLEL LIGHTING**

**LIGHTING CONFIGURATIONS**

tioned to capture direct sunlight are best located in areas such as primary circulation spaces or public lobbies. The designer considering skylights over the stacks or reading areas should detail them to prevent direct sunlight on the library collections and to control glare. North-facing glass or sun-shading devices that deflect direct light are preferable in these situations. Individual reading alcoves near exterior windows offer patrons cozy places for reading, and often become the most popular spots in the building.

## Security Devices

The central location of the checkout area provides a point of visual observation of library visitors entering or leaving the facility. Electronic security devices, using radio frequency identification equipment to detect the presence of a coded tag on the library materials, are typically located at building exits. To prevent unauthorized removal of library materials, these devices emit an audible and/or visual alarm when the tag is within a specified range of the device. Library staff desensitize the tag at the checkout desk, which allows the visitor to exit without setting off the alarm.

The designer should refer to the manufacturer's data for system requirements to properly locate the devices in plan; but, in general, they should be positioned to encourage a traffic pattern that will allow visitors to enter and exit to the right. Minimum separation of the

devices is 36 in. (914 mm), though some manufacturers produce units that can be up to 48 in. (1,219 mm) apart. If the library handles a large volume of patrons, it may be necessary to include turnstiles at the exits to guide visitors, single-file, past the security devices. The use of other security devices such as cameras and monitors should be discussed during the programming phase to determine the level of security and sophistication of devices appropriate for the facility.

## Wiring

Now that electronic information technologies are commonly used, the planning of a library must address the accommodation of the wiring required for these technologies. While the design of the system and its capacity differ for each library, the accommodation of these systems is the same. The designer should consider the arrangement of electrical and data wiring, the placement of the wiring within the infrastructure, the placement of wiring within the casework and the furniture, the accessibility of these systems, the management of these systems, and the possibility for future growth. While future technological advancement will bring wireless technology to the forefront (some libraries already utilize it in limited areas), present-day library design requires the resolution of these wiring issues. For larger libraries, an information technology consultant is often retained for the design and installation of these systems.

## Library Furniture

Durability, functionality, and comfort are fundamental characteristics of good library furniture. Providing custom casework at the checkout desks or other furniture pieces offers an opportunity to bring continuity to interior spaces by incorporating finish materials used elsewhere in the space into the casework design. Alternatively, several manufacturers offer furniture systems designed specifically for library use. Often, by combining prefabricated pieces (such as tables, chairs, study carrels, or shelving at the stacks) with custom-designed casework (such as the checkout desk or other specialty pieces) the designer can be a good steward of the budget, while incorporating custom quality design features into the interior space.

### Seating

Comfortable soft seating, such as upholstered chairs and sofas, is generally best for informal reading or lounge areas. Pull-up chairs with metal or wood arms are typically used at reading tables and carrels. That said, it's important to note that these furniture pieces are subject to extremely heavy wear, and frequent reupholstery is indicated; thus, fabrics should be of the heaviest duty, because they may have a life span of only four to five years. Chairs with mechanically adjustable features are rarely selected for libraries because they are subject to heavy use, hence, potentially frequent maintenance.

### Tables

Reading tables and study carrels often incorporate power outlets and possibly data outlets, depending on the extent of Internet access deemed appropriate in the program, to allow patrons to plug in their laptop computers or other electronic devices. Reading tables and study carrels should be sized large enough for library patrons to spread out their materials, particularly in areas where oversized materials are viewed. The recommended height of study carrel partitions is at least 52 in. (1,320 mm) above the floor to provide privacy within the carrel. Tables or podiums with slanted tops are designed for more convenient reading by slanting the table top toward the viewer. This type of slanted-top table is useful for viewing oversized materials or newspapers.

The selection and arrangement of both seats and tables should be made to meet the requirements of the *Americans with Disabilities Act Accessibility Guidelines* and those of the local codes.

The seminal work of Keyes D. Metcalf, *Planning Academic and Research Library Buildings* (Chicago, IL: American Library Association Editions, 1999), and updated editions of his original work will provide readers with an exhaustive investigation of library design issues.

The designer of a new library can also contact the many library associations for publications and articles on current thinking for planning libraries and their interior spaces. These include the American Library Association (ALA), the Association of College and Research Libraries (ACRL), the Library Administration and Management Association (LAMA), and the International Federation of Library Associations and Institutions (IFLA).

*Jane Clark, AIA; Zimmer Gunsul Frasca Partnership; Seattle, Washington*
*Natasa Jelic; Rhode Island School of Design; Providence, Rhode Island*
*Jim Johnson; Wrightson, Johnson, Haddon & Williams, Inc.; Dallas, Texas*

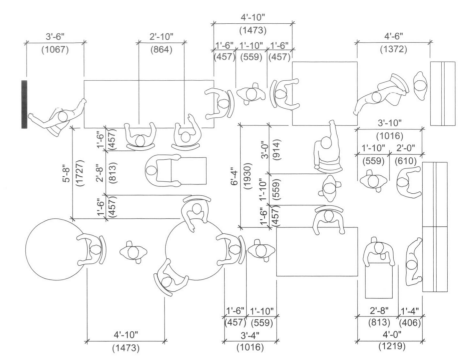

Round tables are not normally recommended for research purposes, but they may be desired in a staff room or in an area designed for light reading.

**LIBARARY READING ROOM TABLE LAYOUT**

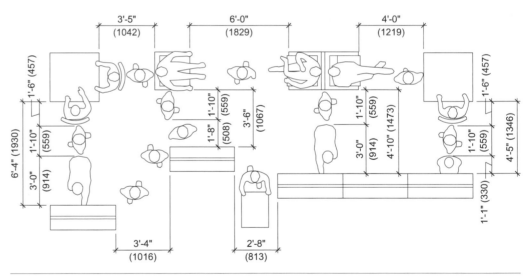

**LOUNGE CHAIRS, TABLES, AND SHELVING LAYOUT**

# CHILD CARE CENTERS

## FIRST CHILD CARE CENTERS

As of the mid-1990s, 30% of all children under the age of five in the United States were enrolled in a child care center. In *Child Care Design Guide,* Anita Rui Olds has calculated that these children "may have spent as many as 12,500 hours in a child care center—the amount of time that most adults have spent in elementary and high school combined." Yet the impact of these environments and this type of care is still not fully understood. Many of the first child care centers were located in renovated buildings and educational wings or basements of churches and synagogues. Structures constructed for the sole purpose of housing child care still comprise a relatively new building type; it is only recently that designers who themselves experienced these environments as children are beginning to bring their perceptions and insights to the planning and design of these facilities.

## DESIGNING ENVIRONMENTS FOR CHILDREN

Designing spaces for children requires an awareness of and sensitivity to the uniqueness of the child as the user within the space. There are both obvious and obscure differences between the perceptions of adults and children regarding spaces, as well as their use of them.

The most obvious difference between adults and children is physical size. An environment whose elements are scaled to the size of the children who will make up the primary user group communicates that their needs were important in the design of the space. For example, windows set at the eye level of children, and lavatory handles that can be reached without standing on stools, indicate that the environment has been designed with children in mind, as opposed to one in which children are forced to adapt to a space that has been designed for adults. Not only does a child-scaled environment help to generate children's sense of control and comfort, it also leads to a higher degree of safety by reducing their need to, for example, stretch awkwardly to reach objects or stand precariously on the edge of furnishings to see over or out.

In the creation of children's spaces, it is also important to remember the very limited experience that children have had with built environments. Whereas adults automatically assume many relationships between and within spaces because they're familiar with the design repetition used in similar spaces, newborns and toddlers cannot, for example, always understand the difference in behavior that is appropriate for the airport and behavior that is appropriate for a religious setting. Likewise, most young children do not always understand the function or purpose of waiting rooms. Children's perceptions of space are also unique. To an adult, a long narrow corridor can be understood as an expedient means of organizing spaces. To the child, it may appear to be a great opportunity for running with no obstructions. Obviously, with repeated exposure and maturity, children become familiar with the organization of spaces, their functions, and expected behaviors within certain types of spaces; but for the designer of children's spaces, it is important to remember the relatively small amount of experience children have engaging with and understanding the built environment.

It is also important that designers remember that signage that is often used in public buildings to orient adults is of little or no value to young children, who lack the ability to read or to understand unfamiliar words. Thus, the use of visual architectural elements and graphics that delineate a course of travel may give a child, even when accompanied by an adult, some sense of control and may help the child to create a means to find his or her way within the built environment.

As users of space, children also represent a vulnerable population. They typically have no power in shaping their environments and, therefore, can only respond to them. Consequently, it is important that they be provided with sensitively designed spaces that will allow them a degree of understanding and sense of control over their surroundings.

## Scale

The prevailing thought of many child care and design professionals is that the child care center environment should present a homelike atmosphere in terms of its organization of spaces and use of building materials, interior furnishings, and finishes. Children often suffer anxiety when separated from their parents, and this anxiety may be alleviated to some degree by environments that engender a feeling of familiarity. Some research has indicated that there may even be a direct relationship between the degree of "homelikeness" of a facility and the tendency for caregivers to respond to the children in a more familial manner.

The optimum maximum size for child care centers is between 60 to 75 children. Centers of this size often feature radial organizations with a commons or multipurpose area that can be shared by the surrounding group rooms placed in the center.

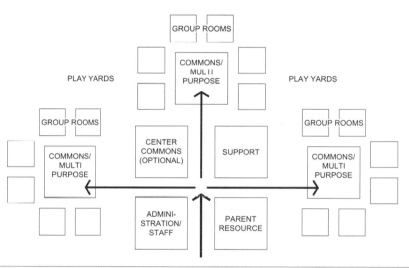

**RADIAL ORGANIZATION OF SPACES FOR A SMALL CHILD CARE CENTER (MAXIMUM OF 60 TO 75 CHILDREN)**

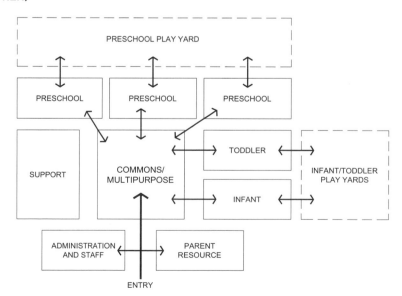

This arrangement features smaller buildings located around a central organizing space. Security at entry to the campus and at each building must be considered. Parent resources and some staff support areas may be duplicated within each building for ease of access.

**CAMPUS PLAN FOR A CHILD CARE CENTER (MORE THAN 75 CHILDREN)**

## Campus-Type Plan

Designers of facilities destined to service more than 75 children should consider using a campus-type plan in an effort to reduce the scale of the facility and the massing of the structures. Smaller-scale environments are more apt to appear homelike and are thought to be less intimidating to a child than larger unfamiliar environments. A campus plan that comprises multiple buildings, each housing fewer children and featuring separate identities and individual entries, is highly desirable. This type of campus plan does, however, require that a mechanism and procedure be developed to ensure security for the entire campus and at each entry to prevent unauthorized and undocumented entry by visitors. If a campus plan is not possible, a building plan that incorporates smaller clusters or pods within a larger building is encouraged.

Within the center of the "campus," great attention should be given to the design of administrative and staff support areas to ensure that they do not overtake or diminish the prominence of the children's areas. This, too, helps to create a warm and exciting child-friendly environment by downplaying those areas that do not directly serve the child.

## SPACES

The day-to-day operations that take place in, as well as the number of children who use, a child care center can greatly impact the type, size, and organization of the required space. The objective of the center can also play a role in the design, hence should be completely understood by the designer prior to beginning design. The sole purpose of some centers is to care for children during the absence of their parents, while other center programs may include an educational objective. The hours of service can also greatly impact the design, especially if the center provides child care for children whose parents may work during night hours. In consultation with the center's owner or director, a list of building area requirements can provide a starting point for discussions that will lead to the delineation of spatial needs and relationships for centers of most any size and program.

An integral part of the design of a child care center is the development of outdoor spaces. Outdoor spaces function best when they are accessible directly from the group rooms. This strengthens the relationship between the indoor and outdoor spaces because it makes them readily available. Both the group room and the outdoor play yard should consist of spaces with many different qualities: spaces that are quiet, spaces that are noisy, spaces that are messy, spaces that are neat, spaces that are cozy, and spaces that are open.

## Group Rooms

The design of group rooms within a child care facility is of great importance, as it is in these spaces that children will spend most of their time. Many activities and functions occur simultaneously within group rooms. It is important to note that the programs of some child care centers will feature multiage groupings, as opposed to a group of same-age children.

## BUILDING AREA REQUIREMENTS FOR CHILD CARE FACILITIES

|  | MINIMUM | ADEQUATE | EXCELLENT |
|---|---|---|---|
| Group Rooms | 55 sq ft/child (5.1 sq m/child) | 65 sq ft/child (6 sq m/child) | 72 sq ft/child (6.7 sq m/child) |
| Support Areas | 15 sq ft/child (1.4 sq m/child) | 20 sq ft/child (1.9 sq. m/child) | 24 sq ft/child (2.2 sq m/child) |
| Circulation/ Service Areas | 18 sq ft/child (1.7 sq m/child) | 25 sq ft/child (2.3 sq m/child) | 29 sq ft (2.7 sq m/child) |
| Total Building Area | 88 sq ft/child (8.2 sq m/child) | 110 sq ft/child (10.2 sq m/child) | 125 sq ft/child (11.6 sq m/child) |
| Outdoor Play Areas | 75 sq ft/child (7 sq m/child) | 125 sq ft/child (11.6 sq m/child) | 200 sq ft/child (18.6 sq m/child) |

*State and local agencies that regulate and license child care centers typically have established minimum space requirements; they should be contacted for more precise calculations of required areas.*

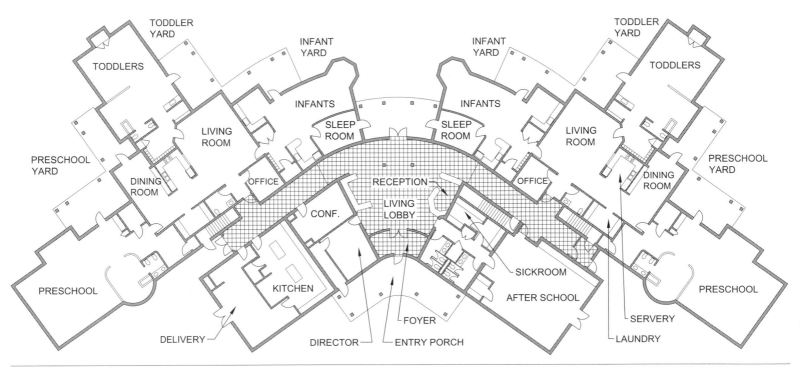

**THE COPPER HOUSE, HUSKY CHILD DEVELOPMENT CENTER; HUSKY INJECTION MOLDING SYSTEMS, LTD.; BOLTON, ONTARIO, CANADA**
*Source: Jacob, Silverstein, Winslow and Deyenhardt Architects; Berkeley, CA*

## Regions and Zones

Within each group room, certain activities function more efficiently when grouped together. These groupings also tend to influence the finishes that may be selected within each area. Group rooms should be divided into two areas: a *wet region* and a *dry region*.

Within the wet region, it is best to create an *entry zone* and a *messy zone*. The entry zone may serve as a "front porch," or transitional area, where the child enters the room; it may be furnished with individual "cubby" storage units for the children, as well as other types of storage. It is also helpful to provide a bench for children to sit on, to, for example, remove rain boots, or for adults, to assist children putting on coats and shoes.

The messy zone should support activities that involve water or where children otherwise cause messes during use, such as art areas and sand play tables. The messy zone is also the best area in which to locate the access to the outdoor play area since dirt and mud may tracked in on the bottom of shoes. Flooring for the wet region is typically a hard flooring that is durable and easy to maintain.

The dry region supports activities that are not as potentially damaging to interior finishes; thus it can be designed to appear much softer in its presentation. The dry region can be further divided into an *active zone* and a *quiet zone*, reflecting the level of energy and noise that may be generated by children playing in each of these areas. The dry region may feature carpeted floors or area rugs that help to further define different play areas.

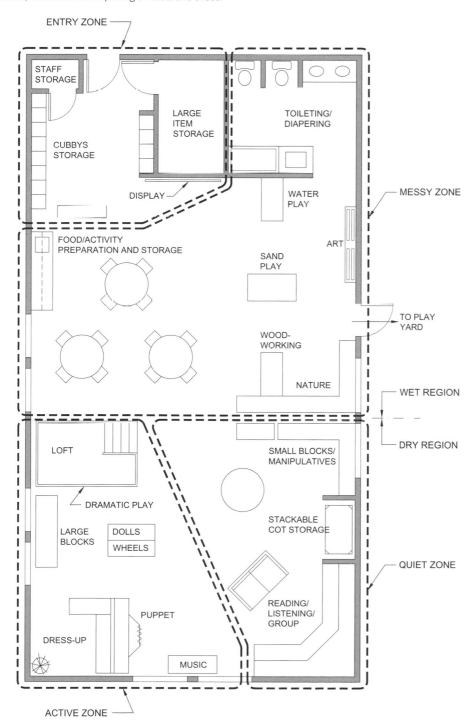

PLAN SHOWING RELATIONSHIPS OF REGIONS AND ZONES WITHIN A TYPICAL TODDLER GROUP ROOM

### ADA Accessibility Guidelines for Building Elements Designed for Children's Use

In 1998, the Architectural and Transportation Barriers Compliance Board (the "Access Board") issued a document (Publication S-30, "Building Elements Designed for Children's Use Final Rule") to provide guidance in the establishment of alternatives for building elements for use by children with disabilities. The document is currently awaiting adoption by the U.S. Justice Department; until it has been formally adopted, the guidelines included in the document are advisory only and are not required or enforceable.

Publication S-30 contains specifications that are based on children's dimensions and anthropometrics and that may be applied to building elements designed specifically for use by children ages twelve and younger. Presently, architects and designers who wish to incorporate these alternatives into their designs for environments may do so through provision 2.2 (Equivalent Facilitation) of the existing *Americans with Disabilities Act Accessibility Guidelines* (ADAAG). This provision permits departures from ADAAG requirements in order to provide equal or greater access. The document not only offers alternatives to various configurations and dimensions of building elements, it also includes, in the appendix, various charts that further break down the information into what is most appropriate according to the age group served.

It is important to note that once the decision has been made to adopt one of the alternative provisions offered by the ADAAG for use in the design of a space for children, all of the alternate provisions must be observed. For example, the decision to use a toilet with a seat height that is allowed under the alternates for children requires that the toilet stall depth, placement of grab bars, and so on, also conform to the alternate provisions for children set for these elements.

The ADAAG provisions that offer child-related alternatives and additional recommendations within the document's appendix include:

4.15 Drinking Fountains and Water Coolers

4.16 Water Closets

4.17 Toilet Stalls

4.19 Lavatories and Mirrors

4.24 Sinks

4.32 Fixed or Built-in Seating or Tables

Additionally, the ADAAG appendix contains helpful information about the following provisions in order to provide more comfortable accessibility for children with disabilities:

4.2.5 and 4.2.6 Forward and Side Reach

4.8.5 Handrails

## PLAYGROUND DESIGN

As in the group rooms, the playground in a child care center will be divided into zones; the most typical are described in the following subsections.

### Entry Zone

The entry zone in the playground should feature a distinctive sense of introduction to the playground area, either by the use of a physical element, such as a gate or entry arch, or via some distinctive change from the surrounding areas. It should provide a neutral zone in which the child can observe the entire playground, gather a sense of its layout, assess the available play opportunities, and make decisions as to when and which activity to engage in first.

This zone may also feature signage that lists rules for playground use and expected behavior, and perhaps any donor boards that list the names of those whose support has made the playground possible. Bike racks should also be located within or near this zone.

### Active/Noisy Play (Gross Motor Play) Zone

The gross motor play zone is where all of the activities traditionally associated with playgrounds take place, such as swinging, sliding, and climbing. It is important to offer a mix of activities that exercise both the lower body (legs) and the upper body (arms). Activities should offer a range of challenge levels. These activities may be provided through manufactured play equipment or custom-designed elements. All equipment should be designed to meet ASTM F1487, *Standard Consumer Safety Performance Specification for Playground Equipment for Public Use,* and this zone should meet the requirements of the ADAAG for play areas.

### Natural Elements Zone

The purpose of including this zone in the playground program is to reduce the tendency to overdevelop the play area. An open grassy area where children can run and play informal ball games is an important part of a successful playground. These large open areas can also provide space for use of large *manipulatives*. Other natural elements, such as gardens, may be located throughout the playground, but plantings should be set in raised planters or located in areas that will not be vulnerable to children running through them to get from one part of the playground to another.

### SPACES FOR CHILD CARE CENTERS

| Group Rooms | Infants |
| | Toddlers |
| | Preschoolers |
| | After-schoolers |
| Indoor Multipurpose | Common Area |
| Administration | Director's Office |
| | Secretary's Office |
| | Receptionist |
| | Reception Area |
| | Conference Room |
| | Sick Child Room |
| | Restrooms |
| Parent Resource Area | Information Center (books, videos, etc.) |
| | Seating Area |
| Staff Area | Workroom |
| | Break Room |
| | Personal Storage (Personal storage and restroom areas may be located in or within close proximity to the group rooms for convenience and continuity of supervision.) |
| Circulation/ Maintenance/Utility Areas | Laundry |
| | Kitchen |
| | Maintenance |
| | Mechanical/Electrical Areas |
| Storage | Curriculum Materials |
| | Art/Craft Materials |
| | Indoor Play Equipment |
| | Buggies/Carriages |
| Outdoor Areas | Infants' Play |
| | Toddlers' Play |
| | Preschoolers' Play |
| | After-schoolers' Play |
| | Outdoor Storage |

Additional landscaping, such as trees located throughout the playground, can provide desirable shade and, with the addition of seating such as tree benches, encourage social interaction. The natural topography of the site should be taken advantage of whenever possible. Varying levels or terraces within a playground can give children a variety of enjoyable perspectives and views. That said, it is important to ensure that the view of responsible adults on-site is not impaired as they supervise the children at play. This is especially important in playgrounds that are to be used by young children.

### GROUP ROOMS FOR CHILD CARE CENTERS

| Infant Room Activities | Sleeping |
| | Rocking |
| | Swinging |
| | Playing |
| | Crawling |
| | Food preparation |
| | Eating |
| | Diapering |
| | Listening |
| | Watching |
| Infant Room Furnishings | Cribs |
| | Adult rocking chairs |
| | Swing seats |
| | Shelf units for toy storage |
| | Crawling mats |
| | Audiovisual equipment and storage |
| | High chairs |
| | Food prep and storage units (including refrigerator) |
| | Adult chairs |
| | Changing tables |
| | Personal infant storage units |
| | Two adult sinks (diapering and food prep) |
| | Adult toilet |
| Toddler Room Activities | Book looking |
| | Rocking |
| | Playing |
| | Building |
| | Arts/crafts |
| | Dramatic play |
| | Food prep |
| | Eating |
| | Diapering and toileting |
| | Sand play |
| | Water play |
| | Music |
| | Listening |
| | Napping |
| Toddler Room Furnishings | Adult rocking chairs |
| | Book stand (front of book visible) |
| | Toy/block shelves |
| | Dramatic play furnishings (e.g., play kitchen, doll furnishings, dress-up, etc.) |
| | Tables and chairs |
| | Changing table |
| | Child-sized toilets (two per 10 to 14 children) |
| | Child hand sinks |
| | Two adult sinks (diapering and food prep) |
| | Easels |
| | Sand table |
| | Water table |
| | Individual cubby storage units |
| | Audiovisual equipment and storage |
| | Food storage and prep units |
| | Art supply storage |
| | Cots (typically stackable) |
| | Audiovisual equipment and storage |
| Preschool Room Activities | (Same as toddler room but without diapering) |
| Preschool Room Furnishings | (Same as toddler room with the following possible additions: Loft Woodworking table) |

*Source: Anita Rui Olds,* Child Care Design Guide; *New York, McGraw-Hill, 2001.*

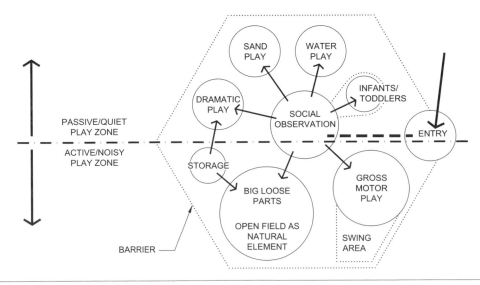

**PLAYGROUND ZONE RELATIONSHIPS**

## Big Loose Parts Zone

Enabling children to build and manipulate an environment to their own design facilitates physical, cognitive, and social development. This zone, therefore, should consist of large so-called manipulatives that can be organized and reorganized by the children in a large open area to create new and different play events at will. Boxes, crates, planks, and boards can be arranged in many configurations, allowing the children to create their own play environment. Big loose parts can consist of found objects such as pieces of wood boards and planks, crates, or large refrigerator boxes. Of course, before such objects are allowed for use by children, responsible adults must check such objects for any safety hazards such as splinters, nails, and staples. Although more costly, manufactured products are also available, and these offer a higher degree of safety and durability.

Notably, the big loose parts zone requires a high degree of supervision to ensure that the children do not create dangerous or unstable constructions, while keeping in mind that the developmental benefits of this type of play are invaluable. Adequate storage should be available in close proximity to store the equipment between uses.

## Passive/Quiet (Dramatic) Play Zone

At the ages of five and six, role-playing in children is at its peak. Whether playing house, store, or fast-food restaurant, reenacting roles that they have seen adults perform is, for many children, the first type of interactive play with other children. This zone, therefore, will feature structures or props that can encourage and enrich this type of play. Built structures can range from the very abstract or generic designs, which allow the children to pretend the structure to be whatever they choose, to the more definitive, such as playhouses. Dramatic play can be further enhanced through the provision of small-scale props such as dress-up clothes, tables and chairs, and empty food boxes. A storage area in close proximity for these items must be available.

It is important to design the dramatic play structures so that children in wheelchairs can access and maneuver within any interior spaces. Many manufactured gross motor play structures include spaces beneath the decks that can be developed as dramatic play areas. However, as a type of passive play, dramatic play is often incompatible with the active and noisy activities of children on the play structure, hence it is best located in a separate area.

## Social Spaces

Areas that support social interaction between children and between children and adults should be located throughout the playground. Social areas should accommodate a range of group sizes from small (two to three) to larger groups of six or more. These areas are often successfully integrated into the playground's landscaping or gardens. If the playground serves a facility, such as a school or child care center, it may be useful to provide an area within the playground that can accommodate a typical class size (12 to 24 children).

## Sand Play Zone

Sand play is a favorite activity, especially for young children. It provides a tactile and creative activity that can be enjoyed by a child playing alone or with other children. Sand play also has high educational value while providing an excellent means of developing manual dexterity.

The sand play area may be contained within a box that is built above grade. For ease of access by children who may have difficulty climbing over a barrier around the sand box, a recessed sand play area that places the top of the sand at grade level and can be walked into may be desirable. For greater play value, locate the sand play area beside or in close proximity to a source of water. For children confined to wheelchairs, sand play may be provided through the use of an elevated table with raised edges. Provisions must be made for the sand to be covered nightly or inspected daily to keep it free from litter, debris, and feline feces.

## Water Play Zone

Children are highly attracted to water. Water play, like sand play, offers children opportunities for play that change with each encounter. Water play facilities can range from a water table that can be filled and drained between each use to large water play structures, similar to those found in water parks. Depending on the extent of water play activities and the type of play anticipated, this area may be located in the active/noisy play zone. However, for playgrounds in which water play is limited to activities during which only the hands and arms get wet, this activity is more suited to the quiet/passive play zone.

The decisions regarding the degree and intensity of water play in the design of a playground should be based on the amount of supervision that will be provided when water play is available and the degree to which caregivers are prepared to allow children and their clothing to become wet. This activity is often located adjacent or near to the sand play area creating the possibility of mixing the two elements together. A nonslip surface should be specified beneath any water play area.

## Hard Surface Zone

Certain activities, such as games that require ball dribbling (e.g., basketball and four-square) and riding wheeled toys, such as tricycles, or propelling toy vehicles, require a hard surface. "Roadways" may function as part of the dramatic play area through the creation of drive-through structures, such as restaurants and banks, and parking spaces. Storage for these vehicles may also be required.

The hard surfaces made be constructed of packed earth, concrete, or asphalt. Packed earth has the advantage of being easier on knees and elbows in the event of falls; however, puddles may form that make the area unusable for long periods of time until it dries out. Concrete, though unforgiving when fallen on, is durable and can be made safer with a light slip-resistant finish. Concrete also causes less strain on knee joints, stays cooler in hot weather than asphalt, and offers a surface on which sidewalk games can be painted and sidewalk chalk can be used. Although the most costly option, rubber-safety surfaces offer the highest degree of safety and comfort.

## Infant and Toddler Zone

If it is anticipated that infants and toddlers (ages two to five) will be using the playground, it is recommended that equipment specifically designed to a smaller scale be used and that activities and surfaces appropriate for crawling babies be included. Separation from zones used by older children is also recommended.

## Playground Amenities for Support, Comfort, and Safety

The playground design also has to incorporate areas for storage, comfort, and safety, as described in the following subsections.

### Storage

Storage areas that either are accessible directly from the playground or are in close proximity to it eliminate the need for a supervising adult to leave the play area in order to retrieve play equipment and items that support the various types of play on the playground. A single storage area may be located in a central location, or multiple, smaller storage areas may be located in direct relationship to the areas of the playground that they serve. Storage is typically required for the dramatic play, big loose parts, and hard surface zones.

Lockable storage is especially critical for playgrounds that will be used in conjunction with a facility such as a school or child care center during the day, and then revert to community use during after-school hours and on weekends. Also important in planning for storage is the location of trash receptacles in the areas of the playground that tend to generate trash, such as around picnic tables and seating areas.

### Comfort and Safety Amenities

Amenities that will provide for the safety of the children and the comfort of both the children and the adult supervisors may include water fountains, misters, seating that offers unobstructed views of the various play areas, and restrooms that either are included in the playground area or are within close proximity. Creating a relaxing setting for the supervising adults, such as a shaded area with tables and comfortable seating that is centrally located for easier supervision, may result in their allowing the children to play for longer periods of time.

### Barriers

In the design of a playground, it is often necessary or desirable to erect physical barriers that either direct a child's movement around certain pieces of playground equipment or that discourage or prevent a child from traveling from one part of the playground to another or from leaving the playground area. These barriers can be made "hard," by the use of fencing, or "soft," with the use of dense landscaping and berms, depending on the degree of separation that is needed. The adult supervisor will be more likely to give children freedom to play and run when there is a barrier that surrounds the play area; also, supervision of the entry and exit areas to the playground will provide confidence that children stay within the confines of the playground.

Within the playground it is also advisable to separate infant and toddler play areas from those of older children for the safety of the younger children. The separation between the two areas does not necessarily have to be a physical barrier. These areas can often be separated simply by creating a sense of passage from one space to the other, so that older children do not accidentally enter the infant/toddler area, and vice versa.

Barriers should also be considered around swings areas to dictate entry into the area from the front, facing the swings, as opposed to from the side, where a child may pass in the trajectory of a swinging child to reach an unoccupied swing seat.

### Guidelines for Floor Finish Selection

- The floor is furniture in child care centers; therefore, make floors warm and inviting to provide many physical and programmatic benefits.
- Use carpet to introduce softness (a prime indicator of center quality) to children's spaces. Good-quality, thick, dense carpet is more durable and responds better to cleaning than thinner carpets of lesser quality. Cut piles are more residential than loop piles.
- Vinyl-backed "peel-and-stick" carpets, which are 100% washable, are ideal for children's group rooms. Installation of carpet squares, as opposed to sheet goods, sometimes facilitates replacement of heavily soiled areas. Large remnants of scrap or mill-end carpets, bound at the edges, can be used to delineate areas in the quiet and active zones if installed carpet is not desired.
- Use 1-in.-sq ceramic tiles to create a nonslippery, water-resistant surface in wet play bays. Large ceramic tiles (12 to 14 in. sq) are slippery in wet areas but excellent for high-use entries and corridors. Scored and colored concrete is equally durable, resists slipping, and lends itself to custom artistic treatment.
- Always choose a carpet tile or linoleum that is mottled or flecked, since solid colors reveal every stain, scratch, and scuff mark. Subdued patterns and colors are preferable to dominant and geometric designs.

*Source: Anita Rui Olds,* Child Care Design Guide; *New York, McGraw-Hill, 2001.*

### Guidelines for Ceiling Design

- Ceiling design is an important contributor to the spirit of a place. Avoid suspended ceilings with 2 ft × 4 ft (200 × 400) grids, which are associated with institutional settings. Vary ceiling heights to signal changes in space use and different levels of intimacy, to provide variety and area definition, and to vary the quality of light and sound. In narrow corridors and small rooms, a high ceiling can minimize feelings of entrapment. Group rooms benefit from two to four different ceiling heights corresponding to the activity levels of the four zones.
- Shape the ceiling to help define the space below. A vaulted ceiling creates a "center" and "edges" to the activities that take place below it.
- Consider incorporating various materials; for example, using plaster, wood, mosaic tile, stucco, and stained glass. Ceiling treatment is especially important where children (infants) will be lying down and looking up.
- Consider a change in ceiling height, coupled with a change in ceiling material; this is particularly powerful in creating a unique sense of "place."
- Where cost is a factor, make creative use of banners to vary ceiling heights and afford aesthetic interest.

*Source: Anita Rui Olds,* Child Care Design Guide; *New York, McGraw-Hill, 2001.*

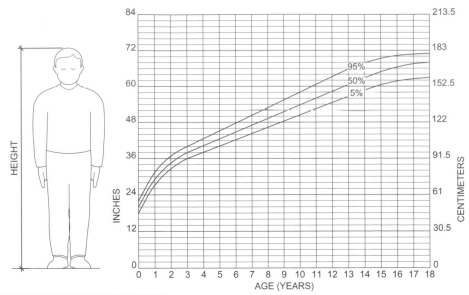

**HEIGHT (INCLUDING INFANT LENGTH)**

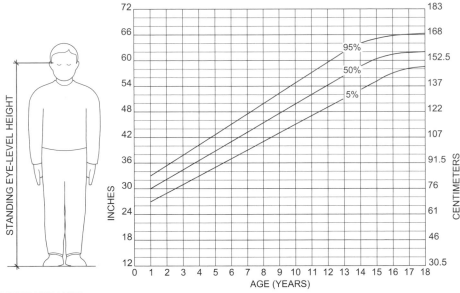

**STANDING EYE LEVEL**

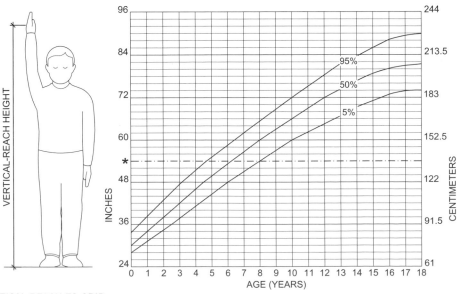

**VERTICAL REACH TO GRIP**

**ANTHROPOMETRIC DATA FOR CHILDREN**

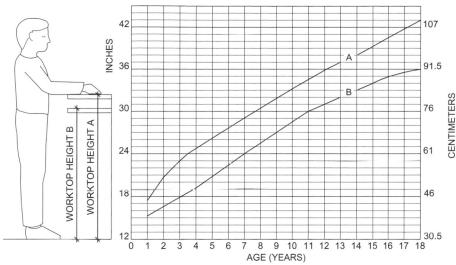

**STANDING WORKTOP HEIGHTS**

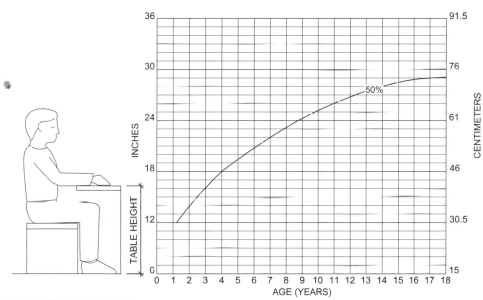

**SEATED WORKTOP HEIGHTS**

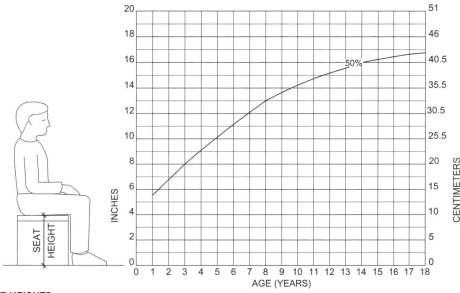

**SEAT HEIGHTS**

**ANTHROPOMETRIC DATA FOR CHILDREN**

**Guidelines for Wall Finish Selection**

- Consider enlivening walls in selected locations by adding wood, stucco, stone, carpet, cork, and brick to enhance their color and tactile qualities.
- Consider glass and glass block walls, in limited quantities, where acoustic but not visual separation is desired.
- Use textures on walls to help control sound clue boundaries and to assist in wayfinding and area definition (as texture and color changes are used on floors).
- Discourage cinder block walls because of their abrasiveness, unfinished feel, and institutional look.
- Incorporate curved walls or curved portions of a wall to break the monotony of straight lines and invite people into a space. This is especially effective in public areas: corridors, stairwells, entrances, and around corners. That said, carefully evaluate the use of curved walls in group rooms because rectangular furniture does not easily fit against a curve.
- Add wood, carpet or handwoven rugs, mirrors, and mosaic tile to architectural elements, such as protruding and freestanding columns, to soften them and add interest.
- Consider using wood in a variety of forms for wall surfaces, baseboards, bumper guards, and handrails.
- Add cove bases at the juncture of walls and floors as another prominent design element. Choose colors and materials that match the walls to make them less prominent and reduce the institutional feel of a space.
- Keep in mind that half-walls and partitions in children's spaces can do most things full walls do: provide platforms, tables and seats, plant ledges, display surfaces, and façades for dramatic play. Remember that partitions need to be stable and nonflammable and should not block any means of egress. Some states require them to be screwed or otherwise affixed to the floor. It is helpful if they have some acoustic insulation properties as well.
- Paint walls; paint is inexpensive and easy to apply and change. Vinyl covered walls provide a slightly more curable surface, but at greater cost and with less flexibility.
- Provide plenty of display space in group rooms and corridors by covering large portions or entire walls with materials such as linoleum, cork, hook-and-loop tape, or fabric that is capable of receiving tape and staples.
- Install mirrors of tempered glass, not plastic, at child height; these resist scratching and clouding.

*Sources: Anita Rui Olds,* Child Care Design Guide; *New York, McGraw-Hill, 2001.*
*Linda Cain Ruth,* Design Standards for Children's Environments; *New York, McGraw-Hill, 2000.*

*Linda Cain Ruth, AIA; College of Architecture Design and Construction; Auburn University, Alabama*

*Conceptual Design: Anita Rui Olds; Anita Olds and Associates; Woodacre, California*
*Architectural Design: Barbara Winslow; Jacobson, Silverstein, Winslow/Degenhardt Architects; Berkeley, California*
*Interior Design: Carla Mathis; Carla Mathis Designs; Menlo Park, California*
*Architect of Record: J.H. Rust; J.H. Rust, Architect; Toronto, Ontario, Canada*
*Landscape Design: Ruedi Hofer; PMA Landscape Architects; Etobicoke, Ontario, Canada*

# ELEMENTARY AND SECONDARY SCHOOLS

## PROGRAMMING AND PLANNING GUIDELINES

Most state departments of education, as well as many organizations, have developed standards to guide the planning, design, and construction of school facilities. These standards vary, reflecting the learning process and curricula for different age groups, as well as for children with special needs. Representative program guidelines for the four most common types of school are included:

- Kindergarten and preschool
- Elementary school
- Middle (or junior high) school
- High school

## DESIGN STANDARDS

In the United States, the primary source of standards—other than state or local regulatory departments—is the National Association for the Education of Young Children (NAEYC) in Washington, DC. NAEYC issues the most widely used accreditation standards for programs for children from birth to eight years, standards that are often higher than state licensing standards.

### Kindergarten and Preschool

Kindergarten typically is a child's first introduction to school, or marks a transition from another preschool program, nursery school, Head Start, certain forms of day care, or any of the many other types of early childhood programs. In most school systems children enter this program at age five or six, but a growing number of states are mandating early childhood programs for younger ages.

Kindergarten generally is defined as a form of preschool education in which children are taught through creative play, social contacts, and natural expression. The concept was originated in Germany in 1837 by Fredrich Froebel. *Kindergarten,* "child's garden," was based on the idea that children's play was significant. Froebel employed games, songs, and stories to address the needs of children (at that time generally ages three to seven). The kindergarten served as a transitional stage from home to school and often was a child's first formal learning experience. In 1861, American educator Elizabeth Palmer Peabody opened the first kindergartens in the United States, in Boston. By the 1920s, kindergartens were included in public schools in most parts of the United States.

Historically, a child's first day at kindergarten was often his or her first formal learning experience away from home, but today more children have been exposed to other forms of preschool programs or child care. Thus, the issue of separation from home and parents must be considered, as well as the transition to a group social environment in which the child usually does not know the other members.

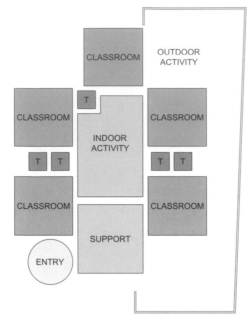

**CLUSTER MODEL—FOCUS ON THE INTERIOR**
The interior cluster model is organized around open play space.

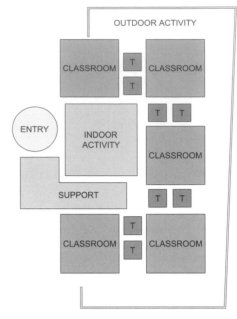

**CLUSTER MODEL—FOCUS ON THE OUTDOORS**
The outdoors cluster model is organized around common services and corridor.

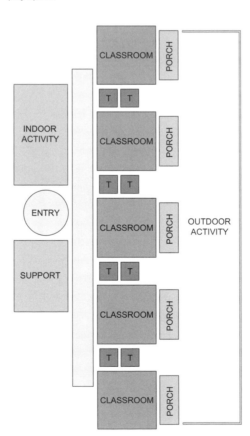

**LINEAR MODEL**
The linear model is organized along an interior spine; focus on the outdoors and covered porches at each classroom.

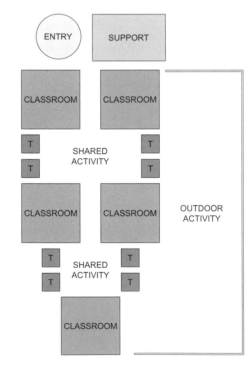

**HYBRID LINEAR MODEL**
The hybrid linear model is organized along a complex spine made up of a series of activity and play spaces.

**KINDERGARTEN AND PRESCHOOL PLAN ORGANIZATIONS**

## DEVELOPMENTAL GUIDEPOSTS FOR CHILDREN AND ADOLESCENTS

| AGE RANGE | PHYSICAL | EMOTIONAL | SOCIAL |
|---|---|---|---|
| Early Childhood (ages 3–5) | • Body growth slows, more adult proportions develop.<br>• At 6, neural development 90% complete.<br>• From 4 to 8 years, lymphoid development increases from 40 to 90%.<br>• Most children are farsighted.<br>• Muscle development begins at 4 years, but larger muscles dominate. | • Tendency to fear imaginary or anticipated dangers.<br>• Crying and tantrums diminish; anger can be expressed in words (often by threatening or yelling).<br>• Anger directed at cause of frustration, retained for longer periods of time; but 4-year-olds begin to seek ways to hide it from others.<br>• Channeling anger and frustration is important. | • Begin to understand concept of taking turns and tend to imitate adults.<br>• 4-year-olds prefer to spend time playing and cooperating with others and can pick up social cues from surroundings.<br>• 5-year-olds prefer to play with others.<br>• May create imaginary playmates if deprived of contact with other children, but most will outgrow these playmates by age 5. |
| Middle Childhood (ages 6–9) | • Apparent difference between growth rate of girls and boys (girls closer to end growth states, boys taller and heavier).<br>• Nearsightedness may begin to develop at 8 years.<br>• 6-year-olds use whole bodies for activities, and large muscles are more developed; 7-year-olds more cautious and show ease with fine motor skills; 8-year-olds develop fine motor skills and have increased attention spans.<br>• Nervous habits begin to appear at age 7 | • 6-year-olds begin to assert independence and demonstrate confidence.<br>• 6-year-olds fear the supernatural.<br>• 7-year-olds are more stable, narcissistic, polite, responsive, empathetic, less aggressive, and can draw connections between cause and effect.<br>• 8-year-olds demonstrate greater independence, vacillate between moods, and begin to sense how others feel about them.<br>• 7- and 8 year olds discover some of their limitations and may hesitate to try new tasks, but 8-year-olds seek to create an external image of competence and confidence. | • Family influence decreases, peers are more important, teachers become authority figures.<br>• 6-year-olds have many internal conflicts, resulting in capriciousness.<br>• 6-year-olds choose playmates on qualities of age and size (not gender or ethnicity); 7-year-olds are more aware of social status or ethnicity differences among themselves.<br>• 7-year-olds are self-critical and often disassociate themselves from frustrations.<br>• 7-year-olds are well mannered unless bored; 8-year-olds are more developed socially.<br>• 7-year-olds are more conscious of position among peers; boys and girls play separately.<br>• 8-year-olds prefer company and approval of peers, and exhibit more self-control and modesty. |
| Late Childhood (ages 9–11) | • More resistance to disease.<br>• Steady increases in body measurements: height and weight (girls more than boys), and muscle growth.<br>• Have fine motor skills.<br>• May feel uncomfortable with scrutiny.<br>• Many girls begin showing signs of puberty. | • Fear exclusion from peers.<br>• Prone to outbursts but try to control them<br>• 10-year-olds are mild tempered, seek reassurance from others; anger comes and goes quickly.<br>• 10-year-olds fear heights and dark.<br>• 11-year-olds fear school, friends, for parents' welfare, strange animals, threatening world events; are more easily angered, often resulting in physical violence, but can control outbursts more appropriately. | • Socialize in exclusive groups with own sex (boys' groups gravitate toward shows of bravado and competition; girls' groups are well structured and more concerned with maturity).<br>• Develop important individual friendships, which are often fluid.<br>• Ties to family less important than ties to peers; adult shortcomings looked at critically, often leading to conflicts. |
| Early Adolescence (ages 12–14) | • Enter pubescence, puberty, and postpubescence.<br>• Activate primary and secondary sex characteristics. | • Emotions vacillate; responses are inconsistent.<br>• 12-year-olds may develop a derogatory sense of humor to control emotions.<br>• 13-year-olds withdraw from others, tending toward secrecy and sullenness<br>• 14-year-olds use derogatory humor as defense and primary form of communication. | • Motivated by desire to fit in with peers, which prevents individual expression but emboldens adolescents to assert independence from home.<br>• Peer groups are exclusive and develop from single-sex to coed.<br>• Intensely drawn to a best friend, believing that only this other person understands. |
| Late Adolescence (ages 15–18) | • Height and weight stabilize.<br>• Girls generally physically mature by 18, boys by 19. | • Feel restrained or controlled by adults.<br>• Have insecure self-image; may fear inadequacy.<br>• Focus attention on opposite sex or close peers.<br>• Feel challenged to find comfortable self-image. | • Assert independence; have power struggles with parents; are most concerned about social life.<br>• If uncomfortable with adulthood, may withdraw to former behaviors. |

As a child grows, he or she typically learns in different ways, and the physical environment of the school should reflect this characteristic.

## KINDERGARTEN DESIGN CONCEPT

The design of schools for early childhood education has always been geared toward comfortable, supportive, and adaptive settings that are conducive to a learning process derived from familiar play and hands-on activities. Specific features associated with home, as well as school, are considered in developing an appropriate transitional setting. The type, size, scale, and variety of more public and private spaces underlie appropriate design and planning.

Much like a house, containing public spaces (living room, parlor, foyer, family room) and more private spaces (kitchen, upstairs bedrooms, bathrooms, etc.), a school should create spaces for comfortable retreat and quiet, reflective play, as well as for small and large group activities. Today, the typical age of children in kindergarten programs ranges from four to six years.

Among the general goals that all early childhood and kindergarten programs should strive to achieve are the following:

- Create a visually rich, fun, and surprising environment.
- Provide spaces and surfaces for display of children's work.
- Provide a variety of settings for work-in-progress.
- Introduce a variety of social settings for small and large groups.
- Make strong connections between the indoors and the outdoors; above all, use daylighting as much as possible.
- Connect spaces to promote communication, orientation, and flexible programming and staffing.
- Build in flexibility of space to accommodate evolving teaching practices.
- Create a distinctive, pleasing entrance.
- Pay special attention to the scale and height of typical elements such as windows, doors, doorknobs and pulls, sinks, toilets, counters, furnishings, mirrors, steps, shelving and storage, light switches, towel dispensers, and other accessories.

Access to kindergarten programs typically is through the public elementary school system, but there are many other options, such as child care centers, day schools, and private elementary schools. Minimum space standards for early childhood education and kindergarten programs have historically been determined by state regulation, often by the U.S. Department of Public Welfare, for child care centers and day schools, or by the U.S. Department of Education, for programs that are components of public schools. Most minimum space standards are based on a square-foot allowance per child, but these standards can vary from state to state.

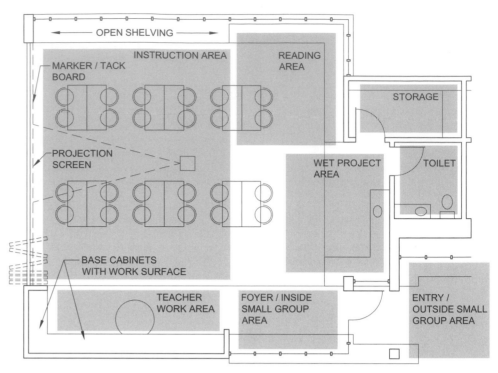

This classroom (1,000 sq ft (92.9 sq m); 24-student capacity) accommodates a variety of group and individual activities with specific areas for instruction, group reading, wet projects, and small groups.

**KINDERGARTEN AND GRADE 1 CLASSROOM**

### The Physical Environment

The indoor and outdoor environments must be safe, clean, attractive, and spacious. There should be enough usable space indoors so children are not crowded (a minimum of 35 sq ft (3.2 sq m) of usable playroom floor space indoors per child and a minimum of 75 sq ft (6.9 sq m) of play space outdoors per child). Program staffs must have access to the designated space and sufficient time to prepare the environment before children arrive.

Activity areas should be clearly defined by spatial arrangement. Space is arranged so that children can work individually, together in small groups, or in a large group. Clear pathways must be provided for children to move from one area to another and to minimize distractions.

### Preschool Design Concept

The space for children three years and older should be arranged to facilitate a variety of small group and individual activities, including block-building, sociodramatic play, art, music, science, math, manipulatives, and quiet reading and writing. Other activities such as sand play and woodworking are also often accommodated. Carpeted spaces as well as hard surfaces, such as wood floors and ample crawling and toddling areas, are typically provided for infants and young toddlers. Sturdy furniture is required to enable nonwalkers to pull themselves up or balance themselves while walking. School-age children should be provided separate space that is arranged to facilitate a variety of age-appropriate activities and permit sustained work on projects.

### Children's Equipment

Age-appropriate materials and equipment of sufficient quantity, variety, and durability should be readily accessible to children and arranged on low, open shelves to promote independent use. Individual spaces for children to store their personal belongings should be provided.

### Private Areas

Private areas should be made available indoors and outdoors so that children can have occasional solitude. Soft elements such as rugs, cushions, or rocking chairs should be provided for the comfort of the child, in addition to sound-absorbing materials to minimize noise.

### Outdoor Areas

Outdoor areas include a variety of surfaces, including soil, sand, grass, hills, flat sections, and hard areas for wheeled toys. Outdoor spaces include shaded, open, and digging area; outdoor equipment should enable riding, climbing, balancing, and individual play. The outdoor area is protected by fences or by natural barriers from access to streets or other dangers.

### Staff Work Area

The work environment for staff should include a place for adults to take a break or work away from children, an adult-size bathroom, a secure place for staff to store their personal belongings, and an administrative area that is separated from the children's areas for planning or preparing materials.

## KINDERGARTEN AREA REQUIREMENTS

The required space standards for kindergartens often fall short of those recommended by social and behavioral research, in both quantity and arrangement of space. Facilities with too little space (less than 35 usable sq ft (3.2 sq m) of space per child) may lead to more aggressive and destructive behavior, fewer friendly contacts, and less solitary learning and play. Conversely, too much space (more than 50 usable sq ft (4.6 sq m) of space per child) can result in reduced attention spans, more supervision required by staff, and an increase in aimless, random behavior.

### Outdoor Activities

The amount of recommended space for outdoor activity can vary significantly. It is best to provide at least the minimum required space, rather than no outside space at all. Compensation for lack of outdoor space with additional indoor activity space, in equal proportion to the outdoor requirement, is acceptable. Given the constraints of building sites, particularly in urban or inner-city locations, outdoor space may not be possible. In such situations, designers must find inventive solutions to enable access to fresh air and sunlight. Any outdoor space, however small, can be important, providing release to the children and offering a broad range of educational opportunities, even if they do not satisfy requirements for an outdoor area.

### Entrance

The main entrance should be a welcoming, spacious area with adequate seating and places for informal visiting. It should be large enough to accommodate small groups of children and adults. This is often the place where children exhibit signs of anxiety over separation from parents. Display areas for bulletins and children's projects can be provided at both adults' and children's eye level. Ideally, the entrance should be close to administrative areas to provide security and to accommodate parent-teacher meetings.

### Administrative Space

Administrative areas should be located near the entrance for easy access by families and for view of the main entrance. Administrative areas usually include a director's office with adequate space for a small meeting table, staff mailboxes, a small meeting room, space for records storage and supplies, space for a small quiet room and first-aid room, and a staff workroom and break area with bathroom.

### Corridors and Transition Spaces

Corridors can be viewed as extensions of activity space. Avoid long, straight hallways by providing nooks and alcoves for sitting, play, and display. Provide space for wall and ceiling-hung projects, and display cases for various art objects. Design open corridor spaces with interior glass windows looking into adjacent classroom and activity spaces; take advantage of borrowed natural light. Avoid designing corridors to have no other use but circulation. Use carpeting or other acoustic materials to reduce noise.

### Classrooms

A well-designed classroom environment is safe for children, supports their emotional well-being, stimulates their senses, and challenges their skills. Subdividing the classroom into well-defined "activity pockets" identifies physical spaces each of which is functionally limited to one activity but not completely closed off from the rest of the classroom or instructor supervision. Observation of preschool children at play suggests that they have a tendency to cluster into small groups of fewer than five, with a mean of about two children. If activity areas are sized for two to five children and an instructor, they should range between 40 and 60 sq ft (3.7 and 5.5 sq m) each. In addition, space should be provided either within the classroom or in a nearby area to allow for an entire class to meet as a single group.

The optimum class size is approximately 20 children per classroom. Select finishes to help reduce noise (think in terms of 20 children at active play). Create areas for distinct activities: for example, group meetings; quiet individual concentration; laboratory and semiactive spaces; workshop and studio spaces for art, drama, blocks, games, and so on. These areas are best created through the use of movable furnishings, shelves, bookcases, and so forth, to promote flexibility and the individual character of each classroom. Rectangular spaces are typically easier to configure than square or oddly shaped areas.

Design space to meet both children's and adult's physical needs. Be sure to provide seating, tables, workspace, and storage suited to both. Provide space for cubbies and lockers, either between classrooms or within classrooms; allow for adult assistance. Provide for display of plants and objects. Take advantage of areas below windows for quiet seating nooks or play areas. Provide a play area specifically suited to wet or messy activities.

### Personalization, Display, and Storage

Providing inventive and creative ways to display the work and projects of the children is essential to support their "habitation" of the space. Every part of the architecture should be thought of as potential display space; use walls, ceilings, floors, and furnishings throughout the facility. Care should be taken to provide a variety of display spaces for two-dimensional flat work and three-dimensional pottery, mobiles, sculpture, and small crafts. The display area should be flexible and allow for quick and easy alteration. A display space should be designed for viewing by both adults and children. Appropriate lighting should emphasize the displays and should be adjustable in both position and intensity. The following are suggestions for display spaces:

- Install picture rails or shelves along walls. Give particular attention to corridor areas, where walls may become repetitive.
- Arrange closed display cases for viewing from one side or from all sides.
- Make use of windowsills or areas in front of windows where natural light and the interplay of light and shadow can enhance the objects viewed.

## RECOMMENDED MINIMUM SPACE REQUIREMENTS FOR KINDERGARTEN AND PRESCHOOL

| | |
|---|---|
| Direct activity/classroom space | 42 sq ft (3.9 sq m)/child |
| Staff support/storage space | 38 sq ft (3.5 sq m)/child |
| Observation space (often used by parents or staff) | 9 sq ft (.83 sq m)/child |
| Subtotal assignable space | 89 sq ft (8.26 sq m)/child |
| Nonassignable space, "multiplier"* | 20 sq ft (1.8 sq m)/child |
| Total facility space/child | 109 sq ft (10 sq m)/child |
| Outdoor activity space | 75–200 sq ft (6.9–18.5 sq m)/child |

*The multiplier is applied to the program area to account for circulation, wall thickness, miscellaneous support spaces, and so forth, but may not include adequate space for mechanical/electrical equipment depending on the system selected.

Source: Campus Child Care News 11(1), January 1996.

## SPACES IN SAMPLE FACULTY PROGRAM FOR KINDERGARTEN

| PROGRAM SPACE | AREA SQ FT (SQ M) |
|---|---|
| Entry area | 200 (18.5) |
| Program assistant's/reception area | 120 (11.1) |
| Administrative assistant's office | 120 (11.1) |
| Director's office | 160 (14.8) |
| Administration copy/supply room | 100 (9.3) |
| Staff workroom/break area/toilet | 350 (32.5) |
| Meeting/parent conference room | 200 (18.5) |
| Quiet room/first aid | 100 (9.3) |
| Kindergarten classrooms (5 @ 800 sq ft (74.3 sq m) each) (Classroom area includes storage, cubbies, kitchen, etc.) | 4,000 (371) |
| Classroom bathrooms (5 @ 80 sq ft (7.4 sq m) each) | 400 (37.2) |
| Central activity/dining area | 1,500 (139.3) |
| Central activity storage | 200 (18.5) |
| Art studio (with kiln) | 500 (46.4) |
| Art studio storage | 60 (5.5) |
| Kitchen/food storage | 600 (55.7) |
| General facility storage | 200 (18.5) |
| Subtotal usable space | 8,810 (818.5) |
| Multiplier for circulation, mechanical area, etc. @ 1.2 | 1,760 (163.5) |
| Total Facility Program (average @ ±106 sq ft (9.8 sq m)/child) | 10,570 (981.9) |

Kindergarten program for 100 children.

### Kitchen and Pantry

A kitchenette can serve a group of classrooms or the entire school area, with counters and cabinets at heights for both children and adults. Locking cabinets should be specified. Locate the kitchenette for easy and secure delivery access and so that it is adjacent to the dining area. If possible, allow for a clear view from the dining area with interior windows, to promote child-staff interaction and learning. Arrange space to allow for display cooking. Ensure that adequate ventilation is provided.

## ELEMENTARY SCHOOLS

Elementary schools typically are defined as including grades 1 through 5 and, sometimes, grade 6. The program criteria set here for grades 1 through 5 can also be used for grade 6, if included in the elementary program. Elementary schools often also include prekindergarten and kindergarten.

### Major Program Elements

The program elements of an elementary school can be categorized in three major areas:

- *Classrooms:* General-purpose classrooms, special education classrooms
- *Specialized program areas:* Music room, science room, art room, computer lab, gymnasium, cafeteria, auditorium, library
- *Administrative and resource areas:* General office, principal's office, guidance office, nurse's office, faculty room, teachers' resource room, specialized resource areas for remediation

It is these three areas that determine the net square footage needed for an elementary school. However, the amount of square footage dedicated to each of these categories can vary greatly from building to building. The number of classrooms is dependent on class size, the applicable standards, and the enrollment projections for each grade level. The amount of square footage dedicated to specialized program areas is somewhat discretionary and depends on how many special programs will be offered. The number of such programs depends, in turn, on the operating budget, the size of the student body, and other factors. However, many school spaces are designed with shared functions, such as a single space used for the gymnasium, auditorium, and cafeteria. The special program areas should not be considered in computing the student capacity of an elementary school. In elementary schools, classroom space determines school capacity. Administration and resource areas are programmed on a school-by-school basis and are dependent on staffing, operating budgets, and other factors.

### TYPICAL MINIMUM CLASSROOM SIZES FOR U.S. ELEMENTARY SCHOOLS

| STATE | REQUIREMENTS |
|---|---|
| New York | The minimum standard for an elementary classroom is 770 net sq ft (71.5 net sq m), based on 27 students. |
| California | Grades 1 through 12 require not less than 960 net sq ft (89.1 net sq m) or an equivalent space that provides not less than 30 sq ft (2.7 sq m) per student. |
| Virginia | Requires 975 sq ft (90.5 sq m) for first grade and 800 sq ft (74.3 sq m) for grades 2 through 5. |
| Florida | Recommends 25 students per classroom for grades 1 through 3, at a range of 36 to 40 net sq ft (3.3 to 3.7 net sq m) per student, and 28 students per classroom for grades 4 through 6, at a range of 30 to 34 net sq ft (2.7 to 3.1 net sq m) per student. |

### Classrooms

For general-purpose classrooms, it is typical to size rooms for approximately 28 students. Note that most schools attempt to keep the number of students per classroom lower than that, usually 22 to 24 students. Nonetheless, unless otherwise established, it is prudent to design for 28 to account for population growth, unbalanced section sizes, and similar contingencies. Classroom sizes typically range from 750 to 1,000 net sq ft (69.6 to 92.9 sq m).

Many states have minimum standards for classroom size. Elementary-age students need to sit either at individual tables and chairs or at group tables. Project areas within the classroom are also needed, which may include areas for science, computer clusters, and other equipment-intensive spaces. In addition, adequate space must be allowed for classroom materials and student storage. Storage should be sized for coats, briefcases, purses, backpacks, and so on. Most elementary schools do not have lockers in corridors, so storage areas must be accommodated within the classroom.

### Specialized Program Areas

The quantity of specialized program areas is determined by the offerings at the school, and varies from school to school. In some cases, multiple functions can be accommodated in a single space, such as a cafeteria and auditorium or a science and art room.

### Community Use

Elementary schools are community facilities—cafeterias, auditoriums, and gyms are commonly used after normal school hours. Therefore, separate entrances, security, and mechanical zones should be considered.

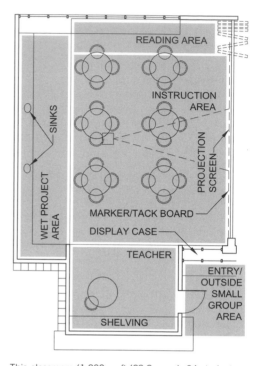

This classroom (1,000 sq ft (29.9 sq m); 24-student capacity) is smaller than the pre-K and K-1 classroom. It accommodates a variety of group and individual activities with specific areas for instruction, group reading, wet projects, and small groups.

**CLASSROOM FOR GRADES 2 THROUGH 5**

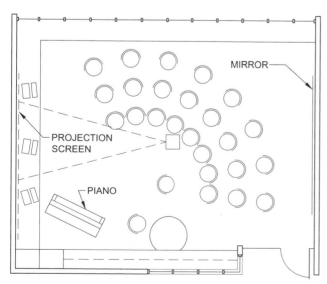

**PERFORMANCE ART SPACE**

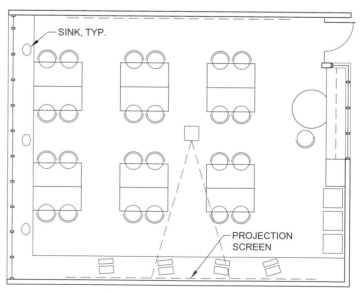

**ART AND MEDIA SPACE**

**SPECIALIZED PROGRAM AREAS**

# MIDDLE SCHOOL AND JUNIOR HIGH SCHOOL

The first middle school emerged as a separate entity early in the twentieth century. Middle schools were established in many areas to provide a mix of vocational and secondary education for the majority of students who quit formal schooling by grade 9. Middle schools are defined here as grades 6 through 8.

Today, for most school districts in the United States, the middle school is still evolving. The middle school experience is intended to provide a transition from the self-contained, nurturing environment of the elementary school to the departmental configuration of the high school. Students are introduced to departmental teaching, interdisciplinary teaching, flexible scheduling, block scheduling, collaborative learning, and flexible groupings.

## Program Elements

The program elements of a middle school can be categorized into four major areas:

- *Classrooms:* General-purpose classrooms, clusters of classrooms (commonly referred to as the "house"), and special education classrooms.
- *Student resource centers:* Technology center, music instruction area, flexible laboratory space, art instruction room, gymnasium, cafeteria, auditorium, library, special-use and club meeting rooms, video technologies, and exhibition space.
- *Teacher support areas:* Conference rooms, common faculty (team teaching) planning and workrooms, faculty dining room, and adult toilet and telephone rooms.
- *School administration:* General offices and waiting area, principal's and assistant principal's suite; guidance, nurse, and custodial offices; and specialized resource rooms for remediation.

Typically, fundamental instruction spaces include general classrooms, library, and gymnasium spaces. In the case of a middle school, 156 sq ft (14.4 sq m) per student is a reasonable planning number for a student population ranging from 500 to 700 students. To deal with financial and other constraints, many school programs include large common areas that have been developed to offer flexible and multifunction opportunities within the same space. Typically, the gymnasium, auditorium, and cafeteria are combined in some fashion (sometimes for two of these functions only). This savings in construction cost must be weighed against the appropriateness of the resultant finishes, acoustic properties, lighting, and scheduling for each of the functions proposed in the multipurpose space.

## Classrooms

General-purpose classrooms typically are designed to accommodate a maximum of 28 students. The permitted maximum number of students per classroom may vary somewhat from state to state. At the middle school level, the typical average class size for both new construction and building additions ranges from 23 to 25 students. This average allows for an increase in the student population of three to five students per classroom without requiring new construction. Extra capacity within the classroom can also accommodate varying class sizes.

## SPACE REQUIREMENTS FOR MIDDLE SCHOOL ADMINISTRATION

| PROGRAM ELEMENT | TYPICALLY REQUIRED BY CODE | NET SQ FT (NET SQ M) RANGE |
|---|---|---|
| **General Office** | | |
| Waiting area | No | 200–400 (18.5–37.1) |
| Secretary's space | No | 75–150 (6.9–13.9) |
| Principal's office | Yes | 250 (23.2) |
| Assistant principal's office | No | 200 (18.5) (requirement based on school population) 600–800 (55.7–74.3) (mail, duplications, processing, etc.) |
| Work area | No | 200–400 (18.5–37.1) |
| Guidance office | Yes | 120 (11.1) per counselor, plus waiting area if clustered (one per 75 students) |
| Nurse's suite | | |
| Waiting room | No | 100–200 (9.2–18.5) |
| Nurse's office | Yes | 150 (13.9) |
| Nurse's assistant area | No | 100 (9.2) (recommended if student population is over 500) |
| Examination area | Yes | 80 (7.4) per station (recommend 1 station/150 students) |
| Rest area | No | 150 (13.9) |
| Toilet room | Yes | 80 (7.4) |
| Specialized resource rooms for remediation | No | 450 (41.8) |
| Custodial space | No | Depends on function; may include paper supply/storage, shop area, cleaning equipment, grounds equipment, etc. |

## SPACE REQUIREMENTS FOR COMMON MIDDLE SCHOOL PROGRAM ELEMENTS

| PROGRAM ELEMENT | TYPICALLY REQUIRED BY CODE | NET SQ FT (NET SQ M) RANGE |
|---|---|---|
| Computer center | No | 850–1,200 (78.9–111.5) (1 per 250 students) |
| Music instruction room | No | 850–1,200 (78.9–111.5) (1 per 250 students) |
| Laboratory spaces | No | 1,000–1,200 (92.9–111.5) (1 per 125 students) |
| Art instruction room | No | 1,000–1,200 (92.9–111.5) (1 per 250 students) |
| Gymnasium | Yes | 3,500 (325) (= one station) (1 station per 250 students) |
| Cafeteria | Yes | School population × 50% × 10 (.92) (recommended) (provides two lunch periods total) |
| Kitchen | No | Depends on food program and equipment; typically equal to one-third the size of dining area |
| Auditorium | No | School capacity × 50% × 7 (.65) (recommended) (based on seating one half of the school population) |
| Library | Yes | 10 (.92 ) per student (recommended) |
| Special use rooms | No | 500–750 (46.4–69.6) per use |
| Media/video center | No | 750–1,000 (69.6–92.9) |
| Exhibition/display areas | No | Standards developed on a school-by-school basis |

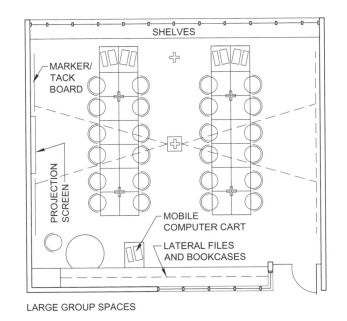

LARGE GROUP SPACES

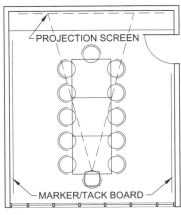

SMALL GROUP SPACES

Classrooms are planned to have integrated technology available in a variety of configurations to enable simulations research and streaming videos. Small group rooms are designed as breakout areas for the shared use of the middle school.

**STUDENT LEARNING SPACES**

## Middle School Design Issues

The middle school experience is intended to provide a transition for students from the self-contained classrooms and nurturing environment of the elementary school to the departmental configuration of the high school. School design has historically been based on the notion that subject-specific classrooms accommodate one teacher, perhaps an assistant, and a group of students for designated periods during the school day. This "cells and bells" approach centers on the idea that the student goes (physically) to the subject.

## Teaming

The increasingly popular middle school educational philosophy of *teaming* has developed as an alternative to the subject-specific classroom. The teaming methodology supports the notion that instructional spaces are flexible and functionally specific. In essence, the subject comes to the student. Cooperative learning, group projects, and team teaching are the main tools that educators use to foster the team philosophy.

## The House Model

Middle school teaming can be defined as an educational program that allows a subset (or house) of students in a specific grade to receive the core of their scholastic instruction from one group of teachers within a small group of flexible classrooms and support spaces. These flexible classrooms are deliberately designed to be function-specific rather than subject-specific.

In this concept, a grade level typically is a *team*. The team is composed of *houses*. A common example of the teaming strategy for a grades 6 to 8 middle school is three teams (one each for sixth, seventh, and eighth grade) of two houses each.

## House Size

Each house in a large middle school may accommodate approximately four classrooms or 100 students. Educators suggest that this diversity in the number of students per grade and other physical discontinuities adds to the middle school experience.

The house approach offers a smaller-size environment within the whole in which a core group of students and teachers can gather, chat, and grow. The house is often the architectural building block of new middle school design.

The great majority of the existing middle schools in the United States were planned and built before the teaming and house methodologies were conceived. As many school districts built new high schools, the old high school was often retrofitted to accommodate the middle school program.

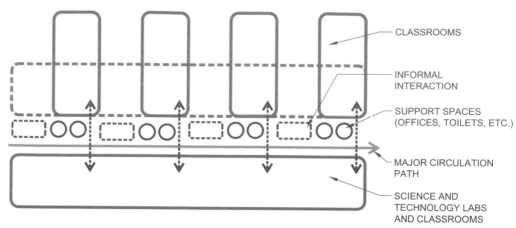

SINGLE LABORATORY SUPPORTING SEPARATE AND DISTINCT CLASSES WITH SHARED SUPPORT SPACES

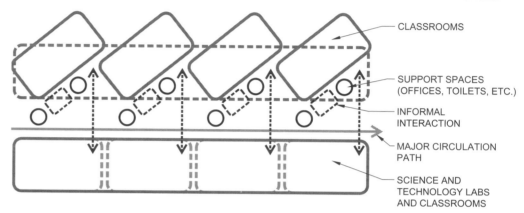

MERGED LABORATORY SUPPORTING SEPARATE AND DISTINCT CLASSES WITH SEPARATE SUPPORT SPACES

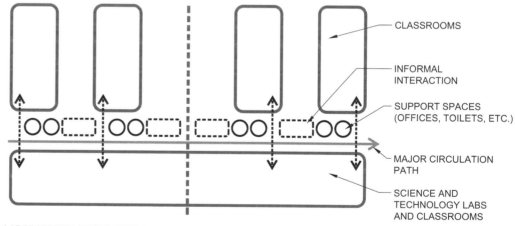

LABORATORIES SUPPORTING TWO CLASSES WITH SHARED SUPPORT SPACES

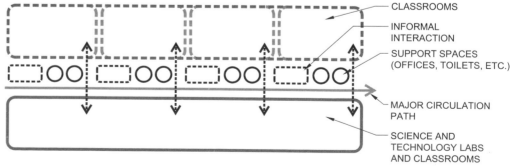

SINGLE LABORATORY SUPPORTING SINGLE MERGED CLASS WITH SHARED SUPPORT SPACES

A variety of configurations can be supported by the house model, while responding to site and architectural issues. A house includes three or four flexible classrooms, a flexible lab space, a computer and technology area, a conference area, and other support spaces.

**HOUSE CONCEPT**

## MATERIAL SELECTION FOR SCHOOLS

Many schools in use today across the country are housed in buildings more than 50 years old. The need for these buildings to withstand the wear and tear from decades of accommodating schoolchildren and various educational programs should be a major factor in the selection of materials. The materials used to construct a school building should be durable and maintainable. They should be capable of withstanding years of use and abuse while continuing to provide an atmosphere conducive to learning.

### Common Material Selections for Primary Spaces

The decisions made regarding material selections, as well as the accessories to protect them, will possibly have the most profound effect on the physical environment and its familiarity to children. We often associate the most institutional and, unfortunately, intimidating settings with endless vinyl tile floors, painted concrete-block walls, cold fluorescent lighting, and numerous wall and corner protection accessories. Although these materials will last a long time, they convey a stronger sense of factory than of home. There are, however, many new products on the market that can provide the durability and maintainability needed without significant compromise of the environment.

### Walls

The use of gypsum board for walls is more than likely, given today's budget considerations, but this material does not provide very suitable impact resistance. Highly susceptible to gouging, dents, and corner damage, standard gypsum products must be enhanced or protected. The use of new high-impact gypsum products now on the market (more commonly specified in public housing projects) or the addition of a "skim coat" of diamond-hard plaster to at least a height of 4 ft (1.2 m), can help to improve the durability of the walls. Painted or ground-face block is a common alternative.

### Floors

Consideration should be given to new carpet materials for use in classrooms and large play areas both to enhance acoustic quality and to reduce injuries associated with slippery, harder surfaces. In many schools, area rugs are used so that they can be moved, replaced, and quickly cleaned. Solution-dyed products with integral moisture backing should be specified to ensure color retention and easy cleanup of soils and spills. In toilet rooms and in areas used for artwork or wet or messy activities, consider the use of VCT or sheet-vinyl products, which provide long-term durability and maintainability as well as many aesthetic options. Some products offer an attractive wood-flooring appearance with 6-ft- (1.8-m-) wide sheets capable of welded seaming and flash cove base details for watertightness.

## CONSIDERATIONS FOR MATERIAL SELECTIONS IN SCHOOLS

| AREA | CONSIDERATIONS |
|---|---|
| Administration | Soft flooring for comfort and acoustics<br>Acoustical barrier walls<br>Cleanable surfaces in workrooms<br>Ventilation for copying area |
| Offices | Acoustical barrier walls for privacy<br>Proper air change and ventilation<br>Durability (not as critical as in student environments) |
| Nurse's area | Sanitary conditions<br>Germ-resistant environment<br>Easy to clean and disinfect<br>Hard, nonporous flooring<br>Smooth, cleanable surfaces<br>Disinfectable sick cots<br>Nonpollutant, nonallergenic environment<br>Proper ventilation, humidity, and temperature levels<br>Fluid-impervious materials |
| Library | Quiet environment<br>Nonglare, nonreflective surfaces for computer use<br>Indirect lighting<br>Controlled moisture and humidity levels |
| Classrooms | Easily cleaned flooring<br>Hard flooring, with a throw-rug option<br>Environment conducive to concentration<br>Glare from windows controlled<br>Work surface/furnishing durability reflective of classroom function<br>Durable shelving and casework<br>Water-resistant walls, cabinets, floors around sink and toilet areas |
| Kitchen | Adherence to sanitation regulations<br>Hard, nonporous, nonslip flooring<br>Ability to withstand heavy daily cleaning with chemicals and disinfectant<br>Seamless surfaces for food preparation and cooking<br>Splash-guard surfaces at sink area<br>Floor and wall surfaces resistant to oil and cooking residues<br>Heat-resistant finishes<br>Smooth surfaces resistant to the growth of bacteria |
| Cafeteria | Hard, nonporous flooring<br>Smooth surfaces resistant to the growth of bacteria<br>Finishes that can be cleaned with disinfectants<br>Hard, smooth wall surfaces for cleaning (at least as a wainscot) |
| Gymnasium | Resilient floor surface that allows true bounce and spring action<br>Hard, durable wall surfaces for ball play<br>Padded wall sections located strategically for game play<br>Noise reduction via acoustical block, ceiling treatments, etc.<br>Durability of all products used: lights, scoreboard, doors, clocks, etc.<br>Vandal-resistant materials |
| Locker Rooms | Nonporous, nonslip flooring<br>Ability to withstand heavy cleaning and student abuse<br>Water- and humidity-resistant materials<br>Mildew-resistant curtains<br>Vandal-resistant materials<br>Proper ventilation at clothing and equipment storage areas<br>Durable lockers and furnishings<br>Moisture-resistant wall surfaces |
| Auditorium | Ease of cleaning beneath the seating area<br>Soft floor finish on walking surfaces to reduce noise<br>Hard and soft wall surfaces placed to achieve the best acoustical properties<br>Vandal-resistant materials<br>Hard surface or cushioned seating, as defined by client<br>Flame-resistant finishes and curtains<br>Resilient stage flooring |
| Technology | Nonglare or antiglare surfaces<br>Static-resistant materials<br>Quiet environment<br>Ability to control exterior light |
| Science | Chemical- and acid-resistant materials<br>Hard, cleanable floor finish<br>Proper ventilation for chemical and gas use<br>Water-resistant work surfaces, cabinetry, walls, and floors<br>Chemical storage |
| Art | Cleanable walls, floors, and ceilings (seamless preferred)<br>Hard, smooth flooring<br>Natural light<br>Heavy-duty storage shelving<br>Fire-resistant kiln area<br>Water-resistant work surfaces, cabinetry, walls, and floors |

## Ceilings

Acoustics should be addressed for each area designed. The use of acoustic ceiling tile in most areas is important, and carpeting should be considered wherever possible. In areas with harder surfaces, such as large expanses of glass wall or hard-tile flooring, acoustic tile ceilings will not be enough. Consideration should be given to the use of acoustic wall treatments such as fabric-wrapped panels. Care should be taken not to locate these panels in high-impact areas, which generally extend up to 4 ft (1.2 m) above the floor.

## Wall Protection

The protection of openings and corners, always a consideration, will ultimately help the facility maintain its appearance. The use of corner guards at key impact areas is recommended; and consideration should be given to recessed guards with carefully coordinated coloring, which helps to blend them with the interior design.

## Trim and Casework

The use of natural wood to enhance the quality of a space is often desirable and can provide a very durable low-maintenance alternative to painted trim and cabinets. Among the common woods used for their durability and affordability are maple and oak. Many manufacturers producing children's furnishings work in maple or other light woods, such as birch or beech. These woods are worth considering in determining the color and aesthetic for trim and casework. If painted cabinets are desired, factory polyester or vinyl paint coatings offer good durability as well as easy cleanup. Unfortunately, colors are often limited to white or almond. Countertops of plastic laminate are quite functional, but cabinet fronts, doors, and drawer fronts on lower cabinetry may peel and delaminate over time. Melamine materials should be used on concealed surfaces only.

The materials selected for a school building should support the educational programs and objectives of the client. The environment should be comfortable for the activities within the space, and the materials chosen should add to the comfort in the children's environment. For example, kindergarten children spend much of their day on the floor, working as groups or in centers, and require a soft play surface such as carpeting. In a high school science classroom, students work at a lab station with chemicals that could be damaging to certain materials. The lab space should have hard, smooth work surfaces; and floor finishes should be easy to clean and chemically resistant.

## OPERATION AND MAINTENANCE

A well-designed school will withstand the expected impacts and abuse from its student populations. The building should be easy for its caretakers to operate and maintain and, ultimately, preserve the financial investment made by the community that authorized its construction. Operations and maintenance issues are different for new construction and existing buildings.

## New School Construction

A new school assignment is an ideal opportunity for an owner and a design team to develop a building that is operations- and maintenance-friendly. The design of the building should be tailored to the requirements of its educational program, consider the abilities of its caretaker, and be easy to operate and maintain. Common sense is usually the best tool for making design decisions that result in a school that is easy to operate and maintain. The designer should consider the following factors related to operations and maintenance:

- The design team's responsibility to advise the community on the best life-cycle strategy for any school construction program
- Sophistication of the building's caretakers
- Durability of building products and equipment
- Special considerations for specific program areas

Throughout the twentieth century, a large percentage of schools used masonry materials for the exterior, in conjunction with masonry, glazed tile, hardwood trim, plaster, and other durable materials for major interior corridors and common areas. The use of robust materials continues to offer the soundest approach for school design today. It is critical for the designer to understand the client's ability to maintain the building and to operate the proposed systems. The skills of a school's staff vary greatly from district to district, and the size of the caretaking staff can range from a single custodian to a team of custodial and facility management people. The size of the staff is, of course, no indicator of its sophistication.

## Protection against Vandalism

The durability of building products and equipment is directly related to the expenditure of maintenance staff hours and the subsequent life-cycle costs of the building's systems. The designer must specify building products that anticipate vandalism, graffiti, and heavy use. The building design should make supervision as easy as possible for the adults who will work in the building. Such a plan includes simple sight lines and provides adult use areas throughout the building—staff meeting rooms and educational resource areas. Sensible location of staff use areas (e.g., closer to the classrooms) can reduce adults' travel time to these spaces and ensure that an adult is always present or nearby in every area of the school. This arrangement can increase adult supervision and reduce vandalism and abuse of the school.

## Durability of Materials

It is common for corridor and classroom partition walls to be built of painted concrete block or glazed masonry units. Because gypsum surfaces are easily scarred, these more durable walls have proven to be easier to maintain. Similarly, terrazzo flooring products have historically provided an attractive and durable floor surface in areas of heavy traffic. Owing to their cost, however, these products have virtually disappeared from new school construction in recent decades. Alternate products such as vinyl composition tile, epoxy tile, and the much more durable media carpet fibers, where appropriate, are typically used today.

## Existing School Buildings

Renovation of an existing school typically involves the correction of existing maintenance and operations problems. For obvious reasons, school districts generally tend to invest most of their financial resources in teaching staff and educational materials (books, technology, athletic equipment, etc.) The physical condition of the school is typically ignored until a problem occurs. Student overcrowding, a leak in the roof, and continuous shorting-out of the electrical power system are examples of such problems. Operations and maintenance considerations for new buildings, as discussed above, should be applied in renovations of existing buildings whenever possible. The designer should consider the following additional factors as they relate to operations and maintenance of an existing school:

- Condition of the mechanical, electrical, and plumbing systems
- Energy conservation through replacement and upgrade of systems
- Sophistication of the building's caretakers
- Typical points of failure
- Identification and mitigation of toxic substances

## Existing Conditions

The design team must survey the school's mechanical, electrical, plumbing, and fire-protection systems. Part of the conditions assessment phase must include estimates of the remaining life of existing equipment. This phase should also include detailed interviews of the caretakers, teaching staff, and administration of the school. These interviews can identify problems that are unique to the particular school building and that recur throughout the school year.

## Mechanical and Electrical Systems

A study of the existing mechanical and electrical systems and the building envelope (windows and typical wall and roof section) can suggest upgrades of the systems through more efficient energy use. The design team will have to compare first costs with savings in utility costs through the payback period. Another area of study includes the building's heating system. Again, the design professional will be asked to determine the cost of a system upgrade in contrast to future utility cost savings.

## Thermal and Moisture Failures

Typical points of failure in the exterior envelope include brick joints, brick joints at windows, and roofing materials. These three areas are among the most neglected in school buildings throughout the country.

## Hazardous Materials

Identification and mitigation of toxic substances are critical to both the project budget and the schedule. It is essential that a qualified environmental engineer complete thorough tests of an existing school as early as possible in the design process. Only the written report by a qualified engineer should be relied upon for determinations in this area. If left undetected until late in the design or construction process, the presence of asbestos or other toxic substances can undermine the construction budget and cause serious delays in the schedule. It can also undermine the architect's credibility with the school board and the community.

Raymond C. Bordwell, AIA, Peter Brown, AIA, and Kathie Engelbrecht; Perkins & Will, Educational Facilities Planning and Research Group; Chicago, Illinois
Text excerpted from: Bradford Perkins (Stephen Klimnet, ed.); Building Type Basics for Elementary and Secondary Schools; New York, John Wiley & Sons, Inc., 2001, pp. 15–217.

PART 4

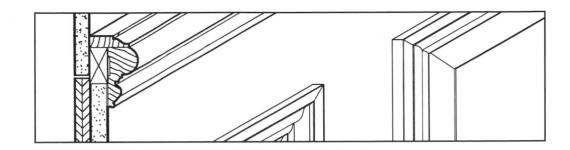

# APPENDIX

Plane and Solid Geometry

Metric System

Uniform Commercial Code

CSI MasterFormat

# PLANE AND SOLID GEOMETRY

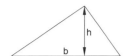

**TRIANGLE**
AREA = ½ any altitude × its base
(altitude is perpendicular distance
to opposite vertex or corner.)

$A = \frac{1}{2} b \times h$

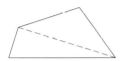

**TRAPEZUM (IRREGULAR
QUADRILATERAL)**
AREA = Divide figure into two
triangles and find areas as above.

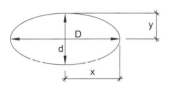

**ELLIPSE**
AREA = .7854 Dd
Approx. perimeter
$= \pi \sqrt{2(x^2 + y^2)}$

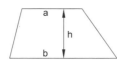

**TRAPEZOID**
AREA = ½ sum of parallel
sides × altitude

$A = \frac{h(a+b)}{2}$

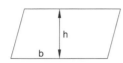

**PARALLELOGRAM**
AREA = either side × altitude

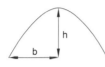

**PARABOLA**
$AREA = \frac{4hb}{3}$

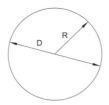

**CIRCLE**
$AREA = \frac{\pi D^2}{4} = \pi R^2$

$CIRCUMFERENCE = 2\pi R = \pi D$
($\pi = 3.14159265359$)

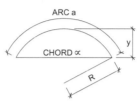

**CIRCULAR SEGMENT**
$ARFA = \frac{(Length\ of\ arc\ a) \times R - \alpha (R - y)}{2}$

$CHORD\ \alpha = 2\sqrt{2yR - y^2}$

$= 2R\ SIN\ \frac{A°}{2}$

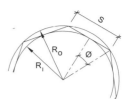

**REGULAR POLYGON**
$AREA = \frac{nSR_1}{2}$
(n = number of sides)

ANY SIDE $S = 2\sqrt{R_0 2 - R_1^2}$

$R = \frac{S}{2\ TAN\ ø}$   $R_0 - \frac{S}{4\ SIN\ ø}$

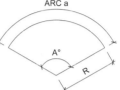

**CIRCULAR SECTOR**
$AREA = \frac{aR}{2}$

$= Area\ of\ circle \times \frac{A°}{360}$

$= 0.0087\ R^2 A°$

$ARC\ a = \frac{\pi R A°}{180°} = 0.0175\ RA°$

## GEOMETRIC PROPERTIES OF PLANE FIGURES

## GEOMETRIC PROPERTIES OF CIRCULAR PLANE FIGURES

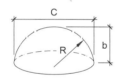

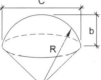

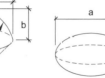

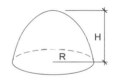

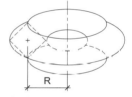

**SPHERE**
$VOLUME = \frac{4\pi R^3}{3}$
$= 0.5236\ D^3$

$SURFACE = 4\pi R^2$
$- \pi D^2$

**SEGMENT OF SPHERE**
$VOLUME = \frac{1\pi b^2(3R - b)}{3}$
(or sector − cone)

$SURFACE - 2\pi Rb$
(not including surface
of circular base)

**SECTOR OF SPHERE**
$VOLUME = \frac{2\pi R^2 b}{3}$

$SURFACE = \frac{\pi R(4b + c)}{2}$
(or: segment + cone)

**ELLIPSOID**
$VOLUME = \frac{\pi abc}{6}$

SURFACE: No simple rule

**PARABOLOID OF
REVOLUTION**
VOLUME = Area of circular
base × ½ altitude

SURFACE: No simple rule

**CIRCULAR RING OF ANY
SECTION**
R = Distance from axis of
ring to true center of section

VOLUME = Area of
section × 2πR

SURFACE = Perimeter of
section × 2πR (consider the
section on one side of axis only)

## VOLUMES AND SURFACES OF DOUBLE-CURVED SOLIDS

### SURFACES OF SOLIDS

The area of the surface is best
found by adding together the areas
of all the faces.

The area of a right cylindrical surface = perimeter of base x length
of elements (average length if other
base is oblique).

The area of a right conical surface
= perimeter of base x ½ length of
elements.

There is no simple rule for the area
of an oblique conical surface or for
a cylindrical one where neither base
is perpendicular to the elements.

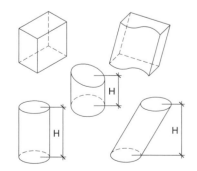

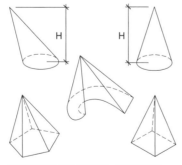

h = ALTITUDE
OF CUT-OFF

H = ALTITUDE
OF WHOLE

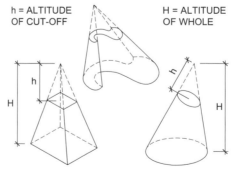

**PRISMS AND CYLINDERS, RIGHT OR
OBLIQUE, REGULAR OR IRREGULAR**
Volume = area of base × altitude

Altitude = distance between parallel bases,
measured perpendicular to the bases.
When bases are not parallel, then:
Altitude = perpendicular distance from
one base to the center of the other.

**PYRAMIDS OR CONES, RIGHT OR
OBLIQUE, REGULAR OR IRREGULAR**
Volume = area of base × ⅓ altitude

Altitude = distance from base to apex,
measured perpendicular to base.

**FRUSTUM OR TRUNCATED PORTIONS
OF THE SOLIDS SHOWN**
Volume = From the volume of the whole
solid; if complete, subtract the volume of
the portion cut off.

The altitude of the cutoff part must be
measured perpendicular to its own base.

*Source: J.R. Hoke, Jr., ed.;*
Architectural Graphic Standards;
*New York, John Wiley & Sons, Inc.*

## VOLUMES AND SURFACES OF TYPICAL SOLIDS

# METRIC SYSTEM

This appendix assimilates metric conversion information to address the appropriate presentation of metric units of measure in construction specifications.

The applicable international metric standard is the International System of Units (SI). The purpose of this appendix is to provide guidance in converting U.S. customary weight and measure units, referred to as inch-pound (IP) units, to metric, and to assist in the proper presentation of metric units in construction documents. Within *Interior Graphic Standards*, text and conceptual drawings provide both IP and SI units, determined by SI conversion standards in order to provide a proportional frame of reference.

Use the tables below to convert the IP units to SI for use in construction documents. In addition, use common sense and professional judgment when converting IP to SI units, as not all conversions are logical or intuitive. Moreover, product manufacturers may have their own policies and procedures for producing metric-sized and IP-sized products.

## CONVERSION RULES

In a *soft conversion*, an exact inch-pound measurement is mathematically converted to its exact (or near-exact) metric equivalent. In a *hard conversion,* a new, rounded, rationalized metric number is created that is convenient to work with and remember.

When converting numbers from inch-pound to metric, round the metric value to the same number of digits as there were in the inch-pound number. In all cases, use professional rounding to determine the exact value.

With professional rounding, the basic module of metric design is 100 mm. Make every effort to keep design dimensions in this increment. Additional multimodules and submodules, in preferred order, are 6,000, 3,000, 1,200, 600, 300, 50, 25, 20, and 10. Example: 1,990 BOCA Article 514.7 requires 36 in. (914 mm) of unobstructed pedestrian walkway width. However, 914 mm is not a clean and rational number, so should be rounded to facilitate the easiest construction possible. Since anything less than 914 mm would not meet the code requirements, the preferred number would be 1,000 mm. Submodules will produce a rounding of 950, 925, or 920 mm.

### Soft Metric

Soft metric means "no physical change." This implies the product need not be physically modified to be used in a metric project. More than 95% of currently used building products will not change. In the future, as standard international metric product sizes are developed by the International Standards Organization (ISO) or another standards organization, these products may undergo modification to be compatible in the world market. Custom products, often made by computer-controlled machinery, can be specified in any size.

### Hard Metric

Hard metric means "product requires physical change." The product must be physically modified to be efficiently used in a metric project, which is planned on a metric grid. A handful of current products must undergo hard metric conversion to new metric sizes.

## HARD METRIC PRODUCTS

| PRODUCT | SIZE (MM) |
|---|---|
| Brick | 90 × 57 × 190[1] |
| Concrete masonry unit | 190 × 190 × 390[1] |
| Drywall | 1,200 × 2,400[2] |
| Raised access flooring | 600 × 600 |
| Suspended ceiling tiles and grids | 600 × 600 and 600 × 1,200 |
| Fluorescent lighting fixtures (lay-in type only) | 600 × 600 and 600 × 1,200 |
| Air diffusers and grilles (lay-in type only) | 600 × 1,200 widths |

[1]*Three vertical courses of metric modular brick with a joint of 10 mm equals 201 mm, which is rounded to 200. Three vertical rows of 200 equal 600 mm; 600 x 600 mm is a preferred nominal module for masonry.*
[2]*Drywall thicknesses remain the same to minimize production impact. The standard thicknesses are 12.7 and 15.9 mm. Standard stud spacing is 400 mm.*

## METRIC PRODUCTS

Construction product manufacturers will determine actual product dimensions and values. Their decisions involve economics and practicality. Factors in their decision include the following:

- Cost of plant and manufacturing conversion, including changes in tooling, retesting and recertification, new literature, and additional marketing
- Economics of single versus double product inventory
- Demand for products from the industry in either system of measure

## USING METRIC UNITS IN SPECIFICATIONS

Metric specifications should use mm for almost all measurements. The use of mm is consistent with the dimensions specified in major codes, such as BOCA and NEC. With the use of mm, the decimal point is used when extreme precision is indicated. Meters may be used only where large, round metric sizes are specified. Centimeters must not be used in specifications. This is consistent with the recommendations of the AIA and ASTM.

## RULES FOR WRITING METRIC SYMBOLS AND NAMES

The following are suggested formats for use in metric terms:

- Print the unit symbol in upright type and in lowercase except for liter (L) or unless the unit name is derived from a proper name.
- Print decimal prefixes in lowercase for magnitudes $10^3$ and lower; print the prefixes in uppercase for magnitudes $10^6$ and higher.
- Leave a space between the numeral and symbol (example: 12 mm).
- Do not use the degree mark with kelvin temperatures.
- Do not leave a space between a unit symbol and its decimal prefix (example: km).
- Do not use the plural of unit symbols, but do use the plural of written unit names (example: kg, kilograms).
- For technical writing, use symbols in conjunction with numerals (example: $10 \text{ m}^2$) and write out unit names if numeral is not used (example: square meters).
- Indicate the product of two or more units in symbolic form by using a dot positioned above the line (example: $\text{kg.;m·s}^2$).

## TABLE COMPARISON OF DRAWING SCALES

| INCH-FOOT SCALES | INCH-FOOT RATIO | METRIC SCALE[1] |
|---|---|---|
| Full size | 1:1 | 1:1 |
| Half size | 1:2 | 1:2 |
| 4 in. = 1 ft 0 in. | 1:3 | |
| 3 in. = 1 ft 0 in. | 1:4 | 1:5 |
| 2 in. = 1 ft 0 in. | 1:6 | |
| 1½ in. = 1 ft 0 in. | 1:8 | 1:10 |
| 1 in. = 1 ft 0 in. | 1:12 | |
| ¾ = 1 ft 0 in. | 1:16 | 1:20 |
| ½ in. = 1 ft 0 in. | 1:24 | 1:25 |
| ¼ in. = 1 ft 0 in. | 1:48 | 1:50 |
| 1 in. = 5 ft 0 in. | 1:60 | |
| ⅛ in. = 1 ft 0 in. | 1:96 | 1:100 |
| 1 in. = 10 ft 0 in. | 1:120 | |
| 1⁄16 in. = 1 ft 0 in. | 1:192 | 1:200 |
| 1 in. = 20 ft 0 in. | 1:240 | 1:250 |
| 1 in. = 30 ft 0 in. | 1:360 | |
| 1⁄32 in. = 1 ft 0 in. | 1:384 | |
| 1 in. = 40 ft 0 in. | 1:480 | 1:500 |
| 1 in. = 50 ft 0 in. | 1:600 | |
| 1 in. = 60 ft 0 in. | 1:720 | |
| 1 in. = 80 ft 0 in. | 1:960 | 1:1,000 |

[1]*Metric drawing scales are expressed in nondimensional ratios. Metric scales 1:2, 1:25, and 1:250 have limited use.*

## DRAWING SHEET DIMENSIONS[1]

| SIZE | SHEET SIZE |
|---|---|
| A0[2] | 1,189 × 841 mm (46.8 × 33.1 in.) |
| A1 | 841 × 594 mm (33.1 × 23.4 in.) |
| A2 | 594 × 420 mm (23.4 × 16.5 in.) |
| A3 | 420 × 297 mm (16.5 × 11.7 in.) |
| A4 | 297 × 210 mm (11.7 × 8.3 in.) |

[1]*The ISO's A-series drawing sizes are preferred metric sizes for design drawings.*

[2]*A0 is the base size with an area of one square meter. Smaller sizes are half the long dimension of the previous size. All A-sizes have a height-to-width ratio of 1 to the square root of 2. Use a 35-mm microfilm frame to reduce these sizes.*

- Do not mix names and symbols (example: N meter).
- Do not use a period after a symbol except when it occurs at the end of a sentence, or for inches (in.) for clarity, so it does not read as the preposition 'in.'
- Always use decimals, not fractions.
- Use a zero before the decimal marker for values less than 1.
- When preparing documentation for use outside the United States, use spaces instead of commas to separate blocks of three digits for any number over four digits (example: 45 138 kg or 0.004 46 kg). In the United States, the decimal marker is a period; in other countries, a comma usually is used.

## USING MEASUREMENT CONVERSION TABLES

These tables present a summary listing of those measurement units normally encountered in construction specifications and drawings. They provide a compilation of a variety of measures from inch-pound (IP) to metric (SI) notations. Generally, the designations identify (from left to right) the following:

- IP measurement unit customarily used
- Exact numerical factor that will derive the exact SI measurement
- SI measurement unit traditionally used

The following listings do not differentiate between soft, hard, or rationalized hard conversions. These listings are examples of customary IP and SI measurement units with the pertinent numerical multiplier.

## METRIC PREFIXES

| MULTIPLES | PREFIXES | SYMBOLS |
|---|---|---|
| $1\ 000\ 000\ 000\ 000 = 10^{12}$ | tera | T |
| $1\ 000\ 000\ 000 = 10^{9}$ | giga | G |
| $1\ 000\ 000 = 10^{6}$ | mega | M |
| $1\ 000 = 10^{3}$ | kilo | k* |
| $100 = 10^{2}$ | hecto | h |
| $10 = 10$ | deka or deca | da |
| $0.1 = 10^{-1}$ | deci | d |
| $0.01 = 10^{-2}$ | centi | c |
| $0.001 = 10^{-3}$ | milli | m* |
| $0.000\ 001 = 10^{-6}$ | micro | m |
| $0.000\ 000\ 001 = 10^{-9}$ | nano | n |
| $0.000\ 000\ 000\ 001 = 10^{-12}$ | pico | p |

*Commonly used with base units in design and construction

## CONVERSION FACTORS

| QUANTITY | FROM INCH-POUND UNITS | TO METRIC UNITS | MULTIPLY BY |
|---|---|---|---|
| Length | mile | Km | 1.609344* |
| | yard | M | 0.9144* |
| | foot | M | 0.3048* |
| | | mm | 304.8* |
| | inch | mm | 25.4* |
| Area | square mile | km² | 2.59000 |
| | acre | m² | 4046.87 |
| | | ha (10 000m²) | 0.404687 |
| | square yard | m² | 0.83612736* |
| | square foot | m² | 0.09290304* |
| | square inch | mm² | 645.16* |
| Volume | acre foot | m³ | 1233.49 |
| | cubic yard | m³ | 0.764555 |
| | cubic foot | m³ | 0.0283168 |
| | | cm³ | 28316.85 |
| | | L (1000 cm³) | 28.31685 |
| | 100 board feet | m3 | 0.235974 |
| | gallon | L (1000 cm³) | 3.78541 |
| | cubic inch | cm³ | 16.387064* |
| | | mm³ | 16387.064* |
| Mass | lb | kg | 0.453592 |
| | kip (1,000 lb) | metric ton (1,000 kg) | 0.453592 |
| Mass/unit length | plf | kg/m | 1.48816 |
| Mass/unit area | psf | kg/m² | 4.88243 |
| Mass density | pcf | kg/m³ | 16.0185 |
| Force | lb | N | 4.44822 |
| Force/unit length | plf | N/m | 14.5939 |
| Pressure, stress, modulus of elasticity | psf | Pa | 47.8803 |
| | psi | kPa | 6.89476 |
| Bending moment, torque, moment of force | ft-lb | N·m | 1.35582 |
| Moment of mass | lb ft | kg·m | 0.138255 |
| Moment of inertia | lb ft² | kg·m² | 0.0421401 |
| Second moment of area | in4 | mm⁴ | 416231 |
| Section modulus | in.3 | mm³ | 16387.064* |
| Mass/area (density) | lb/ft² | kg/m² | 4.882428 |
| Temperature | °F | °C | 5/9(°F-32) |
| Energy, work, quantity of heat | KWh | MJ | 3.6* |
| | Btu | J | 1055.056 |
| | ft lbf | J | 1.35582 |
| Power | ton (refrig) | kW | 3.517 |
| | Btu/s | kW | 1.055056 |
| | hp (electric) | W | 745.700 |
| | Btu/h | W | 0.293071 |
| Heat flux | Btu/f²h | W/m | 3.152481 |
| Rate of heat flow | Btu/s | kW | 1.055056 |
| | Btu/h | W | 0.2930711 |
| Thermal conductivity (k value) | Btu/ft·h·°F | W/m·K | 1.73073 |
| Thermal conductance (U value) | Btu/ft²·h·°F | W/m²·K | 5.678263 |

## BASE UNITS

| PHYSICAL QUALITY | UNIT | SYMBOL |
|---|---|---|
| Length | Meter | m |
| Mass[1] | Kilogram | kg |
| Time | Second | s |
| Electric current | Ampere | A |
| Thermodynamic temperature[2] | Kelvin | K |
| Luminous intensity | Candela | cd |
| Amount of substance[3] | Mole | mol |

[1] "Weight" is often used to mean "mass."

[2] Celsius temperature (°C) is more commonly used than kelvin (K), but both have the same temperature gradients. Celsius temperature is simply 273.15° warmer than kelvin.

[3] Mole is the amount of molecular substance and is used in physics.

## DERIVED UNITS

| QUANTITY | NAME | SYMBOL | EXPRESSION |
|---|---|---|---|
| Frequency | hertz | Hz | $Hz = s^{-1}$ |
| Force | newton | N | $N = kg \cdot m/s^2$ |
| Pressure, stress | pascal | Pa | $Pa = N/m^2$ |
| Energy, work, quantity of heat | joule | J | $J = N \cdot m$ |
| Power, radiant flux | watt | W | $W = J/s$ |
| Electric charge, quantity | coulomb | C | $C = A \cdot s$ |
| Electric potential | volt | V | $V = W/A$ or $J/C$ |
| Capacitance | farad | F | $F = C/V$ |
| Electric resistance | ohm | W | $\Omega = V/A$ |
| Electric conductance | siemens | S | $S = A/V$ or $\Omega^{-1}$ |
| Magnetic flux | weber | Wb | $Wb = V \cdot s$ |
| Magnetic flux density | tesla | T | $T = Wb/m^2$ |
| Inductance | henry | H | $H = Wb/A$ |
| Luminous flux | lumen | lm | $lm = cd \cdot sr$ |
| Illuminance | lux | lx | $lx = lm/m^2$ |

## DECIMAL EQUIVALENTS

| FRACTION | DECIMAL OF AN INCH | DECIMAL OF A FOOT |
|---|---|---|
| 1/64 | 0.15625 | |
| 1/32 | 0.3125 | |
| 3/64 | 0.046875 | |
| 1/16 | 0.0625 | 0.0052 |
| 5/64 | 0.078125 | |
| 3/32 | 0.09375 | |
| 7/64 | 0.109375 | |
| 1/8 | 0.125 | 0.0104 |
| 9/64 | 0.140625 | |
| 5/32 | 0.15625 | |
| 11/64 | 0.171875 | |
| 3/16 | 0.1875 | 0.0156 |
| 13/64 | 0.203125 | |
| 7/32 | 0.21875 | |
| 15/64 | 0.234375 | |
| 1/4 | 0.250 | 0.0208 |
| 17/64 | 0.265625 | |
| 9/32 | 0.28125 | |
| 19/64 | 0.296875 | |
| 5/16 | 0.3125 | 0.0260 |
| 21/64 | 0.328125 | |
| 11/32 | 0.34375 | |
| 23/64 | 0.359375 | |
| 3/8 | 0.375 | 0.0313 |
| 25/64 | 0.390625 | |
| 13/32 | 0.40625 | |
| 27/64 | 0.421875 | |
| 7/16 | 0.4375 | 0.0365 |
| 29/64 | 0.453125 | |
| 15/32 | 0.46875 | |
| 31/64 | 0.484375 | |
| 1/2 | 0.500 | 0.0417 |
| 33/64 | 0.515625 | |
| 17/32 | 0.53125 | |
| 35/64 | 0.546875 | |
| 9/16 | 0.5625 | 0.0469 |
| 37/64 | 0.578125 | |
| 19/32 | 0.59375 | |
| 39/64 | 0.609375 | |
| 5/8 | 0.625 | 0.0521 |
| 41/64 | 0.640625 | |
| 21/32 | 0.65625 | |
| 43/64 | 0.671875 | |
| 11/16 | 0.6875 | 0.0573 |
| 45/64 | 0.703125 | |
| 23/32 | 0.71875 | |
| 47/64 | 0.734375 | |
| 3/4 | 0.750 | 0.0625 |
| 49/64 | 0.765625 | |
| 25/32 | 0.78125 | |
| 51/64 | 0.796875 | |
| 13/16 | 0.8125 | 0.0677 |
| 53/64 | 0.828125 | |
| 27/32 | 0.84375 | |
| 55/64 | 0.859375 | |
| 7/8 | 0.875 | 0.0729 |
| 57/64 | 0.890625 | |
| 29/32 | 0.90625 | |
| 59/64 | 0.921875 | |
| 15/16 | 0.9375 | 0.0781 |
| 61/64 | 0.953125 | |
| 31/32 | 0.96875 | |
| 63/64 | 0.984375 | |
| 1 | 1.00 | 0.0833 |
| 2 | 2.00 | 0.1667 |
| 3 | 3.00 | 0.2500 |
| 4 | 4.00 | 0.3333 |
| 5 | 5.00 | 0.4167 |
| 6 | 6.00 | 0.5000 |
| 7 | 7.00 | 0.5833 |
| 8 | 8.00 | 0.6667 |
| 9 | 9.00 | 0.7500 |
| 10 | 10.00 | 0.8333 |
| 11 | 11.00 | 0.9167 |
| 12 | 12.00 | 1.0000 |

## LINEAR MEASURE

| IP UNIT | MULTIPLY BY | SI UNIT |
|---|---|---|
| mils (1/1,000 in.) | 0.0254 | millimeters (mm) |
| inches | 25.4 | millimeter (mm) |
| feet | 304.8 | millimeter (mm) |
| feet | 0.3048 | meter (m) |
| yards | 914.4 | millimeter (mm) |
| yards | 0.9144 | meter (m) |
| miles | 1.609 344 | kilometer (km) |
| gage[1] | — | millimeter (mm) |
| picks per inch (textiles) | 0.3937 | picks per centimeter (cm) |

*[1]Gage here is a designation for sheet metal thickness or wire diameter. This designation must be transposed from gage to inch thickness or diameter and then converted to an SI unit. There are many gage "standards" used in the metals industry;*

*consult the appropriate gage table for the applicable inch measurement before converting. For galvanized and electroplated zinc-coated steel, the thickness to be used includes the coating; for galvanized metal deck and other structural applications, the thickness of the base metal before coating may need to be specified instead.*

## MASS AND DENSITY

| IP UNIT | MULTIPLY BY | SI UNIT |
|---|---|---|
| grains | 64.79891 | milligram (mg) |
| | 0.06479891 | gram (g) |
| ounces (oz) | 28.349523 | gram (g) |
| | 0.028349523 | kilogram (kg) |
| pounds (lb) | 0.45359237 | kilogram (kg) |
| tons | 0.90718474 | tonne |
| | 907.18474 | kilogram (kg) |
| ounces per linear inch (oz/in.) | 1.11612 | gram/millimeter (g/mm) |
| | 1.11612 | kilogram/meter (kg/m) |
| pounds per linear foot (lb/ft) | 1.48816 | kilogram/meter (kg/m) |
| ounces per square inch (oz/sq in.) | 439.4189 | gram per square millimeter (g/sq mm) |
| | 0.4394189 | kilogram per square meter (kg/sq m) |
| ounces per square foot (oz/sq ft) | 305.15426 | gram per square meter (g/sq m) |
| | 0.3052 | kilogram per square meter (kg/sq m) |
| ounces per square yard (oz/sq yd) | 33.91 | gram per square meter (g/sq m) |
| pounds per square inch (lb/sq in.) | 703.0696 | kilogram per square meter (kg/sq m) |
| pounds per square foot (lb/sq ft) | 4.88243 | kilogram per square meter (kg/sq m) |
| pounds per cubic inch (lb/cu in.) | 27.67990 | gram per cubic centimeter (g/cu cm) |
| pounds per cubic foot (lb/cu ft) | 16.01846 | kilogram per cubic meter (kg/cu m) |
| pounds per cubic yard (lb/cu yd) | 0.5933 | kilogram per cubic meter (kg/cu m) |

## VELOCITY AND RATE OF FLOW

| IP UNIT | MULTIPLY BY | SI UNIT |
|---|---|---|
| inches per minute (in./min.) | 1524 | millimeter per second (mm/s) |
| feet per second (fps) | 0.3048 | meter per second (m/s) |
| feet per minute (fpm) | 0.00508 | meter per second (m/s) |
| miles per hour (mph) | 0.44704 | meter per second (m/s) |
| | 1.609344 | kilometer per hour (km/h) |
| cubic feet per second (cfs) | 28.31685 | liters per second (L/s) |
| cubic feet per minute (cfm) | 0.471947 | liters per second (L/s) |
| cubic feet per hour (cfh) | 7.87 | milliliters per second (mL/s) |
| U.S. gallons per minute (gpm) | 0.06309 | liters per second (L/s) |
| U.S. gallons per hour (gph) | 0.001052 | liters per second (L/s) |
| revolutions per minute (rpm) | Do not convert | |
| steam flow rate (lb/h) at 212 deg F | 0.284 | kilowatts (kW) |

## AREA MEASURE

| IP UNIT | MULTIPLY BY | SI UNIT |
|---|---|---|
| square inches (sq in.) | 6.4516 | square centimeter (sq cm) |
| square feet (sq ft) | 0.0929034 | square meter (sq m) |
| square yards (sq yd) | 0.8361274 | square meter (sq m) |
| acres | 4046.87 | square meter (sq m) |
| | 0.404687 | hectare (ha) |
| square miles (sq mi) | 2.589988 | square kilometer (sq km) |
| | 2.59 | hectare (ha) |
| quantity per square foot (/sq ft) | 10.764 | quantity per square meter (/sq m) |
| quantity per square yard (/sq yd) | 1.196 | quantity per square meter (/sq m) |

## CUBIC MEASURE

| IP UNIT | MULTIPLY BY | SI UNIT |
|---|---|---|
| cubic inches (cu in.) | 16.387064 | milliliter (mL) |
| cubic feet (cu ft) | 0.02831685 | cubic meter (cu m) |
| cubic feet (cu ft) (volume) | 28.32 | liter (L) |
| cubic yards (cu yd) | 0.76455 | cubic meter (cu m) |

## LIQUID MEASURE

| IP UNIT | MULTIPLY BY | SI UNIT |
|---|---|---|
| U.S. gallons (gal) | 3.785412 | liter (L) |
| U.S. quarts | 0.946353 | liter (L) |
| U.S. pints | 0.473176 | liter (L) |
| U.S. fluid ounces (oz) | 29.57353 | milliliter (mL) |

## ENERGY, HEAT, AND WORK

| IP UNIT | MULTIPLY BY | SI UNIT |
|---|---|---|
| British thermal unit (Btu) | 1055.06 | joule (J) |
| | 1.05506 | kilojoule (kJ) |
| Equivalent direct radiation (EDR)—hot water | 44.0 | watt (W) |
| Equivalent direct radiation (EDR)—steam | 70.3 | watt (W) |
| ft-lbf/in. | 53.38 | joule per meter (J/m) |
| foot-pound force (ft × lbf) | 1.355818 | joule (J) |
| | 0.001355818 | kilojoule (kJ) |
| inch-pound force (in. × lbf) (torque or moment) | 0.1130 | N × m |
| kilowatt-hour (kWh) | 3600 | kilojoule (kJ) |
| | 3.6 | megajoule (MJ) |
| horsepower-hour | 2684.52 | kilojoule (kJ) |
| | 2.684 | megajoule (MJ) |
| Btuh (heat) | 0.2930722 | watt (W) |
| ton (refrigeration) | 3.517 | kilowatt (kW) |
| lb(steam)/h at 212 deg F | 0.284 | kilowatt (kW) |
| Btuh × sq ft (heat flow rate) | 3.154591 | watt per square meter (W/sq m) |
| Btu × ft/h × sq ft × deg F (thermal conductivity, k-value) | 1.730735 | W/m × K |
| Btu × in./h × sq ft × deg F (thermal conductivity, K-value) | 0.1442279 | W/m × K |
| Btu/sq ft × h × deg F (thermal conductance, U- or C-value) | 5.678263 | W/sq. m × K |
| deg F × h × sq ft/Btu × in. (thermal resistivity, R-value) | 6.933471 | K × m/W |
| deg F × h × sq ft/Btu (thermal resistance, R-value) | 0.176110 | K × sq m/W |
| perms (23 deg C) (grains/h × sq ft × in. Hg) (vapor permeance) | 57.4525 | ng/Pa × s × sq m |
| perm inches (grains/h × ft × in. Hg) (vapor permeability) | 1.459 29 | ng/Pa × s × m |
| cfm/sq ft of surface area | 5.080 | L/s × sq m |
| | 0.00508 | cu m/s × sq m |

## POWER

| IP UNIT | MULTIPLY BY | SI UNIT |
|---|---|---|
| horsepower (550 ft × lbf/s) (hp) | 745.6999 | watt (W) |
| horsepower (electric) | 746.000 | watt (W) |
| horsepower (boiler) | 9.81 | kilowatt (kW) |
| horsepower (water) | 746.043 | watt (W) |
| foot-pounds force per second | 1.355818 | watt (W) |
| foot-pounds force per minute | 0.02259697 | watt (W) |

## TEMPERATURE

| IP UNIT | MULTIPLY BY | SI UNIT |
|---|---|---|
| Fahrenheit (deg F) | Actual temperature: Subtract 32 degrees then multiply by ⅝ (0.5556) | Celsius (deg C) |
| | Temperature differential: Multiply by ⅝ (0.5556) (Do not subtract 32) | Celsius (deg C) or Kelvin (deg K) |

## ELECTRICITY AND ILLUMINATION

| IP UNIT | MULTIPLY BY | SI UNIT |
|---|---|---|
| candela per square foot (cd/sq ft) | 10.76391 | candela per square meter (cd/sq m) |
| candela per square inch (cd/sq in.) | 1550.0 | candela per square meter (cd/sq m) |
| foot-lamberts | 3.42626 | candela per square meter (cd/sq m) |
| lumens (lm) per square foot | 10.76391 | lux (lx) |
| foot-candles (fc) | 10.76391 | lux (lx) |
| ohms/1,000 feet (wire resistance) | 3.28 | ohms/km |
| degrees (plane angles) | 0.0174 | radians |

## FORCE, PRESSURE, AND STRESS

| IP UNIT | MULTIPLY BY | SI UNIT |
|---|---|---|
| ounces force | 0.278014 | newton (N) |
| pounds force (lbf) | 4.448222 | newton (N) |
| pounds force per foot (lbf/ft) | 14.59 | newton per meter (N/m) |
| kip force | 4448.222 | newton (N) |
| | 4.448222 | kilonewton (kN) |
| tons force | 8896.444 | newton (N) |
| | 8.896444 | kilonewton (kN) |
| tons force per foot | 29187.81 | newton per meter (N/m) |
| pounds force per square inch (lbf/sq in.) (psi) (psig) | 6894.757 | pascal (Pa) or N/sq m |
| | 6.894757 | kilopascal (kPa) or kN/sq m |
| | 0.006894757 | megapascal (MPa) or MN/sq m |
| pounds force per square foot (lbf/sq ft) | 47.88026 | pascal (Pa) or N/sq m |
| | 0.047880 | kilopascal (kPa) or kN/sq m |
| | 0.000047880 | megapascal (MPa) or MN/sq m |
| tons force per square inch | 13789.514 | kilopascal (kPa) |
| | 13.789514 | megapascal (MPa) |
| tons force per square foot | 95760.513 | pascal (Pa) |
| | 95.760513 | kilopascal (kPa) |
| | 0.095760513 | megapascal (MPa) |
| inch water gage (inch wg) at 60 deg F (16 deg C) | 248.84 | pascal (Pa) |
| feet of water column at 60 deg F (16 deg C) | 2.9861 | kilopascal (kPa) |
| inch of mercury column at 0 deg C (32 deg F) | 3386.38 | pascal (Pa) |
| inch of mercury column at 60 deg F (16 deg C) | 3376.85 | pascal (Pa) |

## TABLES OF STANDARD SIZES

### METRIC EQUIVALENTS OF STEEL SHEET METAL GAGES

| NO. | UNCOATED STEEL | | | | GALVANIZED STEEL | |
|---|---|---|---|---|---|---|
| | NOMINAL THICKNESS | | MINIMUM THICKNESS | | NOMINAL THICKNESS | |
| | IN. | MM | IN. | MM | IN. | MM |
| 8 | 0.164 | 4.18 | 0.156 | 3.96 | 0.168 | 4.27 |
| 9 | 0.150 | 3.8 | 0.142 | 3.61 | 0.153 | 3.89 |
| 10 | 0.134 | 3.42 | 0.126 | 3.20 | 0.138 | 3.50 |
| 11 | 0.120 | 3.04 | 0.112 | 2.84 | 0.123 | 3.12 |
| 12 | 0.105 | 2.66 | 0.097 | 2.46 | 0.108 | 2.74 |
| 14 | 0.075 | 1.90 | 0.067 | 1.70 | 0.079 | 2.01 |
| 16 | 0.060 | 1.52 | 0.053 | 1.35 | 0.064 | 1.63 |
| 18 | 0.048 | 1.21 | 0.043 | 1.09 | 0.052 | 1.32 |
| 20 | 0.036 | 0.91 | 0.033 | 0.84 | 0.040 | 1.02 |
| 22 | 0.030 | 0.76 | 0.027 | 0.69 | 0.034 | 0.86 |
| 24 | 0.024 | 0.61 | 0.021 | 0.53 | 0.028 | 0.71 |
| 25 | 0.021 | 0.53 | 0.018 | 0.46 | 0.025 | 0.64 |
| 26 | 0.018 | 0.46 | 0.016 | 0.41 | 0.022 | 0.56 |
| 28 | 0.015 | 0.38 | 0.013 | 0.33 | 0.019 | 0.48 |

Uncoated steel sheet sizes (nominal) are based on the Manufacturers' Standard of the American Iron and Steel Institute (AISI), which is based on the U.S. Standard Gage (a weight gage).

Minimum uncoated steel sizes (inch) are determined by subtracting the tolerances listed in ASTM A568 from nominal sizes. For No. 18 gage and thicker, the tolerances for hot-rolled sheet were used; and for No. 20 gage and thinner, those for cold-rolled sheet were used.

Electrolytic zinc-coated steel is measured by gage listed for uncoated steel not for galvanized steel. The thickness includes the coating, according to ASTM A591, Standard Specification for Steel Sheet, Electrolytic Zinc-Coated, for Light Coating Weight [Mass] Applications.

Galvanized steel thicknesses include the coating (ASTM A653/A653M, Standard Specification for Steel Sheet, Zinc-Coated (Galvanized) or Zinc-Iron Alloy-Coated (Galvannealed) by the Hot-Dip Process, calls for thickness to include the coating). For structural applications, such as metal deck, galvanized steel sheet may be specified by minimum uncoated base metal thickness; in this case, use minimum sizes designated for uncoated steel rather than for galvanized steel.

### SHEET ALUMINUM SIZES

| in.[1] | 0.020 | 0.024 | 0.032 | 0.040 | 0.050 | 0.063 | 0.080 | 0.1 | 0.125 | 0.160 |
|---|---|---|---|---|---|---|---|---|---|---|
| mm[2] | 0.51 | 0.61 | 0.81 | 1.02 | 1.27 | 1.60 | 2.03 | 2.54 | 3.18 | 4.06 |

[1] The preferred inch thicknesses have been established for use in specifying sheet aluminum.
[2] Sizes given in mm are rounded equivalents of the preferred inch thicknesses. For additional preferred thicknesses, see ANSI B32.1 and ANSI B32.3.

### METRIC EQUIVALENTS OF WIRE GAGES

| NUMBER | U.S. STEEL WIRE GAGE OR WASHBURN & MOEN | | AMERICAN WIRE GAGE OR BROWN & SHARPE | |
|---|---|---|---|---|
| | IN. | MM | IN.* | MM* |
| 8 | 0.162 | 4.11 | 0.1285 | 3.264 |
| 9 | 0.148 | 3.76 | 0.1144 | 2.906 |
| 10 | 0.135 | 3.43 | 0.1019 | 2.588 |
| 11 | 0.120 | 3.05 | 0.0907 | 2.304 |
| 12 | 0.106 | 2.69 | 0.0808 | 2.052 |
| 14 | 0.080 | 2.03 | 0.0641 | 1.628 |
| 16 | 0.062 | 1.57 | 0.0508 | 1.290 |
| 18 | 0.048 | 1.22 | 0.0403 | 1.024 |
| 20 | 0.035 | 0.89 | 0.0320 | 0.813 |
| 22 | 0.029 | 0.74 | 0.0253 | 0.643 |
| 24 | 0.023 | 0.58 | 0.0201 | 0.511 |

*Sizes listed in ASTM B3.

### PIPE AND TUBE SIZE DESIGNATIONS

| NPS[1] | DN[2] | NPS | DN | NPS | DN |
|---|---|---|---|---|---|
| ½ | 15 | 2 | 50 | 5 | 125 |
| ⅝ | 18 | 2½ | 65 | 6 | 150 |
| ¾ | 20 | 3 | 80 | 8 | 200 |
| 1 | 25 | 3½ | 90 | 10 | 250 |
| 1¼ | 32 | 4 | 100 | 12 | 300 |
| 1½ | 40 | 4½ | 115 | | |

[1] NPS is the inch-pound designation for nominal pipe size.
[2] DN is the metric designation for diameter nominal.
For pipe sizes more than 12 in., use the conversion factor of 25 mm per inch.

### STAINLESS-STEEL AND NONFERROUS SHEET METAL SIZES

| GAGE | STAINLESS STEEL | | NONFERROUS METALS | |
|---|---|---|---|---|
| | IN. | MM | IN. | MM |
| 8 | 0.172 | 4.37 | 0.128 | 3.26 |
| 9 | 0.156 | 3.97 | 0.114 | 2.91 |
| 10 | 0.141 | 3.57 | 0.102 | 2.59 |
| 11 | 0.125 | 3.18 | 0.091 | 2.30 |
| 12 | 0.109 | 2.78 | 0.081 | 2.05 |
| 14 | 0.078 | 1.98 | 0.064 | 1.63 |
| 16 | 0.062 | 1.59 | 0.051 | 1.29 |
| 18 | 0.050 | 1.27 | 0.040 | 1.02 |
| 20 | 0.038 | 0.95 | 0.032 | 0.81 |
| 22 | 0.031 | 0.79 | 0.025 | 0.64 |
| 24 | 0.025 | 0.64 | 0.020 | 0.51 |
| 26 | 0.019 | 0.48 | 0.016 | 0.40 |
| 28 | 0.016 | 0.40 | 0.012 | 0.32 |

For copper flashing and sheet metal, 10 oz = 0.34 mm, 12 oz = 0.41 mm, 14 oz = 0.48 mm, 16 oz = 0.55 mm, 18 oz = 0.62 mm, 20 oz = 0.7 mm, 24 oz = 0.8 mm, and 32 oz = 1.1 mm.

### GALVANIZED COATING WEIGHTS

| IP DESIGNATION | TRIPLE SPOT TEST (TOTAL BOTH SIDES) | | SI EQUIVALENT* |
|---|---|---|---|
| | OZ/SQ FT | G/SQ M | |
| G01 | N.R. | N.R. | Z001 |
| G30 | 0.30 | 90 | Z90 |
| G40 | 0.40 | 120 | Z120 |
| G60 | 0.60 | 180 | Z180 |
| G90 | 0.90 | 275 | Z275 |
| G115 | 1.15 | 350 | Z350 |
| G140 | 1.40 | 450 | Z450 |
| G165 | 1.65 | 500 | Z500 |
| G185 | 1.85 | 550 | Z550 |
| G210 | 2.10 | 600 | Z600 |
| G235 | 2.35 | 700 | Z700 |
| G300 | 3.00 | 900 | Z900 |
| G360 | 3.60 | 1,100 | Z1100 |

*SI equivalents for coating weights are approximate only; they are the SI designations that are the most nearly equal to the corresponding IP designations.

### SCREW SIZES

| NO. | INCH DIAMETER | METRIC DIAMETER | SI SIZE |
|---|---|---|---|
| 2 | 0.086 | 2.18 mm | M2 × 0.4 |
| 3 | 0.099 | 2.51 mm | M2.5 × 0.45 |
| 4 | 0.112 | 2.84 mm | M3 × 0.5 |
| 6 | 0.138 | 3.51 mm | M3.5 × 0.6 |
| 8 | 0.164 | 4.17 mm | M4 × 0.7 |
| 10 | 0.190 | 4.83 mm | M5 × 0.8 |
| 12 | 0.216 | 5.49 mm | — |
| 14 | 0.242 | 6.15 mm | M6 × 1.0 |
| 16 | 0.268 | 6.81 mm | — |

Number sizes apply to machine, wood, and sheet-metal screws. SI sizes are for machine screws only.

Standard lengths for SI machine screws are 5, 6, 8, 10, 13, 16, 20, 25, 30, 35, and 40 mm.

### LUMBER SIZES

| IN. | NOMINAL SIZE | | ACTUAL SIZE | |
|---|---|---|---|---|
| | DRY | | GREEN | |
| | IN. | MM | IN. | MM |
| 1 | ¾ | 19 | 25/32 | 20 |
| 1¼ | 1 | 25 | 1 1/32 | 26 |
| 1½ | 1¼ | 32 | 1 9/32 | 33 |
| 2 | 1½ | 38 | 1 9/16 | 40 |
| 3 | 2½ | 64 | 2 9/16 | 65 |
| 4 | 3½ | 89 | 3 9/16 | 90 |
| 6 | 5½ | 140 | 5⅝ | 143 |
| 8 | 7¼ | 184 | 7½ | 190 |
| 10 | 9¼ | 235 | 9½ | 241 |
| 12 | 11¼ | 286 | 11½ | 292 |

## COPPER TUBE OD AND SIZE DESIGNATIONS*

| ASTM B88 NOMINAL OR STANDARD SIZE, IN. | ASTM B88M NOMINAL OR STANDARD SIZE, MM | DN DESIGNATION |
|---|---|---|
| ⅛ | 6 | 6 |
| 3/16 | 8 | 7 |
| ¼ | 10 | 8 |
| ⅜ | 12 | 10 |
| ½ | 15 | 15 |
| ⅝ | 18 | 18 |
| ¾ | 22 | 20 |
| 1 | 28 | 25 |
| 1¼ | 35 | 32 |
| 1½ | 42 | 40 |
| 2 | 54 | 50 |
| 2½ | 67 | 65 |
| 3 | 79 | 80 |
| 3½ | — | 90 |
| 4 | 105 | 100 |
| 5 | 130 | 125 |
| 6 | 156 | 150 |
| 8 | 206 | 200 |
| 10 | 257 | 250 |
| 12 | 308 | 300 |

*Correspondence is not exact on any designation. ASTM B88M, Standard Specification for Seamless Copper Water Tube (Metric), presents nominal or standard sizes of 6 mm, 8 mm, and 10 mm that do not correspond with nominal or standard sizes in ASTM B88, Standard Specification for Seamless Copper Water Tube. Sizes 15 mm and larger correspond roughly to the above sizes in ASTM B88.

## METAL ELECTRICAL CONDUIT SIZES TC "METAL ELECTRICAL CONDUIT SIZES"*

| TRADE SIZE (IN.) | METRIC SIZE DESIGNATIONS FOR EMT, IMC, AND GRC | | |
|---|---|---|---|
| ½ | 16 EMT | 16 IMC | 16 GRC |
| ¾ | 21 EMT | 21 IMC | 21 GRC |
| 1 | 27 EMT | 27 IMC | 27 GRC |
| 1¼ | 35 EMT | 35 IMC | 35 GRC |
| 1½ | 41 EMT | 41 IMC | 41 GRC |
| 2 | 53 EMT | 53 IMC | 53 GRC |
| 2½ | 63 EMT | 63 IMC | 63 GRC |
| 3 | 78 EMT | 78 IMC | 78 GRC |
| 3½ | 91 EMT | 91 IMC | 91 GRC |
| 4 | 103 EMT | 103 IMC | 103 GRC |
| 5 | — | — | 129 GRC |
| 6 | — | — | 155 GRC |

*Type of conduit must appear regardless of units of measure selected.

## PLASTIC ELECTRICAL CONDUIT SIZES TC "PLASTIC ELECTRICAL CONDUIT SIZES" *

| IP SIZE (IN.) | METRIC SIZE (MM) | IP SIZE (IN.) | METRIC SIZE (MM) |
|---|---|---|---|
| ½ | 16 | 2½ | 63 |
| ¾ | 21 | 3 | 78 |
| 1 | 27 | 3½ | 91 |
| 1¼ | 35 | 4 | 103 |
| 1½ | 41 | 5 | 129 |
| 2 | 53 | 6 | 155 |

*Type of conduit must appear regardless of units of measure selected.

## SPECIFICATION WRITING RULES

When producing construction specifications and drawings using metric units, address the following:

- Consistent use of terms, abbreviations, and notations
- Standard use of correct terms that properly express the IP and the SI notation
- Guidelines for written statements and numeric expressions

## SUBJECTS NOT ADDRESSED

Several subjects of concern to the specifier, but not included in this appendix, are:

- Building codes and regulations may not contain metric units of measure exclusively. New editions may initially offer dual notation of units and later include only metric units. SI units expressed in codes may not be stated in the unit preferred by product manufacturers or expressed in specifications.
- Fire-tested assemblies and materials that comprise those assemblies are now represented in IP units. When manufacturers change products to standard metric units, those assemblies may need to be retested.
- Land surveys will require conversion from current IP to SI units. Elevations (and inverts) once converted may be expressed in meters above sea level, including the datum. Land title registrations for some states may require descriptions and site or property drawings to be dually annotated depending on their progress of conversion.

## ABBREVIATIONS, SYMBOLS, AND PUNCTUATION OF UNITS OF MEASURE

To standardize both IP and SI units in construction documents:

- Insert a space between the measurement value and the measurement unit except when used as a compound modifier.

  Example: Use 20 MPa, not 20MPa.
  Use 10 lb, not 10lb or 10-lb.

- Use uppercase letters for SI units for the following:

  A for ampere
  C for Celsius
  F for farad
  G for giga
  H for Henry
  J for Joule
  K for Kelvin
  L for liter
  M for mega
  N for Newton
  T for tera
  V for volt
  W for watt

- Do not use exponents to indicate square or cube. Use the abbreviations (sq or cu) in formulas or numeric expressions.

  Example: Use 36 sq ft, not 36 ft².
  Use 36 sq m, not 36 m².
  Example: Use 36 cu ft, not 36 ft³.
  Use 36 cu m, not 36 m³.

- Do not indicate a plural by adding an "s" to metric symbols or names.

  Example: 8 kilograms is 8 kg, not 8 kgs.

- Do not use centimeters (cm) except for square and cubic centimeters. Some metric products, such as imported ceramic tile, may express sizes in cm.

  Example: 10-cm tile should be stated as 100-mm tile.

- Do not mix symbols with words in the same compound expression.

  Example: The correct expression is L/s, not L/second or liter/s.

- When expressing dimensions in IP units, use inch for measurements less than or equal to 1 inch and inches for measurements more than 1 inch. Do not use the inch (") symbol.

  Example: ⅞ inch, 1 inch, 1⅛ inches, 4 inches, unless used as a compound modifier. A 12-inch-high curb compared to a curb that is 12 inches high. Do not use symbols for feet and inches in IP units.

  Example: 3'6" should be stated as 3 ft 6 in.

- Use millimeters (mm) for linear (length, width, and thickness) dimensions.

  Example: 0.0625 in. sheet metal thickness converts to 1.59 mm.

- Avoid using compound numbers, such as the feet and inches designation, in specifications. Use all inches when possible and practical. This will result in like units between IP and SI.

  Example: Use 40 in. (1,016 mm) instead of 3'4", 96 in. (2,438 mm) instead of 8 ft.

- Use millimeter (mm) instead of meter (m) or centimeter (cm). Use millimeters for imported ceramic tile even though manufacturers use centimeters in their product literature. Large linear dimensions, such as building length, may use feet and meters instead of inches and millimeters.

- When using whole numbers plus fractions in IP units, use a hard hyphen between the whole number and numerator of the fraction to keep the terms together.

  Example: 10-5/16 or 2-1/2

- In IP units, do not use keyboard characters for ¼, ½, or ¾, use 1/4, 1/2, or 3/4
- Express values less than 1 in decimal form with a preceding 0.

  Example: Use 0.25, not .25.

- Express decimals only to the degree of accuracy required (unless necessary for consistency).

  Example: Use 29 in., not 29.00 in., unless the value is intended to have a precision of 0.01 in. Use 6 mm, not 6.00 mm, unless the value is intended to have a precision of 0.01 mm.

To delimit numeric expressions:

- For IP units to the left of the decimal, do not delimit whole numbers of four or fewer digits. Use commas in whole numbers having five or more digits by delimiting the digits in groups of three digits with a comma. For SI units, the same rule applies, except use a hard space instead of a comma.

  Example: IP: 1727 ft or 10,000 ft
  SI: 3000 m or 10 000 m

- For IP units to the right of the decimal, do not delimit the digits.

  Example: 0.0004 in. or 0.00055 in.

- For SI units, use prefixes such as kilo or mega to keep values between 0.1 and 9999.
- A few measurement units are common to both IP and SI, such as volts, amperes, and resistance in ohms. Express these values using the SI rules stated above.
- Use a hard space within any numeric expressions to inhibit word-processing software's automatic word wrap.

## MANUSCRIPT RULES

In compound notations, use "by" to indicate the multiplier; do not use a lowercase x. Express multiplication in formulas with a lowercase multiplication symbol "×."

  Example: 12 by 24 in. (300 by 600 mm)
  cfm × sq ft (L/s × sq m)

Exercise care in the proper presentation of IP and SI formulas by using the correct symbols.

  Example: Thermal resistance is expressed in IP units as deg F × h × sq ft/Btu; and in SI units as K × sq m/W.

There are three rules for referencing standards:

If there are two separate standards for inch-pound and metric units, cite them separately, as follows:

  ASTM C 478 (ASTM C 478M)
  (Use hard spaces *both* before and after the C.)

If one standard covers both inch-pound and metric units, and has a slash in the title, cite it as follows:

  ASTM A 366/A 366M

If the reference *also* cites a specific grade, type, class, or other designation, group the information according to units, as follows:

  ASTM A 525/A 525M, G60 (Z180)
  ASTM A 526/A 526M, G60 (Z180)

## DRAWINGS

When converting weight and measure units, consider the relationship of selected units to drawing notes, measurement dimensions, and other expressed units. This relationship is of concern in computer programming developments that will electronically link with specification text. Drawing coordination checklists will address this issue as they are updated or as new ones are created.

An overview of the highlights of metric conversion for construction drawings and specifications comprises the following:

- All linear dimensions are expressed in millimeters (mm) except on-site and civil drawings, where meters (m) with up to three digits to the right of the decimal may be used. Each drawing set should have a definition for the use of SI units to clearly indicate how to differentiate between millimeters and meters.
- Survey elevation measurements use meters (m) above mean sea level, usually with 1 or more digits to the right of the decimal. Floor slab elevations may also use meters (m) above a benchmark or some other reference elevation point.
- Plane angles in surveying are expressed in degrees, minutes, and seconds; or degrees and decimals of a degree.

  Example: 84 degrees 12 minutes 8 seconds or 68.435 degrees. Express slopes as a ratio or percentage. In a ratio, the vertical unit is always to the left of the colon; the horizontal unit is to the right of the colon.

- For slopes less than 45 degrees, the vertical component should be a unitary value.

  Example: A roof slope of 3 in 12 becomes 1:4.

- For slopes greater than 45 degrees, the horizontal component should be a unitary value.

  Example: A steep embankment of 2.5:1.

- For slopes on piping, present as a percentage. List only the percentage with no IP or SI codes and no IP units (percentage is neither IP nor SI).

  Example: ¼ in. in 10 ft becomes 0.2%.

- Express drawing scale to a unitary base.

  Example: ⅛ in. per foot (converts exactly to 1:96) becomes 1:100. (Drawing scales are available in metric divisions.)

- Mechanical and electrical drawings often indicate values and capacities in a variety of single or combined IP units:

  Example: Ceiling diffusers identify cubic feet per minute (cfm) for intended air supply. The metric equivalent liters per second (L/s) must follow the proper metric convention and be consistent with the specification SI (metric) notations.

Converting drawing measurement units, addressing nondimensional issues, and recognizing their effect on drawings are described more thoroughly in NIBS's *Metric Guide for Federal Construction.*

## SOURCES

*American Society for Testing and Materials. ASTM E 380:* Practice for Use of the International System of Units (SI) (the Modernized Metric System) *(West Conshohocken, PA: ASTM), 1993, PCN 03–543189, pp. 34, 35.*

———. *ASTM E 62I:* Practice for Use of Metric (SI) Units in Building Design and Construction (Committee E–6 Supplement to E 380), *1994, p. 30.*

*American Society of Heating, Refrigerating and Air-Conditioning Engineers. SI for HVAC&R; ASHRAE Policy on Units. 7th ed. (Atlanta, GA: ASHRAE), 1992, p. 6.*

*General Services Administration, Office of Design and Construction. Metric Design Guide. Draft, 2nd ed. (Washington, DC: GPO), 1992.*

*Institute of Electrical and Electronics Engineers. IEEE 268:* American National Standard for Metric Practice *(ANSI) (New York: IEEE, 1992), p. 64.*

*International Organization for Standardization; Technical Committee 12. International Standard ISO 1000:* SI Units and Recommendations for the Use of Their Multiples and of Certain Other Units. *3rd ed. (Geneva: ISO 1000), 1992(E), p. 22.*

*National Institute of Building Sciences; the Construction Subcommittee of the Metrication Operating Committee of the Interagency Council on Metric Policy. Metric Guide for Federal Construction (Washington, DC: NIBS), 1991, p. 34.*

*MASTERSPEC®; published by ARCOM; Salt Lake City, Utah, and Alexandria, Virginia.*

# UNIFORM COMMERCIAL CODE – ARTICLE 2 SALES

## 2-101. SHORT TITLE.

This Article shall be known and may be cited as Uniform Commercial Code-Sales.

## 2-102. SCOPE; CERTAIN SECURITY AND OTHER TRANSACTIONS EXCLUDED FROM THIS ARTICLE.

Unless the context otherwise requires, this Article applies to transactions in goods; it does not apply to any transaction which although in the form of an unconditional contract to sell or present sale is intended to operate only as a security transaction nor does this Article impair or repeal any statute regulating sales to consumers, farmers or other specified classes of buyers.

## 2-103. DEFINITIONS AND INDEX OF DEFINITIONS.

(1) In this Article unless the context otherwise requires
- (a) "Buyer" means a person who buys or contracts to buy goods.
- (b) "Good faith" in the case of a merchant means honesty in fact and the observance of reasonable commercial standards of fair dealing in the trade.
- (c) "Receipt" of goods means taking physical possession of them.
- (d) "Seller" means a person who sells or contracts to sell goods.

(2) Other definitions applying to this Article or to specified Parts thereof, and the sections in which they appear are:

"Acceptance". Section 2-606.
"Banker's credit". Section 2-325.
"Between Merchants". Section 2-104.
"Cancellation". Section 2-106(4).
"Commercial unit". Section 2-105.
"Confirmed credit". Section 2-325.
"Conforming to contract". Section 2-106.
"Contract for sale". Section 2-106.
"Cover". Section 2-712.
"Entrusting". Section 2-403.
"Financing agency". Section 2-104.
"Future Goods". Section 2-105.
"Goods". Section 2-105.
"Identification". Section 2-501.
"Installment contract". Section 2-612.
"Letter of Credit". Section 2-325.
"Lot". Section 2-105.
"Merchant". Section 2-104.
"Overseas". Section 2-323.
"Person in position of Seller". Section 2-707.
"Present sale". Section 2-106.
"Sale". Section 2-106.
"Sale on approval". Section 2-326.
"Sale or return". Section 2-326.
"Termination". Section 2-106.

(3) The following definitions in other Articles apply to this Article:

"Check". Section 3-104.
"Consignee". Section 7-102.
"Consignor". Section 7-102.
"Consumer Goods". Section 9-109.
"Dishonor". Section 3-507.
"Draft". Section 3-104.

(4) In addition Article 1 contains general definitions and principles of construction and interpretation applicable throughout this Article.

## 2-104. DEFINITIONS: "MERCHANT"; "BETWEEN MERCHANTS"; "FINANCING AGENCY".

(1) "Merchant" means a person who deals in goods of the kind or otherwise by his occupation holds himself out as having knowledge or skill peculiar to the practices or goods involved in the transaction or to whom such knowledge or skill may be attributed by his employment of an agent or broker or other intermediary who by his occupation holds himself out as having such knowledge or skill.

(2) "Financing agency" means a bank, finance company or other person who in the ordinary course of business makes advances against goods or documents of title or who by arrangement with either the seller or the buyer intervenes in ordinary course to make or collect payment due or claimed under the contract for sale, as by purchasing or paying the seller's draft or making advances against it or by merely taking it for collection whether or not documents of title accompany the draft. "Financing agency" includes also a bank or other person who similarly intervenes between persons who are in the position of seller and buyer in respect to the goods (Section 2-707).

(3) "Between Merchants" means in any transaction with respect to which both parties are chargeable with the knowledge or skill of merchants.

## 2-105. DEFINITIONS: TRANSFERABILITY; "GOODS"; "FUTURE" GOODS; "LOT"; "COMMERCIAL UNIT".

(1) "Goods" means all things (including specially manufactured goods) which are movable at the time of identification to the contract for sale other than the money in which the price is to be paid, investment securities (Article 8) and things in action. "Goods" also includes the unborn young of animals and growing crops and other identified things attached to realty as described in the section on goods to be severed from realty (Section 2-107).

(2) Goods must be both existing and identified before any interest in them can pass. Goods which are not both existing and identified are "future" goods. A purported present sale of future goods or of any interest therein operates as a contract to sell.

(3) There may be a sale of a part interest in existing identified goods.

(4) An undivided share in an identified bulk of fungible goods is sufficiently identified to be sold although the quantity of the bulk is not determined. Any agreed proportion of such a bulk or any quantity thereof agreed upon by number, weight or other measure may to the extent of the seller's interest in the bulk be sold to the buyer who then becomes an owner in common.

(5) "Lot" means a parcel or a single article which is the subject matter of a separate sale or delivery, whether or not it is sufficient to perform the contract.

(6) "Commercial unit" means such a unit of goods as by commercial usage is a single whole for purposes of sale and division of which materially impairs its character or value on the market or in use. A commercial unit may be a single article (as a machine) or a set of articles (as a suite of furniture or an assortment of sizes) or a quantity (as a bale, gross, or carload) or any other unit treated in use or in the relevant market as a single whole

## 2-106. DEFINITIONS: "CONTRACT"; "AGREEMENT"; "CONTRACT FOR SALE"; "SALE"; "PRESENT SALE"; "CONFORMING" TO CONTRACT; "TERMINATION"; "CANCELLATION".

(1) In this Article unless the context otherwise requires "contract" and "agreement" are limited to those relating to the present or future sale of goods. "Contract for sale" includes both a present sale of goods and a contract to sell goods at a future time. A "sale" consists in the passing of title from the seller to the buyer for a price (Section 2-401). A "present sale" means a sale which is accomplished by the making of the contract.

(2) Goods or conduct including any part of a performance are "conforming" or conform to the contract when they are in accordance with the obligations under the contract.

(3) "Termination" occurs when either party pursuant to a power created by agreement or law puts an end to the contract otherwise than for its breach. On "termination" all obligations which are still executory on both sides are discharged but any right based on prior breach or performance survives.

(4) "Cancellation" occurs when either party puts an end to the contract for breach by the other and its effect is the same as that of "termination" except that the canceling party also retains any remedy for breach of the whole contract or any unperformed balance.

## 2-107. GOODS TO BE SEVERED FROM REALTY: RECORDING.

(1) A contract for the sale of minerals or the like (including oil and gas) or a structure or its materials to be removed from realty is a contract for the sale of goods within this Article if they are to be severed by the seller but until severance a purported present sale thereof which is not effective as a transfer of an interest in land is effective only as a contract to sell.

(2) A contract for the sale apart from the land of growing crops or other things attached to realty and capable of severance without material harm thereto but not described in subsection (1) or of timber to be cut is a contract for the sale of goods within this Article whether the subject matter is to be severed by the buyer or by the seller even though it forms part of the realty at the time of contracting, and the parties can by identification effect a present sale before severance.

(3) The provisions of this section are subject to any third party rights provided by the law relating to realty records, and the contract for sale may be executed and recorded as a document transferring an interest in land and shall then constitute notice to third parties of the buyer's rights under the contract for sale.

[Note: *As amended in 1972.*]

## 2-201. FORMAL REQUIREMENTS; STATUTE OF FRAUDS.

(1) Except as otherwise provided in this section a contract for the sale of goods for the price of $500 or more is not enforceable by way of action or defense unless there is some writing sufficient to indicate that a contract for sale has been made between the parties and signed by the party against whom enforcement is sought or by his authorized agent or broker. A writing is not insuffi-

cient because it omits or incorrectly states a term agreed upon but the contract is not enforceable under this paragraph beyond the quantity of goods shown in such writing.

(2) Between merchants if within a reasonable time a writing in confirmation of the contract and sufficient against the sender is received and the party receiving it has reason to know its contents, it satisfies the requirements of subsection (1) against such party unless written notice of objection to its contents is given within 10 days after it is received.

(3) A contract which does not satisfy the requirements of subsection (1) but which is valid in other respects is enforceable

 (a) if the goods are to be specially manufactured for the buyer and are not suitable for sale to others in the ordinary course of the seller's business and the seller, before notice of repudiation is received and under circumstances which reasonably indicate that the goods are for the buyer, has made either a substantial beginning of their manufacture or commitments for their procurement; or

 (b) if the party against whom enforcement is sought admits in his pleading, testimony or otherwise in court that a contract for sale was made, but the contract is not enforceable under this provision beyond the quantity of goods admitted; or

 (c) with respect to goods for which payment has been made and accepted or which have been received and accepted (Sec. 2-606).

## 2-202. FINAL WRITTEN EXPRESSION: PAROL OR EXTRINSIC EVIDENCE.

Terms with respect to which the confirmatory memoranda of the parties agree or which are otherwise set forth in a writing intended by the parties as a final expression of their agreement with respect to such terms as are included therein may not be contradicted by evidence of any prior agreement or of a contemporaneous oral agreement but may be explained or supplemented

 (a) by course of dealing or usage of trade (Section 1-205) or by course of performance (Section 2-208); and

 (b) by evidence of consistent additional terms unless the court finds the writing to have been intended also as a complete and exclusive statement of the terms of the agreement.

## 2-203. SEALS INOPERATIVE.

The affixing of a seal to a writing evidencing a contract for sale or an offer to buy or sell goods does not constitute the writing a sealed instrument and the law with respect to sealed instruments does not apply to such a contract or offer.

## 2-204. FORMATION IN GENERAL.

(1) A contract for sale of goods may be made in any manner sufficient to show agreement, including conduct by both parties which recognizes the existence of such a contract.

(2) An agreement sufficient to constitute a contract for sale may be found even though the moment of its making is undetermined.

(3) Even though one or more terms are left open a contract for sale does not fail for indefiniteness if

the parties have intended to make a contract and there is a reasonably certain basis for giving an appropriate remedy.

## 2-205. FIRM OFFERS.

An offer by a merchant to buy or sell goods in a signed writing which by its terms gives assurance that it will be held open is not revocable, for lack of consideration, during the time stated or if no time is stated for a reasonable time, but in no event may such period of irrevocability exceed three months; but any such term of assurance on a form supplied by the offeree must be separately signed by the offeror.

## 2-206. OFFER AND ACCEPTANCE IN FORMATION OF CONTRACT.

(1) Unless otherwise unambiguously indicated by the language or circumstances

 (a) an offer to make a contract shall be construed as inviting acceptance in any manner and by any medium reasonable in the circumstances;

 (b) an order or other offer to buy goods for prompt or current shipment shall be construed as inviting acceptance either by a prompt promise to ship or by the prompt or current shipment of conforming or non-conforming goods, but such a shipment of non-conforming goods does not constitute an acceptance if the seller seasonably notifies the buyer that the shipment is offered only as an accommodation to the buyer.

(2) Where the beginning of a requested performance is a reasonable mode of acceptance an offeror who is not notified of acceptance within a reasonable time may treat the offer as having lapsed before acceptance.

## 2-207. ADDITIONAL TERMS IN ACCEPTANCE OR CONFIRMATION.

(1) A definite and seasonable expression of acceptance or a written confirmation which is sent within a reasonable time operates as an acceptance even though it states terms additional to or different from those offered or agreed upon, unless acceptance is expressly made conditional on assent to the additional or different terms.

(2) The additional terms are to be construed as proposals for addition to the contract. Between merchants such terms become part of the contract unless:

 (a) the offer expressly limits acceptance to the terms of the offer;

 (b) they materially alter it; or

 (c) notification of objection to them has already been given or is given within a reasonable time after notice of them is received.

(3) Conduct by both parties which recognizes the existence of a contract is sufficient to establish a contract for sale although the writings of the parties do not otherwise establish a contract. In such case the terms of the particular contract consist of those terms on which the writings of the parties agree, together with any supplementary terms incorporated under any other provisions of this Act.

## 2-208. COURSE OF PERFORMANCE OR PRACTICAL CONSTRUCTION.

(1) Where the contract for sale involves repeated occasions for performance by either party with

knowledge of the nature of the performance and opportunity for objection to it by the other, any course of performance accepted or acquiesced in without objection shall be relevant to determine the meaning of the agreement.

(2) The express terms of the agreement and any such course of performance, as well as any course of dealing and usage of trade, shall be construed whenever reasonable as consistent with each other; but when such construction is unreasonable, express terms shall control course of performance and course of performance shall control both course of dealing and usage of trade (Section 1-205).

(3) Subject to the provisions of the next section on modification and waiver, such course of performance shall be relevant to show a waiver or modification of any term inconsistent with such course of performance.

## 2-209. MODIFICATION, RESCISSION AND WAIVER.

(1) An agreement modifying a contract within this Article needs no consideration to be binding.

(2) A signed agreement which excludes modification or rescission except by a signed writing cannot be otherwise modified or rescinded, but except as between merchants such a requirement on a form supplied by the merchant must be separately signed by the other party.

(3) The requirements of the statute of frauds section of this Article (Section 2-201) must be satisfied if the contract as modified is within its provisions.

(4) Although an attempt at modification or rescission does not satisfy the requirements of subsection (2) or (3) it can operate as a waiver.

(5) A party who has made a waiver affecting an executory portion of the contract may retract the waiver by reasonable notification received by the other party that strict performance will be required of any term waived, unless the retraction would be unjust in view of a material change of position in reliance on the waiver.

## 2-210. DELEGATION OF PERFORMANCE; ASSIGNMENT OF RIGHTS.

(1) A party may perform his duty through a delegate unless otherwise agreed or unless the other party has a substantial interest in having his original promisor perform or control the acts required by the contract. No delegation of performance relieves the party delegating of any duty to perform or any liability for breach.

(2) Unless otherwise agreed all rights of either seller or buyer can be assigned except where the assignment would materially change the duty of the other party, or increase materially the burden or risk imposed on him by his contract, or impair materially his chance of obtaining return performance. A right to damages for breach of the whole contract or a right arising out of the assignor's due performance of his entire obligation can be assigned despite agreement otherwise.

(3) Unless the circumstances indicate the contrary a prohibition of assignment of "the contract" is to be construed as barring only the delegation to the assignee of the assignor's performance.

(4) An assignment of "the contract" or of "all my rights under the contract" or an assignment in similar

general terms is an assignment of rights and unless the language or the circumstances (as in an assignment for security) indicate the contrary, it is a delegation of performance of the duties of the assignor and its acceptance by the assignee constitutes a promise by him to perform those duties. This promise is enforceable by either the assignor or the other party to the original contract.

(5) The other party may treat any assignment which delegates performance as creating reasonable grounds for insecurity and may without prejudice to his rights against the assignor demand assurances from the assignee (Section 2-609).

## 2-301. GENERAL OBLIGATIONS OF PARTIES.

The obligation of the seller is to transfer and deliver and that of the buyer is to accept and pay in accordance with the contract.

## 2-302. UNCONSCIONABLE CONTRACT OR CLAUSE.

(1) If the court as a matter of law finds the contract or any clause of the contract to have been unconscionable at the time it was made the court may refuse to enforce the contract, or it may enforce the remainder of the contract without the unconscionable clause, or it may so limit the application of any unconscionable clause as to avoid any unconscionable result.

(2) When it is claimed or appears to the court that the contract or any clause thereof may be unconscionable the parties shall be afforded a reasonable opportunity to present evidence as to its commercial setting, purpose and effect to aid the court in making the determination.

## 2-303. ALLOCATION OR DIVISION OF RISKS.

Where this Article allocates a risk or a burden as between the parties "unless otherwise agreed", the agreement may not only shift the allocation but may also divide the risk or burden.

## 2-304. PRICE PAYABLE IN MONEY, GOODS, REALTY, OR OTHERWISE.

(1) The price can be made payable in money or otherwise. If it is payable in whole or in part in goods each party is a seller of the goods which he is to transfer.

(2) Even though all or part of the price is payable in an interest in realty the transfer of the goods and the seller's obligations with reference to them are subject to this Article, but not the transfer of the interest in realty or the transferor's obligations in connection therewith.

## 2-305. OPEN PRICE TERM.

(1) The parties if they so intend can conclude a contract for sale even though the price is not settled. In such a case the price is a reasonable price at the time for delivery if
   (a) nothing is said as to price; or
   (b) the price is left to be agreed by the parties and they fail to agree; or
   (c) the price is to be fixed in terms of some agreed market or other standard as set or recorded by a third person or agency and it is not so set or recorded.

(2) A price to be fixed by the seller or by the buyer means a price for him to fix in good faith.

(3) When a price left to be fixed otherwise than by agreement of the parties fails to be fixed through fault of one party the other may at his option treat the contract as cancelled or himself fix a reasonable price.

(4) Where, however, the parties intend not to be bound unless the price be fixed or agreed and it is not fixed or agreed there is no contract. In such a case the buyer must return any goods already received or if unable so to do must pay their reasonable value at the time of delivery and the seller must return any portion of the price paid on account.

## 2-306. OUTPUT, REQUIREMENTS AND EXCLUSIVE DEALINGS.

(1) A term which measures the quantity by the output of the seller or the requirements of the buyer means such actual output or requirements as may occur in good faith, except that no quantity unreasonably disproportionate to any stated estimate or in the absence of a stated estimate to any normal or otherwise comparable prior output or requirements may be tendered or demanded.

(2) A lawful agreement by either the seller or the buyer for exclusive dealing in the kind of goods concerned imposes unless otherwise agreed an obligation by the seller to use best efforts to supply the goods and by the buyer to use best efforts to promote their sale.

## 2-307. DELIVERY IN SINGLE LOT OR SEVERAL LOTS.

Unless otherwise agreed all goods called for by a contract for sale must be tendered in a single delivery and payment is due only on such tender but where the circumstances give either party the right to make or demand delivery in lots the price if it can be apportioned may be demanded for each lot.

## 2-308. ABSENCE OF SPECIFIED PLACE FOR DELIVERY.

Unless otherwise agreed
   (a) the place for delivery of goods is the seller's place of business or if he has none his residence; but
   (b) in a contract for sale of identified goods which to the knowledge of the parties at the time of contracting are in some other place, that place is the place for their delivery; and
   (c) documents of title may be delivered through customary banking channels.

## 2-309. ABSENCE OF SPECIFIC TIME PROVISIONS; NOTICE OF TERMINATION.

(1) The time for shipment or delivery or any other action under a contract if not provided in this Article or agreed upon shall be a reasonable time.

(2) Where the contract provides for successive performances but is indefinite in duration it is valid for a reasonable time but unless otherwise agreed may be terminated at any time by either party.

(3) Termination of a contract by one party except on the happening of an agreed event requires that reasonable notification be received by the other party and an agreement dispensing with notification is invalid if its operation would be unconscionable.

## 2-310. OPEN TIME FOR PAYMENT OR RUNNING OF CREDIT; AUTHORITY TO SHIP UNDER RESERVATION.

Unless otherwise agreed
   (a) payment is due at the time and place at which the buyer is to receive the goods even though the place of shipment is the place of delivery; and
   (b) if the seller is authorized to send the goods he may ship them under reservation, and may tender the documents of title, but the buyer may inspect the goods after their arrival before payment is due unless such inspection is inconsistent with the terms of the contract (Section 2-513); and
   (c) if delivery is authorized and made by way of documents of title otherwise than by subsection (b) then payment is due at the time and place at which the buyer is to receive the documents regardless of where the goods are to be received; and
   (d) where the seller is required or authorized to ship the goods on credit the credit period runs from the time of shipment but post-dating the invoice or delaying its dispatch will correspondingly delay the starting of the credit period.

## 2-311. OPTIONS AND COOPERATION RESPECTING PERFORMANCE.

(1) An agreement for sale which is otherwise sufficiently definite (subsection (3) of Section 2-204) to be a contract is not made invalid by the fact that it leaves particulars of performance to be specified by one of the parties. Any such specification must be made in good faith and within limits set by commercial reasonableness.

(2) Unless otherwise agreed specifications relating to assortment of the goods are at the buyer's option and except as otherwise provided in subsections (1)(c) and (3) of Section 2-319 specifications or arrangements relating to shipment are at the seller's option.

(3) Where such specification would materially affect the other party's performance but is not seasonably made or where one party's cooperation is necessary to the agreed performance of the other but is not seasonably forthcoming, the other party in addition to all other remedies
   (a) is excused for any resulting delay in his own performance; and
   (b) may also either proceed to perform in any reasonable manner or after the time for a material part of his own performance treat the failure to specify or to cooperate as a breach by failure to deliver or accept the goods.

## 2-312. WARRANTY OF TITLE AND AGAINST INFRINGEMENT; BUYER'S OBLIGATION AGAINST INFRINGEMENT.

(1) Subject to subsection (2) there is in a contract for sale a warranty by the seller that
   (a) the title conveyed shall be good, and its transfer rightful; and
   (b) the goods shall be delivered free from any security interest or other lien or encumbrance of which the buyer at the time of contracting has no knowledge.

(2) A warranty under subsection (1) will be excluded or modified only by specific language or by circumstances which give the buyer reason to know that the person selling does not claim title in himself or that he is purporting to sell only such right or title as he or a third person may have.

(3) Unless otherwise agreed a seller who is a merchant regularly dealing in goods of the kind warrants that the goods shall be delivered free of the rightful claim of any third person by way of infringement or the like but a buyer who furnishes specifications to the seller must hold the seller harmless against any such claim which arises out of compliance with the specifications.

## 2-313. EXPRESS WARRANTIES BY AFFIRMATION, PROMISE, DESCRIPTION, SAMPLE.

(1) Express warranties by the seller are created as follows:

   (a) Any affirmation of fact or promise made by the seller to the buyer which relates to the goods and becomes part of the basis of the bargain creates an express warranty that the goods shall conform to the affirmation or promise.

   (b) Any description of the goods which is made part of the basis of the bargain creates an express warranty that the goods shall conform to the description.

   (c) Any sample or model which is made part of the basis of the bargain creates an express warranty that the whole of the goods shall conform to the sample or model.

(2) It is not necessary to the creation of an express warranty that the seller use formal words such as "warrant" or "guarantee" or that he have a specific intention to make a warranty, but an affirmation merely of the value of the goods or a statement purporting to be merely the seller's opinion or commendation of the goods does not create a warranty.

## 2-314. IMPLIED WARRANTY: MERCHANTABILITY; USAGE OF TRADE.

(1) Unless excluded or modified (Section 2-316), a warranty that the goods shall be merchantable is implied in a contract for their sale if the seller is a merchant with respect to goods of that kind. Under this section the serving for value of food or drink to be consumed either on the premises or elsewhere is a sale.

(2) Goods to be merchantable must be at least such as

   (a) pass without objection in the trade under the contract description; and

   (b) in the case of fungible goods, are of fair average quality within the description; and

   (c) are fit for the ordinary purposes for which such goods are used; and

   (d) run, within the variations permitted by the agreement, of even kind, quality and quantity within each unit and among all units involved; and

   (e) are adequately contained, packaged, and labeled as the agreement may require; and

   (f) conform to the promise or affirmations of fact made on the container or label if any.

(3) Unless excluded or modified (Section 2-316) other implied warranties may arise from course of dealing or usage of trade.

## 2-315. IMPLIED WARRANTY: FITNESS FOR PARTICULAR PURPOSE.

Where the seller at the time of contracting has reason to know any particular purpose for which the goods are required and that the buyer is relying on the seller's skill or judgment to select or furnish suitable goods, there is unless excluded or modified under the next section an implied warranty that the goods shall be fit for such purpose.

## 2-316. EXCLUSION OR MODIFICATION OF WARRANTIES.

(1) Words or conduct relevant to the creation of an express warranty and words or conduct tending to negate or limit warranty shall be construed wherever reasonable as consistent with each other; but subject to the provisions of this Article on parol or extrinsic evidence (Section 2-202) negation or limitation is inoperative to the extent that such construction is unreasonable.

(2) Subject to subsection (3), to exclude or modify the implied warranty of merchantability or any part of it the language must mention merchantability and in case of a writing must be conspicuous, and to exclude or modify any implied warranty of fitness the exclusion must be by a writing and conspicuous. Language to exclude all implied warranties of fitness is sufficient if it states, for example, that "There are no warranties which extend beyond the description on the face hereof."

(3) Notwithstanding subsection (2)

   (a) unless the circumstances indicate otherwise, all implied warranties are excluded by expressions like "as is", "with all faults" or other language which in common understanding calls the buyer's attention to the exclusion of warranties and makes plain that there is no implied warranty; and

   (b) when the buyer before entering into the contract has examined the goods or the sample or model as fully as he desired or has refused to examine the goods there is no implied warranty with regard to defects which an examination ought in the circumstances to have revealed to him; and

   (c) an implied warranty can also be excluded or modified by course of dealing or course of performance or usage of trade.

(4) Remedies for breach of warranty can be limited in accordance with the provisions of this Article on liquidation or limitation of damages and on contractual modification of remedy (Sections 2-718 and 2-719).

## 2-317. CUMULATION AND CONFLICT OF WARRANTIES EXPRESS OR IMPLIED.

Warranties whether express or implied shall be construed as consistent with each other and as cumulative, but if such construction is unreasonable the intention of the parties shall determine which warranty is dominant. In ascertaining that intention the following rules apply:

   (a) Exact or technical specifications displace an inconsistent sample or model or general language of description.

   (b) A sample from an existing bulk displaces inconsistent general language of description.

   (c) Express warranties displace inconsistent implied warranties other than an implied warranty of fitness for a particular purpose.

## 2-318. THIRD PARTY BENEFICIARIES OF WARRANTIES EXPRESS OR IMPLIED.

[Note: If this Act is introduced in the Congress of the United States this section should be omitted. (States to select one alternative.)]

### Alternative A

A seller's warranty whether express or implied extends to any natural person who is in the family or household of his buyer or who is a guest in his home if it is reasonable to expect that such person may use, consume or be affected by the goods and who is injured in person by breach of the warranty. A seller may not exclude or limit the operation of this section.

### Alternative B

A seller's warranty whether express or implied extends to any natural person who may reasonably be expected to use, consume or be affected by the goods and who is injured in person by breach of the warranty. A seller may not exclude or limit the operation of this section.

### Alternative C

A seller's warranty whether express or implied extends to any person who may reasonably be expected to use, consume or be affected by the goods and who is injured by breach of the warranty. A seller may not exclude or limit the operation of this section with respect to injury to the person of an individual to whom the warranty extends.

[Note: *As amended in 1966.*]

## 2-319. F.O.B. AND F.A.S. TERMS.

(1) Unless otherwise agreed the term F.O.B. (which means "free on board") at a named place, even though used only in connection with the stated price, is a delivery term under which

   (a) when the term is F.O.B. the place of shipment, the seller must at that place ship the goods in the manner provided in this Article (Section 2-504) and bear the expense and risk of putting them into the possession of the carrier; or

   (b) when the term is F.O.B. the place of destination, the seller must at his own expense and risk transport the goods to that place and there tender delivery of them in the manner provided in this Article (Section 2-503);

   (c) when under either (a) or (b) the term is also F.O.B. vessel, car or other vehicle, the seller must in addition at his own expense and risk load the goods on board. If the term is F.O.B. vessel the buyer must name the vessel and in an appropriate case the seller must comply with the provisions of this Article on the form of bill of lading (Section 2-323).

(2) Unless otherwise agreed the term F.A.S. vessel (which means "free alongside") at a named port, even though used only in connection with the stated price, is a delivery term under which the seller must

   (a) at his own expense and risk deliver the goods alongside the vessel in the manner usual in that port or on a dock designated and provided by the buyer; and

   (b) obtain and tender a receipt for the goods in

exchange for which the carrier is under a duty to issue a bill of lading.

(3) Unless otherwise agreed in any case falling within subsection (1)(a) or (c) or subsection (2) the buyer must seasonably give any needed instructions for making delivery, including when the term is F.A.S. or F.O.B. the loading berth of the vessel and in an appropriate case its name and sailing date. The seller may treat the failure of needed instructions as a failure of cooperation under this Article (Section 2-311). He may also at his option move the goods in any reasonable manner preparatory to delivery or shipment.

(4) Under the term F.O.B. vessel or F.A.S. unless otherwise agreed the buyer must make payment against tender of the required documents and the seller may not tender nor the buyer demand delivery of the goods in substitution for the documents.

## 2-320. C.I.F. AND C.& F. TERMS.

(1) The term C.I.F. means that the price includes in a lump sum the cost of the goods and the insurance and freight to the named destination. The term C. & F. or C.F. means that the price so includes cost and freight to the named destination.

(2) Unless otherwise agreed and even though used only in connection with the stated price and destination, the term C.I.F. destination or its equivalent requires the seller at his own expense and risk to

(a) put the goods into the possession of a carrier at the port for shipment and obtain a negotiable bill or bills of lading covering the entire transportation to the named destination; and

(b) load the goods and obtain a receipt from the carrier (which may be contained in the bill of lading) showing that the freight has been paid or provided for; and

(c) obtain a policy or certificate of insurance, including any war risk insurance, of a kind and on terms then current at the port of shipment in the usual amount, in the currency of the contract, shown to cover the same goods covered by the bill of lading and providing for payment of loss to the order of the buyer or for the account of whom it may concern; but the seller may add to the price the amount of the premium for any such war risk insurance; and

(d) prepare an invoice of the goods and procure any other documents required to effect shipment or to comply with the contract; and

(e) forward and tender with commercial promptness all the documents in due form and with any indorsement necessary to perfect the buyer's rights.

(3) Unless otherwise agreed the term C. & F. or its equivalent has the same effect and imposes upon the seller the same obligations and risks as a C.I.F. term except the obligation as to insurance.

(4) Under the term C.I.F. or C. & F. unless otherwise agreed the buyer must make payment against tender of the required documents and the seller may not tender nor the buyer demand delivery of the goods in substitution for the documents.

## 2-321. C.I.F. OR C. & F.: "NET LANDED WEIGHTS"; "PAYMENT ON ARRIVAL"; WARRANTY OF CONDITION ON ARRIVAL.

Under a contract containing a term C.I.F. or C. & F.

(1) Where the price is based on or is to be adjusted according to "net landed weights", "delivered weights", "out turn" quantity or quality or the like, unless otherwise agreed the seller must reasonably estimate the price. The payment due on tender of the documents called for by the contract is the amount so estimated, but after final adjustment of the price a settlement must be made with commercial promptness.

(2) An agreement described in subsection (1) or any warranty of quality or condition of the goods on arrival places upon the seller the risk of ordinary deterioration, shrinkage and the like in transportation but has no effect on the place or time of identification to the contract for sale or delivery or on the passing of the risk of loss.

(3) Unless otherwise agreed where the contract provides for payment on or after arrival of the goods the seller must before payment allow such preliminary inspection as is feasible; but if the goods are lost delivery of the documents and payment are due when the goods should have arrived.

## 2-322. DELIVERY "EX-SHIP".

(1) Unless otherwise agreed a term for delivery of goods "ex-ship" (which means from the carrying vessel) or in equivalent language is not restricted to a particular ship and requires delivery from a ship which has reached a place at the named port of destination where goods of the kind are usually discharged.

(2) Under such a term unless otherwise agreed

(a) the seller must discharge all liens arising out of the carriage and furnish the buyer with a direction which puts the carrier under a duty to deliver the goods; and

(b) the risk of loss does not pass to the buyer until the goods leave the ship's tackle or are otherwise properly unloaded.

## 2-323. FORM OF BILL OF LADING REQUIRED IN OVERSEAS SHIPMENT; "OVERSEAS".

(1) Where the contract contemplates overseas shipment and contains a term C.I.F. or C. & F. or F.O.B. vessel, the seller unless otherwise agreed must obtain a negotiable bill of lading stating that the goods have been loaded in board or, in the case of a term C.I.F. or C. & F., received for shipment.

(2) Where in a case within subsection (1) a bill of lading has been issued in a set of parts, unless otherwise agreed if the documents are not to be sent from abroad the buyer may demand tender of the full set; otherwise only one part of the bill of lading need be tendered. Even if the agreement expressly requires a full set

(a) due tender of a single part is acceptable within the provisions of this Article on cure of improper delivery (subsection (1) of Section 2-508); and

(b) even though the full set is demanded, if the documents are sent from abroad the person tendering an incomplete set may nevertheless require payment upon furnishing an indemnity which the buyer in good faith deems adequate.

(3) A shipment by water or by air or a contract contemplating such shipment is "overseas" insofar as by usage of trade or agreement it is subject to the commercial, financing or shipping practices characteristic of international deep water commerce.

## 2-324. "NO ARRIVAL, NO SALE" TERM.

Under a term, "no sale no arrival" or terms of like meaning, unless otherwise agreed,

(a) the seller must properly ship conforming goods and if they arrive by any means he must tender them on arrival but he assumes no obligation that the goods will arrive unless he has caused the non-arrival; and

(b) where without fault of the seller the goods are in part lost or have so deteriorated as no longer to conform to the contract or arrive after the contract time, the buyer may proceed as if there had been casualty to identified goods (Section 2-613).

## 2-325. "LETTER OF CREDIT" TERM; "CONFIRMED CREDIT".

(1) Failure of the buyer seasonably to furnish an agreed letter of credit is a breach of the contract for sale.

(2) The delivery to seller of a proper letter of credit suspends the buyer's obligation to pay. If the letter of credit is dishonored, the seller may on seasonable notification to the buyer require payment directly from him.

(3) Unless otherwise agreed the term "letter of credit" or "banker's credit" in a contract for sale means an irrevocable credit issued by a financing agency of good repute and, where the shipment is overseas, of good international repute. The term "confirmed credit" means that the credit must also carry the direct obligation of such an agency which does business in the seller's financial market.

## 2-326. SALE ON APPROVAL AND SALE OR RETURN; CONSIGNMENT SALES AND RIGHTS OF CREDITORS.

(1) Unless otherwise agreed, if delivered goods may be returned by the buyer even though they conform to the contract, the transaction is

(a) a "sale on approval" if the goods are delivered primarily for use, and

(b) a "sale or return" if the goods are delivered primarily for resale.

(2) Except as provided in subsection (3), goods held on approval are not subject to the claims of the buyer's creditors until acceptance; goods held on sale or return are subject to such claims while in the buyer's possession.

(3) Where goods are delivered to a person for sale and such person maintains a place of business at which he deals in goods of the kind involved, under a name other than the name of the person making delivery, then with respect to claims of creditors of the person conducting the business the goods are deemed to be on sale or return. The provisions of this subsection are applicable even though an agreement purports to reserve title to the person making delivery until payment or resale or uses such words as "on consignment" or "on memorandum". However, this subsection is not applicable if the person making delivery

(a) complies with an applicable law providing for a consignor's interest or the like to be evidenced by a sign, or

(b) establishes that the person conducting the business is generally known by his creditors to be substantially engaged in selling the goods of others, or

(c) complies with the filing provisions of the Article on Secured Transactions (Article 9).

(4) Any "or return" term of a contract for sale is to be treated as a separate contract for sale within the statute of frauds section of this Article (Section 2-201) and as contradicting the sale aspect of the contract within the provisions of this Article on parol or extrinsic evidence (Section 2-202).

## 2-327. SPECIAL INCIDENTS OF SALE ON APPROVAL AND SALE OR RETURN.

(1) Under a sale on approval unless otherwise agreed
   (a) although the goods are identified to the contract the risk of loss and the title do not pass to the buyer until acceptance; and
   (b) use of the goods consistent with the purpose of trial is not acceptance but failure seasonably to notify the seller of election to return the goods is acceptance, and if the goods conform to the contract acceptance of any part is acceptance of the whole; and
   (c) after due notification of election to return, the return is at the seller's risk and expense but a merchant buyer must follow any reasonable instructions.

(2) Under a sale or return unless otherwise agreed
   (a) the option to return extends to the whole or any commercial unit of the goods while in substantially their original condition, but must be exercised seasonably; and
   (b) the return is at the buyer's risk and expense.

## 2-328. SALE BY AUCTION.

(1) In a sale by auction if goods are put up in lots each lot is the subject of a separate sale.

(2) A sale by auction is complete when the auctioneer so announces by the fall of the hammer or in other customary manner. Where a bid is made while the hammer is falling in acceptance of a prior bid the auctioneer may in his discretion reopen the bidding or declare the goods sold under the bid on which the hammer was falling.

(3) Such a sale is with reserve unless the goods are in explicit terms put up without reserve. In an auction with reserve the auctioneer may withdraw the goods at any time until he announces completion of the sale. In an auction without reserve, after the auctioneer calls for bids on an article or lot, that article or lot cannot be withdrawn unless no bid is made within a reasonable time. In either case a bidder may retract his bid until the auctioneer's announcement of completion of the sale, but a bidder's retraction does not revive any previous bid.

(4) If the auctioneer knowingly receives a bid on the seller's behalf or the seller makes or procures such a bid, and notice has not been given that liberty for such bidding is reserved, the buyer may at his option avoid the sale or take the goods at the price of the last good faith bid prior to the completion of the sale. This subsection shall not apply to any bid at a forced sale.

## 2-401. PASSING OF TITLE; RESERVATION FOR SECURITY; LIMITED APPLICATION OF THIS SECTION.

Each provision of this Article with regard to the rights, obligations and remedies of the seller, the buyer, purchasers or other third parties applies irrespective of title to the goods except where the provision refers to such title. Insofar as situations are not covered by the other provisions of this Article and matters concerning title become material the following rules apply:

(1) Title to goods cannot pass under a contract for sale prior to their identification to the contract (Section 2-501), and unless otherwise explicitly agreed the buyer acquires by their identification a special property as limited by this Act. Any retention or reservation by the seller of the title (property) in goods shipped or delivered to the buyer is limited in effect to a reservation of a security interest. Subject to these provisions and to the provisions of the Article on Secured Transactions (Article 9), title to goods passes from the seller to the buyer in any manner and on any conditions explicitly agreed on by the parties.

(2) Unless otherwise explicitly agreed title passes to the buyer at the time and place at which the seller completes his performance with reference to the physical delivery of the goods, despite any reservation of a security interest and even though a document of title is to be delivered at a different time or place; and in particular and despite any reservation of a security interest by the bill of lading
   (a) if the contract requires or authorizes the seller to send the goods to the buyer but does not require him to deliver them at destination, title passes to the buyer at the time and place of shipment; but
   (b) if the contract requires delivery at destination, title passes on tender there.

(3) Unless otherwise explicitly agreed where delivery is to be made without moving the goods,
   (a) if the seller is to deliver a document of title, title passes at the time when and the place where he delivers such documents; or
   (b) if the goods are at the time of contracting already identified and no documents are to be delivered, title passes at the time and place of contracting.

(4) A rejection or other refusal by the buyer to receive or retain the goods, whether or not justified, or a justified revocation of acceptance revests title to the goods in the seller. Such revesting occurs by operation of law and is not a "sale".

## 2-402. RIGHTS OF SELLER'S CREDITORS AGAINST SOLD GOODS.

(1) Except as provided in subsections (2) and (3), rights of unsecured creditors of the seller with respect to goods which have been identified to a contract for sale are subject to the buyer's rights to recover the goods under this Article (Sections 2-502 and 2-716).

(2) A creditor of the seller may treat a sale or an identification of goods to a contract for sale as void if as against him a retention of possession by the seller is fraudulent under any rule of law of the state where the goods are situated, except that retention of possession in good faith and current course of trade by a merchant-seller for a commercially reasonable time after a sale or identification is not fraudulent.

(3) Nothing in this Article shall be deemed to impair the rights of creditors of the seller
   (a) under the provisions of the Article on Secured Transactions (Article 9); or
   (b) where identification to the contract or delivery is made not in current course of trade but in satisfaction of or as security for a pre-existing claim for money, security or the like and is made under circumstances which under any rule of law of the state where the goods are situated would apart from this Article constitute the transaction a fraudulent transfer or voidable preference.

## 2-403. POWER TO TRANSFER; GOOD FAITH PURCHASE OF GOODS; "ENTRUSTING".

(1) A purchaser of goods acquires all title which his transferor had or had power to transfer except that a purchaser of a limited interest acquires rights only to the extent of the interest purchased. A person with voidable title has power to transfer a good title to a good faith purchaser for value. When goods have been delivered under a transaction of purchase the purchaser has such power even though
   (a) the transferor was deceived as to the identity of the purchaser, or
   (b) the delivery was in exchange for a check which is later dishonored, or
   (c) it was agreed that the transaction was to be a "cash sale", or
   (d) the delivery was procured through fraud punishable as larcenous under the criminal law.

(2) Any entrusting of possession of goods to a merchant who deals in goods of that kind gives him power to transfer all rights of the entruster to a buyer in ordinary course of business.

(3) "Entrusting" includes any delivery and any acquiescence in retention of possession regardless of any condition expressed between the parties to the delivery or acquiescence and regardless of whether the procurement of the entrusting or the possessor's disposition of the goods have been such as to be larcenous under the criminal law.
   [Note: If a state adopts the repealer of Article 6-Bulk Transfers (Alternative A), subsec. (4) should read as follows:]

(4) The rights of other purchasers of goods and of lien creditors are governed by the Articles on Secured Transactions (Article 9) and Documents of Title (Article 7).
   [Note: If a state adopts Revised Article 6-Bulk Sales (Alternative B), subsec. (4) should read as follows:]

(5) The rights of other purchasers of goods and of lien creditors are governed by the Articles on Secured Transactions (Article 9), Bulk Sales (Article 6) and Documents of Title (Article 7).
   [Note: As amended in 1988.]

## 2-501. INSURABLE INTEREST IN GOODS; MANNER OF IDENTIFICATION OF GOODS.

(1) The buyer obtains a special property and an insurable interest in goods by identification of existing goods as goods to which the contract refers even though the goods so identified are non-conforming and he has an option to return or reject them. Such identification can be made at any time and in any manner explicitly agreed to by the parties. In the absence of explicit agreement identification occurs
   (a) when the contract is made if it is for the sale of goods already existing and identified;
   (b) if the contract is for the sale of future goods

other than those described in paragraph (c), when goods are shipped, marked or otherwise designated by the seller as goods to which the contract refers;

(c) when the crops are planted or otherwise become growing crops or the young are conceived if the contract is for the sale of unborn young to be born within twelve months after contracting or for the sale of crops to be harvested within twelve months or the next normal harvest reason after contracting whichever is longer.

(2) The seller retains an insurable interest in goods so long as title to or any security interest in the goods remains in him and where the identification is by the seller alone he may until default or insolvency or notification to the buyer that the identification is final substitute other goods for those identified.

(3) Nothing in this section impairs any insurable interest recognized under any other statute or rule of law.

## 2-502. BUYER'S RIGHT TO GOODS ON SELLER'S INSOLVENCY.

(1) Subject to subsection (2) and even though the goods have not been shipped a buyer who has paid a part or all of the price of goods in which he has a special property under the provisions of the immediately preceding section may on making and keeping good a tender of any unpaid portion of their price recover them from the seller if the seller becomes insolvent within ten days after receipt of the first installment on their price.

(2) If the identification creating his special property has been made by the buyer he acquires the right to recover the goods only if they conform to the contract for sale.

## 2-503. MANNER OF SELLER'S TENDER OF DELIVERY.

(1) Tender of delivery requires that the seller put and hold conforming goods at the buyer's disposition and give the buyer any notification reasonably necessary to enable him to take delivery. The manner, time and place for tender are determined by the agreement and this Article, and in particular

(a) tender must be at a reasonable hour, and if it is of goods they must be kept available for the period reasonably necessary to enable the buyer to take possession; but

(b) unless otherwise agreed the buyer must furnish facilities reasonably suited to the receipt of the goods.

(2) Where the case is within the next section respecting shipment tender requires that the seller comply with its provisions.

(3) Where the seller is required to deliver at a particular destination tender requires that he comply with subsection (1) and also in any appropriate case tender documents as described in subsections (4) and (5) of this section.

(4) Where goods are in the possession of a bailee and are to be delivered without being moved

(a) tender requires that the seller either tender a negotiable document of title covering such goods or procure acknowledgment by the bailee of the buyer's right to possession of the goods; but

(b) tender to the buyer of a non-negotiable document of title or of a written direction to the bailee to deliver is sufficient tender unless the

buyer seasonably objects, and receipt by the bailee of notification of the buyer's rights fixes those rights as against the bailee and all third persons; but risk of loss of the goods and of any failure by the bailee to honor the non-negotiable document of title or to obey the direction remains on the seller until the buyer has had a reasonable time to present the document or direction, and a refusal by the bailee to honor the document or to obey the direction defeats the tender.

(5) Where the contract requires the seller to deliver documents

(a) he must tender all such documents in correct form, except as provided in this Article with respect to bills of lading in a set (subsection (2) of Section 2-323); and

(b) tender through customary banking channels is sufficient and dishonor of a draft accompanying the documents constitutes non-acceptance or rejection.

## 2-504. SHIPMENT BY SELLER.

Where the seller is required or authorized to send the goods to the buyer and the contract does not require him to deliver them at a particular destination, then unless otherwise agreed he must

(a) put the goods in the possession of such a carrier and make such a contract for their transportation as may be reasonable having regard to the nature of the goods and other circumstances of the case; and

(b) obtain and promptly deliver or tender in due form any document necessary to enable the buyer to obtain possession of the goods or otherwise required by the agreement or by usage of trade; and

(c) promptly notify the buyer of the shipment.

Failure to notify the buyer under paragraph (c) or to make a proper contract under paragraph (a) is a ground for rejection only if material delay or loss ensues.

## 2-505. SELLER'S SHIPMENT UNDER RESERVATION.

(1) Where the seller has identified goods to the contract by or before shipment:

(a) his procurement of a negotiable bill of lading to his own order or otherwise reserves in him a security interest in the goods. His procurement of the bill to the order of a financing agency or of the buyer indicates in addition only the seller's expectation of transferring that interest to the person named.

(b) a non-negotiable bill of lading to himself or his nominee reserves possession of the goods as security but except in a case of conditional delivery (subsection (2) of Section 2-507) a non-negotiable bill of lading naming the buyer as consignee reserves no security interest even though the seller retains possession of the bill of lading.

(2) When shipment by the seller with reservation of a security interest is in violation of the contract for sale it constitutes an improper contract for transportation within the preceding section but impairs neither the rights given to the buyer by shipment and identification of the goods to the contract nor the seller's powers as a holder of a negotiable document.

## 2-506. RIGHTS OF FINANCING AGENCY.

(1) A financing agency by paying or purchasing for value a draft which relates to a shipment of goods acquires to the extent of the payment or purchase and in addition to its own rights under the draft and any document of title securing it any rights of the shipper in the goods including the right to stop delivery and the shipper's right to have the draft honored by the buyer.

(2) The right to reimbursement of a financing agency which has in good faith honored or purchased the draft under commitment to or authority from the buyer is not impaired by subsequent discovery of defects with reference to any relevant document which was apparently regular on its face.

## 2-507. EFFECT OF SELLER'S TENDER; DELIVERY ON CONDITION.

(1) Tender of delivery is a condition to the buyer's duty to accept the goods and, unless otherwise agreed, to his duty to pay for them. Tender entitles the seller to acceptance of the goods and to payment according to the contract.

(2) Where payment is due and demanded on the delivery to the buyer of goods or documents of title, his right as against the seller to retain or dispose of them is conditional upon his making the payment due.

## 2-508. CURE BY SELLER OF IMPROPER TENDER OR DELIVERY; REPLACEMENT.

(1) Where any tender or delivery by the seller is rejected because non-conforming and the time for performance has not yet expired, the seller may seasonably notify the buyer of his intention to cure and may then within the contract time make a conforming delivery.

(2) Where the buyer rejects a non-conforming tender which the seller had reasonable grounds to believe would be acceptable with or without money allowance the seller may if he seasonably notifies the buyer have a further reasonable time to substitute a conforming tender.

## 2-509. RISK OF LOSS IN THE ABSENCE OF BREACH.

(1) Where the contract requires or authorizes the seller to ship the goods by carrier

(a) if it does not require him to deliver them at a particular destination, the risk of loss passes to the buyer when the goods are duly delivered to the carrier even though the shipment is under reservation (Section 2-505); but

(b) if it does require him to deliver them at a particular destination and the goods are there duly tendered while in the possession of the carrier, the risk of loss passes to the buyer when the goods are there duly so tendered as to enable the buyer to take delivery.

(2) Where the goods are held by a bailee to be delivered without being moved, the risk of loss passes to the buyer

(a) on his receipt of a negotiable document of title covering the goods; or

(b) on acknowledgment by the bailee of the buyer's right to possession of the goods; or

(c) after his receipt of a non-negotiable document of title or other written direction to deliver, as provided in subsection (4)(b) of Section 2-503.

(3) In any case not within subsection (1) or (2), the risk of loss passes to the buyer on his receipt of the goods if the seller is a merchant; otherwise the risk passes to the buyer on tender of delivery.

(4) The provisions of this section are subject to contrary agreement of the parties and to the provisions of this Article on sale on approval (Section 2-327) and on effect of breach on risk of loss (Section 2-510).

## 2-510. EFFECT OF BREACH ON RISK OF LOSS.

(1) Where a tender or delivery of goods so fails to conform to the contract as to give a right of rejection the risk of their loss remains on the seller until cure or acceptance.

(2) Where the buyer rightfully revokes acceptance he may to the extent of any deficiency in his effective insurance coverage treat the risk of loss as having rested on the seller from the beginning.

(3) Where the buyer as to conforming goods already identified to the contract for sale repudiates or is otherwise in breach before risk of their loss has passed to him, the seller may to the extent of any deficiency in his effective insurance coverage treat the risk of loss as resting on the buyer for a commercially reasonable time.

## 2-511. TENDER OF PAYMENT BY BUYER; PAYMENT BY CHECK.

(1) Unless otherwise agreed tender of payment is a condition to the seller's duty to tender and complete any delivery.

(2) Tender of payment is sufficient when made by any means or in any manner current in the ordinary course of business unless the seller demands payment in legal tender and gives any extension of time reasonably necessary to procure it.

(3) Subject to the provisions of this Act on the effect of an instrument on an obligation (Section 3-802), payment by check is conditional and is defeated as between the parties by dishonor of the check on due presentment.

## 2-512. PAYMENT BY BUYER BEFORE INSPECTION.

(1) Where the contract requires payment before inspection non-conformity of the goods does not excuse the buyer from so making payment unless
(a) the non-conformity appears without inspection; or
(b) despite tender of the required documents the circumstances would justify injunction against honor under the provisions of this Act (Section 5-114).

(2) Payment pursuant to subsection (1) does not constitute an acceptance of goods or impair the buyer's right to inspect or any of his remedies.

## 2-513. BUYER'S RIGHT TO INSPECTION OF GOODS.

(1) Unless otherwise agreed and subject to subsection (3), where goods are tendered or delivered or identified to the contract for sale, the buyer has a right before payment or acceptance to inspect them at any reasonable place and time and in any reasonable manner. When the seller is required or

authorized to send the goods to the buyer, the inspection may be after their arrival.

(2) Expenses of inspection must be borne by the buyer but may be recovered from the seller if the goods do not conform and are rejected.

(3) Unless otherwise agreed and subject to the provisions of this Article on C.I.F. contracts (subsection (3) of Section 2-321), the buyer is not entitled to inspect the goods before payment of the price when the contract provides
(a) for delivery "C.O.D." or on other like terms; or
(b) for payment against documents of title, except where such payment is due only after the goods are to become available for inspection.

(4) A place or method of inspection fixed by the parties is presumed to be exclusive but unless otherwise expressly agreed it does not postpone identification or shift the place for delivery or for passing the risk of loss. If compliance becomes impossible, inspection shall be as provided in this section unless the place or method fixed was clearly intended as an indispensable condition failure of which avoids the contract.

## 2-514. WHEN DOCUMENTS DELIVERABLE ON ACCEPTANCE; WHEN ON PAYMENT.

Unless otherwise agreed documents against which a draft is drawn are to be delivered to the drawee on acceptance of the draft if it is payable more than three days after presentment; otherwise, only on payment.

## 2-515. PRESERVING EVIDENCE OF GOODS IN DISPUTE.

In furtherance of the adjustment of any claim or dispute
(a) either party on reasonable notification to the other and for the purpose of ascertaining the facts and preserving evidence has the right to inspect, test and sample the goods including such of them as may be in the possession or control of the other; and
(b) the parties may agree to a third party inspection or survey to determine the conformity or condition of the goods and may agree that the findings shall be binding upon them in any subsequent litigation or adjustment.

## 2-601. BUYER'S RIGHTS ON IMPROPER DELIVERY.

Subject to the provisions of this Article on breach in installment contracts (Section 2-612) and unless otherwise agreed under the sections on contractual limitations of remedy (Sections 2-718 and 2-719), if the goods or the tender of delivery fail in any respect to conform to the contract, the buyer may

(a) reject the whole; or
(b) accept the whole; or
(c) accept any commercial unit or units and reject the rest.

## 2-602. MANNER AND EFFECT OF RIGHTFUL REJECTION.

(1) Rejection of goods must be within a reasonable time after their delivery or tender. It is ineffective unless the buyer seasonably notifies the seller.

(2) Subject to the provisions of the two following sections on rejected goods (Sections 2-603 and 2-604),
(a) after rejection any exercise of ownership by

the buyer with respect to any commercial unit is wrongful as against the seller; and
(b) if the buyer has before rejection taken physical possession of goods in which he does not have a security interest under the provisions of this Article (subsection (3) of Section 2-711), he is under a duty after rejection to hold them with reasonable care at the seller's disposition for a time sufficient to permit the seller to remove them; but
(c) the buyer has no further obligations with regard to goods rightfully rejected.

(3) The seller's rights with respect to goods wrongfully rejected are governed by the provisions of this Article on seller's remedies in general (Section 2-703).

## 2-603. MERCHANT BUYER'S DUTIES AS TO RIGHTFULLY REJECTED GOODS.

(1) Subject to any security interest in the buyer (subsection (3) of Section 2-711), when the seller has no agent or place of business at the market of rejection a merchant buyer is under a duty after rejection of goods in his possession or control to follow any reasonable instructions received from the seller with respect to the goods and in the absence of such instructions to make reasonable efforts to sell them for the seller's account if they are perishable or threaten to decline in value speedily. Instructions are not reasonable if on demand indemnity for expenses is not forthcoming.

(2) When the buyer sells goods under subsection (1), he is entitled to reimbursement from the seller or out of the proceeds for reasonable expenses of caring for and selling them, and if the expenses include no selling commission then to such commission as is usual in the trade or if there is none to a reasonable sum not exceeding ten per cent on the gross proceeds.

(3) In complying with this section the buyer is held only to good faith and good faith conduct hereunder is neither acceptance nor conversion nor the basis of an action for damages.

## 2-604. BUYER'S OPTIONS AS TO SALVAGE OF RIGHTFULLY REJECTED GOODS.

Subject to the provisions of the immediately preceding section on perishables if the seller gives no instructions within a reasonable time after notification of rejection the buyer may store the rejected goods for the seller's account or reship them to him or resell them for the seller's account with reimbursement as provided in the preceding section. Such action is not acceptance or conversion.

## 2-605. WAIVER OF BUYER'S OBJECTIONS BY FAILURE TO PARTICULARIZE.

(1) The buyer's failure to state in connection with rejection a particular defect which is ascertainable by reasonable inspection precludes him from relying on the unstated defect to justify rejection or to establish breach
(a) where the seller could have cured it if stated seasonably; or
(b) between merchants when the seller has after rejection made a request in writing for a full and final written statement of all defects on which the buyer proposes to rely.

(2) Payment against documents made without reservation of rights precludes recovery of the payment for defects apparent on the face of the documents.

## 2-606. WHAT CONSTITUTES ACCEPTANCE OF GOODS.

(1) Acceptance of goods occurs when the buyer
  (a) after a reasonable opportunity to inspect the goods signifies to the seller that the goods are conforming or that he will take or retain them in spite of their non-conformity; or
  (b) fails to make an effective rejection (subsection (1) of Section 2-602), but such acceptance does not occur until the buyer has had a reasonable opportunity to inspect them; or
  (c) does any act inconsistent with the seller's ownership; but if such act is wrongful as against the seller it is an acceptance only if ratified by him.
(2) Acceptance of a part of any commercial unit is acceptance of that entire unit.

## 2-607. EFFECT OF ACCEPTANCE; NOTICE OF BREACH; BURDEN OF ESTABLISHING BREACH AFTER ACCEPTANCE; NOTICE OF CLAIM OR LITIGATION TO PERSON ANSWERABLE OVER.

(1) The buyer must pay at the contract rate for any goods accepted.
(2) Acceptance of goods by the buyer precludes rejection of the goods accepted and if made with knowledge of a non-conformity cannot be revoked because of it unless the acceptance was on the reasonable assumption that the non-conformity would be seasonably cured but acceptance does not of itself impair any other remedy provided by this Article for non-conformity.
(3) Where a tender has been accepted
  (a) the buyer must within a reasonable time after he discovers or should have discovered any breach notify the seller of breach or be barred from any remedy; and
  (b) if the claim is one for infringement or the like (subsection (3) of Section 2-312) and the buyer is sued as a result of such a breach he must so notify the seller within a reasonable time after he receives notice of the litigation or be barred from any remedy over for liability established by the litigation.
(4) The burden is on the buyer to establish any breach with respect to the goods accepted.
(5) Where the buyer is sued for breach of a warranty or other obligation for which his seller is answerable over
  (a) he may give his seller written notice of the litigation. If the notice states that the seller may come in and defend and that if the seller does not do so he will be bound in any action against him by his buyer by any determination of fact common to the two litigations, then unless the seller after seasonable receipt of the notice does come in and defend he is so bound.
  (b) if the claim is one for infringement or the like (subsection (3) of Section 2-312) the original seller may demand in writing that his buyer turn over to him control of the litigation including settlement or else be barred from any remedy over and if he also agrees to bear all expense and to satisfy any adverse judgment, then unless the buyer after seasonable receipt of the demand does turn over control the buyer is so barred.
(6) The provisions of subsections (3), (4) and (5) apply to any obligation of a buyer to hold the seller harmless against infringement or the like (subsection (3) of Section 2-312).

## 2-608. REVOCATION OF ACCEPTANCE IN WHOLE OR IN PART.

(1) The buyer may revoke his acceptance of a lot or commercial unit whose non-conformity substantially impairs its value to him if he has accepted it
  (a) on the reasonable assumption that its non-conformity would be cured and it has not been seasonably cured; or
  (b) without discovery of such non-conformity if his acceptance was reasonably induced either by the difficulty of discovery before acceptance or by the seller's assurances.
(2) Revocation of acceptance must occur within a reasonable time after the buyer discovers or should have discovered the ground for it and before any substantial change in condition of the goods which is not caused by their own defects. It is not effective until the buyer notifies the seller of it.
(3) A buyer who so revokes has the same rights and duties with regard to the goods involved as if he had rejected them.

## 2-609. RIGHT TO ADEQUATE ASSURANCE OF PERFORMANCE.

(1) A contract for sale imposes an obligation on each party that the other's expectation of receiving due performance will not be impaired. When reasonable grounds for insecurity arise with respect to the performance of either party the other may in writing demand adequate assurance of due performance and until he receives such assurance may if commercially reasonable suspend any performance for which he has not already received the agreed return.
(2) Between merchants the reasonableness of grounds for insecurity and the adequacy of any assurance offered shall be determined according to commercial standards.
(3) Acceptance of any improper delivery or payment does not prejudice the aggrieved party's right to demand adequate assurance of future performance.
(4) After receipt of a justified demand failure to provide within a reasonable time not exceeding thirty days such assurance of due performance as is adequate under the circumstances of the particular case is a repudiation of the contract.

## 2-610. ANTICIPATORY REPUDIATION.

When either party repudiates the contract with respect to a performance not yet due the loss of which will substantially impair the value of the contract to the other, the aggrieved party may
  (a) for a commercially reasonable time await performance by the repudiating party; or
  (b) resort to any remedy for breach (Section 2-703 or Section 2-711), even though he has notified the repudiating party that he would await the latter's performance and has urged retraction; and

  (c) in either case suspend his own performance or proceed in accordance with the provisions of this Article on the seller's right to identify goods to the contract notwithstanding breach or to salvage unfinished goods (Section 2-704).

## 2-611. RETRACTION OF ANTICIPATORY REPUDIATION.

(1) Until the repudiating party's next performance is due he can retract his repudiation unless the aggrieved party has since the repudiation cancelled or materially changed his position or otherwise indicated that he considers the repudiation final.
(2) Retraction may be by any method which clearly indicates to the aggrieved party that the repudiating party intends to perform, but must include any assurance justifiably demanded under the provisions of this Article (Section 2-609).
(3) Retraction reinstates the repudiating party's rights under the contract with due excuse and allowance to the aggrieved party for any delay occasioned by the repudiation.

## 2-612. "INSTALLMENT CONTRACT"; BREACH.

(1) An "installment contract" is one which requires or authorizes the delivery of goods in separate lots to be separately accepted, even though the contract contains a clause "each delivery is a separate contract" or its equivalent.
(2) The buyer may reject any installment which is non-conforming if the non-conformity substantially impairs the value of that installment and cannot be cured or if the non-conformity is a defect in the required documents; but if the non-conformity does not fall within subsection (3) and the seller gives adequate assurance of its cure the buyer must accept that installment.
(3) Whenever non-conformity or default with respect to one or more installments substantially impairs the value of the whole contract there is a breach of the whole. But the aggrieved party reinstates the contract if he accepts a non-conforming installment without seasonably notifying of cancellation or if he brings an action with respect only to past installments or demands performance as to future installments.

## 2-613. CASUALTY TO IDENTIFIED GOODS.

Where the contract requires for its performance goods identified when the contract is made, and the goods suffer casualty without fault of either party before the risk of loss passes to the buyer, or in a proper case under a "no arrival, no sale" term (Section 2-324) then
  (a) if the loss is total the contract is avoided; and
  (b) if the loss is partial or the goods have so deteriorated as no longer to conform to the contract the buyer may nevertheless demand inspection and at his option either treat the contract as avoided or accept the goods with due allowance from the contract price for the deterioration or the deficiency in quantity but without further right against the seller.

## 2-614. SUBSTITUTED PERFORMANCE.

(1) Where without fault of either party the agreed berthing, loading, or unloading facilities fail or an agreed type of carrier becomes unavailable or the

agreed manner of delivery otherwise becomes commercially impracticable but a commercially reasonable substitute is available, such substitute performance must be tendered and accepted.

(2) If the agreed means or manner of payment fails because of domestic or foreign governmental regulation, the seller may withhold or stop delivery unless the buyer provides a means or manner of payment which is commercially a substantial equivalent. If delivery has already been taken, payment by the means or in the manner provided by the regulation discharges the buyer's obligation unless the regulation is discriminatory, oppressive or predatory.

## 2-615. EXCUSE BY FAILURE OF PRESUPPOSED CONDITIONS.

Except so far as a seller may have assumed a greater obligation and subject to the preceding section on substituted performance:

(a) Delay in delivery or non-delivery in whole or in part by a seller who complies with paragraphs (b) and (c) is not a breach of his duty under a contract for sale if performance as agreed has been made impracticable by the occurrence of a contingency the non-occurrence of which was a basic assumption on which the contract was made or by compliance in good faith with any applicable foreign or domestic governmental regulation or order whether or not it later proves to be invalid.

(b) Where the causes mentioned in paragraph (a) affect only a part of the seller's capacity to perform, he must allocate production and deliveries among his customers but may at his option include regular customers not then under contract as well as his own requirements for further manufacture. He may so allocate in any manner which is fair and reasonable.

(c) The seller must notify the buyer seasonably that there will be delay or non-delivery and, when allocation is required under paragraph (b), of the estimated quota thus made available for the buyer

## 2-616. PROCEDURE ON NOTICE CLAIMING EXCUSE.

(1) Where the buyer receives notification of a material or indefinite delay or an allocation justified under the preceding section he may by written notification to the seller as to any delivery concerned, and where the prospective deficiency substantially impairs the value of the whole contract under the provisions of this Article relating to breach of installment contracts (Section 2-612), then also as to the whole,

(a) terminate and thereby discharge any unexecuted portion of the contract; or

(b) modify the contract by agreeing to take his available quota in substitution.

(2) If after receipt of such notification from the seller the buyer fails so to modify the contract within a reasonable time not exceeding thirty days the contract lapses with respect to any deliveries affected.

(3) The provisions of this section may not be negated by agreement except in so far as the seller has assumed a greater obligation under the preceding sections.

## 2-701. REMEDIES FOR BREACH OF COLLATERAL CONTRACTS NOT IMPAIRED.

Remedies for breach of any obligation or promise collateral or ancillary to a contract for sale are not impaired by the provisions of this Article.

## 2-702. SELLER'S REMEDIES ON DISCOVERY OF BUYER'S INSOLVENCY.

(1) Where the seller discovers the buyer to be insolvent he may refuse delivery except for cash including payment for all goods theretofore delivered under the contract, and stop delivery under this Article (Section 2-705).

(2) Where the seller discovers that the buyer has received goods on credit while insolvent he may reclaim the goods upon demand made within ten days after the receipt, but if misrepresentation of solvency has been made to the particular seller in writing within three months before delivery the ten day limitation does not apply. Except as provided in this subsection the seller may not base a right to reclaim goods on the buyer's fraudulent or innocent misrepresentation of solvency or of intent to pay.

(3) The seller's right to reclaim under subsection (2) is subject to the rights of a buyer in ordinary course or other good faith purchaser under this Article (Section 2-403). Successful reclamation of goods excludes all other remedies with respect to them. [Note: *As amended in 1966.*]

## 2-703. SELLER'S REMEDIES IN GENERAL.

Where the buyer wrongfully rejects or revokes acceptance of goods or fails to make a payment due on or before delivery or repudiates with respect to a part or the whole, then with respect to any goods directly affected and, if the breach is of the whole contract (Section 2-612), then also with respect to the whole undelivered balance, the aggrieved seller may

(a) withhold delivery of such goods;

(b) stop delivery by any bailee as hereafter provided (Section 2-705);

(c) proceed under the next section respecting goods still unidentified to the contract;

(d) resell and recover damages as hereafter provided (Section 2-706);

(e) recover damages for non-acceptance (Section 2-708) or in a proper case the price (Section 2-709);

(f) cancel.

## 2-704. SELLER'S RIGHT TO IDENTIFY GOODS TO THE CONTRACT NOTWITHSTANDING BREACH OR TO SALVAGE UNFINISHED GOODS.

(1) An aggrieved seller under the preceding section may

(a) identify to the contract conforming goods not already identified if at the time he learned of the breach they are in his possession or control;

(b) treat as the subject of resale goods which have demonstrably been intended for the particular contract even though those goods are unfinished.

(2) Where the goods are unfinished an aggrieved seller may in the exercise of reasonable commercial judg-

ment for the purposes of avoiding loss and of effective realization either complete the manufacture and wholly identify the goods to the contract or cease manufacture and resell for scrap or salvage value or proceed in any other reasonable manner.

## 2-705. SELLER'S STOPPAGE OF DELIVERY IN TRANSIT OR OTHERWISE.

(1) The seller may stop delivery of goods in the possession of a carrier or other bailee when he discovers the buyer to be insolvent (Section 2-702) and may stop delivery of carload, truckload, planeload or larger shipments of express or freight when the buyer repudiates or fails to make a payment due before delivery or if for any other reason the seller has a right to withhold or reclaim the goods.

(2) As against such buyer the seller may stop delivery until

(a) receipt of the goods by the buyer; or

(b) acknowledgment to the buyer by any bailee of the goods except a carrier that the bailee holds the goods for the buyer; or

(c) such acknowledgment to the buyer by a carrier by reshipment or as warehouseman; or

(d) negotiation to the buyer of any negotiable document of title covering the goods.

(3)

(a) To stop delivery the seller must so notify as to enable the bailee by reasonable diligence to prevent delivery of the goods.

(b) After such notification the bailee must hold and deliver the goods according to the directions of the seller but the seller is liable to the bailee for any ensuing charges or damages.

(c) If a negotiable document of title has been issued for goods the bailee is not obliged to obey a notification to stop until surrender of the document.

(d) A carrier who has issued a non-negotiable bill of lading is not obliged to obey a notification to stop received from a person other than the consignor.

## 2-706. SELLER'S RESALE INCLUDING CONTRACT FOR RESALE.

(1) Under the conditions stated in Section 2-703 on seller's remedies, the seller may resell the goods concerned or the undelivered balance thereof. Where the resale is made in good faith and in a commercially reasonable manner the seller may recover the difference between the resale price and the contract price together with any incidental damages allowed under the provisions of this Article (Section 2-710), but less expenses saved in consequence of the buyer's breach.

(2) Except as otherwise provided in subsection (3) or unless otherwise agreed resale may be at public or private sale including sale by way of one or more contracts to sell or of identification to an existing contract of the seller. Sale may be as a unit or in parcels and at any time and place and on any terms but every aspect of the sale including the method, manner, time, place and terms must be commercially reasonable. The resale must be reasonably identified as referring to the broken contract, but it is not necessary that the goods be in existence or that any or all of them have been identified to the contract before the breach.

(3) Where the resale is at private sale the seller must give the buyer reasonable notification of his intention to resell.

(4) Where the resale is at public sale
   (a) only identified goods can be sold except where there is a recognized market for a public sale of futures in goods of the kind; and
   (b) it must be made at a usual place or market for public sale if one is reasonably available and except in the case of goods which are perishable or threaten to decline in value speedily the seller must give the buyer reasonable notice of the time and place of the resale; and
   (c) if the goods are not to be within the view of those attending the sale the notification of sale must state the place where the goods are located and provide for their reasonable inspection by prospective bidders; and
   (d) the seller may buy.

(5) A purchaser who buys in good faith at a resale takes the goods free of any rights of the original buyer even though the seller fails to comply with one or more of the requirements of this section.

(6) The seller is not accountable to the buyer for any profit made on any resale. A person in the position of a seller (Section 2-707) or a buyer who has rightfully rejected or justifiably revoked acceptance must account for any excess over the amount of his security interest, as hereinafter defined (subsection (3) of Section 2-711).

## 2-707. "PERSON IN THE POSITION OF A SELLER".

(1) A "person in the position of a seller" includes as against a principal an agent who has paid or become responsible for the price of goods on behalf of his principal or anyone who otherwise holds a security interest or other right in goods similar to that of a seller.

(2) A person in the position of a seller may as provided in this Article withhold or stop delivery (Section 2-705) and resell (Section 2-706) and recover incidental damages (Section 2-710).

## 2-708. SELLER'S DAMAGES FOR NON-ACCEPTANCE OR REPUDIATION.

(1) Subject to subsection (2) and to the provisions of this Article with respect to proof of market price (Section 2-723), the measure of damages for non-acceptance or repudiation by the buyer is the difference between the market price at the time and place for tender and the unpaid contract price together with any incidental damages provided in this Article (Section 2-710), but less expenses saved in consequence of the buyer's breach.

(2) If the measure of damages provided in subsection (1) is inadequate to put the seller in as good a position as performance would have done then the measure of damages is the profit (including reasonable overhead) which the seller would have made from full performance by the buyer, together with any incidental damages provided in this Article (Section 2-710), due allowance for costs reasonably incurred and due credit for payments or proceeds of resale.

## 2-709. ACTION FOR THE PRICE.

(1) When the buyer fails to pay the price as it becomes due the seller may recover, together with any inci-

dental damages under the next section, the price
   (a) of goods accepted or of conforming goods lost or damaged within a commercially reasonable time after risk of their loss has passed to the buyer; and
   (b) of goods identified to the contract if the seller is unable after reasonable effort to resell them at a reasonable price or the circumstances reasonably indicate that such effort will be unavailing.

(2) Where the seller sues for the price he must hold for the buyer any goods which have been identified to the contract and are still in his control except that if resale becomes possible he may resell them at any time prior to the collection of the judgment. The net proceeds of any such resale must be credited to the buyer and payment of the judgment entitles him to any goods not resold.

(3) After the buyer has wrongfully rejected or revoked acceptance of the goods or has failed to make a payment due or has repudiated (Section 2-610), a seller who is held not entitled to the price under this section shall nevertheless be awarded damages for non-acceptance under the preceding section.

## 2-710. SELLER'S INCIDENTAL DAMAGES.

Incidental damages to an aggrieved seller include any commercially reasonable charges, expenses or commissions incurred in stopping delivery, in the transportation, care and custody of goods after the buyer's breach, in connection with return or resale of the goods or otherwise resulting from the breach.

## 2-711. BUYER'S REMEDIES IN GENERAL; BUYER'S SECURITY INTEREST IN REJECTED GOODS.

(1) Where the seller fails to make delivery or repudiates or the buyer rightfully rejects or justifiably revokes acceptance then with respect to any goods involved, and with respect to the whole if the breach goes to the whole contract (Section 2-612), the buyer may cancel and whether or not he has done so may in addition to recovering so much of the price as has been paid
   (a) "cover" and have damages under the next section as to all the goods affected whether or not they have been identified to the contract; or
   (b) recover damages for non-delivery as provided in this Article (Section 2-713).

(2) Where the seller fails to deliver or repudiates the buyer may also
   (a) if the goods have been identified recover them as provided in this Article (Section 2-502); or
   (b) in a proper case obtain specific performance or replevy the goods as provided in this Article (Section 2-716).

(3) On rightful rejection or justifiable revocation of acceptance a buyer has a security interest in goods in his possession or control for any payments made on their price and any expenses reasonably incurred in their inspection, receipt, transportation, care and custody and may hold such goods and resell them in like manner as an aggrieved seller (Section 2-706).

## 2-712. "COVER"; BUYER'S PROCUREMENT OF SUBSTITUTE GOODS.

(1) After a breach within the preceding section the buyer may "cover" by making in good faith and without unreasonable delay any reasonable purchase of or contract to purchase goods in substitution for those due from the seller.

(2) The buyer may recover from the seller as damages the difference between the cost of cover and the contract price together with any incidental or consequential damages as hereinafter defined (Section 2-715), but less expenses saved in consequence of the seller's breach.

(3) Failure of the buyer to effect cover within this section does not bar him from any other remedy.

## 2-713. BUYER'S DAMAGES FOR NON-DELIVERY OR REPUDIATION.

(1) Subject to the provisions of this Article with respect to proof of market price (Section 2-723), the measure of damages for non-delivery or repudiation by the seller is the difference between the market price at the time when the buyer learned of the breach and the contract price together with any incidental and consequential damages provided in this Article (Section 2-715), but less expenses saved in consequence of the seller's breach.

(2) Market price is to be determined as of the place for tender or, in cases of rejection after arrival or revocation of acceptance, as of the place of arrival.

## 2-714. BUYER'S DAMAGES FOR BREACH IN REGARD TO ACCEPTED GOODS.

(1) Where the buyer has accepted goods and given notification (subsection (3) of Section 2-607) he may recover as damages for any non-conformity of tender the loss resulting in the ordinary course of events from the seller's breach as determined in any manner which is reasonable.

(2) The measure of damages for breach of warranty is the difference at the time and place of acceptance between the value of the goods accepted and the value they would have had if they had been as warranted, unless special circumstances show proximate damages of a different amount.

(3) In a proper case any incidental and consequential damages under the next section may also be recovered.

## 2-715. BUYER'S INCIDENTAL AND CONSEQUENTIAL DAMAGES.

(1) Incidental damages resulting from the seller's breach include expenses reasonably incurred in inspection, receipt, transportation and care and custody of goods rightfully rejected, any commercially reasonable charges, expenses or commissions in connection with effecting cover and any other reasonable expense incident to the delay or other breach.

(2) Consequential damages resulting from the seller's breach include
   (a) any loss resulting from general or particular requirements and needs of which the seller at the time of contracting had reason to know and which could not reasonably be prevented by cover or otherwise; and

(b) injury to person or property proximately resulting from any breach of warranty.

## 2-716. BUYER'S RIGHT TO SPECIFIC PERFORMANCE OR REPLEVIN.

(1) Specific performance may be decreed where the goods are unique or in other proper circumstances.
(2) The decree for specific performance may include such terms and conditions as to payment of the price, damages, or other relief as the court may deem just.
(3) The buyer has a right of replevin for goods identified to the contract if after reasonable effort he is unable to effect cover for such goods or the circumstances reasonably indicate that such effort will be unavailing or if the goods have been shipped under reservation and satisfaction of the security interest in them has been made or tendered.

## 2-717. DEDUCTION OF DAMAGES FROM THE PRICE.

The buyer on notifying the seller of his intention to do so may deduct all or any part of the damages resulting from any breach of the contract from any part of the price still due under the same contract.

## 2-718. LIQUIDATION OR LIMITATION OF DAMAGES; DEPOSITS.

(1) Damages for breach by either party may be liquidated in the agreement but only at an amount which is reasonable in the light of the anticipated or actual harm caused by the breach, the difficulties of proof of loss, and the inconvenience or nonfeasibility of otherwise obtaining an adequate remedy. A term fixing unreasonably large liquidated damages is void as a penalty.
(2) Where the seller justifiably withholds delivery of goods because of the buyer's breach, the buyer is entitled to restitution of any amount by which the sum of his payments exceeds
   (a) the amount to which the seller is entitled by virtue of terms liquidating the seller's damages in accordance with subsection (1), or
   (b) in the absence of such terms, twenty per cent of the value of the total performance for which the buyer is obligated under the contract or $500, whichever is smaller.
(3) The buyer's right to restitution under subsection (2) is subject to offset to the extent that the seller establishes
   (a) a right to recover damages under the provisions of this Article other than subsection (1), and
   (b) the amount or value of any benefits received by the buyer directly or indirectly by reason of the contract.
(4) Where a seller has received payment in goods their reasonable value or the proceeds of their resale shall be treated as payments for the purposes of subsection (2); but if the seller has notice of the buyer's breach before reselling goods received in part performance, his resale is subject to the conditions laid down in this Article on resale by an aggrieved seller (Section 2-706).

## 2-719. CONTRACTUAL MODIFICATION OR LIMITATION OF REMEDY.

(1) Subject to the provisions of subsections (2) and (3) of this section and of the preceding section on liquidation and limitation of damages,
   (a) the agreement may provide for remedies in addition to or in substitution for those provided in this Article and may limit or alter the measure of damages recoverable under this Article, as by limiting the buyer's remedies to return of the goods and repayment of the price or to repair and replacement of nonconforming goods or parts; and
   (b) resort to a remedy as provided is optional unless the remedy is expressly agreed to be exclusive, in which case it is the sole remedy.
(2) Where circumstances cause an exclusive or limited remedy to fail of its essential purpose, remedy may be had as provided in this Act.
(3) Consequential damages may be limited or excluded unless the limitation or exclusion is unconscionable. Limitation of consequential damages for injury to the person in the case of consumer goods is prima facie unconscionable but limitation of damages where the loss is commercial is not.

## 2-720. EFFECT OF "CANCELLATION" OR "RESCISSION" ON CLAIMS FOR ANTECEDENT BREACH.

Unless the contrary intention clearly appears, expressions of "cancellation" or "rescission" of the contract or the like shall not be construed as a renunciation or discharge of any claim in damages for an antecedent breach.

## 2-721. REMEDIES FOR FRAUD.

Remedies for material misrepresentation or fraud include all remedies available under this Article for non-fraudulent breach. Neither rescission or a claim for rescission of the contract for sale nor rejection or return of the goods shall bar or be deemed inconsistent with a claim for damages or other remedy.

## 2-722. WHO CAN SUE THIRD PARTIES FOR INJURY TO GOODS.

Where a third party so deals with goods which have been identified to a contract for sale as to cause actionable injury to a party to that contract
   (a) a right of action against the third party is in either party to the contract for sale who has title to or a security interest or a special property or an insurable interest in the goods; and if the goods have been destroyed or converted a right of action is also in the party who either bore the risk of loss under the contract for sale or has since the injury assumed that risk as against the other;
   (b) if at the time of the injury the party plaintiff did not bear the risk of loss as against the other party to the contract for sale and there is no arrangement between them for disposition of the recovery, his suit or settlement is, subject to his own interest, as a fiduciary for the other party to the contract;
   (c) either party may with the consent of the other sue for the benefit of whom it may concern.

## 2-723. PROOF OF MARKET PRICE: TIME AND PLACE.

(1) If an action based on anticipatory repudiation comes to trial before the time for performance with respect to some or all of the goods, any damages based on market price (Section 2-708 or Section 2-713) shall be determined according to the price of such goods prevailing at the time when the aggrieved party learned of the repudiation.
(2) If evidence of a price prevailing at the times or places described in this Article is not readily available the price prevailing within any reasonable time before or after the time described or at any other place which in commercial judgment or under usage of trade would serve as a reasonable substitute for the one described may be used, making any proper allowance for the cost of transporting the goods to or from such other place.
(3) Evidence of a relevant price prevailing at a time or place other than the one described in this Article offered by one party is not admissible unless and until he has given the other party such notice as the court finds sufficient to prevent unfair surprise

## 2-724. ADMISSIBILITY OF MARKET QUOTATIONS.

Whenever the prevailing price or value of any goods regularly bought and sold in any established commodity market is in issue, reports in official publications or trade journals or in newspapers or periodicals of general circulation published as the reports of such market shall be admissible in evidence. The circumstances of the preparation of such a report may be shown to affect its weight but not its admissibility.

## 2-725. STATUTE OF LIMITATIONS IN CONTRACTS FOR SALE.

(1) An action for breach of any contract for sale must be commenced within four years after the cause of action has accrued. By the original agreement the parties may reduce the period of limitation to not less than one year but may not extend it.
(2) A cause of action accrues when the breach occurs, regardless of the aggrieved party's lack of knowledge of the breach. A breach of warranty occurs when tender of delivery is made, except that where a warranty explicitly extends to future performance of the goods and discovery of the breach must await the time of such performance the cause of action accrues when the breach is or should have been discovered.
(3) Where an action commenced within the time limited by subsection (1) is so terminated as to leave available a remedy by another action for the same breach such other action may be commenced after the expiration of the time limited and within six months after the termination of the first action unless the termination resulted from voluntary discontinuance or from dismissal for failure or neglect to prosecute.
(4) This section does not alter the law on tolling of the statute of limitations nor does it apply to causes of action which have accrued before this Act becomes effective.

# CSI MASTERFORMAT

## LEVEL TWO NUMBERS AND TITLES

### Introductory Information
00001   Project Title Page
00005   Certifications Page
00007   Seals Page
00010   Table of Contents
00015   List of Drawings
00020   List of Schedules

### Bidding Requirements
00100   Bid Solicitation
00200   Instructions to Bidders
00300   Information Available to Bidders
00400   Bid Forms and Supplements
00490   Bidding Addenda

### Contracting Requirements
00500   Agreement
00600   Bonds and Certificates
00700   General Conditions
00800   Supplementary Conditions
00900   Addenda and Modifications

### Facilities and Spaces
### Systems and Assemblies
### Construction Products and Activities
### Division 1 General Requirements
01100   Summary
01200   Price and Payment Procedures
01300   Administrative Requirements
01400   Quality Requirements
01500   Temporary Facilities and Controls
01600   Product Requirements
01700   Execution Requirements
01800   Facility Operation
01900   Facility Decommissioning

### Division 2 Site Construction
02050   Basic Site Materials and Methods
02100   Site Remediation
02200   Site Preparation
02300   Earthwork
02400   Tunneling, Boring, and Jacking
02450   Foundation and Load-Bearing Elements
02500   Utility Services
02600   Drainage and Containment
02700   Bases, Ballasts, Pavements, and Appurtenances
02800   Site Improvements and Amenities
02900   Planting
02950   Site Restoration and Rehabilitation

### Division 3 Concrete
03050   Basic Concrete Materials and Methods
03100   Concrete Forms and Accessories
03200   Concrete Reinforcement
03300   Cast-in-Place Concrete
03400   Precast Concrete
03500   Cementitious Decks and Underlayment
03600   Grouts
03700   Mass Concrete
03900   Concrete Restoration and Cleaning

### Division 4 Masonry
04050   Basic Masonry Materials and Methods
04200   Masonry Units
04400   Stone
04500   Refractories
04600   Corrosion-Resistant Masonry
04700   Simulated Masonry
04800   Masonry Assemblies
04900   Masonry Restoration and Cleaning

### Division 5 Metals
05050   Basic Metal Materials and Methods
05100   Structural Metal Framing
05200   Metal Joists
05300   Metal Deck
05400   Cold-Formed Metal Framing
05500   Metal Fabrications
05600   Hydraulic Fabrications
05650   Railroad Track and Accessories
05700   Ornamental Metal
05800   Expansion Control
05900   Metal Restoration and Cleaning

### Division 6 Wood and Plastics
06050   Basic Wood and Plastic Materials and Methods
06100   Rough Carpentry
06200   Finish Carpentry
06400   Architectural Woodwork
06500   Structural Plastics
06600   Plastic Fabrications
06900   Wood and Plastic Restoration and Cleaning

### Division 7 Thermal and Moisture Protection
07050   Basic Thermal and Moisture Protection Materials and Methods
07100   Dampproofing and Waterproofing
07200   Thermal Protection
07300   Shingles, Roof Tiles, and Roof Coverings
07400   Roofing and Siding Panels
07500   Membrane Roofing
07600   Flashing and Sheet Metal
07700   Roof Specialties and Accessories
07800   Fire and Smoke Protection
07900   Joint Sealers

### Division 8 Doors and Windows
08050   Basic Door and Window Materials and Methods
08100   Metal Doors and Frames
08200   Wood and Plastic Doors
08300   Specialty Doors
08400   Entrances and Storefronts
08500   Windows
08600   Skylights
08700   Hardware
08800   Glazing
08900   Glazed Curtain Wall

### Division 9 Finishes
09050   Basic Finish Materials and Methods
09100   Metal Support Assemblies
09200   Plaster and Gypsum Board
09300   Tile
09400   Terrazzo
09500   Ceilings
09600   Flooring
09700   Wall Finishes
09800   Acoustical Treatment
09900   Paints and Coatings

### Division 10 Specialties
10100   Visual Display Boards
10150   Compartments and Cubicles
10200   Louvers and Vents
10240   Grilles and Screens
10250   Service Walls
10260   Wall and Corner Guards
10270   Access Flooring
10290   Pest Control
10300   Fireplaces and Stoves
10340   Manufactured Exterior Specialties
10350   Flagpoles
10400   Identification Devices
10450   Pedestrian Control Devices
10500   Lockers
10520   Fire Protection Specialties
10530   Protective Covers
10550   Postal Specialties
10600   Partitions
10670   Storage Shelving
10700   Exterior Protection
10750   Telephone Specialties
10800   Toilet, Bath, and Laundry Accessories
10880   Scales
10900   Wardrobe and Closet Specialties

### Division 11 Equipment
11010   Maintenance Equipment
11020   Security and Vault Equipment
11030   Teller and Service Equipment
11040   Ecclesiastical Equipment
11050   Library Equipment
11060   Theater and Stage Equipment
11070   Instrumental Equipment
11080   Registration Equipment
11090   Checkroom Equipment
11100   Mercantile Equipment
11110   Commercial Laundry and Dry Cleaning Equipment
11120   Vending Equipment
11130   Audio-Visual Equipment
11140   Vehicle Service Equipment
11150   Parking Control Equipment
11160   Loading Dock Equipment
11170   Solid Waste Handling Equipment
11190   Detention Equipment
11200   Water Supply and Treatment Equipment
11280   Hydraulic Gates and Valves
11300   Fluid Waste Treatment and Disposal Equipment
11400   Food Service Equipment
11450   Residential Equipment
11460   Unit Kitchens
11470   Darkroom Equipment
11480   Athletic, Recreational, and Therapeutic Equipment
11500   Industrial and Process Equipment
11600   Laboratory Equipment
11650   Planetarium Equipment

11660    Observatory Equipment
11680    Office Equipment
11700    Medical Equipment
11780    Mortuary Equipment
11850    Navigation Equipment
11870    Agricultural Equipment
11900    Exhibit Equipment

**Division 12 Furnishings**
12050    Fabrics
12100    Art
12300    Manufactured Casework
12400    Furnishings and Accessories
12500    Furniture
12600    Multiple Seating
12700    Systems Furniture
12800    Interior Plants and Planters
12900    Furnishings Restoration and Repair

**Division 13 Special Construction**
13010    Air-Supported Structures
13020    Building Modules
13030    Special Purpose Rooms
13080    Sound, Vibration, and Seismic Control
13090    Radiation Protection
13100    Lightning Protection
13110    Cathodic Protection
13120    Pre-Engineered Structures

13150    Swimming Pools
13160    Aquariums
13165    Aquatic Park Facilities
13170    Tubs and Pools
13175    Ice Rinks
13185    Kennels and Animal Shelters
13190    Site-Constructed Incinerators
13200    Storage Tanks
13220    Filter Underdrains and Media
13230    Digester Covers and Appurtenances
13240    Oxygenation Systems
13260    Sludge Conditioning Systems
13280    Hazardous Material Remediation
13400    Measurement and Control Instrumentation
13500    Recording Instrumentation
13550    Transportation Control Instrumentation
13600    Solar and Wind Energy Equipment
13700    Security Access and Surveillance
13800    Building Automation and Control
13850    Detection and Alarm
13900    Fire Suppression

**Division 14 Conveying Systems**
14100    Dumbwaiters
14200    Elevators
14300    Escalators and Moving Walks
14400    Lifts
14500    Material Handling

14600    Hoists and Cranes
14700    Turntables
14800    Scaffolding
14900    Transportation

**Division 15 Mechanical**
15050    Basic Mechanical Materials and Methods
15100    Building Services Piping
15200    Process Piping
15300    Fire Protection Piping
15400    Plumbing Fixtures and Equipment
15500    Heat-Generation Equipment
15600    Refrigeration Equipment
15700    Heating, Ventilating, and Air Conditioning Equipment
15800    Air Distribution
15900    HVAC Instrumentation and Controls
15950    Testing, Adjusting, and Balancing

**Division 16 Electrical**
16050    Basic Electrical Materials and Methods
16100    Wiring Methods
16200    Electrical Power
16300    Transmission and Distribution
16400    Low-Voltage Distribution
16500    Lighting
16700    Communications
16800    Sound and Video

# GLOSSARY

**above-base building standard** Materials and constructions that are not included in the base building standard.

**absorption** The process of soaking up energy.

**acid-curing finish** A solvent-based wood floor finish.

**acknowledgment** A confirmation of the purchase order, in regard to the purchase orders.

**acrylic** (1) A clear, transparent plastic material widely used for skylights and security glazing. (2) A manufactured fiber composed primarily of acrylonitrile.

**addenda** Contract modifications made to the bidding documents.

**additive** Substance added to another in relatively small amounts to impart or improve desirable characteristics.

**administrative law** That body of law, including decrees and legal decisions, generated by administrative agencies, boards, and commissions. Involves the administration of law by nonjudicial agencies created by the executive or legislative branches of the government.

**agency** A legal agreement between two persons, whereby one is designated the agent of the other.

**agent** A person authorized to act on behalf of another and subject to the other's control in dealing with third parties.

**agreement** The contract document that briefly states the work of the contract, the project time, and the contract sum. It includes other contract documents by reference.

**alkaline** A material having a pH greater than 7.0 in water.

**alkyd** A resin formed by the combination of alcohol and acid.

**alloy** A metal made from mixing various metals to combine their desirable properties.

**annealed glass** Glass cooled under conditions to minimize internal stresses.

**anodize** A finish applied principally to aluminum, which involves passing an electrical current across a solution, most commonly sulfuric acid, in which the aluminum is immersed.

**application rate** The amount of paint that must be applied to a surface to achieve the desired performance, given as the area of substrate in square feet that should be covered by a gallon of paint, or sq ft/gal. For example, an intumescent paint may have to be applied at a rate of 190 sq ft/gal to achieve the required coating thickness, whereas a regular paint may have an application rate of 300 sq ft/gal.

**aramid** A manufactured fiber with low flammability and high strength used in firefighter's apparel, barrier fabrics between upholstery cushions and fabric, and in bullet-resistant vests.

**austenitic** A process by which steel is heated above a certain temperature causing certain components to transform to austentite, making the steel nonmagnetic; named after Sir William Roberts-Austen who invented the process.

**Axminster** A woven carpet in which successive weftwise rows of pile are inserted during the weaving process according to a predetermined arrangement of colors.

**base building** The commercial office building shell and core, including essential services such as the elevator, HVAC system, and toilet rooms.

**base building standard** A package of typical tenant improvements provided by, and sometimes required by, the landlord. Sometimes called the *building standard*.

**beck dyeing** A textile dye method consisting of advancing a continuous loop of textile through a dye bath.

**bill of lading** A document evidencing the receipt of goods for shipment and issued by a person engaged in the business of transporting or forwarding goods.

**bill of sale** A written statement evidencing the transfer of personal property from one person to another.

**blackout lining** A fabric backing used with a drapery to darken a room completely.

**book match** The back of the top wood veneer leaf is matched to the face of the lower leaf, creating a mirror image and continuity in grain, much like the open leaves of a book.

**brass** A copper-zinc alloy.

**bronze** Originally, a copper-tin alloy; today the term is used to identify other alloys with a bronze color.

**building code** A set of laws that set forth the minimum requirements for design and construction to protect public health and safety.

**building gross area** The floor area within the exterior face of the building, including the thickness of the exterior wall.

**bulked continuous filament (BCF)** Continuous strands of synthetic fiber that are formed into yarn bundles without the need for spinning.

**butt master carrier** A drapery carrier that holds the drapery end traversing the rod and joins it to the other drapery end with no overlap. Butt master carriers are often used in roll pleat and stack pleat draperies.

**calendering** A process used to manufacture vinyl wallcovering that squeezes vinyl to the consistency of dough over a series of hot metal rollers, flattening the compound into a sheet.

**calfskin** The hide of a young animal.

**carbon steel** Steel containing up to 1.20% carbon with, generally, no other alloying elements added.

**carrier** A business that undertakes to transport persons or goods or both.

**cascade** A lined window treatment with folds of fabric hanging from the top of a drapery heading.

**casement** A sheer or semisheer fabric window treatment, often used with operable over-drapes or fixed side panels.

**casework** Cabinets, cases, fixtures, or other storage units that are built in or attached to the building.

**cast** Produced by pouring molten material into a mold.

**catalyzed lacquer** A lacquer containing nitrocellulose that dries harder and faster than noncatalyzed lacquer, but cannot be easily touched up.

**cattle hide** The skin of a fully grown cow.

**Ceiling Sound Transmission Class (CSTC)** A value that correlates with the reduction of sound, expressed in increments of 5. The higher the CSTC, the better the sound reduction capability of the ceiling system.

**cementitious backerboard** Smooth, lightweight boards made of portland cement or treated gypsum and lightweight aggregate, and reinforced with glass fiber, that are sometimes used as an underlayment for thinset installations. They are designed to provide a water-resistant base for ceramic tile installations regularly exposed to water (for example, in a shower surround).

**ceramic mosaic tile** Tile with a face area of less than 6 sq in. (150 sq mm).

**change directive** A written contract modification when the consequent alteration of the contract sum or schedule has not yet been agreed upon.

**change order** A written contract modification altering the contract sum. Only the owner can authorize a change order.

**chemical finish** For metals, a finish produced by the reaction of a metal surface to various chemical solutions.

**C.I.F.** Cost, insurance, and freight. Terms instructing a carrier to collect the cost of goods shipped, insurance, and freight charges.

**code** A compilation of statutes; a set of laws.

**C.O.L.** Customer's own leather. Leather that is not supplied by the product manufacturer.

**colorfastness** The capability of a material to retain its original hue.

**color through** A term used to describe high-pressure decorative laminates that are a uniform color throughout the thickness of the sheet.

**colorway** A set of colors for a given pattern or texture. Fabric or wallcovering manufacturers offer a pattern in a variety of colorways to suit different color schemes.

**C.O.M.** Customer's own material. Material, typically fabric, that is not supplied by the product manufacturer.

**common areas** Corridors, lavatories, elevator vestibules, and other areas that tenants share in common.

**common carrier** A company that transports goods or persons for compensation and offers its facilities to the general public without discrimination. Compare *contract carrier*.

**common law** The body of recorded court decisions that courts refer to and rely upon when making legal decisions. Past judicial decisions and reasoning; involves the application of precedent in applying the law.

**compression modulus** An indication of a foam's support, calculated by indenting the foam to 65% of its original height and dividing it by the IFD.

**concealed grid ceiling system** A suspended ceiling system where the grid supporting the ceiling tiles is not visible in the finished ceiling. Also referred to as a *concealed spline system*.

**conditions of the contract** The document that establishes the duties and responsibilities of the construction or FF&E contractor, the owner, and the designer. The conditions of the contract consist of the general conditions and the supplementary conditions.

**conduction** The transfer of heat energy through a substance.

**consideration** In contract law, the mutual promise to exchange benefits and sacrifices between the parties.

**constitution** The basic law of a nation or state.

**constitutional law** That body of law that involves a constitution and its interpretation.

**continuous piece dyeing** A textile dye method in which the greige goods travel through a long production line. First, an applicator spreads dye on the greige goods, then the dye is fixed in a steamer, and the piece is washed and dried.

**contract** An agreement between two or more component parties, based on mutual promises to do or to refrain from doing some particular thing that is neither illegal nor impossible. The agreement results in an obligation or a duty that can be enforced in a court of law.

**contract carrier** A carrier that provides transportation for compensation only to those people with whom it desires to do business. Compare *common carrier*.

**contract documents** The documents that describe the work included in the contract. Contract documents consist of the contract forms (including the agreement, bonds, and certificates) the conditions of the contract, the specifications, the drawings, and the addenda.

**contract for construction** An agreement between the owner and the construction contractor to provide expertise and service.

**contract for FF&E** An agreement between the owner and the FF&E contractor to provide services such as warehousing, delivery, and installation. It is primarily a sale-of-goods contract.

**contract modifications** Changes to the construction or FF&E documents, including addenda, change orders, change directives, and supplemental instructions.

**convection** The transfer of heat energy through air.

**cork** The outer layer of the cork oak tree that is harvested for use as, among other things, resilient flooring.

**crocking** Rubbing off.

**curtain** A hanging textile window treatment. Usually refers to an unlined treatment with a gathered or shirred heading.

**dealer** The local or regional presence of a manufacturer that processes sales and provides various support and follow-up services to the consumer.

**dedicated circuit** An electrical circuit with three conductors, consisting of hot, neutral, and ground, between the final overcurrent device protecting the circuit and the outlets that are reserved for use only with specific equipment.

**delamination** The separation of two materials that had been bonded together.

**delivery** The transfer of possession from one person to another.

**demised premises** That portion of a property covered by a lease agreement, usually defined by the walls and other structures that separate one tenant's space from that of another.

**demising walls** The partitions that separate one tenant's space from another.

**denier** A unit of yarn measurement equal to the weight in grams of 9,000 meters of the yarn.

**density** The mass-per-unit volume.

**descriptive specification** Specifications that detail the requirements for products, materials, and workmanship.

**design-award-build** The traditional approach to a construction contract whereby the designer prepares the contract documents, the contract is awarded to a construction contractor, and the project is built.

**design/build** A construction contract process wherein one party is responsible for both the design and the construction.

**destination contract** A contract under which the seller is required to deliver goods to a place of destination. Title passes to the buyer when the seller delivers the goods.

**dimension stone** Quarried stone with usually one or more mechanically dressed surfaces.

**dimension stone tile** Dimension stone that is less than ¾ in. (19 mm) thick.

**direct glue-down** The most common method of commercial carpet installation, whereby the carpet is glued directly to the floor without a cushion. This is the most dimensionally stable carpet installation method and is often required for stair or ramp applications.

**direct sales force** A selling team that represents the product's manufacturer, not the manufacturer's dealer.

**double glue-down**  A carpet installation method whereby the carpet cushion is adhered to the floor and the carpet is then glued to the cushion.

**drapery**  A hanging, textile window treatment. Usually refers to lined treatments with a stiffened, constructed heading requiring a traversing rod and carriers.

**drawings**  Graphic representations describing the shape and form of the space and the quantities, sizes, and locations of materials and goods. Part of the contract documents.

**drop shipment**  A shipment whereby goods are shipped to a destination different from that of the party who ordered and paid for them.

**dry film thickness (DFT)**  The thickness of the cured paint or coating finish measured in mils (1/1000 in.).

**electrolyte**  A liquid that conducts electricity.

**emissivity**  No or low reflectivity. If a surface has high reflectivity, it has low emissivity.

**end**  A yarn loop in the surface of a carpet.

**end match**  Wood veneers are book matched, then the ends of the sheets are matched, creating a long and wide matching veneer piece.

**exposed grid ceiling system**  A ceiling suspension system of square or rectilinear frames that are visible in the finished ceiling and hold attached or loose laid panels.

**express warranty**  An oral or written statement, promise, or other representation about the quality of a product.

**extruded**  Produced by forcing semimolten material through a die.

**face weight**  The weight of the carpet pile yarn in ounces per square yard; also referred to as *pile weight* or *yarn weight*.

**fast-track**  A construction contract process whereby construction begins before the project design is complete. Separate construction contracts are defined, and contract documents are prepared for each phase. Fast-tracking often increases construction cost due to decreased labor efficiency.

**ferrous**  Consisting mostly of iron; from the Latin *ferrum,* meaning iron.

**FF&E**  Furniture, furnishings, and equipment. Those items included in a project that are considered removable and not part of the construction.

**fiber**  A fine hairlike strand that forms the basis of a yarn.

**fiber cushion**  A carpet cushion made by needlepunching natural fiber, synthetic fiber, or a combination of the two, into a feltlike pad.

**fiberglass**  Glass in fibrous form used in making various products.

**filament fiber**  A long, continuous fiber measured in meters or yards.

**filament yarn**  Continuous strands of silk or of synthetic fiber from a spinerette, twisted together.

**fire-resistant**  A substance that resists the spread of fire by not contributing to the flame.

**flame-retardant**  A substance that slows the rate at which a fire spreads.

**flammability**  The capability to support combustion.

**flammability standard**  A specified level of flammability performance.

**flammability test method**  A group of procedures carried out by a testing laboratory to measure whether a product conforms to the stated acceptance criteria or classification cited by the flammability standard.

**flash cove**  An integral, monolithic wall base for finish flooring.

**flitch**  (1) The section of the wood log ready to be sliced into leaves; (2) the bundle of leaves stacked in sequence after slicing.

**float glass**  Glass sheet manufactured by cooling a layer of liquid glass on a bath of molten tin.

**F.O.B.**  Defined by the UCC as "free on board." It is the place where the title to the goods and risk of loss pass from the seller to the buyer. The buyer pays the transportation costs from the point named in the F.O.B. "place." (UCC 2-319).

**F.O.B. factory-freight prepaid**  Term indicating that the buyer has title to the goods during transit, but the supplier pays the transportation charges to the destination. In this way, the buyer has the convenience of not having to arrange for transportation and the supplier reduces its liability.

**F.O.B. place of destination**  Term indicating the seller is responsible for delivering the goods. The cost of the goods includes shipping charges. If the goods are stolen, damaged, or destroyed in transit, it is the seller's responsibility to recover damages from the carrier (UCC 2-319).

**F.O.B. place of shipment**  Term indicating that the buyer owns the goods at the place of shipment (typically, the manufacturer's factory loading dock). The goods are given to the carrier (typically, a truck), and the seller is no longer responsible for the delivery of the goods or their condition upon arrival. The buyer pays for shipping. If the goods are stolen, damaged, or destroyed in transit, it is the buyer's responsibility to recover damages from the carrier. When the terms of shipment do not specify shipping point or destination, it is assumed to be F.O.B. place of shipment.

**French pleat**  A traditional, folded and stitched drapery heading, sometimes referred to as a *pinch pleat.*

**full-grain leather**  Leather with the original, genuine grain of the hide; the most expensive type of hides.

**fullness**  In reference to draperies and curtains, fullness is the ratio of the total fabric used, less allowances for side hems and seams, to the finished drapery width. For example, a drapery with 100% fullness is 100% wider than the width of the drapery in a closed position, or twice the finished drapery width.

**full warranty**  Under the Magnuson-Moss Warranty Act, a defective product will be fixed or replaced free within a reasonable time after a complaint has been made about the product.

**furnish**  To supply and deliver to the project site, ready for unloading, unpacking, assembly, installation, and similar operations.

**furniture dealer**  The local or regional presence of the furniture manufacturer that processes furniture sales and provides various support and follow-up services.

**fusion-bonded carpet**  A thermoplastic carpet tile manufacturing process whereby yarns are attached to a backing material by means of adhesion rather than tufting or weaving.

**gage**  Measurement according to some standard or system. Also spelled "gauge."

**galvanic corrosion**  Metal corrosion caused by an electrolyte.

**galvanize**  The application of zinc to the surface of cast iron, steel, or steel alloys to prevent corrosion.

**gauge (carpet)**  The measure of the spacing of the tufting needles, center to center, in a tufted carpet.

**gel coat**  A pigmented polyester coating that is applied to the inside surface of a mold and becomes an integral part of a finished piece; for example, a cultured marble countertop.

**general conditions of the contract**  Standardized documents establishing the duties and responsibilities of the construction or FF&E contractor, the owner, and the designer. The general conditions are modified through the supplementary conditions of the contract. See *conditions of the contract.*

**glass-reinforced gypsum (GRG)**  A high-strength, high-density gypsum, reinforced with extruded glass fibers, that is molded to the required shape.

**glazed tile**  A ceramic tile with an impervious finish composed of ceramic materials fused to the face of the tile. The body of a glazed tile may be nonvitreous, semivitreous, vitreous, or impervious.

**gloss**  The relative luminous reflectance. Defined by ASTM D523, *Standard Test Method for Specular Gloss.*

**goods**  All things (including specially manufactured goods) which are movable at the time of identification to the contract for sale other than the money in which the price is to be paid, investment securities, and things in action. (UCC 2-105).

**greige goods**  An unfinished fabric just off the loom or knitting machine.

**gypsum**  Hydrous calcium sulfate.

**gypsum board**  An interior facing panel made from a gypsum core sandwiched between paper faces; also called *drywall, sheet rock,* or *plasterboard.*

**hand**  A fabric's tactile qualities, for example, softness, firmness, drapability, and resiliency.

**hardboard**  A very dense panel product manufactured in a manner similar to medium-density fiberboard (MDF) but under higher pressure, often without adhesive.

**hardwood**  Wood from a deciduous tree.

**heat-strengthened glass**  Glass that has been strengthened by heat treatment, but not to the extent of fully tempered glass.

**heat-treated glass**  Glass that has been strengthened by heat treatment; either fully tempered glass or heat-strengthened glass.

**honed**  A satin smooth stone finish with a dull sheen.

**high-pressure decorative laminate (HPDL)**  Plastic laminate; commonly used for countertops.

**hygrometer**  A device that measures relative humidity.

**Impact Noise Rating (INR)**  A measurement of the sound insulation of a floor and ceiling assembly.

**implied warranty**  A warranty imposed by law rather than by statements, descriptions, or samples given by the seller.

**Indentation Force Deflection (IFD)**  A measure of foam firmness.

**install**  To set up for use or service, including unloading, unpacking, assembly, erection, placing, anchoring, applying, working to dimension, finishing, curing, protecting, cleaning, and similar operations.

**Interzone Attenuation and Articulation Class (AC)**  A single-figure rating measuring the sound-reflective characteristics of ceiling systems in spaces with partial-height walls.

**intumescent**  Swelling and charring when exposed to flame. An intumescent substance expands to form an insulating char when exposed to fire.

**Jacquard loom**  A loom used for figured fabrics such as tapestries, brocades, and damask weaves. Jacquard weaving uses a series of punched cards. Each card perforation controls the action of one warp yarn.

**lacquer**  A coating that dries extremely quickly through the evaporation of a volatile solvent.

**lamb's wool**  Wool sheared from sheep under eight months of age.

**laminated glass**  A glazing material consisting of outer layers of glass laminated to an inner layer of plastic.

**landlord**  A person who owns real property and who rents or leases it to someone else; a lessor.

**law**  A set of rules created by the governing body of a society to ensure the orderly maintenance of that society.

**lease**  A contract granting the use of certain real property to another for a specified period of time in return for payment of rent.

**leaves**  Individual wood veneer slices cut from a log section.

**limited warranty**  Under the Magnuson-Moss Warranty Act, a warranty that is not a full warranty.

**lining**  A fabric backing used to enhance certain qualities of a fabric, for example, drapability, energy performance, and protection from ultraviolet (UV) radiation.

**linoleum**  A resilient flooring material composed of oxidized linseed oil or other resins, mixed with cork or wood flour, mineral fillers, and pigments; derived from the botanical terms for "flax," *linum,* and "oil," *oleum.*

**MasterFormat**  A list of six-digit numbers and titles that classify the materials and requirements of construction and FF&E projects, promulgated by the Construction Specification Institute (CSI).

**mastic**  A pastelike adhesive.

**mechanical finish**  For metals, a finish accomplished by buffing, grinding, polishing, or otherwise texturing the metal surface.

**medium-density fiberboard (MDF)**  A panel product manufactured by breaking down wood particles into fibers by steam pressure, mixing them with adhesive resins, and pressing them into panels.

**mercerization**  A treatment of cotton yarn or fabric to increase its luster and affinity for dyes. The material is immersed under tension in a cold sodium hydroxide solution and is later neutralized in acid. The process causes a permanent swelling of the fiber and thus increases its luster.

**merchant**  A person who deals in goods of the kind sold in the ordinary course of business or who otherwise claims to have knowledge or skills peculiar to those goods.

**mineral tanning**  A leather tanning process using a tanning solution based on chromium salts. Mineral-tanned hides accept dyes well, including rich, vibrant colors. About 90% of leather today is tanned by this method.

**natural fiber**  Textile fiber from animal, plant, or mineral sources.

**needlepunched carpet**  A method of manufacturing carpet by layering tick fiber batts (typically polypropylene) over a support fabric and punching barbed needles through the support fabric.

**Noise Reduction Coefficient (NRC)**  A rating of the sound-absorbing efficiency of a material.

**noncatalyzed lacquer**  An easy-to-apply, touch-up, and recoat solvent-based lacquer, forming a monolithic finish. Sometimes referred to as *standard lacquer.*

**nonferrous**  Containing little or no iron.

**nonvitreous**  An absorption of 7.0% or more when used to describe ceramic tile.

**nonvolatile**  Does not readily evaporate.

**oil-modified polyurethane**  An easy-to-apply, affordable wood floor finish that tends to amber (turn slightly orange) as it ages.

**olefin**  A manufactured fiber of light weight, high strength, and good abrasion resistance. It is used primarily in the manufacture of indoor-outdoor carpet.

**on center**  Spacing measured from the center of one component to the center of the next.

**one-way draw**  A drapery or curtain operation that opens entirely to one side, designated as either *full left* or *full right,* indicating the direction in which the drapery stacks as you face it. For example, if you are looking at an open drapery stacked on the right, it is a right draw.

**ordinance**  A statute or regulation enacted by a municipal (city or town) government.

**oriented strand board (OSB)**  A panel product manufactured from thin, narrow strands of both hardwood and softwood that are blended with adhesive and formed into a multilayer panel.

**overlap master carrier**  A drapery carrier that holds the drapery end traversing the rod and joins it to the other drapery end with an overlap. Overlap master carriers are often used in conventional pleated draperies.

**PageFormat**  A page organization for specifications promulgated by the Construction Specification Institute (CSI).

**panel**  When referring to window treatments, a panel is a single drapery unit of one or more fabric widths.

**parquet**  Wood flooring consisting of small lengths of wood strips, either individual slats or preconfigured into tiles, that are arranged to form patterns.

**particleboard**  A panel product manufactured from wood particles and fibers that are bonded under heat and pressure with an adhesive resin.

**patina**  A thin layer of corrosion resulting from oxidation.

**paver tiles**  Ceramic tiles with a face size of 6 sq in. (1,150 sq mm ) or more.

**performance specification**  Specifications that describe the required results.

**pH**  A numeric scale used to indicate how acidic or basic (alkaline) a solution is.

**piece dyeing**  The dyeing of fabrics after weaving or knitting, as opposed to dyeing in the form of yarn.

**pigment**  An insoluble substance used as coloring.

**pile**  In carpets, the face yarn, as opposed to the backing yarn.

**pile density**  The weight of the pile yarn in a given volume of carpet face.

**pile height** The length of a carpet tuft from the backing to the tip of the tuft.

**pile weight** See *face weight*.

**pinch pleat** A traditional, folded and stitched drapery heading, sometimes referred to as a *French pleat*.

**pitch** The number of ends (yarn loops) in a 27 in. (685 mm) width of carpet.

**plain sawn** Cuts made tangentially to the annual growth ring of a tree. This sawing method produces the least waste and requires the least labor.

**plain weave** One of the three fundamental weaves: plain, satin, and twill. Each weft yarn passes successively over and under each warp yarn, alternating each row.

**plastisol** A method of manufacturing vinyl wallcovering that spreads liquid vinyl onto a backing material as it is rolled by. The materials are then fused together under high temperatures.

**pleat to** The width of the drapery after it has been pleated. For example, if a 48 in. (121.92 cm ) width of fabric is 19 in. (48.26 cm ) after it has been pleated, it is specified as "pleat to 19 in. (48.26 cm)."

**plenum** The space between a finished ceiling and the structure above.

**plywood** A sandwich of wood or wood products between two layers of wood veneer, top and bottom.

**polyester** A manufactured fiber of high strength that is resistant to shrinking and stretching; a quick-drying fiber with good crease retention and wrinkle resistance.

**polymer** A giant molecule composed of many identical simple molecules.

**polymerization** The process by which polymers are formed; the basic formation of plastics.

**polyurethane** A large group of resins and plastic compounds used in varnishes, insulation foam, and sealants.

**precedent** A model case that a court can follow when facing a similar situation.

**prescriptive specifications** Specifications that delineate product or material attributes.

**primer** A substance that prepares a surface for the application of a finish by increasing the surface adhesion.

**private carrier** A company that transports goods or persons under individual contract with those seeking its service. A private carrier is not required to serve all requests, unlike a common carrier.

**project site** The space available to the construction or FF&E contractor for performance of construction or installation activities. The extent of the project site should be shown on the drawings.

**proprietary specifications** Specifications requiring a specific product from a specific manufacturer.

**pro rata** Proportionately.

**provide** To furnish and install, complete and ready for the intended use.

**purchase order** The form used to order goods. It contains a description of the goods, the supplier's catalog identification code, the number of items required, and the price.

**purchase order acknowledgment** A confirmation of the purchase order.

**quarry tile** A tile that is extruded from either natural clay or shale.

**quarter sawn** Cuts made with the growth rings at 60° to 90° angles to the face of the board. This sawing method is not available for all species of wood.

**R-value** The insulating effect of a material; a material's resistance to the flow of heat.

**radiation** The transmission of energy by invisible light waves independent of a substance or air.

**railroading** Fabric applied in a horizontal manner, the way in which it is unrolled from the bolt, with the selvage edge parallel to the seat cushion edge.

**rayon** A manufactured fiber composed of regenerated cellulose; originally known as artificial silk.

**real property** The ground and anything permanently attached to it, including land, buildings, and growing trees and shrubs; the air space above it and the land.

**receipt** Taking physical possession of goods (UCC 2-103).

**reducing strip** An extruded piece that creates a smooth transition and connection between floorings of different types and, possibly, heights.

**reference standard specifications** Specifications based on the requirements set by an accepted authority.

**reflection** Energy bending back from and not penetrating a surface.

**regulation** A governmental order with the force of law.

**rentable area** The floor area that a tenant pays rent on; usually defined as the interior floor area excluding vertical penetrations through the floor, for example, air shafts, elevators, and stairways.

**repeat** Distance between two identical patterns in a length of material, typically fabric or wallcovering.

**resilient flooring** A manufactured sheet or tile of polyvinyl chloride, linoleum, cork, or other material with resilience.

**resin** A nonvolatile (does not readily evaporate) component of paints, coatings, and plastics.

**return** In reference to window treatments, the return is the distance from the traversing rod to the wall or the depth of the projection.

**rift sawn** Cuts made with growth rings at 30° to 60° angles to the face of the board.

**roll pleat** A soft, rounded, uncreased drapery heading.

**rotary cutting** A wood veneer slicing method that produces wide sheets of veneer. The log is mounted on a lathe and the veneer is sliced off as the log spins around.

**rows** The number of ends (yarn loops) per inch in a lengthwise section of Axminster carpet.

**safety glass** Glazing material that complies with ANSI Z97.1, *Safety Glazing Materials Used in Buildings*.

**sale** The passing of title to goods from the seller to the buyer for a price.

**samples** Examples of materials or workmanship.

**satin weave** One of the three fundamental weaves: plain, satin, and twill. The face of the fabric consists almost completely of floating warp yarns. Satin-weave fabrics have a characteristic smooth, lustrous surface.

**SectionFormat** A three-part format for the organization of specification sections, promulgated by the Construction Specification Institute (CSI).

**selvage** (also *selvedge*) The narrow edge of woven fabric that runs parallel to the warp. It is made with stronger yarns in a tighter construction than the body of the fabric, to prevent raveling.

**semivitreous** An absorption of more than 3.0%, but not more than 7.0%, when used to describe ceramic tile.

**sericulture** The growth of silk moths for their silk production.

**setting material** A substance used to fix tile; includes the traditional mortars and the relatively new adhesives.

**shading coefficient (SC)** A measure of a window systems capability to reduce heat gain.

**sheen** The reflectance of a surface.

**shop drawings** Detailed drawings prepared by a fabricator to guide the production of the item, for example, casework.

**silicone** A polymer used for high-range sealants and water repellents.

**skein dyeing** The dyeing of yarn in the form of skeins.

**slip match** Adjacent wood veneer leaves are laid side by side in sequence, in a repeating pattern with no continuity in grain.

**softwood** Wood from a coniferous tree.

**solid surfacing material**  A thick, dense synthetic sheet, uniform through the depth of the material; known by the trade name Corian, manufactured by Du Pont.

**specifications**  Written contract documents that describe the quality of materials and their construction or installation.

**split leather**  Leather made by slicing the hide into two or three layers. The inside layer is often finished as suede.

**sponge rubber cushion**  A carpet cushion made of flat sponge, ripple (waffle) sponge, or reinforced foam rubber. Sponge rubber cushions are generally open-cell forms.

**spun yarn**  Staple fibers twisted together to form a continuous strand.

**stack back**  The width of a window treatment in a fully open position beside the window.

**stack pleat**  A creased drapery heading with the pleat crease sewn front and back for the length of the drapery.

**stain**  A transparent or opaque coating that penetrates and colors a wood surface without masking its inherent grain.

**standard**  A material specification, practice, or test method based on technical research and testing by industry experts.

**staple fiber**  A short fiber, typically measured in centimeters or inches. All natural fibers except silk are staple fibers.

**static generation**  The tendency of a substance to generate static electricity.

**statute**  A law passed by legislature.

**statutory law**  The body of law that includes statutes and ordinances.

**stitches**  The number of ends sewn by the needles down the length of a tufted carpet.

**stretch-in installation**  The traditional method of carpet installation whereby the carpet is stretched over a cushion and attached at the perimeter with a tack strip.

**strike off**  A small printed sample of a custom order for the designer's review and approval.

**stock dyeing**  The dyeing of fibers in staple form.

**subfloor**  The load-bearing surface beneath the finish surface.

**supplemental instructions**  An interpretation or clarification of the contract documents by the designer that does not alter the contract sum or schedule.

**supplementary conditions of the contract**  Customized document modifying the duties and responsibilities of the construction or FF&E contractor, the owner, and the designer, as described in the general conditions. See *conditions of the contract.*

**swag**  A textile window treatment heading with draped soft folds at the tops of drapery.

**synthetic fiber**  Textile fibers that are man-made.

**tempered glass**  Glass that has been heat-treated to increase its toughness and its resistance to breakage.

**tenant**  A person who has temporary possession of an interest in the real property of another.

**tenant improvement**  Materials and construction that form the infill responding to the tenant's needs.

**tenant improvement allowance**  A sum of money allowed for tenant improvements, typically including standard items that will be installed at no cost to the tenant. The quantity of tenant improvements in the allowance is usually described per square foot of rentable space.

**tender**  An offer or performance by one party to a contract which, if unjustifiably refused, places the other party in default and permits the party making the tender to exercise remedies for breach of contract.

**terrazzo**  A floor finish material consisting of concrete with an aggregate of marble chips selected for color and size, which is ground and polished smooth after curing.

**testing laboratory**  An independent entity engaged to perform specific inspections or tests, either at the project site or elsewhere, and to report on and, if required, to interpret the results.

**textile**  Fabric made of fibers, whether woven, knitted, felted, or manufactured by some other means.

**thermal finish**  A stone finish achieved by the application of intense flaming heat to the surface of the stone. Thermal finishes are usually applied to granite.

**thermoplastics**  Plastics that become soft when heated and can be remolded repeatedly without affecting the properties of the plastic.

**thermosets**  Plastics that are permanently hardened after undergoing an irreversible chemical change during processing.

**thick-set**  A ceramic tile setting method using a thick bed of portland cement mortar.

**thinner**  That portion of a paint or coating that is volatile (readily evaporates); the thinner does not become part of the cured film.

**thin-set**  A ceramic tile setting method using a thin layer of dry-set mortar or latex-portland cement mortar.

**title**  The right of ownership to goods. A subdivision of a code containing all the statutes that deal with a particular area of law.

**top-grain leather**  Leather in which the original surface pattern, including scars from barbed wire or brands, is removed by abrasion. This skinless surface is embossed with a pattern, typically resembling the grain of the skin that was removed.

**transmission**  The penetration of energy through a substance.

**tuft**  A cluster of yarns drawn through a fabric or backing and projecting from the surface in the form of cut yarns or loops.

**tuft bind**  The force required to pull a tuft out of a finished carpet. The industry standard for measuring tuft bind is ASTM D 1335, *Standard Test Method for Tuft Bind of Pile Floor Covering.*

**tufted carpet**  Carpet produced by a tufting machine instead of a loom; much as in sewing, the needles are forced through a backing material forming loops, or tufts.

**twill weave**  One of the three fundamental weaves: plain, satin, and twill. A weave characterized by diagonal lines produced by a series of staggered floating warp threads.

**two-way draw**  A drapery or curtain operation that parts drapery panels that meet in the center, opening to either side.

**underlayment**  A panel laid smooth over a subfloor to create a smooth, stiff surface for the application of the finish flooring.

**Uniform Commercial Code (UCC)**  A set of statutory laws relating to certain commercial transactions, including the sale of goods, commercial paper, bank deposits and collections, letters of credit, bulk transfers, warehouse receipts, bills of lading, and secured transactions. Sales law is contained in the UCC.

**upholstered wall system**  A site-constructed wallcovering that stretches fabric taut over a frame and infill material.

**up-the-bolt**  Fabric applied in a vertical manner, with the selvage edge perpendicular to the seat cushion edge.

**usable area**  The floor area that is inhabitable by the tenant.

**variance**  An exemption or an exception permitting a use that differs from those permitted under the existing zoning law.

**varnish**  A slow-drying transparent coating.

**vegetable tanning**  A leather tanning method using a tanning solution based on tree bark, typically oak. The hides are submerged in the solution, and the tannins (tanning materials) from the bark swell the hides.

**vehicle**  That portion of a paint or coating that conveys the ingredients that remain on the substrate after the paint or coating has cured.

**velvet**  (1) A woven carpet in which the pile ends are lifted over wires that are inserted in the same manner as the weft and that cut the pile as they are drawn. (2) A fabric with a short, dense cut pile that produces a rich appearance and soft texture.

**vinyl composition tile (VCT)**  Resilient flooring tiles composed mostly of fillers with a comparatively small amounts of binder and pigments.

**virgin wool**  Wool made into yarn for the first time.

**vitreous**  Glasslike; ceramic tile with an absorption of 0.5% or less.

**volatile**  Readily evaporates.

**volatile organic compounds (VOC)**  Those components of paints and coatings that evaporate readily. VOCs adversely affect human health and the environment.

**wall base**  A strip of material that conceals the joint where a wall meets the floor.

**wall liner**  A nonwoven sheet used under wallcovering where wall surfaces cannot be prepared by conventional means. Wall liners can be used to prevent cracks, holes, and gaps from telegraphing through the wallcovering.

**warehouse**  A building in which any goods, particularly wares or merchandise, are stored.

**warp**  Yarns that run lengthwise and parallel to the selvage in woven fabrics.

**warranty**  A statement, promise, or other representation that an item has certain qualities; also, an obligation imposed by law, that an item will have certain qualities. Warranties made by means of a statement or other affirmation of fact are called *express warranties;* those imposed by law are *implied warranties.*

**warranty of fitness for a particular purpose**  An implied warranty that goods will be fit for a particular purpose. This warranty is given by the seller to the buyer of goods whenever the seller has reason to know of any particular purpose for which the goods are needed, and the buyer relies on the seller's skill and judgment to select the goods.

**warranty of merchantability**  An implied warranty that the goods are fit for the ordinary purpose for which such goods are used. Unless excluded, this warranty is always given by a merchant who sells goods in the ordinary course of business.

**water-based polyurethane**  A low-VOC, nonyellowing, expensive wood floor finish.

**weft**  Yarns that run from selvage to selvage at right angles to the warp in woven fabrics.

**Wilton**  A woven carpet in which the pile yarns are an integral part of the carpet, being held in place by the weft, usually made on a Jacquard loom.

**wire**  The number of ends (yarn loops) per inch in a lengthwise section of Wilton or velvet carpet.

**wired glass**  Glass in which a wire mesh is embedded during the manufacturing process.

**wire height**  The pile height of woven carpet.

**work letter**  A document that describes the improvements to the leased space. It is attached to, and a part of, the lease.

**wrought**  Produced by rolling semimolten material into sheets and punching or cutting out the required shape.

**yarn**  A continuous strand formed by twisting fibers together.

**yarn count**  A relative gauge of a spun yarn's weight; heavier yarns are designated by lower yarn count numbers.

**yarn weight**  See *face weight.*

**zoning law**  A local regulation or ordinance that restricts certain areas to specific uses; for example, areas zoned for residential, commercial, agricultural, industrial or other uses.

# INDEX